Handbook of
Clinical Behavior Therapy
with Children

Handbook of
Clinical Behavior Therapy
with Children

Edited by
Philip H. Bornstein, Ph.D.
and
Alan E. Kazdin, Ph.D.

1985

THE DORSEY PRESS   Homewood, Illinois   60430

ISBN 0-256-03485-0

Library of Congress Catalog Card No. 84–73503

Printed in the United States of America

1 2 3 4 5 6 7 8 9 0 K 2 1 0 9 8 7 6 5

*To Jordie, Hallie, Brette,
Nicole, and Michelle*

Preface

The development and investigation of psychotherapy techniques for children has not progressed as rapidly as the adult treatment literature. This slow progress has been attributed to difficulties in the delineation of childhood problems and ambiguities regarding the need to intervene. Clearly, many childhood problems occur but remit naturally over the course of development. In the last decade, however, remarkable advances have been made in the area of child behavior therapy. Quite simply, for a number of clinical problems, effective or highly promising techniques have emerged.

As a consequence of the above, this *Handbook* attempts to survey the broad and emerging areas of behavioral approaches to treatment with children. The book is intended to be authoritative, comprehensive, and consistent with new developments in psychiatric classification of childhood disorders. Several features of the book are unique. First, psychiatric disorders among children have recently been delineated in the *Diagnostic and Statistical Manual of Mental Disorders* (DSM-III). However, since behavioral researchers/clinicians have tended to reject traditional diagnostic systems, learning-based approaches have not been recognized as widely applicable to psychiatrically classified disorders. As a consequence, there is a need to convey, in an organized manner, the usefulness of behavioral methods to the current psychiatric system of classification. Thus, the *Handbook* demonstrates the relevance of behavioral techniques beyond proponents of behavior therapy and appeals to a diverse group of applied mental health professionals (e.g., psychologists, psychiatrists, social workers). In so doing, the *Handbook* fosters a fuller appreciation of child psychopathology and related treatment instead of rigid adherence to individual therapeutic techniques. It should be noted, however, that while we have selected clinical diagnoses as our framework for organization, this does not imply acceptance of any one model or particular diagnostic system.

Second, the book integrates a scholarly presentation of current research with clinically relevant principles of application. Chapters are designed to present and evaluate behavioral treatment methods. The book is neither intended to serve as a dry academic treatise that reviews experimental research in meticulous detail nor as a mechanical "how-to-do-it" manual. Rather, it provides a state-of-the-art assessment, selectively documented, illustrating theory, research, and practice in child behavior therapy. This multifocus purpose is unique and therefore should be attractive to scientists, practitioners, and a wide audience of students at various levels of training.

Third, the book is broad in scope. Diverse clinical problems, conceptual models, and therapeutic techniques are discussed. Ample coverage is provided for the majority of target problems and behavioral dysfunctions for which children are referred to educational, institutional, and clinical specialists. In addition, a wide range of therapeutic procedures are presented—this includes operant, cognitive, self-control, and other intervention strategies. Wherever possible, chapters describe what progress has been achieved and outline the questions yet to be answered. Indeed, the book should serve a very practical function of directing future efforts by making explicit clinical/research strengths and weaknesses.

Fourth, there is a philosophical movement in clinical psychology that is quite consistent with the overall thrust of the present book. Specifically, professionals are increasingly broadening their scope beyond narrow theoretical and treatment approaches. Those of a behavioral persuasion, for example, are becoming less interested in circumscribed targets of intervention and instead are devoting greater attention to complex forms of human functioning (e.g., social competence). As a result, the present text expands the scope of behavior therapy by addressing the wide concerns of practicing mental health professionals. Indeed, several chapters go well beyond specific child problems. For example, a separate chapter is devoted to the topic of child abuse because of its social and clinical significance to both children and adults. Similarly, preventive-behavioral interventions are included because of promising leads suggested by alternative intervention techniques.

Finally, the book is designed to effect a balance between research and clinical application. Not only is the evidence for alternative treatments provided, but also specific techniques are illustrated via the use of case material. The balance is critical to promote the interface and reciprocal influence of research and practice. This dual focus goes beyond what one can find in other texts in child behavior therapy. Related to the above, child behavior therapy is more than a set of procedures or treatment techniques. The field embraces a particular orientation regarding how clinical problems are viewed and assessed and how treatment techniques are to be evaluated. The approach is not parochial in its conceptual bases. However, it is firm in its commitment to empirical evidence as the basis for identifying effective interventions. This should be clear throughout individual chapters and the book as a whole.

We were unusually fortunate in our recruitment of contributors to find the very top clinical researchers in the field. To help ensure uniformity, we provided editorial feedback and recommended several subtopics and sections across all chapters. However, in deference to the special expertise of contributors and the idiosyncrasies of their individual chapters, guidelines were provided rather than rigidly enforced. The end result is that the contributors have masterfully interwoven clinical research with practice, and we applaud their efforts.

Completion of the book was facilitated greatly by other persons to whom we are indebted. Our secretaries, Linda Richtmyer, Susan Sweet, Lollie Phillip, and Claudia Wolfson helped prepare major portions of the manuscript and overall editorial consistencies. Also, we are grateful to the National Institute of Mental Health (MH00353, MH35408) and the National Institute of Child Health and Human Development (Ref. #5 HD14751-03) for grant support that facilitated completion of the text.

Philip H. Bornstein
Alan E. Kazdin

List of Contributors

Russell A. Barkley, Ph.D.
Chief, Neuropsychology Section
Medical College of Wisconsin

Philip H. Bornstein, Ph.D.
Professor of Psychology
University of Montana

Daniel M. Doleys, Ph.D.
Director, Behavioral Programs
Brookwood Medical Center

Glen Dunlap, Ph.D.
Director of Training and Research,
Autism Training Center
Marshall University

Melissa Finch, M.A.
Research Assistant
Oregon Research Institute

Rex Forehand, Ph.D.
Professor of Psychology
University of Georgia

John P. Foreyt, Ph.D.
Associate Professor, Department
of Medicine
Baylor College of Medicine

Eugene E. Garcia, Ph.D.
Professor, College of Education
Arizona State University

Stephen N. Haynes, Ph.D.
Professor
Illinois Institute of Technology

Hyman Hops, Ph.D.
Research Scientist
Oregon Research Institute

William Jenson, Ph.D.
Assistant Professor, Educational
Psychology
University of Utah

Nadine J. Kaslow, Ph.D.
Postdoctoral Fellow
*University of Wisconsin
School of Medicine*

Alan E. Kazdin, Ph.D.
Professor of Child Psychiatry
& Psychology
*University of Pittsburgh
School of Medicine*

Philip C. Kendall, Ph.D.
Professor of Psychology
Temple University

Robert L. Koegel, Ph.D.
Professor
*University of California/
Santa Barbara*

Cynthia Koehler
Psychology Intern
Neuropsychiatric Institute, UCLA

Albert T. Kondo, Ph.D.
Research Fellow, Department
of Psychology
University of Houston

Benjamin B. Lahey, Ph.D.
Professor, Department of
Psychology
University of Georgia

Johnny L. Matson, Ph.D.
Professor and Director of Research
Department of Learning,
Development, and Special Education
Northern Illinois University

Scott R. McConnell, Ph.D.
Principal Research Associate
*Western Psychiatric Institute
and Clinic*

Timothy J. McIntyre, M.A.
Clinical Intern
Baylor College of Medicine

Ellen Olinger, M.S.
Department of Learning and
Development
Northern Illinois University

Thomas H. Ollendick, Ph.D.
Professor, Department of
Psychology
*Virginia Polytechnic Institute
and State University*

Robert E. O'Neill, M.A.
Research Assistant
*University of California/
Santa Barbara*

H. Kenton Reavis, Ph.D.
Program Specialist
Utah State Office of Education

Lynn P. Rehm, Ph.D.
Professor
University of Houston

John B. Reid, Ph.D.
Research Scientist
Oregon Social Learning Center

George A. Rekers, Ph.D.
Professor of Family and
Child Development
Kansas State University

Ginger Rhode, Ph.D.
Program Consultant, Granite
School District
Salt Lake City

Robyn Ridley-Johnson, Ph.D.
Post-Doctoral Fellow, Department
of Clinical Psychology
University of Florida/Gainesville

Lawrence J. Siegel, Ph.D.
Associate Professor, Department of
Pediatrics
University of Texas Medical Branch

Frank A. Treiber, Ph.D.
Post-Doctoral Clinical Intern
Medical College of Georgia

Richard A. van den Pol, Ph.D.
Associate Director
Montana University Affiliated Program
for Developmental Disabilities
University of Montana

Hill M. Walker, Ph.D.
Professor/Associate Dean
Division of Special Education
and Rehabilitation
University of Oregon

Karen C. Wells, Ph.D.
Associate Professor, Children's
Hospital
*George Washington University School
of Medicine*

Michael D. Wesolowski, Ph.D.
Director of Special Education
and Vocational Rehabilitation
University of Alabama in Birmingham

C. Chrisman Wilson, Ph.D.
Associate Professor
Tulane University

Richard A. Winett, Ph.D.
Professor, Department of Psychology
*Virginia Polytechnic Institute and
State University*

Richard J. Zawlocki, M.A.
Research Instructor
*West Virginia Rehabilitation Research
and Training Center
West Virginia University*

Contents

PART ONE

Conceptual Dimensions in
Child Behavior Therapy

1

Alternative Approaches to the Diagnosis of Childhood Disorders*

Alan E. Kazdin
Western Psychiatric Institute and Clinic
University of Pittsburgh School of Medicine

INTRODUCTION

The delineation of childhood disorders raises a host of issues in research and clinical practice. There is consensus on a few general propositions regarding the study of deviant child behavior. There is agreement that children can evince seriously deviant behavior, that developmental considerations are relevant in viewing behavior, that the context in which children develop (e.g., family, social relations) have bearing on adjustment, and that deviance in childhood may portend problems in adulthood. Beyond the general statements, considerable differences exist in the views of how deviant behavior should be conceptualized, identified, and treated.

Differences in approaches toward childhood disorders are clearly reflected in the area of diagnosis. Diagnosis, defined generally, refers to how problem behaviors will be viewed and delineated. Diagnosis is an initial stage of the clinical process leading to treatment and prediction of outcome. More than that, diagnosis is central to understanding multiple facets of deviance, such as etiology and clinical course. Three general approaches can be identified and include clinically derived, empirically derived, and behavioral diagnosis.

* Completion of this chapter was facilitated by a Research Scientist Development Award (MH00353) and a grant (MH35408) from the National Institute of Mental Health.

The purpose of the present chapter is to discuss these different approaches toward diagnosis of childhood disorders. Within each approach, major diagnostic systems are elaborated to convey basic characteristics and underlying conceptual issues. Major attention is accorded the different purposes to which alternative systems are aimed and the advantages and limitations each reflects. Alternative approaches are also illustrated concretely and discussed in the context of treatment of childhood dysfunction.

CLINICALLY DERIVED PSYCHIATRIC DIAGNOSIS

Clinically derived diagnosis has referred generally to the categorical or typological approach toward classification that has characterized psychiatric diagnosis. The approach relies on clinical observations and experience. From these observations, abstractions are drawn to identify discrete diagnostic entities. Clinically derived systems have been developed by the American Psychiatric Association (APA; 1952, 1968, 1980), the Group for the Advancement of Psychiatry (1966), and the World Health Organization (e.g., Rutter, Shaffer, & Shepherd, 1975). Within the United States, contemporary psychiatric diagnosis is based on the third edition of the *Diagnostic and Statistical Manual of Mental Disorders* (DSM-III, APA, 1980). Disorders and the symptoms of which they are comprised are regarded as present or absent. The task of diagnosis is to identify which symptoms are present, if any, and then to assign and rule out the presence of alternative disorders.

Historical Overview

The historical context and underpinnings of DSM-III entail consideration of the classification of physical and mental disorders more generally, emerging views and treatments of childhood dysfunction, and evolution of the DSM (see Dreger, 1981, 1982; Kazdin, 1983). For present purposes, the historical features that warrant special mention pertain to concerns over the diagnostic process and the events leading to DSM-III.

A continued concern among proponents and critics of the DSM has been the low reliability of psychiatric diagnosis (see Matarazzo, 1983). A major source of unreliability is the variability among practitioners in invoking diagnoses. The task of the clinician in reaching a diagnosis is twofold; namely, to decide what symptoms are present and to apply rules for reaching a diagnosis. Significant advances have emerged in both areas.

Of special relevance to the development of DSM-III are the efforts to develop clear criteria for reaching a diagnosis. In the early 1970s, a group of researchers at Washington University published diagnostic criteria for use in psychiatric research (Feighner et al., 1972). The criteria were designed so that researchers could use a common set of definitions for select disorders. Only a small number of disorders ($n = 16$) were included for which the authors believed that sufficient validity evidence existed. The criteria were proposed to permit identification of homogeneous clinic populations for research. For a particular disorder to be diagnosed, specific core symptoms and a select set of symptoms from a larger list needed to be present.

The significance of the development of the "Feighner criteria," as they came to be called, must be seen in the context of DSM-II in effect at that time. Diagnosis had relied on clinical judgment in matching patients to general descriptions of a disorder. Apart from the unreliability of the procedure, the likelihood of identifying homogeneous populations was remote. The Feighner criteria were expanded with the same goal in mind; namely, to provide investigators with a consistent set of criteria for describing subjects with functional psychiatric disorders. The expanded criteria, referred to as the Research Diagnostic Criteria (RDC; Spitzer, Endicott, & Robins, 1978), have been revised at different points to reflect clinical experience and data from research findings.

The Feighner criteria and RDC were significant developments for different reasons. Both sets of criteria reflect dissatisfaction within psychiatry with the lack of explicit diagnostic criteria and the poor reliability of assigning patients to categories. Specification of the diagnostic criteria attempts to overcome these problems. In addition, the approach of the Feighner criteria and RDC served as the model for developing DSM-III. Specific criteria in DSM-III were adopted from RDC for many diagnostic categories. The same operational model was selected so that a diagnosis depends on the presence of some core symptom(s) plus a subset of additional symptoms from a larger list. The model was adopted for several disorders not covered by RDC.[1] The critical point is that DSM-III followed on the heels of RDC and utilized specific descriptive criteria for reaching psychiatric diagnoses.

The development of specific criteria for applying diagnosis addressed the major source of unreliability in the diagnostic process. Another potential source of unreliability is the means of obtaining the information about the patient's symptoms. DSM-III requires the assessment of many different areas of functioning and the application of inclusion and exclusion criteria to reach a diagnosis. Structured and semistructured interviews have been developed to obtain the necessary information to reach a diagnosis. Prominent among these efforts in assessment with adults have been the Present State Examination (Wing, Cooper, & Sartorius, 1974), the Schedule for Affective Disorders and Schizophrenia (Endicott & Spitzer, 1978), and the Diagnostic Interview Schedule (Robins

---

[1] RDC was developed primarily for researchers and is restricted to a limited set of functional disorders. For research purposes, interest is in studying characteristics of homogeneous groups of patients. High priority is given to minimizing false positives (i.e., identifying cases who do not have the dysfunction). In contrast, DSM-III is designed to address the exigencies and diversity of clinical practice. Hence, DSM-III includes a broad range of diagnostic categories including organic disorders. Also, in DSM-III a diagnosis can be made even if the clinician does not have sufficient information that full criteria are met.

et al., 1981). In the child arena, interviews have emerged, including the Schedule for Affective Disorders and Schizophrenia for School-age Children (Chambers, Puig-Antich, & Tabrizi, 1978), the Diagnostic Interview for Children and Adolescents (Herjanic, 1980), the Child Assessment Schedule (Hodges et al., 1982), and the Diagnostic Interview Schedule for Children (Radloff, 1980). These interviews are designed to obtain information reliably for purposes of diagnosis. Little research has appeared focusing on the reliability of the interviews for diagnosing childhood disorders (Hodges et al., 1982; Orvaschel et al., 1982).

This brief overview highlights the concern and activity within psychiatry over reliability of assessment of psychiatric dysfunction and operationalization of diagnostic criteria. Related efforts to augment reliability of diagnosis could be cited as well, such as the use of computer programs to apply algorithms to reach diagnoses (e.g., Spitzer & Endicott, 1969; Wing et al., 1974) and the use of decision trees to help reach DSM-III diagnoses (APA, 1980), to mention a few.

Characteristics of DSM-III

There are several noteworthy characteristics of DSM-III. First, the system attempts to be generally atheoretical. Emphasis is placed on presenting symptoms rather than presumed etiology.[2] Reference is made to the *descriptive features* and *phenomenology* of the disorder to refer to the symptoms, behaviors, or sources of dysfunction actually presented by the client with minimal interpretation on the part of the clinician. The descriptive features include the current clinical picture as well as the course of the symptoms over time. The non-etiological, descriptive approach is based on the view that clinicians are more likely to agree on presenting symptoms or problems than they are on etiology. Also, a descriptive approach acknowledges that disorders can be explained by diverse conceptual positions. A diagnostic system designed to describe clinical dysfunction should provide basic information compatible with different theoretical views.

Second, an attempt is made to provide a comprehensive description of each disorder by including essential and correlated features, age of onset, course, impairment, predisposing factors, prevalence, familial patterns, and requirements for differential diagnosis. Because DSM-III delineates several new categories of dysfunction, little information is available for many disorders, particularly for children and adolescents.

Third, specific diagnostic criteria are provided for each disorder. The criteria may include different types of information, such as the presence of key symptoms, a subset of additional symptoms, duration of dysfunction, absence of

---

[2] DSM-III does consider etiology in cases in which it is known, as in organic mental disorders and some forms of mental retardation.

other disorders, and so on. The specific criteria for most disorders are based on clinical judgment. Yet, the hope is that specification of the criteria for the disorders will permit self-correction as the evidence accumulates.

Fourth, the system is multiaxial, a major distinguishing characteristic in comparison to previous versions of the DSM. Multiaxial diagnosis recognizes that several different facets of the presenting problem and its related circumstances are clinically relevant. The multiple axes or dimensions are designed to provide a comprehensive way of diagnosing and evaluating disorders, to improve diagnostic agreement by separating different dimensions to direct attention to different facets of the individual, and to facilitate examination of different dimensions in research. The multiaxial system grew out of the work of the World Health Organization (Rutter et al., 1975). Field tests showed that a multiaxial diagnosis was superior to unicategorical diagnosis, especially in diagnosing cases in which psychiatric disorder was associated with physical illness and/or mental retardation. In complex cases in particular, different facets of functioning are likely to be overlooked in favor of florid psychiatric symptoms.

A DSM-III multiaxial diagnosis consists of obtaining information on five axes (see Table 1–1). Axis I (Clinical Psychiatric Syndromes and Other Conditions) includes the majority of "mental disorders" in DSM-III and provides the main delineation of impairment. For Axis I, the clinician must decide if there is a disorder, multiple disorders, or no disorder. The first disorder listed typically is the most prominent area of impairment. Not all Axis I diagnoses are regarded as disorders. Some conditions, not regarded as mental disorders, are coded here if they require treatment attention or account for the basis of referral. Such conditions are delineated as V Codes and include academic problems, parent-child problems, marital problems, malingering, and others. A V code is used if no identifiable disorder is evident but there is a problem that brought the child and/or the parents to treatment.[3]

Axis II (Personality Disorders and Specific Developmental Disorders) is designed to provide information about the prominent personality traits or characteristics that seem relevant to understanding the individual's functioning (e.g., compulsiveness). For children, developmental disorders or specific problems in areas such as reading and arithmetic are listed. This axis is included so that significant aspects of performance other than psychiatric disorders are not overlooked when attention is directed toward the Axis 1 condition that usually accounts for the patient coming to clinical attention.

Axis III (Physical Disorders and Conditions) acknowledges that one's physical health may have important implications for the overall diagnostic picture. Many persons with psychiatric impairment may have organic problems that are relevant for understanding and managing the case (e.g., seizures, diabetes).

---

[3] The V codes are adapted from the International Classification of Diseases (9th ed.).

TABLE 1–1

Multiaxial System Included in DSM III

Axis I Clinical Syndromes and Other Conditions Not Necessarily Attributable to a Disorder but Serve as the Focus of Treatment

This axis includes the majority of disorders with the exception of personality disorders and specific developmental disorders.

Axis II Personality Disorders (usually adults) and Specific Developmental Disorders (usually children and adolescents)

Codes for dominant personality styles or specific developmental problems.

Axis III Physical Disorders and Conditions

Physical health and specific physical disorders or conditions that may be relevant to understanding or managing the case.

Axis IV Severity of Psychosocial Stressors

Psychosocial events that may contribute to the development or exacerbation of the disorder. Problems at home, school, or in social relations; loss of or separation from parents.

Axis V Highest Level of Adaptive Functioning During Past Year

Individuals performance in social relations, school, leisure time that indicate highest level of functioning (for a few month period).

Occasionally, Axis II may reveal complications of Axis I diagnoses (e.g., neurological impairment or gastritis resulting from alcoholism).

Axis IV (Severity of Psychosocial Stressors) identifies psychosocial events that may contribute to the development or exacerbation of the primary diagnosis. The clinician rates the overall severity of stressors judged to be significant contributors to the development or exacerbation of the current disorder. A rating is made on a 7-point scale for severity (1 = none, 7 = catastrophic) based on the number and type of stressful events and their impact. Several stressors are considered, such as loss of a nuclear family member, foster placement, and physical abuse.

Axis V (Highest Level of Adaptive Functioning During Past Year) is designed to reflect how well a person is functioning. Three areas are combined into a single 7-point rating (1 = superior, 7 = grossly impaired). The areas include social relations, occupational or school functioning, and use of leisure time. The rating is designed to assess the highest level of functioning and is included because of its prognostic significance for the person's adjustment.

In general, Axes I and II include all of the mental disorders or dysfunctions. Axis III includes physical disorders and conditions. The first three axes constitute the official diagnostic evaluation. Axes IV and V are designed to provide additional information for planning treatment, managing the case, and predicting outcome.

Critical Underlying Concepts

Diagnostic Levels of Understanding.   Several key concepts underlie psychiatric diagnosis and reflect different levels in the understanding of clinical problems. They are important to make explicit because they are frequently misunderstood and partially serve as the basis for conceptual and professional disputes about the nature of psychiatric diagnosis. The first concept that illustrates the point is that of a *symptom*. In current psychiatric diagnosis, a symptom refers to the presence of a particular overt behavior, affect, cognition, perception, or other sign. Symptoms do not necessarily imply an underlying intrapsychic etiology, a physical disease model, symptom substitution, or related notions. In current use in DSM III, symptoms refer to description of the presenting problem.

Symptoms refer to the lowest level of analysis in the conceptualization of psychiatric dysfunction. Beyond symptoms, the next level of analysis is that of a *syndrome* or constellation of symptoms that occur together and covary over time. A syndrome refers to several symptoms and may involve multiple behaviors, affects, cognitions, and perceptions in any combination. The notion of a syndrome is not based on a disease model but simply refers to the fact that certain behaviors, broadly defined, may co-occur. Whether they do is an empirical matter. Indeed, research has consistently identified multiple behaviors that often go together (e.g., Achenbach & Edelbrock, 1978; Quay, 1979, in press).

A third level of understanding in psychiatric diagnosis is reflected in the notion of *disorder*. The concept is close to that of a syndrome because it refers to a cluster of symptoms that go together. However, more information is needed beyond the clustering of symptoms. The concept of a disorder entails the fact that the syndrome cannot be accounted for by a more pervasive condition. That is, evidence exists that the constellation of symptoms is useful to view as independent of other, more general conditions. The evidence may consist of information about the natural course of the disorder, family history, biological correlates, and response to treatment.

The concept of a disorder depends on the hierarchical organization of diagnosis within DMS-III. Disorders are considered to vary in their inclusiveness of symptoms. Thus, some of the diagnostic classes are organized into hierarchies so that a class higher in the hierarchy may have features found in classes that are lower in the hierarchy (Spitzer & Williams, 1980). For example, affective disorders hierarchically come ahead of anxiety disorders because all of the manifestations of anxiety disorders can occur in persons with affective disorders, but the reverse is not true. Similarly, dementia (an organic brain syndrome) comes hierarchically before schizophrenia because the manifestations of schizophrenia (e.g., delusions, hallucinations) can occur in persons with organic mental disorder, although again, the reverse is not true. The hierarchical arrangement of diagnosis helps define a disorder which consists of a syndrome that cannot be explained or encompassed by a dysfunction of a higher level.

The fourth level of understanding in conceptualizing problems is reflected in the notion of *disease*. Although this is *not* the focus of DSM-III, the concept warrants mention because of the controversy it stirs when discussed in the context of behavior therapy. The notion of disease is invoked for a disorder where there is a specific known etiology and an identifiable underlying (pathophysiological) process. Forms of organic impairment and mental retardation (e.g., Down's syndrome) meet the criteria for disease for the level of understanding of these disorders. In such cases, the criteria for disorder are met along with additional information about the etiology and pathophysiology. The disease concept is not implicit in DSM-III categories with some exceptions mentioned above. DSM-III focuses on syndromes and disorders. There is no presumption inherent in DSM-III that biological abnormalities have caused the conditions that are enumerated. And if a specific and treatable biological etiology were identified, it is likely that the abnormality would be removed from the class of mental disorders and conceptualized as a physical disorder, as in the case of general paresis (Spitzer & Williams, 1980). The main point here is to note that DSM-III is not involved with the classification of diseases and does not assume that disorders do or eventually will meet the criteria of disease.

Dimensions of Dysfunction.　A critical feature of psychiatric diagnosis is the evaluation of multiple dimensions of dysfunction beyond the presenting problem or target behavior. To begin with, diagnosis of psychiatric disorder requires that the person meet criteria for *severity* and *breadth* of dysfunction. Severity may refer to evidence that the person's everyday functioning is impaired or attested to by the duration of dysfunction. Breadth of dysfunction usually is defined by the constellation of symptoms. Both severity and breadth usually go together for a diagnosis to be made. For example, to invoke a diagnosis of major depressive episode in DSM-III, the patient must evince several symptoms (breadth of dysfunction) and evince these symptoms nearly every day for a period of at least two weeks (severity of dysfunction).

For a diagnosis to be applied, information about the *duration* of the problem and nature of its *onset* may also be required. For example, for a diagnosis of conduct disorder, a child must have shown the problem behaviors for at least six months. Similarly, the onset of the dysfunction may be entailed by the diagnosis. For example, depressive symptoms (e.g., sad affect, loss of interest in activities, sleep disorder) would be diagnosed and treated differently if they arose abruptly in response to a clear environmental event (death of a relative), if they developed gradually with no identifiable precipitant, or if they alternated with periods of heightened excitability. As a dimension of dysfunction, the duration of the problem and the manner in which it developed may be relevant to treatment and prognosis (e.g., Gossett et al., 1977).

Contextual and related factors are important to know in diagnosing clinical problems, perhaps especially for children and adolescents because of their dependence on the family, home living conditions, and relations with parents.

Different contextual factors that relate to the presenting problem are entailed by a DSM-III diagnosis. Specific developmental disorders (Axis II), medical problems (Axis III), stressors (Axis IV), and adaptive functioning (Axis V) are considered within the multiaxial diagnosis. Alone or in combination, these dimensions may be relevant for treatment and long-term prognosis. For example, children with a similar Axis I diagnosis may need to be treated differently depending on contextual factors such as stressors (e.g., foster placement, single-parent family, school adjustment).

The above dimensions reflect sensitivity to a variety of factors within psychiatric diagnosis. The dimensions help define the problem, place it into a larger context, and suggest relevant considerations that may have impact for treatment and prognosis. Although consideration of the dimensions is laudatory within current diagnostic practices, the criteria for selecting particular decision-making points and methods for obtaining the relevant information to evaluate various dimensions are wanting. In many cases, fixed criteria are embraced without a clear justification. For example, a child must be of a certain age or have evinced the problem for a particular period to receive a diagnosis. Rigid boundaries for defining disorders are rarely justified on empirical grounds (e.g., one must be three years old to obtain a diagnosis of oppositional disorder). Similarly, the measurement of stressors and highest level of adaptive functioning (Axes IV and V) is not standardized. Thus, reliability of invoking particular ratings, leaving aside their validity and utility, remains in question. Nevertheless, the significant point is that diagnosis embraces several dimensions beyond the presenting target problem. Although there may be great heterogeneity of symptoms within a diagnostic category, invoking an Axis I diagnosis often conveys information about several facets of the problem, such as minimal duration, severity, breadth, and onset. Other axes specify additional factors that are not usually encompassed by other diagnostic systems.

Evaluation of DSM-III

Advantages and Special Features.   There are several advantages to DSM-III and the sort of system it represents for delineating disorders. Briefly, the system considers multiple facets of clinical dysfunction as reflected by the different axes. Also, invoking a particular diagnosis (Axis I) itself conveys considerable information about the dysfunction, such as the severity, breadth, duration, onset, and precipitants of the problem. To be sure, there may be considerable diversity among patients with a given diagnosis. Thus, two conduct disordered children may differ sharply—one may have a 10-year history of firesetting, truancy, and stealing; the other may have a six-month history of physical aggression and tantrums. To many, these dysfunctions may be viewed as fundamentally similar problems. At the concrete level rather than at a higher order level of abstraction, the presenting concerns and target behaviors are quite different. Nevertheless, the diagnosis entails some commonalities and shared parameters. The heterogeneity of the persons with a given diagnosis and various disorder subtypes raises important conceptual and empirical questions yet to be resolved. The important advantage of DSM-III is not that it has identified "true diagnostic" entities for children and adolescents at this time but that the system directs attention to multiple aspects of functioning that are relevant to understanding disorders and their treatment.

Issues and Limitations.   Many limitations and criticisms have been discussed in relation to DSM-III, and these are far too numerous to treat fairly here (see Garmezy, 1978; Rutter & Shaffer, 1980; Schacht & Nathan, 1977). A few major points appear to be fundamental to the goals of DSM-III. To begin with, concerns have been expressed that diagnostic categories continue to proliferate. The present DSM-III includes approximately 265 disorders, a substantial increase over the number in DSM-II (over 180) and DSM-I (over 105). Many of the new disorders have no firm empirical evidence in their behalf. For example oppositional disorder and identity disorder for children and adolescents are proposed. Although the behaviors encompassed by these diagnoses are evident, whether they form a syndrome or disorder is not clear.

A related concern is that DSM-III has been extended into new areas not usually regarded as within the purview of psychiatry. Developmental disabilities (coded in Axis II) relate to delays in areas such as reading, arithmetic, and language. Dysfunctions in these areas typically have not been regarded as "mental disorders" but as special problems within the realm of education and communication. In fact, such delays are occasionally correlated with psychiatric impairment (e.g., reading delays in conduct disorder children). Their inclusion within DSM-III reflects concern that dysfunctional behavior in such areas is often overlooked when attention is devoted to psychiatric symptomatology. Axis II demands that such dysfunctions be considered because they may be relevant to treatment and case management. Nevertheless, a major concern is that children with specific developmental delays might be diagnosed and stigmatized as having mental disorders (Garmezy, 1978; Rutter & Shaffer, 1980).

Another issue pertains to the reliability of reaching a diagnosis, a perennial issue within psychiatric diagnosis. The use of a multiaxial diagnostic system has been shown in field tests of the International Classification of Diseases (ICD, 9th ed.) and DSM-III to enhance clinical agreement, especially in complex clinical cases. However, research on the diagnosis of childhood disorders has not been particularly encouraging to date. Agreement on Axis I diagnosis for children still tends to be relatively low and not clearly superior to that of DSM-II (Cantwell et al., 1979; Mattison et al., 1979; Quay, in press). Consistent with previous research, agreements tend to be higher for major categories within DSM-III (Mattison et al., 1979; Williams & Spitzer, 1980). Reliability data evaluating the ICD-9 suggests that more diagnostic categories are available than can be reliably assessed (Sturge, Shaffer, & Rutter, 1977). DSM-III has even more subdivisions than the ICD-9 and, *a fortiori,* should present greater problems in reliable diagnosis.

A large number of other criticisms and concerns have been levied including the manner in which mental retardation is incorporated into the diagnosis, the definition and assessment of stressors, use of specific but arbitrary diagnostic criteria relating to duration of dysfunction or age of onset when either no evidence or conflicting evidence exists, the failure to consider the child's social functioning more prominently, and others (Benjamin, 1981; Garmezy, 1978; Quay, 1979; Rutter & Shaffer, 1980; Yule, 1981).

General Comments

Overall, DSM-III reflects the state of the art in clinically derived diagnosis. The system has evolved from clinical experience, yet the diagnostic categories themselves have been influenced by research. The special feature of DSM-III to make salient is the importance of research in refining diagnostic categories. By defining disorders in descriptive terms and specifying criteria for reaching a diagnosis, the system can be more readily evaluated and improved upon by research than was heretofore possible.

EMPIRICALLY DERIVED (MULTIVARIATE) DIAGNOSIS

Multivariate approaches to diagnosis are designed to describe the organization of symptoms or behaviors empirically (see Blashfield, 1984). As with nosological classification, a major goal is to identify syndromes. Yet, the underlying approach is quite different. Multivariate approaches are fundamentally dimensional rather than categorical. The degree to which a particular symptom or syndrome (factor) is evident in a child can be specified quantitatively in some way. The assessment approaches do not lead to the statement that a person has a particular diagnostic entity. Rather, one can describe the degree to which several charactertistics are evident. At any point in the quantification of dysfunction, criterion points can be identified to establish groups or to classify nosological types. However, even when typologies are devised, the product is quantitatively based and, in many ways, still reflects a dimensional approach.

Historical Overview

The beginning of empirically based systems for children can be traced to analyses of case history data in the early 1940s (see Dreger, 1981). In a seminal study, Ackerson (1942) identified 125 behavioral problems recorded in the case records of over 3,000 boys and girls (ages 6–17) and computed their intercorrelations. The correlational analyses reflected an initial attempt to identify behaviors that go together. Using this data pool, Jenkins and Glickman

(1946) identified larger groups of symptoms. This was accomplished by computing correlations between symptoms and adding a new symptom to the group if it correlated at some minimal level with the initial items. New items were added to a given group of items only if they continued to meet the criterion. From this method of grouping items, several constellations of symptoms or syndromes emerged (overinhibited, socialized delinquent, unsocialized aggressive, brain injured, and schizoid). Other work using correlational analyses and case history information yielded similar sorts of constellations (e.g., Hewett & Jenkins, 1946).

The application of factor analyses to identify dimensions was an obvious advance (e.g., Achenbach, 1966; Lorr & Jenkins, 1953). Data from case histories and reports by parents, teachers, and mental health workers on standardized measures were increasingly subjected to factor analyses (e.g., Borgatta & Fanshel, 1965; Collins, Maxwell, & Cameron, 1962; Lessing & Zagorin, 1971; Spivack & Levine, 1964). Teachers and parents have been used frequently as raters for these analyses, and individual measures emerged with frequently replicated factor analyses.

As one example, the Behavior Problem Checklist (Quay & Peterson, 1979) is a frequently used measure to evaluate child behavior. The initial investigation leading to the development of the current version was conducted by Peterson (1961) who sampled referral problems of over 400 clinical case records from a child guidance clinic. Items describing deviant behavior were selected for a problem checklist scale and were evaluated by teacher ratings of over 800 normal students (grades K–6). The resulting factor analysis yielded two independent dimensions; namely, conduct problem and personality problem. These reflect major dimensions that may be summarized by aggression and withdrawal, respectively. After several studies across different samples, raters, and settings, the scale has been revised and consists of three replicated factors (conduct problem, personality problem, inadequacy/immaturity). Other factor subscales (socialized delinquency and psychotic behaviors) have been devised for the checklist based on clinic records or *a priori* considerations, but they have not emerged consistently in factor analyses.[4]

A plethora of rating scales and checklists have been administered to parents and teachers to evaluate both nonreferred and clinic samples of children (see Achenbach & Edelbrock, 1978; Dreger, 1982). The measures usually reflect a large spectrum of symptoms. The general approach has been similar, albeit the measures to which it has been applied are numerous. The approach consists of having a rater (parent, teacher, clinician) evaluate children on multiple items of a scale that reflects problems, symptoms, or other characteristics. The results from a large number of children are subjected to factor analysis. The factors that

---

[4] The Behavior Problem Checklist has recently been revised and extended from 55 items to 150 items. The additional items are designed to expand the items of existing factors and to assess new factors (Quay & Peterson, 1983).

are replicated across samples and even factor solutions are regarded as reliable ways of organizing childhood symptoms. Of course, the yield from such analyses can vary as a function of characteristics of the raters or ratees, the measure used, the situation in which performance is evaluated (e.g., school or home), and so on. There have been important consistencies in the results despite the different ways in which the investigations and analyses have been conducted, as discussed below.

Characteristics

Syndromes and Typologies. Multivariate approaches toward classification attempt to determine which behaviors or symptoms go together. These constellations of symptoms or syndromes are derived empirically. Factor analyses identify these syndromes (correlated behaviors) and illustrate the dimensional approach. Rather than determining the presence or absence of a syndrome or disorder, a child can be assigned a position varying in degree on each dimension (factor) of the measure. Since rating scales typically include multiple factors, a child has a score on several dimensions. A profile of the individual child can be determined by looking at the scores on all dimensions.

Factor analysis provides information on the covariation among specific items or behaviors within a particular measure. By itself, the analysis of the factor structure of a given scale does not provide information to characterize individual children. Yet, information on the syndromes obtained from factor analyses can be used as the basis for constructing diagnostic categories or typologies. Cluster analysis is a set of procedures that can be used to move from factor scores to a typology. Through cluster analysis, one can identify persons with similar profiles; i.e., patterns of scores across the different factors or syndromes. Ideally, cluster analysis attempts to identify a finite group of clusters that are mutually exclusive and jointly exhaustive. Once clusters are identified, individuals can be diagnosed (assigned to a cluster type) by assessing the extent to which their profiles resemble a cluster. This match can be evaluated quantitatively (e.g., through correlation). The cluster-based typologies focus on diagnostic entities or disorders somewhat analogous to nosological classification. However, the extent to which an individual's profile on the measure matches cluster type often can be specified as a matter of degree.

Illustration. The number of different measures used for multivariate classification of children is extensive (see Achenbach & Edelbrock, 1978; Quay, in press). The general approach and the informational yield can be conveyed by illustrating recent work on the Child Behavior Checklist (CBCL; Achenbach, 1978; Achenbach & Edelbrock, 1981). The measure has been designed to be completed by parents, although different versions have emerged for teachers and children. The measure includes 118 items that refer to behavior problems, each of which is rated on a 3-point scale (0 = not true, 2 = very or often true). The measure has been evaluated with normal and clinically referred samples. Factor analyses have been completed separately by gender and age groups (4–5, 6–11, and 12–16-years-olds). Thus, although the same items appear in the measure, the factors that emerge vary by these groupings. Apart from the psychopathology scales, the CBCL includes three social competence scales that have been defined *a priori* (activities, social, and school scales). These scales reflect positive social behaviors in which individuals engage.

The factors that have emerged from analyses of boys and girls in the separate age groups are summarized in Table 1–2. The table is organized by second-order (broad-band) factors, referred to as internalizing and externalizing syndromes. First-order factors that comprise these broader dimensions are listed under the headings in the table. For example, for boys ages 6–11, the first-order factors include schizoid, depressed, uncommunicative, obsessive-compulsive, and somatic complaints. These factors reflect overcontrolled or inner-directed problems and load on the broad-band *internalizing* factor. The first-order factors of delinquent, aggressive, and hyperactive reflect undercontrolled or acting-out problems and load on the broad-band *externalizing* factor. (For boys 6–11, the first-order factor of social withdrawal loaded moderately on both internalizing and externalizing scales (Achenbach, 1978) and consequently is considered to reflect mixed psychopathology.)

To provide a complete picture of the child, a profile that consists of the child's score on each of the first-order factors can be drawn. The profile reflects how much of each syndrome (first-order factor) the child shows. Based on normative data from nonclinic and clinic samples, factor scores have been normalized with a mean of 50 and standard deviation of 10. Separate transformed (T) scores are available using normative and clinic samples depending on the interest of the researcher. The T scores can be readily interpreted across age and gender groupings and across factors because of the common metric.

Cluster analyses have been performed for CBCL data to devise a typology based on profile types. Edelbrock and Achenbach (1980) evaluated profiles of over 2,600 children ages 6–16. Using hierarchical clustering procedures, profile types were identified for boys and girls in different age groups. For example, for boys 6–11, the following profile types (clusters) were identified: schizoid-social withdrawal, depressed-social withdrawal, schizoid, somatic complaints, hyperactive, and delinquent. Some of these can be combined to form higher order clusters. A child can be classified (assigned to a cluster) based on his profile. The assignment is determined by objective criteria (in this case, intraclass correlation). The criteria that are used in the analyses to identify clusters initially and to determine assignment of profiles to clusters require judgments. However, once the criteria are set, the process of diagnosis is relatively judgment free.

Consistencies among Alternative Analyses.   Efforts to identify syndromes empirically have utilized a wide array of measures, raters, clinical samples, and

TABLE 1-2

Syndromes Found through Factor Analysis of the Child Behavior Checklist

group	internalizing syndromes*	mixed syndromes	externalizing syndromes*
Boys aged 4–5	1. Social withdrawal 2. Depressed 3. Immature 4. Somatic complaints	1. Sex problems	1. Delinquent 2. Aggressive 3. Schizoid
Boys aged 6–11	1. Schizoid 2. Depressed 3. Uncommunicative 4. Obsessive-compulsive 5. Somatic complaints	1. Social withdrawal	1. Delinquent 2. Aggressive 3. Hyperactive
Boys aged 12–16	1. Somatic complaints 2. Schizoid 3. Uncommunicative 4. Immature 5. Obsessive-compulsive	1. Hostile withdrawal	1. Hyperactive 2. Aggressive 3. Delinquent
Girls aged 4–5	1. Depressed 2. Somatic complaints 3. Schizoid or anxious 4. Social withdrawal	1. Obese	1. Hyperactive 2. Sex problems 3. Aggressive
Girls aged 6–11	1. Depressed 2. Social withdrawal 3. Somatic complaints 4. Schizoid-obsessive		1. Cruel 2. Aggressive 3. Delinquent 4. Sex problems 5. Hyperactive
Girls aged 12–16	1. Anxious-obsessive 2. Somatic complaints 3. Schizoid 4. Depressed withdrawal	1. Immature hyperactive	1. Cruel 2. Aggressive 3. Delinquent

* Syndromes are listed in descending order of their loadings on the second-order internalizing and externalizing factors.

Source: T. M. Achenbach and C. S. Edelbrock, *Manual for the Child Behavior Checklist and revised Child Behavior Profile.* University of Vermont; Author, 1983. (p. 16)

methods of data analyses. Consequently, one might expect few consistencies across studies. However, reviews of multivariate studies have identified several similarities among many different investigations of children (see Achenbach & Edelbrock, 1978; Quay, 1979, in press). Studies have found consistencies both at the level of broad- and narrow-band factors. At the level of broad-band factors, two different types of clusters have consistently emerged that are characterized generally by acting out and inhibited types of performance. These factors have been referred to in diverse ways, such as undercontrolled or externalizing behavior (aggressive, conduct disorder and hyperactive, and delinquent behaviors) and overcontrolled or internalizing behavior (inhibited, shy, depressed, and anxious behaviors). Other broad-band factors have emerged occasionally (e.g., pathological detachment), but they have not been consistently replicated across studies (Achenbach & Edelbrock, 1978).

Among first-order factors, several studies have found syndromes that have been labeled aggressive, delinquent, hyperactive, schizoid, anxiety disorder, depression, social withdrawal, somatic complaints, uncommunicative, immature, and obsessive-compulsive behavior. These syndromes (factors) have been found but are not all equally robust across samples. And, as mentioned previously, the factors that emerge may vary considerably as a function of child age and gender (Achenbach & Edelbrock, 1981). Few studies have reported analyses taking into account these moderating variables. Those factors that have emerged relatively consistently across age and gender and samples that have been identified by Quay (in press) are presented in Table 1–3. The syndromes and six characteristics that reflect the item content of each factor are also illustrated. The most robust syndromes, based on the extent to which they

---

TABLE 1–3

Replicated Dimensions Arising in Multivariate Statistical Analyses with Six Frequently Associated Characteristics of Each

conduct disorder	*socialized aggression*
Fighting, hitting	Has "bad" companions
Disobedient, defiant	Truant from home
Temper tantrums	Truant from school
Destructiveness	Steals in company with others
Impertinent, impudent	Loyal to delinquent friends
Uncooperative, resistant	Belongs to a gang
attention problems	*anxious–depressed withdrawal*
Poor concentration, short attention span	Anxious, fearful, tense
Daydreaming	Shy, timid, bashful
Clumsy, poor coordination	Withdrawn, seclusive
Preoccupied, stares into space	Depressed, sad, disturbed
Fails to finish, lacks perseverance	Hypersensitive, easily hurt
Impulsive	Feels inferior, worthless
motor overactivity	*schizoid–unresponsive*
Restless, overactive	Won't talk
Excitable, impulsive	Withdrawn
Squirmy, jittery	Sad
Overtalkative	Stares blankly
Hams and makes other odd noises	Confused

Source: H. C. Quay, "A Critical Analysis of DSM-III as a Taxonomy of Psychopathology in Childhood and Adolescence," in *Contemporary Issues in Psychopathology,* ed. T. Millon and G. Klerman (New York: Guilford Press, in press).

have emerged across studies, are conduct disorder, attention problems, and anxious-depressed-withdrawal.

The syndromes identified above refer to covariation of items derived through factor analyses. Cluster analyses to identify a typology of childhood disorders have been much less frequently used than factor analyses. Even so, some consistencies have emerged. For example, as noted earlier, Edelbrock and Achenbach (1980) identified the following clusters for boys ages 6–11 based on parent ratings of the CBCL: schizoid-social withdrawal, depressed-social withdrawal, schizoid, somatic complaints, hyperactive, and delinquent. Using the CBCL and sampling children 4- to 15-years-old, Soli et al. (1981) found several clusters for males including learning problems, hyperactive behavior, somatic regulatory deficit, anxiety-depression, delinquency, and rebelliousness. The overlap in clusters related to aggression-delinquency, anxiety-depression, and hyperactivity is particularly encouraging given the differences in clinical samples, methods, and criteria for the cluster analyses.

Using a different parent-completed measure (Institute of Juvenile Research Checklist), Lessing et al. (1982) evaluated normal, inpatient, and outpatient samples of children (ages 4–17). Seven different clusters emerged and included: high asset profile (i.e., no pathology—normal sample), sociopathic-academic problems, moderate asset-egocentric-incontinent, insecure-somaticizing-under-achieving, aggressive-overreactive, schizoid-withdrawn-anxious, and diffuse (mixed) pathology. Again, some clusters corroborated other analyses highlighted above.

There are differences that have emerged from different analyses. For example, Edelbrock and Achenbach (1980) found a cluster for a delinquent type. This cluster did not emerge in the research by Lessing et al. (1982). The clinical facilities from which the samples were drawn in this latter study did not serve delinquents, which no doubt contributed to the different results. Similarly, diffuse psychopathology (mixed syndrome) did not consistently emerge in the analyses by Edelbrock and Achenbach (1980). On the other hand, this cluster emerged in the study by Lessing et al. (1982) and accounted for a sizable portion (25.4 percent) of clinical cases. These differences may have been attributed to the use of inpatient samples in this latter study in that multiple and diffuse symptomatology is more likely than in outpatient cases.

A few considerations need to be acknowledged in highlighting similarities and differences in the factors and clusters that emerge in cross-study comparisons. First, among different studies, similar or identical names for factors and clusters do not necessarily reflect identical content of items or profiles. The labels generally reflect the same sorts of problems but often differ in specific characteristics (Nuechterlein et al., 1981; Soli et al., 1981). Nevertheless, it is important to look beyond the factor and cluster names to understand the genuine consistencies in symptoms across samples. Another point to acknowledge is that factor analyses and cluster analyses can vary widely. The same data (i.e., interitem correlations, profiles on factors) can yield quite different factors or clusters, respectively, based on a variety of decisions, solutions, and criteria selected to perform the analysis. Thus, the absence of similarities among clusters from different studies, for example, does not necessarily reflect a failure to replicate a particular classification scheme. Although these comments suggest the relativity of multivariate solutions to taxonomic questions, they also underscore the significance that might be accorded common findings in factors or clusters across studies.

Evaluation

Advantages and Special Features.   The use of multivariate techniques to describe childhood disorders has many advantages. The manner in which the analyses proceed consists of evaluating each child on a large set of symptoms and syndromes, as a function of the particular checklist or rating scale that is used. Several of the measures for which such analyses are conducted (e.g., Child Behavior Checklist, Behavior Problem Checklist) have been derived from and evaluated with multiple clinical samples to ensure that the range of symptoms is broad. Evaluation of each child on each of several different dimensions (factors) provides a comprehensive examination of dysfunction. With a DSM-III diagnosis, the discrete diagnostic entities that the child evinces are listed on Axis I. Multivariate approaches provide a more comprehensive evaluation in the sense that the child is evaluated for all syndrome (factor) areas.

In DSM-III, a child may be diagnosed as meeting criteria for multiple disorders. The rules for prioritizing the disorders are not clear and depend on judgment about the salience of the problem precipitating contact with the clinic. An inherent feature of a dimensional approach is recognition that a child will have scores on multiple characteristics. The salience of particular areas of dysfunction and the relationship of separate problem areas are determined empirically from the profile data.

The use of standardized rating scales as the basis for multivariate classification has other advantages as well. Psychometric refinement of various checklists and rating scales has proceeded relatively well. Progress has proceeded more rapidly with checklists and rating scales than with diagnostic interviews for nosological classification. Also, checklists have been developed to sample a broad range of symptoms, whereas diagnostic interviews occasionally have emerged with a presupposition of the nature of the disorders that need to be assessed; i.e., they are based on a diagnostic system such as DSM-III. The development of a normative data base has obviously been much easier with checklists and rating scales than with diagnostic interviews. Normative data are important to estimate the extent to which a child at a particular age departs from his or her peers.

Limitations.   Multivariate approaches to diagnosis have problems. As already noted, the factors and clusters that emerge in a given analysis obviously vary as a function of multiple features of the analysis, such as the instrument, item content, clinic sample, rater (teacher, parent, other), and details of the factor and cluster analysis. The dependence of the results on the pool of items and child sample has been recognized in different contexts. For example, a factor for psychotic behavior has not emerged in some multivariate analyses because the relevant items that might load on such a factor were not included in the checklist (e.g., Peterson, 1961). As a general rule, syndromes that have a low frequency are not likely to be identified through factor and cluster analyses (e.g., autism) unless items and patients are specifically included to reflect this dysfunction.

Another issue for multivariate analyses is that they rely heavily on checklists completed by parents and teachers. The basic data are ratings and not direct samples of behaviors. Several considerations are relevant for interpretation of checklist data. To begin with, raters may perceive patterns in the behavior of the children they evaluate. Whether such patterns are evident in actual behavior of the children in the manner they are perceived is unclear. There have been few direct comparisons of overt behavior with parent and teacher checklist ratings to evaluate the validity of the ratings.

A related issue is the extent to which parent or teacher ratings reflect characteristics of the child or the rater. In clinic samples, parents are more likely to suffer from their own dysfunction. Stressors in the home, marital discord, and parental psychopathology may well influence the ratings. For example, research has demonstrated that parent perception and ratings of deviance in the child is directly related to maternal depression (see Griest & Wells, 1983). Subject and demographic characteristics of families may dictate their ratings of the children perhaps somewhat independently of characteristics of the children who are rated (see Kazdin et al., 1983). It is likely that a moderate position on the topic of rater variance is warranted. Ratings probably are influenced by some rater characteristics for some clinical samples of children. The difficulty is that the specific characteristics and the manner in which they might bias factors and clusters obtained through multivariate analysis are not known.

General Comments

Not all of the above concerns are unique to assessment of childhood disorders that utilize checklists and rating scales. For example, data obtained from psychiatric interviews of parents and children presumably are subject to distortions resulting from parental psychopathology. The special difficulty with rating scales is that they often refer to general characteristics that are inferred from behavior over time and across situations. Because the items are based on large samples of performance over extended periods, their accuracy in reflecting performance may be enhanced. On the other hand, the items do not refer to concrete behaviors, making them more subject to rater sources of variance.

Notwithstanding potential problems, the significant feature of multivariate classification has been the consistencies that have emerged among raters (parents, teachers, mental health workers, and children) and clinic populations (inpatient and outpatient samples). Also, many studies have evaluated children by gender and/or age groups; others have not. With all of the diversity in the methods used, the consistencies are even more striking in the factors and clusters that have emerged. The utility of empirically based systems remains to be tested. It is not clear whether the diagnostic entities identified through multivariate techniques will be useful ways of delineating dysfunction, as evaluated in family studies, response to treatment, and longitudinal research. However, the advances made in identifying patterns of childhood deviance and differences over the course of development are especially striking.

BEHAVIORAL DIAGNOSIS

Behavioral diagnosis represents a departure from both nosological and empirically derived methods of classification. The approach seeks to identify the problematic behaviors and the conditions that contribute to those behaviors.[5] Factors in the environment and "in the individual" that can be used to alter behavior are a core part of behavioral diagnosis. A behavioral diagnosis does not identify a disorder or profile of symptoms but provides an analysis of the individual's behavior and factors that might be useful for its modification.

Historical Overview

Behavioral diagnosis does not reflect a single approach or taxonomic system. In fact, within behavior therapy, there has been a disdain for traditional diagnostic approaches. Historically, the attention accorded diagnosis within behavior therapy was heavily weighted with criticism of conventional, clinically derived diagnostic systems rather than with positive contributions toward a viable alternative taxonomy. Early in the development of behavior therapy, psychiatric diagnosis was a frequent target for criticism. The criticisms (directed at the first two editions of the DSM) included the reliance on an implicit disease model of abnormal behavior, the focus on psychodynamic interpretations of presumed etiology, the lack of reliability in reaching diagnoses, the potential stigmatization of labeling individuals as mentally ill, and others (see Kazdin, 1978).

Over time, concern also increased over the ability to classify deviant behavior without consideration of the context in which behavior emerges. Personality research and theory has increasingly recognized the important contribution of

---

[5] At the outset, it is important to clarify that behavioral diagnosis is not necessarily restricted to overt acts of behavior. Behavior is defined broadly to include overt action, affect, cognition, and psychophysiology. The key feature is that the behavior is operationalized through one or more assessment procedures.

situational influences on behavior (e.g., Endler & Magnusson, 1976). Within behavior therapy research, the situational specificity of behavior was reflected in several areas of research (e.g., Bernstein, 1973; Kazdin, 1979; Wahler, 1975). Whether behaviors can be adequately characterized by overriding dispositional labels (e.g., traits, diagnoses of mental disorders), without considering the impact of situational influences, became open for question.

Perhaps the most telling criticism of all by proponents of behavior therapy was that traditional diagnosis seemed to be an enterprise with no clear treatment implications. Even if diagnoses could be reliably reached, the difference it made to the clinician or the patient in a treatment plan remained unclear. Behavioral diagnosis begins with the view that diagnosis should result in a plan for action; i.e., treatment. In fact, behavioral diagnosis focuses very little on diagnosis per se in terms of grouping or classifying persons or their behaviors. The goal is to identify areas of functioning that can be altered or drawn upon for treatment.

Characteristics

Functional Analysis.   There is no single diagnostic system that is universally embraced by proponents of behavior therapy. A general approach that has been advocated in understanding behavior is referred to as a *functional analysis* (Ferster, 1965; Kanfer & Saslow, 1969). Functional analysis consists of identifying the behaviors and the events of which that behavior is a function. These events usually refer to current features in the individual's environment. For example, the behavior of a child who is considered to be hyperactive might be a function of such factors as the way his teacher manages the class, the reactions of peers to the classroom, and events going on at home. Other events than those operative in the immediate present might account for, or contribute to, current behavior (e.g., maternal prenatal care, genetics). However, from the standpoint of treatment and therapeutic change, the issue is what current events sustain performance and can be modified to bring about behavior change.

Behavioral diagnosis begins with the description of behavior in objective and concrete terms. Thus, *hyperactivity* would be too general a focus; the term needs to be defined in terms of behaviors in specific situations that lead or have led to imposition of this label. Apart from defining behavior, the functional analysis consists of looking at factors in the situation or setting that might be related to that behavior. Sometimes the factors appear obvious, as for example, when parents inadvertently provide attention for a child's tantrum. However, in all cases the events that appear to be sustaining behavior merely have the status of hypotheses to be evaluated in the treatment process. Whether a particular set of events in fact controls behavior or effectively alters behavior is eventually evaluated empirically.

To formalize the areas that one examines in behavioral diagnosis, several different components have been identified (Kanfer & Saslow, 1969; Lindsley,

1964). A behavioral-analytic focus examines the stimuli (S), organism (O) or individual client, the responses (R), the contingencies (K), and the consequences (C). The stimuli refer to the antecedent events; the organism refers to those factors in the individual that may be affecting behavior; the responses refer to those observed behaviors that are the focus of treatment; the contingencies refer to the relationships (e.g., various reinforcement schedules) between behaviors and antecedent and consequent events in the environment, and the consequences refer to the specific reinforcing or punishing events that may follow behavior. Not all of the SORKC ingredients may be relevant to a particular problem, but they refer to areas that need to be examined for understanding behavior.

As an illustration, a child may be brought to treatment because of opposition at home. A clinician using functional analyses would first identify exactly what the child does and does not do relating to the concern. The clinician would also ask about the stimuli in the setting that precede the response. Obviously, one stimulus or antecedent is a request or instruction with which the child does not comply. Other events may be critical as well. The behavior may occur only in the presence of one parent, only at certain times of the day, only in certain situations, only when instructions are asked in a particular way, or when siblings or others are present, and so on. All of these components refer to stimuli that might be relevant to the response. The contingency and the consequences will be evaluated by asking or observing directly what events are applied when the child complies or fails to comply with an instruction. For example, noncompliance might result in an argument, attempts from a parent to bribe the child, or simply parent cessation of the request. These consequences are critical and are likely to be modified as part of the treatment. As part of a functional analysis, questions will also be asked about the child, generally to find any factor (e.g., handicap, illness, or events) that may be relevant to behavior.

The focus is on the response and the events with which it may be associated. Many of the issues and concerns in psychiatric diagnosis are all relevant considerations for a functional analysis. Events such as illness, death of a family member, stressors at home, marital discord, parent loss of job, and so on, may be relevant since they serve as the context in which behavior is occurring. An attempt is made to identify those elements of the child's environment so that they can be brought to bear to alter behavior. Some of these events may follow behavior directly; others may exert functional influence over the behavior but be somewhat more removed from particular child behaviors. For example, an important stimulus or setting event that influences child aggressive behavior in the home is maternal social contact outside of the home (Wahler, 1980). Specifically, the number of positive social interchanges mothers have with friends outside the home is inversely related to coercive behaviors they direct toward their children at home. This information may be relevant for designing treatments that are directed at altering parent-child interaction.

The SORKC evaluation grew out of behavioral analysis, an approach within behavior modification that emphasizes the control that the environment exerts on behavior. Early formulations excluded the role of the organism (O) or the individual in this analysis (Lindsley, 1964). The O factor was added to emphasize the relevance of features within the individual that may influence performance (Kanfer & Saslow, 1969). Different sorts of factors of the individual may be relevant. For example, biological limitations, handicap, or conditions that relate to the problem (such as mental retardation) might be critical for purposes of treatment.

Over the last decade, the O portion of the equation has been elaborated greatly in behavior therapy. Specifically, cognitive processes that may influence behavior have received increased attention. These processes refer to thoughts, beliefs, attributes, and self-statements and have been shown to have major roles in many clinical problems. For example, in a cognitive formulation of depression, Beck (1976) accords a central role to the negative expectations that depressed persons show toward themselves, their environment, and their future. Modifying maladaptive cognitions and expectations constitutes the basis for cognitive therapy for depression (Rush, Beck, Kovacs, & Hollon, 1977). Cognitive processes have been accorded a major role in a variety of clinical problems (see Guidano & Liotti, 1983) and therapeutic change techniques (Bandura, 1977).

Whether cognitive processes are causally related to clinical problems or are correlates of the problem is not usually known. The strength and direction of the relationships between cognitive processes and behavior change have been suggested in some studies. For example, Spivack, Platt, and Shure (1976) have repeatedly shown that children who evince adjustment problems at school also suffer deficiencies in specific cognitive processes, that changes in these processes through training are associated with behavior change, and that the degree of change on measures of specific cognitive processes often predicts the degree of behavior change. Such evidence argues strongly for the importance of cognitive processes as part of the functional analysis of behavior.

Classification of Behavior.   Behavioral diagnosis has not been concerned with classification and nosology in the traditional sense. However, there have been some attempts to bring order to the conceptualization of behaviors. Perhaps the most general way to classify behavior has been the consideration of different classes or types of behavior. The different types represent relatively loose diagnostic formulations that are designed to direct attention to what needs to be accomplished in treatment.

Two major classes of behavior generally referred to are *excesses* and *deficits* (Bandura, 1969; Kanfer & Saslow, 1969). *Behavioral excesses* refer to those behaviors in which excessive frequency, intensity, or duration is a special problem. Such behaviors as overactivity in the classroom, fighting, and complaining may be viewed as excesses. Excesses are not merely acting out behaviors but refer to problems in which there may be "too much" of a behavior that, in lower doses, might otherwise be adaptive. For example, avoidance, fear, and obsessions might be conceptualized as excesses because their maladaptive features, at least in part, derive from performing specific behaviors to excess. A goal of treatment is to decrease the frequency or intensity of the behaviors so that they fall within some adaptive or normative range.

Behavioral deficits constitute another class of responses that may be problematic. Here, behavior is a problem because of the failure to occur with sufficient frequency, intensity, or duration. For example, social withdrawal, inassertiveness, apathy, and retardation in academic performance are problematic because of a failure of behavior to occur or a failure to occur at normative levels. The goal of treatment is to develop behaviors so that they are performed at higher rates.

Stimulus control problems form another category of behavioral dysfunction defined in relation to particular stimuli. Behavior may not be controlled by appropriate stimuli when such control is desirable. For example, a child may not respond to instructions of others or adhere to classroom rules. Here, the child may perform the particular behaviors that are of interest, but these behaviors are not under the appropriate control of the environment. Similarly, behavior may be problematic because of the control of inappropriate stimulus. For example, in the case of adults, some forms of sexual deviance, such as pedophilia, are conceptualized as a stimulus control problem because sexual arousal is associated with socially censored sexual stimuli, viz, children.

The above categories reflect a general conceptualization of clinical problems. How behavior is conceptualized is not always clear in relation to these categories. For example, a child who engages in aggressive behavior may have behavioral excesses as defined above. The child may also suffer from deficits; i.e., he or she may lack the appropriate social behaviors to engage others in conversations, to initiate and respond to social overtures, and to express disagreement or anger in an appropriate fashion. It is difficult to know in a given case if aggression also is associated with these deficits. Conceivably, one could eliminate aggressive behavior and see if the person now has a repertoire of socially appropriate behaviors. If not, these behaviors could then be developed. In practice, treatments usually focus simultaneously on the suppression of excesses and development of appropriate prosocial alternative behaviors. The reason has to do with evidence that treatments simultaneously focusing on developing some behaviors, as well as eliminating others, are more effective than those that merely attempt to eliminate behavior (Kazdin, 1984).

Another important feature of the notion of excesses and deficits is the implicit assumption that abnormal behavior is a matter of degree, continuous with normal behavior. In the case of aggressive child behavior, one might say that aggression is in excess of frequency and intensity of normal behavior. Since children normally engage in behavior that can be referred to as aggressive, the extreme cases may seem to be only quantitatively different. Yet, some behaviors are so extreme that they often appear to be qualitatively different, such as self-multilation, self-stimulation (e.g., excessive rocking), or cruelty. Although these can be dismissed as quantitative extremes of ordinary behaviors that most people perform, it is an assumption rather than a fact that these behaviors bear relation to counterparts so labeled in nonclinical samples.

Coding of Behaviors. Reference to problematic behaviors as excesses or deficits is sufficiently general to have relatively broad appeal within behavior therapy. Beyond classification of responses into general categories, there has been no universal way of codifying problem behaviors. One attempt, referred to as the Behavioral Coding System (BCS; Cautela & Upper, 1973), has been developed to help identify target behaviors and to dictate treatment selection.

The BCS refers to clinical problem areas specified in behavioral terms. Twenty-one major categories are included with subdivisions yielding a total of 283 different behaviors. To illustrate the BCS, Table 1–4 provides two categories, namely, eating behaviors and antisocial behaviors. Each general category includes several subcategories to reflect specific problems brought to treatment. Although the terms are behavioral in the sense that they generally refer to specific acts, they are not defined further or operationalized by any particular measurement strategy. Thus, it is not clear what would count as socially unacceptable eating or even stealing in an attempt to code behavior.

The BCS focuses on behavior rather than mental conditions or disorders. Also, presumed etiology or psychological processes embedded in the second edition of DSM (in effect when the coding system emerged) are omitted. Behaviors in the BCS refer to either overt or covert events. Thus, images, thoughts, and feelings are included. In general, the BCS reflects an enumeration of behaviors that often are the focus of treatment.

The conditions for defining a particular behavior are not clear. And there is great room for heterogeneity in defining behaviors that might be subsumed under a particular subcategory. The absence of defining criteria or standard means of assessment are particularly problematic for a system designed to increase objectivity of the diagnostic process. The BCS has not been adopted for use within behavior therapy. The gains achieved from coding behaviors that are not operationally defined are unclear. Finally, the prime focus of identifying treatments once the behavioral problem has been identified has not been achieved. Treatment options are not spelled out for any of the categories.

Another system of coding behaviors has been referred to as the Psychological Response Classification System (PRCS: Adams, Doster, & Calhoun, 1977). The system poses general classes (systems) of responses. As with the BCS, this system attempts to avoid intervening variables and theoretical constructs about presumed causes. The PRCS refers to six general response systems (motor, perceptual, biological, cognitive, emotional, and social) and many response categories within each. Table 1–5 illustrates a sample of the PRCS categories

TABLE 1–4

Sample Responses from the Behavioral Coding System

eating

Eating behavior which occurs with inappropriate frequency or involves inappropriate objects.
Overeating
Eating inadequate amounts
Eating inappropriate objects (specify objects)
Socially unacceptable eating behavior
Not following prescribed diet (e.g., salt-free diet)
Not eating a balanced diet
Excessive drinking of liquids (not alcohol)
Other (specify)

antisocial behaviors

Behaviors which are likely to result in injury to others or which involve depriving others of their property.
Stealing
Physical assault on people
Homicide
Destruction of property
Fire-setting
Writing threatening letters
Making threatening phone calls
Other (specify)

Source: J. R. Cautela and D. Upper, "A Behavioral Coding System," unpublished manuscript, Boston College, 1973, pp. 26–27.

that encompass emotional and social response systems. The information conveys not only the system that may be dysfunctional, but also the types of clinical problems that are included. The focus on defining the systems allows the categories to be nonexhaustive so that particular problems can be categorized as needed.

The system is designed to focus on individual behaviors rather than larger groupings of behavior such as a syndrome. The low level of abstraction and small number of categories are designed to facilitate the diagnostic process. Categorization of the response needs to be followed further by a systematic assessment so that treatment can be applied and evaluated.

Evaluation

Advantages and Special Features.   Behavioral diagnosis represents a general approach toward viewing clinical problems rather than a specific method of classification. The approach is not a substitute for nosological or multivariate

TABLE 1-5

Psychological Response Classification System: Illustrations from Emotional and Social Response Systems

response systems	definition	response categories	definition
Emotional	Activity of tissues and organs innervated by the autonomic nervous system which is associated with specific behavior patterns and specific subjective experiences of the individual	Anxiety Euphoria Dysphoria Anger Affection	
Social	Reciprocal actions of two or more individuals	Coercive	Activities whose intent or effect is the coercion of another
		Coercion eliciting	Activities whose intent of effect is coercion by another
		Submissive	Activities whose intent or effect is compliance (coercion accepting) to another
		Submission resisting	Activities whose intent or effect resists compliance to another
		Nurturance	Activities whose intent or effect is extention of benefits to another
		Nurturance withholding	Activities whose intent or effect is the withholding of benefits from another
		Succorance	Activities whose intent or effect is reception of benefits from another
		Succorance-refusing	Activities whose intent or effect is that of refusing benefits from another

Source: H. E. Adams, J. A. Doster, and K. S. Calhoun, "A Psychologically Based System of Response Classification," in *Handbook of Behavioral Assessment,* ed. A. R. Ciminero, K. S. Calhoun and H. E. Adams (New York: John Wiley & Sons, 1977), pp. 47-78.

classification. Rather, behavioral diagnosis is designed to provide an in-depth analysis of problem behaviors and the conditions that may be useful for changing behavior. The approach is highly individualized. Different clients with similar or identical behaviors may be viewed and treated differently because of the impact and meaning of different stimuli, consequences, and contingencies in which the behaviors are embedded.

An important feature of behavioral diagnosis is its dependence on assessment of problematic behavior prior to and during the course of treatment. Specification of the target responses is designed to help direct assessment strategies so that the problematic behaviors can be measured directly. Measures operationalize the problems that are to be treated and serve as the means by which treatment will be evaluated. Direct observation, psychophysiology, self-report and informant ratings, and other measures alone, but more often in combination, are used to evaluate progress in treatment. The attention accorded assessment and treatment evaluation is a significant strength of the behavioral approach.

Limitations.   The behavioral approach does not provide a systematic means of classifying clinical problems. The two coding systems mentioned earlier (BCS, PRCS) and the general way of classifying problems (excesses, deficits) do not offer a way of codifying behavior. Nor has any of these systems been seriously adopted in research or practice.

The absence of a system of codifying behavior makes the accumulation of knowledge somewhat difficult with this approach. And, without a system of diagnosis, treatment x diagnosis interactions are not easily investigated. At present, emphasis on assessment and treatment is usually on relatively isolated target behaviors. Little attention is accorded to the fact that behaviors often come in packages even though some of the strongest evidence has emerged from behavior therapy research on this topic (Kazdin, 1982; Voeltz & Evans, 1982; Wahler et al., 1979).

Similarly, the behavioral approach is largely ahistorical. The current determinants of behavior, such as environmental contingencies and cognitive processes, are emphasized because they reflect the point at which intervention can be made. Yet, chronicity and onset of behavior may be relevant to designing treatment and, at the very least, should be assessed. Other potentially relevant factors that may relate to treatment outcome, such as severity, onset, and depth of dysfunction, are not systematically codified or assessed as part of behavioral diagnosis. These dimensions might be discussed between client and clinician, but there has been no standard way of reporting this information across clinicians and investigators. Consequently, there is often ambiguity in interpreting the behavior therapy literature in terms of who the clients are in relation to their clinical problem and the severity of their dysfunction (Kazdin, 1983).

Behavioral assessment directs attention toward issues that are directly relevant for treatment. It is important to note, however, that diagnosis and assessment of behavior does not lead inexorably to specific treatment recommendations. There are at least two steps for which no guidelines exist in behavioral diagnosis. First, the client may present several problems. There are no guidelines or consistently followed rules that identify how the practitioner moves from a list of problems to a narrow target focus (Wittlieb, Eifert, Wilson, & Evans, 1978). Second, given the selection of the target focus, there are no clear guidelines for selecting the treatments. Treatments often appear to be based on general classes of problems that individuals evince. For example, individuals who show anxiety of some sort are likely to receive a variation of systematic desensitization, flooding, modeling, or relaxation training. Even though proponents of the behavioral approaches are interested in treatment, there are no decision trees for selecting treatments.

General Comments

In a sense, the behavioral approach toward diagnosis actually begins at the point that clinically derived and multivariate diagnoses leave off. More accurately, behavioral diagnosis circumvents the attempt to classify or to characterize individuals or their problems. The approach usually begins with the symptoms (presenting behaviors) and moves quickly to treatment. The move to treatment is unique among the diagnostic approaches. Yet, the absence of ways of identifying consistencies among clients often obscures who and what is being treated. Nevertheless, behavioral approaches have made marked gains in the area of treatment.

CASE ILLUSTRATION

Background

The information provided by clinically derived, multivariate, and behavioral diagnoses, and their unique features can be conveyed by a case illustration. The case is a 12½-year-old girl named Tammy who was admitted to an 18–bed psychiatric inpatient unit for children, ages 6–12 (Esveldt-Dawson et al., 1982). She was referred for evaluation because of her school failure and the presence of several symptoms including "nervousness," chronic constipation, and abdominal pains. The onset of the symptoms occurred approximately four years earlier and was coincident with the beginning of her alleged sexual molestation by her blind, 75-year-old grandfather. In addition, at this time the child reported that she had been molested sexually by the daughter of her father's girlfriend. The molestation by the grandfather apparently had continued over a period of approximately four years but was recently terminated. Prior to this experience, Tammy's academic performance was above average (B grade average), and her school attendance was excellent. Since the experiences with her grandfather, her performance deteriorated, and her symptoms emerged.

Tammy lived with her parents and four older sisters. She grew up without any significant illness or developmental delays. Her WISC-R IQ was within the normal range (full scale IQ = 95). There had been chronic sources of stress in the home. Her mother had a history of alcohol abuse and attempted suicide. Early in Tammy's development, the father was in the military and frequently away from the home for extended periods. Her mother and father suffered continual marital disharmony followed by divorce and remarriage to each other.

Alternative Diagnoses

Clinical Diagnosis. Prior to admission, information was obtained from direct interviews with Tammy and her parents. Psychiatric evaluation was also completed after admission to the hospital. This included interviews regarding her mental health status, psychosocial and developmental history, and intake assessment batteries that included psychoeducational, psychological, neurological, and medical evaluation. The information was integrated separately by staff to obtain a DSM-III diagnosis.

The information revealed several symptoms including a loss of interest or pleasure in usual activities, feelings of guilt, impairment of functioning at school, and somatic compaints. The most marked and consistent symptoms were feelings of anxiety, marked self-consciousness, avoidance of unfamiliar men, and preoccupation with her past behaviors. She complained that she continued to worry about the future and that she generally felt nervous. Based on DSM-III criteria, Tammy was given an Axis I (Psychiatric Syndrome) diagnosis of Anxiety Disorder, specifically on Overanxious Disorder. Axis II (Developmental Disorders) indicated spastic colon syndrome (related to her constipation) and mild obesity. Axis IV (Psychosocial Stressors) was rated as "extreme" due to severe family disorganization, maternal alcholism, chronic alleged sexual molestation, a sister with a serious disease (cerebral palsy), and other factors. Axis V (Highest Level of Adaptive Functioning) was rated as poor because of impairment in her interpersonal relationships, relative isolation from school and peers, and problems in her school progress.

Multivariate Diagnosis. At admission, Tammy's parents completed the Child Behavior Checklist (CBCL) that provided information across a wide range of symptom areas. For girls ages 12–16, syndromes (factors) on the CBCL include anxiety-obsessive, somatic complaints, schizoid, depressed-withdrawal, immaturity-hyperactivity, delinquency, aggressive, and cruelty. Using a clinic T score (with a $\bar{X}$ of 50 and sd of 10), based on clinically referred girls in this age range, the relative severity in each symptom area could be evaluated. The profile of Tammy's scores is provided in Figure 1–1. Tammy's highest ratings were for schizoid (T = 74, sample item = nightmares), anxiety-obsessive (T = 62, sample item = nervousness), immaturity-hyperactivity (T = 59, sample item = cannot concentrate), and somatic complaints (T = 57, sample item =

FIGURE 1-1

Profile of a 12-Year-Old Girl Based on Parent Child Behavior Checklist Ratings

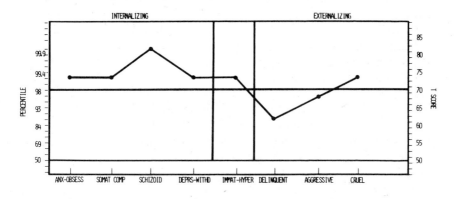

headaches).[6] Cluster analyses of girls 12–16 have yielded a type referred to as anxious-obsessive-aggressive, which is the closest to Tammy's profile (intraclass correlations = .35).

In general, the CBCL information converged with the information obtained for the DSM-III diagnosis. The salient symptoms (item endorsements) that emerged in interviews and parent checklist ratings were similar, with emphasis on fearfulness, avoidance, worry, sadness, and specific somatic complaints. The CBCL sampled a broader range of symptoms and revealed problems not evident from psychiatric interviews (e.g., feeling persecuted, teasing of others, and daydreaming).

Behavioral Assessment.   A behavioral approach was used in the hospital to treat problem areas revealed through the diagnosis. Salient symptom areas were anxiety and avoidance, particularly associated with school and unfamiliar men. In the presence of men, she exhibited withdrawal and severe anxiety that was visibly evident and was attributed to her sexual contact with her grandfather. The selection of anxiety associated with school and unfamiliar men was based on information obtained daily in interaction in the hospital, her impaired functioning, and the relationship of these problems to the clinical picture when she initially was referred for treatment.

---

[6] A T score of 50 is at the 50th percentile; a score of 60 is approximately at the 84th percentile; a score of 70 is approximately at the 98th percentile in comparison to a clinic sample.

To assess anxiety toward school and men, several role-play situations were devised. Those situations pertaining to men included: asking a man for a donation to a hospital, asking a salesman for help in trying on shoes, meeting a new male therapist, welcoming a peer's father on the inpatient unit, and sitting next to a male usher at a dinner. These situations shared the common element of dealing with unfamiliar men. Anxiety pertaining to school situations included: receiving a poor mark on an assignment, being excluded by peers during an art project, speaking in front of class, being unjustly accused of cheating by the teacher, and being sent to the principal for tardiness.

The situations required 15 minutes to complete through a role-play test each day and were administered by a therapist taking the role of the person(s) in the situation; Tammy was encouraged to respond as she normally would. The behaviors Tammy performed while enacting these role-play situations were observed daily from behind a one-way mirror. Several inappropriate and appropriate behaviors relating to anxiety and social functioning were assessed (e.g., nervous mannerisms, stiffness), and Tammy also rated her own level of anxiety. Appropriate behavior such as eye contact, expression of affect, body movement, and overall social skills were also rated.

After several days of assessment across each behavior in the role-play situation, training was initiated by the therapist. Training consisted of providing instructions, therapist modeling, coaching, feedback, and social reinforcement to develop specific behaviors in each role-play situation. Training was introduced in a multiple baseline design across different behaviors. Throughout the course of treatment, behaviors continued to be assessed. The results of training can be seen in Figure 1–2, which shows that inappropriate behaviors decreased and appropriate behaviors increased as training was introduced.

Additional measures were included to evaluate treatment. At five different points over the course of assessment and treatment, an interview was scheduled with an unfamiliar male (one of three males introduced as doctors of the hospital who rotated among the interviews). Each asked mundane questions as part of the brief interview. The interview was rated from behind a one-way mirror to assess nervous mannerisms, stiffness, and other behaviors that also had been rated in the role-play test. Over the course of treatment, these behaviors also reflected reductions in anxiety during the interviews. Finally, ratings of videotapes of baseline and treatment sessions were made by direct-care staff who were blind to the conditions sampled in the tapes. Staff rated Tammy's discomfort as lower and sociability as higher for the treatment tape. Follow-up contact 7 and 21 weeks after treatment had been terminated indicated that school attendance, academic performance, and interactions with adults and peers had improved.

General Comments

The above case conveys the application of alternative diagnostic systems. Within a given setting, the alternative systems may serve different research,

FIGURE 1-2

Rates of Appropriate and Inappropriate Behaviors across Experimental Conditions on Daily Assessments and Probes (indicated by asterisks) by a Second Rater.

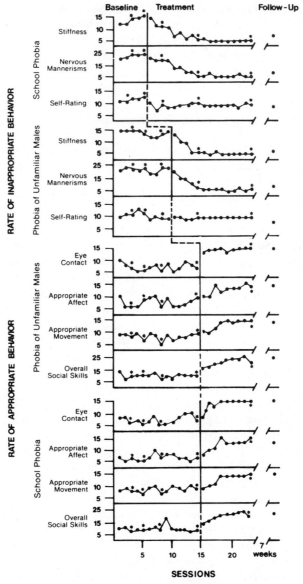

Source: K. Esveldt-Dawson, K. L. Wisner, A. S. Unis, J. L. Matson, and A. E. Kazdin, "Treatment of Phobias in a Hospitalized Child," *Journal of Behavior Therapy and Experimental Psychiatry* 13 (1982), p. 77–83.

clinical, and administrative functions. Although the case conveys the use of different systems, it does not convey their integration. One profitable line of integration would have been to follow up the client with clinical interviews and parent checklist (CBCL) ratings to see if treatment had impact on clinically or empirically derived diagnoses.

More than any diagnostic approach, the case especially illustrates the orientation and focus of behavioral assessment and treatment. The case conveys how assessment and treatment are closely intertwined to operationalize problem areas and to evaluate if therapeutic changes are occurring over the course of treatment.

DIAGNOSIS AND CHILD BEHAVIOR THERAPY

Given the current status of clinically derived and multivariate diagnosis, it is obvious that many basic questions remain to be resolved regarding the organization of childhood disorders. Clarification of disorders immediately enhances and is enhanced by related research on etiology, prognosis, and the natural history of clinical dysfunctions. Given the demands for clinical services, the application of treatments cannot wait for the fundamental diagnostic questions to be resolved. Indeed, it is not clear that resolution of diagnostic questions would even have any immediate benefits on identifying effective treatments.

Concurrent with developments in diagnosis, the treatment literature in child behavior therapy has advanced considerably (Morris & Kratochwill, 1983; Ollendick & Cerny, 1981; Ross, 1981). The advances have resulted from a general approach toward treatment in which clinical problems are translated into target behaviors that are carefully evaluated over the course of treatment. Evaluation helps to focus treatment on problematic behaviors, to see if treatments are achieving their desired outcome, and to make changes in treatment if progress is not made. Moreover, normative data can be brought to bear to examine if the effects of treatment bring the client within the range of behavior of peers who are functioning well in everyday life (Kazdin, 1977).

Advances in treatment have been achieved in most cases in behavior therapy without attention to clinically derived or multivariate diagnoses. But there has been a price for ignoring descriptive diagnosis. The behavior therapy literature is often difficult to integrate into clinical practice. One reason is that there has been no uniform way of describing children in treatment and the level and type of dysfunction to which other areas such as psychiatry can relate. For example, many behavior therapy studies have focused on children who are oppositional and aggressive at home or at school (Kazdin & Frame, 1983). The absence of information about the children or the level, severity, breadth, or chronicity of their dysfunction makes it difficult to estimate to what extent the children might meet criteria for conduct or oppositional disorder. The absence of descriptive material on the populations introduces considerable ambiguity about the clients and the scope of their problems.

The critical feature of clinically derived and multivariate diagnosis is that they provide a standard way of describing clinical populations and their problems. These systems are by no means free from problems. For example, DSM-III provides diagnostic criteria but does not specify the assessment tools to identify symptoms or syndromes. Thus, the way disorders are to be measured and whether different instruments yield the same information is not yet clear. Nevertheless, the limitations of using an existing descriptive system such as DSM-III may be fewer than those associated with avoiding the enterprise entirely.

Proponents of behavior modification have argued that psychiatric diagnosis does not lead to treatment recommendations. Although this is not entirely true (e.g., childhood depression, Puig-Antich & Gittelman, 1982), it stands as a generally accurate characterization. Nevertheless, it does not follow that diagnostic information is irrelevant to treatment. In fact, within behavior therapy, the applicability and efficacy of treatment has been related to the sorts of considerations encompassed by psychiatric diagnosis. For example, for the treatment of conduct problem children, multiple factors, such as parent living conditions, marital discord or divorce, social isolation, and parent psychopathology, may relate to whether treatment can be applied and/or is effective (Patterson, 1982; Wahler et al., 1979). It may be important to know about many of the contextual conditions (e.g., stressors, family life) in which the child's behavior is embedded. DSM-III as a diagnostic system directs attention to many dimensions, albeit the way they are to be assessed is not elaborated. Yet, the use of a diagnostic system that systematically focuses on diverse domains of the child's functioning is likely to be useful for generating effective treatments and hypotheses about the bases of treatment failures.

Behavior therapy has as its hallmark the careful assessment of target behaviors. Relative to diagnostic assessment, identification and measurement of target behaviors has been relatively narrow. Expanded assessment is needed to address broader aspects of clinical problems and the contexts in which they appear. The integration of psychiatric diagnosis into behavioral research has some communicative advantages, but it will not address the major issues in treatment. The dimensions of dysfunction to which psychiatric diagnosis points (e.g., severity, breadth, chronicity, onset of dysfunction) and contextual factors (e.g., family, school functioning, stressors) need to be incorporated into evaluation of clinical problems. Psychiatric diagnosis only sensitizes one to these dimensions; the assessment technology still needs to be developed to measure them in a systematic fashion.

CONCLUSIONS

The chapter has reviewed three general approaches to diagnosis; namely, clinically derived, empirically derived, and behavioral diagnosis. The different approaches were illustrated by elaboration of DSM-III, analyses of parent ratings, and a functional analysis, respectively. The different approaches are often viewed as rivals in the effort to identify the most meaningful way to describe clinical problems. Actually, the approaches accomplish different things differentially well. Clinically derived and multivariate diagnoses provide a standardized way of describing clinical dysfunction. A standard way of describing dysfunction has tremendous significance for many areas of research. Investigating the etiology, family history, and clinical course is likely to profit from the type of approach developed through clinically derived and multivariate diagnosis. Both clinically derived and multivariate diagnoses seek overriding ways of organizing behavior into units. These units (syndromes, disorders) obtain their meaning from other evidence (e.g., family and follow-up studies) that identify stability or predictability of dysfunction.

Behavioral diagnosis does not usually seek overriding similarities among different clients or patients or attempt to understand the organization of dysfunction. Indeed, behavioral analyses of a clinical problem often seek to identify individualized features of the problem and the conditions in which it arises. The major benefit of behavioral assessment is that it can readily move from identification of symptoms to a treatment and to evaluation of treatment outcome.

There is an obvious need to integrate the benefits of different diagnostic systems. Yet, the dilemmas of childhood psychopathology are not resolved simply by adopting all different diagnostic approaches. Childhood diagnosis in general is still relatively underdeveloped; alternative systems have their own problems. The present chapter has discussed major differences among alternative approaches and areas in need of further development.

REFERENCES

Achenbach, T. M. The classification of children's psychiatric symptoms: A factor analytic study. *Psychological Monographs*, 1966, *80* (7, Whole No. 615).

Achenbach, T. M. The Child Behavior Profile: I. Boys aged 6–11. *Journal of Consulting and Clinical Psychology*, 1978, *46*, 478–488.

Achenbach, T. M., & Edelbrock, C. S. The classification of child psychopathology: A review and analysis of empirical efforts. *Psychological Bulletin*, 1978, *85*, 1275–1301.

Achenbach, T. M., & Edelbrock, C. S. Behavioral problems and competencies reported by parents of normal and disturbed children aged four through sixteen. *Monographs of the Society for Research in Child Development*, 1981, *46* (Serial No. 188).

Ackerson, I. *Children's behavior problems: Vol. 2. Relative importance and interrelations among traits.* Chicago: University of Chicago Press, 1942.

Adams, H. E., Doster, J. A., & Calhoun, K. S. A psychologically based system of response classification. In A. R. Ciminero, K. S. Calhoun, & H. E. Adams

(Eds.), *Handbook of behavioral assessment*. New York: John Wiley & Sons, 1977.

American Psychiatric Association. *Diagnostic and statistical manual of mental disorders*. Washington, D. C.: American Psychiatric Association, 1952.

American Psychiatric Association. *Diagnostic and statistical manual of mental disorders* (2nd ed.). Washington, D. C.: American Psychiatric Association, 1968.

American Psychiatric Association. *Diagnostic and statistical manual of mental disorders* (3rd ed.). Washington, D. C.: American Psychiatric Association, 1980.

Bandura, A. *Principles of behavior modification*. New York: Holt, Rinehart & Winston, 1969.

Bandura, A. Self-efficacy: Toward a unifying theory of behavioral change. *Psychological Review*, 1977, *84*, 191–215.

Beck, A. T. *Cognitive therapy and emotional disorders*. New York: International Universities Press, 1976.

Benjamin, L. S. A psychosocial competence classification system. In J. D. Wine & M. D. Smye (Eds.), *Social competence*. New York: Guilford Press, 1981.

Bernstein, D. A. Behavioral fear assessment: Anxiety or artifact? In H. Adams & I. P. Unikel (Eds.), *Issues and trends in behavior therapy*. Springfield: Ill.: Charles C Thomas, 1973.

Blashfield, R. *The classification of psychopathology*. New York: Plenum, 1984.

Borgatta, E. F., & Fanshel, D. *Behavioral characteristics of children known to psychiatric outpatient clinics*. New York: Child Welfare League of America, 1965.

Cantwell, D. P., Russell, T., Mattison, R., & Will, L. A comparison of DSM-II and DSM-III in the diagnosis of childhood psychiatric disorders. I. Agreement with expected diagnosis. *Archives of General Psychiatry*, 1979, *36*, 1208–1213.

Cautela, J. R., & Upper, D. A Behavioral Coding System. Presidental Address presented at the Association for Advancement of Behavior Therapy. Miami, Florida, 1973.

Chambers, W., Puig-Antich, J., & Tabrizi, M. A. *The ongoing development of the Kiddie-SADS (Schedule for Affective Disorders and Schizophrenia for School-age Children*. Paper presented at the American Academy of Child Psychiatry, San Diego, 1978.

Collins, L. F., Maxwell, A. E., & Cameron, K. A factor analysis of some child psychiatric clinic data. *Journal of Mental Science*, 1962, *108*, 275–285.

Dreger, R. M. The classification of children and their emotional problems. *Clinical Psychology Review*, 1981, *1*, 415–430.

Dreger, R. M. The classification of children and their emotional problems: An overview—II. *Clinical Psychology Review*, 1982, *2*, 349–385.

Edelbrock, C. S., & Achenbach, T. M. A typology of Child Behavior Profile patterns: Distribution and correlates for disturbed children aged 6–16. *Journal of Abnormal Child Psychology*, 1980, *8*, 441–470.

Endicott, J., & Spitzer, R. L. A diagnostic interview: The Schedule of Affective Disorders and Schizophrenia. *Archives of General Psychiatry,* 1978, *35,* 837–844.

Endler, N. S., & Magnusson, D. Toward an interactional psychology of personality. *Psychological Bulletin,* 1976, *83,* 856–974.

Esveldt-Dawson, K., Wisner, K. L., Unis, A. S., Matson, J. L., & Kazdin, A. E. Treatment of phobias in a hospitalized child. *Journal of Behavior Therapy and Experimental Psychiatry,* 1982, *13,* 77–83.

Feighner, J. P., Robins, E., Guze, S. B., Woodruff, R. A., Winokur, G., & Munoz, R. Diagnostic criteria for use in psychiatric research. *Archives of General Psychiatry,* 1972, *26,* 57–63.

Ferster, C. B. Classification of behavioral pathology. In L. Krasner & L. P. Ullmann (Eds.), *Research in behavior modification.* New York: Holt, Rinehart & Winston, 1965.

Garmezy, N. DSM-III. Never mind the psychologists: Is it good for the children? *Clinical Psychologist,* 1978, *31,* 3–6.

Gossett, J. T., Barnhart, D., Lewis, J. M., & Phillips, V. A. Follow-up of adolescents treated in a psychiatric hospital: Predictors of outcome. *Archives of General Psychiatry,* 1977, *34,* 1037–1042.

Griest, D. L., & Wells, K. C. Behavioral family therapy with conduct disorders in children. *Behavior Therapy,* 1983, *14,* 37–53.

Group for the Advancement of Psychiatry, Committee on Child Psychiatry. *Psychopathological disorders in childhood: Theoretical considerations and a proposed classification* (Vol. 6). New York: Group for the Advancement of Psychiatry, 1966.

Guidano, V. F. & Liotti, G. *Cognitive processes and emotional disorders: A structural approach to Psychotherapy.* New York: Guilford Press, 1983.

Herjanic, B. *Washington University Diagnostic Interview for Children and Adolescents* (DICA). St. Louis: Washington University School of Medicine, 1980.

Hewitt, L. E., & Jenkins, R. L. *Fundamental patterns of maladjustment: The dynamics of their origin.* State of Illinois, 1946.

Hodges, K., McKnew, D., Cytryn, L., Stern, K., & Kline, J. The Child Assessment Schedule (CAS) diagnostic interview: A report on reliability and validity. *Journal of the American Academy of Child Psychiatry,* 1982, *21,* 468–473.

Jenkins, R. L., & Glickman, S. Common syndromes in child psychiatry. *American Journal of Orthopsychiatry,* 1946, *16,* 244–261.

Kanfer, F. H., & Saslow, G. Behavioral diagnosis. In C. M. Franks (Ed.), *Behavior therapy: Appraisal and status.* New York: McGraw-Hill, 1969.

Kazdin, A. E. Assessing the clinical or applied significance of behavior change through social validation. *Behavior Modification,* 1977, *1,* 427–452.

Kazdin, A. E. *History of behavior modification: Experimental foundations of contemporary research.* Baltimore: University Park Press, 1978.

Kazdin, A. E. Situational specificity: The two-edged sword of behavioral assessment. *Behavioral Assessment*, 1979, *1*, 57–75.

Kazdin, A. E. Symptom substitution, generalization, and response covariation: Implications for psychotherapy outcome. *Psychological Bulletin*, 1982, *91*, 349–365.

Kazdin, A. E. Psychiatric diagnosis, dimensions of dysfunction and child behavior therapy. *Behavior Therapy*, 1983, *14*, 73–99.

Kazdin, A. E. *Behavior modification in applied settings* (3rd ed.). Homewood, Ill.: Dorsey Press, 1984.

Kazdin, A. E., Esveldt-Dawson, K., Unis, A. S., & Rancurello, M. D. Child and parent evaluations of depression and aggression in psychiatric inpatient children. *Journal of Abnormal Child Psychology*, 1983, *11*, 401–413.

Kazdin, A. E., & Frame, C. Treatment of aggressive behavior and conduct disorder. In R. J. Morris & T. R. Kratochwill (Eds.), *The practice of child therapy*. New York: Pergamon Press, 1983.

Lessing, E. E., Williams, V., & Gil, E. A cluster-analytically derived typology: Feasible alternative to clinical diagnostic classification of children? *Journal of Abnormal Child Psychology*, 1982, *10*, 451–482.

Lessing, E. E., & Zagorin, S. W. Dimensions of psychopathology in middle childhood as evaluated by three symptom checklists. *Educational and Psychological Measurement*, 1971, *31*, 175–198.

Lindsley, O. R. Direct measurement and prosthesis of retarded behavior. *Journal of Education*, 1964, *147*, 62–81.

Lorr, M., & Jenkins, R. Patterns of maladjustment in children. *Journal of Clinical Psychology*, 1953, *9*, 16–19.

Matarazzo, J. D. The reliability of psychiatric and psychological diagnosis. *Clinical Psychology Review*, 1983, *3*, 103–145.

Mattison, R., Cantwell, D. P., Russell, A. T., & Will, L. A comparison of DSM-II and DSM-III in the diagnosis of childhood psychiatric disorders. II. Interrater agreement. *Archives of General Psychiatry*, 1979, *36*, 1217–1222.

Morris, R. J., & Kratochwill, T. R. (Eds.). *The practice of child therapy*. New York: Pergamon Press, 1983.

Nuechterlein, K. H., Soli, S. D., Garmezy, N., Devine, V. T., & Schaefer, S. M. A classification system for research in childhood psychopathology: Part II. Validation research examining converging descriptions from the parent and from the child. In B. A. Maher & W. B. Maher (Eds.), *Progress in experimental personality research*. New York: Academic Press, 1981.

Ollendick, T. H., & Cerny, J. A. *Clinical behavior therapy with children*. New York: Plenum Press, 1981.

Orvaschel, H., Puig-Antich, J., Chambers, W., Tabrizi, M. A., & Johnson, R. Retrospective assessment of prepubertal major depression with the Kiddie-SADS-E. *Journal of the American Academy of Child Psychiatry*, 1982, *21*, 392–397.

Patterson, G. R. *Coercive family process.* Eugene, Ore.: Castalia, 1982.

Peterson, D. R. Behavior problems of middle childhood. *Journal of Consulting Psychology,* 1961, *25,* 205–209.

Puig-Antich, J., & Gittelman, R. Depression in childhood and adolescence. In E. S. Paykel (Ed.), *Handbook of affective disorders.* New York: Guilford Press, 1982.

Quay, H. C. Classification. In H. C. Quay & J. S. Werry (Eds.), *Psychopathological disorders of childhood* (2nd ed.). New York: John Wiley & Sons, 1979.

Quay, H. C. A critical analysis of DSM-III as a taxonomy of psychopathology in childhood and adolescence. In T. Millon & G. Klerman (Eds.), *Contemporary issues in psychopathology.* New York: Guilford Press, in press.

Quay, H. C., & Peterson, D. R. *Manual for the Behavior Problem Checklist.* Unpublished manuscript, University of Miami and Rutgers State University, 1979.

Quay, H. C., & Peterson, D. R. *Interim manual for the Revised Behavior Problem Checklist.* Unpublished manuscript, University of Miami and Rutgers State University, 1983.

Radloff, L. *Diagnostic Interview Schedule for Children.* National Institute of Mental Health, Rockville, MD, 1980.

Robins, L. N., Helzer, J. E., Croughan, J., Ratcliff, K. S. National Institute of Mental Health Diagnostic Interview Schedule: Its history, characteristics, and validity. *Archives of General Psychiatry,* 1981, *38,* 381–389.

Ross, A. O. *Child behavior therapy: Principles, procedures and empirical basis.* New York: John Wiley and Sons, 1981.

Rush, A. J., Beck, A. T., Kovacs, M., & Hollon, S. Comparative efficacy of cognitive therapy and pharmacotherapy in the treatment of depressed outpatients. *Cognitive Therapy and Research,* 1977, *1,* 17–37.

Rutter, M., & Shaffer, D. DSM-III. A step forward or back in terms of the classification of child psychiatric disorders? *Journal of the American Academy of Child Psychiatry,* 1980, *19,* 371–394.

Rutter, M., Shaffer, D., & Shepherd, M. *A multi-axial classification of child psychiatric disorders.* Geneva: World Health Organization, 1975.

Schacht, T., & Nathan, P. E. But is it good for the psychologists? Appraisal and status of DSM-III. *American Psychologist,* 1977, *32,* 1017–1025.

Soli, S. D., Nuechterlein, K. H., Garmezy, N., Devine, V. T., & Schaefer, S. M. A classification system for research in childhood psychopathology: Part I. An empirical approach using factor and cluster and conjunctive decision rules. In B. A. Maher & W. B. Maher (Eds.), *Progress in experimental personality research.* New York: Academic Press, 1981.

Spitzer, R. L., & Endicott, J. DIAGNO II: Further developments in a computer program for psychiatric diagnosis. *American Journal of Psychiatry,* 1969, *125,* 12–21.

Spitzer, R. L., Endicott, J., & Robins, E. Research Diagnostic Criteria: Rationale and reliability. *Archives of General Psychiatry,* 1978, *35,* 773–782.

Spitzer, R. L., & Williams, J. B. W. Classification of mental disorders and DSM-III. In H. Kaplan, A. Freedman, & B. Sadock (Eds.), *Comprehensive textbook of psychiatry* (Vol. 1). Baltimore: Williams & Wilkins, 1980.

Spivack, G., & Levine, M. The Devereux Child Behavior Rating Scales: A study of symptom behaviors in latency age atypical children. *American Journal of Mental Deficiency,* 1964, *68,* 700–717.

Spivack, G., Platt, J. J., & Shure, M. M. *The problem-solving approach to adjustment.* San Francisco: Jossey-Bass, 1976.

Sturge, C., Shaffer, D., & Rutter, M. *The reliability of diagnostic categories for child psychiatric disorders in ICD-9.* Paper presented at the Royal College of Psychiatrists, Section of Child Psychiatry, Sterling, Scotland, 1977.

Voeltz, L. M., & Evans, I. M. The assessment of behavioral interrelationships in child behavior therapy. *Behavioral Assessment,* 1982, *4,* 131–165.

Wahler, R. G. Some structural aspects of deviant child behavior. *Journal of Applied Behavior Analysis,* 1975, *8,* 27–42.

Wahler, R. G. The insular mother: Her problems in parent-child treatment. *Journal of Applied Behavior Analysis,* 1980, *13,* 207–219.

Wahler, R. G., Berland, R. M., & Coe, T. D. Generalization processes in child behavior change. In B. B. Lahey & A. E. Kazdin (Eds.), *Advances in clinical child psychology* (Vol. 2). New York: Plenum Press, 1979.

Williams, J. B. W., & Spitzer, R. L. NIMH-sponsored field trial: Interrater reliability. In American Psychiatric Association, *Diagnostic and statistical manual of mental disorders* (3rd ed.) (Appendix F). Washington, D. C.: American Psychiatric Association, 1980.

Wing, J. K., Cooper, J. E., & Sartorius, N. *Description and classification of psychiatric symptoms.* Cambridge, England: Cambridge University Press, 1974.

Wittlieb, E., Eifert, G., Wilson, F. E., & Evans, I. M. Target behavior selection in recent child case reports in *Behavior Therapy. The Behavior Therapist,* 1978, *1* (5), 15–16.

Yule, W. The epidemiology of child psychopathology. In B. B. Lahey & A. E. Kazdin (Eds.), *Advances in clinical child psychology* (Vol. 4). New York: Plenum Press, 1981.

2

Models of Assessment and Treatment in Child Behavior Therapy*

Philip H. Bornstein
University of Montana

Richard A. van den Pol
Montana University Affiliated Program
for Developmental Disabilities

INTRODUCTION

As Kazdin has indicated in the preceding chapter, behavioral assessment does not represent a single approach or unitary concept. Rather, a diversity of behavioral diagnostic methods and models do, in fact, exist. Similarly, there is a wealth of clinical behavior therapy techniques used in the treatment and amelioration of disordered problem behavior. Thus, by way of introduction, we will first discuss some *general issues* related to behavioral assessment and then more specifically present a variety of differing *behavioral assessment models* employed in contemporary clinical practice. A description of *behavioral treatment models* will then be provided. This will be followed by discussion of how behavioral methodology can contribute to a technology of child behavior therapy. Finally, we will conclude with a *case presentation,* hopefully exemplifying the integration of behavioral assessment and treatment paradigms.

_____
* This manuscript was supported in part by grant #G008303567 from the Office of Special Education Programs, U.S. Department of Education. The opinions expressed herein do not necessarily reflect the position or policy of the U.S. Department of Education, and no official endorsement should be inferred.

44

GENERAL ISSUES IN BEHAVIORAL ASSESSMENT

Behavioral assessment is that field of inquiry focused on the identification of target behaviors and their controlling conditions (Nelson & Hayes, 1979). As a consequence, primary emphasis is placed on the selection, definition, and measurement of clinically relevant behaviors. Clearly, however, behavioral assessment extends well beyond the mere specification and objectification of dependent measures. Instead, it can best be characterized as an approach to the study of behavior which utilizes relatively unique assumptions, methods, and goals. In all instances of clinical practice, though, the overriding purpose of assessment is to more fully apprehend behavior with the ultimate goal of effecting change. Thus, it is quite surprising that the child behavior therapy literature has directed such limited attention to this particular topic (Bornstein, Bornstein, & Dawson, 1984). As an initial venture then, let us begin by examining the assumptions which underlie all forms of behavioral assessment.

Assumptions of Behavioral Assessment

A number of basic premises form the foundation of behavioral assessment theory and technique. These are important to note as they, undoubtedly, guide and direct efforts in application. To best understand these underlying concepts, it may be most appropriate to compare behavioral and traditional models of personality assessment. Fortunately, Hartmann, Roper, and Bradford (1979) have already synthesized the major differences between these two approaches (see Table 2–1). They indicate substantial dissimilarity with regard to the nature of personality and presumed causes of behavior. Specifically, traditional approaches infer a personality construct from *within* the individual, i.e., something that he/she has or possesses over time and across situations. Behavioral approaches, on the other hand, tend to place emphasis on social learning history and circumstances *outside* the person—that is, the influence of antecedent and consequent events presently occurring in the environment. Thus, the emphasis is one of "what a person *has* versus what a person *does.*" Second, in the construction of stimulus materials, traditional assessors have not considered selection of test items to be of great conceptual import. To the contrary, behavioral assessors deem that the item pool must be adequately representative of the individual's response to the stimulus situation under study. Third, traditional tests of personality construe test behavior as a sign or correlate of underlying personality. Behavioral tests recognize test behavior as just that—a subset or sample of the behaviors of interest. Fourth, behavioral assessment is unquestionably concerned with the precise specification of dependent measures. Consequently, data collection methods are highly quantifiable in an attempt to increase psychometric accuracy and the identification of target behaviors. This "obsessive" concern for objectification is not found in traditional assessment procedures. Lastly, as alluded to above, the greatest discrepancy between

TABLE 2-1

Differences Between Behavioral and Traditional Approaches to Assessment

	behavioral	*traditional*
I. Assumptions		
1. Conception of personality	Personality constructs mainly employed to summarize specific behavior patterns, if at all	Personality as a reflection of enduring underlying states or traits
2. Causes of behavior	Maintaining conditions sought in current environment	Intrapsychic or within the individual
II. Implications		
1. Role of behavior	Important as a sample of person's repertoire in specific situation	Behavior assumes importance only insofar as it indexes underlying causes
2. Role of history	Relatively unimportant, except, for example, to provide a retrospective baseline	Crucial in that present conditions seen as a product of the past
3. Consistency of behavior	Behavior thought to be specific to the situation	Behavior expected to be consistent across time and settings
III. Uses of data	To describe target behaviors and maintaining conditions	To describe personality functioning and etiology
	To select the appropriate treatment	To diagnose or classify
	To evaluate and revise treatment	To make prognosis; to predict
IV. Other characteristics		
1. Level of inferences	Low	Medium to high
2. Comparisons	More emphasis on intraindividual or idiographic	More emphasis on interindividual or nomothetic
3. Methods of assessment	More emphasis on direct methods (e.g., observations of behavior in natural environment)	More emphasis on indirect methods (e.g., interviews and self-report)
4. Timing of assessment	More ongoing; prior, during, and after treatment	Pre- and perhaps post-treatment, or strictly to diagnose
5. Scope of assessment	Specific measures and of more variables (e.g., of target behaviors in various situations, of side effects, contexts, strengths as well as deficiencies)	More global measures (e.g., of cure, of improvement) but only of the individual

traditional and behavioral assessment may lie in the assessment-treatment relationship.

The goal of traditional assessment has been the description of personality functioning, diagnostic labeling, and prognosis. Only secondarily has assessment led to a specific treatment recommendation. For example, Mischel (1968) and Stuart (1970) have argued that traditional assessment procedures provide little useful information in the selection of appropriate treatment strategies. Behavioral assessment, however, purports to focus on information that is directly relevant to treatment and its evaluation. In fact, behavioral assessment attempts to provide a descriptive analysis of the target behavior and its controlling conditions. In so doing, behavioral assessment operationally defines and functionally analyzes target behaviors of interest. This is conducted across assessment and treatment phases. Thus, behavioral assessment provides ongoing evaluation of client progress and the effects of treatment prior to, during, and following therapeutic intervention.

Purpose of Behavioral Assessment

Having briefly examined the assumptions that underlie behavioral assessment, let us now turn to the reasons why behavioral assessors do, in fact, assess behavior. Bornstein et al. (1984) have outlined four major purposes of assessment: (*a*) to identify problems and select targets of intervention, (*b*) to choose and design a program of treatment, (*c*) to measure the effects of treatment while that program is ongoing, and (*d*) to evaluate the general outcome and efficacy of therapeutic regime. Clearly, the purposes are both broad and extensive. In addition, it must be noted that the actual conduct of assessment will vary, depending on which of the above purposes is (are) to be served. Further, not only will purpose influence conduct, but conduct will reciprocally influence purpose. That is, the manner in which data is collected changes the nature of the "beast" so that different assessment questions are bound to arise. In sum, the assessment-treatment relationship is best conceived of as a dynamic rather than a static enterprise.

Problem Identification and Target Behavior Selection. The purpose of assessment directs the decisions that will be made. If one's purpose is to identify and select target behaviors, then adequacy of problem definition becomes of utmost concern. Unfortunately, a review of the pertinent literature reveals that, while target behaviors may be adequately defined, little information is often presented regarding the manner in which they are first selected. What most typically happens is that parents, teachers, or some other agents of society define the behavior as problematic. But, as Hawkins (1975) has so aptly stated, "Who decided *that* was the problem?" That is, although the behavior has been identified by others, it is not, ipso facto, defined as the target behavior of choice.

If one simply does not accept the presenting complaint as the behavior to be modified, then how is the problem to be identified? Birnbrauer (1978) suggests that a task and situation analysis be performed and, more specifically, that we recognize the behaviors required for success in particular situations, then select as targets only those behaviors that will facilitate better adjustment. For example, let us assume that parent-child observations reveal that 16-year-old Herbie and his parents are frequently arguing with one another. Because it is generally assumed that both Herbie and his family will develop a more effective living situation if arguments were to decrease, the development of communication/ negotiation skills may become the justifiable target behaviors of choice. Furman and Drabman (1981), on the other hand, provide three alternatives to traditional target behavior selection methods. First, using a *normative* approach, data may be collected on the targeted child and some other normative group (typically, this would include agemates and/or classmates). Undesirable behaviors occurring above rate or desirable behaviors occurring below rate are then viable prospects for target behavior selection. Second, *social validation* procedures may be used to identify problems and behaviors of some concern. The identification of relevant behaviors is accomplished by correlating behavioral rates of occurrence with subjective ratings of performance across some larger identified class. Thus, the asking and answering of questions during conversation, for example, may be highly correlated with judges' ratings of social skill effectiveness. Consequently, the asking and answering of questions becomes a likely target behavior of choice. Third, Furman and Drabman (1981) recommend that target behaviors be empirically related to *current and future adjustment*. This approach is very similar to that noted by Birnbrauer (1978) with the exception that Furman and Drabman's emphasis is placed on an empirically derived, decision-making model. In any case, none of the above procedures should serve as the sole criterion for selecting target behaviors. Instead, whenever possible, criteria should be combined in the decision-making process. In so doing, reliability of target behavior selection may increase as the entire process becomes more objective in nature.

As indicated earlier, there often is little detail provided regarding the manner in which child behaviors are targeted for change. In a recent review of child-oriented studies appearing in *Behavior Therapy,* Wittlieb, Eifert, Wilson, and Evans (1979) found that only half of all investigators provided reasons as to why a particular behavior had been selected for treatment. They categorized these reasons into five distinct groupings: (*a*) dangerous to the life or health of the child, (*b*) detrimental to school performance or adjustment, (*c*) socially unacceptable, (*d*) behavior that influences other deviant behaviors, and (*e*) for therapeutic demonstration purposes. Mash and Terdal (1981), on the other hand, list additional conceptual and empirical reasons why behaviors are chosen for treatment. Among these are:

1. Behavior provides an entry point into the natural reinforcement community (i.e., a "behavioral trap").

2. Behavior is positive rather than negative in nature.
3. Behavior is essential to the sequence of normal development (e.g., language, peer relationships).
4. Behaviors create positive environmental reactions to the child.
5. Behaviors are consistent with developmental norms for performance.

The above list is not meant to be exhaustive. However, it should be noted that, regardless of *why* a behavior is chosen, most behavioral assessors will strive toward a number of similar goals: (*a*) develop a functional analysis of the behavior, (*b*) operationally define the behavior, and (*c*) generate a measurement system for the behavior.

Functional analytic concepts have been briefly discussed already. It is sufficient to note that behavioral assessors are most interested in uncovering those variables that control the problem behavior (Nelson & Hayes, 1979). This most frequently takes the form of examining and/or manipulating antecedent, consequent, or organismic conditions. In a related manner, defining the behavior allows the assessor to operationalize his/her analysis of the problem. Finally, measurement provides for a determination of response characteristics (i.e., frequency, intensity, duration measures) and the establishment of a baseline level of performance. In sum, problem identification and target behavior selection is a means by which we increase the probability of effective therapy while simultaneously creating a measure of professional accountability.

Choosing and Designing a Treatment Program.   Once the focus of intervention has been identified, a host of treatment-related decisions follow. Unfortunately, as indicated by Ciminero and Drabman (1977), there is no general model that has been developed to aid in this decision-making process. However, it is generally agreed that treatment selection appears to be a function of numerous factors. These include: (*a*) the assessment information thus far obtained, (*b*) the empirical literature attesting to efficacy of the procedure, (*c*) the therapist's ability to appropriately implement the proposed program of treatment, and (*d*) practical matters relating to an integration of assessment and treatment (e.g., providing the least restrictive alternative). First, as indicated earlier in this chapter, behavioral assessment procedures by their very nature are constructed so as to guide the selection of therapeutic alternatives. Thus, when assessment information reveals that parents do nothing in response to their child's noncompliance, a number of treatment options should immediately become apparent (e.g., time-out, response cost, DRO). Second, not all treatment procedures are equally effective. Moreover, there is growing evidence that some techniques are more appropriate with some clients when administered under certain kinds of conditions. For example, Bornstein, Sturm, Retzlaff, Kirby, and Chong (1981) found that paradoxical instruction dramatically reduced encopretic behavior in a nine-year-old male when soiling was partially the result of exacerbation-based phenomena. Certainly, one might seriously question the use of such paradoxical procedures with other behaviors or under other conditions. Third, not all therapists are equally trained or experienced in the use of a wide band of therapeutic procedures. One of the authors (PHB), for example, was recently supervising a graduate student working with a highly aggressive 13-year-old child. The recommended treatment of choice was a parent-training program for the immediate consequation of inappropriate child behavior. However, behavior analysis revealed that the parents were quite skilled in child management techniques. Further, the child became aggressive and violent in response to what he *considered* to be anger-provoking situations (e.g., not getting what he wanted). More specifically, the child's inappropriate self-statements seemed to precipitate his eventual acting-out behavior. Thus, a cognitively based, anger-control program (Bornstein, Weisser, & Balleweg, in press) seemed to be a viable treatment alternative. Unfortunately, the graduate student was not familiar with such programs and consequently had overlooked its application in this instance. Finally, a variety of practical matters will influence the actual selection of a treatment program. For example, simpler (i.e., less restrictive, less costly, less disruptive) therapeutic procedures are preferred over those of a more complex nature. Similarly, client preference and treatment acceptability are matters that should also be of some concern to the practicing clinician (Bornstein, Fox, Sturm, Balleweg, Kirby, Wilson, Weisser, Andre, & McLellarn, 1983).

Regarding treatment program design, we make the following recommendations: (*a*) targets of intervention should be relatively few in number initially, (*b*) behaviors with a high probability of success should be focused on first, (*c*) therapeutic programs should remain narrow and relatively concentrated (e.g., contingencies applied two hours per day) until a treatment effect is obtained, (*d*) clients should be asked to perform only realistic accomplishments, i.e., do not program failure, and (*e*) data should be collected even as the program is implemented. Appropriately, we now turn to the measurement of behavior during intervention.

Measurement During Intervention.   Systematic data gathering is an essential element of behavior therapy/behavior modification. More specifically, one of the truly unique aspects of clinical behavior therapy is the manner in which assessment extends into the treatment phase. In fact, Keefe, Kopel, and Gordon (1978) have indicated that there are three major ongoing assessment tasks: (*a*) checking on the client's use of therapeutic procedures, (*b*) monitoring the effectiveness of treatment, and (*c*) modifying the treatment program if necessary. Measuring the client's use of therapeutic procedures is actually a compliance-related issue—namely, is the treatment being implemented as prescribed by the clinician? This becomes particularly important in the child behavior therapy area since a great many treatments are, in fact, implemented by parents or other agents of society. Thus, whenever possible, data should be collected on the validity of treatment implementation.

Perhaps the most important measurement function during intervention, however, is related to the monitoring of treatment effectiveness, that is, systematic monitoring of client behavior provides valuable feedback to guide the conduct of treatment. The importance here lies in a number of factors. First, even during treatment, target behaviors continue to be operationally defined and, therefore, objectively monitored. Second, ongoing measurement precludes arbitrary and capricious decisions regarding continuation/noncontinuation of current therapeutic procedures. Third, in most instances, the methods of assessment employed during baseline can also be used during the intervention phase. Thus, the evaluative continuity afforded by systematic monitoring during intervention allows clinicians to modify treatment when inadequate progress occurs. In so doing, minor adjustment or complete modification of therapeutic programs may occur. In either case, however, the process increases the probability of success since inadequate procedures may be replaced by potentially more active treatment techniques.

Lastly, a number of broader issues are also related to measurement during intervention. As alluded to above, recording behavior during treatment results in an increased likelihood of more effective treatment. However, the recording process need not solely pertain to the behavior under study. Rather, treatment itself can also be measured. Yeaton and Sechrest (1981), for example, refer to both the strength and the integrity of treatment. Strength of psychological treatment is analogous to pharmacological "dosage" level, that is, levels of treatment can be applied based on intensity, frequency, or duration of administration. Integrity, on the other hand, refers to the degree that treatment is delivered as intended. Thus, by monitoring the application of treatment with respect to both strength and integrity, we may uncover means by which our therapies become more effective and/or efficient. In addition, continuous monitoring provides a realistic strategy for the attainment of an empirical clinical science. The scientist-practitioner model has been part of clinical psychology for almost 40 years. Never before, however, has this controversial model come closer to realization than through the application of behavior therapy procedures and continuous measurement strategies (Barlow, Hayes, & Nelson, 1984).

Therapeutic Evaluation. As should be obvious from the above, evaluation of therapy outcome is a natural by-product of an integrated assessment-treatment program. This evaluation is usually accomplished by means of a between-group or within-subject design. These designs have been discussed at length in the behavior modification literature (see Hersen & Barlow, 1976; Kazdin, 1982; Kratochwill, 1978). Consequently, they will not be elaborated here. Instead, we will briefly mention that at posttreatment clinicians may want to consider three other forms of outcome evaluation: measures of (*a*) social validity, (*b*) consumer satisfaction, and (*c*) expanded evaluation criteria. Social validity has been discussed earlier in this chapter. Such measures refer to whether the effects of intervention produce changes of clinical or applied significance. These assessments are typically accomplished via social comparison or subjective evaluation methods (Kazdin, 1977). Consumer satisfaction, on the other hand, provides an evaluation of therapeutic outcome as perceived by recipients of the service (Bornstein & Rychtarik, 1983). Finally, expanded outcome criteria refer to a broadening of the evaluation forms used in the assessment of treatment effectiveness. All of the above appear to be of increasing importance in the evaluation of behavior therapy/behavior modification programs.

Methods of Behavioral Assessment

A wealth of behavioral assessment instruments presently exists. Unfortunately, their review is well beyond the purview of this chapter. However, to more fully understand issues related to assessment and treatment paradigms, some limited discussion of behavioral assessment methods is in order. To accomplish this, we will use Cone's (1978) categorization of indirect and direct assessment procedures.

Indirect Methods of Assessment.   Among the indirect methods to be discussed are the behavioral interview, self-report questionnaire, behavioral checklist, peer ratings, and traditional psychological tests. The first method of assessment to be considered is the most widely employed clinical assessment procedure—the behavioral interview. The purpose of the interview is to diagnose, assess, and begin the formulation of treatment plans. Behavioral interviews differ from traditional interviews in that the focus is on specific problem behaviors and environmental variables rather than generic, client-centered forms of questioning. To accomplish this, child, parent, teacher, and significant others may be called upon as informants. Further, these interviews may be of a structured or unstructured nature. Interrater reliability may increase as a result of structured interviews (Herjanic, Herjanic, Brown, & Wheatt, 1975). Alternatively, information relevant to the development of functional analyses may be more readily acquired via unstructured methods. In any case, there are a number of advantages that are attested to by the popularity of the interview as an assessment tool. First, behavioral interviews are flexible enough to allow response to clients' immediate concerns and, therefore, to aid in the establishment of a therapeutic relationship. Second, interviews potentially provide the therapist with a sample of individual and family interactive behavior. Third, interviewing the child allows for the assessment of how behavioral events are cognitively and emotionally processed. This, in turn, may give direction to the evolving individualized treatment plan.

While self-report questionnaires may be of limited utility with very young children, parent behavioral checklists have been widely employed in clinical settings. Granted that self-reports of behavior may be somewhat at variance with alternative modes of assessment, they are nonetheless important. Advantages include: (a) ease of administration, (b) provision of data regarding client's perception of the problem, and (*c*) access to information not otherwise available. Unfortunately, continuing questions remain with respect to subject biases and issues of validity. Similar to self-report questionnaires, behavioral checklists have been used extensively by child behavior therapists. In general, however, checklists have not provided information relevant to the acquisition or maintenance of problem behaviors. Furthermore, items are not always specific and quantifiable enough to aid in formulating behavior change programs. The same is also true of peer sociometric ratings, which provide rather impressionistic ratings of a target child's behavior. However, such ratings appear to be excellent predictors of later, serious psychopathology (Evans & Nelson, 1977).

Traditional personality tests may also be of some usefulness to behavioral clinicians. First, they are apt to provide a more thorough analysis of children's strengths and deficits. Second, such tests broaden the evaluation base and provide a rich sample of potentially relevant information. Third, traditional psychological tests may indicate further areas in need of assessment. Finally, these nonbehavioral instruments often aid in defining the parameters of treatment efficacy. Thus, the authors of this chapter have no argument with traditional psychological tests per se. Our concern is with the manner in which test information has been inappropriately used in the past (i.e., diagnosis, classification). Rather than using traditional tests as measures of underlying personality, they can instead be viewed as part of a broad-based, multifaceted assessment program. In point of fact, since no single measure can be expected to tax all components of a problem behavior, multiple methods of assessment are becoming more the rule than the exception (Bornstein, Bridgwater, Hickey, & Sweeney, 1980).

Direct Methods of Assessment.   Our discussion here will focus on self-monitoring, direct observation, and permanent product measures.

There is ample evidence attesting to the value of self-monitoring in children (Bornstein, Hamilton, & Bornstein, in press). In fact, a number of therapeutic benefits may be derived. First, of course, are the potentially reactive effects of self-monitoring. Second, as an assessment device, self-monitoring is an economical and often informative data collection method. It is not only applicable with a wide range of clients and problems, but often provides information that may otherwise be inaccessible. Third, increased feelings of self-control and responsibility may result from the use of self-monitoring procedures. Unreliability, however, may limit the clinical usefulness of self-monitored data collection methods.

Direct naturalistic observation still remains the hallmark of behavioral assessment. Unfortunately, inadequate psychometric evaluation, lack of normative data, and cost of the procedures often limit application in nonresearch settings. In natural environments, however, significant others can be trained to record the occurrence of specific target behaviors. For example, parents can observe and maintain frequency counts on both appropriate and inappropriate child behavior in the home (Bornstein & Knapp, 1982). Alternatively, direct observation can also be employed in non-naturalistic situations. In fact, analogue observation of both free behavior (e.g., a clinic playroom) and behavior created in response to a role-play situation may have greater practicality for use in clinical settings. One must remain cautious, however, in extrapolating from the laboratory to the natural environment (e.g., see VanHasselt, Hersen, & Bellack, 1981).

Finally, permanent product measures may also serve as behavioral assessment methods. For example, behaviors of interest can be inferred by physical trace erosion or accretion (Webb, Campbell, Schwartz, & Sechrest, 1966). Bornstein and Rychtarik (1978) measured the size of bald spots in a trichotillomanic client. The resulting behavioral by-product provided information with regard to the amount of hair pulled on a weekly basis. Other permanent product measures might include school assignments completed, soiled clothing, weight gain/loss, etc. Archival records may also serve as permanent products. These could include school grades, medical reports, or record of juvenile offenses. Quite frankly, the number and type of unobtrusive measures utilized are limited only by the ingenuity of the behavioral assessor.

In summary, behavioral assessment methods require a careful knowledge of currently available instruments, their psychometric properties, and the cost/practicality of administration. In all instances, however, instruments are used in the service of some conceptual model. Consequently, those models will now be discussed.

BEHAVIORAL ASSESSMENT MODELS

Behavioral assessors have generally rejected traditional methods of assessment and diagnostic classification. Unfortunately, however, no single alternative model has emerged as the "champion" of contemporary behavioral assessment. Instead, a host of conceptual schemes exist. Some of the more frequently employed popular models are presented below. All share in common an attempt to describe the problem behavior, select an appropriate treatment, and evaluate the efficacy of the therapeutic intervention. Moreover, as with all models, each provides a conceptual "superstructure" within which specific behavioral assessment methods may be employed.

Functional Analysis of Behavior

Initially proposed by Peterson (1968), the functional analysis of the behavior model is an empirically based assessment approach. The cardinal features of the method are:

(1) systematic observation of the problem behavior to obtain a response frequency baseline, (2) systematic observation of the stimulus conditions follow-

ing and/or preceding the behavior, with special concern for antecedent discriminative cues and consequent reinforcers, (3) experimental manipulation of
a condition which seems functionally, hence causally, related to the problem
behavior, and (4) further observation to record any changes in behavior which
may occur. (Peterson, 1968, p. 114)

Thus, as noted by Ciminero (1977), the functional analysis of behavior approach is basically an *A-B* experimental design, in which *A* represents baseline
and *B* represents some therapeutic intervention. By manipulating those variables that control the behavior, the efficacy of a particular treatment can be
evaluated. However, while giving direction to early behavioral assessment
efforts, the functional analysis model may be unnecessarily narrow and limited
in applicability (Evans & Nelson, 1977), that is, its emphasis on nonmedi-
ation and the carindal rule of right-wing behaviorism, "thou shalt not infer"
(Mahoney, 1974), may simply be inadequate in this day and age.

Kanfer and Saslow's S-O-R-K-C

The Kanfer and Saslow (1969) S-O-R-K-C model has had great appeal to
behavior modifers. In fact, it probably serves as the "granddaddy" of sophisticated behavioral assessment models. The various elements are as follows:
S (stimulus) refers to antecedent events; O (organism) refers to biological
conditions; R (response) refers to observed behaviors; K (contingency) refers to
schedules or contingency-related conditions; and C (consequence) refers to
events that follow R. Accompanying the S-O-R-K-C framework are seven
specific component areas that theoretically yield information relevant to the
target, treatment, and goals of intervention. These include:

1. *An initial analysis of the problem situation* in which behavioral excesses,
   deficits, and assets are specified.
2. *Clarification of the problem situation* in which affected individuals are
   identified and conditions of occurrence are elaborated.
3. *A motivational analysis* in which incentive and aversive conditions are
   determined.
4. *A developmental analysis* in which biological, sociological, and behavioral
   changes relevant to the problem behavior are specified.
5. *An analysis of self-control* in which situations, limitations, and methods of
   self-regulation are defined.
6. *An analysis of social relationships* in which significant others are identified
   and social resources noted.
7. *An analysis of the social-cultural-physical environment* in which norms,
   settings, and environmental constraints are examined.

While the model is extremely thorough and allows for a wide diversity of
assessment methods, a number of limitations appear. First, it may be so thorough that it becomes clinically impractical. Second, the information obtained

is still interpreted in a subjective manner (Dickson, 1975). Third, the model does not really aid in the selection of the most appropriate treatment strategy. Fourth, embedded within the model is the notion that identification of controlling variables enhances treatment success. In point of fact, this has not been demonstrated yet and may be extremely time-consuming. Lastly, S-O-R-K-C does not specify the "how-what-when-where" of continuous monitoring and evaluation. Still, the model has proven quite useful, especially with its emphasis on multichannel assessment and behavioral asset information.

The BASIC ID

Lazarus' BASIC ID assessment model is an outgrowth of his multimodal treatment program (1973, 1976). Conceptually, he has posited that faulty specification of target behaviors is probably the greatest impediment to successful treatment. Moreover, misidentification of problem behaviors is apt to result from a failure to assess the BASIC ID. The BASIC ID is an acronym specifying the major domains that should be a part of all preintervention assessment: behavior, affect, sensation, imagery, cognition, interpersonal, and drugs (includes organic and physiological processes). In the *behavioral* domain, Lazarus suggests that target characteristics (i.e., frequency, intensity, duration) shall be directly observed with an emphasis on antecedents and consequences of the problem response; here, his emphasis is on overt verbal and motor behaviors. *Affectively,* the clinician should explore those client experiences which give rise to strong emotional response. Some attempt should be made to explore what the client experiences that gives rise to various affective states (i.e., happy, sad). In the domain of *sensation,* physical complaints (e.g., nausea), sensory experience (appetite, odor, etc.), and sensory channel information (e.g., touch, sight, sound) should be examined. In the *imagery* domain, Lazarus calls upon his client to create a series of mental pictures. Image-related tasks are requested and interpreted in a projective-like manner. *Cognitively,* the therapist must identify misconceptions, mistaken beliefs, attributions of self-efficacy, and faulty illogical thinking. The therapist is interested in uncovering both the irrational beliefs and the manner in which these faulty thought processes lead to self-defeating behavior. Regarding *interpersonal relationships,* Lazarus recommends that clients be both heard and observed vis-à-vis their significant relationships with others. Lastly, the domain of *drugs* refers generally to the clients' state of physical being, including appearance, dress, exercise, and diet. The purpose of assessment in this area is to obtain a thorough analysis of the client's physical status and response to his/her environment.

As should be apparent from the above, BASIC ID is a conceptual guideline for the conduct of initial interviews and problem description. Domains are clearly interdependent, and problems can occur both within and across categories. While one need not accept the technical eclecticism of multimodal therapy to do multimodal assessments, there seems to be significant overlap between

FIGURE 2–1

The Behavioral Assessment Grid (BAG); A Taxonomy for Behavioral Assessment

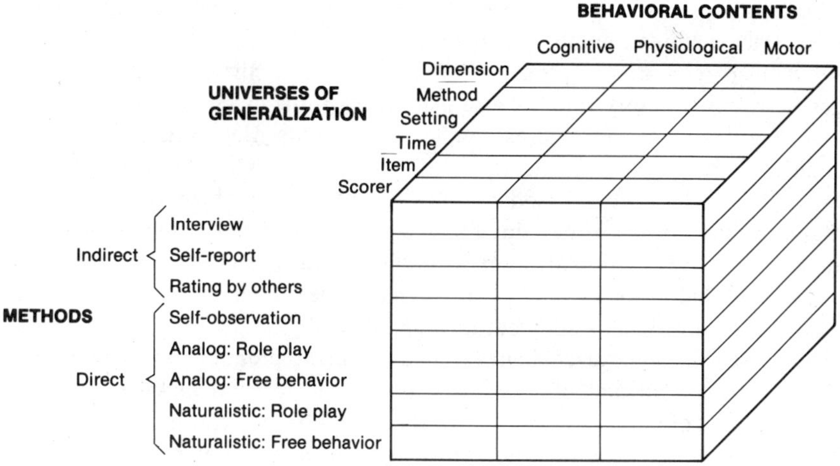

this and the Kanfer and Saslow (1969) S-O-R-K-C model. If differences do exist, they no doubt result from a lack of explicit criteria used in the selection of differing treatments among both models. Thus, the integration of assessment and treatment remains a problem even for some of the more commonly employed behavioral models.

The Behavioral Assessment Grid (BAG)

John Cone (1978) has recently presented a detailed conceptual scheme that may be used as a model for the conduct of behavioral assessments. Cone's model is actually a three-dimensional system for classifying and evaluating behavioral measures. The three aspects of assessment to be simultaneously considered include contents, methods, and types of generalizability. In the content category, Cone is generally referring to cognitive, motor, and physiological domains of behavior. While tripartite assessment is clearly being advocated, a distinction is drawn between the measurement mode and the content area itself, that is, the three domains may be measured by a variety of behavioral techniques or devices. For example, an individual may have self-reported behavioral avoidance (e.g., motor domain). Similarly, motor responses may be assessed via direct observation in laboratory situations. The second dimension, methods, is ordered along a continuum of directness regarding the extent to which these procedures (*a*) measure the clinically relevant target response and (*b*) do so at the time and place of its natural occurrence. At the indirect end of the continuum fall interview, self-report, and rating-by-other methods. Five types of direct observation methods are noted. These include self-observation; analog: role play; analog: free behavior; naturalistic: role-play; and naturalistic: free play. If content and method categories were juxtaposed, a 24-category behavioral taxonomic system results. This is only theoretically possible, however, since a limited number of method categories are available for the measurement of cognitive contents. We will not discuss the third dimension of generalizability at this time because that aspect of the model is more restricted to an evaluation of particular assessment instruments. However, the combined content X method matrix clearly is of relevance in our present discussion. Specifically, Cone's BAG model allows for more comprehensive assessment, that is, behaviors can be measured both across method and content categories. In so doing, greater organization is provided both to the field of behavioral assessment and to the evaluation of the individual client. In fact, if the BAG model were to be widely adopted, it would no doubt facilitate development and evaluation of standardized behavioral assessment programs. Unfortunately, BAG does not, in and of itself, aid in clinical decision making or in the establishment of therapeutic goals. We should not be too critical in this respect, however, as its intended purpose is neither of the above. Rather, it is a system devised for the taxonomic classification and evaluation of behavioral assessment instruments and measures.

Multimethod Clinical Assessment

W. Robert Nay (1979) has proposed a behavioral assessment guide that is perhaps more comprehensive and systematic than any of the models thus far cited. His multimethod clinical assessment strategy provides suggestion regarding the planning, implementation, and utilization of behavioral assessment information. Specifically, the model focuses on five categories of information (referred to as "modalities") and four major methods of assessment. The five modalities and their "facets" (specific information) include:

1. *Description of potential targets* in which attributions and overt/covert referents are defined; furthermore, frequency, duration, and intensity information is obtained.
2. *Conditions of occurrence* in which the target behavior is examined with regard to location, activity, time, antecedents, consequences, and modeling influences.
3. *Historical information* in which case history data is collected with respect to birth, developmental milestones, medical, family, interpersonal, educational, sexual, and occupational history.
4. *Client resources* in which internal (i.e., personal abilities and skills) and external (i.e., environmental) strengths and weaknesses are evaluated;

these may include such areas as intellect, physical abilities, social skills, person support, physical surroundings, finances.

5. *Client motivation* in which information is obtained regarding client's desire to bring about changes in his/her behavior, environment, or both.

While the above modalities refer to *what* is being assessed, the four major methods of assessment refer to *how* it is assessed: interview, written, observation, and physiological. In addition, each of the method categories can be further subdivided into the "facets" of operations, supplier, setting, and sampling components. Thus, a matrix (similar to Cone's [1978] BAG model) can be formed, indicating the various method X modality interactions. Therefore, each cell within such a matrix represents another possible method-modality combination available for the clinical assessment of problem behaviors. Clearly, the above model may potentiate a truly comprehensive assessment. However, if one were to sketch out the complete matrix prior to actually conducting the assessment, the task would simply be overwhelming (see Nay, 1979, Table 12–5). This occurs because each modality and methods "facet" is afforded independent status within the assessment matrix. Of paradoxical interest, however, the reader may note that Nay's method categories are less detailed than Cone's BAG typology. The irony is that, with less methods specifications, Nay's model appears to result in even greater complexity.

BEHAVIORAL TREATMENT MODELS

As reflected by the chapter contents of this text, behavioral interventions with children target a broad array of psychopathologies in an equally wide range of environments. The reader's task of selecting a specific treatment strategy is concomitantly challenging. As the collective authors describe, behavioral treatments have been successfully applied in schools, hospitals, homes, clinics, playgrounds, and institutions with children suffering from medical problems, physical handicapping conditions, developmental disabilities, academic underachievement, social maladjustment, chronic illness, severe psychological disorders (e.g., phobias, autism), as well as with less pervasive psychological distress (e.g., divorce, death of a sibling). For example, behavioral treatments have been widely and effectively used to teach children desirable eating habits, compliance with instructions, classroom deportment, toileting, functional language, and attenuation of depression, aggression, property destruction, and self-injurious behavior.

The robust nature and effectiveness of many behavioral interventions often complicate the clinician's task of selecting and implementing the most appropriate treatment technique, because a variety of behavior therapeutic interventions may have been demonstrated to be effective in treating the same disorder. For example, differential teacher praise, token reinforcement, and token response-cost techniques have all been shown to affect children's classroom performance positively (Iwata & Bailey, 1974; Thomas, Becker, & Armstrong, 1968).

Fortunately, the majority of the following chapters describes not only a range of effective treatments, but also describes outcome comparisons, detailed explanations of various procedures, clinical considerations in implementation, as well as potential problems and their respective solutions. While the present text describes state-of-the-art practices, the field of behavior intervention is certain to continue to grow and evolve. In order to articulate a model for selection of the treatments described here, as well as those yet to be developed, it may be useful to examine some parameters of behavioral intervention. Therefore, one purpose of this chapter is to overview the methodological and empirical underpinnings of behavior therapy in order to arrive at a model for treatment selection, implementation, and evaluation—contributions to the mission of producing a replicable technology of child behavior therapy.

Behavior Therapy and the Experimental Analysis of Behavior

Clinical behavior therapy might be described as the application of the principles of behavioral sciences to the subject matter of traditional psychotherapy. As noted, the distinction between traditional psychotherapy and behavior therapy is not a dichotomous one but one of degree. For example, Bornstein et al. (in press) have noted that behavior therapy currently can be characterized by interdependent functions of assessment and treatment, by an emphasis on quantification, and by attention to current versus historical "causes" of psychopathology. Fifteen years ago, behavior therapy did not enjoy even a qualified identity. Similar to E. G. Boring's (1950) cryptic note that "psychology is what psychologists do," so it might have been argued that, in the past, behavior therapy was whatever behavior therapists did. Indeed, early behavior therapists tended to have backgrounds in the scientific study of the principles of behavior change—both respondent (or Pavlovian) and operant (or Skinnerian) conditioning. However, as knowledge of behavioral intervention effectiveness has become more widespread and interdisciplinary approaches to treatment have been increasingly encouraged (e.g., PL 94–142, ICF-MR regulations), there has been an attendant increase in the number of practitioners who label themselves or their techniques "behavioral" (Branch & Malagodi, 1981). What is less clear are the standards of what actually is "behavioral."

Principles of Behavior Analysis

The Primary Datum: Behavior.   Strictly speaking, a behavior is an action that can be described by its topographic and temporal properties. Traditionally, a behavior was defined as a publicly observable movement through space that had a discrete onset and offset. However, a procedure labeled as behavioral because it measures observable action is incomplete. Additionally, so-called radical behaviorists have begun treating nonpublic events (e.g., thoughts) as operant behaviors, which are subject to consequent effects, control of antecedent stimuli, deprivation, satiation, etc. (Homme, 1965; Skinner, 1974). To the extent that conceptualization of a presenting problem and its attendant intervention are consistent with empiricism and established behavioral principles and methods, we may comfortably study and treat so-called cognitive variables (e.g., thoughts, images, and feelings).

One of the most prevalent cognitive behavioral arenas has been that of *self-control*. As B. F. Skinner (1953) has noted, self-control essentially involves an individual bringing one's own behavior under the influence of an important but weak consequence (e.g., drinking alcohol in moderation to avoid a delayed hangover). To the extent that a clinician may specify the environmental variables that assist an individual to sharpen the control of a "weak" consequence (or weaken an undesirable strong consequence), the behavioral scientific community will be satisfied. However, if the critical independent variable is described as willpower, cognitive-symbolic thinking, or structural changes at interneural synapses, a replicable technology of child behavior therapy is precluded. While each of these constructs may someday prove influential, they are not now empirically accessible to the behaviorally oriented clinician.

Contributions of Respondent and Operant Paradigms.   The two main fields of scientific inquiry that have examined behavior change techniques typically have looked at "controlling variables" that affect the probability of a behavioral occurrence. Respondent paradigms typically measure the effects of stimulus contiguity (i.e., conditioned stimulus-unconditioned stimulus) on "reflexive" behavior. Operant paradigms have assessed so-called voluntary behavior via examining the multiple effects of both antecedent stimuli and strengthening/weakening consequences. Of critical importance, a relatively finite set of behavior change principles has evolved from studies of each paradigm. Depending on whether a clinician-practitioner is targeting respondent or operant behavior, a set of operationally defined principles can be drawn on to develop various empirically testable behavior change procedures. While multiple treatment packages may have been previously applied to any given presenting problem, the idiographic nature of child behavior therapy argues for the creative synthesis of all available resources. As a result, every clinical intervention may in a sense be considered "new." Thus, the distinction between practitioner and researcher becomes less clear; the practitioner-clinician is accordingly obligated to intervene systematically, evaluate assiduously, and speak operationally (i.e., conservatively).

As we begin to extract the defining properties of behavior therapy, we may now note that said interventions encompass:

1. Quantitative analyses of actual performance, including contiguous antecedent and consequent events.

2. The relation between these current environmental variables and the presenting problem.
3. A precise vocabulary for relating the therapeutic intervention performed to established principles of behavior change.

An Evaluative Methodology

An additional critical feature of behavioral intervention is the methodology used to demonstrate the relation between treatment and effect. Typically, behavioral research has utilized intrasubject replication designs (Sidman, 1960). Intrasubject designs characteristically have great internal validity (i.e., they can demonstrate the effects of the independent variable on the dependent measure; Campbell & Stanley, 1963). This power has implications for judging clinical "success." While traditional between-group designs allow judgments of the statistical significance of very slight treatment effects, intrasubject analyses are usually accomplished through visual inspection of frequency polygons or graphs. This conservative methodology increases the probability that demonstrations of experimental success will be both quantitatively and clinically significant (Baer, 1977).

Note, however, that behavioral procedures and methodology do *not* equate to treatment efficacy. Psychoanalysis, client-centered therapy, and other traditional psychotherapies have helped a myriad of clients. However, the strengths of the behavioral approach are that it explicitly attempts to develop a technology of treatments that can be replicated and it provides a quantitative basis for evaluating the degree to which therapeutic effects are reproduced (Johnston & Pennypacker, 1980). That such issues should be of interest to the clinician is predicated on the assumption that most clinical interventions are individualized and that the small N characteristic of even carefully monitored intrasubject designs is an inherent limitation to external validity. That is, the probability of outcome reproduction is directly proportional to the degree to which any given client is similar to the population with which a treatment has been demonstrated. M&M candies may reinforce in-seat behavior of retarded preschoolers but likely will fail as rewards for academic performance from inner-city teens. As behavioral research consistently demonstrates, individual differences among subjects is more the rule than the exception. Thus, every attempt to utilize a documented procedure is, in effect, somewhat of an exploratory endeavor.

Attention to established behavioral research methods can ensure that these endeavors constitute systematic replications of previously researched interventions. Such systematic replications not only enhance external validity by enlarging the population with which a given treatment can be demonstrated effective, but also offer new knowledge critical for the development of a replicable technology of behavioral treatment. Parametric analyses (of treatment intensity), component analyses (of treatment package elements), cost analyses, and consumer satisfaction evaluations may all be incorporated in replications, and they contribute new knowledge to tomorrow's clinicians and their clients. Of course, there are very real limitations inherent in clinical research, and these limitations interact with the treatment model employed. However, utilization of a methodology that successfully blends human service delivery and the experimental analysis of behavior may assist in the development of a basis for treatment selection and implementation.

Contemporary Models of Intervention

The Neobehavioristic Mediational S-R Model.   Eysenck (1982) describes the emphasis of this threatment model as one that attends closely to stimulus-response relations and organismic mediation. Similarly, Agras, Kazdin, and Wilson (1979) note that the S-R treatment model explains classically conditioned S-R relationships by reference to various hypothetical constructs (e.g., anxiety). Thus, this "behavioristic" model is similar but not intended to be as fully consistent with the behavioral parameters discussed above. Basic research supportive of this model includes psychophysiological measurement of activation or arousal phenomena as a function of presentation of actual feared stimuli and symbolic representation thereof. Rather than intervening with cognitions per se, S-R models employ therapeutic respondent conditioning as a means of developing more adaptive S-R links. Ostensibly, therapeutically conditioned S-R relations contribute to improved client adjustment, as in systematic desensitization.

Social Learning Theory.   Bandura (1977) postulates three regulatory systems that interact in the acquisition and maintenance of behavior. *Stimulus contiguity* in the external environment is one system; *external consequences* (e.g., reinforcement) constitute the second. The most influential system, however, involves *cognitive mediation.* Accordingly, the effects of stimulus contiguity are explained by reference to "expectations," and reinforcement provides "information" but does not automatically have an incentive effect. Vicarious learning may occur without active response emission and without external consequences. Therefore, therapy involves the client's self-directed participation in modification of, for example, expectations of personal efficacy. The client is an object of environmental influence but, more importantly, is an active agent of change in the social learning model.

Cognitive Behavior Modification.   Like the social learning model, the cognitive behavioral treatment model also targets thoughts or cognitions, which are viewed as determinants of client behavior. Some authors relate more traditional psychotherapies to cognitive behavior modification (e.g., Agras et al., 1979). Others suggest a more narrow perspective, that is, that the defining property of cognitive behavior modification is the application of behavior modification techniques to thoughts (covert-operants, or "coverants," as per Homme, 1965), in order to bring about clinical change in more publicly accessible behavior.

Applied Behavior Analysis. Agras et al. (1979) suggest that the applied behavior analysis treatment model focuses on consequences and their effects on overt behaviors. These authors mistakenly suggest that this approach is "consistent with Skinner's doctrine of radical behaviorism" (p. 7). To the contrary, this approach is consistent with methodological behaviorism and logical positivism; radical behaviorism explicitly studies "events taking place within the private world within the skin" (Skinner, 1974, p. 16). Of critical importance, however, private events are *not* viewed as causal agents in response emission. Skinner suggests that we view these events as collateral products of environmental and genetic influences—a position compatible with Homme's (1965) conceptualization of the covert operant or "coverant."

Baer (1982) provides a slightly different perspective of applied behavior analysis treatment models. From a position reminiscent of Boring (1950), Baer describes the "model" as the collective verbal behavior of persons who call themselves applied behavior analysts. He further identifies ten dimensions of this collective verbal behavior and suggests that they may be variously combined to produce 255 different treatment models. Four of these (neobehavioristic, social learning, cognitive behavior modification, and what is traditionally referred to as the applied behavior analysis treatment model) have been labeled; 251 remain to be more formally articulated. Consequently, the clinician's task of treatment selection becomes increasingly complex.

A compilation of child behavior therapy treatment models now seems a more formidable task. To review, some authors (e.g., Agras et al., 1979) include traditional psychotherapy in cognitive behavior modification; others (e.g., Baer, 1982) include all previously described models, with an additional 251, within applied behavior analysis. Note that each approach has generated a set of therapeutic interventions that have been successfully replicated by therapists in multiple settings with a variety of clients. With regard to which of the 255 treatment models is actually "correct," the reader is referred to a discussion of complex schedules of reinforcement by Rider (1983), who notes: "[research] findings are incompatible with the notion of a single model of behavior change" (p. 265). In fact, behavior and its determinants are probably far more complex than our collective attempts to account for them verbally. Perhaps the greatest strength of child behavior therapy does not involve subscription to any single treatment model but lies in the methodology used to account for empirically validated treatment effects. This analytic methodology permits utilization of proven procedures, and suggests logical and innovative extensions. A more detailed review of this methodology will underscore how this text and related reviews of effective behavioral procedures can contribute to proven and replicable interventions or to a technology of child behavior therapy.

TOWARD A TECHNOLOGY OF CHILD BEHAVIOR THERAPY

In 1968, Don Baer, Montrose Wolf, and Todd Risley described some of the then current dimensions of applied behavior analysis in an article by the same name. Today, these seven dimensions are still used to judge the quality of applied behavioral research, contributing heavily to the model of clinician as scientist. As Baer, Wolf, and Risley (1968) noted, good research studies should be:

1. Applied (i.e., target a socially or clinically significant problem).
2. Behavioral (i.e., measure actual in vivo performance).
3. Analytic (i.e., changes in performance should be functionally related to treatment).
4. Technological (i.e., operationally or procedurally detailed).
5. Conceptually systematic (i.e., related to established behavior change principles).
6. Effective (i.e., clinically significant change is demonstrated).
7. Generalizable (i.e., over time, across settings, etc.).

In this seminal discussion, Baer, Wolf, and Risley (1968) compared and contrasted "basic" behavioral research with applied behavioral research. Common features included a discovery-oriented focus, careful environmental control of nonmanipulated variables, and demonstration of functional (experimental) relationships. Differences between basic and applied studies were described in terms of degree. Because applied research is constrained to examine socially relevant dependent measures, environmental control of extraneous variables in "real life" settings is necessarily attenuated. Similarly, multiple demonstrations of experimentally controlled behavior change are ethically incompatible with accomplishing clinically significant improvement. High quality applied behavior analysis research can be expected to be less methodologically rigorous than basic research. This loss is accordingly justified by the discovery of knowledge regarding techniques to improve socially relevant behavior.

Applied Behavior Analysis and Behavior Therapy

Early applied behavior analysis investigations typically occurred in settings that, while less controllable than a laboratory setting, offered far greater environmental control than most behavior therapeutic interventions can achieve. For example, early applied behavior analysis investigations were most often accomplished in classrooms, residential institutions, or other restrictive facilities. Often, experimenters had immediate administrative or supervisory responsibility for the delivery of therapeutic interventions (e.g., instruction, training, or behavior deceleration) to clients. Accomplishment of problem-solving research in these settings was a readily appended mission for behaviorally oriented psychologists and demanded only that an appropriate experimental design and reliable data collection methods be superimposed on the treatment paradigm.

The relationship between applied behavior analysis and behavior therapy is not dissimilar to that between basic research and applied behavioral research. That is, while the applied behavior analyst is restricted in his/her ability to control external variables and demonstrate repeated relationships with subjects' performance, the clinician experiences even greater limitations. For example, the clinician rarely has a priori control over antecedent and consequent conditions. The implicit significance of a clinically relevant problem argues against treatment withdrawal or delay, as in a reversal or multiple baseline design. Further, data collection is typically not accomplished by trained observers but by the client or the clients' significant others. In child behavior therapy, these significant others are typically parents and/or teachers who are likely involved in the problem or its remediation and, thus, likely to be less objective and/or reliable in observation. Finally, the clinician rarely has direct control over treatment in child behavior therapy. Instead, the clinician must prepare and monitor others in the delivery of a potentially complex or counterintuitive therapeutic intervention.

The goal of discovery is also common to clinical intervention. However, in clinical intervention there is a relatively greater priority for the discovery of a solution for a specific client problem than there is for demonstration of the functional relation between treatment and performance change. Claims of efficacy are difficult to evaluate fully. Behavior therapy judgments of clinically significant change are typically determined by the client rather than by journal editors or other experts (cf., Kazdin, 1977; Wolf, 1978). And in child behavior therapy, judgments of treatment success are typically one step further removed. That is, the subject of intervention is not the consumer of service. Instead, parents typically decide when a treatment has "worked." Nevertheless, clinical research may discover new knowledge and also may allow specification of those conditions under which well known facts actually do apply. Further, clinical research may clarify basic issues in the principles of behavior. For example, an exciting but not well understood phenomenon concerns decreases in reinforcement in one setting that contribute to performance changes in another setting. Sometimes the performance change in the other setting will be an increase in response rate (*behavioral contrast*); at other times the rate decreases (*induction*). To the extent that clinical researchers can contribute to an understanding of these processes, it may be possible to account for clients' "mood shifts" or aberrant behavior which are not apparently functionally related to immediately observable environmental events.

Conclusion

A model of treatment selection and implementation that prioritizes valid data collection techniques, replicability of treatment, and the functional relation between intervention and clients status will make a genuine contribution to the systematic growth of child behavior therapy. Despite the problems inherent in applied clinical practice, treatment efficacy claims can be corroborated. It is via this empirical treatment model that we truly develop a technology of child behavior therapy.

CASE PRESENTATION

While behavioral assessment and treatment models provide clinicians with data gathering and intervention strategies, they must be placed within the broader context of a thoroughly integrated assessment-treatment framework. Thus, the purpose of this chapter section is to translate the principles and procedures heretofore discussed into practical examples for clinical application. To accomplish this, we will use an actual clinical case reported by Bornstein, Balleweg, McLellarn, Wilson, Sturm, Andre, and van den Pol (1983).

Client and Client History

Josh R., a 10-year-old Caucasian, was referred for treatment by a local physician for encopresis and chronic constipation. Josh had been sucessfully toilet trained at approximately 30 months of age in a manner which appeared quite unremarkable. However, just prior to his fifth birthday and coincidental with the birth of his sister, Josh's toileting behavior became highly irregular. Initially, he would demonstrate extended periods of retentiveness each lasting up to one week. As expected under such conditions (Doleys, 1981), megacolon and fecal impactions occurred. Consequently, Josh was hospitalized on two separate occasions for the removal of these fecal masses. Following this period of retentiveness, Josh remained constipated and began to exhibit a low frequency (approximately one per week) of toileting accidents. However, this frequency progressively increased, and by age eight, Josh soiled at an estimated rate of four to five times per week. At this time, appropriate toileting behavior was occurring approximately once per week.

Behavioral assessment revealed that thorough medical evaluations had been conducted. Obstructive rectal examinations, barium enemas, and dietary intake analyses had all proved negative. As a result, over the course of the five-year period, a variety of treatments had been attempted. These included use of stool softeners and laxatives, environmental manipulations (e.g., placing toys in the bathroom), and a myriad of consultations with local medical specialists. Josh's parents appeared generally quite capable. They had experienced no other serious problems with either child, and a clinical interview revealed that they had manifested considerable competencies regarding the application of parental consequences to child behavior.

Integrated Assessment and Treatment

Given the above information, an intervention plan was formulated and was shared with Mr. and Mrs. R. just prior to the initiation of treatment. It was explained that the soiling may have first developed in response to the birth of Josh's sister. However, it appeared that a new set of circumstances had come to maintain the inappropriate behavior; that is, untimely reinforcement for both constipation and soiling had maintained the problem behavior. Furthermore, moisture from recent fecal masses was being absorbed, producing hard stools and painful defecation. Thus, treatment was directed toward the development of an incentive program for the appropriate elimination of feces. Consequently, the "bathroom game" was presented as a means by which therapy would attempt to reverse contingencies and thereby reinforce nonsoiling behavior.

Experimental Design and Dependent Measures

An ABAB reversal design was utilized to evaluate the efficacy of the therapeutic intervention (Bornstein et al., 1981). During the initial interview, the parents were provided with recording sheets and asked to note all confirmed incidents of soiling and appropriate bowel movements. Incidents of soiling were broadly defined, including both small fecal stains and full bowel movements. Appropriate toileting recorded only when bowel movements occurred as Josh was sitting on the commode. Rather than relying solely on Josh's report, the parents were asked to confirm the occurrence of all appropriate bowel movements. This was accomplished throughout the course of treatment and was recorded by parents on the monitoring sheets that had been provided. Records were collected on a weekly basis and served as the sole source of data presentation.

Procedure

Baseline 1.   This condition was in effect for three weeks, during which time no experimental operations were implemented. The parents were instructed to continue treating Josh in their routine manner, that is, toileting was to be self-initiated, without prompt, and with the continued dosage of one daily tablespoon of mineral oil.

"Bathroom Game 1".   This experimental condition utilized the cards displayed in Figure 2–2. It was explained to Josh that to help him gain control over his toileting behavior, he and the therapist would be playing a game. This game consisted of two identical cards that allowed for the recording of soiling and appropriate toileting incidents. Josh was to have his parents complete the card on a daily basis. If an occurrence of soiling took place, a yes was to be written on that day in the soiling column. Similarly, if a confirmed instance of an appropriate bowel movement were to occur, then a yes was to be scribed in the

---

FIGURE 2-2

Child and Therapist Cards Used in the "Bathroom Game"

Child's Card				Therapist's Card		
Day	Soiling	B.M.		Day	Soiling	B.M.
Mon.				Mon.		*
Tues.				Tues.	*	*
Wed.				Wed.		
Thur.				Thur.	*	*
Fri.				Fri.	*	
Sat.				Sat.		*
Sun.				Sun.		

B.M. column. It was further explained that the therapist's card would have a series of stars on it, and on those days for which the therapist's stars appeared, Josh would have the opportunity to earn financial rewards. Specifically, Josh would earn 50 cents for every starred no in the soiling column and 25 cents for every starred yes in the B.M. column. In addition, Josh was heavily praised by the therapist for all instances of nonsoiling and occurrences of appropriate bowel movements. Starred days were randomly determined by the therapist. During this phase, stars appeared on a variable ratio schedule of one star every two days for both soiling and B.M. columns. The "Bathroom Game 1" condition remained in effect for three weeks.

Baseline 2.   Following the above phase, the family was informed that, since the problem had responded so well to treatment, the "game" could now be terminated and Josh could be expected to maintain the progress achieved. This condition remained in effect for two weeks.

"Bathroom Game 2".   Family members were informed that since withdrawal of the treatment program indicated a reversal of therapeutic effects, it would be necessary to reimplement the "game" procedures. However, beginning with week 11, a programmatic fading scheme was initiated. This was accomplished by progressively leaning out the variable ratio schedule of reinforcement and the mineral oil supplement over the course of the following six weeks (weeks 11–16). Thus, by week 16, only one star appeared on the entire "bathroom card." Beginning with week 17, the "bathroom cards" were no longer utilized, and instead Josh was simply provided with the therapist's social praise, contigent upon continued successful performance. Finally, beginning with week 19, the number of scheduled sessions was decreased, so that only three more sessions were conducted prior to termination at week 28. During this fading of sessions, weekly data were continuously collected through telephone contact with the parents.

Follow-up.   One year after treatment, Mr. and Mrs. R. were recontacted regarding Josh's soiling and appropriate toileting behavior.

Results

Figure 2–3 displays the number of soilings and appropriate bowel movements occurring during all experimental periods. The mean number of weekly soiling incidents across conditions was: Baseline 1 = 4.7, "Bathrom Game 1" = 0.7, Baseline 2 = 3.0, "Bathroom Game 2" = 0.1. Correspondingly, the mean number of appropriate bowel movements per week was: Baseline 1 = 1.03, "Bathroom Game 1" = 3.0, Baseline 2 = 0.5, "Bathroom Game 2" = 4.4. In addition, during follow-up, the parents reported zero incidents of soiling and an average of five appropriate bowel movements per week.

Discussion

The results of this case presentation clearly reveal the effectiveness of the "bathroom game" in the elimination of secondary, retentive encopresis. Func-

---

FIGURE 2–3

Number of Soilings and Appropriate Bowel Movements across Experimental Conditions

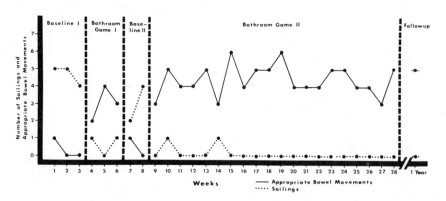

tional control over the frequency of both soiling and appropriate bowel movements was convincingly demonstrated via utilization of a variable ratio schedule of reinforcement in an ABAB reversal design. More importantly, however, was the means by which a thorough behavioral assessment led to the generation of an effective treatment strategy. Furthermore, both evaluation and intervention were based on conceptual behavioral models with clear pragmatic ramifications.

REFERENCES

Agras, W. S., Kazdin, A. E., & Wilson, G. T. *Behavior therapy: Toward an applied clinical science*. San Francisco: W. H. Freeman, 1979.

Baer, D. M. Perhaps it would be better not to know everything. *Journal of Applied Behavior Analysis*, 1977, *10*, 67–172.

Baer, D. M. Applied behavior analysis. In G. T. Wilson & C. M. Franks (Eds.), *Contemporary behavior therapy*. New York: Guilford Press, 1982.

Baer, D. M., Wolf, M. M., & Risley, T. R. Some current dimensions of applied behavior analysis. *Journal of Applied Behavior Analysis*, 1968, *1*, 91–98.

Barlow, D. H., Hayes, S. C., & Nelson, R. O. *The scientist practitioner: Research and accountability in clinical and educational settings*. New York: Pergamon Press, 1984.

Bandura, A. *Social learning theory*. Englewood Cliffs, N.J.: Prentice Hall, 1977.

Birnbrauer, J. S. Some guides to designing behavior programs. In D. Marholin (Ed.), *Child behavior therapy*. New York: Gardner Press, 1978.

Boring, E. G. *A history of experimental psychology*. New York: Appleton-Century-Crofts, 1950.

Bornstein, P. H., Balleweg, B. J., McLellarn, R. W., Wilson, G. L., Sturm, C. A., Andre, J. C., & van den Pol, R. A. The "bathroom game": A systematic program for the elimination of encopretic behavior. *Journal of Behavior Therapy and Experimental Psychiatry*, 1983, *14*, 67–71.

Bornstein, P. H., Bornstein, M. T., & Dawson, B. Integrated assessment and treatment. In T. H. Ollendick & M. Hersen (Eds.), *Child behavioral assessment: Principles and procedures*. New York: Pergamon Press, 1984.

Bornstein, P. H., Bridgwater, C. A., Hickey, J. S., & Sweeney, T. M. Characteristics and trends in behavioral assessment: An archival analysis. *Behavioral Assessment*, 1980, *2*, 125–133.

Bornstein, P. H., Fox, S. G., Sturm, C. A., Balleweg, B. J., Kirby, K. L., Wilson, G. L., Weisser, C. E., Andre, J. C., & McLellarn, R. W. Treatment acceptability of alternative marital therapies: A comparative analysis. *Journal of Marital and Family Therapy*, 1983, *9*, 205–208.

Bornstein, P. H., Hamilton, S. B., & Bornstein, M. T. Self-monitoring procedures. In A. R. Ciminero, H. S. Calhoun, & H. E. Adams (Eds.), *Handbook of behavioral assessment*. New York: John Wiley & Sons, in press.

Bornstein, P. H., & Knapp, M. Self-control desensitization with a multi-phobic boy. *Journal of Behavior Therapy and Experimental Psychiatry,* 1982, *12,* 281–285.

Bornstein, P. H., & Rychtarik, R. W. Consumer satisfaction in adult behavior therapy: Procedures, problems, and future perspectives. *Behavior Therapy,* 1983, *14,* 191–208.

Bornstein, P. H., Sturm, C. A., Retzlaff, P. D., Kirby, K. L., & Chong, H. Paradoxical instruction in the treatment of encopresis and chronic constipation: An experimental analysis. *Journal of Behavior Therapy and Experimental Psychiatry,* 1981, *12,* 167–170.

Bornstein, P. H., Weisser, C. E., & Balleweg, B. J. The assessment and treatment of anger and violent behavior. In M. Hersen & A. Bellack (Eds.), *Handbook of clinical behavior therapy with adults.* New York: Plenum Press, in press.

Branch, M. N., & Malagodi, E. F. Where have all the behaviorists gone? *The Behavior Analyst,* 1980, *3,* 31–38.

Campbell, D. T., & Stanley, J. C. *Experimental and quasi-experimental designs for research.* Chicago: Rand McNally, 1963.

Ciminero, A. R. Behavioral assessment: An overview. In A. R. Ciminero, K. S. Calhoun, & H. E. Adams (Eds.), *Handbook of behavioral assessment.* New York: John Wiley & Sons, 1977.

Ciminero, A. R., & Drabman, R. S. Current developments in the behavioral assessment of children. In B. B. Lahey & A. E. Kazdin (Eds.), *Advances in clinical child psychology* (Vol. 1). New York: Plenum Press, 1977.

Cone, J. D. The behavioral assessment grid (BAG): A conceptual framework and taxonomy. *Behavior Therapy,* 1978, *9,* 882–888.

Dickson, C. R. Role of assessment in behavior therapy. In P. McReynolds (Ed.), *Advances in psychological assessment* (Vol. 3). San Francisco: Jossey-Bass, 1975.

Doleys, D. M. Encopresis. In M. Ferguson & B. Taylor (Eds.), *The comprehensive handbook of behavioral medicine.* New York: Spectrum, 1981.

Evans, I. M., & Nelson, R. O. Assessment of child behavior problems. In A. R. Ciminero, K. S. Calhoun, & H. E. Adams (Eds.), *Handbook of behavioral assessment.* New York: John Wiley & Sons, 1977.

Eysenck, H. J. Neobehavioristic (S-R) theory. In G. T. Wilson & C. M. Franks (Eds.), *Contemporary behavior therapy.* New York: Guilford Press, 1982.

Furman, W., & Drabman, R. S. Methodological issues in child behavior therapy. In M. Hersen, R. M. Eisler, & P. M. Miller (Eds.), *Progress in behavior modification* (Vol. II). New York: Academic Press, 1981.

Goldfried, M. R. Behavioral assessment in perspective. In J. D. Cone & R. P. Hawkins (Eds.), *Behavioral assessment: New directions in clinical psychology.* New York: Brunner/Mazel, 1977.

Hartmann, D. P., Roper, B. L., & Bradford, D. C. Some relationships between behavioral and traditional assessment. *Journal of Behavioral Assessment,* 1979, *1,* 3–21.

Hawkins, R. P. Who decided *that* was the problem? Two stages of responsibility for applied behavior analysis. In W. S. Wood (Ed.), *Issues in evaluating behavior modification*. Champaign, Ill.: Research Press, 1975.

Herjanic, G., Herjanic, M., Brown, F., & Wheatt, T. Are children reliable reporters? *Journal of Abnormal Child Psychology*, 1975, *3*, 41–48.

Hersen, M., & Barlow, D. H. *Single-case experimental designs: Strategies for studying behavior change*. New York: Pergamon Press, 1976.

Homme, L. E. Perspectives in psychology: XXIV. Control of coverants, the operants of the mind. *Psychological Record*, 1965, *15*, 501–511.

Iwata, B. A., & Bailey, J. S. Reward *versus* cost token systems: An analysis of the effects on students and teachers. *Journal of Applied Behavioral Analysis*, 1974, *7*, 567–576.

Johnston, J. M., & Pennypacker, H. S. *Strategies and tactics of human behavioral research*. Hillsdale, N.J.: Lawrence Erlbaum Associates, Inc., 1980.

Kanfer, F. H., & Nay, W. R. Behavioral assessment. In G. T. Wilson & C. M. Franks (Eds.), *Contemporary behavior therapy: Conceptual and empirical foundations*. New York: Guilford Press, 1982.

Kanfer, F. H., & Saslow, G. Behavioral diagnosis. In C. M. Franks (Ed.), *Behavior therapy: Appraisal and status*. New York: McGraw-Hill, 1969.

Kazdin, A. E., Assessing the clinical or applied significance of behavior change through social validation. *Behavior Modification*, 1977, *1*, 427–452.

Kazdin, A. E. *Single-case research designs: Methods for clinical and applied settings*. New York: Oxford, 1982.

Kazdin, A. E., & Wilson, G. T. *Evaluation of behavior therapy*. Cambridge, Mass.: Ballinger, 1978.

Keefe, F. J., Kopel, S. A., & Gordon, S. B. *A practical guide to behavioral assessment*. New York: Springer, 1978.

Kratochwill, T. R. (Ed.). *Single-subject research: Strategies for evaluating change*. New York: Academic Press, 1978.

Lazarus, A. A. Multimodal behavior therapy: Treating the "BASIC ID". *Journal of Nervous and Mental Disease*, 1973, *156*, 404–411.

Mahoney, M. J. *Cognition and behavior modification*. Cambridge, Mass.: Ballinger, 1974.

Mash, E. J., & Terdal, L. G. Behavioral assessment of childhood disturbance. In E. J. Mash & L. G. Terdal (Eds.), *Behavioral assessment of childhood disorders*. New York: Guilford Press, 1981.

Mischel, W. *Personality and assessment*. New York: John Wiley & Sons, 1968.

Nay, W. R. *Multimethod clinical assessment*. New York: Gardner Press, 1979.

Nelson, R. O., & Hayes, S. C. The nature of behavioral assessment: A commentary. *Journal of Applied Behavior Analysis*, 1979, *12*, 491–500.

Ollendick, T. H., & Cerny, J. A. *Clinical behavior therapy with children*. New York: Plenum Press, 1981.

Peterson, D. R. *The clinical study of social behavior.* New York: Appleton-Century-Crofts, 1968.

Rider, D. P. Preference for mixed versus constant delays of reinforcement: Effect of probability of the short, mixed delay. *Journal of the Experimental Analysis of Behavior,* 1983, *39,* 257–266.

Sidman, M. *Tactics of scientific research.* New York: Basic Books, 1960.

Skinner, B. F. *Science and human behavior.* New York: Macmillan, 1953.

Skinner, B. F. *About behaviorism.* New York: Alfred A. Knopf, 1974.

Stuart, R. B. *Trick or treatment: How and when psychotherapy fails.* Champaign, Ill.: Research Press, 1970.

Thomas, D. R., Becker, W. C., & Armstrong, M. Production and elimination of disruptive classroom behavior by systematically varying teacher's behavior. *Journal of Applied Behavioral Analysis,* 1968, *1,* 35–45.

VanHasselt, V. B., Hersen, M., & Bellack, A. S. The validity of role play tests for assessing social skills in children. *Behavior Therapy,* 1981, *12,* 202–216.

Wade, T. C., Baker, T. B., & Hartmann, D. P. Behavior therapists' self-reported views and practices. *The Behavior Therapist,* 1979, *2,* 3–6.

Webb, E. J., Campbell, D. T., Schwartz, R. D., & Sechrest, L. *Unobtrusive measures: Nonreactive research in the social sciences.* Chicago: Rand McNally, 1966.

Wittlieb, E., Eifert, G., Wilson, F. E., & Evans, I. M. Target behavior selection in recent child case reports in behavior therapy. *The Behavior Therapist,* 1979, *1,* 15–16.

Wolf, M. M. Social validity: The case for subjective measurement on how applied behavior analysis is finding its heart. *Journal of Applied Behavior Analysis,* 1978, *11,* 203–214.

Yeaton, W. H., & Sechrest, L. Critical dimensions in the choice and maintenance of successful treatments. Strength, integrity, and effectiveness. *Journal of Consulting and Clinical Psychology,* 1981, *49,* 156–168.

3

Outcome Evaluation in Child Behavior Therapy: Methodological and Conceptual Issues*

Philip C. Kendall
Temple University

Cynthia Koehler
Neuropsychiatric Clinic, UCLA

Unfortunately, progress in the evaluation of child behavior therapy has not kept pace with the evaluation of behavior therapy in general. To date, there is comparatively little good controlled outcome research on any form of therapy for children. Efforts need to be made "to resist the trend toward making children parapeople who receive paraservice based on results from pararesearch" (Barrett, Hampe, & Miller, 1978). Investigations of behavioral techniques have been at the forefront of efforts to remedy the dearth of well-designed child therapy outcome evaluations.

Outcome research with children presents a number of special challenges not encountered in the evaluation of therapy outcome for adults. First, it is difficult to determine whose opinions about the behavior changes desired should be considered. Parents, teachers, and peers are all likely to have different opinions from those of the child who actually receives therapy. In addressing ethical issues of research in behavior therapy, Stolz expressed the following opinion:

* Completion of this manuscript was facilitated by a National Institute of Mental Health Research in Psychopathology Training fellowship (#1T32MH17069–01) awarded to the second author.

"It seems to me that it is pertinent to ask who will benefit from the 'control' that results from the intervention. Is the child's behavior being changed for the benefit of the school, of the parent, of the experimenter, or of the child?" (1975, p. 246). These are not easy questions to answer, but they are important questions to ask, and will be incorporated into our discussion of the appropriate criteria for evaluating child behavior therapy.

Another factor complicating the evaluation of child behavior therapy outcome is that behavioral programs for children frequently involve a number of aspects of the child's environment. It is therefore possible that changes might take place not only in the child's behavior, but also in the operation of a number of systems within which the child interacts. Interventions that are capable of affecting entire classrooms or family units may be exceptionally potent and efficacious, but this generalized impact makes evaluations difficult. How do we compare the efficacy of a technique that seems to have decreased significantly a child's behavior problems in school with one that has decreased the child's school behavior problems to a somewhat lesser degree, but also has had a positive influence on the way other members of the class respond to the target child? This is just one example of the type of question the evaluator of treatments for children must face.

One final major concern for the evaluation of behavior change in children has to do with separating change due to treatment from the natural course of development of children. Normal developmental issues must be carefully delineated and controlled for in research, because most children's behavior changes through maturation at a much quicker pace than that of adults.

EARLY EFFORTS AND RUMBLINGS OF DISSATISFACTION

Case studies have been a traditional means by which therapy outcome has been reported. These studies usually consist of fairly detailed descriptions of the client, the treatment, and the "results." Although case studies often deal with topics of much clinical interest, numerous methodological shortcomings prevent them from being a dependable source of treatment efficacy conclusions. Ross (1981b) has described case studies as high on clinical relevance but low on scientific rigor.

The first limitation of the case study is that it is almost exclusively those cases that were "successful" or impelling by virtue of being idiosyncratic that are published. While unrepresentative publishing procedures are certainly not unique to the case study method, they do present special problems for the case study method, because combined with the lack of other kinds of experimental control, they prevent reliable conclusions from being drawn. Another limitation of the case study is that even the most sincere clinician's self-report about self-evaluated therapeutic improvement is subject to question. Moreover, many case studies include a number of different treatment approaches within the one case, preventing identification of the "active" treatment. One of the most serious limitations of the case study is that one simply cannot generalize from an accumulation of case studies and make summary evaluative statements (Browning & Stover, 1971). Despite numerous limitations, case studies may be useful for generating hypotheses and for suggesting potentially beneficial areas for controlled research.

Early group-comparison outcome studies were designed to answer questions such as, "Does therapy work?" and "Which therapy works best?" Many researchers have expressed dismay at the numerous unwarranted assumptions underlying these questions. In 1966, Kiesler delineated some "myths" of psychotherapy research, which were serving to "weaken research designs and confuse the interpretation of research findings" (1966, p. 110). Most relevant to the present discussion are his uniformity assumption myths, as applied both to patients and therapists. These assumptions cause researchers to ignore the heterogeneity of patients and therapists and to attempt to make sweeping summary statements about the effects of psychotherapies in general, rather than recognizing that specific therapeutic techniques may be differentially effective for different clients, especially as they are provided by different types of therapists. Efforts have been made to remedy some of these research design deficiencies, but many journal articles still end with the plea for more factorial research that incorporates a number of diverse characteristics of therapies, clients, and therapists. Kiesler's proposed solution was the adoption of a factorially designed *grid model* (1971), which attacks uniformity assumptions by including in every outcome study design at least one client characteristic variable, at least one therapist characteristic variable, at least two different outcome measures, and a variable time of outcome assessment for different clients. This model deserves continued attention.

Paul has been a behavioral critic of the manner in which conventional outcome research had been conducted. He stated, "The initial question posed, 'Does psychotherapy work?' is virtually meaningless" (1967, p. 111). Marshall (1980) reports that VandenBos, a policy official at the American Psychological Association, responded to that question by retorting, "It is a stupid question. It's like asking 'Does surgery work?' Does surgery work in treating the common cold?" Clearly, the question as usually posed is not sufficiently specific to allow for meaningful answers. Kiesler (1966) and, more quotably, Paul proposed that, "The question towards which all outcome research should ultimately be directed is the following: *What* treatment, by *whom* is most effective for *this* individual with *that* specific problem, and under *which* set of circumstances?" (1967, p. 111). This question directly attacks the uniformity myths as discussed by Kiesler (1966) and merits the continued reiteration that it has received (e.g., Gottman & Markman, 1978; Greenspan & Sharfstein, 1981; Kendall & Norton-Ford, 1982a).

Unfortunately, the initial rush to compare therapies was premature. Studies documenting the efficacy of specific therapeutic techniques must precede any comparisons of otherwise unproven methods (Rachman & Wilson, 1980). Kazdin and Wilson wrote: "The comparison is only important when each technique is known to be effective in some specific area and presents an alternative to an existing treatment with similar evidence" (1978b, p. 158).

There were also some early efforts to evaluate *behavior therapy* as if it were a single "monolithic entity" (Kazdin & Wilson, 1978b, p. 174). As mindful practitioners and contemporary researchers know, neither behavior therapy, behavior therapy for children, cognitive-behavioral therapy for children, nor the general term *psychotherapy* can be meaningfully evaluated as wholes. The strategies encompassed by each of these global labels are numerous and diverse, requiring focused consideration. Although researchers have recently reported more circumscribed comparisons and evaluations, some published discussions of the effects and procedures of therapy continue to mask numerous strategic variations (e.g., Ellis, 1980). Increasingly loud rumblings of dissatisfaction with this problem and other unwarranted assumptions have helped to clarify the questions asked and the strategies employed in the evaluation of child behavioral interventions.

CULPRITS OF EXPERIMENTAL INADEQUACY

Well-controlled experimentation in behavior therapy consists of the manipulation of one or more independent variables, while other variables are held constant to keep them from influencing the results—the goal being to determine that the independent variable was responsible for changes observed in the dependent variable. Mahoney has summarized the "10 most common culprits in experimental inadequacy" (also referred to as *threats to internal validity*) (1978, p. 663).

Internal Validity

For the purposes of treatment outcome evaluation, the most crucial task is to determine that it was the treatment, and no other extraneous factors, that was responsible for changes observed in the child's behavior. To the extent that an experiment can accomplish this, it is said to have internal validity. The other extraneous variables are referred to as factors that jeopardize internal validity (Campbell & Stanley, 1963). Kendall and Norton-Ford (1982b, pp. 438–439) have developed a table that shows the manner in which these sources of internal invalidity potentially affect therapy outcome research (see Table 3–1).

The two therapy outcome research strategies that will be described and advocated are single-subject designs and between-group designs, both of which achieve experimental control by employing specific procedures designed to counteract sources of internal invalidity. For example, in between-group designs, the inclusion of a no-treatment control group allows for the examination of client changes over time and the impact of various events in everyday

TABLE 3-1

Sources of Internal Invalidity as Related to Therapy Outcome Research

source	definition	examples	
		general	specific instance
History	Events other than therapy that occur during the time period when therapy is provided; simultaneous occurrence of extratherapy events	Informal counseling by peers; important lifestyle change	A long phone call from a former roommate relieves a client's depression and gives a new meaning to his life. The phone call comes about the time that the therapist begins an important part of treatment. The depression is relieved.
Maturation	Psychological or biological changes that appear to occur naturally with the passage of time	Children's development of the capacity for abstract thought; menopausal effects	The normal cognitive development of a child may result in an increased ability to take another person's perspective, and therefore behave in a more sensitive and empathic manner. The child displays less aggression.
Testing	The impact of repeated exposure to the assessment measures	Increased skill due simply to the practice provided by repeated testing; reduced anxiety due to repeated exposure to the feared stimulus; increased self-disclosure due to multiple instances of asking personal questions	A client becomes more interpersonally skilled in social situations as a result of the researcher's role-play tests. Performing the role-play tests over and over has beneficial effects. The client more comfortably interacts with members of the opposite sex.
Instrumentation	Decay in the sensitivity-accuracy of the assessment instruments	Fatigue on the part of observers; decreased sensitivity of psychophysiological equipment due to usage	Children's attentiveness in the classroom appears to show less off-task behavior due to the observers paying less attention after having been an observer for several weeks. The observers are not seeing or recording the off-task behavior. The child appears to be paying more attention, but only because the off-task behavior is not being noticed.
Statistical regression	The tendency for persons whose initial scores on assessment measures are extreme (high or low) to have later scores that drifted toward the mean	Extreme depression (bottom of the scale) is more likely to rise, since it cannot drop further; hyperactive children are more likely to show less activity	A client who scores particularly high on a measure of anxiety before therapy is statistically more likely to score nearer the mean on a second testing than to score even higher.

TABLE 3–1 (concluded)

		examples	
source	*definition*	*general*	*specific instance*
Mortality	Attrition of participants-clients	Clients who drop out from therapy and for whom posttherapy assessments are not available	Clients in a study of the treatment of depression terminate prematurely. Their data are lost, even though they may have terminated because of a sense of already achieved relief. The client has not returned to complete the assessments.
Selection	Utilization of participants-clients who might appear to change simply because of personal factors that predispose them to do so rather than due to the intervention	Clients who volunteer for a therapy program advertised in a local newspaper may be on the verge of changing due to a high level of personal motivation.	Using adolescents in studies of peer pressure or persuasion. The characteristics of adolescent subjects tends to make them especially susceptible to peer pressure and persuasive maneuvers.

life. Inclusion of such a group permits statements to be made about the impact of treatment over and above threats to internal validity such as history and maturation.

External Validity

After demonstrating that the manipulated independent variable produced changes in the dependent variable(s) of interest, a second goal of therapy outcome research is to extend the results of the experiment beyond the immediate experiment: to generalize. Factors that prevent the results of therapy outcome studies from being generalized to actual clients or to therapists and clients with different characteristics are referred to as *threats to external validity* (Campbell & Stanley, 1963). These potential threats are described in Table 3–2.

Since any characteristic of the evaluation may later be found to be related to its results, factors that may decrease the generalizability of results cannot be identified until replications are attempted, which vary some of the factors of the initial study (Kazdin, 1980). One paradox of therapy outcome experimentation is that the main strategy for increasing external validity is to use a more heterogeneous group of clients, therapists, settings, methods, and measures to make the experiment as much like the natural therapeutic situation as possible. The problem is that the closer experimental conditions are to natural situations, the greater the number of uncontrolled factors that will pose threats to internal validity. Striking the proper balance is the challenge of clinical research.

TABLE 3-2

Threats to External Validity as Related to Therapy Outcome Research

threat	definition	*examples* general	specific instance
Interactions of the environment and testing	Preintervention assessments may sensitize clients to the intervention, thus potentiating the intervention's influence.	When clients who are to receive a therapy for fear are asked to role play the feared situation, this action may increase their motivations to change.	An otherwise ineffective treatment may appear to alleviate fear, but the fear reduction is due to increased motivation from some aspect of the study. This increased motivation would not be present when the treatment is provided outside the context of a study and would then be ineffective.
Interaction of selection and intervention	If all clients selected are a special subgroup who are particularly amenable to participation, thse clients cannot be considered comparable to the rest of the population.	If only two of the four clinics that are asked to be involved in a therapy outcome study agree to do so, the results cannot be generalized to all clinics. The two that refused might be significantly different from the two that agreed.	A project designed to compare psychological therapy, medications, and a control condition for the treatment of hyperactivity requires parents to give their informed consent. Many parents refuse to participate, not wanting their child assigned to the control condition. This selection problem reduces the researcher's ability to generalize the results to all hyperactive children.
Reactive arrangements	Clients may change due to a reaction to the fact of participating in a novel experience, rather than due to the therapy interaction.	Clients may change due to an expectancy on their parts or on the part of their therapist. Therapy must, or should, cause change, and clients change simply because they expect they ought to.	A father's physical abuse of family members is reduced by therapy not as a result of the therapist's actions, but a function of the father's belief that going to therapy will make him stop being abusive.
Multiple intervention interference	When several kinds of intervention are combined in one experience, the total effect may be very different than the outcome of any one of them in isolation.	Clients involved in multi-component therapies may fail to change because the plethora of intervention obscures the positive impacts of each separate component.	A child's acting-out, aggressive behavior pattern elicits aggression from his father, rewarding attention from his mother and his peers, and attempts at rational discussion by school authorities. A single consistent approach designed to reduce the aggression would be more effective when not interfered with by other efforts.

Generally, demonstration of internal validity is given precedence over external validity, primarily because "one must first have unambiguously demonstrated a finding before one can ask about its generality" (Kazdin, 1980, p. 51). However, for demonstrations of therapeutic efficacy, in which the "real" client is ultimately the main concern, external validity must be given serious consideration. A favored solution is a compromise in which experimental control is clearly demonstrated through an internally valid study, with further studies conducted to address questions of external validity, carefully extending the results to new clients, different therapists, a variety of dependent measures, and diverse settings.

The Integrity of the Independent Variable

A recent article (Peterson, Homer, & Wonderlich, 1982) addressed the threats to both reliability and validity posed by inaccurate or incomplete descriptions of the independent variable. Clear evaluation of therapy outcome results depends on clear knowledge of exactly what is being evaluated. The need for greater precision in variable description and for independent variable manipulation accuracy has been acknowledged by many (Fiske, Hunt, Luborsky, Orne, Parloff, Reiser, & Tuma, 1970; Kazdin & Wilson, 1978b; Kendall & Norton-Ford, 1982b, Kiesler, 1966). Mahoney has proposed the moral: "Don't take the independent variable for granted" (1978, p. 665). Clear, comprehensive description of the treatment is the first step, but the second crucial step is checking to be sure treatment was implemented as planned.

A variety of options exist for conducting checks on the manipulation. At minimum, therapists must be thoroughly trained according to a detailed protocol, with occasional checks made on the therapist during treatment (Peterson et al., 1982). A solution, which is methodologically more sound and which provides additional useful information, is to make tape recordings of therapy sessions. These can be rated for accuracy of the manipulation and can later be examined for the quality of therapy (Kendall & Hollon, 1983), as well as used to check for comparability of treatment in different studies (Kendall & Norton-Ford, 1982b).

It is highly recommended that a number of other specific aspects of treatment be evaluated and recorded. Fiske et al. (1970) have suggested many factors that could likely have an impact on therapy results and that are frequently ignored or not reported. The following is a sample of their thorough list: number of sessions missed, description of the treatment location, cost of treatment, and source of payment. Characteristics of the therapist and ratings of his or her in-therapy behavior can also add useful information. A thorough description of the client should obviously include age, education, sex, socioeconomic status, severity of problems, and diagnosis, if available. We add that details of any past or concurrent psychological or related treatment should be noted. With children, it is especially important to note the source of referral and details of the child's family situation. Although suggestions such as these may sound over-whelming to the investigator, this type of information is usually obtained fairly readily and is crucial for eventually reaching the ultimate goal of therapy outcome research, namely, documentation of the differential efficacy of specific techniques for particular types of individuals with unique problems.

SINGLE-SUBJECT DESIGNS

Single-subject designs are based on comparisons of the individual's behavior across time. These design strategies are suited to the evaluation of the impact of treatment of particular children rather than to an evaluation of average group effects. The strategy maintains the focus on the individual, similar to the case study, but it far surpasses the uncontrolled case study in empirical rigor and allows causal relationships to be identified (Kazdin, 1982b).

Single-subject designs require the continuous assessment of the child's be-havior over a period of time so that changes in behavior can be compared with changes in treatment conditions (Hayes, 1981). Most single-subject designs begin with a *baseline* phase, in which the child's behavior(s) targeted for change are observed and recorded. This baseline period provides a description of the extent of the problem behavior, allows for comparisons of the behavior after treatment is initiated, and allows the investigator to predict the course over time that the behavior would take if treatment were not initiated. Proper methodology suggests that the collection of baseline data be continued until the target behav-ior is exhibited at a stable rate. While real world factors often interfere with this methodological mandate, stable baselines are necessary so that changes in behavior after the introduction of treatment can be attributed to treatment rather than to natural behavioral fluctuation. Kazdin explains that "a projection of baseline performance into the future is the implicit criterion against which treatment is eventually evaluated" (1982b, p. 462).

Different phases of single-subject designs are typically identified by capital letters, with *A* characteristically denoting the baseline condition, and *B* repre-senting the first treatment. If more than one treatment is applied, each is represented by successive capital letters (C, D, etc.) (Ross, 1981a). A number of single-subject designs exist, and most of the major designs include a number of variations. Five basic designs are summarized below. For more detailed discussions, see Barlow and Hayes (1979), Hersen and Barlow (1976), Kazdin (1980; 1982a; 1982b) and Kazdin and Hartmann (1978).

Specific Designs

ABAB Design. The ABAB design, also called the reversal design, provides the simplest demonstration of the single-subject design rationale. Initial baseline information is gathered *(A);* the intervention *(B)* is introduced until a new stable trend emerges; the baseline contingencies are reintroduced to determine if the behavior reverses to its previous pattern and level; then, the treatment intervention is reestablished. If the behavior returns to a level close to that found during the initial treatment phase and departs considerably from the reintroduced baseline level, the investigator is provided with a fairly straightforward demonstration of the effect of the intervention.

The ABAB design can be illustrated by reference to a five-year-old participant in a treatment program to suppress self-stimulatory behavior (Harris & Wolchik, 1979). This particular example is actually a somewhat complex version of the basic reversal design, because it includes the application of more than one treatment. It should be noted that contemporary illustrations of simple ABAB designs are rare. Researchers are currently much more likely to combine the basic ABAB design with facets of other types of single-subject designs, as in the example that follows, or not to employ the ABAB design in favor of another single-subject strategy. In Harris and Wolchik's study, baseline and treatment conditions occurred in the day school usually attended by the child, Matt. Initial baseline data on the number of self-stimulatory responses were gathered during 15-minute periods approximately nine times per day for nine days. Following baseline conditions, three different treatments were implemented: time-out, overcorrection, and differential reinforcement of other behavior (DRO), with a baseline period preceding each new treatment condition. Baselines were continued until self-stimulation had returned to pretreatment levels, and treatment was continued until self-stimulation had been noticeably suppressed or until five days had passed.

The results clearly demonstrate the differential effectiveness of the three treatments (see Figure 3–1). Both time-out and overcorrection were very effective in reducing self-stimulatory behavior in relation to baselines, but DRO actually increased self-stimulation. A return to a more successful treatment, such as overcorrection, would have been desirable before the termination of the program.

In the ABAB design, a causal relation is said to be demonstrated when behavior approaches initial baseline level after treatment is withdrawn. In this manner, changes in the child's behavior are shown to be due to the intervention rather than to some confounding source of internal invalidity. Unfortunately, the reversal aspect of this design, which demonstrates the causal role of the treatment manipulation, is also precisely the aspect of the design that presents the greatest ethical and practical limitations for the clinician interested in employing this single-subject design.

From an ethical standpoint, it may appear unwarranted to withdraw a treatment that appears to be efficacious. From a practical standpoint, certain behaviors may not return to baseline after treatment is withdrawn, for a variety of reasons. This occurred with another child in the study reported by Harris and Wolchik (1979). The performance of certain behaviors may be followed by naturally reinforcing consequences that reduce the likelihood of the improved

FIGURE 3–1

Matt's Mean Number of Self-Stimulatory Responses per Session across all Treatment Conditions

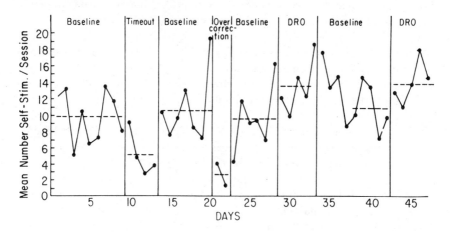

behavior returning to baseline levels simply because treatment has been discontinued.

Although the ABAB design frequently provides clear demonstration of the impact of treatment on performance, the problems inherent in the reversal design have led most researchers working in clinical settings to adopt alternative designs.

Multiple Baseline Designs.   Multiple baseline designs demonstrate the impact of treatment by showing that behavior changes as a function of the intervention being introduced at different points in time. Data are gathered on two or more baselines. When treatment is introduced, it is applied to only one of the baselines. The untreated baseline serves as a control for potentially confounding sources of invalidity being responsible for changes in behavior rather than the intervention. Treatment efficacy is demonstrated when each baseline changes only after the intervention has been applied to it, and not before. There are three main types of multiple baseline designs, each employing a different baseline criterion. Baselines can consist of different responses for an individual, the same response across different individuals, or the same response for an individual across different situations. These three variations are referred to as mutiple baseline *across responses, across subjects,* [1] and *across situations,* respectively.

---

[1] The multiple baseline across subjects design is one design that illustrates that the term *single-subject design* is somewhat a misnomer. A number of single subject designs can, in fact, be used with more than one subject.

An interesting application of the multiple baseline design across settings was reported by Singh, Winton, and Dawson (1982). An institutionalized, profoundly retarded girl was treated for excessive screaming with facial screening. Baseline and treatment conditions were conducted in three areas of the institution in which the girl normally spent time: the lobby, a courtyard, and the dayroom. Baseline data were gathered for a specific number of days in each location: 6 days in the lobby, 12 in the courtyard, and 18 in the dayroom. Facial screening (blocking her face with a bib) was implemented, in sequence across the three locations contingent on screaming behavior. Treatment was discontinued following no screaming for six consecutive days in all three locations. The effects of treatment are clear: screaming decreased dramatically in each of the settings after facial screening was implemented and was entirely absent after a few days. (see Figure 3-2).

The main advantage of multiple baseline designs is that a reversal phase in which treatment is withdrawn is not necessary to document treatment control. (Note, however, that a reversal can be used for the last baseline of a multiple baseline design, since no untreated baselines are available). Another advantage is that frequently an optimal goal of treatment is to alter more than one behavior across more than one individual or situation (Kazdin & Marholin, 1978). Kazdin and Marholin further point out that the multiple baseline design may be well suited to providing a small-scale test of a particular treatment with either a few clients or a few behaviors to test for the practicality of attempting a large-scale application.

The limitations of this design include the difficulty of finding several independent behaviors to treat, the problems with identifying two or more different behaviors that can be readily treated with the same technique, and the fact that all baselines must be stable before any treatment is implemented, which is potentially a time-consuming dilemma if the problem behaviors need immediate intervention (Gelfand & Hartmann, 1975). If baselines are interdependent, then some generalization of changed behavior is expected, even before the intervention has been formally applied to the second baseline. Although this may be a desired result from a clinical standpoint, it makes the demonstration of experimental control difficult; thus, another design might be more appropriate.

Changing-Criterion Design. The effect of treatment in the changing-criterion design is demonstrated by showing that behavior changes will correspond to specified performance criteria that change over the course of treatment. The design again starts with a baseline phase that, after stabilization, is followed by an intervention that includes the specification of the number of responses which is required in order for the child to receive a specified response consequence. This design has typically been employed for easily quantifiable behaviors, such as number of cigarettes smoked, calories consumed, or positive social interactions attempted. The criterion level changes throughout intervention, usually becoming increasingly stringent. If behavior consistently changes to match the most recent criterion, it is postulated that the intervention and criterion change

FIGURE 3-2

Number of Screams per Hour across Settings during Baseline and Facial Screening

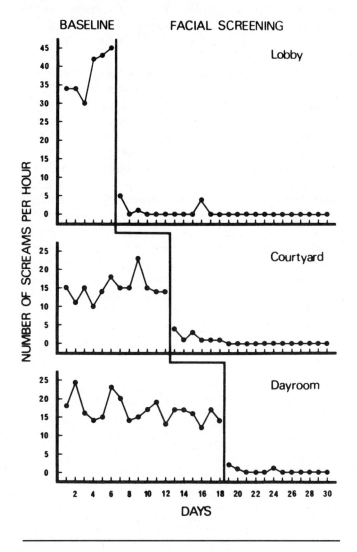

are responsible for the change in target behavior rather than any confounding external influence.

One advantage of this design is that the goal of gradually improved perform-ance is a very acceptable one to clinicians and clients alike. However, this design is not particularly useful for behaviors that would be likely to show abrupt rather than gradual changes. It is potentially a less powerful demonstration of treatment control than that afforded by other designs because there is less assurance that extraneous events may not account for a unidirectional change. Unambiguous results are obtained only if performance matches the criteria very closely and if criteria are repeatedly changed. One possible strategy for eliminating some ambiguity is to introduce some criterion changes that do not continue in the previous unidirectional manner. Obviously, some behaviors do not lend themselves to such reversals, even if they are small.

Alternating and/or Simultaneous-Treatment Designs. The alternating and/ or simultaneous-treatment designs (Barlow & Hayes, 1979; Kazdin & Hartmann, 1978) differ from the other single-subject designs discussed thus far in that they are said to allow for the comparison of two or more different treatments within a single individual. Although different treatments are sometimes compared in extensions of the ABAB design, as was the case in the Harris and Wolchik study (1979), treatments are thereby confounded with sequence or order effects. In the alternating and/or simultaneous-treatment designs, treatments are administered within a single phase in such a manner that sequencing is said not to be a confound. Furthermore, treatment comparisons can be made more rapidly than with the ABAB design. The first phase of the design is a baseline period in which behavior is observed during at least two separate occasions each day, under different observation periods. Application of treatment is varied daily so that each treatment is balanced across each observation period. Treatment is continued until the behavior stabilizes across all treatment conditions. If one treatment has been found to be more effective than the others, it can be implemented in the final phase. Confidence in treatment control will be bolstered if this final phase results in performance superior to that of any previous phase.[2]

---

[2] There is no clear consensus in the literature as to whether or not the alternating-treatments design and the simultaneous-treatment design are the same or different designs. Barlow and Hayes (1979) distinguished between the two, writing that in the simultaneous-treatment design, two or more treatments are concurrently available to the subject, whose choice of one of them is used as the means for comparing treatments. In contrast, Barlow and Hayes describe the alternating-treatments design as one in which the baseline period is followed by the implementation of two rapidly alternating treatments, with the relative effects of the two treatments on a single behavior being observed. They propose that this design is appropriate for comparing the effect of a treatment with no-treatment (baseline), as well as for comparing the effects of two or more different treatments for an individual. These authors suggested that only one true simultaneous treatment design has been published, and that many studies being labeled as such were in fact alternating-treatment designs. The confusion between these two designs becomes apparent when one finds the simultaneous-treatment design described as presenting "different interventions that are implemented in an 'alternating' fashion" (Kazdin & Hartmann, 1978). The title of one recent article referred to the design as "Simultaneous-or Alternating-Treatments Design" (Shapiro, Kazdin, & McGonigle, 1982, p. 105). At best, the simultaneous-treatment design is used infrequently, and it does not seem necessary to resolve the controversy in this chapter. Rather, relevant methodological and conceptual issues that could pertain to either one or to both designs, depending on the manner in which the designs are defined, will be presented.

These designs can be altered to extend to interventions balanced across different treatment administrators as well as across different times of the day. This variation may be particularly appropriate for residential settings in which it is important that improved client behavior generalize across staff members. Conditions such as setting, treatment, administrator, and time of day of treatment are counterbalanced with each treatment. The resulting behavior is plotted separately for each of the treatments, and because potentially confounding factors have been counterbalanced, differences in the plots of behavior change for different conditions can be attributed to the treatments themselves.

Despite the positive features, some difficulties exist with regard to the implementation of these designs. First, if too many treatments are compared, then it becomes difficult to balance them across time periods. Second, the types of treatments employed must not have any carry-over effects, which would mask the impact of the other treatment(s) administered that same day. Thus, drugs are not a form of treatment appropriate for this type of evaluation. Treatments must also be sufficiently dissimilar in order to produce differential responding. As noted earlier, checks on the treatment manipulation would be helpful. Finally, the behaviors targeted for change must be capable of rapid shifts so that differential responsiveness to treatments is possible.

The problem of multiple-treatment interference in these designs is that the effect of one treatment may be determined in part by the other treatment with which it is compared (Barlow & Hayes, 1979). Shapiro, Kazdin and McGonigle (1982) examined the effects of token reinforcement compared with baseline behavior versus token reinforcement compared with response-cost contingencies. They found that, for the five mentally retarded, behaviorally disturbed children they studied, on-task behavior during the implementation of token reinforcement was much more variable when the alternative condition was one of response-cost, rather than simply of baseline. On-task behavior was also found to be affected by the order in which the two interventions were presented. This study demonstrated that juxtaposing different treatments in the same phase may result in client behavior that is different from behavior when treatments are presented in independent phases.

An example of the alternating-treatment design is presented by Ollendick, Shapiro, and Barrett (1981), who compared physical restraint and positive practice overcorrection to a no-treatment condition for their effects on the stereotypic hand movement behaviors of three mentally retarded, emotionally disturbed children. After baseline observations during three time periods each day, the two treatment and the one no-treatment conditions were introduced in a counterbalanced order by a single therapist for the same three time periods as baseline conditions. The treatment that produced the greatest reduction in stereotypic behavior was implemented during all time periods as the last phase of the study. Both treatment conditions were found to reduce stereotypic behavior for all three children, while the no-treatment condition did not reduce stereotypies. The two treatments were found to be differentially effective for the three children. This finding illustrates an advantage of the alternating-treatments design, namely, the ability to determine on an individual basis what treatments are most effective for which children (see Figure 3–3).

The authors (Ollendick et al., 1981) suggest that an alternative strategy to including a no-treatment condition in the alternations, which allowed the children to engage in untreated stereotypic behaviors during sessions, would be to employ a periodic no-treatment probe during the study. This probe would initially serve the purpose of demonstrating treatment control and could later explore treatment maintenance.

Special Considerations

Kazdin (1982b) has discussed a number of important design requirements that must be addressed when considering the use of single-subject designs. These requirements include the presence of trends in the data, the degree of variability, and phase shifting criteria. In a number of the designs, clear demonstration of treatment control depends on a relatively stable baseline. If trends are present during the baseline phase, especially in the therapeutic direction, then the true impact of treatment may be difficult to separate from the preexisting trend. Recommended is the withholding of treatment until the baseline stabilizes; but this strategy may not be feasible in many clinical settings. The multiple baseline designs are less dependent on stable baselines for a demonstration of treatment control since the presence of two or more baselines acts as a control. Finally, various statistical procedures, such as time-series analysis (Glass, Willson, & Gottman, 1975), can be used to address whether changes in the behavior after the introduction of treatment are significantly greater than changes that might have been expected on the basis of the baseline trends. Recently, Tryon (1982) has described a simplified time-series analysis that requires fewer data points than the standard analysis and that employs much less complex mathematical calculations.

Another potential complication for interpreting the effects of treatment arises when there is substantial variablility in the data, making predictions of expected future behavior difficult. Successive data points may be averaged to reduce the appearance of variability. However, Kazdin (1982b) delineates the advantages of attempting to identify some of the sources of variability, as this can then be information applied to the development of the most appropriate treatment.

An important facet of single-case designs is the investigative approach necessary for individual development of the designs for each child. Decisions about when to shift phases can be made most appropriately only after data have begun to be collected. It is important to shift phases in such a manner that all phases are given equal opportunity to "work." Furthermore, a new phase should be introduced only after the behavior trend has become clear, relatively stabilized, and not excessively variable. Interpretation of the data can be unambiguous

FIGURE 3-3

Stereotypic Hair Twirling and Accurate Task Performance for Tim across Experimental Conditions

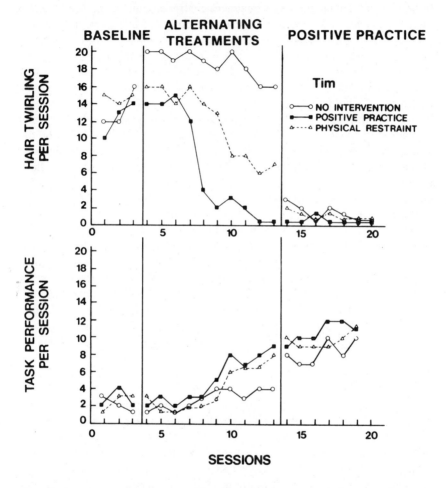

The plotted data are an average of the three daily time periods. The three different treatments were presented only during the alternating-treatments phase. During the last phase, positive practice overcorrection was used during all three daily time periods.

only if clear patterns are present in each phase. Thus far, carry-over effects have been mentioned only with regard to simultaneous-treatment designs. However, residual effects in shifting from one phase of a single-subject design to other phases are potentially a confound for most single-subject designs.

Kendall (1981a, 1982, 1984) has addressed the issue of the balance between desired demonstration of treatment control and the suggestion of a lack of generalization in single-subject designs. Kendall delineates the dilemma by asking: "When the behavior does not reverse, or when baselines other than the one being treated show variation with a treatment, is this due to the generalization of the treatment to no-treatment conditions (which would be a therapeutically favorable event), or is it due to a lack of treatment control where the intervention is not having an effect?" (1981a, p. 309). In suggesting ways to answer this question, Kendall differentiates *stimulus generalization,* in which changes in behavior transfer to other settings from where the behavior was treated, from *response generalization,* in which treating one specific behavior also has an impact on other behaviors. A methodology is proposed that allows for the demonstration of both treatment control and generalization by assessing changes in stimuli *or* behaviors to document treatment control and then by exploring generalization effects in the other domain.

More specifically, stimulus generalization could be addressed when a multiple baseline design across behaviors is employed; response generalization could be evaluated when the design used to demonstrate experimental control is either reversal, multiple baseline across situations, or alternating and/or simultaneous-treatments designs. Johnson and Cuvo (1981) provide a demonstration of this strategy for teaching mentally retarded adults to cook, using a multiple baseline across subjects to demonstrate experimental control and a multiple baseline across responses to investigate response generalization.

Evaluation of the Data

Three main options for single-subject evaluation are open to the investigator: nonstatistical visual evaluation, statistical evaluation, and clinical evaluation.

Nonstatistical Evaluation. Nonstatistical evaluation of the data from single-subject designs typically refers to visual inspection of plots of the data to insure that only those effects that are strong and easily noted will be considered meaningful. This has been the most widely employed method for single-subject evaluation. The rationale for this procedure is that single-case designs seek to identify potent treatment effects, rather than those that are merely statistically significant; most clients will not be satisfed with being informed their improvement is statistically significant if they still feel terrible.

One problem with visual inspection is that different judges may not be particularly reliable. DeProspero and Cohen (1979) collected ratings of the "experimental control" of 36 different simulated ABAB reversal figures from each of 114 reviewers for behavioral journals. The judges were found not to be very reliable, producing a median interrater agreement of 0.61. Except for a few clear graphs, a consistently wide range of ratings was obtained for each graph.

Visual inspection will no doubt continue to be an important mode of data evaluation, and its dependence on the presence of strong treatment effects documents clinical utility. However, problems with interrater agreement, as well as with baselines evidencing trends, suggest that, in some circumstances, it may be useful to combine visual inspection with either statistical or clinical evaluation as well.

Statistical Evaluation. Critics argue that the use of statistical tests for the evaluation of single-case data may result in treatments being lauded as effective because they produce behaviors that, from a statistical standpoint, are significantly different from untreated behaviors, but that do not, in fact, represent powerful treatment effects. However, statistical evaluation may contribute important information in certain circumstances (see Kazdin, 1980). First of all, in exploratory research, which is attempting to investigate the effects of new treatment components, those variables that produce statistically significant results would be the most productive ones to include in future treatment packages. Kazdin further writes that statistical techniques "act as a filter, however imperfect, for discriminating among the many variables that might be investigated further" (1980, p. 363). Statistical techniques are also useful for identifying treatment effects, which may be somewhat weak for immediate clinical application but, nevertheless, are theoretically important. Finally, statistical techniques may be imperative to employ in cases in which the design requirements necessary for visual inspection were not met (i.e., when a stable baseline was not achieved).

A number of researchers have abandoned the debate about whether or not statistical evaluation of single-subject data should be conducted, and they have begun to address the important question of which tests should be applied to which designs and under what circumstances (see Glass et al. [1975], Kazdin [1976], and Kratochwill [1978], for descriptions of specific statistical techniques). Recently, additional considerations concerning the appropriate statistical analyses for the simultaneous and alternating-treatment designs have been described (Kratochwill & Levin, 1980). These authors recommend nonparametric, randomization tests instead of analysis of variance procedures.

A few factors should be kept in mind if statistical tests are to be used. First, a larger number of instances of recorded behavior will be necessary to allow for a demonstration of statistical significance. The application of randomization tests (Edington, 1980) requires that treatment times be randomly assigned to treatments. In addition, Kazdin (1982b) makes the crucial point that treatment control in most single-subject designs is demonstrated by the pattern of behavior across phases. Thus, it is not sufficient to statistically compare only one treatment phase with one baseline phase. Statistical procedures, which analyze the complete pattern of results, must be employed. Because of the impact of variability within phases on ultimate interpretation of results, treatment reports must include either descriptive statistics of within-phase variability or graphical representation of all the data (Birnbrauer, 1976).

Clinical Evaluation. As previously mentioned, sole reliance on statistical evaluation may fail to adequately address the clinical significance of treatment effects. Visual inspection, while tending to emphasize potent behavioral changes, does not necessarily consider the clinical impact, either. Self-destructive behavior provides a frequently used example (Kazdin, 1977, 1980, 1982a) of the necessity for considering clinical significance. A decrease in self-destructive behavior, which achieves statistical significance and which looks to be a dramatic change via visual inspection, remains comparatively unacceptable from a clinical standpoint as long as self-destructive behavior persists.

Kendall and Norton-Ford define clinical significance as "the meaningfulness of the magnitude of change, the remediation of the presenting problem to the point that it is no longer troublesome" (1982b, p. 449). The determination of clinical significance is frequently more difficult than either visual or statistical evaluation can adequately address because, as Kazdin has noted: "For many behaviors focused upon in therapy, the *level* of the behavior, rather than its presence or absence, dictates whether it is socially acceptable" (1977, pp. 429–430).

There are two main strategies for evaluating clinical significance: normative comparisons and subjective evaluation methods. The *normative comparison* method (Kendall & Norton-Ford, 1982b) relies on the identification of appropriate "nondeviant" peers of the child and comparison of the child client's target behavior both before and after treatment with the behavior of the nondeviant peers. For example, Patterson's (1974) evaluation of treatment for boys with conduct problems included matching deviant families for SES, age of the "target" child, number of children in the family, and father presence or absence, with other families who had not sought treatment. Baseline observations were conducted in the homes of both sets of families, and a range of "normal" behavior scores was delineated on the basis of the nondeviant target child. A normal range of behavior scores was also identified on the basis of the behavior of "nonproblem" peers from the same classrooms as the target children. Patterson could thereby demonstrate treatment control as well as address the clinical meaningfulness of the change, by employing analysis of variance for repeated measures and visual inspection of the data for the presence of marked graphical changes from baseline to treatment phase.[3]

---

[3] Statistical tests can be used to determine whether the treated group is significantly different from the normative group. In these comparisons, it is desirable that the differences at posttreatment be nonsignificant—no meaningful differences between treated and normative samples. Based on

Another example of the use of normative comparisons is provided by Matson (1981). Three mentally retarded girls, treated for severe fear of adult strangers, were matched on age and on degree of mental retardation with girls evidencing a "normal" level of fearfulness. The scores of these normally fearful girls on the dependent measures used in the study were considered the level of clinically significant treatment results. This study is especially important because it addresses one of the potential problems with normative comparison, namely, the identification of the appropriate normative group. In many cases, it would not be reasonable to insist that the behavior of retarded persons move into the behavior range of nonretarded "normals." Selection of the appropriate normative group remains a difficult decision. For instance, to whom should chronic psychiatric patients be compared? If the goal is to make them less blatantly distinguishable from nonpsychiatric patients, then that might seem the proper comparison group. However, that may be an unrealistic goal. Other difficult issues include the appropriate variables on which subjects should be matched, and the extent of the range of "normal" subjects' behavior that will be considered normal or acceptable.

Another method for evaluating the clinical importance of the change achieved is *subjective evaluation* (Kazdin, 1977). This method entails a global evaluation of how well the child is functioning by persons who are likely to remain in contact with the child and who are either in a position of expertise or who have some relationship with the child. Appropriate evaluators would include parents, teachers, and peers. The goal is for these persons to report whether treatment has made a noticeable qualitative impact on the daily functioning of the child.

To help eliminate biases, some studies have employed ratings by individuals not familiar with the child. Unfortunately, what is gained in objectivity is lost in the ability of these judges to address the perceived impact for this particular child's functioning. For example, Schreibman, Koegel, Mills, and Burke (1981) had undergraduates rate videotapes of the free play of autistic children before and after therapy to determine if the judges would form more positive global impressions of the autistic children after therapy and to examine the correlation of the degree and direction of behavior change as scored by objective measures with the subjectively perceived degree and direction of change.

Despite the usefulness of subjective evaluation, its potential limitations must be considered. First, global ratings, as opposed to more specific measures, present a number of problems that will be addressed in a later section of the chapter. Subjective evaluations are the source of a great variety of biases, many of them relatively idiosyncratic and unidentifiable. The choice of whose subjective evaluation to consider may make a large difference in the reported perception of change and is likely to be a dual function of the evaluator's needs as well as the child's behavior.

---

these results, the average treated child is not meaningfully different on the measure used from average normal subjects, and the investigator can make more encouraging claims about the *impact* of the treatment.

A change that can be perceived by an outside observer may still not be a substantial enough change to be clinically significant, and it may be more a function of perceived *global* change than actual change in the target behavior. This would argue for the usefulness of employing both normative comparisons and subjective evaluations. Another suggestion may be to choose persons to serve as subjective evaluators who are directly affected by the problem behavior of the child. For instance, if a child has difficulties staying in his or her seat in school and talks out of turn, then an evaluation by the teacher obviously would be appropriate. The fact that biases may enter into the rating is not really a confounding factor, since the teacher's perceptions remain the standard for whether or not the child's behavior is considered a problem. Sociometric assessments have also been proposed as a potential measure of the clinical impact of therapy (Kendall, Pellegrini & Urbain, 1981) and as a normative criterion (Gottman, Gonso, & Rasmussen, 1975).

Clearly, normative comparisons and subjective evaluation of single-subject designs add crucial information about the impact of treatment. However, it is essential to realize that the assessment of clinical significance cannot replace statistical techniques and visual inspection in the evaluation of the effects of treatment because demonstration of clinical significance does not demonstrate treatment control. Kazdin and Wilson wrote, "Of course, the issue of the magnitude of change is only meaningfully raised after there is empirical evidence that a procedure demonstrates change" (1978b, p. 40). Clinical relevance and treatment control can be considered together.

Pros and Cons of Single-Subject Designs

Single-subject designs lend themselves particularly well to applied investigations in which the ultimate question is how to best help individual children. A number of design options are available, and one is likely to be useful for most every clinical situation. These designs are particularly useful for the study of rare clinical problems in which group-comparison research would be impossible and as an initial test of treatment effectiveness before a large-scale program is begun (Kazdin, 1982a). Another useful function served by these designs is the demonstration of negative results to raise questions about generally accepted hypotheses (Dukes, 1965).

These designs do have limitations, however. First, although single-subject designs adequately address questions of whether the treatment employed was effective with the subject(s) treated, these designs are unable to answer clearly a number of other evaluative questions, such as which components of the treatment accounted for the change, which variations may be more effective, and how a treatment interacts with client characteristics (Kazdin, 1982a). The generality of results also presents problems for this class of designs. Ross has written: "If one wants to know whether that treatment would also be effective in the hands of other therapists, with other cases, and in different settings, that is if one wants to generalize from one's results, the approach has limitations" (1981a, p. 25).

Cognitive-behavioral interventions are being increasingly employed in the treatment of childhood behavior and learning problems. These newer methods demand efficacy evaluation as much as the more traditional behavioral techniques but can present special methodological dilemmas for the evaluator. Specifically, certain types of single-subject designs are not readily applicable to cognitive-behavioral therapy. The ABAB design appears particularity inappropriate because the effects on cognitions of training a child to make specific types of self-statements cannot be reversed. However, the effects of cognitive-behavioral interventions do lend themselves nicely to evaluation by the multiple baseline designs.

Presently, there is a paucity of well-developed methods for assessing cognitions as the dependent variable (see Kendall & Urbain, 1981). Thus, at least for the present time, behaviors remain the most appropriate dependent variable for the evaluation of cognitive-behavioral therapy. For example, Bernard, Kratochwill, and Keefauver (1983) employed rational emotive therapy and self-instructional training in the treatment of chronic hair-pulling. The number of hairs the subject pulled out while studying was the dependent variable, rather than any cognitive measure. Clearly, for several reasons (Kendall, 1981b), it will be most useful for advances to be made in methods for assessing changes in cognitions. In the meantime, however, methods related to cognitive frequency counts could be employed. For instance, a depressed adolescent client could be instructed to keep track of negative self-statements with a golf counter. The frequency of these statements could then be plotted in terms of the different phases of the intervention and evaluation design, with baseline to posttreatment changes in cognition and behavior being the dependent measures of interest.

BETWEEN-GROUP DESIGNS

Group comparison methodologies may be used to compare the effects of a particular therapy with no therapy, to compare the relative effectiveness of two or more therapies, or to compare different techniques or components of one specific therapy. In any of these comparisons, the goal is to isolate the effects of therapy from behavior changes that may be due to other variables. The general strategy is to control these extraneous factors by purposely ensuring that they are included in the proper control group(s) or condition(s) (Kendall & Norton-Ford, 1982b). Typically, comparable subjects are randomly assigned to one of the conditions. While random assignment of subjects to conditions is crucial to ensure that every subject has an equal probability of being assigned to any of the conditions in the study, this method of subject assignment is only likely to ensure the comparability of control and treatment groups on variables important to the study. Unwanted differences between conditions become progressively more likely as sample size decreases. Consequently, a recommended alternative procedure is *randomized blocks assignment,* in which subjects are placed into subgroups that are highly comparable with regards to important factors, such as initial level of problem behavior, and that contain the same number of subjects as the number of experimental conditions (e.g., three subjects per subgroup if the study contains one control condition and two treatment conditions). Subjects from each subgroup are then randomly assigned to one of the experimental conditions.

A partial function of random selection of subjects is the generality of results to different persons. This refers to each member of the population to which one is interested in generalizing having an equal probability of being selected for the study—a truly representative sample. Frequently, this is an impractical and often impossible achievement, requiring initial studies to evaluate the treatment effect and subsequent studies that are specifically designed to assess the generality of the results.

The choice of the appropriate control group is another important decision in between-group designs. Specific controls are selected to reduce the threats to internal validity that would prevent the experimenter from being able to make causal statements about the effects of treatment. A number of different types of control conditions are available, each with its own advantages, limitations, and most appropriate applications.

The one design requirement all control groups share is that subjects be randomly assigned to either the experimental or control group. An important recommendation is that demographic information and important variables of interest be collected from all clients so that the true comparability of groups can be determined. While it is not a requirement for control group strategies, this procedure helps with subsequent data interpretation.

A no-treatment control group is assessed at the same points in time as the experimental group but does not receive the independent variable. This group controls for threats to internal validity, such as the effects of assessment, history, and maturation (Campbell & Stanley, 1963), but it does not control for such factors as anticipation of change due to therapy, expectancy of change, and visits to a therapist—independent of what the therapist actually does (Kendall & Norton-Ford, 1982b).

One solution to some of these uncontrolled factors, as well as to the higher attrition rate usually encountered in no-treatment control groups, is the waiting-list control group. Subjects in this group receive therapy after posttherapy assessments have been completed with the treated subjects but serve as a no-treatment control group until that time. The time between pretherapy and posttherapy assessment periods must be the same for the two groups. One potential difficulty with the waiting-list control group is that clients will sometimes attempt to receive alternative treatment during the waiting period.

In an effort to distinguish behavior changes that are the result of a particular therapeutic intervention from changes that could result from a person receiving any type of therapy, nonspecific-treatment controls, or *placebo controls,* are designed and implemented. The placebo control group undergoes the same assessment procedures as the treatment group and attends the same number of sessions as the treatment group. However, this control group is provided only with a therapeutic rationale and attention from and contact with a therapist. Assuming the procedure is credible to participants, inclusion of this group in a between-group design can control for expectancy and contact effects.

It must be noted that the successful inclusion of a control group of this type is more complex than it may sound. First, clients must be informed that they may receive a treatment believed to be psychologically inert. Second client expectations for positive results as well as therapist conviction in treatment may be difficult to sustain over a number of sessions. Finally, it is possible that over the course of the non-specific (placebo) treatment contact, therapeutic processes may spontaneously develop, which are, in fact, active therapeutic ingredients. O'Leary and Borkovec (1978) have questioned ethical, practical, and methodological features of placebo control groups and have endorsed other options. For instance, researchers could employ "best available" alternative treatment comparisons.

The main function of any type of control condition must be to rule out specific threats to internal validity. However, depending on the treatment questions of interest, certain types of control groups can be adapted to also help identify the specific factors in the treatment manipulation that are accounting for behavior changes.

Specific Types of Designs

There are several between-group experimental designs employed in child behavior therapy. The following section provides a brief discussion of the more frequently used methods. This section draws heavily from the classic text by Campbell and Stanley (1963). This source, as well as Kazdin (1980) and Kendall and Norton-Ford (1982b), can be consulted for more detailed expositions.

Pretest-Posttest Control Group Design.   This is the between-group design used most frequently in therapy evaluation (Kazdin, 1980). A group that receives treatment is compared with a group that does not, but both groups are assessed with identical dependent measures before and after the therapeutic manipulation so that the effects of repeated assessment can be monitored. The pretest provides a check on within-group variability, as well as information about the variability between groups. However, pretests may sensitize clients to the treatment, that is, the pretest and treatment may interact, making generalization to subjects who do not receive preassessment invalid.

Factorial Designs.   Frequently, the investigator is interested in more complex questions than can be addressed by the pretest-posttest design. Earlier in the chapter, it was pointed out that therapy outcome research cannot rest on uniformity myths (Kiesler, 1966). The multifaceted questions that must eventually be asked require factorial designs that permit two or more variables to be simultaneously analyzed within one research project.

Factorial designs allow the separate as well as interactive effects of different variables to be explored. An interaction occurs when the intervention produces results that are different for different levels of other independent variables. Interaction effects are exciting, since they provide the basis for prescriptive interventions. Have you ever asked an instructor or workshop presenter to address a question such as "Does treatment A work with problem B children?" Having been told that the procedure has produced gains for problem C children, you want to generalize for your clientele. The presentee responds, "It depends." While this response may frustrate those who want a simple answer to the question, it is, when based on meaningful interaction effects, a most satisfactory answer. For instance, treatment A may be effective with children who have a cognitive capacity for mediational thinking (e.g., criterion IQ score) but may be ineffective with lower-functioning children. Factorial designs offer the opportunity for identifying interactions and for making sensible and prescriptive "it depends" statements.

There is no single factorial design. Rather, factorial designs may include different numbers and types of variables, as well as different levels within each variable. Factorial designs can also accommodate both within-groups and between-groups manipulations. For instance, the repeated measurements that are required for the evaluation of clinical intervention include assessments before treatment, after treatment (and perhaps during), and at a follow-up point. This is a within-group comparison—the same subjects compared over time. The comparison of several groups of subjects (different clients) treated differently is the between-groups comparison. Such a mixed factorial design allows for the identification of differential changes over time due to different types of treatment.

Although factorial designs can provide valuable information, their interpretation can be complex if a very large number of interactions are found to be significant. Also, the inclusion of extra factors in a design requires that additional groups be employed—a requirement that can become costly and impractical. Nevertheless, Paul (1967) has expressed the opinion: "the factorially designed experiment with no-treatment and attention-placebo controls is the only approach which offers the establishment of antecedent-consequent relationships for specific treatments without possible confounding" (p. 116). The factorial design is most common among therapy researchers in general and deserves prominence within the child behavior therapy literature as well.

Quasi-experimental Designs. Quasi-experimental designs are those in which the requirements for a true control group as required for an experiment cannot be met. These quasi-experimental designs have also been labeled *nonequivalent control group* designs (Campbell & Stanley, 1963), which describe the most common situations in which subjects are not randomly assigned to treatment and control groups. This is a commonly encountered dilemma for research in clinical settings in which children's treatments cannot be freely manipulated or when groups of interest are already in existence. Various threats to internal validity will interfere with clear interpretation of data in quasi-experimental designs. However, strategies, such as conducting pretests of both treatment and control groups, can at least address issues of group comparability.

Posttest-only and Solomon Four-group Designs. The posttest-only design consists of a group that receives treatment and one that does not, but the effects of treatment are assessed only after its conclusion. This design prevents the investigator from having information available about any possible differences between groups prior to treatment. Also, without initial assessment of the therapy group members, it cannot be statistically evaluated whether they changed significantly over the course of therapy. As a result, few studies with this design appear in the literature—the absence of a pretest would be one reason that a reviewer would recommend that the study not be published. The advantage of this design is that the potential threat to external validity created by the administration of a pretest is eliminated. If the assessment procedures are very costly, time-consuming, or stressful, it might be considered useful to omit the pretest. However, this argument is generally regarded as weak—pretests are very important and should not be omitted unless absolutely necessary.

The Solomon four-group design addresses the same concerns as the posttest-only design (i.e., preassessment sensitization), but it overcomes the weaknesses of the posttest-only approach. The Solomon design requires at least four groups, half of which receive the treatment and half of which do not. One of the experimental groups and one of the control groups receive both a pretest and a posttest, and the other two receive only a posttest. This design controls both for the effects of testing and for the effects of treatment. It also provides replication of treatment and control conditions. The main drawback of this procedure is that it is potentially very costly and requires twice the usual sample size. The fact that this design is used rarely, as is true for the posttest-only design, indicates that therapy evaluators are most likely unconcerned with the sensitization due to pretesting.

Data Evaluation

Unlike the visual inspection of single-subject designs, data from between-group designs are routinely submitted to statistical analyses. Group averages are compared by statistical tests, such as analysis of variance, and a treatment outcome is declared to be statistically significant if the mean treatment difference is greater than that which could have occurred just by chance. However, statistical and clinical significance are not synonymous. Fiske et al. (1970) suggest that after a treatment has been declared statistically significant, the proportion of variance accounted for must be considered. Kendall (1982) underscores the merits of normative comparisons. An example of such an application is provided by Rickel and Lampi (1981), who report a follow-up study of a preschool intervention program in which the differences between high-risk and low-risk children were compared for statistical significance by multivariate analysis of variance but in which a comparison to the functioning of the "normal" control group was considered as the appropriate criterion for clinically significant change. Statistical significance and meaningful clinical change can be examined cooperatively.

Ross has referred to between-group designs with the phrase: "learn much about many, know little about one" (1981b, p. 321). Indeed, the clear advantage of experimentally controlled between-group designs is that general statements can be made about the influence of treatment on groups of people. However, Kazdin (1980) has pointed out that the potent effects required for visual inspection of single-subject designs may, in the long run, have greater generality than the results of between-group studies, which are designed primarily to meet the requirements for statistical significance. Nevertheless, more detailed reporting of group data, such as the percentage of subjects reaching predetermined outcome criteria, would seem to offer the best of both strategies.

CRITERIA FOR EVALUATING THERAPY OUTCOME

The evaluation of behavior therapy outcome for children is perhaps more complex than it is for adults. This is primarily because the child, the child's parents, the therapist, society, and a number of other significant persons in the child's life are all likely to have somewhat different treatment goals and, therefore, different opinions regarding the appropriate criteria for treatment outcome evaluation. Whose opinion should matter most for outcome criteria? This is an exceptionally value-laden issue and not one that the researcher or therapist can or should attempt to answer alone. Should therapy be evaluated in terms of the child's subjective sense of happiness, the parents' contentment with the results, the therapists's perception of therapy "success," "objective" standardized ratings of the child's behavior, the teacher's ability to tolerate the child in the classroom, or should other standards be used for decisions about treatment effects? As for the selection of dependent measures, probably the optimal solution is to give credence to a combination of these factors. However, this is not always practical, and the clinician frequently is required to make difficult choices as to the manner in which treatment will be evaluated. The sections that follow address the importance of acknowledging that the diverse values and perspectives of persons evaluating child behavior therapy outcome will affect those evaluations. In addition, a model is described that differentiates two types of outcome assessments and that provides a useful way of evaluating the role played by a variety of dependent measures.

The Role of Values and Perspectives

A vocal advocate for recognition of the role played by values in judgments of outcome has written:

> It is a common finding that outcome assessments by patients, peers, indepen-
> dent clinicians, and therapists correlate only moderately. One may attribute
> this to the imperfection of the instruments and the fallibility of raters, but one
> should also be aware of the fact that raters bring different perspectives to bear
> and that the relative lack of correlation partially results from legitimate di-
> vergences in their vantage points. . . . Values influence and suffuse every
> judgment of outcome. (Strupp, 1978, p. 8)

Strupp and Hadley (1977) proposed a tripartite model for the evaluation of therapy that suggests that outcome should be simultaneously viewed from the perspectives of the individual, society, and the mental health professional. The three perspectives are included because of the diverse aspects of a person's functioning that each of these viewpoints considers important. They wrote: "If one is interested in a *comprehensive* picture of the individual, evaluations based on a single vantage point are inadequate and fail to give necessary consideration to the *totality* of an individual's functioning" (1977, p. 190). The diverse perspectives of different outcome raters is explicated by Mintz (1977). The client is most likely to evaluate treatment results in relation to other experiences, the therapist in comparison to other clients, and the researcher in terms of a variety of factors in the study, especially other clients and therapists. Bergin (1971) has proposed that a conceptual and methodological improvement would be the specification of the different variables that enter into clients' and therapists' therapy outcome ratings so that the role of values can be somewhat partialled out from other aspects of change.

Dual-Level Outcome Criteria

Recognition of the role played by values and differential perspectives in therapy outcome evaluation is not sufficient unto itself. The effectiveness of behavior therapy with children must also be evaluated by more detailed measures. A burden is therefore placed on researchers to be exceptionally clear in conceptualizing exactly what effects of therapy they are assessing with different measures and different evaluators. Assessments of therapy outcome might be construed within a model that considers two levels: the *specifying level* and the *general impact level* (Kendall, Pellegrini, & Urbain, 1981). The goal of specifying level assessments is to establish what specific changes the treatment did and did not produce. Specific skills and specific behaviors are evaluated at this level. The goal of impact level assessments is to determine whether or not the treatment had a conspicuous impact, relating to whether the change produced by treatment makes a *noticeable* difference in the child's behavioral impact on others.

The different types of outcome criteria addressed by these two levels will be described, followed by a presentation of appropriate dependent measures, which are categorized by level.

Kazdin describes some basic requirements for the dependent measures: a direct relationship to the construct under study, sensitivity to the type and extent of change expected, and allowance for a wide range of responses (1980, pp. 219–221). Additionally, Nelson (1981) suggests that the selected dependent measures accurately reflect the therapeutic objectives. Also, since most treatment outcome experimental designs require that the same dependent measures be repeatedly employed, the measures should be suitable to this repeated administration. This is most feasible when alternate forms of the same measure are available.

Specifying Level Assessments

As previously mentioned, specifying level assessments are concerned with clear delineation of the skills the child has learned and identification of the behavior that was modified. Appropriate dependent measures for this level include direct observations of behavior, self-report measures, and various task performance measures.

Direct Observations of Behavior.   Behavioral observations at the specifying level focus on such things as rates of behavior and labeling of specific desirable and undesirable events. In direct observations of the child's behavior, the focus is placed on the child's overt behavior, either in the natural environment or in a situation designed to be relevant for assessment of the variables of interest. The behavior can be observed and coded as it occurs, or it can be audio/video taped and subsequently coded. Especially if observations are conducted in the natural environment, then questions about the generalization of treatment can be answered directly, and fewer inferences need to be made.

Despite the many positive features of behavioral measures, especially for the evaluation of behavior therapy, they do have limitations. First, new observational systems are usually designed for every outcome study, making comparisons between studies difficult. As a partial remedy, it has been suggested that researchers attempt to employ some of the same observational codes. A second problem has to do with the potential reactive influence that being observed can have on the child's behavior, as well as with questions about the representativeness of the behavior sample observed. "Direct samples of relevant behaviors of interest in everyday situations may not necessarily provide information about how behavior is performed during the nonobserved periods" (Kazdin, 1980, p. 237). For example, certain low-rate behaviors, such as "fire setting" and "stealing" may occur very infrequently during the scheduled periods of observation.

If direct behavioral observation is employed, then the investigator must be concerned with interrater reliability—the degree to which ratings of observers who independently score the child's behavior agree. Gelfand and Hartmann (1968) suggested that observers should be naive as to the treatment employed and that high interobserver reliability shoud be established before actually beginning treatment. When treatment extends over several months, then random reliability checks are needed to confirm the original levels of agreement.

Self-report Measures. Kendall and Braswell have written, "Sole reliance on the child-client is not desirable; however, self-reports can help specify the effect of the intervention" (1982, p. 25). A wide variety of self-report measures is available, such as self-ratings, questionnaires, and self-monitoring procedures (Nelson, 1981). Some of the obvious advantages of these measures are that the child has access to personal information that no one else can rate, and that these measures are generally convenient and cost efficient. Most important, the way the child evaluates his or her own behavior change may be crucial information to obtain. For instance, a study by Braswell, Kendall, and Koehler (1982) examined the relationship between children's attributions regarding behavior change and treatment outcome following cognitive-behavioral intervention for non-self-controlled behavior (see Kendall & Braswell, 1984, for detailed description of the cognitive-behavioral treatment). Children's attributions of positive behavior change to personal effort were found to be associated with increasingly positive teacher ratings of behavior change. Also, the greater the positive change on teacher ratings, the less likely a child was to attribute his or her success to luck.

One must be very cautious with self-report measures, however, since developmental level affects the child's ability to understand the instructions, the scale items, and the nature of the self-report task. Additional potential limitations of self-report can include social desirability, the "hello-goodbye" effect, and the potential of not reliably measuring the behaviors of interest. For instance, in studies of anxiety in children, as assessed by self-report measures, the distinction between states and traits was often noted. That is, while adults could meaningfully separate how they feel at the present time (state) from how they usually or generally feel (trait), children have difficulty making this distinction. In one study, children's self-reported trait scores changed, due to a manipulation of an emotional state (Finch, Kendall, Montgomery & Morris, 1975).

It is desirable to assess treatment outcome by a variety of techniques. However, incorporating both the direct observation of children's behavior and their self-reports may, at times, result in the need for reconciliation of disparate conclusions about treatment effects. If the desired behavior changes are evident upon direct observations but not acknowledged in self-reports, it is reasonable and likely that the validity of the nonsupportive self-report data will be questioned. Researchers and clinicians must resist the temptation to place sole emphasis on assessments confirmatory of treatment gains when additional data are not fully supportive of that conclusion.

Task Performance. The specifics of behavior change can be evaluated by assessing children's task performance on various skills measures, such as skills in impersonal problem solving, interpersonal problem solving, and social cognition (see Kendall et al., 1981; Kendall & Braswell, 1982). The choice of the most appropriate measure(s) will depend on the types of skills the therapy was intended to develop and enhance—interpersonal task performance for social skills training, academic performance for educational training, job performance for vocational training.

Impact Level Assessments

The specifying level is not in and of itself an adequate criterion for decisions about treatment effect. The degree of impact from those behavior changes is also crucial to consider. Most studies based on between-group designs address the question of the statistical significance of change by reporting the mean differences between control and treatment groups on one or a variety of outcome measures. As previously discussed, group mean differences do not provide sufficient information for making decisions about the proportion of individuals who might be expected to change. The proportion of clients who actually improve must be more frequently reported. Kazdin and Wilson explain, "Selecting a treatment that produces improvements in the largest number of clients maximizes the probability that a given client will be favorably affected by treatment" (1978a, p. 409).

The extent of the improvement, that is, the range of behaviors affected by the treatment, is another important impact-related criteria. In attempting to make causal attributions, one must be careful not to confound assessments of specific behaviors with assessments of their impact. For example, Birnbrauer (1976) justifiably warns against making statements about clients' accomplishments after completing treatment and then evaluating therapy on the basis of those achievements. Unless these reports of the clients' performance are made by someone not involved with the therapy, they are likely to be seriously biased by the impact those changes have had on the person evaluating the behavior. Also, causal conclusions obviously cannot be drawn from such anecdotal reports.

Impact level assessments should evaluate the importance of the behavior changes, both to the client and to significant others. The acceptability of a given therapeutic intervention must also be considered. Therapy ineffectiveness will be more or less guaranteed if, for one reason or another, the client is not comfortable with the mode of treatment. With children, the scope of opinions that must be considered extends to parents, frequently to teachers and peers, and sometimes to siblings.

Discussions of deterioration effects (Bergin & Lambert, 1978) and relapse rates (Gottman & Markman, 1978) are sometimes avoided in the treatment outcome literature, but they must be made a part of the evaluation criteria package. Furthermore, any negative side effects produced as a function of treatment must also be weighed in making treatment choice decisions. Finally, consideration must be given to the emotional cost of treatment to the child and collaterals. Although one should not necessarily choose the treatment that is the least stressful, it is one of the many factors that must be weighed in the treatment choice decision.

Dependent measures appropriate for assessing impact level include teacher and parent ratings, sociometric evaluations, archival data, and normative comparisons. Normative comparisons will not be described since they have been covered earlier. It should be noted that many of the issues previously discussed in terms of subjective evaluations of single-subject designs are equally applicable to the current discussion of teacher and parent ratings as impact level assessments.

Rating Scales.   Global ratings of the child by those who are in the most direct contact with the child, such as parents, teachers, and therapists, have been frequently used for therapy outcome evaluation. The popularity of this technique can be attributed to its simplicity as well as to its adaptability to almost any topic of interest. Mintz (1977) offers a number of arguments in favor of including therapists' global ratings in therapy outcome research: the therapist is an expert in this area, knows the patient and the case, is likely to be more objective than the child or child's family, and has access to all the clinical data that have been gathered. The liabilities of therapists' global ratings are also acknowledged by Mintz. Specifically, therapists are likely to be biased toward rating their therapy as successful, their knowledge base frequently does not extend beyond clinical information, and they cannot rate no treatment controls with whom they have not had contact.

Further inadequacies of global assessments (Kazdin, 1980; Kazdin & Wilson, 1978b) include that the investigator has lack of control over the variables the rater permits to enter into his or her ratings; the fact that criteria for the ratings may change over time, apart from any actual changes in the child's behavior; that global ratings across raters and across studies are very difficult to compare; and that detail and specificity are lost by the very nature of the assessment. The goal of the therapy evaluation must be considered in deciding whether or not to include a global rating as a dependent measure. As mentioned in the discussion of subjective evaluations as a form of assessing clinical significance, if one is interested in knowing how those people who are most affected by the child's behavior problems perceive the posttherapy behavior changes, then the biases inherent in global ratings become less a methodological dilemma and more a source of information. Ratings need not necessarily be global. A number of scales are available which make explicit the behavior changes that are of interest. Inclusion of rating scales designed to assess certain behavior patterns, especially when gathered in methodologically sound fashion, provide valuable impact-level data.

Sociometric Evaluations.   The opinions of a child's peers are another resource for evaluating whether or not treatment produced a conspicuous impact. Kendall et al. (1981) describe three main types of sociometrics: peer nominations, rating scales, and descriptive matches. In peer nominations, children identify the peers whom they most prefer and most dislike, or choose other children to be in groups with themselves. Peer rating scales are basically developmental and role-appropriate versions of parent and teacher rating scales. Descriptive matching requires that children identify their peers by being presented with behavioral descriptors. These various sociometric methods can provide a useful adjunct to evaluations of the child by adults.

Archival Data.   A more longitudinal evaluation of therapy outcome may possibly be obtained by reference to archival data. Although not prominent in past assessments of behavior therapy impact, archival data provide suggestive information that may be gathered, for example, from the number of visits to the principal in a school intervention or the number of negative court contacts following a program for delinquent youths.

Multiple Measures

The conclusion of most discussions of the appropriate dependent variables for therapy outcome research is that, since change is multidimensional, multiple measures should be employed[4] (Bergin & Lambert, 1978; Fiske et al., 1970; Kazdin, 1980; Kazdin & Wilson, 1978b; Kendall, 1982; Mahoney, 1978; Nelson, 1981).

There is a degree of overlap between specifying level and impact level assessments. Some measures may, in fact, potentially address both levels. For instance, depending on the extent of the direct observation of the child's behavior, it may be possible to answer questions about what exactly changed and to make statements about the observed impact of those changes on various facets

---

[4] Rosen and Proctor (1981) have written, "The use of general and/or similar outcome measures for a broad range of clients, problems, and therapies is likely to result for some clients in use of outcomes that may have no relevance either to the conduct of their treatment or to its evaluation" (pp. 422–423). Two individualized measures of psychotherapy outcome are extensively discussed by Mintz and Kiesler (1982): the Target Complaints strategy, and Goal Attainment Scaling. The Target Complaints assessment strategy employs each client's spontaneously presented target complaint as its criteria for evaluating the impact of treatment. Goal Attainment Scaling is a strategy for devising individualized, multivariable scaled descriptions of goals against which treatment efficacy can be compared. Neither strategy has received detailed attention in the child behavior therapy literature.

of the child's functioning and interactions. This area of overlap, while complicating easy classification of measures as either one level of assessment or another, need not be a cause for dismay. Rather, this gray area illustrates the importance of not focusing on one level to the exclusion of the other. As stated elsewhere, "Multiple measures make it possible to know not only the impact of treatment but also what specific cognitive and behavioral changes are responsible for the impact" (Kendall & Braswell, 1982, p. 28). It would be unreasonable to assume that one measure could be the "true" measure either of the child's initial problems or of the ultimate gains. Most children are treated for more than a single discrete problem, and different problems are best assessed by different measures.

The use of multiple measures can potentially provide convergent validity for conclusions about the impact of treatment. However, the results of different measures should not necessarily be expected to coordinate exactly, since they may measure different effects of treatment and different perspectives on outcome and since behavior changes might be specific to certain assessment modalities. Thus, multiple measures can provide us with information about the way treatment has influenced an array of the child's functioning.

Cost and efficiency require attention as well. The cost of treatment and the efficiency with which change can be instigated do not supplant the criteria of utmost importance (namely, those that affect the client most directly), but they do have an important indirect effect on the client. From both a practical and ethical standpoint, the least expensive and most efficient treatment is obviously preferred, other factors being equal. Cost-related criteria include cost in terms of money, client and therapist time, and any necessary equipment. Efficiency criteria include the amount of time necessary to impact change and the manner in which treatment can be effectively administered (e.g., in groups versus individually) (Kazdin, 1980; Kazdin & Wilson, 1978a).

FOLLOW-UP INVESTIGATIONS

Ross (1978) has labeled the short-term follow-up assessments of child behavior therapy as "the most frequent shortcoming," and states, "the fact that researchers using other treatment approaches have no good follow-up data either can hardly serve as a reason not to correct our own deficiencies" (p. 614). Deciding how long after treatment children should be reassessed will depend on the type of behavior treated, the goals of therapy, and a number of logistical factors, but investigations of the maintenance of behavior change clearly need to extend beyond the currently standard few weeks to few months time period.

The greatest problem for follow-up investigations is attrition—loss of subjects either because of an inability to locate them or their refusal to participate in further assessment. Attrition creates interpretative difficulties because the group of subjects followed up may not be representative of the original groups.

Gottman and Markman (1978) recommend investigating differential attrition by blocking follow-up subjects on pre to post therapy gains. Their rationale is that it may be primarily those subjects who improved who are willing to be assessed at follow-up—clearly confounding the conclusions of the follow-up investigation. Kendall and Norton-Ford (1982b) further suggest that information be obtained from the client about experiences, such as additional treatment, that have intervened between the end of therapy and the follow-up assessment period.

Another methodologically important procedure for follow-up investigations is for comparable dependent measures to be employed immediately after treatment and during the follow-up investigations (Gottman & Markman, 1978; Kendall & Norton-Ford, 1982b). This requirement means that the dependent measures chosen must be suitable for repeated application. Furthermore, if the period of time from pretreatment to follow-up is long enough that the child's age will change during the study, then the dependent measures need to be carefully evaluated for their developmental-level appropriateness. A key problem for child intervention evaluation is the need to be concerned with measurement equivalence (see Baltes, Reese, & Nesselroade, 1977). Interventionists must ask and attempt to answer the following query: should the same assessment device be used at pretreatment, posttreatment, and follow-up (i.e., at different ages) or should a different but age-appropriate measure be used to assess the identical concept? The same behaviors could be observed at the different ages, but will the same behaviors have similar meanings at the different ages? A reduction in aggressive behavior may be confused with developmental change. That is, there may be fewer fights with peers, but more abusive verbal language toward adults. If only peer-fighting behaviors are observed, then developmental change masks the intervention evaluation.

One proposed solution would be to use multiple measurements—essentially a combination of both options noted earlier. If and when desired changes are produced on identical assessments over time, the therapeutic benefit could only be determined when comparisons are made against changes produced (a) by development alone and (b) by the repeated assessments. Appropriate control conditions provide the needed methodology. If and when desired changes are produced on the age-appropriate (but nonidentical) measures, therapeutic benefit must also be gleaned from comparisons over time with proper controls. By using both approaches to assessment, the evaluator can determine whether or not the outcome was dependent on the type of measurement strategy employed. In cases in which changes are apparent on *both* measurement strategies, the findings will be impressive (Kendall, Lerner, & Craighead, 1984).

One final note about follow-ups: are our expectations about the long-term effects of our interventions reasonable? Are we not asking too much when we expect that a treatment will continue to have desired effects long after its discontinuation? This expectation appears especially unrealistic if a maintenance program was not included in the treatment plan. We specifically propose that, while follow-ups should consistently be assessed and reported, the efficacy of the intervention must be judged against more reasoned expectations for maintenance. The longer and more comprehensive the intervention, the greater the expectations for maintenance at follow-up can be. However, one must keep in mind that maintenance may follow a different theoretical explanation than did the original behavior change.

NONSPECIFICS

Therapy outcome research is usually designed to consider the effects of various kinds of treatment on various types of clients. The client, the therapist, the therapeutic techniques, and time are all recognized variables that must enter into treatment evaluation. However, not only are these four factors much more complex than they might at first appear, but a number of "nonintentional influences" (Lazarus, 1980) may also have a potential impact on therapy outcome. Fiske et al. (1970) summarize the dilemma well:

> A major problem in assessing the outcome of therapeutic treatment is determining the effects contributed by sources other than the treatment, the therapist, and the patient himself. The nature of the patient's environment during therapy, the attitudes of significant others toward him and his treatment, and the occurrence of changes in the patient's life-situation and of any special events or traumas should be known. In general, it is likely that such sources of effects will be controlled by truly random assignment of subjects to treatment groups. It seems advisable, however, to gather data on these matters to ensure that they do not have systematic effects which bias the findings. (p. 26)

Carefully constructed designs control for a number of potentially confounding variables. Most of these have been discussed in terms of control groups. A number of other variables that may influence treatment outcome are not as easily eliminated as confounds via the use of control groups. These variables have typically been referred to as *nonspecific factors*. They include therapeutic relationship, therapist enthusiasm, client's motivation, and the potential for spontaneous remission. This list is not intended to be exhaustive, but it is important to recognize the potential for nonspecific factors to cloud clear interpretation of treatment effects as being a direct function of therapeutic techniques alone. These nonspecific factors typically require direct manipulation as independent variables and purposeful inclusion as factors to examine in the study. Cross and Sheehan (1981) have proposed the factors, which have usually been labeled nonspecific, be identified, referred to as *secondary variables,* and be directly studied. They write: "If no attempt is made to include a range of both primary and secondary variables likely to be involved in therapy and no attempt is made to distinguish between them, then there must necessarily be a lack of confidence in asserting what actually produced the therapeutic change that has been observed" (1981, p. 350). It does not appear warranted to conclude, as some have done (Bergin & Lambert, 1978; Hynan, 1981), that the nonspecific factors are the only actively effective constituents of therapy.

The interaction of a particular child with a particular therapist may be another avenue warranting further exploration (Kendall & Norton-Ford, 1982b). Dougherty (1976) has taken an empirical approach to client-therapist matching, creating regression equations to predict on the basis of multiple measures which types of therapists would be most and least suited for which types of clients. The viability of these predictions were later tested by client assignments to specific therapists. Kendall and Norton-Ford (1982b) suggest that this type of procedure could be followed in other clinics, with the benefit of assured effective client-therapist matching through continued use of the technique.

COMPOSITE STUDIES OF THERAPY OUTCOME

Researchers have attempted to gather the results from a number of different therapy outcome studies in order to perform cumulative analyses and to make summary statements about the efficacy of different types of therapies and different specific techniques. Considerable controversy exists as to whether or not these between-study comparisons should be conducted (Agras & Berkowitz, 1980) and, if so, with what methods. The two approaches most employed are the *box-score strategy* (e.g., Luborsky, Singer, & Luborsky, 1975), and *meta-analysis* (e.g., Landman & Dawes, 1982; Smith & Glass, 1977). The box-score strategy is primarily a tally of the number of studies favoring each of a number of different kinds of treatments. Typically, these studies tabulate statistically significant versus not statistically significant results across a number of studies and conclude that one type of treatment is either "better than," "worse than," or "no different" from other types of treatment.

Meta-analyses depend on the calculation of "effect sizes" for the dependent variables in the studies and then on an analysis of the various effect sizes to determine the degree to which treated subjects changed in comparison to control subjects. Effect sizes are generally calculated in one or two ways. The mean score of one group can be subtracted from that of another, and the difference can be divided by one or both groups' standard deviation. Alternatively, expected mean squares can be calculated from analysis of variance data. In either case, the resulting effect sizes can be compared for different types of therapy, as well as for different dependent variables.

A number of criticisms have been launched against both of these cumulative techniques. First, the box-score method gives an unwarranted advantage to studies with large sample sizes that produce statistically significant but nevertheless weak results. Second, there is a strong probability that true differences between treatments will get lost as the results from a large number of unrelated studies are indiscriminately collated. Other limitations include the manner in which techniques within a single therapy are collapsed, as well as the grouping of different clients, therapists, behavior problems, and assessment methods (Kazdin & Wilson, 1978b).

One of the criticisms launched against the box-score strategy applies equally well to many meta-analyses. This is that the quality of summary conclusions reached can only be as good as the quality of the original studies entered into the summary (Kazdin & Wilson, 1978b; Kendall & Norton-Ford, 1982b). Kendall (1984) delineates a number of important criteria for those studies included in the meta-analysis, cautioning especially for details of the treatment and control groups to be specified, since, for example, "one researcher's attention control might be similar to another researcher's treatment condition" (p. 80). One recent proposal (Kendall & Hollon, 1983) suggests that therapy outcome researchers tape therapy sessions and then archive the tapes, making them available to other investigators. Tapes could be subsequently calibrated for quality, as well as for providing a much-needed check on the true comparability of identically labeled treatments.

Recently, Wilson and Rachman (1983) have challenged the notion that meta-analysis removes much of the subjectivity and bias present in other modes of aggregating treatment outcome results. Subjective decisions are made as to which studies to include in the analysis, as well as how to classify and code the therapy constituents. The controversy concerning the appropriate use of meta-analysis is heated.[5] As with box-score methods, a number of statistical problems also exist for meta-analyzers, but some of these have been recognized and remedied in more recent studies (Landman & Dawes, 1982).

Meta-analyses have not yet been conducted with child therapy outcome research. While a number of limitations of meta-analysis have been identified, it is nevertheless useful and important to have available composite studies that the clinician can employ to assist with the selection of the most efficacious treatment for a particular child. Between-study analyses of the child therapy outcome literature could serve a very useful purpose, as long as the conclusions drawn are not global but address results of specific techniques for specific clients with particular kinds of problems. In this instance, researchers conducting meta-analyses would do well to take into account the practical needs of the clinician. If that effectively transpired, the clinician might be more willing to base treatment choice decisions on empirical grounds, and new avenues for interactive benefit will have been paved. It is hoped that the development of useful composite studies of child treatment outcome can be hastened by knowledge gained from shortcomings in the initial cumulative analyses of adult therapy outcome studies.

---

[5] A recent issue of *Journal of Consulting and Clinical Psychology* (1983) included a special section with seven articles about meta-analysis. The reader wishing to pursue further exploration of this topic is referred to that special section, as well as to some of the actual analyses (Landman & Dawes, 1982; Shapiro & Shapiro, 1982; Smith & Glass, 1977). Kendall (1984) provides a "second look" at meta-analyses, evaluating them following a first round of improvements and Kendall and Maruyama (in press) comment on the future of meta-analysis.

THE INTERFACE BETWEEN RESEARCHERS AND CLINICIANS

Although most of this chapter has been devoted to methodological and conceptual issues in therapy outcome research, the topics discussed are intended to be applicable to the clinician as well as to the researcher and student. Ross (1978) has noted that the three stages of assessment necessary for therapy outcome research are of similar importance to the clinician providing treatment. Adequate provision of behavior therapy requires that behavioral information be obtained before beginning treatment so the clinician has knowledge about the appropriate starting points of intervention. The monitoring of target behaviors should continue throughout treatment to ensure treatment is having some positive impact and no deleterious effects. The third stage required for therapy outcome evaluation is assessment following treatment and optimally at some later times to investigate maintenance. While this last stage has not always been included in clinical work, the practical benefits of doing so can be easily recognized.

Hayes (1981) has suggested a number of design and methodological adaptations that he believes should allow the clinician to successfully conduct outcome research. While Wilson (1982) has disagreed that the proper "tools" will eradicate the research/practice split, many behaviorists (e.g., Ross, 1978) contend that the division need not be as wide. Spevak and Gilman (1980) have illustrated one system of extensive dependent variable collection to monitor the results of behavior therapy techniques as conducted in a clinic. The authors appear optimistic about the role of the system in the determination of the actual clinical efficacy of a variety of behavioral techniques. On balance, Mannarino, Michelson, Beck, and Figueroa (1982) offer a report of their difficulties in establishing treatment outcome studies in a child psychiatric clinic.

Agras and Berkowitz (1980) have aptly identified some of the impediments to extended programs of clinical research in behavior therapy. "Unfortunately, as we have seen, the major rewards in clinical research have less to do with the product, a more effective therapy, than with the rewards of the academic market place—publications, promotions, and tenure. This is in sharp distinction from other forms of technologic progress where the rewards for those involved in development are most closely tied to how well the product works" (p. 486).

Since many research articles end with a plea for therapists and researchers to join hands, it would appear necessary to evaluate the economic and social factors preventing this union from occurring more readily. One of the major pressures, in our opinion, is triggered by the "required choice" that is made when seeking and selecting employment. Jobs are written and advertised for *either* researchers or practitioners, and while most if not all candidates are trained to function in both roles, the employer often divides the roles. More job descriptions should be geared specifically to the person interested in doing half-time clinical work and half-time research, and should coordinate efforts from those two areas as much as possible.

By now, the harried clinician might be at a loss with regard to exactly how to effectively don multiple hats and be simultaneously adept at making treatment choice decisions and treatment efficacy evaluations. We fully recognize that practical realities may make suggestions that the clinician conduct outcome studies appear absurd. Nevertheless, we suggest that it is possible and necessary to integrate research data within clinical practice.

The clinician can be an effective user of other's published data, perhaps being most interested in data from group comparison studies to assist in making decisions as to the most appropriate kind of treatment for a particular kind of child client. It is understandable that there might be a reluctance to assume that the successful results reported for a single-subject design study would necessarily generalize to a client with different characteristics. Group comparison studies include a group of subjects, with a stronger likelihood that positive results are not idiosyncratic to one particular type of subject. Also, because clinicians may be less likely to search for a number of replicated single-subject design results than to read the results of one group comparison study, the importance of these latter studies reporting data of clinical significance as well as statistical significance is reemphasized. Percentage of subjects who improved, the characteristics of those subjects, and normative comparisons should all be evaluated and reported in group comparison studies.

In contrast to the clinician as the consumer of research, when the clinician is the producer, single-subject designs usually will be most appropriate. An assessment of the effectiveness of the particular treatment techniques eventually chosen and employed by the clinician usually will be most practically, readily, and successfully conducted by single-subject designs rather than by group comparison methods. Yet, when evaluation is examined clinic-wide, group studies are appropriate.

RECOMMENDATIONS FOR FUTURE RESEARCH IN CHILD BEHAVIOR THERAPY OUTCOME

Behavior therapy has been a leader in the strategy of focusing on a specific disorder and of systematically examining the comparative efficacy of a number of different types of treatment methods (Gelder, 1976). This type of therapy evaluation is most useful to the clinician wishing to make accurate and specific recommendations. This should continue and should be expanded to treatment of some types of behavior problems not generally given empirical evaluation. It would appear wise for any future cumulative studies that are conducted to focus on summarizing the efficacy results of one particular type of treatment or on comparing a variety of methods for the treatment of a single disorder.

Given the current emphasis on therapy accountability, further investigation of cost effectiveness is recommended. For example, some of the techniques usually used individually could be evaluated for appropriateness in group therapy.

The rigid dichotomization of process studies and outcome studies may be unnecessary. Outcome researchers must incorporate exploration of the therapeutic process into their assessments. The rationale for this statement is that sole reliance on pre and posttreatment assessment may provide an inaccurate picture of therapeutic change. The possibility of curvilinear change functions would be important to explore, rather than resting on assumptions of monotonic change (Kiesler, 1971).

An interest in the *mechanisms* of behavior change would suggest the need to integrate assessment of cognitions into the evaluation of behavior therapy outcome (Kendall, 1982; Kendall & Norton-Ford, 1982b). The widening application of cognitive-behavioral interventions necessitates that concentrated efforts go into careful evaluation of appropriate dependent measures of cognitions to supplement the better developed behavioral measures (see Kendall & Urbain, 1981, for an illustration of the combined application of cognitive and behavioral evaluation measures).

Current strategies for the evaluation of child behavior therapy outcome must become more integrated, with more sincere attempts to coordinate past and future studies, as well as the employment, whenever possible and appropriate, of dependent measures that overlap with those of other studies (Fiske et al., 1970).

Ross (1981b) repeats a suggestion of Hersen and Barlow (1976) to gather substantial information about all individuals participating in a between-group design, so that after the group comparison data are analyzed, results can be plotted in relation to each individual child and his or her unique characteristics. This method would allow a clinician to compare characteristics of the client with those of children in the study according to their differential responses to treatment. Ross has labeled this the *tracer method* and stated that it has not been previously used in child behavior therapy research.

The *deviant case analysis* is another interesting strategy for broadening the applications of therapy outcome research. Initially proposed by Ross in 1963, it also has not been implemented. Basically, it entails conducting an outcome study using a standard between-group design but, immediately after statistical analysis of the data, recontacting any children whose data run counter to group trends. A great deal can be learned from those cases that refute our hypotheses.

Therapy outcome evaluation with children must take into account normal developmental processes. The results of therapy cannot be properly evaluated without the existence of well-established developmental norms that can be used as outcome criteria and for planning appropriate intervention (Kendall et al., 1981). Base rates must be developed for a number of common behaviors, such as temper tantrums, bed wetting, and nightmares. Further, the developmental course of a number of behavior problems should be charted to allow clinicians to compare therapeutic results with changes expected simply through maturation. Knowing more about the duration of different problem behaviors would also provide us with information for deciding if an intervention should be implemented, or if the natural course of development should be left to run its course.

REFERENCES

Agras, W., & Berkowitz, R. Clinical research in behavior therapy: Halfway there? *Behavior Therapy,* 1980, *11,* 472–487.

Baltes, P. B., Reese, H. W., & Nesselroade, J. R. *Life-span developmental psychology: Introduction to research methods.* Monterey, Calif.: Brooks/Cole Publishing, 1977.

Barlow, D., & Hayes, S. Alternating treatments design: One strategy for comparing the effects of two treatments in a single subject. *Journal of Applied Behavior Analysis,* 1979, *12,* 199–210.

Barrett, C., Hampe, E., & Miller, L. Research on psychotherapy with children. In S. Garfield & A. Bergin (Eds.), *Handbook of psychotherapy and behavior change: An empirical analysis* (2nd ed.). New York: John Wiley & Sons, 1978.

Bergin, A. The evaluation of therapeutic outcomes. In A. Bergin & S. Garfield (Eds.), *Handbook of psychotherapy and behavior change: An empirical analysis.* New York: John Wiley & Sons, 1971.

Bergin, A., & Lambert, M. The evaluation of therapeutic outcomes. In S. Garfield & A. Bergin (Eds.), *Handbook of psychotherapy and behavior change: An empirical analysis* (2nd ed.). New York: John Wiley & Sons, 1978.

Bernard, M., Kratochwill, T., & Keefauver, L. The effects of rational-emotive therapy and self-instructional training on chronic hair pulling. *Cognitive Therapy and Research,* 1983, *7,* 273–279.

Birnbrauer, J. Mental retardation. In H. Leitenberg (Ed.), *Handbook of behavior modification and behavior therapy.* Englewood Cliffs, N.J.: Prentice-Hall, 1976.

Braswell, L., Kendall, P., & Koehler, C. *Children's attributions of behavior change: Patterns associated with positive outcome.* Paper presented at the annual meeting of the Association for Advancement of Behavior Therapy, Los Angeles, Calif., November 1982.

Browning, R., & Stover, D. *Behavior modification in child treatment: An experimental and clinical approach.* Chicago: Aldine-Atherton, 1971.

Campbell, D., & Stanley, J. *Experimental and quasi-experimental designs for research.* Chicago: Rand McNally, 1963.

Cross, D., & Sheehan, P. Classification of variables in psychotherapy research: Therapeutic change and the concept of artifact. *Psychotherapy: Theory, Research and Practice,* 1981, *18,* 345–353.

DeProspero, A., & Cohen, S. Inconsistent visual analyses of intrasubject data. *Journal of Applied Behavior Analysis*, 1979, *12*, 573–579.

Dougherty, F. Patient-therapist matching for prediction of optimal and minimal therapeutic outcome. *Journal of Consulting and Clinical Psychology*, 1976, *44*, 889–897.

Dukes, W. N=1. *Psychological Bulletin*, 1965, *64*, 74–79.

Edington, E. Random assignment and statistical tests for one-subject experiments. *Behavior Assessment*, 1980, *2*, 19–28.

Ellis, A. Rational-emotive therapy and cognitive behavior therapy: Similarities and differences. *Cognitive Therapy and Research*, 1980, *4*, 325–340.

Finch, A., Kendall, P., Montgomery, L., & Morris, T. Effects of two types of failure on anxiety in children. *Journal of Abnormal Psychology*, 1975, *84*, 583–585.

Fiske, D., Hunt, H., Luborsky, L., Orne, M., Parloff, M., Reiser, M., & Tuma, A. Planning of research on effectiveness of psychotherapy. *Archives of General Psychiatry*, 1970, *22*, 22–32.

Gelder, N. Research methodology in psychotherapy––Why bother? *Proceedings of the Royal Society of Medicine*, 1976, *69*, 505–508.

Gelfand, D., & Hartmann, D. Behavior therapy with children: A review and evaluation of research methodology. *Psychological Bulletin*, 1968, *69* 204–215.

Gelfand, D., & Hartmann, D. *Child behavior analysis and therapy*. New York: Pergamon Press, 1975.

Glass, G., Willson, V., & Gottman, J. *Design and analysis of time-series experiments*. Boulder, Colorado: Associated University Press, 1975.

Gottman, J., Gonso, J., & Rasmussen, B. Social interaction, social competence, and friendship in children. *Child Development*, 1975, *46*, 709–718.

Gottman, J., & Markman, H. Experimental designs in psychotherapy research. In S. Garfield & A. Bergin (Eds.), *Handbook of psychotherapy and behavior change: An empirical analysis* (2nd ed.). New York: John Wiley & Sons, 1978.

Greenspan, S., & Sharfstein, S. Efficacy of psychotherapy: Asking the right questions. *Archives of General Psychiatry*, 1981, *38*, 1213–1219.

Harris, S., & Wolchik, S. Suppression of self-stimulation: Three alternative strategies. *Journal of Applied Behavior Analysis*, 1979, *12*, 185–198.

Hayes, S. Single case empirical design and empirical clinical practice. *Journal of Consulting and Clinical Psychology*, 1981, *49*, 193–211.

Hersen, M., & Barlow, D. *Single-case experimental designs: Strategies for studying behavior change*. New York: Pergamon Press, 1976.

Hynan, M. On the advantages of assuming that the techniques of psychotherapy are ineffective. *Psychotherapy: Theory, Research, and Practice*, 1981, *18*, 11–13.

Johnson, B., & Cuvo, A. Teaching mentally retarded adults to cook. *Behavior Modification*, 1981, *5*, 187–202.

Journal of Consulting and Clinical Psychology, 1983, *51,* 3–75.

Kazdin, A. Statistical analysis for single-case experimental designs. In M. Hersen & D. Barlow (Eds.), *Single case experimental designs: Strategies for studying behavior change.* New York: Pergamon Press, 1976.

Kazdin, A. Assessing the clinical or applied importance of behavior change through social validation. *Behavior Modification,* 1977, *1,* 427–452.

Kazdin, A. *Research design in clinical psychology.* New York: Harper & Row, 1980.

Kazdin, A. Methodological strategies in behavior-therapy research. In G. Wilson & C. Franks (Eds.), *Contemporary behavior therapy: Conceptual and empirical foundations.* New York: Guilford Press, 1982 (a).

Kazdin, A. Single-case experimental design. In P. Kendall & J. Butcher (Eds.), *Handbook of research methods in clinical psychology.* New York: John Wiley & Sons, 1982 (b).

Kazdin, A., & Hartmann, D. The simultaneous-treatment design. *Behavior Therapy,* 1978, *9,* 912–922.

Kazdin, A., & Marholin, D. Program evaluation in clinical and community settings. In D. Marholin (Ed.), *Child behavior therapy.* New York: Gardner Press, 1978.

Kazdin, A., & Wilson, G. Criteria for evaluating psychotherapy. *Archives of General Psychiatry,* 1978, *35,* 407–416 (a).

Kazdin, A., & Wilson, G. *Evaluation of behavior therapy: Issues, evidence, and research strategies.* Cambridge, Mass.: Ballinger, 1978 (b).

Kendall, P. C. Assessing generalization and the single-subject design. *Behavior Modification,* 1981, *5,* 307–319 (a).

Kendall, P. C. Assessment and cognitive-behavioral interventions: Purposes, proposals and problems. In P. Kendall & S. Hollon (Eds.), *Assessment strategies for cognitive-behavioral interventions.* New York: Academic Press, 1981 (b).

Kendall, P. C. Behavioral assessment and methodology. In C. Franks, G. Wilson, P. Kendall, & K. Brownell, *Annual review of behavior therapy* (Vol. 8). New York: Guilford Press, 1982.

Kendall, P. C. Behavioral assessment and methodology. In G. Wilson, C. Franks, K. Brownell, & P. Kendall, *Annual review of behavior therapy* (Vol. 9). New York: Guilford Press, 1984.

Kendall, P. C., & Braswell, L. Assessment for cognitive-behavioral interventions in the schools. *School Psychology Review,* 1982, *11,* 21–31.

Kendall, P. C., & Braswell, L. *Cognitive-behavioral therapy for impulsive children.* New York: Guilford Press, 1984.

Kendall, P. C., & Hollon, S. D. Calibrating the quality of therapy: Collaborative archiving of tape samples from therapy outcome trials. *Cognitive Therapy and Research,* 1983, *7,* 199–204.

Kendall, P. C., Lerner, R., & Craighead, W. Human development and intervention in childhood psychopathology. *Child Development,* 1984, *55,* 71–82.

Kendall, P. C., & Maruyama, G. Meta-analysis: On the road to synthesis of knowledge? *Clinical Psychology Review*, in press.

Kendall, P. C., & Norton-Ford, J. *Clinical psychology: Scientific and professional dimensions*. New York: John Wiley & Sons, 1982 (a).

Kendall, P. C., & Norton-Ford, J. Therapy outcome research methods. In P. Kendall & J. Butcher (Eds.), *Handbook of research methods in clinical psychology*. New York: John Wiley & Sons, 1982 (b).

Kendall, P. C., Pellegrini, D. S., & Urbain, E. S. Approaches to assessment for cognitive-behavioral interventions with children. In P. C. Kendall and S. D. Hollon (Eds.), *Assessment strategies and cognitive-behavioral interventions*. New York: Academic Press, 1981.

Kendall, P. C., & Urbain, E. Cognitive-behavioral intervention with a hyperactive girl: Evaluation via behavioral observations and cognitive performance. *Behavioral Assessment*, 1981, *3*, 345–357.

Kiesler, D. Some myths of psychotherapy research and the search for a paradigm. *Psychological Bulletin*, 1966, *65*, 110–136.

Kiesler, D. Experimental designs in psychotherapy research. In A. Bergin & S. Garfield (Eds.), *Handbook of psychotherapy and behavior change*. New York: John Wiley & Sons, 1971.

Kratochwill, T. (Ed.). *Single-subject research: Strategies for evaluating change*. New York: Academic Press, 1978.

Kratochwill, T., & Levin, J. On the applicability of various data analysis procedures to the simultaneous and alternating treatment designs in behavior therapy research. *Behavioral Assessment*, 1980, *2*, 353–360.

Landman, J., & Dawes, R. Psychotherapy outcome: Smith and Glass's conclusions stand up under scrutiny. *American Psychologist*, 1982, *37*, 504–516.

Lazarus, A. Toward delineating some causes of change in psychotherapy. *Professional Psychology*, 1980, *11*, 863–870.

Luborsky, L., Singer, B., & Luborsky, L. Comparative studies of psychotherapies: Is it true that "everyone has won and all must have prizes"? *Archives of General Psychiatry*, 1975, *32*, 995–1008.

Mahoney, M. Experimental methods and outcome evaluation. *Journal of Consulting and Clinical Psychology*, 1978, *46*, 660–672.

Mannarino, A., Michelson, L., Beck, S., & Figueroa, J. Treatment research in a child psychiatric clinic: Implementation and evaluation issues. *Journal of Clinical Child Psychology*, 1982, *11*, 50–55.

Marshall, E. Psychotherapy works, but for whom? *Science*, 1980, *207*, 506–508.

Matson, J. Assessment and treatment of clinical fears in mentally retarded children. *Journal of Applied Behavior Analysis*, 1981, *14*, 287–294.

Mintz, J. The role of the therapist in assessing psychotherapy. In A. Gurman & A. Razin (Eds.), *Effective psychotherapy: A handbook of research*. Oxford: Pergamon Press, 1977.

Mintz, J., & Kiesler, D. Individualized measures of psychotherapy outcome. In P. Kendall & J. Butcher (Eds.), *Handbook of research methods in clinical psychology.* New York: John Wiley & Sons, 1982.

Nelson, R. Realistic dependent measures for clinical use. *Journal of Consulting and Clinical Psychology,* 1981, *49,* 168–182.

O'Leary, K., & Borkovec, T. Conceptual, methodological, and ethical problems of placebo groups in psychotherapy research. *American Psychologist,* 1978, *33,* 821–830.

Ollendick, T., Shapiro, E., & Barrett, R. Reducing stereotypic behaviors: An analysis of treatment procedures utilizing an alternate treatments design. *Behavior Therapy,* 1981, *12,* 570–577.

Patterson, G. Interventions for boys with conduct problems: Multiple settings, treatments, and criteria. *Journal of Consulting and Clinical Psychology,* 1974, *42,* 471–481.

Paul, G. Strategy of outcome research in psychotherapy. *Journal of Consulting and Clinical Psychology,* 1967, *31,* 109–119.

Peterson, L., Homer, A., & Wonderlich, S. The integrity of independent variables in behavior analysis. *Journal of Applied Behavior Analysis,* 1982, *15,* 477–492.

Rachman, S., & Wilson, G. *The effects of psychological therapy.* Oxford: Pergamon Press, 1980.

Rickel, A., & Lampi, L. A two-year follow-up study of a preventative mental health program for preschoolers. *Journal of Abnormal Child Psychology,* 1981, *9,* 455–464.

Rosen, A., & Proctor, E. Distinctions between treatment outcomes and their implications for treatment evaluation. *Journal of Consulting and Clinical Psychology,* 1981, 49, 418–425.

Ross, A. Behavior therapy with children. In S. Garfield & A. Bergin (Eds.), *Handbook of psychotherapy and behavior change: An empirical analysis* (2nd ed.). New York: John Wiley & Sons, 1978.

Ross, A. *Child behavior therapy: Principles, procedures, and empirical basis.* New York: John Wiley & Sons, 1981 (a).

Ross, A. Of rigor and relevance. *Professional Psychology,* 1981, *12,* 318–327 (b).

Schreibman, L., Koegel, R., Mills, J., & Burke, J. Social validation of behavior therapy with autistic children. *Behavior Therapy,* 1981, *12,* 610–624.

Shapiro, E., Kazdin, A., & McGonigle, J. Multiple-treatment interference in the simultaneous- or alternating-treatments design. *Behavioral Assessment,* 1982, *4,* 105–115.

Shapiro, D. A., & Shapiro, D. Meta-analysis of comparative therapy outcome studies: A replication and refinement. *Psychological Bulletin,* 1982, *92,* 581–604.

Singh, N., Winton, A., & Dawson, M. Suppression of antisocial behavior by facial screening using multiple baseline and alternating treatments designs. *Behavior Therapy,* 1982, *13,* 511–520.

Smith, M. & Glass, G. Meta-analysis of psychotherapy outcome studies. *American Psychologist*, 1977, *32*, 752–760.

Spevak, M., & Gilman, S. A system for evaluative research in behavior therapy. *Psychotherapy: Theory, Research and Practice*, 1980, *17*, 37–43.

Stolz, S. Ethical issues in research on behavior therapy. In S. Wood (Ed.), *Issues in evaluating behavior modification: Proceedings of the first Drake conference on professional issues in behavior analysis, March 1974.* Champaign, Ill.: Research Press, 1975.

Strupp, H. Psychotherapy research and practice: An overview. In S. Garfield & A. Bergin (Eds.), *Handbook of psychotherapy and behavior change: An empirical analysis* (2nd ed.). New York: John Wiley & Sons, 1978.

Strupp, H., & Hadley, S. A tripartite model of mental health and therapeutic outcomes: With special reference to negative effects in psychotherapy. *American Psychologist*, 1977, *32*, 187–196.

Tryon, W. A simplified time-series analysis for evaluating treatment interventions. *Journal of Applied Behavior Analysis*, 1982, *15*, 423–429.

Wilson, G. Psychotherapy process and procedure: The behavioral mandate. *Behavior Therapy*, 1982, *13*, 291–312.

Wilson, G., & Rachman, S. Meta-analysis and the evaluation of psychotherapy outcome: Limitations and liabilities. *Journal of Consulting and Clinical Psychology*, 1983, *51*, 54–64.

PART TWO

Disorders Arising during
Childhood

4

Mental Retardation

Johnny L. Matson
Ellen Olinger
Northern Illinois University

Mental retardation has a long tradition. For example, in ancient Greece and Rome as well as in the medieval periods, persons with severe cognitive deficits were treated as objects of scorn, ridicule and persecution (Rosen, Clark, & Kivitz, 1976). At best, they were court jesters and clowns; at worst, they were considered a burden to the family and, consequently, destroyed. In Rome, these children were frequently drowned in the Tiber River. Even as recently as the Reformation, John Calvin and Martin Luther referred to the mentally retarded as being filled with Satan. Their fate ranged from marginal tolerance to imprisonment or burning at the stake. Only in recent times have these persons been elevated to the level of human beings worthy of consideration, care, and deserving of human rights and equality. Progress has been substantial, particularly in recent years, and changes continue. Currently a revolution is occurring in the legal and philosophical domains as they relate to the mentally retarded. As a result, normalization and mainstreaming, which espouse the rights of the mentally retarded to participate as fully as they are capable, have emerged and are sweeping the Western world (see Matson & Mulick, 1983). Litigation, such as the landmark Wyatt-Stickney case, which has been argued in the courts for over 10 years, has been introduced to support these views (Marchetti, 1983). Among the points that have emerged and that bear directly on the treatment of the mentally retarded are the right to an individual habilitation plan, an update of intellectual functioning and annual consideration of treatment, care in the least restrictive setting, the provision of adequate and appropriately trained staff, sufficient living space and privacy, and the concept of employing the least restrictive and least aversive treatment that is likely to be effective. (Behavioral approaches are generally considered less restrictive/aversive than medications by the courts.) These factors are likely to have a continuing impact on the types of behaviors treated and the procedures that are used for some time to come.

Conceptualization

Given the numerous and multifaceted causes of mental retardation, it is impossible to note here all the factors contributing to its development and the many reasons for mental retardation—particularly for the milder forms where causes are unknown. (Rather than attempt to discuss all the conditions that constitute this disorder, the reader is referred to Matson & Mulick [1983] and MacMillan [1982].) A similar problem exists even with particular problems commonly exhibited by mentally retarded persons, such as self-injurious behavior (Baumeister & Forehand, 1976). In this instance, a number of possible causes exist, including psychodynamic, behavioral and physiological theories. The bulk of the existing evidence supports the behavioral and physiological hypotheses, but much is yet to be learned before definitive statements about specific causative agents and the magnitude of their impact on particular conditions can be made.

A number of factors can predispose one to mental retardation. As noted, researchers cannot tell at this time what the exact effect of each of these variables are in each case, whatever genetic and birth-related variables are among those that impact most heavily on the mental development of children. For example, mothers above the age of 40 are much more likely to have a Down's syndrome child than a mother of 25, assuming all other factors are equal, and a number of various types of mental retardation run in families.

As noted, familial variables also seem to be involved to a large extent. It is noted that the highest rates of mental retardation are found in children who are culturally disadvantaged, culturally different or culturally deprived (MacMillan, 1982). Some examples may help to further demonstrate this point. Studies of twins have been used to show that conditions relative to environment may be highly influential. One finding is that twins score 4 to 7 points lower on IQ tests than children born one at a time. This finding would seem to suggest that the extra attention afforded by adults to children whose birth is spaced over time may be critical (Vanderberg, 1968). Similarly, this holds true for scholastic achievement, and these effects are noted across all social classes. Additionally, under conditions in which a low level of stimulation is afforded children by adults, negative and dramatic differences are noted. Perhaps the classic study exemplifying this point is the report of Skeels and Dye (1939). They placed 13 orphaned children younger than three years old in wards of an institution for the mentally retarded with female, mentally retarded adults; 12 other children were left in the orphanage. Contact in the former group between adult and child was frequent, whereas in the latter group, it occurred only when biological needs were evident. At the beginning of the study, IQs of the groups were 64 and 87, respectively. Assessments of IQ at 21 and 43 months showed increases in IQ for children with surrogate mentally retarded mothers and decrements in IQ for children left in the orphanage. In a follow-up 20 years later, all but two of the children with surrogate mothers had been adopted, while all 12 children from the orphanage remained institutionalized. Marked differences in the two groups remained, with those in the community having an average of 12 years of education and obtaining jobs, such as clerks and teachers (Skodak, 1965).

Data such as these suggest that progress is being made in identification of the many factors that contribute to mental retardation. Although research on pre-natal and perinatal influences has been particularly striking, it has been found that parents only infrequently are aware of or take action based on the data. As a result, genetic counseling strategies are greatly needed, and it is one area in which behavior therapists could have a marked impact (see Matson & Mulick, 1983 for a discussion of the topics noted above).

Definition

For purposes of the present review, the definition of mental retardation provided by the American Association on Mental Deficiency (AAMD) will be used (Grossman, 1983). The characteristics of the assessment are threefold. First, the problem must be identified before age 18. Second, the person must be classified as mentally retarded on adaptive behavior with a well recognized scale, generally the American Association on Mental Deficiency Adaptive Behavior Scale or Vineland Social Maturity Scale. Third and finally, a standard-ized intelligence test (either a Weschler scale or Stanford Binet) should be administered. Unfortunately, for behavior therapists in particular, adaptive be-havior for measuring treatment effects is rarely used in practice for such classi-fication (Breuning & Barrett, 1983).

The AAMD system separates the mentally retarded into four groups: mild, moderately, severely, and profoundly mentally retarded. The mild and mod-erately mentally retarded are ambulatory, have rudimentary speech, are infre-quently identified as having a specific genetic or physiological condition caus-ing the problem, and constitute approximately 98 percent of all mentally retarded persons. The severely and profoundly mentally retarded almost invar-iably have identifiable organic pathology leading to their condition, frequently have very few self-help skills, and typically have other handicaps, such as lack of or malformed limbs, hearing or visual impediments, and seizure disorders. There is considerable controversy as to the current value and overall potential of behavior therapy with those more seriously impaired (Ellis, 1981).

To be classified as mentally retarded on an intelligence test, the person's performance must be two standard deviations or more below the mean. There-fore, by definition (see normal probability curve), approximately 2.5 or 3 percent of the United States population (roughly 6 million persons) are mentally retarded. Because this group is very large, it is one that deserves much consideration in the development of treatment programs.

Behavior therapy with the mentally retarded has a long tradition relative to other populations studied. Along these same lines, the variety of methods that have been employed is considerable, compared to what has been demonstrated with other groups (excluding college sophomores). Of course, some procedures have been used more frequently than others, with a decided bent toward the more operantly based methods, such as overcorrection, time-out, and the use of tangible reinforcers. In the near future, however, there is likely to be a dramatic increase in more cognitively based methods, such as self-control procedures. (See Shapiro, 1981 for a review of this literature of the mentally retarded.) Similarly, methods that employ cognitive imagery have been proposed (Doubros, 1966).

Definitions of behavior therapy with the mentally retarded have varied considerably. For example, Doubros (1966) has stated that the aim of behavior therapy with mildly and moderately mentally retarded persons "is twofold: (*a*) to generate self-control and (*b*) to increase socially acceptable behaviors" (p. 229). These goals certainly are a major facet of behavior therapy with this segment of the mentally retarded population. For purposes of the present review, however, any use of learning based treatment procedures is subsumed under behavior therapy with the mentally retarded. Thus, the term *behavior therapy* must include a rather liberal interpretation with the mentally retarded, since many of the treatment procedures do not occur in the therapy room and deal with many problems that could be characterized as outside the realm of psychiatric problems, such as self-help skills training.

How and under what conditions did such developments occur? Perhaps those in clinical psychology and psychiatry who have espoused psychodynamic views of treatment are most responsible for behavior therapy's singular impact on the mentally retarded. The reason is that proponents of the psychodynamic approach have routinely stated that mentally retarded children do not have the necessary cognitive skills for obtaining insight or having sufficient ego development to deal effectively with the complex problems and issues that emerge in the therapist-patient relationship. Another problem encountered by the traditional psychotherapist was that the efforts that were made with this group did not prove to be particularly effecitve ones. Furthermore, many of the problems presented by the mentally retarded were not particularly pleasant (e.g., defecating in one's pants, engaging in self-injurious behavior, and getting into fights). Fortunately for these afflicted persons, behaviorally oriented psychologists were willing to take up the challenge.

Perhaps the earliest applied study with the mentally retarded was conducted by Norman Ellis (1963) at the Pinecrest State Hospital, a large facility for the mentally retarded in Pineville, Louisiana. Prior to this study, there had been a number of basic research questions addressed with the mentally retarded, one of which involved a human-size operant chamber similar to a Skinner Box. In these studies, reinforcement schedules and other related issues of interest were investigated (see studies by Ellis, 1962; Ellis & Pryer, 1958; Girardeau, 1962). Ellis' classic toilet training study was a success, settting the tone for many applied behaviorally oriented research studies that appeared in the ensuing years. Common elements of these early studies were that research typically was performed with institutionalized persons, involved basic self-help, showed self-injurious or aggressive behavior, and often involved both punishment and reinforcement components in the training programs. Common treatments, such as the token economy (Ayllon & Azrin, 1968) and overcorrection (see Ollendick & Matson, 1976), were employed for the first time with the mentally retarded. Additionally, the effects of the treatment programs were rapid, although the generalization and maintenance of gains in many of these programs is still somewhat open to question. The lack of broad and longstanding gains has been a major point of criticism from those who profess different theoretical approaches. However, it is generally the case that with these other approaches there is little or no empirical basis to support that even the most meager initial treatment effects occur (Matson & Barrett, 1982). Despite these problems, behavior therapy is certainly as firmly entrenched with the mentally retarded as with any population, and this trend is likely to continue.

Range of Procedures and Problems Treated

As noted, toilet training (Ellis, 1963) was the first problem behavior of the mentally retarded successfully treated with behavioral procedures. Since then, a wide range of problems have been effectively modified. These behaviors include: role modeling, social reinforcement, performance feedback (Matson & Stephens, 1978; Matson, Kazdin, & Esveldt-Dawson, 1980), contingent lemon juice (Becker, Turner, & Sajwaj, 1978), time-out and reinforcement (Bostow & Bailey, 1969), overcorrection (Azrin & Wesolowski, 1975), response cost (Burchard & Barrera, 1972), contingent music (Davis, Wieseler, & Hinzel, 1980), water mist (Dorsey, Iwata, Ong, & McSween, 1980), and contingent exercise (Luce, Delguardi, & Hall, 1980). The problems treated are similarly wide ranging. Some of these are rapid eating (Favell, McGimsey, & Jones, 1980), public disrobing (Foxx, 1976), self-stimulation (Foxx & Azrin, 1973), self-injury (Lovaas & Simmons, 1969), vomiting and rumination (Luckey, Wilson, & Musick, 1968), masturbation in public (Luiselli, Helfel, Pemberton, & Reisman, 1977), and pedestrian skills (Matson, Ollendick & Adkins, 1980). While all of these studies were not with children, all the behaviors noted could be treated with young persons, and it further demonstrates the voluminous amount of data that has accrued in a short period of time.

ASSESSMENT

While Bornstein outlines models of assessment in child behavior therapy as a whole in the second chapter of this book, the present chapter will describe the principles and procedures of behavioral assessment that relate specifically to mentally retarded children. The approach taken is that an ideal assessment of these children involves multiple measures of many different operationally defined behaviors under various circumstances and settings. Many types of data are potentially pertinent since medical, developmental, cognitive, emotional, social, and environmental factors all interact in complex ways. In other words, the professional who seeks to accurately assess mentally retarded children behaviorally must possess a repertoire of skills, a battery of tools, and a conceptual and empirically justified framework.

The relationship of behavioral assessment to mental retardation is strong and growing, and it spans the entire developmental period and range of severity in cognitive deficits detailed earlier. While behavioral assessment is an emerging and rapidly developing area, Nelson and Hayes (1981) summarize the major goals. These include the identification of target behaviors and suitable methods of measurement, determination of environmental and organismic controlling variables, selection of an intervention strategy that is likely to work, and evaluation of intervention effectiveness.

The present discussion is meant to be more methodological than theoretical, and it is centered around behavioral assessment in the home, school, and community. However, the objectives summarized by Nelson and Hayes (1981) are implicit throughout the discussion. In addition, techniques and principles that are applicable in one setting may be useful in other settings. A discussion of treatment procedures relevant to mentally retarded children follows an emphasis on assessment; for, while the achievement of sophisticated theoretical harmony is yet in progress in behavioral assessment, "there is a consensus regarding the need for viewing the development of effective assessment strategies not as an endpoint but rather as a necessary prerequisite for improving and evaluating services for children" (Mash & Terdal, 1981, p. 4).

In the Home

The relationship between assessment and the home is important for several reasons. First, recent legislation and litigation, such as Public Law 94–142, require active parental participation in education and treatment. Bateman and Herr (1981), Martin (1979), and Turnbull III and Turnbull (1978) provide comprehensive reviews of relevant litigation and landmark legislation. Second, working with parents of handicapped children is now an area of professional activity in its own right. For example, current textbooks for use in training teachers may devote an entire chapter to this topic (e.g., Lerner, Mardell-Czudnowski, & Goldenberg, 1981), and professionals are encouraged to develop specific skills in counseling parents (Stewart, 1978). Third, the importance of the home environment in child development is essential. As Matson and Beck (1981) note, it is difficult to think of child assessment without family evaluation. Fourth, parents may be helpful in treating problems that occur in the home and in promoting the generalization of new skills. Matson (1981), for example, used participant modeling by mothers to successfully treat fears of three moderately mentally retarded girls. The mothers served as primary therapists, and the reductions in their children's fears were important since the phobic response had resulted in reduced family social interactions. Fifth, children do not typically refer themselves for assessment; therefore, a trained professional should look at the child's environment to better understand reasons for referral (Wells, 1981). Finally, people in general are often observed to behave differently under different assessment conditions and settings. This factor is technically referred to as situational specificity (Kazdin, 1979). For example, environmental variables, such as reinforcement schedules, may be such that a child is well behaved at home but not at school. The reason for this can only be determined through assessment in both settings.

Kazdin (1980) discusses the strengths and limitations of several modalities of assessment, including global ratings by others, questionnaires, and direct measurement of specific behaviors. With respect to gaining clinically useful information concerning home variables, behavioral interviews are often used. However, empirical research in the use of the interview is far from comprehensive and conclusive. Wells (1981), for example, notes that the paucity of research on the behavioral interview is out of proportion to the frequency of its use, and Haynes and Jensen (1979, p. 98) point out that it is used for screening and diagnosis "without sufficient evaluation of its validity for making such decisions."

Despite existing conditions, the behavioral interview may be the only possible way to gain knowledge of relevant home factors and basic medical and developmental data. Moreover, parental reports are valuable indices of parental characteristics, such as attitudes and knowledge of child development, that are not always assessable through observation of parental behavior (Parke, 1978). Others in the home environment, such as children (given some language functioning) and relatives, may also work along with the parents and may be asked to complete an adaptive behavior scale on the child. Mothers, however, are usually the primary informants (Mash & Terdal, 1981).

Behavioral interviewing is a skill that must be developed and it includes listening, questioning to identify and delimit problem behaviors, knowledge of ethical issues, and the ultimate goal of obtaining functional analyses of treated behaviors (Morganstern & Tevlin, 1981). Regarding mentally retarded children, the interviewer should obtain information concerning relevant medical, historical, behavioral, and developmental factors. For example, the ages at which the child walked independently, became self-sufficient in dressing and toileting, and began to use language in a functional manner is information especially relevant in the assessment and treatment of mental retardation. In addition, it is important to determine naturally occurring antecedents and consequences in the home for performance or nonperformance of such skills. However, the interviewer must be advised that inaccuracies that cast parental practices in a more favorable light can occur (Matson & Beck, 1981).

Morganstern and Tevlin (1981) state that observation in natural settings may be a supplement to the interview. Behavioral observation involves measuring directly the occurrences of overt behaviors and is a multifaceted methodology (see Kazdin, 1980, 1981). With respect to the present discussion, parents can be trained to keep a record of behaviors that are important to the improved functioning of their mentally retarded child. For example, self-help skills often need to be more specifically trained in this population, and parents can help in their assessment by learning to record the number of times per day the child independently toilets, dresses, eats, etc. In addition, the involved professional can request permission to personally observe in the home, although the child and family may behave differently when an observer is present (see Haynes & Horn, 1982, for a review of reactive effects.) For example, positive reinforcement may be used with greater frequency in the presence of observers.

When a child is observed in the home, or in *any* setting, an analysis of the interaction between the child and the environment is essential if assessment is to approach exhaustiveness. Berkson (1978), for example, states that ecological methods of observation, which involve direct observation of environment-behavior interactions, should be applied to the study of mental retardation. From the clinician or researcher's point of view, then, it is important to delineate contingencies and behavioral expectations in the home and other environments, and the interactions that are likely to occur in these various environments.

In School

Because more people are identified as mentally retarded in later school years (Berkson, 1978), behavioral assessment in school is especially critical. For example, a child who demonstrated no significant problems as a toddler may later be diagnosed as mildly mentally retarded when faced with the increasing complexities of the elementary school environment. Learning to read, add and subtract, and interact with large numbers of peers on the playground may present challenges that cannot be met without special education. Thus, assessment in schools is closely related to the delivery of services. School assessment is complex and involves an array of persons, including parents and guardians, administrators, psychologists, special and regular education teachers, and social workers. According to PL 94–142 and Sec. 504, the evaluation team must include a teacher or other professional knowledgeable in the area of the suspected handicap (see Turnbull III & Turnbull, 1979, for regulations which cover testing, classification, and placement). The relevant point for this discussion is that specialists in the assessment and treatment of mental retardation are legal as well as educational necessities. The present chapter describes a number of assessment methods that the professional may wish to include in a comprehensive assessment approach to school skills. The end goal is appropriate and effective experiences for children.

Testing Considerations

Many published assessment tools of varying degrees of quality are available, and, thus, becoming a competent consumer of them is a task in and of itself. It is important to use a test for its stated purpose. Similarly, tests with inadequate reliability and validity data should be given less weight in the decision-making process. The Bayley Scales of Infant Development (Bayley, 1969), however, are an example of a norm-referenced comprehensive developmental scale with a highly respected technical adequacy (Bagnato & Neisworth, 1981). As developmental factors are paramount in mental retardation, the Bayley Scales are frequently used, especially with severe and profound levels of impairment. The three major subscales—the mental scale, the motor scale, and the infant behavior record—encompass over 244 tasks and characteristics. The 2 to 30-month age range for children of normal development is represented. However, development with mentally retarded persons is slower; thus, with the most seriously profoundly mentally retarded individuals, the Bayley may be the test of choice for adults as well.

With respect to testing mentally retarded children, an important consideration is the possible effects of reinforcement and testing conditions upon performance on standardized tests. Young, Bradley-Johnson, and Johnson (1982), for example, found that mentally retarded children performed differently on the WISC-R when provided with more systematic and immediate reinforcement for correct responding than is recommended by the testing manual. In this study, 30 white mildly mentally retarded students, who ranged in age from 7 to 12 years (x = 10.5) and included 19 boys and 11 girls, were randomly selected and then randomly assigned to three experimental groups—controls, delayed reinforcement, and immediate reinforcement. The reinforcement groups received tokens at different times for correct responses, in addition to the social reinforcement for effort as prescribed in the manual. The control group received the social reinforcement only. While all children were administered the WISC-R, the children in the control group were tested first to decrease the influence of knowledge about token conditions. Based on Slosson IQ scores, results showed no statistical differences between groups before the WISC-R testing under different reinforcement conditions; however, a significant difference between groups was found on the full scale IQ, WISC-R scores. Both token reinforcement groups scored higher than the control group, although no differences were found between the reinforcement groups. Given that IQ scores play a major role in diagnosis and placement, the possible effects of reinforcement in standardized testing with mentally retarded children are highly relevant. Interestingly, only one child in the control group scored above the mentally impaired level, while half of the children in the token groups scored above this level. Young, Bradley-Johnson, and Johnson (1982) reason that since PL 94–142 mandates least restrictive placements, then regular class placements with the use of tangible reinforcers may be preferable over special education classes that do not use these reinforcers for some mildly mentally retarded children.

In addition, the effects of incentives and feedback on social skills performance have been demonstrated. For example, Kazdin, Matson, and Esveldt-Dawson (1981) studied these effects with normal and psychiatric inpatient children and found that their social skills performance during testing was consistently enhanced by reinforcement. These results are relevent to mental retardation in some individuals (Matson & Barrett, 1982). Furthermore, there are strong programmatic implications; presumably, individuals who do not possess given skills should be taught differently than those who possess the skills but do not demonstrate them under certain conditions (Kazdin, et al., 1981). These individuals can only be separated from one another through attempts to elicit their best performance by systematically varying assessment conditions and then by comparing the data from these conditions.

Behavioral Observations.   Direct behavioral observations should be considered a primary method of evaluating particular critical responses in the mentally retarded child's repertoire. It is generally believed by behavior therapists that nothing substitutes for behavioral observations because they can be used to pinpoint target behaviors and to identify antecedent and consequent events that may influence the occurrence or nonoccurrence of specific responses (Matson & Beck, 1981). The major strength of behavioral observations is that they entail direct observation and recording of responses as they occur naturally in everyday settings. Moreover, direct observations are often continuous over a period of time and, thus, can provide a larger sample of behavior than assessments that occur during limited and perhaps contrived therapy sessions or environmental contexts. For example, if a child's interaction with peers on the playground is a problem area, then that child can be observed directly in that setting over several days. Responses that can be recorded include the duration of time the child can successfully interact with others, the number and characteristics of peers, teacher reactions to responses, the specific activities engaged in, and the frequency and intensity of undesired behaviors such as physical outbursts. Gottlieb (1978) stresses the interactive nature of behavior in the examination of the mentally retarded child's social adaptation to school; hence, the child's observable behavior is expressed within a context of peer and teacher characteristics and responses. An unanswered question is the degree to which the mentally retarded child's behavior is similar across settings and in the responses it elicits from other persons (Gottlieb, 1978).

Comprehensive behavioral observations in school include attention to academic responding. For example, the frequency, accuracy, and duration of oral and written responses in the various content areas can be measured in order to gain an understanding of the child's daily academic functioning. Knowledge of a child's actual performance in the curriculum used in his/her school is likely to be more revealing than a score on a standardized achievement test. For instance, an observational analysis of a child's math skills may show a greater proficiency in math facts when the response mode is oral than when it is written or when certain reinforcement contingencies are in effect. This type of information is especially helpful to the classroom teacher, as it carries programmatic implications. In the case of the math example, then, the child who has difficulty writing numbers can more efficiently memorize math facts through the use of flashcards. Instruction in writing skills can proceed in a way that does not confound with other skills.

Ratings. Rating scales, sociometric devices, and problem checklists are currently receiving significant empirical attention. These assessment methods include self-report inventories and ratings by significant others, such as teachers and students. Self-report measures allow assessment of responses that are not readily observable through other means (Kazdin, 1980). If the child is cognitively capable of participating in self-reports, then (s)he can offer information concerning behaviors and perceptions in a number of settings across time. Similarly, a parent or a teacher sees a great deal of the child's behavior and they may be able to provide a broad and rich amount of information that only comes from long and close examination.

Parent and teacher rating scales and behavioral checklists, which are proliferating and a number of relevant studies in this area, are described by Achenbach and Edelbrock (1978). In general, these devices involve having someone who is sufficiently familiar with the child rate his/her behaviors in terms of the degree to which behaviors, such as hyperactivity, compliance, and toileting skills, are problems. These assessments are obviously easier to obtain than are reliable and representative direct observations. However, checklists and rating scales rely on human judgments and are also susceptible to observer biases. Ary, Jacobs, and Razavich (1979) therefore suggest pooling or averaging several independent ratings of a person. In school, for example, the ratings of teachers, principals, social workers, school psychologists, and so forth could be used in concert to arrive at judgment. In addition, a compelling area of research is that of empirical comparisons between direct observations and rating scales (Cullinan, Epstein, & Dembinski, 1979).

Finally, checklists and rating scales do not provide fine-grained analyses of behavior. They can, however, be used to identify potential problem areas, and thus, delimiting the assessment field in an economical and efficient manner. Furthermore, it should be pointed out that most checklists to date, unlike direct behavioral observations, have been used almost exclusively with children of normal intelligence. Modification with mild and moderately mentally retarded persons may only have to be minor. However, with the extremely cognitively impaired children such as the profoundly mentally retarded, who may often have very little or no verbal skills and a very limited cognitive capacity, fewer scales are available. Also, in most instances and for obvious reasons self-report measures would be completely out of the question. Two scales that are used widely with the extremely cognitively impaired population are the American Association on Mental Deficiency Adaptive Behavior Scale for Children and Adults (Nihira, Foster, Shellhaas, & Leland, 1975) and the Vineland Social Maturity Scale, which was recently renormed. There is also a version of the AAMD Adaptive Behavior Scale for use in public schools (Nihira, et al., 1975). As Meyers, Nihira, and Zetlin (1979) point out, adaptive behavior instruments in general are being developed in increasing numbers. Briefly, the adaptive behavior construct at the minimum refers to a subject's competencies in adjustment to the culture as compared with normal age expectations, and it is typically considered to be a "loose construct" (p. 433). In general, adaptive behavior scales secure information by third-party informants on a variety of skills. For example, the AAMD Adaptive Behavior Scale (Nihira, et al., 1975) samples such domains as independent functioning, physical development, economic activity, language development, vocational activity, responsibility, stereotyped behavior, psychological disturbances, and antisocial behavior. Because the third-party informant method of assessment is indirect, the data collected should be verified by direct observation whenever possible. Furthermore, Meyers, et al., (1979) caution that (a) it is important to take individual differences in developmental rates of growth into consideration, especially with mentally retarded individuals; (b) different developmental trends can be recognized in different adaptive behavior components; and, (c) the data do not support a unitary trait description of adaptive behavior. With respect to this latter point, a subject should not be characterized by a single adaptive behavior score, but by data from many sources.

In Community

Professionals working with mentally retarded children are particularly challenged since, by definition, these children's potential for success in the community under normal conditions is very limited. It would seem to make sense, then, for key persons in the home, school, and community to share assessment data and to develop an ongoing interactive problem strategy. Furthermore, as noted earlier in this chapter, considerable emphasis on mainstreaming and integrating these children into the community seems to be a primary mandate. For instance, if a child is involved in a local park district program, it will be useful for the child's teacher to know what social skills the child needs to learn in order to have a successful community experience. Communication between a child's coach, for example, and the teachers and parents is desirable. Among other concerns, they could work toward consensus on how key behaviors should be consequated and on what skills should receive instructional priority. Mentally retarded children generally require more structure and consistency in learning and discipline than do normal children. Therefore, coordination between the home, school, and community is invaluable in terms of both assessment and treatment. Many of the assessment methods already discussed are applicable here; hence, interviews, certain adaptive behavior scales, and direct observations may prove amenable.

With respect to the community, vocational and leisure skills training among the mentally retarded are necessarily the focus of more professional concern and research. As Sitlington (1981) states, vocational programming in least restrictive environments is part of the federal special education mandate. Furthermore, mentally retarded students must be prepared for work experiences in the community in a more systematic manner, and educational goals in vocational skills must be developed just as they are for the basic academic skills. Stokes and Baer (1977) stress that generalization must be actively programmed; therefore, potential work environments must also be assessed in order to specifically prepare mentally retarded students to function productively and appropriately in them (Wehman & Pentecost, 1983). Adequate leisure skills are also essential to normalization, and Cheseldine and Jeffree (1981) recommend that leisure time activities receive the benefit of the same techniques used in work skills training. This approach is also called for in working with the mentally retarded. For example, according to a survey of 214 families conducted by these authors in England, the most often reported activities of mentally handicapped adolescents were solitary, passive, and/or oriented towards the family, and not outside friends. Social skills assessment and training is a related area, and leisure and social skills are currently the focus of considerable research with the mentally retarded (e.g., Adkins & Matson, 1980; Matson & Marchetti, 1980; Matson, et al., 1980). This area is especially pertinent to the community, as mentally retarded individuals must be able to relate to their co-workers (Wehman & Pentecost, 1983).

Summary

Several behavioral assessment procedures have been discussed in terms of their applicability to mentally retarded children in home, school, and community settings. The practical value and face validity of these procedures may be apparent, but more empirical research is needed before a sufficient range of empirically based instruments is available. This situation is the case throughout the various subpopulations of handicapped children, but it is no more striking than with mentally retarded children.

In addition to scale development, other factors are needed. For example, the interrelationships between assessment measures that evaluate both similar and different domains are not fully understood (Kazdin, 1981). Also, as we have alluded to, attention needs to be given specifically to the assessment of children, and strategies that are specific to defined subpopulations must be developed empirically (Mash & Terdal, 1981). In other words, comprehensive behavioral assessment packages that are tailored specifically to mentally retarded children and other subpopulations would be highly useful in a range of settings. The factors that delineate subpopulations should also be studied empirically. It is certainly the case, for example, that the variation in the behavioral repertoire of mildly to profoundly retarded persons is much greater than the variation of mildly mentally retarded children compared to nonhandicapped children. Thus, certain assessment batteries on social behavior, for example, might hypothetically incorporate mildly mentally retarded children, while moderately and severely mentally retarded children constitute another group, and profoundly mentally retarded children constitute yet another group. Until such developments are made, however, the assessor must draw from a variety of sources and seek for repeated and independent verifications of data.

DIFFERENTIAL DIAGNOSIS

The issue of diagnosis and classification of children is complex and often controversial, for different theoretical models lead to different methods and classification systems. Behaviorists typically have ignored traditional systems because of their poor reliability and validity and because of disagreements concerning interpretations of symptoms (Matson & Beck, 1981). In most cases, behaviorists have not been arguing against diagnosis per se, but the methods used to arrive at a diagnosis (Matson & Beck, 1981). There is a need for a classification system that professionals can use to further the diagnosis and treatment of children. According to Taylor (1983), the third edition of the *Diagnostic and Statistical Manual* (DSM-III) (American Psychiatric Association, 1980), its shortcomings notwithstanding, should be more acceptable to behavior therapists than DSM-II (American Psychiatric Association, 1968). Of course, mental retardation is included in DSM-III. Some of the shortcomings of DSM-III identified by Taylor include insufficient reporting of epidemiological data, operational criteria not previously used, and the pseudospecificity of many of the criteria. However, strengths such as the use of field trials are noteworthy, and Taylor (1983) suggests that behavioral assessors use DSM-III so behavioral assessment will fall within the overall context of research and clinical practice.

Differential diagnosis in the mentally retarded is currently receiving more empirical attention. Too often, if a person is diagnosed as mentally retarded, this event reduces the probability that other possible disorders will be identified and properly treated. For example, emotional problems and mental retardation may both be present in a single individual, yet the emotional problems may not be properly assessed once a diagnosis of mental retardation is made. Obviously, if they are not properly assessed, they are not likely to be specifically treated. One explanation for this phenomenon has been termed *diagnostic overshading* (Reiss, Levitan, & Szysko, 1982). Levitan and Reiss (1983) report data from an empirical study that suggest that diagnostic overshading is not specific to a particular professional but is characteristic of the wide range of mental health workers. Matson and Barrett (1982) have also been seeking to develop a theoretical and empirical base for understanding psychopathology in mentally retarded persons. They point out that different subgroups within mental retardation may benefit from entirely different treatment approaches. An obvious contrast is between the mildly mentally retarded and profoundly mentally retarded, nonambulatory child. Thus, differential diagnosis is intended to lead to differential treatments that are appropriate for the individual under assessment. Mental retardation encompasses, or may be associated with, a variety of cognitive and social characteristics.

TREATMENT

Range of Treatments

A range of empirically validated treatment procedures now exists to improve the cognitive and social functioning of mentally retarded children. However, based on empirical findings, there may be disparity among techniques concerning their effectiveness. The various approaches include positive and negative reinforcement, overcorrection, shaping, social learning methods such as modeling, time-out, physical punishment, and differential reinforcement of other behavior (DRO). Cognitively oriented treatments are increasing in prevalence. Self-help skills, academic functioning, language acquisition, social skills, stereotypic behaviors, and leisure skills are some of the responses commonly treated with the mentally retarded person. Increasingly, complex forms of behavior, such as social competence, are addressed in addition to molecular responses such as "in seat".

Treatment of mental retardation is a broad area that is increasing in its sophistication. There are a number of recommended sources that together can cover far more than what we are able to do in one chapter. Therefore, many sources should be consulted concurrently in working with mentally retarded children (e.g., Ellis, 1979; Forehand & Baumeister, 1976; Haywood, Meyers, & Switzky, 1982; Matson, in press; Sulzer-Azaroff & Mayer, 1977). In addition, several journals are helpful for their reporting of current research (e.g., see *Applied Research in Mental Retardation, American Journal of Mental Deficiency, Behavior Therapy, Behavior Modification, Behaviour Research and Therapy, Journal of Applied Behavior Analysis,* and the *Journal of Behavior Therapy and Experimental Psychiatry*). Some of the procedures to be described are generally considered positive and nonaversive, some aversive, and others relatively neutral. There are ethical and legal considerations involved in the selection and implementation of treatments, and these are reviewed more fully elsewhere (e.g., Martin, 1975). Researchers and practitioners are advised to be well aware of these considerations, especially in this current age of legislation and litigation. This trend is nowhere more evident than with mentally retarded children. Specific empirical demonstrations of major treatment procedures are

described shortly, following a discussion of nuances and practical considerations to keep in mind when choosing specific treatments.

Nuances and Implementation Issues

Although general principles of learning are reasonably well documented and aid
us in predicting what will work for whom and under what conditions, no one
approach can ever be considered optimal in every situation and/or can be
expected to work in all instances as initially planned. There are several reasons
for stating this qualification. First, newly trained personnel must be advised that
therapies do not proceed in textbook fashion in naturalistic settings. Fire drills,
staff shortages, unexpected family problems, a new child in class, illness, and
so forth can all act as confounding variables. Knowledge of this ahead of time
may possibly help ward off frustration and encourage professional patience.
Second, characteristics of children vary, and it is always an empirical question
which of these characteristics is interacting with a given treatment. Sex, age,
and IQ are often stressed, but other variables, such as a child's reinforcement
history, may also be very important. Third, instructional settings vary greatly;
thus, what is possible and desirable in one setting may not be workable in
another. Practical constraints challenge professionals to be creative and to make
the best of every setting for the sake of the child's progress. Fourth, some
procedures, such as overcorrection, are fairly complex and should be taught
specifically to therapists. In cases such as these, a person in the field can learn
of new techniques from professional reading in books and journals but is
advised to seek professional training and supervision before applying what is
read to a subject (see Matson & Ollendick, 1977). To do otherwise is to increase
the probability of mistakes. Fifth, some treatments may not work by themselves
and may need to be used in combination with other treatments. In fact, a great
deal of research is needed to understand how treatments may interact. Positive
reinforcement, for example, is commonly effective in conjunction with other
methods. Sixth, behaviorists are paying increasing attention to a fuller analysis
of the complexity of the environment. Rogers-Warren and Warren (1977), for
example, stress ecological perspectives in the analysis of behavior. A more
comprehensive environmental analysis is likely to produce more explanatory
data concerning both success and failures of treatments.

   Staff training is an area intimately and obviously related to treatment procedures. Gottlieb (1981), for instance, asks what type and amount of inservice
training is necessary in order to provide regular and special educators with the
requisite skills for instructing educable mentally retarded children in mainstream classes. Questions concerning how to best train staff are empirical, and
they are the focus of specific studies. Goncalves, Iwata, and Chiang (1983), for
example, conducted a study in the assessment and training of supervisors in an
educational facility for severely retarded students ages 5–25. They used a
multiple baseline design across two groups of supervisors who, according to

baseline data, did not provide adequate feedback to therapists and who often modeled incorrect usage of technical terms during brief weekly meetings with 18 therapists. The experimenter played a tape recording of supervisor-therapist interaction and commented on the positive and negative aspects of the supervisor's behavior. Treatment data reflected improvements in evaluative statements and technical terms for the group of supervisors overall; however, the data reflect mean performances, and thus, statements concerning individual supervisors cannot be made. Goncalves, et al., (1983) also hypothesize that reactivity and modeling may have contributed to the feedback and direct social reinforcement given to the supervisors by the experimenter. In addition, possible effects on the students themselves are in need of specific assessment.

Another example concerning staff behavior and mentally retarded children is provided by Ivancic, Reid, Iwata, Faw, and Page (1981). This supervision study involved the direct care, evening shift staff from a unit of a state retardation facility. The unit served multihandicapped and profoundly mentally retarded young children, and five of these children (three to seven years old) were involved in the study. A multiple baseline study across staff behaviors was used to increase their language training behaviors during bath routines at night. Specifically, in-service meetings and a series of prompting and feedback procedures were used to train staff. Explanations of language behavior, modeling, reminders, vocal and written feedback, and public posting were all incorporated into the procedure. A maintenance condition was also implemented. Results showed an increase in staff language training behavior that did not interfere with their task of bathing the children. However, Ivancic et al., (1981) caution that reactivity may have contributed to the results. In addition, conclusive statements concerning the children cannot be made; for, although one child's vocalizations increased over baseline, there were no consistent changes across children. Language training with severely impaired subjects, however, is complex (see Jones & Robson, 1979). Finally, the acquired staff skills generalized to dressing activities.

A related area to staff training is parent training. Parents may also be able to function as supportive therapists for their children, although parents may vary greatly in their abilities and desires to function in this capacity. Clark, Baker, and Heifetz (1982) conducted a follow-up study of 49 families who voluntarily participated in a training program for parents of mentally retarded children. The study occurred 14 months after the parents completed the program, and it involved mothers, who were the primary teachers in all instances. The authors attempted to develop prediction models for the results of parent training in behavior modification, and the outcome variables used were posttraining knowledge and follow-through programming. Contrary to typical expectations, child variables were not related to the outcome measures. Follow-though programming was related to performance during the program, but previous experience with behavior modification did not predict long-term results. A word of qualification is that the parents in the sample were volunteers; the assumption cannot be made that all parents of mentally retarded children are equally willing to learn behavioral principles. As Stewart (1978) stresses, learning to accept and cope with the diagnosis of a handicap can be difficult.

Comparative Analysis and Treatments of Choice

Several studies that illustrate these procedures with mentally retarded children are now described. As Sulzer-Azaroff and Mayer (1977) explain, the treatments of choice are those that are effective but also minimally intrusive. To the maximum extent possible, clients should have input and control over treatments they receive. Furthermore, reinforcement procedures should be preferred over punishment when both are likely to be effective. This approach is particularly important with children and certainly with those with mental retardation, since the latter group is rarely competent to give informed consent.

Reinforcement Procedures

Numerous studies support the validity of positive reinforcement and explore various schedules, or plans, for delivery of reinforcers. For example, Hopkins (1968) worked with a mentally retarded boy (Exp. II of the study), who exhibited an abnormally low rate of smiling. Continuous candy reinforcement was used to increase the rate of smiling to a normal range, and progressively lean reinforcement schedules were then used to fade out the candy without a resultant decrease in smiling. Social interactions successfully replaced the candy in this study—a desirable outcome as this is a move from primary to secondary reinforcers.

Currently, many positive reinforcement procedures with mentally retarded children are used in conjunction with other treatments. For instance, Matson, Esveldt-Dawson, and Kazdin (1982) treated spelling deficiencies in mildly and borderline mentally retarded children. Raising the academic levels of this subpopulation increases the likelihood of successful experiences in mainstreamed classes. The learning environment of mentally retarded children generally needs to be more specifically structured in order to progress toward this goal. In treating spelling deficits, then, Matson, et al. (1982) compared overcorrection (positive practice) with overcorrection plus reinforcement. The positive reinforcement involved stars or stickers and praise for correct spelling. Different single-case designs were used to examine treatment effectiveness with each of the subjects. For two of the subjects, performance in spelling was improved when reinforcement was added to the practice procedure. These results indicate the possibility of combining reinforcement procedures with other treatment approaches in order to maximize effectiveness in teaching.

Reinforcement procedures, such as differential reinforcement of other behavior (DRO) and of incompatible behavior (DRI), are used to reduce maladaptive responding in a nonaversive manner. Self-injurious behavior (SIB) is of serious concern in the severe and profound levels of mental retardation, as is stereotypic behavior. For example, Tarpley and Schroeder (1979) compared DRO with DRI on rate of suppression of self-injurious behavior. The subjects were three profoundly mentally retarded individuals, 24, 8, and 24-years old. A multiple schedule within-subjects design was used to compare the treatments, and baseline involved complete extinction with the exception of the first 10 seconds. For two of the subjects, SIB was reduced to near zero levels, and DRI was more effective than DRO. Tarpley and Schroeder (1979) state, however, that degree of response incompatibility may be a parameter that should be further investigated in the use of DRI procedures.

Developmental lags in language are common in mental retardation, and since language is a pivotal and complex skill that affects responses in both academic and social areas, it receives considerable emphasis. Jones and Robson (1979) review operant language training in the severely mentally handicapped, Welch (1981) reviews behavioral research in teaching generative grammar to mentally retarded children, and Kerr and Lambert (1982) review behavior modification of written language with children from various populations. Reinforcement is a vital component of structured language training with mentally retarded children (Jones & Robson, 1979). Clark, Boyd, and MaCrae (1975) trained written language in mentally retarded subjects with a procedure that incorporated tokens (see Kazdin, 1982b, for a discussion of the token economy). Training also included copying models and correction procedures. The subjects were four male and two female delinquent or mildly mentally retarded adolescents who were enrolled in a prevocational class. Training involved the completion of job application forms that required nine items of biographical information, and a multiple baseline design across the items was used to evaluate the program. In all cases, the adolescents achieved high correct usage on an item only after being trained on it.

Punishment

In a classic study on the effects and side effects of punishment, Risley (1968) treated the autistic behaviors of a six-year-old severely deviant, nonverbal girl who showed no imitative behaviors. The child exhibited persistent climbing behavior that was dangerous. Although time-out for climbing in the home, along with reinforcement for incompatible behavior, was initially tried, these procedures did not suppress the behavior. Punishment with shock and a verbal reprimand, No!, for climbing were used first in the laboratory and then in the home, and the shock procedure successfully eliminated climbing. Initially, the effects were limited to the stimulus conditions of the experimenter in the laboratory room. In order to approximate more normal child-rearing practices, shock was used to "back up" time-out in a chair contingent upon climbing. Autistic rocking was eliminated by the contingent and concurrent application of shouting and shaking the child, which was a punishing stimulus for rocking but apparently not for climbing. The most important side effect was the increase in eye contact produced by reinforcement when climbing was suppressed. Reinforcement, however, was ineffective as long as the child was climbing. Risley (1968) suggests that elimination of deviant behaviors may be an essential prerequisite to training new and desired behaviors; however, he does not advocate blanket use of punishment. In this study, shock was used only after other treatments to suppress climbing had failed.

Barrett, Matson, Shapiro, and Ollendick (1981) used an alternating treatments design with pictoral condition-specific discriminative stimuli to compare punishment and DRO procedures in reducing the stereotypic behaviors of two moderately mentally retarded and behaviorally disturbed children who were in a short-term residential program. Praise for good behavior, scoldings, spankings by parents, verbal redirection, systematic attention, and ignoring by staff had all proven ineffective in reducing the stereotypic behaviors of the children. The DRO procedure involved primary reinforcers, and the subjects were awarded them contingent on 10 consecutive seconds of absence of stereotypy. Punishment for one child, who engaged in finger sucking, involved visual screening that entirely shielded her vision until 10 consecutive seconds of nondisruptive and nonstereotypic behavior elapsed. For the other child, who engaged in tongue protrusion, punishment involved lightly placing a manufactured sterile wooden blade against the tongue until 10 consecutive seconds of tongue retraction occurred. In both cases, therapists nonverbally motioned to the children to resume designated activities following punishment. A no-treatment control condition was also used in the experimental design. Barrett et al., (1981) found that punishment was the most effective procedure for both children in reducing tongue protrusion and finger sucking. Six-month follow-up data were collected on both subjects, and the behaviors remained at near zero rates. The authors state that the results should not be taken to mean that DRO is an ineffective procedure but that very persistent stereotypic behaviors may be more successfully treated with aversive procedures.

Time-Out

Time-out from positive reinforcement, which is another procedure used to decrease maladaptive responding, may take different forms, such as totally removing the child from the environment or restricting the child from participation in activities. Johnson and Baumeister (1981) point out that the effects of time-out must be related to the richness of the "time-in environment" and that behaviors, such as self-injurious responding, are inappropriate for treatment with time-out. A common use of time-out is for disruptive behavior at school. Foxx and Shapiro (1978) used a nonexclusionary procedure that does not entail the removal of children from the classroom; therefore, it is a procedure likely to receive greater social acceptance than exclusionary time-out. Five boys who were severely, profoundly, or moderately to severely mentally retarded served as subjects. The setting was a special education class in a state institution. The frequency and type of misbehavior was high, including running in the room, yelling, banging and throwing objects, and out-of-seat behavior. The experimental design (ABCBC) involved the sequence of baseline, reinforcement, time-out plus reinforcement, reinforcement, and time-out plus reinforcement. In order to achieve a rich "time-in" environment, positive reinforcement was used alone first. The children wore ribbons during reinforcement, and the nonexclusionary time-out procedure involved removal of the ribbon and a subsequent three-minute deprivation from positive reinforcement. The ribbon was then returned to the child to signal that time-in had resumed. The teacher was trained by one of the experimenters. The results showed that the nonexclusionary time-out procedure was effective in the reduction of disruptive behavior in these students. A one-day probe the following school year showed that the teacher had learned to manage the procedure independently and that disruptive behaviors remained at low levels with the use of the ribbon program. However, Foxx and Shapiro (1978) recommend that an exclusionary time-out room be available as a backup in case the ribbon procedure is not effective.

Overcorrection

Overcorrection has become an ambiguous and muddled area due to problems of definition and misconception (Foxx & Bechtel, 1982). According to Foxx and Bechtel (1982), it represents a strategy that unifies behavioral principles, such as punishment, extinction, and negative reinforcement. The major components of overcorrection—restitution and positive practice—were used in a complex toileting program with mentally retarded adults (Azrin & Foxx, 1971). Research in this area has since proliferated, and an extensive review is provided by Foxx and Bechtel (1982). One study by Matson, Horne, Ollendick, and Ollendick (1979) compared the two distinct components of overcorrection. Twenty young children were referred by their teachers for disruptive behavior. Although these children were not specifically diagnosed as mentally retarded, the disruptive behavior they displayed is common in various populations of mentally retarded persons in various settings. In this study, children were treated on an individual basis within one of three experimental groups. A no-treatment control group, a restitution-only group, and a positive-practice-only group were used. Both active treatment components were equally effective in the treatment of disruptive behavior, and the study shows that the components can be effective separately. Interestingly, in a follow-up questionnaire, 19 of the 20 children reported that overcorrection was preferable to removal from class, yelling, and spanking.

Durability of treatment effects is an important concern in behavior therapy, and this is as true of overcorrection as of any other technique. Matson, Ollendick, and Martin (1979) provide one-year follow-up data on eight profoundly mentally retarded adults who had been treated with overcorrection in order to reduce self-stimulatory behavior. Results were inconsistent, as suppression of the target behavior was maintained at a near zero level for two subjects but approached pretreatment levels for the other six subjects. The authors suggest that maintenance be enhanced by the use of procedures, such as reinforcement of alternate or incompatible behaviors.

Social Learning

There is an increasing emphasis on the role of cognition in treatment. Social-learning theory places more emphasis on covert events, which are directly observable by the subject (Nelson, 1977). According to Cautela (1970) and Homme (1965), similar mechanisms most likely control both overt and covert processes. Thus, covert processes may also be subjected to experimental analysis and manipulation. External stimuli have an effect upon covert processes. Bandura (1971), for example, states that in social-learning theory behavior is regulated both by external consequences directly experienced and by vicarious reinforcement and self-reinforcement. Because of the emphasis on both covert and overt events, a diversity of methods such as modeling, observational learning, self-evaluation, self-reinforcement, and role playing are utilized to enhance social skills, cognitive learning, and so forth.

Self-regulation is an area that is receiving more consideration in the treatment of mental retardation, as self-regulation procedures may be used to promote independent functioning and a higher overall rate of adaptive behavior. Shapiro (1981) reviews self-control procedures with the mentally retarded and states that the procedures should be used routinely to reduce the dependency often observed in mentally retarded individuals. An example of a study in this area is provided by Shapiro and Klein (1980). Four mentally retarded and emotionally disturbed children (mean IQ = 54) in a psychiatric hospital school program were the subjects, and fading procedures were used to teach self-management. The dependent variables were on-task behavior, disruptive behavior, and task performance and accuracy. A token program was initially used to increase on-task behavior, and self-management was then gradually taught to the children, as the verbal and physical prompts involved in self-assessment were systematically faded. The children were ultimately taught to manage themselves using the token program, and classroom behavior improved for most subjects.

Litrownik, Freitas, and Franzini (1978) also substantiate the application of self-management techniques to mentally retarded persons. They taught these skills to 30 moderately mentally retarded children in a laboratory setting using a demonstration training program. The children were divided into three groups and were matched on sex, IQ, chronological age, and mental age. The groups were then randomly assigned to experimental conditions that were labeled training, attention control, and no-contact control. Bowling, seatwork, and self-monitoring responses were the dependent variables. The training condition involved live demonstrations, a training tape, and training in self-monitoring. The subjects in the attention-control group were yoked to the subjects in the training group and also had the opportunity to perform the various responses and to view models. However, no training in self-monitoring was provided to the attention-control group. The group taught to self-monitor performed better on all tasks.

Summary

A brief review of the few comparative studies made with mentally retarded children has been provided. As can be readily seen, there are very few studies of this type, and the data are far from complete. However, the lack of comparative studies between treatments is far from specific to mentally retarded children. This is the case because of the expense and difficulty in conducting group studies large enough to incorporate at least two major treatment modalities. Similarly, the single-case strategies, such as the multielement design, may not prove very useful with mentally retarded children, since they are unlikely to be able to discriminate between two separate treatment regimes used with them for the same problem.

With these problems and limitations aside, a few broad generalizations are possible, taking into account the few sample studies mentioned here as well as the additional available research. Punishment procedures are generally more effective than reinforcement procedures for highly recalcitrant, socially undesirable behaviors, such as self-injurious and aggressive behaviors. Group studies are at a minimum, but there are numerous single-case studies in which reinforcement was tried and proved ineffective, and then one of a number of punishment procedures did prove effective. (See Matson & DiLorenzo, 1983, for an extensive review of this topic.) As noted previously, we recommend the use of reinforcement whenever punishment is employed. Such an approach would seem to be particularly important with mentally retarded children, since they are less likely to have established various types of appropriate responding. Thus, when inappropriate behaviors are suppressed, the new behaviors displayed are also likely to be highly inappropriate.

Some single-case comparative studies analogous to those described above for punishment compared to reinforcement have also been made. However, the results of these studies are much more unclear. All of these data should, however, be interpreted very tentatively. As noted, many more comparative treatment studies are needed.

Clinical Considerations

There are several generally agreed upon characteristics of the therapeutic procedure that apply to the mentally retarded as well as to all persons, and the reader is referred to Martin (1975) for an explanation of the legal issues and requirements in behavior modification usage. First, there are legal mandates, such as equal educational opportunities, informed consent, and an emphasis on specific goal setting and documented individualization (i.e., the IEP) in treatment programs. Mentally retarded persons are not to be considered (wrongly) as a homogeneous group, but as the individuals they are. Each mentally retarded child brings unique characteristics, such as reinforcer preferences and past learning histories to the treatment process. While research enables us to identify procedures likely to work, individual characteristics always add variables to the implementation process. Therefore, while general principles of learning and treatment apply, individualization is a legal and clinical necessity. This does not mean, however, that children are never to be taught in groups; for it is possible and desirable to work in group settings with several children who have the same programming needs.

Second, behavioral assessments must be conducted on an ongoing individual basis in goal setting and must identify socially meaningful target behaviors for treatment and the antecedents and consequences that control them. Direct observation and measurement are desirable methodologies, as are other methods reviewed earlier. Several techniques should be used in concert to explore different facets of problems and to reduce bias and error. Data collection and treatments should occur in the subject's daily settings as much as possible. In addition, assessment should be continued throughout treatment to carefully monitor programs. The emphasis is on clinical objectivity in treatment; thus, the use of numerical data and clinical judgment is intended to increase the probability that decisions concerning interventions are more scientific than subjective, and more systematic than arbitrary.

Third, treatments should be introduced in a planned, highly organized manner. The practitioner is advised to become familiar with basic designs for group research (Kazdin, 1980) and for single-subject research (Hersen & Barlow, 1976; Kazdin, 1982a) in clinical psychology, educational psychology, psychiatry, and special education. These designs explain how a research component can be added to a treatment plan to examine carefully the effects of treatment. Again, the goal for our decisions concerning children is to be objective and data based.

Fourth, the issue of generalization and maintenance of treatment effects remains in need of much empirical attention. For example, if a child learns better social skills in school, will (s)he also exhibit them at home? In general, transfer of gains to new settings must be specifically programmed. In addition, will gains in social skills achieved be maintained over time? The latter question can only be answered through follow-up assessments, but such data are seldom collected. Matson and Breuning (1982), for example, surveyed a large sample of applied research in mental retardation published from 1975–1980 and reported that, among 171 treatment studies reviewed, only six studies had six months of follow-up or more.

Fifth, the therapeutic procedure should entail measurement of multiple behaviors since the treatment(s) used may have multiple, and perhaps unanticipated, effects. There is a need to explore the area of response interrelationships; hence, a systematic effort to assess multiple effects of interventions directed toward single target behaviors is absent.

Sixth, social validation methodology should be used to identify relevant target behaviors and to identify levels of treatment gains that are practically and socially meaningful (Kazdin & Matson, 1981). Social validation information in the form of norm peer comparison is especially helpful in determining when mentally retarded children can successfully function in less restrictive settings (Barton, Brulle, & Repp, 1982).

Case Example

There are such a large number of conditions that constitute mental retardation in children and such a wide range of cognitive levels and behavioral repertoires that a description of one case would hardly be representative of the field. However, as a means of providing a more broadly applicable example, a study by Matson (1981) of a moderately retarded girl (estimates are that 90–96 percent of mentally retarded persons are in the mild to moderate range) will be provided.

The girl, 10-years-old was evaluated on intellectual ability using a standardized intelligence test and test of adaptive behavior. Informed consent was obtained, and the treatment data was to be used later for her IEP (see point one above). She had been referred because of excessive fear of strangers. She was evaluated on how closely she would approach a strange adult speaking to strangers and on self-report of fear. Additionally, the girl was evaluated on pervasiveness of fear using the Louisville Fear Survey Schedule. The fear behavior of this child had important practical ramifications because it markedly inhibited the child's socialization and the parent's social lives (see point two above). The child refused to stay with a babysitter or to engage in social outings her parents undertook with friends. To establish a criterion for success, the teacher and teacher's aides were asked to rank in order the same sex peers as the girl receiving treatment on fear of strangers; ranking of the children further showed that the child selected for treatment was exhibiting behaviors in need of remediation (see point six above).

Treatment was provided using participant modeling—a method that, based on the limited experimental data available, is the most effective procedure for eliminating fears of children. During the training sessions, the mother would explain that a strange adult was going to come into the room where they currently stood but that she (the mother) would be with her daughter at all times. Next, the mother talked about what her daughter could say to the adult, and then they would practice their verbal responses. Next, the mother and daughter would approach this strange adult. If necessary, the mother provided a prompt to the child as to what she should say and had her repeat it. The mother would repeat the procedure with the child as necessary (see point three and four above). A number of verbal and nonverbal behaviors were measured (see point five above). Treatment proved effective, demonstrating the potential utility of modeling, instructions, and related procedures for enhancing appropriate behavior and skill of mentally retarded children.

Summary

In conclusion, the behavior therapy procedure employed should involve: (*a*) the collection of behavioral assessment data; (*b*) the matching of treatment to child behavior on a documented individualized basis; (*c*) systematic introduction of interventions; (*d*) continuous and follow-up data collection to monitor the degree of program success; (*e*) evaluation of effectiveness using principles of research; (*f*) a plan to monitor other behaviors for unanticipated effects; and, (*g*) social validation. Approaches such as this should markedly enhance an already substantial and encouraging behavioral technology to date in the treatment of mentally retarded children.

REFERENCES

Achenbach, T. M. & Edelbrock, C. S. The classification of child psychopathology: A review and analysis of empirical efforts. *Psychological Bulletin*, 1978, *85*, 1275–1301.

Adkins, J., & Matson, J. L. Teaching institutionalized mentally retarded adults socially appropriate leisure skills. *Mental Retardation*, 1980, *18*, 249–252.

American Psychiatric Association. *Diagnostic and statistical manual of mental disorders (2nd ed.)*. Washington, D.C.: Author, 1968.

American Psychiatric Association. *Diagnostic and statistical manual of mental disorders (3rd ed.)*. Washington, D.C.: Author, 1980.

Ary, D., Jacobs, L. C., & Razavich, A. *Introduction to research in education*. New York: Holt, Rinehart & Winston, 1979.

Ayllon, T. & Azrin, N. H. *The token economy*. New York: Appleton-Century-Crofts, 1968.

Azrin, N. H. & Foxx, R. M. A rapid method of toilet training the institutionalized retarded. *Journal of Applied Behavior Analysis*, 1971, *4*, 89–99.

Azrin, N. H. & Wesolowski, M. D. Eliminating habitual vomiting in a retarded adult by positive practice and self-correction. *Journal of Behavior Therapy and Experimental Psychiatry*, 1975, *6*, 145–148.

Bagnato, S. J., & Neisworth, J. T. *Linking developmental assessment and curricula, prescriptions for early intervention*. Rockville, Mary.: Aspen Systems Corporation, 1981.

Bandura, A. *Social learning theory*. Morristown, N.J.: General Learning Press, 1971.

Barrett, R. P., Matson, J. L., Shapiro, E. S., & Ollendick, T. H. A comparison of punishment and DRO procedures for treating stereotypic behavior of mentally retarded children. *Applied Research in Mental Retardation*, 1981, *2*, 247–256.

Barton, L. E., Brulle, A. R. & Repp, A. C. The social validation of programs for mentally retarded children. *Mental Retardation*, 1982, *20*, 260–265.

Bateman, B. D. & Herr, C. M. Law and special education. In J. M. Kauffman & D. P. Hallahan (Eds.), *Handbook of special education*. Englewood Cliffs, N.J.: Prentice-Hall, 1981.

Baumeister, A. A. & Forehand, R. Deceleration of aberrant behavior among retarded individuals. In M. Hersen, R. M. Eisler & R. P. Miller (Eds.), *Progress in behavior modification*. New York: Academic Press, 1976.

Bayley, N. *Manual for the Bayley Scales of Infant Development*. New York: Psychological Corporation, 1969.

Becker, J. V., Turner, S. M. & Sajwaj, T. E. Multiple behavioral effects of the use of lemon juice with a ruminating toddler-age child. *Behavior Modification*, 1978, *2*, 267–278.

Berkson, G. Social ecology and ethology of mental retardation. In G. P. Sackett (Ed.), *Observing behavior, Vol. 1, Theory and applications in mental retardation*. Baltimore: University Park Press, 1978.

Bostow, D. E. & Bailey, J. S. Modification of severe disruptive and aggressive behavior using brief timeout and reinforcement procedures. *Journal of Applied Behavior Analysis*, 1969, *2*, 31–37.

Breuning, S. E. & Barrett, R. P. Intelligence. In J. L. Matson & S. E. Breuning (Eds.), *Assessing the mentally retarded*. New York: Grune and Stratton, 1983.

Burchard, J. R. & Barrera, F. An analysis of time-out and response cost in a programmed environment. *Journal of Applied Behavior Analysis*, 1972, *5*, 271–282.

Cautela, J. R. Covert reinforcement. *Behavior Therapy*, 1970, *1*, 33–50.

Cheseldine, S. E., & Jeffree, D. M. Mentally handicapped adolescents: Their use of leisure. *Journal of Mental Deficiency Research*, 1981, *25*, 49–59.

Clark, D. B., Baker, B. L. & Heifetz, L. J. Behavioral training for parents of mentally retarded children: Prediction of outcome. *American Journal of Mental Deficiency*, 1982, *87*, 14–19.

Clark, H. B., Boyd, S. B., & MaCrae, J. W. A classroom program teaching disadvantaged youth to write biographic information. *Journal of Applied Behavior Analysis*, 1975, *8*, 67–75.

Cullinan, D., Epstein, M. H., & Dembinski, R. J. Behavior problems of educationally handicapped and normal pupils. *Journal of Abnormal Child Psychology*, 1979, *1*, 495–502.

Davis, W. B., Wieseler, N. A. & Hinzel, T. E. Contingent music in management of rumination and out-of-seat behavior in a profoundly mentally retarded institutionalized male. *Mental Retardation,* 1980, *18,* 43–47.

Dorsey, M. F., Iwata, B. A., Ong, P. & McSween, T. E. Treatment of self-injurious behavior using a water mist: Initial response suppression and generalization. *Journal of Applied Behavior Analysis,* 1980, *13,* 343–354.

Doubros, S. G. Behavior therapy with high level, institutionalized, retarded adolescents. *Exceptional Children,* 1966, *32,* 229–233.

Ellis, N. The Partlow case: A reply to Dr. Ross. *Law and Psychology Review,* 1981, *5,* 15–49.

Ellis, N. R. Amount of reward and operant behavior in mental defectives. *Journal of Comparative and Physiological Psychology,* 1962, *6,* 595–599.

Ellis, N. R. Toilet training the severely defective patient: An S-R reinforcement analysis. *American Journal of Mental Deficiency,* 1963, *68,* 99–103.

Ellis, N. R. (Ed.). *Handbook of mental deficiency, psychological theory and research,* (2nd ed.). Hillsdale, N.J.: Lawrence Erlbaum Associates, Inc., 1979.

Ellis, N. R. & Pryer, M. Primary versus secondary reinforcement in simple discrimination learning of mental defectives. *Psychological Reports,* 1958, *4,* 67–70.

Favell, J. E., McGimsey, J. F. & Jones, M. L. Rapid eating in the retarded: Reduction by non-aversive procedures. *Behavior Modification,* 1980, *4,* 481–492.

Forehand, R., & Baumeister, A. A. Deceleration of aberrant behavior among retarded individuals. In M. Hersen, R. M. Eisler, & P. M. Miller (Eds.), *Progress in behavior modification.* New York: Academic Press, 1976.

Foxx, R. M. The use of overcorrection to eliminate the public disrobing (stripping) of retarded women. *Behaviour Research and Therapy,* 1976, *14,* 53–61.

Foxx, R. M. & Azrin, N. H. The elimination of autistic self-stimulatory behavior by overcorrection. *Journal of Applied Behavior Analysis,* 1973, *6,* 1–14.

Foxx, R. M., & Bechtel, D. R. Overcorrection. In M. Hersen, R. M. Eisler, & P. M. Miller (Eds.), *Progress in behavior modification,* (Vol. 13). New York: Academic Press, 1982.

Foxx, R. M., & Shapiro, S. T. The timeout ribbon: A nonexclusionary timeout procedure. *Journal of Applied Behavior Analysis,* 1978, *11,* 125–136.

Girardeau, F. L. The effects of secondary reinforcement on the operant behavior of mental defectives. *American Journal of Mental Deficiency,* 1962, *67,* 441–449.

Goncalves, S. J., Iwata, B. A., & Chiang, S. J. Assessment and training of supervisors' evaluative feedback to their staff in an operant learning program for handicapped children. *Education and Treatment of Children,* 1983, *6,* 11–20.

Gottlieb, J. Observing social adaptation in schools. In G. P. Sackett (Ed.), *Observing behavior, Vol. I, Theory and applications in mental retardation.* Baltimore: University Park Press, 1978.

Gottlieb, J. Mainstreaming: Fulfilling the promise? *American Journal of Mental Deficiency,* 1981, *86,* 115–126.

Grossman, H. *Manual and terminology and classification in mental retardation.* Washington, D.C.: American Association on Mental Deficiency, 1983.

Haynes, S. N. & Horn, W. F. Reactivity in behavioral observation: A review. *Behavioral Assessment,* 1982, *4,* 369–385.

Haynes, S. N. & Jensen, B. J. The interview as a behavioral assessment instrument. *Behavioral Assessment,* 1979, *1,* 97–106.

Haywood, H. C., Meyers, C. E., & Switzky, H. N. Mental retardation. In M. R. Rozenzweig (Ed.), *Annual review of psychology* (Vol. 33). Palo Alto, Calif. Annual Reviews Inc., 1982.

Hersen, M., & Barlow, D. H. *Single Case experimental designs: Strategies for studying behavior change.* New York: Pergamon Press, 1976.

Homme, L. E. Perspectives in psychology: XXIV control of coverants, the operants of the mind. *The Psychological Record,* 1965, *15,* 501–511.

Hopkins, B. L. Effects of candy and social reinforcement, instructions, and reinforcement schedule learning on the modification and maintenance of smiling. *Journal of Applied Behavior Analysis,* 1968, *1,* 121–129.

Ivancic, M. T., Reid, D. H., Iwata, B. A., Faw, G. D., & Page, T. J. Evaluating a supervision program for developing and maintaining therapeutic staff-resident interactions during institutional care routines. *Journal of Applied Behavior Analysis,* 1981, *14,* 95–107.

Johnson, W. L., & Baumeister, A. A. Behavioral Techniques for decreasing aberrant behaviors of retarded and autistic persons. In M. Hersen, R. M. Eisler, & P. M. Miller (Eds.), *Progress in behavior modification* (Vol. 13). New York: Academic Press, 1981.

Jones, A., & Robson, C. Language training the severely mentally handicapped. In N. R. Ellis, (Ed.), *Handbook of mental deficiency, psychological theory and research* (2nd ed.). Hillsdale, N.J.: Lawrence Erlbaum Associates, Inc., 1979.

Kazdin, A. E. Behavioral observation. In M. Hersen & A. S. Bellack (Eds.), *Behavioral Assessment.* New York: Pergamon Press, 1981.

Kazdin, A. E. *Single-case research designs, methods for clinical and applied settings.* New York: Oxford University Press, Inc., 1982(a).

Kazdin, A. E. Situational specificity: The two-edged sword of behavioral assessment. *Behavioral Assessment,* 1979, *1,* 57–75.

Kazdin, A. E. *Research design in clinical psychology,* New York: Harper & Row, 1980. Copyright by A. E. Kazdin.

Kazdin, A. E. The token economy: A decade later. *Journal of Applied Behavior Analysis,* 1982, *15,* 431–445(b).

Kazdin, A. E. & Matson, J. L. Social validation in mental retardation. *Applied Research in Mental Retardation,* 1981, *2,* 39–53.

Kazdin, A. E., Matson, J. L., & Esveldt-Dawson, K. Social skill performance among normal and psychiatric inpatient children as a function of assessment conditions. *Behaviour Research and Therapy,* 1981, *19,* 145–152.

154 CHAPTER 4

Kerr, M. M., & Lambert, D. L. Behavior modification of children's written language. In M. Hersen, R. M. Eisler, P. M. Miller (Eds.), *Progress in behavior modification* (Vol. 13). New York: Academic Press, 1982.

Lerner, J., Mardell-Czudnowski, C., & Goldenberg, D. *Special education for the early childhood years.* Englewood Cliffs, N.J.: Prentice-Hall, 1981.

Levitan, G. W. & Reiss, S. Generality of diagnostic overshadowing across disciplines. *Applied Research in Mental Retardation,* 1983, *4,* 59–64.

Litrownik, A. J., Freitas, J. L., & Franzini, L. R. Self-regulation in mentally retarded children: Assessment and training of self-monitoring skills. *American Journal of Mental Deficiency,* 1978, *82,* 499–506.

Lovaas, O. I. & Simmons, J. Q. Manipulation of self-destruction in three retarded children. *Journal of Applied Behavior Analysis,* 1969, *2,* 143–157.

Luce, S. C., Delguardi, J. & Hall, R. V. Contingent exercise: A mild but powerful procedure for suppressing inappropriate verbal and aggressive behavior. *Journal of Applied Behavior Analysis,* 1980, *13,* 583–594.

Luckey, R. E. Wilson, C. M. & Musick, J. K. Aversive conditioning as a means of inhibiting vomiting and rumination. *American Journal of Mental Deficiency,* 1968, *73,* 139–142.

Luiselli, J. K. Helfen, C. S., Pemberton, B. W. & Reisman, J. The elimination of a child's in-class masturbation by overcorrection and reinforcement. *Journal of Behavior Therapy and Experimental Psychiatry,* 1977, *8,* 201–204.

MacMillan, D. L. *Mental retardation in school and society* (2nd ed.). Boston: Little, Brown, 1982.

Marchetti, A. G. Wyatt v. Stickney: A historical perspective. *Applied Research in Mental Retardation,* 1983, *4,* 189–206.

Martin, R. *Educating handicapped children: The legal mandate.* Champaign, Ill. Research Press, 1979. Copyright by Reed Martin.

Martin, R. *Legal challenges to behavior modification, trends in schools, corrections, and mental health.* Champaign, Ill.: Research Press, 1975.

Mash, E. J. & Terdal, L. G. Behavioral assessment of childhood disturbance. In E. J. Mash & L. G. Terdal (Eds.), *Behavioral assessment of childhood disorders.* New York: Guilford Press, 1981.

Matson, J. L. Assessment and treatment of clinical fears in mentally retarded children. *Journal of Applied Behavior Analysis,* 1981, *14,* 287–294.

Matson, J. L. Treating the problems of mentally retarded children. In R. G. Morris & T. R. Kratochwill (Eds.), *Practice of therapy with children: A textbook of methods.* New York: Pergamon Press, in press.

Matson, J. L. & Barrett, R. P. *Psychopathology in the mentally retarded,* New York: Grune and Stratton, 1982.

Matson, J. L. & Beck, S. Assessment of children in inpatient settings. In M. Hersen & A. S. Bellack (Eds.), *Behavioral assessment.* New York: Pergamon Press, 1981.

Matson, J. L., & Bruening, S. E. A review and analysis of applied research in mental retardation: 1975–1980. *Applied Research in Mental Retardation*, 1982, *3*, 185–189.

Matson, J. L., & DiLorenzo, T. *Punishment and behavior modification. New Perspectives and alternatives.* New York: Springer, 1983.

Matson, J. L., Esveldt-Dawson, K., & Kazdin, A. E. Treatment of spelling deficits in mentally retarded children. *Mental Retardation*, 1982, *20*, 76–81.

Matson, J. L., Horne, A. M., Ollendick, D. G., & Ollendick, T. H. Overcorrection: A further evaluation of restitution and positive practice. *Journal of Behavior Therapy and Experimental Psychiatry.* 1979, *10*, 295–298.

Matson, J. L., Kazdin, A. E., & Esveldt-Dawson, K. Training interpersonal skills among mentally retarded and socially dysfunctional children. *Behaviour Research and Therapy*, 1980, *18*, 419–427.

Matson, J. L. & Marchetti, A. A comparison of leisure skills training procedures for the mentally retarded. *Applied Research in Mental Retardation*, 1980, *1*, 113–122.

Matson, J. L. & Mulick, J. A. *Handbook of mental retardation.* New York: Pergamon Press, 1983.

Matson, J. L. & Ollendick, T. H. Issues in toilet training. *Behavior Therapy,* 1977, *8*, 549–553.

Matson, J. L., Ollendick, T. H., & Adkins, J. A comprehensive dining program for mentally retarded adults. *Behaviour Research and Therapy*, 1980, *18*, 107–112.

Matson, J. L., Ollendick, T. H. & Martin, J. E. Overcorrection revisited: A long-term follow-up. *Journal of Behavior Therapy and Experimental Psychiatry,* 1979, *10*, 11–13.

Matson, J. L. & Stephens, R. M. Increasing appropriate behavior of explosive chronic psychiatric patients with a social-skills training package. *Behavior Modification*, 1978, *2*, 61–76.

Meyers, C. E., Nihira, K., & Zetlin, A. The measurement of adaptive behavior. In N. R. Ellis (Ed.), *Handbook of mental deficiency, psychological theory and research* (2nd ed.). Hillsdale, N.J.: Lawrence Erlbaum Associates, Inc., 1979.

Morganstern, K. P. & Tevlin, H. E. Behavioral interviewing. In M. Hersen & A. S. Bellack (Eds.), *Behavioral assessment.* New York: Pergamon Press, 1981.

Nelson, R. O. Assessment and therapeutic functions of self-monitoring. In M. Hersen, R. M. Eisler, & P. M. Miller (Eds.), *Progress in behavior modification* (Vol. 5). New York: Academic Press, 1977.

Nelson, R. O. & Hayes, S. C. Nature of behavioral assessment. In M. Hersen & A. S. Bellack (Eds.), *Behavioral assessment.* New York: Pergamon Press, 1981.

Nihira, K., Foster, R., Shellhaas M., & Leland, H. *AAMD adaptive behavior scale.* Washington, D.C.: American Association on Mental Deficiency, 1975.

Ollendick, T. H. & Matson, J. L. Overcorrection: An overview. *Behavior Therapy,* 1976, 410–412.

Parke, R. D. Parent-infant interaction: Progress, paradigms, and problems. In G. P. Sackett (Ed.), *Observing behavior, Vol. 1, Theory and applications in mental retardation*. Baltimore: University Park Press, 1978.

Reiss, S., Levitan, G. W. & Szysko, J. Emotional disturbance and mental retardation: Diagnostic overshadowing. *American Journal of Mental Deficiency*, 1982, *86*, 567–574.

Risley, T. R. The effects and side effects of punishing the autistic behaviors of a deviant child. *Journal of Applied Behavior Analysis*, 1968, *1*, 21–34.

Rogers-Warren, A., & Warren, S. F. *Ecological perspectives in behavior analysis*. Baltimore: University Park Press, 1977.

Rosen, M., Clark, G. R. & Kivitz, M. S. (Eds.). *The history of mental retardation: Collected papers* (Vol. 1). Baltimore: University Park Press, 1976.

Shapiro, E. S. Self-control procedures with the mentally retarded. In M. Hersen, R. M. Eisler, & P. M. Miller (Eds.), *Progress in behavior modification*, (Vol. 12). New York: Academic Press, 1981.

Shapiro, E. S., & Klein, R. D. Self-management of classroom behavior with retarded/disturbed children. *Behavior Modification*, 1980, *4*, 83–97.

Sitlington, P. L. Vocational and special education in career programming for the mildly handicapped adolescent. *Exceptional Children*, 1981, *47*, 592–598.

Skeels, H. M. & Dye, H. B. A study of the effects of differential stimulation on mentally retarded children. *Proceedings of the American Association on Mental Deficiency*, 1939, *44*, 114–136.

Skodak, M. Adult status of individuals who experience early intervention. In B. W. Richards (Eds.), *Proceedings of the 1st congress of the association for the scientific study of mental deficiency*. Reigate, England: Michael Jackson, 1965.

Stewart, J. C. *Counseling parents of exceptional children*. Columbus, Ohio: Bell & Howell Co., 1978.

Stokes, T. F., & Baer, D. M. An implicit technology of generalization. *Journal of Applied Behavior Analysis*, 1977, *10*, 349–367.

Sulzer-Azaroff, B., & Mayer, G. K. *Applying behavior-analysis procedures with children and youth*. New York: Holt, Rinehart & Winston, 1977.

Tarpley, H. D., & Schroeder, S. R. Comparison of DRO and DRI on rate of suppression of self-injurious behavior. *American Journal of Mental Deficiency*, 1979, *84*, 188–194.

Taylor, C. B. DSM-III and behavioral assessment. *Behavioral Assessment*, 1983, *5*, 5–14

Turnbull III, H. R. & Turnbull, A. P. *Free appropriate public education Law and implementation*. Denver: Love Publishing Co., 1978.

Vandenberg, S. G. The nature and nurture of intelligence. In D. D. Glass (Ed.), *Genetics*. New York: Rockefeller University Press, 1968.

Wehman, P., & Pentecost, J. H. Facilitating employment for moderately and severely handicapped youth. *Education and Treatment of Children*, 1983, *6*, 69–80.

Welch, S. J. Teaching generative grammar to mentally retarded children: A review and analysis of a decade of behavioral research. *Mental Retardation*, 1981, *19*, 277–284.

Wells, K. C. Assessment of children in outpatient settings. In M. Hersen & A. S. Bellack (Eds.), *Behavioral assessment*. New York: Pergamon Press, 1981.

Young, R. M., Bradley-Johnson, S., & Johnson, C. M. Immediate and delayed reinforcement on WISC-R performance for mentally retarded students. *Applied Research in Mental Retardation*, 1982, *3*, 13–20.

5

Attention Deficit Disorders*

Russell A. Barkley
*Departments of Neurology
and Psychiatry
Medical College of Wisconsin*

INTRODUCTION

The term *Attention Deficit Disorder* (ADD), with or without hyperactivity, is only the most recent relabeling of a set of childhood behavioral characteristics that has had many diagnostic labels applied to it over the past 80 years. These characteristics, elaborated later, consist of short attention span, poor concentration, impulsivity, restlessness, and difficulties with rule-governed behavior that are all inappropriate for the child's age (Barkley, 1981a; Ross and Ross, 1976, 1982). While the children so characterized may have many other associated features, these are felt to be the primary problems that plague all of the children in this diagnostic group. Incredibly vast literature has been written about ADD children, making them one of the most well-studied disorders of childhood over the past 25 years. The present chapter will not attempt to review all of the research conducted on hyperactive or Attention Deficit Disorder children, but will highlight the most recent understanding of this disorder and show how intelligent, effective treatment strategies may flow from these current conceptualizations. The reader interested in a more thorough review of this literature is referred to the scholarly texts by Ross and Ross (1976, 1982). A

*The author is grateful to Cheryl Ucaker for preparation of the manuscript and to Seymour Weingarten, Editor-in-Chief, The Guilford Press, for permission to reprint many tables and figures from my text (Barkley, 1981a).

more detailed approach to clinical practice with ADD children is available in my text (Barkley, 1981a) and the earlier one by Safer and Allen (1976).

In this chapter, the term Attention Deficit Disorder will be used to refer to both DSM-III categories (with and without hyperactivity) and will be used interchangeably with previously related terms, such as *hyperkinetic reaction of childhood* or *hyperactive child syndrome*. No distinction is made here between the two categories of ADD in the DSM-III since there is no evidence to show that this is a valid or useful distinction. While the term *hyperactive* technically refers to excessive levels of motor activity, it has generally been used to refer to a cluster of behavioral attributes in a child that go beyond mere activity level to include the other symptoms mentioned earlier.

History

Many investigators credit Still (1902) with being the first to fully recognize the separate existence of a group of children whose major difficulties were in the control of their own behavior as distinguished from children with delays in intellectual development or brain damage. Still argued persuasively that these children typically were of at least normal intelligence and that their behavioral problems could not be explained simply on the basis of poor child rearing by their parents. While Still described these children as restless, inattentive, impulsive, and frequently more emotional, aggressive, and destructive than their normal peers, he felt the major defect to be in the moral control of behavior or in *volitional inhibition*. That is, their most distinguishing attribute was their inappropriate social conduct wherein they often failed to follow rules, etiquette, norms, or direct instructions given by others. Still also recognized that the disorder had an early onset, appeared to be chronic, was more often seen in males than females, and that such children often had an increased number of minor deformities in appearance or minor physical anomalies. While he described cases in which these behavioral disorders were clearly the direct result of neurological disease or damage, Still noted that many other cases had no history of neurologic damage or disease, and some even appeared to be familial in nature. Nonetheless, biological rather than environmental causes were felt to be the primary etiologies of the disorder.

Research on the disorder showed a resurgence in the 1940s in the works of Strauss, Lehtinen, and Leviri (see Ross and Ross, 1976). They described children whose greatest problems were in restlessness, overactivity, impulsivity, distractibility, and poor attention span. They attributed the problems to brain injury, although direct evidence of brain damage was weak or nonexistent in many children. Serious and sustained scientific interest did not appear until the late 1950s in the studies of Laufer, Denhoff, and Solomons (1957) and those of Werry (1968, Werry and Sprague, 1970) and clinical descriptions by Chess (1960). Children who clinicians earlier in the century had called postencephalitic behavior disorder, organic driveness, or brain injured were now described as hyperactive, hyperkinetic, or as having minimal brain damage or dysfunction. Emphasis was placed on excessive activity level as the major symptom, with the disorder believed to be limited to the childhood years (Laufer, 1971; Laufer and Denhoff, 1957).

In the early 1970s, Douglas and her students at McGill University reported a series of studies on these children using a variety of objective laboratory measures of attention, concentration, impulsivity, and activity level. The subjects were selected using more operational criteria than had been used by previous investigators, and efforts were made to exclude retarded, brain damaged, psychotic, or gross sensory-impaired children. The results of these studies (see Douglas, 1972, 1974, 1980; Douglas and Peters, 1979) suggested that overactivity was not the only or even the primary problem of these children. Instead, Douglas emphasized the deficiencies in sustained attention and impulse control as being the most important symptoms. Later studies (Barkley, 1977b; Barkley and Ullman, 1975; Routh and Schroeder, 1976; Ullman, Barkley and Brown, 1978) using multiple objective measures of these and other behavior and cognitive functions would further document the serious deficits these children displayed in attention, concentration, and impulse control. Excessive activity level was also documented (see Barkley and Cunningham, 1978) but not in all settings or in all types of activity. The greatest problems with activity level were seen more in structured situations demanding restraint by the child rather than in free-play situations. At the same time, studies in classrooms also noted significant problems for these children in on-task behavior (Ayllon and Rosenbaum, 1977; Jacob and O'Leary, 1978; Whalen, Collins, Henker, Alkus, Adams and Stapp, 1978). By the end of the last decade, the disorder was renamed Attention Deficit Disorder in the latest revision of the *Diagnostic and Statistical Manual of Mental Disorders* (APA, 1980), so as to emphasize attentional problems as the most salient symptom.

At the same time, Campbell began to study systematically the family interactions decribed in the earlier reports by Battle and Lacey (1972). In a well-executed series of studies, Campbell (1973, 1975) demonstrated that the mother-child interactions of hyperactive children differed considerably from those of normal or learning disabled children. Hyperactive children were observed to be more noncompliant, attention seeking, and negative, while their mothers were more directive of the children and provided greater structure, supervision, and encouragement as compared to normal mother-child dyads. Later, Barkley and Cunningham (1979, 1980) replicated these results and demonstrated that the use of stimulant drugs significantly alters these interaction patterns so that they are more like those of normal children. Like Humphries, Kinsbourne, and Swanson (1978), these investigators interpreted their results to suggest that the commanding, negative, and directive interactions of the mothers were more a reaction to, than a cause of, the child's symptoms. In addition to extending the study of ADD symptoms to the social context in which they normally occur, these studies demonstrated that noncompliance is also a major difficulty of hyperactive children. Furthermore, they suggest that it may be this problem that parents find the most distressing and that leads to the referral of the children for treatment (Barkley, 1981b, 1982; Barkley and Cunningham, 1980).

Historically, we seem to have come back to the earlier notions of Still (1902), perhaps with much greater confidence, that problems with self-control, compliance, adherence to social rules, or volitional inhibition are primary deficits in ADD children besides their obvious inattention, restlessness, and impulsivity. Whether the problems with noncompliance and self-control are merely the social secondary effects of the deficits in attention or are, themselves, primary deficits in rule-governed behavior (Barkley, 1981a, 1982) has not been resolved. What is obvious is that interaction problems exist for ADD children not only in their interactions with their mothers, but also with their fathers (Tallmadge and Barkley, 1983), siblings (Mash and Johnston, 1983b), peers (Cunningham, Siegel and Offord, 1980; Whalen, Henker, Collins, Fink, and Dotemoto 1979), and teachers (Whalen, Henker and Dotemoto, 1980). These interaction problems exist in both hyperactive girls and boys (Befera and Barkley, 1984), and while their severity may decline with age, they continue to remain abnormal into preadolescence or even longer (Barkley, Karlsson and Pollard, 1984; Barkley, Karlsson, Strzelecki, and Murphy, 1984; Mash and Johnston, 1982).

In summary, hyperactive or ADD children have been recognized as a separate, clinical entity since at least the beginning of this century. Diagnostic labels and theories of the nature and etiologies of the disorder have varied greatly over time, depending on the professional identity of the investigators, the cultural and historical milieu in which they worked, the assessment methods available at the time, and the treatment approaches desired to be employed. While it was initially felt to be a defect in moral control of behavior, emphasis shifted to overactivity as the primary symptom and brain damage (often without evidence) as its suspected cause. Over time, greater importance was placed on inattention and impulsivity as the more salient symptoms. More recently, social interaction conflicts and problems with compliance and rules have been added to these symptoms.

Prevalence/Incidence

The ability to specify the prevalence of a childhood disorder within the population with any degree of confidence largely depends on how specific and reliable the definition of the disorder happens to be. As I have discussed elsewhere (Barkley, 1982), despite the long and colorful history of ADD in children, there have been few attempts to define the disorder operationally until only recently. Many experts in this field accept a prevalence estimate of 3 to 5 percent of the school-age population, but we know this varies considerably, depending on the degree of consensus among the parent(s), teacher, and physician (Lambert, Sandoval and Sassone, 1978), the symptoms one wishes to include (Lapouse and Monk, 1958; Werry and Quay, 1971), and whether an arbitrary cut-off score is used on a child behavior rating scale (Trites, Dugas, Lynch & Ferguson, 1979). The sex of the child, socioeconomic status, and geographic region also affect the extent to which children may be diagnosed hyperactive (Ross and Ross, 1982; Trites, 1979). Thus, prevalence rates may vary from less than 1 percent to more than 45 percent, depending on these factors.

The disorder, no matter how defined, seems to occur more often in boys than in girls, with ratios ranging from 3 to 1 to 9 to 1, depending on the study (Ross and Ross, 1976). A generally accepted ratio of 6 to 1 is often used, but this can be affected by cultural beliefs on the differential referral of boys and girls to child mental health programs and on the acceptability of the symptoms in either sex. Referral rates may also be influenced by the degree of marital dysfunction in the family, which is known to occur more often in the parents of boys than girls (Oltmanns, Broderick, and O'Leary, 1977) and to be highly correlated with the severity of childhood problems as rated by parents (Forehand and McMahon, 1981). Family stress, maternal isolation from social networks, sex of parent, and maternal depression may all affect the prevalence rates since they are known to differentially affect the degree to which boys and girls are viewed as deviant by their parents (Befera and Barkley, 1983; Mash, in press; Mash and Johnston, 1983a; Wahler, 1976). The reasons for the greater prevalence of males with this disorder is not at all clear but may ultimately relate to the same reasons boys are more likely to have learning disorders, psychosis, mental retardation, and other psychological disorders.

DESCRIPTION

Primary Characteristics

As already noted, ADD children appear to display major difficulties in: (a) attention, (b) impulsivity, (c) regulation of activity levels, and (d) rule-governed behavior. These characteristics are defined as deviant relative to the child's age (especially mental age) and sex. The problem is not that they cannot do these things, but that their level or quality of performance in these areas is not acceptable for their current developmental stage. While many authors speak of these symptoms as if they were well defined, homogeneous, unidimensional, and easily measured, such is hardly the case. The unfortunate reality is that there exist many different dimensions of attention (see Douglas and Peters, 1979), impulsivity (see Paulsen and Johnson, 1980), activity level (see Barkley, 1977b) and rule-governed behavior (see Barkley, 1982; Skinner, 1954) that greatly complicate attempts to conceptualize this disorder. Furthermore, many different methods of assessing these behaviors exist, limited mainly by the creativity and perseverance of the investigator; yet, most of the methods are not readily applicable in clinical settings where the need for them is greatest. While this chapter will treat the disorder as a single diagnostic entity for ease and brevity of presentation, the actual complexity and heterogeneity of the disorder(s) should not be far from our thoughts.

The belief that ADD children have primary difficulties with their *attention* stems from repeated demonstrations that such children have problems sustaining their response to assigned tasks or target stimuli for as long a time period as their normal peers. When required to sit and attend to an assigned activity, they appear to engage in competing activity sooner than other children, shift their attention away from the task more readily, lose interest in continued performance at the task, and even attend to less relevant dimensions of the task than normal children. Therefore, their duration of "time on task" is shorter than other children's, and they make more mistakes (usually omissions of responses) than their peers (see Douglas, 1972). Hence, the span or length of their attention is said to be short.

It is perhaps worth recalling at this point what Skinner (1954) noted 30 years ago: attention, in and of itself, is not a thing or entity but merely a way of describing a functional relation between a given stimulus and a desired response from the individual. We say a child is inattentive when his persistence at responding is less or the quality of his response is less desirable than others of his age group. Rather than fault the child, we could just as easily fault the stimulus by concluding that it failed to elicit the desired response and failed to keep the child responding to it for a desired length of time. Viewed this way, we can treat inattention not directly but indirectly by making the consequences for sustaining response to a task more powerful or salient or by enhancing various parameters (attractiveness) of the stimulus or task itself. "Attention" will vary, then, as a function of the nature of a stimulus and the response consequences. To truly appreciate the nature of ADD children, we must ask to what types of stimuli (tasks) do ADD children have the greatest difficulty maintaining response and what types of task consequences are least effective in this regard? Unfortunately, research is only beginning to explore this issue. Thankfully, some research has shown us that ADD children are not inattentive to all things or unaffected by all consequences. Therefore, there is much hope in pursuing a behavioral analysis of the problem.

Similarly, ADD children are described as lacking in reflection, or as being *impulsive*. This is demonstrated in tasks in which the child is asked to respond to some set of stimuli (a problem), but in which emitting the correct response is made more likely if the child withholds an answer momentarily to search the stimulus array more carefully for cues that help him to discriminate the correct response (see Douglas, 1972). Tasks measuring impulsivity often use arrays of stimuli that are initially similar to each other but that differ along less obvious dimensions. Two scores are usually derived from such tasks, which are the time to the first response and the correctness of the response. Children who respond more quickly, yet less accurately, than normal are called impulsive. Like attention, impulsivity is not a thing but a description of a functional relation between a stimulus and a response. Also like attention, it seems to be a problem in a temporal relation (time interval), but whereas inattention involves the length of time a child responds to a task, impulsivity is the length of time between the presentation of a stimulus and the onset of the attempt at a correct response. Both inattention and impulsivity relate to problems in temporal relations between stimuli (cues) and responses (behavior), which may help us to one day understand why ADD children often have both problems.

Overactivity, or restlessness, has been extensively studied (see Ross and Ross, 1976), and few doubt that hyperactive or ADD children are more active, in certain situations, than normal children. The greatest differences from normal children occur in settings that require restraint and self-control by the child (Barkley, 1977a; Barkley and Cunningham, 1978). Like normal children, ADD children display greater levels of activity during preschool years than their middle or late childhood years, and by adolescence, restlessness rather than gross motor overactivity may be the most obvious problem with their activity levels. As with the other symptoms, overactivity is not usually manifested everywhere, and knowing how it fluctuates across settings may help us to better understand the disorder. Routh (1978) has suggested that the difficulty involved here is not necessarily one of overactivity per se but a deficiency in regulating activity level to adhere to situational demands. The problem is more clearly viewed as one of inhibition or self-control and can only be appreciated relative to some social context and the degree to which it demands restraint.

In thinking about each symptom described so far, it is no coincidence that the ADD child's greatest problems arise in highly structured, restrictive settings that demand the most restraint from the child. More to the point, the child's problems are more salient in settings requiring compliance with commands, directions, previously taught rules, or guidelines for social etiquette. For this reason, I have previously argued (Barkley, 1981a, 1981b, 1982) that a deficiency in rule-governed behavior is also a primary problem of ADD children. Rule-governed behavior refers to the stimulus control of child behavior by language or, more specifically, language that conveys information as to how to respond in a situation. Its opposite is contingency-shaped behavior (Skinner, 1954), wherein a child's behavior is shaped and controlled by natural consequences occurring in the present situation, rather than the child responding to a social rule as to how to behave. Like the other symptoms, ADD children are not completely deficient in this ability but are less capable of controlling their behavior by rules than others their own age. It appears to be to rules that ADD children have the greatest trouble sustaining their responses.

Skinner (1954) has eloquently argued that there are at least three overlapping, hierarchical stages in developing rule-governed behavior—compliance, self-control, and problem solving. In its simplist form, compliance is a child's response to a command or directive given in the immediate situation.

Self-control is the compliance to a rule previously taught to the child and probably relies heavily on subvocal or internal speech (our memory for rules). Problem solving is the child's ability to engage in self-directed questioning, deriving a rule to comply with in a situation for which he has not previously learned how to respond. All of the stages involve the control of behavior by linguistic stimuli, either verbalized or subvocalized (internally represented speech). There is growing evidence to show that ADD children have problems in all three areas of rule-governed behavior (see Barkley, 1982). In short, the control of behavior by rules in ADD children is weak compared to normal children, and it is probably weakest in governance by internal speech (self-control and problem solving).

Presently, research results cannot tell us whether the problems with rule-governed behavior are secondary to the problems with attention and impulsivity, whether the opposite is the case, or whether they are partially interacting but equally primary problems. Until further research is available to address this issue, the author has chosen to view the problems with rule-governed behavior as a primary symptom, the one that, more than the others, creates the greatest problems for the ADD child in his social interactions. Assessment and treatment will focus primarily on this symptom, although the other symptoms and the associated features receive some attention (see below).

Range of Severity

The primary problems of the ADD child fluctuate to some degree, depending on a number of factors. Similar to other childhood disorders, there is probably a range of severity of ADD in children. Stated bluntly, some ADD children are worse than others, and perhaps this relates simply to biological (or biosocial) variation. Beyond this, some evidence suggests that the severity of symptoms, at least as reported by parents, varies with socioeconomic status (Paternite and Loney, 1980), sex of the child (Befera and Barkley, 1984), sex of the parent interacting with the child (Barkley, 1981a; Goyette, Conners and Ulrich, 1978; Tallmadge and Barkley, 1983), and the presence or absence of a sibling in the social situation (Mash and Johnston, 1983b). The number of demands placed on the child in a given situation, the degree of familiarity of the child with a situation, and whether the child is involved in a one-to-one situation with an adult also seem to affect the severity of problem behaviors (Barkley, 1977a; Cunningham and Barkley, 1979; Jacob, O'Leary, and Rosenblad, 1978; Ross and Ross, 1982). Mash and Johnston (1983a) have also shown that the level of parenting stress reported by mothers correlates with the severity of ADD symptoms as reported by her and the degree of interaction problems she has with the ADD child.

That ADD children display situational variation in behavior is illustrated in Table 5–1 and Figure 5–1. Table 5–1 shows the percentage of 30 ADD children compared to 30 normal children having problems in various home

TABLE 5–1

Percentage of Hyperactive and Normal Children Displaying Problems in 14 Home Situations and the Mean Severity Rating in Each Setting

situation	hyperactive		normal	
	percent	mean severity*	percent	mean severity
While playing alone	40.0	4.3	0.0	0.0
Playing with others	90.0	5.4	10.0	1.6
Mealtimes	86.7	4.7	13.3	3.0
Getting dressed	73.3	6.1	10.0	2.3
Washing/bathing	43.3	5.1	16.7	1.2
When parent is on phone	93.3	6.6	33.3	1.3
While watching television	80.0	5.0	3.3	2.0
When visitors are in home	96.7	6.1	30.0	1.6
When visiting others	96.7	5.4	13.3	1.5
Public places	96.7	5.4	23.3	2.7
When father is at home	73.3	3.9	6.7	2.5
When asked to do chores	86.7	5.6	36.7	2.0
At bedtime	83.3	5.0	20.0	1.5
While riding in the car	73.3	4.8	20.0	1.7

* Severity was rated by parents on a scale from 1 (mild) to 9 (severe)
Source: Barkley, *Hyperactive Children: A Handbook for Diagnosis and Treatment.* (New York: Guilford Press, 1981). Reprinted with permission. © 1981 by Guilford Press.

settings. Figure 5–1 further illustrates the rated severity of these behavior problems. ADD children appear to show fewer problems while playing alone, while bathing, or while their fathers are home, yet they have greater difficulties in settings calling for them to restrict their behavior to allow their parents to interact with others in that situation (i.e. meals, phone, with visitors) or to allow parents to attend to a chore or activity (phone, shopping). The more the setting requires the child to comply with commands, rules, and restrictions, the more the ADD children have problems in those settings and the more severe the problems seem to be.

Associated Features

Children selected on the basis of their ADD symptoms appear to be more likely than normal children to manifest a variety of other difficulties. Not all ADD children have these problems, nor are all children who have these associated problems likely to be diagnosed as ADD. Nevertheless, ADD children have a higher than normal occurrence of these problems. An unanswered issue, however, is whether ADD children are more likely to have these problems than other groups of clinic referred children.

FIGURE 5-1

Mean Severity Rating by Parents for 30 Hyperactive and 30 Normal Children across 14 Home Situations

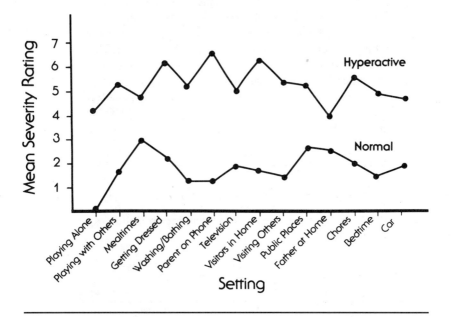

Some hyperactive children appear to be more distractible than normal children, but the point remains controversial (Radosh and Gittelman, 1981). Less controversial is the association of aggression and conduct disorders (i.e., lying, stealing, destructiveness) with ADD in children. Recent studies (Loney, Langhorne and Paternite, 1978; Stewart, Cummings, Singer and DeBlois, 1981) suggest that as many as 67 percent of ADD children have problems with aggression and conduct but that the symptoms do not covary. That is, degree of ADD does not predict degree of aggression or vice versa. Parents report that ADD children take more risks, respond less to discipline and consequences, and may have a higher pain tolerance than normal children, although research has yet to document these reports using more objective measures.

Socially, ADD children have considerable problems in peer relations (Campbell and Paulauskas, 1979; Cunningham, Siegal and Offord, 1980; Whalen et al., 1979), and they are often viewed by peers as being immature, self-centered, and easily frustrated. Parents often state that their children tend to play with younger children, have few if any close friends, and tend to play with toys characteristic of younger children; yet, again, research supporting these results has not been done. Certainly, ratings of personality characteristics distinguish hyperactive from normal children or other psychiatric groups. Figure 5–2 shows the profile of 60 ADD children (Barkley, 1981a) on the Achenbach Child Behavior Checklist (Achenbach, 1978).

While the scores on all scales of the profile are higher than normal, peak scale elevations occur on those scales assessing aggression, hyperactivity delinquency, and motor restlessness (obsessive-compulsive). Figure 5–3 shows similar results for 26 ADD boys (Breen and Barkley, 1983), using the Personality Inventory for Children (Wirt, Lachar, and Klinedinst, 1977). The results of that study showed ADD boys to have highest elevations on scales measuring general maladjustment, delinquency, hyperactivity, social skills, and emotional liability (psychosis scale) compared to normal children. A subsequent study (Breen and Barkley, 1984) found these same scales to differentiate ADD boys from those with learning disabilities.

FIGURE 5–2

Profile for 60 Hyperactive Boys on the Achenbach Child Behavior Checklist

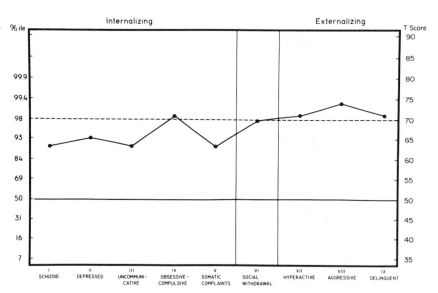

Source: R. Barkley, *Hyperactive Children: A Handbook for Diagnosis and Treatment.* (New York: Guilford Press, 1981). Reprinted with permission. © by Guilford Press.

FIGURE 5-3

Profile for 26 Hyperactive and 26 Normal Children on the Personality Inventory for Children

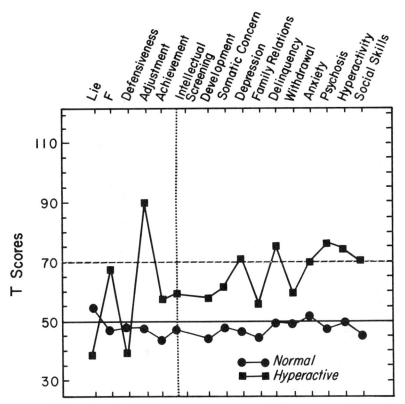

Source: M. Breen & R. Barkley, "The Personality Inventory for Children: Its Clinical Utility with Hyperactive Children," *Journal of Pediatric Psychology*, 1983, 8, 359–366. Reprinted with permission. © by Plenun Press.

In their academic performance, ADD children show numerous problems. Off-task behavior, noisiness, and disruption are common, as are problems completing classwork and homework. Parents and teachers complain of underachievement by the child, and some reports suggest that more than 20 percent of ADD children also have specific learning disabilities (Safer and Allen, 1976). Some evidence indicates ADD children are less intelligent than children from the same neighborhood (Safer and Allen, 1976), normal children (Mash and Johnston, 1982), or their siblings (Tarver-Behring, Barkley, and Karlsson, 1983). Loney (1974; Loney and Milich, 1981; Milich and Loney, 1979) suggests that ADD children are likely to show a characteristic pattern on the WISC-R, known as the ACID profile (low scores on arithmetic, coding, information, and digit span). Whether this indicates problems with attention, concentration, short-term memory, or other mental functions is not clear.

Both research and clinical lore suggest that ADD children are more accident prone, have more allergies, more upper respiratory infections and otitis media, more minor physical anomalies, are more physically immature, have underreactive patterns on evoked potential tests or electroencephalogram studies, and are more uncoordinated than other children (see Hastings & Barkley, 1978; Ross and Ross, 1982; Rosenthal and Allen, 1978; and Trites, Tryphonas and Ferguson, 1980 for reviews). They may also have a higher incidence of enuresis and encopresis, eating problems, and sleeping disorders than normal children. What remains to be shown is whether these distinguish ADD children from those having other psychiatric disorders.

Onset and Course

The age at which the first symptoms of ADD are discovered in children vary considerably, although the research that has examined the issue indicates that more than 90 percent are problematic by entry into formal school (Barkley, 1982; Stewart et al., 1981). Certainly, it would be difficult to diagnose ADD in children prior to 18 months of age using the criteria of either the DSM-III or those I have justified elsewhere (Barkley, 1981a, 1982) and outlined later in this chapter. According to parental reports, probably 50 to 60 percent of ADD children manifest their symptoms by two to three years of age but may not be referred until several years later. Most researchers would agree that the onset of ADD after six to seven years of age is rare (see APA, 1980; Barkley, 1982) and probably is secondary to central nervous system trauma or disease. Such children may be said to have "acquired" ADD if their behavioral symptoms persist beyond 6 to 12 months.

Although the formal primary symptoms of ADD may not be manifest until two to three years of age at their earliest, up to 30 percent may be described as having been difficult to care for since birth or early infancy (Carey and McDevitt, 1978; Stewart et al., 1981). Parents often describe the ADD child's temperament as an infant as difficult, irritable, colicky, or hard to manage. Temperament refers to a cluster of behavioral characteristics comprising five groups: emotionality, sociability, regularity of habit, response to stimulation, and activity level. Research by Chess, Thomas, Rutter and Birch (1963) with infants and by Chamberlin (1977; McIvery and Chamberlin, 1978) with infants and toddlers point to "difficult" temperament in infants as being not only a stable feature of the child's response style to his environment, but also a good predictor of later behavior problems and hyperactivity. Thus, some ADD children may show difficulties in their mother-infant interactions from an early age due to difficulties with temperament (Campbell, 1979).

By two to three years of age, ADD children are usually at their peak of gross motor overactivity. Parents must supervise them almost constantly lest they get into mischief, damage property, or harm themselves or others. Problems with noncompliance to parental commands have begun at this age, and parents may wonder if the "terrible two's" will ever end. Some ADD children may show sleeping problems, eating difficulties (picky eaters, etc.), or be very hard to toilet train. Parents may find themselves fatigued due to the chronic attention they must give to the child. Many find their social activities being curtailed, due to the inability to take the child places without his creating a disturbance or to the unwillingness of others to babysit the child.

In the nursery school or kindergarten years, problems with overactivity and noncompliance persist. By now, parents are complaining of a lack of self-control by the child (can't be trusted, doesn't follow rules, etc.). Peer problems have often emerged by now (Campbell and Paulauskas, 1979), with ADD children described as physically and verbally aggressive to others, selfish, prone to tantrums, bullying others, unable to share or cooperate, and emotional. For some, bed wetting or soiling (encopresis) remains a problem.

By school age, the symptoms may have changed in form to some degree, or the social and academic effects have become more salient. Now, teachers also complain of noncompliance as well as out of seat, off-task, disruptive, and immature behavior. Learning disabilities are noted in some ADD children, while most will be classified as underachievers. At home, children with ADD continue to be noncompliant and poorly self-controlled. Coercive interaction patterns are well entrenched by now (see Patterson, 1976), and the children have learned how to escape or avoid many responsibilities or chores expected of others. Getting homework done or getting ready for school may be major confrontations in the household. Complaints from neighbors concerning the child's conduct problems in the community may emerge, if they haven't already.

By late childhood or preadolescence, patterns of poor school achievement, difficult parent-child interactions, poor peer relations, and immature self-control are well established. Both the children and their mothers may show symptoms of clinical depression, low self-esteem, and feelings of poor competence in their respective roles. Although compliance to direct commands has improved, the child's self-control, trustworthiness, and acceptance of responsibility remain problematic. Motor overactivity has declined, but the children lag behind in sustained attention and impulse control especially in school. Those with patterns of earlier aggression and conduct problems are likely to persist in these difficulties throughout this stage of adolescence.

In adolescence, those with only ADD symptoms seem to have their greatest problems in school. The children may have friends by now, although they are not always desirable ones. The ADD teenager still has less-than-normal responsibilities at home, but parents may have given up by now trying to get greater compliance from the child. Difficulties with curfew, driving privileges, and drinking under age may arise. School failure, retention in grade, or even truancy are likely to have occurred now if not earlier. Aggressive ADD adolescents may have even poorer social acceptance now, and lying, stealing, fighting, and juvenile status offenses may be occurring.

The young adulthood of these children is not as easily described, for there are few adequate studies following ADD children to this age. Those that have (Weiss, Hechtman and Perlman, 1978; Weiss, Hechtman, Perlman, Hopkins and Wener, 1979) suggest that ADD symptoms have diminished considerably in their intensity but still may be enough to distinguish them from other young adults. Many have feelings of sadness and despair over their childhoods. They may be working and viewed by employers as satisfactory, yet they may be underemployed relative to siblings and peers. Alcoholism is a problem for some. Peer acceptance may still be a problem for those who have had chronic, past difficulties in this area. In sum, the problems of adolescence persist into adulthood for many, though not all, ADD children.

A related issue is the discovery of variables that predict differential outcomes within this group. The work of Loney and her colleagues (see Paternite and Loney, 1980) has been one of the most rigorous and fruitful series of studies on predicting adolescent outcome in hyperactive children. Other than socioeconomic status, one of the best predictors of adolescent adjustment is aggression during childhood. ADD children who were also aggressive were more likely to show problems with antisocial behavior, poor school performance, and poor peer acceptance. ADD children without aggression were likely to have problems primarily in school performance during adolescence. This outcome seems to exist regardless of earlier stimulant drug treatment or psychological interventions. The extent to which the fathers of ADD children exerted control over them during childhood was also predictive of adolescent outcome, with those whose fathers were less controlling showing a poorer prognosis. Like Loney, Weiss and her colleagues (Weiss et al., 1978, 1979) also found aggression, poor parent-child relations, and mental health of other family members to be predictive of both adolescent and young adulthood outcome.

It is worth remembering that the findings with respect to developmental course and prediction of outcome in ADD are not well established. Many follow-up studies are fraught with methodological problems that confound their results. Some used poorly defined subjects; others failed to separate the effects of different symptoms on outcome (i.e., ADD versus aggression), and others still used inadequate measures of outcome. The greatest problem affecting the majority of studies was the failure to use a control group of clinic referred non-ADD children, so as to decipher what outcomes are specific to ADD children and what are simply general outcomes of any deviant child. As a result, much of what was described above, while characterizing the ADD child's development as best as current research permits, may not be specific to ADD children but general to psychiatric referrals. A further problem with such research has been its relatively high rate of loss of subjects for follow-up evaluation. Where attrition rates are high, there is some evidence to suggest that those subjects who are evaluated differ from those lost to follow-up, in that the latter may have worse outcomes. If so, current follow-up research may reflect a better outcome of ADD children than is actually the case (see Paternite and Loney, 1980; Ross and Ross, 1982 for further discussion).

Given these limitations, it seems fair to conclude that, for now at least, the evidence suggests that most ADD children have difficulties throughout childhood and adolescence with respect to the primary behavioral symptoms: inattention, impulsivity, restlessness, and poor rule-governed behavior. Others may develop further problems that stem from chronic maladjustment, such as depression, poor peer relations, and academic failure. The outcome of the ADD child appears to be related to the extent of aggression and conduct disorders in childhood as well as to family mental health factors and socioeconomic status. Where these factors are problematic, outcome will be less satisfactory. Degree of ADD symptoms, by themselves, seem to predict only a continuation of the symptoms, poor educational adjustment and eventual educational level in adolescence. Clearly, more and better designed follow-up research is warranted before even this summation can be accepted as accurate.

CONCEPTUALIZATION

Definition

From the literature on ADD children, I have culled the following definition of ADD, or hyperactivity, which has been described and defined elsewhere (Barkley, 1981a, 1982):

> A disorder in children of age inappropriate attention span, impulse control, restlessness, and rule-governed behavior that arises early in childhood (prior to age six years), is significantly pervasive or cross-situational, is usually chronic throughout development, and is not the direct result of severe emotional disturbance, gross sensory impairment, demonstrated gross neurological damage, severe language delay, or mental retardation.

This definition does not imply that children who are autistic, psychotic, deaf, blind, delayed in language, or retarded, cannot have ADD but that, in the clinician's judgment, the symptoms of ADD are not simply secondary to these conditions. Brain injured children may also have ADD symptoms that coexist with but do not stem from the neurologic damage. In those cases in which previously non-ADD children develop ADD symptoms after neurologic disease or damage, the child may be labeled as having *acquired ADD secondary to* _____, with the neurologic disease identified (i.e. acquired ADD secondary to frontal lobe damage or head trauma). Such children may well be different in course, outcome, response to treatment, and so on from ADD children whose symptoms are of the developmental idiopathic sort without evidence of early neurologic damage. Furthermore, rather than distinguishing between ADD with or without hyperactivity, research findings suggest that ADD with or without aggression (conduct disorders) may be a far more useful distinction from the standpoint of prognosis and perhaps even response to treatment.

Diagnostic Criteria

As noted elsewhere (Barkley, 1982), this definition can be translated into seven clinical criteria for identifying children as ADD, and these differ, to some extent, from the less specific, less developmentally referenced, and more liberal criteria set forth in the DSM-III.

1. Parent or teacher complaints of short attention span, impulsivity, restlessness, and poor rule-governed behavior (compliance and self-control).

2. Ratings by parents or teacher on well-standardized child behavior rating scales, assessing factors reflecting the symptoms in #1. These ratings must place the child two standard deviations above the mean for normal children of the same age and sex.

3. Ratings using the Home Situations Questionnaire that indicate behavior problems by the child in eight or more of 16 situations, suggesting significantly pervasive behavior difficulties.

4. Onset of symptoms before six years of age as reported by parents.

5. Duration of symptoms of 12 months as reported by parents or teachers.

6. Normal intelligence or, if the child is mentally retarded, the ratings in #2 are compared to children of similar mental age to establish deviance.

7. Exclusion of children with autism, psychosis, deafness, blindness, or severe language delay if these conditions are felt to be the direct cause of the child's behavioral problems. If brain damage is demonstrable and felt to be causal of the symptoms, the term *acquired ADD secondary to* _____ *is used* and the disease or damage is specified.

By definition, these criteria limit the diagnosis to 2 or 3 percent of children and insure that such children have problems of early onset that are pervasive and typically chronic. In some instances, the criteria are arbitrary or arguable; yet, some criteria must be specified now to reduce the diagnostic quagmire created by the idiosyncratic, unjustified, subjective, and unreliable clinical opinions in use to date. Future theoreticians and clinicians will no doubt improve upon or change these criteria. For now, they offer relatively clear-cut, reliably defined conditions to be met that can be easily explained to parents, teachers, and others with a need to know how a diagnosis was reached.

Etiology

Research in this area has begun to increase in the past decade, and its results are suggestive or as yet only incomplete. Serious methodological problems plague previous studies, and limitations of experimental designs or measurement techniques continue to hamper present studies of the subject. As a result, the etiologies of ADD are not especially clear or well documented. Without undertaking an extensive, detailed review of each study in this area, it seems reasonable to discuss briefly the proposed etiologies on which there has been some research of a reasonable caliber. The reader is referred to Ross and Ross (1976, 1982) for more detailed discussion.

One of the earliest proposed causes of ADD was brain damage or disease (Still, 1902; Strauss and Lehtinen, 1947), and many felt this accounted for the majority of ADD children. It is certainly possible for neurologic damage to lead to ADD-like symptoms in children, especially if such damage occurs to the prefrontal cortex and specifically, the orbital surfaces (Hecaen and Albert, 1978; Heilman and Valenstein, 1979; Mattes, 1980). However, most children with brain damage do not develop ADD symptoms (Rutter, 1977, 1982), and most ADD children do not have "hard" or unequivocal signs or histories of brain damage (Rie and Rie, 1980; Rutter, 1977; Taylor and Fletcher, 1983). While brain damage may cause ADD in some children, it hardly seems to be its primary etiology.

The notion that ADD children are neurologically immature has been offered by some (Kinsbourne, 1977) and supported by substantial *indirect* evidence. ADD children appear to be like younger normal children in their attention spans, impulsivity, activity level and social interactions (Barkley, Karlsson and Pollard, 1984; Cunningham, Siegel and Offord, 1980; Routh and Schroeder, 1976; Routh, Schroeder, and O'Tuama, 1974). Some show patterns on various psychophysiological measures (i.e., EEG, evoked potentials), suggestive of immature cortical activation of the brain (Hastings and Barkley, 1978; Rosenthal and Allen, 1978). The notion of immaturity does not imply a developmental lag that eventually catches up to normal but may refer to chronically immature behavior patterns that improve with age but are always delayed relative to normal same-age children. The causes of such immaturities are not known and might conceivably be related to familial-hereditary patterns of development, obstetrical or pregnancy complications, malnutrition, physical abuse, or other as yet unrecognized causes.

Deficiencies or imbalances in neurotransmitters in the brain have, at times, been entertained as causes of ADD in children. Much of this evidence stemmed from the response of ADD children to stimulant drugs, implying that a deficit in the neurotransmitters affected by these drugs might be the cause of the behavioral symptoms (Wender, 1971). The later demonstrations that normal children respond in a similar direction to stimulants as ADD children called this line of reasoning into serious doubt (Rapoport, Buchsbaum, Zahn, Weingartner, Ludlow and Mikkelsen, 1978). More direct research on measuring the by-products of central neurotransmitters have been conflicting (see Ross and Ross, 1982) as to whether and what neurotransmitters are affected. The recently recognized relationship between Gilles de la Tourette Syndrome, believed to be a dopamine disorder in the basal ganglia, and ADD symptoms in the early histories of many children with Tourette's Syndrome (Golden, 1982) may refuel interest in this area of research.

Toxic reactions to certain environmental substances have been proposed as possible etiologies. Increased body lead burdens in children have been suggested by some (David, Clark, and Voeller, 1972) but disputed by others (Milar, Schroeder, Mushak and Bonne, 1981). Ross and Ross (1982) believe this to be a promising area of research on one possible cause of ADD in some children. Certainly, the idea that ADD is caused by toxic reactions to additives (Feingold, 1975) has been amply refuted (Conners, 1980; Taylor, 1979), and while a few children may show mild behavioral changes if given high doses of food dyes, one can hardly view this as a major, primary cause of ADD as its proponents believe. Some children may, as side effects, show behavioral problems resembling ADD in response to anticonvulsants, such as phenobarbital or Dilantin (Wolf and Forsythe, 1978); but, considering that most ADD children are not using anticonvulsants, this, too, must be viewed as a minor cause.

Allergies continue to be offered up as primary causes of ADD (Taylor, 1980), with little research support (see Ross and Ross, 1982). Even less evidence exists for theories of vitamin or protein deficiencies as causes of ADD (Smith, 1976). While few experienced clinicians doubt that allergic reactions might exacerbate preexisting behavioral disorders, the role of allergies as primary etiologies must be viewed as doubtful with the burden of scientific proof falling upon those who would espouse such ideas.

Similarly, there is a dearth of evidence for purely environmental causes of ADD. Some suggest that poor child management skills in parents lead to ADD in their children (Willis and Lovaas, 1977). While the parents of ADD children do show greater levels of commands, discipline, and negative interactions with their children (Barkley, in press; Barkley and Cunningham, 1980), and these do improve after parent training programs (Pollard, Ward, and Barkley, 1983), this does not prove a causal connection. Drug studies intimate that these interaction patterns by parents may be more a reaction to than a cause of the child's behavioral problems (Barkley and Cunningham, 1979). More than likely, preexisting temperamental styles (Campbell, 1979) or cognitive characteristics (i.e., inattention) lead to certain immature or inappropriate social behaviors by the ADD child, which may provoke control reactions from adults. Such reactions may hinder the child's problems under certain circumstances, further exacerbating the child's negative behavior, and culminating in a bidirectional, escalating pattern of negative social exchanges between parents and ADD children (Bell & Harper, 1977; Patterson, 1976). Once learned by the child, these coercive social behaviors may generalize to other people or settings outside the home (Patterson, 1982) in which they may result in further controlling reactions by others, such as teachers (Whalen, Henker and Dotemoto, 1980), or peers (Cunningham et al., 1980; Whalen et al., 1979), or simply to avoidance and ostracism. While this does not explain the initial cause of the cognitive deficits or temperament of the ADD child, it may explain the development of the social interaction pattern seen in families of ADD children or in their peer and teacher social exchanges. Other environmental causes, such as modeling or imitation (Copeland and Weissbrod, 1977), have not been adequately developed into an acceptable theory of ADD, although it is possible such factors might exacerbate the already existent ADD symptoms in a child.

One of the most exciting areas of research is on possible hereditary causes of ADD. Much evidence exists to show that parents and other relatives of ADD children are more likely to have been ADD themselves or to have shown a higher rate of psychiatric problems than is seen in normal children (Cantwell, 1975, 1978; Morrison and Stewart, 1971, 1973a, 1973b, 1974; Morrison, 1980). However, boys with conduct disorders show similar family patterns (Stewart, deBlois, and Cummings, 1980; Stewart and Leone, 1978), suggesting that it may be the conduct problems rather than ADD symptoms per se that are related to this pattern of familial distribution. Adequate twin studies are lacking, and possible chromosomal location studies such as those recently done with reading disabilitites (Smith, Kimberling, Pennington and Lubs, 1983) remain to be done. Nonetheless, many experts strongly suspect a genetic predisposition in some children to their ADD symptoms, but their optimism awaits more definitive evidence.

Biological variation, or the normal distribution of characteristics within a population, has been suggested as one possible contributor to ADD in children (Kinsbourne, 1977). This notion suggests that the frequency of symptoms of ADD in humans occur in a bell-shaped distribution, much like other physical or cognitive features. Children who happen to place at the extreme lower end of the distribution will have difficulty in adjusting in society and will be considered deviant. Such children may be labeled ADD, not due to brain damage or dysfunction but simply due to their placement on an extreme end of the normal curve of phenotypes for attention and impulsivity in the population. Given our use of arbitrary statistical cut-off scores on child behavior rating scales as part of the diagnosis, some children who could be identified as ADD are simply variants of the normal curve.

The author has come to view the causes of ADD much like we view the causes of mental retardation. There are probably multiple causes, many biologic, some environmental-social, and others a mixture of both (phenotypic). These causes lead to the diagram shown in Figure 5–4 of two overlapping distributions of differential size. The larger distribution reflects the phenotypic variation of ADD symptoms in the population. The curve reflects phenotypes that are, to varying degrees, mixtures of genetic and environmental influences that have lead to the child's current characteristics. Children at the lower extreme of this distribution of attention span, reflection, and rule-governed behavior will have great difficulty adjusting to the demands of our present rule-oriented, educated society. Such ADD children are part of a continuum of normal variation but are deviant to the degree that their characteristics create conflicts, maladjustment, and negative interactions with others. Still, other ADD children are truly "organic" or "neurologic" in the etiology of the symptoms, and they occupy the smaller distribution in the left side of Figure 5–4. These children probably had normal genotypes for their cognitive characteristics, but pre-, peri-, or postnatal complications or later trauma or disease occurred, leaving them afflicted with ADD symptoms that often are more severe than those seen with the "normal" phenotypic distribution. If we say that ADD is identified as being the extreme end of a normal curve of childhood characteristics, then we will find children in that range of diagnosis whose causes are multiple, such as we see in mental retardation.

FIGURE 5–4

The Theoretical Distribution of Attention Span and Impulse Control within the General Population

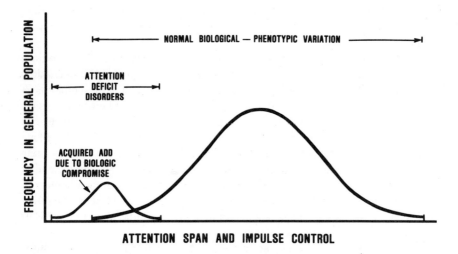

The large curve represents the normal variation within the population while the smaller curve represents that distribution secondary to biological compromise of a child.

Predisposing Influences

Only recently have studies begun to focus on the issue of what factors may predispose children toward the development of significant attentional deficits or hyperactivity, or toward the likelihood of their referral by parents to child mental health clinics. Much of what will be summarized here remains tentative and worthy of replication. Still, some promising variables have emerged that appear to increase or decrease the probability of a child being diagnosed as hyperactive or ADD. One factor mentioned earlier is socioeconomic status (SES), in that both the frequency/prevalence of ADD as well as the severity of symptoms covary to some extent with the SES of the child's family (Paternite and Loney, 1980; Trites, 1979). Infants with higher numbers of minor deviations in appearance or anomalies may be more likely to develop ADD or behavioral disorders in general (Rapoport, Quinn, Berg and Bartley, 1979), although they may not be specific predictors of ADD alone but of a broad range of developmental problems (Firestone, Peters, Rivier and Knights, 1978). Research on infant temperament suggests that babies with more difficult dispositions, irregularity of habits, excessive activity, and overreaction to stimulation may be more likely to develop ADD by school age than those infants without such difficult temperaments (Carey, 1972; McInerny and Chamberlin, 1978). Results of the Perinatal Collaborative Project (Nichols, 1980) intimate that maternal smoking during pregnancy, as well as father absence from the home, correlate to a significant, although low, degree with later ADD and, hence, may serve as predisposing factors.

Several factors seem to be associated with ADD in children or with the likelihood of referral for treatment, but they have not been demonstrated as yet to be predisposing factors toward ADD. Parental conduct problems, alcohol abuse, hysterical personality, maternal depression, and marital dysfunction are all more frequent in the families of ADD children (see Ross and Ross, 1982). But, these factors have not been used to select children with such family characteristics for prospective follow-up to assess their value as predictors of ADD. Mash and Johnston (1982) have shown that parental stress is predictive of greater directiveness by mothers and noncompliance by ADD children in task situations: again, this suggests that family characteristics may be either predisposing or exacerbating factors in ADD. Clearly, this is an area deserving greater research emphasis than has been seen to date.

Family Patterns

It was mentioned earlier that parent-child and sibling-child interactions in ADD children are different from those seen in the interactions of normal or learning disabled children. ADD children are less compliant, more negative, less able to sustain compliance, and more talkative and disruptive than normal children during interactions with their mothers and fathers, especially during periods when the children must accomplish tasks (Barkley, Cunningham, and Karlsson, 1983; Campbell, 1973, 1975; Cunningham and Barkley, 1979; Mash and Johnston, 1983; Tallmadge and Barkley, 1983). Their parents are more directive, commanding and negative, and less responsive to the children's interactions than is seen in normal parent-child dyads. In short, there exists much conflict in the family interaction patterns of ADD children. While drug studies suggest that the parental interaction patterns of children are mainly a reaction to the child's difficult behavior (Barkley and Cunningham, 1979; Cunningham and

Barkley, 1978; Humphries et al., 1978; Pollard et al., 1983), this does not preclude the possibility that parental reactions futher exacerbate the behavioral problems of the ADD child (Bell, 1981; Bell and Harper, 1977; Mash and Johnston, 1982).

Patterson (1976) has developed, elaborated, and extensively studied (Patterson, 1982) a theory of how such interaction patterns might develop in families of behavior disordered children. Known as *coercion theory,* it states that noncompliant, aggressive, or aversive child behaviors serve to coerce others into acquiescing to the child's demands or to giving up on enforcing commands or limits on child behavior. Aversive behavior by the child permits him to escape from or avoid unpleasant situations (i.e., chores), which serves to negatively reinforce further occurrences of such behavior by the child because of its success. Parents may also use coercive behaviors against the child to get him to acquiesce to their demands and, thereby, negatively reinforcing parental control reactions with the child. The result is that in high demand settings, such as task periods, negative interactions by both parent and child escalate rapidly in a mutually coercive fashion so as to get the other person to capitulate. At various times, both are successful, so both persist in using high rate, intense, and negative interactions to control the other. When paired with Bell's model of reciprocal, bidirectional influence in parent-child interactions, a powerful theory emerges for conceptualizing the family interaction patterns of noncompliant, aggressive, or behavior problem children.

Although these patterns may develop through the child imitating the coercive interactions of other family members (Patterson, 1976), there is no reason why ADD children might not be prone to engage in or to learn such behaviors because of the children's impulsivity, greater control by immediate consequences, and short attention spans. Once initiated by the ADD child, such behavior may succeed at coercing and controlling others, which would lead to its continued use by the child. While many non-ADD children can learn and exhibit coercive interaction patterns, ADD children may be more prone to develop such patterns because of their behavioral symptoms. Furthermore, it is also possible that the parents of ADD children are more likely to assist inadvertently in the development of coercive behavior by the child because of their own greater impulsiveness, conduct problems, inattention, and use of coercive behaviors with others (Morrison and Stewart, 1971).

Despite the fact that no research seems to be available on the issue, an idea that has been advanced by Meichenbaum (personal communication 1983) has great conceptual and intuitive appeal and might further explain the deterioration of parent-child interaction patterns. Meichenbaum suggests that normal children seem to employ certain behaviors that serve to *de-escalate* negative behavior by the parent toward the child. Children may employ humor, laughter, satire, facial expressions, or even "submissive" behavior (sobbing, pouting, etc.) at times when parents may be angry with them. These may serve to decrease parental negative or punitive behavior. It may prove to be that ADD children are deficient in employing such de-escalating behavior during parental negative interactions or that the parents themselves are less responsive to such behaviors by the children. Whichever is the case, the end result is that negative, angry, coercive exchanges between parent and child escalate further than would be seen in normal family patterns of interaction. Related to this may be the likelihood that not only do parents of ADD children praise or reinforce appropriate child behavior less than those of normal children, but ADD children may show less appreciation and reinforcement of more positive parent reactions toward them. Needless to say, some research on these hypotheses would be important.

It appears that the families of hyperactive or ADD children are fraught with frequent and, at times, intense conflict among family members. Compared to normal, such families engage in more coercive, negative exchanges with high rates of commands by parents and noncompliance by ADD children. Punishment and inconsistent consequences for child behaviors occur more than is normal, while rates of social reinforcement and perhaps even de-escalating responses to conflict are deficient. While the child's symptoms may predispose both the child and the family toward this form of coercion and conflict, there is little doubt that family characteristics, especially parental ones, play a modulating role in the severity or exacerbation of these symptoms.

Relationship to Conduct and Learning Disorders

Probably one of the most controversial areas of exchange among scientists working in this field is whether ADD is simply a part of the general diagnostic category of conduct disorders or is distinguishable from it in certain respects. Shaffer and Greenhill (1979) have argued that both disorders occur more in males, have similar etiologies, have a greater occurrence of family psychiatric disorders, and lead to later maladjustment, alcoholism, academic failure, delinquency, and antisocial behavior to the same extent. Others (Lahey, Green, and Forehand, 1980; Sandberg, Rutter and Taylor, 1978; Shaffer, McNamara, and Pincus, 1974; Stewart, deBlois, and Cummings, 1980) seem to express a similar view or at least some doubt as to the existence of ADD as a separate disorder. In contrast, Barkley (1982), Loney and her colleagues (1980; Paternite and Loney, 1980) and Ross and Ross (1982) view the two disorders as separate yet overlapping conditions wherein the presence of both in a child predicts poorer outcome than if either is alone.

If we accept the definition set forth herein as well as the conceptualization of the disorder offered here and by Douglas (1972, 1980), then it is possible for some degree of separation to exist between these disorders. ADD is viewed as a cognitive handicapping condition of poor attention, impulse control, and the governance of behavior by rules. Conduct disorders involve repetitive and persistent patterns of aggression, antisocial behavior (lying, stealing, destructiveness), violation of social norms, rules, or laws, and usually a disregard for the feelings or well being of others. As Loney has shown (Loney, Langhorne and Paternite, 1978; Loney and Milich, 1981; Milich and Loney, 1979), it is possible for children to have either disorder alone, although as many as 67 percent of ADD children may also display conduct disorders. Others (Campbell, 1975; Firestone and Martin, 1979) provide further evidence of the separability of the disorders. At present, it would seem premature to consider these to be the same disorder when there may prove to be not only a difference in prognosis (Paternite and Loney, 1980), behavioral characteristics (Roberts, Milich, Loney and Caputo, 1981), and early childhood predisposing factors (Sandberg et al., 1978), but also in response to treatment (Loney, Prinz, Mishalow and Joad, 1978).

Similarly, ADD in children may be distinct from, yet overlap with, specific learning disabilities (LD) in children (Safer and Allen, 1976). If one views LD in children as a significant delay in academic achievement relative to expected grade level (Barkley, 1981c; Gaddes, 1980), then it is quite obvious that a child can have LD without ADD, as in dyslexia (Benton and Perl, 1978), or can have ADD without LD, as is often the case (Loney, 1974; Safer and Allen, 1976). Breen and Barkley (1984) have shown that ADD children with or without LD are quite distinguishable from children with only LD in their personality characteristics, while others have shown these two diagnostic groups to differ in mother-child interactions (Campbell, 1975), attentional deficits (Douglas and Peters, 1979), adolescent drug usage (Blouin, Bornstein, and Trites, 1978), and response to stimulant drug therapy (Rie, Rie, Stewart and Ambuel, 1976). For now, it seems worthwhile to view ADD, LD, and conduct disorders as separate psychopathological disorders in childhood that frequently overlap yet have differing effects on adjustment, prognosis, and response to treatment. Some children may have only one disorder, others may have two, and still others may have all three disorders in combination.

ASSESSMENT

Given the view espoused here, the focus of assessment will be on the need to identify the existence of the four primary symptoms (inattention, impulsivity, restlessness, and poor rule-governed behavior), as well as the other defining criteria outlined earlier. A behavioral approach to assessment, viewed as the most efficacious in gathering information (see Barkley, 1981a, 1981b), requires a functional analysis of behavior that is undertaken through interviews and observations. This permits the establishment of the frequency of occurrence of the problem behaviors as well as their situational contexts, antecedents, and consequences (see Mash and Terdal, 1981). Historical information is also sought to assist in differential diagnosis and to establish the duration of problem behaviors. Finally, norm-referenced rating scales are used to establish deviance of the child from developmental patterns of normal children in attention, impulse control, activity level, and compliance/self-control. It is my personal view that the problems with rule-governed behavior are the most salient in creating distress for the child, family, and others, and so they receive the greater emphasis during the evaluation. A brief overview of assessment is provided here, since I have detailed elsewhere (Barkley, 1981a) the purpose and procedures involved. In most cases, the evaluation occurs in a clinic setting but is augmented, when feasible, by direct observations in the home or classroom or by data collected by parents or teachers in those environments.

Interviews

An essential element of the evaluation of ADD children is a thorough interview with the parents, since they or other adults are clearly the ones distressed by the child's behavior and have sought the clinic referral. It is worthwhile to remember in this process that the distress experienced by the parent of an ADD child is not entirely related to the actual severity of that child's problems. In part, marital distress, maternal depression, social isolation (Wahler, 1980), parental psychiatric status, stress in the parental role (Mash and Johnston, 1982), and other setting factors (Wahler and Fox, 1981) will contribute to parent perceptions of child deviance yet may not stem directly from the child's problems. Effort should be made to try to tease out the relative contribution of such factors to the current status of the child and family.

Once the usual demographic data and developmental-medical history of the child are obtained, the clinician spends time with the parents to discuss their primary complaints about the child and is sure to assist parents in specifying precisely what aspects of the child concern them. Parents tend to express vague, general classes of complaints that must be probed in detail to decipher the essential problems the child is posing for the family, classroom, or community. The interview then shifts to a detailed discussion of parent-child interactions in the home during common situations (see Table 5–2), or the parents are given the Home Situations Questionnaire (Table 5–3), which is then discussed with them. The purpose here is to evaluate the degree of compliance problems the child presents and the manner in which the parents respond to them, not to mention the types of rules or commands likely to pose problems for the child. A similar interview occurs with the teacher, using the School Situations Questionnaire (Table 5–4) as a guide to a discussion of social behavior by the child and problems with noncompliance.

In the parental interview, time is spent reviewing the parent's own history and current status as well as that of other children in the family. Does either parent have a history of LD, ADD, conduct disorders, depression, drug abuse or other psychiatric condition? What is the current status of the marriage? What other stress events exist in the family? What is the psychological status of the siblings of the ADD child? How do the siblings interact with the ADD child? These and other questions should be pursued to clarify the family context in which the child interacts.

TABLE 5-2

Parental Interview Format*

situations to be discussed with parents	follow-up questions for each problematic situation
General—overall interactions	1. Is this a problem area? If so, then proceed with questions 2 to 9.
Playing alone	
Playing with other children	2. What does the child do in this situation that bothers you?
Mealtimes	
Getting dressed in morning	3. What is your response?
During washing and bathing	4. What will the child do next?
While parent is on telephone	5. If the problem continues, what will you do next?
While watching television	
While visitors are at home	6. What is usually the outcome of this interaction?
While visiting others' homes	
In public places (supermarkets, shopping center, etc.)	7. How often do these problems occur in this situation?
While mother is occupied with chores or activities	8. How do you feel about these problems.
When father is at home	9. On a scale of 0 to 10 (0 = no problem; 10 = severe problem), how severe is this problem to you?
When child is asked to do a chore	
At bedtime	
Other situations (in car, in church, etc.)	

* Adapted from C. Hanf, University of Oregon Health Sciences, 1976.
Source: R. Barkley, "Hyperactivity," *Behavioral Assessment of Childhood Disorders*, ed. E. Mash & L. Terdal (New York: Guilford Press, 1981). Reprinted with permission. © 1981 by Guilford Press.

TABLE 5-3

Home Situations Questionnaire

NAME OF CHILD _____

NAME OF PERSON COMPLETING THIS FORM _____

Does this child present any behavior problems in any of these situations? If so, indicate how severe they are.

situation	yes/no (circle one)		if yes, how severe? (circle one) mild								severe
While playing alone	YES	NO	1	2	3	4	5	6	7	8	9
While playing with other children	YES	NO	1	2	3	4	5	6	7	8	9
Mealtimes	YES	NO	1	2	3	4	5	6	7	8	9
Getting dressed	YES	NO	1	2	3	4	5	6	7	8	9
Washing/bathing	YES	NO	1	2	3	4	5	6	7	8	9
While you are on the telephone	YES	NO	1	2	3	4	5	6	7	8	9
While watching TV	YES	NO	1	2	3	4	5	6	7	8	9
When visitors are in your home	YES	NO	1	2	3	4	5	6	7	8	9

TABLE 5-3 (concluded)

situation	yes/no (circle one)	mild								severe
					if yes, how severe? (circle one)					
When you are visiting someone else	YES NO	1	2	3	4	5	6	7	8	9
In supermarkets, stores, church, restaurants, or other public places	YES NO	1	2	3	4	5	6	7	8	9
When asked to do chores at home	YES NO	1	2	3	4	5	6	7	8	9
At bedtime	YES NO	1	2	3	4	5	6	7	8	9
While in the car	YES NO	1	2	3	4	5	6	7	8	9
Father at home	YES NO	1	2	3	4	5	6	7	8	9

Sources: R. Barkley, *Hyperactive Children: A Handbook for Diagnosis and Treatment.* (New York: Guilford Press, 1981). © 1981 by Guilford Press.

TABLE 5-4

School Situations Questionnaire

NAME OF CHILD_____

NAME OF PERSON COMPLETING THIS FORM_____

Does this child present any behavior problems for you in any of these situations? If so, indicate how severe they are.

situation	yes/no (circle one)	mild								severe
					if yes, how severe? (circle one)					
While arriving at school	YES NO	1	2	3	4	5	6	7	8	9
During individual desk work	YES NO	1	2	3	4	5	6	7	8	9
During small group activities	YES NO	1	2	3	4	5	6	7	8	9
During free play time in class	YES NO	1	2	3	4	5	6	7	8	9
During lectures to the class	YES NO	1	2	3	4	5	6	7	8	9
At recess	YES NO	1	2	3	4	5	6	7	8	9
At lunch	YES NO	1	2	3	4	5	6	7	8	9
In the hallways	YES NO	1	2	3	4	5	6	7	8	9
In the bathroom	YES NO	1	2	3	4	5	6	7	8	9
On field trips	YES NO	1	2	3	4	5	6	7	8	9
During special assemblies	YES NO	1	2	3	4	5	6	7	8	9
On the bus	YES NO	1	2	3	4	5	6	7	8	9

Source: R. Barkley, *Hyperactive Children: A Handbook for Diagnosis and Treatment.* (New York: Guilford Press, 1981). Reprinted with permission. © 1981 by Guilford Press.

Some time is always taken to interview the child, although the value of such an interview is limited by the frequent lack of appreciation or insight ADD children have about their problems. Nonetheless, the child's view of school, home, and community problems is important to obtain when possible. Such an interview also permits a brief observation of physical, language, and social characteristcs about the child that are gleaned from this first-hand interaction.

Rating Scales

Parents and teachers are then requested to complete several child behavior rating scales, which have factors that appear to assess the major symptoms of the ADD child. I am likely to use the Conners Parent Questionnaire (Goyette, Conners, and Ulrich, 1978), the Home Situations Questionnaire (Barkley, 1981a), and the Child Behavior Profile (Achenbach, 1978), which the parents complete. Other scales, such as the Werry-Weiss-Peters Activity Rating Scale (see Barkley, 1981a), the Personality Inventory for Children (Wirt, Lachar and Klinedinst, 1977), and many others could be used, although their information is redundant to some extent with the other rating scales noted above. Teachers are given the Conners Teacher Questionnaire (Goyette et al., 1978) and the School Situations Questionnaire (Barkley, 1981a). These parent and teacher questionnaires are used primarily to establish the child's deviance from normal in the behaviors of concern as well as to clarify their situational contexts and pervasiveness. They may also be readministered periodically throughout treatment to assess degree of change and continued deviance from normal children. Further discussion on the use of these scales can be found in Barkley (1981a).

Many behavioral clinicians and scientists recognize the role of contextual factors in child behavior problems (Wahler and Fox, 1981), yet these may be difficult to assess. I have found it useful to evaluate marital discord, level of maternal depression, stress in the parental role, and key stress events in the family through the use of parent completed rating scales. The Beck Depression Inventory (Beck, 1972), the Marital Adjustment Inventory (Manson and Lerner, 1962), the Parent Stress Index (Abidin and Burke, 1978), and the Family Problems Inventory (Barkley, 1981a) have been useful in this regard, although other similar questionnaires could be substituted.

Direct Observations

When time and resources permit, it is often helpful to obtain direct behavioral observations of the problem behaviors of concern to the family or teacher. In this case, observations of the child's interactions with his parents, especially during task accomplishment periods, is useful in revealing the rate, intensity, style, and other aspects of the child's noncompliance and difficulties with sustained attention as well as the parent's manner of reacting to these problems. We would observe mothers with their ADD children in a clinic playroom and provide the mother with a list of commands to have her child perform. Observations are made via a one-way mirror or are video taped. Often, introducing another parent or a sibling into the room with the mother and child can elicit further interaction problems from the ADD child. This clinic analogue setting is discussed more fully in Barkley (1981a).

Behavioral recording methods that are used focus on commands, praise, and negative behaviors by the parent and compliance, play, and disruptive behavior by the child. I have found the recording procedures of Mash, Terdal and Anderson (1973) and those of Forehand and McMahon (1981) to be quite useful in assessing these interactions. These observations can also be taken in the home during times when problem behaviors are most likely to occur. The Home Situations Questionnaire can help in selecting which settings are the most problematic and the best to observe.

These same procedures can be used to directly observe the interactions of the child with his teacher. However, the Stony Brook Coding System is often more useful (see Tonick, Friehling, and Warhit, 1973; Abikoff, Gittelman-Klein and Klein, 1977) in sampling child behaviors that are likely to prove distressing to the teacher and that can be construed as forms of noncompliant behavior. Such categories as interference, off-task, gross motor movement, out-of-seat, aggression, day dreaming, extended verbalization, and others are recorded using a 15-second time-sampling procedure. The system has satisfactory intercoder agreement and is sensitive to drug and behavior therapies.

Parent/Teacher Recordings

One of the most efficient ways of getting frequent information on child behavior, especially as interventions are implemented and progress, is to request parents or teachers to use simple record-keeping methods to track the target behavior(s) of interest. Parents may keep a diary of child noncompliance to parent commands in a specific home situation, such as getting dressed for school, having been asked to do chores, etc. The parent may record the command given, the number of times it had to be repeated, and what the parent eventually did (if anything) to gain compliance. Teachers may keep similar diaries of on-task behavior during individual seat work, number of problems completed during math or reading, or any other behavior of interest. Sometimes, parents or teachers may tape record a given interaction with a child each day for later decoding by the examiner. This has the added advantage of capturing the intensity of a negative or noncompliant interaction with the child rather than just the frequency data.

Psychometric Tests

ADD children often display below average academic performance, making it necessary to determine whether specific learning disabilities may also be present, which further affect school performance. It is not the purpose of this chapter to discuss the assessment of learning disabilities in children. The reader is referred to Barkley (1981c), Gaddes (1980), or the chapter by Lahey in this text for a further discussion of this issue. Suffice it to say here that ADD children may require assessment with intellectual, academic, motor, spatial, and drawing-copying tests to assist in determining the contribution of potential academic deficits to current adjustment problems.

Assessment: Summary

The above should suggest that the evaluation of ADD children combines a variety of different assessment methods not only to gain a functional analysis of the current behavior problems, but also to establish their age of onset, duration, and deviation from normal development. Parent, teacher, and child interviews are combined with child behavior rating scales, questionnaires on parent and family characteristics, and direct observations of the child's social behavior with others so as to appreciate the social context in which the child's problem behaviors occur. Parents and teachers may also collect behavioral data using diaries, structured data collection forms, or even tape recordings of interactions of interest. Of course, these assessment methods will be taken periodically throughout therapy to determine the success of the interventions.

TREATMENTS

To date, research on the long-term effects of various interventions for ADD have proven most disappointing in altering the outcome of the child and family. Many interventions can produce short-term gains or improvements, but these may dissipate by follow-up one or two years later. Many experts now accept the fact that ADD is a chronic disorder that presently is not likely to be cured by current therapies. Nonetheless, substantial reductions in ADD symptoms, especially noncompliance, can be achieved, provided that parents and teachers have time and motivation to continue using the procedures after training is complete.

Numerous therapies for ADD children have been proposed, but many have not withstood close experimental scrutiny. Dietary treatments, biofeedback, relaxation training, elimination of allergies or fluorescent lighting, and other interventions of this sort either have not been experimentally validated, or, where they have been studied, have been found to produce minimal or no therapeutic change (Barkley, 1981a; Conners, 1980; Ross and Ross, 1976, 1982). The most useful treatments at this time involve training parents in child behavior management principles and techniques, stimulant medication, classroom behavior therapy methods (see chapters by Walker and Lahey in this volume), and self-control training of the child. These will be reviewed briefly below. (Each is more thoroughly discussed in the text by Barkley [1981a], and research on them is reviewed in some detail by Ross and Ross, [1976, 1982]).

Stimulant Drug Treatment

Stimulant drugs are frequently used to treat ADD children. As many as 600,000 children each year are given stimulant drugs for behavior management (Cantwell and Carlson, 1978, Gadow, 1981), making it the most frequently used therapy for ADD in children. In many cases, however, drugs are used as part of a treatment package that involves training parents to use different approaches in managing child behavior and/or alteration of the child's educational program to more effectively teach the child. In other cases, these additional therapies are lacking, and the child is left with prescriptions as the only form of intervention. (The reader interested in detailed information on drug therapy is referred to the excellent text by Werry [1978] and the specific chapter by Cantwell and Carlson [1978]. Other reviews are available by Barkley [1976, 1977a], Conners and Werry [1979], Sroufe [1975], and Whalen and Henker [1976]).

The most commonly used drugs for ADD are Ritalin (methylphenidate), Dexedrine (D-amphetamine), and Cylert (pemoline). They are rapidly acting compounds that begin to produce changes in behavior between 20 and 60 minutes after oral ingestion; peak within 90 minutes to three hours; and finish therapeutic effects generally within four to eight hours, depending on which drugs are used and whether the slow release spansules or standard versions are employed. Side effects from the drugs may persist beyond eight hours after ingestion but are usually over within 24 hours.

The major effect of these drugs is on concentration and sustained attention. As a result, compliance with requests and parent-child interactions may also improve, especially during task situations (Barkley and Cunningham, 1980). Decreases in impulsiveness are frequently seen, as are decreases in disruptiveness and task-irrelevant activity level. Intelligence or academic achievement (knowledge) are not usually improved (Barkley, 1977a; Barkley and Cunningham, 1978), although time-on-task and academic productivity may increase (Ayllon, Layman and Kandel, 1975) in some cases. The drugs seem most useful as managers of disruptive behavior and have not, as yet, been shown to affect the adolescent or young adult outcome of ADD children (Cantwell and Carlson, 1978; Paternite and Loney, 1980). The drugs may be used throughout childhood and adolescence, although their use seems to diminish as children approach adolescence. Perhaps this is the result of the unfounded belief by many clinicians that ADD children outgrow their problems by adolescence or that stimulant drugs are no longer effective at this age. My own experience suggests that getting adolescents to use the drug, especially on any consistent basis, is quite difficult, and many, given the choice, seem to prefer not to use them. The effects of stimulants on ADD children are no longer believed to be paradoxical since normal children show changes in behavior in the same direction as ADD children (Rapoport et al., 1978). Interest in using these drugs with adults with a chronic history of behavior disorders suggestive of ADD is increasing with the recent demonstration by Wender and his colleagues (Wender, Reimherr and Wood, 1981), which showed that many such adults might respond well to stimulant drugs.

Research on predicting drug responding (Barkley, 1976; Ross and Ross, 1982) suggests that degree of inattention is the most consistently useful predictor of a positive response. However, factors, such as family disorganization, number of other problems associated with ADD in the child, level of intelligence, presence of neurological damage, and presence of nervous tics may, with more careful research on the issue, be shown to be related to drug response. Some evidence is accruing that indicates that level of anxiety in the ADD child predicts a poorer response to stimulants (Fish, 1971; Voelker et al., 1983).

All of the stimulants produce side effects, and some are unique to each drug that is employed. Insomnia and decreased appetite are the most commonly cited. Late afternoon irritability, dysphoric mood, tics, nervous habits, headaches, stomachaches, and a proneness to crying also develop in some children. The number and severity of side effects seems to be dose related, although the development of tics may also be related to duration of therapy. Positive responses to the drugs appear age related: few children younger than four years of age respond well, while 75 percent of those over five years of age show a positive response. Side effects are also likely to be age related, although few studies have looked at age as a variable in drug responding.

Some studies have examined the utility of combining stimulants with behavior therapy procedures or of the comparative efficacy of each used alone. The results are related to the rigor of the design of these studies as well as to the types of measures examined. Both procedures appear to be equally effective at improving restlessness and attention span in the classroom, as well as compliance to parental requests and ratings of child behavior in the home (Gittelman-Klein, Abikoff, Pollack, Klein, Katz and Mattes, 1980; Pollard, Ward and Barkley, 1983; Wolraich, Drummond, Soloman, O'Brien, and Sivage, 1978). However, behavior therapy techniques appear more useful at increasing academic accuracy and productivity (Ayllon et al., 1975), as well as parental reinforcement of appropriate child behavior (Pollard, et al., 1983). As others have stated (Mash and Dalby, 1979), the issue is not simply which behavior therapies are better, but which may be more useful for what types of children, of what ages, in what situations, and for what types of behavior.

Parent Training Program

Although there have been many demonstrations that behavior modification applied directly to ADD children by experimenters can produce short-term improvements in ADD symptoms, most serious investigators now recognize that parents and teachers in the child's natural environment should be the ones to learn and use these methods with the ADD child (see Barkley, 1981a; Mash and Dalby, 1979; Ross and Ross, 1982). Many different programs exist for training parents in child management skills (Mash, Handy and Hamerlynck, 1976a, 1976b), but all seem to have in common the belief that teaching parents a more consistent, immediate, and appropriate use of consequences following appropriate or inappropriate child behavior is the best method. Most of these programs have not been applied to children specifically diagnosed as ADD, so their effectiveness with this group is hard to judge. Clearly, the methods to be taught to parents and the target behaviors for which they are to be used depend on what the core difficulties of the ADD child are thought to be by the clinician. As noted earlier, I believe noncompliance or poor rule-governed behavior to be a primary deficit in these children, and so, our program focuses heavily on this problem. The reader is referred to Mash and Dalby (1979) for a critical review of behavior therapy for ADD children, to the text by Ross and Ross (1982) for a review of most therapeutic approaches to this disorder, and to Barkley (1981a) for a detailed explication of the parent training program outlined below.

The principles of the program we employ in our clinic derive from the work of Hanf (1969) and of Forehand and his students (see Forehand and McMahon, 1981 for a review) on training parents to improve child compliance to commands and rules. The procedures have been elaborated and slightly modified for the particular problems of ADD children but, in many respects, parallel the original program (see Wells and Forehand chapter in this text). There are essentially 10 steps in the program, and each builds on the previous ones. The goals of the program are to increase parents' knowledge of ADD in children, parent-child relations, and behavior change techniques. Obviously, through teaching, practice, and homework, it is hoped that actual improvements in child behavior will occur. A similar program, modified for classroom behavior problems, may also be taught to regular or special education teachers.

Step 1: Information on ADD. We believe that parents, more than anyone, require accurate up-to-date information on the nature, etiology, course, prognosis and treatments for ADD in children. Much of what is available to them through the popular media and press is inaccurate and emphasizes recent fads for treating ADD. We believe parents need an opportunity to discuss questions, misconceptions, rumors, etc. with an *informed* professional who has stayed reasonably well read about the disorder. At the very least, clinicians undertaking this program should be familiar with the texts by Ross and Ross (1976, 1982). This first session follows a lecture-discussion format acquainting parents with the information available on ADD.

Step 2: Understanding Parent-Child Relations. Next, parents are provided with a discussion on Bell's theory (Bell and Harper, 1977) of parent-child interactions to better understand how family interactions have reached their current status. Patterson's theory (1976, 1982) is also integrated with Bell's to discuss how children learn to coerce parents out of placing demands on them and why simply ignoring such coercive behaviors often does not succeed at changing them. Bell's theory is presented in laypersons terms, using illustrations from the text by Barkley (1981a). It discusses the role of parental expectations or limits in determining how and when parents will respond to unacceptable child behavior. The notion that certain classes of child behavior elicit from parents certain types of control reactions toward the child is also reviewed. This often helps parents to see why, many times, they react to a difficult child with more control, direction, and supervision than is used with a normal child. The role played by background or family factors in potentially exacerbating parent-ADD child relations is discussed, and an inventory is taken with the parents of potential stressors in the current family situation. Parents are encouraged to make plans as to how they will address, resolve, or cope with the identified stress events. Following Patterson's view, parents are instructed as to how a typical coercive interaction with a child might progress and why such exchanges become more frequent if the child is even partially successful at avoiding commands or undesired situations.

Step 3: Developing and Enhancing Parental Attention to Child Behavior. Patterson (1976) has shown that parental praise, attention, and other types of reinforcement are not especially valuable to a deviant child and are unlikely to be successful in altering child behavior if used as a consequence. Forehand (Forehand and McMahon, 1981) has also shown that parents of deviant children profit from training in differentially attending to appropriate versus inappropriate child behavior. This session, therefore, focuses on teaching parents better methods and styles of commenting upon, praising, and attending to child behavior. Through practice during play each day with the child, parents learn to attend to positive behavior while ignoring less acceptable behavior by the child.

Step 4: Reinforcing Compliance and Independent Play. Once parents demonstrate the ability to attend effectively to child behaviors during play, they are asked to begin using this method of attending to other types of child behavior (dressing, eating, chore performance, child-sibling interactions, etc.). Specifically, parents are taught how to give effective commands to the child and how to praise and attend to compliance when it occurs. However, no instruction is given yet in how to deal with noncompliance other than to ignore it and to focus on other commands the child does follow. Parents are simply being taught to differentially attend to compliance by the child.

One form of noncompliance parents often complain of is the ADD child's inability to play alone for a certain time, permitting parents to complete chores or projects (talking on the phone, cooking, speaking to visitors, reading, etc.). To deal with this, parents are specifically trained to attend to, shape, and further develop independent play by the child when parents are busy with activities. The process is simply a differential reinforcement of low rates (DRL) schedule, in which parents initially provide frequent praise to the child for short periods of not interrupting (independent play). Praise is then provided progressively less often as the period in which children must play by themselves to get the attention is gradually lengthened.

Step 5: Establishing the Home Token System. This session is included in training because praise and attention are not always sufficiently motivating to an ADD child to increase compliance. Furthermore, parents are not especially effective or consistent in allotting privileges and other reinforcers to the ADD child. Setting up a home token system is a simple matter that draws upon virtually all privileges available to the child to reinforce compliance and also serves to reduce the arbitrariness by which parents dispense privileges to an ADD child. In other words, it can be a very effective way to better organize parental reactions to child behavior.

The system used is similar to that by Christophersen, Barnard and Barnard (1981) in which children between the ages of four and seven are given plastic poker chips for compliance and other desirable behavior, which are then exchanged for privileges. Children eight years and older are provided points for compliance, which are recorded in a notebook kept like a checkbook register. These children spend their points for privileges, and the points are deducted from the book. The therapist assists parents and children in drawing up a list of chores and a separate list of privileges. The amount to be paid for each chore is determined as is the price for each privilege. Parents may also give bonus chips or points to the child for his attitude while doing a chore or command, for not engaging in a particular antisocial behavior (not lying, stealing, no aggression, etc.) during a fixed period of time, and for doing jobs or chores without being formally told to do so. The chips or points are not to be taken away as penalties in this step for inappropriate behavior.

Step 6: Using Time-Out and Response Cost for Noncompliance. In this session, parents are now permitted to deduct chips/points for noncompliance or inappropriate behavior. Previously, if the child failed to comply, he simply earned no chips or points. Now, noncompliance results in penalties or deductions in chips/points. Parents are instructed in how to use this response-cost procedure fairly and effectively.

Then, parents are trained in the use of a time-out technique, similar to that used by Forehand (Forehand and McMahon, 1981) and discussed in detail in the text by Barkley (1981a). Initially, parents focus on using time-out for only one or two types of noncompliance in the home (aggression, not dressing for school, not picking up toys, etc.), preventing the child from excessive punishment and allowing the parent to practice the technique without being overwhelmed with the job of addressing all forms of misbehavior at once.

Step 7: Extending Time-Out to Other Noncompliant Behavior at Home.
This session merely extends the method taught in step 6 to other misbehaviors
occurring at home. If there remain multiple types of misbehavior by the child
or if parents do not seem to be satisfactorily using time-out as directed, they may
be permitted to use it with only one or two additional misbehaviors by the child.
Otherwise, they may now extend its use to any noncompliance at home they
believe warrants this consequence, remembering that the response cost method
is available for minor transgressions.

Step 8: Coping with Public Misbehavior by the Child.   This session teaches
parents how to slightly modify the previously taught methods for use in stores,
restaurants, church, others' homes, or other public places. Here, emphasis is
placed on teaching parents to anticipate what type of misbehavior may occur and
how they will deal with it *before* going into the public place. For instance,
before entering a store, the parent and child remain on the sidewalk while: (1)
the parent reviews the rules of behavior the child is to follow; (2) the child
repeats them back; (3) the parent explains to the child the incentive to be given
for compliance (praise, chips, etc.); and (4) the parent explains the punishment
that will be used for noncompliance. The parent and child now enter the store
and the parent immediately begins differentially attending to compliance with
rules.

Step 9: Review of Methods and Principles.   This session is used to review
with parents the key procedures and concepts of the program and to assist them
in trouble-shooting continuing interaction problems they may be having, as well
as to have *them* think of how these methods could be used to address the
problem. In brief, this session focuses on making parents problem-solvers when
noncompliant behavior begins to emerge now or in the future with an ADD
child.

Step 10: Booster Session.   One to two months later, parents are asked to return
for follow-up to assess how well the methods continue to be used and whether
the chips/points system should be continued or be gradually faded out.

Limitations of the Program.   The process explained above relies heavily on
the therapist's ability to communicate the procedures and concepts to the parents
in simple, understandable terms without relying too much on reading by the
parents. Where applicable, the therapist also models the method under discussion in that session, and gets parents to practice the procedure in the session.
Homework is then assigned, and parents may have some simple record-keeping
to do to insure the homework is done.

There are, admittedly, certain families that are less likely to succeed in such
a program. Research by Wahler (1980), Forehand and McMahon (1981), Patterson (1976, 1982), and many others (see Mash et al., 1976a, 1976b) suggest

certain predictors of failure in parent training programs. The extent to which mothers are isolated from typical community and social support networks, low socioeconomic status, severe marital discord, maternal depression, serious parental psychopathology, severe antisocial behavior by the child, and severe stress in the parental role all correlate to varying degrees with outcome in parent training. In fact, research by Firestone (Firestone and Witt, 1982) suggests that published reports of treatment efficacy for parent training and stimulant medication may be overly optimistic since these studies often fail to report the extent of subject attrition during treatment. As a result, those families finishing therapy can be expected to have a better outcome or to have been more responsive to training initially. The data on those who fail to complete training go unreported, and these are often the more refractory cases. An excessively positive report of treatment effectiveness is often the result.

Our experience with this parent training program suggests it can be used with children as young as two years of age (excluding the chip system) and for most children up to 10 to 12 years of age, with some clinical judgment and common sense being used with older children. Beyond this age, it is often necessary to involve the child as an active participant in family therapy, as opposed to the methods taught to the parents with the child as a passive recipient. For ADD adolescents, we will frequently use the program developed by Robin (1981) that trains both the parents and teenager in problem-solving skills to be used in reducing family conflict. The reader is also directed to writings on Achievement Place (Kirigin, Braukmann, Atwater and Wolf, 1982) for further suggestions in dealing with this quite difficult age group.

In conjunction with parent training, parents may need to receive marriage counseling, stress management training, psychotherapy or medications for their personal psychiatric problems given the increased occurrence of family psychopathology in ADD children. For a variety of reasons, some ADD children are so severe in their deviant behavior that outpatient therapy simply will not suffice. Such children may require placement in foster care, day psychiatric hospitals, or inpatient residential treatment centers. Once their behavior comes under greater control and efforts are made to reintegrate them with the family, this parent training program might then be employed.

Training in Self-Control

Another approach to treating ADD children has been direct instruction in learning to control their own behavior. Self-control training of this sort often involves teaching the child to:

1. Recognize problem situations.
2. Delay responding in the problem setting.
3. Engage in self-directed speech to help the child:
    a. Further clarify and define the problem.

    b. Generate possible solutions.
    c. Consider short- and long-term consequences for the solutions.
    d. Select the most effective solution.
4. Implement the best solution.
5. Evaluate his performance.
6. Engage in self-reinforcement for displaying self-control.

Theoretically, such an approach would seem to address part of the problems ADD children have with rule-governed behavior, i.e., self-control and problem solving. The research to date, however, has shown mixed or even disappointing results. The reader is referred to the work of Camp (1980), Douglas (1980), Kendall (1981), and Ross and Ross (1982) for further elaboration or critical reviews of this research. Most of the studies have used direct instruction of the child in these methods by the experimenter or by a teacher in an experimental classroom. To date, none have tried to teach parents how to train their children in such procedures and how to sustain its use by the children. Early reports (Bornstein and Quevillon, 1976; Meichenbaum and Goodman, 1971; Palkes, Stewart and Kahana, 1968) were quite positive in demonstrating improved behavior and self-control in impulsive children, especially on laboratory or academic tasks. Later reports (Barkley, Copeland and Sivage, 1980; Cohen, Sullivan, Mincle, Novak and Helwig, 1981; Douglas, Parry, Marton and Garson, 1976) have found few or no lasting results from such programs and little generalization outside of the training situation.

Failures in these training procedures can result from a number of circumstances that deserve more research attention than they have received to date. As Ross and Ross (1982) have noted, many programs are too narrow in scope, fail to teach the child the concept of self-control other than simple exercises in it, and often do not use the methods in the actual settings in which self-control is a problem for the child (i.e. regular classroom, playground, neighborhood). The age of the child, level of mental development, presence of environmental consequences for self-control, and other variables may be important in how well a child acquires these skills (see Copeland, 1981; Harris and Ferrari, 1983 for reviews).

Space does not permit the complete elaboration of how to train ADD children in these procedures. However, two approaches to self-control are outlined in Tables 5–5 and 5–6 as developed by Douglas (1980) and Kendall (1981), respectively. Obviously, such programs are complex and intensive, requiring a skilled therapist to be successful. The cost effectiveness of such procedures is an issue yet to be investigated. It would seem that if such procedures could be simplified sufficiently so that parents could be trained to implement them with the ADD child, more enduring results might be forthcoming.

One issue related to these procedures, yet without any research to date, is the idea described earlier from Meichenbaum (personal communication) that ADD children as well as their parents may be less skilled in the ways that normal

TABLE 5-5

Levels of Training Children in Self-Control

*Level I. Helping children understand the nature of their deficits and
the ways in which training can help.*

1. Providing an explanation of the nature of the children's attentional, inhibitory, and arousal-modulating deficits.
2. Helping the children recognize how these deficits affect their daily functioning and create problems for them.
3. Convincing them that the deficits can be modified and motivating them to share actively in the process.
4. Introducing the children to the basic elements of the cognitive training approach.

*Level II: Strengthening the children's motivation and capacity to deal with
the problem-solving role.*

1. Providing success experiences within the training sessions by the following means:
    Breaking tasks into component parts.
    Presenting tasks in gradually increasing order of difficulty.
    Tailoring teaching material to children's individual capacities.
    Providing systematic reviews of material covered.
2. Arranging success experiences at home and school by doing the following:
    Helping parents and teachers organize demands made on children to coincide with their ability to meet these demands successfully.
    Encouraging parents and teachers to reward genuine attempts at mastery, as well as successes.
3. Teaching the children general rules for approaching tasks, including the following:
    Defining task demands accurately.
    Assessing one's own relevant knowledge and/or the available cues in a situation or problem.
    Considering all possible solutions.
    Evaluating relative effectiveness of solutions considered.
    Checking work carefully.
4. Discouraging passivity and encouraging independent effort by doing the following:
    Addressing children with titles like "Chief Problem Solver"
    Discouraging undue dependence on trainers.
    Discouraging mimicking of trainers' strategies or parroting of instructions; encouraging children to produce their own strategies and to restate instructions in their own words.
    Shifting responsibility for correcting work and administering rewards to children themselves.
    Helping children learn to differentiate between careless errors and errors that reflect genuine problems with understanding.
5. Making children aware of any behaviors and attitudes on their part that interfere with problem solving:
    Drawing their attention to flagging attention or "hyped up" behavior.
    Discouraging excessive talking.
    Reminding them to "work beyond" superficial aspects of a situation or problem.
    Discourage unreasonably low criteria for success.

Level III: Teaching specific problem-solving strategies.

1. Modeling and teaching strategies directed toward improving attention and concentration. These strategies might include the following:
    Organized and exhaustive scanning techniques.
    Focusing strategies.
    Checking for critical factors.
    Careful listening for essential information.
2. Teaching strategies and offering management suggestions directed toward increasing inhibitory control and developing organizational skills. This might be accomplished by doing the following:

TABLE 5-5 (*concluded*)

Teaching the children to sit on their hands until they have thought through possible solutions.
Encouraging parents and teachers to provide special places for keeping important materials and helping the children remember to use them.
Encouraging the use of special notebooks for classroom assignments; keeping notebooks in special places.
Modeling the use of lists for events or assignments to be remembered, necessary materials to be assembled for projects, clothes and books to be laid out for following day.
3. Teaching strategies and offering management suggestions directed toward improved control of the children's level of alertness and arousal. These might include the following:
Labeling of arousal states
Teaching the children to exhort or calm themselves using verbal self-commands.
Suggesting interesting "breaks" between periods of concentrated work.
Being sensitive to the fact that children may need stimulation to combat boredom.
4. Teaching other specific strategies children have failed to learn:
Rehearsal strategies and mnemonic devices.
Strategies required for particular academic activities (e.g., steps involved in adding fractions or in writing an essay).

Source: V. I. Douglas, "Treatment and Training Approaches to Hyperactivity: Establishing Internal or External Control," *Hyperactive Children: The Social Ecology of Identification and Treatment*, Eds. C. K. Whalen & B. Henker (New York: Academic Press, 1981). Reprinted with permission. © 1980 by Academic Press.

TABLE 5-6

Description of the Task and Highlights of the 12-Session Cognitive-Behavioral Program for Self-Control

session	task	highlights
1	"Which one comes next?"	Introduction to self-instructions, response-cost contingency, self-evaluation and bonus chip systems, and reward menu; overt Verbal Self-Instruction (VSI); concrete labeling of response cost; assign homework project.
2	"Following directions"	Review self-instructions and homework project; overt VSI for majority of session, begin fading process to whispered VSI with final 2–3 tasks; concrete labeling.
3	"Specific skills series"	Review self-instructions (especially coping statements) and homework

TABLE 5–6 (*concluded*)

session	task	highlights
		assignment; encourage rephrasing of VSI to curb rote memorization, continue fading process with whispered VSI, some overt; begin conceptual labeling with final 1–2 errors.
4	"The little professor math skills"	Encourage rephrasing of VSI and note additional step possible with a new task; whispered VSI, conceptual labeling; child begins self-evaluation.
5	"The little professor math games"	First interpersonal task; homework project reviewed: example of when the child actually used the 5 steps outside of therapy; whispered VSI, begin fading to covert VSI; conceptual labeling.
6	"Tangram puzzles"	Continue fading from whispered to covert VSI; conceptual labeling; emphasis on coping model, copying statements during diffcult tasks.
7	Checkers	Covert, occasionally whispered VSI; conceptual labeling; inquiry into specific classroom/home problems.
8	"Cat and mouse"	Last of interpersonal-play sessions; homework assignment for next time: example of using VSI in social/ interpersonal situation; covert; occasionally whispered VSI; conceptual labeling.
9	Identifying emotions	First session related directly to interpersonal problem-solving; mixture of VSI (i.e., overt and covert), modification of steps; probing by therapist when necessary; conceptual labeling.
10	Hypothetical situations: "What would happen if?"	Rephrasing/adjustment of VSI for new problem-solving situation; mixture of VSI; conceptual labeling.
11	Role playing: hypothetical situations	Role-playing of social situations, both "created" and "real"; mixture of VSI; conceptual labeling.
12	Role playing: real-life situations	Role-playing of child's real problems; mixture of VSI; conceptual labeling; child pretends to teach therapy procedures to another child.

Source: P. Kendall, "Cognitive-behavioral interventions with children," *Advances in Clinical Child Psychology*, Vol. 4. Eds., B. Lahey & A. Kazdin (New York: Plenum Press, 1981). Reprinted with permission. © 1981 by Plenum Press.

children and parents use to de-escalate a potentially negative, explosive, or intensely emotional situation with each other. Perhaps training children to use smiles, praise, affection, appreciation, regretful remarks and so on toward their parents might serve to defuse potentially escalating and negative encounters. Training parents to do similar things when confronted with inappropriate child behavior might also serve to keep emotional reactions under control so that more rational approaches to the problem could be contemplated and exercised. In short, how do normal children avert or de-escalate negative encounters with parents, how do normal parents similarly de-escalate confrontations toward children, and can these be taught to ADD children and their parents?

Home-Based Reinforcement Methods

All of the procedures described above require a certain degree of adult supervision of the child in the situation in which the child's problems occur. But how might one attempt to control behaviors that occur outside of adult supervision? It is assumed that self-control training might be internalized by the child and used elsewhere, but support for this idea is weak. One way is to provide the child with a record or evaluation form that goes with him and is completed by others who will be involved in the setting where the child is going. Virtually all such previous procedures have involved the child being evaluated at school with a report card sent home; parents then provide consequences based on the quality of the evaluation by the teacher. Atkinson and Forehand (1979) have provided a critical review of this method deserving of the reader's attention if such procedures are to be used.

An example of a home-based reinforcement program used in our clinic is displayed in Figure 5–5. The child takes this report card to school each day and is evaluated by each teacher or at the end of each class or subject. Four areas of behavior are evaluated, although others can be added or made more specific to the type of problem the child has in that setting. Teachers are to initial the card and make comments on the back if necessary. Each area of behavior is rated on a scale of 1 (excellent) to 5 (terrible). When taken home, the card is reviewed by the parents and discussed with the child. Points or chips then are awarded or taken away for each number on the card, and the net points earned is then used by the child to purchase privileges at home, similar to the home token system discussed earlier. The more positive the rating, the more points are given. Ratings of four or five usually result in deducted points. Penalties exist for failure to get all teachers to fill out the card, for forgeries, or for failure to bring the card home.

There is no reason why similar report cards could not be used when the child leaves home to play at a friend's home, to go to a club or organization meeting, or to go to sports practice. The behavior categories to be rated by others could be made specific to the setting where the child goes and the kinds of problems

FIGURE 5-5

A Daily School Report Card Used as Part of a Home-based Reinforcement Program for Improving Classroom Behavior in Hyperactive Children

DAILY STUDENT RATING CARD

NAME _____ DATE _____

Please rate this child in each of the areas listed below as to how he performed in school today using ratings of 1 to 5. 1 = excellent, 2 = good, 3 = fair, 4 = poor, 5 = terrible or did not work.

AREA	CLASS PERIODS / SUBJECTS					
	1	2	3	4	5	6
participation						
class work						
handed in homework						
interaction with other children						
teacher's initials						

Place comments on back if needed:

Source: R. Barkley, *Hyperactive Children: A Handbook for Diagnosis and Treatment* (New York: Guilford Press, 1981). Reprinted with permission. © by Guilford Press.

previously shown there. Such a procedure can obviously be used in conjunction with any or all of the treatments just discussed.

CASE ILLUSTRATION

Sean, six years, 11 months old, was referred by his teacher and pediatrician for evaluation of behavior problems and poor school performance. He was attending a parochial school and was in the middle of his first-grade year. The parents were both 33 years of age, with the father having a high school education and the mother having quit school after 10th grade. The father was employed as a toolmaker, and the mother was a housewife. There was an older daughter, 14 years of age, said to be satisfactorily adjusted.

The developmental history was remarkable for occasional use of Librium by the mother during pregnancy. The child was born one month postmature at 9 pounds, 10 ounces without significant delivery complications. Medical history in early childhood was significant only for frequent upper respiratory infections. Walking unassisted developed by 14 months. Speech was late, emerging at two and a half years for simple words but rapidly developing thereafter. The child first showed signs of overactivity, restlessness, and difficulty "settling down" between two to three years of age. By the mother's report, the child had little trouble with kindergarten but was viewed as immature, inattentive, overactive, and hard to control by entry into the first grade.

Both at home and school, Sean was quite noncompliant, obeying less than 2 out of 10 commands on the average when initially requested of him. Instructions and rules were repeated often to Sean with minimal compliance occurring. The parents often found themselves interacting with the child in a high rate, negative, and intense manner, with Sean frequently throwing tantrums in response to a request. Low tolerance for frustration as well as proneness to anger and crying were also reported. In addition to compliance problems, Sean was enuretic nightly and encopretic with an average frequency of two to three soiling accidents per week.

The scores on the child behavior rating scales placed Sean over two standard deviations above the mean on the Hyperactivity Index of the Conners Parent and Teacher Questionnaires. The profile on the Child Behavior Checklist indicated significantly deviant elevations on scales assessing hyperactivity, aggression, delinquency, and social withdrawal. On the Home Situations Questionnaire, Sean was rated by his parents as posing behavior problems in 12 of the 16 situations, with the most severe occurring while parents were on the telephone, when visitors were in the home, in public places (i.e. stores), and when visiting others. His mean severity score across all behavior problem settings was 5.9 on a scale of 0 (no problem) to 9 (severe problem).

Psychometric testing done by the school staff indicated Sean had an IQ estimate of 125, falling in the superior range of abilities. Academic tests revealed the child to be at or above current grade level in math, reading, spelling, and handwriting with no evidence of specific learning disabilities. Teacher reports indicated Sean was underachieving in class relative to his actual abilities, with the greatest problems of failure to finish assignments, short attention span, talking out in class at inappropriate times, demanding of attention from teacher, restlessness, and disruptive of other children's activities. Despite his intellect, he was viewed as childish, immature, self-centered, and prone to temper tantrums in the class and at recess. If his behavior did not improve, the parochial school staff would recommend transfer of Sean to a program for emotionally disturbed children in the public school.

The mother's self-report ratings on the Beck Depression Inventory were significantly deviant, as were both her and her husband's ratings on the Marital

Satisfaction Inventory. Marital discord was particularly salient in those areas related to child rearing issues. Stress events in the family appeared to be health problems with the mother (obesity, gallbladder disorders, ulcers), employment issues with the father (risk of job layoff), financial matters (overextension on credit cards and bank loan), and problems with relatives (criticism of family's approach to handling Sean's problems). There was no evidence of alcohol or drug abuse in the parents, and they both seemed to have some social activities and friends outside the home, despite a reduction in these activities caused by Sean's unmanageable behavior.

The mother and child were observed for 15 minutes of free play and 25 minutes of task accomplishment in a clinic playroom with observation facilities. Table 5–7 shows the measures derived from the Response Class Matrix as well as the mean and standard deviation on each measure for local, normal children of this age. The results suggest that, in free play, the child was less responsive to his mother's interactions, less compliant with her request or commands, and more negative than normal children. His mother was more directive than normal and more controlling of the child's play. In the task period, problems with noncompliance by the child, lower durations of compliance, and higher levels of maternal commands were quite problematic. From this, it is clear that significant interaction problems existed, especially in situations in which commands were given to the child. The mother was quite controlling of the child's behavior and play, and the child was quite noncompliant and even less responsive to the general interactions initiated by his mother.

The child was given a diagnosis of ADD with hyperactivity and was felt to have significant problems with enuresis, encopresis, and aggression. Multiple interventions were recommended and eventually employed with Sean and his parents. Sean was initially tested in a drug-placebo examination procedure in which weekly clinic observations and parent and teacher ratings were used to evaluate two doses of Ritalin (0.3 mg/kg and 0.5 mg/kg given twice daily) against a placebo. Each drug condition lasted one week. Results indicated Sean to be maximally responsive to the 0.3 mg/kg dose given twice daily, and this was conveyed to his pediatrician who initiated drug treatment of Sean at this dose.

The parents received instruction in the parent training program discussed above. A home point system for behavior management was also implemented. By the end of treatment, Sean was rated on the Conner's Parent Questionnaire as still being above the mean for normal children on the Hyperactive Index but with a score considerably less than prior to training. On the Home Situations Questionnaire, Sean was viewed as a problem in only 6 of 16 settings with a rated severity of 1.2—much reduced from ratings before therapy.

Despite medication, some problems continued to occur at school with finishing class assignments and peer interactions. The daily report card described earlier was initiated with the child earning additional points at home for satisfactory daily classroom ratings. This resulted in a dramatic improvement in

TABLE 5-7

Mother-Child Interaction Measures for a Six-Year, 11-Month-Old Boy with Attention Deficit Disorder with Hyperactivity Taken during Free Play and Task Settings

measures*	ADD-H child† free play	mean and (S.D.) norms for same-age local boys‡	
Mother interacts	60	67.5	(14.1)
Child responds	63	92.3	(5.7)
Mother questions	15	11.5	(7.4)
Child responds	93	94.5	(10.1)
Mother praises	0	1.0	(1.3)
Mother negative	3	0.8	(0.3)
Mother directs	20	3.4	(3.5)
Child complies	50	93.1	(12.5)
Child interacts	81	89.2	(9.2)
Mother responds	78	87.3	(8.1)
Child plays	18	9.7	(9.9)
Mother controls play	26	1.4	(4.9)
task			
Mother directs	52	19.4	(8.5)
Child complies	42	94.5	(6.2)
Duration of compliance	2.2	5.7	(2.0)
Mother praises	0	4.2	(4.2)
Mother negative	5	0.6	(1.4)
Child negative	8	0.4	(0.9)

* Measures are derived from the Response Class Matrix and are expressed as percentages of occurrence of total interactions during the free play or task periods. Duration of compliance is the mean number of coded intervals of child compliance divided by the number of maternal commands.

† ADD-H refers to Attention Deficit Disorder with Hyperactivity.

‡ Source: R. Barkley, J. Karlsson, and S. Pollard. "Developmental Changes in the Mother-Child Interactions of Hyperactive and Normal Children," Unpublished manuscript, Medical College of Wisconsin, 1983.

class conduct, although occasional behavioral transgressions still occurred. The child remained on this card system until the end of that school year when both it and the Ritalin dosage were discontinued for the summer vacation.

After the daily school report card had been introduced and stabilized, the parents were taught the use of a behavior training procedure to treat Sean's encopresis. The program is described in the paper by Walker (1978), and employs a combination of cathartics, regular daily elimination, and incentives for successful bowel elimination by the child. After three months, the child was completely self-initiating bowel elimination five times per week with no soiling accidents having occurred throughout the past month.

The enuresis was treated using a bell and pad device designed to awaken the child from sleep at the first sign of urination in bed. Sean was also placed on 25 mg of Tofranil, given prior to bedtime. After the drug was eliminated in one month, only the bell and pad device as well as a point system continued to be used for reinforcement of dry nights. At a three-month follow-up, Sean had been dry each night for the past month. The treatment methods were then gradually faded out with no symptom recurrence. After summer vacation, the child returned to his parochial school for second grade. He was placed on the 20 mg slow release Ritalin spansule as well as the daily report card system. The latter was discontinued after four weeks with no behavioral deterioration. Presently, the child remains on Ritalin, and enuresis and encopresis have not recurred. The parents are seen occasionally (every four to six months) for follow-up visits to review child management procedures in the home. The parents rated the marriage as better, since greater control over Sean has developed. Referral of the parents to a credit counseling service proved of some assistance to them, as did referral of the mother to an internal medicine specialist for treatment of her gallbladder and ulcer conditions. Certainly, continued counseling and intervention with the child and family will be provided periodically as needed throughout Sean's development.

CONCLUSION

This overview of the nature, course, etiology, assessment and treatment of ADD children suggests that this is a disorder of attention, self-control, and social conduct that arises early in childhood, persists at varying degrees into young adulthood, and cannot as yet be quickly or completely ameliorated. Assessment focuses on the primary deficits of poor attention span, impulsivity, restlessness, and especially on problems with rule-governed behavior. Emphasis is given to understanding the social interactions of the child with parents, teachers, siblings, and others so as to appreciate the context in which the problems of the child occur. Interviews, rating scales, direct observations and parent/teacher collected data are used with the results of psychometric tests and medical exams, when necessary, to fully evaluate the constellation of the child's primary and related problems. Treatment currently remains symptomatic but tries to address the deficits in compliance and self-control, which are felt to be the most problematic. Multiple interventions involving psychological, medical, and educational personnel are often required at various points in the child's developmental course to assist the child and his family in effectively coping with the difficulties of the ADD child.

REFERENCES

Abidin, R. R. & Burke, W. T. *Parenting Stress Index*. Unpublished manuscript, Department of Foundations of Education, University of Virginia, 1978.

Abikoff, H., Gittelman-Klein, R., & Klein, D. F. Validation of a classroom observation code for hyperactive children. *Journal of Consulting and Clinical Psychology,* 1977, *45,* 772–783.

Achenbach, T. M. The Child Behavior Profile. I. Boys aged 6–11. *Journal of Consulting and Clinical Psychology,* 1978, *46,* 478–488.

American Psychiatric Association, *Diagnostic and Statistical Manual of Mental Disorders* (3rd Ed.). Washington, D.C.: 1980.

Atkinson, B. M. & Forehand, R. Home-based reinforcement programs designed to modify classroom behavior: A review and methodological evaluation. *Psychological Bulletin,* 1979, *86,* 1298–1308.

Ayllon, T., Layman, D., & Kandel, H. J. A behavioral-educational alternative to control of hyperactive children. *Journal of Applied Behavior Analysis,* 1975, *8,* 137–146.

Ayllon, T. & Rosenbaum, M. S. The behavioral treatment of disruption and hyperactivity in school settings. In B. Lahey & A. Kazdin (Eds.), *Advances in child clinical psychology* (Vol. 1). New York: Plenum Press, 1977.

Barkley, R. A. Predicting the response of hyperkinetic children to stimulant drugs: a review. *Journal of Abnormal Child Psychology,* 1976, *4,* 327–348.

Barkley, R. A. A review of stimulant drug research with hyperactive children. *Journal of Child Psychology and Psychiatry,* 1977 *18,* 137–165(a).

Barkley, R. A. The effects of methylphenidate on various measures of activity level and attention in hyperkinetic children. *Journal of Abnormal Child Psychology,* 1977, *5,* 351–369(b).

Barkley, R. A. *Hyperactive children: A handbook for diagnosis and treatment.* New York: Guilford Press, 1981(a).

Barkley, R. A. Hyperactivity. In E. Mash & L. Terdal (Eds.), *Behavioral assessment of childhood disorders.* New York: Guilford Press, 1981(b).

Barkley, R. A. Learning disabilities. In E. Mash & L. Terdal (Eds.), *Behavioral assessment of childhood disorders.* New York: Guilford Press, 1981(c).

Barkley, R. A. Guidelines for defining hyperactivity in children (Attention Deficit Disorder with Hyperactivity). In B. Lahey & A. Kazdin (Eds.), *Advances in child clinical psychology* (Vol. 4). New York: Plenum Press, 1982.

Barkley, R. A. The social interactions of hyperactive children: effects of age, sex, medication, and sex of parent. In R. McMahon & R. Peters (Eds.), *Childhood disorders: behavioral-developmental approaches.* New York: Brunner/Mazel, in press.

Barkley, R. A., Copeland, A., & Sivage, C. A self-control classroom for hyperactive children. *Journal of Autism and Developmental Disorders,* 1980, *10,* 75–89.

Barkley, R. A. & Cunningham, C. E. Stimulant drugs and activity level in hyperactive children. *American Journal of Orthopsychiatry,* 1978, *49,* 491–499.

Barkley, R. A. & Cunningham, C. E. The effects of methylphenidate on the mother-child interactions of hyperactive children. *Archives of General Psychiatry,* 1979, *36,* 201–208.

Barkley, R. A. & Cunningham, C. E. The parent-child interactions of hyperactive children and their modification by stimulant drugs. In R. Knights & D. Bakker (Eds.), *Treatment of hyperactive and learning disordered children.* Baltimore, Md.: University Park Press, 1980.

Barkley, R. A., Cunningham, C. E. & Karlsson, J. The speech of hyperactive children and their mothers: comparisons with normal children and stimulant drug effects. *Journal of Learning Disabilities,* 1983, *16,* 105–110.

Barkley, R. A., Karlsson, J., & Pollard, S. Developmental changes in the mother-child interactions of hyperactive children. Unpublished manuscript, Medical College of Wisconsin, 1983

Barkley, R. A., Karlsson, J., Strzelecki, E. & Murphy, J. The effects of age and Ritalin dosage on the mother-child interactions of hyperactive boys. *Journal of Consulting and Clinical Psychology,* 1984, in press.

Barkley, R. A. & Ullman, D. G. A comparison of objective measures of activity level and distractibility in hyperactive and nonhyperactive children. *Journal of Abnormal Child Psychology,* 1975, *3,* 213–244.

Battle, E. S. & Lacey, B. A context for hyperactivity in children, over time. *Child Development,* 1972, *43,* 757–773.

Beck, A. T. *Depression: causes and treatment.* Philadelphia: University of Pennsylvania Press, 1972.

Befera, M. & Barkley, R. A. The mother-child interactions, personality characteristics, and family psychiatric status of hyperactive and normal girls and boys. *Journal of Child Psychology and Psychiatry,* 1984, in press.

Bell, R. Q. Four new research approaches to socialization: an evaluation of their advantages and disadvantages. *Journal of Abnormal Child Psychology,* 1981, *9,* 341–346.

Bell, R. Q. & Harper, L. V. *Child effects on adults.* New Jersey: Lawrence Erlbaum Associates, Inc., 1977.

Benton, A. & Pearl, D. *Dyslexia: an appraisal of current knowledge.* New York: Oxford University Press, 1978.

Blouin, A. G. A., Bornstein, R., & Trites, R. Teenage alcohol use among hyperactive children: a 5-year follow-up study. *Journal of Pediatric Psychology,* 1978, *3,* 188–194.

Bornstein, P. H. & Quevillon, R. P. The effects of a self-instructional package on overactive preschool boys. *Journal of Applied Behavior Analysis,* 1976, *9,* 179–188.

Breen, M. & Barkley, R. A. The Personality Inventory for Children (PIC): Its clinical utility with hyperactive children. *Journal of Pediatric Psychology,* 1983, *8,* 359–366.

Breen, M. & Barkley, R. A. A comparison of hyperactive, learning disabled, and hyperactive-learning disabled children on the Personality Inventory for Children. *Journal of Clinical Child Psychology*, 1984, in press.

Camp, B. W. Two psychoeducational treatment programs for young aggressive boys. In C. Whalen & B. Henker (Eds.), *Hyperactive children: the social ecology of identification and treatment*. New York: Academic Press, 1980.

Campbell, S. B. Mother-child interaction in reflective, impulsive, and hyperactive children. *Developmental Psychology*, 1973, *8*, 341–349.

Campbell, S. B. Mother-child interaction: A comparison of hyperactive, learning disabled, and normal boys. *Anerican Journal of Orthopsychiatry*, 1975, *45*, 51–57.

Campbell, S. B. Mother-infant interaction as a function of maternal ratings of temperament. *Child Psychiatry and Human Development*, 1979, *10*, 67–76.

Campbell, S. B. & Paulauskas, S. Peer relations in hyperactive children. *Journal of Child Psychology and Psychiatry*, 1979, *20*, 233–246.

Cantwell, D. P. Genetics of hyperactivity. *Journal of Child Psychology and Psychiatry*, 1975, *16*, 261–264.

Cantwell, D. P. Hyperactivity and antisocial behavior. *American Academy of Child Psychiatry*, 1978, *17*, 252–262.

Cantwell, D. P. & Carlson, G. A. Stimulants. In J. Werry (Ed.), *Pediatric psychopharmacology*. New York: Bruner/Mazel, 1978.

Carey, W. B. Clinical applications of infant temperament measurements. *Journal of Pediatrics*, 1972, *81*, 823–828.

Carey, W. B. & McDevitt, S. C. Stability and change in individual temperament diagnosis from infancy to early childhood. *American Academy of Child Psychiatry*, 1978, *17*, 331–337.

Chamberlin, R. W. Can we identify a group of children at age two who are at risk for the development of behavioral or emotional problems in kindergarten or first grade? *Pediatrics*, 1977, *59*. (Supplement)

Chess, S. Diagnosis and treatment of the hyperactive child. *New York State Journal of Medicine*, 1960, *60*, 2379–2385.

Chess, S., Thomas, A., Rutter, M., & Birch, H. G. Interaction of temperament and environment in the production of behavioral disturbances in children. *American Journal of Psychiatry*, 1963, *120*, 142–148.

Christophersen, E. R., Barnard, S. R., & Barnard, J. D. The family training program manual: the home chip system. In R. Barkley, *Hyperactive children: a handbook for diagnosis and treatment*. New York: Guilford Press, 1981.

Cohen, N. J., Sullivan, S., Minde, K. K., Novak, C., & Helwig, C. Evaluation of the relative effectiveness of methylphenidate and cognitive behavior modification in the treatment of kindergarten aged hyperactive children. *Journal of Abnormal Child Psychology*, 1981, *9*, 43–54.

Conners, C. K. *Food additives and hyperactive children.* New York: Plenum Press, 1980.

Conners, C. K. & Werry, J. S. Pharmacotherapy of psychopathology in children. In H. Quay & J. Werry (Eds.), *Psychopathological disorders of childhood* (2nd ed.). New York: John Wiley & Sons, 1979.

Copeland, A. P. The relevance of subject variables in cognitive self-instructional programs for impulsive children. *Behavior Therapy,* 1981, *12,* 520–529.

Copeland, A. P. & Weissbrod, C. S. Effects of modeling on hyperactivity related behavior. Paper presented at the meeting of the American Psychology Association, San Francisco, 1977.

Cunningham, C. E. & Barkley, R. A. The interactions of normal and hyperactive children with their mothers in free play and structured task. *Child Development,* 1979, *50,* 217–224.

Cunningham, C. E., Siegel, L., & Offord, D. Peer relations among hyperactive children. Paper presented at the meeting of the American Psychological Association, Montreal, September 1980.

David, O. J., Clark, J., & Voeller, K. Lead and hyperactivity. *Lancet,* 1972, *2,* 900–903.

Douglas, V. I. Stop, look, and listen: the problem of sustained attention and impulse control in hyperactive and normal children. *Canadian Journal of Behavioural Science,* 1972, *4,* 259–282.

Douglas, V. I. Sustained attention and impulse control: implications for the handicapped child. In J. Swets & L. Elliott (Eds.), *Psychology and the handicapped child.* Washington, D.C.: U.S. Department of Health, Education and Welfare, DHEW Pub., 1974. (No. (OE) 73–05000)

Douglas, V. I. Treatment and training approaches to hyperactivity: Establishing internal or external control. In C. Whalen & B. Henker (Eds.), *Hyperactive children: the social ecology of identification and treatment.* New York: Academic Press, 1980.

Douglas, V. I., Parry, P., Marton, P., & Garson, C. Assessment of a cognitive training program for hyperactive children. *Journal of Abnormal Child Psychology,* 1976, *4,* 389–410.

Douglas, V. I. & Peters, K. G. Toward a clearer definition of the attentional deficit in hyperactive children. In G. A. Hale & M. Lewis (Eds.), *Attention and the development of cognitive skills.* New York: Plenum Press, 1979.

Feingold, B. F. *Why your child is hyperactive.* New York: Random House, 1975.

Firestone, P. & Martin, J. E. An analysis of the hyperactive syndrome. A comparison of hyperactive, behavior problem, asthmatic, and normal children. *Journal of Abnormal Child Psychology,* 1979, *7,* 261–263.

Firestone, P., Peters, S., Rivier, M. & Knights, R. M. Minor physical anomalies in hyperactive, retarded, and normal children and their families. *Journal of Child Psychology and Psychiatry,* 1978, *19,* 155–160.

Firestone, P. & Witt, J. E. Characteristics of families completing and prematurely discontinuing a behavioral parent-training program. *Journal of Pediatric Psychology*, 1982, *7*, 209–222.

Fish, B. The "one child, one drug" myth of stimulants and hyperkinesis. *Archives of General Psychiatry*, 1971, *25*, 193–203.

Forehand, R. & McMahon, R. *The noncompliant child.* New York: Guilford Press, 1981.

Gaddes, W. H. *Learning disabilities and brain function: A neuropsychological approach.* New York: Springer-Verlag, 1980.

Gadow, K. D. Drug therapy for hyperactivity: treatment procedures in natural settings. In K. D. Gadow & J. Loney (Eds.), *Psychosocial aspects of drug treatment for hyperactivity.* Boulder, Colo.: Westview, 1981.

Gittelman-Klein, R., Abikoff, H., Pollack, E., Klein, D. F., Katz, S. & Mattes, J. A controlled trial of behavior modification and methylphenidate in hyperactive children. In C. Whalen & B. Henker (Eds.), *Hyperactive children: The social ecology of identification and treatment.* New York: Academic Press, 1980.

Golden, G. S. Movement disorders in children: tourette syndrome. *Developmental and Behavioral Pediatrics*, 1982, *3*, 209–216.

Goyette, C. H., Conners, C. K., & Ulrich, R. F. Normative data on Conners Parent and Teacher Rating Scales. *Journal of Abnormal Child Psychology*, 1978, *6*, 221–236.

Hanf, C. A two stage program for modifying maternal controlling during mother-child interaction. Paper presented at the Western Psychological Association Meeting, Vancouver, B.C., 1969.

Harris, S. L. & Ferrari, M. Developmental factors in child behavior therapy. *Behavior Therapy*, 1983, *14*, 54–72.

Hastings, J. E. & Barkley, R. A. A review of psychophysiological research with hyperkinetic children. *Journal of Abnormal Child Psychology*, 1978, *6*, 413–447.

Hecaen, H. & Albert, M. L. *Human neuropsychology,* New York: John Wiley & Sons, 1978.

Heilman, K. M. & Valenstein, E. *Clinical neuropsychology.* New York: Oxford University Press, 1979.

Humphries, T., Kinsbourne, M., & Swanson, J. Stimulant effects on cooperation and social interaction between hyperactive children and their mothers. *Journal of Child Psychology and Psychiatry*, 1978, *19*, 13–22.

Jacob, R. G., O'Leary, K. D., & Rosenblad, C. Formal and informal classroom settings: effects on hyperactivity. *Journal of Abnormal Child Psychology*, 1978, *6*, 47–59.

Kendall, P. C. Cognitive-behavioral interventions with children. In B. Lahey & A. Kazdin (Eds.), *Advances in clinical child psychology* (Vol. 4). New York: Plenum Press, 1981.

Kinsbourne, M. The mechanism of hyperactivity. In M. Blaw, I. Rapin, & M. Kinsbourne (Eds.), *Topics in child neurology*, New York: Spectrum, 1977.

Kirigin, K. A., Braukmann, C. J., Atwater J. D., & Wolf, M. M. An evaluation of Teaching-Family (Achievement Place) group homes for juvenile offenders. *Journal of Applied Behavior Analysis*, 1982, *15*, 1–16.

Lahey, B. B., Green, K. D., & Forehand, R. On the independence of ratings of hyperactivity, conduct problems, and attention deficits in children: a multiple regression analysis. *Journal of Consulting and Clinical Psychology*, 1980, *48*, 566–574.

Lambert, N. M., Sandoval, J., & Sassone, D. Prevalence of hyperactivity in elementary school children as a function of social system definers. *American Journal of Orthopsychiatry*, 1978, *48*, 446–463.

Lapouse, R. & Monk, M. A. An epidemiologic study of behavior characteristics in children. *American Journal of Public Health*, 1958, *48*, 1134–1144.

Laufer, M. W. Long-term management and some follow-up findings on the use of drugs with minimal cerebral syndromes. *Journal of Learning Disabilities*, 1971, *4*, 55–58.

Laufer, M. W. & Denhoff, E. Hyperkinetic behavior syndrome in children. *Journal of Pediatrics*, 1957, *50*, 463–474.

Laufer, M. W., Denhoff, E., & Solomons G. Hyperkinetic impulse disorder in children's behavior problems. *Psychosomatic Medicine*, 1957, *19*, 38–49.

Loney, J. The intellectual functioning of hyperactive elementary school boys: a cross-sectional investigation. *American Journal of Orthopsychiatry*, 1974, *44*, 754–762.

Loney, J., Langhorne, J. E., & Paternite, C. E. An empirical basis for subgrouping the Hyperkinetic/MBD syndrome. *Journal of Abnormal Psychology*, 1978, *87*, 431–441.

Loney, J. & Milich, R. S. Hyperactivity, inattention and aggression in clincial practice. In M. Wolraich & D. K. Routh (Eds.), *Advances in Behavioral Pediatrics* (Vol. 2). Greenwich, Conn.: JAI Press, 1981.

Loney, J., Prinz, R. J., Mishalow, J., & Joad, J. Hyperkinetic/aggressive boys in treatment: predictors of clinical response to methylphenidate. *American Journal of Psychiatry*, 1978, *135*, 1487–1491.

Manson, M. P. & Lerner, A. *The Marriage Adjustment Inventory Manual*. Los Angeles: Western Psychological Services, 1962.

Mash, E. J. Families with problem children. In A. Doyle, D. Gold, & D. Moscowitz (Eds.), *Children in families under stress*. San Francisco: Jossey-Bass, in press.

Mash, E. J. & Dalby, J. T. Behavioral interventions for hyperactivity. In R. Trites (Ed.), *Hyperactivity in children: Etiology, measurement and treatment implications*. Baltimore, Md.: University Park Press, 1979.

Mash, E. J., Hamerlynck, L. A. & Handy, L. C. (Eds.), *Behavior modification and families*. New York: Brunner/Mazel, 1976a.

Mash, E. J., Hamerlynck, L. A., & Handy, L. C. (Eds.), *Behavior modification approaches to parenting*. New York: Brunner/Mazel, 1976b.

Mash, E. J. & Johnston, C. A comparison of the mother-child interactions of younger and older hyperactive and normal children. *Child Development*, 1982, *53*, 1371–1381.

Mash, E. J. & Johnston, C. Parental perceptions of child behavior problems, parenting self-esteem, and mothers' reported stress in younger and older hyperactive and normal children. *Journal of Consulting and Clinical Psychology*, 1983a, *51*, 86–99.

Mash, E. J. & Johnston, C. Sibling interactions of hyperactive and normal children and their relationship to reports of maternal stress and self-esteem. *Journal of Clincal Child Psychology*. 1983b, *12*, 91–99.

Mash, E. J. & Terdal, L. *Behavioral assessment of childhood disorders*. New York: Guilford Press, 1981.

Mash, E. J., Terdal, L., & Anderson, K. The Response Class Matrix: a procedure for recording parent-child interactions. *Journal of Consulting and Clinical Psychology*, 1973, *40*, 163–164.

Mattes, J. A. The role of frontal lobe dysfunction in childhood hyperkinesis. *Comprehensive Psychiatry*, 1980, *21*, 358–369.

Meichenbaum, D. H. Personal communication, March 22, 1983.

Meichenbaum, D. H. & Goodman, J. Training impulsive children to talk to themselves: a means of developing self-control. *Journal of Abnormal Psychology*, 1971, *77*, 115–126.

McInerny, T. & Chamberlin, R. W. Is it feasible to identify infants who are at risk for later behavioral problems? *Clinical Pediatrics*, 1978, *17*, 233–238.

Milar, C. R., Schroeder, S. R., Mushak, P., & Boone, L. Failure to find hyperactivity in preschool children with moderately elevated lead burden. *Journal of Pediatric Psychology*, 1981, *6*, 85–96.

Milich, R. The differential validity of impulsivity measures among boys with externalizing disorders. Paper presented at the 15th Annual Banff International Conference, Banff, Canada, March 1983.

Milich, R. & Loney, J. The factor composition of the WISC for hyperkinetic/MBD males. *Journal of Learning Disabilities*, 1979, *12*, 491–495.

Morrison, J. R. Adult psychiatric disorders in parents of hyperactive children. *American Journal of Psychiatry*, 1980, *137*, 825–827.

Morrison, J. R. & Stewart, M. A. A family study of the hyperactive child syndrome. *Biological Psychiatry*, 1971, *3*, 189–195.

Morrison, J. R. & Stewart, M. A. Evidence for polygenetic inheritance in the hyperactive child syndrome. *American Journal of Psychiatry*, 1973a, *130*, 791–792.

Morrison, J. R. & Stewart, M. A. The psychiatric status of the legal families of adopted hyperactive children. *Archives of General Psychiatry,* 1973b, *23,* 888–891.

Morrison, J. R. & Stewart, M. A. Bilateral inheritance as evidence for polygenicity in the hyperactive child syndrome. *Journal of Nervous and Mental Diseases,* 1974, *158,* 226–228.

Nichols, P. L. Early antecedents of hyperactivity. *Neurology,* 1980, *30,* 439.

Oltmanns, T. F., Broderick, J. E. & O'Leary, K. D. Marital adjustment and the efficacy of behavior therapy with children. *Journal of Consulting and Clinical Psychology,* 1977, *45,* 724–729.

Palkes, H. S., Stewart, M. A. & Kahana B. Porteus Maze performance of hyperactive boys after training in self-directed verbal commands. *Child Development,* 1968, *39,* 817–826.

Paternite, C. E. & Loney, J. Childhood hyperkinesis: relationships between symptomatology and home environment. In C. K. Whalen & B. Henker (Eds.), *Hyperactive children: The social ecology of identification and treatment.* New York: Academic Press, 1980.

Patterson, G. R. The aggressive child: victim and architect of a coercive system. In E. J. Mash, L. A. Hamerlynck, & L. C. Handy (Eds.), *Behavior modification and families.* New York: Brunner/Mazel, 1976.

Patterson, G. R. *Coercive family process.* Eugene, Ore.: Castalia, 1982.

Paulsen, K. & Johnson, M. Impulsivity: a multidimensional concept with developmental aspects. *Journal of Abnormal Child Psychology,* 1980, *8,* 269–278.

Pollard, S., Ward, E., & Barkley, R. The effects of parent training and methylphenidate on the parent-child interactions of hyperactive boys. *Child and Family Behavior Therapy,* 1983, *5,* 51–69.

Radosh, A., & Gittelman, R. The effect of appealing distractors on the performance of hyperactive children. *Journal of Abnormal Child Psychology,* 1981, *9,* 179–190.

Rapoport, J. L., Buchsbaum, M. S., Zahn, T. P., Weingartner, H., Ludlow, C., & Mikkelsen, E. J. Dextroamphetamine: cognitive and behavioral effects in normal prepubertal boys. *Science,* 1978, *199,* 560–563.

Rapoport, J. L., Quinn, P. O., Burg, C., & Bartley, L. Can hyperactives be identified in infancy? In R. Trites (Ed.), *Hyperactivity in children.* Baltimore, MD: University Park Press, 1979.

Rie, H. E. & Rie, E. D. *Handbook of minimal brain dysfunctions: a critical review.* New York: John Wiley & Sons, 1980.

Rie, H. E., Rie, E. D., Stewart, S., & Ambuel, J. P. Effects of methylphenidate on underachieving children. *Journal of Consulting and Clinical Psychology,* 1976, *44,* 250–260.

Roberts, M. A., Milich, R., Loney, J., & Caputo, J. A multi-trait multi-method analysis of variance of teachers' ratings of aggression, hyperactivity, and inattention. *Journal of Abnormal Child Psychology,* 1981, *9,* 371–380.

Robin, A. L. A controlled evaluation of problem-solving communication training with parent-adolescent conflict. *Behavior Therapy,* 1981, *12,* 593–609.

Rosenthal, R. H. & Allen, T. W. An examination of attention, arousal, and learning dysfunctions of hyperkinetic children. *Psychological Bulletin,* 1978, *85,* 689–715.

Ross, D. M. & Ross, S. A. *Hyperactivity.* New York: John Wiley & Sons, 1976.

Ross, D. M. & Ross, S. A. *Hyperactivity* (2nd Edition). John Wiley & Sons, 1982.

Routh, D. K. Hyperactivity. In P. Magrab (Ed.), *Psychological management of pediatric problems* (Vol. 2). Baltimore, Md.: University Park Press, 1978.

Routh, D. K. & Schroeder, C. S. Standardized playroom measures as indices of hyperactivity. *Journal of Abnormal Child Psychology,* 1976, *4,* 199–207.

Routh, D. K., Schroeder, C. S., & O'Tuama, L. Development of activity level in children. *Developmental Psychology,* 1974, *10,* 163–168.

Rutter, M. L. Brain damage syndromes in childhood: concepts and findings. *Journal of Child Psychology and Psychiatry,* 1977, *18,* 1–21.

Rutter, M. L. Syndromes attributable to minimal brain dysfunction in childhood. *American Journal of Psychiatry,* 1982, *139,* 21–33.

Safer, D. & Allen, R. *Hyperactive children: diagnosis and management.* Baltimore, Md.: University Park Press, 1976.

Sandberg, S. T., Rutter, M., & Taylor, E. Hyperkinetic disorder in psychiatric clinic attenders. *Developmental Medicine and Child Neurology,* 1978, *20,* 279–299.

Shaffer, D. & Greenhill, L. A critical note on the predictive validity of "the hyperkinetic syndrome." *Journal of Child Psychology and Psychiatry,* 1979, *20,* 279–299.

Shaffer, D., McNamara, N., & Pincus, J. H. Controlled observations on patterns of activity, attention, and impulsivity in brain-damaged and psychiatrically disturbed boys. *Psychological Medicine,* 1974, *4,* 4–18.

Skinner, B. F. *Science and human behavior.* New York: Macmillan, 1954.

Smith, L. *Your child's behavior chemistry.* New York: Random House, 1976.

Smith, S. D., Kimberling, W. J., Pennington, B. F., & Lubs, H. A. Specific reading disability: identification of an inherited form through linkage analysis. *Science,* 1983, *219,* 1345–1347.

Sroufe, L. A. Drug treatment of children with behavior problems. In F. D. Horowitz (Ed.), *Review of child development research* (Vol. 4). Chicago: University of Chicago Press, 1975.

Stewart, M. A., Cummings, C., Singer, S., & deBlois, C. S. The overlap between hyperactive and unsocialized aggressive children. *Journal of Child Psychology and Psychiatry,* 1981, *22,* 35–45.

Stewart, M. A., deBlois, C. S., & Cummings, C. Psychiatric disorder in the parents of hyperactive boys and those with conduct disorder. *Journal of Child Psychology and Psychiatry,* 1980, *21,* 283–292.

Stewart, M. A. & Leone, L. A family study of unsocialized aggressive boys. *Biological Psychiatry*, 1978, *13*, 107–118.

Still, G. F. Some abnormal psychical conditions in children. *Lancet*, 1902, *1*, 1008–1012, 1077–1082, 1163–1168.

Strauss, A. A. & Lehtinen, L. E. *Psychopathology and education of the brain-injured child.* New York: Grune & Stratton, 1947.

Tallmadge, J. & Barkley, R. A. The interactions of hyperactive and normal boys with their mothers and fathers. *Journal of Abnormal Child Psychology*, 1983, in press.

Tarver-Behring, S., Barkley, R., & Karlsson, J. The mother-child interactions of hyperactive boys and their normal siblings. Unpublished manuscript, Medical College of Wisconsin, 1983.

Taylor, E. Food additives, allergy, and hyperkinesis. *Journal of Child Psychology and Psychiatry*, 1979, *20*, 357–363.

Taylor, H. G. & Fletcher, J. M. Biological foundations of "specific development disorders": methods, findings and future directions. *Journal of Clinical Child Psychology*, 1983, *12*, 46–65.

Taylor, J. F. *The hyperactive child and the family.* New York: Everest House, 1980.

Tonick, I., Friehling, J., & Warhit, J. Classroom observation code. Unpublished manuscript. State University of New York at Stony Brook, 1973.

Trites, R. *Hyperactivity in children.* Baltimore: University Park Press, 1979.

Trites, R., Dugas, F., Lynch, G., & Ferguson, H. B. Incidence of hyperactivity. *Journal of Pediatric Psychology*, 1979, *4*, 179–188.

Trites, R., Tryphonas, H., & Ferguson, H. B. Diet treatment for hyperactive children with food allergies. In R. M. Knights & D. Bakker (Eds.), *Treatment of hyperactive and learning disordered children.* Baltimore: University Park Press, 1980.

Ullman, D. G., Barkley, R. A., & Brown, H. W. The behavioral symptoms of hyperkinetic children who successfully responded to stimulant drug treatment. *American Journal of Orthopsychiatry*, 1978, *48*, 425–437.

Voelker, S., Lachar, D., & Gdowski, C. The Personality Inventory for Children and response to methylphenidate: preliminary evidence for predictive validity. *Journal of Pediatric Psychology*, 1983, *8*, 161–169.

Wahler, R. G. Deviant child behavior within the family: developmental speculations and behavior change strategies. In H. Leitenberg (Ed.), *Handbook of behavior modification and behavior therapy.* Englewood Cliffs, N.J.: Prentice-Hall, 1976.

Wahler, R. G. The insular mother: her problems in parent-child treatment. *Journal of Applied Behavior Analysis*, 1980, *13*, 207–219.

Wahler, R. G. & Fox, J. J. Setting events in applied behavior analysis: toward a conceptual and methodological expansion. *Journal of Applied Behavior Analysis*, 1981, *14*, 327–338.

Walker, C. E. Toilet training, enuresis, and encopresis. In P. Magrab (Ed.) *Psychological Management of Pediatric Problems*. Baltimore: University Park Press, 1978.

Weiss, G., Hechtman, L., & Perlman, T. Hyperactives as young adults: school, employer, and self-rating scales obtained during ten-year follow-up evaluation. *American Journal of Orthopsychiatry*, 1978, *48*, 438–445.

Weiss, G., Hechtman, L., Perlman, T., Hopkins, J., & Wener, A. Hyperactive children as young adults: a controlled prospective 10 year follow-up of the psychiatric status of 75 hyperactive children. *Archives of General Psychiatry*, 1979, *36*, 675–681.

Wender, P. *Minimal brain dysfunction in children*. New York: John Wiley & Sons, 1971.

Wender, P., Reimherr, F. W., & Wood, D. R. Diagnosis and drug treatment of attention deficit disorder (minimal brain dysfunction) in adults: a replication. *Archives of General Psychiatry*, 1981.

Werry, J. S. Developmental hyperactivity. *Pediatric Clinics of North America*, 1968, *15*, 581–599.

Werry, J. S. *Pediatric psychopharmacology*. New York: Brunner/Mazel, 1978.

Werry, J. S. & Quay, H. The prevalence of behavior symptoms in younger elementary school children. *American Journal of Orthopsychiatry*, 1971, *41*, 136–143.

Werry, J. S. & Sprague, R. L. Hyperactivity. In C. G. Costello (Ed.), *Symptoms of psychopathology*. New York: John Wiley & Sons, 1970.

Whalen, C. K., Collins, D. E., Henker, B., Alkus, S. R., Adams, D., & Stapp, J. Behavior observations of hyperactive children and methylphenidate (Ritalin) effects in systematically structured classroom environments: Now you see them, now you don't. *Journal of Pediatric Psychology*, 1978, *3*, 177–187.

Whalen, C. K. & Henker, B. Psychostimulants and children: a review and analysis. *Psychological Bulletin*, 1976, *83*, 1113–1130.

Whalen, C. K. & Henker, B. (Eds.), *Hyperactive children: the social ecology of identification and treatment*. New York: Academic Press, 1980.

Whalen, C. K., Henker, B., Collins, B. E., Finck, D., & Dotemoto, S. A social ecology of hyperactive boys: medication effects in systematically structured classroom environments. *Journal of Applied Behavior Analysis*, 1979, *12*, 65–81.

Whalen, C. K., Henker, B., & Dotemoto, S. Methylphenidate and hyperactivity: effects on teacher behaviors. *Science*, 1980, *208*, 1280–1282.

Willis, T. J. & Lovaas, I. A behavioral approach to treating hyperactive children: the parent's role. In J. G. Millichap (Ed.), *Learning disabilities and related disorders*. Chicago: Year Book Medical Publishers, 1977.

Wirt, R. D., Lachar, D., Klinedinst, J. K., & Seat, P. D. *Multidimensional descrip-*

tion of child personality: a manual for the Personality Inventory for Children. Los Angeles: Western Psychological Services, 1977.

Wolf, S. M. & Forsythe, A. Behavior disturbance, phenobarbital, and febrile seizures. *Pediatrics,* 1978, *61,* 728–731.

Wolraich, M. L., Drummond, T., Soloman, M. K., O'Brien, M. L., & Sivage, C. Effects of methylphenidate alone and in combination with behavior modification procedures on the behavior and academic performance of hyperactive children. *Journal of Abnormal Child Psychology,* 1978, *6,* 149–161.

6

Conduct and Oppositional Disorders

Karen C. Wells
Children's Hospital National Medical Center
George Washington University School of Medicine

Rex Forehand
University of Georgia

Aggressive behavior can be traced throughout humanity's recorded history. Paralleling the observations of its own aggressive behavior, the human race has postulated various explanatory models to account for it. Most early historical models attributed the behavior to spirits or substances that were beyond personal control. Biblical civilization was often overcome by "evil spirits" compelling them to rage and aggression. Elizabethan and Victorian society were at the mercy of vile circulating humors that caused evil tempers and antisocial behavior. In more recent history, Sigmund Freud was so disturbed by his observations of wartime atrocities in World War I that he incorporated a "death instinct" into his drive theories of human behavior (Freud, 1922).

Modern approaches to the explanation, prediction, and treatment of aggression continued in the search for internal variables to account for aggressive behavior. Rather than evil spirits or vile humours, however, the search evolved to investigations of biological, genetic, and cognitive variables in the etiology of aggression (Kohlberg, 1976; Lewis, 1981; Mednick, 1981). In addition, there has been a much greater emphasis on the effects of the family and social and community environments in shaping and maintaining aggressive behavior. Indeed, one of the most important contributions of the social and behavioral sciences in the past 50 years has been the systematic explication of environmental variables that directly relate to the development of aggression. In the final analysis, we will undoubtedly find that aggressive behavior can only be understood completely as the final outcome of a multiplicity of biological, genetic, environmental, and social variables, any one or more of which may exert an influence in any given individual.

The purpose of this chapter is to review issues in classification, etiology, assessment, and treatment of aggressive behavior in children living within a family context. As alluded to above, emphasis will be placed on an interactional model that views aggression as the result of a confluence of variables, each potentially contributing some proportion of the variance in explaining aggressive behavior. Most attention, however, will be given to those variables that are potentially modifiable, given our current knowledge, technology, and armamentarium of treatment strategies.

DESCRIPTION OF CONDUCT AND OPPOSITIONAL DISORDERS

The most widely used system for classifying childhood psychopathological disorders in the United States is the Diagnostic and Statistical Manual of Mental Disorders—third edition, or, the DSM-III (American Psychiatric Association, 1980). In spite of the questionable reliability of the diagnostic categories in the childhood disorders section of the DSM-III, it is nevertheless an administrative necessity in most child mental health settings in this country (Wells, 1981). Consequently, behavior therapists are compelled to understand the relationship between DSM-III categories of Conduct and Oppositional disorders and syndromes of aggressive behavior identified in the empirical literature.

DSM-III Syndromes of Aggressive Behavior

There are two major types of aggressive behavior disorders relevant to children in DSM-III: *Conduct Disorders* and *Oppositional Disorders*. The Conduct Disorder category includes four subtypes: undersocialized, aggressive; undersocialized, nonaggressive; socialized, aggressive; and socialized, nonaggressive. As can be seen, the four subtypes vary along two dimensions: aggressive-nonaggressive and socialized-undersocialized.

A child classified with one of the aggressive subtypes is characterized by a repetitive and persistent pattern (at least six months) of aggressive conduct in which the rights of others are violated, which is evidenced by physical violence against persons or property or by thefts outside the home involving confrontation with a victim. The nonaggressive conduct disorders involve rule violations, such as truancy, substance abuse, lying and stealing, which are nonviolent and do not involve confrontation with a victim.

The socialized-undersocialized dimension refers to the child's capacity for feelings of guilt and attachment to other persons. A child classified with one of the socialized subtypes shows evidence of regard for and attachment to one or more peer-group friends and/or shows remorse for wrongdoing. A child with one of the undersocialized subtypes has failed to establish a normal degree of affection, empathy, or bond with others. The DSM-III represents an advancement over previous systems of classification in that it provides specific criteria for making decisions relevant to these diagnoses.

The second major syndrome of aggressive behavior in children is Oppositional Disorder. According to DSM-III, the essential feature is a pattern of disobedient and provocative opposition to authority figures, primarily the parents but sometimes extending to teachers and other children as well. The essential behavioral characteristics are temper tantrums, argumentativeness (back talk), stubbornness, and violations of minor rules. The diagnosis is not made for children who violate the basic rights of others or break major social norms or rules. In these cases, Oppositional Disorder is ruled out, and the child is said to have a Conduct Disorder (American Psychiatric Association, 1980).

In spite of greater specificity and objectivity for DSM-III compared to its predecessors (DSM-I and DSM-II), the reliability of DSM-III child diagnostic categories is poor. The overall agreement among clinicians' diagnoses in the first field trials was .52 using Kappa, a statistic that corrects for chance agreements (American Psychiatric Association, 1980). Even this low-agreement coefficient was obtained only by calling any diagnosis of Conduct Disorder, regardless of subtype, an agreement. Subsequent studies, in which clinicians were provided with the same case materials on which to base their diagnoses, reported even *poorer* reliability (Mattison, Cantwell, Russell, & Will, 1979; Mezzich & Mezzich, 1979). Interestingly, reliability of diagnosis appears much better for adult than for child diagnostic categories.

Regarding validity, very few studies have been conducted. One recent study (Henn, Bardwell, & Jenkins, 1980) examined the predictive validity of subtypes of Conduct Disorder by following up three groups of children 10–12 years after their discharge from a juvenile detention facility. The three groups were diagnosed as undersocialized, aggressive; undersocialized, nonaggressive; and socialized, aggressive. Evidence for predictive validity was found particularly for the socialized-undersocialized distinction in diagnosing Conduct Disorder. Socialized delinquents had fewer returns to the training school and did better on parole than those in the undersocialized groups. Socialized delinquents also had better adult outcomes than their undersocialized counterparts in terms of adult criminal activity. The likelihood of a conviction on an adult charge and the chance of going to prison or jail as an adult were significantly higher for undersocialized delinquents.

Evidence for predictive validity for the aggressive-nonaggressive distinction also was found within the undersocialized groups. Subjects in the aggressive groups were arrested as adults for more *violent* crimes, including assault, rape, and murder than the unaggressive group, although the total *number* of arrests and convictions did not differ. Nonaggressive subtypes were more likely to be arrested for less confrontive, less hostile crimes, such as contributing to the delinquency of a minor and malicious injury to a building.

Although results of the Henn et al.(1980) study suggest that there may be some predictive validity in the DSM-III subcategories of Conduct Disorder, particularly within adjudicated populations, no other validity studies of the DSM-III diagnostic categories are available, and as we have already seen, evidence for reliability is poor. Wells (1981) and Achenbach (1982) have suggested that the reason for this may be that the childhood diagnostic categories were developed via discussion and concensus/opinion of DSM-III committee members rather than through empirical research. It is necessary, therefore, to consider empirical research efforts relevant to classification as they relate to Conduct and Oppositional disorders and to evaluate the extent to which DSM-III syndromes do or do not correspond to empirically identified syndromes of childhood disorders.

Empirically Derived Syndromes of Aggressive Behavior

Empirical classification systems take a dimensional, not a categorical, approach to childhood psychopathology (Quay, 1979). This approach assumes that all children's behavior varies along a finite number of behavioral dimensions. Each dimension is relatively independent and consists of a cluster of behaviors, which covary with one another but not with behaviors from other dimensions. In this dimensional model, a "syndrome" is not viewed in the medical model sense as something the child *has,* but as a group of behaviors found to be statistically associated with one another. A clinic-referred child is not characterized best by a single diagnostic label that attempts to type him/her as an individual, but in terms of his/her position along each possible behavioral dimension as compared to children in the normal population (Wells, 1981).

Quay (1979) has reviewed the empirical factor-analytic studies of childhood psychopathology and concluded that, despite great diversity across studies with respect to assessment instruments, type of population and type of respondent, four major orthogonal factors account for the largest percentage of the variance. Of interest to the topic of this chapter are the two factors related to aggressive behavior, labeled *Conduct Disorder* and *Socialized Aggressive Disorder* by Quay (1979). In an independent review, Achenbach and Edelbrock (1978) essentially reached the same conclusion, finding evidence for two major antisocial behavior syndromes labeled *Aggressive* and *Delinquent.* These correspond to Quay's Conduct Disorder and Socialized Aggressive Disorder, respectively.

Quay (1979) has provided tables of the behavioral characteristics most frequently found across studies for each of the disorders. Adaptations from these tables of the major characteristics are presented in Table 6–1. In contrast to DSM-III diagnostic categories, evidence for good reliability and validity of the

TABLE 6-1

**Behavior Characteristics of Conduct Disorder
and Socialized Aggressive Disorder**

conduct disorder	socialized aggressive disorder
1. Fighting, hitting, assaultive	1. Has "bad" companions
2. Temper tantrums	2. Steals in company with others
3. Disobedient; defiant	3. Loyal to delinquent friends
4. Destructiveness	4. Belongs to a gang
5. Impertinent	5. Truant from school
6. Uncooperative	6. Stays out late at night
7. Disruptive, interrupts	
8. Negative; refuses direction	
9. Restless	
10. Boisterous, noisy	
11. Irritable	
12. Attention seeking	

Source: H. C. Quay, "Classification," in *Psychopathological Disorders of Childhood* (2nd ed.), eds. H. C. Quay and J. Werry (New York: John Wiley & Sons, 1979), pp. 17 and 21.

two major antisocial behavior syndromes has been found in numerous studies (see Quay, 1979, for a review).

Achenbach (1980) has examined the relationship between DSM-III diagnostic categories and empirically derived categories. Some DSM-III categories roughly correspond to the empirically derived categories, whereas other DSM-III syndromes have no counterparts in the empirical literature. This correspondence is presented in Table 6-2.

Based on the Achenbach and Edelbrock (1978) and Quay (1979) reviews, there appears to be incontrovertible empirical evidence for the existence of at least two separate antisocial behavior syndromes in children. If one accepts Achenbach's (1980) conclusion that the difference between socialized, aggressive and socialized, nonaggressive Conduct Disorder is fundamentally a sex difference, then these empirical syndromes correspond to three DSM-III diagnostic categories. Looking across all the factor analytic studies, there is no clear-cut evidence for the existence of a separate, independent syndrome of oppositional behavior that is clearly discriminable from Conduct Disorder. In most factor analytic studies, behaviors appearing under DSM-III Oppositional Behavior Disorder (e.g., temper tantrums, stubbornness) correlate with and are subsumed by the Conduct Disorder factor (American Psychiatric Association, 1980).

It should be noted that some behavioral theorists (e.g., Herbert, 1978) believe that there *may* be at least three separate dimensions of antisocial behavior in children; this, along with the results of a few studies, suggests that the door

TABLE 6–2

Correspondence of DSM-III and Empirically Derived Categories of Aggressive Disorders

DSM-III diagnostic category	*empirically derived category*
1. Undersocialized, aggressive Conduct Disorder	1. Conduct disorder (Quay) Aggressive (Achenbach)
2. Undersocialized, nonaggressive Conduct Disorder	2. No counterpart
3. Socialized, aggressive Conduct Disorder	3. Socialized Aggressive Disorder (Quay) Delinquent (boys) (Achenbach)
4. Socialized, nonaggressive Conduct Disorder	4. Delinquent (girls) (Achenbach)
5. Oppositional Disorder	5. No counterpart

Source: T. M. Achenbach, "DMS-III in Light of Empirical Research on the Classification of Child Psychopathology," *Journal of the American Academy of Child Psychiatry,* 19 (1980), pp. 395–412.

should be left open on this question at the present time. For example, in a recent hierarchical cluster analysis of parent-observed behavior problems using a checklist developed by Patterson (see Patterson, Reid, Jones, & Conger, 1975), Chamberlain (1980) found three clusters relevant to antisocial behavior. These clusters were labeled *Aggressive, Unsocialized,* and *Immature.* The Aggressive and Unsocialized clusters correspond to the two aggressive behavior dimensions described by Quay and Achenbach. The third cluster, Immature, was comprised of the following behaviors: complain, whine, irritable, pout, temper tantrums, and negative.

In another study from Patterson's research group (Lorber & Patterson, 1981), Guttman Scalogram analyses were applied to the presenting problems of children referred to the Oregon Social Learning Center (OSLC), which specializes in the treatment of aggressive children. This analysis revealed three potential progressions of behavior problems obtained from case referral symptoms. The first progression has been labeled *Stealer* by Patterson (1982) mainly because stealing was the primary referral problem of these children. The other two progressions were labeled *Social Aggressive* and *Immature.* Of considerable interest was the fact that each of the three discrepant progressions had one important aspect in common—each began with noncompliance as the highest rate intake symptom, as illustrated in Table 6–3.

Patterson and his group have speculated that these three patterns of behavioral progression in children referred for aggressive behavior may have differential clinical implications, may arise from different etiologic factors, and may have different prognoses and responses to treatment (Lorber & Patterson, 1981). For example, Moore, Chamberlain and Mukai (1979) followed two

TABLE 6-3

**Behavioral Progressions of Three Types
of Aggressive Behavior**

stealer	*social aggressive*	*immature*
Noncomply	Noncomply	Noncomply
↓	↓	↓
Lie	Fights with sibs	Whine
↓	↓	↓
Run around	Tease	Yell
↓	↓	↓
Steal	Temper	Bed wet
↓	↓	
Sets fire	Hits	
	↓	
	High rate of observed deviant behavior	

Source: R. Lorber and G. R. Patterson, "The Aggressive Child: A Concomitant of a Coercive System," *Advances in Family Intervention, Assessment and Theory,* 2 (1981), pp. 47–87.

groups of children initially referred to Patterson's group for treatment of aggressive behavior. Children classified as Stealers had a significantly higher rate of court-recorded offenses two to nine years later, compared to children classified by Patterson as Aggressive, whose rates of court-recorded offenses did not differ from a normative sample. This study appears to provide evidence for validity of the Stealer versus Aggressive subtypes of antisocial behavior identified by Patterson's research group. Results of this study are also interesting when compared to those of Henn et al. (1979) reported earlier. It would appear that Patterson's Stealer category corresponds roughly to a DSM-III diagnosis of Undersocialized Conduct Disorder (either aggressive or nonaggressive, depending on the violent or nonviolent nature of offenses), whereas Patterson's Aggressive category corresponds roughly to a DSM-III category of Socialized Aggressive Conduct Disorder or Oppositional Disorder, depending on the nature and intensity of physical violence displayed by the child.

Further evidence from Patterson's group for the validity of the Stealer versus Aggressive distinction comes from Patterson's analysis of MMPI profiles of the mothers of both Stealers and Aggressives. Mothers of Stealers had profiles characterized by peaks on the Psychopathic Deviate, Hypomania and Schizophrenia scales, whereas mothers of Aggressives had profiles consisting of a more neurotic pattern, for example, angry, depressed, rigid, withdrawn and distanced from others (Patterson, 1980). These differences would suggest different genetic, family environment, and/or parenting style influences in the development of the two subtypes of antisocial disorder in children. The third potential subtype of antisocial disorder identified by Patterson, Immature, is not well understood at this time. There are no studies on differential treatment, prognosis, or family variables for this category from Patterson's group.

Finally, a few factor analytic studies find some evidence for at least three potential dimensions of antisocial behavior in children. In factor analyses of behavior ratings of boys institutionalized for delinquent behavior, Quay (1964) found three patterns, which he labeled *Socialized-Subcultural Delinquency, Unsocialized-Psychopathic Delinquency* and *Disturbed-Neurotic Delinquency.* Similar results for three different factors of antisocial behavior were reported by Wolff (1967) in a primary school age population of clinic-referred children. Langner, Gerston, McCarthy, Eisenberg, Green, Herson and Jameson (1976), in a cross-sectional survey of Manhattan households, also found evidence for three antisocial behavior dimensions in 6–18-year-old children. These were labeled *Conflict with Parents, Fighting,* and *Delinquency.*

In summary, there are undoubtedly at least two separate dimensions or syndromes of antisocial behavior in children. Evidence is accumulating that these two syndromes are associated with different sets of etiologic influences, require different treatment approaches, and have different long-term prognoses. There is equivocal evidence that there may be a third dimension of antisocial behavior in children, although it is not well understood. Some authors who have identified a third dimension believe it represents a developmental immaturity dimension (Patterson, 1982), or perhaps Attention Deficit Disorder (ADD). For example, it would not be surprising that some children with ADD and associated behavior problems might be referred to Patterson's research and treatment center, since 75 percent of ADD children have secondary conduct problems (Safer & Allen, 1976). On the other hand, a third dimension of antisocial behavior, Conflict with Parents, which was identified in a large scale epidemiological survey (Langner et al., 1976), appears to correspond more closely to an oppositional behavior syndrome. Clearly, more research will be needed to definitively answer the question of multiple subtypes of antisocial behavior in children.

Associated Features

Reading Disability. That children who display antisocial behavior often have reading problems is a frequently documented clinical and empirical observation. In the Isle of Wight study (Rutter, Tizard, Yule, Graham, & Whitmore, 1976), a large scale epidemiological survey of the entire child population of an island off the coast of England, one third of the children with specific reading retardation (defined as a 28-month or more lag in reading ability of normal IQ children) also showed clinically significant antisocial behavior. Conversely, one third of children with antisocial behavior also had reading retardation. Lewis, Shanok, Balla and Bard (1980) reported that, in an incarcerated delinquent population, poorer reading was correlated with more violent behavior. The precise nature of the relationship between antisocial behavior and reading problems is unclear at the present time.

Social Skills Deficits.   The inclusion of a socialized-undersocialized dimension underlying subtypes of Conduct Disorder in DSM-III implies that at least some of these children have severe deficits in social skills and abilities, resulting in poor adult and peer relationships. Lorber and Patterson (1981) reported that 72 percent of children referred for treatment to the Oregon Social Learning Center (OSLC) had "poor peer relations" as a symptomatic behavior reported by their parents. Recent research in behavioral assessment of social skills has documented significantly poorer social skills of delinquents compared to nondelinquent boys (Freedman, Rosenthal, Donahoe, Schlundt, & McFall, 1978) and girls (Gaffney & McFall, 1981). The former study showed that social skills discriminate subgroups *within* a delinquent population as well. Delinquent boys who were highly "disruptive" (i.e., more occurrences of violent behavior and significant rule violations) had poorer social skills than less disruptive delinquent boys. There appears to be a direct relationship between aggressive behavior and social skills deficits.

Depression.   There is accumulating evidence for an association between aggressive behavior and depression in children, especially boys. In a postmortem clinical study of adolescents who committed suicide, Shaffer (1974) found that three fourths of the sample had engaged in antisocial behaviors. Chiles, Miller and Cox (1980) reported that 23 percent of 13–15-year-old adolescent delinquents admitted to a correctional facility met research diagnostic criteria for a major affective disorder. Conversely, Puig-Antich (1982) reported that one third of his sample of children, having been referred to a child depression clinic and meeting research diagnostic criteria for a major depressive disorder, also met DSM-III criteria for Conduct Disorder. This finding was unanticipated.

Puig-Antich (1982) is cautious in his interpretations of these findings, indicating that it was not clear if this represented more than a chance association of these two disorders. However, Edelbrock and Achenbach (1980) conducted a cluster analysis of behavior profiles of children referred for mental health services. Cluster analysis allows for identification of groups of individuals showing similar behavior patterns (Achenbach, 1982). In this empirical study, a profile pattern labeled *Depressed-Social Withdrawal-Aggressive* was identified, representing a group of children (7.6 percent of the total sample) who showed this cluster of syndromes. Edelbrock and Achenbach (1980) point out that these children would probably receive a DSM-III diagnosis of Undersocialized Aggressive Conduct Disorder. However, empirical methods demonstrate that these children may be equally deviant on depression and social withdrawal dimensions.

In the opinion of the present authors, it is incumbent upon child psychologists and psychiatrists to be more sensitive to the possible association between aggressive disorders and depression than we have been in the past. We will come back to this point in our discussion of assessment.

EPIDEMIOLOGY OF AGGRESSIVE DISORDERS

Results of any studies on epidemiology of aggressive disorders are dependent on and influenced by the methodology employed in the study, particularly the subject population from which the sample is drawn, the method of labeling the child as having an antisocial disorder, and the ages of the children in the subject sample at the time of the study. Nevertheless, comparing across several studies, some generalizations regarding prevalence and sex distribution can be made.

Prevalence

Studies on the prevalence of aggressive disorders in clinic-referred populations (Cerreto & Tuma, 1977; Speer, 1971; Wolff, 1961; Wolff, 1971) indicate that these children are the most common referrals to mental health centers. From one third to three quarters of all child referrals concern these kinds of problems (see Table 6–4).

A perusal of Table 6–4 reveals some additional interesting findings regarding prevalence rates. Wolff (1961, 1971) found that the total proportion of clinic-referred children with antisocial behavior increased as age increased. Rutter et al. (1976) found that 4 percent of the *total* 10–11-year-old child population on the Isle of Wight had a diagnosable conduct problem. However, of all children who had a psychiatric disorder of any type, 70 percent had a conduct disorder. Trites, Dugas, Lynch and Ferguson's (1979) results, indicating approximately a 3 percent prevalence rate in a total school population sample using a statistical approach to diagnosis, roughly corresponds to the Rutter et al. (1976) 4 percent prevalence rate using clinical diagnostic methods and the World Health Organization's ICD-9 system of nomenclature. The correspondence found in these two studies is a reflection of the empirical tradition in British psychiatry and stands in sharp contrast to the results of Cerreto and Tuma (1977) using the American DSM-II. In spite of the availability of Unsocialized Aggressive and Delinquent Reaction diagnostic categories in the DSM-II, American psychiatrists grossly underutilized these categories, tending to view these children's behavior as an expression of a reactive adjustment problem.

Sex Distribution

Table 6–4 also provides data regarding sex distribution of antisocial behavior disorders. Again, although results differ slightly from study to study, it is clear that boys are much more likely to display antisocial behavior than girls. This finding holds true regardless of the sample or age of the children.

TABLE 6-4

Prevalence of Conduct Disorders

study	sample	age	method of classification	percent label	percent of total	percent boys	percent girls
Wolff, 1961	Clinic	2–5 yrs.	Clinical diagnosis	Aggressive	47%	65%	35%
Wolff, 1971	Clinic	5–12 yrs.	Empirical factor	Aggressive/ Acting-out Antisocial	74%	62%	38%
Speer, 1971	Clinic	5–13+ yrs.	Empirical factor	Conduct disorder	34%	72%	28%
				Social delinquency	08%	71%	29%
Cerreto & Tuma,	Clinic	2–19 yrs. X = 11.7	DSM-II	Unsocialized aggressive	08%		
				Delinquent Reaction	003%		
				Adjustment Reaction	38%	58%	42%
Rutter, et al., 1976	Total population survey	10–11 yrs.	Precursor of WHO-ICD-9	Antisocial, conduct mixed conduct- emotional disorder	4% (70%)		
Trites, et al., 1979	School population survey	3–12+ yrs.	Empirical factor	Conduct disorder	2.9%	73%	27%

Course

Follow-up studies of antisocial children generally demonstrate the stability of antisocial behavior over time; that is, a significant proportion of antisocial children continue to display antisocial behavior in adulthood. However, antisocial behavior is not the only adult outcome. Some of these children go on to present other forms of psychiatric disorder as adults, and a small subset have normal adult functioning in terms of good adjustment in the family, job, and community. Results of a select number of follow-up studies are presented in Table 6–5. As can be seen, the most common adult diagnosis for individuals who were antisocial as children is Sociopathic or Antisocial Personality Disorder. The remainder fall out among the various emotional and personality disorders with a small percentage having some type of psychotic disorder as adults. Undoubtedly, some of these individuals labeled as psychotic would today receive diagnoses of bipolar affective disorder.

Results presented here concur with those of Robins (1970) in her review of 23 follow-up studies. She also found that approximately 40 percent of antisocial children showed antisocial or sociopathic personality disturbance as adults, compared with only 10 percent for adults who were not antisocial children. The remaining children fell into other adult diagnostic categories, including psychoses, anxiety disorders, and nonaggressive personality disturbances.

The studies reviewed above evaluated the adult psychiatric status of children with aggressive behavior disorders. Other investigators have evaluated the course of aggressive disorders by examining the stability of aggressive behavior across time, and two separate reviews of this literature have recently appeared (Loeber, 1982; Olweus, 1979). Olweus (1979) examined 16 longitudinal studies, following children from one to 18 years, and found an average correlation of .63 between measurements of aggression at two time intervals. Loeber (1982) refined the analysis by showing that children who initially display higher rates of aggressive behavior, a greater variety of aggressive behaviors, an earlier onset of aggressive behavior, and who were aggressive in more than one setting, are more likely to persist in this behavior than children who are less extreme on these parameters. These reviews prompted Lorber and Patterson (1981) to postulate an aggressive behavior "trait" for some children, referring to "an individual's mode of responding which is expressed in a stable fashion across both time and settings" (p. 65). Combining results of studies on stability and natural history of aggressive behavior disorders, it would appear that the most likely outcome of aggressive child behavior is aggressive or antisocial adult behavior.

ETIOLOGY OF AGGRESSIVE DISORDERS

As mentioned earlier, it is becoming increasingly apparent that aggressive behavior in children cannot be understood fully from a unidimensional perspective but, that in many cases, it represents the final outcome of predisposing constitutional or biological influences in conjunction with forces within the social and family contexts. This polygenic perspective on etiology of aggressive behavior is consistent with the behavioral-analytic approach to the understanding and assessment of psychological disorders explicated by Kanfer and Saslow (1969). In their now classic monograph, Kanfer and Saslow proposed an S-O-R-K-C model of assessment of individual cases that greatly expanded the more limited, traditional S-R analysis used by behavioral analysts up to that time. In this expanded model, Kanfer and Saslow clearly outlined the importance of the biological condition of the organism (the O variable in the functional analytic model) in etiology and assessment. Some authors (Kohlberg, 1976; Meichenbaum, 1977) have expanded the O variable to include cognitive or attitudinal variables that the individual brings to the situation. Furthermore, rather than limiting analysis of behavior problems to immediate

TABLE 6–5

Natural History of Conduct Disorders

study	method	subject sample	beginning age	study period	beginning diagnosis	terminal diagnosis
Annesley, 1961	Follow-up	Inpatient psychiatry unit	12–18 yrs.	2–5 years	"Behavior disorder" (violence, stealing, truancy)	40% behavior disorder 1% schizophrenia
Morris, et al., 1955	Follow-up	Inpatient unit	4–15 yrs. X = 10	To adulthood	Aggressive behavior disorder (unsocialized aggressive	59% "poor social adjustment" (18% committed crimes) 20% schizophrenia 21% normal
O'Neal & Robins, 1958	Follow-up	Psychiatry clinic	13 yrs.	30 years	Delinquent	37% Sociopathic personality 14% Neuroses 6% Psychoses 11% ill; no diagnosis 14% Normal 9% Alcoholism

Pritchard & Graham, 1966	Child and adult psychiatry clinic attenders	Psychiatry clinic	5-16 yrs. $X = 11.6$	4-28 yrs. $X = 10.8$	Aggressive/antisocial (No court contact)	6% Sociopathic personality 30% Neuroses 30% Psychosis 4% Ill; no diagnosis 14% Normal
					Delinquency	37% Antisocial personality 19% Inadequate personality 19% Neurose 15% Immature & schiziod personality 11% Psychotic disorders
					Conduct disorder	30% Antisocial personality 30% Neuroses 30% Inadequate personality 10% Immature & schiziod personality 0% Psychotic disorders

antecedent (the S variable) and consequent (the C variable) events, the expanded model emphasized the importance of the larger environmental context within which behavior is shaped and maintained. According to Kanfer and Saslow (1969), "since the patient operates in a complex of systems, not only psychological events but all events, including biologic, economic, and social, must be admitted as potential variables in the analysis, without prior judgment about their order of importance" (p. 426).

This expanded model of behavioral diagnosis, proposed almost 15 years ago, opened the door for behavioral theorists to incorporate data collected within the biological and social sciences for a more complete understanding of the etiology of aggressive behavior. Accordingly, we will now briefly consider some of the research on potential constitutional, biological, and social variables in etiology of aggression, followed by a review of the more familiar research on psychological and family system influences.

Constitutional and Biological Predisposing Influences

Child Temperament.   As reviewed earlier, recent analyses by Lorber and Patterson (1981) indicate that aggressive behavior in many children appears at an early age and is expressed in a stable fashion across both time and settings, prompting these authors to postulate an aggressive behavior "trait". Such reviews converge with recent increased interest among child researchers in the *child's* contribution to parent-child interaction patterns that, once they are established, directly increase aggressive behavior within the family (Emery, Binkoff, Houts & Carr, 1983). Along these lines, Thomas, Chess and Birch (1968) have described the "temperamentally difficult" baby who, from the outset, is an intense, irregular, negative and nonadaptable child, and who is more likely to contribute adversely to the mother-child interaction. Rutter, Birch, Thomas and Chess (1964) showed that these children are more likely to be referred for treatment of temper tantrums and aggressive behavior at age six than nontemperamental children. Regarding aggressive behavior, Webster-Stratton and Eyberg (1982) demonstrated positive correlations between parent-reported child conduct problems, child temperament and mother-child interactions. Furthermore, in a causal analysis of familial and temperamental determinants of aggressive behavior using path analysis techniques, Olweus (1980) found that boys' temperament contributed substantially to the additive statistical model in the prediction of aggressive behavior. However, temperament variables did not contribute as much to the explanatory variance as family variables.

Medical Variables.   Shanok and Lewis (1981) compared the medical histories of matched samples of nonincarcerated delinquent girls, incarcerated delinquent girls, and nondelinquent girls. In general, delinquent girls were found to have had significantly more accidents and injuries up until age 21 than non-delinquent girls. Across the delinquent samples, incarcerated (and presumably more aggressive) girls had more perinatal difficulties, more head and face injuries, more neurologic abnormalities, and a greater likelihood of having been abused (and presumably injured) as young children. In an earlier study comparing large samples of delinquent to nondelinquent children, Lewis and Shanok (1977) had shown that the differences in hospital visits was greatest before age four and between ages 14 and 16.

Findings regarding neurological abnormalities were also reported in another study from Lewis' research group (Lewis, Shanok, Pincus & Glaser, 1979). In this study, more violent, incarcerated delinquent boys were differentiated from less violent, incarcerated delinquent boys on symptoms of psychomotor epilepsy, minor neurological impairment signs, and grossly abnormal EEGs and/or a history of grand mal epilepsy. It should be noted that these children were selected only on the basis of their aggressive behavior and not on the basis of suspected neurological disorder.

The potential association between violent aggressive behavior and EEG abnormalities in children coincides with medical researchers' claims regarding a causal relationship between temporal lobe epilepsy and violence in adults. A recent study evaluated the manifestations of 33 epileptic attacks in 19 patients with documented histories of psychomotor seizure disorder (temporal lobe epilepsy) and aggressive behavior (Delgado-Escueta, Mattson, King, Goldensohn, Spiegel, Madson, Crandall, Dreifuss & Porter, 1981). In this study, aggressive behavior was clearly observed during the height of epileptiform paroxysms, ranging from nondirected aggressive movements to mild to moderate violence directed toward other persons or objects. While these and other authors are not yet willing to conclude that temporal lobe epilepsy results in violent crime, they do conclude that epileptic automatism can be manifested as *directed* violence and aggression.

Extending this research to children, Lewis, Pincus, Shanok and Glaser (1982) performed neuropsychiatric and electroencephalographic evaluations on 97 adjudicated delinquent boys at a state correctional facility. These authors found that 78 percent of the boys studied had one or more symptoms of temporal lobe epilepsy, and 46 percent had three or more symptoms. Independent review of the clinical records by two clinicians (a psychiatrist and a neurologist), who used preestablished diagnostic criteria, indicated that 18 percent of the sample met full criteria for psychomotor seizure disorder. As in a previous study, these children were selected only on the basis of their extreme aggressive behavior and not on the basis of suspected neurological disorder. From this study, the authors concluded that psychomotor epilepsy is far more prevalent in delinquent populations than in the general population. The uncontrolled, nonblind nature of the study leads us to be considerably more cautious. Nevertheless, this study, along with others reviewed in this section, suggests that neurological dysfunction may be more prevalent in highly aggressive than in normal populations and may be etiologically related to extreme aggression and violence in some cases. Further methodologically sound research is clearly needed in this area.

Social Influences

A few studies have identified social context variables that are related to the development and maintenance of aggressive and delinquent behavior. Those that are identified most frequently across studies are low socioeconomic status, large sibship size, and broken homes (Robins, 1966; Rutter, Tizard & Whitmore, 1970; West & Farrington, 1973). However, in her recent analysis of the effects of these variables, Robins (1979) concluded that the effects of the two variables, low socioeconomic status and broken homes, are actually attributable to processes within the family. For example, in studies holding social class constant and examining differences between parents of delinquents and nondelinquents, parents of delinquents have been found to be less adequate in terms of overall social adjustment. They are less educated, make less use of available health services, and show less ability to obtain and hold a job. According to Robins (1979), because of their poorer social coping abilities, these individuals are more likely to occupy positions in the lower socioeconomic class and are also more likely to show poor parenting abilities, directly resulting in aggressive child behavior. Regarding the effects of broken homes, Robins (1966) and Hetherington, Cox, and Cox (1979) have suggested that it is not broken homes per se, but problems in the parents *leading* to divorce or separation that is the critical predictive factor.

The nature of the relationship between family size and aggressive behavior is unclear. However, one might speculate that the larger the family, the less parental attention and supervision that is available for each child. Therefore, most of the evidence seems to be pointing to processes within the family, rather than social variables per se, as the more powerful etiologic factors in development of aggression in children. We will now turn to a consideration of these factors.

Family Patterns

Parenting Behavior.   Over the past 20 years, systematic behavioral research from several research laboratories has identified child and parent behaviors that differentiate families of aggressive from families with normal children. Comparing across studies, parents of aggressive children can be differentiated from parents of normal children by the rate of topography of commands delivered to their children: parents of aggressors give significantly more commands than parents of normals. More specifically, they deliver a higher rate of poorly formulated, nonspecific, or vague commands in a threatening, angry, or nagging manner. Parents of aggressors have also been demonstrated to criticize their children at a higher rate and to respond with a greater proportion of negative behavior in general than parents of normals. All of these findings have been demonstrated empirically in naturalistic observations in the homes of aggressive and normal children, using reliable and valid behavioral coding systems. (For reviews of this literature see Rogers, Forehand & Griest, 1981; Wells & Forehand, 1981).

The findings from behavioral assessment research regarding poor parenting behaviors in aggressive families are substantiated by sociological research as well. In a large scale study that attempted to identify predictors of delinquent behavior, Glueck and Glueck (1972) found the following parent variables to be more common among delinquent than nondelinquent families: lack of family cohesiveness, indifference or hostility toward the delinquent child and unsuitable supervision and discipline. McCord, McCord, and Zola (1959) reported that certain combinations of parent variables were highly predictive of delinquency. The most important of these parent variables were parent quarrelsomeness, hostility, neglectfulness, laxity in discipline, and lack of maternal love.

In a more recent study from Norway that investigated early familial and temperamental factors in the development of aggression, Olweus (1980) used an experimental design, allowing a causal model for development of aggressive behavior in boys to be formulated and empirically tested. In this study, four factors in the model contributed in an additive fashion to the development of aggression. These variables were mother negativism, mother's permissiveness for aggression, mother's and father's use of power-assertive methods, and boy's temperament. The first two factors accounted for the greatest causal impact. Child temperament contributed significantly, but less substantially than parent variables. In discussing these results, Olweus (1980) concludes that "if the mother is negative, rejecting, and indifferent to the boy when he is young, this is likely to result in the adolescent boy becoming relatively more aggressive and hostile toward his environment" (p. 651). Regarding maternal permissiveness, he concluded, "A highly accepting, tolerant or lax attitude without clear limits for the boy's aggressive behavior contributes substantially to the development of an aggressive reaction pattern in the boy" (p. 651).

In reviewing the results of studies, such as those reported above, from behavioral, social, and psychological research, it is striking that one finding is consistent across studies—the extreme importance in the etiology of aggression of parental, particularly maternal, hostility and negativism toward the child, and/or the lack of consistent limits and consequences for negative behavior. These parenting variables appear to underlie the effects of social variables, such as social class or broken homes (Robins, 1979). Likewise, they appear to contribute more to the explanatory variance than child temperament variables (Olweus, 1980). Therefore, it is important to understand the learning mechanisms whereby these parenting behaviors contribute to the development and maintenance of aggressive behavior in children.

The most systematic explanation of the relationship between parent behavior and child aggressive behavior has been offered by Patterson (1976; 1980). Patterson emphasizes the coercive or controlling nature of many aggressive behaviors and has developed the "coercion hypothesis" to account for their escalation and maintenance. According to this hypothesis, most young children employ aversive behaviors in interactions with their mothers. Such behaviors (e.g., crying) are intially adaptive, that is, they quickly shape the mother in the skills necessary for the young child's survival (i.e., feeding, temperature control). However, while most children decrease aversive behaviors as they grow older, other children continue to employ aversive control strategies, because their parents fail to model and positively reinforce more appropriate prosocial skills, and/or because they continue to reinforce the child's coercive behaviors. As far as this latter point is concerned, Patterson (1976; 1980) has emphasized the extreme importance of negative reinforcement in the escalation and maintenance of coercive behaviors. In the negative reinforcement model, coercive behavior on the part of one family member is reinforced when it results in the removal of an aversive event that is applied by another family member. The following examples illustrate negative reinforcement processes occurring between parent and child.

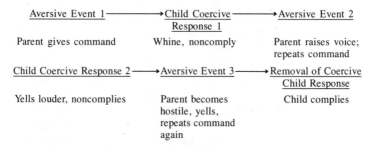

In the example, the child's coercive behaviors are negatively reinforced when the parent withdraws the aversive stimulus (command). In the following example, coercion escalates:

In this example, the parent's increasing hostility, and threatening behaviors are negatively reinforced by the child's eventual compliance.

In the preceding examples, it is apparent how negative reinforcement functions to increase the probability of aggressive behavior by both parent and child. In addition, as this "training" occurs over long periods of time, significant increases in rate and intensity of these coercive behaviors occur as both family members are reinforced for higher amplitude aggression. Thus, in this system, the child is reinforced for engaging in coercive behaviors since these behaviors sometimes "work" in removing aversive parental behaviors. The parents are reinforced for increases in their negative, hostile, threatening, or nagging behaviors since these parental responses sometimes "work" in terms of removing *immediate* aggressive child behaviors. However, the long-term consequences for the family are increases in aggressive behavior, a negative family climate, increases in feelings of anger and hostility or, conversely, depression and withdrawal, and a decrease in positive interactions among family members (Patterson, 1976; 1980; Patterson & Reid, 1970; Wells & Forehand, 1981).

Loeber (1982) and Patterson (1982) have suggested that there may be parenting style differences in families of children displaying overt aggression (fighting, arguing, noncompliance) versus families of children displaying covert aggression (stealing). According to these authors, covert antisocial behaviors may be associated with the parents' lack of monitoring of the child's behavior (i.e., lack of supervision), whereas overt aggression may be associated primarily with coercive interactions among parents and child and disruptions in the parents' discipline. At the present time, evidence is scant, and these speculations should be viewed as hypotheses to be tested. However, if parenting style differences between aggressive and predelinquent children can be demonstrated, then it would have significant implications for differential etiology and treatment of the two major subtypes of child antisocial behavior disorder.

Marital Discord and Conflict. Studies on the relationship between marital dissatisfaction in parents and aggressive behavior in children have produced equivocal results. A relationship has been found in some (e.g., Ferguson & Allen, 1978; Johnson & Lobitz, 1974; Oltmanns, Broderick & O'Leary, 1977; Porter & O'Leary, 1980) but not all samples (e.g., Griest, Forehand, Wells, & McMahon, 1980), and when there is a significant relationship, it is sometimes weak. For example, in their study of clinic-referred conduct disordered children, Oltmanns, et al. (1977) found that one third of the parents had unsatisfying marriages. The relationship is usually weaker in nonclinic families.

However, more recent research in the area of marital conflict and divorce indicates that the methodology used in earlier studies may be part of the reason for confusion in this area. Most early studies employed the Locke-Wallace Marriage Inventory (Locke & Wallace, 1959) in investigating the relationship between child behavior and marital dysfunction. This assessment device provides a general measure of satisfaction with marriage. However, a study by Porter and O'Leary (1980) found no significant correlations between marital satisfaction (measured by the Locke-Wallace questionnaire) and child behavior problems, whereas significant correlations were found between *marital hostility* and child behavior problems. Furthermore, data from Hetherington's research project on the effects of divorce on children lend credence to the hypothesis that it is marital hostility and conflict, not general marital dissatisfaction, that is more directly related to child behavior problems. She found that children of divorced parents who continue to have conflicts after the divorce have more behavior problems than do children from conflict-free divorces (Hetherington, Cox & Cox, 1976). These data have prompted Hetherington, et al. (1979), Emery (1982), and others to speculate that children from broken or intact homes characterized by open interparental conflict are at greater risk for behavior problems than are children from relatively harmonious broken or intact homes. The effect of marital turmoil appears to be much greater on boys than on girls (Emery & O'Leary, 1982; Porter & O'Leary, 1980; Rutter, 1971) and to relate to more pervasive problems in older compared to younger boys. Porter and O'Leary (1980) found significant correlations between overt marital hostility and Conduct Disorder in 5–10-year-old boys. However, in older boys (aged 10–16) significant correlations were found between marital hostility scores and behavior problem subscale scores of Personality Disorder, Inadequacy-Immaturity and Socialized Delinquency using Quay's (1977) Behavior Problem Checklist.

While it appears from recent research that a relationship does exist between interparental conflict and aggressive child behavior, particularly in boys, most of the studies have been correlational; therefore, direction of causation cannot be concluded. While it is often assumed that marital discord causes or exacerbates child behavior problems, it may be equally likely that having a problem child serves as a precursor to marital conflict or that other variables contribute to both (Griest & Wells, 1983). In this regard, our earlier discussion of parenting variables related to etiology of aggression appears relevant. In that section, we found that parental hostility, quarrelsomeness, criticism, and negativism directed to the child are related significantly to development of aggressive behavior in children. These same behaviors occurring *between parents* also appear to be related to child aggression. Thus, it seems that parents who may be generally hostile, negative, and critical, and families who generally lack affective attachments and cohesiveness among their members, produce aggressive behavior in children. This behavior pattern in adults may produce a disruption in many interpersonal relationships, including adult-adult and adult-child.

Parent Psychopathology.   The psychiatric literature is replete with studies demonstrating a relationship between parent psychopathology and child behavior problems (Griest & Wells, 1983). Recent studies have aimed specifically at identifying those dimensions of parent psychopathology related to aggression in children.

In a sample of families whose children were referred to a clinic specifically for treatment of conduct disorders, Johnson and Lobitz (1974) found significant correlations between *fathers'* elevated MMPI scores (particularly on the *Hy, Pd,* and *Sc* scales) and observed deviance level of the target child. In a more recent study by Patterson (1980), *mothers* of children classified in Patterson's system as Stealers (DSM-III: Undersocialized Conduct Disorder; aggressive or nonaggressive) had MMPI peaks on Psychopathic Deviate, Hypomania and Schizophrenia scales, whereas mothers of children classified as Aggressive (DSM-III: Socialized Aggressive Conduct Disorder or Oppositional Disorder) showed elevations on scales indicating depression, rigidity, and social introversion. As Patterson (1980) points out, the MMPI profile for mothers of Stealers corresponds to the classic profile for juvenile delinquents, whereas the pattern for mothers of Aggressives is a more neurotic pattern.

Recent studies from our research group extend Patterson's findings on mothers of aggressive, oppositional children. In our studies, maternal depression and anxiety have repeatedly been identified as factors that discriminate mothers of oppositional from mothers of normal children (Griest et al., 1980), that negatively affect mothers' perceptions of their children (Forehand, Wells, McMahon, Griest, & Rogers, 1982; Griest, Wells, & Forehand, 1979), and that predict attrition rates during parent training treatment (McMahon, Forehand, Griest, & Wells, 1981) and during follow-up (Griest, Forehand & Wells, 1981).

In summary, certain forms of parent psychopathology are significantly related to two types of aggressive disorders in children. However, the mechanisms whereby parent psychopathology may be etiologically related to child deviance is unclear, as the relationship may reflect genetic, family environment, and/or parenting style influences in development of aggression. For example, there is evidence that genetic factors play some role in the etiology of delinquent and criminal behavior (Cadoret & Cain, 1980; Hutchings & Mednick, 1974). On the other hand, parents who are elevated on hypomania and paranoid dimensions of behavior may be more likely to be irritable, negative, hostile and blaming; hence, as we have seen, these parenting behaviors are directly related to development of aggression in children. It appears that the etiologic relationship of parent psychopathology to child aggressive disorders is likely to be complex.

Some Tentative Conclusions on Etiology of Aggression

As our review indicates, speculations regarding the significance of a wide range of social, biological, constitutional, behavioral, and family environment influences in the etiology of aggressive behavior in children have been offered by various researchers and theorists. Variables within each of these realms have been related to child aggression. However, because most researchers design and conduct studies within their particular area of interest and expertise, no large scale studies exist that combine all possible variables into one research design that investigates the unique and combined predictive significance of these variables to the etiology of aggression. Until such a large scale project is conducted, we can only speculate as to the relative etiologic significance of social, behavioral, constitutional, and biologic influences. However, by examining individual studies that have been conducted, some tentative speculations can be made.

First, it is very clear that at least two subtypes of aggressive behavior exist in children and that these are presumably associated with different combinations of etiologic influences. Almost all of the studies on biologic, genetic, and neurological influences in aggression have been conducted with delinquent, usually incarcerated, populations (DSM-III: Undersocialized Aggressive Conduct Disorder) with the most violent and aggressive children showing the greatest evidence of neurological abnormality, physical insults, or genetic contribution. There is little evidence for significant contribution of these variables to etiology of milder forms of conduct or oppositional disorders (DSM-III: Socialized Nonagressive Disorder or Oppositional Disorder).

The effects of social variables seem to be important insofar as they mediate processes with the family, particularly the parents, relating to aggression in children. These parenting and family influences have been found to be present in both severe delinquent and mild nondelinquent forms of conduct disorder. Specifically, it is the interpersonal processes between parents (i.e., marital hostility) and among parents and child that appear to be *directly* and *causally* related to aggression in children. Parent-parent and parent-child relationships characterized by high rates of hostility, negativism, criticism, indifference among family members, low rates of family cohesiveness and positive attention, and/or laxity in supervision and effective consequences for negative child behavior appear to result in aggression. In this regard, one of the most significant contributions of behavioral research has been the systematic explication of modeling and negative reinforcement processes that define the learning mechanisms whereby child and parent aggressive behaviors are shaped and maintained in the family context (i.e., coercion theory).

The effects of parent psychopathology on severe forms of child aggression or delinquent behavior may result from genetic, modeling and/or parenting influences. For milder forms of child aggression or oppositionalism, there is little evidence for genetic transmission. Rather, depression and anxiety in parents of mild conduct disordered children may result in aggressive behavior in one of several ways, as recently outlined by Griest and Wells (1983). First, due to symptoms associated with depression (i.e., agitation, irritability, difficulty concentrating, insomnia), parent depression may result in lowered tolerance of normal variations in child behavior, causing increased hostility, negativism, and use of punishment by the parent. In addition, parental depression manifesting a decreased energy level, hypersomnia, feelings of despair and hopelessness may result in decreases in parental positive attention and supervision— conditions that have also been related to child aggression. Finally, parents who view their children's behavior as aversive, uncontrollable, and unmanageable may experience "learned helplessness," which further exacerbates parent depression and withdrawal from the child (Seligman, 1975).

In summary, in mild forms of aggressive, oppositional behavior, it is likely that parenting and family interaction influences are the most etiologically significant variables. As aggressive behavior becomes more extreme, violent, or pervasive, it may be more and more likely that additional biological, neurological, or genetic variables also contribute to the explanatory variance. Even in these more extreme cases, however, it is clear that processes within the family continue to play an important role. It is extremely important that prevention and treatment programs for aggressive children include a comprehensive assessment of variables reviewed above, with particular emphasis on parenting and family assessment, since processes within the parents and family predict mild as well as severe forms of aggressive disorder.

ASSESSMENT

Assessment of aggressive behavior disorders of children must take into account the primary features of the disorder as well as associated features that may be present. As we have seen, aggressive children are characterized primarily by high rates of disobedient, disruptive, assaultive, and/or destructive behaviors. In addition, they may display reading or other academic difficulties, emotional problems (primarily depression), social skills deficits, and social withdrawal. Their parents may display marital conflict/dissatisfaction and adjustment problems of their own, including depression, irritability, and/or antisocial behavior. Because each of these child and family variables may contribute directly to the child's behavior disorder, the assessment process must include evaluation of each of these variables. In addition, because extreme aggression or violent behavior may be associated with neurological abnormality, referral for a medical evaluation may be necessary in some cases.

A complete review of assessment strategies for each of the dimensions outlined above is beyond the scope of this chapter, and the reader is referred to several technical reviews (Barlow, 1981; Hersen & Bellack, 1981; Mash & Terdal, 1981). We shall briefly describe assessment strategies that provide for evaluation of dimensions of child and family functioning in the settings where these are displayed.

In the Home

The most frequently used method for assessing problems occurring in the home setting is the clinical interview. Several structured interviews relevant to description and diagnosis of home problems recently have been developed and tested in research settings. However, most clinicians rely on unstructured interviews in the initial stages of assessment.

Interviews should be conducted with certain goals in mind. First and foremost, the interview should serve as a vehicle for establishing rapport with the parent (and child) and for communicating that the therapist is concerned and knowledgeable about the types of problems occurring in the family and has a genuine desire to help. Thereafter, questioning should focus on a description of the child's major problems in the home setting, as well as information relevant to a functional analysis. For example, the interviewer should ask the parent to describe the child's primary problem behaviors, social relationships, and whether the child ever seems depressed, sad, or withdrawn. The parent also should be asked to describe the situations in which problems occur at home and the parents' typical ways of responding to the problems. Once current behavior and emotional patterns are discussed, the interviewer should ask questions regarding the child's early development, particularly early temperamental patterns. The parent might be asked, for example, if the child was a difficult, irritable baby, had irregular sleep, had irregular eating and/or behavior patterns, or if the child was even-tempered and easy to manage as a baby.

The interviewer also should attempt to evaluate the general emotional climate in the home, particularly with regard to hostility and negativism between and among parents and children. Questions would focus on the parents' feelings toward the target child and toward each other in the case of a two-parent home.

Finally, a discussion of the emotional adjustment of the parent(s) should take place, particularly focusing on feelings of depression, anxiety, or social withdrawal of the parent. If the parent answers affirmatively, the interviewer might ask how the parent believes his/her personal difficulties affect his/her interactions with and management of the child.

In addition to the interview, several behavior checklists and rating scales are available to aid in the assessment of home problems. Child behavior checklists developed by Quay (1977), Conners (1970), and Achenbach (1978) can be completed by parents. These checklists yield factor scores on aggression, depression, and social withdrawal behavior dimensions, allowing a statistical comparison of the referred child to children in the normal population (see Wells [1981] for a review of child behavior checklists). Parents' marital adjustment and marital conflict can be assessed using the Locke-Wallace Marriage Inventory (Locke & Wallace, 1959) and the O'Leary-Porter Scale, a 20-item inventory designed to measure marital hostility (Porter & O'Leary, 1980). Finally, parent emotional adjustment and psychopathology relevant to child behavior problems can be assessed using the MMPI (Dahlstrom & Welsh, 1960), the Beck Depression Inventory (Beck, Ward, Mendelsohn, Mock, & Erbaugh, 1961), and the State-Trait Anxiety Inventory-Trait form (Spielberger, Gorsuch, & Lushene, 1970), as well as a number of other questionnaires (See Hersen & Bellack, 1981).

A final method of assessing home behavior problems involves direct behavioral observations. While considerable research effort has gone into the development of complex behavior coding systems for measuring disruptive child and family behavior in the home (see Wells [1981] for a review of these coding systems), this approach to assessment is used primarily in research settings. Recent attempts have been made to develop more practical approaches to direct home observation, such as having parents observe and record behavior in the home (e.g., Wells, Griest, & Forehand, 1980) and using audiotaped recordings in the home that can be scored later (e.g., Christensen, 1979; Johnson, Christensen, & Bellamy, 1976). While these approaches to home observation show promise, their clinical utility, reliability, and validity have not been adequately demonstrated.

An alternative to direct observations in the home is direct observation of parent-child interactions in the clinic through a one-way mirror. In most clinic observation procedures, parents are instructed to interact with their children in an unstructured situation (e.g., free play with toys) and in a structured situation (e.g., parent gives commands to engage in certain tasks, such as play tasks, clean-up tasks, or academic work tasks). An observer codes parent and child behaviors from an adjoining observation room using one of the coding systems alluded to earlier. Forehand and his colleagues have demonstrated that clinic observation data discriminate between aggressive and normal children and their parents; in addition, treatment effects observed in the clinic coincide with treatment effects observed in the home (Griest et al., 1980; Forehand, King, Peed, & Yoder, 1975; Peed, Roberts, & Forehand, 1977). For these reasons, clinic observations represent a viable alternative to direct home observations (Atkeson & Forehand, 1981).

In the School

As already noted, children with aggressive behavior disorders frequently display problems observable in the school setting. Interviews with the parent and teacher, teacher-recorded behavior, and behavioral observations by independent observers frequently will reveal that the child does not follow classroom rules, does not obey the teacher, and often disrupts the classroom routine (see Atkeson & Forehand, 1981, for a review of these procedures). Several teacher-completed checklists also have been developed to further delineate and quantify the nature of classroom problems. The most frequently used questionnaire, the Conners Teacher Rating Scale (CTRS) (Conners, 1969), provides factors relevant to conduct disorders, anxiety, and social adjustment in the classroom, allowing a statistical comparison to normal children (Goyette, Conners, & Ulrich, 1978).

In addition to observations of classroom behavior, children with aggressive behaviors should be screened to determine their level of academic achievement, particularly in reading. The teacher should be interviewed regarding the child's previous school failure and current achievement in academic subjects relative to the child's age peers. In addition, standardized achievement tests, such as the Peabody Individual Achievement Test (PIAT) or the Wide Range Achievement Test (WRAT), might be administered to screen for academic difficulties. Because children with aggressive behavior often have reading problems, they may need to be referred for special tutoring or resource room intervention.

Finally, screening should include an examination for possible visual and hearing difficulties. An interview with the teacher and/or child and, when deemed necessary, referral to a specialist can be utilized to eliminate these potential contributors to school problems.

In the Community

The importance of assessment of the family's community interactions comes from a growing body of data linking parents' interpersonal relationships outside the family to child behavior problems (Griest & Wells, 1983). In his recent work in this area, Wahler (1980) has identified two types of families with aggressive children: insular and noninsular. Insular families are typically characterized by low income, poor education, and most importantly, few social contacts. When social contacts do occur, they are likely to be aversive. In contrast, noninsular families are typically middle-class and have frequent positive social contacts outside the family.

The importance of assessing family insularity derives from its association to child behavior problems. Leske, Afton, Rogers, and Wahler (1978) reported that as a mother's frequency of positive social contacts increases, positive interactions within the family also increase. Similarly, Wahler (1980) reported negative daily covariations between mothers' friendly extrafamilial contacts and occurrence of oppositional child behavior. Finally, family insularity bears directly on generalization of treatment effects for aggressive children. Insular mothers continue to engage in global, blame-oriented descriptions of their children, even after direct observation methods indicate that the child has improved. Not surprisingly, these families fail to maintain positive gains after treatment compared to noninsular families (Wahler & Afton, 1980).

Because of the importance of family insularity in the display and treatment of aggressive child behavior, this variable should be included in the assessment process. For this purpose, Wahler has developed a Community Insularity Checklist, currently used in clinical and research studies and obtainable from the author.

Like the parents, the aggressive child may also display difficulties in social relationships outside the family within the peer group. Assessment of this problem area also should occur. [The reader is referred to several recent comprehensive reviews of assessment of children's social skill (Green & Forehand, 1980; Hops & Greenwood, 1981; Michelson & Wood, 1980; Van Hasselt, Bellack, Hersen, & Whitehill, 1979)]. The major methods of assessment include: Rating scales, such as the Walker Behavior Problem Checklist, which has a factor labeled *Disturbed Peer Relations* (Walker, 1970); sociometric ratings, in which classroom peers are asked to rate children with whom they would most like to play, work, or be with; role-playing tests, such as the Behavioral Assertiveness Test for Children (Bornstein, Bellack, & Hersen, 1977) and the Behavioral Assertiveness Test for Boys (Reardon, Hersen, Bellack & Foley, 1979); and behavioral observations in the natural environment. Rating scales and sociometric techniques are most useful in initially identifying socially isolated or unskilled children. Role-play tests and naturalistic observations are helpful in isolating particular components of social skills for incorporation into treatment programs.

TREATMENT

In a review of treatment strategies by the present authors through 1980 (Wells & Forehand, 1981), we found that four major approaches to treatment of conduct disordered children had received the most research evaluation to that time. These approaches included: reprogramming the social environment via parent behavioral training, use of token economies in the home, behavioral contracting, and conflict resolution skills training (see Wells & Forehand, 1981, for a methodological review of studies in these areas). By far, the treatment approach that has received most research attention is reprogramming the social environment via parent behavioral training. This approach often includes use of token economies or behavioral contracting as part of an overall program.

Parent training involves the child's parents or caregivers as behavior change agents or as administrators of the treatment program in the home setting. Thus, this treatment was developed primarily for children living in a family context. In addition, parent training interventions initially were applied to children with any and all forms of aggressive behavior, ranging from mild oppositional difficulties in the home to antisocial behavior in the community (e.g., stealing). No attempts were made to subclassify children with different types of aggressive behavior disorders or to develop treatments that were differentially effective with different subclasses of disorder.

Since 1980, several advances have been made in parent training research. First, because behavioral parent training was developed and tested in research laboratory settings, the question of whether these technologies could be applied effectively in community-based clinical settings remained unanswered. This question has now been addressed. Secondly, although parent training treatment had been compared to no-treatment control groups (e.g., Wiltz & Patterson, 1974), no studies previously existed comparing behavioral parent training to other forms of active treatment. Data bearing on this question of comparative efficacy are now available. Thirdly, as our knowledge of subclasses of aggressive behavior disorder becomes clearer, it has also become clear that different approaches to treatment will be required for different subclasses. Finally, several studies recently have been conducted refining our knowledge of effective treatment implementation and investigating procedures to enhance generalization of treatment effects obtained from parent training. As each of the questions bears directly on clinical treatment of aggressive behavior in children, we will briefly review each of these areas.

Community Dissemination

Until recently, most parent-training programs reported in the psychological literature were developed and implemented in University based behavioral laboratories. Their usefulness in natural settings was unclear. However, in 1975, the Oregon Social Learning Center (OSLC) was asked to assist in establishing a community based, clinical service to treat aggressive children in Helena, Montana. In a recent report of the first two and a half years of that facility's operation, Fleischman and Szykula (1981) showed that parent training for families of aggressive children can be effectively implemented in community-based clinical settings by professional therapists trained in social learning treatment. Furthermore, results obtained in this community project paralleled results obtained in research settings; that is, significant treatment effects were found for Total Aversive Behavior measured in the home, parent-collected daily behavior data, and global ratings of improvement by parents at treatment termination. The cost of treatment per family was $776 in the third year of the project, and referrals to the center from the community were steadily increasing. These data indicate that parent-training approaches can be implemented effectively in clinical settings in an efficient and cost-effective manner.

Comparative Efficacy

Prior to 1980, four studies existed that compared parent training treatment to waiting list control groups (Karoly & Rosenthal, 1977; Peed, et al., 1977; Wiltz & Patterson, 1974) or to an attention placebo control group (Walter & Gilmore, 1973). These studies appeared to demonstrate that behavioral parent training was superior to no-treatment or inert treatments for aggressive children. However, two studies have recently been conducted comparing parent training to active nonbehavioral treatments. In the first of these studies, Bernal, Klinnert and Schultz (1980) compared parent training to "client-centered parent counseling," involving exploration of feelings, attitudes, and experiences in the family and using student therapists. Parent report, parent-completed behavior rating scales, and parent satisfaction measures showed superior treatment effects for behavioral parent training compared to client-centered counseling. No differential treatment effects were found on Overall Deviant Behavior or Noncompliance measured in the home by trained home observers, although effects for Overall Deviant Behavior approached significance. In addition, superiority of behavioral parent training over client-centered counseling was not maintained at a six-month follow-up, although both groups showed continuing improvement.

In the second study, Patterson, Chamberlain and Reid (1982) compared behavioral parent training conducted at the Oregon Social Learning Center (OSLC) by experienced professional therapists to community based treatment. Families in the comparison group were randomly referred to community agencies or to psychologists and psychiatrists in private practice. Thus, this study represents the first true comparison of parent training to treatments typically offered in the community. Results showed that parent behavioral training was clearly superior to community based treatment on Total Aversive Behavior, measured in the home by objective home observers, and on parents' general level of satisfaction with treatment. Differences in parent daily report data were generally in favor of parent behavioral training but were not statistically significant.

How does one account for the differences in results of these two studies, and what conclusions can be drawn regarding comparative efficacy? In the Bernal et al. (1980) study, treatments were administered in 10, one-hour therapy sessions by graduate student therapists. In the Patterson et al. (1982) study, behavioral parent training was administered for an average of 17 hours by full-time staff employed by OSLC for up to five years and trained by Patterson. This raises the question if only individuals trained and supervised by Patterson can obtain positive behavioral treatment effects in parent training. The answer seems to be that treatment effects are *not* specific to Patterson, as Fleischman (1981) has replicated Patterson's positive results in a different setting, using therapists who had never been trained or supervised by Patterson. As in Patterson et al. (1982), however, Fleischman's therapists were professional staff with up to six years of experience in social learning treatment.

These studies suggest that, in order for parent training to show clearly superior effects compared to other forms of treatment, treatment must be open-ended and based on the idiosyncratic progress of each particular family, each with up to an average of 17 hours of treatment time, as is done at OSLC. Programs that attempt to impose a predetermined, limited number of therapy sessions on families may not respond to the unique characteristics of families that determine their progress. In addition, these studies indicate that parent training is not a casual undertaking that can be administered effectively by relatively inexperienced therapists, but that it should be done by individuals willing to make a serious commitment to acquire the requisite skills through reading, training, and supervision.

Patterson has anecdotally reported in recent articles (Patterson & Fleischman, 1979; Patterson, et al., 1982; Patterson, Reid & Chamberlain, 1981) that several additional "treatment ingredients," not emphasized in previous research, also may be required in order to obtain clearly superior results from parent training. These include clinical skills for dealing with resistance to therapeutic instructions (Patterson et al., 1981) and direct attention to marital conflicts and other parent problems. These speculations converge with the recent model of behavioral family therapy for aggressive children outlined by Griest and Wells (1983). We reviewed studies that lead to the conclusion that, in families in which the parents are experiencing marital, psychological, or social maladjustment, parent training alone represents incomplete and inadequate treatment. For these families, parent training will be most effective when accompanied by interventions to address marital, psychological, and social dysfunction.

In summary, in studies comparing behavioral parent training to other forms of therapy, parent training has been demonstrated to be equally efficacious or superior, depending on the outcome measure being evaluated and the assessment interval (i.e., posttreatment or follow-up). In no case have other forms of therapy been found to be superior to parent training.

Differential Treatment Effectiveness

In early parent training research for conduct disordered children, all children referred for aggressive or antisocial behavior were included in experimental groups and received the same treatment interventions. However, we have reviewed several studies in this chapter indicating that at least two subtypes of aggressive disorder exist, and a recent study indicated that these two subtypes are associated with differential treatment effectiveness from traditional parent training. Moore, Chamberlain and Mukai (1979) found that young stealers had a much poorer long-term prognosis compared to nonstealers who engage in more direct, face-to-face social aggression and oppositional behavior with their parents. Stealers were five times more likely to become involved with the police or juvenile court two to nine years after treatment as compared to Social Aggressives. This study confirmed earlier observations of Reid and Hendriks (1973) and Reid and Patterson (1976) that families characterized by low-rate but highly aversive child behavior and for whom *stealing* was part of the referral problems had significantly poorer response to treatment.

These studies have prompted recent additions to the standard parent training approach when the target child is displaying predelinquent, antisocial behavior, particularly stealing. Changes in treatment are based on the fact that stealing is a covert behavior, which is normally concealed from parents and is less likely to be monitored by them. After learning standard parenting skills, parents of Stealers are taught to apply specific negative consequences whenever a *suspicion* of stealing has occurred. This approach stands in contrast to typical behavior therapy approaches that emphasize consequences for overt behavior and place the burden on the child to refrain from stealing *and* to remain above suspicion.

Reid, Hinojosa-Rivera and Lorber (1980) have evaluated the effectiveness of modified parent training for children who steal. In this study, 28 families of Stealers received treatment at OSLC. Outcome measures consisted of: (*a*) parents' reports of stealing; (*b*) parents' reports of other referral problems; and (*c*) Total Aversive Behavior, a summary behavioral category derived from home observations conducted by trained, independent observers. Results indicated significant decreases in parents' reports of stealing events and other referral problems from pre to posttreatment and at a six-month follow-up. Total Aversive Behavior decreased nonsignificantly. However, as might be expected, aversive social behaviors in the family were not high to begin with in this sample of Stealers.

While the results of the Reid et al. (1980) study are suggestive, the main effects on stealing were assessed from parental report measures, raising questions regarding the validity of the findings. Further research is under way at OSLC that is expanding the measurement system to include outside assessments of covert aggression, such as juvenile court and police records. However, at the present time, the modified treatment approach of Reid et al. (1980) represents the first systematic attempt to address covert aggressive behaviors in children and to improve the rather poor results obtained for this population of children from standard parent training. Therefore, we will describe both of these treatment approaches in detail.

Treatment of Aggressives. Two programmatic approaches to treatment of overtly aggressive or oppositional children have been developed and systematically researched. One approach, primarily used with younger children (2-8-years old), was developed by C. Hanf and was subsequently evaluated by Forehand in a systematic research program. This approach focuses on modifying general parent-child interaction patterns as well as specific target behaviors. The second approach developed by Patterson, primarily for use with older children (5-13-years old), emphasizes point systems and token economies administered by the parents at home. Both approaches are based on principles of social learning theory.

In the Hanf-Forehand parent training program, treatment is divided into two distinct phases. During Phase I, parents learn a specific set of "attending and following" skills that can be used in general positive interactions with children, as well as when the parent "catches the child being good." These skills are modeled for the parent who subsequently practices them with the therapist and then with the child in therapy sessions. In addition, the parent is taught to reduce commands, questions, and criticisms directed to the child. After training in attending and following, parents learn to give verbal rewards (e.g., "you did such a good job of picking up the blocks.") and physical rewards (e.g., hugs, pat on the head). Daily homework assignments are given to the parent to spend at least one 15-minute period with the child, attending and rewarding appropriate behavior. In addition, one or two prosocial behaviors (e.g., compliance, playing well with siblings) are targeted, and the parent is instructed to "catch" the child engaging in these prosocial behaviors and to attend and reward on these occasions. Finally, the skill of ignoring (extinction) is taught for application to minor or nondestructive behaviors.

Many younger children will show decreases in oppositional or minor aggressive behavior after the parents learn Phase I skills. However, for severe or longstanding oppositional or aggressive behavior, Phase I skills will not be sufficient to reduce these behaviors. Thus, in Phase II, parents are taught a specific punishment procedure for use initially with noncompliance and, later, for other aggressive behaviors. First, parents are taught the importance of good commanding behavior. They are taught to give clear, concise commands with no more than one or two at a time. They are also taught not to repeat any given command more than once. Noncompliance by the child is followed by a warning of impending consequences. Following noncompliance to the warning, the parent is taught to administer a three to five minute time-out procedure (confinement to a chair in a corner). Lastly, the parent learns to take the child back to the original command situation and issue the initial instruction again. In daily homework practice, the parent implements time-out with the child for noncompliant behavior; subsequently, time-out is applied to other aggressive behaviors. (See Forehand & McMahon, 1981, for an extended explication of this parent training program).

Patterson's treatment program, for children in an older age range, can be divided into three phases, with progression to each phase contingent upon successful completion of the one before. The first phase of treatment focuses on teaching parents the basic concepts and language of social learning theory. Parents are asked to read one of two texts (Patterson, 1975; Patterson & Guillion, 1968) and answer questions on each chapter. During the second phase, parents are taught to define, track, and record behavior and are asked to delineate two deviant and two prosocial behaviors of their child. The parents then record these behaviors in the home for a three day period. Daily phone calls to the home occur during this time to prompt parents to collect their data for the day.

In the third phase, the parent is trained to develop intervention programs beginning with two or three easily tracked behaviors. A point system is set up whereby the child earns and loses points contingent on positive and negative behaviors, respectively. Points are exchanged *daily* for back-up rewards selected by the child. In addition, parents are taught to use positive social reinforcers, such as verbal labeled rewards for positive behaviors, and to implement a time-out procedure for negative behaviors. Thus, the child is earning multiple reinforcers for positive behaviors (e.g., praise and points for compliance) and multiple negative consequences for deviant behavior (e.g., loss of points and time-out for noncompliance) (Patterson, et al., 1975; Wells & Forehand, 1981).

As the reader can observe, these two approaches to treatment of aggressive children attempt to modify exactly those family interpersonal processes identified in behavioral and sociological research as directly contributing to development of aggressive behavior in children. The Hanf-Forehand program most directly accomplishes this by targeting poor commanding behavior and criticisms by the parent (i.e., nagging, threatening, inappropriate commands) and by replacing these behaviors with more positive general interaction skills (i.e., attending and rewarding). The result is a decrease in the general level of hostility and negativism in the family directed toward the child. In addition, both approaches modify specific learning processes that have served to shape and maintain aggressive behavior (i.e., coercive family interaction) and teach parents effective skills for setting consequences on deviant child behavior. To the extent that parent training or any other therapeutic approach will be effective, it is these parent and child behaviors that must be changed.

Treatment of Stealers. Parent training treatment for children who engage in "predelinquent" behaviors, such as stealing, is complicated by the fact that the primary referral problems are highly aversive but occur at a relatively low frequency compared to in-home aggression and may not be observed immediately by parents. In fact, many stealers generally are not supervised closely by their parents, making detection and timely consequences for positive or negative child behaviors impossible (Reid & Patterson, 1976).

To address these difficulties, an adaptation of traditional parent training programs that has been designed by Reid and Patterson (1976) is based on the assumption that firsthand, immediate detection of all stealing events is not a feasible goal (Reid et al., 1980). In this adaptation, parents are first taken through the fundamental parent training program of Patterson et al. (1975). Following this, a specific program for dealing with covert stealing is taught to parents. First, "stealing" is defined as the child's possession of anything for which s/he can not account, an accusation of stealing by an informed other that the parents have reason to believe, or the parents' clear and considered suspicion that the child has taken something (Reid et al., 1980). Thus, emphasis is placed on the report of *suspicion* of stealing rather than actual stealing behavior.

Secondly, a mild consequence for an occurrence of the target behavior (as defined above) is negotiated to be assigned and completed immediately. Usually this is one or two hours of hard work around the home. Parents are taught to ignore the child's denial of stealing, thus making it the child's responsibility not only to refrain from stealing, but also to remain above suspicion. Thirdly, in order to improve monitoring and parental supervision of the child, a check-in system is negotiated, with a schedule that depends on the age of the child. Daily phone calls are made to the home by the therapist to support the parents and to remind them to apply consequences for each and every suspected stealing event, no matter how minor or insignificant. This is undoubtedly an extremely important component of treatment.

As indicated earlier, Reid et al. (1980) have evaluated this approach to treatment of aggressive children who steal. While results appear encouraging, there is no assurance that the primary dependent variable, parent-reported stealing, accurately reflects the actual frequency of stealing events, as Reid et al. (1980) freely admit. Instead of teaching children to reduce their stealing behavior, this program may have taught children to conceal their stealing more effectively. Only long-term follow-up studies analyzing rates of police records and court-recorded offenses for treated and untreated children will answer this question. Nevertheless, this approach represents the first systematic program for treating predelinquent stealers living within the family, and further research is indicated.

Implementation and Generalization

Technique Refinements.   Recently, research efforts have been directed toward refining component skills taught to parents in parent training programs and identifying those components associated with optimal treatment effects. Since child noncompliance is the most frequently reported referral problem for aggressive children, most studies have examined differential effects of various components of treatment on this target behavior. These studies have refined our understanding of the most effective techniques for reducing child aggressive behavior.

While parental attending and rewarding skills are important for improving a negative family climate, these parenting behaviors may not, by themselves, alter noncompliance or other child aggressive behaviors (Budd, Green, & Baer, 1976; Roberts, Hatzenbuehler, & Bean, 1981). Rather, it appears that immediate parental antecedents and consequences to child aggression are most important in breaking the coercive cycle between parent and child and in reducing these behaviors. Regarding parental antecedents, commands or instructions given by the parent play a very important role in decreasing child aggression. Roberts, McMahon, Forehand, and Humphreys (1978) demonstrated that command training alone resulted in significant increases in child compliance. This and other studies have prompted extensions in the amount of therapeutic time spent on teaching parents good "commanding skills." In their treatment manual, Forehand and McMahon (1981) have outlined classes of poor commands that parents are systematically taught to identify and modify. Parents are then taught to give clear, concise, direct instructions, no more than one or two at a time, and to allow the child sufficient time to comply before going on to the next command. Increasing the amount of therapy time spent on role playing, modeling, and practice of good commanding skills will undoubtedly improve treatment effectiveness.

Another extremely important component of most parent training programs is a time-out procedure implemented by parents contingent on child aggression. However, in order for time-out to be most effective, it must be implemented with a knowledge of certain important parameters. Hobbs, Forehand, and Murray (1978) demonstrated that, while very short durations of time-out decrease deviant child behavior, longer durations (up to five minutes) produce greater response suppression and more effectively maintain the suppression when time-out contingencies are removed. Therefore, most programs teach parents to implement time-out from 5 to 15 minutes in duration. Roberts (1982) has shown that, while warned and unwarned time-out procedures are equally effective in increasing child compliance, warned procedures are associated with fewer actual time-outs (i.e., more efficient learning). For this reason, parents should be taught to give a clear warning of impending time-out following noncompliance to an initial command. The warning usually follows an "if . . . then" format (e.g., "if you do not pick up your blocks, then you will have to sit in the corner for five minutes"). Time-out is implemented contingent on noncompliance to this warning.

The rules defining how and by whom the child is released from time-out are also important. Bean and Roberts (1981) showed that when parents determined release contingencies, clinically significant increases in child compliance were obtained compared to children who were in charge of releasing themselves from time-out. For the latter children, some improvements in compliance were noted but were clinically insignificant. For this reason, release from time-out should be controlled by the parent following the minimum duration criterion established for that child (e.g., five minutes), only if the child is quiet at the end of that time. Yelling, whining, or crying results in an extension of the time-out criterion, and the child may come out only upon a statement from the parent (e.g., "since you are quiet now, you may come out"). After release from time-out, the parent should reissue the original command.

Programming Generalization. In the early days of social learning treatment for aggressive children, the primary concern of clinicians and researchers was demonstration of the immediate effects of parent training on children's aggressive target behaviors. The main approach to issues of generalization of treatment effects was what Stokes and Baer (1977) referred to as "train and hope;" that is, parents were trained in the clinic to modify their children's behavior, and clinicians hoped that treatment effects would generalize from the clinic to the home, to behaviors other than the primary target behaviors, to other problem children in the home and, perhaps most importantly, across time.

Several reviews of generalization of treatment effects obtained with parent training indicate that despite our best hopes and intentions, treatment effects do not always maintain after treatment is terminated, or generalize to other behaviors, siblings, or settings (Forehand & Atkeson, 1977; Sanders & James, 1983). For this reason, it is becoming more and more common to incorporate into the treatment plan strategies that are specifically designed to promote generalization of treatment effects, particularly temporal generalization (i.e., maintenance of therapeutic effects after treatment is terminated).

Wells, et al. (1980) demonstrated that teaching parents self-control skills of self-monitoring, self-evaluation, and self-reinforcement resulted in continued improvements in child behavior following termination of treatment compared to children whose parents did not receive instructions in self-control skills. In this approach, training in self-control skills is incorporated into the parent training program. After learning standard attending, reinforcement, and time-out skills, parents are taught to self-monitor these behaviors on a counting device (e.g., wrist counter), and they then practice parenting behavior *and* self-monitoring during therapy sessions. After completing treatment, parents contract with the therapist to continue in daily homework practice of parenting skills with their child, daily self-monitoring during practice periods, and daily self-reinforcement for good parenting. Parents also "call in" self-monitored data to an answering service (or secretary) on a decreasing schedule of occurrence in order to gradually fade from external control to self-control. As indicated above, these self-control strategies may not only help maintain treatment effects, but also may enhance treatment effects obtained with parent training alone (Wells et al., 1980).

McMahon, Forehand, and Griest (1981) evaluated another approach to programming generalization of treatment effects. These investigators showed that formal training in principles and concepts of social learning theory results in maintenance of treatment effects obtained with parent training compared to a treatment consisting of parent training without formal instruction in social learning principles.

In this approach, parents are given reading assignments and receive didactic instruction in social learning principles prior to learning parenting techniques. Reading material is taken from behavioral parenting manuals (e.g., Becker, 1971), and parents periodically must pass brief tests during treatment to indicate that they understand the social learning principles. Not only does this formal training in principles of social learning theory enhance maintenance of treatment, but it also increases parents' satisfaction with treatment (McMahon et al., 1981).

In a more recent evaluation from our research group, Griest, Forehand, Rogers, Breiner, Furey, and Williams (1982) investigated the effectiveness of "parent enhancement training" in facilitating temporal generalization. Parent training plus parent enhancement therapy maintained treatment effects compared to parent training alone.

Perhaps the efficacy of parent enhancement therapy relates to the fact that it was designed to address the personal, marital, and community adjustment issues identified in the empirical literature as contributing to child aggressive behavior. In this treatment, emphasis is placed on the fact that parents play a tripartite role, which consists of adequate functioning as a parent, spouse/partner, and individual adult, and that the three roles are integrally interrelated. Parents engage in discussions, role playing, and homework assignments relating to their expectations and perceptions of child behavior, their own mood or psychological adjustment, spouse/partner communication and problem solving, and interactions with friends and extended family members. While interventions may not be necessary in *each* of these areas for *all* families, the data seem to indicate that assessment and treatment of *all* areas of potential dysfunction in families of aggressive children improves treatment effects obtained with parent training alone and enhances generalization of treatment effects. For this reason, it is predicted that the next decade will see clinical and research efforts aimed at aggressive children, moving away from a unidimensional parent training model and toward a more comprehensive model of behavioral family therapy (Griest & Wells, 1983).

CASE EXAMPLE

Doug S., a seven-year-old white male child, was brought to the psychology clinic by his mother for assessment and treatment of increasing difficulties in the areas of noncompliance, belligerence, and argumentativeness, primarily with his mother in the home. Upon interview, Doug's mother indicated that he never obeyed her, always wanted to control things, and picked fights with his younger brother. Mrs. S. described Doug as having "always been a handful, from day one." He was an irritable, fussy, noncuddly baby and continued to have temper tantrums at age seven. Mrs. S. was afraid that his temper and aggressive behavior would alienate him from his peers in the neighborhood and at school. Indeed, a telephone interview with the second grade teacher revealed that Doug was instigating fights at school and was having difficulty reading at a second grade level.

Factor scores on the Conners Parent Rating Scale and the Walker Behavior Problem Checklist confirmed Doug's problems in the areas of conduct and peer relationships. Cognitive and achievement testing showed that he had normal intelligence but was a year behind in reading skills.

Further interview with his mother revealed no history of major accidents or injuries. A medical report from Doug's pediatrician confirmed this, indicating that Doug's vision and hearing were normal.

In conducting the family assessment, several important facts were revealed. Mrs. S., a single parent, was unemployed and had limited income. She was presented as a rather depressed, overwhelmed woman who seemed to have marginal coping skills. She had no extended family members living nearby and could not name a friend with whom she had regular, friendly contact.

Clinical observations revealed very little positive interaction between mother and son. When asked by the clinician to have Doug clean up the toys in the playroom, Mrs. S. was unsuccessful in doing so. Doug defiantly refused to pick up the toys, and Mrs. S. finally picked them up herself. Formal scoring of the coded mother-child interaction revealed a high rate of poor commands that were repeated many times by mother and a high rate of noncompliance, whining, and yelling (back talk) by Doug. It appeared that Doug was on the verge of a temper tantrum when Mrs. S. began picking up the toys. Based on the above interviews, observations, and testing, it appeared that Doug probably had been a temperamentally difficult baby who had not been very reinforcing of his mother's initial attempts at attachment and parenting. By the time they reached the clinic, Mrs. S. seemed somewhat withdrawn from Doug and interacted with him mainly when she was forced to discipline him. She had many stresses associated with running her family on a limited income and few social supports.

Based on these observations, it was decided to employ the Hanf-Forehand parent training approach with Mrs. S. and to seek special tutoring for Doug through the school. This was done to increase positive interactions between

Mrs. S. and Doug, to teach her more effective methods of discipline and to help Doug in his reading skills. The therapist spent several sessions with Mrs. S. on each parenting skill, with a great deal of encouragement and support for between-session practice. The therapist took care not to place excessive demands on Mrs. S., but to pace the skills and homework assignments at an acceptable rate.

Throughout training, Mrs. S. learned to self-monitor new parenting skills, particularly attending, rewarding, and positive reinforcement skills. During the initial treatment phase, the therapist phoned Mrs. S. twice a week between sessions to add further support and answer questions. Over the next six months, the therapist gradually faded telephone calls to once a month. Throughout Mrs. S.'s association with the clinic, a social worker advised her in her negotiations with social agencies, helped her with applications, and aided her in finding appropriate job opportunities.

With the above treatment program, extending over a nine-month intensive treatment and follow-up period, Doug's noncompliant and aggressive behavior in the home diminished. He continued to have some problems in the classroom until a teacher consultation took place. He received one hour of daily one-to-one tutoring in reading throughout the second grade and was recommended for continued tutoring in the third grade.

SUMMARY

Aggressive behavior disorders of childhood represent the most frequent referrals to child mental health facilities. If left untreated, aggressive behavior persists across time, and the long-term prognosis for these children is poor.

In this chapter, we have reviewed recent literature relevant to etiology, assessment, and treatment of aggressive, conduct disordered children. Results of this review appear to indicate that aggressive behavior can be caused by one or more genetic, constitutional, social, or behavioral variables and may be associated with other clinical symptoms in the child or family (i.e., depression, social dysfunction, social skills deficits). Assessment of aggressive children and their families must include attention to each of these variables.

Regarding treatment, we have directed most of our comments to interventions that have received the most systematic research evaluation and that show greatest evidence for positive treatment effects. These include social learning based treatments for modifying parent behaviors and child behaviors in the home and community. Thus, most of our discussion regarding treatment focused on nonadjudicated children living within a family context. Because the outcome of treatment for older delinquent and/or adjudicated antisocial children is poor (e.g., Kirigin, Braukmann, Atwater, & Wolf, 1982; Lewis, Lewis, Shanok, Klatskin, & Osborne, 1980), it seems important to identify children for treatment as early as possible and to treat them within the context of their families.

Current evidence indicates that such treatment can significantly change dysfunctional family processes and child antisocial behavior, particularly for younger children who engage in overt aggression in the family context. Research is currently being directed toward development and evaluation of more effective treatment programs for predelinquent children whose antisocial behaviors may be covert. Because aggressive children represent such a large proportion of the child psychiatric population, continued clinical and research efforts expanding our knowledge of etiology, our clinical assessment procedures, and our treatment methodologies for these children will continue to be important tasks facing child clinicians and researchers.

REFERENCES

Achenbach, T. M. The Child Behavior Profile: I. Boys aged 6 through 11. *Journal of Consulting and Clinical Psychology,* 1978, *46,* 478–488.

Achenbach, T. M. DSM-III in light of empirical research on the classification of child psychopathology. *Journal of the American Academy of Child Psychiatry,* 1980, *19,* 395–412.

Achenbach, T. M. *Developmental psychopathology* (2nd ed.). New York: John Wiley & Sons, 1982.

Achenbach, T. M. & Edelbrock, C. S. The classification of child psychopathology: A review and analysis of empirical efforts. *Psychological Bulletin,* 1978, *85,* 1275–1301.

American Psychiatric Association. *Diagnostic and statistical manual of mental disorders* (3rd ed.). Washington, D.C.: American Psychiatric Association, 1980.

Annesley, P. T. Psychiatric illness in adolescence: Presentation and prognosis. *Journal of Mental Science,* 1961, *107,* 268–278.

Atkeson, B. M., & Forehand, R. Conduct disorders. In E. J. Mash & L. G. Terdal (Eds.), *Behavioral assessment of childhood disorders.* New York: Guilford Press, 1981.

Barlow, D. H. *Behavioral assessment of adult disorders.* New York: Guilford Press, 1981.

Bean, A. W., & Roberts, M. W. The effect of time-out release contingencies on changes in child noncompliance. *Journal of Abnormal Child Psychology,* 1981, *9,* 95–105.

Beck, A. T., Ward, C. H., Mendelsohn, M., Mock, J., & Erbaugh, J. An inventory for measuring depression. *Archives of General Psychiatry,* 1961, *4,* 561–571.

Becker, W. C. *Parents are teachers: A child management program.* Champaign, Ill.: Research Press, 1971.

Bernal, M. E., Klinnert, M. D., & Schultz, L. A. Outcome evaluation of behavioral parent training and client centered parent counseling for children with conduct problems. *Journal of Applied Behavior Analysis,* 1980, *13,* 677–691.

Bornstein, M. R., Bellack, A. S., & Hersen, M. Social skills training for un-assertive children: A multiple baseline analysis. *Journal of Applied Behavior Analysis,* 1977, *10,* 183–195.

Budd, K. S., Green, D. R. & Baer, D. M. An analysis of multiple misplaced social contingencies. *Journal of Applied Behavior Analysis,* 1976, *9,* 459–470.

Cadoret, R. J., & Cain, C. Sex differences in predictors of antisocial behavior in adoptees. *Archives of General Psychiatry,* 1980, *37,* 1171–1175.

Cerreto, M. C., & Tuma, J. M. Distribution of DSM-II diagnoses in a child psychiatric setting. *Journal of Abnormal Child Psychology,* 1977, *5,* 147–155.

Chamberlain, P. *Standardization of a parent report measure.* Unpublished doctoral dissertation, University of Oregon, 1980.

Chiles, A., Miller, M. L. & Cox, G. B. Depression in an adolescent delinquent population. *Archives of General Psychiatry,* 1980, *37,* 1179–1184.

Christensen, A. Naturalistic observation of families: A system for random audio recordings in the home. *Behavior Therapy,* 1979, *10,* 418–422.

Conners, C. K. A teacher rating scale for use in drug studies with children. *American Journal of Psychiatry,* 1969, *126,* 152–156.

Conners, C. K. Symptom patterns in hyperactive, neurotic and normal children. *Child Development,* 1970, *41,* 667–682.

Dahlstrom, W. G. & Welsh, G. S. *An MMPI handbook: A guide to use in clinical practice and research.* Minneapolis: University of Minnesota Press, 1960.

Delgado-Escueta, A. V., Mattson, R. H., King, L., Goldensohn, E. S., Spiegel, H., Madson, J., Crandall, P., Dreifuss, F., & Porter, R. J. The nature of aggression during epileptic seizures. *New England Journal of Medicine,* 1981, *305,* 711–716.

Edelbrock, C. & Achenbach, T. M. A typology of child behavior profile patterns: Distribution and correlates for disturbed children aged 6–16. *Journal of Abnormal Child Psychology,* 1980, *8,* 441–470.

Emery, R. E. Interparental conflict and the children of discord and divorce. *Psychological Bulletin,* 1982, *92,* 310–330.

Emery, R. E., Binkoff, J. A., Houts, A. C. & Carr, E. G. Children as independent variables. Some clinical implications of child-effects. *Behavior Therapy,* 1983, *14,* 398–412.

Emery, R. E., & O'Leary, K. D. Children's perceptions of marital discord and behavior problems of boys and girls. *Journal of Abnormal Child Psychology,* 1982, *10,* 11–24.

Ferguson, L. R., & Allen, D. R. Congruence of parental perceptions, marital satisfaction, and child adjustment. *Journal of Consulting and Clinical Psychology,* 1978, *46,* 345–346.

Fleischman, M. J. A replication of Patterson's "Intervention for boys with conduct problems." *Journal of Consulting and Clinical Psychology,* 1981, *49,* 342–351.

Fleischman, M. J., & Szykula, S. A. A community setting replication of a social learning treatment for aggressive children. *Behavior Therapy,* 1981, *12,* 115–122.

Forehand, R., & Atkeson, B. M. Generality of treatment effects with parents as therapists: A review of assessment and implementation procedures. *Behavior Therapy,* 1977, *8,* 575–593.

Forehand, R., King, H. E., Peed, S., & Yoder, P. Mother-child interactions: Comparison of a noncompliant clinic group and a nonclinic group. *Behaviour Research and Therapy,* 1975, *13,* 79–84.

Forehand, R., & McMahon, R. J. *Helping the noncompliant child: A clinician's guide to parent training.* New York: Guilford Press, 1981.

Forehand, R., Wells, K. C., McMahon, R. J., Griest, D. L., & Rogers, T. Maternal perceptions of maladjustment in clinic-referred children: An extension of earlier research. *Journal of Behavioral Assessment,* 1982, *4,* 145–151.

Freedman, B. J., Rosenthal, L., Donahoe, C. P., Schlundt, D. G., & McFall, R. M. A social-behavioral analysis of skill deficits in delinquent and nondelinquent adolescent boys. *Journal of Consulting and Clinical Psychology,* 1978, *46,* 1448–1462.

Freud, S. Beyond the pleasure principle (1922). In *Standard edition of the complete works of Sigmund Freud* (Vol. 7). London: Hogarth Press, 1953.

Gaffney, L. R. & McFall, R. M. A comparison of social skills in delinquent and nondelinquent adolescent girls using a behavioral role-playing inventory. *Journal of Consulting and Clinical Psychology,* 1981, *49,* 959–967.

Glueck, S. & Glueck, E. *Identification of pre-delinquents: Validation studies and some suggested uses of Glueck Tables.* New York: Intercontinental Medical Book Corp., 1972.

Goyette, C. H., Conners, C. K., & Ulrich, R. F. Normative data on revised Conners parent and teacher rating scales. *Journal of Abnormal Child Psychology,* 1978, *6,* 221–236.

Green, K. D., & Forehand, R. Assessment of children's social skills: A review of methods. *Journal of Behavioral Assessment,* 1980, *2,* 143–158.

Griest, D. L., Forehand, R., Rogers, T., Breiner, J., Furey, W., & Williams, C. A. Effects of parent enhancement therapy on the treatment outcome and generalization of a parent training program. *Behaviour Research and Therapy,* 1982, *20,* 429–436.

Griest, D. L., Forehand, R. & Wells, K. C. Follow-up assessment of parent behavioral training: An analysis of who will participate. *Child Study Journal,* 1981, *11,* 221–229.

Griest, D. L., Forehand, R., Wells, K. C., & McMahon, R. J. An examination of differences between nonclinic and behavior-problem clinic-referred children and their mothers. *Journal of Abnormal Psychology,* 1980,*89,* 497–500.

Griest, D. L., & Wells, K. C. Behavioral family therapy with conduct disorders in children. *Behavior Therapy,* 1983, *14,* 37–53.

Griest, D. L., Wells, K. C., & Forehand, R. An examination of predictors of maternal perceptions of maladjustment in clinic-referred children. *Journal of Abnormal Psychology,* 1979, *88,* 277–281.

Henn, F. A., Bardwell, R., & Jenkins, R. L. Juvenile delinquents revisited: Adult criminal activity. *Archives of General Psychiatry,* 1980, *37,* 1160–1163.

Herbert, M. *Conduct disorders of childhood and adolescence: A behavioral approach to assessment and treatment.* New York: John Wiley & Sons, 1978.

Hersen, M. & Bellack, A. S. *Behavioral assessment: A practical handbook* (2nd ed.). New York: Pergamon Press, 1981.

Hetherington, E. M., Cox, M., & Cox, R. Divorced fathers. *Family Coordinator,* 1976, *25,* 417–428.

Hetherington, E. M., Cox, M. & Cox, R. Family interaction and the social, emotional and cognitive development of children following divorce. In V. Vaughn & T. Brazelton (Eds.), *The family: Setting priorities.* New York: Science and Medicine, 1979.

Hobbs, S. A., Forehand, R., & Murray, R. G. Effects of various durations of time-out on the noncompliant behavior of children. *Behavior Therapy,* 1978, *9,* 652–656.

Hops, H., & Greenwood, C. R. Social skills deficits. In E. J. Mash & L. G. Terdal (Eds.), *Behavioral assessment of childhood disorders.* New York: Guilford Press, 1981.

Hutchings, B. & Mednick, S. A. Registered criminality in the adoptive and biological parents of registered male criminal adoptees. In S. A. Mednick, F. Schulsinger, J. Higgins, & B. Bell (Eds.), *Genetics, environment, and psychopathology.* Amsterdam: North Holland/Elsevier, 1974.

Johnson, S. M., Christensen, A., & Bellamy, G. T. Evaluation of family intervention through unobstrusive audio recordings: Experiences in "bugging" children. *Journal of Applied Behavior Analysis,* 1976, *9,* 213–219.

Johnson, S. M. & Lobitz, G. K. The personal and marital adjustment of parents as related to observed child deviance and parenting behavior. *Journal of Abnormal Child Psychology,* 1974, *2,* 192–207.

Kanfer, F. H. & Saslow, G. Behavioral diagnosis. In C. M. Franks (Ed.), *Behavior Therapy: Appraisal and status.* New York: McGraw-Hill, 1969.

Karoly, P., & Rosenthal, M. Training parents in behavior modification: Effects on perceptions of family interaction and deviant child behavior. *Behavior Therapy,* 1977, *8,* 406–410.

Kirigin, K. A., Braukmann, C. J., Atwater, J. D., & Wolf, M. M. An evaluation of teaching-family (Achievement Place) group homes for juvenile offenders. *Journal of Applied Behavior Analysis,* 1982, *15,* 1–16.

Kohlberg, L. Moral stages and moralization: The cognitive developmental approach. In T. Lickona (Ed.), *Moral development and moral behavior.* New York: Holt, Rinehart, & Winston, 1976.

Langner, T. S., Gersten, J. C., McCarthy, E. D., Eisenberg, J. G., Green, E. L., Herson, J. H. & Jameson, J. D. A screening inventory for assessing psychiatric impairment in children 6 to 18. *Journal of Consulting and Clinical Psychology*, 1976, *44*, 286–296.

Leske, G., Afton, A., Rogers, E. S., & Wahler, R. G. *The interpersonal functioning of insular and noninsular families: Factors related to treatment success and failure*. Unpublished manuscript, University of Tennessee, 1978.

Lewis, D. O. *Vulnerabilities to delinquency*. New York: Spectrum, 1981.

Lewis, D. O., Pincus, J. H., Shanok, S. S. & Glaser, G. H. Psychomotor epilepsy and violence in a group of incarcerated adolescent boys. *American Journal of Psychiatry*, 1982, *139*, 882–887.

Lewis, D. O. & Shanok, S. S. Medical histories of delinquent and nondelinquent children: An epidemiological study. *American Journal of Psychiatry*, 1977, *134*, 1020–1025.

Lewis, D. O., Shanok, S. S., Balla, D. A., & Bard, B. Psychiatric correlates of severe reading disabilities in an incarcerated delinquent population. *Journal of the American Academy of Child Psychiatry*, 1980, *19*, 611–622.

Lewis, D. O., Shanok, S. S. Pincus, J. H., & Glaser, G. H. Violent juvenile delinquents: Psychiatric, neurological, psychological and abuse factors. *Journal of the American Academy of Child Psychiatry*, 1979, *18*, 307–319.

Lewis, M., Lewis, D. O., Shanok, S. S., Klatskin, E., & Osborne, J. R. The undoing of residential treatment: A follow-up study of 51 adolescents. *Journal of the American Academy of Child Psychiatry*, 1980, *19*, 160–171.

Locke, H. J. & Wallace, K. M. Short marital-adjustment and predictor tests: Their reliability and validity. *Marriage and Family Living*, 1959, *21*, 251–255.

Loeber, R. The stability of antisocial and delinquent child behavior: A review. *Child Development*, 1982, *53*, 1431–1446.

Lorber, R. & Patterson, G. R. The aggressive child: A concomitant of a coercive system. *Advances in family intervention, assessment and theory*, 1981, *2*, 47–87.

Mash, E. J. & Terdal, L. G. *Behavioral assessment of childhood disorders*. New York: Guilford Press, 1981.

Mattison, R., Cantwell, D. P., Russell, A. T. & Will, L. A comparison of DSM-II and DSM-III in the diagnosis of childhood psychiatric disorders. *Archives of General Psychiatry*, 1979, *36*, 1217–1222.

McCord, W., McCord, J. & Zola, I. K. *Origins of crime*. New York: Columbia University Press, 1959.

McMahon, R. J., Forehand, R. & Griest, D. L. Effects of knowledge of social learning principles on enhancing outcome and generalization in a parent training program. *Journal of Consulting and Clinical Psychology*, 1981, *49*, 526–532.

McMahon, R. J., Forehand, R., Griest, D. L. & Wells, K. C. Who drops out of therapy during parent behavioral training? *Behavioral Counseling Quarterly*, 1981, *1*, 79–85.

Mednick, S. A. The learning of morality: Biosocial bases. In D. O. Lewis (Ed.), *Vulnerabilities to delinquency*. New York: Spectrum, 1981.

Meichenbaum, D. *Cognitive behavior modification*. New York: Plenum Press, 1977.

Mezzich, A. C. & Mezzich, J. E. Diagnostic reliability of childhood and adolescent behavior disorders. Presented at American Psychological Association, New York, September 1979.

Michelson, L., & Wood, R. Behavioral assessment and training of children's social skills. In M. Hersen, P. Miller, & R. Eisler (Eds.), *Progress in behavior modification* (Vol. 9). New York: Academic Press, 1980.

Moore, D. R. Chamberlain, P., & Mukai, L. H. Children at risk for delinquency: A follow-up comparison of aggressive children and children who steal. *Journal of Abnormal Child Psychology*, 1979, *7*, 345–355.

Morris, H. H., Escoll, P. J., & Wexler, R. Aggressive behavior disorders of childhood: A follow up study. *American Journal of Psychiatry*, 1956, *112*, 991–997.

Oltmanns, T. F., Broderick, J. E., & O'Leary, K. D. Marital adjustment and the efficacy of behavior therapy with children. *Journal of Consulting and Clinical Psychology*, 1977, *45*, 724–729.

Olweus, D. Stability of aggressive reaction patterns in males: A review. *Psychological Bulletin*, 1979, *86*, 852–857.

Olweus, D. Familial and temperamental determinants of aggressive behavior in adolescent boys: A causal analysis. *Developmental Psychology*, 1980, *16*, 644–660.

O'Neal, P. & Robins, L. N. The relation of childhood behavior problems to adult psychiatric status: A 30-year follow-up study of 150 subjects. *American Journal of Psychiatry*, 1958, *114*, 961–969.

Patterson, G. R. *Families*. Champaign, Ill.: Research Press, 1975.

Patterson, G. R. The aggressive child: Victim and architect of a coercive system. In E. J. Mash, L. A. Hammerlynck & L. C. Handy (Eds.), *Behavior modification and families*. New York: Brunner/Mazel, 1976.

Patterson, G. R. Mothers: The unacknowledged victims. *Monographs of the Society for Research in Child Development*, 1980, *45*(5, Serial No. 186).

Patterson, G. R. *Coercive family process*. Eugene, Ore.: Castalia, 1982.

Patterson, G. R., Chamberlain, P., & Reid, J. B. A comparative evaluation of a parent-training program. *Behavior Therapy*, 1982,*13*, 638–650.

Patterson, G. R., & Fleischman, M. J. Maintenance of treatment effects: Some considerations concerning family systems and follow-up data. *Behavior Therapy*, 1979,*10*, 168–185.

Patterson, G. R., & Guillion, M. E. *Living with children: New methods for parents and teachers*. Champaign, Ill.: Research Press, 1968.

Patterson, G. R. & Reid, J. B. Reciprocity and coercion: Two facets of social systems. In C. Neuringer & J. Michaels (Eds.), *Behavior modification in clinical psychology.* New York: Appleton-Century-Crofts, 1970.

Patterson, G. R., Reid, J. B. & Chamberlain, P. *Beyond technology.* Paper presented at the XII Annual Banff International Conference on Behavior Modification, April 1981.

Patterson, G. R., Reid, J. B., Jones, R. R. & Conger, R. E. *A social learning approach to family intervention: Families with aggressive children.* Eugene, Ore.: Castalia, 1975.

Peed, S., Roberts, M., & Forehand, R. Evaluation of the effectiveness of a standardized parent training program in altering the interactions of mothers and their noncompliant children. *Behavior Modification,* 1977, *1*, 323–350.

Porter, B. & O'Leary, K. D. Marital discord and childhood behavior problems. *Journal of Abnormal Child Psychology,* 1980, *8*, 287–295.

Pritchard, M. & Graham, P. An investigation of a group of patients who have attended both the child and adult departments of the same psychiatric hospital. *British Journal of Psychiatry,* 1966, *112*, 603–612.

Puig-Antich, J. Major depression and conduct disorder in prepuberty. *Journal of the American Academy of Child Psychiatry,* 1982, *21*, 118–128.

Quay, H. C. Personality dimensions in delinquent males as inferred from the factor analysis of behavior ratings. *Journal of Research in Crime and Delinquency,* 1964, *1*, 33–36.

Quay, H. C. Measuring dimensions of deviant behavior: The Behavior Problem Checklist. *Journal of Abnormal Child Psychology,* 1977, *5*, 277–287.

Quay, H. C. Classification. In H. C. Quay & J. Werry (Eds.), *Psychopathological disorders of childhood* (2nd ed.). New York: John Wiley & Sons, 1979.

Reardon, R. C., Hersen, M., Bellack, A. S., & Foley, J. M. Measuring social skill in grade school boys. *Journal of Behavioral Assessment,* 1979, *1*, 87–105.

Reid, J. B., & Hendriks, A. F. C. J. A preliminary analysis of the effectiveness of direct home intervention for treatment of predelinquent boys who steal. In L. A. Hamerlynck, L. C. Handy & E. J. Mash (Eds.), *Behavior therapy: Methodology, concepts and practice.* Champaign, Ill.: Research Press, 1973.

Reid, J. B., Hinojosa-Rivera, G., & Lorber, R. *A social learning approach to the outpatient treatment of children who steal.* Unpublished manuscript, Oregon Social Learning Center, 1980.

Reid, J. B., & Patterson, G. R. The modification of aggression and stealing behavior of boys in the home setting. In A. Bandura & E. Ribes-Inesta (Eds.), *Behavior modification: Experimental analyses of aggression and delinquency.* Hillsdale, N.J.: Lawrence Erlbaum Associates Inc., 1976.

Roberts, M. W. The effects of warned versus unwarned time-out procedures on child noncompliance. *Child and Family Behavior Therapy,* 1982, *4*, 37–53.

Roberts, M. W., Hatzenbuehler, L. C. & Bean, A. W. The effects of differential attention and time out on child noncompliance. *Behavior Therapy,* 1981, *12*, 93–99.

Roberts, M. W., McMahon, R. J., Forehand, R., & Humphreys, L. The effects of parental instruction-giving on child compliance. *Behavior Therapy,* 1978, *9,* 793–798.

Robins, L. N. *Deviant children grown up.* Baltimore: Williams & Wilkins, 1966.

Robins, L. N. The adult development of the antisocial child. *Seminars in Psychiatry,* 1970, *2,* 420–434.

Robins, L. N. Follow-up studies. In H. C. Quay & J. Werry (Eds.), *Psychopathological disorders of childhood* (2nd ed.). New York: John Wiley & Sons, 1979.

Rogers, T. R., Forehand, R. & Griest, D. L. The conduct disordered child: An analysis of family problems. *Clinical Psychology Review,* 1981, *1,* 139–147.

Rutter, M. Parent-child separation: Psychological effects on the children. *Journal of Child Psychology and Psychiatry and Allied Disciplines.* 1971, *12,* 233 260.

Rutter, M., Birch, H. G., Thomas, A. & Chess, S. Temperamental characteristics in infancy and the later development of behavioural disorders. *British Journal of Psychiatry,* 1964, *110,* 651–661.

Rutter, M., Tizard, J. & Whitmore, K. *Education, health and behaviour.* London: Longmans, 1970.

Rutter, M., Tizard, J., Yule, W., Graham, P. & Whitmore, K. Research report: Isle of Wight studies, 1964–1974. *Psychological Medicine,* 1976, *6,* 313–332.

Safer, D. J. & Allen, R. P. *Hyperactive children: Diagnosis and management.* Baltimore: University Park Press, 1976.

Sanders, M. R., & James, J. E. The modification of parent behavior: A review of generalization and maintenance. *Behavior Modification,* 1983, *7,* 3–27.

Seligman, M. E. P. *Helplessness: On depression, development, and death.* San Francisco: W. H. Freeman, 1975.

Shaffer, D. Suicide in childhood and early adolescence. *Journal of Child Psychology and Psychiatry,* 1974, *15,* 275–291.

Shanok, S. S. & Lewis, D. O. Medical histories of female delinquents: Clinical and epidemiological findings. *Archives of General Psychiatry,* 1981, *38,* 211–213.

Speer, D. C. The Behavior Problem Checklist (Peterson-Quay): Baseline data from parents of child guidance and nonclinic children. *Journal of Consulting and Clinical Psychology,* 1971, *36,* 221–228.

Speilberger, C. D., Gorsuch, R. L., & Lushene, R. E. *STAI manual for the state-trait anxiety inventory.* Palo Alto, Calif.: Consulting Psychologists Press, 1970.

Stokes, T. F., & Baer, D. M. An implicit technology of generalization. *Journal of Applied Behavior Analysis,* 1977, *10,* 349–367.

Thomas, A., Chess, S. & Birch, H. G. *Temperament and behavior disorders in children.* New York: University Press, 1968.

Trites, R. L., Dugas, E., Lynch, G., & Ferguson, H. B. Prevalence of hyperactivity. *Journal of Pediatric Psychology,* 1979,*4,* 179–188.

Van Hasselt, V. B., Hersen, M., Bellack, A. S., & Whitehill, M. B. Social skill assessment and training for children: An evaluative review. *Behaviour Research and Therapy*, 1979,*17*, 413–438.

Wahler, R. G. The insular mother: Her problems in parent-child treatment. *Journal of Applied Behavior Analysis*, 1980, *13*, 207–219.

Wahler, R. G., & Afton, A. D. Attentional processes in insular and noninsular mothers: Some differences in their summary reports about child problem behavior. *Child Behavior Therapy*, 1980,*2*, 25–41.

Walker, H. M. *The Walker Problem Behavior Identification Checklist: Test and manual*. Los Angeles: Western Psychological Services, 1970.

Walter, H., & Gilmore, S. D. Placebo versus social learning effects in parent training procedures designed to alter the behaviors of aggressive boys. *Behavior Therapy*, 1973, *4*, 361–377.

Webster-Stratton, C., & Eyberg, S. M. Child temperament: Relationship with child behavior problems and parent-child interactions. *Journal of Clinical Child Psychology*, 1982, *11*, 123–129.

Wells, K. C. Assessment of children in outpatient settings. In M. Hersen & A. S. Bellack (Eds.), *Behavioral assessment: A practical handbook* (2nd ed.). New York: Pergamon Press, 1981.

Wells, K. C. & Forehand, R. Childhood behavior problems in the home. In S. M. Turner, K. S. Calhoun, & H. E. Adams (Eds.), *Handbook of clinical behavior therapy*. New York: John Wiley & Sons, 1981.

Wells, K. C., Griest, D. L., & Forehand, R. The use of a self-control package to enhance temporal generality of a parent training program. *Behaviour Research and Therapy*, 1980,*18*, 347–353.

West, D. J. & Farrington, D. P. *Who becomes delinquent?* London: Heinemann, 1973.

Wiltz, N. A. & Patterson, G. R. An evaluation of parent training procedures designed to alter inappropriate aggressive behavior of boys. *Behavior Therapy*, 1974, *5*, 215–221.

Wolff, S. Symptomatology and outcome of pre-school children with behaviour disorders attending a child guidance clinic. *Journal of Child Psychology and Psychiatry*, 1961, *2*, 269–276.

Wolff, S. Behavioural characteristics of primary school children referred to a psychiatric department. *British Journal of Psychiatry*, 1967, *113*, 885–893.

Wolff, S. Dimensions and clusters of symptoms in disturbed children. *British Journal of Psychiatry*, 1971, *118*, 421–427.

7

Anxiety Disorders of Childhood and Adolescence

Lawrence J. Siegel
University of Texas Medical Branch

Robyn Ridley-Johnson
University of Florida

In modern society, anxiety and fear are a pervasive part of the human condition. Every individual experiences fear or anxiety at some time in life, and, as such, it may be seen as a "normal" emotional response. The etiological significance of fear and anxiety in childhood disorders was established early in this century by Freud's work on the case of Little Hans (Freud, 1909) and was followed shortly, thereafter, by the single case studies of Watson and Rayner (1920) and Jones (1924) on the development and treatment of phobias in young children within a learning theory framework.

Fears are a common problem of normal childhood. As many as nine out of 10 children develop specific fears sometime during their early years (Lapouse & Monk, 1959; MacFarlane, Allen, & Honzik, 1954). These fears take many forms, including fears of physical injury, natural events, and social and achievement situations (Miller, Barrett, Hampe, & Noble, 1972). Childhood fears are often quite transient and tend to dissipate with age; therefore, all fearful or anxious behaviors may not warrant professional intervention. However, tenacious or severely debilitating fears, such as school phobia, which can interfere with the child's daily functioning and social development, often necessitate therapeutic intervention. Because the prognosis for children who develop specific fears or phobias appears to be rather good (Miller, 1983), treatment approaches that are short term, inexpensive, and practical are highly desirable. As such, behavioral treatment methods have been used extensively in the treatment of children's fears and phobias and have been shown to have sufficient empirical support to warrant their systematic use in numerous clinical and applied settings with children.

This chapter reviews the various behavioral techniques that have been applied to the treatment of numerous anxiety or fear-related disorders in children. A description and critical evaluation of each procedure is provided, and developmental, demographic, and etiological factors relevant to anxiety disorders in children are addressed. Finally, issues in the diagnosis and assessment of anxiety and fear-related problems in children are briefly reviewed.

DEFINITIONS OF ANXIETY, FEAR, AND PHOBIA

A useful starting point in exploring the assessment and treatment of children's anxiety disorders is to define the terms *anxiety, fear,* and *phobia.* One definition of anxiety and fear distinguishes them by the degree to which a response is differentiated and in terms of the eliciting stimulus. Thus, anxiety is defined as a diffuse response often without ostensible cause, whereas fear is a more differentiated response to a specific object or situation (Johnson & Melamed, 1978). Phobias constitute a subset of fears that are "pathological."

An alternative definition used by Miller (1983) is that anxiety is a response to internal cues. Typically, no external situation that elicits the anxious response can be identified. When anxiety does occur in response to a situation or object that is objectively nonthreatening, the response is referred to as a phobia. Fear, in contrast to anxiety, is defined as a normal physiological reaction to a genuine threat.

Anxiety has also been defined as a psychological entity rather than as a response. Defining anxiety as a construct (Morris & Kratochwill, 1983) leads to trait or dispositional explanations of behavior, whereby anxiety "causes" the behavior. The clinician may question the utility of definitional distinctions among these terms; hence, from a social learning viewpoint, the practical significance of precisely differentiating anxiety and fear has not been demonstrated. For example, Johnson and Melamed (1978) contend that, for the behaviorist, the assessment procedures that are used to identify eliciting stimulus conditions for a behavior bear little relationship to which descriptive term is employed. Similarly, Barrios, Hartmann, & Shigetomi (1981) argue that the descriptive labels fail to predict behavior and, therefore, are of low information value to the clinician.

In keeping with the trend of the social learning literature on anxiety disorders, anxiety and fear will be treated in this chapter as responses of the same class. The term *fear* will generally be used to refer to this class of responses. Phobias are also regarded as responses of the same class but, as discussed below, are viewed as more severe in nature.

PATHOLOGICAL VERSUS NORMAL FEARS IN CHILDREN

Diagnosing an Anxiety Disorder

Expressions of fear are most often normal, adaptive responses. Appropriate diagnosis of an anxiety disorder depends on the clinician's consideration of several issues. First, the clinician will want to assess the function of the behavior manifesting the child's fear. Analysis of the meaning of a behavior involves theoretical considerations that are discussed later. Other information essential to diagnosis includes the duration of the problem, severity of the problem, and degree of maladaptiveness of the behavior (Barrios et al., 1981; Graziano, DeGiovanni, & Garcia, 1979; Marks, 1969; Morris & Kratochwill, 1983; Richards & Siegel, 1978). The degree to which a fear actually disrupts a child's life also needs to be assessed (Kennedy, 1965). For example, one may question whether to treat a child with a severe and persistent fear of an object or situation that is, however, rarely encountered in the child's life.

Miller, Barrett, and Hampe (1974) addressed the above diagnostic issues in outlining eight criteria which define a phobia, as opposed to normal fears. Their criteria state that a phobia:

1. Is out of proportion to the demands of the situation.
2. Cannot be explained or reasoned away.
3. Is beyond voluntary control.
4. Leads to avoidance of the feared situation.
5. Persists over an extended period of time.
6. Is unadaptive.
7. Is not age or stage specific (p. 90).

Richards and Siegel (1978) observed that diagnosis of any anxiety disorder rests on points similar to the Miller et al. (1974) criteria, especially points 1, 5, 6, and 7. Application of the label *behavior disorder,* then, requires more than documentation of fear-related behavior—it requires a judgment that the behavior exceeds certain limits of severity and disruptiveness characteristic of normal fears.

Developmental Changes in the Content of Children's Fears

Developmental theory is incorporated into the assessment process in the seventh of the Miller et al. (1974) criteria for a phobia: "Is not age or stage specific." Cognitive and emotional development are reciprocal processes, so the incidence and content of children's fears varies at differing stages of development. Fear results from understanding the significance of stimuli; consequently, the types of fear-eliciting stimuli change from infancy through adolescence.

Based on parent ratings, factor analytic studies have identified content categories of children's fears. Miller et al., (1972) identified three factors in a factor analytic study using the Louisville Fear Survey Schedule: (*a*) fears of physical injury or personal loss (e.g., having an operation, being kidnapped, parental divorce); (*b*) fears of natural and supernatural dangers (e.g., fear of the dark, storms, monsters, and ghosts); and (*c*) fears reflecting "psychic stress," related most often to interpersonal relationships (e.g., school attendance, fears of making mistakes). Miller (1983) cites a more recent factor analysis of the same instrument by Staley and O'Donnell, who found five similar factors for ages 6–16. These were fears of: (*a*) public physical injury; (*b*) animals; (*c*) school related; (*d*) night; and (*e*) public places.

The range of fear-eliciting stimuli broadens with increasing age (Morris & Kratochwill, 1983). Infants show fear reactions to excessive or unexpected sensory stimuli and strangers; separation anxiety becomes evident around the first year of age (Miller, 1983). Preschoolers' fears tend to focus on animals, the dark, and imaginary creatures (Bauer, 1976; Jersild & Holmes, 1935; Miller, 1983). As children grow older, coinciding with both school entrance and the development of concrete operational thought, their fears are predominately of school, of injury, and social fears, while the earlier fears of animals, the dark, and imaginary creatures decline (Jersild & Holmes, 1935; Lapouse & Monk, 1959; Morris & Kratochwill, 1983). During adolescence, social fears become more complex, including anxieties concerning social alienation and the macabre (Miller, 1983.).

Thus, in distinguishing between a normal and clinical fear in children, the developmental appropriateness of the fear content needs to be assessed. Treatment for age-appropriate fears is most often not indicated, as developmental data suggest the fear may spontaneously decrease with age.

Incidence of Normal and Excessive Fears in Children

Developmental data show that the incidence rate of fears in childhood is quite high. In a study of children from age two until adolescence, MacFarlane, Allen, and Honzik (1954) found that 90 percent of the children had at least one specific fear in their first 14 years. Kennedy (1983) estimates that 50 percent of children experience significant, although not phobic, fears. Jersild and Holmes (1935) reported that younger children, ages 2-6, experience several concurrent fears (4.6 per child). Lapouse and Monk (1959) found that almost half of older children, ages 6-12, similarly had several fears (seven or more). The literature suggests, however, that children's reports of fears generally decline from early childhood to late adolescence (Graziano et al., 1979). This general decline is broken by a peak in reported fears at age 11—around the onset of adolescence (MacFarlane et al., 1954). This peak likely reflects the emergence or predominance of social fears and concerns in adolescence. It also coincides with a transitional period of cognitive development, which is the approximate age of the emergence of formal operational thought. Thus, the content of adolescents' fears reflects increasingly abstract thought processes.

In contrast to looking at the numbers of fears reported by children, Miller et al. (1974) looked at the intensity of children's fears in response to different stimuli included in the Louisville Fear Survey Schedule. They reported that most of the stimuli elicited no fear in most children (about 85 percent), normal fear reactions in about 10 percent of children, and excessive fear reactions in 5 percent or less of children, as reported by their parents.

Incidence rates of phobias in the child population are dramatically lower than are incidence rates of normal fears. Reports consistently indicate that .5 to 2 percent of the children have specific clinical fears (Agras, Sylvester, & Oliveau, 1969; Kennedy, 1965; Miller et al., 1974; Rutter, Tizard, & Whitmore, 1970). Reports of school phobias incidence rates have ranged from around 2 percent (Kennedy, 1965) to up to 8 percent (Kahn & Nurstein, 1962) of all children. In comparison to incidence rates of children's specific fears, Johnson (1979) reports the incidence of the broader disorder of social withdrawal to be much higher, with estimates ranging between 10 to 20 percent of school-age children (Evers & Schwarz, 1973; O'Conner, 1972). These children are described as anxious, socially isolated, hypersensitive, self-conscious, and seclusive.

In child psychiatric populations, specific phobias account for 3 to 8 percent of referrals (e.g., Graziano et al., 1979; Marks, 1969). Of these children, 1 to 2 percent are school phobics (Chazan, 1962). The higher rate of social withdrawal than specific phobias in the general child population is reflected in a correspondingly higher percentage of socially withdrawn children in referrals to child mental health clinics. Johnson (1979) estimates this percentage at 25 percent.

Sex Differences in Incidence Rates

Where sex differences in incidence rates of anxiety disorders have been found, the rates have been higher among girls than boys. Girls appear to have more fears and phobias than boys (e.g., Bauer, 1976; Jersild & Holmes, 1935; Lapouse & Monk, 1959), although boys and girls are equally represented in the incidence rate of school phobia (Johnson, 1979). It is not clear whether girls are in fact more fearful than boys or whether they (or their parents) are simply more willing to admit to their fears.

Development of Anxiety Disorders

Psychoanalytic and learning theory are the two major theoretical positions that address the development of anxiety disorders and the etiology of anxiety; additionally, learning theory addresses the issue of maintenance of disordered behavior. Since successful clinical intervention depends on attention to the current influences on behavior and fears, with perhaps only an indirect relationship to etiological considerations, the learning position offers a more powerful guide for the clinician than does psychoanalytic theory.

Psychoanalytic Theory. Anxiety is a central concept in psychoanalytic theory. According to Freud, the emotional discomfort experienced as anxiety is the result of intrapsychic conflict between the id, ego, and superego—the three functional divisions of the personality. Anxiety serves as a warning signal to which the ego responds by mobilizing defense mechanisms, which are the unconscious processes that keep unacceptable impulses from being directly expressed. Some distortion of reality is characteristic of normal psychological functioning because of the indirect nature in which we express and examine our feelings and fears. Overreliance on defense mechanisms, however, leads to neurotic behavior; reality is then so distorted that the individual can no longer function normally. Freud viewed childhood phobic behavior as a defense mechanism by which anxiety is displaced onto an external object or situation that is symbolic of unacceptable unconscious impulses (i.e., the oedipal conflict). Although it is unrealistic, avoidance behavior, then, reduces anxiety. It is apparent that treatment of an anxiety disorder from a psychoanalytic conceptualization requires attention to the motivational processes underlying behavior, rather than to the behavior itself. To date, little or no evidence other than that obtained through case studies has been provided to support this position.

Learning Conceptualization. A conceptualization of anxiety disorders that emphasizes learning has at least four separate sources of theoretical contribution. As such, a single theoretical statement regarding the development of anxiety disorders is lacking. Perhaps, the strength of the learning conceptualization lies in the successful interventions it offers, rather than in etiological explanations per se. The success of these interventions derives from careful analysis of the current influences maintaining behavior.

Trauma is one obvious causal variable in the development of children's excessive fears. A respondent conditioning paradigm explains the fear as a conditioned response elicited by a conditioned stimulus—a neutral stimulus that was present when the original trauma involving fear (an unconditioned response to an unconditioned stimulus) occurred. A precipitating traumatic event cannot, however, be identified in many clinical cases of children's fears (Solyom, Beck, Solyom, & Hugel, 1974). Seligman and Johnston (1973) have noted that avoidance behavior is not always mediated by fear. Therefore, classical conditioning alone cannot account for children's fears.

Operant conditioning may often be a causal process in the acquisition of fearful behavior and is usually a critical component of its maintenance. Fearful behavior is developed and/or supported by reinforcing environmental consequences. For example, the child may be rewarded for exhibiting fearful behavior by receiving solicitous attention from others. The child's behavior may also be negatively reinforced by avoidance behavior that generates anxiety reduction.

Modeling may be a process involved in the acquisition of children's fears. A fear may be vicariously classically conditioned if a child observes a model that undergoes a fearful experience (Bandura & Rosenthal, 1966); or, through operant processes, a child may acquire fearful behavior by observing a model reinforced for the behavior. Parental fearful behavior and anxiety appear to be an especially potent factor in the acquisition and maintenance of children's fears (e.g., Bandura & Menlove, 1968; Shaw, 1975; Solyom et al., 1974).

Respondent and operant conditioning, either directly or by modeling, thus represent learning conceptualizations of children's anxiety disorders. In addition, influential explanations of children's fears, which have been offered by Mowrer (two-factor learning theory, 1960) and Wolpe, explain the fear acquisition via classical conditioning and the subsequent maintenance of the avoidance response by instrumental or operant conditioning. Although intuitively satisfying, empirical data have not supported this position. In addition to the criticisms of the classical conditioning explanation that were previously noted, one problem with the two-factor theory is the resistance of avoidance responses to extinction (Marks, 1969).

It is most likely that etiology differs across cases of children's fearful and anxious behavior. Classical or operant processes, modeled or direct, may be contributors to varying degrees and in varying combinations among children in the acquisition of the behavior. Certainly, learning processes help to sustain fearful behavior and are useful in this modification.

Predisposing Influences

Hereditary factors may possibly predispose some children to the development of an anxiety disorder. As noted by Johnson and Melamed (1979), individual differences in arousal and habituation to stimulation may be related to children's acquisition of fears. Individual differences in temperament have been demonstrated in infancy (e.g., Thomas, Chess, Birch, Hertzig & Korn, 1963), and infants' abilities to regulate their physiological states is considered an important index of their adaptability and developmental status. Thus, from birth, children vary in their reactivity and ability to adjust to environmental stimulation. In addition, some researchers have reported that psychiatric problems are more common in the families of patients with anxiety disorders (Solyom et al., 1974).

Certain stimuli appear more likely to elicit fear in humans than others (e.g., fears of animals are more common than fears of objects), suggesting a genetic basis for increased reactivity to some stimuli. As previously discussed, the content of children's fears changes over the developmental course, suggesting that sensitivity to stimuli varies developmentally as well.

Rachman and Hodgson (1974) have postulated that fears can be innate and maturational, such as fear of the dark, sudden noises, and presence of strangers. Similarly, Seligman (1971) has proposed an evolutionary approach that focuses on human fears and phobias as a form of "prepared classical conditioning." He believes that there is a selective process in the development of fear-related behaviors that have an evolutionary basis. Thus, fears or phobias may be conceptualized along a dimension of preparedness. On the one extreme of the preparedness dimension are fear responses that occur instinctively, followed by responses that occur after only a few pairings. Next are responses that occur after many pairings (unprepared responses). Responses on the other extreme of the continuum are what Seligman refers to as *contraprepared* (i.e., responses that occur only after a large number of pairings). While there is some support for this model of fear-related behaviors in adults (Hugdahl, Fredrikson, & Ohman, 1977; McNally & Reiss, 1982; Ohman, Eriksson & Olofsson, 1975), there has been no research conducted on the preparedness of children's fears or phobias.

Family characteristics and child-rearing practices may foster the development of children's anxiety disorders. The importance of modeling and reinforcement contingencies has already been noted. The mother-child relationship and family disturbances are viewed as especially important in some cases of school phobia (Johnson, 1978), although in others, problems in school itself seem to be the focus of the problem. Weissman (in press) has found that children of phobic mothers also show concurrent anxiety disorders. Children between the ages of 6 and 17, whose mothers were diagnosed as depressed and either agoraphobic or manifesting panic disorder, were diagnosed as having high rates of depression, separation anxiety, and other categories of anxiety disorders. While these findings are interesting, they should be interpreted cautiously since the individuals who rated the children's behavior were not blind with respect to parental pathology.

Prognosis

The prognosis for children who develop fears is good (Johnson & Melamed, 1979; Miller, 1983; Richards & Siegel, 1978). Even in the absence of therapeutic intervention, most fears remit spontaneously; furthermore, the more specific and focused the fear is the better the prognosis. It appears that adjustment difficulties in adulthood may be more likely to occur with the broader-based or more severe childhood anxiety disorders. For example, Poznanski (1973) reported excessive fears in children to be more persistent, and some investigators have reported a poorer prognosis for school phobic children than for children with other fears. In this regard, the DSM-III description of the childhood anxiety disorder, Overanxious Disorder, in which anxiety is described as generalized, states that the disorder may persist into adulthood, described possibly as Generalized Anxiety Disorder or a Social Phobia.

ASSESSMENT OF ANXIETY DISORDERS

Historically, anxiety has been characterized within a behavioral framework as a complex array of responses rather than as a single, clearly defined response. That is, anxiety may manifest itself as one or more of three basic classes of responses, including physiological (changes mediated by the autonomic nervous system), skeletal-muscular (overt motor behavior), and verbal (cognitive) behavior (Lang, 1968). Consider, for example, a nine-year-old boy who exhibits an extreme fear of thunder storms. The child's thoughts may be expressed verbally through statements such as, "I am afraid of the loud noise and lightning and scared that it will hurt me." The child's anxiety also may be defined behaviorally by avoidance or escape behaviors (e.g., hiding under the bed covers) or through motoric responses, such as physically trembling during a storm. Finally, anxiety may be expressed as physiological arousal in which the child who is fearful of thunder storms manifests an increase in heart rate, tenses his or her muscles, and perspires excessively.

There is an impressive body of research that suggests that measures of fear and/or anxiety do not correlate very highly with one another (Lang, Melamed & Hart, 1970; Martin & Sroufe, 1970). Because this is particularly prevalent in measures of childhood anxiety (Melamed & Siegel, 1980; Ruebush, 1963), it is important to sample all response modes that may reflect a child's anxiety. For example, the child's self-report of subjective experience may not be congruent with how he or she actually behaves in the fearful situation. The physiological response to fear-inducing stimuli may indicate increased visceral activation, yet the child exhibits few problematic motor responses or avoidance responses. Which system do we believe? There is no research data to suggest that any one of these three systems deserves primary consideration. Furthermore, different measures of behavior within a single system may vary. For instance, heart rate and skin conductance may not equally reflect physiological arousal. As such, anxiety should not be inferred on the basis of a single indicator of autonomic arousal (Lacey, 1967). Instead, it is the pattern of relationships between responses that defines the meaning of anxiety or fear. Individuals may differ in their tendency to exhibit certain patterns of responses in different systems or in the same system at different times. It has also been observed that the discordance between systems may appear because of differential rates of change in the problem behaviors. This suggests that it is important to sample the behaviors at different time periods within the same setting.

Multidimensional Assessment Procedures

Because the child's anxiety-related problems may be reflected in several response systems, it is important to assess the target behavior in each system that is practical or relevant. Furthermore, since the three response modalities do not always show change at the same rate or in a consistent manner across systems, it is beneficial to assess as many diminsions of the target behavior as possible in order to insure maximum treatment effectiveness. In fact, predictions regarding the choice of the treatment approach may best be made by examining the discrepancies between these systems within the individual (Lang, 1977).

It is beyond the scope of this chapter to provide a detailed discussion of the various approaches for the assessment of anxiety disorders and fear-related behaviors in children. Excellent reviews of this area include the following: Barrios et al. (1981), Johnson and Melamed (1979), and Morris and Kratochwill (1983).

Numerous assessment techniques have been used for evaluating the cognitive, motoric, and physiological components of fears and anxiety in children. Each of these response systems is briefly discussed below.

Cognitive Response Modalities. The child's subjective experience of distress associated with anxiety or fearful situations is assessed through client self-report. Self-report data may be obtained through an interview or from the child's response to structured questionnaires or inventories. The interview attempts to elicit information from the child regarding the stimuli that currently trigger the anxiety or fear-related behaviors.

Self-report measures of children's fears and anxieties typically ask the child to rate the extent to which specific symptoms or events are experienced in particular settings and situations. In addition, the child may rate the intensity of their subjective feelings of anxiety or fear based on their general experiences or during or immediately following exposure to the anxiety-evoking stimulus. A distinction further may be made between measures of trait and state or situational anxiety (Cattell & Scheier, 1961; Spielberger, 1966). Measures of trait anxiety are presumed to assess a more stable or generalized characteristic of the child, while situational measures tend to assess a transitory state that presumably varies over time and across situations and occurs in response to specific stimuli.

Motor Response Modalities. Direct or indirect sampling of the child's motor or overt behaviors that are considered to reflect anxiety or fear-related responses, such as avoiding or escaping from the situation, impaired performance or inhibition of behavior, and numerous discrete motor behaviors is another major component of the multiple response systems assessment process. Direct observation of the child in the natural environment, such as the home or school or in a laboratory or clinic setting, are used to obtain information about overt manifestations of anxiety disorders in children. One of the most common procedures for obtaining observational data about a child's fears that are associated with highly specific stimuli, such as dogs, is the *Behavioral Avoidance Test*. In this technique, the child is asked to perform a graded series of approach behaviors toward the feared object, and the child's behavior is scored along a number of dimensions, such as distance moved toward the feared object and amount of time spent in the presence of this stimulus (Lang & Lazovik, 1963).

If the anxiety-related problems occur regularly in the child's environment, it may be useful to obtain naturalistic observations. Individuals who are trained to use specific observational coding systems developed to assess behaviors that are presumably associated with anxiety or behavioral distress typically record the presence or absence of each behavior during a particular time interval.

Some anxiety-related problems may occur at times or in particular settings that may not be readily available for observation by a highly trained observer, such as at bedtime. In such instances, it may be useful to obtain information from significant persons in the child's natural environment, such as parents or teachers. Several specific behavior checklists and global rating scales have been developed for use by persons who are familiar with the child. These measures require that the rater check the occurrence or nonoccurrence of particular behavioral indices of fear or anxiety, which is based on current or past observations of the child's behavior. In addition, the child's behavior may be rated on a scale ranging from low to high frequency.

Physiological Response Modalities.   Numerous indices of autonomic nervous system activity, such as heart rate, blood pressure, muscle tension, skin conductance, and respiration, have been used as measures of the physiological component of anxiety and fear (Nietzel & Bernstein, 1981). Typically, these physiological responses are monitored by highly sophisticated psychophysiological equipment. Less complex procedures for assessing physiological activity also have been used, including radial pulse rate, the palmar sweat index (Melamed & Siegel, 1975), and other easily observable behaviors considered to reflect physiological arousal, such as nausea, diarrhea, frequent urination, and profuse sweating. While there have been numerous reports of the use of physiological measures of anxiety and fear in adults, there have been relatively few empirical studies of this approach with children (Barrios et al., 1981; Melamed & Siegel, 1980).

There is considerable research evidence that marked desynchrony often occurs between different physiological measures. Thus, each individual has his or her own idiosyncratic pattern of responses such that some persons may be primarily heart rate responders, while others may primarily respond on measures of electrodermal activity (Lacey & Lacey, 1968). As a result, it is highly recommended that more than one physiological measure of anxiety and fear be used in order to evaluate the different patterns of responses within each individual.

Goals of Assessment

A functional analysis is the framework within which behavioral assessment is undertaken. Its purpose is to identify the problem behaviors in such a way that treatment can be clearly prescribed and objectively evaluated. A functional analysis attempts to determine the relationship between the anxiety or fear-related behavior that the child exhibits and the events in the environment that control the appearance and/or maintenance of the behavior. Once the relationship between the environmental events and the anxiety or fear responses have been determined, these events can be systematically altered to produce a desired change in the problem behaviors.

In the assessment of children's fears and related problems, it is particularly important to identify the stimuli that elicit the anxiety or fearful responses. These stimuli can be external events or objects, such as dogs or the doctor, or they can be internal events, such as thoughts or images including maladaptive cognitions that inappropriately define an experience or event as unsafe (Borkovec, Weerts & Bernstein, 1977).

Because anxiety responses also may be maintained or controlled by their consequences in the environment, it is important to identify events that systematically follow their occurrence. For example, a child might receive social reinforcement, such as attention from others when he or she exhibits the fear-related behaviors.

Finally, it is important to evaluate the extent to which skill deficits in the child's repertoire contribute to the anxiety disorders. A child's fear-related reactions might be mediated, in part, because the child does not know what is expected or what to do in the situation. Therefore, an effective treatment program might be needed to help the child develop new skills in his or her repertoire, in addition to eliminate the fearful behaviors. For example, a child who is anxious about taking exams may not have the prerequisite skills for preparing for and taking tests in school. Similarly, the child who exhibits anxiety reactions in social situations or exhibits avoidance behaviors with peers may not have the appropriate social and communication skills to interact in an effective manner with other children.

Diagnosis and Classification of Anxiety Disorders

In the most recent edition of the *Diagnostic and Statistical Manual of Mental Disorders* (DSM-III) of the American Psychiatric Association (1980), three disorders of childhood and adolescence are included in which anxiety is the primary clinical feature: *Separation Anxiety Disorder, Avoidant Disorder of Childhood or Adolescence,* and *Overanxious Disorder.* DSM-III specifies that in the former two disorders, anxiety is focused on specific situations. In the latter disorder, anxiety is presumed to have generalized to a variety of situations.

In addition to the Anxiety Disorders of Childhood and Adolescence, DSM-III provides four types of anxiety disorders that may be used in the diagnosis of both children and adults. This group of anxiety disorders is *Panic Disorder, Generalized Anxiety Disorder, Phobic Disorder,* and *Obsessive Compulsive Disorder.* Anxiety is said to be a predominant feature of the former two disorders, whereas in the latter two disorders, anxiety is experienced as a consequence of the individual's attempts to control or master the symptoms. Three types of phobic disorders are listed: *Agoraphobia, Social Phobia,* and *Simple Phobia.*

DSM-III represents a clinically derived rather than an empirically devised system of classifying behavior disorders. While DSM-III offers a more systematic approach for purposes of communication and the taxonomy of behavior disorders than its predecessors, it currently provides little or no empirical guidelines for the individual assessment and behavioral treatment of children with anxiety or fear-related problems. In DSM-III, symptoms indicating each disorder are presented with a specified number of symptoms that need to be presented for the diagnosis to be established. For example, among the diagnostic criteria for a Separation Anxiety Disorder is the presence of at least three of nine possible symptoms. However, within a behavioral framework, the clinician is concerned primarily with the extent to which any particular symptom might interfere with the child's adaptive functioning in the environment rather than the extent to which a particular symptom might appear along with a constellation of other symptomatic behaviors. Therefore, the behavior therapist would attempt to develop an intervention program for one of the symptoms specified under Separation Anxiety Disorder that indicates a "persistent reluctance or refusal to go to sleep without being next to a major attachment figure or to go to sleep away from home" (p. 53), whether or not this problem is presented along with the other symptoms that are listed for this disorder. Such an approach to diagnosis and assessment is useful to the behavior therapist to the extent that it provides the type of information that will enable the therapist to develop a treatment program and to guide the treatment process with anxiety-related disorders in children. At the present time, empirical evidence is lacking in this area with respect to the anxiety disorders included in DSM-III.

BEHAVIORAL TREATMENT OF ANXIETY DISORDERS

This section presents the behavioral treatment procedures that have been frequently used with children who exhibit anxiety and fear-related disorders. In addition, some recently developed procedures, which have not yet experienced widescale use but that show considerable promise, are also discussed. The clinical and research literature in this area has undergone considerable growth in recent years (see Gelfand, 1978; Graziano et al., 1979; Hatzenbuehler & Schroeder, 1978; Morris & Kratochwill, 1983; Richards & Siegel, 1978). The behavioral treatment of children's fears and anxieties has typically involved procedures that include one or more of the following approaches: counterconditioning procedures, operant techniques, modeling procedures, and self-control procedures. Each of these treatment methods will be described in detail below, including a discussion of issues to be considered in implementing each procedure. In addition, evidence regarding the therapeutic efficacy of each method of the treatment of children's fear-related disorders is presented.

Counterconditioning Procedures

A widely used behavioral technique for treatment of anxiety-related disorders is systematic desensitization that is based on the principle of counterconditioning. This procedure can be traced to some of the earliest accounts of the application of learning-based techniques to the treatment of fear in young children (Jones, 1924).

Wolpe (1958) is primarily associated with the development of systematic desensitization. He assumed that the process underlying this procedure was reciprocal inhibition. Essentially, he proposed that anxiety or fear could be reduced or inhibited by replacing the maladaptive anxiety response with an adaptive response. According to Wolpe (1958), "If a response antagonistic to anxiety can be made to occur in the presence of anxiety-evoking stimuli so that it is accompanied by a complete or partial suppression of the anxiety responses, the bond between these stimuli and the anxiety responses will be weakened" (p. 71). Thus, the association between a particular stimulus and the anxiety response that it elicits can be broken or counterconditioned by presenting the stimulus while the anxiety response is prevented from occurring. While the relaxation response, which is induced through deep muscle relaxation (Jacobson, 1938), is the most frequently used anxiety-inhibiting response, other responses have also been identified as incompatible with anxiety including eating, assertion, and sexual arousal (Wolpe, 1958). While the exact mechanisms underlying the effects of desensitization procedures remain open to empirical validation (Davison & Wilson, 1972; Goldfried, 1971), there is considerable evidence for the effectiveness of systematic desensitization as a method for reducing anxiety-related responses.

Systematic desensitization involves three basic components: (*a*) training in a response that is incompatible with anxiety, such as deep muscle relaxation; (*b*) construction of a hierarchy of anxiety-related evoking situations, and (*c*) counterposing relaxation while the child is exposed to the anxiety-evoking stimuli either imaginally or in vivo. Each of these components will be elaborated upon below.

Relaxation Training. The most common method of relaxation training is the procedure developed by Jacobson (1938) to induce deep muscle relaxation. After the child is placed in a comfortable position in a reclining chair, he or she is instructed to alternately tense and relax various muscle groups (i.e., face, neck, arms, legs), while concentrating on the feelings of tension and relaxation. Each muscle group is tensed for approximately 10 seconds and relaxed for about 30 seconds. The therapist enhances sensations of relaxation by using suggestions of warmth and relaxation. Every muscle group is tensed and relaxed a minimum of two times or until the child reports complete relaxation of the muscle group.

Deep muscle relaxation training takes approximately three sessions to complete. The child is encouraged to practice the relaxation at home for a brief period at least twice each day. Following sufficient practice, the child should be capable of inducing total relaxation in just a few minutes. Variations of muscle relaxation training procedures for use with children are outlined in detail by Cautela and Groden (1978) and Koeppen (1974).

Anxiety Hierarchy Construction. An anxiety hierarchy consists of a number of statements of specific situations that relate to the child's fears. Each item or statement is elaborated upon in sufficient detail to enable the child to vividly imagine the event or experience. Information about the specific components of the child's fear and stimulus characteristics unique to the feared object or event is obtained from data gathered during the assessment process described earlier in the chapter. With the assistance of the therapist and significant others, such as parents and teachers, a series of situations that result in increasing amounts of anxiety or discomfort for the child are ordered from least to most anxiety arousing. Each item in the hierarchy should be arranged in such a way that the child perceives only a small increase in anxiety over the previous item.

The length of a hierarchy for a particular child varies, depending on a number of factors, such as the range of stimuli that are involved and the intensity of the child's fear. In addition, hierarchies can vary across several dimensions. Some hierarchies are spatial-temporal, varying along space and/or time dimensions. Thematic hierarchies, on the other hand, involve items that have a similar theme but differ in the extent to which they are anxiety-arousing. Many hierarchies represent a combination of these two forms (Paul & Bernstein, 1973).

Systematic Desensitization. Once the child has learned to achieve a state of deep relaxation and the anxiety hierarchy has been developed, desensitization can begin. Typically, the child is first instructed to relax; then, the therapist presents each item from the hierarchy and asks the child to vividly imagine each scene. While visualizing each scene, the child is asked to remain as relaxed as possible. If the child experiences even the slightest anxiety, he or she is instructed to signal the therapist by raising a finger. At that point, the child is told to stop imagining and to continue relaxing. After the child is relaxed, the same scene is attempted again. If anxiety is not signaled, a second opportunity to visualize the scene is provided. The next scene is then presented, following three consecutive successes. This process is followed until the most anxiety-evoking scene can be imagined without experiencing anxiety. Three to four items are usually presented during each therapy session.

The stepwise progression of substituting relaxation for anxiety generalizes from low-anxiety situations to higher-anxiety situations, so eventually, the child can imagine the most feared activity with little distress. The generalization to real-life fear situations is facilitated by assigning tasks involving the performance of those items imagined without anxiety.

There are a number of variations of systematic desensitization that have been developed (Morris & Kratochwill, 1983). One of the most frequently used of these variations is called *in vivo desensitization*. This procedure is similar to the imaginal desensitization described above except that the hierarchy items are presented in the actual situation rather than through imagination. In addition to the relaxation training, the therapist's presence serves as an anxiety-inhibiting factor through his reassurance and encouragement.

Another procedural modification of desensitization that has been adopted specifically for use with children is called *emotive imagery*. Lazarus and Abramovitz (1962) used "emotive" images as an anxiety-inhibiting response with fearful children. This type of imagery was designed to "arouse feelings of self-assertion, pride, affection, mirth, and similar anxiety-inhibiting responses" (Lazarus & Abramovitz, 1962; p. 191). They described the steps in this procedure as follows: (*a*) develop a graduated hierarchy of the child's fears; (*b*) determine the child's hero image, such as Superman; (*c*) have the child imagine a series of credible events within which is woven a story about his or favorite hero; (*d*) carefully arouse the child's affective responses with the story; (*e*) when the positive emotions have been aroused, introduce each hierarchy item until the entire hierarchy has been completed without distress.

Stedman (1976) provides an interesting case study of systematic desensitization with a school phobic child. Alice, a nine-year-old, became extremely anxious in any school situation that required her to perform a new or poorly mastered academic task in front of a class. Reading class and music class were two such situations, and she was avoiding these anxiety-producing situations by leaving school before these classes.

Behavioral interventions for Alice's refusal to attend reading and music class included two desensitization programs: a standard systematic desensitization program using an imagined hierarchy, and an in vivo desensitization program implemented by a teacher in the school setting. A contingency contracting system in which her parents reinforced Alice's school attendance was also implemented. Treatment involved 16 sessions with Alice and her parents and two meetings with school personnel.

· The systematic desensitization program followed the standard procedure outlined earlier and was aimed at the main precipitant of Alice's present school avoidance—music class. Alice was successfully trained in deep muscle relaxation; a hierarchy was developed that focused on music class and had a general theme on performance of unfamiliar or complex school work in front of peers and teachers. Excerpts from this hierarchy are presented in Table 7–1. Systematic desensitization was begun in the third therapy session and continued through the 14th session, with Alice progressing through the hierarchy while

TABLE 7–1

**Excerpts from a Music Class and Academic Hierarchy
Used in a Systematic Desensitization Program***

1. I am at home at night thinking about sitting in music class watching the others play their recorders . . .
5. I am in music class with the teacher by herslf. I am playing an easy, familiar tune on my recorder, and the teacher looks pleased . . .
9. I am in music class with the teacher by herself. I am playing a hard tune on which I make many mistakes, and the teacher looks slightly displeased . . .
14. I am in music class with the teacher and all the students. I am plc ,ing an easy tune in front of the class, with the teacher watching me . . .
18. I am in front of the music class, playing a fairly hard tune on which I make many mistakes, and several students smile and laugh . . .
22. I have played poorly in front of the music class, and the teacher corrects me after class for a poor performance . . .
26. I am in reading class, and the teacher calls on me to stand up and read. I stumble over words, while several students laugh at me and the teacher looks impatient . . .
29. I am in reading class, and the teacher calls on me to stand up and read. I stumble over words, and the teacher asks me to sit down and comments that I should know the work. The whole class laughs.

* Source: J. M. Stedman, "Family Counseling with a School-Phobic Child," in *Counseling Methods*, eds. J. D. Krumboltz and C. E. Thoresen (New York: Holt, Rinehart & Winston, 1976), p. 285. Reprinted with permission. © 1976 by Holt, Rinehart & Winston.

deeply relaxed and reporting increasing anxiety reduction as she moved through the hierarchy.

Starting conjointly with the eighth therapy session, Alice's teachers were incorporated into an in vivo desensitization program, which ran concurrently with the imagery-based systematic desensitization treatment. This in vivo program was carried out in or near the school setting and included the following steps: (*a*) Alice's music teacher would tutor her outside the school until she reached a level of skill similar to that of her class; (*b*) Alice would reenter music class for 10-minute periods but would not be required to play her recorder, (*c*) Alice would remain in music class for the full time and would play the recorder (Stedman, 1976; p. 285).

This multifaceted treatment program was successful, and Alice started attending all of her classes regularly and reported little further anxiety in doing so. A two-year follow-up evaluation indicated that this successful outcome had been maintained, and Alice was even leading her classmates in singing at the school.

An interesting variation of systematic desensitization is reported by Wish, Hasazi, and Jurgela (1973) in the treatment of an 11-year-old male who had a fear of loud noises. These fears centered around noises, such as fire-crackers, thunder, or jet engines. The child was able to learn muscle relaxation and assisted in the construction of a fear hierarchy, which consisted of a list of the sounds arranged in the order of their anxiety-evoking properties. An audiotape was then made of the sounds from the hierarchy with his favorite music super-imposed. The child was instructed to relax in a dark room and to listen to the tape with the volume gradually increased during the eight-day (three sessions per day) treatment period. Following treatment, he could comfortably listen to the previously feared sounds. A nine-month follow-up showed that his tolerance for previously feared noises was maintained.

Forced Exposure Procedures.   In addition to systematic desensitization, there are several other methods for modifying respondently conditioned anxiety responses. These techniques are called *flooding* and *implosion* and are based on the notion that anxiety responses can be extinguished through repeated presentation of the anxiety-evoking stimuli (in vivo or in imagination) in a safe setting until the distressing stimuli no longer elicit anxiety (Marshall et al., 1979). Thus, unlike desensitization in which the child imagines a fearful scene while attempting to remain relaxed, these methods have the child imagine the scene for prolonged periods of time without engaging in relaxation training.

Flooding typically involves the repeated exposure of distressing stimuli either in imagination or in vivo. As an anxiety reaction occurs, the therapist attempts to intensify the client's reaction by elaborating on the anxiety-arousing aspects of the scene. This procedure continues until the anxiety is completely dissipated.

Implosive therapy is similar in procedure to flooding. Implosive therapy, however, often presents fear-related stimuli that are more intense and has the client imagine extreme and aversive consequences as a result of exposure to these stimuli (Stampfl & Levis, 1973). Usually, the scenes are presented in a highly exaggerated and dramatic manner.

Ollendick and Gruen (1972) provide an illustration of a flooding procedure in the treatment of an eight-year-old boy with an extreme fear of bodily injury. His fears considerably restricted his activity such that he refused to go to school for fear of becoming injured while playing, and he had difficulty sleeping every night. An example of the flooding scenes used in treatment included the following:

> You are alone walking through a forest going to a lake to fish, and you hear weird noises and see strange things. The wind begins blowing very hard, and you trip and hit your head on a rock. When you get up, blood trickles down your forehead into your eyes, nose, and mouth . . . (Ollendick & Gruen, 1972, p. 391).

Following two therapy sessions, the child's fears considerably decreased, and the number of sleepless nights reduced to two episodes per week. At a six-month follow-up, the child reported less fear, and he was no longer experiencing sleep difficulties. In addition, despite a recent hospitalization for a bicycle accident, he was no longer exhibiting concerns about being hurt.

Clinical and Research Issues

While systematic desensitization procedures appear to be relatively simple, on the surface they are, in fact, quite complex and require considerable skill on the part of the therapist. This is particularly true in the use of desensitization procedures and its variants in the treatment of young children. Systematic desensitization requires a degree of cooperation and enthusiasm that children may not always be inclined to give, and sometimes it is difficult to teach young children the deep muscle relaxation training. In addition, young children may be unable to achieve sufficiently vivid imagery to use in imaginal desensitization (Ollendick, 1979). It is partly with this in mind that related but alternative fear-reduction techniques, such as emotive imagery or in vivo desensitization, often are utilized with children.

While the in vivo exposure to anxiety-arousing stimuli may be an usual alternative to imagery-based procedures, all fears (e.g., fear of injury) are not readily amenable to in vivo treatment approaches. As a result, it may be necessary to adapt imagery-based procedures that can be used with young children. For example, with a young dog phobic child, Kissel (1972) used a series of graduated tasks that included looking at picture books of dogs and making up stories about dogs to enhance the child's visualization of anxiety-arousing stimuli.

Hierarchy construction must be done very carefully and is an essential component of all desensitization procedures. A graded hierarchy should be developed in such a manner that each scene that is presented to the child is sufficiently weak in its anxiety-arousing properties so as to induce little or no distress in the child.

Insufficient assessment of factors contributing to the child's fear-related problems may lead to the ineffective use of systematic desensitization. The therapist must insure that the child has the prerequisite skills appropriate to the previously avoided situation. Sometimes the child is fearful, at least in part, simply because he or she does not know what to do in the situation. In addition, because the child has avoided a situation for so long, he or she might not have learned the necessary skills that most children would have naturally developed. This would particularly be the case in children who exhibit extreme forms of social withdrawal.

Systematic desensitization with adults has received considerable research attention, and its effectiveness has been well demonstrated. While this procedure enjoys considerable case study support for use with anxious and fearful children, there have been few controlled experimental studies with this population (Graziano et al., 1979; Hatzenbuehler & Schroeder, 1978). The few controlled studies that do exist with children do not argue strongly for the *superiority* of systematic desensitization over other behavioral treatment procedures (Richards & Siegel, 1978). However, the findings from the case studies and controlled experimental investigations do suggest that systematic desensitization, when combined with other techniques, such as positive reinforcement, and when tied to eventual in vivo exposure and practice with the feared situation, can be a potentially useful method for reducing a variety of anxiety-related problems in children (Morris & Kratochwill, 1983; Ollendick, 1979).

There have been few reports of the use of flooding or forced exposure procedures with children. Evidence for their effectiveness with fearful children is based only on several uncontrolled case studies (Morris & Kratochwill, 1983).

The use of flooding procedures with children has been somewhat controversial, and a number of writers have cautioned against their routine use (Gelfand, 1978; Graziano, 1975). Because of the stress-arousing nature of these procedures, Gelfand (1978), for example, suggests that the treatment setting may become sufficiently aversive for the child, thus, leading to avoidance of therapy sessions. Others have proposed that prolonged exposure to highly anxiety-arousing imagery may, in some instances, exacerbate the client's fear (Marshall et al., 1979). Given these possible concerns, it is suggested that flooding procedures be used with considerable caution.

Modeling Procedures

Learning by observing or imitating the behavior of others is an important process in the acquisition of many behaviors for children. Modeling techniques are based primarily on the principles of observational learning, which can produce a number of behavioral changes. Through observing a model's behavior, an individual:

> may learn new, appropriate behavior patterns, and modeling may thus serve an *acquisition* function. More likely, the observation of a model's behavior in various situations may provide social *facilitation* of appropriate behaviors by inducing the client to perform these behaviors, of which he was previously capable, at more appropriate times, in more appropriate ways, or toward more appropriate people. Modeling may lead to *disinhibition* of behaviors that the client has avoided because of fear or anxiety. And while disinhibiting behaviors, modeling may promote *vicarious* and *direct extinction* of the fear associated with person, animals, or object toward which the behavior was directed. (Rimm & Masters, 1979; pp. 103–104)

In observational learning or therapeutic modeling, the child (or observer) is exposed to the behavior of a model (i.e., therapist, peer) and the consequences that may accrue to the model's behavior. It is not essential that the child actually engage in any overt responses or that he or she receive direct consequences for that behavior. The model may be physically present or may be presented through filmed or imaginal (symbolic) techniques.

Bandura (1969, 1971) makes a distinction between the acquisition and performance of a response. Through a model's behavior, the observer forms symbolic responses (imaginal representations) similar to those responses performed by the model; these symbolic mediators have cue-producing properties that later modify and guide the observer's behavior. Whether an individual actually performs the modeled behavior depends on a number of factors, such as the consequences to the model's behavior and whether there are adequate incentives for the observer to perform the behavior.

There is currently a substantial amount of literature regarding the use of modeling procedures in the treatment of children's anxiety and fear-related behaviors. Modeling techniques have been used primarily with common childhood fears, such as fear of animals and water, and fears of medical and dental treatment. The typical procedure is to have the fearful child observe one or several models approach and interact with the feared event or stimulus with no adverse consequences and/or positive consequences resulting for the model's approach behavior. In addition, the model's approach behavior usually occurs in a graduated manner in which the model engages in increasingly more anxiety-arousing interactions with the feared stimulus or event (Perry & Furukawa, 1980). The model is presumed to teach new response patterns to the child or to permit the performance of previously established behaviors by reducing the fear-evoking capacity of the situation and, thereby, disinhibiting approach behaviors (Bandura, 1969).

Three variations of modeling procedures have been used in the treatment of anxiety and fear in children: live modeling, symbolic modeling, and participant modeling (Ollendick, 1979). Each type of modeling procedure varies to the extent to which the model's behavior is presented in the actual presence of the fearful child and to which the model interacts with the child.

Live Modeling.   In live modeling, the child observes an actual or live model engage in the fear-related activity. The model performs the graduated approach behavior in the child's presence; however, the child is not required to interact with the feared object or event. Live modeling was used in a classic study by Bandura et al., (1967) to increase the approach behaviors of 48 children, three to five years old, who had demonstrated fear of dogs. The two models were four-year-old males who were not fearful in the presence of dogs. The fearful children were divided into four groups. In the first condition, modeling plus positive context, the children observed a model fearlessly approach and interact with a dog in the context of a highly enjoyable party-like atmosphere. Children in the modeling plus neutral context simply observed the model approach the dog without a party. The third group, exposure plus neutral context, attended a party with the dog present; however, no approach behavior was modeled for the fearful children. In the final condition, positive context, the children participated in a party in which neither the dog nor the model were present.

Children in each group were exposed to eight, 10-minute treatment sessions over four consecutive days. In the two model conditions, the model performed a series of graded interactions with the dog, including a gradual change in the physical restraints on the dog, the closeness of the model's approach behaviors, and the duration of the model's contact with the dog. For example, during the first treatment session, the dog was confined to a playpen, and the model periodically talked to and petted the dog. By the fifth session, the model walked the dog on a leash outside of the playpen. In the last session, the model climbed into the playpen and fed, hugged, and petted the dog.

The effectiveness of each group in increasing approach behaviors in the fearful children was assessed by a Behavioral Avoidance Test at pre and post-treatment and again at a follow-up session. Children in the two modeling groups demonstrated significantly more approach behaviors at posttreatment and follow-up assessment periods than the children in the two control groups. In addition, children in the two modeling conditions were able to perform significantly more often than the other two groups the terminal task in the Behavioral Avoidance Test, which required the child to remain alone in the room with dog.

With children who exhibited fearful behaviors that interfered with dental treatment, White and Davis (1974) investigated the relative effectiveness of live modeling, familiarization with dental equipment in the absence of a model, and a no-treatment control condition. The subjects were 15 children between four and eight years of age. In the live modeling group, five children, from behind a one-way mirror, observed a child-model undergoing dental treatment. The five children in the familiarization group merely observed the dentist and his assistant name and handle the same dental equipment used in the model condition but without the presence of a model. Children in the control group had no opportunity to observe the instruments or a model's behavior prior to dental treatment. The children in the first two conditions received the experimental interventions during six sessions over a three-week period. The results indicated that approach behaviors, ranging from "walking down the hall" to "allowing of restoration" was not different between the live model and familiarization groups. Both of these treatments produced significantly greater approach behavior than the no-exposure group, both at the immediate dental treatment session and at a six-month follow-up period. In addition, children in the modeling group exhibited fewer hiding and refusal of treatment behaviors than the exposure group. Children in the exposure-only group also requested that a significant other (i.e., mother, sibling) be present during dental treatment, whereas no similar requests were made by any child in the modeling group.

Symbolic Modeling. A second type of modeling, referred to as *symbolic modeling*, typically involves the presentation of a model through film or video-tape. Another type of symbolic modeling, called *covert modeling*, consists of an individual picturing, through imagination, various approach behaviors of the "model" with the feared event. While covert modeling procedures have been investigated with adults, there have been only minimal reports of this technique with children (Chertock & Bornstein, 1979).

The use of filmed modeling in the treatment of fearful children is illustrated in a study reported by Bandura and Menlove (1978). This study was similar to the investigation of dog avoidant children by Bandura et al. (1967) except that the model in this study was presented via film. One group of children observed a film that depicted a fearless five-year-old male engage in increasingly greater contacts with a dog. A second group observed a film that showed several male and female peer models interact with a number of dogs of different sizes. In a control group, children observed a film about Disneyland, which was similar in length to the other two films but had no dogs depicted. Children in both film modeling groups were found to significantly increase their approach behaviors on a Behavioral Avoidance Test compared to the control group. No significant differences were observed on approach behaviors between the two experimental groups. The multiple model condition was, however, somewhat more effective than the single model group in their performance of remaining alone in the room with the dog.

In an attempt to assist children in their efforts to cope with the normal and reality-based fears of medical treatment and hospitalization, Melamed and Siegel (1975) explored the effectiveness of filmed modeling as a method for reducing anxiety in children who were hospitalized for surgery. The participants in this study were 60 children between the ages of 4 and 12 who were admitted to a pediatric hospital for elective surgery. These children had no prior history of hospitalization and were scheduled for tonsillectomies, hernia operations, or urinary-genital tract surgery. Thirty children matched for age, sex, race, and type of operation were assigned to the experimental and control groups. Numerous self-report, physiological, and behavioral outcome measures were used to assess state and trait anxiety in the children. These measures were given before and after the children viewed the film, the evening before surgery, and at a one-month follow-up examination after the child's discharge from the hospital. In addition, parents completed a measure of childhood behavior problems prior to hospitalization and again at follow-up.

Prior to their admission to the hospital, children in the experimental and control groups viewed one of the two films described below:

> The experimental film, entitled *Ethan Has An Operation,* depicts a 7-year-old white male who has been hospitalized for a hernia operation. This film is 16 minutes in length, consists of 15 scenes showing various events that most children encounter when hospitalized for elective surgery from time of admission to time of discharge, including the child's orientation to the hospital ward and medical personnel such as the surgeon and anesthesiologist; having a blood test and exposure to standard hospital equipment, separation from the mother; and scenes in the operating and recovery rooms. In addition to explanations of the hospital procedures provided by the medical staff, various scenes are narrated by the child, who describes his feelings and concerns that he had at each stage of the hospital experience. Both the child's behavior and verbal remarks exemplify the behavior of a coping model so that while he exhibits some anxiety and apprehension, he is able to overcome his initial fears and complete each event in a successful and nonanxious manner . . .

The subjects in the control group were shown a 12-minute film entitled, *Living Things Are Everywhere*. The control film was similar in interest value to the experimental film in maintaining the children's attention but was unrelated in content to the hospitalization. It presents the experiences of a white preadolescent male who is followed on a nature trip in the country. (Melamed & Siegel, 1975; pp. 514–515)

The results indicated that state measures of anxiety showed a significant reduction of preoperative and postoperative fear arousal for children who observed the peer-modeling film, but not for the children who observed the control film. Children in the filmed modeling group evidenced lower sweat-gland activity, fewer self-reported medical fears, and less anxiety-related behaviors than children in the control group. These results were obtained both the night before surgery and at a one-month postsurgical examination. Moreover, only children in the control group were reported by their parents to have exhibited an increase in the frequency of behavior problems following hospitalization. These findings suggest that filmed modeling procedures may have important preventive implications by helping children to cope more effectively with potentially stressful experiences and by preventing possible fearful reactions from occurring.

Participant Modeling. Bandura (1976) has argued that a particularly potent modeling procedure, referred to as *participant modeling,* involves a combination of modeling and guided reinforced practice. Participant modeling provides an opportunity for the fearful child to observe a model demonstrate approach behaviors to the feared object and then, after observing the model, to make direct contact with the feared object. This procedure involves a carefully structured and graduated process in which modeled performances by the therapist (or some other model) are immediately imitated and practiced by the child under gradually more difficult and real-life conditions. The therapist initially provides extensive encouragement, physical or verbal prompts, information feedback, and positive reinforcement for the child's practice attempts until the therapist's participation is gradually faded out, and the child can engage in the previously feared activity without the therapist's assistance (Bandura, 1976). Bandura and his associates have also found that behavior change can be accelerated and generalization can be enhanced with participant modeling procedures by the use of adjunctive procedures that they call *response-induction aids* (e.g., prompts, joint performance with the therapist, gradually increasing time of exposure to the feared object), and *self-directed performance* (e.g., additional self-directed practice with a variety of situations following the initial participant modeling session) (Bandura, Jeffrey, & Gajdos, 1975; Bandura, Jeffrey, & Wright, 1974).

Lewis (1974) examined the effectiveness of a participant modeling procedure in reducing children's fear of water activities. The relative effectiveness of participation plus filmed modeling, filmed modeling alone, participation alone, and a no-treatment control condition were investigated with 40 children who exhibited a fear of swimming at a summer camp. The children, who were between 5 and 12 years of age, were administered a 16-item Behavioral Avoidance Test that required increasingly more difficult swimming behaviors, including climbing into a three-foot deep pool and putting their face in the water. Based on their performance on this test, they were matched for levels of avoidance and were assigned to one of the four groups. In the modeling plus participation group, each child was shown an eight-minute film of three peer-models performing graded tasks in the swimming pool similar to the behavioral avoidance test. The film also included a narration in which the models described their performance and how they were feeling and praised themselves for their activities in the water. Immediately after viewing this film, an experimenter accompanied each child to the pool for 10 minutes and physically assisted each in practicing the items on the avoidance test, giving praise for any activity that was attempted or completed. Children in the modeling alone condition saw the eight-minute film and, instead of practicing in the pool with the experimenter, played a 10-minute game of checkers at the side of the pool. The children in the participation only group saw an eight-minute neutral film (cartoons) that had no themes of water activities; they were then taken to the pool and were exposed to the participation component in which they attempted the items on the avoidance test with the physical assistance and encouragement of the experimenter. Finally, children in the control group viewed the neutral film and then played checkers with the experimenter by the pool. The results demonstrated that all three treatment groups exhibited less fear and engaged in more water activities than the control group. Children in the modeling plus participation group, however, exhibited greater reductions in fear of the water and more improvements in their swimming abilities than any other group.

Finally, the treatment of several patients with severe needle phobias through participant modeling is illustrated in a study by Taylor, Ferguson, and Wermuth (1977). The patients were hospitalized for diagnostic tests or surgery that necessitated multiple insertion of needles or intravenous catheters for the withdrawal of blood samples or injection of medication. However, because of their intense fear of needles, they fainted or refused to cooperate with the medical procedures.

A participant modeling approach was used in which the patients were given an instrument tray containing intravenous equipment, including syringes, covered needles, and alcohol swabs. When the patient was able to tolerate having the tray in the room, the therapist identified and handled each item and gave it to the patient. The patient was then instructed to handle the equipment until it felt comfortable to do so. In addition, the patient was asked to handle increasingly larger covered needles. This was continued until the patient no longer reported feeling anxious, at which time the covers were removed from the needles. When the patient was able to hold the syringe and open needle in a comfortable manner, the therapist demonstrated touching the needle to his own skin, moving the needle up and down his arm. The patient was then asked to imitate this behavior. A syringe was then filled with medication, and the patient was asked to copy the therapist's behavior of injecting medication into an orange. The patient continued to practice this until anxiety was no longer reported. Finally, the therapist stuck the needle into his own arm to demonstrate that there were no adverse consequences. The treatment session culminated in the therapist drawing the patient's blood. This procedure, which lasted approximately one hour, significantly reduced the patient's anxiety and distress, and enabled them to engage in the previously feared medical procedures.

Clinical and Research Issues

In the application of modeling procedures to the treatment of fears and anxiety-related problems in children, there are a number of factors that the therapist must consider to enhance the effectiveness of the modeling process (Marlatt & Perry, 1975; Melamed & Siegel, 1980; Perry & Furukawa, 1980). Among these factors is an important consideration of the characteristics of the model. Models who are prestigious, warm and friendly, competent, and of an appropriate age usually facilitate the modeling effect (Gelfand, 1978; Perry & Furukawa, 1980). Perceived similarity between the observer and the model also generally increases modeling effects, as does the use of multiple models (Bandura, 1971; Thelen, Fry, Fehrenbach, & Frautschi, 1979).

There is some evidence to suggest that coping models who are initially anxious but subsequently overcome their fears to complete the task in a confident and competent manner may be preferable in some instances in the treatment of fear-related problems than are mastery models who exhibit no fear or concern (Meichenbaum, 1971; Rachman, 1972; Thelen et al., 1979). In a similar manner, Gelfand (1978) notes that, in the treatment of socially withdrawn and socially avoidant children, effective modeling demonstrations have typically used peers who were initially similar to the socially withdrawn observers, but who later demonstrate increasingly assertive and competent responses.

How the model is presented also has important treatment implications:

> The model should be presented so as to maximize the observer's *attention* to and *retention* of the model's behavior. Attention may be aided by choosing an appropriate context free from distraction, and by highlighting the model's behavior through the use of preliminary instructions and narrations of the key features of the model's performance. If the model is engaging in behaviors which are likely to make the observer anxious, supplementary instructions in relaxation may enhance attention to the model. The observer is also more likely to attend to the model if he is *uncertain* about how to perform the behavior himself and needs information in order to respond appropriately. (Marlatt & Perry, 1975, p. 153)

Indeed, an important function of modeling is the information that it provides to the child, such as information regarding the exact nature of the feared stimulus and suggestions for alternative patterns of responding to such situations. The extent to which this information serves to facilitate skills acquisition versus disinhibition of anxiety-mediated approach behaviors has yet to be investigated.

The choice of live or filmed modeling also needs to be considered by the therapist. At the present time, there is not clear evidence to suggest that one type of modeling is more effective than the other. Use of live models may increase the attention, involvement, and motivation of the observer and may provide flexibility by enabling the model to modify behavior as is appropriate for a given child. On the other hand, symbolic or filmed models offer the advantages of efficiency, standardization, and increased therapist control over presentation (Perry & Furukawa, 1980). Films or videotapes afford the opportunity for editing whenever necessary, and they can be used repeatedly.

Currently, there is a substantial amount of literature of controlled investigations of modeling in the treatment of childhood fears and anxiety-related behaviors (Gelfand, 1978; Graziano et al., 1979; Melamed & Siegel, 1980; Richards & Siegel, 1978; Thelen et al., 1979). Some investigators have suggested that modeling approaches may be the most effective means of fear reduction in children (Bandura, 1976; Gelfand, 1978). Ollendick (1979) has summarized the research literature in this area by noting that the short-term efficacy of modeling procedures has been adequately demonstrated in the treatment of circumscribed fears. In particular, participant modeling appears to be a rather powerful treatment procedure that induces rapid behavior change.

There have been few comparative studies of the various types of modeling procedures (i.e., Ritter, 1968), and therefore, it is not possible at this time to draw definitive conclusions regarding the relative efficacy of each approach in the treatment of fearful children. In addition, there have been few reports of the long-term maintenance of treatment effects with modeling procedures.

Finally, further research is needed with children who manifest more clinically significant fears and anxiety disorders. Many of the controlled experiments have been analogue studies that may limit the generalizability of the findings to children who have excessive and persistent fears (Morris & Kratochwill, 1983; Ollendick, 1979).

Operant Procedures

A number of contingency management techniques, based on operant conditioning principles, have been used in the treatment of fears and anxiety-related disorders in children. Operant procedures involve the manipulation of antecedent events and consequences of behavior in order to increase or decrease the frequency of certain behaviors. The most frequently used operant procedures in the treatment of children's fears and avoidance behaviors are positive reinforcement, shaping, and stimulus fading.

Positive Reinforcement. A procedure in which a positive event contingently follows a behavior and increases the frequency of that behavior is called *positive reinforcement.* Positive reinforcement is perhaps the most basic technique of behavior therapy and typically is used with other contingency management procedures, such as shaping, stimulus fading, prompting, and operant extinction.

Ayllon, Smith, and Rogers (1970) used positive reinforcement procedures combined with several other contingency management approaches in the treatment of an eight-year-old, school phobic girl. She had been increasingly absent from school during second and third grade and would exhibit violent temper tantrums when her mother attempted to take her to school. The treatment program essentially involved the use of positive reinforcement for school attendance and a decrease in reinforcement for school avoidance.

One facet of the intervention program involved a home-based motivational system with a charting system implemented in which each day of voluntary school attendance was noted with a star. Each such day resulted in several pieces of candy, and a week of starred days resulted in a special event, such as having her cousin stay overnight. At the same time, the mother attempted to provide as little positive reinforcement as possible for school avoidant behaviors, such as excuses of illness and complaining. This intervention resulted in a dramatic increase in the child's voluntary school attendance. Follow-up assessments at six and nine months after treatment indicated that she was voluntarily going to school each day with no tantrums.

Positive reinforcement was also used by Leitenberg and Callahan (1973) to reduce children's fear of the dark. Fourteen children with an average age of six years were assigned to a treatment or control group. The treatment method involved a procedure that was termed *reinforced practice*. Each child was seen individually for two sessions each week for a maximum of one month. Treatment sessions consisted of the therapist providing feedback on the length of time the child remained in a darkened room. In addition, they were praised and received tangible reinforcers for each time they remained in the dark longer than the previous trial. Compared to the no-treatment controls, the treated children were able to remain in an unfamiliar dark room for a significantly greater length of time.

Shaping. Closely related to positive reinforcement is the technique of *shaping*. Shaping consists of reinforcing successive approximations to the target behavior, with each approximation being slightly closer to the final one. For example, a school phobic child initially might be reinforced for walking halfway to school, then three fourths of the way, then all the way, then all the way and remain at school for five minutes, then all the way plus a half hour, and so on until this gradual process leads to the child remaining at school for the entire day. A program similar to this was used by Tahmisian and McReynolds (1971) to treat school avoidance in a 13-year-old girl. The treatment procedure involved the parents, who spent increasing amounts of time walking around school before and after class with the child. Sessions with the parents were alternated, with having the child walk around the school by herself. Within three weeks, the child was able to attend all of her classes on a regular basis. This improvement was maintained at a four-week follow-up period.

Some children cannot be reinforced for a desired behavior because they do not engage in that behavior at all. A prompting technique may be used to initiate the behavior. Once the behavior occurs, it is reinforced and then shaped to some target response. A shaping procedure was used along with prompting in a case study by Nordquist and Bradley (1973). A classmate was used to initiate or prompt interaction with a socially isolated child who never talked to or played with peers. The teacher then attended to and socially reinforced increasing social interactions between the socially withdrawn child and other children in the class. Over time, this procedure increased the child's cooperative play and verbalizations to an appropriate level.

Stimulus Fading.   A procedure that attempts to change behavior by focusing on the antecedent events of the behavior is *stimulus fading*. This technique involves a gradual change of the stimulus controlling a child's performance to another stimulus, usually with the intention of maintaining the performance without a loss or alteration under the new conditions. As in shaping, stimulus fading has a gradual approach; in shaping, the response requirements are gradually changed, whereas in stimulus fading the stimulus conditions controlling a response are gradually changed.

Stimulus fading often is combined with contingency management techniques, as in the treatment of a case of elective mutism reported by Wulbert, Nyman, Snow, and Owen (1973). The child was a six-year-old electively mute girl who had not spoken in one year of preschool, in kindergarten, or in three years of Sunday school. At home, she was fluent and eagerly spoke with her mother. A treatment program was implemented in which the child and her mother came to a clinic three times a week. The two of them would interact in various games and activities that required both motor and verbal responses from the child. An unfamiliar adult was very gradually faded into the room and eventually into the activities with the child and mother. At this point, the child's mother was faded out, and another unfamiliar adult was faded in. Finally, the teacher and some of the child's classmates were faded in. The steps used in fading the first therapist into stimulus control of the child's behavior are presented in Table 7–2. In addition, a time-out procedure was used when the child did not respond to requests for verbalizations from other unfamiliar adults.

This intervention was very effective; the stimulus fading procedure was shown to be a necessary component of the treatment program. Following treatment, the child would raise her hand when the teacher asked a question of the class and, if called on, would give a loud, clear verbal response.

Clinical and Research Issues

A prerequisite to the use of operant-based contingency management procedures is a careful assessment of the child's fear-related behaviors in the context of the

TABLE 7–2

Graded Steps of Closeness Used in Fading an Experimenter into Stimulus Control in a Stimulus Fading Program*

0. Neither visible nor audible
   a. Neither visible nor audible
   b. Not visible but audible over radio
      (saying, "ask Emma question #1 or give Emma direction #17")
   c. Not visible but audible both over radio and from hall
1. Visible at door
   a. Visible and audible standing in hall, turned 180° away from Emma
   b. Visible and audible standing in doorway, turned 180°
   c. Visible and audible standing inside room, with door closed, turned 180°
   d. Visible and audible inside room, door closed, turned 135°
   e. Visible and audible inside room, door closed, turned 90°
   f. Visible and audible inside room, door closed, turned 45°
   g. Visible and audible facing with dark glasses on
   h. Inside room with door closed, facing, radio off
2. Inside room halfway to chair
3. Inside room standing at chair
4. Inside room sitting in chair
5. Reading questions in unison with person already in stimulus control
   a. Inside room reading task items in unison with mother and/or handing cards together
   b. Inside room reading the critical element of the task item alone and/or handing cards together except mother drops hand before Emma takes
   c. Inside room reading the critical element of task alone, handing cards alone
6. Reading questions alone while person in stimulus control remains seated at table
   a. Inside room reading all the directions alone, holding and handing cards
   b. Inside room mother silent, but watching
   c. Inside room mother reading at table
7. Reading questions alone while person in stimulus control moves away from the table
   a. Inside room mother reading with chair away from table
   b. Inside room mother reading with chair beside door
   c. Inside room mother in doorway
   d. Inside room mother in hallway
8. Inside room mother absent

* Source: M. Wulbert, B. A. Nyman, D. Snow, and Y. Owen, "The Efficacy of Stimulus Fading and Contingency Management in the Treatment of Elective Mutism: A Case Study," *Journal of Applied Behavior Analysis* 6, 1973, p. 437. Reprinted with permission. © 1973 by the Society for Experimental Analysis of Behavior, Inc.

setting in which the problem occurs. For the procedures to be effective, the therapist must be able to identify the environmental stimuli (both antecedent events and consequences) that have a controlling relationship to the child's fear.

Particularly when combined with techniques such as shaping and stimulus fading, positive reinforcement can be an effective approach for increasing desired behaviors. It can also be used indirectly to decrease maladaptive behaviors by reinforcing behavior that is incompatible with the undesirable behavior.

Shaping is a versatile behavior change procedure. It can be used to acquire responses in new environments gradually and to reinforce the child for gradually approaching feared objects or situations. Eventual exposure to the anxiety-arousing stimuli appears to be a key component of successful treatment programs for fearful children (Miller et al., 1974). Shaping requires considerable clinical skill since the therapist must decide how to break up the target behavior into progressive steps and how rapidly to progress from one step to the next. The child should experience clear success (and minimal anxiety) at one step before progressing onto the next one. These issues are also applicable to the use of stimulus fading techniques.

Most reports of the use of contingency management procedures in the treatment of children's fears involve uncontrolled case studies. The controlled studies that have been reported typically involve single-subject reversal designs. Controlled studies of operant approaches using group comparisons are almost nonexistent (Richards & Siegel, 1978). Finally, the outcome measures in this area have focused exclusively on overt avoidance behaviors. There has been no attempt to integrate a more comprehensive assessment that includes the three response modalities discussed earlier (Morris & Kratochwill, 1983). Consequently, the use of operant procedures for the treatment of fearful children should be considered speculative at this time.

Self-Control Procedures

Unlike the behavioral techniques discussed so far in this chapter, behavioral self-control embodies a more general approach and treatment strategy rather than a specific technique (Kanfer, 1980; Richards & Siegel, 1978). Self-control has been defined as a procedure that helps the client "to become one's own therapist and teacher by making specific responses that modify other personal responses" (Richards, 1976; p. 462). Thus self-control is not so much identified with a particular technique as it is with a treatment strategy that endeavors to teach clients how to think and behave like therapists and how to apply these thoughts and behaviors to their self-improvement (Goldfried & Merbaum, 1973; Kanfer, 1980; Thoresen & Mahoney, 1974).

Self-control strategies involve the same systematic manipulation of environmental events as do external contingency management procedures; the only difference is that the individual is responsible for the control of these events. One advantage of self-control procedures is that they permit the client to engage in a variety of responses to modify maladaptive behaviors in the specific settings in which the behaviors occur. This is particularly useful for maladaptive behaviors that may not be readily accessible to the therapist.

There are a variety of self-control techniques that are used either alone or in combination with other behavioral intervention approaches. Particular techniques that are frequently taught to clients within a self-control framework include self-monitoring, stimulus control, relaxation, self-reinforcement, self-punishment, self-instruction, and problem-solving strategies.

Self-control techniques that have been used in the treatment of anxiety and fears primarily have involved the teaching of cognitive or thinking skills to the client. Once these skills have been acquired, the client is instructed in their use under those conditions in which they are confronted with the feared stimulus.

Kanfer, Karoly, and Newman (1975) investigated the effectiveness of verbal self-control procedures for reducing children's fear of the dark. Forty-five children, five to six years of age, who evidenced strong fear of the dark participated in the study. The program was conducted in a schoolroom equipped with rheostat illumination controls, covered windows, and an intercom system. The children were randomly assigned to one of three groups and were taught one of the following verbal cues: (*a*) sentences that emphasized the child's active control or competence of the dark (competence group), (*b*) sentences that focused on reducing the aversive qualities of the dark (stimulus group), and (*c*) sentences that had a neutral content (control group). The children were trained in a well-lit room and then were tested in a totally dark room, with duration of darkness tolerance and terminal light intensity (children could increase the illumination) serving as outcome measures.

Children were trained individually in the experimental room, with the trainer communicating to them from another room via an intercom. They were instructed to listen to and repeat exactly what the trainer said. The self-instructional sentences were as follows:

> In the *competence group* the children were told to say "I am a brave boy (girl). I can take care of myself in the dark." In the *stimulus group* the special words were, "The dark is a fun place to be. There are many good things in the dark." In the *neutral group* they were, "Mary had a little lamb. Its fleece was white as snow." (Kanfer et al., 1975; p. 253)

Once the child had learned the appropriate sentences, the trainer returned to the room, praised the child, and gave further instructions for elaborating statements to accompany the initial statements.

The results demonstrated that the competence-focused treatment condition was superior to the other groups. Self-instructional sentences that emphasized the child's competence to cope with the anxiety-inducing experience of being in a dark room resulted in the longest tolerance times. Self-instructional sentences that emphasized the positive aspects of the dark were less effective, whereas neutral sentences had no appreciable effect. Hence, self-instructions focusing on active coping and competence with the feared stimulus may be an important component in enabling children to confront anxiety-arousing experiences.

Siegel and Peterson (1980) examined the effectiveness of a self-control treatment package on anxiety reduction in preschool aged children undergoing dental treatment. Forty-two children were assigned to one of three conditions. In the self-control coping skills group, the children were taught cue-controlled muscle relaxation in which they repeated the words "calm and nice." With the assistance of the experimenter, each child also was taught to use pleasant imagery, which they selected, such as a pleasant scene or favorite place to think about. Finally, the child was instructed to use calming self-talk by repeating the phrase, "I will be alright in just a little while. Everything is going to be all right." Children assigned to a sensory information condition were presented with the typical sights, sounds, and sensations that they would experience during restorative dental treatment. Finally, children in the control group were read a story that was unrelated to the dental experience. The results indicated that both the self-control coping skills training and the sensory information were significantly more effective than the control condition in reducing disruptive behaviors, ratings of anxiety and discomfort, and physiological arousal, and in increasing the children's cooperation during the dental procedures. There were no significant differences between the two treatment groups. These treatment effects were maintained at a second dental treatment session approximately one week after exposure to the experimental conditions (Siegel & Peterson, 1981).

Clinical and Research Issues

The use of self-control approaches with children has increased during the past several years, particularly with children who are verbally adept. Therapy can be conceptualized as an apprenticeship in problem solving (Mahoney, 1974), and if this is the orientation a therapist plans to take, it should be made very explicit to the child. The child must be reasonably motivated and see the treatment goals as desirable if self-control training is to be effective. Self-control procedures often focus on cognitive factors, and as a result, the child must have the verbal skills necessary to use the intricate verbal components of these procedures.

Few well-controlled outcome studies on the use of self-control procedures in reducing anxiety and fears in children are available. In addition, self-control approaches have been used with only a small number of fears and anxiety-related problems in children. While these methods appear to be promising, further research is needed to permit a more definitive evaluation of the efficacy of this approach in the treatment of children's fears.

CASE EXAMPLE

A detailed case example is provided below to illustrate the use of a multifaceted treatment program developed by MacDonald (1975) in the treatment of a particularly troublesome and complex dog phobia. This case nicely demonstrates the manner in which the various facets of the treatment program are carefully coordinated with one another and implemented in a planned, sequential fashion.

History and Presenting Problem

The client was an 11-year-old male who had been severely dog phobic for eight years. His extreme fear and consequent adaptation to that fear had clearly set him apart from his peers. His parents had to drive him everywhere because he feared contact with dogs. In addition, he did not participate in any school activities because they were held in locations where dogs might be present. As MacDonald (1975) noted, "his social and personal development had been markedly restrained by his phobia" (p. 317). A number of incidents were identified as contributing to the development of his fear of dogs, including being bitten and having been knocked down by several dogs.

A series of assessment sessions indicated that the boy's dog phobia was maintained by multiple supports, including conditioned anxiety to dogs, parental expectations and prompting of dog avoidance, and the boy's discretionary use of these parental expectations to modify situations to conform to his needs. MacDonald (1975) detailed the rationale and goals of the multifaceted treatment program she developed for this child:

> Because of the intricate interplay between the phobia's various mutually supportive elements, a "multiple" treatment strategy was indicated—a combination of learning-based approaches used in concert to alter a specified set of targets and induce a specified set of interdependent outcomes. The targets included the child's conditioned emotional reaction to dogs, his deficit in appropriate animal handling skills, his social supports for fearful behavior, and his rather general social skill deficiency resulting from the prolonged role of "dog phobic." The goal included unemotional and skillful interactions with dogs, a social environment supportive of non-fearful behavior, an increase in the amount of emotionally uneventful time spent outdoors, and the development of solitary and group outdoor play skills. (p. 318)

Treatment Program

The complexity and sequential nature of the treatment program are illustrated in Table 7–3. The program began with relaxation training and hierarchy construction. Over a period of 11 treatment sessions, a 37-item hierarchy was constructed. As is illustrated in Table 7–4, extensive item prompts were used to increase therapist control over visualized scenes. Systematic desensitization ran from the eighth to 17th sessions. Adjunctive procedures, such as emotive imagery techniques, homework assignments involving relaxation practice, and concomitant exposure to tape recordings of barking dogs, were implemented in a sequentially planned fashion during the course of therapy (sessions 5, 8, 10, and 12).

Training in dog handling skills was initiated early in the therapy program (sessions 4–7). The boy learned how to interpret dog body language, read several dog handling manuals, and engaged in a participant modeling sequence (using a stuffed animal) to teach him dog petting skills. Modeling procedures were employed during the middle and latter stages of the treatment program (sessions 5, 8, and 10–17), affording the opportunity for graduated exposure to the phobic stimulus and further instruction in dog handling skills. Finally, social environmental restructuring (sessions 5, 6, 8, 10, and 11; e.g., teaching the

TABLE 7-3

Summary of Treatment Procedures Used in a Multifaceted Therapy Program for a Child's Dog Phobia*

procedure

Relaxation training	X-X-X-X-X-X-X-X-X
Hierarchy construction	X-X-X-X-X-X-X-X-X-X-X
Systematic desensitization	X-X-X-X-X-X-X-X-X-X
Desensitization adjuncts	X-X-------X---X
Dog skill training	X-X-X-X
Modeling	X-----X---X-X-X-X-X-X-X
Programmed outdoor activity	X-X-X-X-X-X-X
Social environmental restructuring	X-X---X---X-X

```
└┴┴┴┴┴┴┴┴┴┴┴┴┴┴┴┴┘
 2   4   6   8  10  12  14  16
      treatment session
```

* Source: M. L. MacDonald, "Multiple Impact Behavior Therapy in a Child's Dog Phobia," *Journal of Behavior Therapy and Experimental Psychiatry* 6, 1975, pp. 317–322. Reprinted with permission. © 1975 by Pergamon Press.

TABLE 7-4

Illustrative Imaginal Desensitization Hierarchy Items Used in a Multifaceted Therapy Program for a Child's Dog Phobia*

*item
number*   *item†*

2 Standing on the front porch in the late afternoon with your Dad, about ready to go inside, looking down the block and seeing a Beagle three houses away minding his own business and trotting toward you.

10 Sitting in the _____ family's kitchen with the rest of your family, hearing Mr. _____ say, "He surely was a hard egg, wasn't he?" and watching Dumplin', who's lying down at the kitchen entrance, look at you, get up, and trot around the table to a spot three feet from you.

11 Standing in your Gramma and Grampa's front yard playing ball with your Dad and Sister and watching a Schnauzer exploring about 50 feet away.

31 Sitting in your back yard, alone, playing with your G.I. Joe and looking up to see an unfamiliar collie running down your driveway and past the garage.

* Source: M. L. MacDonald, "Multiple Impact Behavior Therapy in a Child's Dog Phobia," *Journal of Behavior Therapy and Experimental Psychiatry* 6, 1975, pp. 317–322. reprinted with permission. © 1975 by Pergamon Press.
† All items were introduced with the phrase "Alright, (name), I'd like you to imagine. . ."

parents not to prompt avoidance behaviors) and programmed outdoor activity (sessions 10–16; e.g., assignments to walk progressively greater portions of the route to school) were implemented toward the middle and latter portions of the treatment program, respectively.

MacDonald (1975) summarizes the results of this program as follows:

> At the six treatment session, the child reported staying outdoors without worrying about dogs for the first time in his memory. At the eleventh session he spontaneously stated that he had told his classmates that he had "gotten over his problem." He and his parents were reporting appropriate reactions in benign as well as threatening dog encounters regularly by the fourteenth treatment session. Just prior to termination, the child demonstrated his mastery and skill to his family at an outdoor "recital." (pp. 321–322)

At a two-year follow-up evaluation, these treatment effects had been maintained.

SUMMARY AND CONCLUSIONS

The decision to select a given treatment strategy is based largely on the information obtained during the assessment process and on the goals that have been identified for each child. In examining the antecedent events and consequences of the maladaptive behavior within the context of a functional analysis, the therapist attempts to identify the factors that contribute to and maintain the child's anxiety responses. If social skills deficits play a prominant role in the anxiety disorder, the child would benefit more from a treatment approach that focuses on helping him or her acquire alternative responses or more appropriate use of the skills the child already has. If the anxiety response is primarily associated with excessive arousal elicited by cognitive stimuli, treatment approaches that help the child to modulate the visceral system through imaginal techniques, such as systematic desensitization, might be appropriate. To the extent that maladaptive cognitions appear to mediate the anxiety-related behaviors, treatment might focus on self-control techniques, such as self-instructional procedures that help the child control the anticipatory experience of the anxiety or fear. It should be noted that it is often necessary to use several behavioral techniques concurrently in a treatment program in order to change most effectively the maladaptive behavior and insure persistence of behavior change.

Regardless of the behavioral treatment approach for anxiety disorders, it would appear that direct exposure to the anxiety-arousing stimuli is an essential component of all effective intervention programs. These procedures differ primarily in the manner and timing of the direct exposure.

It is interesting to note that significant others (parents, teachers, etc.) in the child's environment have been enlisted as primary change agents in a number of behavioral treatment programs of children's anxiety disorders. Under the guidance of the therapist, significant others were trained to modify successfully a variety of anxiety and fear responses in the natural environment of the child. In those cases in which environmental contingencies were identified as contributing to the child's fearful behavior, the participation of significant others in the treatment program often is essential.

Notably lacking are well-controlled experimental studies. Many of the treatment programs reported in the literature on children's anxiety and fear represent single case studies that do not even include systematic single-case study methodology. In addition, there are few studies of the comparative efficacy of these various behavioral procedures. Finally, a few long-term follow-up studies have been reported in the behavioral treatment of children's fear-related disorders. This area is clearly in need of further outcome studies that are well controlled, long term, and carried out in real-life settings with clinically anxious and fearful children.

Despite these limitations, behavioral treatment approaches to children's fears hold considerable promise. The preliminary findings are sufficiently encouraging to warrant continued investigation of the procedures presented in this chapter.

REFERENCES

Agras, W. S., Sylvester, D., & Oliveau, D. The epidemiology of common fears and phobias. *Comprehensive Psychiatry,* 1969, *10,* 151–156.

American Psychiatric Association. *Diagnostic and statistical manual of mental disorders* (3rd ed.). Washington, D.C.: American Psychiatric Association, 1980.

Ayllon, T., Smith, D., & Rogers, M. Behavioral management of school phobia. *Journal of Behavior Therapy and Experimental Psychiatry,* 1970, *1,* 125–138.

Bandura, A. *Principles of behavior modification.* New York: Holt, Rinehart, & Winston, 1969.

Bandura, A. Psychotherapy based upon modeling principles. In A. E. Bergin & S. L. Garfield (Eds.), *Handbook of psychotherapy and behavior change.* New York: John Wiley & Sons, 1971.

Bandura, A. Effecting change through participant modeling. In J. D. Krumboltz & C. E. Thoresen (Eds.), *Counseling methods.* New York: Holt, Rinehart & Winston, 1976.

Bandura, A., Grusec, J., & Menlove, F. Vicarious extinction of avoidance behavior. *Journal of Personality and Social Psychology,* 1967, *5,* 16–23.

Bandura, A., Jeffrey, R. W., & Gajdos, E. Generalizing change through self-directed performance. *Behaviour Research and Therapy,* 1975, *13,* 141–152.

Bandura, A., Jeffrey, R., & Wright, C. Efficacy of participant modeling as a function of reponse induction aids. *Journal of Abnormal Psychology,* 1974, *83,* 56–64.

Bandura, A., & Menlove, F. Factors determining vicarious extinction of avoidance behavior through symbolic modeling. *Journal of Personality and Social Psychology,* 1968, *8,* 99–108.

Bandura, A., & Rosenthal, T. Vicarious classical conditioning as a function of arousal level. *Journal of Personality and Social Psychology,* 1966, *3,* 54–62.

Barrios, B. A., Hartmann, D. P., & Shigetomi, C. Fears and anxieties in children. In E. J. Mash, & L. G. Terdal (Eds.), *Behavioral assessment of childhood disorders.* New York: Guilford Press, 1981.

Bauer, D. An exploratory study of developmental changes in children's fears. *Journal of Child Psychology and Psychiatry,* 1976, *17,* 69–74.

Borkoveck, T. D., Weerts, T. C., & Bernstein, D. A. Assessment of anxiety. In A. R. Ciminero, K. S. Calhoun, & H. E. Adams (Eds.), *Handbook of behavioral assessment.* New York: John Wiley & Sons, 1977.

Cattell, R. B., & Scheier, I. H. *The meaning and measurement of neuroticism and anxiety.* New York: Ronald Press, 1961.

Cautela, J. R., & Groden, J. *Relaxation: A comprehensive manual for adults, children, and children with special needs.* Champaign, Ill.: Research Press, 1978.

Chazan, M. School Phobia. *British Journal of Educational Psychology,* 1962, *32,* 209–217.

Chertock, S. L., & Bornstein, P. H. Covert modeling treatment of children's dental fears. *Child Behavior Therapy,* 1979, *1,* 249–255.

Davison, G. C., & Wilson, G. T. Critique of "desensitization: Social and cognitive factors underlying the effectiveness of Wolpe's procedure." *Psychological Bulletin,* 1972, *78,* 28–31.

Evers, W. L., & Schwarz, J. C. Modifying social withdrawal in preschoolers: The effects of filmed modeling and teacher praise. *Journal of Abnormal Child Psychology,* 1973, *31,* 248–256.

Freud, S. (1909) The analysis of a phobia in a five-year-old boy. *Standard edition of the complete psychological works of Sigmund Freud* (Vol. 10). London: Hogarth Press, 1963.

Gelfand, D. M. Behavioral treatment of avoidance, social withdrawal and negative emotional states. In B. B. Wolman, J. Egan, & A. O. Ross (Eds.), *Handbook of Treatment of Mental Disorders in Childhood and Adolescence.* Englewood Cliffs, N.J.: Prentice-Hall, 1978.

Goldfried, M. Systematic desensitization as training in self-control. *Journal of Consulting and Clinical Psychology,* 1971, *37,* 228–234.

Goldfried, M. R., & Merbaum, M. A perspective on self-control. In M. R. Goldfried, & M. Merbaum (Eds.), *Behavior change through self-control.* New York: Holt, Rinehart & Winston, 1973.

Graziano, A. M. (Ed.), *Behavior therapy with children* (Vol. 2). Chicago: Aldine Publishing, 1975.

Graziano, A. M., DeGiovanni, I. S., & Garcia, K. A. Behavioral treatments of children's fears: A review. *Psychological Bulletin*, 1979, *86*, 804–830.

Hatzenbuehler, L. C., & Schroeder, H. E. Desensitization procedures in the treatment of childhood disorders. *Psychological Bulletin*, 1978, *85*, 831–844.

Hugdahl, K., Fredrikson, M., & Ohman, A. "Preparedness" and "arousability" as determinants of electrodermal conditioning. *Behaviour Research and Therapy*, 1977, *15*, 345–353.

Jacobson, E. *Progressive relaxation*. Chicago: University of Chicago Press, 1938.

Jersild, A. T., & Holmes, F. B. Children's fears. *Child Development Monograph*, 1935 (No. 20).

Johnson, S. B. Children's fears in the classroom setting. *School Psychology Digest*, 1979, *8*, 382–396.

Johnson, S. B., & Melamed, B. G. The assessment and treatment of children's fears. In B. Lahey, & A. Kazdin (Eds.), *Advances in child clinical psychology*. New York: Plenum Press, 1978.

Jones, M. C. The elimination of children's fears. *Journal of Experimental Psychology*, 1924, *7*, 382–390.

Kahn, J., & Nurstein, J. School refusal: A comprehensive view of school phobia and other failures of school attendance. *American Journal of Orthopsychiatry*, 1962, *32*, 707–718.

Kanfer, F. H. Self-management methods. In F. H. Kanfer, & A. P. Goldstein (Eds.), *Helping people change* (2nd ed.). New York: Pergamon Press, 1980.

Kanfer, F. H., Karoly, P., & Newman, A. Reduction of children's fear of the dark by confidence-related and situational threat-related verbal cues. *Journal of Consulting and Clinical Psychology*, 1975, *43*, 251–258.

Kennedy, W. A. School phobia: Rapid treatment of fifty cases. *Journal of Abnormal Psychology*, 1965, *70*, 285–289.

Kennedy, W. A. Obsessive-compulsive and phobic reactions. In T. H. Ollendick, & M. Hersen (Eds.), *Handbook of child psychopathology*. New York: Plenum Press, 1983.

Kissel, S. Systematic desensitization therapy with children: A case study and some suggested modifications. *Professional Psychology*, 1972, *3*, 164–168.

Koeppen, A. S. Relaxation training for children. *Elementary School Guidance and Counseling*, 1974, *9*, 14–21.

Lacey, J. I. Somatic response patterning and stress: Some revisions of activation theory. In M. H. Appley, & R. Trumbull (Eds.), *Psychological stress: Issues in research*. New York: Appleton-Century-Crofts, 1967.

Lacey, J. I., & Lacey, B. B. Verification and extension of the principle of autonomic response stereotypy. *American Journal of Psychology*, 1968, *71*, 50–73.

Lang, P. J. Fear reduction and fear behavior: Problems in treating a construct. In J. M. Shlier (Ed.), *Research in psychotherapy* (Vol. 3). Washington D.C.: American Psychological Association, 1968.

Lang, P. J. Physiological assessment of anxiety and fear. In J. D. Cone, & R. P. Hawkins (Eds.), *Behavioral assessment: New directions in clinical psychology.* New York: Brunner/Mazel, 1977.

Lang, P. J., & Lazovik, A. D. Experimental desensitization of a phobia. *Journal of Abnormal and Social Psychology,* 1963, *66,* 519–525.

Lang, P. J., Melamed, B. G., & Hart, J. Automating the desensitization procedure: A psychophysiological analysis of fear modification. *Journal of Abnormal Psychology,* 1970, *76,* 220–234.

Lapouse, R., & Monk, M. A. Fears and worries in a representative sample of children. *American Journal of Orthopsychiatry,* 1959, *29,* 803–818.

Lazarus, A. A., & Abramovitz, A. The use of emotive imagery in the treatment of children's phobias.*Journal of Mental Science,* 1962, *108,* 191–195.

Leitenberg, H., & Callahan, E. J. Reinforcement practice and reductions of different kinds of fears in adults and children. *Behaviour Research and Therapy,* 1973, *11,* 19–30.

MacDonald, M. L. Multiple impact behavior therapy in a child's dog phobia. *Journal of Behavior Therapy and Experimental Psychiatry,* 1975, *6,* 317–322.

MacFarlane, J. W., Allen, L., & Honzik, M. P. A developmental study of the behavior problems of normal children between 21 months and 14 years. Berkeley: University of California Press, 1954.

Marks, I. M. *Fears and phobias.* New York: Academic Press, 1969.

Marlatt, G. A., & Perry, M. A. Modeling methods. In F. H. Kanfer, & A. P. Goldstein (Eds.), *Helping people change.* New York: Pergamon Press, 1975.

Marshall, W. L., Gauthier, J., & Gordon, A. The current status of flooding therapy. In M. Hersen, R. M. Eisler, & P. M. Miller (Eds.), *Progress in behavior modification* (Vol. 7). New York: Academic Press, 1979.

Martin, B., & Sroufe, L. A. Anxiety. In C. G. Costello (Ed.), *Symptoms of psychopathology.* New York: John Wiley & Sons, 1970.

McNally, R. J., & Reiss, S. The preparedness theory of phobias and human safety-signal conditioning. *Behaviour Research and Therapy,* 1982, *20,* 153–159.

Meichenbaum, D. Examination of model characteristics in reducing avoidance behavior. *Journal of Personality and Social Psychology,* 1971, *17,* 298–307.

Melamed, B., & Siegel, L. Reduction of anxiety in children facing hospitalization and surgery by use of filmed modeling. *Journal of Consulting and Clinical Psychology,* 1975, *43,* 511–521.

Melamed, B. G., & Siegel, L. J. *Behavioral medicine: Practical applications in health care.* New York: Springer, 1980.

Miller, L. C. Fears and anxiety in children. In C. E. Walker, & M. C. Roberts (Eds.), *Handbook of clinical child psychology.* New York: John Wiley & Sons, 1983.

Miller, L. C., Barrett, C. L., & Hampe, E. Phobias of childhood in a prescientific era. In A. Davids (Ed.), *Child personality and psychopathology: Current topics. New York: John Wiley & Sons, 1974.*

Miller, L. C., Barrett, C. L., Hampe, E., & Noble, H. Revised anxiety scales for the Louisville Behavior Check List. *Psychological Reports,* 1971, *29,* 503–511.

Miller, L. C., Barrett, C. L., Hampe, E., & Noble, H. Factor structure of childhood fears. *Journal of Consulting and Clinical Psychology,* 1972, *39,* 264–268.

Morris, R. J., & Kratochwill, T. R. *Treating children's fears and phobias: A behavioral approach.* New York: Pergamon Press, 1983.

Mowrer, O. H. *Learning theory and behavior.* New York: John Wiley & Sons, 1960.

Neitzel, M. T., & Bernstein, D. A. Assessment of anxiety and fear. In M. Hersen, & A. S. Bellack (Eds.), *Behavioral assessment: A practical handbook* (2nd ed.). New York: Pergamon Press, 1981.

Nordquist, V., & Bradley, B. Speech acquisition in a nonverbal isolate child. *Journal of Experimental Child Psychology,* 1973, *15,* 149–160.

O'Connor, R. D. Relative efficacy of modeling, shaping and the combined procedures for modification of social withdrawal. *Journal of Abnormal Psychology,* 1972, *79,* 327–334.

Ohman, A., Eriksson, A., & Olofsson, C. One-trial learning and superior resistance to extinction of autonomic responses conditioned to potentially phobic stimuli. *Journal of Comparative and Physiological Psychology,* 1975, *88,* 619–627.

Ollendick, T. H. Fear reduction techniques with children. In M. Hersen, R. M. Eisler, & P. M. Miller (Eds.), *Progress in behavior modification* (Vol. 8). New York: Academic Press, 1979.

Ollendick, T. H., & Gruen, G. E. Treatment of a bodily injury phobia with implosive therapy. *Journal of Consulting and Clinical Psychology,* 1972, *38,* 389–393.

Paul, G. L., & Bernstein, D. A. *Anxiety and clinical problems: Systematic desensitization and related techniques.* Morristown, N.J.: General Learning Press, 1973.

Perry, M. A., & Furukawa, M. J. Modeling methods. In F. H. Kanfer, & A. P. Goldstein (Eds.), *Helping people change* (2nd ed.). New York: Pergamon Press, 1980.

Poznanski, E. O. Children with excessive fears. *American Journal of Orthopsychiatry,* 1973, *43,* 428–438.

Rachman, S. Clinical applications of observational learning, imitation and modeling. *Behavior Therapy,* 1972, *3,* 379–397.

Rachman, S., & Hodgson, R. Synchrony and desynchrony in fear and avoidance. *Behaviour Research and Therapy,* 1974, *12,* 311–318.

Richards, C. S. Improving study behaviors through self-control techniques. In J. D. Krumboltz, & C. E. Thoresen (Eds.), *Counseling methods.* New York: Holt, Rinehart & Winston, 1976.

Richards, C. S., & Siegel, L. J. Behavioral treatment of anxiety states and avoidance behaviors in children. In D. Marholin II (Ed.), *Child behavior therapy.* New York: Gardner Press, 1978.

Rimm, D. C., & Masters, J. C. *Behavior therapy: Techniques and empirical findings*. New York: Academic Press, 1979.

Ritter, B. The group desensitization of children's snake phobias using vicarious and contact desensitization procedures. *Behaviour Research and Therapy*, 1968, *6*, 1–6.

Ruebush, B. K. Anxiety. In H. W. Stevenson (Ed.), *Child psychology*. The sixty-second yearbook of the National Society for the Study of Education. Chicago: University of Chicago Press, 1963.

Rutter, M., Tizard, J., & Whitmore, K. *Education, health and behavior*. New York: John Wiley & Sons, 1970.

Seligman, M. E. P. Phobias and preparedness. *Behavior Therapy*, 1971,*2*, 307–320.

Seligman, M., & Johnston, J. A cognitive theory of avoidance learning. In J. McGuigan, & B. Lumsden (Eds.), *Contemporary approaches to conditioning and learning*. New York: John Wiley & Sons, 1973.

Shaw, O. Dental anxiety in children. *British Dental Journal*, 1975, *139*, 134–139.

Siegel, L. J., & Peterson, L. Stress reduction in young dental patients through coping skills and sensory information. *Journal of Consulting and Clinical Psychology*, 1980, *48*, 785–787.

Siegel, L. J., & Peterson, L. Maintenance effects of coping skills and sensory information on young children's response to repeated dental procedures. *Behavior Therapy*, 1981, *12*, 530–535.

Solyom, I., Beck, P., Solyom, C., & Hugel, R. Some etiological factors in phobic neurosis. *Canadian Psychiatric Association Journal*, 1974, *19*, 69–78.

Spielberger, C. D. Theory and research on anxiety. In C. D. Spielberger (Ed.), *Anxiety and behavior*. New York: Academic Press, 1966.

Stampfl, T. G., & Levis, D. J. *Implosive therapy: Theory and Technique*. Morristown, N.J.: General Learning Press, 1973.

Stedman, J. M. Family counseling with a school-phobic child. In J. D. Krumboltz & E. C. Thoresen (Eds.), *Counseling methods*. New York: Holt, Rinehart & Winston, 1976.

Tahmisian, J., & McReynolds, W. The use of parents as behavioral engineers in the treatment of a school phobic girl. *Journal of Counseling Psychology*, 1971, *18*, 225–228.

Taylor, C. B., Ferguson, J. M., & Wermuth, B. M. Simple techniques to treat medical phobias. *Postgraduate Medical Journal*, 1977, *53*, 28–32.

Thelen, M., Fry, R. A., Fehrenback, P. A., & Frautschi, N. M. Therapeutic video-tape and film modeling: A review. *Psychological Bulletin*, 1979, *86*, 701–720.

Thomas, A., Chess, S., Burch, H., Hertzig, M., & Korn, S. *Behavioral individuality in early childhood*. New York: New York Univeristy Press, 1963.

Thoresen, C. E., & Mahoney, M. J. *Behavioral self-control*. New York: Holt, Rinehart & Winston, 1974.

Watson, J. B., & Rayner, R. Conditioned emotional reactions. *Journal of Experimental Psychology,* 1920, *3,* 1–14.

Weissman, M. M. The epidemiology of anxiety disorders: Rates, risks, and familial patterns. In H. Tuma, & J. Maser (Eds.), *Anxiety and anxiety disorders.* Hillsdale, N.J.: Lawrence Erlbaum Associates, Inc., in press.

White, W. C., & Davis, M. T. Vicarious extinction of phobic behavior in early childhood. *Journal of Abnormal Child Psychology,* 1974, *2,* 25–37.

Wish, P. A., Hasazi, J. E., & Jurgela, A. R. Automated direct deconditioning of a childhood phobia. *Journal of Behavior Therapy and Experimental Psychiatry,* 1973, *4,* 279–283.

Wolpe, J. *Reciprocal inhibition therapy.* Stanford, Calif.: Stanford Univeristy Press, 1958.

Wulbert, M., Nyman, B. A., Snow, D., & Owen, Y. The efficacy of stimulus fading and contingency management in the treatment of elective mutism: A case study. *Journal of Applied Behavior Analysis,* 1973, *6,* 435–441.

8

Eating Disorders*

John P. Foreyt
Department of Medicine
Baylor College of Medicine

Albert T. Kondo
Department of Psychology
University of Houston

This chapter describes the etiology, assessment, and treatment of a number of disorders characterized by gross disturbances in eating behavior. These disorders include bulimia, anorexia nervosa, pica, rumination disorders of infancy, and obesity. All of these disturbances except obesity are classified as "eating disorders" in the *Diagnostic and Statistical Manual of Mental Disorders, Third Edition* (DSM-III) (American Psychiatric Association, 1980). Simple obesity is included in the clinical modification of the World Health Organization's International Classification of Diseases, 9th Revision (ICD-9-CM) (World Health Organization, 1978) as a physical disorder and is not included in the eating disorders section of the DSM-III because "it is not generally associated with any distinct psychological or behavioral syndrome" (p. 67). When psychological dynamics are significant in either the etiology or the course of an individual's obesity, these are indicated as "psychological factors affecting physical condition" (DSM-III 316.00). However, because obesity is a major problem among children and adolescents, we have also included it in this chapter.

* This chapter was supported by Grant No. HL 17269 from the National Heart, Lung, and Blood Institute, National Institutes of Health, Bethesda, Maryland. Dr. Kondo is a Research Fellow in Behavioral Medicine at the University of Houston, supported by the National Heart, Lung, and Blood Institute Grant No. 1 T32 HL07258-01A1.

BULIMIA

Bulimia is defined as "Episodic binge eating accompanied by an awareness that the eating is abnormal, fear of not being able to stop eating voluntarily, and depressed mood and self-deprecating thoughts following the eating binges" (American Psychiatric Association, 1980). In addition to these characteristics, the presence of any three are required:

1. Consumption of high-caloric, easily ingested food during a binge.
2. Inconspicuous eating during a binge.
3. Termination of such eating episodes by abdominal pain, sleep, social interruption, or self-induced vomiting.
4. Repeated attempts to lose weight by severely restrictive diets, self-induced vomiting, or use of cathartics or diuretics.
5. Frequent weight fluctuations greater than 10 pounds due to alternating binges and fasts.

The bulimic episodes must not be caused by anorexia nervosa or any other physical disorders. Thus, bulimia is thought to be separate from anorexia nervosa. This stance has raised some controversy as many clinicians and researchers have found it to occur with anorexia (e.g., Bruch, 1973; Feighner, Robins, Guze, Woodruff, Winokur, & Munoz, 1972; Russell, 1979).

Bulimia is, therefore, binge eating with associated symptomatology. It is this symptomatology that separates the condition from the occasional excessive eating experienced by many people.

A confusion appears to have developed around the use of the term *bulimia*. The popular press, electronic media, clinicians, and researchers have used it to connote the practice of binge eating followed by purging, usually through vomiting or the use of laxatives. For example, a recent paper stated, "The DSM-III now identifies the entity of bulimia as an eating disorder characterized by the binge-purge cycle" (Grinc, 1982). Purging, whether it occurs through vomiting, cathartics, or diuretics, can be a part of this syndrome, but bulimia's existence is not defined by the accompanying presence of purging. Individuals may be classified as bulimic if their cycles are characterized by binge eating followed by termination due to abdominal discomfort. Individuals who are bulimic in this manner have a greater tendency to be overweight as compared to their anorexic or normal weight counterparts.

In addition to a definitional problem, the confusion concerning bulimia has been further fueled by the many terms that have appeared in the literature to describe it, including *bulimarexia* (Boskind-Lodahl & Sirlin, 1977), *abnormal normal weight control syndrome* (Crisp, 1981–82), *dietary chaos syndrome* (Palmer, 1979), *compulsive eating* (Green & Rau, 1974), and *bulimia nervosa* (Russell, 1979). This proliferation of terms suggests its popularity in the scientific literature and, as a corollary, our limited present state of knowledge.

Prevalence

The prevalence of bulimia is largely unknown (American Psychiatric Association, 1980). It is a condition usually practiced alone, and the proportion of those afflicted who do not come for treatment is difficult to estimate. Surveys conducted in recent years, however, suggest, that it may be a reasonably prevalent condition. One survey (Hawkins & Clement, 1983) found that one half of the men and two thirds of the women in a college sample reported having engaged in binge eating. One third of each group further noted that they binged at least once a week. Another survey (Strangler & Prinz, 1980) reported that 3.8 percent of a sample of university students seen at a psychiatric clinic were diagnosed as bulimic. Among anorexics, the proportion showing evidence of bulimia varies from study to study, ranging from 10 percent (Halmi, 1974) to 47 percent (Casper, Eckert, Halmi, Goldberg, & Davis, 1980).

Data obtained on obese patients at treatment clinics suggest that bulimia may be fairly common among this population. Loro & Orleans (1981) indicated that 28.6 percent of their obese clients reported binge eating at least two times per week, and approximately 51 percent reported this behavior at least once per week. Jackson and Ormiston (1977) found that 27 percent of their obese clientele reported binge eating from two to seven times per week. While these data are not based on large surveys, they are suggestive of an appreciable prevalence of bulimia in our society.

Personal Characteristics

The unknown prevalence of bulimia and its presence among all weight groups (i.e., underweight, normal weight, and overweight) make characterization of the bulimic difficult. Generalizations have been derived primarily from clinical populations. As such populations may represent a biased sample of the total, the information obtained must be regarded as questionable. With this limitation in mind, the bulimic has been characterized as:

1. Primarily of normal weight, though some may be slightly underweight, and others may be overweight.
2. Predominantly females.
3. Usually an adolescent or young adult.
4. Frequently substance abusers, most often barbiturates, amphetamines, or alcohol.
5. Frequently concerned over body image and appearance.
6. Often feeling that their lives are dominated by conflicts about eating (American Psychiatric Association, 1980).

Etiology

At this time, there is no widely accepted etiology for bulimia. This lack is quite understandable as our general knowledge of this condition is in its formative stages. One particular problem with finding a cause is that researchers are not in agreement as to its nature. The basis of this confusion exists around the issue of whether bulimia is a symptom of another disorder or a separate syndrome in and of itself. In DSM-III, bulimia is presented as a syndrome with its own set of diagnostic characteristics and its own etiology. However, some have suggested that bulimia is a symptom of patients who are anorexic or obese. Guiora (1967), for example, indicated that bulimia and anorexia nervosa are poles of the same disorder, not separate syndromes. Taking a slightly different perspective, Beumont, George, and Smart (1976) proposed that anorexia nervosa exists in two clinical forms: one characterized by starvation dieting and the other by vomiting or purging. Russell (1979) viewed bulimia as a variant of anorexia nervosa with a number of comparable features, including a similar psychopathology. He found that bulimia appeared as a progression in the clinical course of anorexia for a number of his patients. Bulimics were those who were unable to withstand prolonged starvation and periodically succumbed to binge eating.

Bulimia has also been implicated as an eating disorder contributing to the problem of obesity (Loro & Orleans, 1981; Stunkard, 1959; Wilson, 1976). As an eating pattern among the obese, bulimia is assumed to differ from that seen in anorexic or normal weight individuals. Vomiting or purging is probably less frequent in the obese as compared to the others.

There is also a wide range of theories concerning its etiology. Bruch (1973) felt that this eating disorder was the result of a confusion between the sensation of hunger and particular affective states. She theorized that the existence of such confusion set the stage for excessive and inappropriate eating. Thus, anxiety or depression may precipitate an eating binge that temporarily assuages the feelings confused with hunger. Taking a more classically psychoanalytic perspective, others saw bulimia as a mechanism to fulfill underlying needs, including pregnancy (Nemiah, 1950) and self-mutilation (Nogami & Yobana, 1977). White and Boskind-White (1981), recognizing that bulimia (or "bulimarexia," as they refer to it) was largely a disorder of females, suggested that it occurs because of the need for some women to fit into the role of "stereotyped femininity." In living this role, they seem to take on characteristics that may serve as the basis for bulimia, including an excessive concern for appearance and thinness, passivity, helplessness, and a need to please others.

In recent years, a psychobiological explanation has developed. Because much of compulsive or binge eating appears to occur after dietary restriction, the rapid consumption of food at such times suggests an organismic reaction to deprivation. Russell (1979) hypothesized that the bulimic's compulsion to eat derives from a deprived state characterized by a body weight less than optimal. This concept of an optimal weight for humans was proposed by Nisbett (1972) as set point theory that states that individuals have an equilibrium weight they will defend. Rising above or falling below this weight places the body in a state of disequilibrium and sets into motion mechanisms that return it to its former state. For many bulimics, excess weight has to be avoided at all costs. However, such avoidance may work in opposition to their biologically characteristic weight or set point weight. Thus, their heroic efforts to diet may be sabotaged by the "equilibrium returning" mechanism of the binge.

The etiology of bulimia is assuredly multifactorial. It is probable that this disorder is caused by biological, psychological, social, familial, and cultural factors that are all present in particular proportions and manner to create the conditions for its appearance. Hawkins and Clements (1983) attempted to illustrate the complex interactions leading to the onset of bulimia by means of a conceptual model. Though their model is primarily heuristic, it suggests that the involved nature of the problem will indeed make the efforts toward determining causation a difficult one.

Behavior

The bulimic syndrome is best characterized as episodic binge eating. This kind of eating differs from the "hearty" variety in that it is often followed by self-deprecation and depression.

The binge eating patterns vary widely, with frequencies ranging from 1 to 2 times per week to 5 to 10 times per day (Orleans & Barnett, in press). Though the selection of foods during these episodes may be idiosyncratic, ingestion of high-caloric, sweet items that require little chewing seems to be favored. During these binges, the amount of food consumed may be prodigious. Russell (1979) reported a subject who said she ingested between 15,000 and 20,000 calories during an evening episode.

A binge may be terminated by abdominal fullness, pain, sleep, purging, or social interruption. Purging, in the form of laxatives, vomiting, and diuretics, is a frequent practice. Pyle, Mitchell, and Eckert (1981), for example, found that of the 34 bulimics they studied, 94 percent engaged in vomiting behavior, while 53 percent were found to abuse laxatives.

In some cases, several associated behaviors exist as part of the condition; most commonly, these are stealing, alcoholism, and drug abuse (Casper et al., 1980; Pyle et al., 1981). Stealing may serve a functional purpose for many bulimics, such as helping defray the costs of their expensive eating habits.

Treatment

Without a determined etiology, treatment of bulimia remains problematic. Despite this handicap, however, a number of treatment methodologies have been attempted. Green and Rau (1974) found abnormal EEG readings among 10 bulimic patients. To correct this problem, they administered the drug diphenylhydantoin. Nine of the 10 patients were reported to have symptom remission after this application. Further studies conducted with this drug have produced equivocal results (Mitchell & Pyle, 1981). Various forms of psychotherapy have been used, suggesting that the problem may be effectively treated through resolution of the underlying psychological issues (Bruch, 1973; Dally & Gomez, 1979; White & Boskind-White, 1981). Thus far, there have not been enough controlled studies to establish the efficacy of these psychotherapeutic approaches.

The work of several investigators (Herman & Polivy, 1975; Spencer & Fremouw, 1979) suggested that the compulsive eating of bulimics may be caused, in part, by their dietary restraint. Further, it appeared that certain conditions could trigger a binge episode among the restrained: (*a*) a cognition that any infraction of dietary "rules" is a sign of having "blown it," and (*b*) emotional distress. In both instances, particular therapeutic interventions may assist in alleviating the problem. Cognitive restructuring strategies might help the restrained eater from binge eating after the initiation of inappropriate consumption.

Behavioral interventions have also been reported in the treatment of bulimia. Monti, McCrady, and Barlow (1977) employed positive reinforcement, informational feedback, and contingency contracting to treat a bulimic anorexic female. Treatment resulted in both increased weight and caloric intake, and results were reported to have been maintained at six months following treatment. Smith (1981) used exposure and response prevention to treat an overweight binge eater. The patient was exposed to favored foods and then was prevented from binging. This strategy diminished the patient's compulsive eating behaviors, and, concomitantly, resulted in weight loss. Somewhat similar is the *programmed binge* advocated by Loro and Orleans (1981). Programmed binging involves replicating a binge episode under therapeutic supervision. The client is requested to binge on problematic food items in a particular manner and perspective. Instead of a binge episode, the process is reframed as a structured learning experience, one in which the client is encouraged to understand. The client is also instructed to experience and taste the food by eating slowly and deliberately.

We have worked with a number of bulimics and favor a multidimensional, experimental approach to treating bulimia. This orientation toward treatment has been taken by others (e.g., Fairburn, 1981; Loro & Orleans, 1981; Orleans & Barnett, 1983), though empirical studies have yet to demonstrate its effectiveness. The basic elements of the multidimensional treatment we suggest include:

1. *Self-monitoring* of binge eating topography, associated thoughts and feelings, presence or absence of others, and the particular environment involved.

2. *Stimulus control strategies* to limit or negate the environmental cues that lead to inappropriate eating. These include removal of binge foods from the household and avoidance of problematic eating situations (e.g., particular restaurants or being alone in the house during specific hours).

3. *Antecedent control* of factors preceding the binge. These factors often

include particular feeling states (e.g., boredom or anxiety), difficulty with interpersonal relationships, and dietary deprivation.

4. *Cognitive restructuring* for alleviating the cognitive distortions frequently associated with bulimia (Beck, 1976).

5. *Social skills training* for many bulimics. Deficits are frequently observed in this group with respect to assertiveness, interpersonal communication, and basic problem-solving capabilities. Improving such skills may be necessary for the patient to develop a greater sense of self-control and become more effective in living.

6. *Flexibility and sensitivity* as the cornerstone of the treatment philosophy and methodology. Our approach to treatment is experimental. We determine the needs of the bulimic on an individual basis and proceed with treatment based on this information. These needs are monitored continuously so that the treatment protocol remains appropriate and effective. This flexible orientation toward treatment requires sensitivity on the part of the therapist and the development of a high degree of trust with the bulimic.

The need for flexibility in treatment is imperative, especially when one considers the wide range of variables associated with the bulimic syndrome. Bulimics may be underweight, normal weight, or obese. This weight categorization of patients is further complicated by the variances that may occur within a given category. For example, bulimia may occur in anorexia nervosa as a concurrent symptom of this condition or as a progression of the disorder after weight gain has occurred (Mitchell & Pyle, 1982). Therefore, treatment among patients must differ.

There is a wide age range of individuals with bulimia. Although this disorder usually begins in late adolescence or early adult life, it may appear at other ages as well. Loro and Orleans (1981) reported the following age data for 280 patients treated at their clinic during a 15-month period: (*a*) for males, an age range of 22 to 76 years with a mean age of 44.1 years, and (*b*) for females, an age range of 18 to 78 years with a mean age of 41.7 years. Pyle, et al. (1981) treated 34 bulimics over a one-year period. The median age of their clients was 24 years with an age range of 19 to 51 years. With such wide age differences among bulimics, the therapist must be ready to adapt treatment methodologies to the varying life conditions presented by each client. For example, the bulimic anorexic is often an adolescent female living within the household of her parents. The dynamics of her problem may differ considerably from a single, bulimic woman in her late 20s or an obese male in his 40s who is the head of his household.

Treatment of bulimia may also differ depending on whether or not some form of purging is part of the symptomatology. Those who purge (i.e., through vomiting and/or use of laxatives or diuretics) with their binge eating frequently have more physical and psychological difficulties than those who only binge eat. The binge-purgers often recognize the aberrancy of the practice, and this awareness typically results in low self-esteem, diminished sense of self-control, social isolation, and depression.

We suggest that the treatment of bulimia should proceed with two overlapping goals: to reduce or eliminate the problem behaviors, and to rectify underlying or resultant feelings, cognitions, and social relationships associated with the syndrome. We advocate giving concurrent attention to both goals, since each is frequently found in association with the other. For example, many bulimics appear to fall into deep levels of depression because of their inability to control their behaviors in relation to food and eating. In such cases, clinical progress is often somewhat dependent on the client's capability to regain control in this area of life.

Besides changing the behaviors associated with bulimia, the therapist must consider treatment of the factors causing and perpetuating the disorder. Wilson (1976) indicated a similar philosophy when he stated that treatment of binge eating should emphasize "self-acceptance and more effective coping skills, in which clients are encouraged to abandon the self-defeating concept of self-worth defined by body weight" (p. 701). Improvement in behaviors and course of treatment appear to be the consequence of better adjustment and not a precondition (Wilson, 1976).

Case Study

Linda was a 19-year-old female referred by a therapist she had been seeing in Massachusetts. She had been working as a waitress, living with her mother, sister, and brother, but decided to follow her 21-year-old boyfriend, Bill, to Houston and move in with him. She was 5 feet 6 inches tall and weighed 125 pounds.

She had become particularly concerned about her weight at age 17 when her high school gym coach told her that she looked a little overweight. She learned from a classmate how to induce vomiting by sticking her fingers into her throat.

For two years, she had vomited after almost all of her eating episodes. As her vomiting increased, binge eating also increased. When binging, Linda would eat any food available in her apartment and usually would binge alone after her boyfriend left for work. Linda was aware that her binging was abnormal, although she said that she could not stop eating until all the food available to her was gone.

Treatment consisted of several steps. First, Linda was asked to self-monitor in a diary all the food she ingested. She also wrote down the time it was ingested, place, amount, who she was with, how she was feeling, and associated thoughts.

The food diary served as the basis for defining problem areas and for designing environmental strategies to reduce the probability of engaging in binge eating. We first worked on finding Linda a job, and she took one with a travel agency. Since the couple had one car, both ate breakfast together and left for work together, with Bill dropping Linda off. Lunch was eaten with her new co-workers, usually at a nearby soup and salad restaurant, and dinner was eaten with Bill. Shopping for food was scheduled on a weekly basis to be done with Bill. Meal planning and proper diet were carefully discussed during treatment.

Linda's upbringing was reviewed in great detail. Linda recalled that her father was an abusive man who literally terrorized his children. Meal times had been especially traumatic for Linda because her father demanded that she always eat everything on her plate. Thus, dinner often became a battle of wills. Linda recalled one meal when she was about eight years old, and her father insisted that she eat a piece of meat. When Linda refused, her father said that she was not to leave the table until she had eaten it. About 30 minutes after the meal, he returned to the table and saw that she was gone. When he learned that Linda's mother had let her go without eating the meat, he demanded that the meat be taken out of the dirty dish water and eaten. At that point, the mother intervened. Dealing with Linda's feelings about her parents, particularly her father, was especially important for her to see how much of her current behavior was related to her upbringing.

Linda's previous therapist had done excellent work with her, helping her build social skills, develop better problem-solving ability, and become more assertive. Considerable time and effort were spent in her present treatment to continue her improvement in these areas.

As Linda's understanding of her current behavior as a reflection of her past increased, especially with respect to her strong negative feelings about her father, and as her ability to use her problem-solving skills improved, her bulimia began to diminish, although improvement was slow. First, she had some evening meals and then some breakfasts without vomiting. Linda has spent 20 months (about 75 hours) in therapy, and although she remains in treatment, her condition has substantially improved.

ANOREXIA NERVOSA

Anorexia nervosa has undoubtedly existed for hundreds of years. Its recognized existence as a clinical entity, however, has been a relatively recent occurrence. In 1689, Richard Morton referred to a condition of "nervous consumption" with characteristics similar to our present day diagnosis of anorexia nervosa (Bruch, 1978). The first description of this condition did not appear in the medical literature until the 1870s. At that time, Charles Laseque in France and Sir William Gull in England provided Western medicine with the first clinical view of this perplexing illness, and Gull was the first who referred to this condition as anorexia nervosa (Giannini, 1981–82).

Although we have progressed far since the pioneering work of Laseque and Gull, our knowledge of the etiology and treatment of anorexia remains in its infancy. We are not sure what causes it, nor have we settled upon an effective treatment. In this time of search and development, behavioral psychology has become a substantial contributor to the armamentarium of clinicians treating the problem.

Problem Characteristics

Anorexia nervosa has several diagnostic criteria that define its presence, with the most notable being the severe loss of weight experienced by the afflicted. A weight loss of at least 25 percent of original weight, without a physical cause for such loss, is the accepted standard for this condition. Other diagnostic criteria include disturbed body image, intense fear of becoming obese, and a refusal to maintain body weight within the normal weight range for the individual's age and height (American Psychiatric Association, 1980). While the term *anorexia nervosa* literally means a nervous loss of appetite, it has been suggested (Bruch, 1973, 1978; Dally, 1979; Garfinkel, 1974) that normal or even exaggerated hunger continues. The reduction of food intake appears to result from the desire to be thin rather than from a loss of hunger.

A number of physical symptoms are frequently associated with the occurrence of anorexia nervosa. Aside from the marked weight loss, the most consistent physical finding is amenorrhea among females. Other symptoms, which are similar to those found in starving, undernourished organisms, include low metabolic rate, low blood pressure, cold intolerance, insomnia, bradycardia, and pathological EEG patterns (Bemis, 1978). In severe cases, the life of the anorexic becomes a major issue, and hospitalization is required.

Personal Characteristics

Anorexia nervosa is a problem primarily of females; studies have shown that the percentage of anorexics who are female generally range from between 70 percent (Kay & Leigh, 1954) to 95 percent (American Psychiatric Association, 1980).

Anorexics generally have families that are both affluent and well-educated (Crisp, Kalucy, Lacy, & Harding, 1977; Halmi, Goldberg, Eckert, Casper, & Davis, 1977). Within this setting, they are perceived by their parents as being perfectionistic, well-behaved, achieving, and competitive (Halmi et al., 1977). The anorexic child is often described by mothers and fathers as the pride of their brood and the child who has given them the least difficulty and greatest satisfaction. When the illness of the child becomes evident, most parents are astonished that such turmoil existed within their sweet and loving exterior (Bruch, 1978).

Personality characteristics include shyness, anxiety, and obsessive-compulsive traits (Bemis, 1978). Concerns about bodily perceptions are also typically present. Anorexics generally have a distorted image of their bodies, perceiving themselves to be larger and fleshier than they actually are. This misperception is often accompanied by an inordinate fear of obesity and an incessant drive toward thinness (Garner & Garfinkel, 1981–82).

The intrapsychic distortions of the anorexic translate into a characteristic set of behaviors. The concomitant desire for thinness and fear of fatness leads them to engage in a number of activities in their single-minded pursuit of slenderness. Severe food restriction is the most common behavior found in this group; others include excessive exercise, laxative abuse, and self-induced vomiting (Bemis, 1978).

Etiology

Many theories exist regarding the etiology of anorexia nervosa, ranging from those of a biological orientation (e.g., Katz et al., 1976; Marks & Bannister, 1963) to intrapsychic ones (e.g., Bruch, 1973, 1978). Bruch (1977) suggested that the psychological disturbances that lead to anorexic behavior derive from the individual's defective self-awareness and disturbed interpersonal relationships, placing substantial emphasis on familial values and interactional patterns. The anorexic family, appearing to be perfect in a superficial sense, is one in which the children are well cared for, well-dressed, and have an array of cultural and educational advantages. However, this exterior of perfection may also be accompanied by the values and behaviors that engender anorexia in the susceptible:

> The parents may be described as overprotective, overconcerned, and over-ambitious. They overvalue their children and expect obedience and superior performance in return. (Bruch, 1977; pp. 2–3)

Rosman, Minuchin, Baker, and Liebman (1977) saw similar characteristics in families of anorexics and noted that those commonly observed included enmeshment, overprotectiveness, rigidity, and lack of conflict resolution.

Bruch (1977) further suggested that the confusion in hunger awareness and fears concerning lack of inner self-control derive from the anorexic's earliest experiences. In this regard, she placed particular emphasis on the early mother-child feeding relationship. If disturbances in this relationship occur intensely and frequently enough, then problems for the child may extend into adulthood. In particular, some children and adults develop a confusion over the signals of true biological hunger and the discomfort of other emotional and physical assaults. Such confusion forges the path of anorexia nervosa.

Garner and Bemis (1982) have developed an etiological model of anorexia nervosa based on the anorexic's compelling conviction to become thin. Unlike Bruch, their model primarily looks at the proximal sources of this conviction instead of those that derive from early childhood. They suggest that young women who have poor self-concept and feel excluded from the acceptance of their peers may conclude that the answer to their problem lies in the achievement of an enviable figure. Efforts to achieve this goal (through dieting and exercise) are additionally reinforced by feelings of greater self-control, autonomy, and spiritual purity. For young women entrapped in the anorexic's distorted perceptions, life is thought to be ruled by two powerful contingencies: the positive reinforcement of weight loss and the terrifying fear of weight gain.

The culture, values, and beliefs of a particular society assuredly are influences in the etiology of anorexia nervosa. A society that places high value on the attainment of a slender figure can expect to have a higher prevalence of this malady than one that values it less. In the Western nations, the standard of slenderness appears to have greater influence on women than men. It is probable that the higher expectation for attractiveness (and therefore slenderness) in women is partial cause of this result (Al-Issa, 1980; Garner, Garfinkel, Schwartz & Thompson, 1980). As indicated earlier, it is estimated that women exceed men in becoming anorexic by a ratio of approximately 9 to 1.

Treatment

There are many approaches to treating anorexia nervosa, including pharmacological, psychoanalytic, family centered, behavioral, and eclectic (Bemis, 1978). None of these has demonstrated universal application or success. This result suggests the perplexing nature of the condition as well as our lack of knowledge concerning its etiology. Clinical treatments for anorexia proceed, based on the therapist's theoretical orientation and/or methods developed through experience with patients. The remainder of this discussion will concentrate on the behavioral approaches that have been developed for treating anorexia nervosa.

The use of behavior modification in the treatment of anorexia nervosa first appeared in the experimental literature in 1965 (Bachrach, Erwin & Mohr, 1965). Since that time, a substantial number of articles have been published supporting the benefits of this approach (Garfinkel, Moldofsky & Garner, 1977). In this regard, operant conditioning methods have been the most frequently reported form of treatment, though systematic desensitization (Hallsten, 1965) and aversive counter conditioning (Kenny & Solyom, 1971) have also been used.

The use of operant conditioning in the treatment of anorexia can take a number of varied courses. Typically, however, it involves the use of positive and negative contingencies in association with a performance criterion. In the case of anorexia, the performance criterion is generally a predetermined daily weight gain. The patient may obtain valued social and material rewards for achievement of a prescribed weight gain or loss of normal privileges for failure to do so.

Supporters of operant strategies note such advantages as rapid weight gain and lack of deleterious side effects often experienced with the pharmacologic agents. The advantage of rapid weight gain, however, appears to be temporary. Garfinkel et al. (1977) reviewed the use of behavior modification in the treatment of anorexia nervosa and concluded that little evidence exists that indicates its superiority over other therapies for longer term weight gain. Further, they suggested that it be used with some care because of the anorexic's sensitivity to weight gain and loss of control over the eating process. Bruch (1974) voiced a similar caution and further indicated that the application of behavior modification with these patients may be "dangerous."

A number of behavioral researchers and therapists have recognized that the singular use of operant conditioning in treating the anorexic is insufficient. Bemis (1978), for example, suggested that, while operant conditioning has proven to be an excellent technique in restoring the patient's weight, it is not appropriate for handling the intrapsychic distortions and relationships that maintain the problem behaviors. It is probable that these limitations explain the poor record shown by operant methods in sustaining initial weight gains. In order to rectify these deficiencies, several approaches used in conjunction with operant techniques have been suggested or attempted. Agras and Werne (1977) used social skills training, assertiveness training, relaxation exercises, and video techniques as part of their treatment protocol. Geller (1975) combined operant conditioning and psychoanalytic therapy. He suggested that this combination addressed the dual requirements of rapid initial weight gain and treatment of the underlying psychological difficulties. In a similar vein, Garner and Bemis (1982) suggested the use of cognitive-behavioral interventions to achieve similar goals. Rosman et al. (1977) have claimed unusual success in treating anorexic patients by combining family therapy and operant conditioning. In their paradigm of causation, the family milieu and interactional patterns are considered critical in the etiology of the adolescent's anorexia. Therefore, treatment must be directed at both the patient and family if lasting results are to be expected.

We advocate a treatment approach to anorexia based on three characteristics: (1) multidisciplinary, (2) multidimensional, and (3) flexibility. We also feel that a treatment of this nature is appropriate for this exceedingly complex illness. A brief description of each characteristic of treatment is presented in the discussion below.

Anorexia nervosa is a medical, psychological, and nutritional problem. As such, its treatment requires the involvement of specialists from each discipline. Their involvement must be a coordinated team effort if it is to have greatest benefit to the patient. Russell (1977) advocated the use of a team in treating anorexics in an inpatient psychiatric facility. In this regard, he emphasized that members of the team be knowledgeable of the psychological characteristics of the condition and exhibit sensitivity in their interactions with patients. Therefore, the team must have some commitment to the treatment of the anorexic patient since its effectiveness may be contingent on additional training.

It is desirable that one person serve as the primary individual with whom the anorexic interacts. The presence of such a person provides continuity and focus during the entire treatment process. In certain instances, this person can become the coordinator of treatment in providing information regarding the course that it is taking and for answering questions.

In conjunction with the multidisciplinary treatment of anorexia, we favor a treatment that is multidimensional. This perspective has been advocated by other clinicians and researchers (Bruch, 1978; Garner, Garfinkel & Bemis, 1982; Hersen & Detre, 1980). Multidimensional treatment may include such diverse elements as drug therapy, operant conditioning, family therapy, social skills training, and illness-related education.

Our rationale for using a multidimensional treatment format derives from our view of the etiology of anorexia as well as the needs presented by most patients. There is no known etiology for this condition. However, we feel that certain factors play some role in the development of this illness in most cases: social standards for appearance, cognitive distortions and disturbances, maladaptive familial interaction patterns and standards, and a diminished sense of self. These and other factors then become the foci for treatment. With each patient, the emphasis placed on each factor will vary, depending on the degree to which it is perceived to contribute to the maintenance of the problem behaviors. Thus, we advocate an experimental, fact-finding approach to the treatment of the anorexic patient.

The methods used to treat the various factors contributing to this condition will depend on the skills and background of the therapist. For the behaviorally oriented therapist, however, we feel that certain problems of the anorexic are logically handled with particular interventions. For example, it is often found that the primary need of the anorexic entering treatment is to gain weight. This action may be necessary to preserve the patient's physical health as well as to diminish the psychological disturbances frequently observed in human starvation. To aid the anorexic in achieving weight gain, operant techniques are both effective and efficient. The cognitive distortions characteristic of the anorexic can effectively be treated by using cognitive behavioral methodologies. A substantial amount of literature (e.g., Foreyt & Goodrick, 1981a; Mahoney & Arnkoff, 1978) is available that describes specific techniques. Garner and Bemis (1982) recently suggested a therapeutic structure for the treatment of anorexia nervosa based on cognitive behavioral interventions. Using these interventions, a number of distortions and misperceptions may be treated, including incorrect body image, erroneous beliefs and assumptions, and a distortion of environmental "messages."

The cornerstone of the treatment approach we advocate lies in flexibility. Each patient is an individual with a particular intrapsychic and environmental schema associated with the illness. Therapists must, therefore, work with their clients in finding the most helpful combination of treatment strategies. Flexibility is imperative as the therapeutic regime will assuredly differ in emphasis and kind for each patient.

Case Study

When Kim's father telephoned, he sounded desperate, stating that he wanted to hospitalize his daughter immediately. He said that Kim was anorexic, and because his insurance was expiring in a month, he wanted his daughter's problem "taken care of." When Kim, age 21, came to her first outpatient session, she weighed 93 pounds (her height is 5 feet, 4 inches). She said that she has been afraid of becoming obese for the past four years, and she felt that at her current weight she was "somewhat overweight" and was not particularly upset about her father's concern over her health. Although she once had weighed as much as 120 pounds, she had been in the 90-pound weight range for almost two years and had menstrual irregularity since that time. Her physician had not found any physical problems to account for her weight loss.

Kim grew up in Wisconsin and attended a Catholic school run by strict nuns for her first eight grades. She then attended one year of public high school in Wisconsin at which time Kim's father was transferred to Houston, Texas. Kim said that she was depressed and cried the first two years in Houston. Although always an excellent student, she did not make many friends until her junior year. At 16 years of age, she was involved in a serious car accident in which a boyfriend was killed. Her own injuries kept her out of school for six months. After she returned to school, she became more active and involved in class activities. A very attractive blue-eyed blonde, Kim was a cheerleader her last year in high school and a class officer. Her father described her as a perfect daughter, well-liked, and never any problem to the family.

Because Kim's anorexia was not life-threatening at the time, we did not hospitalize her but worked closely with her physician and saw her in intensive weekly outpatient therapy. Kim kept a detailed food diary, including each time she vomited. A nutritious eating plan was developed and gradually implemented. Considerable time was spent discussing the role of her family with respect to the development and maintenance of her current behavior. Although Kim was attending a local college, she was still living with her parents. It was learned that Kim's father was a very overprotective disciplinarian; her mother was an alcoholic who had been physically abusive to Kim and her younger brother and sister during their childhood. Her mother currently drank most of the day and was almost always intoxicated each evening when Kim arrived home from school or her job.

During therapy, Kim developed a more complete understanding about herself and her anorexia. Cognitive distortions about her physical state and her belief that she was the cause of much of her mother's unhappiness were dealt with at length. After eight months of therapy, Kim decided to leave home and move into an apartment near her school. Although Kim is still in therapy, she is now seen only twice a month, and her anorexic symptoms have diminished. After treatment for 14 months, Kim's weight is now in the average range for her height, and her outlook for the future is optimistic.

PICA

The term *pica* derives from the name of a bird whose Latin reference is "Pica pica." This bird is notorious for its habit of stealing objects not considered edible (Bicknell, 1975). Pica among humans is defined as the ingestion of nonnutritive substances. The wide range of items that are typically consumed include paint, hair, cloth, bugs, earth, leaves, and fecal matter (American Psychiatric Association, 1980). Pica is generally a disorder of infancy and early childhood; however, on occasion, it may continue into adolescence and adulthood. Among adults, the occurrence of pica has been associated with malnourishment, extreme adversity, and the influence of particular cultural practices and beliefs (Bicknell, 1975).

Chronic pica behavior can have detrimental social and physical consequences. As a behavior outside the norm, pica causes consternation and puzzlement among caretakers and medical personnel. If the child is old enough to have frequent interaction among age peers, the aberrancy of this behavior may influence the nature of these relationships and subsequent perceptions of self.

Pica behavior can also produce harmful physical problems. These include lead poisoning (Madden, Russo, & Cataldo, 1980), intestinal parasites (Foxx & Martin, 1975), and intestinal blockages (Ausman, Ball, & Alexander, 1974). Lead poisoning is perhaps the most frequently observed medical consequence of pica behavior. Children raised in substandard, old (i.e., prior to 1940) housing are particularly susceptible to this malady, since housing may have the deteriorated remnants of original paint work. Because early paint was lead based, fallen and peeling chips pose an environmental hazard to the pica prone child. Screening programs in deteriorated urban housing areas uncovered a high proportion (15 percent to 40 percent) of children with abnormally large concentrations of lead in their bodies (Madden, et. al., 1980). Excessive lead concentrations in the body can lead to neurological damage and death (Woody, 1971).

There is no accurate information with regard to the prevalence of pica, except that it is rare (American Psychiatric Association, 1980). Research has suggested, however, that this problem tends to concentrate among those socially and economically disadvantaged. The susceptibility of this group to pica is thought to be associated with parental lack of awareness, poor child supervision, overcrowding, insufficient stimulation, and a disorganized familial life (Bicknell, 1975).

Etiology

The etiology of pica is not known. Physiological, social, and psychological theories exist. The interested reader may find detailed descriptions of them in the literature (e.g., Bicknell, 1975). For purposes of this chapter, only the psychological theories will be discussed.

The two major psychological theories derive from the psychodynamic and behavioral paradigms. The psychodynamic view suggests that pica is a child's mode of compensation for an inadequate mother-child relationship (Bicknell, 1975). Behavioral psychologists, on the other hand, view pica as learned maladaptive behavior. The initial ingestion of inedible objects by a child might occur for a variety of reasons, including curiosity and chance. If this behavior is rewarded, it is likely that it will be repeated. For an emotionally neglected child, the parental attention produced by this behavior may be sufficient reward to induce a later repetition (Woody, 1971).

Pica is also found frequently among the mentally retarded. Some suggest that this behavior is among the many indicative of their retarded development. Others feel that the pica behavior itself can contribute to the development of the retardation, that is, the ingestion of items containing lead can produce lead poisoning, which is a known causative factor in mental retardation. The accumulated research evidence, however, does not suggest that pica of this kind is a significant contributor to the development of retardation (Bicknell, 1975).

Treatment

The most widely used treatment for pica behavior is environmental alteration. Thus, if a child has developed lead poisoning through the ingestion of paint chips, environmental solutions to this problem include moving to another house or a restoration of the current one. This solution has the drawbacks of cost and of whether or not such action cures the problematic behavior. With respect to the latter, altering the environment may not resolve the psychosocial factors that precipitated the behavior (Woody, 1971).

At this time, much of the work on the behavioral treatment of pica has been experimental and with institutionalized mentally retarded individuals. The treatments have focused on operant conditioning methodologies to eliminate pica behavior. These methodologies include the use of brief physical restraint (Bucher, Reykdal, & Albin, 1976), a mouthwash overcorrection procedure (Foxx & Martin, 1975), and a combined time-out and reinforcement of other behavior techniques (Ausman et al., 1974). While the studies demonstrated substantial reduction in pica behavior, their applicability to a non-institutionalized population has yet to be evaluated. Additionally, the long-term maintenance of the new behaviors has not been systematically documented. Thus, it is not clear at this time if these approaches have long-term effectiveness.

Finney, Russo, and Cataldo (1982) developed a treatment approach for pica, intending to have broader utility than those described above. Their treatment methodology stressed three factors: (1) developmental progress of the child, (2) learning of new behaviors and their generalization to many settings, and (3) ethical considerations in treatment. Four children with pica related lead poisoning were treated. Treatment consisted of the use of increasingly more restrictive alternatives, from the use of a discrimination procedure to differential reinforcement of behaviors other than pica to, finally, an overcorrection procedure. Thus, the child receiving the punishment oriented overcorrection procedure would have had extensive treatment with the other methods without observable improvement. The treatment method was found to substantially reduce pica behavior in the four children studied. Though no follow-up information was reported, the investigators noted that two of the parents continued to use the procedures at home and indicated their effectiveness.

As suggested above, treatment of pica behavior must take into account the particular patient and factors associated with the problem. The following questions have pertinence with respect to the treatment course taken:

Is the patient mentally retarded?

Is the patient institutionalized?

Is the patient in physical danger (e.g., through lead poisoning)?

How old is the patient?

Are there predisposing environmental factors involved (e.g., crowded conditions, deteriorating housing, and lack of environmental stimulation)?

Are there familial difficulties which may have contributed to the onset of the problem?

What is the relationship of the mother with the child?

The answers to these questions are pertinent to the design of a treatment protocol for a particular patient. Because of the multifactorial nature of pica, it is our bias to use a broad spectrum approach to treatment.

Treatment of pica with behavioral methodologies would appear to be most useful in eliminating the behavior. However, clinicians need to evaluate the utility of the methods in maintaining the newly formed behaviors. For example, one might question how easy the techniques may be taught, learned, and used by parents. In institutional settings, a similar question may be posed for the caretakers of the child.

If the assessment of the patient's behavior uncovers various environmental and social factors contributing to the problem, these should be addressed as well. For example, an environment that is lacking the stimulation and the provisions for appropriate play may lead a child to experiment and mouth undesirable items. In such cases, environmental enrichment is an obvious partial answer to the problem. Madden et al. (1980) found that pica in the children in their study reduced with the addition of toys into a previously impoverished environment.

Familial factors may contribute to the onset and maintenance of pica in a child (Woody, 1971). Familial tensions, lack of affection from the mother, and disturbances during the feeding process are all possibly associated with the undesired behavior. Thus, counseling of the family may be a necessary and integral part of treatment.

Woody (1971) termed the eclectic approach suggested above *environmental-psycho-behavioral*. He felt that a broad approach of this kind was necessary for a problem of such multiple causes. Treatment should be multidisciplinary, treated by both medical and mental health personnel.

RUMINATION

Rumination is characterized by the self-induced regurgitation of previously ingested food. Though this condition can begin at almost any age, it usually begins in infancy (Sheinbein, 1975). Occurrence of this problem among older children and adults is generally without adverse health consequences (Kanner, 1972); this is not the case for infants. Chronic rumination among infants can lead to lowered resistance to disease, electrolyte disturbance, undernutrition, and sometimes death (Sheinbein, 1975). Gaddini and Gaddini (1959) noted that one death occurred in the six cases they examined, while Kanner (1957) indicated that 11 of 52 ruminating infants died.

Rumination among infants is generally considered to be voluntary and pleasurable (Sajwaj, Libet, & Agras, 1974). Prior to regurgitation, infants typically engage in active tongue movements, abdominal contractions, and digital stimulation of the mouth and throat (O'Neil, White, King, & Corek, 1979). The food brought up to the mouth is accomplished without apparent nausea or disgust. After reaching the mouth, food is then either reswallowed or ejected (Kanner, 1972).

No information is currently available regarding the prevalence of ruminative behavior, though it is thought to be very rare (American Psychiatric Association, 1980).

Etiology

There is no consensus of agreement concerning the causes of rumination. The two predominant interpretations of this disorder derive from psychoanalytic and behavioral psychology.

From psychoanalytic theory, ruminative behavior in infants is associated with a disturbed mother-child relationship (Richmond, Eddy, & Green, 1958; Fullerton, 1963; Stein, Rausen, & Blau, 1959). Mothers of afflicted infants are characterized as dependent, immature, and incapable of providing warm and intimate care for the infant (Richmond et al., 1958). Their inability to relate appropriately to the infant is most notable during times of feeding and fondling. As these occasions generally provide most of the comfort and gratification babies experience, disturbances at such times may produce psychological problems. Fullerton (1963) suggested that infantile depression is sometimes associated with ruminative behavior, while Stein et al. (1959) reported diagnoses of infantile anxiety neurosis and depression in an afflicted eight-month-old boy. With the presence of a disturbed psychological state, rumination is interpreted as the related somatic response (Richmond et al., 1958; Fullerton, 1963).

Behavioral psychology views rumination as a learned phenomenon. It may begin as an incidental response that later becomes habitual, or it may arise as a result of disturbance in the infant's psychosocial environment (Lavigne, Burns, & Cotter, 1981). Regardless of the manner in which it begins, ruminative behavior may be reinforced through selective attention by parents and others (Cunningham & Linscheid, 1976; Sheinbein, 1975; Toister, Condron, Worley, & Arthur, 1975).

Treatment

A wide range of procedures has been attempted to treat infantile rumination, including surgery, medications, mechanical chin straps, arm restraints, esophagus blocks, thickened feedings, electroshock, and the use of massive attention (Lavigne et al., 1981; Murray, Keele, & McCarver, 1977). Of these alternatives, massive attention has been the most effective. Its use has been reported primarily in the psychoanalytic literature. As this perspective presumes that a disturbed relationship between mother and infant is at the root of the ruminative behavior, treatment is directed towards providing the nurturant care that the infant needs but has not received. This is accomplished by substantial attention given to the baby by a surrogate mother, usually a nurse, aide, or volunteer. While this treatment is given to the infant, concurrent treatment is given to the mother. Its purpose is to examine and reduce the intrapsychic disturbances associated with the maladaptive mother-child interaction (Lavigne et al., 1981). While this approach has demonstrated effectiveness, it has drawbacks as well. The application of massive attention requires a substantial investment of human resources, which may be difficult to establish, coordinate, and maintain, especially in a busy hospital setting.

Until recently, much of the behavioral treatments for rumination focused on the use of punishment for preruminatory behavior. Hence, when visible indications of imminent vomiting were observed, punishment was applied. These punishments have included electroshock (e.g., Cunningham & Linscheid, 1976; Lang & Melamed, 1969) and the use of aversive taste consequences, including lemon juice (e.g., Sajwaj et al., 1974) and tabasco sauce (e.g., O'Neil et al., 1979). Of these procedures, electroshock appears to be the most effective in eliminating ruminative behavior, though the taste aversion techniques have demonstrated their utility as well (Lavigne et al., 1981). The major disadvantage of these methodologies is the negative reaction of both parents and professionals to their use. Because many individuals are reluctant to apply a punishment procedure to an infant, elicitation of the necessary cooperation is often difficult to obtain.

Problems associated with methodologies using aversive techniques have been largely alleviated with the development of treatments that rely on social contingencies. Treatments of this nature attempt to establish a desired behavior (i.e., the absence of rumination) through the provision of social reinforcement (e.g., holding or affectionate attention) when it is observed. This reinforcement is withdrawn if the undesired behavior (i.e., rumination) commences. This procedure was used successfully in the treatment of a ruminating nine-month-old girl (Wright, Brown, & Andrews, 1978). Cessation of rumination was maintained at a 435-day follow-up.

Several researchers (Sheinbein, 1977; Murray et al., 1976; O'Neil et al., 1979) have used social contingencies in conjunction with other techniques. For example, Sheinbein (1975) applied a negative reinforcer (i.e., arm restraints) along with the removal of social attention when rumination began. Murray et al. (1977) placed tabasco sauce on the infant's tongue with the first signs of rumination in addition to the cessation of affectionate holding.

In general, treatments emphasizing social contingencies have yielded positive outcomes, with infants treated in this manner showing rapid weight gains (Lavigne et al., 1981). As this approach is not objectionable by most parents, treatment gains may be solidified by further application in the home. This factor may be important in order to shorten hospital stays and enhance the probabilities for maintenance.

A substantial amount of empirical work is needed to determine the treatment or treatment combination that yields the most satisfactory results. This effort, however, is complicated by the need to use a methodology that is humane as well as effective. As noted above, professionals and parents alike often object to treatments that appear overly aversive to the infant.

The use of social contingencies in treating rumination seems to be an effective and acceptable method. It has a further advantage in that it may be applied without use of added equipment or extensive training.

Because the treatment of rumination is without established methodologies or guidelines, the clinician must approach this problem with an air of experimentation. Consideration of the severity of the problem, infant's level of physical distress, philosophy and knowledge of the attending physician, cooperation of hospital staff, and the attitudes of the parents should be involved in the development of a treatment protocol. Treatment itself may require alteration if improvement is not apparent over a reasonable period of time. For example, a social contingency methodology may be supplemented by a mildly aversive procedure (e.g., the application of lemon juice on the tongue) or the inclusion of differential reinforcement. O'Neil et al. (1979) used differential reinforcement to encourage periods of nonruminative behavior in a 26-month-old girl. When the child did not ruminate for a specified period of time, her behavior was rewarded with tastes of honey.

The complete treatment of rumination should consider the factors that will maintain or diminish the progress obtained during hospitalization. In this regard, investigation of the family milieu is critical. Some feel that the cause of rumination may reside in dysfunctional parent-infant interactions (Fullerton, 1963; Richmond et al., 1958). This factor, however, does not appear to be present in all cases of rumination. Lavigne et al. (1981) found disordered relationships in four of the nine cases they investigated. Nevertheless, the clinician should be aware of the possibility and its implications for maintenance.

OBESITY

Obesity is the state of having excessive adipose tissue. For many, childhood obesity is the precursor to later adult obesity and the health risks that accompany it. More than 80 percent of overweight children become overweight adults (Abraham & Nordsieck, 1960). If overweight continues through adolescence, the odds against the child becoming a normal weight adult are 28 to 1 (Stunkard & Burt, 1967).

For the child, perhaps the most difficult aspect of obesity involves its social and psychological consequences. Contemporary industrialized societies prize slenderness; it has been portrayed by the mass media to be associated with a number of positive attributes: youth, intelligence, energy, activity, and attractiveness. The obese child is frequently seen as deviant and the object of scorn and prejudice. The continual exposure to derisive attitudes concerning the child's physical appearance can easily affect self-image and self-esteem.

Problem Characteristics and Assessment

Childhood obesity has two characteristics that require consideration: excessive adiposity and its psychological aspects. Generally, both factors contribute to the overall difficulties experienced by the child, and both need to be assessed and treated.

Assessment of the presence of excessive fat is most easily done by visual inspection and self-report. However, it is useful to have an objective measure of adiposity as well, since fat loss is one way of assessing the progress of treatment.

Weight is the most commonly used indirect measure of excessive adiposity. Because it does not measure fat content directly, it is only suggestive of its presence. When applied to children, weight must be used with care. Comparing a child's weight with established norms must take into account such factors as sex, age, height, and body build. Omitting one or more factors in assessing proper weight level can lead to substantial error. A mesomorphic boy, for example, may be overweight but within established norms for fat (Foreyt & Kondo, 1983).

Other means of measuring body fat also exist. Among the more practical and available are skinfold measures and densitometry. Both are standard procedures for the measurement of fat, and established norms are readily available. Descriptions of their use with children may be found elsewhere (Foreyt & Goodrick, 1981b).

For behavior therapists, excessive accuracy in the measurement of fat is probably not necessary. As indicated earlier, visual inspection can provide much information regarding the extent of the problem and the progress of treatment.

For most obese children and adolescents, the problem extends beyond the physical. They are often the objects of ridicule and prejudice. Unless they are quite unusual, one can expect that fat children will have poor self-image and low self-esteem (Mayer, 1975). Other psychological and social difficulties may also exist that serve to not only diminish the child's enjoyment of life, but also to exacerbate the overweight condition. Many children face ostracization from peers and withdraw from social contact and activity. They learn to entertain and console themselves in solitary, often sedentary ways. Functioning in this manner reduces caloric expenditure and leads to further weight gain.

Assessment of the child's psychosocial difficulties requires involvement of the child and parents. Family attitudes concerning obesity may add to the child's psychological burden since the child's obesity may be as much a parental problem as it is the child's. In such cases, the therapist needs to determine who has the motivation for the child's treatment.

Etiology

At its most basic level, the cause of obesity is simple: overweight children eat too much and do too little. An energy imbalance exists, but unfortunately, along with this simple paradigm of causation are numerous intervening variables that ultimately make explanation exceedingly complex.

Recent research suggests that fat children (and adults) achieve their condition by factors other than a sole propensity to gluttony. Many have a genetic tendency so that their obesity is a combined result of both "nature and nurture" (Weil, 1977). An individual's body type (or somatotype) may influence the tendency towards fatness or thinness. Obese people tend to have an endomorphic structure, i.e., a somatotype characterized by a barrel chest and short limbs. Obesity is rare among those whose somatotype is predominantly ectomorphic, i.e., those having elongated skeletal structures. In an observational study of fat and thin babies, Mayer (1975) observed that thin babies actually consumed more food than their fat counterparts. However, the thin babies were also more active and tense, while the fat babies tended to be placid and inactive. Perhaps even the predisposition to activity and placidity may be a heritable characteristic. Thus, the inactivity observed among many obese may be as much a cause of their condition as it is a result of it.

The possibility that nature plays a role in the etiology of obesity has been given support during the past decade by the *set point theory* (Nisbett, 1972). This theory suggests that individuals have an ideal biological weight and that deviation from it sets into motion mechanisms that will cause eventual return to the equilibrium state. In a manner similar to the action of a thermostat, it has been theorized that the body has a "ponderstat" that returns body weight to the set point level when change occurs (Bradley, 1982). Proponents of this theory suggest that dieters who reduce their body weight face a losing battle because of the inexorable pressures of the set point mechanisms. The existence of set point has been supported in various human and animal research. Most notable among them are the starvation studies of Keys, Brozek, Henschel, Mickelson, and Taylor (1950) and the overfeeding investigation of Sims and Horton (1968). In both studies, set point mechanisms appeared to operate, and when normal feeding patterns returned, pre-experimental body weights followed.

Along with physiological influences, environmental factors also function in the etiology and maintenance of the obese state. The extent of their influence, however, is not known at this time. For children, the social and physical environments that shape their eating patterns are multiple, including parents, peers, school, and the mass media. During the child's early years and decreasing as time passes, parents are the most powerful influencing factors. Parental dietary customs and patterns are the literal template by which children fashion their own. If this template is one that encourages the selection and consumption of high-caloric foods, then the likelihood of obesity is high.

There appears to be a self-perpetuating cycle of obesity that occurs in many families: obese parents tend to produce obese children (Charney, Goodman, McBride, Lyon, & Pratt, 1976). If neither parent is obese, the probability of having an obese child is 7 percent. However, if one parent is obese, the probability increases to 40 percent, and if both parents are obese, the probability grows to 80 percent (Mayer, 1975).

Treatment

As it has been the experience with adults, treatment of obesity with children and adolescents has been relatively ineffective. This holds true whether treatment has emphasized diet, anorectic drugs, exercise, behavior modification, or even enforced starvation (Brownell, 1982; Coates & Thoresen, 1978). Some of these approaches produce substantial short-term losses, but the maintenance has been consistently poor (Coates & Thoresen, 1981). This result may have been due partially to the tendency to treat the presenting problem (i.e., obesity) and not the conditions that support it (i.e., the psychological, social, and physical factors).

Review of Behavioral Treatment.   Behavioral treatment of childhood obesity has been the subject of increasing research during the past decade, though the studies remain too few in number to make sound evaluations. However, results to date indicate weight losses ranging between 4 to 13 pounds, with substantial variability between subjects and poor maintenance (Brownell, 1982).

The use of behavior modification in treating obesity among children and adolescents has been largely a case of shifting programs aimed at adults to this younger population. Treatments have emphasized modifying the variables that are assumed to have association with maladaptive eating. These include consideration of eating rate, availability of problematic foods in the home, and reducing unstructured eating. Studies using these approaches have shown good weight losses (e.g., Aragona, Cassady, & Drabman, 1975; Gross, Wheeler, & Hess, 1976; Kingsley & Shapiro, 1977). While these studies have suggested that behavior modification has utility, its limitations cannot be overlooked. As in the case of adults (Foreyt, Goodrick, & Gotto, 1981; Wilson & Brownell, 1980), these strategies do not appear powerful enough to produce clinically significant weight losses, nor are they maintained.

In an effort to produce better results, the movement in behavioral treatments appears to be toward multifaceted programs (Brownell & Stunkard, 1980; Epstein, Wing, Koeske, Ossip, & Beck, 1982). In addition to the components (e.g., stimulus control, eating topography control, and self-monitoring) that have become standard in behavioral treatment, newer programs are including cognitive therapy, exercise, social skills training, and family involvement. The hope has been that the addition of these elements will correct previously recognized deficiencies.

Assessment. Treatment should begin with a thorough assessment of the child's physical and psychological condition. In some cases, it may be necessary to consult with the family physician so that physical causes of obesity may be ruled out. Examination of the child's psychological status may include assessment of self-esteem, physical image, personal capabilities, and social competence. Involvement of the parents is essential in this assessment process because they can provide another view of the child's psychological and social functioning, and they can give the therapist insights concerning family interaction processes. We particularly look for such matters as:

Who is motivated to have the child lose weight?

How is overweight viewed by the parents?

Do family eating patterns seemingly support the child's problem?

How much is the family willing to help the child in the effort to lose weight and keep it off?

These questions are important in assessing the prospects for successful weight loss and maintenance.

Goals. The goals of our treatment are twofold: (*a*) to reduce the child's body fat, and (*b*) to improve psychosocial functioning. Our emphasis on body fat reduction as a goal, as opposed to weight loss, reflects our conservative approach to treating childhood obesity. As children are often in various phases of growth, added weight is a natural by-product of the process. Therefore, using weight as the standard by which treatment progress is measured may be inappropriate. Fat reduction, on the other hand, does not have a similar disadvantage. Also, improvement in psychosocial functioning is often as important as body fat reduction as a goal of treatment. Many children enter treatment with low self-esteem and poor self-image. Some show signs of depression, a tendency toward isolation, and immaturity in their social skills. These kinds of problems are often associated with the weight problem, and their resolution is essential to long-term success.

Age.   The age of the child is an important variable. Age is largely associated with degree of independence, cognitive development, ability to self-manage, and capability towards personal expression. These variables structure almost every facet of treatment from the manner in which it is conducted in the office to the homework assignments given. Presence or absence of parents during consultation, for example, is an important matter in treatment that has relationship to age. Young children need the presence of parents as a source of assurance and to assist in treatment. Older children may require private sessions with the therapist without the presence of parents, but in such situations, it is useful to have periodic meetings with both parents and children. By so doing, active involvement of the parents can be maintained.

Behavioral Strategies.   Our approach to treatment is loosely fashioned after the behavioral programs that have become somewhat standard in obesity treatment. Four elements are central: self-monitoring, stimulus control, eating management, and contingency management. Detailed descriptions of these elements and their application may be found elsewhere (Ferguson, 1976; Stuart & Davis, 1972). We suggest use of these elements based on their applicability to individually determined problems. If a child overeats because of maladaptive eating habits (e.g., eating too rapidly or placing large quantities of food on utensils), then eating management strategies are used. Determination of the child's food and eating problems is essential to this process, and this requires a thorough assessment at the initiation of and during treatment (Foreyt & Goodrick, 1981b).

Exercise.   Along with the behavioral eating management strategies, encouragement of exercise and physical activity is integral to our approach. Some overweight children do not eat more than their normal weight peers, but they are less active (Dwyer, Feldman, & Mayer, 1967; Huenemann, 1972, 1974; Mayer, 1975). Each child is assessed regarding baseline physical activity levels, personal history with respect to sports and exercise, and current attitudes regarding participation.

Often, assessment reveals that the child has had negative experiences with physically oriented activities. Many have faced ridicule because of their size and lack of athletic capabilities. There is little that is more painful, embarrassing, and esteem-reducing as the experience of being selected last when teams are chosen. Once the teams are selected, the negative experience does not end. Overweight children are frequently placed in positions that emphasize their size and lack of athletic capabilities. These include the traditional "fat boy" positions: batting last and catcher in baseball, and tackle and center in football. With negative experiences of these kinds, the reticence for involvement in physical activity is understandable.

Encouraging exercise should be an ongoing part of therapy. Its many benefits, including reduction of stress and tendency to make one feel better, should be emphasized. Addition of exercise to the life of the physically reticent child should occur in a slow yet progressive fashion. This takes the form of adding activity to present life patterns. For example, walking to various locations is substituted for a ride in the car or bus when feasible, and needed household chores, such as grass cutting or running errands, are included. As the child becomes more confident, structured exercise and sports activities may be added. These, however, are not attempted until the child indicates a reasonable readiness.

Cognitive Interventions. As indicated earlier, our goals include improving the child's psychological and social functioning. In working toward these goals, we rely heavily on the use of cognitive interventions (Foreyt & Kondo, 1983).

Cognitive methodologies are applied in many ways in weight control programs. Mahoney and Mahoney (1976) described some of their applications in a program designed for adults. With children, the use of these strategies is similar: to determine the presence of cognitive distortions and to correct them. For obese children, distortions occur in a number of areas, including beliefs regarding food, perceptions of self, and their value within the family schema. Price and Geronilla (1981) indicated how food and emotions can be inappropriately linked:

> Eating may be used to soothe tensions, calm anxiety, and to compensate for frustrations. Symbolically, food can become a substitute for love between a parent and child, a chosen means to express love they find difficult to express in any other way. (p. 193)

We find that treating the child's maladaptive cognitions is best done with the help and cooperation of both parents. It has been our experience that cognitive change with children cannot be successfully done through office visits alone, but that the new learnings need to be reiterated and reinforced throughout the week with parental guidance. Training the parents is an integral part of this phase of therapy. Our frequent experience is that many parents require change in their own distortions if they are to help their children. Many parents are overweight, and they have their share of maladaptive beliefs concerning food, eating, and themselves. They frequently serve as the source of some of the beliefs adopted by their children. Helping the child often becomes, by necessity, a familial process. It should be noted that some parents are reluctant to see themselves as having a problem. In such cases, we work within the constraints of the situation.

A number of cognitive intervention methods are applicable to the treatment of the obese child, including problem solving (Mahoney, 1977), cognitive restructuring (Ellis, 1979), and self-instructional training (Meichenbaum, 1977). Therapists must use judgment and experimentation to determine the readiness of the child for a given intervention and its applicability. The recent review by Kendall (1981) is an excellent resource of the methods and uses of this intervention for children.

Social Skills Training.   Another integral portion of our treatment of childhood obesity is social skills training. As the object of considerable prejudice, many obese children tend to be isolated, withdrawn, and lacking in the social skills appropriate to their age. Often, it appears that these conditions exacerbate their inappropriate eating, that is, food becomes both a gratification and solace from the feelings of loneliness.

As in other aspects of treatment, we use an eclectic, experimental approach to improving social skills. After assessment of the child's difficulties, our method is to apply techniques appropriate to the particular need. This includes the use of behavioral assignments, aspects of assertiveness training, and development of personal competence to help the child develop self-esteem through growth-involved skill areas. Additional benefits may accrue from this process if the skills are also seen as valuable by the child's peers.

Case Study

At intake, Becky, a 13-year-old female, was 61 inches tall and weighed 191 pounds. Triceps skinfold was 34 mm. We first consulted with a dietitian and determined an adequate caloric intake. This amount was divided into food groups, and we permitted a specific number of food exchanges from each food group each day. We then taught the food groups and serving sizes of various foods to Becky and her parents. Responsibility for monitoring food variety and portion size was initially shared between Becky and her mother. As Becky showed that she could handle more responsibility, we gradually shifted the task to her. We gave Becky a laminated card listing the food groups and showed her how to use it. Each food group was color coded on the card: meat (red), vegetables (green), fruits (orange), breads and cereals (yellow), milk and milk products (white), and a miscellaneous category (brown). The number of exchanges for each group was represented by a colored circle for each exchange. As food was eaten, we told Becky to draw an X over the circle for the appropriate exchange to keep a record of food eaten for that day. The card was then wiped clean each evening.

Becky also kept a brief food diary that we reviewed at each session. Several problems were identified from the diary. Although Becky was a fairly active person, she also enjoyed a considerable number of between-meal snacks, particularly ice cream, "Little Debbies," and candy bars. With Becky and her mother, we jointly set a goal of reducing her snacking to one time per day. Other foods could be added to her eating plan, as long as they were vegetables or fruits. These were allowed because of her activity level, her frequent binges, and to help her develop a liking for these foods. During the first two weeks, Becky cut her inappropriate snacking in half from about four per day to two per day. After a month Becky had reduced her snacking to once a day.

According to her mother, Becky also tended to eat rapidly at mealtimes. We involved the family to help her slow down her eating, having the family play a game at the evening meal called "tasting the ingredients and textures." This game involved a conscious exploration of the food that is eaten. Members of the family are asked to name what spices make up a particular sauce and to describe the texture of various foods as they are eaten.

During therapy with Becky, it became obvious that she had a very poor self-image. We dealt with her negative feelings about herself by giving her support and encouragement and reinforcing her musical talents. As Becky discussed specific negative thoughts about herself, we helped her change those thoughts to more positive ones. For example, Becky was not invited to a pajama party by one of her classmates. She thought that she had not been asked to the party because of her weight and because she would be an embarrassment to her classmate. She added that she understood because she would not want to be around a fat girl like herself either. We discussed the situation in great detail, giving other possible explanations for her not being invited. We also helped Becky understand that whatever the reason, brooding about it was not useful and that she should get busy in other activities with friends; consequently, Becky called a friend and invited her to the movies.

Becky did well during 26 weekly sessions of treatment, lowering her weight from 191 pounds to 176 pounds. Her triceps skinfold was 28 mm (her height was 61.25 inches). Becky and her parents were pleased with the 15-pound weight loss, and they planned to continue using the laminated card. Becky's family was very supportive in the program and their encouragement helped her during difficult periods.

SUMMARY

The treatment of eating disorders is an especially challenging area. These disorders are often quite serious (in the case of anorexia, sometimes fatal) and are highly resistant to treatment. The need for good research to develop more effective treatment strategies is critical. To improve treatment, researchers and clinicians should carefully examine the processes leading to and maintaining the eating disorder. Although behavioral strategies have added considerably to our success at treating these conditions, narrow definitions of behavioral treatment, including self-monitoring, stimulus control, and contingency management, have usually not been sufficient to effect long-term changes. Multidimensional treatment, including family therapy, social skills training, cognitive-behavioral procedures, and drug therapy are often required. Along with behaviorally trained clinicians, other professionals, including physicians, exercise physiologists, and dietitians, are required as integral members of a multidisciplinary treatment team. With the expertise of these disciplines working together, we should maximize our chances of success in the treatment of these refractory conditions.

REFERENCES

Abraham, S., & Nordsieck, M. Relationship of excess weight in children and adults. *Public Health Reports,* 1960, *75,* 263–273.

Agras, S., & Werne, J. Behavior modification in anorexia nervosa: Research foundations. In R. A. Vigersky (Ed.), *Anorexia nervosa.* New York: Raven Press, 1977.

Al-Issa, I. *The psychopathology of women.* Englewood Cliffs, N.J.: Prentice-Hall, 1980.

American Psychiatric Association. *Diagnostic and statistical manual of mental disorders* (3rd ed.). Washington, D.C.: American Psychiatric Association, 1980.

Aragona, J., Cassady, J., & Drabman, R. Treating overweight children through parental training and contingency contracting. *Journal of Applied Behavior Analysis,* 1975, *8,* 269–278.

Ausman, J., Ball, T. S., & Alexander, D. Behavior therapy of pica with a profoundly retarded adolescent. *Mental Retardation,* 1974, *12,* 16–18.

Bachrach, A. J., Erwin, W. J., & Mohr, J. P. The control of eating behavior in an anorexic by operant conditioning techniques. In L. P. Ullmann & L. Krasner (Eds.), *Case studies in behavior modification.* New York: Holt, Rinehart & Winston, 1965.

Beck, A. T. *Cognitive therapy and emotional disorders.* New York: International Universities Press, 1976.

Bemis, K. M. Current approaches to the etiology and treatment of anorexia nervosa. *Psychological Bulletin,* 1978, *85,* 593–617.

Beumont, P. J. V., George, G. C., & Smart, D. E. "Dieters" and "vomiters and purgers" in anorexia nervosa. *Psychological Medicine,* 1976, *6,* 617–622.

Bicknell, J. *Pica: A childhood symptom.* London: Butterworth, 1975.

Boskind-Lodahl, M., & Sirlin, J. The gorging-purging syndrome. *Psychology Today,* 1977, *10,* 50–52; 82–85.

Bradley, P. J. Is obesity an advantageous adaptation? *International Journal of Obesity,* 1982, *6,* 43–52.

Brownell, K. D. Obesity: Understanding and treating a serious, prevalent, and refractory disorder. *Journal of Consulting and Clinical Psychology,* 1982, *50,* 820–840.

Brownell, K. D., & Stunkard, A. J. Behavioral treatment of obese children and adolescents. In A. J. Stunkard (Ed.), *Obesity.* Philadelphia: W. B. Saunders, 1980.

Bruch, H. *Eating disorders: Obesity, anorexia nervosa, and the person within.* New York: Basic Books, 1973.

Bruch, H. Perils of behavior modification in treatment of anorexia nervosa. *Journal of the American Medical Association,* 1974, *230,* 1419–1422,

Bruch, H. Psychological antecedents of anorexia nervosa. In R. A. Vigersky (Ed.), *Anorexia nervosa*. New York: Raven Press, 1977.

Bruch, H. *The golden cage: The enigma of anorexia nervosa*. Cambridge: Harvard University Press, 1978.

Bucher, B., Reykdal, B., & Albin, J. B. Brief physical restraint to control pica in retarded children. *Journal of Behavior Therapy and Experimental Psychiatry*, 1976, *7*, 137–140.

Casper, R. C., Eckert, E. D., Halmi, K. A., Goldberg, S. C., & Davis, J. M. Bulimia: Its incidence and clinical importance in patients with anorexia nervosa. *Archives of General Psychiatry*, 1980, *37*, 1030–1035.

Charney, E., Goodman, H. C., McBride, M., Lyon, B., & Pratt, R. Childhood antecedents of adult obesity. *New England Journal of Medicine*, 1976, *295*, 6–9.

Coates, T. J., & Thoresen, C. E. Treating obesity in children and adolescents: A review. *American Journal of Public Health*, 1978, *68*, 143–151.

Coates, T. J., & Thoresen, C. E. Treating obesity in children and adolescents: Is there any hope? In J. M. Ferguson & C. B. Taylor (Eds.), *The comprehensive handbook of behavioral medicine (Vol. 2)*. New York: Medical and Scientific Books, 1981.

Crisp, A. H. Anorexia nervosa at normal body weight! The abnormal normal weight control syndrome. *International Journal of Psychiatry in Medicine*, 1981–82, *11*, 203–233.

Crisp, A. H., Kalucy, R. S., Lacey, J. H., & Harding, B. The long term prognosis in anorexia nervosa: Some factors predictive of outcome. In R. A. Vigersky (Ed.), *Anorexia nervosa*. New York: Raven Press, 1977.

Cunningham, C. E., & Linscheid, T. R. Elimination of chronic infant ruminating by electric shock. *Behavior Therapy*, 1976, *7*, 231–234.

Dally, P. J. *Anorexia nervosa*. New York: Grune and Stratton, 1979.

Dally, P. J., & Gomez, J. *Anorexia nervosa*. London: William Heinlemann, 1979.

Dwyer, J. T., Feldman, J. J., & Mayer, J. Adolescent dieters: Who are they? Physical characteristics, attitudes, and dieting practices of adolescent girls. *American Journal of Clinical Nutrition*, 1967, *20*, 1045–1056.

Ellis, A. Rational emotive therapy. In R. J. Corsini (Ed.), *Current psychotherapies* (2nd ed.). Itasca, Ill.: Peacock, 1979.

Epstein, L. H., Wing, R. R., Koeske, R., Ossip, D., & Beck, S. A comparison of lifestyle change and programmed aerobic exercise on weight and fitness changes in obese children. *Behavior Therapy*, 1982, *13*, 651–665.

Fairburn, C. A cognitive behavioral approach to the treatment of bulimia. *Psychological Medicine*, 1981, *11*, 707–711.

Feighner, J., Robins, E., Guze, S., Woodruff, R. A., Winokur, G., & Munoz, R. Diagnostic criteria for use in psychiatric research. *Archives of General Psychiatry*, 1972, *26*, 57–63.

Ferguson, J. M. *Habits, not diets: The real way to weight control.* Palo Alto, Calif.: Bull Publishing Company, 1976.

Finney, J. W., Russo, D. C., & Cataldo, M. F. Reduction of pica in young children with lead poisoning. *Journal of Pediatric Psychology,* 1982, *7,* 197–207.

Foreyt, J. P., & Goodrick, G. K. Cognitive behavior therapy. In R. J. Corsini (Ed.), *Handbook of innovative psychotherapies.* New York: John Wiley & Sons, 1981(a).

Foreyt, J. P., & Goodrick, G. K. Childhood obesity. In E. Mash & L. G. Terdal (Eds.), *Behavioral assessment of childhood disorders.* New York: Guilford Press, 1981(b).

Foreyt, J. P., Goodrick, G. K., & Gotto, A. M. Limitations of behavioral treatment of obesity: Review and analysis. *Journal of Behavioral Medicine,* 1981, *4,* 159–174.

Foreyt, J. P., & Kondo, A. T. Cognitive-behavioral treatment of childhood and adolescent obesity. In A. Ellis & M. E. Bernard (Eds.), *Rational–emotive approaches to the problems of childhood.* New York: Plenum Press, 1983.

Foxx, R. M., & Martin, E. D. Treatment of scavenging behavior (coprophogy and pica) by overcorrection. *Behaviour Research and Therapy,* 1975, *13,* 153–162.

Fullerton, D. T. Infantile rumination: A case report. *Archives of General Psychiatry,* 1963, *9,* 593–600.

Gaddini, R., & Gaddini, E. Rumination in infancy. In C. Jessner & E. Pavenstadt (Eds.), *Dynamic psychopathology in childhood.* New York: Grune and Stratton, 1959.

Garfinkel, P. E. Perception of hunger and satiety in anorexia nervosa. *Psychological Medicine,* 1974, *4,* 309–315.

Garfinkel, P. E., Moldofsky, H., & Garner, D. M. The outcome of anorexia nervosa: Significance of clinical features, body image, and behavior modification. In R. A. Vigersky (Ed.), *Anorexia nervosa.* New York: Raven Press, 1977.

Garner, D. M., & Bemis, K. M. A cognitive behavioral approach to anorexia nervosa. *Cognitive Therapy and Research,* 1982, *6,* 123–150.

Garner, D. M., Garfinkel, P. E., Schwartz, D., & Thompson, J. Cultural expectations of thinness in women. *Psychological Reports,* 1980, *47,* 483–491.

Garner, D. M., & Garfinkel, P. E. Body image in anorexia nervosa: Measurements, theory, and clinical implications. *International Journal of Psychiatry in Medicine,* 1981–82, *11,* 263–284.

Garner, D. M., Garfinkel, P. E., & Bemis, K. M. A multidimensional psychotherapy for anorexia nervosa. *International Journal of Eating Disorders,* 1982, *1,* 3–46.

Geller, J. L. Treatment of anorexia nervosa by the integration of behavior therapy and psychotherapy. *Psychotherapy and Psychosomatics,* 1975, *26,* 167–177.

Giannini, J. A. Anorexia nervosa: A retrospective view. *International Journal of Psychiatry in Medicine,* 1981–82, *11,* 199–202.

Green, R. S., & Rau, J. H. Treatment of compulsive eating disturbances with anticonvulsant medication. *American Journal of Psychiatry,* 1974, *131,* 428–432.

Grinc, G. A. A cognitive behavioral model for the treatment of chronic vomiting. *Journal of Behavioral Medicine,* 1982, *5,* 135–141.

Gross, I., Wheeler, M., & Hess, K. The treatment of obesity in adolescents using behavioral self control. *Clinical Pediatrics,* 1976, *15,* 920–924.

Guiora, A. Z. Dysorexia: A psychopathological study of anorexia nervosa and bulimia. *American Journal of Psychiatry,* 1967, *124,* 391–393.

Hallsten, E. A. Adolescent anorexia nervosa treated by desensitization. *Behaviour Research and Therapy,* 1965, *3,* 87–91.

Halmi, K. A. Anorexia nervosa: Demographic and clinical features in 94 cases. *Psychosomatic Medicine,* 1974, *36,* 18–26.

Halmi, K. A., Goldberg, S. C., Eckert, E., Casper, R., & Davis, J. M. Pretreatment evaluation in anorexia nervosa. In R. A. Vigersky (Ed.), *Anorexia nervosa.* New York: Raven Press, 1977.

Hawkins, R. C., II, & Clement, P. F. Binge eating syndrome: The measurement problem and a conceptual model. In R. C. Hawkins II, W. Fremouw, & P. F. Clement (Eds.), *The binge-purge syndrome.* New York: Springer, 1983.

Herman, C. P., & Polivy, J. Anxiety, restraint, and eating behavior. *Journal of Abnormal Psychology,* 1975, *84,* 666–672.

Hersen, M., & Detre, T. The behavioral psychotherapy of anorexia nervosa. In T. B. Karasu & L. Bellak (Eds.), *Specialized techniques in individual psychotherapy.* New York: Brunner/Mazel, 1980.

Huenemann, R. L. Food habits of obese and nonobese adolescents. *Postgraduate Medicine,* 1972, *51,* 99–105.

Huenemann, R. L. Environmental factors associated with preschool obesity. *Journal of the American Dietetic Association,* 1974, *64,* 488–491.

Jackson, J. N., & Ormiston, L. H. Diet and weight control clinic: A status report. Unpublished manuscript, Stanford University, 1977.

Kanner, L. *Child psychiatry* (3rd ed.). Springfield, Ill.: Charles C Thomas, 1957.

Kanner, L. *Child psychiatry* (4th ed.). Springfield, Ill.: Charles C Thomas, 1972.

Katz, J. L., Boyar, R. M., Weiner, H., Gorzynski, G., Roffwarg, H., & Hellman, L. Toward an elucidation of the psychoendocrinology of anorexia nervosa. In E. J. Sochar (Ed.), *Hormones, behavior, and psychopathology.* New York: Raven Press, 1976.

Kay, D. W. K., & Leigh, D. The natural history, treatment and prognosis of anorexia nervosa, based on a study of 38 patients. *Journal of Mental Sciences,* 1954, *100,* 411–431.

Kendall, P. C. Cognitive behavioral interventions with children. In B. Lahey & A. Kazdin (Eds.), *Advances in clinical child psychology.* New York: Plenum Press, 1981.

Kenny, F. T., & Solyom, L. The treatment of compulsive vomiting through faradic disruption of mental images. *Canadian Medical Association Journal*, 1971, *105*, 1071–1073.

Keys, A., Brozek, J., Henschel, A., Mickelson, O., & Taylor, H. S. *The biology of human starvation* (Vols. 1 and 2). Minneapolis: University of Minnesota Press, 1950.

Kingsley, R. G., & Shapiro, J. A comparison of three behavioral programs for control of obesity in children. *Behavior Therapy*, 1977, *8*, 30–36.

Lang, P. J., & Melamed, B. G. Avoidance conditioning therapy of an infant with chronic ruminative vomiting. *Journal of Abnormal Psychology*, 1969, *74*, 1–8.

Lavigne, J. V., Burns, W. J., & Cotter, P. D. Rumination in infancy: Recent behavioral approaches. *International Journal of Eating Disorders*, 1981, *1*, 70–82.

Loro, A. D., & Orleans, C. S. Binge eating in obesity: Preliminary findings and guidelines for behavioral analysis and treatment. *Addictive Behaviors*, 1981, *6*, 155–166.

Madden, N. A., Russo, D. C., & Cataldo, M. F. Behavioral treatment of pica in children with lead poisoning. *Child Behavior Therapy*, 1980, *2*, 67–81.

Mahoney, M. J. Personal science: A cognitive learning therapy. In A. Ellis & R. Grieger (Eds.), *Handbook of rational emotive therapy*. New York: Springer, 1977.

Mahoney, M. J., & Arnkoff, D. B. Cognitive and self control therapies. In S. L. Garfield & A. E. Bergin (Eds.), *Handbook of psychotherapy and behavior change: An empirical analysis*. New York: John Wiley & Sons, 1978.

Mahoney, M. J., & Mahoney, K. *Permanent weight control: A total solution to the dieter's dilemma*. New York: W. W. Norton, 1976.

Marks, V., & Bannister, R. G. Pituitary and adrenal function in undernutrition and mental illness (including anorexia nervosa). *British Journal of Psychiatry*, 1963, *109*, 480–484.

Mayer, J. Obesity during childhood. In M. Winick (ed.), *Childhood obesity*. New York: John Wiley & Sons, 1975.

Meichenbaum, D. *Cognitive behavior modification*. New York: Plenum Press, 1977.

Mitchell, J. E., & Pyle, R. L. The bulimic syndrome in normal weight individuals: A review. *International Journal of Eating Disorders*, 1982, *1*, 61–63.

Monti, P. M., McCrady, B. S., & Barlow, D. H. Effect of positive reinforcement, informational feedback and contingency contracting on a bulimic anorexic female. *Behavior Therapy*, 1977, *8*, 258–263.

Murray, M. E., Keele, D. K., & McCarver, J. W. Treatment of ruminations with behavioral techniques: A case report. *Behavior Therapy*, 1977, *8*, 999–1003.

Nemiah, J. C. Anorexia nervosa: A clinical psychiatric study. *Medicine*, 1950, *29*, 225–268.

Nisbett, R. E. Hunger, obesity, and the ventromedial hypothalamus. *Psychological Review*, 1972, *79*, 433–453.

Nogami, Y., & Yobana, F. On Kibarashi-gui (binge eating). *Folia Psychiatrica et Neurologica Japonica*, 1977, *31*, 159–166.

O'Neil, P. M., White, J. L., King, C. R., & Corek, D. J. Controlling childhood rumination through differential reinforcement of other behavior. *Behavior Modification*, 1979, *3*, 355–372.

Orleans, C. S., & Barnett, L. R. Binging and purging: Guidelines for behavioral assessment and treatment. In R. C. Hawkins II, W. Fremouw & P. F. Clement (Eds.), *The binge-purge syndrome*. New York: Springer, 1983.

Palmer, R. L. The dietary chaos syndrome: A useful new term? *British Journal of Medical Psychology*, 1979, *52*, 187–190.

Price, J. H., & Geronilla, L. A. Childhood obesity: A review. *Health Values: Achieving High Level Wellness*. 1981, *5*, 192–198.

Pyle, R. L., Mitchell, J. E., & Eckert, E. D. Bulimia: A report of 34 cases. *Journal of Clinical Psychiatry*, 1981, *42*, 60–64.

Richmond, J. B., Eddy, E., & Green, M. Rumination: A psychosomatic syndrome of infancy. *Pediatrics*, 1958, *22*, 49–55.

Rosman, B. L., Minuchin, S., Baker, L., & Liebman, R. A family approach to anorexia nervosa: Study, treatment, and outcome. In R. A. Vigersky (Ed.), *Anorexia nervosa*. New York: Raven Press, 1977.

Russell, G. General management of anorexia nervosa and difficulties in assessing the efficacy of treatment. In R. A. Vigersky (Ed.), *Anorexia nervosa*. New York: Raven Press, 1977.

Russell, G. Bulimia nervosa: An ominous variant of anorexia nervosa. *Psychological Medicine*, 1979, *9*, 429–448.

Sajwaj, T., Libet, J., & Agras, S. Lemon juice therapy: The control of life-threatening rumination in a six-month-old infant. *Journal of Applied Behavior Analysis*, 1974, *7*, 557–563.

Sheinbein, M. Treatment for the hospitalized infantile ruminator: Programmed brief social behavior reinforcers. *Clinical Pediatrics*, 1975, *8*, 719–724.

Sims, E. A. H., & Horton, E. S. Endocrine and metabolic adaptation to obesity and starvation. *American Journal of Clinical Nutrition*, 1968, *21*, 1455–1470.

Smith, G. R. Modification of binge eating in obesity. *Journal of Behavior Therapy and Experimental Psychiatry*, 1981, *12*, 333–336.

Spencer, J. A., & Fremouw, W. J. Binge eating as a function of restraint and weight classification. *Journal of Abnormal Psychology*, 1979, *88*, 262–267.

Stein, M. L., Rausen, A. R., & Blau, A. Psychotherapy of an infant with rumination. *Journal of the American Medical Association*, 1959, *171*, 2309–2312.

Strangler, R. S., & Prinz, A. M. DSM-III: Psychiatric diagnosis in a university population. *American Journal of Psychiatry*, 1980, *137*, 937–940.

Stuart, R. B., & Davis, B. *Slim chance in a fat world*. Champaign, Ill.: Research Press, 1972.

Stunkard, A. J. Eating patterns and obesity. *Psychiatric Quarterly,* 1959, *33,* 284–295.

Stunkard, A. J., & Burt, V. Obesity and body image II. Age at onset of disturbances in the body image. *American Journal of Psychiatry,* 1967, *123,* 1443–1447.

Toister, R. P., Condron, C. J., Worley, L., & Arthur, D. Faradic therapy of chronic vomiting in infancy: A case study. *Journal of Behavior Therapy and Experimental Psychiatry,* 1975, *6,* 55–59.

Weil, W. B. Current controversies in childhood obesity. *Journal of Pediatrics,* 1977, *91,* 175–187.

White, W. C., & Boskind-White, M. An experimental-behavioral approach to the treatment of bulimarexia. *Psychotherapy: Theory, Research, and Practice,* 1981, *81,* 501–507.

Wilson, G. T. Obesity, binge eating, and behavior therapy: Some clinical observations. *Behavior Therapy,* 1976, *7,* 700–701.

Wilson, G. T., & Brownell, K. D. Behavior therapy for obesity: An evaluation of treatment outcome. *Advances in Behaviour Research and Therapy,* 1980, *3,* 49–86.

Woody, R. H. Controlling pica via an environmental-psychobehavioral strategy: With special reference to lead poisoning. *Journal of School Health,* 1971, *41,* 548–555.

World Health Organization. *Mental disorders: Glossary and guide to their classification in accordance with the ninth revision of the International Classification of Diseases.* Geneva: World Health Organization, 1978.

Wright, D. F., Brown, P. A., & Andrews, M. E. Remission of chronic ruminative vomiting through a reversal of social contingencies. *Behaviour Research and Therapy,* 1978, *16,* 134–146.

9

Stereotyped Movement Disorders*

Michael D. Wesolowski
The Sparks Center for Developmental and Learning Disorders
University of Alabama in Birmingham

Richard J. Zawlocki
West Virginia Rehabilitation Research and Training Center
West Virginia University

INTRODUCTION

Stereotyped movements are repetitive, persistent, nonfunctional behaviors exhibited by almost everyone. Some people pace, while others tap their toes or pencils. Cigarette smoking, overeating, and overdrinking could be considered stereotyped behaviors in the broad sense. Stereotyped movements only become disorders requiring treatment when they interfere with learning, result in an unattractive appearance, inhibit social interaction, or cause tissue damage. We will only address those disorders classified as *stereotyped movement disorders* by the *Diagnostic and Statistical Manual of Mental Disorders* (DSM-III).

These include transient tics, chronic motor tics, Tourette's syndrome, and atypical stereotyped movement disorders. Stereotyped movement disorders are primarily characterized by DSM-III as involving tics. For the purpose of this chapter, we will define tics as any involuntary, repetitious, spasmodic muscle contraction.

---

* The preparation of this chapter was supported by the National Institute of Handicapped Research through the West Virginia Rehabilitation Research and Training Center, West Virginia University, Morgantown, W. V. 26506. The authors would like to express their gratitude to Deborah J. Hendricks and Janet Boyles for their assistance in the preparation of this manuscript.

Transient Tic Disorders

Transient tics are involuntary, repetitive, and rapid movements. The duration of the tic is at least one month, but not more than one year. Surveys of school-children have reported that from 12 to 24 percent of the children have had some kind of tic. Although most children exhibit some stereotyped movement, the frequency of such behavior diminishes as the nervous system develops (Yates, 1970). Tics are more common in children than in adults (Hersen & Eisler, 1973) and affect males three times more often than females (Tapia, 1969).

Chronic Motor Tic Disorders

Chronic motor tics usually involve no more than three muscle groups at one time, and the duration is at least one year. Most published studies combine estimates of prevalence for both tics and Tourette syndrome (TS). An estimate for TS and chronic motor tic disorders is 1.6 percent (Baron, Shapiro, Shapiro, & Rainer, 1981), meaning that 1.554 percent of the U.S. population or about 2,428,800 people have chronic motor tics (since the estimate for TS is about 0.046 percent).

The most commonly treated tic in the behavioral literature is spasmodic torticollis, and most authors classify torticollis as a form of torsion dystonia. Paterson (1945) found an incidence of spasmodic torticollis of about 1 percent among psychiatric admissions and .02 percent among general hospital admissions. Marsden (1976), however, points to the lack of evidence that the incidence for psychiatric disorders in dystonic patients is any greater than in the normal population.

Because the neck is usually the most affected area in dystonia, the earliest cases in the literature were referred to as spasmodic torticollis, although other parts of the body were affected by the disorder, as is shown in sketches (Gowers, 1888). The tendency to diagnose this disorder as spasmodic torticollis, despite involvement of other areas, still persists today (Hirschmann & Mayer, 1964). The first cases of dystonia were thought to have hysterical or neurotic bases. Again, the tendency today is to regard individuals in the early stages of the disorder as having a functional rather than organic illness (Eldridge, Riklan, & Cooper, 1969). According to Coleman (1970), dystonia is a rare syndrome but may be one of the most ancient; for example, the German literature contains a paper on severe torticollis, or dystonic twisting, of the neck in dinosaurs.

In 1911, Oppenheim coined the term *dystonia musculorum deformans*. Unfortunately, this term, which is most popular in the United States, is not accurate because muscles are not the basic problem and deformity is not present, especially in early stages; hypertonia is the only abnormality. In the same year, Flatau and Sterling (1911) suggested another label, *progressive torsion spasm of childhood*, which may be the most accurate description for the disorder (Eldridge, 1970).

Tourette's Syndrome (TS)

Descriptions of TS date back to 1489 when a priest was described as having motor and phonic tics and was thought to be a Satanic possession. Charcot (1885) named the disease after one of his students, Gilles de la Tourette (1885), who described the symptoms and course in detail. Once considered a rare clinical phenomenon, TS has been reported with increasing frequency in the past 15 years (Hersen & Eisler, 1973). The estimate of prevalance by the Tourette Syndrome Association is about 0.046 percent, or 100,000 TS patients in the United States. The male to female sex ratio is 3 to 1 for both tics and TS.

Atypical Stereotyped Movement Disorders

These disorders involve unusual mannerisms by retarded and autistic individuals. Stereotypy has been observed in the majority (about 65 percent) of institutionalized developmentally disabled children (Berkson & Davenport, 1962). Body rocking, head rolling, and hand waving occurred in 66 percent, 63 percent, and 57 percent, respectively, of Kaufman & Levitt's (1965) sample of 83 institutionalized retarded persons. Other kinds of stereotyped behavior among this population include eye poking, head banging, body twirling, face slapping, object spinning, and digit sucking.

DESCRIPTION

Stereotyped movement disorders have four major characteristics in common: (1) they are repetitive, (2) nonfunctional, (3) persistent, and (4) some voluntary control can be maintained over the movement. Tics may occur in various forms throughout the body, including blinking, twitching, or squinting of the eyes; facial grimaces; nasal wheezing; trembling of the hands; jerking of the arms, elbows, head, shoulders, legs, feet, mouth, or cheeks; and contractions of the stomach (Hersen & Eisler, 1973). The movements can be voluntarily suppressed for minutes to hours. The intensity varies over weeks or months in transient tics but remains constant in chronic tics. The most common transient tic is an eye blink or other facial tic; however, the whole head, torso, or limbs may be involved. All tics are exacerbated by stress or anticipation but disappear during sleep and may be attenuated during absorbing activities.

The age of onset for transient tics is always during childhood or early adolescence and may begin as early as two years of age. Chronic motor tics usually begin in childhood but may occur after age 40. When the onset is in adult life, the tic tends to be limited to a single muscle group.

Dystonia has a distinct clinical picture, although variations exist that are associated with different etiologies. Torticollis and retrocollis are present. One or more extremities become affected, making it difficult to walk and/or write.

Truncal movements take the form of scoliosis and lordosis. Orofacial spasms with retrocollis may make it difficult to swallow and talk. Dystonic movements are generally slow, sustained, involuntary, and twisting. They may sometimes be rapid, repetitive, and jerky, in which case they are termed *dystonic spasms*. Dystonic movements may be generalized (affecting the entire body), segmental (affecting the neck and one or two limbs), or focal (affecting localized muscle groups). Symptoms may begin anywhere and exhibit a rapid and steady progression. The principal clinical abnormality in dystonia is cocontraction of antagonistic muscles, occurring first during voluntary movement and later during attempts to maintain posture or during rest. These symptoms are aggravated by stress, attempts at hand-eye coordination (e.g., writing, eating, dressing), and locomotion. In the early stages, another symptom is an inability to fall asleep. The dystonic symptoms are completely abolished once the person is asleep. Studies of EEG patterns suggest an imbalance between rapid eye movement (REM) sleep and non-REM sleep (Coleman & Barnet, 1969).

Cooper (1970) presents points that suggest a diagnosis of dystonia: (1) normal birth delivery and uneventful development during the first years of life; (2) insidious appearance of symptoms, usually between the ages of 7 and 13 years, with steady progression in severity; (3) absence of other neurological or psychological abnormalities; (4) presence of similar disease in other family members or history of Jewish ancestry or both. Symptoms may remit after adolescence or actually improve. A feature associated with dystonia reported by several authors is superior intelligence.

The following description of Tourette syndrome is largely taken from a translation of Tourette's original 1885 article by Goetz and Klawans (1982). The condition usually starts at a young age, between 2 and 13 years. Movements begin in the face (eye squinting, grimaces, masseter contractions) or upper extremities. The arms will shake, extend, and contract, and then the neck muscles become involved, flinging the head from one side to the other. The lower extremities eventually are affected, with the whole leg or both legs moving. The most common movement is a jump; hence, the term for those afflicted is *jumpers*. In the majority of cases, all movements are executed simultaneously. The movements may vary, but they maintain these general characteristics in all subjects. Two characteristics are the *abruptness* with which the movements appear and their *rapidity*. Facial and upper extremity movements recur every few minutes, while larger body movements, such as jumps, may only be seen every 15 minutes to an hour. During sleep, the tics cease.

Patients can experience spontaneous periods of remission when tics become minimal. This period can last for years, and the patients may consider themselves cured, until they find the tics have suddenly recurred.

The disease may be limited to the motor tics, but in the majority of cases the movements are followed by other signs more characteristic of TS. At the height of a movement, the patient will shout an inarticulate sound and then echo something just spoken by another individual. This echolalia is often accompanied by echopraxia, or imitating actions. Palilalia, or repeating one's own words or phrases, may also be present. The last symptom to evolve is co-prolalia, or the use of obscene words. More than half of TS patients have coprolalia, with the most common words reported in several surveys to be "fuck" and "shit." The phenomenon of coprolalia has been the keystone of the argument for the psychogenic basis of TS (Abuzzahab & Anderson, 1979).

Nuwer (1982) presents three reasons as to why coprolalia is organic. First, coprolalia occurs in other neurological disorders. Second, the verbalizations in TS differ from ordinary exclamations since they are of unusual cadence, pitch, volume, and imprecise pronunciation of phonemes. And third, the specific words uttered in coprolalia are often the same ones produced when a computer joins English phonemes in a pseudo-random fashion. Other associated features may be nonspecific EEG abnormalities, soft neurological signs, hyperactivity, or perceptual problems during infancy and childhood. These occur in about half of the individuals with TS.

The range of severity in stereotyped movement disorders varies depending on the particular topography, intensity, and development. In mentally retarded or autistic individuals, for example, stereotyped movement disorders typically occur as innocuous forms of self-stimulation, including body rocking, head rolling, or hand waving. In its extreme form, however, stereotypy may become self-injurious (Azrin & Wesolowski, 1980; Carr, 1977; Wesolowski & Zaw-locki, 1982). Self-injury causes tissue damage and may take many forms, such as head banging, eye poking, biting, scratching, or hitting oneself. Chronic motor tics may not only be a source of social embarrassment, but also of severe physical disabilities.

CONCEPTUALIZATION

Most stereotyped movement disorders probably have similar origins whether they are exhibited by autistic, retarded, or "normal" persons. In many cases, stereotyped acts often start as behavior presenting few problems for the individual or others. Many tic syndromes may have a neurological basis, but environmental factors may increase severity as the tic becomes more evident and chronic. Some people may begin a habit by imitating the behavior of a family member or friend.

Stereotyped movements usually begin at low rates and gradually increase in frequency over a period of months or years. Little annoyance or inconvenience usually results with infrequent stereotypy. As the habit begins occurring more frequently, the individual becomes accustomed to the inconvenience of the habit, and it then becomes a real problem.

Habits typically become so inculcated into people's everyday activities that affected individuals do not notice them. Furthermore, once a tic becomes well established, people may not react to it because they feel they will embarrass the person. In addition, people with a tic sometimes deny its existence, thereby fostering further inhibition in other individuals.

Several hypotheses have been put forth by learning theorists to explain stereotyped movement disorders, especially with respect to retarded and autistic populations (see reviews by Baumeister & Forehand, 1973; Carr, 1977; Frankel and Simmons, 1976; and Russo, Carr, & Lovaas, 1980). They have concluded stereotypy is usually a learned response controlled by its effects on the individual and others. This conclusion is based on data supporting three major hypotheses.

The positive reinforcement hypothesis views stereotypy as a means of obtaining social attention. Thus, stereotyped behavior should decrease when social consequences are withdrawn. The negative reinforcement hypothesis views stereotypy as a means of avoiding unpleasant or demanding situations. For example, an adult might require less of a child with a stereotyped movement disorder. The self-stimulation hypothesis states that some forms of stereotypy are caused and maintained by its sensory stimulation. This hypothesis assumes that an optimal level of stimulation is needed for each individual and that stereotypy occurs when stimulation is at insufficient levels. Numerous animal experiments and studies with retarded individuals have demonstrated higher rates of stereotypy in impoverished conditions (Berkson & Mason, 1964; Berkson & Davenport, 1962; Harlow & Harlow, 1971).

There is a great deal of evidence supporting organic bases for stereotypy. For example, Luria (1973) has related the location of brain lesions to different kinds of behavioral disturbances. In particular, Luria (1973) noted, "The inability of patients with massive lesions of the frontal lobes to carry out an assigned programme is . . . replaced by *uncontrollable floods of inert stereotypes*" (p. 206). Thus, when persons with lesions of the frontal lobes perform a series of tasks roughly equal with respect to difficulty, they tend to exhibit similar activity or some repetitive behavior in subsequent tasks.

Stevens and Blanchley (1966) have suggested that TS is a metabolic disturbance involving a central nervous system enzyme or neurotransmitter dysfunction. The reports of often dramatic relief by the administration of certain drugs indicate that an organic basis cannot be ruled out and that a biochemical anomaly may be present (Thomas, Abrams, & Johnson, 1971). Drugs providing relief for patients with TS are dopamine receptor blocking agents, while levodropa, a precursor to dopamine, aggravates TS symptoms. This suggests that TS might result from overactivity in one or more central dopaminergic systems of the basal ganglia. Friedhoff (1982) presents evidence that the locus of the pathology is the striated dopaminergic membrane receptors. Because of its early onset, TS appears to be a disorder of maturation of one or more aspects of the central nervous system (Friedhoff, 1982).

The question of organic impairment has been raised not only for TS but also for tics in general. Studies of families of patients with TS have shown a high frequency of chronic motor tics as well as an increased frequency of TS among relatives (Kidd & Pauls, 1982; Shapiro, Shapiro, Bruun, & Sweet, 1978). Thus, there is evidence that tics and TS are hereditary, although the genetic transmission is extremely complex.

Although tics and TS occur in all racial and ethnic groups, several studies indicate that TS is more prevalent among people of East European Jewish ancestry (Shapiro & Shapiro, 1982a; Shapiro, et al., 1978; Wassman, Eldridge, Abuzzahab, & Nee, 1978).

Dystonia has been found to be related to disturbances in the basal ganglia, but the dysfunction seems to result from underactivity in the dopaminergic system. Most dystonias have a genetic basis, although some may result from environmental influences, for example, encephalitis. Eldridge (1970) surveyed neurological centers throughout the United States between 1967 and 1969 and ascertained 578 families with one or more members having torsion dystonia, for example, 0.299 per 100,000 people. Among the Jewish population, however, 148 families of the total 578 (25 percent) had dystonia, or 2.52 per 100,000 people. The prevalence of dystonia among Jews is about eight times that of all other ethnic groups combined.

Lesch-Nyhan syndrome is an example of an X-linked genetic disorder occurring exclusively in males (Nyhan, 1968). Symptoms of the disease include muscle spasticity, athetoid cerebral palsy, mental retardation, hyperuricemia, and a deficiency of the enzyme hypoxanthine guanine phosphoribosyl transferase, which results in the failure of purine metabolism (Lesch & Nyhan, 1964). Self-injurious behavior is also part of the syndrome and takes the form of compulsive, repetitive biting of the lips, tongue, and fingers (Dizmang & Cheatham, 1970). The similarity in stereotyped behaviors and biochemistry led Shapiro, Shapiro, Bruun, Sweet, Wayne, and Solomon (1976) and Coleman (1976) to conclude that the same genetic mechanism is involved in Lesch-Nyhan syndrome, dystonia, and Tourette's syndrome.

Cornelia de Lange syndrome (de Lange, 1933) is diagnosed by a myriad of physical characteristics, including mental retardation, retarded growth, low birth weight, hirsutism, a small nose, long eyelashes, turned-down lips, micrognathia, and relative diminutiveness of the face and hands (Bryson, Sakati, Nyhan, & Fish, 1971). Karyotypic examinations have shown the presence of chromosomal segments in the cells of some of these children, but their contribution is unclear at this time (Jervis & Stimson, 1963). The topographies of stereotyped self-injury in children with this disease include self-scratching, hitting their faces, biting their fingers, lips, shoulders, and knees, and picking at their eyelids (Shear, Nyhan, Kirman, & Stern, 1971). There does not appear to be a definite pattern of stereotypy seen across children with this disorder, and no phenotypic differences have been found between children exhibiting self-injury and those who do not (Bryson et al., 1971). The lack of an identifiable genetic basis for the disorder, the variability in the topography of the stereotyped self-injury, and the successful treatment of the behavior by operant conditioning (Shear et al., 1971) all suggest that stereotyped self-injury in Cornelia de Lange syndrome may be a product of organic abnormality influenced by environmental factors (Russo et al., 1980).

Self-injury also may accompany otitis media, a painful middle ear infection commonly found in pediatric populations. De Lissovoy (1963) found a higher incidence of otitis media in the head-banger group (6 out of 15) than in the control group (1 out of 15) and concluded that head banging was a form of pain relief. The data are difficult to interpret, however, because some of the children who did not have otitis media banged their heads anyway (Carr, 1977).

Self-stimulatory behavior may be performed to induce symptoms of underlying pathological conditions, such as epileptic seizures. Fabish and Darbyshire (1965) have described self-induced seizures in epileptic patients by hyperventilation. Wright (1973) reported self-induced seizures resulting from rapid hand movements in front of the eyes or blinking. Certain frequencies of photic stimulation are powerful reinforcers for autistic children, but repetitive light does not seem to be as potent a reinforcer for retarded children (Frankel, Freeman, Ritvo, Chikami, & Carr, 1976). Children with certain visual impairments may press their fingers into their eyes to produce phosphene (Franceschetti, 1947), which is the sensation of light resulting from the stimulation of the retina or optic nerve produced either by mechanical or electrical means. The topography of this digito-occular phenomenon may vary somewhat, but all children press their fingers into their eyes, sometimes causing tissue damage to the orbital structures or the eyelids (Franceschetti, 1947). Landwirth (1964) also reported stereotyped behavior in children with visual sensory neuropathy and retinitis pigmentosa.

Stereotypy appears to occur more frequently in children with developmental disorders, such as mental retardation, autism, brain damage (Carr, 1977), sensory neuropathy, dysautonomia (Franceschetti, 1947; Landwirth, 1964), and childhood schizophrenia (Frankel & Simmons, 1976). It appears that organic pathology and environmental factors predispose these populations to increased risk for stereotyped movement disorders.

ASSESSMENT

Information used in the behavioral assessment can come from a variety of sources through two general methods: direct and indirect observation. Direct observation refers to immediately recording the stereotyped behavior by an observer. Walls, Haught, and Dowler (1982, p. 132) have identified four direct observation recording strategies: (1) event recording—counting the number of times the target behavior occurs in a specified amount of time; (2) interval recording—noting whether or not the target behavior occurs during each successive interval (typically of fairly short duration); (3) time-sampling recording—noting whether or not the target behavior occurs in short observation intervals separated by nonobservation periods. (4) outcome recording—counting the number of objects or behavioral products at the end of a specific period. Indirect observation, on the other hand, refers to gathering information from self-reports of the client by such techniques as interviews, questionnaires, and self-monitoring.

Direct Observation

Practitioners are more likely to use direct observation since confidence in the validity of the data resulting from direct observation is usually greater than data derived from other procedures (Haynes, 1978). Direct observation is used primarily to identify and quantify stereotypy, its determinants and covariants, and to evaluate treatment outcomes.

In most cases, direct observation of the stereotypy in the natural environment yields valid indices of that behavior and the variables of which it is a function. Stereotyped movements that are less reactive and more observable are preferable, and hence, they are more amenable to direct observation. It may be necessary, however, to attempt to measure other less accessible stereotyped behavior through more indirect methods.

There are several characteristics of stereotypy that may affect direct observation in natural environments. These include the rate of the behavior, situations in which it is most likely to occur, the social value of the behavior, and the cost of such observations. It is impractical and expensive to observe behaviors that do not occur frequently in the natural environment unless the observation is carried out by the clients. Some stereotyped behaviors occur in situations, e.g., the home, that make it difficult to use direct observation. Other behaviors, such as the sounds and movements associated with tic syndromes, are most readily recorded through self-monitoring. Stereotypy most conducive to direct observation are those occurring at relatively high frequencies in situations that permit more intrusive forms of observation. The stereotyped acitivty of autistic or retarded individuals is responsive to this kind of assessment since it often occupies a major portion of their behavioral repertoires. The use of rate measures, derived from direct observation in studies on stereotyped activity, has generated a large body of literature. Sensory extinction was designed originally as an assessment technique for determining the specific sensory consequences maintaining self-stimulatory behavior. Sensory extinction has been shown to be a useful assessment and treatment approach for self-stimulation in developmentally disabled children (Rincover, 1978; Rincover, Cook, Peoples, & Packard, 1979; Rincover & Devany, 1982).

Several technologies have been developed to provide information on stereotypy. These technologies involve types of automatic measurement devices, including a special seat with microswitches attached to runners or with a hinged back that breaks a beam of light; a mercury switch that may be fixed to a person's shoulder; a system of levers, guides, pulleys, and string; a telemetric helmet; an ultrasonic motion detector; and a stabilimetric cushion. Attempts to devise more precise ways of recording stereotypy produce more information on parameters of the behavior besides rate, for example, topography, duration of each response, intervals between responses, and magnitude. Demonstrating that the rate of a stereotyped movement disorder can be affected by some intervention is not always sufficient (Baumeister & Forehand, 1973). The use of a measurement technology that produces the maximum amount of information about a stereotyped movement disorder permits an accurate determination of factors responsible for the stereotypy.

Technology has also been applied to the assessment of torticollis. Brierly (1967) used a headgear with a mercury switch to measure deviations of the head. Bernhardt, Hersen, and Barlow (1972) had a client sit with his profile against grid markings on a wall to measure movements of the head. Whenever tic syndromes are being assessed, film or videotape should be used prior to, during, and after intervention to provide permanent records of the movement.

A primary factor affecting the applicability of observation procedures is reactivity. The presence of an observer or equipment alters the stimulus properties of the environment and yields data of questionable reliability. In such cases, the use of self-monitoring or hidden equipment can usually minimize disruption and the effects of reactivity. In addition, nonprofessional observers (e.g., family members, friends, teachers) may be used to gather data in a more economical and less reactive manner, provided they are properly trained and that their performance is monitored on occasion. Disorders occurring infrequently or in particular settings can be measured more efficiently by individuals in the environment. In cases where the stereotypy occurs frequently, however, it may be more desirable to use professionally trained observers or videotape to ensure objectivity.

The amount of time necessary to monitor a particular stereotyped movement adequately often varies inversely with the magnitude and variability of the disorder. Thus, when the rate varies between sessions or occurs infrequently, then more observation time is required to derive a reliable estimate of the typical rate. Usually, time sampling or interval recording is used in these circumstances. Sessions should be divided into smaller intervals to increase the likelihood that the data obtained will provide a valid index of stereotypy and the factors influencing it.

Creating an environment that provides certain information is another valuable strategy for several reasons. Structured environments may increase the probability of the occurrence of certain stereotyped movement disorders, and may reduce the variability of data. Structured environments can provide sensitive measures of the effects of particular intervention programs. The type of environment employed in the assessment will be a function of the goals of the observation, characteristics of the patient and the stereotypy, and hypotheses of interest. Such situations can involve the use of minimal structure in the natural environment as well as the use of a highly structured setting, such as a laboratory or clinic. Since observations of family interactions in the home are sometimes interrupted by telephone calls, television, or visitors, constraints may be placed on family members when observers are present so that data obtained in this setting are more reliable. The most frequent structures imposed in this situation are limiting the family to a few rooms, restricting phone calls and visitors, and keeping the television off. In hospital settings, routine interruptions, for example, taking of vital signs and visitation, may be controlled to prevent interference. These kinds of restrictions make it more likely that the data obtained will be as valid as possible.

The most frequently used structured environment is a clinic or hospital as a laboratory setting. This setting is used since it is where direct service often takes place. Care can be taken to employ as many familiar people and circumstances as possible so that the behavior may occur in a setting approximating the natural environment. In this contest, the patient is asked to do certain tasks either alone or with a family member while relevant data are recorded.

The laboratory or clinic usually presents the most favorable circumstances for implementing physiological assessment techniques. A client is seated in a controlled room with transducers attached to those areas that can be monitored for the physiological event under consideration. An adaptation period decreases the likelihood that data are confounded by the novel environment. After adaptation, the client is presented with various auditory or visual stimuli, exposed to some intervention, or asked to engage in various activities while being monitored.

Many behavior therapy procedures, including aversion conditioning, systematic desensitization, covert sensitization, relaxation training, and biofeedback, focus on either direct or indirect control of physiological variables. Modification of these physiological events is sometimes the primary goal of treatment. Interventions designed to reduce muscle tension, as in cases of movement disorders, represent one example. In other cases, treatment may be conceptualized as the modification of a mediating variable, for example, anxiety, thereby producing a reduction in stereotypy.

By their very nature, stereotyped movement disorders involve the contraction of muscles. Electromyography (EMG) measures electrical activity generated when muscles contract with the placement of surface or needle electrodes along a muscle to allow the changes in muscle action potential to be monitored in specific regions. Monitoring EMG levels of muscles associated with stereotypy during implementation of techniques, such as relaxation training or systematic desensitization, provides feedback to the clinician and client. This information aids the practitioner and client in planning, monitoring, and reformulating intervention.

Electrodermal activity also may be useful in monitoring intervention programs. When measured from palmar areas, electrodermal responses change as a function of cognitive activity and stress. Decreased skin resistance and increased skin potential is a reflection of increased sympathetic arousal or stress (Pinkerton, Hughes & Wenrich, 1982; Wesolowski & Deichmann, 1980). This approach is of value since most stereotyped movement disorders are characterized by excessive arousal of the sympathetic division of the autonomic nervous system either during or before symptom onset.

Several technologies offer promise in obtaining information about stereotyped movement disorders, including evoked potential (EP), regional cerebral blood flow (rCBF), and nuclear magnetic resonance (NMR)—all of which represent futuristic assessment technologies. These methods have limitations and require refinement as precise measurement systems for physiological functioning (e.g., neuronal activity in the brain, metabolic processes in muscles). Yet, they do represent a valuable means for assessing children's capacities for receiving and processing sensory input, since it can be problematic to adequately evaluate children with traditional perceptual tests and neurological exams.

The goal of EP techniques is the extraction of weak signals within the electrical activity of the brain, correlating with the presentation of certain stimuli. There are correlations between autistic children and abnormal brainstem auditory evoked responses (Sohmer & Student, 1978). Squires, Buchwald, Liley, and Strecker (1982) described the results of two studies demonstrating differences in the brainstem auditory evoked responses of retarded adults from those of nonretarded individuals.

Regional cerebral blood flow (rCBF) technology was designed to permit a quantitative and topographic examination of alterations of blood flow in the brain as a result of differential neuronal activity associated with various stimuli. The temporal resolution of rCBF is greater than EP procedures, but EP techniques do not provide a reliable and comprehensive topographical analysis of relationships between brain functioning and tasks as shown in rCBF studies (Thatcher & Maisel, 1979). An aspect of rCBF is the use of a radioactive isotope (e.g., Xenon 133), which is either inhaled or injected into the person's bloodstream. Thus, rCBF is more intrusive than EP, which employs surface electrodes.

Nuclear magnetic resonance (NMR) techniques have been applied to medical research only recently (Hoult, 1981). This technology makes it possible to ascertain the movement and structure of molecules. NMR has been adapted to monitor blood flow and to produce images as in brain tomography (Hawkes, Holland, Moore, & Worthington, 1980). There is little evidence showing any danger in using NMR technology, but the risks associated with NMR may not be known for years (Hoult, 1981). Although the application of NMR to medicine is relatively new, it appears to be potentially the most valuable diagnostic tool for practitioners concerned with a wide variety of disorders. The three technologies EP, rCBF, and NMR may represent invaluable assessment methodologies capable of making significant contributions in the clarification of etiology of numerous human disorders.

Indirect Assessment

The interview is probably the oldest and most frequently used assessment procedure. The purpose of the interview is to obtain preliminary information pertinent to the stereotyped movement disorder and variables responsible for it. This information provides an overview of the client's problem and should suggest areas in which more rigorous assessment will be appropriate. The interview has a significant influence on the client's expectations as well as on the outcome of intervention since it typically occurs during the initial meeting between patient and practitioner.

The format of the interview can vary from being highly structured to open, depending on the specific goals. Structured interviews are more likely to be employed in conjunction with interventions designed around physiological problems or in situations in which the interviewer has been informed of the referral problem. An unstructured interview imposes mimimal constraints on the subjects discussed, since the interviewer follows cues provided by the client and does not restrict questioning. Unstructured interviews are more likely to be used when clients have multiple behavior problems or when disorders have not been indicated prior to the interview. Practitioners often use it as a follow-up to the structured interview to obtain additional information about the disorder.

Questionnaires are often used in conjunction with the initial interview. They can be self-administered, thereby requiring little time to interpret, and can yield quantitative data relevant to the stereotyped behavior. Questionnaires usually do not deal directly with the assessment of specific physiological dysfunctions but may be useful in determining certain components of the problem (e.g., levels of stress and anxiety). Information also may be acquired through questionnaires designed to measure assertiveness, depression, and choices of reinforcement.

Self-monitoring consists of clients' self-observation and systematic recording of their problem. The observations usually focus on the topography of the stereotypy as well as on the antecendents and consequences of this behavior. There are several advantages to self-monitoring. First, the process can be used as a means of educating the client, as an intervention strategy to facilitate behavior change, and as a way to assess the effectiveness of intervention. Second, this technique may be a more efficient assessment method than other procedures for infrequent stereotyped behaviors. Third, covert behaviors also can be more validly assessed through self-monitoring. Finally, self-monitoring may be useful when other methods are ineffective, produce reactive effects, require an extensive amount of time, or are simply invalid.

There are numerous methods by which a client can monitor stereotypy. Some techniques that have been used involve wrist counters, index cards, data-recording forms, slips of paper, and notebooks. Contiguity between the stereotyped behavior and its recording seems to affect the accuracy of self-monitoring, and therefore, the recording device should remain easily accessible to the client. The client also should be instructed to make a record of the stereotypy immediately after its occurrence. Practitioners can increase the probability that self-report data will be an accurate representation if time is taken to ensure that the patient can identify the target behavior, understand the recording methods, and appreciate the importance of accurate records.

There is sufficient evidence to indicate that the act of self-monitoring itself may change the rate or topography of the monitored behavior. Factors affecting the degree of reactivity to self-monitoring include recording data prior to or following the emission of the behavior, recording either occurrence or non-occurrences, the contiguity between the behavior and its recording, the schedule of self-monitoring, social contingencies associated with self-monitoring, self-administered contingencies, and personal and social value associated with the monitored behavior. Data derived from self-monitoring may be an accurate reflection of the current rate, but not of the rate prior to self-monitoring or when self-monitoring is not occurring. Nevertheless, in the case of tics, it may be the assessment procedure of greatest utility.

TREATMENT

Similar behavioral treatments have been employed on stereotyped movement disorders. They include operant techniques of reinforcement and punishment, training incompatible responses, response prevention and interruption, self-monitoring, and biofeedback. Medical treatments have emphasized drugs and/ or surgery depending on the disorder.

Transient Tic Disorder

The fact that transient tics are characterized by a duration of not more than one year suggests that there may not be a need for treatment. The child's tic should be ignored and not ridiculed or imitated. The child also should not receive special assistance because of the tic. However, if the whole head, limbs, neck, or torso is affected, it may be the first symptom of dystonia or other chronic motor tic syndrome. Treatment should then be pursued as early as possible, since the data suggest more promising outcomes if treatment begins during the first year after onset. The treatment in these cases should be a combination of biofeedback training and habit reversal. These treatments are explained in detail in the next section.

Chronic Motor Tic Disorders

One of the earliest approaches was mechanical control of localized tics. Metal bands were used for torticollis, and orthopedic casting was used for affected limbs (Eldridge, 1970). Hypnosis was also one of the earliest methods for treating chronic tics but is of limited value (Flatau & Sterling, 1911). Electro-convulsive therapy was attempted but has no place in the treatment of chronic tics (Eldridge et al., 1969).

Neurosurgery has a long history with movement disorders. Newer techniques, such as cryosurgery and stereotactic surgery, have provided significant relief for many patients (Cooper, 1969). Differences in the age of patients, types of disorder, techniques employed, sights in the brain attacked, and definitions of improvement make it difficult to compare the results of various studies. As reported by Eldridge (1970), of the 257 patients who have undergone neurosurgery, 180 (70 percent) were said to have beneficial long-term results; 63 were described as having no benefit or as having their conditions worsen; and 14 were reported as having improved during the short term they were observed. The most effective operative sight is the region of the ventral left nucleus of the thalmus. In a 20-year follow-up on 208 patients (Cooper, 1976), 69.7 percent were rated improved; 18.3 percent were about the same; and 12 percent were worse. Cooper predicted that 84 percent of the patients would have been worse if they had not had surgery. In general, thalamic surgery seems to be of most benefit when there is little in the way of torticollis or truncal involvement. In contrast, the greatest risks and poorest results may be in those cases in which axial involvement predominates. Risks include weakness, paresis, sensory dysfunction, and pseudobulbar complications.

Waltz and Davis (1983) have investigated the use of spinal cord stimulation in the treatment of movement disorders, i. e., cerebral palsy, multiple sclerosis, spasticity, athetosis, and dystonia. A system of four electrodes is incorporated into a fine, thin catheter assembly that can be installed through a single epidural needle into the cervical area between C2 and C4. There are 18 different combinations in the four electrode system, and patients respond to a specific electrode combination. Results vary according to disorders, but reports show that between 70 and 85 percent of the patients have marked improvements.

Numerous pharmacologic agents have been tried in treating chronic tics. Among the earliest were magnesium sulfate and the combination of morphine and scopolamine. Later, the successful use of quinine and vitamins E and B6 were reported enthusiastically by several authors. The physiotherapy accompanying these treatments was reported by patients to be at least as helpful as the chemical agents. In recent years, claims have been made for the use of orphenadrine, ACTH, large doses of chloropromazine, and diazepam in treating chronic tic disorders (Eldridge, 1970). Diazepam (valium) has been the most useful drug, but response has varied. Several patients had dramatic improvement that, unfortunately, lasted only a few days. Many helped by diazepam report that periodically changing the dose or time schedule has improved the efficacy of the drug. Burke and Fahn (1983) have concluded that trihexyphenidyl has a benefit for patients, especially children, with torsion dystonia. Haloperidol has been reported to aggravate symptoms when used alone for torsion dystonia but has been effective for facial dyskinesia (Gilbert,

1972) and Tourette's syndrome (Shapiro & Shapiro, 1968). More recently, haloperidol has improved torsion dystonia (Mandell, 1970).

For the past 15 years, there has been great interest in the use of L-dopa in dystonia. In 1964, L-dopa was reported to have benefited a patient with torticollis, but progressive dystonic symptoms in other parts of his body suggested generalized torsion dystonia (Hirschmann & Mayer, 1964). Since then, there have been several reports of the usefulness of L-dopa in treating various forms of dystonia (Coleman & Barnet, 1969). With therapeutic dosages of L-dopa, 20 percent of the patients may benefit, while others may experience exacerbation (Barbeau, 1970; Colemen, 1970).

There is wide variation in the basic physiologic properties of the drugs used, but a feature common to most is that they promote relaxation and reduce anxiety. This also may explain why many clients with chronic tics are reported to be addicted to alcohol or other drugs. Failure of any drug to help an individual with chronic tics does not rule out the possibility that the drug might be helpful at a different stage or to an individual with another form of chronic tic (Eldridge, 1970).

Massed or negative practice, a technique in which the client voluntarily reproduces the movement rapidly and repeatedly, has been the oldest and most popular behavior therapy used for chronic tics (Dunlap, 1932). Continual responding or practice produces fatigue, making further performance of the movement uncomfortable. Resting or engaging in behavior other than the abnormal movement is reinforced by reduction of fatigue or muscular discomfort. Thus, the client becomes less able to voluntarily produce the abnormal behavior, thereby experiencing a reduction in the involuntary movement. In addition, the movement is practiced in new situations, weakening its connection with the usual eliciting stimuli. Videotape may facilitate the reproduction of the behavior because the client can repeatedly study the movements in detail. The videotapes also can be replayed at a later date in treatment when the improved performance may serve as added feedback (Hersen & Eisler, 1973).

Practice periods can range from very brief intervals, such as Yates' (1958) procedure (five one-minute trials interspersed with one-minute rest intervals), to protracted periods (up to six hours with a rest period of up to several weeks). A cue, such as a metronome, may facilitate training (Clark, 1963). Conclusive evidence determining the optimal length of practice is not available, but Yates (1970) suggests prolonged practice is more effective than brief periods. As with any behavior therapy, practice should occur in social situations approximating those in which the movement has been a problem so as to facilitate generalization. For example, other people can be brought into the therapy room (Wesolowski, 1982; Yates, 1970), and the patient can practice at home. Smelling salts (Knepler & Sewall, 1974) and punishing incorrect responses with shock (Clark, 1963) have been used in conjunction with negative practice.

A number of reports have attested to the effectiveness of negative practice in treating tics (Agras & Marshall, 1965; Chapel, 1970; Clark, 1963; Nicassio,

Liberman, Patterson, Ramirez, & Sanders, 1972; Rafi, 1962; Walton, 1961; Yates, 1958; 1970). Less positive results, such as no improvements (Savicki & Carlin, 1972), negative practice not working as well as other behavior therapies (Azrin, Nunn, & Frantz, 1980), or problems associated with its use (Feldman & Werry, 1966; Lahey, McNees, & McNees, 1973) have also been noted.

Azrin et al. (1980) compared negative practice with habit reversal in treating chronic tics. Figure 9–1 shows that habit reversal eliminated most of the symptoms in one week, while negative practice initially reduced tics by about 40 percent. However, the average rate increased by 10 percent and leveled off.

FIGURE 9–1

Reduction of Tics by Two Treatment Methods

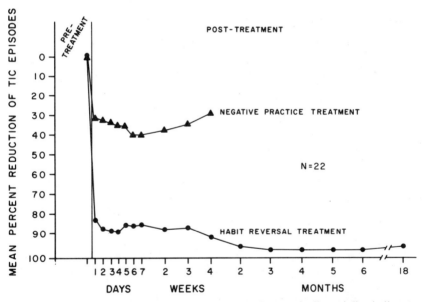

The tic frequency is expressed as the average percentage reduction relative to the pre-treatment frequency, which is 0 percent reduction by definition. The vertical dotted line designates the time when treatment was given. Time since treatment is expressed in days for the first week, in weeks for the first month, and in months thereafter plus an 18-month follow-up. The day designated "0" is when treatment was given. The upper curve is for the patients receiving negative practice and the lower curve is for those receiving habit reversal treatment.

Source: N. H. Azrin, R. G. Nunn, and S. E. Frantz, "Habit Reversal vs. Negative Practice Treatment of Nervous Tics," *Behavior Therapy* 11 (1980), pp. 169–178. Reprinted with permission.

One problem of negative practice is that it is a tedious procedure and may be unpleasant for the therapist and client (Lahey et al., 1973). Another major problem is the emotional reaction sometimes accompanying this procedure. The tic represents a conditioned, emotional response to anxiety and a source of anxiety, which creates a vicious cycle. Negative practice tries to break this cycle at the point of the tic but may cause more anxiety and actually prove detrimental (Feldman & Werry, 1966). Muscle relaxation or medication may be used in conjunction with or as preparation for negative practice training with particularly anxious patients. Frederick (1971), for example, treated a woman with an eye blink tic by preliminary sessions of systematic desensitization to stimuli that bore little relationship to the tic. Once the hierarchy was completed, negative practice was begun, although the tic had already shown marked improvement. Medication, such as meprobamate (Turner, Hersen, & Alford, 1974) or barbituates (Yates, 1970), also may serve to break the anxiety cycle and facilitate negative practice.

Feedback, in a variety of forms, has been used successfully to treat movement disorders. Barrett (1962) found that contingent white noise and interruption of music reduced multiple violent tics. Brierly (1967) cured two clients of torticollis by administering shock to their wrists when their heads were not in a normal position as measured by a headgear with a mercury switch. Bernhardt et al. (1972) eliminated torticollis using a different kind of feedback. Their clients sat with their profiles against grid markings on a wall, and a light was turned on whenever they moved their heads upward to a certain degree. The light was terminated only after the client's head returned to a specific position. Ericksen & Huber (1975) eliminated torticollis by having their client fixate on a point on the wall and make small head movements in synchronization to the beat of a metronome.

One of the most promising behavior therapies for torticollis and dystonia is electromyographic (EMG) feedback. The first application of EMG feedback in the treatment of spasmodic torticollis was reported by Cleeland (1973). Auditory EMG feedback from the sternocleidomastoid muscle was combined with mild shocks to the fingertips during spasms of this muscle. Nine of 10 subjects showed a 77 percent reduction is spasm frequency after treatment. At an 18-month follow-up, six of these nine clients showed further spasm reduction.

Cleeland (1979) has consistently found lower spasm frequency in trials using both shock and feedback than using either technique by itself. Shock is set at a level between 3 and 5 milliamps, which patients usually describe as unpleasant but not painful. This led Cleeland to question the aversive nature of the shock and to believe it was a type of tactile biofeedback. Spasm contingent shock is not used until the head initially moves. The sternocleidomastoid muscle on the side of the neck opposite to the direction of head turning demonstrates the greatest spasmodic activity. Electrodes are placed approximately 1 centimeter apart along the belly of this muscle. Patients are hospitalized for two to three weeks and receive 45 minutes of biofeedback sessions daily Monday through Friday. Physical therapy accompanies biofeedback training to increase the range of motion of the head. Since the degree of spasm is often increased by tasks involving hand-eye coordination, patients may spend time working on individualized projects and occupational therapy. Movement disorders, especially torticollis, are usually exacerbated by walking. Patients work on spasm control while walking, using portable EMG devices. Patients are seen on an outpatient schedule on a decreasing basis (e.g., two days per week for the first month, and one day per week for the second and third outpatient month) after discharge from the hospital.

Of 52 patients at the end of training, 8 of them showed minimum or no benefits, 28 showed moderate success, and 16 showed marked improvement. At a follow-up of 30.5 months, 11 showed little or no success, 18 exhibited some benefits, and 8 showed substantial changes, with 15 patients lost to follow-up. The most dramatic improvements were shown in patients who had symptoms for less than 12 months. Of those patients ($n = 10$), 70 percent showed moderate to marked improvement. As with other movement disorder studies, the more rapidly biofeedback and other behavioral interventions can occur, the greater the likelihood of a successful outcome (Cleeland, 1979).

Cleeland's work parallels that of Brudny and his colleagues (Brudny, Grynbaum & Korein, 1974; Brudny, et al., 1976; Korein, et al., 1976). Brudny's biofeedback training differs from Cleeland's in several respects. First, Brudny does not use shock contingent on muscle spasms. Second, Brudny uses visual as well as audio feedback. Third, Brudny uses 8 to 12 weeks of therapy with 1/2 hour sessions scheduled three times a week. Fourth, Brudny makes no mention of occupational or physical activities in his reports.

Brudny et al. (1974) reports having treated 13 patients with torticollis and five patients with dystonia (the primary problem was torticollis). All the patients receiving feedback could maintain head positions in neutral states for the duration of the session with minor fluctuations; of those without feedback, nine could maintain the neutral head positions for significant periods. In the five cases with more complete dystonia, results were less satisfactory. Later, Brudny et al. (1976) treated 48 patients with torticollis and 7 patients with more complete dystonia. Of the 48 patients with torticollis, 20 had significant improvement. At follow-up (Korein et al., 1976), 19 of the 48 patients (40 percent) maintained significant long-term improvement. Six of the seven patients with dystonia involving extremities showed improvement after EMG feedback training, but three of these regressed during the follow-up period. Comparisons of Brudny's and Cleeland's long-term results show little difference. At follow-up, 50 percent of Cleeland's group in comparison to 40 percent of Brudny's group maintained improvement.

Azrin and Nunn (1973) have successfully used habit reversal to reduce torticollis and other tics. This procedure requires clients to become extremely aware of the movement by observing its occurrence in the mirror, learning what

ILLUSTRATION 9–1

NERVOUS HABIT OR TIC			COMPETING EXERCISE
SHOULDER-JERKING			SHOULDERS DEPRESSED
SHOULDER-JERKING ELBOW-FLAPPING			SHOULDERS AND HANDS PRESSURE
HEAD-JERKING			TENSING NECK
HEAD-SHAKING			TENSING NECK
EYELASH-PLUCKING			GRASPING OBJECTS
FINGERNAIL-BITING			GRASPING OBJECTS
THUMB-SUCKING			CLENCHING FISTS

(Left) Pictorial representation of the various types of nervous tics or habits. (Right) Type of competing exercise used for corresponding tic or habit. The arrows show the direction of isometric muscle contraction being exerted by the client.

Source: N. H. Azrin and R. G. Nunn, "Habit-Reversal: A Method of Eliminating Nervous Habits and Tics," *Behaviour Research and Therapy* 11 (1973), pp. 619–628. Reproduced with permission.

movements are precursors for the tic, and discovering what situations seem to produce the movement.

A competing response consisting of an isometric exercise incompatible to the tic should be developed to replace the tic (see Illustration 9–1). In the case of torticollis, a competing response of holding the chin tightly against the sternum for three to five minutes is practiced whenever the tic or the urge to perform the tic occurs. This isometric exercise also may be performed at various times throughout the day. Isotonic exercises are often used in conjunction with isometric exercises to strengthen flacid atrophied sternocleidomastoid muscles and to stretch out hypertrophied trapezius muscles. The client's family, friends, and co-workers also are asked to remind the client to perform the exercise and reinforce the client for not performing the tic. These persons sometimes have to be brought into the treatment room to see that the client can control the tic. As shown in figure 9–2, symptoms were eliminated in 14 days with a promising follow-up at five months.

The treatment of choice for chronic tics depends on the age of the patient and the progression of the disorder. If the patient is a young child, anticholinergic drugs (trihexyphenidyl or ethopropazine) may be beneficial. Thalamic neurosurgery is not recommended, given the findings of Waltz and Davis (1983) with spinal cord stimulation. In general, surgical techniques are not recommended for young children.

Behavior therapy is the treatment of choice to avoid surgery and drugs and especially if treatment is begun within 12 months of onset. Some type of broad spectrum behavior therapy with a combination of biofeedback training and habit reversal training should be employed. The intensive biofeedback training coupled with mild electric shock would not only teach the client how to relax the involved muscle, but also make the patient aware of the movement by providing contingent shock. The inclusion of physical and occupational therapy as an adjunct to biofeedback training would increase its efficacy. Another way to increase the awareness of the tic is awareness training in habit reversal. The competing response practice provides the client with a "fail-safe" response when the tic or the urge to perform the tic occurs. This enables the client to control the movement, gives an alternative to the tic, makes the client more aware of the movement, and strengthens atrophied muscles antagonistic to the abnormal movement.

Tourette's Syndrome

The earliest treatment for TS—exorcism—was sometimes successful, and afflicted individuals avoided being burned at the stake. Used throughout the centuries, exorcism, which was recently rejuvenated by the book and movie *The Exorcist* (based on an exaggerated description of a patient with TS), has apparently lost its effectiveness, since most of the two dozen patients who currently admit to using it have not been cured (Shapiro & Shapiro, 1982a).

FIGURE 9-2

Mean Percentage Reduction of Nervous Habits following Treatment by the Habit Reversal Method

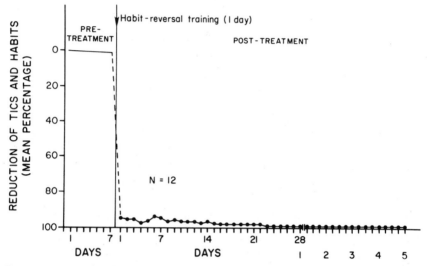

The pretreatment level is designated as 0% reduction and was obtained for the 7-day period immediately preceding treatment. The habit reversal training required about 2 hours on the day designated by the arrow and dotted line. The post-treatment data points are given daily for the first 28 days and monthly thereafter. Each data point is the average reduction relative to the pretreatment level. The data points are for all 12 clients up to Day 21, for 11 clients for 7 weeks, for 9 clients for 2 months, and for 7 clients for 5 months.

Source: N. H. Azrin and R. G. Nunn, "Habit-Reversal: A Method of Eliminating Nervous Habits and Tics," *Behaviour Research and Therapy* 11 (1973), pp. 619–628. Reproduced with permission.

A review of the literature until 1973 indicated that 89 percent of TS patients were improved after six months of treatment with the drug haloperidol, compared with 29 percent of those receiving various other therapies (Abuzzahab & Anderson, 1979). A subsequent review similarly found that of 137 patients given haloperidol, 82.5 percent were treated successfully, 8.3 percent had partial success, and 8.3 percent failed to benefit (Shapiro et al., 1978). Despite the success of haloperidol, many people would rather suffer the disabling TS symptoms than suffer the disabling side effects of the drug. The short-term side effects are drowsiness, apathy, depression, dystonic reactions, and pseudo-parkinsonism. More ominous are the potential long-term side effects, namely, tardive dyskinesia (Borison, et al., 1982), which is a drug induced syndrome consisting of persistent abnormal involuntary movements and persistent akathisia (motor restlessness). Prolonged exposure to antipsychotic drugs, such as phenothiazines or britayrophenones, causes tardive dyskinesia (Fahn, 1983).

Many researchers have recently tried to find a suitable substitute drug for haloperidol. Borison et al. (1982) compared haloperidol with clonidine, fluphenazine, trifluperazine, and lithium. Lithium was of little value, but neuroleptics, such as fluphenazine, produced fewer side effects than haloperidol. A non-neuroleptic, clonidine, was as efficacious as haloperidol and was without the adverse reactions. Shapiro and Shapiro (1982b) compared haloperidol to primozide, penfluridol, and clonidine. All drugs were judged as equal to or better than haloperidol in treating TS and with fewer side effects. Bruun (1982) treated 20 TS patients with clonidine. Ten patients received more benefits than with haloperidol, three preferred haloperidol, four had no relief, and three experienced side effects (irritability, nightmares, insomnia, and racing thoughts), causing them to discontinue clonidine. The most frequently reported side effects of clonidine are transient hypotension, drowsiness, and dry mouth. These appear to be dose related and usually subside during treatment.

A variety of behavioral procedures have been used to treat TS. Frequencies of the tics reported regularly to the therapist, for example, once a day by phone, provided multiple opportunities to reinforce these counts (Thomas et al., 1971). Hutzell, Platzek and Logue (1974) reduced the symptoms of TS in an 11-year-old child by having him count the tics on a hand counter and incorporate this into a game played with the therapist. Negative practice has been found to be somewhat effective with TS (Clark, 1966). Tophoff (1973) used negative practice, relaxation, and assertion training to successfully treat TS; nevertheless, the efficacy of negative practice is questionable, given the findings of Azrin et al. (1980), Feldman and Werry (1966), Lahey et al. (1973), and Savicki and Carlin (1972). Miller (1970) successfully treated TS in a child using time-out and differential reinforcement. Reinforcement of incompatible behavior has been found useful with tic syndromes (Browning & Stover, 1971; Longin, Kohn, & Macurik, 1974). Browning and Stover (1971) successfully treated a young boy with TS by extinction, substituting the explosive bark with a verbal phrase (e.g., "pay attention to me"), and reinforcement for periods of control.

The treatment of choice for TS should be a broad spectrum approach. The patient should see a neurologist to see if a drug or combination of drugs would be helpful. In our review, clonidine appears to be the best drug to try first. Along with drug therapy, relaxation training and habit reversal (Azrin & Nunn, 1973) would be beneficial. These treatments exemplify the use of awareness training, teaching incompatible responses, reinforcing periods of tic control, and involving other people in the therapeutic procedure.

Atypical Stereotyped Movement Disorders

A large number of treatments for stereotyped movement disorders have been employed with autistic and retarded individuals. There have been a number of reviews describing the effectiveness of behaviorally oriented therapeutic efforts in reducing self-injury and self-stimulatory behavior (e.g., Baumeister & Forehand, 1973; Forehand & Baumeister, 1976; Frankel & Simmons, 1976; Luiselli, 1981; Picker, Poling, & Parker, 1979; Russo et al., 1980).

Procedures used to eliminate or reduce self-stimulatory and self-injurious behavior of autistic and retarded children include such punishment techniques as electric shock, hair pulling, shouting and shaking, slapping, aromatic ammonia, mouthwash, water mist, isolation, brief immobilization or physical restraint, response interruption, overcorrection, sensory extinction, and sensory time-out techniques like facial screening. Reductions in self-injury and self-stimulation of retarded and autistic children also have been achieved through differential reinforcement of other behavior (DRO) (Repp, Deitz, & Speir, 1974) and differential reinforcement of incompatible behavior (DRI) (Tarpley & Schroeder, 1979). The administration of different tranquilizing drugs, including chlorpromazine (Hollis, 1968) and thoridazine (Davis, Sprague, & Werry, 1969), has produced reductions in self-stimulation in retarded persons. Nevertheless, the use of drugs at dosage levels not totally debilitating has not been demonstrated to be effective in decreasing self-injury (Picker et al., 1979).

The treatment of choice for retarded and autistic children exhibiting stereotyped movement disorders will vary depending on several factors. The most important consideration concerns the consequences of stereotypy. Behavior resulting in severe damage obviously requires more drastic intervention. In selecting an intervention, it is essential to determine whether resources are available to carry out the treatment. Another factor influencing the selection of treatment is the acceptability of the intervention to the child, persons responsible for the child, and those implementing the procedure. The rate of stereotypy is also important. Self-injury (producing little damage) and infrequent self-stimulation require different treatment than does stereotypy that precludes learning or that is harmful. Maintenance of treatment gains over time and across settings represents an important aspect of any intervention. Finally, positive and negative side effects associated with any treatment should be taken into account.

The most effective treatment of stereotyped movement disorders is a combination of punishment and reinforcement procedures. Although reinforcement has been demonstrated to decrease self-injury and self-stimulation in retarded children (e.g., Repp et al., 1974; Tarpley & Schroeder, 1979), stereotypy usually occurs at such high rates that it is necessary to use punishment in combination with reinforcement. Many punishers effective in controlling stereotypy (e.g., electric shock, shaking, slapping, isolation) are not acceptable, due to legal and ethical constraints. Thus, the preferred approach in modifying stereotyped movement disorders should be the least aversive procedure effective in reducing the problem and a reinforcement program to increase more appropriate activity.

When stereotypy is self-injurious, the most pressing concern is to eliminate this behavior as quickly as possible. Electric shock is the treatment choice because it has been demonstrated to produce immediate and substantial reductions in self-injury (Corte, Wolf, & Locke, 1971). The use of shock, however, has disadvantages. Most people find shock undesirable, and it can be easily abused, especially in institutional settings. The effects of shock also are situation specific, i.e., the reductions of stereotypy tend to occur only where treatment is carried out. Finally, there is equivocal evidence to substantiate the likelihood of positive or negative side effects of shock. The maintenance of reductions in stereotypy also is enhanced when reinforcement is used. Therefore, electric shock and DRI is the treatment of choice for self-injury that is harmful and remains impervious to other forms of treatment.

More acceptable types of punishment, such as overcorrection in conjunction with reinforcement, have been used to eliminate self-injury and self-stimulation in autistic or retarded children (e.g., Azrin, et al., 1975; Foxx & Azrin, 1973; Wesolowski & Zawlocki, 1982). Overcorrection is preferable to electric shock since it has been demonstrated to be effective and is more socially acceptable. There are differential reports of positive and negative side effects and the maintenance of reductions in stereotypy achieved with this procedure. The drawbacks in using overcorrection are its cost in execution time and the difficulties in implementing it with older, stronger, resistive children.

Continuous physical restraint has been one of the most popular methods of dealing with persons whose self-injuries occur at high rates (Forehand & Baumeister, 1976). There are several disadvantages with the use of restraint, including the possibility of physical damage (e.g., shortening tendons, demineralization), the prevention of participation in more adaptive activities, the failure to alter those circumstances responsible for the self-injury, and the unacceptability of restraint (Picker et al., 1979). Brief immobilization contingent on stereotypy, with or without reinforcement, has been shown to reduce atypical stereotyped movement disorders (Azrin & Wesolowski, 1980; Rapoff, Altman, & Christophersen, 1980; Shapiro, Barrett, & Ollendick, 1980).

Response interruption stops the undesirable response for a couple of seconds, and only a few studies have examined response interruption on stereotypy. The procedure employed by Wesolowski and Zawlocki (1982) to treat eye gouging consisted of only momentarily stopping the behavior. Their use of response interruption produced a decrease (about 35 percent) in eye gouging in one subject, while it resulted in an initial increase (about 26 percent) in the second subject that returned to the previous baseline rate (see Figures 9–4 and 9–5). Although their data do not demonstrate response interruption to be an effective technique, employing reinforcement with response interruption might have produced better results. This was shown by Richmond (1983) who eliminated hand mouthing in three retarded women by pulling their hand down for two or three seconds. Each woman received praise and ice cream following specified intervals without mouthing.

Azrin and Wesolowski (1980) first reported substantial reductions in the self-stimulation of profoundly retarded adolescents and adults using a reinforcement plus interruption method as shown in Figure 9–3. Their response-interruption technique initially consisted of a verbal reprimand followed by guiding the trainees' hands to their lap for a two-minute period. If they were trying to self-stimulate or misbehave during the last 10 seconds of the two-minute period, the period was extended until the client was calm. When the trainee had not exhibited stereotypy for a 30-minute interval, the two-minute

FIGURE 9–3

Stereotyped Behavior in a Special Class of Seven Profoundly Retarded Adults Whose Stereotypy Was Resistant to Displacement

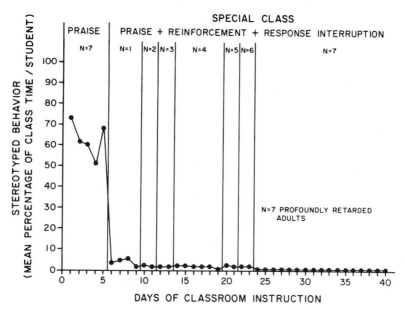

Each data point shows the mean percentage of 10-sec. observation intervals during which stereotypy was exhibited per trainee. During the first 5 days, the instructor provided praise, instruction and manual guidance for correct behaviors in the class. Each of the seven trainees was given intensive individual instruction entailing reinforcement for correct responses and interruption of stereotypic behaviors during sessions occurring at the first vertical line. The data for those sessions do not appear in the figure. The trainees were added one at a time to the class as indicated by the changing N size after each vertical line. After the intensive individual training, the class provided snack reinforcement for correct behavior and interruption of stereotyped responses in addition to the praise.

Source: N. H. Azrin and M. D. Wesolowski, "A Reinforcement Plus Interruption Method of Eliminating Behavioral Stereotypy of Profoundly Retarded Persons," *Behaviour Research and Therapy* 18 (1980), pp. 113–119. Reprinted with permission.

interruption period was halved until it finally consisted of only a verbal warning. If two instances of self-stimulation occurred in a 30-minute period, then the response-interruption period was reset to two minutes. Reinforcement consisted of presenting snack treats, stroking, and praise for correct responses (e.g., putting blocks in a bucket, giving eye contact).

There is evidence showing that stereotypy can be reduced merely by presenting retarded persons with objects or toys (Berkson & Mason, 1964; Davenport & Berkson, 1963; Moseley, Faust, & Reardon, 1970). Social interaction has been shown to be an important factor responsible for the reductions in stereotypy (Berkson & Mason, 1964; Moseley et al., 1970). Thus, simple and acceptable interventions can be effective in modifying some kinds of stereotyped movement disorders.

The self-stimulation hypothesis states that a given amount of stimulation must be present to avoid stereotypy. Theoretically, if the level of stimulation was increased in children displaying stereotypy, the behavior should decrease. Wells and Smith (1983) tested this theory by providing increased sensory integration (Ayers, 1972) to four retarded people who exhibited stereotyped self-injurious behavior. The noncontingent stimulation consisted of vibration, rocking in a hammock, and rolling the subjects over a ball. Self-injury was reduced in all four subjects.

Two promising treatments for stereotypy are sensory extinction and sensory time-out. Sensory extinction removes or masks specific sensory consequences for self-stimulation (Rincover, 1978). For example, if a child's self-stimulation consisted of tapping objects on hard surfaces and was maintained by its auditory consequences, then sensory extinction might involve carpeting the hard surfaces. Sensory time-out, on the other hand, is a technique in which the stimulus input of a sensory modality is decreased or terminated for a specific period that is contingent on a response (Wesolowski & Zawlocki, 1982). For instance, a child's head banging might be eliminated by covering the child's eyes. Thus, distinctions between sensory extinction and sensory time-out are based on different behavioral principles. Sensory extinction has been used to eliminate self-stimulation (Rincover, 1978; Rincover et al., 1979) and self-injury (Rincover & Devany, 1982) of developmentally disabled children. Sensory time-out (Wesolowski & Zawlocki, 1982) and facial screening (Zegiob, Alford, & House, 1978) also have suppressed stereotypy in retarded children.

The effectiveness of sensory time-out with and without a DRO, of response interruption, and of overcorrection with a DRO in controlling an injurious, self-stimulatory behavior (eye gouging) in blind retarded twin girls were investigated by Wesolowski and Zawlocki (1982). The sensory time-out consisted of placing shooter's earmuffs on the children for two minutes. If the girls were crying or struggling in the last 10 seconds of this period, then it was extended by 10 second intervals. A small amount of apple juice was delivered contingent on a two-minute period without self-injury. As depicted in Figures 9–4 and 9–5, sensory time-out and DRO resulted in the suppression of the eye gouging, and at a two-month follow-up, the behavior was still absent. Figures 9–6 and

FIGURE 9-4

The Mean Percentage of Time that Subject I Spent Eye Gouging over Baseline, Time-Out from Auditory Stimuli, Response Interruption, and Sensory Time-Out plus DRO Conditions of the Study

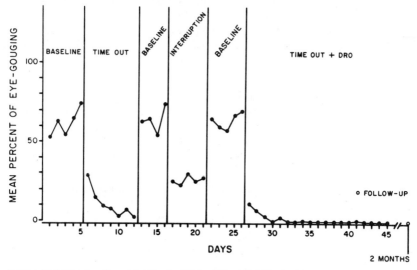

Source: M. D. Wesolowski and R. J. Zawlocki, "The Differential Effects of Procedures to Eliminate an Injurious Self-Stimulatory Behavior (Digito-ocular sign) in Blind Retarded Twins," *Behavior Therapy* 13 (1982), pp. 334–345. Reprinted with permission.

9–7 show that eye gouging was occurring at slightly higher levels about a year later, and an overcorrection and DRO treatment was implemented on the same twins. The treatment involved having the girls perform an exercise after a verbal warning ("Name, if you put your hands in your eyes, we will have to practice moving our hands.") and removing their hands from their eyes. Their arms were extended out from their sides in a position parallel to the floor for about three to five minutes, they were given instructions ("arms up," "arms to the side," and "arms down"), and if necessary, were guided through in moving their arms to the three positions for about 15 minutes. The DRO consisted of delivering food after a 10-second interval without eye gouging and was gradually lengthened to a five-minute period. This overcorrection and DRO was carried out over an eight-hour day. Eye gouging was eliminated with the overcorrection and DRO and was not observed by the staff about a year later (see Figures 9–6 and 9–7).

Six factors were selected as important considerations in selecting a treatment for atypical stereotyped movement disorders. These include (*a*) consequences of the stereotypy, (*b*) feasibility, (*c*) acceptability, (*d*) persistence of stereotypy,

FIGURE 9-5

The Mean Percentage of Time that Subject II Spent Eye Gouging over Baseline, Time-Out from Auditory Stimuli, Response Interruption, and Time-Out plus DRO Conditions of the Study

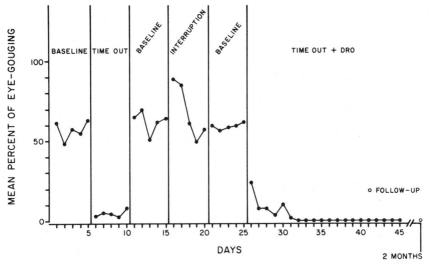

Source: M. D. Wesolowski and R. J. Zawlocki, "The Differential Effects of Procedures to Eliminate an Injurious Self-Stimulatory Behavior (Digito-ocular sign) in Blind Retarded Twins," *Behavior Therapy* 13 (1982), pp. 334–345. Reprinted with permission.

(*e*) maintenance, and (*f*) side effects. On the basis of these six factors, several procedures were suggested as choices for treatment.

Electric shock with a DRO or overcorrection and DRO are to be used as a last resort in many instances but are the treatment of choice in severe self-injury. In conjunction with reinforcement, brief immobilization, sensory extinction, and sensory time-out offer promising means for controlling less severe self-injury and many types of self-stimulation. Data on maintenance are not well established with these interventions. These procedures have the advantages of being easy to implement and of providing little potential for abuse. They also represent more desirable alternatives in modifying some forms of stereotypy since they are less aversive and more acceptable. Although negative side effects have not been reported in connection with these procedures, there have been only a few studies employing such techniques.

The most important daily consideration in using these procedures is careful monitoring to ensure that they are not abused and that any necessary adjustments are made. The goal of any treatment for stereotypy should be to strengthen more adaptive activity and to eliminate the stereotyped behavior.

FIGURE 9-6

The Mean Percentage of Time that Subject I Spent Eye Gouging over Baseline and Overcorrection plus DRO Conditions of the Study

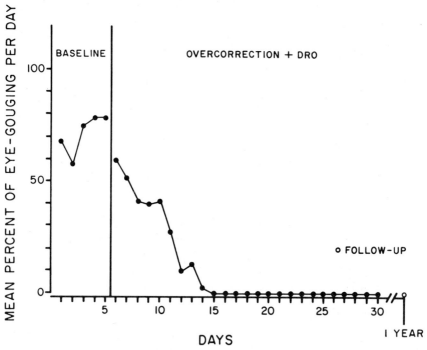

Source: M. D. Wesolowski and R. J. Zawlocki, "The Differential Effects of Procedures to Eliminate an Injurious Self-Stimulatory Behavior (Digito-ocular sign) in Blind Retarded Twins," *Behavior Therapy* 13 (1982), pp. 334–345. Reprinted with permission.

Thus, an essential component is a plan to enrich autistic or retarded childrens' environments by providing ample opportunities for stimulation and reinforcement. Natural reinforcement (praise and activities the child likes) should be used when possible. Finally, punishment should be reduced and terminated at the earliest opportunity.

CASE EXAMPLES

Two case examples are provided to give the reader clinical pictures of at least two of the wide variety of stereotyped movement disorders dealt with in this chapter.

FIGURE 9-7

The Mean Percentage of Time that Subject II Spent Eye Gouging over Baseline and Overcorrection plus DRO Conditions of the Study

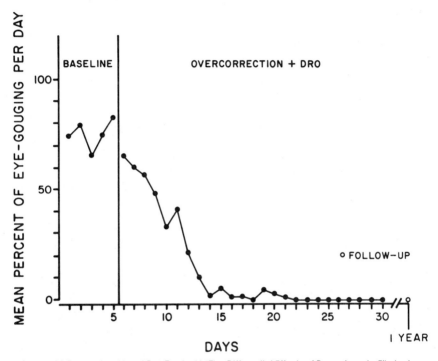

Source: M. D. Wesolowski and R. J. Zawlocki, "The Differential Effects of Procedures to Eliminate an Injurious Self-Stimulatory Behavior (Digito-ocular sign) in Blind Retarded Twins," *Behavior Therapy* 13 (1982), pp. 334–345. Reprinted with permission.

Case One: Torsion Dystonia

A boy of East European, non-Jewish ancestry with no family history of nervous disease had a normal birth and normal physical and mental development until age 15. At that time (June 1963), he began to drag his left leg. After being taped for one month, the leg improved but not to the original state.

In March 1964, the first signs of torticollis appeared and worsened rapidly. The patient saw many physicians, but they all said there were no organic problems and suggested a psychiatric disorder. In February 1965, the patient was referred to a university medical center and was diagnosed as having spasmodic torticollis. He was told that he must learn to relax but not told how.

Over the next few months, movements spread to the upper extremities, and the diagnosis was changed to dystonia musculorum deformans. The patient was given valium and was told to increase the dosage until he was taking 80 mg a day. The symptoms were progressing rapidly. Torticollis, retrocollis, and oromandibular spasms made swallowing difficult. Cocontractions throughout the right arm made writing and holding a glass of fluid nearly impossible, and the affected deltoid muscle of the left arm made its use difficult. The left leg dragged, and with retrocollis, walking was difficult. Only the massive doses of valium reduced the symptoms for short periods.

In April 1966, a left cryothalamotomy was performed, and the symptoms disappeared from the right arm. Torticollis and retrocollis were reduced but not eliminated. A right cryothalamotomy, done a few months later, resulted in complete elimination of all symptoms for about one month. Slowly, the movements returned to the left arm and neck. Two more right cryothalamotomies were attempted in the next year without success.

In 1969, the patient tried L-dopa therapy. The dosage was increased to 12 grams a day, and with the 80 mg a day of valium, it produced drowsiness sufficient to reduce the symptoms. Side effects of L-dopa were nausea and vomiting.

In April 1972, a right stereotactic thalamotomy produced a reduction of dystonic movements in the left arm, but the surgical side effects included blindness in the left visual field and paresis of the left side of the body. Vision returned to normal in about a week, but the paresis caused worsening of speech and loss of function in the left hand and leg. Torticollis and retrocollis were unaffected.

In January 1974, the patient began habit reversal therapy. The treatment focused on torticollis and retrocollis. The regimen included awareness training, incompatible response training (chin on the sternum), and a series of exercises designed to strengthen atrophied muscles (sternocleidomastoid) and to stretch hypertrophied muscles (trapezius). The chin was to be held tightly against the sternum for three to five minutes whenever retrocollis occurred, and this position was to be assumed whenever the patient engaged in reading. For 20 minutes twice a day, he was to perform isometric exercises to strengthen and stretch neck muscles. He also was supposed to ask friends and co-workers to praise him for holding his head straight and to remind him to perform the incompatible response if retrocollis occurred. He found this very difficult to do, and he ignored the instruction.

When he started habit reversal, the patient immediately discontinued L-dopa and reduced the dose of valium from 80 mg to 10 mg a day. Habit reversal greatly reduced torticollis and retrocollis for the next four months, but the patient always had to hang his head down, especially when walking. Although habit reversal almost entirely eliminated torticollis and retrocollis, the patient found the regimen difficult to maintain, and he stopped the exercises in 1977.

Since 1977, retrocollis and lordosis have worsened, making it difficult to walk and write, but all other symptoms remain static. The patient continues taking 10 mg valium per day. In September 1983, the patient underwent cervical cord stimulation. After 24 hours of stimulation, there was a 34.4 percent reduction of overall muscle tension as measured by evoked potential. There is a slight improvement in all the symptoms. Spinal cord stimulation has a cumulative effect, and therefore, it is impossible to tell at this time how much improvement will be gained.

This case example was chosen for several reasons. First, it typifies the usual course of the dystonia. Second, several treatments are illustrated, including thalamic surgery, drug therapy (valium and L-dopa), habit reversal, and spinal cord stimulation. Third, the accuracy of this case can be attested to by the fact that it is of one of the authors; yet, such a statement of its accuracy may reflect subjective opinion.

Case Two: Self-Injury

Dickie, an 11-year-old developmentally disabled boy, had displayed two different atypical stereotyped movement disorders for the past eight years. These behaviors consisted of biting his arms and waving his fingers in front of his eyes. They were first noticed when Dickie was about three-years old and around a year after he had been institutionalized by his parents. These stereotyped movements had not been a source of major concern to the staff of the institution until the last couple of years. The stereotypy had begun increasing in both magnitude and frequency during this time, despite attempts by the staff to control this behavior. These efforts by the staff consisted primarily of telling him to stop waving his fingers or biting his arms, making him go to his room for at least 15 minutes when he continued the stereotypy, and finally establishing periods of physical restraint. As a last resort, drugs were used. Unfortunately, none of these methods worked very well, and the harmful effects of Dickie's behavior presently include infections and substantial damage to the skin on his arms. In addition, Dickie has been excluded from several training and educational programs because of the problems posed by his stereotypy, i.e., it was disruptive to the ongoing activities, and he was not considered a responsive student.

Two other treatments also have been tried with varying success in the past six months. The first treatment used by the staff was an overcorrection procedure based on restitution for the self-injury and positive practice for the self-stimulatory behavior. More specifically, the staff had Dickie perform the following activity every time he bit his arm: (a) get a clean washcloth and hand towel, (b) wash and dry the bite mark, (c) place the washcloth and towel in the dirty laundry, (d) go to the nurse and obtain a cotton ball and antiseptic, (e) clean the bite mark with the cotton and antiseptic, and (f) return the antiseptic to the nurse and properly dispose of the cotton ball. The positive practice component for the hand waving consisted of a set of exercises in which Dickie was required to put his arms out from the sides of his body (in a position parallel to the floor), straight up in the air over his head, back out to the sides, down to the sides of his legs, and then back out to the horizontal position. This cycle of exercises was repeated for a 10-minute period every time Dickie waved his fingers in front of his eyes. A differential reinforcement of other behavior (DRO) procedure was employed in conjunction with overcorrection. This DRO procedure involved rewarding Dickie with a token for five-minute periods without the occurrence of the stereotypy. Although this treatment produced some noticeable improvements in Dickie's behavior, it was eventually terminated by the staff after about a week since it proved to be too time-consuming and impractical.

The second treatment implemented for Dickie's stereotypy involved a sensory time-out procedure, facial screening, and a DRO. The staff began requiring Dickie to wear a terrycloth bib, and they raised the bib to cover his face for two minutes whenever he bit his arms or waved his fingers in front of his eyes. The bib was not removed from Dickie's face if he was struggling, trying to perform the stereotypy, or attempting to take the bib off during the last 10 seconds of the two-minute period. This two-minute period was extended by 10 second intervals until Dickie remained quiet for 10 seconds. In addition, Dickie was reinforced with a token for five-minute periods without the stereotypy. This treatment was started about four months ago, and after approximately three weeks, Dickie's stereotypy was completely suppressed. He has exhibited the hand waving behavior on only two occasions since the sensory time-out or facial screening procedure was discontinued about three months ago. Dickie also has not bitten his arms for about 3.5 months, or approximately two weeks after the start of treatment. The DRO procedure has been modified so that Dickie is currently rewarded every hour with a token for not engaging in stereotypy. In addition, Dickie has become involved in some special eduation activities, and the staff has made a special effort to spend more time interacting with Dickie in various ways (e.g., playing games, training different skills). Finally, Dickie was gradually taken off medication (i.e., tranquilizers) during treatment and has not required the administration of drugs for over three months.

CONCLUSIONS

Stereotyped movement disorders were defined as being involuntary, repetitious, persistent, nonfunctional, and capable of having some voluntary control exerted on them. In an effort to comply with DSM-III, the disorders that were focused on were transient tic disorders, chronic motor tic disorders, Tourette's syndrome, and atypical stereotyped movement disorders.

Transient tic disorders affect up to 24 percent of children and only last up to one year. Since they are short-lived and usually involve only facial muscles, transient tics should be ignored. If these tics affect the whole head, neck, and shoulders, however, then treatment should be pursued in the form of biofeedback training in combination with habit reversal.

Chronic motor tics last more than one year and involve up to three muscle groups simultaneously. The chronicity of these tics and the fact that they can be quite debilitating make these tic syndromes important to treat. Massed or negative practice has been used, but it is not the treatment of choice. The recommended treatment is a combination of habit reversal, relaxation training, and biofeedback (EMG) training. New discoveries indicate that cervical spinal cord stimulation may be warranted for many movement disorders.

Tourette's syndrome involves multiple motor and phonic tics. The course of the disease is complicated, but once it starts (usually in the face), it insidiously progresses in a characteristic manner. Although it occurs in all racial and ethnic groups, there is evidence for a genetic predisposition toward Jews. The treatment of choice is a combination of the drug clonidine with broad spectrum behavior therapy involving habit reversal and relaxation training.

Atypical stereotyped movement disorders are unusual mannerisms displayed by most retarded and autistic individuals. They range from innocuous movements to self-injury. The treatment of choice depends on several factors but should always proceed from the least aversive alternative and should include reinforcement to increase more adaptive activities.

In reviewing the literature, several facts become evident. The origin of most stereotyped movement disorders may be genetic and/or have a neurological basis. However, this does not affect the treatment of choice that in most cases, involves the use of behavior therapy. In some cases, the behavior therapy may be augmented by medical procedures.

REFERENCES

Abuzzahab, F. S., & Anderson, F. O. (Eds.) *Gilles de la Tourette's syndrome.* St. Paul, Minn.: Mason Publishing Company, 1979.

Agras, S., & Marshall, C. The application of negative practice to spasmodic torticollis. *American Journal of Psychiatry,* 1965, *122,* 579–582.

Ayres, A. J. *Sensory integration and learning disorders.* Los Angeles: Western Psychological Services, 1972.

Azrin, N. H., Gottlieb, L., Hughart, L., Wesolowski, M. D., & Rahn, T. Eliminating self-injurious behavior by educative procedures. *Behaviour Research and Therapy,* 1975, *13,* 101–111.

Azrin, N. H., & Nunn, R. G. Habit-reversal: A method of eliminating nervous habits and tics. *Behaviour Research and Therapy,* 1973, *11,* 619–628.

Azrin, N. H., Nunn, R. G., & Frantz, S. E. Habit reversal vs. negative practice treatment of nervous tics. *Behavior therapy,* 1980, *11,* 169–178.

Azrin, N. H., & Wesolowski, M. D. A reinforcement plus interruption method of eliminating behavioral stereotypy of profoundly retarded persons. *Behaviour Research and Therapy,* 1980, *18,* 113–119.

Barbeau, A. Rationale for the use of L-dopa in the torsion dystonias. *Neurology,* 1970, *20,* 96–102.

Baron, M., Shapiro, E., Shapiro, A. K., & Rainer, J. D. Genetic analysis of Tourette syndrome suggesting major gene effect. *American Journal of Human Genetics,* 1981, *33,* 767–775.

Barrett, B. H. Reduction in rate of multiple tics by three operant conditioning methods. *The Journal of Nervous and Mental Disease,* 1962, *135,* 187–195.

Baumeister, A. A., & Forehand, R. Stereotyped acts. In N. R. Ellis (Ed.), *International review of research in mental retardation* (Vol. 6). New York: Academic Press, 1973.

Berkson, G., & Davenport, R. K., Jr. Stereotyped movements of mental defectives: I. Initial survey. *American Journal of Mental Deficiency,* 1962, *66,* 849–852.

Berkson, G., & Mason, W. A. Stereotyped movements of mental defectives: IV. The effects of toys and the character of the acts. *American Journal of Mental Deficiency,* 1964, *68,* 511–524.

Bernhardt, A. J., Hersen, M., & Barlow, D. H. Measurement and modification of spasmodic torticollis: An experimental analysis. *Behavior Therapy,* 1972, *3,* 249–297.

Borison, R. L., Ang, L., Chang, S., Dysken, M., Comaty, J. E., & Davis, J. M. New pharmacological approaches in the treatment of Tourette syndrome. In A. J. Friedhoff & T. N. Chase (Eds.), *Advances in neurology: Gilles de la Tourette syndrome* (Vol. 35). New York: Raven Press, 1982.

Brierly, H. The treatment of hysterical spasmodic torticollis by behavior therapy. *Behaviour Research and Therapy,* 1967, *5,* 139–142.

Browning, R. M., & Stover, D. O. *Behavior modification in child treatment.* Chicago: Aldine-Atherton, 1971.

Brudny, J., Grynbaum, B. B., & Korein, J. Spasmodic torticollis: Treatment by feedback display of EMG. *Archives of Physical Medicine and Rehabilitation,* 1974, *55,* 403–408.

Brudny, J., Korein, J., Grynbaum, B. B., Friedmann, L. W., Weinstein, S., Sachs-Frankel, G., & Belandres, P. V. EMG feedback therapy: Review of treatment of 114 patients. *Archives of Physical Medicine and Rehabilitation,* 1976, *57,* 55–61.

Bruun, R. D. Clonidine treatment of Tourette syndrome. In A. J. Friedhoff & T. N. Chase (Eds.), *Advances in Neurology: Gilles de la Tourette syndrome* (Vol. 35). New York: Raven Press, 1982.

Bryson, V., Sakati, N., Nyhan, W. L., & Fish, C. H. Self-mutilative behavior in the Cornelia de Lange syndrome. *American Journal of Mental Deficiency,* 1971, *76,* 319–324.

Burke, R. E., & Fahn, S. Double-blind evaluation of trihexyphenidyl in dystonia. In S. Fahn, D. B. Calne, & I. Shoulson (Eds.), *Advances in neurology: Experimental therapeutics of movement disorders* (Vol. 37). New York: Raven Press, 1983.

Carr, E. G. The motivation of self-injurious behavior: A review of some hypotheses. *Psychological Bulletin,* 1977, *84,* 800–816.

Chapel, J. L. Behavior modification techniques with children and adolescents. *Canadian Psychiatric Association Journal,* 1970, *15,* 315–318.

Charcot, J. M. Intorno ad alcuni casi di tic convulsive con coprolalia ed ecolalia, reported by G. Melotti. *La Riforma Medica,* 1885, 184–186.

Clark, D. F. The treatment of hysterical spasm and agoraphobia by behavior therapy. *Behaviour Research and Therapy,* 1963, *1,* 245–250.

Clark, D. F. Behavior therapy of Gilles de la Tourette's syndrome. *British Journal of Psychiatry,* 1966, *112,* 771–778.

Cleeland, C. S. Behavioral techniques in the modification of spasmodic torticollis. *Neurology,* 1973, *23,* 1241–1247.

Cleeland, C. S. Biofeedback and other behavioral techniques in the treatment of disorders of voluntary movement. In J. V. Basmajian (Ed.), *Biofeedback — principles and practice for clinicians.* Baltimore: Williams & Wilkins, 1979.

Coleman, M. Preliminary remarks on the L-dopa therapy of dystonia. *Neurology,* 1970, *2,* 114–121.

Coleman, M. Effect of nicotinamide administration in a patient with an extra-pyramidal movement disorder and hyperuricemia: A double-blind crossover study. In R. Eldridge & S. Fahn (Eds.), *Advances in neurology: Dystonia* (Vol. 14). New York: Raven Press, 1976.

Coleman, M. P., & Barnet, A. L-dopa reversal of muscular spasms, vomiting, and insomnia in a patient with an atypical form of familial dystonia. *Transactions of the American Neurological Association,* 1969, *94,* 91–95.

Cooper, I. S. *Involuntary movement disorders.* New York: Hoeber, 1969.

Cooper, I. S. Neurosurgical treatment of dystonia. *Neurology,* 1970, *20,* 133–148.

Cooper, I. S. 20-year follow-up study of the neurosurgical treatment of dystonia musculorum deformans. In R. Eldridge & S. Fahn (Eds.), *Advances in neurology: Dystonia* (Vol. 14). New York: Raven Press, 1976.

Corte, H. E., Wolf, M. M., & Locke, B. J. A comparison of procedures for eliminating self-injurious behavior of retarded adolescents. *Journal of Applied Behavior Analysis,* 1971, *4,* 201–213.

Davenport, R. K., Jr., & Berkson, G. Stereotyped movements of mental defectives: II. Effects of novel objects. *American Journal of Mental Deficiency,* 1963, *67,* 879–882.

Davis, K. V., Sprague, R. L., & Werry, J. S. Stereotyped behavior and activity level in severe retardates: The effect of drugs. *American Journal of Mental Deficiency,* 1969, *73,* 721–727.

de Lange, C. Sur un type nouveau de degeneration (Typus Amstelodamensis). *Archives de Medicine des Enfants,* 1933, *36,* 713–719.

de la Tourette, Gilles. Etude sur une affection nerveuse caracterisee par de l'incoordination motrice accompagnee de echolalie et de coprolalie. *Archives of Neurology,* 1885, *9,* 19–42.

de Lissovoy, V. Head banging in early childhood: A suggested cause. *Journal of Genetic Psychology*, 1963, *102*, 109–114.

Dizmang, L. H., & Cheatham, C. F. The Lesch-Nyhan syndrome. *American Journal of Psychiatry*, 1970, *127*, 671–677.

Dunlap. K. *Habits: Their making and unmaking.* New York: Liveright, 1932.

Eldridge, R. The torsion dystonias: Literature review and genetic and clinical studies. *Neurology*, 1970, *20*, 1–78.

Eldridge, R., Riklan, M., & Cooper, I. S. The limited role of psychotherapy in torsion dystonia: Experience with 44 cases. *Journal of the American Medical Association*, 1969, *21*, 705–708.

Ericksen, R. A., Huber, H. Elimination of hysterical torticollis through the use of a metronome in an operant conditioning paradigm. *Behavior Therapy*, 1975, *6*, 405–406.

Fabish, W., & Darbyshire, R. Report on an unusual case of self-induced epilepsy with comments on some psychological and therapeutic aspects. *Epilepsia*, 1965, *6*, 335–340.

Fahn, S. High-dosage anticholinergic therapy in dystonia. In S. Fahn, D. B. Calne, & I. Shoulson (Eds.), *Advances in neurology: Experimental therapeutics of movement disorders* (Vol. 37). New York: Raven Press, 1983.

Feldman, R. B., & Werry, J. S. An unsuccessful attempt to treat a tiquer by massed practice. *Behaviour Research and Therapy*, 1966, *4*, 111–117.

Flatau, E., & Sterling, W. Progressiver torsionspasms bie kindern. *Z. Gesamte Neurologie Psychiatric*, 1911, 77, 586–612.

Forehand, R., & Baumeister, A. A. Deceleration of aberrant behavior among retarded individuals. In M. Hersen, R. M. Eisler, & P. M. Miller (Eds.), *Progress in behavior modification* (Vol. 2). New York: Academic Press, 1976.

Foxx, R. M., & Azrin, N. H. The elimination of autistic self-stimulatory behavior by overcorrection, *Journal of Applied Behavior Analysis*, 1973, *6*, 1–14.

Franceschetti, A. Rubeole pendant la grossesse et cataracte congenitals chez l'enfant, accompagnee du phenomene digito-oculaire. *Ophthalmoloqica*, 1947, *114*, 332–339.

Frankel, F., Freeman, B. J., Ritvo, E., Chikami, B., & Carr, E. Effects of frequency of photic stimulation upon autistic and retarded children. *American Journal of Mental Deficiency*, 1976, *81*, 32–40.

Frankel, F., & Simmons, J. G. Self-injurious behavior in schizophrenic and retarded children. *American Journal of Mental Deficiency*, 1976, *80*, 512–522.

Frederick, C. J. Treatment of a tic by systematic desensitization and massed response evocation. *Journal of Behavior Therapy and Experimental Psychiatry*, 1971, *2*, 281–283.

Friedhoff, A. J. Receptor maturation in pathogenesis and treatment of Tourette syndrome. In A. J. Friedhoff & T. N. Chase (Eds.), *Advances in neurology: Gilles de la Tourette syndrome* (Vol. 35). New York: Raven Press, 1982.

Gilbert, G. I. The medical treatment of spasmodic torticollis. *Archives of Neurology,* 1972, *27,* 503–506.

Goetz, C. G., & Klawans, H. L. Gilles de la Tourette on Tourette syndrome. In A. J. Friedhoff & T. N. Chase (Eds.), *Advances in neurology: Gilles de la Tourette syndrome* (Vol. 35). New York: Raven Press, 1982.

Gowers, W. R. *A manual of diseases of the nervous system.* Philadelphia: Blakiston, 1888.

Harlow, H. F., & Harlow, M. K. Psychopathology in monkeys. In H. D. Kimmel (Ed.), *Experimental psychopathology.* New York: Academic Press, 1971.

Hawkes, R. C., Holland, G. N., Moore, W. S., & Worthington, B. S. Nuclear magnetic resonance (NMR) tomography of the brain: A preliminary clinical assessment with demonstration of pathology. *Journal of Computer Assisted Tomography,* 1980, *4,* 577–586.

Haynes, S. N. *Principles of behavioral assessment.* New York: Gardner Press, 1978.

Hersen, M., & Eisler, R. M. Behavioral approaches to study and treatment of psychogenic tics. *Genetic Psychology Monograms,* 1973, *87,* 289–312.

Hirschmann, J., & Mayer, K. Zur Beeinflussung der Akinese und anderer extrapyramidal-motorischer S torungen mit L-dopa. *Deutch Medica Wescheren,* 1964, *89,* 1877–1884.

Hollis, J. H. Chlorpromazine: Direct measurement of differential behavior effect. *Science,* 1968, *159,* 1487–1489.

Hoult, D. I. *An overview of NMR in medicine.* Washington, D.C.: National Center for Health Care Technology, 1981.

Hutzell, R. R., Platzek, D., & Logue, P. E. Control of symptoms of Gilles de la Tourette's syndrome by self-monitoring. *Journal of Behavior Therapy and Experimental Psychiatry,* 1974, *5,* 71–76.

Jervis, G. A., & Stimson, C. W. De Lange syndrome. *Journal of Pediatrics,* 1963, *63,* 634–645.

Kaufman, M. E., & Levitt, H. A study of three stereotyped behaviors in institutionalized mental defectives. *American Journal of Mental Deficiency,* 1965, *69,* 467–473.

Kidd, K. K., & Pauls, D. L. Genetic hypotheses for Tourette syndrome. In A. J. Friedhoff & T. N. Chase (Eds.), *Advances in neurology: Gilles de la Tourette syndrome* (Vol. 35). New York: Raven Press, 1982.

Knepler, K. N., & Sewall, S. Negative practice paired with smelling salts in the treatment of a tic. *Journal of Behavior Therapy and Experimental Psychiatry,* 1974, *5,* 189–192.

Korein, J., Brudny, J. Grynbaum, B., Sachs-Frankel, G., Weisinger, M., & Levidow, L. Sensory feedback therapy of spasmodic torticollis and dystonia: Results in the treatment of 55 patients. In R. Eldridge & S. Fahn (Eds.), *Advances in neurology: Dystonia* (Vol. 14). New York: Raven Press, 1976.

Lahey, B., McNees, M. P., & McNees, M. C. Control of an obscene "verbal tic" through timeout in an elementary school classroom. *Journal of Applied Behavior Analysis*, 1973, *6*, 101–104.

Landwirth, J. Sensory radicular neuropathy and retinitis pigmentosa. *Pediatrics*, 1964, *34*, 519–524.

Lesch, M., & Nyhan, W. L. A familial disorder of uric acid metabolism and central nervous system function. *American Journal of Medicine*, 1964, *36*, 561–570.

Longin, H. E., Kohn, J. P., & Macurik, K. M. The modification of choreal movements. *Journal of Behavior Therapy and Experimental Psychiatry*, 1974, *5*, 263–265.

Luiselli, J. K. Behavioral treatment of self-stimulation: Review and recommendations. *Education and Treatment of Children*, 1981, *4*, 375–392.

Luria, A. R. *The working brain: An introduction to neuropsychology.* New York: Basic Books, 1973.

Mandell, S. The treatment of dystonia with L-dopa and haloperidol. *Neurology*, 1970, *20*, 103–106.

Marsden, C. D. The problem of adult-onset idiopathic torsion dystonia and other isolated dyskinesias in adult life. In R. Eldridge & S. Fahn (Eds.), *Advances in neurology: Dystonia* (Vol. 14). New York: Raven Press, 1976.

Miller, A. L. Treatment of a child with Gilles de la Tourette's syndrome using behavior modification techniques. *Journal of Behavior Therapy and Experimental Psychiatry*, 1970, *1*, 319–321.

Moseley, A., Faust, M., Reardon, D. M. Effects of social and nonsocial stimuli on the stereotyped behaviors of retarded children. *American Journal of Mental Deficiency*, 1970, *74*, 809–811.

Nicassio, F. J., Liberman, R. P., Patterson, R. L., Ramirez, E., & Sanders, N. The treatment of tics by negative practice. *Journal of Behavior Therapy and Experimental Psychiatry*, 1972, *3*, 281–287.

Nuwer, M. R. Coprolalia as an organic symptom. In A. J. Friedhoff & T. N. Chase (Eds.), *Advances in neurology: Gilles de la Tourette syndrome* (Vol. 35). New York: Raven Press, 1982.

Nyhan, W. L. Lesch-Nyhan syndrome: Summary of clinical features. *Federation Proceedings*, 1968, *27*, 1034–1041.

Oppenheim, J. Ueber eine eigenartige Krampf krankheit des kindlichen und jugendlichen Alters (dysbasia lordotica progressiva, dystonia musculorum deformans). *Neurologie Centralblar*, 1911, *30*, 1090–1107.

Paterson, M. T. Spasmodic torticollis: Results of psychotherapy in 21 cases. *Lancet*, 1945, *2*, 556–559.

Picker, M., Poling, A., & Parker, A. A review of children's self-injurious behavior. *The Psychological Record*, 1979, *29*, 435–452.

Pinkerton, S., Hughes, H., & Wenrich, W. W. *Behavioral medicine.* New York: John Wiley & Sons, 1982.

Rafi, A. A. Learning theory and the treatment of tics. *Journal of Psychosomatic Research*, 1962, *6*, 71–76.

Rapoff, M. A., Altman, K., & Christophersen, E. R. Elimination of a retarded blind child's self-hitting by response-contingent brief restraint. *Education and Treatment of Children*, 1980, *3*, 231–236.

Repp, A. C., Deitz, S. M., & Speir, N. C. Reducing stereotypic responding of retarded persons by the differential reinforcement of other behavior. *American Journal of Mental Deficiency*, 1974, *79*, 279–284.

Richmond, G. Evaluation of a treatment for a hand-mouthing stereotypy. *American Journal of Mental Deficiency*, 1983, *87*, 667–669.

Rincover, A. Sensory extinction: A procedure for eliminating self-stimulatory behavior in developmentally disabled children. *Journal of Abnormal Child Psychology*, 1978, *6*, 299–310.

Rincover, A., Cook, R., Peoples, A., & Packard, D. Sensory extinction and sensory reinforcement principles for programming multiple adaptive behavior change. *Journal of Applied Behavior Analysis*, 1979, *12*, 221–233.

Rincover, A., & Devany, J. The application of sensory extinction procedures to self-injury. *Analysis and Intervention in Developmental Disabilities*, 1982, *2*, 67–81.

Russo, D. C., Carr, E. G., & Lovaas, O. I. Self-injury in pediatric populations. In J. M. Ferguson & C. B. Taylor (Eds.), *The comprehensive handbook of behavioral medicine. Extended applications & issues* (Vol. 3). New York: Spectrum, 1980.

Savicki, V., & Carlin, A. S. Behavioral treatment of Gilles de la Tourette's syndrome. *International Journal of Child Psychotherapy*, 1972, *1*, 97–108.

Shapiro, A. K., & Shapiro, E. Treatment of Gilles de la Tourette's syndrome with haliperidol. *Journal of Psychiatry*, 1968, *144*, 345–350.

Shapiro, A. K., & Shapiro, E. Tourette syndrome: History and present status. In A. J. Friedhoff & T. N. Chase (Eds.), *Advances in neurology: Gilles de la Tourette syndrome* (Vol. 35). New York: Raven Press, 1982a.

Shapiro, A. K., & Shapiro, E. Clinical efficacy of haloperidol, pimozide, penfluridol, and clonidine in the treatment of Tourette syndrome. In A. J. Friedhoff & T. N. Chase (Eds.), *Advances in neurology: Gilles de la Tourette syndrome* (Vol. 35). New York: Raven Press, 1982b.

Shapiro, A. K., Shapiro, E., Bruun, R. D., & Sweet, R. D. (Eds.) *Gilles de la Tourette syndrome*. New York: Raven Press, 1978.

Shapiro, A. K., Shapiro, E. S., Bruun, R. D., Sweet, R., Wayne, H., & Solomon, G. Gilles de la Tourette's syndrome: Summary of clinical experience with 250 patients and suggested nomenclature for tic syndromes. In R. Eldridge & S. Fahn (Eds.), *Advances in neurology: Dystonia* (Vol. 14). New York: Raven Press, 1976.

Shapiro, E. S., Barrett, R. P., & Ollendick, T. H. A comparison of physical restraint and positive practice overcorrection in treating stereotypic behavior. *Behavior Therapy*, 1980, *11*, 227–233.

Shear, C. S., Nyhan, W. L., Kirman, B. H., & Stern, J. Self-mutilative behavior as a feature of the de Lange syndrome. *Journal of Pediatrics,* 1971, *78,* 506–509.

Sohmer, H., & Student, M. Auditory nerve and brainstem evoked responses in normal, autistic, minimal brain dysfunction and psychomotor retarded children. *Electroencephalogram Clinical Neurophysiology,* 1978, *44,* 380–388.

Squires, N., Buchwald, J., Liley, F., & Strecker, J. Brainstem auditory evoked potential abnormalities in retarded adults. In J. Courjon, F. Mauguiere, & M. Revol (Eds.), *Clinical applications of evoked potentials in neurology.* New York: Raven Press, 1982.

Stevens, J. R., & Blanchley, P. H. Successful treatment of Maladie des Tics: Gilles de la Tourette's syndrome. *American Journal of Diseases of Children,* 1966, *112,* 541–545,

Tapia, F. Haldol in the treatment of children with tics and stutterers—and an incidental finding. *Psychiatric Quarterly,* 1969, *43,* 647–649.

Tarpley, H. D., & Schroeder, S. R. Comparison of DRO and DRI on rate of suppression of self-injurious behavior. *American Journal of Mental Deficiency,* 1979, *84,* 188–194.

Thatcher, R. W., & Maisel, E. B. Functional landscapes of the brain: An electrotopographic perspective. In H. Begleiter (Ed.), *Evoked brain potentials and behavior.* New York: Plenum Press, 1979.

Thomas, E., Abrams, K., & Johnson, J. Self-monitoring and reciprocal inhibition in the modification of multiple tics of Gilles de la Tourette's syndrome. *Journal of Behavior Therapy and Experimental Psychiatry,* 1971, *2,* 159–171.

Tophoff, M. Massed practice, relaxation and assertion training in the treatment of Gilles de la Tourette's Syndrome. *Journal of Behavior Therapy and Experimental Psychiatry,* 1973, *4,* 71–73.

Turner, S. M., Hersen, M., & Alford, H. Effects of massed practice and meprobamate on spasmodic torticollis: An experimental analysis. *Behaviour Research and Therapy,* 1974, *12,* 259–260.

Walls, R. T., Haught, P., & Dowler, D. *How to train new skills: Planning, teaching, evaluating.* Dunbar, W.V.: West Virginia Rehabilitation Research and Training Center, 1982.

Walton, D. Experimental psychology and the treatment of a ticquer. *Journal of Child Psychology and Psychiatry,* 1961, *2,* 148–155.

Waltz, J. M., & Davis, J. A. Cervical cord stimulation in the treatment of athetosis and dystonia. In S. Fahn, D. B. Calne, & I. Shoulson (Eds.), *Advances in neurology: Experimental therapeutics of movement disorders* (Vol. 37). New York: Raven Press, 1983.

Wassman, E. R., Eldridge, R., Abuzzahab, F. S., & Nee, L. Gilles de la Tourette syndrome: Clinical and genetic studies in a Midwestern city. *Neurology,* 1978, *28,* 304–307.

Wells, M. E., & Smith, D. W. Reduction of self-injurious behavior of mentally retarded persons using sensory-integrative techniques. *American Journal of Mental Deficiency,* 1983, 87, 664–666.

Wesolowski, M. D. Collateral reduction of muscle tension and self-reported anxiety in a cerebral palsied child using EMG feedback. *American Journal of Clinical Biofeedback,* 1982, *5*, 138–144.

Wesolowski, M. D., & Deichmann, J. Physiological activity and attitudes toward disabled persons. *Rehabilitation Counseling Bulletin,* 1980, *23*, 218–226.

Wesolowski, M. D., & Zawlocki, R. J. The differential effects of procedures to eliminate an injurious self-stimulatory behavior (digito-ocular sign) in blind retarded twins. *Behavior Therapy,* 1982, *13*, 334–345.

Wright, L. Aversive conditioning of self-induced seizures. *Behavior Therapy,* 1973, *4*, 712–713.

Yates, A. J. The application of learning theory to the treatment of tics. *Journal of Abnormal Social Psychology,* 1958, *56*, 175–182.

Yates, A. J. *Behavior Therapy.* New York: John Wiley & Sons, 1970.

Zegiob, L., Alford, G. S., & House, A. Response suppressive and generalization effects of facial screening on multiple self-injurious behavior in a retarded boy. *Behavior Therapy,* 1978, *9*, 688.

10

Speech and Language Disorders

Eugene E. Garcia
Arizona State University

INTRODUCTION: LANGUAGE ACQUISITION

The study of language continues to unfold increasingly complex wrinkles in theories of linguistics and psychology. What was once a study of linguistic structure has become today an interlocking study of linguistic, psychological, and social domains, each important in its own right but together converging in broader attempts to construct and reconstruct the nature of language. These converging perspectives acknowledge the multi-faceted nature of social interaction.

Within the last few years, research in normal language acquisition has shifted from the study of one native language (Brown, 1973; Gonzalez, 1969) to the comparative study of children from diverse linguistic societies (Bowerman, 1975; Braine, 1976). The present chapter deals with the study of young children acquiring the native language of English and the therapeutic treatment of those children identified as language disordered. Therefore, the present treatment of speech and language disorders includes a general discussion regarding language acquisition as well as a more specific discussion of speech and language clinical intervention.

Native Language Acquisition: A Task Analysis

Within the last few decades, interest in language acquisition has been intense and has consistently resulted in a multiplicity of methods, terms, and, of course, research publications. I will in no way attempt to do justice to this immense body of literature, but I will attempt to succinctly summarize and discuss major trends in this field in as much as they relate to the basic topic of interest here. For more detailed reviews of monolingual language acquisition, several other publications (some technical, others not as technical) are recommended: Menyuk, 1971; Cazden, 1972; Brown, 1973; Lenneberg & Lenneberg, 1975; Braine, 1976; Bloom, 1978; Bates, 1976; DeVilliers & DeVilliers, 1978.

When we consider the observation and documentation of language, it seems appropriate to conclude that "languages are composed of speech sounds, syllables, morphemes and sentences, and meaning is largely conveyed by the properties and particular use of these units" (Menyuk, 1971; p. 21). Therefore, language can be seen as a regularized system wherever it occurs. Native speakers of language can make judgments concerning this regularity by considering whether or not any utterance makes "sense." Although the emphasis has been placed on languages' structural regularity, additional evidence (Bates, 1976) clearly indicates that structure cannot stand alone. That is, the meaning of an utterance is conveyed by both its formal structure and the specific environment in which it occurs. Therefore, for any verbal signal to make "sense," we must be considerate of the physical and social characteristics of the surrounding environment.

Moreover, particular physical characteristics of the utterance itself (the intonation, stress, speed, etc., of the utterance) are important. These characteristics become increasingly significant during the study of early language acquisition when the structure of the child's utterance is limited, yet the functioning of verbal communication is quite complex. In sum, the effect of any verbal signal depends on its linguistic, physical character in conjunction with its actual context.

Children's acquisitions of their native linguistic competence can be characterized as a contiuum, moving from simple one-word utterances to more complex word combinations (syntax). If one ignores the functional use of crying as the beginning of communicative competence, then single-word utterances, usually very idiosyncratic (e.g., "papa" for *food*), mark the first distinguishable stage of formalized language development. To move beyond this early stage, the child faces tasks associated with phonology, morphology, syntax, and semantics.

Phonology. This form of information available to the infant is characterized by articulatory and acoustic features of speech sounds. Therefore, any word's (or utterance's) basic physical constituent is the sound or combination of sounds. The specific distinctive features and the rules for using these features are not evident at this time and are a source of continuous investigation. Evidence of phonological discrimination in infants, four to six weeks of age, is available (Morse, 1974), although the exact nature of such discrimination as it is related to linguistic development is unclear (Eimas, 1974; Fergusen & Garnica, 1975; Morse, 1974). An international alphabet of phonemes categorizes the various individual speech sounds that are found throughout the world. Therefore, phonologists can transcribe or code the sounds of language, and, in some cases, mechanically duplicate these sounds. It is the task of the child to differentiate between the sounds in his environment, much like the phonologist, and then duplicate and structure these sound systems into communicative networks. At this level, it seems crucial for the child to receive phonological input since he/she does not come preprogrammed for any one class of sound systems.

Morphology.   Morphemes can be considered the smallest meaningful unit of speech (Cazden, 1972). *Free morphemes* are the first to occur in early language, and these units can stand alone, such as "mommy," "daddy," etc. *Blend morphemes* are later in developing and cannot occur alone but must be attached to other morphemes. These include verb inflections like *ed* and *ing* and noun inflections like *s* (for pluralization and possession). Extensive studies that have traced the development of certain morphemes longitudinally in the same children have detailed a seemingly reliable order of development for specific morphemes in English speakers (Brown, 1973; De Villiers & De Villiers, 1973). The use of morphemes development as an index of developmental language complexity is best exemplified by work with the now famous Cambridge children: Adam, Eve, and Sarah. Of significance in this detailed longitudinal study was the clear rise in linguistic ability as measured over time by the Mean Length of Utterance (MLU) and the individual differences across subjects in this rise.

Syntax.   Syntactic rules identify sequential relationships of verbal units and, in doing so, describe one further systematic regularized character of language. In English, we are accustomed to word strings that begin with a subject (a noun or noun phrase), followed by a verb or verb phrase, and terminated with an object (a noun or noun phrase related to the verb). Of course, this description is only an ideal mapping of pieces we call sentences. Utterances in typical human discourse frequently exclude one or more of these units and rely on the context of the utterance to convey the proper meaning. For example, the utterance "Bill," under particular circumstances, may be restated as one of a number of fully formed sentences: "Come in the house, Bill;" "Bill, look at me;" "Bill, open the door;" etc.

Semantics.   The semantic component of language might be best characterized as an individual or community dictionary of a specific individual's language or of the language of several individuals. Just as I have attempted to define phonology, syntax, and semantics in these pages, each unit(s) of speech must be defined in order to serve any meaningful function. Definitions of any linguistic unit(s) may not be formalized in the spoken language of young children, yet they are as important to the functioning of language as formal definitions are in written prose. For instance, a child's utterance of "cucu" may be defined both for him and his audience by its function, "asking for a cookie." Confusions in definition often occur due to the differential experience with a particular unit of speech. It is clear that this same sort of definitional confusion is also operating among adults. (In most regions of the United States, the term *coffee regular* indicates the absence of cream or sugar; in parts of New England, this same term specifies the addition of cream). Countless examples such as these are readily available to each of us.

Therefore, interpretations of a sentence, such as "The girl jumped rope," requires knowledge concerning the properties of each constituent part: girl, jumped, and rope. Yet, the string of these parts placed together in the sentence are just as important a facet of the sentence as its individual parts. That is, the *syntagmatic* relationship of these parts (how they are placed in sequence) reveals significant information concerning the relationship of these parts.

Linguistic Variability. Two terms are frequently used to describe the major diversity of language: *idiolect* and *dialect*. The first term is used to recognize each person's unique linguistic experiences and how they shape that person's individual language. A group of similar idiolects that differs from other groups with respect to phonology, morphonology, etc. identifies a dialect. Therefore, it is the case that similar dialects usually make up an identifiable language group, which in turn suggests the nonexistence of a "pure" language. Theoretically, non-standard dialects can be assumed to be equally well developed and systematic. Independent from its theoretical validity, the nation of dialect equivalence with regard to development and regularization receives empirical support from the extensive research on black dialect patterns (Labov, 1970). Labov and his colleagues have pointed out several systematic differences between black English and what is normally identified as the dialect of standard English. The research describes the verb form *be* "to indicate generally repeated action, or existential state in sentences such as 'He be with us;' 'They be fooling around' " (Labov & Cohen, 1967; p. 76). An additional study by Henrie (1969) found that urban black children used unconjugated *be* ("He's always be there.") to express habitual meaning in a task requiring them to retell a story they had heard in standard English.

Physical, geographic separation is one variable that accounts for such linguistic diversity. Although this is a common and clearly observable explanation, dialects occur under other circumstances. For instance, the speech of mothers (or any adult) to young children differs significantly from adult speech. Snow and Ferguson (1977) have documented and discussed this interesting and consistent form of linguistic differentiation as more simple and more redundant. In fact, the overall speech of young children might be considered a dialect as it is presently defined here. (It is important to note that the term *dialect* is usually constrained to the description of adult, "fully-mature," speech competencies.) Of major significance is that speakers develop diverse linguistic repertoires and that this is the norm, not the exception.

Due to its importance in the investigation of social class differences in speech usage, another concept related to linguistic diversity needs to be raised here: speech code. Historically, the concept of speech code can be traced to early work of Basal Bernstein, an English sociologist who was concerned with the different linguistic styles of middle class and working class children in England (Bernstein, 1961). The speech of these children was reportedly classified into *restricted codes* and *elaborated codes*. Restricted code was characterized by indexical speech, which is speech that presumes some high degree of shared knowledge. Therefore, this speech was described as usually much shorter (in terms of utterance length) and less specific in character. The elaborated code, on the other hand, was more formal in the sense that no shared knowledge was presumed. This speech made use of more adjectives, adverbs, and clauses. Lower class children were described as using only a restricted code, while middle class children could switch between codes depending on the environmental demands. Although these formulations are clearly still a major focus of controversy, they are discussed here to serve as an introduction to the form of linguistic diversity referred to as *codes*. Hymes (1974) has explicitly detailed some of the variables that must be considered in determining the code or style of the speaker and the ability of the listener to make sense of the variations:

Setting
Where and when the speech act is taking place. Children are generally allowed to be louder outside than in, for instance, and may already have learned they are supposed to whisper (or not talk at all) in church.

Participants
Age, sex, kinship, social class, education, or occupation may make a difference. An English speaker would seldom have difficulty identifying the listener in a conversation with a young child by the speaker's grammar, word choice, and intonation (although the same style is sometimes used with pets). Many languages have different pronominal forms to indicate social distance, and the sex of a speaker, to some extent, determines appropriate word choice.

Ends
Style sometimes depends on purpose, whether the speech act is a request, demand, query, warning, or more statement of information.

Act sequence
This refers to the prescribed form a speech act takes when it is closely controlled by the culture, as is usually the case with prayers, public speeches of lectures, and jokes. It also refers to what may be talked about in each, what can be appropriately prayed about in contrast to what can be appropriately joked about.

Key
The same words may express various tones, moods, manner (serious, playful, belligerent, sarcastic). The signal may be nonverbal, such as wink or gesture, or conveyed by intonation, word choice, or some other linguistic convention.

Instrumentalities
Different verbal codes may be selected. Even a monolingual will have a choice of registers (varieties along a formal-informal continuum). Many speakers are able to choose among regional and social dialects as well. The choice is usually an unconcious one and may indicate respect, insolence, humor, distance, or intimacy.

Norms
Norms of interaction and interpretation in a speech act include taking turns in speaking (if appropriate in the speaker's culture), knowing the proper voice level to express anger, and sharing understandings about such things as what to take seriously and what to discount. It includes knowing polite greeting forms and other "linguistic manners," like what not to talk about at the dinner table.

Genres
Some speech acts may be categorized in formal structures: poem, myth, tale, proverb, riddle, curse, prayer, oration, lecture, editorial. Even children are often expected to know a few of the forms appropriate to their culture, including the "Once upon a time . . ." of middle-class English. (Hymes, 1974; pp. 47–48)

Native Language Acquisition: Theoretical Perspectives

It is with this multifaceted nature of language that the speech and language clinicians come face to face when assisting children in achieving communicative competence. It is possible to conclude that normal children by a very early age, have mastered a large segment of their linguistic environment. That is, a child has developed a significant portion of linguistic and social interaction competency within the first five to six years of his/her life. The child is able to understand and produce complex forms of language at this time. (Complexity is defined here in terms of the linguistic features discussed earlier: phonology, morphology, syntax, and semantics.) In addition, the child is capable of code switches, or shifts, which serve to further clarify his speech productions and his understanding of his/her social interactions.

How does the child tackle this myriad of tasks? How is this related to the task of the clinician? Chomsky (1965) considers language as dichotomous in nature, consisting of linguistic *competence* and linguistic *performance*. The first attribute of language is concerned with the speaker's linguistic knowledge; the second, with the speaker's actual linguistic productions. Chomsky relegates the duties of the child to that of a linguist: the child must determine from relevant linguistic information in his environment the underlying systems of rules in order to generate appropriate linguistic performances. As indicated earlier in the chapter, it does not seem appropriate to restrict our interest in language to a pure structural analysis. Yet, Chomsky's definition served as a theoretical base for much of the research presently available on young children (Bloom, 1978; De Villiers & De Villiers, 1978; Menyuk, 1971). The structure of children's speech and their ability to perform transformations has been of prime interest. It is true that any analysis of language acquisition must account for the almost miraculous performance of young children with respect to generative speech. That is, any theoretical or conceptual treatment of language acquisition must account for the clear performance of children in understanding and producing utterances that they themselves have never heard. As Cazden (1981) has argued, acquisition of language does not seem to be related to environmentally oriented interactions that focus on the mechanisms of modeling or speech correction. This theoretical perspective would hold the genetic base for language development as most important and is reflective of a larger nativistic perspective reflected in Chomsky's (1965) view of language. Within this theoretical view, the clinician has a minor role in language training.

An alternative environmental assistance, learning perspective, has concentrated significantly on the mechanism of modeling and environmental feedback in considering the acquisition of language (Baer, 1976; Miller & Dollard, 1941; Sherman, 1971; Skinner, 1957). This conceptualization of language has had a significant effect on research that is clinically concerned with language training of language deviant and deficient populations (Garcia & DeHaven, 1980; Goetz, Schular, & Sailor, 1980). This research has indicated the effectiveness of training specific instances of morphology and syntax using a training package that includes (*a*) shaping, (*b*) fading, and (*c*) differential reinforcement. Central to these training efforts has been the utilization of imitation of "correct" speech forms and the generalized use of trained speech beyond the specific stimulus/response parameters receiving attention during training. For instance, Guess (1968) trained a speech deficient child first to imitate singular and plural labels and then to label specific singular and plural instances of stimulus arrays without plural sets; hence, the subject was able to label correctly never-before-trained plural stimulus arrays. Training on series of plural arrays produced a generalized plural response class. Within this theoretical conceptualization, the clinician is of critical import.

In contrast to the linguistic and learning conceptualization of language, a more recent theoretical alternative has received research attention. Within the developmental area, there exists an ongoing controversy over whether language influences cognition or cognition influences language. Piaget (1952) has long recognized that complex cognitive functioning occurs in young children who have yet to develop only the simplest of linguistic skills. He has proposed that language is a subset of cognitive and symbolic functioning. Morehead and Morehead (1974) have directly related Piaget's cognitive development conceptualization to the process of language acquisition. Vygotsky (1962), on the other hand, argues that higher levels of cognition originate in language. He proposed that certain concepts cannot be developed until language has "developed the capacity" to deal with these concepts. He holds that, after the age of two years, emotions, perceptions, and social behavior are intimately related with linguistic experience. Independent of the locus of control (i.e., language influences cognition or cognition influences language), there is a growing agreement that the two symbolic processes are intricately related (De Villiers & De Villiers, 1978).

Prutting (1979) selectively reviews literature related to this cognitive-language interaction perspective. She summarizes and organizes the developmental of phonological, morphological, syntactic, and pragmatic communicative behaviors in six stages from prelinguistic to the adult level. She argues that the ontogeny of linguistic behavior is directly related to the cognitive processes that the child is capable of at various stages of development. Although such a conclusion leaves the specific causal relationship between cognition and language unresolved, it clearly provides a conceptualization of language development cognizant of the relationship. Moreover, much like Piaget (1952), this stage-process position holds that the child is an active participant in his/her own development. The exact implications of this theoretical conceptualization for speech and language intervention has only recently been addressed (Morehead & Morehead, 1974). The role of the clinicians might best be described as a "cognitive facilitator" with less concern for direct linguistic training.

In sum, native language acquisition must presently be considered within several conceptual domains. It seems most appropriate to acknowledge at least three major theoretical orientations: (*a*) linguistic, (*b*) learning, and (*c*) cognitive. It seems just as appropriate to emphasize that each position possesses its supporters and detractors; yet, empirical research generated by each position has clearly advanced our understanding of language acquisition by emphasizing the empirical phenomenon and alternative processes that account for these phenomenon. It seems evident that language acquisition is systematic. It can be described as a developmental phenomenon, with its present character dependent on its past character and its development significantly related to environmental interaction. Although the descriptive account of its developmental character is unfolding, the exact causal relationship between environmental, cognitive, and linguistic parameters continue to be explored. With this general introduction to the complexities of language, the remainder of this chapter will deal with the specific environmental variables identified as significant in enhancing communication in language delayed populations.

DESCRIPTION OF THE DISORDERS

Give the complex definition of language, a similar complex problem surfaces in defining a language/speech disorder. The American Speech-Language-Hearing Association reports that some 5 percent of school-age children are language impaired (De Villiers & De Villiers, 1978). Some 80 percent of these language impaired children are identified as possessing articulation disorders. More recent speech intervention thinking suggest that articulation disorders are the most treated but not necessarily the most handicapping condition related to severely impaired communication (Goetz, et al., 1979). That is, clinical intervention too often is aimed at disorders that least effect communicative competence.

Given the prior definition of language, it is conceivable that a disorder may result both in the receptive and expressive domain, in language form (phonology, morphology, or syntax), in the paralinguistic character of speech (stuttering, false starts, intonation, speed, etc.), in language discourse, or in some combination of the above. It is not clear whether some disorders are likely to occur as a group and others as more isolated. It is clear that experimental treatment of disorders does occur most often in isolation. For this reason, the following review of treatment demonstrations is divided into isolated language modalities.

RECEPTIVE SPEECH

The stimulus control of words (i.e., receptive language) has been continually emphasized in the behavioral development of children and in general language training programs (Baron, Kaufman, & Stauber, 1969; Gesell & Thompson, 1934). However, receptive language control (e.g., pointing to objects when requested, following instruction) has received little examination in reference to procedures for establishing such control. Zimmerman, Zimmerman, and Russell (1969) conducted one of the initial studies concerning the development of instruction-following behavior with retarded individuals. Using a single subject design, Zimmerman et al. found that token reinforcement could generate and maintain a high frequency of instruction-following behavior. The study illustrated an effective procedure of increasing instruction-following responses for at least some of the retarded subjects, while emphasizing the importance of providing objective, quantitative information about developing such behavior. Operant training techniques have also been applied in establishing receptive language generalization with an autistic child (Craighead, O'Leary, & Allen, 1973). These authors found that instruction-following could be developed across instructions that had not been presented in training.

Several studies (e.g., Guess, 1969; Guess & Baer, 1973) have continued to examine procedures for establishing receptive language and for producing generalization with severely language delayed populations. Focusing on plural morphemes, these investigators illustrated that generalization of receptive speech can occur with this population. Frisch and Schumaker (1974) have extended this research area by enamining generalized prepositional usage in retarded children. These investigators applied prompting and reinforcement procedures in training a request to place various objects next to, under, or on top of other objects. Five requests were designed in each prepositional category along with using the different objects, which allowed for several different combinations of requests for each preposition examined. Their results indicated that, as training on requests of each prepositional category developed, correct responses to untrained requests of that category occurred. Receptive generalization within prepositional categories (responses) was clearly evident as a result of the operant techniques applied in the study. Frisch and Schumaker also found that it seemed necessary to train and produce generalization in each category separately before training concurrently between categories. The results of this study further support past research as well as provide an additional basis for further investigation.

Other studies involving normal and retarded populations do not support the previous results in obtaining generalization. Striefel and Wetherby (1973) used a combination of positive reinforcement and prompting and fading procedures to train a profoundly retarded boy to follow specific instructions. Operant techniques were shown to establish and control instruction-following with over 20 different verbal instructions that underwent training. However, generalization did not occur to nontrained verbal instructions, nor did all verbal components of the instructions control the specific responses.

Multiple cues, many times, are an ingredient found within stimulus-control training procedures. Receptive training procedures using multiple cues (such as pointing a finger and simultaneously providing the verbal cue "bring me the doll") have been demonstrated as effective (Striefel, Bryan, & Aikins, 1974). In most instances, establishing stimulus control of a single element cue (verbal requests) has been achieved by the use of fading techniques and is often the first step in training receptive speech.

PRODUCTIVE SPEECH

Being able to *produce* appropriate speech is extremely important for children. Contrasted with receptive speech, productive speech encompasses those verbal signals which the child can say and use. Kaye, Kaye, Whelan, and Hopkins (1968) reported one of the first studies on generalized productive speech. The training focussed on the use of verbal greetings with withdrawn mental patients. It was found that generalization across persons only occurred after a number of therapists were included in training that behavior. Lyon (1971) also demonstrated generalization effects with hospitalized schizophrenics. The subjects were reinforced for answering a number of everyday questions, such as "What's your name?" and "What are you doing?" The same questions in settings where the therapist did not reinforce this response substantially improved only after the therapist utilized various settings for training.

Although acquired language may often spontaneously generalize (Craighead, et al., 1973; Johnston & Johnston, 1972), a therapist should not rely totally on this phenomenon (Wincze, Leitenberg, & Agras, 1972). Indeed, an analysis of those procedures that are beneficial in facilitating this phenomenon should be stressed and continually programmed. An initial study relating to this issue with nonverbal, retarded children was completed by Garcia (1974). Garcia established a conversational speech form through the use of differential reinforcement (e.g., shaping and fading techniques) and imitation. The speech form consisted of three responses, each involving a three-word sentence. Three experimenters assigned to three different settings were involved in the study. The use of the conversational speech form was observed by the third experimenter, who had never trained the speech form, only after the first two experimenters had conducted training in their assigned areas. This evidence would indicate that variation in training situations and/or the use of more than one speech therapist would enhance generalized speech usage.

Generalized conversational speech (e.g., questioning) has also been investigated with retarded individuals within a training setting. Twardosz and Baer (1973) provide such research in training two retarded boys to ask an appropriate question about those items that they could not label. In analyzing the applied techniques, Twardosz and Baer found that modeling alone had no significant effects. However, when the children were prompted and rewarded for appropriate questioning (i.e., saying "what letter?"), they began to ask questions about the nontrained stimulus objects. This study further illustrates that generalized speech usage can be obtained by means of operant training techniques and that the development of this phenomenon can occur with the retarded population.

Generative Response Class

The term *generative response class* has emerged to describe a group of responses affected by both stimulus and response generalization. Baer and Guess (1973) have suggested that such patterns of generalization could be termed *generative*. That is, specific training procedures not only changed the target responses, but also developed an array of responses generated from the training program. This pattern of generalization may be exemplified when children begin to generate several untrained responses to a set of untrained stimulus items. Generative response classes have usually been discussed in reference to the development of imitation and language.

Imitation. Imitation generally entails the behavior of matching a modeled response (Sloane & MacAulay, 1968). Because imitation may entail a wide range of responses, it is frequently used to explain the development of a vast array of children's behaviors and is considered a basic behavioral mechanism in the childhood learning process (Peterson, 1968).

Baer and Sherman (1964) reported one of the first studies on generalized imitation with preschool children. These researchers applied operant techniques in developing motor imitative responses and observed the control of untrained imitative responses as a function of the training procedures. Generalized motor imitation has received considerable attention with autistic as well as retarded children since this early study. Metz (1965) systematically reinforced an autistic child's responses that were topographically similar to the trainer's modeled demonstrations. By saying "good" and providing food after each correct response, Metz demonstrated that operant training techniques could establish and maintain imitative responses to demonstration both involved and not involved in training. Therefore, the child who underwent training learned to generate new, untrained modeled demonstrations. Stimulus generalization occurred in this study because novel, nontrained demonstrations were followed. Response generalization occurred because novel responses that were not trained were also established. Baer, Peterson, and Sherman (1967) reported similar findings with three severely retarded children. Employing operant training procedures, Baer, et al. (1967) found that the children would begin to imitate untrained, modeled responses after several different responses had been trained. As a result, these investigators illustrated that a generalized imitative repertoire could be developed with institutionalized retardates and that such a phenomenon could be a possible goal in therapeutic services.

Although several studies have investigated these generalization effects, the boundaries of generalization effects have received little attention. Imitation, for example, may not be one large response class but a set of different, topographically separate subclasses that may limit the overall generative effects of imitation. Garcia, Baer, and Firestone (1971) analyzed the boundaries of imitative response classes with retarded children. The operant training techniques applied in establishing generalized imitation were effective but within restricted topographical boundaries (i.e., small motor, large motor, short vocal, and long vocal). Thus, training each topographical-imitative response set resulted in developing a corresponding imitative response class.

Language Repertoires. In addition to establishing simple vocal imitations (e.g., Lovaas, Berberich, Perloff, & Schaeffer, 1966), more complex forms of verbal behavior have been developed with retarded children. One of the initial studies in this area was completed by Guess, Sailor, Rutherford, and Baer (1968). The authors examined the generative use of the plural morpheme in a severely retarded girl. The training procedures involved reinforcing the girl for imitating the experimenter's correct verbal label of a single object or pair of objects. As a result of the operant training procedures, the subject began to label new, never-before-trained objects in the plural form. The training of generative grammar has been demonstrated by studies using operant techniques for developing usage of noun suffixes, verb inflections, rules of syntax, and prepositional usage (Shumaker & Sherman, 1970; Wheeler & Sulzer, 1970).

Garcia, Guess, and Byrnes (1973) have further expanded the research on generative language by demonstrating the development and generalized use of a singular and plural declarative sentence with a retarded girl. The training procedures in this study included modeling and differential reinforcement. The study examined training a response to a question when a picture was presented. Reinforcement was contingent on correct responding. Not only was correct responding established, but a generative use of syntax occurred. Generative speech usage was obtained and covaried with the modeled sentence form that was reinforced. The study by Garcia, et al., (1973) supports earlier techniques involved in obtaining generative speech (i.e., shaping, fading, modeling, prompting) as well as demonstrating the importance of differential reinforcement in establishing the generative usage of syntax with a speech deficient child.

Zimmerman and Rosenthal (1974) have reported that rule-governed behavior, including Piagetian conservation responses, problem-solving strategies, and creative behavior, can be developed by modeling procedures in normal children. Training techniques, such as physical prompting, shaping, and reinforcement are not necessary for developing such complex responses with normal children. In fact, using guided practice (prompting) as well as providing verbal instruction can be far less effective with normal children than to simply present a model (Rosenthal & Zimmerman, 1973; Rosenbaum, 1967). However, the differential effectiveness of training procedures found in teaching normal children may not hold true by teaching the same behaviors with retarded children. Indeed, retarded children may require a combination of training procedures rather than an isolated technique, such as modeling, for establishing generative or rule-governed skills.

Forehand and Yoder (1974) completed one of the first comparative studies in establishing generalization with 36 normal and 36 retarded children. By examining the acquisition and transfer of conceptual learning with varied training procedures, these investigators found that such consequences as tangible and social rewards were not effective with either group of children. The combined procedures of modeling and modeling plus verbal cues facilitated conceptual learning in both groups. It was also reported the IQ level was not a factor influencing training or transfer. Forehand and Yoder concluded that retarded and normals, matched on mental age, equally profited from the training procedures for both the original learning and transfer of that learning.

Clinton and Boyce (1975) also failed to find any significant differences between normal and retarded children. These investigators found that both groups of children produced more plurals during the experimental phase when exposed to modeling and appropriate statements about the production of plurals than when exposed simply to modeling. Clinton and Boyce suggest that the experimental task and the developmental level of the subjects may be attributed to the failure to find any differences between the normal and retarded groups of children. Further research is certainly needed for determining what factors do interact and produce differential effects of generalization with normal and retarded populations.

Studies reporting only limited generalization effects with retarded individuals seem to indicate that a combination of training procedures is important. Guess

(1968) exemplifies this problem in developing simple language responses. This researcher utilized feedback, verbal cues (instructions and questions), non-verbal cues, and reinforcement procedures in teaching retarded children the receptive and productive usage of the plural morpheme. In examining the relationship between receptive and productive language, Guess found a lack of generalization effects across the two speech modalities. That is, the children did not generalize to the productive modality after being taught in the receptive modality and vice-versa. This study indicated that, although a combination of training procedures may be successfully used in establishing simple forms of language, training may be required across a wide range of responses before establishing extensive generalization effects with retarded children. Mann and Baer (1971) investigated the relationship of receptive training to correct productive language usage with normal functioning children. Their findings indicated that training in the receptive modality facilitated the correct articulation of words, and therefore, generalization across modalities was obtained with normal children.

Guess and Baer (1973) taught four severely retarded children to use appropriate pluralization rules (i.e., concurrently training both productive and receptive speech). The study involved training productive usage of the plural ending *s* and training receptive usage of the plural ending *es* with two of the subjects. Although a generative rule of usage occurred within receptive and productive modalities, generative usage across modalities was demonstrated by only one of the four subjects. The occurrence of generalization across receptive and productive speech even when the plural morpheme was extremely similar (i.e., *es* versus *s*) was demonstrated to be the exception rather than the rule. Although there are instances in which receptive and productive language have been independent (Guess, 1968), these two behavioral classes may still be functionally related (Mann & Baer, 1971). Guess and Baer (1973) concluded that speech therapists should probably train retarded children in both receptive and productive modalities to ensure a complete and appropriate use of pluralism rules. The exact variables (e.g., baseline performance levels of subjects) affecting receptive and productive speech as an entire response class remain to be thoroughly examined. It should be assumed that such research, as well as investigations on how a response may be added or subtracted from an established response class, is valuable. The educator as well as the clinician involved in developing and breaking down response classes and in developing generative response classes could surely benefit from such research (Peterson, 1968).

RELATED ISSUES: MAINTENANCE

Recently, serious interest has been directed toward related issues of therapeutic maintenance of trained speech and language. From an applied perspective, it might be of benefit to consider the maintenance of training effects as a special instance of generalization. In this case, maintenance might be considered, at the most simplest of levels, generalization across time. As with the previously discussed types of generalization, maintenance effects do not negate the simultaneous presence of a training procedure in some form. Traditionally, maintenance effects have been considered separate from ongoing training procedures and are only temporarily linked to any previous history of training. If maintenance of behavior can be viewed systematically as a generalization (reviewed above), then data does not predict much, if any, maintenance. Instead, this data suggests that a systematic study of maintenance effects is necessary to identify relevant training variables that possibly are applied on a varied temporal basis, which would be functionally related to a maintenance phenomenon.

Therefore, the normal follow-up study is in need of functional expansion. Instead of asking if behavior occurs sometime after training is terminated, the question should take a functional form by asking how to insure that the behavior will occur sometime after an initial training procedure is terminated. From a therapeutic perspective, this last issue seems as important as the one concerned with the original change or acquisition of behavior.

The need for follow-up in applied behavior analysis has continued to be emphasized over the years (Gelfand & Hartmann, 1968; Reese & Filipczak, 1980). However, very little follow-up information has been reported, especially over any long-term period. For instance, in reviewing three major behavioral publications, Keeley, Shemberg & Carbonell (1976) indicate that only 12 percent of all sampled studies provided follow-up information for at least six months after intervention. The need for follow-up measures becomes extremely important when considering the extensive application of behavior modification with the mentally retarded.

Clinical studies reporting follow-up information have varied in their length of follow-up. Some studies have focused on relatively short-term follow-up in a few months (Herbert & Baer, 1972); others on long-term follow-up of several years (Lovaas, Koegel, Simmons & Long, 1973). Investigating imitation training with autistic children, Koegel and Rincover (1977) found that some of the children would generalize what had been taught across settings but did not maintain their acquired skill over a relatively short period. Follow-up and the use of intermittent reinforcement schedules in training and noncontingent reinforcement in the nontraining settings influenced the maintenance of the acquired skill. Hall and Tomblin (1978) studied the long-term effects of speech training interventions. Language-impaired and articulation-impaired subjects were located some 13 to 20 years after initial contact with a speech pathologist. Language-impaired subjects achieved at lower levels than the articulation-impaired subjects on standardized educational measures.

Follow-up research by Lovaas et al. (1973) has demonstrated that the significant differences in the therapeutic outcomes for autistic children depend on the posttreatment environment. Children who remained in an institutional environment following extensive therapy tended to regress to pretreatment levels, but children who returned home with their parents trained in behavior modification techniques actually improved markedly. A more important finding by Lovaas et al. showed that reinstating therapy briefly reestablished much of the original therapeutic gains with the children. Therefore, the study supports the view that once a skill has been taught, it is much easier to reinstate that skill.

Both the short-term and long-term research suggest that a trained skill may not be maintained. In addition, maintenance may be related to variables that are different from those factors influencing generalization across settings but associated with (a) the posttreatment environment and (b) the severity of the communication disorder.

Garcia and DeHaven (1980) report a six-year follow-up study that provides direct observational measure of an institutionalized profoundly retarded youth. The original research with the target subject involved training generalized conversational speech (DeHaven & Garcia, 1974). There were two objectives of this long-term follow-up. The first objective was to obtain a direct observational assessment of the youth's performance to determine how much functional speech had been retained. If the subject had lost the generalized skill, it was assumed that a minimum amount of training would be necessary to reestablish the previously acquired repertoire of functional speech. The second objective then was to determine the amount of training necessary to reestablish the previously taught speech. The results of the study indicated that the subject did not maintain the previously trained generalized skill. However, training was effective in reestablishing the generalized speech usage, but much more training was necessary than was initially expected. Once a skill has been taught it is not, at least in this case, easier to reinstate with the same training procedures.

From an applied point of view, the results, of follow-up studies continue to add to our knowledge of generalization and therapeutic efforts with the language disorder. It seems all too clear that generalization over time is an elusive phenomenon. A wide range of motivational factors and other variables (e.g., drugs, institutional conditions) may have contributed to the nonmaintenance effects and possibly to the extensive amount of retraining necessary. These studies do provide encouragement for developing long-term maintenance programs, because without such a component language training would become something only researchers would practice. This would be an extreme disservice to the therapists and clients who are in need of this important applied technology.

Variables that Influence Generalization

Another issue that is related to generalization effects focuses on several variables that potentially influence the occurrence of generalization, namely, training procedures, the type of population, and the nature of the responses selected for training.

Training. Language training packages (Baer & Sherman, 1964; Risley & Wolf, 1967) have included such components as the presentation of verbal or visual discrimination stimuli, guided practicing (prompting), shaping and fading procedures, and contingent reinforcement for correct responding. Variations include immediate delivery of reinforcers (Frisch & Schumaker, 1974), delayed reinforcement (Schwartz & Hawkins, 1970), the use of primary reinforcers (Garcia, et al., 1973), and the use of token procedures (Wheeler & Sulzer, 1970).

While providing an enriched technology of behavior analysis, the array of language training procedures has clouded the investigation of training effects. The effects are in no doubt influenced by the training procedures that are utilized; however, at this point, it is not possible to indicate what those specific influences are.

Populations. Much of the research on language training has been completed with extreme populations, usually retarded or severely disturbed individuals; however, there has been little effort to discover differences in generalization effects that can be attributed to the population factor alone. Two comparative studies between normal and retarded children have failed to indicate any significant difference in the generalization of language behavior (Clinton & Boyce, 1975; Forehand & Yoder, 1974).

Responses. In training both receptive and productive language behaviors, many levels of response difficulty have been selected. The range includes a simple hand wave response (Stokes, Baer & Jackson, 1974) and the use of sentences (Garcia, 1974) and questions (Twardosz & Baer, 1973). The most meaningful unit of analysis of training effects would seem to be the comparison of the difficulty level of the response and the population with which that response was trained. It is apparent that more research is needed in this area.

A CLINICAL CASE: SUSAN

Susan was referred to the Speech Audiology Department upon her admittance to kindergarten. Her parents and her teacher reported that she had a "minimum use of verbal behavior with a tendency to imitate other's speech." She had never received speech or language therapy. The following briefly describes the procedures that were utilized in determining and implementing a therapeutic language program.

Diagnosis

Keeping in mind that language is more than the correct usage of phonology, morphology, and syntax, Susan was administered standard diagnostic instruments along with a systematic classroom and home observation. Moreover, interviews with the parents and each sibling, combined with a similar interview with her teacher, were conducted. Each of these indices of Susan's language behavior was utilized in determining therapeutic goals as well as treatment characteristics. For example, language form and vocabulary measures indicated Susan's (*a*) minimal knowledge (based on the norm) of rudimentary lexicon, morphology, and syntax, and (*b*) no serious problems with phonology. However, Susan's use of language was restricted to brief requests and responses-to-requests by other children. She rarely initiated discourse, nor did she contribute to discourse once it was initiated by others.

Training

The above evaluative characteristics suggest a particular training emphasis relating to social discourse. That is, a training program was developed to enhance Susan's ability to:

1. utilize verbal requests, especially verbal requests relating to a "natural" call for requests by others (such as, "what do you want?", "where do you want to go?") Examples include: "Give me _____;" "I want _____;" "I want to go to _____." This training illustrates the use of examplars with functional categories. Its goal was to train these exemplars with the issue of generative response class in mind.

2. initiate discourse by use of common greetings and initiations. Examples are: "Hi, what are you doing?"; "Hi, you want to play?" Please note that the form of the language was not an issue but that the initiating function was the focus.

Generalization

The parents and the teacher, along with siblings and school peers, participated in this aspect of training. Parents were enlisted to conduct a minimum of 25 formal training trials daily and to be cognizant of and utilize natural instances of requesting and discourse initiating. A similar arrangement was established with the classroom teacher. Moreover, Susan's older brother and two of her classmates spent a minimum of 10 minutes daily in a requesting exercise developed by the therapist. All of these training sessions supported the therapist's daily 20-minute session with Susan.

Outcomes

Although there was no experimental evaluation of the therapeutic effects of this intervention, the following data was reported:

1. *Therapeutic Session.* Susan's responses to request and initiation trials increased to nearly 100 percent over a period of 25 sessions.

2. *Home Sessions.* Susan's response to request and initiation trials increased to nearly 75 percent correct over this same temporal period. Susan consistently failed to respond correctly to one of the request trials (each trial was presented five times). Her parent's reported: "language ability is much better. Suzie speaks more often and she usually tells us what she wants now."

3. *Classroom Session.* Susan's response to request and initiation trials during classroom session was 100 percent correct. The teacher reported Susan's parallel increase in general verbal responding to her requests.

(No data was collected for sibling and peer training sessions.)

Summary

The above example of the training program for Susan identifies several issues raised in the main body of this chapter. The diagnostic evaluation was concerned with both form and function, and the training designed and implemented considered generative response class research procedures to establish a broad sector of verbal responding. Moreover, generalization to other settings, e.g., individuals, was incorporated into the therapeutic goals and intervention strategy. Some ongoing evaluation of Susan's language usage, both formally and informally obtained in each of the settings, was evident. Although this example does not include clinical adaptation of all the phenomenon noted by research in this area, it is an example that incorporates our most recent understanding of a language disorder treatment based on a body of empirical research.

SUMMARY AND CONCLUSIONS

This review indicates that speech and language enhancement effects can be obtained with language disabled children and that generalization may occur across both stimulus and response modalities. Studies reported in this manuscript have employed various behavior change procedures with several types of populations. In addition, these studies have been carried out across a wide range of situations and settings. Because of the diversity of variables included in this group of studies, a strong conclusion can be made—training can be successfully programmed, and it can be deliberately developed within a technology of behavioral change procedures.

Researchers have generally used a combination of training procedures in modifying specific responses and in facilitating transfer of training. Reasons for combining these procedures have frequently focused on clinical considerations, including such factors as (*a*) a priority of obtaining positive and beneficial effects, (*b*) the complexity of the target behaviors involved in training, and (*c*) an emphasis on maximizing the speed in assisting the child.

Yet, investigators have been successful in isolating and comparing variables that influence language training effects. With normal children, the use of modeling procedures along with varying nonrelevant task aspects can be sufficient for developing skills and for producing generalization. More extensive training procedures (including a greater amount of training) are usually required in order to obtain generalization with retarded individuals. In addition, the types of training techniques employed may vary in their efficiency of producing generalization. And finally, how the behavior change techniques are combined and applied during training (e.g., across a variety of settings or concurrently to a variety of responses) can be a critical factor in facilitating transfer of training. As a result, the extent of training effects is dependent on a combination of variables, including the subject population undergoing training, the specific procedures used, and the target behavior.

REFERENCES

Baer, D. M. The organism as host. *Human Development,* 1976, 19, 87–98.

Baer, D. M., Peterson, R. F., & Sherman, J. The development of imitation by reinforcing behavioral similarity to a model. *Journal of the Experimental Analysis of Behavior,* 1967, *10,* 405–416.

Baer, D. M., & Sherman, J. Reinforcement control generalized imitation in young children. *Journal of Experimental Child Psychology,* 1964, *1,* 34–49.

Baron, A., Kaufman, H., & Stauber, K. A. Effects of instructions and reinforcement feedback on human operant behavior maintained by fixed interval reinforcement. *Journal of Experimental Analysis of Behavior,* 1969, *12,* 701–712.

Bates, E. *Language and context.* New York: Academic Press, 1976.

Bernstein, B. Social class and linguistic development: A theory of social learning. In A. H. Halsey, J. Floud, and C. A. Anderson (Eds.), *Education, economy and society.* New York: Free Press, 1961.

Bloom, L. *Readings in language development.* New York: John Wiley & Sons, 1978.

Braine, M. D. S. Children's first word combinations. *Monographs of the Society for Research in Child Development,* 1976.

Bowerman, M. Crosslinguistic similarities at two stages of syntactic development. In E. Lenneberg and E. Lenneberg (Eds.), *Foundations of language development.* London: UNESCO Press, 1975.

Brown, R. A. *A first language: The early stages.* Cambridge, Mass.: Harvard University Press, 1973.

Cazden, C. B. *Child language and education.* New York: Holt, Rinehart & Winston, 1972.

Cazden. C. B. Language development and the preschool environment. In C. B. Cazden (Ed.), *Language in early childhood education* (Rev. ed.). Washington, D.C.: NAWYC, 1981.

Chomsky, N. *Aspects of the theory of syntax*. Cambridge, Mass.: MIT Press, 1965.

Clinton, L., & Boyce, K. D. Rule-governed imitative verbal behavior as a function of modeling procedures. *Journal of Experimental Child Psychology*, 1975, 19, 115–121.

Craighead, W. E., O'Leary, K. D., & Allen, J. S. Teaching and generalization of instruction following in an "autistic" child. *Journal of Behavior Therapy and Experimental Psychiatry*, 1973, *4*, 171–176.

DeHaven, E. D., & Garcia, E. E. Continuation of training as a variable influencing the generalization of speech in a retarded child. *Journal of Abnormal Child Psychology*, 1974, *2*, 217–227.

De Villiers, J., & De Villiers, P. *Language acquisition*. Cambridge, Mass.: Harvard University, 1978.

Eimas, P. D. Linguistic processing of speech by young infants. In R. L. Schiefelbush and L. L. Lloyd (Eds.), *Language prespectives*. Baltimore: University Park Press, 1974.

Ferguson, C. A., & Garnica, O. K. Theories of phonological development. In E. Lenneberg and E. Lenneberg (Eds.), *Foundations of language development*. London: UNESCO Press, 1975.

Forehand, R., & Yoder, P. Acquisition and transfer of conceptual learning by normals and retardates: The effects of modeling, verbal cues, and reinforcement. *Behavior Research and Therapy*, 1974, *12*, 199–204.

Frisch, S. A., & Schumaker, J. B. Training generalized receptive prepositions in retarded children. *Journal of Applied Behavior Analysis*, 1974, *7*, 611–622.

Garcia, E. The training and generalization of a conversational speech form in nonverbal retardates. *Journal of Applied Behavior Analysis*, 1974, *7*, 137–151.

Garcia, E., Baer, D. M., & Firestone, I. The development of generalized imitation within topographically determined boundaries. *Journal of Applied Behavior Analysis*, 1971, *4*, 101–113.

Garcia, E. & DeHaven, E. Use of operant techniques in the establishment and generalization of language: A review and analysis. *American Journal of Mental Deficiency*, 1980, *79*, 169–178.

Garcia, E., Guess, D., & Byrnes, J. Development of syntax in a retarded girl using procedures of imitation, reinforcement, and modeling. *Journal of Applied Behavior Analysis*, 1973, *6*, 189–298.

Gelfand, D. M. & D. P. Hartmann. Behavior therapy with children: A review and evaluation of research methodology. *Psychological Bulletin*, 1968, *69*, 204–215.

Gesell, A., & Thompson, H. *Infant behavior: Its genesis and growth*. New York: McGraw-Hill, 1934.

Goetz, L., Schular, A., & Sailor, W. Teaching functional speech to the severely handicapped: New directions. *Journal of Austism and Behavior Disorders*, 1980, *1*, 135–151.

Gonzalez, G. *The phonology of Corpus Christi Spanish.* Austin: Southwest Educational Development Laboratory, 1969.

Guess, D. An experimental analysis of linguistic development: The productive use of the plural morpheme. *Journal of Applied Behavior Analysis,* 1968, *1*, 297–306.

Guess, D., & Baer, D. M. An analysis of individual differences in generalization between receptive and productive language in retarded children. *Journal of Applied Behavior Analysis,* 1973, *6*, 311–331.

Guess, D., Sailor, W., Rutherford, G., & Baer, D. M. An experimental analysis of linguistic development: The productive use of the plural morpheme. *Journal of Applied Behavior Analysis,* 1968, *1*, 297–306.

Hall, P. K., & Tomblin, J. B. A follow-up study of children with articulation and language disorders. *Journal of Speech and Hearing Disorders,* 1978, *43*, 277–291.

Henrie, S. N., Jr. A study of verb phrases used by five-year-old nonstandard English-speaking children. Unpublished doctoral dissertation, University of California, Berkeley, 1969.

Herbert, E. W. & Baer, D. M. Training parents as behavior modifiers: self recording of contingent attention. *Journal of Applied Behavior Analysis,* 1972, 5, 139–150.

Hymes, D. *Foundations in sociolinguistics: An ethnographic approach.* Philadelphia: University of Pennsylvania Press, 1974.

Johnston, J. M., & Johnston, G. T. Modification of consonant speech-sound articulation in young children. *Journal of Applied Behavior Analysis,* 1972, *5*, 233–246.

Kaye, R. J., Kaye, J. H., Whelan, P. A., & Hopkins, B. L. The effects of reinforcement on the modification, maintenance, and generalization of social responses of mental patients. *Journal of Applied Behavior Analysis,* 1968, *1*, 307–317.

Keeley, S. M., Shemberg, F. M., & Carbonell, J. Operant clinical intervention: behavior management or beyond? Where at the data? *Behavior Therapy,* 1976, *7*, 292–305.

Koegel, R. L., & Rincover, A. Research on the difference between generalization and maintenance in extra-therapy responding. *Journal of Applied Behavior Analysis,* 1977, *10*, 1–12.

Labov, W. *The study of nonstandard English.* Urbana, Ill.: National Council of Teachers of English, 1970.

Labov, W., & Cohen, P. Systematic relations of standard and nonstandard rules in grammars of Negro speakers. *Project Literacy Reports No. 8.* Ithaca, N.Y.: Cornell University, 1967.

Lenneberg, E., & Lenneberg, E. (Eds.). *Foundations of language development* (Vol. 1 and 2). London: UNESCO Press, 1975.

Lovaas, I. O., Beberich, J. P., Perloff, B. F., & Schaeffer, B. Acquisition of imitative speech in schizophrenic children. *Science,* 1966, *151*, 705–707.

Lovaas, O. I., Koegel, R., Simmons, J. Q., & Long, J. S. Some generalizations and follow-up measures on autistic children in behavior therapy. *Journal of Applied Behavior Analysis,* 1973, *6,* 131–166.

Lyon, V. L. Conditioning and generalization of a verbal response in hospitalized schizophrenics. Unpublished doctoral dissertation, University of Kansas, 1971.

Mann, R., & Baer, D. M. The effects of receptive language training on articulation. *Journal of Applied Behavior Analysis,* 1971, *4,* 291–299.

Menyuk, P. *The acquisition and development of language.* New York: Prentice-Hall, 1971.

Metz, J. R. Conditioning generalized imitation in autistic children. *Journal of Experimental Child Psychology,* 1965, *2,* 389–399.

Miller, N. E., & Dollard, J. *Social learning and imitation.* New Haven, Conn.: Yale University Press, 1941.

Morehead, K. M., & Morehead, A. From signal to sign: A Piagetian view of thought and language during the first two years. In R. L. Shiefelbusch and L. L. Lloyd (Eds.), *Language perspectives: acquisition, retardation and intervention.* Baltimore: University Park Press, 1974.

Morse, P. A. Infant speech perception: A preliminary model and review of literature. In R. L. Schiefelbusch and L. L. Lloyd (Eds.), *Language perspectives: acquisition, retardation and intervention.* Baltimore: University Park Press, 1974.

Peterson, R. F. Some experiments on the organization of a class imitative behaviors. *Journal of Applied Behavior Analysis,* 1968, *1,* 225–235.

Piaget, J. *The origins of intelligence in children.* New York: W. W. Norton, 1952.

Prutting, C. A. Process/'pras/,ses/n: The action of moving forward progressively from one point to another on the way to completion. *Journal of Speech and Hearing Disorder,* 1979, *26,* 185–198.

Reese, S. C., & Filipczak, J. Assessment of skill generalization: measurement across setting, behavior, and time in educational setting. *Behavior Modification,* 1980, *4,* 209–224.

Risley, T. R., & Wolf, M. Establishing functional speech in echolalic children. *Behaviour Research and Therapy,* 1967, *5,* 73–88.

Rosenbaum, M. E. The effect of verbalization of correct responses by performers and observers on retention. *Child Development,* 1967, *38,* 615–623.

Rosenthal, T. L., & Zimmerman, B. J. Organization, observation and guided practice in concept attainment and generalization. *Child Development,* 1973, *44,* 606–613.

Schwartz, M., & Hawkins, R. Application of delayed reinforcement procedures to the behavior of an elementary school child. *Journal of Applied Behavior Analysis,* 1970, *3,* 85–96.

Sherman, J. Imitation and language development. In H. W. Reese and L. P. Lippset (Eds.), *Advances in child development and behavior.* New York: Academic Press, 1971.

Shumaker, J., & Sherman, J. A. Training generative verb usage by imitation and reinforcement procedures. *Journal of Applied Behavior Analysis*, 1970, *3*, 273–287.

Skinner, B. F. *Verbal behavior.* New York: Appleton-Century-Crofts, 1957.

Sloane, H. N., & MacAulay, B. D. *Operant procedures in remedial speech and language training.* Boston: Houghton Mifflin, 1968.

Snow, C. & Ferguson, C. *Talking to children.* Cambridge, Mass.: University Press, 1977.

Striefel, S., Bryan, K. S., & Aikins, D. G. Transfer of stimulus control from motor to verbal stimuli. *Journal of Applied Behavior Analysis*, 1974, *7*, 123–137.

Striefel, S., & Wetherby, B. Instruction-following behavior of a retarded child and its controlling stimuli. *Journal of Applied Behavior Analysis*, 1973, *6*, 663–670.

Stokes, T. F., Baer, D. M., & Jackson, R. L. Programming the generalization of greeting response in four retarded children. *Journal of Applied Behavior Analysis*, 1974, *7*, 599–611.

Twardosz, S., & Baer, D. M. Training two severely retarded adolescents to ask questions. *Journal of Applied Behavior Analysis*, 1973, *6*, 655–661.

Vygotsky, L. S. *Thought and language.* Cambridge, Mass.: MIT Press, 1962.

Wheeler, A. J., & Sulzer, B. Operant training and generalization of a verb response form in a speech-deficient child. *Journal of Applied Behavior Analysis*, 1970, *3*, 137–147.

Wincze, J. P., Leitenberg, H., & Agras, H. S. The effects of token reinforcement and feedback on the delusional verb behavior of chronic paranoid schizophrenics. *Journal of Applied Behavioral Analysis*, 1972, *5*, 247–262.

Zimmerman, B. J., & Rosenthal, T. L. Observational learning of rule-governed behavior by children. *Psychological Bulletin*, 1974, *81*, 29–42.

Zimmerman, E. H., Zimmerman, J., & Russell, C. D. Differential effects of token reinforcement on instruction-following behavior in retarded children. *Journal of Applied Behavior Analysis*, 1969, *2*, 101–112.

11

Enuresis and Encopresis

Daniel M. Doleys
Behavioral Medicine Services
Brookwood Medical Center
Divison of AMI
Birmingham, Alabama

ENURESIS

Definition and Incidence

The term *enuresis* is derived from Greek terminology and roughly translates to mean "to make water." Enuresis is a common problem among children. There are basically two types: daytime (diurnal) and nighttime (nocturnal) wetting. Both types can be further subdivided into continuous (primary) and discontinuous (secondary). The continuous enuretic has never achieved total urinary continence, while the discontinuous enuretic has demonstrated at least six months of urinary continence. However, the six-month criteria is arbitrary, since any duration of continence that is considered long enough to have provided evidence of control of bladder functioning would be sufficient to differentiate between the continuous and discontinuous enuretic. A third differentiation is between children who have functional enuresis and those with neurologic or urologic pathology (Doleys, 1977, 1978). Some definitions have incorporated the term *involuntary passage of urine*. Whether or not the passage of urine is voluntary or involuntary seems to be a judgment made by the researcher or clinician rather than based in fact. To the extent that *involuntary* implies the presence of underlying *organic pathology,* the latter term would seem more descriptive. In fact, there has been renewed interest in the application of behavioral procedures to the treatment of urinary incontinence secondary to urologic or neurologic pathology (Parker & Whitehead, 1982). In addition, there has been some examination of adjustment problems in individuals with urological disorders (Laurence & Beresford, 1975). Enuresis is not only a very common problem, but also has been identified as being associated with child abuse (Kempe & Helfer, 1972). Lund (1963) has enumerated approximately 90 different types of urinary incontinence. It is interesting to note that about 90 percent of these fall into the "functional" category and nearly 80 percent into the continuous type. These data imply that most enuretics have no organic or physical basis for their problem and that they progress from infancy into childhood without having acquired urinary control. This fact may be accounted for by inappropriate and/or inadequate training procedures, which vary considerably (Doleys & Dolce, 1982).

The age at which a child can be considered enuretic varies, because there are considerable cultural differences (Doleys & Dolce, 1982). Most estimates for the age of enuretics fall in the range of three to five years, but it is rare for a child less than five years of age to be treated. Statistics show that approximately 20 percent of five-year-olds wet their beds frequently enough to be considered enuretic (Cohen, 1975; Oppell, Harper, & Rider, 1968). This percentage decreases, with about 5 percent of 10-year-olds and 2 percent of 12-to-14-year-olds known to be enuretic. Of those enuretic, approximately 80 percent of younger children and 50 percent of older children tend to be of the continuous type, and males outnumber females by about 2 to 1. *Spontaneous remission* has been estimated to occur in about 13.5 percent of children in the age category of 7½ to 12 years and in 14 to 16 percent of children in the age category of 5 to 19 years (Forsythe & Redmond, 1974).

The rationale for treating the younger enuretic child is self-evident. The term *spontaneous remission* is a misnomer and tends to reflect our lack of understanding and knowledge as to exactly how and why these children become continent. It would not be unreasonable to expect that in many cases it is a function of unsystematically applied aversive contingencies, including punitive treatment by the parents, ridicule of peers, and restriction of social interactions. Given the variety of effective behavioral approaches available, little sound rationale can be found for admonishing concerned parents to simply wait and allow the child an opportunity to outgrow the incontinence.

Etiology

There has been considerable debate and controversy regarding the etiology of enuresis (Doleys, 1977, 1978; Doleys, Schwartz, & Ciminero, 1981; Shaffer, 1977; Walker, 1978). Sleep has been indicated as a major factor in enuresis and has been referred to as an *arousal disorder* (Finley, 1971; Perlmutter, 1976). Recent data, however, have not been supportive of this position (Mikkelsen, Rapoport, Nee, Gruenau, Mendelsen, & Gillin, 1980). These researchers were unable to find any association between enuresis and stage of sleep. These investigations have been confounded by a lack of differentiation between depth of sleep, as defined by electroencephalographic data, and arousability. Children may sleep deeply simply because they have never been taught to do otherwise. Data comparing enuretics to nonenuretics on the dimension of arousability are conflicting (Bostack, 1958; Boyd, 1960; Braithwaithe, 1956; Kaffman & Elizur, 1977).

Higher concordance rates have been found among monozygotic twins, as compared to dizygotic. In addition, a higher incidence of enuresis has been found among children from families with one or more members who were enuretic. These findings, though open to many interpretations, have frequently been regarded as evidence of genetic predisposition as a factor in enuresis (Bakwin, 1973; Cohen, 1975; Faray, 1935).

A psychodynamic or psychoanalytic approach to the etiology of enuresis would speculate that the problem behavior is a symptom suggesting the presence of some underlying conflicting anxiety or emotional stress (Pierce, 1972; Sperling, 1965). This hypothesis suggests that the elimination of the problem of enuresis would result in symptom substitution unless the underlying conflict was remedied. Examinations of treatment outcomes, however, have not shown this to be the case. In fact, children who are relieved of the problem of enuresis often appear much better adjusted, happier, and content (Baker, 1969; Dische, 1971; Werry & Cohrssen, 1965).

Gerrard and his colleagues (Esperanca & Gerrard, 1969; Zaleski, Gerrard, & Shokeir, 1973) have suggested that enuretic children tend to have smaller functional bladder capacity than nonenuretics. It is hypothesized that this smaller capacity may be a result of inadequate cortical inhibitions or is indicative of some type of allergenic reaction whereby the bladder is maintained in spasm, thus preventing it from accommodating larger volumes or urine. The data in this area are not entirely consistent, because there appears to be a considerable overlap between functional bladder capacities between nonenuretics and enuretics of the same age (Rutter, 1973). Additionally, as will be noted later, increasing functional bladder capacity seems neither necessary nor sufficient to produce continence. However, it should be pointed out that allergies do play a very specific role in some enuretic children, especially those with nocturnal enuresis, and thus, they should be ruled out in assessment.

The learning behavioral model of enuresis describes the behavior as a habit deficiency resulting from inadequate learning experiences and/or inappropriate reinforcement contingencies (Atthowe 1973; Lovibond & Coote, 1970; Young, 1965a). This model interprets bladder fullness as a stimulus that has acquired discriminative properties in the continent child. That is, bladder fullness results in an inhibitory response that delays or postpones urination until the proper time or place. Several conditioning based procedures have grown out of this model, including the bell-and-pad, or urine-alarm (Mowrer and Mowrer, 1938), and dry-bed training (DBT: Azrin, Sneed, & Foxx, 1973, 1974).

Assessment

Assessment of the enuretic child need not be particularly time-consuming or expensive but must be systematic and comprehensive. It should incorporate a clinical interview and collection of behavioral data covering a two-to four-week period of time. A clinical interview should be used to gain (1) history and description of the problem, (2) family and medical history, (3) knowledge of other problems in the family or with the child, (4) impression of the home and family environment, and (5) information about previous treatment attempts (Doleys, 1978, 1979b; Doleys et al., 1981). Although enuresis is a well-defined and rather specific problem, it does in fact occur within the context of the family and the child's general psychological environment—a factor that must be considered prior to implementing treatment. Patterns of enuretic behavior should be noted by the collection of data relevant to (*a*) time and frequency of enuretic episodes, (*b*) diurnal patterns of voiding, and (*c*) bladder capacity. Assessment of bladder capacity can be obtained relatively easily using the water-loading procedure (Zaleski, et al., 1973), which can be done in the home or the office (Harris & Purohit, 1977). Although a medical examination is recommended to screen for potential problems, a general physical, urinalysis, and urine culture to rule out renal pathology and infection are usually sufficient. More intrusive procedures, such as voiding cystourethrogram, cystoscopy, or execretory urograms, should be reserved for those children who display symptoms suggestive of organic pathology or who have been recalcitrant to the most systematic of treatments (Campbell, 1970; Perlmutter, 1976). Urinary tract infections are more common among females than males and should be watched for, although they seem to occur in only about 10 percent of cases (Jones, Gerrard, Shokeir, & Houston, 1972). Daytime voiding patterns characterized by frequency, inadequate retention, and abnormal stream may be indicative of such infections (Arnold & Ginsberg, 1975; Smith, 1967).

This baseline evaluation period serves several functions. First, it provides an assessment of parent and child motivation and ability to follow directions. Second, it yields data descriptive of the child's current functioning. Third, it provides a baseline against which the effects of treatment may be assessed. Too often clinicians ignore relevant factors that may aid them in assessing the efficacy of treatment because proper assessment procedures are not followed. For example, some children are multiple wetters, that is, they wet more than once during the night. If this is not detected and the therapist only examines the number of wet nights per week, a treatment may be discarded early as being ineffective because the child continues to wet every night during the week and it would not be recognized that the number of wets per night was possibly decreasing. Similarly, noting and recording the size of the wet spot may be used to gauge the effectiveness of treatment. Some children will not cease wetting entirely during the early part of treatment but will void smaller and smaller amounts of urine, which is suggestive of the gradual acquisition of inhibitory control mechanisms. Obtaining these types of data may be very helpful in maintaining motivation of parents and children in the early part of treatment.

Treatment

Drugs. A variety of stimulants, anticholinergics, and tranquilizers, and antidepressants have been used in the treatment of nocturnal enuresis. The most frequently used and effective of the lot appears to be imipramine hydrocholoride (Tofranil). The specific mechanism of action of this medication is not understood, though its effects are often attributed to mood elevation, lightening of sleep, anticholinergic effects, and/or increase in voluntary control via urethral sphincter (Blackwell & Currah, 1973; Mahony, Laferte, & Mahoney, 1973). However, when compared with other approaches, the use of this medication does not seem to be the most effective or efficient. Increase in urinary control is generally observed in about 85 percent of the cases during the first two weeks of treatment, but total continence is recorded in only about 30 percent of cases with up to 95 percent relapsing following withdrawal of the medication (Blackwell & Currah, 1973; Kardash, Hillman & Werry, 1968; Shaffer, 1977; Stewart, 1975).

Bladder Expansion. As noted above, a small functional bladder capacity has been indicted as an important etiological consideration in enuresis. Bladder expansion, or retention control training (RCT), exercises generally involve the children consuming gradual increases in amounts of liquid and asking them to refrain from voiding for gradually extended periods of time. One early study found that only six of 83 children practicing on a daily basis became continent (Starfield & Mellits, 1968). Other studies by Kimmel and Kimmel (1970) and Paschalis, Kimmel and Kimmel (1972) reported much different data, indicating that 17 of 38 children became dry within 21 days using RCT. This outcome has not been replicated (Allen, 1976; Harris & Purohit, 1977; Raeburn, Gemming, Lowe, & Dowrick, 1977). In fact, retention control, or bladder extension, training has been shown to be less effective than the urine-alarm (Fielding, 1980) and dry-bed training (Doleys, Ciminero, Tollison, Williams & Wells, 1977). Retention training does, however, seem to be a potentially useful technique with daytime enuretics.

Urine-Alarm. Perhaps the most frequently used technique for the treatment of nighttime enuresis is the urine-alarm. This procedure utilizes a urine sensing device that rests on the child's bed or, in some cases, is small enough to be attached to the inside of clothing. A bell or buzzer of some type is triggered by the closing of a circuit upon the onset of voiding. Once awakened, the child toilets himself and returns to bed. Theoretically, it is suggested that conditioning occurs with repeated association of the alarm and voiding. Through this process, the child comes to impose an inhibitory response upon voiding, thus sleeping through the night; or, alternatively, bladder distension cues may acquire discriminative properties that result in the child being aroused by bladder distention, which enables voiding to occur in the bathroom rather than in the bed.

Early studies with this procedure (Seiger, 1952) noted rates of remission up to 80 percent, while recent remission rates of 80 to 90 percent have been reported with relapse rates approximately 30 percent. A review article by Doleys (1977) summarized studies conducted between 1960 and 1975. The data covered over 600 subjects and revealed a rate of remission of 75 percent, with treatment ranging from 5 to 12 weeks. The average relapse rate was 41 percent. Nearly 68 percent of subjects retreated after relapse became continent. The most frequently cited reasons for relapse included noncompliance of parents or child, early withdrawal from treatment, and inconsistent application of the technique. Inadequate intensity of the auditory stimulus does appear to be a factor in the initial rate of acquisition but may or may not be related to relapse.

In comparative studies, the urine-alarm has been found to be more effective than nighttime awakening (Catalina, 1976), placebo tablets (White, 1968), no treatment (DeLeon & Mandell, 1966), verbal psychotherapy (Novick, 1966), imipramine (McConaghy, 1969; Young, 1965b), and retention control training (Allen, 1976). Little work has been done to examine the potential utility of a combination of the urine-alarm with imipramine. Some children are multiple wetters and respond rather slowly to the urine-alarm and other techniques. It might be clinically very useful to place these children on a combination of the urine-alarm and imipramine, since the rather immediate effects of imipramine may intensify motivation. Gradual withdrawal of the imipramine might result in the onset of some wetting, but with the heightened motivation on the part of the parent and the child, conditioning with the urine-alarm might prove to be quite successful.

Equipment failure is a major concern with the urine-alarm. Some of the sandwich type alarms, in which the construction involves two sheets separated by some type of absorbent pad, can result in false alarms when the two sheets slide and make contact with one another. The use of this type of an apparatus also requires more care on the part of the parent and the child to ensure that it is set up correctly. Alarm systems are also a problem. Although most children might be aroused by alarms in the area of 85 decibels, some will require much more intense alarms, perhaps to 100 or 105 decibels (Finley & Wansley, 1976). Of course, the durability of the alarm system is of course of great concern. Many of the alarms commercially available through mail-order houses do not appear to maintain high reliability under repeated and sustained use. There has been considerable modification in the design of urine-alarm devices (Finley & Smith, 1975). Modification of the devices have virtually eliminated the possibility of "buzzer ulcers."

In an attempt to reduce frequency of relapse, two modifications of the urine-alarm procedures as described above have been examined. The first involves the use of an intermittent schedule. Under this protocol, the alarm is programmed to operate on a given schedule, usually 50 to 70 percent of the wets. Theoretically, it is assumed that this is analogous to a partial reinforcement schedule. Experiments in learning have shown that acquisition of responding under partial reinforcement has been more resistant to extinction than under continuous reinforcement. There is some question, however, as to the "goodness of fit" of this model to enuresis, but nonetheless, the data are quite encouraging (Finley, Besserman, Bennett, Clapp & Finley, 1973; Finley & Wansley, 1976; Finley, Wansley & Blenkarn, 1977). However, not every attempt at the use of an intermittent schedule has been successful in yielding data showing improvement over that of a continuous schedule (Taylor & Turner, 1975; Turner, Young & Rachman, 1970). Differences might be accountable for by the schedule presentation, degree of parental compliance, and apparatus used as well as criteria for dryness. The Finley, et al. (1977) study noted impressive statistics. Using a 70 percent intermittent variable schedule with 80 enuretics, continence (14 consecutive dry nights) was achieved by 94 percent of the subjects completing treatment with an average duration of seven weeks. Overall relapse rate was 25 percent, with relapses varying from 5.25 percent for seven to eight-year olds to 50 percent for 9 to 10-year olds.

A second modification to the standard urine-alarm is the use of *overlearning*. Overlearning involves the consumption of 10 to 32 ounces of liquid (depending on the age and weight of the child and the predilections of the clinician and researcher) prior to bedtime after initial dryness has been achieved through the standard urine-alarm. It has been assumed that relapses may occur because of the absence of generalization of conditioning to a broad range of bladder fullness and degree of distention (Young & Morgan, 1972). Increasing the amount of liquid at night will have the effect of creating greater degrees of bladder fullness, therefore testing the original conditioning and presenting an opportunity to reward the occurrence of continence in the presence of a broader range of bladder fullness and detrusor muscle detention. Its overall effectivenss is likely to be enhanced by the gradual introduction and increase of nighttime liquids in a one to three week period of time. Early studies in this area (Jehu, Morgan, Turner & Jones, 1977; Taylor & Turner, 1975; Young & Morgan, 1972) reported beneficial effects. Young and Morgan (1972), for example, noted lower relapse rates for overlearning versus the standard urine-alarm procedure (13 versus 35 percent, respectively). In a study by Jehu, et al. (1977) 95 percent of 90 children achieved continence with an average treatment duration of 12 weeks. It is likely that this technique bears further consideration.

Dry-Bed Training. Dry-bed training (DBT) is a multifaceted program employing the application of social contingencies. This was introduced as an alternative to the urine-alarm by Azrin, et al. (1973, 1974). DBT incorporates the use of positive practice, positive reinforcement, retention control training, nighttime awakening, negative reinforcement, and full-cleanliness training. It has been shown to be useful with children of normal intellectual capacity as well as with mentally retarded children. The approach has been the basis for the development of a toilet training manual (*Toilet Training in Less Than a Day;* Azrin & Foxx, 1974). A manual to be used by parents of nonretarded, nocturnally enuretic children has also been developed (Azrin & Besalel, 1979). Evaluation of this approach in the manual was undertaken by 13 parents who carried out the procedure without professional assistance. Enuresis was reduced from 68 percent of nights during baseline to 27 percent of nights at the end of one week and to 10 percent at the end of three months. The average number of wets for children achieving the 14 consecutive dry nights criterion was six, with one child failing to achieve this criterion within six months (Besalel, Azrin, Thienes-Hontos, McMorrow, 1980).

Attempts at the replication of the original dry-bed training procedure has yielded inconsistent results. Doleys, et al., (1977) noted DBT to be more effective than retention control training, but the rate of remission was not nearly as high as that noted in the previous studies by Azrin. A two-year follow-up indicated that five of the eight children who had achieved dryness through DBT continued to be continent (Williams, Doleys, & Ciminero, 1978). Bollard and his colleagues have undertaken an extensive examination of dry-bed training (Bollard, 1982; Bollard & Nettelbeck, 1981; Bollard, Nettelbeck & Roxbee, 1982; Bollard & Woodroofe, 1977). In brief, these studies revealed that, first, although DBT seemed somewhat superior to the urine-alarm, this difference was not statistically significant; second, DBT was not nearly as effective when a urine-alarm system that noted when the wets occurred was not present; third, DBT was equally effective when administered by the parents, a trainer in the child's home, or a trainer in the hospital. In doing a component analysis of DBT, it was noted that the awakening schedule was probably the single most effective component. In the DBT, the child is awakened at specific times during the night and is encouraged to toilet if the urge to void is present. This awakening is gradually faded as acquisition is achieved. Positive practice and retention control did not seem to aid significantly in its effectiveness. It appears as though any one of these techniques utilized by itself does not greatly enhance the overall effects of the standard urine-alarm procedure. However, they do have a cumulative effect in that the three of them added to the urine-alarm procedure does improve effectiveness, but not statistically so. One must weigh the additional demands on the parent and the child's time as compared to the urine-alarm procedure against the identified improvement in clinical effectiveness.

ENCOPRESIS

Definition and Incidence

Functional encopresis can be defined as the passage of fecal material into the clothing or any generally unacceptable area in the absence of organic pathology after the age of three (Doleys, 1980a). Terms such as *fecal incontinence* or *psychogenic megacolon* have also been utilized. Psychogenic megacolon perhaps is most appropriately applied to those cases in which incontinence is, at least in part, a result of an enlarged colon. As one might expect, there is a variety of definitions for encopresis (Levine, 1975, 1982; Pierce, 1975; Yates, 1970). The most frequently noted qualifying factors include age, pattern of toileting, and etiology (Fitts & Mann, 1977). It is often difficult to differentiate between the child who in encopretic and one who has not been toilet trained. Knowledge of general developmental rate, prior attempts at toilet training, and presence of bladder control may all help to influence which label is applied. It is generally agreed, however, that under normal circumstances children should have achieved bowel control by the age of four.

Encopresis may result from dietary factors, allergic reactions to foods and other substances, infections, disease and abnormalities in the anatomy and physiology. Levine (1982) has identified a number of potentiators of encopresis and associated them with certain periods of life. For example, during the infancy and toddler years simple constipation, colonic inertia, contingenital anorectal problems, parental overconcern, and course of medical interventions are identified. During the ages between two and five years, psychosocial stresses during training, coercive or overly permissive training, toileting fears, and painful or difficult defecation may arise. During the early school years, avoidance of school bathrooms, prolonged or acute gastroenteritis, frenetic lifestyles, food intolerances, etc. seem to be more prevalent.

Several attempts have been made to develop a classification system (Doleys et al., 1981; Levine & Bakow, 1976), with an emphasis on recognizing two major factors. The first is the degree of incontinence, which may vary from less than weekly (very infrequent) to daily (very severe). The second factor involves a degree of constipation. This ranges on a continuum from retention for a couple of days with defecation that requires straining and results in the depositing of hard stools to severe retention that may persist to 14 days and is characterized by abdominal distention, impactions, and a diffused enlarged colon. Functional encopresis may also be subdivided into continuous (primary) and discontinuous (secondary). The continuous encopretic has not demonstrated bowel control for at least six months. A second useful subdivision is that of *retentive* versus *nonretentive* (Gavanski, 1971; Walker, 1978). The retentive encopretic will show a history of constipation and frequent bowel movements and regular use of purgatives. In some cases, this may be brought about by a fear of defecation (toilet phobia, Doleys, 1979a), and other such children may present with what Berg and Jones (1964) call a *pot refusal syndrome.* Smearing of feces (copraphagia) or stress incontinence may also be observed. The majority of encopretics will have some degree of constipation.

One subcategory that demands attention is *overflow incontinence.* Overflow incontinence, or "paradoxical diarrhea" (Davidson, 1958), refers to the leakage of fecal material about an impaction created by bowel retention or constipation.

This can be seen in children who have been known to retain for long periods of time. Casual observation implicates the presence of diarrhea, but the use of constipating agents would obviously compromise the problem. This condition is often seen in children who have very odorous stools, frequent yet small amounts of soiling, soiling that appears diarrhea-like in nature, and total unawareness of a desire to defecate.

Estimates of the incidents of functional encopresis vary from 1.5 to 7.5 percent of children. Levine (1975) and Yates (1970) cite 3 percent and Levine (1982) notes that about 1.5 percent of second graders are encopretic. Bellman (1966) reported 8.1 percent of three-year olds soiled their pants, 2.4 percent of four-year-olds, and 2.2 percent of five-year-olds. Newson and Newson (1968) report figures of 2.3 percent of males seven to eight years of age and .7 percent of females of the same age. Percentages appear to drop with age, such that 1.2 and .3 percent of males and females respectively from ages 10 to 12 are encopretic (Rutter, Tizard, & Whitmore, 1970). The problem is substantially more common in males than females, with ratios ranging up to 6 to 1, and is often found in children who show developmental delays in other areas (Stein & Susser, 1967).

Levine (1975) examined 102 encopretics. Eighty seven were between the ages of 4 and 13, 85 percent were male, and 50 percent were incontinent during the day and at night. Most denied awareness of the urge to defecate and complained of abdominal pain, poor appetite, and lethargy. Impactions were noted in 75 percent; 40 percent were classified as continuous. Familial, marital, and behavioral pathologies were not major contributing factors. These, however, have been reported as associated problems when enuresis is present along with the encopresis (Hersov, 1977; Wolters, 1974 a, b). Quality of parental interaction, coerciveness during toilet training, and ambivalence of parents have been cited as leading factors in the development of encopresis (Anthony, 1957; Pinkerton, 1958). Constitutional predispositions, circumstances of the environment, and critical life events all appear to have impact on the development of functional encopresis (Levine, 1982).

Physiology

The physiology of continence and defecation has been elaborated in a number of sources (Anthony, 1963; Gaston, 1948). The process is basically reflexive in nature. Initiated by stimulation of receptors in the rectal mucosa, defecation occurs in response to distention of the rectum produced by mass peristalsis of fecal material out of the colon. Filling and distention of the rectum results in (a) increased colonic peristalsis, (b) reflexive relaxation of internal anal sphincter, and (c) the desire to defecate. Voluntary contraction of thoracic and abdominal muscles and the relaxation of external sphincter bring about defecation. If defecation is inhibited, rectal stretch receptors adapt to existing pressure, and the urge to defecate diminishes. Subsequent urges may not occur for an additional 24 hours when peristalsis begins. During this time, moisture from the fecal mass is absorbed, producing a hard stool and thus more painful defecation.

It is not difficult to understand from this description how children are able to retain for extensive periods of time. Normal defecation is a very active, not a passive, process. Muscular contractions and external anal sphincter relaxation must be a coordinated movement. Excessive pressure via demand for performance during toileting can interfere with this process through anxiety and/or fear-mediated muscle contractions. Any abnormality in structural, sensory, or motor components of the system can interfere with development of normal continence.

Etiology

Psychodynamically oriented approaches to encopresis conceptualize it as a symptom of unconscious conflict. The underlying conflicts may result from lack of parental love, guilt value of the feces, separation anxiety, fear of loss of feces, pregnancy wishes, aggression against a hostile world, response to familial dysfunction, and traumatic separation from mother between oral and anal stages of psychosexual development (Lehman, 1944; Pierce, 1975; Silber, 1969). Some have focused on the "power struggle" that presumably develops between parent and child during the course of toilet training (Anthony, 1957; Hersov, 1977; Hilburn, 1968). That inappropriate or coercive training methods can contribute heavily to the development of encopresis seems incontrovertible. The hypothesizing of unconscious conflicts has been of little heuristic value and relatively nonproductive when applied clinically. In particular, it appears to have little utility in the management of the development of the disabled child.

A second rather common approach to accounting for the development of encopresis is a medical-constitutional model. This emphasizes a neurodevelopmental approach that focuses on the potential lack of neurological integrity, inappropriate functioning of a physiological mechanism, and/or anatomical malfunctions as casual factors. While this approach cannot be discarded because many cases of encopresis do have some organic component to them, the presence of organic pathology does not preclude the utilization of a nonmedical (i.e., behavioral) treatment. Epstein and McCoy (1977) applied behavioral procedures to a child who was diagnosed with Hirschsprung's Disease. In this case, it is known that nerve innervation is inadequate for the detection or production of normal peristaltic movement (Silber, 1969). Surgical corrections of anatomical abnormalities, such as an ectopic anuses (Leape & Ramenofsky, 1978), do not always result in the immediate resumption of normal toileting. While it is important to rule out anatomical and physiological abnormalities and to correct them when they are present, it is important to maintain vigilance regarding the impact of environmental contingencies and circumstances even in the presence of such.

The learning-behavioral model is, of course, the third approach to etiology. This model emphasizes inadequate or inappropriate learning experiences as being of major etiological significance. In the case of the primary enuretic or encopretic, the therapist would evaluate the presence of prerequisite skills, such as undressing, and the amount of reinforcement for proper toileting. It is often assumed that cues resulting from rectal distention and internal anal sphincter relaxation have not become discriminative for temporary retention followed by bowel movements into the commode. For the continuous encopretic, avoidance conditioning principles are often invoked. It is postulated that pain or fear arousing events have been associated with the onset of encopresis. Therefore, retention becomes negatively reinforced by the postponement of pain. The behavior (retention) may persist in spite of the fact that when the child ultimately does have a bowel movement the pain is present and oftentimes to a higher degree than it would have been without retention. Alternatively, from this same theoretical approach, a child could inadvertently be conditioned to display encopresis by receiving untimely reinforcement via parental attention when soiling occurs.

Within the learning-conditioning model a functional analysis (Doleys, et al., 1981) is used to identify contributing and environmental contingencies. Modification of contingencies is the focus of therapy. It is important to realize that one set of circumstances or contingencies may be present in promoting the development of encopresis, but a second set of circumstances may be maintaining it. For example, a child may have a period of soiling associated with illness or diet. Parental attention associated with these accidents may be highly reinforcing and, thus, comes to maintain the behavior at a high frequency. For this reason, an exacting analysis of current conditions is often seen as more critical than a comprehensive understanding of the patient's early history.

Assessment

Comprehensive assessment of the encopretic child should include a medical evaluation, clinical interview, and behavioral recording (Doleys, et al., 1981; Levine, 1982). Medical examinations often include a medical history, rectal examination, barium enema, or biopsy as required. A complete physical examination should be undertaken. A sensory examination and careful neurological assessment may be needed to rule out such conditions as Crohn's Disease. Barium enemas are seldom, if ever, needed, and anal manometry is sometimes used to evaluate sphincter function. On rare occasions, rectal biopsies may be needed to identify ganglionic abnormalities. Girls frequently suffer from urinary tract infections and should be examined carefully for this complication (Levine, 1982). Radiographic studies may be indicated in children with long-standing problems. Congenital hypothyroidism, anorectal abnormalities, and Hirschsprung's must be ruled out. Such problems are often identifiable through a careful medical history (Hendren, 1978; Leape & Ramenofsky, 1978; Ravitch, 1958). Other common factors include a constitutional predisposition, dietary intake, difficulty in passing large, hard stools because of failure to provide leverage, presence of pain, and involuntary resistance in the presence of fecal impactions (Davidson, 1958). In cases with severe retention, one must examine and consider the degree of megacolon. Differentiating between irritable bowel syndrome and malabsorption to determine what, if any, laxative or stool softeners might be required may be necessary. In summary, medical consultation becomes an indispensable part of the assessment.

In the clinical interview, the therapist must (a) differentiate among the various types of encopresis, (b) determine contributing environmental contingencies and circumstances, and (c) obtain data-relevant behavioral-emotional competencies of the parents or caregivers. Shortcuts in the assessment generated by the clinician's hunches or intuitions are to be avoided. It is not uncommon that clinicians "tend to find what we look for" (Wright, 1978). Similarly, narrowness in conceptualization and treatment of encopresis can result in cases that seem much more identical than they actually are. This does not imply that the clinician need to bring to bear incompatible theoretical approaches regarding the etiology of encopresis, but that the treatment be dictated by the assessment data rather than preconceived notions of the origin of the problem.

Behavioral records are an invaluable aspect of the assessment. Establishing patterns of soiling, determining ability of parent and child to maintain such records, assessing motivation, and developing a baseline against which to assess the treatment effectiveness can all be accomplished with these recordings. Records should include the frequency of soiling, the magnitude of each accident, when and where the episode occurred, and whether or not appropriate toileting has occurred. Unfortunately, many therapists focus only on the soiling episodes, ignoring whether or not the child shows appropriate toileting behavior. Assessment of the role of fear should be given special priority in light of the documented presence of "toilet phobias" (Ashkenazi, 1975; Doleys & Arnold, 1975; Gelber & Mayer, 1965). Gavanski (1971) describes a pot refusal syndrome associated with coercive toilet-training procedures. This syndrome is characterized by the child refusing to sit on the commode. In assessment it is also important to talk with the child regarding his/her sensation and perception of the urge to defecate. Children should be asked to demonstrate how they push or try to go to the bathroom. Developing rapport with the child and the parents may be very beneficial in helping to insure cooperation and compliance, both of which have been associated with successful treatment (Levine & Bakow, 1976). Bornstein, Sturm, Retzlaff, Kirby, and Chong (1981) demonstrated the use of paradoxical instruction in inducing anxiety in a nine-year-old encopretic.

Once treatment is begun, evaluation should be ongoing. Frequency of appropriate toileting, percentage of toileting that is self-initiated, frequency of accidents, degree of assistance or prompts required, situational generality of toileting skills, and frequency of laxatives, stool softeners, or other medications should be monitored. A false sense of accomplishment can be achieved by attending only to frequency of accidents, since it is possible for a child to reduce the frequency of encopretic episodes by retaining. One must monitor appropriate toileting to insure that the desirable behavior is being developed and/or maintained.

Treatment

Medical Devices. A variety of medical devices have been developed for the treatment of encopresis, including a number of commercially available devices, as Foxx and Azrin (1973) list. Logan and Garner (1971) describe a device useful with deaf children. A transistorized device allowing for the transmission of a signal noting inappropriate elimination is detailed by Van Wagenen and Murdock (1966) and Fried (1974). Potty chair devices are rather common (Cheney, 1973; Watson, 1968). Hopkinson and Lightwood (1966) describe the application of an electrical device surgically implanted in the anal area, which maintains normal sphincter tone in patients with retroprolapse, a condition resulting in nearly continual passage of feces due to the absence of appropriate anal-sphincter contraction. Kohlenberg (1973) and Engle (1978) describe apparatuses that can be inserted in the rectum and used for conditioning of sphincter activity.

Medical Treatments. Medical treatments typically rely on the use of purgatives (laxatives and enemas) and dietary manipulation (Nisley, 1976; Ravitch, 1958; Silber, 1969). The utilization of these procedures must consider (a) obtaining and maintaining parental compliance, (b) the acquisition of appropriate toileting skills, and (c) long-term maintenance of desirable behaviors. In some cases, imipramine (Tofranil) has been applied because of its anti-spasmodic property. This medication apparently influences the frequency of bowel movements through its inhibitory effect on internal anal sphincters. Gavanski (1971) reports on the successful application of Tofranil and psychotherapy, cautioning, however, that imipramine should be used only for temporary relief of high frequency soiling, should be applied only to the nonretentive encopretic, and should always be used in conjunction with appropriate adjunctive therapies.

Berg and Jones (1964) have provided a rather useful view of the literature in this area. They indicate that relief of soiling achieved by these mechanical methods tends to be temporary. One of the more successful procedures is reported by Davidson, Kugler, and Bauer (1963). These investigators applied a three-part program to 119 encopretics. The program was initiated by utilizing mineral oil to induce regular bowel movements. In a second phase, laxatives were gradually withdrawn, and during the third phase, parental counseling and monitoring of the child's behavior through periodic contacts was undertaken. The results showed that 75 percent, or 90 patients, completed the program. Eighty were identified as successfully treated (67 of the total sample and 89 percent of completors). A careful examination of the procedures, however, makes it clear that counseling, feedback, self-monitoring, physician contact, and support and encouragement were extensively used along with the laxatives and enemas.

In a very systematic and rational fashion, Levine (1982) has outlined an approach to the management of childhood encopresis. The emphasis is on the management of frequency of bowel movements through the use of purgatives that are gradually faded over time. He also discusses "demystification" of the problem. The importance of removing blame and establishing a good rapport are obvious. A detailed account of follow-up procedures, when and under what conditions to use abdominal X rays, and hospitalization is presented. The approach incorporates the use of counseling and referral for associated psychosocial and developmental issues. This is perhaps one of the most detailed approaches to the medical management of encopresis and certainly has the potential for blending extremely well with the application of behavioral techniques to help insure compliance, development, and maintenance of appropriate toileting behaviors.

Verbal Psychotherapy. A number of studies have reported on the application of verbal psychotherapy and play therapy in the treatment of encopresis with varying rates of success (Gavanski, 1971; McTaggert & Scott, 1959; Pinkerton, 1958). In a review of 70 cases, Berg and Jones (1964) noted that rate of remission among children receiving psychotherapy was not statistically significantly different from those who had not. Ashkenazi (1975) reports that three children who had previously failed in treatment with psychotherapy and play therapy later became continent when treated through behavioral therapy emphasizing regular potting, induction of defecation, and positive reinforcement. Pinkerton (1958) reported on the use of verbal psychotherapy with 30 encopretics. Treatment was carried out in part through the parents and emphasized reduction of parental fear and prejudices, thereby permitting insight into the emotional origins of the problem and encouraging them to become indifferent to the symptoms. Treatment with the child included hospitalization when parental counseling was ineffective. Play therapy was employed, first, to penetrate the child's defensive facade and establish adequate depths of contact with him; second, to define his fundamental problems for him through the medium of projective play techniques; third, to promote the working through of his difficulties with associated release through play of his pent-up hostilities; and fourth, to restore his emotional stability following the restoration of these difficulties. Reportedly, 17 of 30 cases became continent with follow-up studies ranging up to three and a half years.

It is difficult to specify the aspects or qualities of verbal psychotherapy that may be related to its therapeutic outcome. Comparative studies have not been undertaken and a component analysis of the therapeutic procedure is lacking. The techniques also seem to incorporate a variety of behavioral procedures, including self-monitoring and systematic reinforcement in addition to the use of purgatives.

Behavioral Procedures.   Behavioral approaches in the treatment of functional encopresis have emphasized the arrangement of environmental consequences so as to encourage the development and maintenance of appropriate toileting behavior. In designing such a program, one must keep in mind that defecation in the commode is the final act in a long chain of behaviors. Unless each component of the chain is performed successfully, including undressing, locating the appropriate facility, detecting of the need to defecate, etc., accidents are likely to occur. Assessment of the encopretic child that does not consider whether or not and to what degree these prerequisite behaviors are present will likely lead to an ineffective or, at the very least, an inefficient treatment. For this reason, the target behaviors must be individualized on the basis of the child's existing repertoire. The continuous encopretic will require somewhat of a different type of treatment approach than the discontinuous encopretic. Similarly, differential treatments are likely to be required for the retentive versus the nonretentive encopretic. The utilization of some type of desensitization procedure may be necessary for the child who displays a toilet phobia or such fear and anxiety that interfere with desirable performance. And finally, the goal of treatment is for the child to demonstrate appropriate independent toileting behaviors. In many instances, researchers and clinicians have merely focused on the frequency of accidents rather than the presence of appropriate behavior as the indication of therapeutic effectiveness.

Doleys (1978, 1979a, 1980a), Walker (1978), and Schaefer (1979) have each provided rather thorough reviews of behavioral treatments of encopresis. Doleys has chosen to categorize these treatments into four groups: type I reinforcment, type II reinforcement, punishment, and type III. The type I procedures generally employ positive reinforcement contingent on appropriate bowel movements, which usually is the emphasis of the program. Several studies have documented the effectivenss of this approach (Bach & Moylan, 1975; Neale, 1963; Young, 1973; Young & Goldsmith, 1972). In these cases, reinforcement was delivered when the child evidenced a bowel movement while sitting on the commode. In some instances, laxatives and enemas were used in the early stages of treatment to help promote the desirable behavior. Perhaps one of the better controlled studies is that of Young (1973), in which 24 children, 4 to 10 years of age, were utilized. Many of the subjects had diminished sensation of the need to defecate resulting from dilatation of the internal anal sphincter. Treatment was initiated by removal of any impaction or accumulated fecal material, then a regimen of daily toileting in the morning, utilizing a warm drink or food to help initiate bowel movements, was begun. Movements into the commode were reinforced. Twenty of the 24 children were given Senokot (a laxative/stool softener) nightly to insure defecation in the morning. Nineteen of the subjects were treated successfully as indicated by the absence of feces in the rectum, having 28 consecutive clean days with an average treatment duration of five months.

The type II reinforcement procedure schedules positive reinforcement contingent on clean pants as opposed to appropriate toileting. Several studies in the area (Ayllon, Simon, & Wildman, 1975; Logan & Garner, 1971; Pedrini & Pedrini, 1971) have shown some success with this approach. Logan and Garner (1971) described a pant-alarm, or buzzer, that sounded off contingent upon soiling and that was used with a seven-year-old, partially deaf child. Points were awarded within a token economy program for each hour the child kept the buzzer silent. Although these few studies have shown some success, the type II reinforcement is not generally encouraged for development of appropriate defecation habits. Because the emphasis is on retaining clean pants, it may come about either through appropriate defecation or may result in children retaining for longer periods of time in an attempt to obtain a reinforcement.

A few studies have illustrated the use of punishment in the treatment of encopresis (Edelman, 1971; Freinden & VanHandel, 1970). In the first of these studies, a 30-minute time-out in the bedroom followed soiling episodes of a 12-year-old female. A second study utilized cleaning of soiled clothes by washing with strong soap and cold water as a consequence. Success was reported in 41 and 20 weeks respectively for the two studies. Application of similar techniques is not encouraged because of the potential for punishment to elicit emotional responses, to promote negative parent-child interactions, and to lead to excessive retention. By the time a child has reached the clinician, he/she has usually been exposed to a good deal of reprimanding, time-out, withholding of privileges, embarrassment, spanking, etc. The application of punishment to human behavior has received well-deserved recent attention (Axelrod & Apschi, 1983) and should be used most judiciously.

The fourth category of programs is referred to as the type III. These techniques are comprehensive and usually involve a combination of positive reinforcement and punishment. Laxatives and stool softeners are often employed. Programs are generally implemented with the use of procedures designed to promote frequent bowel movement whether they occur in the pants or in the commode. Levine (1982) has provided a very detailed and comprehensive outline of how this can be achieved and documented. Three studies (Doleys, Adams, & Rice, 1980; Doleys & Arnold, 1975; Doleys, McWhorter, Williams & Gentry, 1977) have examined the use of a three-part program, including (a) periodic pant checks, (b) full-cleanliness training contingent on soiling, and (c) positive reinforcement for appropriate toileting. Pant checks were scheduled from one to two hours apart, depending on the age of the child. Positive verbal reinforcement was contingent on clean pants. Younger children and those who were given to excessive retention were prompted to toilet themselves and placed on the commode for 15 minutes after each pant check. Accidents were followed by full-cleanliness training (FCT; Foxx, Azrin, 1973), involving (*a*) parents' expression of displeasure, (*b*) child washing underpants and trousers for 20 minutes, and (*c*) child taking a bath and washing for 20 minutes in cool water. Parents were instructed to be nonchalant in the execution of FCT and to repeatedly verbalize the reason for the child having to go through these maneuvers and that this could be avoided with proper toileting. Children were not released from FCT if they were being disruptive, so parents were prevented from negatively reinforcing this behavior. The third aspect of the program involved the use of token reinforcement in the form of stars or colored squares on a chart, which were provided for self-initiated bowel movements. Accumulation of tokens was followed by the presentation of a back-up reinforcer that was obtained prior to the onset of the program and kept in the bathroom in the sight of the child to aid in strengthening motivation. Reinforcers were generally inexpensive, and the initial contract established that the child would receive one within the first two weeks of treatment. The initial four subjects were treated within 10 weeks, with one demonstrating relapse and follow-up due to parental noncompliance.

The replication of this study (Doleys, et al., (1980) added laxatives and suppositories when appropriate. Twenty subjects ranging from 4 to 12 years of age (an average of 7.5 years) were used. Fourteen were male, and six were female; eleven were primary encopretics and nine were secondary. Nine of the children were retentive. Baseline soilings ranged from 1.5 to 8 per week. Frequency of bowel movements ranged from 0 to 7 per week. Twelve children completed the treatment program as defined by participating in the program for 12 weeks or more, following the prescribed treatment, and providing data. Ten of the children were considered successfully treated as evidenced by averaging one soiling episode or less per month during follow-up, parental report of lack of a problem, and regular bowel movements in the commode. Results showed the treatment duration did not significantly vary between male and female, but continuous encopretics took approximately five weeks longer in treatment than discontinuous encopretics. Retentive encopretics also showed a longer treatment duration. Follow-up averaged 17.6 months and was available on 9 of 10 subjects. Eight of nine children demonstrated a frequency of soiling of less than two per month on the average, and each continued to have three bowel movements in the commode per week. Suppositories and laxatives that were used with three of the four retentive subjects were gradually faded out and found to be helpful in promoting bowel movements that could be reinforced. Prolonged use of such purgatives can produce a pattern of passive defecation, in which the child makes a few attempts on his/her own but simply sits passively and relies on the artificial production of a bowel movement. The use of laxatives and purgatives is very helpful and often a necessity with the retentive encopretic but must be applied judiciously and in consultation with a physician.

Similar programs to the one described above have been reported by several researchers and clinicians (Ashkenazi, 1975; Wright, 1973; Wright, 1975; Wright & Walker, 1976). The use of intermittent reinforcement schedule involving rewards for nonsoiling and appropriate bowel movements is described by Bornstein, et al., (1983).

More direct conditioning of anal sphincter activity has been demonstrated by Kohlenberg (1973) and Engle, Nikoomanesh, and Schuster (1974). In the first of these studies, a balloon-type apparatus was inserted in the rectum and was attached to a tube filled with cold water to provide feedback to the subject. Constriction of anal sphincter raised the level of the fluid, resulting in monetary reinforcement. The treatment was effective with a 13-year-old discontinuous encopretic, who demonstrated consistent toileting due to dilated sphincter. In the second approach, seven patients were exposed to a similar procedure. Follow-up ranged from six months to five years, and revealed the maintenance of acquired continence in five of seven cases.

It has been suggested that 30 percent of encopretic children may also display enuresis. Work by Doleys, et al., (1977) and Edelman (1971) suggested that the two problems were functionally independent, that is, modification of one did not necessarily affect the other. Epstein and McCoy (1977) did, however, notice an increase in bowel movements in a three-year-old child with Hirschsprung's disease following the use of retention control training for enuresis. Although there are no specific rules for which problem to treat first when both exist simultaneously, some guidelines have been presented (Doleys, et al., 1981).

CASE STUDY

The patient was a five-year-old white female who was a continuous encopretic. She had shown a long history of constipation followed by episodes of frequent soiling. Bowel movements became quite painful, which simply exacerbated the constipation since the pain was avoided by retention. The child experienced significant abdominal distention secondary to the retention. She had been examined medically, and no organic pathology could be found, though there was some suspicion of megacolon. Assessment of the family noted them to be upper middle-class with no significant familial disruption. Toilet training had progressed in an uncomplicated and uneventful fashion, and the child had acquired urinary control without difficulty. She has never acquired bowel control but the problems were greatly exacerbated when her younger sister was born. The child was noted to be precocious and somewhat a behavioral problem.

Initial treatment involved the application of full-cleanliness training, regular potting, use of token reinforcement for appropriate bowel movements in the commode, dry and clean pants, and utilization of Senokot at night. The Senokot was gradually faded as the child demonstrated greater frequency of bowel movements. The application of the program over a six-month period of time virtually resolved the problem and reduced episodes of soiling to less than once a month. These episodes were highlighted by rather small stains as opposed to the passage of fecal material to the clothes.

The patient was seen three years after initial treatment. At this time, she continued to have bowel movements but showed an increase in frequency of soiling. The soiling episodes were marked by the passage of small amounts of fecal material usually not well formed. The episodes ranged from small staining to what would appear to be nearly a full bowel movement. The episodes of soiling would come and go, and no other evidence of GI or GU problems was present. Baseline recording noted that the patient was unable to detect many of the episodes in which she passed fecal material into her clothes. The episodes would happen at various times during the day. A dietary intake was also obtained, and it was determined to be excessive for caffeine and sugar and to have a low amount of fiber and fruit.

Final evaluation of the patient suggested the presence of partial megacolon based on her apparent inability to be aware of the need to defecate, the periodic passing of small amounts of stool even after having a bowel movement on the commode, and passive defecation characterized by merely sitting on the commode and waiting for the bowel movement to occur. The dietary intake also showed a complicating factor of too much caffeine, which is known to stimulate motility and, in a child with megacolon, may result in more frequent defecation or the passage of stool than would be desirable. The treatment for this child involved (a) diet modification, (b) periodic potting during the day for no less than 10 minutes and instructions in applying abdominal pressure to promote bowel movement, and (c) the reapplication of token reinforcement for appropriate bowel movements. This strategy was effective in regaining control of her soiling.

This particular case study is presented for several reasons. First, it illustrates the importance of long-term follow-up in encopretic children. In the case of the child above, the soiling was resolved in the first round of treatment but reappeared in part for different reasons. Second, it suggests the importance of a rather detailed baseline assessment regarding the pattern and severity of the soiling so as to determine the possibility of underlying organic pathology; in this case, it was suspected megacolon. The presence of megacolon does imply treatment modifications over the strategy that would be implemented in a child not thusly affected. Third, this case helped to highlight the importance of a multidisciplinary assessment. The dietary records were reviewed by a nutritionist who quickly identified the problem with the caffeine.

All too often, behaviorally oriented clinicians become satisfied with six to eight-month follow-up data of the type that are frequently presented in the applied and research literature. In clinical practice, long-term maintenance and follow-up is essential since many patients do not return with reappearance of the problems but will try to implement what they remember of old strategies, ignoring the fact that the circumstances of the problem may have been changed.

SUMMARY

Some significant advances have been made in our understanding of functional nocturnal enuresis. The development of new techniques continues, but further work is required for determining mechanisms involved in relapse. It would appear at this juncture that one may have to sacrifice a short treatment duration in order to improve relapse rates. Perhaps those treatments that produce the fastest results may not produce the most longlasting. An entirely new technology is being developed to look at other types of enuresis, specifically those that have some accompanying organic pathology. More work needs to be done in the analysis and treatment of diurnal enuresis and bladder dysfunctioning. The use of a multidisciplinary team of professionals may prove invaluable.

Encopresis continues to be a somewhat difficult problem to manage. It may be a function of not having adequately defined the various categories of encopresis and thus treating each the same. Classification of children as continuous, discontinuous, retentive, etc., is being seen with a higher degree of regularity. Hopefully, this will produce data relevant to differential treatment and a long-term maintenance. Present research has suffered from a variety of inadequacies, including absence of adequate description of the problem and subjects, use of small numbers of subjects, lack of comparative, well-controlled studies, and lack of attention to the relationship between treatment success and subject characteristics. The more comprehensive behavioral programs seem to show the greatest promise.

REFERENCES

Allen, R. B. *Bladder capacity and awakening behavior in the treatment of enuresis.* Unpublished doctoral dissertation, University of Vermont, 1976.

Anthony, C. P. *Textbook of anatomy and physiology* (6th ed.). St. Louis: Mosby, 1963.

Anthony, E. G. An experimental approach to the psychopathology of childhood encopresis. *British Journal of Medical Psychology,* 1957, *30,* 146–175.

Arnold, S. J., & Ginsburg, A. Understanding and managing enuresis in children. *Postgraduate Medicine,* 1975, *58,* 73–82.

Ashkenazi, Z. The treatment of encopresis using a discriminative stimulus and positive reinforcement. *Journal of Behavior Therapy and Experimental Psychiatry,* 1975, *6,* 155–157.

Atthowe, J. M. Nocturnal enuresis and behavior therapy: A functional analysis. In R. B. Rubin, J. Henderson, H. Fensterheim, & L. P. Ullmann (Eds.), *Advances in behavior therapy* (Vol. 4). New York: Academic Press, 1973.

Axelrod, S., & Apsche, J. *The effects of punishment on human behavior.* New York: Academic Press, 1983.

Ayllon, R., Simon, S. J., & Wildman, R. W. Instructions and reinforcement in the elimination of encopresis: Case study. *Journal of Behaviour Therapy and Experimental Psychiatry*, 1975, *6*, 235–238.

Azrin, N. H., & Besalel, V. A. *Parent's guide to bedwetting control: A step-by-step method*. New York: Simon & Schuster, 1979.

Azrin, N. H., & Foxx, R. M. *Toilet training in less than a day*. New York: Simon & Schuster, 1974.

Azrin, N. H., Sneed, T. J., & Foxx, R. M. Dry bed: a rapid method of eliminating bedwetting (enuresis) of the retarded. *Behaviour Research and Therapy*, 1973, *11*, 427–434.

Azrin, N. H. , Sneed, T. J., & Foxx, R. M. Dry-bed training: Rapid elimination of childhood enuresis. *Behaviour Research and Therapy*, 1974, *12*, 147–156.

Bach, R., & Moylan, J. M. Parent-administered behavior therapy for inappropriate urination and encopresis: A case study. *Journal of Behaviour Therapy and Experimental Psychiatry*, 1975, *6*, 147–156.

Baker, B. L. Symptom treatment and symptom substitution in enuresis. *Journal of Abnormal Psychology*, 1969, *74*, 42–49.

Bakwin, H. The genetics of enuresis. *Clinics in Developmental Medicine*, 1973, *48–49*, 73–77.

Bellman, M. Studies on encopresis. *Acta Paediatrica Scandinavica* (Supplement No. 70), 1966.

Berg, I., & Jones, K. V. Functional fecal incontinence in children. *Archives of Disease in Childhood*, 1964, *39*, 465–472.

Besalel, V. A., Azrin, N. H., Thienes-Hontos, P., & McMorrow, M. Evaluation of a parent's manual for training enuretic children. *Behaviour Research and Therapy*, 1980, *18*, 358–366.

Blackwell, B., & Currah, J. The pharmacology of nocturnal enuresis. In I. Kolvin, R. C. McKeith, & S. R. Meadow (Eds.), *Bladder Control and enuresis*. Philadelphia: W. B. Saunders, 1973.

Bollard, J. *A systematic modification of dry-bed training for the treatment of nocturnal enuresis*. Doctoral dissertation, University of Adelaide, Adelaide, South Australia, 1982.

Bollard, J., & Nettlebeck, T. A comparison of dry-bed training and standard urine-alarm conditioning treatment of childhood bedwetting. *Behaviour Research and Therapy*, 1981, *19*, 215–226.

Bollard, J., & Nettlebeck, T. A component analysis of dry-bed training for treatment of bedwetting. *Behaviour Research and Therapy*, 1982, *20*, 383–390.

Bollard, J., Nettlebeck, R., & Roxbee, L. Dry-bed training for childhood bedwetting: a comparison of group with individually administered parent instruction. *Behaviour Research and Therapy*, 1982, *20*, 209–217.

Bollard, R. J., & Woodroffe, P. The effect of parent-administered dry-bed training on nocturnal enuresis in children. *Behaviour Research and Therapy*, 1977, *15*, 159–165.

Bornstein, P. H., Balleweg, B. J., McLellarn, R. W., Wilson, G. L., Sturm, C. A., Andre, J. C., Van Den Pol, R. A. The "bathroom game," a systematic program for the elimination of encopretic behavior. *Journal of Behavior Therapy and Experimental Psychiatry*, 1983, *14*, 67–71.

Bornstein, P. H., Sturm, C. A., Retzlaff, P. D., Kirby, K. L. & Chong, H. Paradoxical instruction in the treatment of encopresis and chronic constipation: an experimental analysis. *Journal of Behavior Therapy and Experimental Psychiatry*, 1981, *12*, 167–170.

Bostack, J. Exterior gestation, primitive sleep, enuresis and asthma: A study in aetiology. *Medical Journal of Australia*, 1958, *149*, 185–192.

Boyd, M. M. The depth of sleep in enuretic school children and in non-enuretic controls. *Journal of Psychosomatic Research*, 1960, *4*, 274–281.

Braithwaithe, J. V. Some problems associated with enuresis. *Proceedings of the Royal Society of Medicine*, 1956, *49*, 33–39.

Campbell, M. F. Neuromuscular uropathy. In M. F. Campbell & T. H. Harrison (Eds.), *Urology* (Vol. 2). Philadelphia: W. B. Saunders, 1970.

Catalina, D. A. Enuresis: The effects of parent contingent wake-up. *Dissertation Abstracts*, 1976, *37*, 28–025.

Cheney, C. D. Mechanically augmented human toilet training or the electric potty chair. In R. L. Schwitzgebel & R. H. Schwitzgebel (Eds.), *Psychotechnology: Electronic control of mind and behavior.* New York: Rinehart & Winston, 1973.

Cohen, M. W. Enuresis, *Pediatric clinics of North America*, 1975, *22*, 545–560.

Davidson, M. D. Constipation and fecal incontinence. In H. Bakwin (Ed.), *Pediatric clinics of North America.* Philadelphia: W. B. Saunders, 1958.

Davidson, M. D., Kigler, M. D., & Bauer, C. H. Diagnosis and management in children with severe protracted constipation and obstipation. *Journal of Pediatrics*, 1963, *62*, 261–266.

DeLeon, G., & Mandell, W. A comparison of conditioning and psychotherapy in the treatment of functional enuresis. *Journal of Clinical Psychology*, 1966, *22*, 326–330.

Dische, S. Management of enuresis. *British Medical Journal*, 1971, *2*, 33–36.

Doleys, D. M. Behavioral treatments for nocturnal enuresis in children: A review of the recent literature. *Psychological Bulletin*, 1977, *84*, 30–54.

Doleys, D. M. Assessment and treatment of enuresis and encopresis in children. In M. Hersen, R. Eisler, & P. M. Miller (Eds.), *Progress in behavior modification.* New York: Academic Press, 1978.

Doleys, D. M. Assessment and treatment of childhood encopresis. In A. J. Finch & P. C. Kendall (Eds.), *Treatment and research in child psychopathology.* New York: Spectrum, 1979(a).

Doleys, D. M. Assessment and treatment of childhood enuresis. In A. J. Finch & P. C. Kendall (Eds.), *Treatment and research in child psychopathology.* New York: Spectrum, 1979 (b).

Doleys, D. M. Enuresis. In J. Ferguson & C. B. Taylor (Eds.), *Advances in behavioral medicine*. New York: Spectrum, 1980 (a).

Doleys, D. M., Adams, R., & Rice, J. *Behavioral treatment of encopresis*. Paper presented at Association for Advancement of Behavior Therapy, New York, November 1980.

Doleys, D. M., & Arnold, S. Treatment of childhood encopresis: Full cleanliness training. *Mental retardation*, 1975, *13*, 14–16.

Doleys, D. M., Ciminero, A. R., Tollison, J. W., Williams, C. L., & Wells, K. C. Dry-bed training and retention control training: A comparison. *Behavior Therapy*, 1977, *8*, 541–548.

Doleys, D. M., & Dolce, J. J. Toilet training and enuresis. *Pediatric clinics of North America*, 1982, *29*, 297–313.

Doleys, D. M., McWhorter, A. Q., Williams, S. C., & Gentry, R. Encopresis: Its treatment and relation to nocturnal enuresis. *Behavior Therapy*, 1977, *8*, 77–82.

Doleys, D. M., Schwartz, M. S., & Ciminero, A. R. Elimination problems: Enuresis and encopresis. In E. J. Mash & L. G. Terdal (Eds.), *Behavioral assessment of childhood disorders*. New York: Guilford Press, 1981.

Edelman, R. F. Operant conditioning treatment of encopresis. *Journal of Behavior Therapy and Experimental Psychiatry*, 1971, *2*, 71–73.

Engle, B. The treatment of fecal incontinence by operant conditioning. *Automedica*, 1978, *2*, 101–108.

Engle, B., Nikoomanesh, D., & Schuster, M. M. Operant conditioning of rectosphincteric responses in the treatment of fecal incontinence. *New England Journal of Medicine*, 1974, *290*, 646–649.

Epstein, L. H., & McCoy, J. F. Bladder and bowel control in Hirschsprung's disease. *Journal of Behavior Therapy and Experimental Psychiatry*, 1977, *8*, 97–99.

Esperanca, M., & Gerrard, J. W. Nocturnal enuresis: Comparison of the effect of imipramine and dietary restriction of bladder capacity. *The Canadian Medical Association Journal*, 1969, *101*, 721–724.

Faray, L. G. Enuresis: A genetic study. *American Journal of Diseases of Childhood*, 1935, *49*, 557–578.

Fielding, D. The response of day and night wetting children and children who wet only at night to retention control training and the enuresis alarm. *Behaviour Research and Therapy*, 1980, *18*, 305–317.

Finley, W. W. An EEG study of the sleep of enuretics at three age levels. *Clinical Electroencephalography*, 1971, *2*, 46–50.

Finley, W. W., Besserman, R. L., Bennett, L. F., Clapp, R. K., & Finley, P. M. The effect of continuous, intermittent, and "placebo" reinforcement on the effectiveness of the conditioning treatment for enuresis nocturna. *Behaviour Research and Therapy*, 1973, *11*, 289–297.

Finley, W. W., & Smith, H. A. A long-life, inexpensive urinedetection pad for conditioning of enuresis nocturna, *Behaviour Research Methods and Instrumentation*, 1975, *7*, 273–276.

Finley, W. W., & Wansley, R. A. Use of intermittent reinforcement in a clinical-research program for the treatment of enuresis nocturna. *Journal of Pediatric Psychology*, 1976, *4*, 24–27.

Finley, W. W., Wansley, R. A., & Blenkarn, M. M. Conditioning treatment of enuresis using a 70% intermittent reinforcement schedule. *Behaviour Research and Therapy*, 1977, *15*, 419–427.

Fitts, M. D., & Mann, R. A. Encopresis: An historical and behavioral perspective of definition. *Journal of Pediatric Psychology*, 1977, *4*, 31–38.

Forsythe, W. I., & Redmond, A. Enuresis and spontaneous cure rate. *Archives of Diseases of Childhood*, 1974, *49*, 259–263.

Foxx, R. M., & Azrin, N. N. *Toilet training the retarded*. Champaign, Ill.: Research Press, 1973.

Freinden, W., & VanHandel, D. Elimination of soiling in an elementary school child through application of aversive technique. *Journal of School Psychology*, 1970, *8*, 267–269.

Fried, R. A device for enuresis control. *Behavior Therapy*, 1974, *5*, 682–684.

Gaston, E. A. The physiology of fecal continence. *Surgery, gynecology, and obstetrics*, 1948, *87*, 280–290.

Gavanski, M. The treatment of non-retentive secondary encopresis with imipramine and psychotherapy. *Canadian Medical Association Journal*, 1971, *104*, 227–231.

Gelber, H., & Meyer, V. Behavior therapy and encopresis: The complexities involved in treatment. *Behaviour Research and Therapy*, 1965, *2*, 227–231,

Harris, L. S., & Purohit, A. P. Bladder training and enuresis: A controlled trial. *Behaviour Research and Therapy*, 1977, *15*, 485–490.

Hendren, W. H. Constipation caused by anterior location of the anus and its surgical correction. *Journal of Pediatric Surgery*, 1978, *13*, 505–512.

Hersov, L. Fecal soiling. In M. Rutter and L. Hersov (Eds.), *Child psychiatry: Modern approaches*, Philadelphia: Blackwell Scientific Publications, 1977.

Hilburn, W. B. Encopresis in childhood. *Journal of Kentucky Medical Association*, 1968, *66*, 978.

Hopkinson, B. R., & Lightwood, R. Electrical treatment of anal incontinence. *The Lancet*, February 1966, 297–298.

Jehu, D., Morgan, R. T. T., Turner, R. K. & Jones, A. A controlled trial of the treatment of nocturnal enuresis in residential homes for children. *Behaviour Research and Therapy*, 1977, *15*, 1–6.

Jones, B., Gerrard, J. W., Shokeir, M. K., & Houston, C. S. Recurrent urinary infections in girls: Relation to enuresis. *Canadian Medical Association Journal*, 1972, *106*, 127–130.

Kaffman, M. & Elizur, E. Infants who become enuretic: A longitudinal study of 161 kibbutz children. *Child Development Monographs*, 1977. (No. 42).

Kardash, S., Hillman, E., & Werry, J. Efficacy of imipramine in childhood enuresis: A double-blind control study with placebo. *Canadian Medical Association Journal*, 1968, *99*, 263–266.

Kempe, C. H., & Helfer, R. E. *Helping the battered child and his family.* Oxford, England: Lippincott, 1972.

Kimmel, H. D., & Kimmel, E. C. An instrumental conditioning method for the treatment of enuresis. *Journal of Behavior Therapy and Experimental Psychiatry*, 1970, *1*, 121–123.

Kohlenberg, R. J. Operant conditioning of human anal sphincter pressure. *Journal of Applied Behavior Analysis*, 1973, *6*, 201–208.

Laurence, K. M., & Beresford, A. Continence, friends, marriage, children, in 51 adults with spina bifida. *Developmental Medicine and Child Neurology*, 1975, *17*, 123–128.

Leape, L. L., & Ramenofsky, M. L. Anterior ectopic anus: A common cause of constipation in children. *Journal of Pediatric Surgery*, 1978, *13*, 627–630.

Lehman, E. Psychogenic incontinence of feces (encopresis) in children. *American Journal of Diseases of Childhood*, 1944, *68*, 190–198.

Levine, M. D. Children with encopresis: A descriptive analysis. *Pediatrics*, 1975, *56*, 412–416.

Levine, M. D. Encopresis: its potentiation, evaluation, and alleviation. *Pediatric clinics of North America*, 1982, *29*, 315–330.

Levine, M. D., & Bakow, H. Children with encopresis: A study of treatment outcome. *Pediatrics*, 1976, *58*, 845–852.

Logan, D. L., & Garner, D. G. Effective behavior modification for reducing chronic soiling. *American Annals of the Deaf*, 1971, *116*, 382–384.

Lovibond, S. H., & Coote, M. A. Enuresis, In C. G. Costello (Ed.), *Symptoms of psychopathology.* New York: John Wiley & Sons, 1970.

Lund, C. J. Types of urinary incontinence. In C. J. Lund (Ed.), *Clinical obstetrics and gynecology.* New York: Harper & Row, 1963.

Mahony, D. T., Laferte, R. O., & Mahoney, J. E. Observations on sphincter-augmenting effect of imipramine in children with urinary incontinence. *Urology*, 1973, *1*, 317–323.

McConaghy, N. A controlled trial of imipramine, amphetamine, pad-and-bell conditioning and random wakening in the treatment of nocturnal enuresis. *Medical Journal of Australia*, 1969, *2*, 237–239.

McTaggert, A., & Scott, M. A review of twelve cases of encopresis. *Journal of Pediatrics*, 1959, *54*, 762–768.

Mikkelsen, E. J., Rapoport, J. L., Nee, L., Gruenau, C., Mendelsen, W., & Gillin, C. Childhood enuresis: I. Sleep patterns and psychopathology. *Archives of General Psychiatry*, 1980, *37*, 1139–1144.

Mowrer, O. G., & Mowrer, W. M. Enuresis—A method of its study and treatment. *American Journal of Orthopsychiatry,* 1938, *8,* 436–459.

Neale, D. H. Behavior therapy and encopresis in children. *Behaviour Research and Therapy,* 1963, *1,* 139–149.

Newson, J., & Newson, E. *Four-year-old in the urban community.* London: Allen & Unwin, 1968.

Nisley, D. D. Medical overview of the management of encopresis. *Journal of Pediatric Psychology,* 1976, *4,* 33–34.

Novick, J. Symptomatic treatment of acquired and persistent enuresis. *Journal of Abnormal Psychology,* 1966, *71,* 363–368.

Oppel, W. C., Harper, P. A., & Rider, R. V. The age of attaining bladder control. *Pediatrics,* 1968, *42,* 614–626.

Parker, L., & Whitehead, W. Treatment of urinary and fecal incontinence in children. In D. C. Russo and J. W. Varni (Eds.), *Behavioral Pediatrics: Research and practice.* New York: Plenum Press, 1982.

Paschalis, A. P., Kimmel, H. D., & Kimmel, E. Further study of diurnal instrumental conditioning in the treatment of enuresis nocturna. *Journal of Behavior Therapy and Experimental Psychiatry,* 1972, *3,* 253–256.

Pedrini, B. C., & Pedrini, D. T. Reinforcement procedures in the control of encopresis: A case study. *Psychological Reports.* 1971, *28,* 937–938.

Perlmutter, A. D. Enuresis. In R. Kelalis (Ed.), *Clinical pediatric urology.* Philadelphia: W. B. Saunders, 1976.

Pierce, C. M. Enuresis. In A. M. Freedman & H. I. Kaplan (Eds.), *The child: His psychological and cultural development* (Vol. I). New York: Athenum Publishers, 1972.

Pierce, C. M. Enuresis and encopresis. In A. M. Friedman, H. I. Kaplan, & B. J. Sadock (Eds.), *Comprehensive textbook of psychiatry,* II. Baltimore: Williams & Wilkins, 1975.

Pinkerton, P. Psychogenic megacolon in children: The implications of bowel negativism. *Archives of Diseases in Childhood,* 1958, *33,* 371–380.

Raeburn, J. M., Gemming, J. S., Lowe, B., & Dowrick, P. W. *The Kimmel and Kimmel technique for treating nocturnal enuresis: Two controlled studies.* Unpublished manuscript, University of Auckland Medical School, Auckland, New Zealand, 1977.

Ravitch, M. M. Pseudo Hirschsprung's disease. *Annals of Surgery,* 1958, 148, 781–795.

Rutter, M. Indication for research. In I. Kolvin, E. C. MacKeith, & S. R. Meadow (Eds.), *Bladder control and enuresis.* Philadelphia: J. B. Lippincott, 1973.

Rutter, M., Tizard, J., & Whitmore, K. (Eds.), *Education, health and behavior.* London: Longmans, 1970.

Schaefer, C. R. *Childhood encopresis and enuresis: Causes and therapy.* New York: Van Nostrand Reinhold, 1979.

Seiger, H. W. Treatment of essential nocturnal enuresis. *Journal of Pediatrics,* 1952, *49,* 738–749.

Shaffer, D. Enuresis. In M. Rutter & L. Hersov (Eds), *Child psychiatry: Modern approaches.* Philadelphia: Blackwell Scientific Publications, 1977.

Silber, D. L. Encopresis: Discussion of etiology and management. *Clinical Pediatrics,* 1969, *8,* 225–231.

Smith, E. D. Diagnosis and management of the child with wetting. *Australian Pediatric Journal,* 1967, *3,* 193–205.

Sperling, M. Dynamic considerations and treatment of enuresis. *Journal of the American Academy of Child Psychiatry,* 1965, *4,* 19–31.

Starfield, B., & Mellits, E. D. Increase in functional bladder capacity and improvements in enuresis. *Journal of Pediatrics,* 1968, *72,* 483–487.

Steing, Z. A., & Susser, M. The social dimensions of a symptom: A social-medical study of enuresis. *Social Science and Medicine,* 1967, *1,* 183–201.

Stewart, M. A. Treatment of bedwetting. *Journal of the American Medical Association,* 1975, *232,* 281–283.

Taylor, P. D., & Turner, R. K. A clinical trial of continuous, intermittent and overlearning "bell and pad" treatments for nocturnal enuresis. *Behaviour Research and Therapy,* 1975, *13,* 281–293.

Turner, R. K., Young, G. C., & Rachman, S. Treatment of nocturnal enuresis by conditioning techniques. *Behaviour Research and Therapy,* 1970, *8,* 368–381.

Van Wagenen, R. K., & Murdock, E. E. A transistorized signal package for the toilet training of infants. *Journal of Experimental Child Psychology,* 1966, *3,* 312–314.

Walker, C. E. Toilet training, enuresis, encopresis. In P. R. Magrad (Ed.), *Psychological management of pediatric problems* (Vol. 1). Baltimore: University Park Press, 1978.

Watson, L. S. Application of behavior shaping devices to training severely and profoundly mentally retarded children in an institutional setting. *Mental Retardation,* 1968, *6,* 21–23.

Werry, J. S., & Cohrssen, J. Enuresis: An etiologic and therapeutic study. *Journal of Pediatrics,* 1965, *67,* 423–431.

White, M. A thousand consecutive cases of enuresis: Results of treatment. *The Medical Officer,* 1968, *120,* 151–155.

Williams, C. L., Doleys, D. M., & Ciminero, A. R. A two-year follow-up of enuretic children treated with dry bed training. *Journal of Behavior Therapy and Experimental Psychiatry,* 1978, *9,* 285–286.

Wolters, W. H. G. *Kinderin mit encopresia, een psychosomatische benadering.* Utrecht: Elinhivyk, 1974 (a).

Wolters, W. H. G. A comparative study of behavioral aspects in encopretic children. *Psychotherapy and psychosomatics,* 1974, *24,* 86–79(b).

Wright, L. Handling the encopretic child. *Professional Psychology,* 1973, *4,* 133–144.

Wright, L. Outcome of a standardized program for treating psychogenic encopresis. *Professional Psychology,* 1975, *6,* 453–456.

Wright, L. Psychogenic encopresis. *Ross Timesaver: Feelings and their Medical Significance,* 1978, *20,* 11–16.

Wright, L., & Walker, C. E. Behavioral treatment of encopresis. *Journal of Pediatric Psychology,* 1976, *4,* 35–37.

Yates, A. J. *Behaviour therapy.* New York: John Wiley & Sons, 1970.

Young, G. C. The aetiology of enuresis in terms of learning theory. *The Medical Officer.* January 1965, pp. 19–23 (a).

Young, G. C. Conditioning treatment of enuresis. *Developmental Medicine and Child Neurology,* 1965, *7,* 557–562 (b).

Young, G. C. The treatment of childhood encopresis by conditioned gastroileal reflex training, *Behaviour Research and Therapy,* 1973, *2,* 499–503.

Young, G. C., & Morgan, R. T. T. Overlearning in the conditioning treatment of enuresis. *Behaviour Research and Therapy,* 1972, *10,* 419–420.

Young, I. L., & Goldsmith, A. D. Treatment of encopresis in a day treatment program. *Psychotherapy: Theory, Research and Practice,* 1972, *9,* 231–235.

Zaleski, A., Gerrard, J. W., & Shokeir, M. H. K. Nocturnal enuresis: The importance of a small bladder capacity. In I. Kolvin, R. C. MacKeith, & S. R. Meadow (Eds.), *Bladder control and enuresis.* Philadelphia: W. B. Saunders, 1973.

12

Sleep Disorders

C. Chrisman Wilson
Tulane University

*Stephen N. Haynes**
Illinois Institute of Technology

In recent years, behavior therapists have shown an increased interest in developing treatment strategies for several of the sleep-related problem behaviors evidenced in children, including sleepwalking (e.g., Clement, 1970; Framer & Sanders, 1980), sleep terrors (Framer & Sanders, 1980; Kellerman, 1979), nightmares (Haynes & Mooney, 1975; Roberts & Gordon, 1979), and insomnia (Anderson, 1979; Weil & Goldfried, 1973). Sleepwalking (somnambulism) frequently involves the child (without full consciousness or later memory for the episode) leaving the bed and walking about. Sleep terrors (night terrors) involve repeated episodes of sudden, intense arousals from NREM sleep that are associated with behavioral manifestations of intense anxiety but for which there is little or no recall upon awakening. Nightmares, in contrast, involve awakening from REM sleep, often with vivid recall of an unpleasant dream episode. Insomnia typically involves unsatisfactory sleep due to extended sleep onset latencies, frequent awakenings during the night, or premature morning awakenings. In spite of the disturbing nature of some of these problems to the child and to others in the child's environment, interventions with these problems thus far have received insufficient attention from behavior therapists. Contributing to the limited attention paid to these disturbances is the fact that sleep problems are

---

* The authors would like to thank Gail C. Wilson and Wesley J. Hansche for their helpful comments in the preparation of this chapter.

441

often conceptualized as *secondary* components or manifestations of other childhood behavior problems (Dollinger, 1982) and are sometimes considered trivial in comparison to other disorders (Anders, 1982). Another contributing factor to the lack of attention to such problems seems to be a lack of definitive information concerning characteristics and parameters of these disorders.

In addressing the behavioral treatment of sleep disorders in children, the current chapter focuses first on diagnostic classification systems and then describes the normal sleep pattern in children. Next, general issues related to the conceptualization of sleep disorders are considered, along with assessment strategies and issues. Subsequent chapter sections focus on specific sleep disorders, i.e., sleepwalking (somnambulism), night terrors (pavor nocturnus), dream anxiety attacks (nightmares), and insomnia. For each, behavioral characteristics, etiological conceptualizations, and behavioral intervention strategies are presented. The chapter concludes with suggestions for the focus of assessment of children's sleep disorders and a discussion of unique and continuing issues in the assessment and treatment of these disorders.

DIAGNOSTIC CLASSIFICATION SYSTEMS

The recent development and publication of the *Diagnostic Classification of Sleep and Arousal Disorders* (DCSAD) by the Association of Sleep Disorders Centers and the Association for the Psychophysiological Study of Sleep (ASDC & APSS, 1979) provides a much-needed structure for the accurate classification of sleep disorders. It should also be noted that, where sleep related disorders are addressed in the *Diagnostic and Statistical Manual, 3rd Edition* (DSM-III) of the American Psychiatric Association (1980), these designations correspond to the DCSAD; an outline of the DCSAD is contained in Appendix E of DSM-III (APA, 1980). Where appropriate, subsequent sections of this chapter cite both classification systems with respect to the disorders addressed.

Within the DCSAD system (ASDC & APSS, 1979), the disorders of sleepwalking (somnambulism), sleep terror (pavor nocturnus), and dream anxiety attacks (nightmares) are presented as "Dysfunctions Associated with Sleep, Sleep Stages, or Partial Arousals (Parasomnias)." Insomnia is treated within the DCSAD system as a "Disorder of Initiating and Maintaining Sleep (DIMS)."

Dream anxiety attacks (nightmares) and insomnia are not addressed specifically in DSM-III. Sleepwalking disorder and sleep terror disorder are treated in DSM-III as "Disorders Usually First Evident in Infancy, Childhood or Adolescence (APA, 1980)."

NORMAL SLEEP STRUCTURE

Normal sleep patterns are characterized by REM and NREM sleep stages. REM sleep is more often associated with reports of dreaming than is NREM sleep.

The NREM period can be further subdivided (Dement & Kleitman, 1957) into four stages according to electroencephalogram activity. The REM and NREM stages constitute two distinct states of neurophysiologic activity, with the REM state involving activation, and the NREM state representing inhibition. NREM Stages 1–4 reflect changes from very light to very deep sleep, respectively. The child in Stage 1 sleep in easily awakened, while the child in Stage 4 sleep may even be picked up without awakening. Thus, terms such as *deep* and *light* sleep are behavioral ones that relate to the ease with which the individual may be awakened.

The typical adult sleep cycle begins with "descending" NREM sleep stage shifts through Stage 1 to Stage 4; following is an "emergent" shift through Stages 3 and 2 to a REM period; then the cycle is repeated (Anders & Weinstein, 1972). Ordinarily, a night's sleep involves four to six cycles of REM/NREM sleep. Typically, the child will fall asleep in 15-20 minutes and will progress through Stages 1 to 3, arriving at Stage 4 approximately 15-20 minutes after falling asleep (Williams, Karacan, & Hursch, 1974). One to two hours after sleep onset, the first REM period will appear. While the first REM period may be relatively brief (e.g., five minutes), subsequent REM periods are usually 15-20 minutes long. Following the first REM period, NREM sleep begins again and the cycle continues (Williams, Karacan, & Hursch, 1974).

Although differing in minor detail, the sleep patterns of infants and adults alternate between an aroused and an inhibited state. At birth, the REM and NREM states may be differentiated via psychophysiological measures, such as the electroencephalogram (EEG) and the electrooculogram (EOG). The neonatal sleep onset pattern changes so that the pattern of transitions from the waking state to the REM state (i.e., REM onsets) is later replaced by the adult pattern of transitions from wakefulness to the NREM state (at approximately 6-12 months of age) (Anders, 1982). In children older than the age of two, the characteristics of physiological sleep measures have largely assumed adult forms, although sleep stage *proportions* have not yet achieved adult ratios (Anders & Weinstein, 1972). However, changes in the organization of these sleep states are found to continue through adolescence. Thus, for most age groups it is possible to observe periods of REM sleep alternating with periods of NREM sleep.

It is of interest that children not only progress rapidly through sleep Stages 3 to 4 following sleep onset, but they also spend a considerably greater period of time in these phases (Coates & Thoresen, 1981b; Kales & Kales, 1974), a factor which may be of etiological significance in the greater frequency of sleepwalking and night terrors in child, as compared with adult, populations. It is also of note that several of the more behaviorally remarkable of the childhood sleep disorders (i.e., sleepwalking and sleep terrors) appear out of NREM sleep Stages 3–4. Except for dream anxiety attacks (nightmares), few sleep disorders appear during the REM period (Ware & Orr, 1983). As it will become apparent in subsequent sections, the stage of sleep (REM or NREM) during which sleep attacks occur is important to the differential diagnosis of night terrors from nightmares.

SLEEP DISORDERS IN PERSPECTIVE

As indicated by Coates and Thoresen (1981a; 1981b), the term *sleep disorder* usually refers to (1) behavioral patterns or responses occurring during or associated with sleep, (2) complaints by the individual attributed to excessive or inadequate sleep, (3) a dysfunction in sleep-control processes, or (4) pathologies directly associated with sleep. For the assessment of and intervention with such problems, these authors have emphasized the appropriateness of a 24-hour perspective that would go beyond sleep activity itself. That is, REM sleep, NREM sleep, and wakefulness are linked and interdependent components of overall circadian cycles. Thus, the assessment and treatment of sleep disorders require that *daytime* as well as *nighttime* variables be considered (Coates & Thoresen, 1981a). While problem behaviors are associated with sleep, controlling factors may be associated with waking states as well (Coates & Thoresen, 1981a), which is a perspective having important implications for assessment and intervention.

ASSESSMENT STRATEGIES FOR SLEEP DISORDERS

As indicated previously, adequate preintervention assessment is a necessity in the development of effective treatment programs, and behavioral assessment serves a variety of interdependent functions (Haynes, 1984; Haynes & Wilson, 1979). For example, assessment provides descriptions of the problem and identification of those desirable or undesirable client behaviors upon which to focus intervention (Wilson & Evans, 1983). It further allows identification of those alternative behaviors that might reduce the probability or functional utility of the problem behaviors (Goldfried, 1982). One of the most important functions of assessment is that it facilitates identification of causal variables (i.e., antecedent and consequent controlling factors), which are frequently the target of intervention (Haynes, 1984). Behavioral assessment allows for a functional analysis (i.e., a functional integration of results from preintervention assessment), which ultimately determines intervention goals and strategies. Thus, preintervention assessment has an important impact on the design of intervention programs—intervention programs will vary within and across classes of behavior as a function of characteristics and determinants of the behavior (Haynes, in press, 1984). The evaluation of changes in the principle target behavior (intervention outcome), as well as the side effects and generalization of intervention strategies, are facilitated by the assessment process. Further, ongoing assessment during intervention allows for decisions as to the necessity or appropriateness of intervention modification. Functions of behavioral assessment also include provision of data for differential diagnosis, provision of historical data on clients and behavior problems, and provision of demographic and epidemiological data (Haynes, 1984).

For the differential diagnosis or evaluation of children's sleep disorders, as well as for treatment planning, preintervention assessment should begin with the derivation of a behaviorally specific description of the sleep behavior or complaint. Also included should be a systematic examination of physiological, environmental, and psychological factors that may function as causative or maintaining variables in the problem behavior.

Methods of Assessment

Among the approaches having utility for the assessment of sleep disorders in children are (1) self-reports and reports by others (e.g., interviews, self-monitoring, next-day reports, and sleep diaries), (2) direct observation of sleep behaviors in naturalistic or analogue settings by participant or external observers, (3) automated recordings of sleep behaviors (via audio or videotape recordings), and (4) physiological sleep recordings.

Self-reports and Reports by Others. Probably the most frequently used behavioral assessment instrument is the *behavioral interview* (Haynes & Wilson, 1979; Linehan, 1977). In order to obtain information regarding the characteristics of the problem sleep behavior, it is essential that interviews be conducted with the child, parents, and other significant individuals in the child's environment for the purposes of specifying the problem behavior and to gain information about possible correlates and controlling factors. Such interviews are frequently used in the assessment of children's sleep disorders and are a cost effective means of information acquisition. It should be further noted, however, that in spite of its widespread use and potential utility, the interview remains the instrument least subjected to empirical evaluation (Haynes & Wilson, 1979). For example, because of the self-report nature of information obtained, it could be expected that factors such as demand and bias could influence reports, thus requiring that the information be interpreted with caution.

The specific goals of the interview are to gather information on (1) the topography of the sleep problem, (2) quantitative indices (e.g., frequency, duration, intensity, and in particular, the probability that a particular behavior will occur given the occurrence of other events [*conditional probability*]), (3) the child's developmental status (e.g., physical, cognitive, social, emotional), (4) history and previous attempts at intervention, (5) antecedent factors that might be associated with its occurrence (e.g., stressors, diet, exercise, illness), (6) parental reactions to the episodes, and (7) the child's perceptions of and reactions to the sleep problem.

Self-monitoring involves the systematic self-observation and recording of the occurrence (or nonoccurrence) of specified behaviors and events (Ciminero, Nelson, & Lipinski, 1977; Haynes & Wilson, 1979; Nelson, 1977). Self-monitoring procedures may provide useful information regarding the characteristics and correlates of sleep disorders. For example, for children complaining of insomnia, it might be requested that recordings be made at each awakening. Additionally, monitoring could focus on activity prior to bed, frequencies of ruminations over difficulty going to sleep, etc. For the case of nightmares, children might be asked to record anxiety-producing events during waking hours and parental responses to the nightmare episodes. While self-monitoring has been successfully employed with children (Haynes & Wilson, 1979) in the assessment of academic and school-related behaviors (e.g., Bornstein, Hamilton, & Quevillon, 1977; Nelson, Lipinski, & Boykin, 1978), little is known of the utility of self-monitoring with children's sleep disorders. Self-monitoring is one of the more cost efficient of the behavioral assessment instruments and allows for data acquisition in the natural environment. While it may prove a rich source of information regarding children's sleep problems, several sources of error (e.g., observer bias, reactivity, methods of sampling, contingencies, the reaction of the child's social environment) must be considered in data interpretation.

Another approach to the reporting of sleep behaviors has employed formats known as *next-day reports* that include the use of sleep diaries. Next-day reports of sleep behaviors associated with insomnia (e.g., estimated latencies to sleep onset, number of awakenings, cognitive activity) have been utilized (Haynes, Adams, West, Kamens, & Safranek, 1981; Haynes & Mooney, 1975), as have sleep diaries that require individuals to record events, cognitions, and moods regardless of any presumed association with sleep (Coates & Thoresen, 1977). Such formats, with some modifications, might be used by children or by their parents to report on sleep behavior. While such approaches involve structured reporting formats, they are not truly questionnaires. Instead, in some cases they more closely approximate self-monitoring procedures, and in others (e.g., when parents use them to report on children's behaviors), data collection may involve interview procedures by parents (e.g., as parents attempt to ascertain cognitive content or recall asssociated with nightmare activity). While questionnaires are probably the second most frequently used behavioral assessment instrument (Emmelkamp, 1981), none have been specifically developed for assessment of children's sleep behaviors, and the relevancy and utility of questionnaires for this purpose remains unclear. Although questionnaries are inexpensive to administer and often have face validity and focus on specific behaviors and events, questionnaires often are more rationally than empirically derived (Jensen & Haynes, in press). Similarly, the same sources of error (e.g., demand factors and bias) associated with questionnaires are also likely associated with the next-day reports and diaries thus far employed. Accordingly, interpretation must be approached with caution.

Interviews, self-monitoring, and next-day reports represent a cost-efficient means of deriving information about the target behavior. However, these strategies are not without certain problems. For example, self-reports may or may not correspond closely to physiological or behavioral measures obtained (Coates & Thoresen, 1981a). With the use of self-report formats, it is important that individuals and the client provide data. For example, children who experience night terrors during sleep obviously could not be expected to report on behavioral manifestations occurring during sleep. Similarly, while the mental content during a nightmare episode may be recounted, it again would be difficult for the child to report on other activities during the sleep period. Thus, information from others in the child's environment may be invaluable to the assessment process.

Observation of Ongoing Sleep Behavior. Direct observation may also provide valuable information on the characteristics and correlates of childhood sleep problems. These observations may involve home or laboratory environments and external or participant (i.e., persons from the natural environment) observers (Bootzin & Engle-Friedman, 1981). Naturalistic observation using external observers (those not normally part of the environment) is the assessment procedure most congruent with a behavioral construct system (Hartmann & Wood, 1982). Such measures can provide information on the conditional probabilities of behaviors and represent the most powerful method of intervention outcome evaluation for a variety of behavior problems (Haynes, 1984). Participant observation in the natural environment, however, has the advantages of minimizing change in the environment and being less costly; additionally, it is more frequently used with children than with adults. For any observational strategies, however, sources of error must be considered in the interpretation of data. Investigators (e.g., Baum, Forehand, & Zeigob, 1979; Foster & Cone, 1980; Haynes, 1984; Haynes & Horn, 1982; Haynes & Wilson, 1979; Price & Haynes, 1980) have suggested sources of error associated with observation, including (1) reactivity, (2) observer bias, (3) variations in situational context (e.g., presence in a sleep laboratory may influence sleep behavior), (4) the extent of observer training, and (5) the degree of specificity contained in behavioral codes. Another difficulty associated with direct observation of children's sleep behavior involves the availability of external or participant observers for the time periods necessary to conduct observations. For low frequency behaviors, the time demands could be considerable. While episodes of sleep terror may awaken parents (as may episodes of somnambulism and nightmares) so that they are present to observe behaviors and outcomes once the episodes have begun, critical information regarding behavioral chains leading to the episode or antecedent behaviors may go unobserved unless continuous and systematic observations are made during the child's sleep cycle.

Automated Recording of Ongoing Sleep Behaviors. Approaches that circumvent the difficulties associated with observer availability include the audio and videotape monitoring of sleep behavior. To the extent that the child can acclimatize to the presence of such equipment, these strategies have considerable utility in data collection because they provide ongoing records of behavioral events while minimizing the reactive effects of observation. They also provide permanent records of behavior for analysis at later times.

Audio recordings from tape recorders or dictaphones may have benefit in monitoring verbal behaviors associated with nightmare, night terror, or somnambulistic episodes. In addition, they provide a convenient means of patient self-monitoring of episodes of awakening associated with insomnia. To the degree that the child or adolescent is able, cognitions, ruminations, and feelings can be self-reported on tape. In those cases in which all-night recordings are required, provision should be made for the extended recording times, since cassette tapes typically will not provide greater than two hours of recording time. Reel-to-reel recorders, however, can be employed for up to six hours of recording. In the use of videotape recordings, time of recording is less of a dilemma since the more recent Beta formats provide for up to six hours of recording time. However, in the use of videotape recording, lighting requirements present problems, and provision must be made accordingly. A related strategy for automated recording in the natural environment involves *critical event sampling* (Haynes, 1978; Margolin, 1981). For example, children or parents might actuate recorders at those times when there is a high probability of problematic episodes. While such automated recording can be cost and time efficient and can represent a rich source of information, it is infrequently used, with no psychometric evaluation of this assessment procedure. Thus, the sources and degree of error can only be estimated, although factors such as reactivity might be expected to operate (Haynes, 1984).

Physiological Sleep Recordings.   Owing to the increased involvement of behavior analysts in the evaluation and treatment of psychosomatic and medical-psychological disorders (Davison & Davison, 1980; Haynes & Gannon, 1981) and to the fact that many behavioral interventions are aimed at modification of some aspect of physiological functioning, there has been an increased emphasis on psychophysiological measurement. Although costly, measures such as all-night polysomnographic recordings of sleep activity, which typically involve electroencephalogram (EEG), electrooculogram (EOG), and electromyogram (EMG) measures, can be useful in the differentiation of sleep disorders and in intervention planning. For example, EEG and EOG measures, which reflect the presence of NREM or REM periods, facilitate the differentiation between night terror and nightmare episodes. EEG and EMG recordings may be found to be helpful in pinpointing disturbances leading to complaints of insomnia.

Interpretations of all-night laboratory sleep recordings are hindered because of their potentially reactive effects on the individual's sleep pattern. The novelty and/or demand factors associated with the sleep laboratory setting may alter sleep patterns, especially for children, thus qualifying the generalizability of such measures. However, there is ample evidence that laboratory derived measures have satisfactory discriminant validity and clinical utility.

In an effort to more directly measure sleep patterns in the natural environment, procedures have been developed for polysomnographic monitoring in the home. For example, Coates, Rosekind, and Thoresen (1978) reported the development of a system for transmitting EEG measures from individuals' homes via telephone. Unfortunately, while all-night sleep measures are highly desirable in the assessment of sleep problems, the necessary instrumentation and its operation is expensive and typically is not available to a majority of behavior therapists faced with sleep disorders as a presenting problem. Fortunately, at least among adults, there are reasonably high correlations between self-reported and polysomnographically monitored sleep patterns (e.g., Haynes, et al., 1981). Again, however, sources of error (e.g., sensitivity, movement artifact, sensor placement, surface resistance) must be considered in evaluating physiological data.

DYSFUNCTIONS ASSOCIATED WITH SLEEP, SLEEP STAGES, OR PARTIAL AROUSALS (PARASOMNIAS)

The parasomnias consist of a constellation of clinical problems representing undesirable physical phenomena that either appear exclusively during sleep (e.g., night terrors) or are exacerbated by sleep (ASDC & APSS, 1979). According to the DCSAD, these episodes are manifestations of central nervous system activation. In this section, three of the parasomnias are addressed, i.e., sleepwalking, night terrors, and nightmares. Sleepwalking and night terror episodes are found to occur in association with NREM sleep Stages 3 and 4 (deep sleep), during the early portion of the night (ASDC & APSS, 1979; Broughton, 1968). Nightmares (anxiety dream attacks) are regarded as REM sleep phenomena (i.e., an awakening from REM sleep or sometimes from light NREM sleep (ASDC & APSS, 1979). However, the association between specific sleep disorders and specific sleep stages is inconsistent.

The parasomnias are suggested to be the most common of the childhood sleep disorders (Anders & Weinstein, 1972; Ware & Orr, 1983), and they characteristically elicit considerable parental attention, although they are generally benign in that they typically are not symptomatic of more significant pathology (Ware & Orr, 1983).

SLEEPWALKING DISORDER (SOMNAMBULISM)

Sleepwalking is a problem involving a complex sequence of behaviors that frequently involve the child leaving the bed and walking about without full consciousness or later memory. It usually occurs 30 to 200 minutes after sleep onset (during the first one third of the night) and is most frequently associated with Stages 3 and 4 of NREM sleep (deep sleep). The duration of the episode is typically from a few minutes to half an hour.

The characteristics and typical sequence of behavior have been described by several authors (Anders, 1982; Broughton, 1968; Coates & Thoresen, 1981a; Kales & Kales, 1974; Kellerman, 1979; Schroeder, Gordon, & Hawk, 1983; Weitzman, 1981) and are also indicated in the DCSAD (ASDC & APSS, 1979) and in the DSM-III (APA, 1980). Specific diagnostic criteria contained in these classification systems are based on the description which follows.

Sleepwalking involves the child quietly sitting up in bed and then carrying out perseverative motor movements. This is followed by performance of more complex sequences of motor behavior, which may include dressing, opening doors, etc. The child evidences a blank, staring face and behaviorally is relatively unresponsive to communication from others. Although the child is able to see and manuever around objects in his/her path, the child can be awakened only with great difficulty and evidences poor coordination. Sleepwalking may terminate spontaneously by awakening (typically accompanied by disorientation), by returning to bed, or by lying down elsewhere without awakening. Amnesia for the episode is typical. The EEG shows quite high amplitude in Stage 4 just preceding the episode, with flattening (i.e., arousal) just before the episode and a combination of NREM stages and lower amplitude EEG alpha activity as walking begins.

It is estimated that from 1 to 6 percent of the child population at some time experiences chronic sleepwalking problems, with as many as 15 percent of all children experiencing isolated episodes. The disorder occurs more commonly in males than in females, and Broughton (1968) suggested that males outnumber females in a 4 to 1 ratio. Sleepwalking episodes may vary from infrequent to one to four times per week in severe cases. A higher than normal incidence of other episodic disorders associated with deep NREM sleep (e.g., nocturnal enuresis, sleep terror disorder) are found to accompany cases of sleepwalking. As contrasted with adults evidencing this disorder, sleepwalking does not appear to be reliably associated with other behavior disorders.

The onset of sleepwalking disorder may occur anytime after walking is learned, but it usually appears between the ages of 6 and 12 years. Adult sleepwalkers usually give a history of childhood onset, followed by a remission. Sleepwalking in children and adolescents usually lasts several years, regardless of episode frequency. A majority of child sleepwalkers are asymptomatic by their 20s.

While the behavior itself may not be a major concern, complications associated with sleepwalking disorder include (*a*) the possibility of accidental injury since sleepwalkers do not always transverse their environments in perfect safety and (*b*) the possibility that repetitive episodes may lead to problems in interpersonal relationships. For example, the child may begin to avoid situations (such as staying overnight with friends) in which others might become aware of the symptomatology. It is important to note that, aside from these issues, the disorder is considered to have a benign course.

Etiological Conceptualizations

Among the factors that potentially play an etiological role in sleepwalking are (1) arousal factors, (2) developmental and maturational factors, (3) genetic factors, (4) daily stressors, (5) medical illness and physical stress, and (6) medication effects.

Sleepwalking is most frequently conceptualized as a *disorder of arousal* (Anders, 1982; Broughton, 1968; Coates & Thoresen, 1981b) involving an abrupt increase in motor activity under circumstances of incomplete central nervous system (CNS) arousal (ASDC & APSS, 1979). Investigators further suggest that this arousal disorder is associated etiologically with *developmental/maturational factors* in the form of CNS immaturity (Anders, 1982; Broughton, 1968; Guilleminault & Anders, 1976; Kales & Kales, 1974; Kales, Kales, Soldatos, Chamberlin, & Martin, 1979). The fact that this disorder is usually outgrown is consistent with a developmental immaturity conceptualization (Kales, Kales, Soldatos, Caldwell, Charney, & Martin, 1980). Furthermore, an immaturity factor (i.e., a sudden rhythmical high-voltage, slow-wave activity) that persists to a later age than in nonsomnambulistic children has been noted in the sleep EEGs of these children (Kales, Soldatos, Caldwell, Kales, Humphrey, Charney, & Schweitzer, 1980).

Parents who were sleepwalkers have a greater than expected number of children who are sleepwalkers. Further, concordance for sleepwalking has been reported to be as much as six times greater for monozygotic than for dizygotic twins (Anders & Weinstein, 1972). This has led some investigators (e.g., Kales, Kales, Soldatos, Chamberlin, & Martin, 1979) to propose a *genetic* etiological component to the disorder. At this point, it should be noted that physiological, rather than psychological components, seem to be primary when onset occurs in childhood (in adulthood, psychopathology may be a more likely factor), although variables, such as environmental stressors, may significantly influence its course.

Dollinger (1982) suggested that such disorders may be associated with *daily stressors*, such as severe anxiety. Support for an association between anxiety and sleepwalking has also been suggested by Meyer (1975) and by Clement (1970). Meyer (1975) reported the onset of sleepwalking in an adult male as a function of stress (test anxiety), and Clement (1970) suggested anxiety associated with nightmares as a precursor.

The reports from several authors (e.g., Anders & Weinstein, 1972; Coates & Thoresen, 1981b; Framer & Sanders, 1980; Kales & Kales, 1974; Kurtz & Davison, 1974; Nagaraja, 1974) seem to suggest that sleepwalking may be associated with stressful and other environmental factors. For example, sleepwalking episodes can be provoked by abruptly standing the child upright during NREM Stages 3 or 4 (Kales & Kales, 1974), suggesting the role of external stimuli in the disorder. Likewise, Anders and Weinstein (1972) and Anders

(1982) indicate the potential influence of environmental factors in that episodes may occur less frequently in the laboratory than in the home environment. Kurtz and Davison (1974) reported that the onset of sleepwalking disorder followed a traumatic event; furthermore, Nagaraja (1974) reported that the onset in one child occurred subsequent to separation from his father. A dyssynchrony in circadian and sleep-wake cycles has also been suggested as an etiological factor (Coates & Thoresen, 1981b); that is, the demands for bedtime routine and other correlates of external demands for the child's sleep behavior may not be consistent with the child's circadian cycle, thus affecting the probability of the occurrence of episodes. Thus far, however, no empirical data is available to confirm or disconfirm this hypothesis.

Sleepwalking episodes have also been noted to occur in conjunction with *physical stress and illness*. Kales, Kales, Soldatos, Chamberlin, & Martin (1979) reported that with elevated body temperature (especially during NREM Stages 3 or 4) sleep becomes fragmented and total sleep time is reduced. They also noted that Stages 3 or 4 sleep have been shown to decrease significantly when fever is experimentally induced. These authors hypothesized that this initial suppression may be followed by a rebound in sleep Stages 3 or 4, which may set the stage for the occurrence of disorders of arousal from slow-wave sleep. They reported the cases of five children who demonstrated onset of sleepwalking either during the active (i.e., high fever) or recovery stages from febrile illness. Sleep patterns may also be affected by factors such as fatigue or prior sleep loss (APA, 1980; ASDC & APSS, 1979; Kales, Kales, Soldatos, Chamberlin, & Martin, 1979). In further regard to physiological factors, Broughton (1968) reported that patients manifest other constellations of physiological change that differ from normals and that these changes may occur during episodes and at other times as well (e.g., the individual will make movements that are independent of attacks and are complex and gestural, and these may occur with EEG slow-wave activity). Such changes may differentially contribute to sleep disorders of a given type, and changes may be enhanced during some nights that culminate in an episode.

Regarding *medication usage,* the rebound effect associated with suppression of Stages 3 or 4 sleep is relevant to the evaluation of some pharmacological treatments that have been employed to ameliorate sleepwalking episodes. Drugs, such as Diazepam, might reduce sleepwalking by suppressing Stage 4 sleep (Glick, Schulman, & Turecki, 1971). However, a rebound in sleepwalking might be noted when pharmacological intervention is withdrawn.

Intervention with Sleepwalking Disorder

The development of intervention strategies should reflect etiological considerations. Strategies will thus vary as a function of hypotheses derived from preintervention assessment. Because any specific behavior disorder (e.g., sleepwalking) will demonstrate across-subject variance in etiology, approaches to intervention will also vary. Based on current etiological conceptualizations of sleepwalking, interventions could be expected to focus on modifications of the individual's arousal level and/or on modifications of environmental stressors and psychological factors. To date, there have been few behavioral interventions with somnambulistic episodes. Although some interventions with other disorders (e.g., sleep terror) have been reported to have had peripheral effects on accompanying episodes of sleepwalking, these reported effects have not been systematically evaluated. Accordingly, those interventions are considered in other sections of this chapter. Reported here are those applications for which somnambulism has been the primary target behavior.

Intervention Strategies. Behavioral interventions with Sleepwalking Disorder in children generally fall into the domains of (1) response interruption, (2) systematic desensitization, (3) behavioral contracting, (4) instructions, and (5) environmental alteration.

With regard to response interruption approaches, Clement (1970) reported on the efficacy of an awakening procedure in the treatment of sleepwalking in a seven-year-old boy. In this case, the child was awakened by his mother upon each occurrence of a recurring nightmare (the nightmare was identified as a characteristic precursor of the sleepwalking episodes). The awakening procedure was based on the assumption that the nightmare had become a classically conditioned stimulus for sleepwalking episodes (possibly via heightened arousal accompanying the dream material) and that the awakening procedure should serve to break up the existing stimulus response association. In addition, the child was given pictures of the "black bug," which was the fear stimulus in the dream content, and was instructed to hit and tear up the pictures each time he was awakened from the nightmare. Further, the mother was instructed to reinforce his verbal expression of anger. However, it is unclear whether the primary treatment effects were a function of an interruption of the response chain, anxiety reduction, or both.

In the case of a 13-year-old male experiencing sleepwalking and nightmare episodes, Framer and Sanders (1980) employed a family contingency contracting system to reduce stress presumed to be related to the child's disturbed sleep behavior. Because of family conflicts over the child's behavior, formal if-then contracts were negotiated between the parents and the child. These contracts involved increased compliance to parental requests in return for increased activities and privileges. While significant improvements in the behavior were noted, factors such as increased parental reinforcement of appropriate sleep behavior cannot be ruled out as contributing components to the behavioral change.

Several investigators (Kales & Kales, 1974; Kales, Kales, Soldatos, Chamberlin, & Martin, 1979; Kales, Soldatos, Caldwell, Kales, Humphrey, Charney & Schweitzer, 1980) have suggested that the primary treatment concern in cases of sleepwalking is the safety of the child during the episodes. Accordingly, it is important that the child's environment be modified so as to reduce the possibility of injury. This may include making sure that the child sleeps on the ground floor of the home, removing objects that could cause harm from the sleep environment, and providing door and window locks, etc. (Kales, Soldatos, Caldwell, Kales, Humphrey, Charney, & Schweitzer, 1980). These investigators also suggested that interruption of the sleepwalking episode may be contraindicated if such an intervention might result in confusion or fright. They also noted the importance of instructions to parents (e.g., that the child can be gently led back to bed) to reassure them that the episodes are not ordinarily a sign of psychopathology and that they are usually outgrown (Kales & Kales, 1974, 1975).

An additional consideration in the formulation of treatment strategies involves the appropriateness of medications in the management of sleepwalking. As already indicated, drug treatments (e.g., Diazepam) have been employed to reduce the rate of sleepwalking episodes (Glick, Schulman, & Turecki, 1971). However, considering the findings of Kales, Kales, Soldatos, Chamberlin, & Martin (1970) that suppression of Stage 4 sleep (associated with Diazepam) may result in a rebound effect that may set the stage for such episodes, the use of medications that suppress Stage 4 sleep should be carefully evaluated. Should the behavior analysis reveal that such drugs are being used, then collaboration with the child's physician is highly desirable.

SLEEP TERROR DISORDER (PAVOR NOCTURNUS)

Also referred to as "night terrors," Sleep Terror Disorder involves repeated episodes of intense, sudden arousal during sleep that involves behavioral manifestations of intense anxiety. Although involving a partial arousal response, the child remains asleep during the episode. Episodes typically occur between 30 and 200 minutes after sleep onset (during the first one third of the night), which is the interval of Stages 3 or 4 NREM sleep (deep sleep) containing slow-wave delta activity. The sleep episode is typically from one to five minutes in duration, although some episodes may last up to 20 minutes. In some cases, episodes may occur more than once during the same night.

The characteristics and typical sequence of behavior have been described by several authors (i.e., Anders, 1982; Broughton, 1968; Carlson, White & Turkat, 1982; Glick, Schulman, & Turecki, 1971; Kales & Kales, 1974, 1975; Kellerman, 1979; Roberts & Gordon, 1979; Schroeder, Gordon, & Hawk, 1983; Ware & Orr, 1983; Weitzman, 1981) and are also described in the DCSAD (ASDC & APSS, 1979) and in the DSM-III (APA, 1980). Specific diagnostic criteria contained in these classification systems are based on the description which follows.

Typically, the episode begins with an intense scream as the child abruptly sits up in bed. Intense behavioral manifestations of anxiety are reflected in the child's frightened expression, dilated pupils, and vocalizations (e.g., moans, groans, cries for help). Also characterizing the episodes are profuse perspiration, a quickened pulse, rapid breathing, piloerection, and agitated and perseverative motor movement (automatisms). During the episode, the child is generally unresponsive to parental efforts to calm him/her or to interrupt the attack, while appearing inconsolable (a particularly perplexing feature of the disorder to parents). Following awakening, the child immediately falls to sleep. Some episodes may progress into sleepwalking, especially if vigorous attempts are made to interrupt the episode by standing the child upright. Upon awakening, the child may recount a sense of terror and fragmentary dream content but rarely will be able to report complete dream sequences. Morning amnesia for the episode is common. Prior to difficult episodes, sleep EEG delta waves may be higher in amplitude than usual for NREM phases, and breathing and heart rates are slower. The onset of the episode may be accompanied by significant increases in heart rate, and the EEG quickly assumes an alpha pattern.

It is estimated that from 1 to 4 percent of the child population at some time experiences this disorder. The disorder is more common in males than in females and is more common in children than in adults. Sleep terror episodes may vary from infrequent to successive nightly occurrences. Further, it is suggested that severity of the episodes may be proportional to the duration of the preceding Stage 3 or 4 sleep periods. A higher than normal incidence of other episodic disorders associated with deep NREM sleep (e.g., somnambulism, nocturnal enuresis) are observed to accompany cases of sleep terror. Although psychopathology has been associated with cases of sleep terror in adults, this relationship has not been found in cases of sleep terror in children.

The onset of sleep terrors usually appears between the ages of 4 and 12 years, and adults with the disorder may similarly give a history of childhood onset. Episodes may be extremely variable in frequency, ordinarily being separated by days or weeks but occasionally occurring on successive nights. Sleep terrors usually disappear in adolescence. The course of Sleep Terror Disorder may involve longer periods of time than that of Sleepwalking Disorder. While no major complications are suggested in DSM-III (APA, 1980) or in the DCSAD (ASDC & APSS, 1979), this disorder may lead to secondary disturbances in normal family life, and the individual may begin to avoid normal activities and situations where the episodes might draw attention from others.

Etiological Conceptualizations

As with sleepwalking, factors such as (1) arousal, (2) development and maturation, (3) genetic influences, (4) environmental stressors, (5) medical illness and physical stress, and (6) drugs have been implicated in the etiology of sleep terrors, as have (7) environmental contingencies.

Sleep Terror Disorder is basically conceptualized as a *disorder of arousal* (Broughton, 1968; Kales, Kales, Soldatos, Caldwell, Charney, & Martin,

1980), which, like other Stages 3 or 4 sleep disorders, involves abrupt physiological activation under conditions of incomplete arousal (Ware & Orr, 1983). In this regard, it has been suggested that the confusion and disorientation characteristic of the parasomnias is due to arousal from Stages 3 or 4 sleep and that such arousal might be considered a normal event that sets the stage for the episodes. These post-arousal confusional states may explain the many common symptoms between sleepwalking and sleep terror episodes, such as disorientation and amnesia for episodes (Broughton, 1968). Along these lines, some investigators have suggested that sleep terror and sleepwalking episodes may represent points on the same continuum, with the former representing the most intense manifestations and with the latter representing a more moderate form (Fisher, Kahn, Edwards, & Davis, 1973; Kales, Kales, Soldatos, Caldwell, Charney, & Martin, 1980). On the other hand, Broughton (1968) suggested that preexisting patterns of physiological change (e.g., relative tachycardia during slow-wave sleep in cases of sleep terror) may be associated with particular types of sleep problems (e.g., sleep terror versus sleepwalking episodes).

Also implicated as etiological factors in Sleep Terror Disorder have been *developmental and maturational factors*, such as central nervous system immaturity (Anders, 1982; Kales, Kales, Soldatos, Caldwell, Charney, & Martin, 1980; Kales, Soldatos, Caldwell, Kales, Humphrey, Charney, & Schweitzer, 1980). For example, maturation of the child's central nervous system early in life is accompanied by increases in the proportions of time spent in sleep Stages 3 or 4. Additionally, the duration of the first NREM period is comparatively large in the early years. However, with increased age (beyond the age of two years), the relative proportion of time spent in the initial phase of NREM sleep is reduced. Thus, while increases in proportions of delta sleep may help set the stage for the parasomnias (Anders, 1982; Anders & Weinstein, 1972), maturational/developmental lags could delay reductions in the time spent in the initial NREM phase (Kales & Kales, 1974; Ware & Orr, 1983) and, thus, may play a role in the significantly higher rates of this disorder in childhood. Developmental or maturational immaturity might thus account for both the higher frequency in childhood and the fact that children seem to outgrow episodes by adolescence (Anders, 1982; Kales, Kales, Soldatos, Caldwell, Charney, & Martin, 1980). The fact that sleep terror episodes may persist longer in life than sleepwalking episodes has also led investigators to propose that developmental factors, at least in the continuation of episodes, may be less important than in Sleepwalking Disorder (Kales, Kales, Soldatos, Caldwell, Charney & Martin, 1980). Thus far, however, research documentation of such relationships is lacking.

Sleep Terror Disorder has been found to be more common among those with a family history of it than in the general population (APA, 1980; ASDC & APSS, 1979; Youkilis, & Bootzin, 1981), leading some investigators to postulate a *genetic* etiological component in the disorder (Carlson, White, & Turkat, 1982; Hallstrom, 1972; Kales, Kales, Soldatos, Chamberlin, & Martin, 1979;

Kales, Weber, Charney, Bixler, & Ladd, 1977). For example, in a study of sleep terrors over three familial generations, Hallstrom (1972) reported that at least 20 percent of those adult sleep terror sufferers indicated an immediate family history. However, the possibility that social learning factors contribute to such findings cannot be excluded (Carlson, White, & Turkat, 1982). Although physiological factors may play an important role in sleep terrors, factors that control their occurrence have not been clearly identified, and these physiological formulations do not provide clear explanations as to those factors/events that provoke sleep terror episodes.

A variety of *daily stressors* may affect the conditional probability of sleep terrors, as may environmental stimuli. Anxiety associated with stressful life events, for example, may play a role. Kellerman (1979) reported on occurrences of sleep terrors in the case of a child suffering from acute leukemia. In that case, it was suggested that anxiety resulting from necessary separation from the mother (for hospitalization and treatment procedures) and from the medical procedures themselves contributed to onset of the episodes. While not clearly associated with anxiety, significant (stressful) life events have been reported by adults with histories of sleep terrors to be associated with the onset of episodes (Kales, Kales, Soldatos, Caldwell, Charney, & Martin, 1980), although these were self-reports of events that had occurred several years in the past. In another case, Kellerman (1980) suggested that anxiety resulting from viewing a frightening film played a causative role in the onset of sleep terrors, and Marshall (1975) and Roberts and Gordon (1979) suggested anxiety associated with physical trauma to be etiologically related to sleep terrors.

Stressful social relationships (e.g., problem family interactions) may also be associated with the occurrence of sleep terrors. For example, Framer and Sanders (1980) reported on the elimination of sleep terror episodes following treatment that reduced family stress. Because this was not a controlled study, however, these findings must be cautiously interpreted. External stimuli, such as noises, have been implicated in the occurrence of sleep terrors. Fisher, Kahn, Edwards, and Davis (1973) reported that a buzzer could serve to elicit an episode when sounded during sleep Stages 3 or 4. This suggests that auditory or other external environmental stimuli occurring during sleep may elicit episodes. Internal stimuli may also be related to sleep terrors. Ware and Orr (1983) reported on the elimination of sleep terror episodes in an enuretic child. In that case, having the child void his bladder prior to sleep onset resulted in decreases in sleep terror episodes, leading the authors to hypothesize that they might have been stimulated by a full bladder. Taken together, the findings reviewed suggest that the conditional probability of sleep terrors may be related to the influence of external or internal environmental stressors on children's arousal responses.

Cognitive activity also may be an important precipitant in sleep terrors. One line of support for this hypothesis comes from several investigators (e.g., Fisher, Kahn, Edwards, Davis, & Fine, 1974; Kales, Caldwell, Soldatos, Kales, & Russell, 1977) who found that the fragmented recall of the content of sleep terror episodes involved fearful scenes, such as being physically attacked or of falling. However, while some content may suggest common themes, it remains unclear as to how ongoing thought is related to occurrences (Carlson, White, & Turkat, 1982). Regarding cognitive activity, Broughton (1968) suggested that, as a result of internal stimulation produced from arousal, the individual may label such interoceptive stimulation as anxiety or terror. Similarly, Keith (1975) has suggested that any elaborated cognitive content may result from the episodes' neurological underpinnings. However, it is also the case that cognitive activity can affect neurophysiological processes.

In summary, the relationship between cognitions or anxiety and sleep terror episodes is unclear. Anxiety may increase the probability or intensity of episodes, may be an outcome of sleep terrors, or, once associated with episodes triggered by other factors, anxiety may then serve to evoke further episodes. While children may become afraid of these episodes or afraid to go to sleep because of them, empirical evidence for such a phenomenon is lacking.

Physical illness, stress, or fatigue may also play an etiological role in sleep terrors. Evidence supporting this possibility comes from several investigators (Anders & Weinstein, 1972; Kales & Kales, 1974; Kales, Kales, Soldatos, Caldwell, Charney & Martin, 1980; Kales, Kales, Soldatos, Chamberlin, & Martin, 1979; Marshall, 1975; Roberts & Gordon, 1979). In five cases of febrile illness involving temperatures of 104 degrees or more, the onset of sleep terrors occurred concurrently with the illness (Kales, Kales, Soldatos, Chamberlin, & Martin, 1979). In four of those cases, the symptoms disappeared as the physical illness was brought under control. In the fifth case, the symptoms continued for several months. As already indicated, Marshall (1975) reported the onset of sleep terrors associated with a case of physical trauma, and Kales and Kales (1974) suggested that pain or physical discomfort may be linked etiologically to sleep terror episodes. Although Roberts and Gordon (1979) postulated that anxiety was the critical component in the onset of sleep terrors in the case of a burn trauma, such a trauma might result in episodes as a result of neurophysiological changes. Also implicated in the etiology of sleep terrors are factors that contribute to a deepening of nighttime sleep, such as prior sleep loss or fatigue (Anders & Weinstein, 1972; Kales, Kales, Soldatos, Caldwell, Charney & Martin, 1970), which may set the stage for occurrences through subsequent rebounds in NREM sleep.

While not empirically evaluated thus far, findings reported in these preceding investigations suggest the importance of a *systems approach* for intervention with sleep terrors, i.e., strategies that do not approach the behavior problem in isolation from family interactions.

The use of *drugs* also may be related to episodes of sleep terror. It has been suggested that drugs, such as tricyclics and neuroleptics (e.g., imipramine, amitriptyline hydrochloride), can evoke sleep terror episodes as in the Flemenbaum investigation (1976), although it was not clear whether the episodes were truly sleep terrors in that investigation. Kales and Kales (1975) suggested caution in the use of Diazapam with children because of the possible rebound effects that might precipitate sleep terror episodes.

Environmental contingencies may play an etiological role in episodes. In the case previously discussed by Kellerman (1980), it was also suggested that the problem episodes were reinforced by contingent parental attention to the episodes.

Based on the findings reviewed, it is apparent that the etiology of sleep terrors involves multiple interacting factors. Physiological factors, such as the child's level of central nervous system development, may interact with factors such as anxiety, stress, fatigue, illness or medication usage in the initiation and/or maintenance of the disorder.

Differentiation of Sleep Terrors and Nightmares. Family members, clinicians, and researchers alike have confused sleep terror episodes with nightmare episodes, and in some instances have used the term *nightmare* in referring to both occurrences. However, Sleep Terror Disorder and Dream Anxiety Attacks (nightmares) differ on a number of dimensions. These include differences in (1) EEG characteristics, (2) time of the night during which they occur, (3) behaviors associated with the episodes (i.e., verbal, physiological, and motor), (4) arousability and responsiveness to the environment, (5) memory for dream content, (6) post-awakening mental state, and (7) incidence.

As already indicated, EEG patterns associated with sleep terror episodes are indicative of NREM Stages 3 or 4, while EEG patterns associated with nightmares are indicative of REM sleep (APA, 1980; ASDC & APSS, 1979; Carlson, White, & Turkat, 1982; Keith, 1975). Furthermore, sleep terror episodes typically occur in the first one third of the night, while nightmares predominate in REM sleep periods during the middle and latter portions of the night (APA, 1980; ASDC & APSS, 1979; Carlson, White, & Turkat, 1982; Hersen, 1972). The onset of the sleep terror episode is typically signalled by a cry or scream and such verbalizations are almost always present during the episode (Keith, 1975), while verbalizations during nightmare episodes, if present, tend to be subdued.

A significant heightening of physiological activity accompanies sleep terror episodes (e.g., a greatly increased heart rate, profuse sweating, pupil dilation, piloerection), indicating intense physiological arousal, while, in the case of nightmares, there is only a gradual increase in pulse rate and only moderate arousal (ASDC & APSS, 1980; Carlson, White, & Turkat, 1982; Keith, 1975). Motorically, extreme activity is present in sleep terror episodes and may progress to sleepwalking. Additionally, the child may thrash around in bed. In contrast, decreased muscle tone is more typical of the nightmare episode, and sleepwalking does not occur (Keith, 1975). During sleep terror episodes, the child is quite difficult to arouse and tends to be unresponsive to the environment (APA, 1980; ASDC & APSS, 1979; Broughton, 1968; Carlson, White & Turkat, 1982), while during nightmare episodes, the child is more easily aroused and tends to be responsive to the environment (ASDC & APSS, 1982; Carlson, White, & Turkat, 1982).

Memory or recall of the content of sleep terror episodes typically is extremely limited, and the child may be amnesic for the episode the next morning (APA, 1980; ASDC & APSS, 1979; Broughton, 1968; Carlson, White, & Turkat, 1982). In contrast, children typically report clear and vivid memories of the dream content occurring in nightmare episodes (Keith, 1975). If the child is awakened from a sleep terror episode, the child's mental content is typically one of confusion and disorientation (ASDC & APSS, 1980; Broughton, 1968). However, when children are awakened from nightmare episodes, they typically become lucid very abruptly and can be calmed without great difficulty (Keith, 1975). Finally, sleep terror and nightmare episodes may be distinguished in terms of incidence, i.e., Sleep Terror Disorder is somewhat rare (1–4 percent of the population), while nightmares are quite common.

Intervention with Sleep Terror Disorder

Owing to the range of factors potentially contributing to the initiation and maintenance of sleep terrors, interventions can involve multiple components to modify the child's arousal responses, drug intake, nighttime stimuli, and daily stressors. Again, because etiological factors vary across children, treatment packages would vary as a function of suspected controlling variables.

While several published studies on the treatment of sleep terrors have involved multicomponent strategies, the components were not necessarily derived from a systematic behavioral assessment. Additionally, the interventions reported in the literature are case reports, and thus, there is no clear evidence as to the relative efficacy of the treatment packages or of the specific components. Further confounding interpretation is the fact that in several of the reported cases no clear determination can be made as to whether the behavior targeted for intervention would be classified as sleep terror episodes, nightmare episodes, or combinations of the two.

Intervention Strategies.   Behavioral treatment strategies reported in the sleep terror literature generally fall into the domains of (1) contingency management (e.g., behavioral contracting and reinforcement for sleep-appropriate and non-anxious behaviors), (2) instructional procedures, (3) anxiety reduction via desensitization or incompatible response training, and (4) response prevention/interruption.

With regard to behavioral contracting, Framer and Sanders (1980) reported on the case of a 13-year old experiencing sleepwalking and sleep terror episodes (it is unclear whether episodes would be classified as sleep terrors or nightmares). Assuming the episodes to be associated with antecedent environmental (family) stress, these investigators negotiated if-then contracts between the parents and child to reinforce compliance and to improve interactions. While this strategy was reported effective in eliminating sleep terrors, the authors appropriately urged caution in interpreting the results because the impact of other factors (e.g., parental attention and reinforcement for appropriate sleep behaviors) was not evaluated in this A-B design.

Approaches involving instruction generally constitute what Carlson, White, & Turkat (1982) have described as *conservative management*. Several investigators (e.g., Guilleminault & Anders, 1976; Kales & Kales, 1974, 1975) have emphasized that sleep terror episodes occur so infrequently and are so typically outgrown that reassurance to parents of the fact that such occurrences in childhood do not typically represent indices of psychopathology may often be sufficient.

Kellerman (1979) reported on the behavioral treatment of sleep terrors in a three-year-old suffering from acute leukemia. In this case, it was hypothesized that anxiety associated with separation from the mother and with the trauma of the required medical procedures was the critical etiological factor. The strategies employed involved (1) progressive muscle relaxation training for the mother so that she could control her own anxiety and remain in the treatment room with her daughter, (2) an in vivo desensitization procedure involving opportunities for the child to play with some of the medical instruments and dolls, (3) positive reinforcement provided by the mother contingent on the absence of sleep terror episodes on the previous night, and (4) reductions in attention paid by the parents to the sleep terror episodes. While this program was effective, the contribution of specific components cannot be determined.

In another case of sleep terrors presumed to be associated with anxiety, Kellerman (1980) employed a treatment package to reduce fear responses assumed to have originated from viewing a frightening Dracula film. Employing incompatible response training, he had the child practice drawing pictures of Dracula, displaying anger, and tearing up the drawings (a procedure similar to that reported by Clement [1970] as a treatment of sleepwalking problems). Further, angry verbal responses were modeled by the author and imitated by the child, and the child was encouraged to use them whenever he noticed the slightest amount of fear. Additionally, the parents were instructed to reinforce sleep appropriate behaviors and to minimize attention for sleep terror episodes. While this intervention was effective, two issues should be noted. First, the contribution of individual components again cannot be determined. Second, whether episodes would most appropriately be classified as sleep terrors, nightmares, or combinations of the two is unclear.

Roberts and Gordon (1979) reported on a multicomponent treatment strategy for sleep terrors in a five-year-old suffering from a burn trauma. These authors viewed the episodes as an indicator of anxiety aroused by specific stimuli during waking hours and further hypothesized that the problem episodes might be reinforced by attention from nurses and parents. Roberts and Gordon chose against an extinction approach because the wild thrashing during the episode might increase risk to the child (a good example of a case in which treatment decisions were directly related to the characteristics of the problem behavior). Instead, the parents used a response prevention procedure by interrupting the episodes at the first sign of occurrence. Additionally, parents were instructed to respond to her in a neutral manner when arousing her to reduce potential reinforcement for the problem behavior. Interestingly, the awakening procedure at first increased the frequency of the sleep terror episodes. This increase, however, was then followed by reductions in the problem behavior. It should also be noted that in contrast to extinction procedures that would require attention to be withheld (e.g., by not going to the child when they became alerted to the episode), this procedure required that the parents be in proximity to the child so that they could awaken her and also protect her against injury. When the child was subsequently rehospitalized, episodes recurred. At that point, the authors successfully employed a program combining exposure to a hierarchy of fire-related stimuli (i.e., pictures taken from magazines) presented by the mother with opportunities for the child to play with toys following exposure.

As previously indicated, drug treatments involving tricyclics and neuroleptics have been successfully employed in the treatment of sleep terrors in adults (Fisher, Kahn, Edwards, & Davis, 1973), although it has been suggested elsewhere that such medications may be associated with a post-withdrawal increase in the frequencies of episodes (Flemenbaum, 1976). Likewise, Diazepam has been suggested to be the drug of choice (Glick, Schulman, & Turecki, 1971), while other findings suggest that Stage 3 or 4 suppressions may result in problematic rebounds. Should the behavior analysis reveal the the child is currently receiving such medications, careful monitoring and cooperation with the child's physician would be desirable.

DREAM ANXIETY ATTACKS (NIGHTMARES)

Dream Anxiety Attacks (nightmares) may be viewed as awakenings from REM sleep (or, on occasion, from light NREM sleep) with clear and detailed recall of an extended, disturbing dream. Like Sleepwalking and Sleep Terror Disorders, nightmares are classified in the DCSAD (ASDC & APSS, 1979) as a parasomnia, although in contrast to the others, nightmares are not viewed as disorders of partial arousal. Because of the significantly different behavioral and physiological features of Sleep Terror and Dream Anxiety Attacks, the DCSAD classification committee recommended that the term *nightmare* be reserved for the latter in spite of the tradition of applying the term to both conditions. While this distinction in usage could contribute to a reduction in confusion with respect to diagnosis and treatment of the two disorders, it remains unclear as to whether sleep terrors and nightmares represent etiologically different disorders or whether they represent two forms of the same disorder.

A number of investigators have described the characteristics and typical sequence of behavior (Anders, 1982; Cellicci & Lawrence, 1978; Coates & Thoresen, 1981a, 1981b; Hersen, 1972; Keith, 1975; Schroeder, Gordon, & Hawk, 1983; Weitzman, 1981; Youkilis & Bootzin, 1981). The DCSAD (ASDC & APSS, 1979) also provides a description of the disorder. Specific diagnostic criteria contained in that classification system are consistent with the description that follows.

Nightmares are characterized by an awakening from REM sleep (or sometimes light NREM sleep Stage 1) in the middle to latter portion of the sleep period, and, upon arousing, the individual is aware of having had a disturbing dream episode. Thus, the manner of awakening appears to be dissimilar to that of sleep terrors. For nightmare episodes (as contrasted with sleep terror episodes), there is typically rather elaborate, vivid dream recall, and the dream content commonly involves an immediate and credible threat to the individual's self-esteem, security, or survival. Such characteristic themes of the 20th century as death, injury, and conflict have been contrasted by Hersen (1972) with those of the Middle Ages (e.g., demons and devils) to illustrate variation in content across time. Although dream content may be vague, reports of threat in the dream typically involve fear, shock, or a defensive/retaliatory response, which is often accompanied by an abrupt motor response in the dream and which ordinarily is also expressed in actual physical movement. It is this active movement that seems to precipitate reentry into the waking state. Thus, the nightmare has been operationally defined by Hersen (1972) as a frightening dream that awakens the dreamer, although the utility of this definition would seem limited in that sleep terrors might also satisfy this model.

During the nightmare episode, the individual remains responsive to the environment and is easily aroused. The episode provokes moderate to intense anxiety and is characterized by slight autonomic fluctuations. While some movement may occur, it tends to be minimal. Similarly, there may be some increase in pulse rate, but in neither case do these responses approach the levels of autonomic arousal seen in sleep terror episodes. Also in contrast to sleep terrors, nightmare episodes are not usually accompanied by vocalization.

While nightmares are a particularly distressing problem for a small proportion of the population (i.e., 5 to 7 percent), occasional nightmares are otherwise common in the general population. Based on self-reports of nightmare episodes, Hersen (1972) pointed out that females admitted experiencing more frequent nightmares than did males. However, it remains unclear whether females react more fearfully than males or whether a social desirability factor may operate in that males may be less inclined to admit to the experience than are females (Hersen, 1972). No significant age differences have been demonstrated in the frequency of nightmares, and they appear to be experienced at all ages and by virtually all people. As with other parasomnias, nightmare experiences may range in frequency from nightly episodes to infrequent occurrences. In addition to the typical nighttime occurrence, nightmares may also be experienced during naps lasting an hour or more.

Because nightmares are not confined to any age level, there is no particular age that would predict onset or offset. Complications of nightmares include (1) the possibility that they may disrupt normal sleep patterns and (2) the possibility that sleep phobias might develop. Knowledge of the course of this disorder remains quite limited.

Etiological Conceptualizations

While the development of a theoretical framework to successfully account for the characteristics and occurrences of nightmares has proven difficult (Haynes & Mooney, 1975), etiological formulations have focused on (1) anxiety associated with a variety of daily stressors (e.g., cognitive, physiological, environmental), (2) environmental contingencies, (3) pharmacological effects, and (4) physiological characteristics.

Anxiety has been the most frequently implicated factor in the etiology of nightmares (e.g., Dollinger, 1982; Haynes & Mooney, 1975; Hersen, 1971, 1972; Roberts & Gordon, 1979). While not directly involving child populations, Feldman and Hersen (1967) reported a significant positive relationship between fears of death and frequencies of nightmares, although this finding was not corroborated in investigations by Lester (1969). Significant correlations between manifest anxiety scores and nightmare frequency have been reported by Hersen (1971) for psychiatric inpatients and by Haynes and Mooney (1975) for college undergraduates. Dollinger (1982) has suggested that nightmares (as well as other parasomnias) may have their etiology in severe anxiety that is poorly controlled during sleep, while Fisher, Byrne, Edwards, and Kahn (1969) suggested nightmares involve controlled anxiety (as compared with sleep terrors). It should be noted that the distinction implied by reference to "controlled" or "uncontrolled" anxiety appears to be primarily based on the degree of anxiety associated with a particular episode. The DCSAD (ASDC & APSS, 1979) suggests nightmares to be associated with anxiety disorders in children and adults.

Cognitive and learning parameters have been implicated as etiological factors in nightmares. In a series of three investigations, Haynes & Mooney (1975) commented on the explanatory utility of learning conceptualizations with regard to the occurrence and frequency of nightmare episodes. One of the models addressed involves the view that nightmares may serve an anxiety reducing function in that through repeated cognitive exposure to fear-producing stimuli extinction of anxiety would occur. In such a model, it is presumed that physiological arousal is conditioned to specific dream stimuli, and that, accordingly, the nightmare (involving sustained, intense fear stimuli) would produce a reduction in physiological responses to those stimuli (a conceptualization consistent with the flooding treatment model). Haynes and Mooney (1975) further suggested that, while sustained exposure should result in anxiety extinction, awakening during the episode would interrupt such an effect and could be expected to result in recurrences of the episodes, which could account for nightmare parameters such as frequency. Accordingly, they argued that awakening could be conceptualized as an escape response, which would restrict the anxiety reduction features of the nightmare. Finally, a higher frequency of awakening at night and during nightmares might be predicted because of the sleep-incompatible nature of arousal levels associated with Dream Anxiety Attacks. The finding of significant positive relationships between nightmare frequency/ nighttime awakenings and manifest anxiety reported by Haynes and Mooney is consistent with an anxiety-extinction model, while their failure to find a significant relationship with regard to the physiological index of anxiety employed (i.e., EMG levels) left this interpretation in question. Accordingly, it was suggested that, until further evidence is obtained, a more parsimonious interpretation than that of the anxiety-extinction model may be that nightmare frequency is a direct manifestation and correlate of anxiety.

Related to the formulations addressed by Haynes & Mooney, Kellerman (1980) suggested that, while most children are exposed to fear-producing stimuli, most engage in self-curative behaviors via self-paced exposure to the particular fear stimuli. However, some events such as parental protectiveness might serve to restrict children's opportunities to engage in such counter-anxious behavior and, in this sense, parental protectiveness might serve as a maintaining factor in such disorders (Kellerman, 1980). Thus, variables such as awakenings during nightmare episodes (Haynes & Mooney, 1975) and parental behaviors (Kellerman, 1980) might serve to interrupt anxiety reduction processes and protract occurrences of the episodes. Consistent with an anxiety formulation of nightmares, the rate and content of nightmares may be related to antecedent stimuli in the waking environment. In this regard, Silverman and Geer (1968) indicated that the content of specific nightmares was the same as daytime phobias or chronic fears and thus could be manipulated in the same manner as fears experienced in the waking state (see also Geer & Silverman, 1967). These authors further suggested that persons who manifest chronic fears through recurrent dream anxiety attacks also engage in obsessive thinking and that recurrent daytime ruminations and recurrent nightmares may represent walking and sleeping counterparts of the same mode of adjustment. Although it is not clearly associated with anxiety, Framer and Sanders (1980) suggested environmental stress (i.e., problem social interactions) to be a precipitating factor in nightmare and sleepwalking disorders.

Roberts & Gordon (1979) reported on episodes of nightmares and sleep terrors in a five-year-old subsequent to a burn trauma and indicated that the child had developed a strong phobic reaction to a wide range of fire-related stimuli. In conceptualizing nightmares as a function of anxiety that is aroused by specific stimuli occurring during the waking hours, Roberts and Gordon (1979) viewed each nightmare as a resensitization trial in which the imaginal conditioned stimulus (i.e., fire) was paired with the imaginal unconditioned stimulus (i.e., pain). Thus, it was speculated that the image of fire would continue to elicit anxiety, and naturally occurring stimuli in the environment could serve as resensitization cues to maintain the problem episodes. It should be noted that this conceptualization of nightmare episodes as resensitization trials, which would serve to maintain the sleep problem, is in contradiction to the model proposed by Haynes and Mooney (1975), in which continued exposure to fear-producing stimuli would serve an anxiety-extinction function.

In addition to anxiety associated with cognitive and antecedent environmental factors, *environmental consequences* associated with Dream Anxiety Attacks may also influence their occurrences. For example, Roberts and Gordon (1979) suggested that operant factors, such as the attention paid to episodes by hospital personnel, parents, or others in the child's environment, might serve to maintain or intensify subsequent episodes.

Nightmares may also result from *pharmacological effects*. A reduction in or a withdrawl of REM sleep suppressing agents can lead to a rapid recovery or rebound of REM sleep (e.g., REM sleep ratios of 30 to 50 percent) often associated with nightmare-like episodes (ASDC & APSS, 1979; Fisher, Byrne, Edwards, & Kahn, 1970), which is a feature of abrupt withdrawal from sleeping pills or alcohol (ASDC & APSS, 1979). However, rebounds in REM sleep following non-drug related sleep loss are less correlated with Dream Anxiety Attacks.

Associated with *physiological characteristics*, Anthony (1959) suggested that mental imagery might play an important role in sleep disorders. He postulated that (1) differences in manifestations in sleep disorders lie in individual differences in capacity for imagery, and (2) the capacity for night imagery is related to the capacity for day imagery. Presuming visualizing capacity to be normally distributed in the population, Anthony proposed that extreme visualizing tendencies at one tail of the distribution might account for the pathological development of sleep attacks such as nightmares or sleep terrors. That is, when the visualizing apparatus is hypersensitive, there is increased discharge into visual pathways. However, no empirical evidence is available to support this hypothesis. By itself, this would not account for differences between nightmare and sleep terror phenomena. Further, application of this formulation to sleepwalking and sleep terrors is confounded by the fact that the two may exist concurrently and that those children who develop sleepwalking early may often have sleep terrors several years later, with sleep terror episodes becoming the more predominant.

In conceptualizing etiologies in the parasomnias, an interactional model that takes into account multiple causality (e.g., developmental, physiological, and environmental variables) may have greater utility than univariate ones in accounting for the conditional probability that some children, but not others, would evidence these problems.

Intervention with Dream Anxiety Attacks

As with treatment strategies discussed in previous sections of this chapter, most published reports of the treatment of nightmares have been limited to case study reports. However, the interventions reviewed in this section have, to a much greater extent, been developed as a function of conceptualizations and analyses of the unique characteristics of the individual problem behaviors.

Intervention Strategies.　In accord with the conceptualization of nightmares as having their principle basis in anxiety, the majority of behavioral treatments have involved anxiety reduction. These approaches have targeted either dream content or fear stimuli occurring during the waking hours, depending on the individual behavioral analyses.

Included among the treatments employed with nightmares, either singly or in combination, have been systematic desensitization (Cavior & Deutsch, 1975; Clement, 1970; Roberts & Gordon, 1977), flooding (Handler, 1972; Kellerman, 1980), and thought stopping (Handler, 1972). Additionally, behavior rehearsal (Handler, 1972; Kellerman, 1980), response prevention (Clement, 1970; Roberts & Gordon, 1977), incompatible response procedures (Clement, 1970; Kellerman, 1980), and manipulation of reinforcement contingencies (Clement, 1970; Kellerman, 1980; Roberts & Gordon, 1979) have been utilized to ameliorate nightmares. Likewise, contingency contracting (Framer & Sanders, 1980) has been used to modify supposed antecedent environmental stressors.

Investigators have reported on the effects of desensitization procedures in the treatment of nightmares in child populations. (Cavior & Deutsch, 1975; Clement, 1970; Roberts & Gordon, 1977). While it is unclear whether an adolescent (16-year-old) prisoner's "aversive dream," which was related to real events, constituted a nightmare, Cavior and Deutsch (1975) first taught a standard relaxation response and divided the client's dream into 12 hierarchical imaginal scenes. Each scene was sequentially introduced with the suggestion to relax. In addition, the client was instructed to practice the procedures outside the treatment sessions. Surprisingly, these investigators reported that no further anxiety occurred in response to the dream, although the dream itself continued, and suggested that the obtained effect resulted from extinction via exposure to the dream-related material. Nevertheless, the reported continuation of the dream in the absence of anxiety constitutes a confusing finding.

In a case of intervention with recurrent nightmares and sleepwalking in a seven-year-old boy, Clement (1970) reported on the success of a multi-component strategy that in part involved repeated exposure to fear stimuli while engaging in anxiety-incompatible behaviors. As with other studies, it is unclear whether nightmares or sleep terrors constituted the actual problem behavior. Roberts & Gordon (1979) employed desensitization with a five-year-old who had been traumatized by burns. The child was exposed to a hierarchy of 10 magazine pictures of fires representing a wide variety of settings and uses. Following each exposure the child was allowed to play with toys.

In an intervention reported to be successful with a child experiencing nightmares containing monster themes, Handler (1972) first assured the child that he would protect him and help him get rid of the monster. Then, holding the child on his lap, Handler asked him to close his eyes and to imagine the monster's presence in the room (a technique similar to flooding). Handler next modeled an assertive behavior that involved banging his fist on the desk and yelling at the imaginary monster to leave the child alone. This was followed by verbalizations of "leave me alone." Then, the child was requested to imitate the same behavior. After repeated rehearsals, the behavior was then carried out with the room lights turned off. It should be noted here that aspects of the procedure are somewhat reminiscent of thought-stopping to the degree to which the procedure might terminate ruminations over the fear stimuli.

Additionally, in a treatment program containing components similar to flooding procedures, Kellerman (1980) exposed a five-year-old to dream fear stimuli in the form of pictures of Dracula, with the instruction to tear up the pictures and verbalize anger (as modeled by the therapist). As in the Handler (1972) investigation, a component of this procedure also involved behavior rehearsal of counter-anxious responses.

Components of treatment programs for nightmare episodes have also included response prevention/interruption procedures (Clement, 1970; Roberts & Gordon, 1977), incompatible response strategies (Clement, 1970; Kellerman, 1980), and manipulation of reinforcement contingencies (Clement, 1970; Kellerman, 1980; Roberts & Gordon, 1979). For example, Clement (1970) included an awakening procedure with an incompatible response procedure (performance of aggressive verbalizations and behaviors directed at the fear stimulus) and parental reinforcement for these counter-anxious behaviors in order to interrupt nightmares and sleepwalking behaviors in a seven-year-old boy. Clement also took steps to remove parental attention to the problem behavior under the assumption that this attention served as a reinforcer to maintain the behavior. Similarly, Kellerman (1980) employed an incompatible response strategy (e.g., anger in the presence of the fear stimulus, turning on the lights or radio, going to the refrigerator) for a five-year-old on occasions when the child felt anxious. In addition to desensitization, Roberts and Gordon (1979) employed response prevention with a five-year-old experiencing nightmares and sleep terrors. In that case, the mother was instructed to interrupt early elements of the behavioral sequence by using the child's clutching of her nightgown as the cue to intervene. Additionally, the behavior analysis suggested that nurses and parents might be reinforcing the behavior through their responses to the episodes, and steps were taken to eliminate this potential reinforcement.

An additional intervention strategy employed with nightmares and sleep-walking is that of family contingency contracting. This was used by Framer and Sanders (1980) with the assumption that antecedent environmental stressors in the form of problem family interactions served as controlling variables for episodes in a 13-year-old male. In that procedure, formal if-then contracts were implemented to increase the child's compliance to parental requests in return for increased privileges.

As is obvious from the previous discussion, little is known of the differential efficacy of treatment strategies or of the contribution of the various components included in those intervention packages for intervention with nightmares. Both systematic desensitization and techniques similar to flooding have been suggested to be effective. However, in several studies, the confounding of additional treatment components has occurred, thus making differential evaluations difficult.

CONTINUING ISSUES

In spite of the etiological conceptualizations presented for the parasomnias, it is fair to say that, to date, etiological factors for sleepwalking, sleep terrors, or nightmares have not been conclusively identified. Contributing to the lack of understanding is the fact that many of the etiological hypotheses offered have not been empirically verified and are subject to interpretation. For example, the presumed relationship between sleepwalking or sleep terrors and NREM sleep stages is confounded by the issue of conditional probability. While children typically evidence these episodes early in the night (during sleep Stages 3 or 4), the proportion of Stages 3 and 4 sleep is also greater earlier than later in the night. Therefore, associations between particular disorders and sleep stages may simply reflect chance associations, or they may be somehow causally related.

While anxiety is a commonly postulated etiological factor in the parasomnias, their relationship remains unclear. For example, while sleep terrors may follow trauma or stress, they might in fact result from neurophysiological changes. Accordingly, anxiety might play a role in maintenance, while other factors might serve as critical events for onset. So, anxiety might increase the probability or intensity of episodes, it might be an outcome of episodes, or, once associated with episodes triggered by other factors, it might serve to maintain sleep problems. One additional point to be made with regard to our limited knowledge of these disorders, however, is the fact that experimental manipulations that could validate the various etiological hypotheses are often constrained by ethical considerations.

Thus, our knowledge of etiological factors, as well as our knowledge of the effectiveness of various treatment strategies, has largely been derived from case studies that are correlational in nature and that, in some cases, lack adequate controls. While case studies can allow for differentiation of the contribution of treatment components if undertaken in a controlled manner, those reviewed here provide little evidence as to the relative contribution of individual components to treatment effectiveness. Further, treatments of interest, such as anxiety reduction techniques (e.g., systematic desensitization), typically have been employed as a part of intervention packages utilizing other components such as modeling, cognitive self-instruction, behavioral contracting, or contingency management so that no differential evaluations of individual components can be made. In many of these cases, other variables such as changes in parental reinforcement have not been evaluated when deriving conclusions about the effectiveness of a particular treatment. Further confounding evaluations of the relevancy or effectiveness of particular treatments, such as desensitization, is the fact that we do not know whether a factor such as anxiety is a consistent component of particular disorders across individuals. Additionally, it is not clear in many cases whether nightmares, sleep terrors, or combinations of the two have represented the targets of intervention.

Finally, while those applications with nightmares have largely been developed as a function of conceptualizations and analyses of the unique characteristics of the individual problem, those reviewed for sleepwalking and sleep terrors typically have not. Thus, definitive conclusions regarding the appropriateness and efficacy of particular behavioral strategies remain inferential and must await systematic, comparative evaluations.

DISORDERS OF INITIATING AND MAINTAINING SLEEP (INSOMNIAS)

The Disorders of Initiating and Maintaining Sleep (DIMS) represent a heterogeneous set of conditions (ASDC & APSS, 1979) characterized by a chronic inability to sleep efficiently as a function of (1) delays in the onset of sleep, (2) frequent arousals during sleep, and (3) premature awakening in the morning hours (ASDC & APSS, 1979; Bootzin & Engle-Friedman, 1981; Bootzin & Nicassio, 1978; Borkovec, 1982; Coates & Thoresen, 1981a). Sleep efficiency may be thought of as the ratio of time in bed to time asleep. It should be further noted that since insomnia is largely a subjective phenomenon, attempts to establish an objective definition have thus far met with only limited success.

Within the DCSAD nosology, nine subtypes of insomnia are identified, with several of those interpreted as secondary to environmental, medical, or psychiatric conditions. The DCSAD also emphasizes that when such insomnias have continued for several months or more, a learning (behavioral) component often may aggravate the condition (ASDC & APSS, 1979). Such components may thus require direct intervention, even though the basic etiology may have been nonbehavioral (Borkovec, 1982). As indicated by Borkovec (1982), most of the published behavioral literature has focused on sleep-onset insomnia, possibly because of the predominance of this complaint. However, in individual patients, symptomatology is not necessarily limited to one factor (such as sleep-onset problems) and in some cases may include both sleep-onset and sleep-maintenance problems. As would be expected based on the recent development of the DCSAD nosology for DIMS, researchers and clinicians have not typically categorized disorders in a manner consistent with the classification system. Accordingly, the published literature does not fit well with the current sub-categories. Nevertheless, inspection of the literature suggests that most re-ported clinical complaints variously share features with the DCSAD categories of (1) Persistent Psychophysiological DIMS (i.e., a sleep-onset and sleep-maintenance insomnia presumed to be associated with physiological arousal and conditioning factors), (2) subjective DIMS complaints without objective find-ings (i.e., complaints of insomnia that are at variance with polysomnographic data), and in some cases, (3) childhood-onset DIMS (i.e., a sleep-onset and sleep-maintenance insomnia involving inefficient sleep that develops before puberty and persists into adulthood), with a majority of reported etiological and treatment studies involving Persistent Psychophysiological DIMS. As noted by Borkovec (1982), the psychophysiological and subjective forms of insomnia are those predominantly associated with psychological factors.

The remainder of this chapter employs the framework of persistent psycho-physiological DIMS as a structure for discussion. Insomnias associated with drug use, medical problems, and psychiatric problems, while not emphasized, are also addressed. An outline of the DCSAD nosology for DIMS is contained in the appendix of DSM-III (APA, 1980).

PERSISTENT PSYCHOPHYSIOLOGICAL DIMS

Persistent Psychophysiological DIMS represents a sleep-onset and sleep-maintenance insomnia that presumably develops as a result of interacting fac-tors such as physiological arousal and inappropriate conditioning experiences associated with sleep (ASDC & APSS, 1979). These factors may serve an additive function with respect to arousal and, in interaction, may serve to perpetuate the condition. The disorder may develop from Situational Psycho-physiological DIMS (i.e., a brief period of sleep disturbance often elicited by acute emotional arousal or conflict) when that condition persists for more than three weeks (ASDC & APSS, 1979). While some patients may evidence only one or the other of these factors, others may demonstrate variations of both (ASDC & APSS, 1979).

The characteristics of sleep-onset and sleep-maintenance insomnias have been described by a number of investigators (e.g., Anders, 1982; Bixler, Kales, & Soldatos, 1979; Bootzin & Engle-Friedman, 1981; Bootzin & Nicassio,

1978; Borkovec, 1982; Coates & Thoresen, 1981a, 1981b; Erickson, 1982; Haynes et al., 1981; Hyde & Pegram, 1982; Kales & Kales, 1974; Kamens, Haynes, Franzen, & Hamilton, 1983; Knapp, Downs, & Alperson, 1976; Knopf, 1979; Ross, 1981; Ware & Orr, 1983; Youkilis & Bootzin, 1981), and are presented in the DCSAD (ASDC & APSS, 1979). Specific diagnostic criteria contained in that classification system correspond to the description that follows.

Children, like adults, may lie in bed for extended periods without going to sleep (sleep-onset latencies of greater than 30 minutes are the usual criterion level for sleep-onset problems). In some cases, this may be followed by the child approaching the parents with complaints of being unable to go to sleep. In other cases, the parents may discover the difficulty when checking on the child subsequent to putting him/her to bed. Multiple nighttime awakenings may also constitute a difficulty for the child. In either instance, it is common for the child to leave the bed and report to the parents that "I woke up" or "I can't sleep." These complaints may be accompanied by requests to stay up with the parents (when the child's bedtime is earlier than that of the parents), or by requests that the parents stay with the child or that they give permission for the child to sleep with them (when the parents have already retired for the night). Often it is difficult to determine whether these complaints by the child represent true sleep-onset and sleep-maintenance difficulties, or whether they represent attempts to put off bedtime or to avoid being alone at night. Accordingly, some cases of insomnia in children may go unidentified if misinterpreted by parents; in others, insomnia-like complaints may be unrelated to difficulty in initiating or maintaining sleep. Further, because children may not identify an inability to go to sleep or to remain asleep as a problem, such difficulties may go unidentified unless noted by parents.

Although adult complaints of insomnia include reports of poor sleep quality or quantity, this is not necessarily the case with children. That is, while children also experience difficulties in sleep efficiency (i.e., a reduced proportion of sleep time relative to time in bed), children may not make such specific complaints, although this may vary as a function of the child's ability to identify sleep problems. Similarly, it is unclear whether the inability to sleep becomes as significant a concern to children as it may to adults, and the conditional probability of such effects may be related to the child's capacity to conceptualize sleep problems as such.

Persistent Psychophysiological DIMS in both children and adults is characterized by heightened physiological arousal that involves behavioral manifestations such as increased muscle tension. Children experiencing insomnia often are described by their parents as being "light sleepers" (in some cases, children may provide similar descriptions of themselves). Children experiencing insomnia may present multiple somatic complaints, although these complaints may be vague and may consist of reports such as feeling sick, uptight, or restless. While both child and adult insomniacs may report worrisome cognitive content prior to sleep onset, it is unclear whether worries over the inability to sleep are a part of that content for most children. More often, characteristic content involves ruminations over experiences during the day, whether the next day's homework is completed, difficulties with peers, fears of being alone in the dark, etc. Situational specificity may be reflected in children's sleep difficulties since problems in sleep onset or sleep maintenance may not be experienced when in locations other than in the child's own bed or bedroom (e.g., when sleeping with parents or when visiting friends overnight). Additionally, children's sleep-onset and maintenance problems may be reduced in association with reductions in stress (e.g., school holidays or vacations).

While information on the prevalence in children is unclear, child psychiatrists' responses to a national survey conducted by Bixler, Kales, and Soldatos (1979) indicated that approximately 60 percent of their patients reported sleep problems with insomnia being one of the most frequent (Kales & Kales, 1974). No evidence has appeared that would suggest sex differences associated with the disorder. The severity of Persistent Psychophysiological DIMS must be considered in terms of the characteristic complaint as well as by subjective reports of distress. For example, owing to its classification as a persistent DIMS, it is to be expected that in severe cases the complaints of delayed sleep onset may represent a nightly occurrence. Additionally, sleep-onset latency in severe cases may be an hour or more. In those cases in which a portion of the complaint rests upon frequent nighttime awakenings from sleep, severe cases may involve multiple occurrences during the night's sleep period. Reflective of poor sleep efficiency, patients with severe cases may be able to sleep only three to five hours per night, which may also result in impairment of daytime functioning.

Persistent Psychophysiological DIMS is observed in all age groups, including children. While insomnia complaints are less frequent in early childhood populations, there is an increased incidence of these disorders in adolescence (Anders, 1982). Insomnia may continue undiagnosed or untreated for a number of years and may be complicated by the individual's concern over the sleep problem. In this regard, the probability of complaints of insomnia may, for young children, be influenced by several factors. For instance, until sleep cycles are more firmly established (as in the case of adolescents and adults), problems in sleep onset and maintenance may not be recognized by the child. Also, since DIMS complaints involve a subjective component, the child's cognitive developmental level may preclude such complaints until the child reaches a level at which s/he can conceptualize difficulties in initiating or maintaining sleep as such. It may also be the case in some instances that other factors associated with delayed sleep onset or awakenings in children, such as fears of going to sleep (associated with nightmares) or awakenings associated with sleep terrors, may mask what might otherwise be identified as insomnia complaints. That is, expressed fears or fearful awakenings may overshadow the fact that sleep onset is delayed or that frequent awakenings are occurring and instead may lead to a focus on the fear component. In some ways, these factors might account for the lower reported incidence of insomnia complaints in young children.

Etiological Conceptualizations

A variety of factors may play a role in the etiology of insomnia, including (1) heightented physiological arousal, (2) conditioning factors, (3) poor sleep habits, (4) cognitive activity, (5) daily stressors, (6) psychological character-istics, (7) pharmacological factors, and (8) medical and physical factors.

Among the factors implicated etiologically with this disorder is *heightened physiological arousal* (Borkovec, 1982; Coates & Thoresen, 1981b; Haynes, Follingstad, & McGowan, 1974; Hyde & Pegram, 1982; Kales & Kales, 1974, 1975). To the degree that individuals maintain higher resting arousal levels or respond physiologically to environmental or cognitive stimuli, this might set the stage then for difficulties in sleep onset or maintenance. While the hypothesized relationship between physiological hyperactivity and sleep difficulty is an intu-itively attractive one, the exact role of physiological arousal in the disorder remains unclear. For example, Haynes, Follingstad, and McGowan (1974) did not find sleep-onset latency to be correlated with EMG levels, and Haynes, Sides, and Lockwood (1977) found no relationship between relaxation training and subjective or objective measures of sleep improvement. However, more recently, Haynes (unpublished manuscript) found that insomniacs exhibited retarded adaptation to physiological arousal when awakened. Those subjects' heart rates returned to normal at a slower rate than those of noninsomniac subjects, indicating that recovery from stress may be an important determinant, especially for the inability to go back to sleep again.

Regarding *conditioning factors,* stimuli in the sleep environment may become associated with arousal responses and may result primarily in difficulties falling asleep (Bootzin, 1972; Bootzin & Nicassio, 1978; Borkovec, 1982; Coates & Thoresen, 1981b; Hauri, 1979; Haynes, Adams, & Franzen, 1981; Haynes, Adams, West, Kamens, & Safranek, 1982; Youkilis & Bootzin, 1981). Thus, aspects of the sleep environment, instead of serving as cues for sleep, may serve to evoke physiological and/or cognitive arousal and may contribute to sleep disruption. Other variables potentially contributing to this situation include loud noises, movement, and other sensory stimulation, thus reflecting the potentially multiple, idiosyncratic determinants of insomnia.

Operant factors may also play etiological or maintenance roles in complaints of insomnia. For example, Bergman (1976) suggested parental attention con-tingent on poor sleep behaviors and their complaints may serve to reinforce and thus maintain the problem behavior. However, no empirical evidence exists to support this hypothesis.

Insomnia may be conditioned in association with other problems, such as psychiatric disturbance, drug use or withdrawal, or other medical conditions (ASDC & APSS, 1979; Kales & Kales, 1975; Monroe & Marks, 1977; Youkilis

& Bootzin, 1982), and in some cases, such associated features may lead to the diagnosis of other subtypes of insomnia under the DCSAD system, depending on the weighting of such factors.

Poor sleep habits may also play an etiological role in insomnia. For example, disruptions in the sleep-wake cycle may be contributed to by inconsistencies in bedtimes, napping, or remaining in bed past the ordinary morning hour for arising (Hauri, 1979; Coates & Thoresen, 1981a, 1981b).

It also appears that *cognitive activities* play an etiological role in this disorder. For example, Coates & Thoresen (1981b) suggested that persons complaining of insomnia may experience continuing cognitive activity that could either prevent sleep or that could contribute to the subjective impression of not sleeping when physiological measures (e.g., EEG measures) would suggest the individual to be asleep. If cognitive hyperactivity is presumed, then chronic, worrisome, and uncontrollable thoughts may lead to heightened central nervous system arousal, which in turn could disrupt sleep (Borkovec, 1982; Coates & Thoresen, 1981b; Youkilis & Bootzin, 1981).

Other cognitive components of this disorder might be associated with variability and efficacy with respect to sleep patterns and expectations for sleep. For example, Coates and Thoresen (1981b) suggested that a marked variability in sleep across subsequent nights may be central to complaints of insomnia. Such variability may lead to perceptions of helplessness (lack of control over sleep), and the individual may interpret sleep as a highly unpredictable phenomenon. To the degree that sleep is perceived as unpredictable, this may then become something to worry over and may, in fact, represent the basis for subjective complaints (Borkovec, 1982). Subjective complaints may also be associated with a distorted time sense, i.e., insomniacs typically overestimate sleep-onset latency through self-reports (Borkovec, 1982). Further, in the sleep laboratory, insomniacs often report that they were not sleeping when they are awakened from Stage 2 sleep, which also suggests a perceptual distortion.

Daily stressors can also contribute to the etiology of insomnia, although the relationship of presleep stress to sleep-onset latency is unclear. For example, Haynes, Adams, and Franzen (1981) found higher physiological arousal to stress among sleep-onset insomniacs, although this was associated with decreased instead of increased latency. Performance anxiety in the sleep situation may also contribute to sleep-onset difficulties (Ascher & Efran, 1978; Hauri, 1979; Relinger & Bornstein, 1979). That is, a history of sleep-onset or sleep-maintenance difficulties may be associated with ruminations about possible sleep difficulties (Bornstein, 1977; Ribordy & Denney, 1977) or may produce a conditioned physiological arousal to the sleep situation. Thus, cognitive apprehensions over the inability to sleep because of previous unsuccessful attempts may result in heightened central nervous system arousal, which is a state incompatible with sleep (Hyde & Pegram, 1982).

Also implicated in the etiology of this disorder have been *psychological characteristics* of insomniacs (Coates & Thoresen, 1981b; Guilleminault & Anders, 1976; Ware & Orr, 1983; Youkilis & Bootzin, 1981). For example, characteristics such as mild depression and chronic worry have been found to be correlated with the disorder (Bertelson & Monroe, 1979; Borkovec, 1982; Coates & Thoresen, 1981a; Coursey, Buchsbaum, & Frankel, 1975; Haynes, Follingstad, & McGowan, 1974; Hyde & Pegram, 1982; Shealy, Lowe, & Ritzler, 1980; Ware & Orr, 1983). While the relationship between psychological characteristics and Persistent Psychophysiological DIMS is unclear, psychological conflict or anxiety may play a role by generating physiological arousal levels that are incompatible with sleep (Karacan, Ilaria, Ware, Thornby, & Chambliss, 1978). However, it is also possible that both are the products of stress or cognitive factors.

It is important to note that pharmacological, medical and/or physical factors can influence this disorder, and these include diet, medications, various hormonal dysfunctions, and CNS dysfunctions. *Pharmacological effects,* such as tolerance or withdrawal from CNS depressants or the sustained use of CNS stimulants, can contribute to Persistent Psychophysiological DIMS (Guilleminault & Anders, 1976; Hyde & Pegram, 1982), as may a variety of *medical or physical conditions,* such as sleep apnea, toxic conditions, or pain (ASDC & APSS, 1979; Hyde & Pegram, 1982; Kales & Kales, 1974, 1975). It has also been suggested that the individual's awakening threshold may play a role in insomnia (Bonnet & Johnson, 1978a, 1978b; Bootzin & Engle-Friedman, 1981).

Although many of these etiological inferences are derived from investigations with adults, it is assumed that they also hold true for children. In conceptualizing etiologies in the insomnias, an interactional model that takes into account multiple causality (e.g., learning, physiological and environmental variables) may have greater utility than univariate ones in accounting for the fact that some children, but not others, would evidence these problems.

Differentiation of Persistent Psychophysiological DIMS. As indicated by the DCSAD (ASDC & APSS, 1979), Persistent Psychophysiological DIMS is difficult to classify diagnostically, owing to the long-standing combination of inappropriate learning and emotional factors. Thus, the diagnostic approach taken for this disorder is in large part a process of exclusion. Conditions that must be excluded in establishing this diagnosis (a task that is difficult because of the common features shared between this and other disorders) include DIMS associated with psychiatric disorders, medical disorders that may lead to DIMS, disorders of excessive somnolence (e.g., narcolepsy), childhood-onset DIMS, sleep-related (nocturnal) myoclonus, circadian rhythm disturbances, and DIMS with atypical polysomnographic features (ASDC & APSS, 1979).

In DIMS associated with psychiatric disorders, the insomnia tends to fluctuate directly with the onset and offset of the particular disorder, while in Persistent Psychophysiological DIMS, the insomnia tends to be more fixed (ASDC & APSS, 1979). Persistent Psychophysiological DIMS can ordinarily be distinguished from excessive somnolence by a long-term sleep latency and by the absence of sleep apnea and narcolepsy. Those individuals with childhood-onset DIMS often present symptoms highly similar to Persistent Psychophysiological DIMS, and the differentiation appears to be made depending on whether the pattern is most parsimoniously explained by factors such as associative conditioning and physiological arousal. The childhood-onset type tends to be more constant through a variety of emotional circumstances (ASDC & APSS, 1979). Sleep-related (nocturnal) myoclonus may be differentiated from Persistent Psychophysiological DIMS via polysomnographic measures. With respect to circadian rhythm disturbances, the DCSAD points out considerable difficulty in differentiation from Persistent Psychophysiological DIMS. However, it is suggested that the long sleep latency, the unbroken nature of sleep once onset occurs, and the extended period of sleep when achieved may lead to the diagnosis of delayed sleep phase. Finally, in DIMS with atypical polysomnographic features, the atypical characteristics of the polysomnogram continue even when unbroken sleep occurs, in contrast to Persistent Psychophysiological DIMS in which atypical polysomnographic features tend to disappear once the condition improves.

With these factors in mind, diagnosis of Persistent Psychophysiological DIMS would be based on findings of (1) sleep-onset latencies of 30 minutes or longer, frequent awakenings from sleep (e.g., two or more times per night), or both, (2) the persistence of sleep problems for three or more weeks following resolution of any precipitating events, (3) physiological arousal (e.g., muscle tension), (4) repetitive awakenings associated with worried, ruminative thoughts, (5) improved sleep associated with stress removal (e.g., vacation times), (6) reduced difficulty in sleeping when in sleep environments other than his/her own, and (8) apprehension over the ability to fall asleep.

Intervention with Insomnia

Behavioral approaches would appear to be the most appropriate for the treatment of psychophysiological and subjective insomnias (Borkovec, 1982). Based on the etiological conceptualizations of Persistent Psychophysiological DIMS, treatment applications have focused on arousal reduction and interruption of previous conditioning influences. Applications with children, however, have been quite limited.

Intervention Strategies. Behavioral treatments employed with insomnia have included relaxation procedures (Levine, 1980; Porter, 1975; Weil & Goldfried, 1973) and the modification (removal) of suspected contingent external reinforcement for problem sleep behaviors (Anderson, 1979; Bergman, 1976). Among the most frequently recommended behavioral interventions for insomnia are relaxation procedures (Borkovec, 1982). These procedures are based on the premise that if the individual can learn to be relaxed at bedtime, then s/he will fall asleep faster (Nicassio & Bootzin, 1974; Youkilis & Bootzin, 1981). Relaxation procedures have been suggested to reduce complaints of subjective insomnia and both the objective and subjective problems in psychophysiological DIMS (Borkovec, 1982).

In treating cases of insomnia in two children (aged three and eight), Levine (1980) utilized guided fantasy suggestions embedded in a fairy tale (an audiotaped bedtime story), which was designed to elicit progressive relaxation through images of being warm, heavy, relaxed, and secure. This procedure was suggested to aid in the control of anxiety and in coping with stressors, reflecting the fact that insomnia is often associated with other life problems of children. The procedure involved listing the child's likes and dislikes (e.g., favorite fantasy figures) and then creating a fairy tale in which the favorite items were woven into a plot wherein the fantasy figure interacted with the child and demonstrated effective ways of dealing with identified stressors (a procedure similar to covert guided modeling). It was suggested at the end of the story that the fantasy figure falls asleep on the child's lap and the child must sleep so as not to disturb his/her friend. The child was also informed that listening to the recording would make it easier to sleep. While this program was reported to be effective, the guided fantasy aspect was confounded with modeling procedures and expectations (demand factors). Thus, a direct evaluation of the individual effect of guided fantasy cannot be made. Porter (1975) also employed a guided fantasy procedure like that utilized by Levine (1980). While both reported significant effects for treatment, neither investigation employed controls so that interpretations had to be made with caution. Nevertheless, these strategies demonstrate the construction of age-appropriate treatment procedures for children.

In another investigation involving an 11-year-old child, Weil and Goldfried (1973) used relaxation instructions to intervene with sleep-onset complaints. Assessment revealed that the child experienced ruminations and difficulty in falling asleep, a reluctance to stay at home when his parents went out, and a sensitivity to external sounds. Relaxation instructions were presented first by the therapist and later by tape recording in the client's bedroom and consisted of alternate tensing and relaxing of muscles (note that from a stimulus control conditioning view, the encouragement of tensing responses in bed would seem questionable). Two weeks later, they shifted from the tensing portion of the instructions and provided a tape with only relaxation instructions. They then gave instructions that whenever in bed the child was not to focus on the noise and ruminations but was to concentrate on relaxation.

Several explanations have been offered for the effectiveness of relaxation procedures with insomnia. For example, the effect may be a result of muscle tension release (Borkovec, 1982); it may result from reduced physiological arousal; the focus of attention on physiological sensations might be incompatible with worrisome thoughts (Borkovec, 1982); or it may be that the individual learns a new way of behaving (Hauri, 1979).

Environmental consequences have also been modified in cases when reinforcement was hypothesized to play a role in maintaining or shaping problem sleep behaviors. Although not clearly representing sleep-onset insomnia, Bergman (1976) interpreted a seven-year-old's resistance to go to bed and to sleep in his own room (he would instead remain awake until the parents had gone to bed and then would go to their room to sleep with them) to be related to parental reinforcement in the form of allowing the child to sleep with them. In viewing the "insomnia" as an operant shaped by the parents, Bergman instructed the parents not to let the child sleep with them and to tell him to go back to his room every time he came to their room to sleep. This was to be carried out with a minimum of conversation, and the child was to be returned physically to his own room if necessary. It was reported that within two weeks the child was sleeping soundly through the night in his own room.

Anderson (1979) employed a treatment program that included relaxation training and a reduction of parental attention in the case of a 13-year-old with a four-month history of insomnia. In that case, the child was reported to become agitated after dinner and to pace the floor and occasionally cry. Thus, his mother would sit up with him until late in the evening. He would then go to bed and lie awake for several hours. Additionally, he would wake up during the night and then would go to the parents' bedroom, verbalizing vague somatic complaints. Although the father would stay in bed, the mother would arise and sit with the child in the living room until he finally returned to bed. Along with relaxation, training focused on the child's agitation and tension levels; Anderson also reduced the attention and involvement of the mother, under the assumption that her responses were reinforcing sleep-incompatible behaviors. Thus, the procedure in the first week involved the mother staying in the living room with the child for a reduced period of time. In the second week, she was to go into the bathroom so as to avoid interacting with the child if he came into their bedroom. During subsequent weeks, she was to remain in bed and was to tell him to return to his room and to do the relaxation exercises. Over an eight-week period, insomnia episodes were reported to drop to negligible levels.

CONTINUING ISSUES

There are a number of remaining issues concerning the etiology, assessment, and treatment of childhood DIMS. Perhaps the most striking deficiency in this literature is the lack of controlled studies on the etiology of the disorder. While numerous controlled group factorial designs have been employed in the study of adult DIMS, none have been conducted with children. The uncontrolled case studies that have been the primary mode of study cannot satisfactorily address issues of etiology and treatment effectiveness. In particular, large group polysomnographic studies of insomniac and noninsomniac children are needed to delineate the sleeping patterns associated with this disorder.

As with other childhood sleep disorders, multiple interacting etiological factors are probably involved. However, the individual case reports have tended to invoke univariate models of causality, which preclude a more comprehensive examination of etiology. In particular, the role of environmental stressors (e.g., family, school) and presleep ruminative cognitive activity in delaying sleep onset requires further examination.

A second deficiency relates to the treatment strategies utilized. Specifically, a number of major adult treatment procedures simply have not received application with child populations. This would include stimulus control procedures (Bootzin, 1972), biofeedback (Haynes, Sides, & Lockwood, 1977), and paradoxical instruction (Relinger & Bornstein, 1979).

Subtypes of childhood DIMS need further study. Some of the reports reviewed suggested that, for some children, DIMS may be associated with actual difficulty in attaining or maintaining sleep (similar to *psychophysiological* insomnia). Others appear to be able to attain and maintain sleep but do not, or report not being able to, for varying reasons. Again, large group polysomnographic analysis would be helpful.

Similarly, confidence in treatment efficacy, the relationship between etiological hypotheses and treatment strategies, and individual differences in responses to specific treatments remain to be investigated.

THE FOCUS OF ASSESSMENT

In most cases, treatment must reflect etiological conceptualizations of a target behavior and thus will vary as a function of controlling variables and client characteristics. Further, any specific sleep problems will demonstrate across-subject variance, thus dictating variance in appropriate treatments. Accordingly, the effectiveness of intervention programs can be expected to vary as a function of the adequacy of preintervention assessment. Based on etiological conceptualizations of the various sleep problems addressed in this chapter, a comprehensive assessment will include: (1) a behavioral description of the sleep disorder, (2) information on historical factors, (3) the child's characteristics (e.g., maturational status, adjustment level, physiological arousability), (4) the child's daytime and presleep behaviors, (5) an evaluation of daily stressors, (6) environmental contingencies, (7) medical illnesses and other physical factors, and (8) pharmacological factors. Such information is important in the differential diagnosis of sleep disorders, in determinations of the existence of multiple-sleep problems (e.g., sleepwalking and sleep terrors are sometimes found to coexist), in the identification of controlling and maintaining variables, in the derivation of effective treatment strategies, and in the acquisition of baseline information against which intervention outcomes can be compared.

Behavioral Description

A behavioral description of the problem sleep behavior should include *specification of the content and sequence of events* comprising the problem sleep episodes as well as information on characteristics, such as frequencies of occurrence, temporal features (e.g., duration of episodes, time to or time from sleep onset), episode intensity, the child's arousability and sensitivity to environmental stimuli, cognitive content associated with the episodes (e.g., dream content, recall, and clarity; worrisome ruminations; anticipatory fears), and the presence of other sleep disorders. Among other things, a thorough behavioral description can help to identify early elements in behavioral chains as the targets for intervention. For the parasomnias and insomnias, information on episode *frequency and intensity* can have utility in determining the need for treatment and, in some cases, may reflect covariation between the sleep problem and controlling variables (e.g., environmental stressors).

Temporal features, such as time from sleep onset, may reflect associations between REM or NREM sleep stages in the differentiation of sleep terrors from nightmares. For complaints of insomnia, the time to sleep onset is important, as is the time from sleep onset in cases of multiple or premature awakenings. Likewise, assessment should include estimates of the time taken to return to sleep once awakened (Haynes, Sides, & Lockwood, 1977). Similarly, the sleep stage associated with the time of awakening can be of importance (e.g., insomniacs awakened from Stage 2 sleep may report that they were not asleep—a feature possibly contributing to subjective complaints of insomnia). Factors such as total sleep time, movement during sleep, and awakening threshold also may be of importance. At this point, two indexes of sleep behavior should be noted. Borkovec (1982) described an index (ratio) of the total time asleep versus the total time in bed for the assessment of insomnia, and Haynes, Sides, and Lockwood (1977) described an index in which the number of times awake are multiplied by the time needed to go to sleep as a measure of sleep behavior. This latter index would change as either of the two variables changed.

The child's *arousability and sensitivity* to the environment can provide important information with regard both to differential diagnosis and to controlling factors in childhood sleep disorders. For example, it is difficult to awaken the child from sleepwalking and sleep terror episodes, while this is not the case for nightmares. In cases of insomnia and possibly in the parasomnias where partial arousals are found to occur, sleep incompatible arousal responses may be associated with environmental stimulation. Further, arousability and the degree of sensitivity to environmental stimuli may not only contribute to the conditional probability of episodes, but also may be related to the conditioning of sleep-incompatible behaviors that can serve a maintenance function.

Cognitive content, such as fear-producing stimuli in dream content, may provide clues as to environmental stressors that might contribute to the parasomnias. Similarly, worrisome ruminations associated with daytime experiences or anticipated difficulties in falling asleep are of interest in cases of insomnia. Such information may suggest targets for intervention, as well as intervention strategies. Descriptions of the characteristics and sequences of the child's sleep problem can also provide information as to the *presence of other sleep problems*. For example, in some cases sleepwalking and sleep terrors are found to occur together. Additionally, it is possible that insomnia in childhood may be masked and/or contributed to by anticipatory fear responses associated with nightmare episodes.

Historical Factors

Historical factors of interest include the child's age at the first occurrence of episodes and the duration of the sleep problem, significant events associated with the initial occurrence of episodes, and the family history of sleep problems. Information regarding the *age of onset* is of interest because the occurrence of sleepwalking typically is most frequent between the ages of 6 and 12 years, and sleep terrors most commonly occur between the ages of 4 and 12 years. While the occurrence of episodes within these age ranges has been speculated to involve developmental factors, their occurrence beyond these ranges may reflect other problems. Nightmares, on the other hand, are not associated with any particular age level. Insomnia, while representing a less common complaint in early childhood, becomes a more frequent complaint in adolescence. From an historical standpoint, diagnosis of Persistent Psychophysiological DIMS will require continuation of the condition for at least three to four weeks.

For the parasomnias and insomnias, the time of first occurrence may also provide clues as to *significant life events* that may play an etiological role, although such factors need not be the same as those currently maintaining the disorder. While no greater incidence of nightmares within families (as compared with the general population) has been reported, sleepwalking, sleep terrors, and insomnia do show an increased incidence within families. Thus, information on the *family history* of sleep problems, including the similarity of parents' sleep problems to the child's problem, the course of those disorders, and the parents' reactions to their own sleep problems, can contribute to our understanding of the conditional probabilities of the occurrence and course of sleep disorders and to the relative contributions of maturational or developmental factors for the etiology and maintenance of the disorder.

Child's Characteristics

The child's current age and developmental/maturational status, the child's psychological characteristics and current level of adjustment, and the child's physiological responsivity are important to assessment. The child's *developmental status* is important in that both sleepwalking and sleep terror episodes have been hypothesized to be linked etiologically to an immaturity factor with respect to central nervous system development. While not addressed in the literature, delays in other areas of development might covary with these disorders. Although nightmares are not hypothesized to be a developmental phenomenon, developmental information may be useful in differentiating nightmare complaints from sleep terrors. The child's *psychological adjustment* is also of interest in that evidence of unsatisfactory adjustment may reflect the child's inability to deal effectively with stressors that, in turn, might set the stage for nighttime sleep problems. Also, significant levels of anxiety resulting from frequent nightmare episodes may interfere with the capacity to deal with stressors. Insomnias, in some cases, may be associated with psychological problems such as depression (Coates & Thoresen, 1981b; Youkilis & Bootzin, 1981). Also important to assessment is the child's *arousal level or arousability.* For example, heightened physiological arousal is a factor implicated in the etiology of insomnia, and arousability may also play an etiological role in the parasomnias. If possible, the child's sleep patterns and sleep cycles should be monitored via polysomnographic recordings.

Child's Daytime and Presleep Behaviors

The child's daytime activities, performance levels and deficits in school and elsewhere, changes from previous behaviors, and bedtime and sleep routines may provide information as to etiological and maintaining variables in children's sleep disorders, as well as information on the effects of sleep problems. *Daytime activities,* such as exercise (insufficient or excessive amounts), may influence sleep behaviors. For example, too little exercise may result in heightened arousal incompatible with sleep, while excessive physical exertion can result in sleep problems via fatigue. While little attention has been given to the effects of sleep problems on daytime *performance levels,* sleep problems (such as sleep loss associated with insomnia) may be reflected in reduced school performance and other behavioral changes (Bootzin & Engle-Friedman, 1981). To the degree that nightmares are reflective of anxiety, such anxiety could be expected to produce daytime behavioral effects as well. In turn, such effects might serve as precursors to subsequent episodes. *Changes from previous behavior* are also of note. Next-day performance may help pinpoint the presence of lessened sleep versus perceived sleep loss (presuming, of course, that subjective impressions of sleep loss would not adversely affect performance on subsequent days). Such information may contribute to decisions as to the necessary scope of treatment, and performance levels may have utility as dependent measures in ongoing assessment and treatment.

Children's *bedtime routines and schedules* may provide information as to avoidance behaviors associated with fears of falling asleep and of experiencing nightmares or may suggest factors contributing to heightened physiological arousal at bedtime. For some cases of insomnia, demands for bedtime and sleep may be out of phase with the child's normal sleep cycle (Coates & Thoresen, 1981b), resulting in unsuccessful sleep attempts when the child is not sleepy. Attempts to go to sleep may inhibit sleep onset (Borkovec, 1982; Relinger & Bornstein, 1979; Youkilis & Bootzin, 1981). Inconsistent bedtimes and other poor sleep habits may also serve as contributing variables. In the assessment of children's sleep behaviors, the evaluation of children's afternoon naps may have discriminant validity in identifying sleep problems and may be good measures of such behaviors as sleep-onset latencies, awakenings, and responses to stressors, thus serving as a particularly useful and cost-efficient assessment procedure with children.

Evaluation of Daily Stressors

Assessment should include attention to a variety of potential stressors that can play an etiological or maintaining role in children's sleep disorders. These include significant life events, social interactions, cognitive activities, and other internal and external stimuli. *Significant life events* (Haynes, Adams, & Franzen, 1981; Haynes, Adams, West, Kamens, & Safranek, 1982), such as the death of relatives, traumas, exposure to fear-producing stimuli, or situations during waking hours, may contribute to sleep problems (e.g., the presumed association between anxiety and nightmares). Similarly, stressful *social interactions* with parents, siblings, or others in the social environment may serve as etiological or maintaining variables for insomnia and the parasomnias.

Children's *cognitive activities,* including fearful ruminations or performance anxiety, may serve as stressors to negatively influence sleep. Negative school experiences, demands for performance, teasing from other children, or anxiety over future punishment all can contribute to worrisome cognitive activity and, perhaps in turn, to sleep-incompatible arousal states associated with insomnia. Similarly, stories about the boogie man and frightening movies or television programs may contribute to anticipatory fears of bed and sleep and possibly to nightmare content or insomnia. Daily stressors may be of particular importance in nightmares because of the hypothesized relationship between nightmare content and fear stimuli in the waking state. It is of note that nightmare conceptualizations have involved both classical and operant factors as contributors to heightened levels of anxiety and fear. Phobic stimuli occurring during waking hours may increase anxiety levels. Anticipatory fear responses developing as a result of previous nightmare episodes may set the stage for subsequent episodes.

Internal stimuli, such as pain, feelings of nausea, or bladder distention, may contribute to arousal responses in the parasomnias and insomnia, and *external stimuli* in the sleep environment (Coates & Thoresen, 1981b; Haynes, Adams, West, Kamens, & Safranek, 1982; Weil & Goldfried, 1973; Youkilis & Bootzin, 1981), such as noise, heat, or light, may likewise be important. Familiar objects under low-light conditions may appear unfamiliar and threatening to the child, resulting in fear responses and arousal incompatible with sleep. The presence of television sets or stereos may, through association, also contribute to sleep incompatible responses. When sleepwalking is a problem, assessment of the sleep environment with respect to factors that might pose a danger to the child is also important. For example, a child whose sleeping quarters are situated on the upper bunk of a bunkbed may be at risk. Likewise, sleeping quarters on the upper floors of the home may be hazardous. Objects in the sleep environment (e.g., heaters, fans, sharp objects) should also be considered in any environmental assessment and modification.

Evaluation should also be made of the relationship between the occurrence of stressors and the frequencies or intensity of problem sleep episodes. Assessment of such relationships can provide valuable information regarding the conditional probability of the occurrence of episodes and may suggest environmental manipulations to reduce those probabilities. Finally, while stress is a frequently employed explanation and one which is logically related to sleep disorders, it should be noted that this relationship thus far lacks clear empirical validation.

Environmental Contingencies

Reactions by others in the child's environment to the problem sleep behaviors are also important in the analysis of controlling variables. For example, parent-delivered contingencies may maintain or increase sleep problems. Sleepwalking, sleep terrors, and nightmares can have the effect of significantly increasing both physical and verbal parental attention to the child. Contingent verbal and/or physical efforts to comfort the child upon awakening from a nightmare may intensify post-episode fear responses, which then may contribute to fears over sleeping. Parent-delivered contingencies may also contribute to sleep-avoidant behaviors (e.g., attempts to put off bedtime or instances of lying awake in bed) in cases in which parents acquiesce to such attempts. Likewise, the child's fears of being alone at night may be reinforced when parents allow the child to leave his/her own bedroom and sleep with them (contingent on verbalizations of fear by the child). Also of interest in terms of parental reaction to the child's sleep problems is the question of whether the child's concern over the problem is comparable to that of the parents (Ware & Orr, 1983).

Medical Illnesses and Other Physical Factors

A variety of physical and medical problems (e.g., pain, fatigue, febrile illness, epilepsy) can be associated with sleep problems. High fever has been implicated as a precursor to some sleepwalking episodes in children. Sleep-related epileptic seizures may be accompanied by nightmare-like dreams. Because sleep disorders may be primary or may be secondary to a physical disorder, Coates & Thoresen (1981a) suggested that when presenting a complaint involving a sleep problem a medical examination is needed. Further, Guilleminault,

Korobkin, Anders, & Dement (1977) suggested that a normal physical examination would suffice and that the sleep problem may be presumed to be primary if no physical illness is obvious.

Pharmacological Factors

Assessment should include attention to pharmacological agents, which may influence the child's sleep behaviors. The previous or current use of drugs is important since tolerance or withdrawal from CNS depressants or the chronic use of CNS stimulants can lead to sleep disruptions (Coates & Thoresen, 1981b; Guilleminault & Anders, 1976). In general, any substance that affects central nervous system functioning adversely affects sleep patterns (e.g., alcohol, barbiturates, numerous recreational drugs, amphetamines, caffeine, a variety of prescription medications, contents of certain foods). Prescription drugs such as Diazepam may contribute to reductions in the duration of NREM sleep periods. Withdrawal of the drug may be related to episodes of sleepwalking and sleep terror via a rebound in NREM sleep and a protraction of the time spent in that stage. Likewise, tricyclics or neuroleptics may influence the occurrence of sleep terrors. Withdrawal from drugs, such as the barbiturates, may produce REM rebounds accompanied by severe nightmares. The content of food or beverages may also influence children's sleep behaviors. Some cases of insomnia may be related to ingestion of caffeinated beverages, such as certain soft drinks, which can produce heightened physiological arousal.

CLINICAL ISSUES IN INTERVENTION IMPLEMENTATION

Several issues should be noted with respect to the implementation of treatment strategies with children's sleep disorders. These include, but are not limited to, (1) mediators of treatment, (2) monitoring of treatment effects, (3) identification of episode occurrences, (4) reactions by significant others to episodes, and (5) the necessity of treatment.

Because episodes are limited to nighttime hours and occur in a limited setting, the behavior analyst would ordinarily not be present in the home to observe or apply treatment strategies contiguously with problem sleep episodes. This also means that the analyst ordinarily would not be present to directly observe the implementation of procedures by others. Thus, a family member (or others, such as hospital staff members) often must serve as the mediator for treatment strategies employed with the sleep problems and must be appropriately trained. Accordingly, it is desirable to have parents rehearse the procedure(s) with feedback provided from the behavior analyst. This may be done either within an analogue clinic setting with parents role playing the behaviors or through several initial visits in the home.

Also necessary is a means of deriving adequate measures of the problem behavior during preintervention and treatment periods to assess the effects of treatment. Because the problem episodes typically occur in a limited setting and at limited times, critical event sampling can have particular utility (Haynes, 1984b). While continuous videotape monitoring of child behaviors would be most desirable from an observational standpoint, cost factors, requirements for lighting, and the obtrusiveness of such equipment may argue against such strategies. Audiotape recordings, however, are inexpensive, are unobtrusive, and do not create problem lighting requirements. Recordings can be obtained continuously throughout the night, or parents could turn on recorders once they become aware of an episode. But, while audiotaping can be useful in monitoring episodes accompanied by verbalizations (e.g., sleep terrors), they are of little help in monitoring episodes such as sleepwalking or insomnia (unless in the latter case the individual is asked to verbally report ongoing cognitive activity associated with attempts to go to sleep). It is also important to monitor the treatment program and parental implementation of it on a continuing basis. If it is suspected that the parents may be inconsistent, then the encouragement of daily reports of treatment compliance can be helpful. To the degree that treatment strategies require verbal interaction or the lack of it (e.g., withholding or minimizing attention), tape recordings again may serve to evaluate compliance and continuity of treatment. However, unless audio or other recordings are collected continuously throughout the night, such procedures only allow evaluation once episodes have begun and do not provide information as to immediate antecedents of episodes.

Because many of the episodes associated with children's sleep problems (e.g., sleepwalking, sleep terrors, nightmares) represent low frequency events that occur at night, it can be difficult for parents to be present at each occurrence for purposes of observation or intervention. In many cases, parents become alerted to the occurrence (if they do at all) once the episode has begun. For a problem of sleepwalking in an adult, Meyer (1975) adjusted a couple's sleeping arrangement so, in order to get out of bed, the patient had to crawl across his wife. While such environmental manipulations can provide a signaling system to alert an individual to the episode, they still do not guarantee awareness of the onset of an episode or antecedent patient behaviors.

Parental reactions can affect the child's behaviors associated with problem sleep episodes. If the parents are overly concerned with or frightened by the particular episodes (e.g., sleepwalking, sleep terrors), then when they awaken the child, they might also convey their anxiety or fear to the child and contribute to the child's apprehension or confusion. Accordingly, instructions to parents in responding to episodes and reassurance to allay their fears are important. Because of the possibility that heightened arousal contributes to these disorders, care should be taken that parents are able to respond in a calm manner so that their own discomfort is not communicated to the child, thus heightening the child's arousal. Also, fears over episodes may influence the parents' ability to carry out treatment suggestions. For example, features such as the apparent inconsolability of the child during sleep terror episodes may frighten parents and contribute to their feelings of being unable to successfully intervene. Thus, it is important to assess parents' feelings about episodes and their abilities to follow intervention procedures so that neither they nor the child are subjected to unnecessary anxiety.

An additional issue is that of whether or not the sleep problem warrants specialized treatment beyond that of conservative management (i.e., parental assurance and environmental modification for the safety of the child). Some investigators (e.g., Kales & Kales, 1974) have suggested that the most appropriate treatment in cases of sleepwalking and sleep terrors is simply reassurance to parents that children will typically outgrow the episodes and that steps should be taken in the meantime to avoid injury. However, intervention decisions must be based on the frequency, severity, and duration of the disorder and the degree of discomfort of both the parents and child produced by the disorder.

A CASE EXAMPLE: NIGHTMARE INTERVENTION

Roberts and Gordon (1979) described a case of a five-year-old girl who, following an accident in which she received burns covering 20 percent of her body, experienced nightmares and sleep terror episodes at a high freqeuncy (i.e., 15–20 times per night). The course of assessment and treatment involved interviews with the parents to obtain a history of the problem, the collection of questionnaire data that involved both the characteristics of the child and of her parents (i.e., questionnaires employed included the Louisville Behavior Checklist, the Walker Problem Behavior Identification Checklist, and the Locke-Wallace Marital Adjustment Inventory), a discussion with the parents regarding the rationale for treatment, continued monitoring and evaluation of treatment progress, modification of treatment strategies, and a six-month follow-up that included parental reports of the child's behavior and a readministration of the original questionnaires.

The burn trauma occurred eight weeks prior to the first clinic visit. Her nightgown had caught on fire while she and her younger brother were playing with matches in the bedroom. She was hospitalized on the night of the accident and had remained there for approximately six weeks, during which time she had several skin graft operations. The child began having nighmares on the first night in the hospital, and the nightmares (note that the authors did not clearly distinguish between nightmares and sleep terrors) followed a specific sequence that suggested that she was dreaming of the fire. The nightmare episode began with the child clutching her nightgown and moving her hands upward over her body in the direction in which the most severe burns occurred. She would then begin to scream and kick until awakened by the hospital staff. The authors also reported that at no time was the child able to remember the content of the nightmares.

Following each episode in the hospital, the nurses would calm the child by providing ice cream and offering her reassurances. The nightmares continued at a high rate for two weeks after the child returned home. The parents attempted to calm her after nightmare episodes by giving her something to drink. She was also allowed to come into the parents' bedroom and sleep with them. Thus, some nightmares occurred in her room, and others occurred in the parents' room. Information obtained by the authors from the parents indicated that she had no other major behavior problems. Baseline information was obtained via the parents' monitoring frequencies of episodes (in the hospital, the nursing staff had recorded instances on the child's hospital chart). An episode was recorded by the mother each time the child was heard to scream.

Based on the initial behavior analysis, Roberts and Gordon felt that potentially reinforcing consequences for nightmares were provided by the nursing staff and the parents. They further distinguished between these maintaining factors and initiating variables (i.e., the original trauma). This conceptualization suggested the efficacy of extinction by removal of all potentially reinforcing consequences. However, the authors pointed out that this was contraindicated because the wild thrashing that occurred during episodes posed the risk of harm to the child. Accordingly, the authors decided to use a response prevention procedure instead and to interrupt the behavioral sequence at an early stage and with a minimum of parental contact. The mother was instructed to arouse the child but not to talk with her; instead, she was to allow the child to go back to sleep immediately.

As reported by the authors, the awakening procedure initially increased the rate of nightmares, although the risk of physical injury was removed. Soon, however, this trend was reversed, and nightmare rate declined significantly (i.e., less than one per night after the first week of treatment). After four weeks, the child was readmitted to the hospital for further surgery, and the nightmares recurred. The authors suggested that this resulted because the nursing staff had not received any instructions regarding appropriate responses to the episodes (note that a stimulus control explanation might also account for this phenomenon). Once the child returned to her home, the episodes continued at the rate of approximately two per night.

At that point, the parents also reported that the child was becoming increasingly fearful of fire-related stimuli, which suggested the need for an alternate treatment. Thus, systematic desensitization was instituted. And, because of her age, pictorial stimuli rather than imaginal stimuli were employed. To that end, the authors created a hierarchy of 10 magazine pictures that represented fire in a wide variety of settings and uses. The child's mother served as the therapist in exposing the child to the fear stimuli. Following each exposure, the child was allowed to play with her favorite toys. The length of trials was gradually increased from 15 seconds to one minute, and the hierarchy was presented every day for three weeks until the picture at the top of the hierarchy was finally reached and rated as not scary. Follow-up results, as reported by Roberts and Gordon, indicated that there had been no recurrences of the nightmares or sleep terrors, even though she had once again been hospitalized for skin graft procedures. Additionally, the parents indicated no behavioral disturbances at that time.

SUMMARY

Based on recent advances in the assessment of sleep behaviors, including physiological and behavioral measures, and on suggestive findings for the efficacy of behavioral intervention strategies for sleep problems in both children and adults, it is expected that the increased focus on children's sleep disorders will continue. At present, however, our knowledge of the behavioral assessment and treatment of children's and adolescents' sleep disorders is quite limited.

Sleep disorders may have their origins in factors other than those that maintain them. Thus, in consideration of etiology, it is important to remember that a variety of those factors discussed may interact to establish and maintain the particular disorder. Any could serve to initiate the disorder for some children, while the same factors might play a maintenance role for other children if primary etiological factors were other than those currently maintaining the behavior.

REFERENCES

American Psychiatric Association. *Diagnostic and statistical manual of mental disorders* (3rd ed.). Washington, D.C.: American Psychiatric Association, 1980.

Anders, T. F. Neurophysiological studies of sleep in infants and children. *Journal of Child Psychology and Psychiatry and Allied Disciplines*, 1982, *23*, 75–83.

Anders, T. F., Carskadon, M. A., Dement, W. C., & Harvey, K. Sleep habits of children and the identification of pathologically sleepy children. *Child Psychiatry and Human Development*, 1978, *9*, 56–63.

Anders, T. F., & Guilleminault, C. The pathophysiology of sleep disorders in pediatrics: Sleep in infancy. *Advances in Pediatrics*, 1976, *22*, 137–150.

Anders, T. F., & Weinstein, P. Sleep and its disorders in infants and children: A review. *Journal of Pediatrics*, 1972, *50*, 311–324.

Anderson, D. R. Treatment of insomnia in a 13-year-old boy by relaxation training and reduction of parental attention. *Journal of Behavior Therapy and Experimental Psychiatry*, 1979, *10*, 263–265.

Anthony, E. J. An experimental approach to the psychopathology of childhood: Sleep disturbances. *British Journal of Medical Psychology*, 1959, *32*, 19–37.

Ascher, L. M. Paradoxical intention. In A. Goldstein & E. R. Foa (Eds.), *Handbook of behavioral interventions*. New York: John Wiley & Sons, 1980.

Ascher, L. M., & Efran, J. S. Use of paradoxical intention in a behavioral program for sleep onset insomnia. *Journal of Consulting and Clinical Psychology*, 1978, *46*, 547–550.

Ascher, L. M., & Turner, R. M. A comparison of two methods for the administration of paradoxical intention. *Behaviour Research and Therapy*, 1980, *18*, 121–126.

Ascher, L. M., & Turner, R. M. Paradoxical intention and insomnia: An experimental investigation. *Behaviour Research and Therapy*, 1979, *17*, 408–411.

Association of Sleep Disorders Centers and the Association for the Psychophysiological Study of Sleep. Diagnostic classification of sleep and arousal disorders (1st ed.). *Sleep*, 1979, *2*, 1–137.

Baum, C. G., Forehand, R., & Zeigob, L. E. A review of observer reactivity in adult-child interactions. *Journal of Behavioral Assessment*, 1979, *1*, 167–177.

Bergman, R. L. Treatment of childhood insomnia diagnosed as hyperactivity. *Journal of Behavior Therapy and Experimental Psychiatry*, 1976, *7*, 199.

Bertelson, A. D., & Monroe, L. J. Personality patterns of adolescent poor and good sleepers. *Journal of Abnormal Child Psychology*, 1979, *7*, 191–197.

Bixler, E. O., Kales, A., & Soldatos, C. R. Sleep disorders encountered in medical practice: A national survey of physicians. *Behavioral Medicine*, 1979, *2*, 13–21.

Bixler, E. O., Kales, J. D., Scharf, M. B., Kales, A., & Leo, L. A. Incidence of sleep disorders in medical practice: A physician survey. *Sleep Research*, 1976, *5*, 62.

Bonnet, M. H., & Johnson, L. C. Relationship of arousal thresholds to sleep stage distribution and subjective estimates of depth of sleep. *Sleep*, 1978, *1*, 161–168.

Bonnet, M. H., Johnson, L. C., & Webb, W. B. The reliability of arousal threshold during sleep. *Psychophysiology*, 1978, *15*, 412–416.

Bootzin, R. R. A stimulus control treatment for insomnia. *Proceedings of the American Psychological Association*, 1972, 395–396.

Bootzin, R. R., & Engle-Friedman, M. The assessment of insomnia. *Behavioral Assessment*, 1981, *3*, 107–126.

Bootzin, R. R., & Nicassio, P. M. Behavioral treatments for insomnia. In M. Hersen, R. Eisler, & P. Miller (Eds.), *Progress in behavior modification* (Vol. 4). New York: Academic Press, 1977.

Bootzin, R. R., & Nicassio, P. M. Behavioral treatments for insomnia. In M. Hersen, R. M. Eisler, & P. M. Miller (Eds.), *Progress in behavior modification* (Vol. 6). New York: Academic Press, 1978.

Borkovec, T. D. Insomnia. *Journal of Consulting and Clinical Psychology*, 1982, *50*, 880–895.

Borkovec, T. D. Psuedo- (experiential) insomnia and idiopathic (objective) insomnia: Theoretical and therapeutic issues. *Advances in Behavior Research and Therapy,* 1979, *2,* 27–55.

Borkovec, T. D., & Fowles, D. C. Controlled investigation of the effects of progressive and hypnotic relaxation on insomnia. *Journal of Abnormal Psychology,* 1973, *82,* 153–158.

Bornstein, P. H., Hamilton, S. B., & Quevillon, R. P. Behavior modification by long distance: Demonstration of the functional control over disruptive behavior in a rural classroom setting. *Behavior Modification,* 1977, *1,* 369–380.

Broughton, R. J. Sleep disorders: Disorders of arousal? *Science,* 1968, *159,* 1070–1078.

Broughton, R. J. The incubus attack. In E. Hartmann (Ed.), *Sleep and dreaming,* Boston: Little, Brown, 1970.

Carlson, C. R., White, D. K., & Turkat, I. D. Night terrors: A clinical and empirical review. *Clinical Psychology Review,* 1982, *2,* 455–468.

Carskadon, M. A., Harvey, K., & Dement, W. C. Acute restriction of nocturnal sleep in children. *Perceptual and Motor Skills,* 1981, *53,* 103–112.

Cautela, J. R. Behavior therapy and the need for behavioral assessment. *Psychotherapy,* 1968, *5,* 175–179.

Cavior, N., & Deutsch, A. Systematic desensitization to reduce dream induced anxiety. *Journal of Nervous and Mental Disease,* 1975, *161,* 433–435.

Ciminero, A. R., Nelson, R. O., & Lipinski, D. P. Self-monitoring procedures. In A. R. Ciminero, K. S. Calhoun, & H. E. Adams, (Eds.), *Handbook of behavioral assessment.* New York: John Wiley & Sons, 1977.

Clement, P. W. Elimination of sleepwalking in a seven-year-old boy. *Journal of Consulting and Clinical Psychology,* 1970, *34,* 22–26.

Coates, R. J., Rosekind, M. R., & Thoresen, C. E. All night sleep recordings in clients' homes by telephone. *Journal of Behavior Therapy and Experimental Psychiatry,* 1978, *9,* 157–162.

Coates, T. J., & Thoresen, C. E. Sleep disturbance in children and adolescents. In E. J. Mash & L. G. Terdal (Eds.), *Behavioral assessment of childhood disorders.* New York: Guilford Press, 1981 (a).

Coates, T. J. & Thoresen, C. E. Treating arousals during sleep using behavioral self-management. *Journal of Consulting and Clinical Psychology,* 1979, *47,* 603–605.

Coates, T. J., & Thoresen, C. E. Treating sleep disorders: Few answers, some suggestions and many questions. In S. M. Turner, K. S. Calhoun & H. E. Adams (Eds.), *Handbook of clinical behavior therapy.* New York: John Wiley & Sons, 1981 (b).

Coursey, R., Buchsbaum, M., & Frankel, B. Personality measures and evoked responses in chronic insomniacs. *Journal of Abnormal Psychology,* 1975, *84,* 239–249.

Davidson, P. O., & Davison, S. M. *Behavioral medicine: Changing health lifestyles.* New York: Brunner/Mazel, 1980.

Dollinger, S. J. On the varieties of childhood sleep disturbance. *Journal of Clinical Child Psychology,* 1982, *11,* 107–115.

Emmelkamp, P. M. G. The current and future status of clinical research. *Behavioral Assessment,* 1981, *3,* 249–253.

Feldman, M. J., & Hersen, M. Attitudes toward death in nightmare subjects. *Journal of Abnormal Psychology,* 1967, *72,* 421–425.

Feldman, M. H., & Hyman, E. Content analysis of nightmare reports. *Psychophysiology,* 1968, *5,* 221.

Fisher, C., Byrne, J. V., & Edwards, A. NREM and REM nightmares. *Psychophysiology,* 1968, *5,* 221–222.

Fisher, C., Byrne, J. V., Edwards, A., & Kahn, E. A psychophysiological study of nightmares. *Journal of the American Psychoanalytic Association,* 1970, *18,* 747–782.

Fisher, C., Byrne, J., Edwards, A., & Kahn, E. REM and NREM nightmares. *Psychophysiology,* 1969, *6,* 252.

Fisher, C., Kahn, E., Edwards, A., & Davis, D. M. A psychophysiological study of nightmares and night terrors. *Journal of Nervous and Mental Disease,* 1973, *157,* 75–76.

Fisher, C., Kahn, E., Edwards, A., Davis, D. M., & Fine, J. A psychophysiological study of nightmares and night terrors. *Journal of Nervous and Mental Disease,* 1974, *158,* 174–188.

Flemenbaum, A. Pavor nocturnus: A complication of single daily tricyclic or neuroleptic dosage. *American Journal of Psychiatry,* 1976, *134,* 570–572.

Foster, S. L., & Cone, J. D. Current issues in direct observation. *Behavioral Assessment,* 1980, *2,* 313–338.

Framer, E. M., & Sanders, S. H. The effects of family contingency contracting on disturbed sleeping behaviors in a male adolescent. *Journal of Behavior Therapy and Experimental Psychiatry,* 1980, *11,* 235–237.

Glick, B. S., Schulman, D., & Turecki, S. Diazepam (Valium) treatment in childhood sleep disorders: A preliminary investigation. *Diseases of the nervous System,* 1971, *32,* 565–566.

Goldfried, M. R. Behavioral assessment: An overview. In A. S. Bellack, A. Kazdin, & M. Hersen (Eds.), *International handbook of behavior modification and therapy.* New York: Plenum Press, 1982.

Guilleminault, C., & Anders, T. F. The pathophysiology of sleep disorders in pediatrics: Sleep disorders in children. *Advances in Pediatrics,* 1976, *22,* 151–174.

Guilleminault, C., Eldridge, F. L., Simmons, F. B., & Dement, W. C. Sleep apnea in eight children. *Pediatrics,* 1976, *58,* 23–30.

Guilleminault C., Korobkin, R., Anders, T. A., & Dement, W. C. Nocturnal disturbances in children: NREM dyssomnia or other? *Sleep Research,* 1977, *6,* 169.

Hallstrom, T. Night terrors in adults through three generations. *Acta Psychiatrica Scandinavica,* 1972, *48,* 350–352.

Handler, L. The amelioration of nightmares in children. *Psychotherapy: Theory, Research and Practice,* 1972, *9,* 54–56.

Hartmann, D. P., & Wood, D. D. Observation methods. In A. S. Bellack, A. Kazdin, & M. Hersen (Eds.), *International handbook of behavior modification and therapy.* New York: Plenum Press, 1982.

Hartmann, E. A note on the nightmare. In E. Hartmann (Ed.), *Sleep and dreaming.* Boston: Little, Brown, 1970.

Hauri, P. Behavioral treatment of insomnia. *Medical Times,* 1979, *107,* 36–47.

Haynes, S. N. Behavioral assessment in the design of intervention programs. In R. O. Nelson, & S. Hayes (Eds.), *Conceptual foundations of behavioral assessment.* New York: Guilford Press, in press.

Haynes, S. N. Behavioral assessment of adults. In M. Hersen, & Goldstein (Eds.), *Handbook of psychological assessment.* New York: Pergamon Press, 1984.

Haynes, S. N. *Principles of behavioral assessment.* New York: Gardner Press, 1978.

Haynes, S. N., Adams, A., & Franzen, M. The effects of presleep stress on sleep-onset insomnia. *Journal of Abnormal Psychology,* 1981, *90,* 601–606.

Haynes, S. N., Adams, A. E., West, S., Kamens, L., & Safranek, R. The stimulus control paradigm in sleep-onset insomnia: A multimethod assessment. *Journal of Psychosomatic Research,* 1981, *26,* 333–339.

Haynes, S. N., & Chavez, R. The interview in the assessment of marital distress. In E. E. Filsinger (Ed.), *A sourcebook of marriage and family assessment.* Beverly Hills, Calif.: Sage Publications, 1983.

Haynes, S. N., Follingstad, D. R., & McGowan, W. T. Insomnia: Sleep patterns and anxiety level. *Journal of Psychosomatic Research,* 1974, *18,* 69–74.

Haynes, S. N., & Gannon, L. R. *Psychosomatic disorders: A psychophysiological approach to etiology and treatment.* New York: Praeger Publishers, 1981.

Haynes, S. N., & Horn, W. F. Reactive effects of behavioral observation. *Behavioral assessment,* 1982, *4,* 369–386.

Haynes, S. N., & Jensen, R. J. The interview as a behavioral assessment instrument. *Behavioral Assessment,* 1979, *1,* 97–106.

Haynes, S. N., & Mooney, D. K. Nightmares: Etiological, theoretical, and behavioral treatment considerations. *The Psychological Record,* 1975, *25,* 225–236.

Haynes, S. N., Price, M. G., & Simons, J. B. Stimulus control treatment of insomnia. *Journal of Behavior Therapy and Experimental Psychiatry,* 1975, *6,* 279.

Haynes, S. N., Sides, H., & Lockwood, G. Relaxation instructions and electromyographic biofeedback intervention with insomnia. *Behavior Therapy*, 1977, *8*, 644–652.

Haynes, S. N., & Wilson, C. C. *Behavioral assessment: Recent advances in methods, concepts, and applications*. San Francisco: Jossey-Bass, 1979.

Haynes, S. N., Woodward, S., Moran, P., & Alexander, D. Relaxation treatment of insomnia. *Behavior Therapy*, 1974, *5*, 555–558.

Hersen, M. Nightmare behavior: A review. *Psychological Bulletin*, 1972, *78*, 37–48.

Hersen, M. Personality characteristics of nightmare sufferers. *Journal of Nervous and Mental Disease*, 1971, *153*, 27–31.

Hyde, P., & Pegram, V. Sleep, sleep disorders, and some behavioral approaches to treatment of insomnia. In D. M. Doleys, R. L. Meredith, and A. R. Ciminero (Eds.), *Behavioral medicine: Assessment and treatment strategies*. New York: Plenum Press, 1982.

Jacobson, E. *Progressive relaxation*. Chicago: University of Chicago Press, 1938.

Kales, A., Caldwell, A., Soldatos, C. R., Kales, J. D., & Russell, E. Clinical and psychological characteristics of parents with night terrors. *Sleep Research*, 1977, *6*, 172.

Kales, A., & Kales, J. D. Sleep disorders: Recent findings in the diagnosis and treatment of disturbed sleep. *New England Journal of Medicine*, 1974, *299*, 487–497.

Kales, A., Soldatos, C., Caldwell, A., Kales, J., Humphrey, F., Charney, D., & Schweitzer, P. Somnambulism. *Archives of General Psychiatry*, 1980, *37*, 1406–1410.

Kales, A., Weber, G., Charney, D. S., Bixler, E. D., & Ladd, R. Familial occurrence of sleepwalking and night terrors. *Sleep Research*, 1977, *6*, 177.

Kales, J. D., & Kales, A. Nocturnal psychophysiological correlates of somatic conditions and sleep disorders. *International Journal of Psychiatry in Medicine*, 1975, *6*, 43–62.

Kales, J. D., Kales, A., Soldat s, C. R., Caldwell, A. B., Charney, D. S., & Martin, E. D. Night terrors: Clinical characteristics and personality patterns. *Archives of General Psychiatry*, 1980, *37*, 1413–1417.

Kales, J. D., Kales, A., Soldatos, C. R., Chamberlin, K., & Martin, E. D. Sleepwalking and night terrors related to febrile illness. *American Journal of Psychiatry*, 1979, *136*, 1214–1215.

Karacan, I., Ilaria, R., Ware, C., Thornby, J., & Chambliss, S. Is the poor sleep of insomniacs due to anxiety? *Sleep Research*, 1978, *7*, 236.

Keith, P. R. Night terrors: A review of the psychology, neurophysiology, and therapy. *Journal of Child Psychiatry*, 1975, *14*, 477–489.

Kellerman, J. Behavioral treatment of night terrors in a child with acute leukemia. *Journal of Nervous and Mental Disease*, 1979, *167*, 182–185.

Kellerman, J. Rapid treatment of nocturnal anxiety in children. *Journal of Behavior Therapy and Experimental Psychiatry,* 1980, *11,* 9–11.

Knapp, T. J., Downs, D. L., & Alperson, J. R. Behavior therapy for insomnia: A review. *Behavior Therapy,* 1976, *7,* 614–625.

Kurtz, H., & Davidson, S. Psychic trauma in an Israeli child: Relationship to environmental security. *American Journal of Psychotherapy,* 1974, *28,* 438–444.

Lester, D. Fear of death and nightmare experiences. *Psychological Reports,* 1969, *25,* 437–438.

Levine, E. S. Indirect suggestions through personalized fairy tales for treatment of childhood insomnia. *American Journal of Clinical Hypnosis,* 1980, *23,* 57–63.

Lindsley, O. Operant behavior during sleep: A measure of depth of sleep. *Science,* 1957, *116,* 1290–1291.

Margolin, G. Practical applications of behavioral marital assessment. In E. E. Filsinger, & R. A. Lewis (Eds.), *Assessing marriage: New behavioral approaches.* Beverly Hills, Calif.: Sage Publications, 1981.

Marshall, J. R. The treatment of night terrors associated with the posttraumatic syndrome. *American Journal of Psychiatry,* 1975, *132,* 293–295.

Miller, L. C. Fears and anxiety in children. In C. E. Walker and M. C. Roberts (Eds.), *Handbook of clinical child psychology.* New York: John Wiley & Sons, 1983.

Nagaraja, J. Somnambulism in children. *Child Psychiatry Quarterly,* 1974, *7,* 18–19.

Nelson, R. O. Methodological issues in assessment via self-monitoring. In J. D. Cone, & R. P. Hawkins (Eds.), *Behavioral assessment: New directions in clinical psychology.* New York: Brunner/Mazel, 1977.

Nelson, R. O., Lipinski, D. P., & Boykin, R. The effects of self-recorders' training and the obtrusiveness of the self-recording device on the accuracy and reactivity of self-monitoring. *Behavior Therapy,* 1978, *9,* 200–208.

Nicassio, P., & Bootzin, R. A comparison of progressive relaxation and autogenic training as a treatment of insomnia. *Journal of Abnormal Psychology,* 1974, *83,* 253–260.

Nicassio, P. M., & Buchanan, D. C. Clinical application of behavior therapy for insomnia. *Comprehensive Psychiatry,* 1981, *22,* 512–521.

Porter, J. Guided fantasy as a treatment for childhood insomnia. *Australian and New Zealand Journal of Psychiatry,* 1975, *9,* 169–172.

Price, M. G., & Haynes, S. N. The effects of participant monitoring and feedback on marital interaction and satisfaction. *Behavior Therapy,* 1980, *11,* 134–139.

Relinger, H., & Bornstein, P. H. Treatment of sleep onset insomnia by paradoxical instruction: A multiple baseline design. *Behavior Modification,* 1979, *3,* 203–222.

Reynolds, C. F., Shubin, R. S., Coble, P. A., & Kupfer, D. J. Diagnostic classification of sleep disorders: Implications for psychiatric practice. *Journal of Clinical Psychiatry,* 1981, *42,* 296–299.

Ribordy, S. C., & Denney, R. The behavioral treatment of insomnia: An alternative to drug therapy. *Behaviour Research and Therapy,* 1977, *15,* 39–50.

Rickard, H. C., & Elkins, P. D. Behavior therapy with children. In C. E. Walker and M. C. Roberts (Eds.), *Handbook of clinical child psychology.* New York: John Wiley & Sons, 1983.

Roberts, R. N., & Gordon, S. B. Reducing childhood nightmares subsequent to a burn trauma. *Child Behavior Therapy,* 1979, *1,* 373–381.

Ross, A. O. *Child behavior therapy: Principles, procedures and empirical basis.* New York: John Wiley & Sons, 1981.

Ross, R. R., Meichenbaum, D. H., & Humphrey, C. Treatment of nocturnal head-banging by behavior modification techniques: A case report. *Behavior Research and Therapy,* 1971, *9,* 151–154.

Russo, R. M., Gururaj, V. J., & Allen, J. E. The effectiveness of diphenhydramine HCl in pediatric sleep disorders. *Journal of Clinical Pharmacology,* 1976, *16,* 284–288.

Schroeder, C. S., Gordon, B. N., & Hawk, B. Clinical problems of the preschool child. In C. E. Walker and M. C. Roberts (Eds.), *Handbook of clinical child psychology.* New York: John Wiley & Sons, 1983.

Shealy, R. C., Lowe, J. D., & Ritzler, B. A. Sleep Onset Insomnia: Personality characteristics and treatment outcomes. *Journal of Consulting and Clinical Psychology,* 1980, *48,* 659–661.

Shorkey, C., & Himle, D. P. Systematic desensitization treatment of a recurring nightmare and related insomnia. *Journal of Behavior Therapy and Experimental Psychiatry,* 1974, *5,* 97–98.

Sines, J. O., Pauker, J. D., & Sines, L. K. *Missouri Children's Picture Series Manual.* Iowa City, Iowa: Psychological Assessment and Services, 1974.

Turner, W. M., & Ascher, L. M. Controlled comparison of progressive relaxation, stimulus control, and paradoxical intention therapies for insomnia. *Journal of Consulting and Clinical Psychology,* 1979, *47,* 500–508.

Ware, J. C., & Orr, W. C. Sleep disorders in children. In C. E. Walker and M. C. Roberts (Eds.), *Handbook of clinical child psychology.* New York: John Wiley & Sons, 1983.

Webb, W. B., & Agnew, H. The effects of a chronic limitation of sleep length. *Psychophysiology,* 1974, *11,* 265–274.

Weil, G., & Goldfried, M. R. Treatment of insomnia in an eleven-year-old child through self-relaxation. *Behavior Therapy,* 1973, *4,* 282–284.

Weitzman, E. D. Sleep and its disorders. *Annual Review of Neuroscience,* 1981, *4,* 381–417.

Wiener, T. M. *Psychopharmacology in childhood and adolescence.* New York: Basic Books, 1977.

Wilkinson, R. T., & Mullaney, D. Electroencephalogram recording of sleep in the home. *Postgraduate Medical Journal*, 1976, *52*, 92–96.

Williams, R. L., Karacan, I., & Hursch, C. J. *Electroencephalography (EEG) of human sleep: Clinical applications*. New York: John Wiley & Sons, 1974.

Wilson, F. E., & Evans, I. M. The reliability of target-behavior selection in behavioral assessment. *Behavioral Assessment*, 1983, *5*, 15–32.

Yen, S., McIntire, R. W., & Berkowitz, S. Extinction of inappropriate sleeping behavior: Multiple assessment. *Psychological Reports*, 1972, *30*, 375–378.

Youkilis, H. D., & Bootzin, R. R. A psychophysiological perspective on the etiology and treatment of insomnia. In S. N. Haynes & L. Gannon (Eds.), *Psychosomatic disorders: A psychophysiological approach to etiology and treatment*. New York: Praeger Publishing, 1981.

13

Pervasive Developmental Disorders*

Glen Dunlap
Marshall University

Robert L. Koegel
Robert O'Neill
University of California, Santa Barbara

INTRODUCTION

The major diagnostic category in the DSM-III section concerning Pervasive Developmental Disorders is that of Infantile Autism (p. 87). Another category, Childhood Onset Pervasive Developmental Disorder, is discussed more briefly and is characterized as an extremely rare disorder. This chapter will focus on the characteristics and treatment of infantile autism, the major category in the DSM-III section. We will begin with a description of the disorder and a brief summary of predominant conceptualizations. The chapter will then outline methods of behavioral assessment and behavioral treatment approaches. In order to clearly illustrate the process of a broad-based behavioral intervention, a large portion of the chapter has been reserved for a detailed case description of an autistic child's participation in our behaviorally oriented treatment program.

---

* Preparation of this chapter and portions of the research described here were supported by U.S. Public Health Service Research Grants, MH 28210 and MH 28231 from the National Institute of Mental Health, and Research Contract No. 300-82-0362 from the U.S. Department of Education— Special Education Program. Appreciation is expressed to Lynn Koegel for her provision of the photographs used in this article.

Infantile autism first began to be delineated as a clinical syndrome by Leo Kanner who, in 1943, published a paper describing a group of 11 withdrawn atypical children who exhibited a set of unusual symptoms. Kanner used the term *early infantile autism* to label the set of clinical features displayed by these children. This form of severe childhood disorder was differentiated from other childhood psychoses and disorders that had a later onset (in late childhood or adolescence) and different symptoms. A specific description of the current diagnostic criteria and behavioral characteristics associated with the disorder is presented in following sections of this chapter.

A number of studies with different population groups in a variety of countries have identified prevalence ratios from 2 to 4 cases of autism per 10,000 children utilizing fairly strict criteria (American Psychiatric Association, 1980; Csapo, 1979; Wing, 1976) to up to 10 to 20 cases per 10,000 children utilizing broader based definitions (cf. Warren, 1983; Wing & Gould, 1979). The differing prevalence ratios reported could be due to a number of factors. For example, a study based only on reported diagnosed cases would probably yield lower prevalence rates than investigations that involve actual population screenings (Janicki, Lubin, & Friedman, 1983).

A higher incidence of infantile autism in male children has been reported by several investigators, with the ratios usually being 3 or 4 males to 1 female (Janicki, et al., 1983). It is generally accepted that the disorder is roughly three times more common in males than in females. It has been speculated that this is due to biological factors (Tsai, Stewart, & August, 1981), however, the specific factors that may be involved have not been identified at this point.

A description of behavioral characteristics associated with infantile autism is presented in the next section.

DESCRIPTION

The essential features of autism according to DSM-III (APA, 1980) are a lack of responsiveness to other people, gross impairment of communicative skills, and bizarre responses to various aspects of the environment, all developing within the first 30 months of age. These characteristics have been discussed, with varying points of emphasis, by numerous diagnosticians and researchers (cf. Schopler, 1978). Two of the most frequently cited discussions of the diagnostic criteria have been advanced by Rutter (1978) and by Ritvo and Freeman (1978). It is interesting to note that each of these authors emphasized slightly different aspects of the definition. For example, Rutter emphasized four criteria: (1) an onset before the age of 30 months; (2) impaired social development that has a number of special characteristics and is out of keeping with the child's intellectual level; (3) delayed and deviant language development that also has certain defined features and is out of keeping with the child's intellectual level; and (4) insistence on sameness, as shown by stereotyped play patterns, abnormal preoccupations, or resistance to change. Ritvo and Freeman, on the other hand, stressed five slightly different criteria: (1) signs and symptoms present before 30 months of age; (2) disturbances of developmental rate and/or sequences; (3) disturbances of responsiveness to sensory stimuli; (4) disturbances of speech, language, and cognitive capacities; and (5) disturbances of relating to people, events, and objects.

Behaviorally Specific Characteristics of the Disorder

While various professionals have chosen to emphasize different aspects of the definition, one who observes a group of autistic children will find that numerous specific behaviors are quite prevalent. Johnson and Koegel (1982) listed seven groups of behaviors that are likely to be exhibited in varying combinations by any large group of autistic children:

1. Autistic children exhibit a profound failure to relate to other people, which is often apparent from birth. They may show an absent or delayed social smile, and may not reach upwards in anticipation of being picked up. Some children fail to form emotional attachments to significant people in their environment, for example, not showing distress when their mother leaves the room. Similarly, a child might play in the vicinity of other children without interacting or participating with them.

2. Autistic children commonly show various levels of impaired or delayed language acquisition and comprehension. Many autistic children are nonverbal and others may show echolalia. For example, a child may repeat numerous phrases or conversations previously heard without indication that the words convey meaning. Immature grammar, pronoun reversal, and/or the inability to use abstract terms may also be apparent.

3. Many children show apparent sensory dysfunction, as if they do not see or hear some environmental events. They may exhibit under- or overresponsiveness to touch, light, sound, or pain. For instance, the child may not exhibit a startle response to a loud disturbance, but may respond to the sound of a candy wrapper, or may tantrum excessively every time a siren goes by.

4. Many autistic children show inappropriate and/or flat affect. They may not display appropriate facial expression and may not exhibit fear in dangerous situations, such as crossing the street. They may respond to even simple requests with severe, prolonged tantrums. They may also laugh and giggle uncontrollably in the absence of any apparent eliciting stimuli, or cry inconsolably for hours.

5. Typically, autistic children will occupy themselves for hours in stereotyped, repetitive self-stimulatory behaviors, which serve no apparent purpose other than providing the child with sensory input. Commonly, self-stimulatory behaviors take the form of manipulation of hands or fingers in front of the eyes, eye crossing, repetitive, meaningless vocalizations

(e.g., "aeh, aeh, aeh . . ."), suspending or spinning objects in front of the eyes, mouthing objects, hand tapping, body rocking, and other stereotyped behavior. Such behaviors have been found to significantly impair learning in autistic children (Koegel & Covert, 1972).

6. Autistic children often fail to develop normal, appropriate play. They may forsake toys altogether, preferring instead to spin a lampshade or flick a light switch on and off. If they do interact with toys, they may do so in an abnormal manner. For instance, the child may arrange, stack, or sort stimuli repetitively, over and over in the same pattern, and may show extreme disruption if the pattern is altered. Or they may turn a truck over and spin the wheels rather than roll it on the ground. Social play with peers may develop spontaneously, but usually does not.

7. Finally, autistic children commonly show obsessive, ritualistic behaviors which have been characterized as a profound resistance to change in the environment or normal routines. Familiar bedtime routines, insistence on one type of food, one type of furniture arrangement, and particular routes to familiar places are examples of routines which, when altered even in minor fashion, can create extreme disruptions in a child's behavior.

Associated Features

In addition to these characteristics noted above, it has been observed that autistic children are very atypical with respect to their intellectual functioning. That is, while most autistic children function overall in the mentally retarded range (i.e., IQ below 70), they typically show extreme variability in subareas of intellectual functioning with several isolated areas usually at or above normal levels. For example, while performance may be extremely low in areas involving symbolic thought (such as language), it may be extremely high (sometimes approaching genius) in areas involving rote memory, mathematics, and/or music (cf. Applebaum, Egel, Koegel, & Imhoff, 1979).

With respect to physical characteristics, no features have yet been identified. In fact, it has frequently been noted that no particular physical characteristics appear to accompany the disorder in childhood. It has, however, been commented that years of atypical responding, including behaviors such as poor eating habits, abnormal posturing, and/or teeth grinding may result in physical abnormalities by adulthood.

With respect to associated neurological features, few specific characteristics have been identified. However, it is beginning to be noted that as the children age, epileptic seizures frequently begin to occur (Rutter, 1970). In addition, increasing evidence is beginning to point to impairment in the language dominant hemisphere; although, it is possible that autistic children who receive early treatment may overcome this characteristic to some extent (Wetherby, Koegel, & Mendel, 1981).

Range of Severity

It is important to note that all children who are diagnosed autistic do not show all of the above characteristics, nor do they show the characteristics to the same degree. As such, there is an extremely wide range of severity for this disorder. We feel this has led to many unfortunate circumstances, since most professionals have a tendency to treat autistic children as if they are all much the same and as if they are all *severely* handicapped. The DSM-III describes the disorder (as if there were only one) as extremely incapacitating, with special education facilities almost always being necessary. In our experience, however, we have observed the differences among the children to be frequently greater than their similarities. For example, while it is clear that educational programs can have an extensive impact on autistic children, some autistic children require years of intensive training before they reach the level at which other children first enter treatment (cf. Russo & Koegel, 1977). Further, we have observed some autistic children who, with treatment, have completely overcome their disorder to the point where absolutely no identifiable remnant existed; and we have observed others who, after years of treatment, are still severely handicapped (although improved over their original state).

Differential Diagnosis

Differential diagnosis can be viewed either from a behavioral perspective (see below) or from a more traditional perspective as discussed in this section. Johnson and Koegel (1982) have discussed the fact that untrained individuals might easily confuse a number of other diagnostic categories with autism. As such, some commentary related to several of these disorders seems appropriate. Johnson and Koegel discussed these issues as described below.

From a purely traditional perspective, autism has many characteristics in common with several other global disorders. For example, the major differentiating factor between the traditional autistic disorder and mental retardation relates to evidence of the uneven developmental delays discussed above (Ritvo & Freeman, 1978). While the stereotypic retarded child shows relatively even deficits in all functioning areas, the classic autistic child should evidence isolated, "splinter" aptitudes for high-level functioning in areas such as mechanical, mathematical, or musical abilities (Applebaum, et al., 1979; Rimland, 1978).

In the past, the terms *autism* and *childhood schizophrenia* have often been confused. With the advent of the DSM-III, these categories are being more explicitly defined. The major differences are as follows: (1) Childhood schizophrenia and related categories usually have an older age of onset (5–12 years), while the autistic syndrome appears to be present from birth and is readily apparent prior to 30 months of age; and, (2) Schizophrenic individuals commonly show higher levels of language ability characterized by thought disorder or word salad, while autistic individuals exhibit a very limited use of language (typically mutism or echolalia, as noted previously).

Because autistic children commonly show disturbances or irregularities in their responses to sensory stimuli, they have often been mistakenly diagnosed as deaf or blind. The distinction from actual deafness or blindness is best noted in the variable nature of the presumed sensory deficit. For instance, the child's apparent threshold level for an auditory stimulus may differ dramatically when the stimulus is neutral as compared to when the auditory stimulus has been associated with reinforcement (Koegel & Schreibman, 1976).

In differentiating traditional autism from central disorders of language processing (aphasia), we look for language delays that are accompanied by disturbances in responses to sensory stimuli and/or inappropriate relations to people and objects (Ritvo & Freeman, 1978).

Age of Onset, Course, and Complications

As noted above, the age of onset is, by definition, very young, and children diagnosed as autistic can exhibit varying symptoms and degrees of severity of the disorder. This is also true for the course of the children's development. While the disorder is considered chronic, children with autism will show different patterns of development and improvement of symptomatology (DeMyer, 1979). Several authors have presented and reviewed evidence that suggests that between two thirds and three quarters of the autistic population have a poor prognosis, in that they will not become socially and vocationally independent (DeMyer, 1979; Lotter, 1978). However, Lotter (1978), in his review of follow-up and outcome studies, points out that the range of outcomes is quite wide and variable. Also, methodological and procedural differences between studies makes it somewhat difficult to come up with clear conclusions.

A large variable in this area is treatment (Koegel & Dunlap, 1981). Many follow-up studies compare children who have received varying amounts and types of therapies, making it difficult to ascertain their contribution to the children's current functioning. There is not a great deal of information on the progress children can make if they are involved in long-term intensive treatment programs. For example, Lovaas, Koegel, Simmons, and Long (1973) presented follow-up data on 20 children who had been treated with behavioral procedures for one or more years. Their results demonstrated that children who were placed in nontreatment environments following therapy regressed to pretreatment levels, while children who were placed with their parents (who had been trained to continue therapy procedures) maintained or increased their gains. This finding suggests that with long-term, thorough treatment and education the prognosis for many of these children could perhaps be greatly improved.

Research in this area is progressing rapidly, such that previously "incurable" aspects of the disorder are one by one falling subject to remediation. As such, a child who may appear severely incapacitated today may be extremely treatable tomorrow. Because of this rapidly advancing progress through research, we feel it is best to emphasize the course of progress of the disorder when subjected to treatment and analysis, rather than to focus on static aspects that do not receive treatment.

CONCEPTUALIZATION

The etiology of autism has not been discovered at this point. While a great deal of research supports theories concerning an underlying neurological basis of the disorder (DeMyer, 1979; Rutter & Schopler, 1978; Wetherby, et al., 1981), the exact nature of the dysfunction is as yet unknown. Wetherby, et at. (1981) reviewed and presented evidence suggesting that a primary or secondary cortical impairment could be responsible, with possible involvement of auditory brainstem nuclei.

DeMyer (1979) suggested that the nature of the brain dysfunction is probably static, with an initial traumatic event resulting in the death or maldevelopment of brain cells. However, the brain is still capable of anatomic growth. As mentioned previously, the research by Wetherby, et al. (1981) demonstrated improvements in measurements of central auditory function as a result of treatment and/or brain cell development, suggesting an interaction of neural plasticity and treatment variables. Specific studies concerning neurological, electrophysiological, and biochemical variables are thoroughly reviewed in Ritvo, Freeman, Ornitz, and Tanguay (1976), and Rutter and Schopler (1978), as well as the literature cited above.

In relation to etiology, a number of researchers and authors have hypothesized possible genetic predispositions and influences (DeMyer, 1979; Folstein & Rutter, 1978; Spence, 1976). It is unclear whether a genetic factor alone is sufficient to cause the disorder or what the factor might be. Research has shown that a variety of disorders, such as congenital rubella, meningitis, and encephalitis, can be involved as predisposing influences (American Psychiatric Association, 1980; Folstein & Rutter, 1978). The interaction of such environmental and genetic influences remains a question, in terms of how they might each contribute to the disorder. More research is needed to answer these questions.

In the early stages of the identification and conceptualization of autism as a distinct disorder, emphasis was placed on a psychogenic model of etiology, with the parents of the children being characterized as cold and rejecting, thus causing their children's aberrant behavior (Bettelheim, 1967; Kanner, 1943). This type of thinking was very prevalent through the 1960s and continues even now to some extent. However, a great deal of research has demonstrated that parents of autistic children *do not* differ from parents of normal children in terms of demonstrating more psychopathology, less warmth, or more abnormal patterns of interaction with their children (Cantwell, Baker, & Rutter, 1978;

DeMyer, 1979; Koegel, Schreibman, O'Neill, & Burke, 1983; Schopler & Reichler, 1971). In fact, parents are now often integrated into the treatment program for their child—an approach which will be further discussed in a later section.

As discussed above, research to date has failed to specifically delineate causative variables in autism. This has led those who are trying to develop effective treatments to focus on manipulating environmental variables to eliminate inappropriate behavior and teach those that are more appropriate. This type of approach characterizes those who have utilized a behavior analysis and modification approach to understanding and treating autism (Koegel, Rincover, & Egel, 1982; Lovaas, 1977; Lovaas, Schreibman, & Koegel, 1974; Schreibman & Koegel, 1981). Such a behavior analytic approach emphasizes the careful assessment of behavioral variables prior to and throughout treatment. This type of assessment approach as applied to the treatment of autism is discussed in the next section.

BEHAVIORAL ASSESSMENT

As noted above, there is considerable heterogeneity among children who are diagnosed autistic. As a result, many behaviorally oriented researchers have begun to focus on more functional assessments of individual behaviors exhibited by the children, even if a particular behavior under question is not present in all autistic children and whether or not the behavior is also exhibited by other children who are not diagnosed autistic. Behavioral assessment differs from traditional assessment in three important ways (Johnson & Koegel, 1982).

First, each child receives an individual assessment based on the specific behaviors that the child exhibits, rather than as grouped (classified) with many children exhibiting the highly variable characteristics of the syndrome of autism. Second, the assessment of specific behaviors and their controlling variables suggests specific and empirical directions in treatment and allows continuous evaluation of treatment effectiveness. Finally, the behavioral assessment allows prognostic inferences based on the empirically determined treatment methods; that is, when the variables controlling a behavior are known, the prognosis is good. For behaviors for which controlling variables are undefined, the prognosis is more guarded (Schreibman & Koegel, 1981). The detailed procedures used in behavioral assessment are explained below.

Defining Target Behaviors

Every response identified for treatment must be operationally defined, including topography of the response, its relative frequency of occurrence, its duration, and its occasion for occurrence.

Measurement

The test of an adequate definition is whether or not it facilitates the reliable and valid measurement of the behavior in question. Accurate measurement serves to quantify the initial severity of the target behavior and to allow daily evaluation of teaching procedures and effectiveness. Discrete events, such as isolated vocalizations or instances of eye contact, can be tallied to provide a frequency count. Behaviors such as self-stimulation or appropriate play, which occur intermittently, can be quantified on an interval or time-sampling basis. Other measurement procedures, including trial-by-trial recordings and measurement of permanent products, can also be used to quantify child improvement during treatment programs.

The integrity of the behavioral definition should be clearly established by assessing the reliability of the recording procedures. That is, two observers using the same behavioral definition should be able to independently measure the same behavior at the same time with a high degree of agreement.

Designing a Treatment Intervention

Following the reliable definition and measurement of the child's responding, the therapist is left with a relatively specific and detailed inventory of the child's target behaviors. This inventory describes the child in terms of a conglomeration of the individual behaviors exhibited and allows for a very individualized approach to treatment development and evaluation. Hence, the heterogeneity of the autistic population presents a lesser problem than it does with traditional assessment because, with a behavioral assessment, every child has an individual assessment of problem areas and needs. In this manner, behavioral assessment leads directly into individualized treatment development.

Use of Previous Research. Once target behaviors are selected, defined, and measured, the therapist proceeds to determine the environmental conditions supporting the behavior and then to manipulate the environment to alter the behavior in the desired direction (Schreibman & Koegel, 1981). The first step in this procedure often involves a literature search since many difficult behaviors have already been extensively studied. For example, much is known about self-destructive behavior and the variables that control it (Carr, 1977). In such cases, treatment programs that have already been developed can be utilized.

Isolating Controlling Variables. If, however, the literature has not isolated the variables or if more than one variable may influence the child's responses, the therapist may want to attempt to isolate specific controlling variables. This typically involves a systematic examination of the events immediately preceding and following problem behaviors. For example, it might be found that the child is being reinforced by attention to inappropriate behavior. Or, it might be suspected that one type of instruction is more effective than another instruction for a particular child (cf. Koegel, Dunlap, Richman, & Dyer, 1981). In any case, as environmental influences on an increasing variety of behaviors are understood, those behaviors that have similar controlling variables may be grouped into functional units. Treatment can then be applied to all the behaviors of that group, resulting in the modification of large aspects of the child's functioning in reduced periods of time.

Assessment in the Home, School, and Community. Through the processes of parental interview and direct observation of the child in his/her home, school, future classroom, or any other location, a therapist will be able to assess the environmental demands placed on the child currently and those that will be present in the future. A functional, chronological age-appropriate type of skill delineation can be facilitated by placing the handicapped individual in the future environment and defining and measuring the exact behaviors needed to facilitate independent functioning. For example, an important aspect of independent community function is the ability to secure appropriate transportation. By accompanying the student on a bus ride, the therapist can carry out an analysis such as that just described. The variety of natural environments in which the activity will occur might include trips to the grocery store, the record store, the library, a job, etc. The subenvironments in which the student will be required to function will include the bus stop, the entrance door, the fare box, the aisles, the seated or standing position on the bus, and the rear or front exit door. The activities required in each subenvironment can then be easily delineated. For instance, at the bus stop, the student should be able to locate the bus stop, sit or stand quietly awaiting the bus, and should choose the bus that will take him/her to the destination. At the fare box, the student should greet the bus driver, ask how much the fare is, if necessary, and count out the correct amount and deposit it. At each step in the process, the component, requisite activities will become clear. Each of these activities will require specific skills, some more advanced than others. The exact skills that the student will need to learn will be evident by his/her baseline or untreated responding in each subenvironment.

An example of the use of current functioning abilities and deficits in the determination of treatment programs has been provided by Russo and Koegel (1977). In this study, an autistic child's normal public school educational placement was in jeopardy because of her maladaptive and inappropriate behaviors. The experimenters assessed the target behaviors in terms of what behaviors were necessary for that child to function productively and to remain in that classroom. The three sets of behaviors targeted for the performance of appropriate activities in the classroom were increased social interaction, decreased self-stimulation, and increased verbal response to the teacher's questions and instructions. The activities, including group and individual working, story time, and peer playtime, were similar to those in any kindergarten class. The design and implementation of treatment programs utilized token reinforcement to influence the target behaviors in the desired direction. The important consideration is that the evaluation of the child took place in the actual environment and situation in which she needed to develop appropriate functioning.

In summary, Johnson and Koegel (1982) consider the important questions when determining target behaviors to be: (a) Can learning situations be tailored to increase the chances of the behavior or concept being applied by the child to the natural environments? (b) Will this target behavior help the child fit in with age-appropriate peers? (c) Will this behavior, skill, or concept promote age-appropriate, independent functioning?

Differential Diagnosis with Respect to Behavioral Assessment

As might be inferred from the above discussion, when one conducts a behavioral assessment, differentiation of autism from disorders such as mental retardation, schizophrenia, etc. becomes much less important. For example, one could eliminate self-injurious behavior in much the same manner, regardless of whether the child was or was not diagnosed autistic. In a behavioral assessment, the point of primary importance is the identification of the variables controlling any of the abnormal behavior patterns and then changing these variables to influence the behavior patterns. This approach cuts across traditional diagnostic boundaries, making the behavioral approach to treatment applicable across a very broad range of traditional diagnostic categories.

TREATMENT

A large number of theories have been proposed concerning the cause and development of autistic behavior. In turn, these have led to a large number of treatment approaches aimed at alleviating the disorder. Presently, the majority of these treatment approaches can be grouped into three major categories: (1) the psychoanalytically based approach; (2) programs based on sensory-deficit models; and (3) the behavior analysis and modification approach, discussed previously (Egel, Koegel, & Schreibman, 1980). These approaches have been discussed in detail by Egel, et al. (1980) and will be presented briefly here.

As discussed in the section on family patterns, early psychodynamically oriented clinicians hypothesized that the autistic child's behavior was caused by the pathology of the parents (Bettelheim, 1967). Treatment is aimed at developing the child's self-concept and eliminating inappropriate behavior by encouraging the child to engage in any behavior they want to in order to express their autonomy. Exposure to such a nondemanding environment lessens the child's fear and need to display inappropriate defensive behaviors.

This approach has been criticized for a number of reasons. As mentioned above, there is no real evidence that parents of autistic children cause their children's disorder. The main reports of success with this approach have been mainly subjective evaluations, with a lack of empirical evaluation and specific treatment descriptions. Also, empirical studies have shown the psychoanalytic approach produces poorer results than structured, educational approaches (Egel, et al., 1980).

Other researchers have proposed theories regarding deficiencies in perceptual and sensory processing and integration (Ornitz & Ritvo, 1968). This approach is related to the neurological theories, in that problems with certain structures (such as the reticular formation), which deal with sensory input and stimulation, are hypothesized. Such theories are used to explain deficits in attention and such symptoms as self-stimulatory behavior.

Treatment programs based on this approach have emphasized a variety of techniques, such as an initial emphasis on pleasurable, gratifying sensory experiences, graduated exposure to sensory input and stimulation, and the use of tasks to develop awareness of body coordination. The research in this area has been equivocal, with different studies confirming different aspects of the theory. As with the psychoanalytic approach, there is a lack of specifically described and empirically evaluated treatment programs, thus making evaluation difficult.

In contrast to the above approaches, the behavior analysis and modification paradigm has not posited specific, underlying causes of the disorder, but has focused instead on developing treatment approaches that strengthen or weaken behaviors through environmental manipulations. As discussed above, programs using this approach, regardless of the behaviors targeted, have a number of characteristics in common, such as careful operational definitions, objective measurements of observable behaviors, and manipulations of antecedent and consequent variables to produce positive behavior change. Many of the techniques listed below are common in a behavioral treatment program and are described in some detail in the case history portion of this chapter.

Oftentimes, the initial focus is on reducing disruptive and maladaptive behaviors (tantrums, self-stimulatory and self-injurious behavior, etc.), which can interfere with learning. A variety of procedures have been developed to control these behaviors, such as time-out (Bostow & Bailey, 1969; Solnick, Rincover, & Peterson, 1977), overcorrection (Foxx & Azrin, 1973), paced instruction (Plummer, Baer, & LeBlanc, 1977), and extinction and the use of punishment (Lovaas & Simmons, 1969; Rincover, Cook, Peoples, & Packard, 1979). While such behaviors are being suppressed, work is begun also on teaching new behaviors and stimulus functions. This is usually first carried out in a structured situation to enhance the development of initial learning and control. Teaching interactions are structured, involving the use of clear instruction, prompts (if needed), and functional reinforcers and punishers (Schreibman & Koegel, 1981). The use and characteristics of such discrete trial techniques have been discussed in detail by Koegel, Egel, and Dunlap (1980), Koegel, et al. (1982), Koegel, Russo, and Rincover (1977), Lovaas (1977), and others. Through techniques such as shaping and chaining (Schreibman & Koegel, 1981), discrete trials can be used to teach a great variety of behaviors, some of them quite complex, such as functional speech (Lovaas, 1977).

The behavior analysis approach, in contrast to the psychoanalytic and sensory-deficit models, has the support of a great deal of empirical research documenting its effectiveness. The emphasis on careful behavioral definitions and descriptions of treatment procedures also allows for the replication and use of the techniques with children in a variety of settings and locales, as discussed in the assessment section.

While such treatment has been shown to be effective, there are some drawbacks to the approach. For example, the treatment can be expensive, requiring quite a bit of one-to-one therapy with trained clinicians, particularly in the early stages (although many autistic children can eventually be taught in groups, as shown by Koegel and Rincover, 1974). For this reason, ways of maximizing the efficiency of therapy are important. The use of parents as therapists has been a major advance along these lines. The study described above by Lovaas, et al. (1973) was one of the first demonstrations of the utility of parents in carrying out treatment programs with their children.

Since then, a number of investigations have presented empirically based procedures for training parents (Koegel, Glahn, & Nieminen, 1978). The efficiency of the approach was illustrated by a study described by Koegel, Schreibman, Britten, Burke, & O'Neill (1982). Two groups of families were assigned to either a parent training or clinic treatment program for one year. A large variety of measures, including paper and pencil measures of the children's social functioning as well as direct observational measures of behavior in clinic and home settings, were taken prior to, throughout, and following treatment. Essentially, the results demonstrated that equal initial gains and, in some areas, more durable gains were obtained with 25 to 50 hours of parent training, as opposed to 225 hours of direct clinic treatment. In addition to these direct results, further work in our experimental clinics has investigated other positive collateral effects of parent training, such as a greater amount of leisure time for families involved (Burke, 1982; Koegel, Schreibman, Johnson, O'Neill, & Dunlap, in press).

In addition, research has demonstrated the feasibility of training siblings of autistic children to utilize behavioral teaching procedures (Schreibman, O'Neill, & Koegel, 1983). This has the potential to further enhance treatment gains. The incorporation of parents and other family members in the children's treatment is fast becoming the rule, rather than the exception, and promises to continue to be a highly useful approach to minimizing the cost and maximizing the efficiency of therapy for autistic children.

Another potential avenue towards more efficient treatment programs involves the targeting and modification of global, or pivotal, response classes in the children's behavior (Lovaas, et al., 1973). This involves modifying particular behaviors or responses in the children's repertoire that affect large areas of their responding. For example, many autistic children display stimulus over-selectivity, a tendency to respond to only a very restricted portion of the stimuli in their environment, which can greatly hinder their learning (Lovaas, Schreibman, Koegel, & Rehm, 1971; Lovaas, Koegel, & Schreibman, 1979). Research has demonstrated that, with training, autistic children can learn to respond on the basis of multiple cues (Koegel & Schreibman, 1977). This would help them to be able to respond to and learn from their environment in a more normal manner, which could affect a large number of behaviors, such as language and social behavior. This could produce widespread changes with limited intervention.

Motivation is another pivotal response class that has been discussed in the literature (Dunlap, 1984; Dunlap & Egel, 1982; Dunlap & Koegel, 1980; Koegel & Egel, 1979). A variety of methods for increasing and maintaining the children's responding in learning situations have been developed, including prompting correct task completion (Koegel & Egel, 1979) and systematically varying antecedent and consequent stimuli (Dunlap & Egel, 1982). The establishment of high levels of motivation, as evidenced by high rates of responses and response attempts, would be very adaptive in helping the children get the most benefit from learning situations. High rates of responding would allow the children to come into maximal contact with environmental contingencies that could help establish and maintain their behavior. The continued investigation of such pivotal response classes could greatly enhance the effectiveness of behavioral treatments in the future.

The basics of behavioral approaches to treatment have been presented, along with issues relating to their implementation. Some clinical considerations concerning their application will be discussed next.

Clinical Considerations: Generalization

When one conducts treatment with behavior modification, one is taking advantage of the human organism's incredible capacity to adapt to the environment by learning. Thus, when the therapist systematically teaches a new behavior by manipulating environmental conditions, the environmental contingencies become obvious, resulting in at least two major effects: (1) learning is greatly facilitated, with the acquisition of new behaviors occurring very rapidly, and (2) the organism easily discriminates the treatment contingencies, thereby typically learning the new behavior(s) only under those treatment conditions and not generalizing the new skill to other circumstances. Thus, when a therapist conducts behavior modification with autistic children, it is important to specifically plan for the following types of generalization:

1. One should plan for stimulus generalization, or the performance of the behavior in settings outside of the treatment environment. For example, Rin-

cover & Koegel (1975) demonstrated that stimulus generalization by autistic children can be enhanced if similar cues are present in both training and extra-therapy environments. However, if one conducts the initial assessment in the target environment (as suggested in the assessment sections above) or if one conducts treatment in the target environment, as in parent training, then it is probable that these problems would be greatly reduced.

2. Response generalization also needs to be planned. Thus, it is important to insure that the specific behaviors being taught during treatment are relevant and directly related to the target objective. For example, if one teaches a child to count blocks arranged in a row on a table in a clinic setting, it is not very likely that the child will generalize this skill to calculating the amount of money needed to purchase a comic book in a store. In other words, the specific target behaviors being taught need to be planned in relation to the final objectives the child needs to attain for successful functioning in the natural environment.

3. Generalization over time (or maintenance) is also important. Much research now has shown that if a target behavior is taught under very structured, artificial conditions, then it is not likely to maintain after the child is discharged from treatment. Therefore, variables known to influence maintenance need to be manipulated. Thin schedules of reinforcement in treatment settings (cf. Koegel, Egel, and Williams, 1980; Koegel & Rincover, 1977) and the use of natural reinforcers (cf. Williams, Koegel, & Egel, 1981) that are likely to be present in the final target environments have been suggested to be extremely important in this regard.

A great deal of research in these areas has been reviewed and possible solutions to such problems have been presented by Stokes & Baer (1977).

CASE HISTORY

Preface

As the label implies, a pervasive developmental disorder such as autism requires a comprehensive treatment program directed at the remediation of diverse behavioral deficiencies and excesses. Behavioral objectives typically include the establishment of complex communication, social, and community living skills, as well as the elimination of bizarre, anti-interactive responses such as stereotypies and abnormal emotional behaviors. For these reasons, the case to be described in the following pages represents a complex and diverse treatment process directed at so comprehensive a collection of behaviors that it is not unreasonable to view the treatment of autism as the habilitation of a person, rather than an intervention which targets a limited set of behaviors.

Pervasive developmental disorders is a heterogenous category. It is impossible to identify any one case that is totally representative. The case we have selected, however, may be viewed as typical in many respects. The boy entered treatment with a firm diagnosis of autism from two major diagnostic centers. He presented neither an extremely negative nor an overwhelmingly positive set of prognostic indicators. We have selected his case for illustration because his is among the most representative available and because our continuing involvement over a period of more than two years permits a detailed exposition of treatment efforts and progress.

While the boy's behaviors may be common as far as the syndrome of autism is concerned, the overall intervention to be described is probably less typical in certain respects. First, the vast majority of treatment efforts were provided without cost for the family due to their participation in our externally funded experimental clinic and training programs and due to the generosity and concern of many individuals and agencies in the Santa Barbara community. Second, many of the interventions were experimental in nature and represented efforts to forge new ground in the efficiency and effectiveness of therapeutic endeavors. The fact that several of the interventions were conducted in the context of research meant that some of the programs entailed procedures that transcended standard clinical practice and that, at times, the resources provided for assessment and evaluation exceeded those that are normally available.

One final note of preface is in order. This case description was written from the perspective of our clinical research team at the University of California at Santa Barbara and consists of information primarily derived from our own notes, reports, data, programs, and recollections. Thus, it may appear to some readers as if the boy's treatment and progress was attributable to our efforts alone. This was not the case. Many concerned service providers contributed to various aspects of intervention, including some of the programs described below and areas that are not described in detail. While these service providers will remain nameless, we would like to acknowledge the special efforts of certain educators, social service workers, and volunteers. Above all, the boy's mother and father have been instrumental in all aspects of treatment. They have shouldered the considerable burden of identifying appropriate services and, in many instances, of actually implementing the treatment programs. In short, the community-based treatment of pervasive developmental disorders requires contributions from a multiplicity of concerned service providers. It would be inappropriate to proceed with this case description without explicit recognition of this important fact.

Intake

Ernie (a pseudonym) was first seen at our clinic when he was four years and four months of age. An only child, his parents had recently moved to the Santa Barbara area in order to be in the immediate vicinity of specialized services for pervasive developmental disorders. Only a few months prior to the family's relocation, Ernie had received a firm diagnosis of autism from one of the country's foremost centers for assessment and diagnosis of childhood disorders.

The specialists at the diagnostic center had recommended that the parents seek early, behaviorally oriented intervention and had specifically indicated our program at the University of California at Santa Barbara.

Although Ernie's birth was a complicated affair due to a medical involvement of his mother and although his birth was premature, there was no evidence that his developmental disability was in any way a function of birth trauma. There has been no hard sign of neurological impairment. Ernie's parents did not detect any particular disorder until he was about 15 months old when a delay in the development of eye gaze and other attending responses became apparent. By the age of two years, Ernie's failure to acquire speech and his excessive tantrums were sources of major concern. At this time, Ernie's parents began to actively seek specialized diagnostic and treatment services. Autism was first suggested as a diagnosis when he was 30 months old, although confirmation was not provided until shortly after Ernie turned three. The next year consisted largely of a search for appropriate services.

When we first met Ernie and his family, both parents were in their early 30s. Ernie's father was slowly recuperating from a serious physical incapacitation, and his mother, a former professional dancer, was becoming weakened due to a progressive kidney ailment. Despite these handicaps, both parents were completely devoted to the well-being of their son and readily expressed their affection and love for him. The family unit was (and remains) cohesive and supportive, in spite of the major difficulties that occur in the process of raising a severely handicapped child.

Ernie's first appearance at our clinic occurred shortly after the family's move to Santa Barbara when an opening developed, due to an expansion of our clinic capabilities. Ernie was brought to the clinic by both of his parents. Our first meeting was conducted in the context of a preadmission intake interview, during which the parents described the boy's developmental history, his current behaviors (abilities and disabilities), and their short and long-term plans and aspirations. During this meeting, our staff closely observed Ernie's behavior as he was presented with a variety of toys and materials, as he was asked questions and given instructions, and as he was provided opportunities to interact with his parents and with a number of other individuals.

Our observations of Ernie's behavior during this first meeting, and from a series of preintervention videotapes recorded shortly following intake, confirmed a clear diagnosis of autism according to DSM-III criteria. In addition to onset prior to 30 months of age and evidence of a general and uneven developmental disturbance, a vast majority of characteristic behavioral symptoms were in evidence.

First, Ernie's language development was profoundly delayed. Although he used a number of recognizable words, these verbalizations were rarely appropriate to the social context and were most commonly immediate or delayed echoes. Almost all of his context-appropriate words were simple responses to common questions (e.g., "What is your name?") that his mother had taught him at home.

He was also capable of labeling approximately 40 to 50 common objects such as a chair and an apple. Most often, he would repeat the question (e.g., "What is this?") or portions of the question without showing evidence that a different sort of reply was desired. His most frequent type of speech involved repetitive echoes of jingles that he had overheard from the television. For example, Ernie was often observed to sit in a corner flapping his hands and musically intoning, "Da da, da da . . . Superman." Although he was capable of imitating parts of adult speech, he almost never did so. His spontaneous, socially appropriate speech was almost nonexistent, although he would, on rare occasions, climb onto his mother's lap and request "tickle" while giggling.

Ernie's language comprehension at intake was more advanced than his verbal expression. He was able to follow a number of simple requests (e.g., "stand up," "show me your hands") and identify particular objects from an assortment when asked, for example, "Where is the crayon?" During our first observations, Ernie's inconsistent responding and preoccupation with self-directed stimulation made it somewhat difficult to obtain a completely reliable assessment of his language comprehension; however, it was nevertheless apparent that he was able to respond to much more than he could express. It was also apparent that he displayed a number of behaviors that interfered with his responsivity to communicative interaction.

Ernie's social development was marked by an absence of attention to most other people; however, in contrast to many other autistic children, he also appeared to enjoy contact with some individuals, especially his parents. He smiled when his mother cuddled him and, at times, approached her for affection. Still, he spent most of his time away from interaction, instead preferring solitary and typically stereotypic activities. He never initiated social interactions with other children or with adults he was not familiar with. While he did not ordinarily show great resistance to interaction with unfamiliar people, he would often engage in loud and violent tantrums if those people placed demands or restrictions on his behavior. For example, if an unfamiliar clinician asked him to respond to a series of test instructions, he might cry loudly and persistently until he was permitted to leave the test situation.

Our observations, which were consistent with parental reports, indicated that Ernie's most common activity was to engage in stereotypic and seemingly self-stimulatory behavior. His most frequent stereotypies included arm flapping, strumming a stick with his fingers, rocking, and repetitively singing television jingles. These responses were typically accompanied by a state of unresponsiveness to other stimuli. For example, while engaged in such behaviors, he rarely acknowledged instructions and had to be physically prompted to respond. At such time, he appeared to be deaf, although his hearing on other occasions was clearly within normal limits.

Unlike some other autistic children, Ernie did not display any serious self-injurious or aggressive behaviors. He did display loud tantrums, usually when a demand was placed upon him or occasionally when he was asked to deviate from a familiar routine, such as when he was asked to taste an unfamiliar food.

Physically, Ernie was a very attractive, well-groomed boy. He had none of the physical deformities characteristic of some forms of retardation. His fine and gross motor movements were coordinated, although he lacked some of the skills at throwing balls and drawing pictures that are ordinarily acquired by children who regularly practice such activities. He was beginning to use eating utensils and to put on some articles of clothing, but he was not toilet trained nor had he acquired any other self-care skills. On the Vineland Social Maturity Scale, Ernie's overall level of functioning prior to our intervention was estimated to be slightly below that of a typical three-year-old.

In short, at intake Ernie displayed most of the common characteristics of autism. His language and social development were severely delayed, he displayed violent tantrums and frequent self-stimulation, and his behavior was characterized by an overall lack of responsivity to environmental events. Although his symptoms clearly indicated a diagnosis of autism, this case also presented signs that suggested a probability that some relatively rapid progress could be achieved as a result of intervention. Among the positive indications were the presence of some speech that was controlled by appropriate stimuli, the suggestion that some social stimulation appeared to be reinforcing, and the fact that Ernie's parents were committed and available to contribute to his habilitation.

Clinical Assessment

Ernie was enrolled in a half-day preschool program for handicapped children when he began treatment at our clinic. Therefore, initial clinic sessions were scheduled for three afternoons per week with 90 minutes per session. The first few sessions were devoted to the completion of an assessment designed to identify initial target behaviors and potential reinforcers. The process by which such a behavioral assessment is conducted has been described in an earlier section of this chapter. Thus, the present description will be limited to the details that were most central to Ernie's treatment. It must also be recognized that the process of assessment and analysis is, by necessity, ongoing. A continuous reevaluation of treatment goals, reinforcers, and programs is a hallmark of behavioral intervention and is probably a particularly important component when addressing as complex and pervasive a disorder as autism.

In the case of Ernie, we decided to conduct our initial assessments and intervention within the confines of our clinic facilities in order to maximize control of the environment and, thus, hasten the establishment of stimulus control over behavior. It was decided, however, that the bulk of intervention would be rapidly transferred to settings in the natural environment.

In order to identify potential reinforcers for use in clinic sessions, we constructed a list of stimuli in the following manner. First, we asked Ernie's parents to carefully specify the things he most preferred to do at home. During this interview, we sought in particular to identify those activities that he actually spent a good deal of time with. Second, we directly observed Ernie during free-play situations in several contexts and with a wide variety of stimuli, ranging from toys to foodstuffs. From these sources, we were able to build a list of many potential reinforcers. Among the stimuli or activities that seemed to have the strongest potential were pictures or objects associated with the super-heroes, especially Superman; recordings of certain children's songs; fruit juice and soft drinks; and mild tickling and jostling. During the first two clinic sessions, we tested these stimuli and found that each appeared to be reinforcing for certain behaviors because Ernie typically repeated the behavior that was immediately followed by a presentation of the stimulus.

Our identification of initial target behaviors involved a similar process (i.e., discussion with parents and direct observation) and was also facilitated by our clinical experience and by reports from the literature (e.g., Koegel & Covert, 1972; Lovaas, 1977). These sources indicated that learning would be extremely difficult if we did not begin by gaining control over Ernie's self-stimulation and disruptive behavior. For the same reasons, we determined to establish a high rate of compliance and responsive performance, so that we could anticipate an attempt to succeed on virtually every clinic trial. In short, our initial objectives were to establish instructional control in the clinic sessions. Such instructional control would permit an efficient instruction in speech and language, pre-academic skills, and other areas. In addition, such control would be a logical prerequisite for the later transfer of treatment programs to natural environment settings, such as Ernie's home and classroom.

Establishing Instructional Control

Ernie's treatment began in a small room in our clinic, in the Speech and Hearing Center at UCSB. Ernie sat in a chair facing a clinician from our staff. Also present in the room was a student data recorder, who was also available to provide physical guidance if necessary. In Ernie's case, it was never necessary for two clinicians to provide treatment simultaneously (although with some lower functioning or extremely disruptive children, it has sometimes been an advantage for two clinicians to work together during the early stages of inter-vention). A variety of instructional materials and reinforcers were placed on a nearby table for ready access by the clinician. After the first two treatment sessions, a second table was placed between Ernie and his clinician on which instructional materials were presented. Instructional periods lasted about 15 minutes, with breaks of 5 to 10 minutes separating each period.

The first treatment session was designed to establish control over very basic attending responses. Using simple requests (e.g., "Put your hands in your lap"), Ernie was instructed to sit quietly and to look at the clinician. When he complied with these instructions, he was given praise (e.g., "Good job!", "That's right") and a brief presentation of one of the reinforcers. The rein-forcers were varied from trial to trial (Egel, 1982) and were initially presented on a CRF schedule. As compliance increased, the schedule of reinforcement was gradually thinned, although praise continued to be provided for at least one out of every three successful occurrences. When Ernie did not respond correctly to the instruction, the clinician said "No" and quickly repeated the request. If Ernie failed on three consecutive trials, the clinician manually prompted compliance. If he engaged in self-stimulatory behavior (e.g., hand flapping, repetitive singing), he was admonished with a stern No! and was given immediate manual guidance to resume the desired posture.

Soon after initiation of these treatment procedures, Ernie began to tantrum by screaming and flailing his arms. As our earlier observations had suggested that such disruptions appeared to be reinforced by escape from demanding situations (cf. Carr, Newsom & Binkoff, 1980), the clinician treated the tantrum with paced instructions (Plummer, et al., 1977), a procedure that serves to put escape responses on extinction. The clinician ignored the tantrum and continued to

FIGURE 13–1A

Here, Ernie is pictured in a very early stage of clinic treatment. The clinician is prompting Ernie to sit quietly with his hands in his lap (Figure 13–1A). In a latter session (Figure 13–1B), full attention has been established.

FIGURE 13-1B

present instructions while manually prompting compliance. After approximately two minutes, the tantrum subsided, and the instruction progressed. Additional tantrums occurred, but each was of shorter duration, and soon they declined so that fewer than one occurred per session.

As soon as the basic attending posture was established (within 15 minutes), a variety of other instructions was introduced. At this early stage, these were also responses that were strongly suspected of being within Ernie's repertoire. They included requests for nonverbal imitation (e.g., "Do this" followed by a modelled behavior), verbal imitation (e.g., "Say, 'This is a ball'"), and compliance with simple commands (e.g., "Stand up," "Touch your head"). These instructions were presented in a random order with no more than three instructions for a particular task presented in succession (Dunlap & Koegel, 1980). This varied task format was employed to alleviate boredom and to encourage responsivity to specific task requirements. During these first few sessions, instruction was restricted to very simple activities that could be readily accomplished. If Ernie failed on a specific task for more than five trials in a row (while he was successful on the other tasks), the task was put aside until a later session.

After two treatment sessions, Ernie responded correctly on over 90 percent of the trials and tantrummed very infrequently. Therefore, during the third session, a variety of new (or acquisition) tasks were introduced. These included increasingly complex imitation (e.g., repeating a series of rhythmic taps on the table), two- and three-part instructions (e.g., "Touch your head, then your feet"), and identification of numerous objects (e.g., "Which is the screw-driver?"). At this point, the focus of treatment had changed subtly from the establishment of control to establishing control within a learning context. As this one-to-one clinic phase continued, Ernie's self-stimulation and disruptive behavior were rapidly reduced, and his ability to imitate, follow instructions, and identify common objects increased. We then began to focus more directly on developing appropriate speech and language.

Establishing Functional Speech and Language

Ernie began treatment with a small repertoire of functional communicative responses. He was able to say his first name upon request and could verbally label between 40 to 50 common objects. He also showed a large amount of delayed and, more significantly for treatment purposes, immediate echolalia. The presence of immediate echolalia meant that, during the earliest stages of treatment, he was able to mimic, in a parrot-like manner, the words uttered by his clinician. When a clinician would say, "This is a tennis shoe," Ernie would typically respond with the exact same statement. He would similarly reply to questions, such as "What is this?" or "Where do you live?" by repeating part or all of the question (e.g., "Where do you live?" or perhaps, just "live").

After the first few weeks of treatment, during which time Ernie's responsivity to instruction had been substantially elevated, it became clear that his verbal repertoire contained a number of qualities that augured well for future progress. First, his verbal responses, even though they were mainly echolalic, were reliable and distinct. On nearly every trial, Ernie would repeat with clear articulation what he had heard. Second, he rarely echoed those questions or requests for which he had previously been taught a more appropriate response. For example, he did not repeat "Stand up," "Look at me," or "What is your name?" Instead, he answered with the appropriate response. Another positive sign was that he seemed to learn these more appropriate behaviors very rapidly. For example, within only a few trials, he learned to "clap hands," and there-after, he did not echo that phrase.

Our initial objectives were to rapidly expand Ernie's vocabulary and, in so doing, reduce echolalia. In subsequent sessions, we provided instruction on structures for phrasing requests (e.g., "I want _____," "May I have _____?"), for describing actions (e.g., "The boy/girl/etc. is

_____"), and for physical stimuli (e.g., "This is a _____").
As these skills were developed, we introduced training on various abstractions
(e.g., prepositions, sequences), attributes (e.g., shapes, size), negation and
affirmation, and conversational conventions. The process of language instruction is, of course, complex and lengthy (and, for Ernie, is still continuing).
No attempt will be made here to detail the vast amount of programming involved. Rather, readers are referred to a number of helpful sources (Lovaas,
1977; Fay & Schuler, 1980). However, we would like to illustrate some of the
steps with the following vignettes.

Labeling Objects and Actions.   Ernie proved to be quite adept at acquiring
labels for common objects and actions. Within one month of clinic treatment he
had learned to reliably communicate with well over one hundred such labels.
The instruction made use of Ernie's echolalia in the following manner. In order
to teach the word "jumping" in an appropriate context, an assistant began to
jump up and down, while the clinician asked "What is she doing?" and immediately prompted in a distinct voice, "jumping." Ernie repeated "jumping" and
was praised for doing so. On subsequent trials, the volume and clarity of the
clinician's prompt ("jumping") was faded. Soon, Ernie was able to describe the
action of jumping up and down as "jumping" without any prompt at all. When
the label was reliably produced in the clinic room, the response was then
requested in different settings (e.g., in the hallway, outside the clinic building)
and by different trainers (e.g., the clinic supervisor) in order to assure generalization and appropriate stimulus control (cf. Rincover & Koegel, 1975). In
this manner, Ernie rapidly learned the names for a number of objects and
actions.

Providing Information.   As Ernie gained facility with labels, instruction began on information that is frequently sought in the natural environment. Ernie
was already able to give his first name upon request; however, he had not
learned to state his address, telephone number, age, or other details. Instruction
in this area was conducted in a manner very similar to the teaching of labels.
For example, he was first taught to recite his address (e.g., "1023 South Main
Street") and was then taught when to say it, (e.g., when asked "Where do you
live?" or "What is your address?"). With this _transfer of stimulus-control_
paradigm (from the clinician's model, which was echoed, to the appropriate
discriminative stimulus), Ernie learned his phone number, last name, and other
pertinent information.

  When target questions had very similar topographies, instruction proved
more difficult and time-consuming. For example, in order to respond correctly
to the questions "How are you?" and "How old are you?", Ernie had to reliably
detect the discriminative word "old." This instruction was accomplished by
exaggerating the distinctive feature of the discrimination. In establishing stimulus control over the response "four years old," the clinician asked "How _old_

are you?" by greatly emphasizing the key word, and prompting the correct response. These trials were interspersed with "How are you?" trials, and gradually, the distinctive prompt was de-emphasized. After many trials and a very systematic fading procedure, Ernie learned to regularly differentiate the questions. The fading procedure had to be partly replicated when additional clinicians presented the questions.

Basic Phrases and Sentence Structures. During the third month of treatment, sentence structures were added to labeling responses and request forms. Through imitation and chaining procedures, object labels were augmented with "This is a _____," "It's a _____," and other structures. Action labels were augmented with "The boy/girl/etc. is _____." Request forms included "I want a _____" and "May I have a _____." Initial training on object phrasing, for example, focused on a single structure, such as "This is a _____." As this structure began to be used with regularity, the alternative structures were introduced in order to avoid robotic responding. In subsequent training trials, any of the alternative structures were reinforced with equal enthusiasm.

Abstractions-Prepositions. Ernie's vocabulary, knowledge of sentence structures and responsivity to verbal stimuli quickly expanded such that, within a few months, he was well prepared to begin instruction on a variety of abstractions. Ernie was taught to distinguish between and express qualities and attributes of objects (e.g., color, shape, size, texture), to use pronouns (e.g., you, she, I) and to describe placements with prepositions (e.g., under, in, between, behind, with). As an example of instruction on such abstract concepts, let us look at the process by which Ernie was taught to distinguish "on" and "under". Initial training addressed the ability to distinguish the operations receptively. Using a variety of materials, instructions were given to place an object (e.g., a toy car) on or under another object (e.g., a table, a piece of paper). When he was successful, the clinician said, "That's right! Where is the (car)?" and Ernie was prompted to respond, "*on* the table". As the prompts were removed, Ernie began to reliably respond with correct placements. The clinician then began to intersperse trials with which the object was placed on or under and, without any other instruction, Ernie was asked to describe its location. The clinician placed the object either on or under another object and asked Ernie to express, "The (car) is on/under the (table)." These trials were repeated with a variety of stimuli, including the clinician and Ernie himself. For example, some trials contained questions such as "Where is my hand?" (reply: under the table) and "Where are you sitting?" (reply: on the chair). As Ernie gained competence with these and other prepositions, he was taken to other settings for continued instruction. On one occasion in the play yard directly outside of the clinic building, he correctly described a ball's location as "under the bush" and the fact that he was standing "on the bench." As he was lifted back to the pavement, he spontaneously stated that he was now "on the street," overgeneralizing a previously used term.

Need for Training in the Natural Environment

The first four months of our treatment programs for Ernie took place within the controlled environment of the UCSB clinic. With the exception of some transfer programming and generalization testing, instruction had been provided in the context of one-to-one interaction, with consistent access to powerful reinforcers and optimal stimulus arrangements. Ernie had made very rapid progress in the areas of compliance, attention and responsivity, and speech and language development. Although he still displayed a small amount of self-stimulation, he rarely tantrummed, and overall, he appeared to be much less autistic than when he entered our program. However, many of these positive effects were seen only in the clinic setting and in the presence of his treatment providers—a common problem as noted in previous sections of this chapter.

While his parents and other familiar contacts reported growth in Ernie's language at home and elsewhere, there was little change reported in other vital areas of functioning. He remained concompliant at home and continued to display tantrums and very high rates of self-stimulation in other community settings. He was not yet toilet trained and was not showing adequate gains in other self-care and community living skills.

The discrepancy between Ernie's performance and rate of learning in the clinic and elsewhere made it clear that a focus on training in the natural environment was becoming increasingly necessary. The instructional control that had been gained in the clinic provided a source of optimism regarding the potential success of such an orientation. Therefore, beginning with the fifth month of treatment, the emphasis of our intervention was directed at the development of adaptive behavior in natural community settings. While Ernie continued to be seen in our clinic once or twice per week, our efforts were increasingly focused on his behavior at home, in his school placements, and in other community-based locations.

Parent Training

As discussed previously, the training of parents to implement behavior modification programs with their children has been repeatedly demonstrated to be one of the most, if not *the* most, important components of intervention for developmentally disabled children (Lovaas, et al., 1973; Sanders & James, 1983). Without such training, generalization and maintenance of treatment gains are rarely observed, and intervention in the most relevant environments is rarely provided and is typically done so at great expense. Our project at the University of California, Santa Barbara, in collaboration with Dr. Laura Schreibman's program at Claremont McKenna College and the University of California, Santa Barbara, has been one of several centers for parent-training research across the country. The results of this research and the specific procedures involved have been reported in several recent publications (e.g., Koegel, et al., 1982; Koegel, et al., 1983). The following description of the training of Ernie's parents will not repeat these procedures in detail; however, interested readers are referred to the previously mentioned sources.

Although formal parent training in this case did not commence until the fifth month of treatment, this is not to imply an absence of parent involvement. From the beginning, Ernie's mother and father accompanied Ernie to his clinic appointments and usually observed the entire session through one-way windows, or, on occasion, by sitting in the treatment room. In addition, treatment programs were always designed in consultation with the parents, in regards both to target behaviors and procedures. Finally, the primary clinicians and supervisors had visited Ernie's home prior to intervention and, on several occasions, during the early months of treatment. Over this period of time, both parents had read articles, engaged in numerous conversations with clinic personnel, and had gained familiarity with the behavioral approach to developmental disorders.

Formal, hands-on training in behavior modification began immediately following the collection of videotaped assessments of the parents' interactions with their son. Assessments were conducted in the context of an instructional interaction and in the context of routine activities in the home. These assessments served to highlight the particular strengths of each parent's pretraining interaction as well as to shed light on the areas that would require some additional consideration.

The assessments revealed that both parents displayed many positive interactional behaviors. For example, both parents interacted with Ernie frequently, and both provided a large amount of praise and other reinforcers. The areas that were highlighted as particular targets for training were those that typically stand out in untrained individuals. Specifically, these areas included the delivery of clear instructions and the establishment and implementation of clear contingencies of reinforcement (Koegel, et al., 1978; Koegel, et al., 1977).

Training commenced with the presentation of an instructional videotape that displayed several examples of correct and incorrect use of behavioral techniques. This was followed by several sessions of practice with feedback, during which each parent sought to teach Ernie needed skills (e.g., shoe tying, identifying numerals) in the clinic environment. The feedback to the parents was specifically designed to teach correct usage of the discrete trial components, each of which has been identified as crucial to the instructional process. After a number of sessions, both parents were able to employ the discrete trial teaching procedures above 80 percent correct criterion and were similarly successful in teaching new skills to their son.

When criterion in the clinic-instructional context was achieved, training was transferred to the home. At this point, specific behavior problems (e.g., tantrums) and instructional targets (e.g., dressing) were identified, and the trainer began to serve as a consultant for the parents' planning and implementation of behavioral programs. Initially, the trainer provided frequent advice and corrections but quickly retreated to permit the parents autonomy and to develop confidence in their independent ability to plan and carry through interventions.

One of the first programs to be conducted by Ernie's parents involved the violent tantrums that Ernie displayed when his parents asked him to perform a behavior, such as turning the television set off. Previously, the tantrums would often result in the television staying on for a period of time or a different, but equally favored, activity being substituted. After training, the parents determined that a certain level of compliance was necessary and that having the TV off at a designated hour was not unreasonable. They further recognized that Ernie's tantrums might have been reinforced by postponing the end of TV or by the presentation of the substitute event. Therefore, they resolved to put the tantrums on an extinction schedule, to be certain that their instructions would be complied with, and to be sure that compliance would be reinforced. In this manner, with the support of the trainer-consultant, these instances of tantrums in the home were sharply reduced. Subsequent interventions, concerning both instructional and behavior management programs, were also successful.

Although parent training equipped Ernie's parents with additional skills needed to promote education and manage behavior and although Ernie's behavior was much improved as a function of his parents' behavioral interaction, it is important to recognize that not all of Ernie's behavior problems were immediately remediated. Ernie continued to display some stereotypic behaviors and tantrums, although at a much lower level. However, Ernie did learn to be much more cooperative, and as a function of his parents' instruction, he began to learn domestic living behaviors at a much more rapid pace. Consistent with results obtained from other families (Koegel, et al., 1983), Ernie's family routines and interactions have come to resemble much more closely those of families without handicapped children. An important effect of parent training is that community integration has become a much more feasible objective, due to behavioral improvements resulting from parental control and instruction. In Ernie's case, as well as in numerous others, we have observed that the improved relations are not always related to specifically planned interventions but may be more a function of the strengthened interactional techniques (including clear instruction and contingencies), which occur on a regular and ongoing basis and which are principal targets of thorough training in behavior modification procedures.

Self-Care: Toilet Training

The first systematic program that our UCSB staff implemented in Ernie's natural nonclinic surroundings, conducted prior to the completion of parent training, involved toilet training. Ernie had experienced no success in previous toilet training efforts and had worn diapers since birth. We had not attempted to conduct a toilet training program from our clinic operation because, in previous experience, we had found that rapid success with severely developmentally disordered children depended on establishing a consistent approach that accounted for the child's waking hours (Dunlap, Koegel, & Koegel, in press). After four months of clinic intervention, we were able to work with Ernie's parents and other care providers to create a comprehensive and consistent program for toilet training across Ernie's daily routine.

Although Ernie had never been toilet trained, he demonstrated a number of behaviors that may be considered prerequisite for efficient and thorough training. He was fully ambulatory, he could grasp and pull his pants up and down, and he was sufficiently verbal to be taught to tell people (e.g., school teachers) when he needed to use the bathroom.

Toilet training was initiated after each of Ernie's primary care providers (parents, teachers, clinicians, etc.) had been contacted and had agreed to implement the training procedures. The procedures included the following: (1) providing regular opportunities for Ernie to use the toilet, (2) rewarding Ernie for any successful elimination in the toilet, (3) implementing a positive practice contingency (Foxx & Azrin, 1973b) immediately following the detection of an accident (note: for many handicapped children, we have found that a signaling device is necessary for immediate detection; however, this was not needed in Ernie's case), and (4) periodically rewarding Ernie for having dry pants. In addition, a data sheet was prepared for Ernie to carry to each of his daily environments. For a detailed description and documentation of these procedures, interested readers are referred to Dunlap, et al. (1983).

In order to complete as much of the early training as possible in a well-controlled stable setting, the program was initiated on a Saturday morning in Ernie's home. Ernie's father and two of our clinic staff began the procedure by offering liquids and, after 10 minutes, prompting Ernie to walk to the toilet, pull his pants down, and sit. When nothing occurred after another 10 minutes, he was prompted to return to his chair and was offered more juice, water, and/or milk. After another 10 minutes, he was again prompted to use the toilet, and this time, he urinated a small amount in the bowl. He was praised with great enthusiasm, offered potato chips and more liquids, and was again prompted to return to his position on the chair. Soon, he urinated in his pants and was required to engage in the positive practice procedures. These procedures have been thoroughly described in the literature (Dunlap, et al., in press; Foxx & Azrin, 1973b) and involved requiring Ernie to repetitiously follow the correct toileting sequence. During the next four hours, Ernie had two more successes and several more accidents. During the fifth hour, he displayed his first self-initiated movement to the toilet and completion of the entire toileting sequence. At this point, he began to participate in a variety of activities around the house. After another self-initiated success, he wet his pants again. It appeared to his trainers that he was engaged in self-stimulatory hand flapping and forgot to control his bladder. He proceeded through the positive practice procedure and had no more accidents the rest of the day.

On Sunday, Ernie wet his pants once in the morning, was instructed through the positive practice procedure by his father, and had no more accidents and a number of self-initiated successes during the remainder of the morning and afternoon. Throughout the rest of the week, all of Ernie's care providers partic-ipated in the intervention as Ernie followed his normal routine and was self-initiating in every environment. As the data in Figure 13–2 illustrate, Ernie quickly acquired successful toilet skills in all of his daily environments.

With the completion of toilet training and the training of Ernie's parents, Ernie soon approached the normal range of functioning in the area of self-care. His parents were able to teach him most of the expected dressing, grooming, and eating behaviors such that, by the age of five, he was not notably deficient in these self-care areas. These gains were significant in that Ernie's parents, unlike the parents of some other developmentally delayed children, could ad-dress other areas of development rather than spending long hours with basic child-care activities and could feel much more free to expose Ernie to the experiences of societal integration. Not very long after toilet training was

FIGURE 13-2

Results of the toilet training program which was implemented throughout all of Ernie's daily environments. The toilet training procedures are described briefly in the text and in greater detail in Dunlap, Koegel, and Koegel, in press.

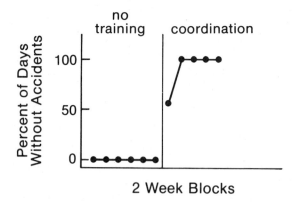

completed, Ernie spent his first night away from his parents at the home of a trusted friend.

Responsivity

At five and a half years of age, Ernie had been in treatment for nearly one year. He had shown substantial progress in most areas of functioning, including self-care, speech and language, and compliance. His disruptive behavior had been sharply reduced and, largely through his school activities, he had displayed an aptitude for number concepts and other preacademic behaviors. To many people with whom he came into contact, Ernie was regarded as a cute boy with a delightful smile and a number of engaging characteristics. With his increased language facility, Ernie had developed a pleasant singing voice and, although he was often shy with strangers, he could often be prompted to perform a popular song, such as the theme from "Annie." Like many children, he had come to adore several TV personalities, ranging from the Greatest American Hero to the Incredible Hulk. Overall, Ernie had rapidly overcome many of the profound deficiencies with which he had entered treatment. However, Ernie was still a long way from being normal. Despite his considerable repertoire of adaptive skills, in most environments Ernie continued to display an abnormal lack of responsivity to surrounding events. Frequently associated with increasingly subtle self-stimulatory behaviors (e.g., gazing, stereotypic humming), this tuning- or spacing-out served to disassociate him from many group activities, events of his classroom, and the social community in general.

At the request of his parents and advocates, Ernie's school placement had been moved from a preschool classroom for handicapped children to a community-based private school, which primarily served normally functioning children between the ages of four and six years old. The director and the staff of this school program were familiar with developmental disabilities and were extremely receptive to the objective of maximizing Ernie's educational integration. When the school's scheduling permitted individualized instruction, Ernie performed well, showing encouraging progress in primary reading, number concepts, and pencil manipulations. It was in classroom and outdoor group activities that Ernie's unresponsivity was particularly troublesome. Although a student aide from UCSB was often present to prompt responding in these group activities, when the aide withdrew or was not present in the immediate vicinity, Ernie typically failed to attend to group instructions or activities. Instead, he would usually hum a repetitive tune or silently tap a stick or other object within his grasp. It became obvious that this persistent lack of attention would endanger his continued placement in the integrated setting.

Ernie continued to be seen at our UCSB clinic on one or two occasions per week. At this time, we focused our efforts on the analysis and development of techniques for increasing responsivity in natural environments. In previous work with Ernie and other children, we had identified a number of methods for elevating responsiveness in the context of direct instruction (e.g., Dunlap, 1984; Dunlap, Dyer, & Koegel, 1983; Egel, 1980; Egel, 1981; Koegel, Dunlap, & Dyer, 1980; Koegel & Williams, 1980; Williams, et al., 1981). However, promoting a general reduction of tuned-out behavior, without the presence of a treatment provider, was a different and more difficult problem. This issue of generalization and maintenance has, of course, been described as one of the most important and pervasive concerns in the field of behavior modification (Carr, 1980; Egel, 1982; Horner, Bellamy, & Colvin, 1983; Stokes & Baer, 1977). The problem has been particularly intransigent when the behavior occurs very frequently, requires deceleration (like self-stimulation), and is probably, in some sense, self-reinforcing (cf. Devany & Rincover, 1982).

As a research unit concerned with Ernie's (and other children's) responsivity, we initiated preliminary analyses of several clinical techniques designed to produce a generalized increase in responsive performance. As discussed above, we have been involved in attempts to develop pivotal behaviors that might serve to positively influence, in an indirect manner, a broad range of additional responses. In short, we were seeking to equip Ernie with certain skills that would enable him to acquire much more information from his daily interactions. From one perspective, this research may be viewed as an attempt to directly affect the constructs known as *attention, motivation,* and *responsivity.* Clearly, a major and generalized impact on such functioning would have a significant impact on the symptomatology of autism in particular and, more generally, the classification of pervasive developmental disorders.

While studies conducted over the past 10 to 15 years have contributed greatly toward an understanding of such pivotal characteristics (see Koegel, et al., 1980; Lovaas & Newsom, 1976), we are still distant from an understanding that is sufficient to produce a fully generalized and durable improvement in such broad characteristics. Indeed, the analyses that were piloted with Ernie are too preliminary to be reported with confidence at this point in time. However, it might be instructive to illustrate some aspects of this approach by describing our efforts to heighten Ernie's observational learning (or observational re-sponsivity) in classroom and unstructured settings.

It has been previously mentioned that, unless Ernie was engaged in individ-ualized instruction, he typically did not take notice of events or activities that occurred around him. For example, when he and another child sat at a table facing a teacher, he did not attend to the child's responses, and thus, he learned nothing from these potentially informative interactions. We began intervention on this deficiency by replicating such a classroom situation. Ernie and another child set facing a teacher, while Ernie's therapist sat is close proximity. As the teacher asked the other child to perform a task (e.g., to draw a triangle), Ernie's therapist prompted Ernie to quietly respond to important aspects of the relevant stimuli (cf., Koegel, et al., 1981). The teacher then asked Ernie to relate what had just occurred. If Ernie responded correctly (for example, by saying, "Judy drew a triangle "), he was reinforced. As Ernie achieved increasing success, the therapist's prompts were faded and eventually withdrawn. After a number of sessions, Ernie was able to observe and talk about his partner's responding.

Ernie's observational responsivity was also addressed in a less structured setting, that is, when he was unoccupied with any specific task requirement. In this paradigm, Ernie was left alone for a period of time when an event occurred that a normally responsive child would undoubtedly notice. For example, a co-therapist, Freddy, would suddenly throw a ball across the room. Ernie was then asked, "What did Freddy do?" Before training, Ernie almost never responded correctly. However, after treatment (with prompting and reinforcement), Ernie was able to reliably report on such surrounding activities.

While this kind of research is still at too preliminary a stage to report on generalization or maintenance, we have been encouraged by some of the early treatment results because they appear to target one of the central characteristics of autism, i.e., responsivity to external events. In Ernie's case, we found that he was capable of responding to a variety of external events that he had not previously done. This is a very promising indicator, suggesting that a breakthrough in the treatment of responsivity may not be far away.

Developing Durable Appropriate Behavior in School

When Ernie turned six years old, it became increasingly clear that two patterns of behavior would pose threats to his opportunity to participate in integrated school placements. First, he continued to interact with a level of responsivity that could effectively exclude him from many group activities. Second, during unstructured recess periods and occasionally in large-group activities, he displayed stereotypic behaviors that were viewed as bizarre by unfamiliar observers. While these types of behavior are sometimes tolerated in the earliest grades of school, they are clearly unacceptable in later years and would serve to expel Ernie from regular exposure to normally developing peers. Ernie's parents, teachers, and UCSB staff agreed that remediation of these behavior problems was critical.

It was determined that the interaction should fulfill certain criteria. First, the treatment should be implemented in the context of Ernie's normal school routine; and second, the auxiliary treatment agents should be eventually faded such that their presence in the classroom would not be continually required. In other words, the intervention was to be conducted in the natural environment in order to obviate concerns regarding generalization and was to be durable so that improved performance would not be dependent on the availability of a costly and conspicuous classroom aide.

The program that was decided upon was a recently developed model (Dunlap, Johnson, Koegel, & O'Neill, 1983) based on research on the use of delayed contingencies (e.g., Fowler & Baer, 1981) to promote generalization and maintenance. In this program, intervention began in Ernie's school setting, with a well-trained aide providing a dense schedule of reinforcers for adaptive on-task responding and for immediate reprimands contingent on stereotypic and unresponsive performance. Gradually, the reinforcer schedule was thinned. When reinforcers were provided approximately once every five minutes, the aide began to systematically delay the delivery of reprimands. Initially, the aide allowed one second to elapse between the offending behavior (e.g., self-

FIGURE 13-3

Ernie Relaxing after a Job Well Done in his School Training Program

stimulation) and the delivery of the reprimand. As the delay was gradually extended, the aide concurrently moved further and further away from Ernie. At the same time, the reinforcers were provided less and less frequently. Thus, three operations were working simultaneously: (1) the reinforcement schedule was decreased; (2) the delay of reprimands was gradually extended; and, (3) the physical presence of the aide was gradually removed.

At the time of this writing, the positive reinforcers and reprimands are being faded, and the program is gradually being transferred to the regular classroom teachers. At this point, Ernie's on-task responding continues to be displayed at a very high level. Based on our experiences with other children who evidenced similar classroom difficulties, we are optimistic that the treatment effects will prove to be durable (Dunlap, et al., 1983).

Current Status and Objectives

Ernie is now six and a half years old and has been in treatment for slightly more than 30 months. Over this period of time, he has made a great deal of progress in almost every area of functioning. His deviant behaviors, such as tantrums and self-stimulation, have been markedly reduced such that in most situations, he no longer appears to be substantially different from other children his age. His deficiencies in skill areas, such as self-care, communication, and intellectual functioning have also been largely overcome. He is progressing with his class-mates in academic achievement, is fully toilet trained, is at or near age level in other self-help skills, and is advancing rapidly in his ability to communicate with verbal language. However, there are still areas that will require continued intensive intervention before Ernie can be considered to have advanced beyond a diagnosis of autism.

The most notable area of deficiency continues to be social interaction. While Ernie has acquired many social skills, he still tends to be by himself unless directly prompted to play or otherwise interact with other children and un-familiar adults. On the school play yard, while other children play together, Ernie will typically engage in solitary activities. The interactions that do occur are simple and very brief. We have recently observed that such opportunities for interaction are frequently terminated prematurely, due to the social avoidance behaviors (e.g., removal of eye contact, walking away), which Ernie continues to display. As Dyer, Koegel, and Bell (1983) have noted, many autistic children utilize strategies for aborting social contact, especially when the topics of interaction are not idiosyncratically preferred or when they involve demands (Carr, Newsom & Binkoff, 1976; 1980). Unfortunately, for Ernie and other autistic children, such topics that evoke avoidance responses appear to be extremely numerous, far outnumbering those affecting normally developing youngsters.

The goal of increasing social interaction is one that has recently been ad-dressed by a number of applied researchers (e.g., Gaylord-Ross, Haring,

Breen, & Pitts-Conway, 1982; Strain, 1981). The techniques reported in their studies, as well as the products from our own analyses, will be used in the coming months to promote a more rapid development in this critical area. Social interaction is a complex area that must take into account the diverse realm of communicative abilities (including syntax, semantics, and pragmatics), pivotal response characteristics (e.g., the constructs or attention and motivation), and the pervasive concern of generalization and maintenance.

An objective that is centrally related to the promotion of increased socialization pertains to the need to maintain Ernie's participation in truly integrated school and community activities. As described above, Ernie is now enrolled in an integrated school setting, and recent intervention appears to be assuring the success of that placement at the present time. We are continuing to monitor the effects of that intervention and are prepared to reintroduce specialized assistance if the need arises. Based on years of observation and evaluation, we are convinced that much of Ernie's continued progress will be dependent on the opportunity to participate in and benefit from the experiences that affect the socialization of all community members. Given a continuation of these opportunities and given continued access to informed treatment and evaluation services, we are optimistic that Ernie will continue his rapid habilitative progress and, perhaps, develop into a productive, fulfilled, and fully integrated member of our society.

SUMMARY

This chapter has examined the diagnostic classification of pervasive developmental disorders. Focusing on the principal manifestation, autism, we have provided a description of the disorder, outlined various conceptualizations, and discussed methods of assessment and intervention. In order to illustrate the course and effects of a broad-based treatment approach, we have devoted much of the chapter to a description of our work with Ernie, a young boy who entered treatment with a firm diagnosis of autism. We have attempted to show how a comprehensive program of clinical and community involvement can serve to overcome the pervasive disabilities implied by the autism label. In so doing, we hope to have conveyed the message that a diagnosis of autism is not a sentence to a life of irrevocable disability. Rather, with the efforts of family and community and the products of scientific analysis, the symptoms of autism are increasingly vulnerable to treatment.

REFERENCES

American Psychiatric Association. *Diagnostic and statistical manual of mental disorders* (3rd ed.). Washington, D.C., APA, 1980.

Applebaum, E., Egel, A. L., Koegel, R. L., & Imhoff, B. Measuring musical abilities of autistic children. *Journal of Autism and Developmental Disorders*, 1979, *9*, 279–285.

Bettelheim, B. *The empty fortress*. New York: Free Press, 1967.

Bostow, D. E., & Bailey, J. B. Modification of severe disruptive and aggressive behavior using brief timeout and reinforcement procedures. *Journal of Applied Behavior Analysis*, 1969, *2*, 31–38.

Burke, J. C. *Collateral effects of parent training on the daily interactions of families with autistic children*. Unpublished masters thesis, University of California, Santa Barbara, 1982.

Cantwell, D. P., Baker, L., & Rutter, M. Family factors. In M. Rutter and E. Schopler (Eds.), *Autism: A reappraisal of concepts and treatment*. New York: Plenum Press, 1978.

Carr, E. The motivation of self-injurious behavior: A review of some hypotheses. *Psychological Bulletin*, 1977, *84*, 800–816.

Carr, E. G., Newsom, C. D., & Binkoff, J. A. Stimulus control of self-destructive behavior in a psychotic child. *Journal of Abnormal Child Psychology*, 1976, *4*, 139–153.

Carr, E., Newsom, C. D., & Binkoff, J. A. Escape as a factor in the aggressive behavior of two retarded children. *Journal of Applied Behavior Analysis*, 1980, *13*, 101–117.

Csapo, M. Prevalence and needs assessment study of autistic children in British Columbia. *British Columbia Journal of Special Education*, 1979, *3*, 159–191.

DeMyer, M. K. *Parents and children in autism*. Washington, D.C.: Winston and Sons, 1979.

Devany, J., & Rincover, A. Self-stimulatory behavior and sensory reinforcement. In R. L. Koegel, A. Rincover, & A. L. Egel (Eds.), *Educating and understanding autistic children*. San Diego, Calif.: College-Hill Press, 1982.

Dunlap, G. The influence of task variation and maintenance tasks on the learning and affect of autistic children. *Journal of Experimental Child Psychology*, 1984, *37*, 41–64.

Dunlap, G., Dyer, K., Koegel, R. L. Autistic self-stimulation and intertrial interval duration. *American Journal of Mental Deficiency*, 1983, *88*, 194–202.

Dunlap, G., & Egel, A. L. Motivational characteristics. In R. L. Koegel, A. Rincover, and A. L. Egel (Eds.), *Educating and understanding autistic children*. San Diego, Calif.: College-Hill Press, 1982.

Dunlap, G., Johnson, J., Koegel, R. L., & O'Neill, R. E. Maintaining responsive performance with delayed contingencies. Presented at the Annual Convention of the American Psychological Association, Anaheim, California, 1983.

Dunlap, G., & Koegel, R. L. Motivating autistic children through stimulus variation. *Journal of Applied Behavior Analysis*, 1980, *13*, 619–628.

Dunlap, G., Koegel, R. L., & Koegel, L. Continuity of treatment: Toilet training in multiple community settings. *Journal for the Association for the Severely Handicapped,* in press.

Dyer, K., Koegel, R. L., & Bell, L. Generalized reduction of social avoidance behavior in autistic children. Presented at the 91st Annual Convention of the American Psychological Association, Anaheim, California, 1983.

Egel, A. L. The effects of constant versus varied reinforcer presentation on responding by autistic children. *Journal of Experimental Child Psychology,* 1980, *30,* 455–463.

Egel, A. L. Reinforcer variation: Implications for motivating developmentally delayed children. *Journal of Applied Behavior Analysis,* 1981, *14,* 345–350.

Egel, A. L. Programming the generalization & maintenance of treatment gains. In R. L. Koegel, A. Rincover, & A. L. Egel (Eds.), *Educating and understanding autistic children.* San Diego, Calif.: College-Hill Press, 1982.

Egel, A. L., Koegel, R. L., & Schreibman, L. A review of educational-treatment procedures for autistic children. In L. Mann and D. Sabatino (Eds.), *Fourth review of special education.* New York: Grune and Stratton, 1980.

Fay, W. H., & Schuler, A. L. *Emerging language in autistic children.* Baltimore: University Park Press, 1980.

Folstein, S., & Rutter, M. A twin study of individuals with infantile autism. In M. Rutter and E. Schopler (Eds.), *Autism: A reappraisal of concepts and treatment.* New York: Plenum Press, 1978.

Fowler, S., & Baer, D. M. "Do I have to be good all day?" The timing of delayed reinforcement as a factor in generalization. *Journal of Applied Behavior Analysis,* 1981, *14,* 13–24.

Foxx, R., & Azrin, N. The elimination of autistic self-stimulatory behavior by overcorrection. *Journal of Applied Behavior Analysis,* 1973, *6,* 1–14 (a).

Foxx, R. M., & Azrin, N. *Toilet training the retarded.* Champaign, Ill.: Research Press, 1973(b).

Gaylord-Ross, R., Haring, T., Breen, C., & Pitts-Conway, V. (Eds.). *The social integration of autistic and severely handicapped students.* San Francisco: San Francisco State University, 1982.

Horner, R. H., Bellamy, G. T., & Colvin, G. T. Responding in the presence of non-trained stimuli: Implications of generalization error patterns. Unpublished manuscript, University of Oregon, 1983.

Janicki, M. P., Lubin, R. A., & Friedman, E. Variations in characteristics and service needs of persons with autism. *Journal of Autism and Developmental Disorders,* 1983, *13,* 73–85.

Johnson, J., & Koegel, R. L. Behavioral assessment and curriculum development. In R. L. Koegel, A. Rincover, and A. L. Egel (Eds.), *Educating and understanding autistic children.* San Diego, Calif.: College-Hill Press, 1982.

Kanner, L. Autistic disturbances of affective contact. *Nervous child,* 1943, *3,* 217–250.

Koegel, R. L., & Covert, A. The relationship of self-stimulation to learning in autistic children. *Journal of Applied Behavior Analysis,* 1972, *5,* 381–388.

Koegel, R. L. & Dunlap, G. Descriptions of families in a large research project. A review of parents and children in autism, by Marian K. DeMyer. *Merrill-Palmer Quarterly,* 1981, *21,* 69–77.

Koegel, R. L., Dunlap, G., & Dyer, K. Intertrial interval duration and learning in autistic children. *Journal of Applied Behavior Analysis,* 1980, *13,* 91–99.

Koegel, R. L., Dunlap, G., Richman, G., & Dyer, K. The use of specific orienting cues for teaching discrimination tasks. *Analysis and Intervention in Developmental Disabilities,* 1981, *1,* 187–198.

Koegel, R. L., & Egel, A. L. Motivating autistic children. *Journal of Abnormal Psychology,* 1979, *88,* 418–426.

Koegel, R. L., Egel, A. L., & Dunlap, G. Learning characteristics of autistic children. In W. S. Sailor, B. Wilcox, and L. J. Brown (Eds.), *Methods of instruction with severely handicapped students.* Baltimore: Brookes Publishers, 1980.

Koegel, R. L., Egel, A. L., & Williams, J. A. Behavioral contrast and transfer across settings in teaching autistic children. *Journal of Experimental Child Psychology,* 1980, *30,* 422–437.

Koegel, R. L., Glahn, T. J., & Nieminen, G. S. Generalization of parent-training results. *Journal of Applied Behavior Analysis,* 1978, *11,* 95–109.

Koegel, R. L., & Rincover, A. Treatment of psychotic children in a classroom environment. I. Learning in a large group. *Journal of Applied Behavior Analysis,* 1974, *7,* 45–59.

Koegel, R. L., & Rincover, A. Some research on the difference between generalization & maintenance in extra-therapy settings. *Journal of Applied Behavior Analysis,* 1977, *10,* 1–16.

Koegel, R. L., Rincover, A., & Egel, A. L. *Educating and understanding autistic children.* San Diego, Calif.: College-Hill Press, 1982.

Koegel, R. L., Russo, D. C., & Rincover, A. Assessing and training teachers in the generalized use of behavior modification with autistic children. *Journal of Applied Behavior Analysis,* 1977, *10,* 197–205.

Koegel, R. L., & Schreibman, L. Teaching autistic children to respond to simultaneous multiple cues. *Journal of Experimental Child Psychology,* 1977, *24,* 299–311.

Koegel, R. L., & Schreibman, L. Identification of consistent responding to auditory stimuli by a functionally "deaf" autistic child. *Journal of Autism and Childhood Schizophrenia,* 1976, *6,* 147–156.

Koegel, R. L., Schreibman, L., Britten, K., Burke, J. C., & O'Neill, R. E. A comparison of parent training to direct child treatment. In R. L. Koegel,

A. Rincover, and A. L. Egel (Eds.), *Educating and understanding autistic children*. San Diego, Calif.: College-Hill Press, 1982.

Koegel, R. L., Schreibman, L., Johnson, J., O'Neill, R. E., & Dunlap, G. Collateral effects of parent training on families with autistic children. In R. Dangel and R. Polster (Eds.), *Behavioral parent training: Issues in research and practice*. New York: Guilford Press, in press.

Koegel, R. L., Schreibman, L., O'Neill, R. E., & Burke, J. C. Parental and family interaction characteristics of families of autistic children. *Journal of Consulting and Clinical Psychology*, in press.

Koegel, R. L., & Williams, J. A. Direct vs. indirect response reinforcer relationships in teaching autistic children. *Journal of Abnormal Child Psychology*, 1980, *8*, 537–547.

Lotter, V. Follow-up studies. In M. Rutter and E. Schopler (Eds.), *Autism: A reappraisal of concepts and treatment*. New York: Plenum Press, 1978.

Lovaas, O. I. *The autistic child: Language development through behavior modification*. New York: Irvington Press, 1977.

Lovaas, O. I., Koegel, R. L., & Schreibman, L. Stimulus overselectivity in autism: A review of research. *Psychological Bulletin*, 1979, *86*, 1236–1254.

Lovaas, O. I., Koegel, R. L., Simmons, J. Q., & Long, J. S. Some generalization and follow-up measures on autistic children in behavior therapy. *Journal of Applied Behavior Analysis*, 1973, *6*, 131–166.

Lovaas, O. I., & Newsom, C. D. Behavior modification with psychotic children. In H. Leitenberg (Ed.), *Handbook of behavior modification and behavior therapy*. Englewood Cliffs, N.J.: Prentice-Hall, 1976.

Lovaas, O. I., Schreibman, L., & Koegel, R. L. A behavior modification approach to the treament of autistic children. *Journal of Autism and Childhood Schizophrenia*, 1974, *4*, 111–129.

Lovaas, O. I., Schreibman, L., Koegel, R. L., & Rehm, R. Selective responding by autistic children to multiple sensory input. *Journal of Abnormal Psychology*, 1971, *77*, 211–222.

Lovaas, O. I., & Simmons, J. Q. Manipulation of self-destruction in three retarded children. *Journal of Applied Behavior Analysis*, 1969, *2*, 143–157.

Ornitz, E. M., & Ritvo, E. R. Perceptual inconstancy in early infantile autism. *Archives of General Psychiatry*, 1968, *18*, 76–98.

Plummer, S., Baer, D. M., & LeBlanc, J. M. Functional considerations in the use of procedural time-out and an effective alternative. *Journal of Applied Behavior Analysis*, 1977, *10*, 689–705.

Rimland, B. Inside the mind of an autistic savant. *Psychology Today*, 1978, *12*, 68–80.

Rincover, A., Cook, R., Peoples, A., & Packard, D. Using sensory extinction and sensory reinforcement principles for programming multiple adaptive behavior change. *Journal of Applied Behavior Analysis*, 1979, *12*, 221–233.

Rincover, A., & Koegel, R. L. Setting generality and stimulus control in autistic children. *Journal of Applied Behavior Analysis*, 1975, *8*, 235–246.

Ritvo, E. R., & Freeman, B. J. National Society for Autistic Children definition of the syndrome of autism. *Journal of Autism and Childhood Schizophrenia*, 1978, *8*, 162–167.

Ritvo, E. R., Freeman, B. J., Ornitz, E. M., & Tanguay, P. E. (Eds.), *Autism: Diagnosis, current research, and management*. New York: Spectrum, 1976.

Russo, D. C., & Koegel, R. L. A method for integrating an autistic child into a normal public school classroom. *Journal of Applied Behavior Analysis*, 1977, *10*, 579–590.

Rutter, M. Diagnosis and definition of childhood autism. *Journal of Autism and Childhood Schizophrenia*, 1978, *8*, 139–161.

Rutter, M. Autism: Educational issues. *Special Education*, 1970, *59*, 6–10.

Rutter, M., & Schopler, E. (Eds.), *Autism: A reappraisal of concepts and treatment*. New York: Plenum Press, 1978.

Sanders, M. R., & James, J. E. The modification of parent behavior: A review of generalization and maintenance. *Behavior Modification*, 1983, *1*, 3027.

Schopler, E. On confusion in the diagnosis of autism. *Journal of Autism and Childhood Schizophrenia*, 1978, *8*, 137–138.

Schopler, E., & Reichler, R. J. Developmental therapy by parents with their own autistic child. In M. Rutter (Ed.), *Infantile autism: Concepts, characteristics, and treatment*. London: Churchill Livingstone, 1971.

Schreibman, L., & Koegel, R. L., A guideline for planning behavior modification programs for autistic children. In S. M. Turner, K. S. Calhoun, and H. E. Adams (Eds.), *Handbook of clinical behavior therapy*. New York: John Wiley & Sons, 1981.

Schreibman, L., O'Neill, R. E., & Koegel, R. L. Behavioral training for siblings of autistic children. *Journal of Applied Behavior Analysis*, 1983, *16*, 129–138.

Solnick, J. V., Rincover, A., & Peterson, C. Some determinants of the reinforcing and punishing effects of time-out. *Journal of Applied Behavior Analysis*, 1977, *10*, 415–424.

Spence, M. A. Genetic studies. In E. Ritvo, B. J. Freeman, E. Ornitz, and P. E. Tanguay (Eds.), *Autism: Diagnosis, current research and management*. New York: Spectrum, 1976.

Stokes, T. F., & Baer, D. M. An implicit technology of generalization. *Journal of Applied Behavior Analysis*, 1977, *10*, 349–368.

Strain, P. S. (Ed.), *The utilization of peers as behavior change agents*. New York: Plenum Press, 1981.

Tsai, L., Stewart, M. A., & August, G. Implication of sex differences in the familial transmission of infantile autism. *Journal of Autism and Developmental Disorders*, 1981, *11*, 165–173.

Warren, F. Personal communication, 1983.

Wetherby, A., Koegel, R. L., & Mendel, M. Central auditory nervous system dysfunction in echolalic autistic individuals. *Journal of Speech and Hearing Research*, 1981, *24*, 420–429.

Williams, J. A., Koegel, R. L., & Egel, A. L. Response-reinforcer relationships and improved learning in autistic children. *Journal of Applied Behavior Analysis*, 1981, *14*, 53–60.

Wing, L. *Early childhood autism*. New York: Pergamon Press, 1976.

Wing, L., & Gould, J. Severe impairments of social interaction and associated abnormalities in children: Epidemiology and classification. *Journal of Autism and Developmental Disorders*, 1979, *9*, 11–29.

PART THREE

Disorders Commonly
Associated with Childhood

14

Social Skills Deficits*

Hyman Hops
Melissa Finch
Oregon Research Institute

Scott McConnell
Western Psychiatric Institute and Clinic

INTRODUCTION

The Importance of Peer Relationships

Social interaction is unquestionably an inherent and vital human function. The ability to form effective and meaningful social relationships has long been considered critical to development. In the past, peer relationships in early childhood have received less attention than familial relationships for at least two reasons. First, the dominance of psychoanalytic theory resulted in the attribution of singular importance to parent-child (especially mother-child) relationships for later social and psychological functioning (Lewis & Rosenblum, 1975). Secondly, the growth of the Piagetian movement, with its emphasis on the egocentric nature of infants and preschoolers, precluded interest in the study of meaningful social relationships among this population (Rubin & Ross, 1982). Within the last decade, however, increased interest in this topic has led to a plethora of research showing that the development of peer relationships is

* This manuscript was prepared with the assistance of NIMH Grant #MH33205, Hyman Hops, Principal Investigator.

The authors wish to acknowledge the assistance of Virginia Osteen and Agatha McLean in the preparation and typing of the manuscript and Linda Rangus for graphics. Appreciation is also extended to Lew Lewin and Pat Rogers for the use of the case study presented here and Antonia Forster for her critique of an earlier draft.

a critical determinant of later adaptive functioning (Hartup, 1983). Furthermore, recent research suggests that early relationships among infants and toddlers may provide opportunities for young children to acquire social-affective behavior that will not be learned in interactions with their parents (Mueller, 1972).

The unique components of peer relations appear to be (*a*) the egalitarian nature of the relationships and (*b*) the equivalence of the developmental levels (Hartup, 1983; Mueller & Vandell, 1979). Parents exercise greater control than peers in their interactions with their children, for example, by initiating the majority of interactions. Among peers, however, the frequency of initiation is likely to be equal (Greenwood, Walker, Todd, & Hops, 1979; Mueller & Vandell, 1979). Furthermore, parents may be frustrated and bored by the length and repetitive nature of many children's games. The same repetitious repertoires among children, however, provide them with the opportunity to practice and achieve mastery of specific skills (Hartup, 1983). Peer interaction may also promote the development of more mature social and cognitive schemes, such as those found in fantasy play (Rubin, 1980).

Disturbances in Peer Relationships

From a clinical perspective, disturbances in peer relationships have been shown to be one of the best predictors of psychiatric, social, and other adjustment difficulties later in life. Rejection by the peer group has predicted delinquency (Roff, Sells, & Golden, 1972), dropping out of school (Ullman, 1957), bad conduct discharges from military service (Roff, 1961), and mental health referrals up to 13 years later (Cowen, Pederson, Babigian, Izzo, & Trost, 1973). Taken together, the evidence strongly suggests that social competence is essential to normal healthy development, that social behavior is relatively stable, and that children who demonstrate consistent patterns of socially problematic behavior are likely to show later social, psychological, scholastic, and occupational difficulties. Certainly, the adult literature has consistently demonstrated relationships between low social competence and various forms of adult psychopathology (Bellack & Hersen, 1979; Kazdin, 1979; Bellack & Morrison, 1982).

Current Interest in Peer Relations

The current interest in children's social behavior is reflected in the extensive development of diagnostic assessment and treatment procedures for socially problematic children of all ages. For example, the updated Diagnostic and Statistical Manual of Mental Disorders (DSM-III), published by the American Psychiatric Association, has increased from one to three the number of categories that include social withdrawal as a major symptom group (American Psychiatric Association, 1980). In addition, there has been an epidemic increase in the number of social skills training programs developed for children from preschool to adolescence (see reviews by Conger & Keane, 1981; Hops, 1982, 1983; Wanlass & Prinz, 1982).

This increase in the availability of social skills training procedures has resulted from the clinical perception of the need for treatment. As has sometimes been the case in clinical psychology, the field has developed backwards, with treatment procedures being implemented before they have been experimentally validated. This order of events accounts for the fact that, while treatment procedures proliferate, researchers have not yet agreed on definitions of social competence or social skills deficits in children. Thus, there continues to be a confound in the assessment and treatment of social disorders among children, and clinicians are guided more by their theoretical orientation than by empirical results. A major objective of future researchers is to empirically identify those specifiable deficits that require intervention.

CONCEPTUALIZATION

This chapter will consider socially problematic behavior from a skill deficit perspective. To do so, it is important first to distinguish between the concepts of social competence and social skill. While they have been used interchangeably in the child and adult literature (Hops, 1983; McFall, 1982), a more precise use of these concepts can assist our discussion of the assessment and treatment of socially problematic children.

The Relationship between Social Competence and Skill

Definitions of social competence in children abound. This simply reflects our inability to agree on the criteria for competence (Anderson & Messick, 1974; Zigler & Trickett, 1978), i.e., to identify specific social behaviors or skills that account for competent performance in social situations. In the absence of objective, specifiable, external criteria by which to judge the competence of social behavior, the impact of the behavior on the social agents in the environment is used instead. Thus, the assessment of social competence is generally based on the global judgments of a child's peers (Hops & Lewin, 1984), parents (Achenbach & Edelbrock, 1982), or teachers (Walker, McConnell, Holmes, Todis, Walker, & Golden, 1983). Parents' ratings have discriminated between children referred to mental health centers for treatment and nonreferred children (Achenbach & Edelbrock, 1981). Peer ratings have demonstrated long-term predictive validity for a variety of social adjustment problems (Cowen et al., 1973; Roff, et al., 1972). Not surprisingly, these measures are not highly correlated (Hops & Finch, 1982), reflecting the different criteria each of these groups uses as the bases for their judgments. Thus, it may be necessary to use multiple measures of social competence to reflect an individual's performance across social settings and agents. Identifying the criteria used by each of the social agents may provide some of the answers in our attempts to delineate the specific social skills that underlie judgments of social competence.

A Skill Deficit Perspective

A social skill deficit perspective assumes that specific identifiable skills form the basis for socially competent behavior and that interpersonal difficulties may arise as a function of a faulty behavioral repertoire (Bellack & Hersen, 1979; McFall, 1982). Treatment and assessment are inexorably tied together because treatment is aimed at precisely those social skill deficits that have been identified in the assessment process, thus ensuring an efficient and cost-effective intervention. Unfortunately, we have not yet determined the specific deficits that require remediation.

A skill deficit perspective does not necessarily assume that the absence of such skills is a function of a faulty learning history, i.e., that children low in social competence have not been taught the specific skills that are essential prerequisites for socially adaptive functioning. There is insufficient data available in support of such a hypothesis.

Predisposing Factors.   Impairments in social skills may be due to a variety of other factors. For example, a developmental delay in language acquisition is highly likely to affect the extent and quality of a child's social interaction (Hops, 1983; Finch & Hops, 1982). Children with language and comprehension difficulties may be hampered in their ability to communicate and interact with the peer group, especially as they grow older.

Similarly, motor skills take on increasing importance with increasing age. High-status compared to low-status children in fourth grade had significantly higher scores on physical fitness and muscular strength that were maintained over a three-year period (Broekhoff, 1976, 1977). Data for preschool children are similar. Significant relationships were found between performance on tests of physical strength, agility, and coordination, and levels of social interaction observed in free play (Hops & Finch, 1982). Popularity was also significantly correlated with levels of motor performance; significant differences in popularity were found between high- and low-performing five- and six-year-olds (Steigelman, 1981).

Parenting behavior may also affect a child's social development. Increasingly, the case is made that the social competence of children is in part accounted for by the level of the parents' child management or parenting skills (Sherman & Farina, 1974; Patterson & Reid, 1970; Patterson, 1982). Snyder (1977), for example, found that parents of nonproblem children were less likely to reward and more likely to punish displeasing child behavior. In contrast, parents of problem children dispensed consequences in almost random fashion.

Supporting this finding are data from our laboratory indicating that parents of withdrawn children showed significantly reduced rates of prosocial behavior directed to the children compared to either average or highly competent children (Finch, 1984).

Remediation of Skill Deficits. The skill deficit perspective assumes that impaired functioning can be corrected regardless of etiology. For example, developmental delays in language may be due to anoxia at birth. But, direct instruction in the specific areas of deficit can result in improvements in language with severely and profoundly handicapped children (Becker, Engelmann, Carnine, & Maggs, 1982). Similarly, improvements in social responding can be obtained using powerful intervention techniques aimed directly at the specific components of social interaction (Ladd, 1981; Walker, Greenwood, Hops, & Todd, 1979).

DESCRIPTION

Social skills deficits differ from other psychosocial problems of childhood in several important ways. First, there is no clear age of onset; rather, dysfunction in the development of appropriate social behaviors can occur, with devastating effects, from infancy (Lewis & Rosenblum, 1975) through adolescence (LeCroy, 1982). Second, as we shall see, prevalence estimates for social skills deficits are inconsistent and appear to vary as a function of the measurement procedures used to identify the children needing treatment. Finally, the associated features of social skills deficits vary widely, including such diverse constellations of child characteristics as motor behaviors (Steigelman, 1981), language skills (Hops & Finch, 1982), socioeconomic status (Gottman, Gonso, & Rasmussen, 1975), and parent-child interaction patterns (Finch & Hops, 1981; Patterson, 1982).

Target Population

Children with social skills deficits are not a homogeneous group. Indeed, it is our opinion that social skills deficits cut across multiple clinical populations as traditionally conceived. For example, learning disabled children have been shown to lack social competence and are less accepted by their peers (Bryan, 1974; Bryan & Bryan, 1978). Disruptive and solitary behavior has also been associated with hyperactivity (Cohen, Sullivan, Minde, Novak, & Helwig, 1981; Pelham & Bender, 1982). In fact, children whose diagnosis is Schizoid Disorder of Childhood, Childhood Onset Pervasive Developmental Disorder, Atypical Pervasive Developmental Disorder, or Avoidant Disorder, according to DSM-III criteria (American Psychiatric Association, 1980), are, by definition, likely to be deficient in social skills.

If researchers and clinicians in the field were able to agree on a precise definition of social competence and to articulate its underlying skill components, then social skills deficits would be attributed to any children who fail to engage in socially appropriate or competent behavior. Furthermore, social skills training would be considered an essential ingredient of any intervention program designed to help these children.

However, because no such definition of social competence currently exists, children have been selected by researchers and/or referred to clinicians largely on the basis of their socially *inappropriate* behavior, which is more easily specified (e.g., social withdrawal, aggression, autistic behaviors,). Thus, in practice, target populations have been described, disorders delineated, and treatment packages developed mainly on the basis of the *type* of inappropriate behavior exhibited.

While our conceptualization of social skills deficits as a disorder cuts across these traditionally defined populations, the primary target group for social skills interventions at this time has been the withdrawn, isolated, and unassertive child (Conger & Keane, 1981; Hops, 1982, 1983; Wanlass & Prinz, 1982). This population may include children who could be diagnosed as Schizoid Disorder of Childhood or Adolescence (DSM-III) on the basis of their inability to make friends, avoidance of nonfamilial social contacts, and lack of reinforcement from peer interaction. The field has only relatively recently begun to see the applicability of social skills treatment packages for other clinical groups of children: socially aggressive (Walker, Hops, & Greenwood, 1981); educationally handicapped (Walker, McConnell, Holmes et al., 1983), unassertive (Bornstein, Bellack, & Hersen, 1977), delinquent (Spence & Marzillier, 1978), or at risk to begin smoking (Biglan, Severson, Bavry, & McConnell, 1983).

While efforts will be made to include the findings of research conducted on various child populations, reflecting the available literature, this chapter will emphasize primarily the assessment and treatment of the socially unresponsive child. We further narrow our chapter to focus on childhood social skills deficits that pertain mainly to peer interaction rather than to sibling or parent-child interaction for several reasons. First, the adequacy of peer relations appears to have the greatest long-term predictive validity for social adjustment. Secondly, the majority of research on childhood social competence and social interaction has been conducted in the preschool and elementary school settings where the opportunity for direct observation is the greatest. Third, while a child's relationships with siblings are likely to be important in their own right, their impact on peer interaction remains equivocal at this time (Pepler, Corter, & Abramovitch, 1982).

Prevalence and Sex

Estimating the prevalence of children with social skills deficits is an impossible task at this stage of conceptual and methodological development in the field.

First, as discussed above, social behavior is so pervasive a contributor to adaptive functioning that social skills deficits are likely to occur in the majority of traditional diagnostic or clinical subgroups.

Secondly, there are no guidelines consistently adhered to in the assessment of children with problems in peer social interaction. Assessment is partially confounded, for example, by the type of diagnostic instrument used (Hops & Greenwood, 1981; Hops & Lewin, 1984). When direct observation is used to select for treatment children who are socially withdrawn, the rates of identified children have varied from 1 to 28 percent of the population. When sociometric instruments have been used in the diagnostic process, 16 to 50 percent of children in classrooms have been called isolated and targeted for treatment (Hops & Greenwood, 1981; Hops, 1983).

Indexes of social difficulties have also varied when parent reporting has been examined (Achenbach & Edelbrock, 1981). Approximately 10 percent of parents report social withdrawal in their children. Shyness is reported in about 50 percent of four- to five-year-olds, decreasing to approximately 30 percent by 16 years of age. Similarly, loneliness is indicated in about 30 percent of four- to five-year-olds, decreasing to approximately 15 percent in midadolescence. However, without precise behavioral definitions of withdrawal, shyness, and loneliness, these data do little to clarify the boundaries of the field.

The relative proportions of boys and girls exhibiting social skills deficits have not been established either. Such data depend to a large extent on the type of deficit assessed. It is generally believed that girls are more likely to be socially withdrawn, and boys socially aggressive. While there is considerable evidence for the latter (Hops, Walker, Fleischman, Nagoshi, Omura, Skindrud, & Taylor, 1978), there is simply no evidence in support of the former. A review of children selected as withdrawn on the basis of social interaction levels does not clearly indicate that females predominate (Hops & Greenwood, 1981). Achenbach and Edelbrock (1981) found differences in parent reporting only for a loneliness item on children over 12 years of age: 20 percent of girls were reported to be lonely, compared to 10 percent of boys.

All these data, regardless of their source, must be viewed cautiously since they do not indicate which children are in need of treatment or at risk for future social adjustment problems. Certainly, given the limited treatment resources available, we must select prudently only those children who are most in need of treatment. More longitudinal research is needed to assess the short- and long-term impact of specific social skills deficits on children at various levels of deficit.

Behavioral Characteristics of the Socially Incompetent

As noted above, empirical efforts to describe the nature and breadth of social skills deficits have only recently been initiated. To date, these investigations have been largely exploratory, highlighting significant correlation relationships but failing to demonstrate causal links between measures of social behavior and more general assessments of social competence. Nonetheless, these studies do provide the initial foundations for a further understanding of the nature and develôpment of social skills deficits.

In an early and seminal study, Hartup, Charlesworth, and Glazer (1967) examined the relationship between direct observation measures of children's social behavior and more general measures of their social competence (i.e., positive and negative peer nomination sociometrics). These investigators obtained positive and significant correlations between (a) subjects' rates of positive social interaction with peers and the number of positive sociometric nominations they received, and (b) subjects' rates of negative interactions with peers and the number of negative sociometric nominations received. Thus, Hartup et al. (1967) offered early evidence of a significant, albeit general, relationship between children's observed social behavior and their status on more general measures of social competence.

Gottman and his colleagues (Gottman et al., 1975; Gottman, 1977a,b) further contributed to the description of social skills deficits, comparing groups of popular and unpopular children on a wide range of social cognition and social skill variables. Differences were identified in subjects' performance as a function of socioeconomic status and grade level. In addition, unpopular students when compared to popular students (a) scored significantly lower on a word-guessing task designed to sample referential communication skills, (b) scored lower on a role-play test of friendship making, (c) spent more time alone and off task, and (d) distributed less positive attention and received less positive attention from their peers.

Greenwood, Walker, Todd, and Hops (1981) conducted a descriptive analysis of preschool children's social interactions. Rather than using sociometric status as the criterion for identifying social skills deficits, as done by Hartup et al. (1967) and Gottman et al. (1975), Greenwood and his colleagues examined the relationship between several classes of directly observed social behavior and a summative measure of interactive frequency.

In addition to normative analyses of interaction rate by age and sex, Greenwood et al. (1981) compared high-, medium-, and low-rate interactors. For both males and females, low-rate interactors (a) made significantly less initiations to peers and (b) had significantly lower sociability ratios, indicating that these children initiated to peers relatively less often than peers initiated to them. In addition, female low-rate interactors were significantly less likely to respond to others' initiations than were medium- or high-rate interacting girls.

The findings of Greenwood et al. (1982) were extended to more detailed descriptions of subjects' social interactions by Greenwood, Todd, Hops, and Walker (1982). Again comparing low-rate interactors within preschool classrooms to medium- and high-rate interactors, Greenwood et al. (1982) further demonstrated that children who spent little time in social interaction (a) made fewer social initiations, (*b*) received fewer initiations from peers, (*c*) were less likely to respond to peer initiations, (*d*) talked less, (*e*) spent less non-interactive time in proximity to peers, and (*f*) spent more free-play time alone with a task, observing other children, or interacting with adults.

Data from our laboratory further embellish the nature of social competence in young children (Hops & Finch, 1982). A comprehensive measure of social competence was developed, combining parent ratings, teacher ratings, peer judgments of social behavior via a sociometric procedure, and a global measure based on direct observation. This measure was found to be relatively stable over a two-year period. Two factors emerged: coordination, which is a motor skill factor, and a social skills factor, which combined positive verbalizations and initiations. These two factors accounted for 35 percent and 40 percent of the variance in the social competence of boys and girls, respectively.

As noted above, efforts to empirically describe the nature and development of social skills deficits have only recently been initiated. To date, this research has been almost exclusively correlational and has focused on preschool and elementary school children during their interactions at school. As yet, we have little or no information regarding causal relationships between varying rates of specific behaviors and status on general measures of social competence. The identification of significant correlates is, however, a necessary first step; experimental investigations to evaluate these causal relationships must now proceed. We turn now to a discussion of the assessment of childhood social competence and social skills deficits.

ASSESSMENT

Concurrent with the increasing interest in peer relationships noted earlier is a rapid expansion in the attention and effort devoted to procedures for assessing children's social competence and interactive behavior (cf. Asher & Hymel, 1981; Greenwood, Walker, & Hops, 1977; Hops & Greenwood, 1981). This has led to development and psychometric evaluation of a wide variety of behavioral assessment procedures, including (*a*) peer sociometric status (e.g., Asher, Singleton, Tinsley, & Hymel, 1979; Cohen & Van Tassel, 1978; Hops, Finch, & Stevens, 1983), (*b*) teacher ratings of children's competence, popularity, and interactive behavior (e.g., Connolly & Doyle, 1981; Greenwood, Walker, Todd, & Hops, 1976, 1979; Greenwood, Todd, Walker, & Hops, 1978), and (*c*) observational procedures for the precise specification of children's social interactions (e.g., Hops, & Stevens, 1977; Garrett, Stevens, & Walker, 1978).

Limitations of Research-Based Measures

To date, however, many of these behavioral assessment measures have been developed for research, rather than clinical, applications (Emmelkamp, 1981;

Foster & Hoier, 1983). In reviewing the current status of procedures available for the behavioral assessment of social skills deficits, Foster and Hoier (1983) have identified three potential problems associated with the application of research-based procedures in the clinical assessment of individual cases. First, with the exception of questionnaires and behavioral checklists, such measures may be too costly or time-consuming for use in applied settings. For instance, in the authors' current research, a paired-comparison sociometric rating procedure is used to assess individual children's popularity and mutual friends (see Hops & Finch, 1982; Hops & Lewin, 1984). Although superior in reliability (Cohen & Van Tassel, 1978), it is a costly procedure requiring a lengthy administration, expensive materials (i.e., multiple photographs of each child), and elaborate calculations to yield essential scores. Although the paired-comparison sociometric is uniquely suited to important research issues, this and other sociometric assessment procedures may not be cost effective in clinical settings (Greenwood et al., 1979; Hops & Greenwood, 1981; Hops & Lewin, 1984; McConnell & Odom, in press).

Second, measures and norms derived in social skills research may not be appropriate for a given client. Assessing an individual client's similarity to a norm sample is often hindered by investigators' failure to report and adequately describe within-group variability (Foster & Hoier, 1983). Further, available measures of social skill do not extend to all ages or stimulus settings. Much of the normative and descriptive data available to date has been collected in preschool (e.g., Greenwood et al., 1976, 1977, 1981; Tremblay, Strain, Hendrickson, & Shores, 1981) or elementary school (e.g., Gottman et al., 1975; Walker & Hops, 1973; Walker, McConnell, & Clarke, 1983) free-play settings. There is, however, some evidence that interactions during free play at school may not be generalizable to children's interactions in other settings (Foster & DeLawyer, 1983; Hops et al., 1979). In addition, the extrapolation of social skill norms and criteria from one age group to another has been widely criticized as inappropriate (Strain, Odom, & McConnell, in press). Further, we do not yet know which classes of social behavior vary widely by setting or person and which represent more stable cross-setting and cross-person critical competencies (Hops, 1983; Puttallaz, 1982).

Third, many assessment procedures used in research settings yield scores that are too global or inclusive to have utility in clinical settings. These global scores do not help the clinician identify specific behaviors that must be targeted in treatment, nor do they assist in the development of functional analyses once these behaviors are identified. When information about discrete behaviors can be garnered from these global measures, the reliability of these "part scores" is often unknown.

The therapist's task is further complicated by the relative paucity of validated procedures for assessing children with social skills deficits in home or community settings. To date, the vast majority of empirical evaluations of social skills assessment and training has been conducted in schools or residential care facilities. This does not discount the importance of a child's social relationships with parents, siblings, and others in nonschool settings (cf. Hops, 1983; Lewis & Rosenblum, 1975). Rather, it reflects (a) our current emphasis on the interactions of children with same-aged peers (Hops, 1983; Lougee, Grueneich, & Hartup, 1977) and (b) the nature of social skills deficits, in that such deficits may not be evident until the child comes in contact with a heterogeneous peer group.

What, then, is a clinician interested in assessing and treating children's social skills deficits to do? Behavior therapists are faced with a need to conduct reliable, complete, and useful assessments of individual children in a way that is maximally cost effective. Fortunately, some attention has been given to the development of measures that meet these requirements. In particular, procedures have been developed for (a) screening large groups of children to identify individuals at risk for social adjustment, (b) determining whether referred or identified children are in need of social skills training, and (c) summarizing or describing, in rather broad terms, identified individuals' social behavior in naturalistic settings.

Beyond these available methods, the therapist must rely on the more general behavioral assessment funnel (Hawkins, 1979; Mash & Terdal, 1974, 1981) to plan and conduct appropriate assessments. This funnel includes procedures for (a) *diagnosis* to identify children in need of treatment and describe the nature of the difficulty, (b) *design* to specify the behaviors to be included in treatment, and (c) *evaluation* to monitor the child's progress during treatment and the effectiveness of behavior change after treatment. For the remainder of this section, we will review selected examples of available measures and procedures for assessing children's social skills deficits within this conceptual framework.

Diagnosis

The first step in a behavioral assessment of children's social skill deficits is to determine whether or not a child's behavior is problematic. This process can involve (a) *screening* to identify children who may be experiencing difficulty and for whom more thorough assessment is necesssary and (b) *problem definition*, which is a more detailed examination and description of the child's behavioral dysfunction. We shall now examine typical screening procedures and those required to better define the problem.

Screening

Generally, screening is used to identify two groups of children: (a) those already experiencing social skills deficits or (b) those at risk for later deficits (Hops & Greenwood, 1981). Children in the first group are likely to come in contact with treatment providers through direct referral by parents or teachers. The latter group is identified only by the rare occurrence of systematic broad-based early identification assessments as used in primary prevention programs (Rolf & Hasazi, 1977).

Referral.   Referral by parents or teachers is perhaps the most frequent method for initiating assessment and treatment of children with a wide range of deviant behaviors. To date, however, the reliability and validity of the referral process has received little systematic attention within behavioral assessment (Hops & Greenwood, 1981).

The authors' experience has shown that parents and teachers may not always refer withdrawn, socially isolated children for treatment. Withdrawn children may spend little time in proximity to adults or peers, may rarely initiate interactions with others, or may acquiesce during social interactions; adults in many settings may not detect these phenomena or may not evaluate them as being reason for concern (Hops, 1982; McConnell & Walker, 1983). In contrast, the aggressive, acting out child exhibits behaviors that require excessive attention from adults (Walker, 1979). In our work in the schools, we have found it necessary to provide teachers with specific prompts to refer withdrawn or isolate children. Examples of two programs that have included formats designed to increase the utility of teacher referrals by increasing their attention to important, but subtle, aspects of children's behavior are *Procedures for Establishing Effective Relationships Skills (PEERS)* (Hops et al., 1979) and *A Curriculum for Children's Effective Peer and Teacher Skills (ACCEPTS)* (Walker, McConnell, Holmes et al., 1983).

There are two benefits to using referrals by parents or teachers for the assessment of social skills deficits. First, extended contact with an individual child provides a richness of data that is very useful in the initial stages of a behavioral assessment. Second, referring agents (particularly teachers) often have a great deal of experience and knowledge regarding the social interactions of children similar in age to the one being referred. This experience can provide a set of norms and standards against which child behavior can be evaluated and inappropriate development or performance identified.

However, adult referrals should not serve as the sole means of identifying children with social skills deficits. Teachers assign significantly less importance to appropriate social skills for overall success in school than they do to academic skills and the absence of behavioral excesses (Hersh & Walker, in press; Walker, McConnell, Walker et al., 1983). Further, there is a relative lack of knowledge of the reliability and validity of these referrals. Further research is needed to identify the relationship of referrals to observed child behaviors, the accuracy of referrals for identifying at-risk children, or the specific variables that contribute to the decision to refer.

In summary, while parent and teacher referrals can provide important information for the identification and assessment of children with social skills deficits, such referrals cannot be relied on as the sole source for initiation of treatment. To guarantee the identification of children who will benefit from training, more thorough screening procedures are needed.

Rankings.   To benefit from the wide range of observations available to teachers or parents, while eliminating the shortcomings of open-ended referrals, researchers have recently developed ranking procedures for systematically screening intact groups of children. Rather than relying on adults to decide to refer an individual child, rankings prompt them to evaluate and compare the social behavior or competence of *all* children in a given group. On the basis of these relative evaluations, students requiring more thorough assessment and possible treatment can be identified.

Teacher rankings of the *frequency* of children's verbal interactions form the initial step in a comprehensive identification and assessment program for socially withdrawn preschool children (Greenwood et al., 1978). Rankings for a class of 18 to 25 children take no more than 20 minutes and can be easily completed with only written instructions. Greenwood and his colleagues (Greenwood et al., 1976, 1978, 1979) found the procedure to be (*a*) stable across a one-month period, (*b*) significantly correlated with directly observed rates of individual students' social interactions, and (*c*) surprisingly accurate at identifying the child with the lowest rate of interaction in each classroom.

Like other screening measures, however, teacher rankings are of limited utility in specifying the nature of the problem or the discrete behaviors that must be addressed in treatment. Further, ranking measures have been applied only in preschool (Connolly & Doyle, 1981; Greenwood et al., 1976, 1979) and elementary school (McConnell, 1982) settings. As yet, we do not have a comparable low-cost screening measure for identifying children with social skills deficits in home or community settings. Thus, therapists must rely on parent referrals, with all of their attendant shortcomings, or more detailed and expensive assessments to identify children with specific deficits outside the school setting.

Sociometrics.   Although not as cost effective as teacher rankings, peer judgments can also be used to tentatively identify socially problematic children in school settings. Data obtained from sociometric procedures have been shown to be predictive of later adjustment and mental health status (e.g., Cowen, et al., 1973; Roff et al., 1972; Ullman, 1952). Consequently, it has been suggested that sociometric status is the most valid criterion for the measurement of social competence (Asher, Oden, & Gottman, 1976; Gottman, 1977a; Gresham, 1983).

The partial ranking, or restricted nomination procedure, and peer ratings are the two most commonly used sociometric measures (Hops & Lewin, 1984). The partial ranking procedure requires children to pick a fixed number of classmates (usually three) in terms of some established referent (e.g., "Who do you most like to play (work) with," or "Who is your best friend?"). The percent of nominations received for each referent situation provides a measure of popularity or acceptance by the peer group. Negative nomination procedures (e.g., "Who do you *not* like to play with?") have also been used to indicate the level of peer rejection. Both positive and negative nominations are required to precisely diagnose socially problematic children without confusing *neglected* (few positive or negative nominations) and *rejected* (few positives and many negatives) children. Recent research suggests that different interventions may be required for each of these types of socially deficient children (Coie & Kupersmidt, 1983; Dodge, 1983). The neglected may require instruction in initiation skills, while rejected children may have to learn to control aggressive behavior and increase their positive responding. Further research is needed to experimentally validate these preliminary findings.

The peer rating method asks each child to rate all of his/her classmates on a three to seven-point Likert scale, according to the criterion specified in the referent situation (e.g., "How much do you like to play with _____?"). The mean rating received provides an index of each child's likeability (Singleton & Asher, 1977). Peer rating scales require equal consideration for *all* members of the group and yield more evenly distributed scores (Hops & Greenwood, 1981).

In summary, measures of sociometric status can provide valuable screening data for the assessment of social skills deficits. Used properly, they can discriminate between children who are neglected or rejected by their peers. Such measures also have two distinct limitations for use in screening. First, the instruments are relatively more expensive to administer than many other screening measures. Their administration may require clearance from school district administrators and permission from students' parents, especially when negative nominations are used. Second, reliabilities are generally higher for older children. Therefore, obtaining reliable information from preschool children may require more time-consuming assessment procedures, such as picture-sociometrics or paired comparisons (Hops & Greenwood, 1981; Hops & Lewin, 1984).

Defining the Problem

After identifying potential treatment candidates, it is necessary to (*a*) confirm that a given child requires treatment and (*b*) define more precisely the nature of the problem. Typical questions answered during this phase of assessment include: (*a*) Is this child's social behavior sufficiently atypical that treatment is warranted? (*b*) Is the problem associated with a behavioral excess or deficit? (*c*) Is the problematic behavior setting specific, and if so, in what settings is the problem evident? (*d*) What general implications are there for further assessment and treatment?

Problem definition, like referral and screening, is a relatively general, low-cost assessment procedure in which measures of the child's behavior are indirectly or directly compared to some set of outside criteria. Indirect comparisons are typically made via standardized behavior rating scales or checklists. Direct evaluations of child behavior may be accomplished by collecting summative direct observation measures of relevant child behavior and comparing these data to available norms (e.g., Greenwood et al., 1978; Walker & Hops, 1976).

Behavior Rating Scales and Checklists. Behavior rating scales and checklists are commonly completed by referring parents or teachers to describe the behavioral excesses or deficits of the identified child. These scores are then compared to normative data to determine whether or not, on the basis of adult evaluation, the child's behavior is deviant. Several examples of such instruments follow.

The Walker Problem Behavior Identification Checklist, or WPBIC (Walker, 1983), is a 50-item checklist with five empirically derived scales: (*a*) Acting Out, (*b*) Distractibility, (*c*) Disturbed Peer Relations, (*d*) Withdrawal, and (*e*) Immaturity. Norms are available for boys and girls from preschool/kindergarten to grade six (Walker, 1983). There is some evidence that the WPBIC yields similar results when completed by parents and teachers (Strain, Steele, Ellis, & Timm, 1982).

The WPBIC has a high degree of utility in the initial assessment of social skills deficits. The instrument has been shown to be very stable over time and to effectively discriminate between boys referred for mental health/special education services and a matched sample of male classmates (Walker, 1983). Further, the withdrawal scale has been shown to be sensitive to treatment (Weinrott, Corson, & Wilchesky, 1979) and related to social interaction rates (Greenwood et al., 1976).

Other checklists and rating scales that produce general factors related to social competence that may be useful in this stage of assessment are the *Child Behavior Checklist* (CBC) (Achenbach & Edelbrock, 1982) and the *Social Competence Scale and Problem Checklist* (SCS) (Kohn, 1977). The CBC has been developed for use by both parents and teachers to identify problem behavior in children aged 4 to 16. Specific factors of possible interest include Social Withdrawal, Aggressive, and Schizoid. The SCS is a teacher rating scale used primarily with preschool and primary grade children that provides two factors of interest: Interest-Participation versus Apathy-Withdrawal and Cooperation-Compliance versus Anger-Defiance. While there is evidence for the reliability and construct validity of these scales, the predictive validity for children with social skills deficits has not been established for the CBC and is only minimal for the SCS (Connolly & Doyle, 1981; Kahn & Hoge, 1983). More research for the applications discussed here is needed.

The senior author and his colleagues developed several teacher ratings scales specifically designed for identifying children with social skill deficits and excesses. The *Social Interaction Rating Scale* (SIRS) was developed as part of the PEERS program, a treatment package for socially withdrawn children in the elementáry grades (Hops et al., 1978). The eight-item scale is significantly correlated with observed positive social behavior and successfully discriminates referred from nonreferred children with 90 percent correct classification (Hops et al., 1978).

The *Social Behavior Rating Scale Positive* (SBR+) was developed as one component of SAMPLE, a screening/assessment package for socially withdrawn preschoolers (Greenwood et al, 1978). Both individual scores and the total scale score are significantly correlated with (*a*) observed rates of interaction and (*b*) sociometric acceptance. Children's scores may indicate the need for further assessment and possible treatment.

The *Social Behavior Rating Scale* (SBRS) is part of the assessment process in RECESS, a treatment package for socially aggressive elementary school children (Walker, Street, Garrett, Crossen, Hops, & Greenwood, 1978). A seven-item Negative Social Behavior Scale was found to discriminate between aggressive children and their normal peers.

Although further research is required to experimentally validate these rating scales, their empirical development suggests that they can be presently useful in the problem definition stage of assessment.

Direct Observation. Measures collected via direct observation have provided the primary dependent variables in most treatment studies of children with social skills deficits (e.g., Hops et al., 1979; Ladd, 1981; Strain, Shores, & Timm, 1977; Walker, McConnell, Walker et al., 1983). Direct observation measures vary from simple, summative procedures to complex, highly descriptive ones and are appropriately used throughout the assessment process (Hawkins, 1979; Hops & Greenwood, 1981).

During the problem definition phase of assessment, relatively simple, summative direct observation measures can be useful for confirming information collected by adult ratings or referrals. This pre-baseline observation can also aid the therapist in tentatively identifying target behaviors that must be included in treatment. At this stage of assessment, a direct observation measure must (*a*) be relatively simple to complete in a reliable, yet cost-effective, way and (*b*) provide appropriate norms (e.g., Walker & Hops, 1976) or other standards (cf. Hops, 1983; Van Houten, 1979) against which the child's behavior can be evaluated.

Perhaps the most direct and simple observational measure is the percent of time a child spends in appropriate social interaction with others. While rate of interaction measures have been criticized as a sole measure of social competence (Asher et al., 1976; Gottman, 1977a), there are a number of reasons to suggest their use in the assessment of social skills deficits. First, overall rates of social interaction, which are largely positive (Hops, 1983), have been shown to be significantly related to the rates of occurrence of a wide variety of discrete social skills (see Description section). Second, normative standards for evaluating children's rates of interacting with peers are available (e.g., Greenwood et al., 1976, 1979; Hops et al., 1979; Walker, McConnell, Clarke, 1983).

Finally, social interaction rates can be easily and reliably collected in naturalistic settings by therapists, teachers, peers, or others (Strain, McConnell, & Cordisco, 1983).

The Consultant Social Interaction Code (CSIC), also part of the PEERS Program for the socially withdrawn (Hops et al., 1979), was developed for the observational assessment of social behavior in playground settings. The instrument was designed for use by teacher-consultants (e.g., counselors, school psychologists).

The CSIC is a five-second interval, time-sampling procedure with five categories of child social behavior. Two of the categories, Positive Social and Negative/Alone, form a mutually exclusive and exhaustive summary of the observed child's social interactions. The three remaining categories of observed behavior, Start (i.e., initiate interaction), Answer (e.g., respond to a peer's initiation), and Talk, describe significant topographic elements of the observed child's interactions with others.

Normative data for these and other social interaction variables are available for both preschool (Greenwood et al., 1982) and primary grade (Hops et al., 1978) children. These data can assist the therapist in making decisions about (*a*) the presence or absence of social skills deficits and (*b*) the general areas, or response classes, on which treatment must focus (Kazdin, 1977; Walker & Hops, 1976). In addition to evaluating a child's behavior against national norms, evaluations can be based on normative data collected in the same setting in which the child is observed (Hops et al., 1979; Patterson, 1974; Walker & Hops, 1976). This latter procedure offers some control over fluctuations in setting variables that may affect social behavior (Hops & Greenwood, 1981) and may provide a more appropriate referent for the identification of deviant behavior (Nelson & Hayes, 1979).

An alternative to interval recording is to collect general ratings of child behavior on the basis of periods of direct observation in relevant settings. Moses and McConnell (1982), following the work of Weinrott, Reid, Bouske, and Brummett (1981), developed the *Observer Impression Assessment Scale* (OIAS) for rating the free-play interactions of elementary school children. The OIAS is a 15-item, 5-point Likert-type scale designed to be completed immediately following a six-minute observation in school free-play settings. Item content covers normative comparisons (e.g., "The child talks at the same volume as his peers"), social participation (e.g., "The child takes turns talking"), and peer responses (e.g., "The peers interacting with the child appear to be having fun").

The OIAS was included as one measure in an evaluation of procedures for assessing social skills among grade school boys (McConnell, 1983). In addition to a total score, three scale scores were empirically derived by factor analysis: Verbal and Social Competence, Cooperative Play, and Social Participation.

Each of the four scales was found to be internally consistent, stable across observation sessions, and significantly related, in expected directions, to relevant direct observation measures of the boys' behavior. Further, with the exception of the Verbal and Social Competence score, they individually discriminated between referred and nonreferred groups. To date, however, there is only limited evidence of the utility of the OIAS in clinical settings. As used by McConnell (1983), this instrument (*a*) was completed by individuals who had received specific training in the observational assessment of social interactions, and (*b*) was not validated against treatment outcome. While direct observation rating scales may hold promise for increasing the efficiency and validity of problem definitions in social skills assessment, their validation in clinical work is still needed.

Summary.   The problem definition phase of assessment yields a description of the child's strengths and weaknesses and indicates general response classes on which subsequent assessment and treatment must focus. Instruments employed in this phase of assessment are typically more behavior-specific than referral or screening measures yet may still rely on indirect or summative sampling procedures to evaluate a child's performance.

Behavioral researchers have made numerous contributions to problem definition procedures in clinical settings. As we have reviewed, researchers have developed both checklists (Achenbach & Edelbrock, 1982; Greenwood et al., 1978; Hops, et al., 1978; Walker, 1983) and direct observation procedures (Hops et al., 1978; McConnell, 1983) for recording relevant information. Further, each of these researchers has provided some normative basis for evaluating child outcomes. Thus, cost-effective means for sampling a broad range of child behaviors are available in clinical settings.

Design

The relationship between behavioral assessment and treatment becomes most clear during the design phase of assessment. Here, specific behaviors to be targeted in treatment are identified, and specific intervention procedures are planned. Frequently, this design phase may continue in an alternating fashion with treatment; target behaviors related to the defined problem are identified, treatment is initiated, and the general problem area is reevaluated. If the child is not yet performing at acceptable or expected levels, then new target behaviors are identified, and the process begins again.

The primary objective of the design phase of assessment is to identify highly specific behaviors and setting events on which treatment will focus. As such, narrow-band, high-fidelity assessment procedures must be employed (Cronbach, 1970; Mash & Terdal, 1974). The behaviors specified by these instruments should be those that significantly contribute to the alleviation of problems identified by earlier phases of assessment.

Assessment procedures to aid in identifying target behaviors and selecting treatment procedures will next be discussed.

Rating Scales

Rating scales elicit parents', teachers', or other adults' evaluations of the child's performance on well-defined response classes (e.g., "Responds verbally to others' initiations"). Several rating scales (e.g., Greenwood et al., 1978; Hops et al., 1978; Walker, et al., 1978) consist of items shown to be correlated with direct observation measures of children's behavior in free-play settings. While these behavior-specific ratings are typically summed into scale scores, they may also contribute individually to the specification of target behaviors for treatment.

We must be cautious, however, in relying heavily on interpretation of individual item scores. While there is some evidence that adults are more accurate when rating behavior-specific items (Bolstad & Johnson, 1977; Hops & Greenwood, 1981), there is also evidence that agreement between adults decreases as specificity of items increases (Evans & Nelson, 1977). Further, while the response classes rated by adults can be correlated with external criteria, these ratings are often too general to relate directly to the design of treatment. For instance, knowing that a child does not respond verbally to the initiations of peers is important; it does not, however, tell the therapist which specific behaviors the child must learn.

In summary, rating scales can provide a therapist with critical knowledge regarding a child's functioning in diverse settings (e.g., at home, in the classroom, on the playground). Further, these rating scales can provide valuable information regarding response classes in which the child's performance is problematic. This information is not, however, generally sufficient for the specification of target behaviors for treatment. More fine-grained measurement is usually necessary.

Behavior Role Play Tests

Behavioral assessment is distinguished from traditional assessment by its focus on *samples* of clinically significant behaviors. One of the difficulties in the assessment of social skills, however, is that critical behaviors may occur (*a*) in settings beyond the therapist's office (e.g., at home, in the classroom, or at the grocery store) or (*b*) irregularly (e.g., responding to the physical aggression of an agemate). To increase therapists' ability to sample such behaviors, several investigators have attempted to develop assessment procedures in which critical child behaviors are elicited and evaluated in analogue situations. Carefully selected social situations are presented to the child who responds to a confederate, as though the situation were real.

The *Behavioral Assertiveness Test for Children* (BAT-C) (Bornstein et al., 1977), based on a similar test for adults (Eisler, Hersen, Miller & Blanchard, 1975), is a set of nine analogue situations in which an assertive response is thought to be most socially appropriate. In administering the BAT-C, a narrator presents a short description of the scene to the child, and a confederate provides an explicit, standardized prompt to which the child responds. The child's response is scored for (*a*) duration of eye contact, (*b*) duration of speech, and (*c*) requests for new behavior.

Several other behavioral role play tests have been developed for assessing children's social behaviors. Reardon, Hersen, Bellack, and Foley (1979) expanded the BAT-C to include an equal number of items eliciting positive assertive and negative assertive responses from the child. Edelson and Rose (1978) assess a wider range of children's social behavior, sampling interactions at school, at home, and with peers in the community.

Scores on role play tests have successfully discriminated between groups of children rated as high- or low-assertive by their teachers (Reardon et al., 1979), as well as between children who have and have not received social skills training (Bornstein et al., 1977; Walker, McConnell, Walker et al., 1983). To date, however, there is little evidence of their external validity (i.e., their relationship to a child's performance in the natural environment) (Van Hasselt, Bellack, & Hersen, 1981). Walker, McConnell, Walker et al., (1983) report only low to moderate correlations between role play scores and direct observation measures of elementary school children's social behavior. Further, Kazdin and his associates have demonstrated that children's performance on role play tests can vary significantly as a function of assessment conditions (Kazdin, Matson, & Esveldt-Dawson, 1981) and preassessment experiences (Kazdin, Esveldt-Dawson, & Matson, 1982). It appears obvious that further research into variables controlling the psychometric quality and external validity of role play tests is warranted.

In summary, behavioral role play tests offer therapists one means of assessing a wide variety of social behaviors in an efficient and standardized manner. They can be used to effectively identify target behaviors for treatment (Bornstein et al., 1978). However, the analogue situations used may bear little or no similarity to the settings in which the child's social behavior is problematic. Thus, under optimal conditions, behavioral role play tests may only indicate whether specific skills are in a child's repertoire.

Direct Observation

The extent to which specific skills are exhibited in natural settings, the quality with which they are performed, and their functional antecedents and consequences can only be determined by some form of direct observation in the relevant home, community, and school settings. Recently, procedures for directly observing in schools and other structured environments have received greater attention and have been better developed. Observational methods applied to home and community settings have included self-monitoring (McConnell, Biglan, Severson, 1984) and daily telephone contact with parents (Jones, 1974).

One example of a school-based direct observation system is the CSIC (Hops et al., 1978), previously discussed in the "Problem Definition" section. It consists of two summative and three topographic categories of social interaction and can easily and reliably be applied by school personnel in a wide range of social settings. Although the CSIC focuses on the targeted behaviors included in the PEERS treatment package, the scores derived from this measure (e.g., percent of time in social interaction and rate of positive social initiations) may be appropriate for other client-specific applications. Further, given the strong relationship between general measures of social interaction and rates of specific social behaviors (Greenwood et al., 1982), the CSIC may be especially appropriate for use in a wide range of treatment programs.

To obtain data about specific social skills using more informal observations, Walker, McConnell, Walker et al. (1983) developed a summative rating form to be completed by therapists, teachers, or paraprofessional playground supervisors. Three scores are collected: (*a*) an estimate of time spent in social interaction, based on ratings of whether the child spent at least 50 percent of each five-minute period appropriately, (*b*) checks on the occurrence or non-occurrence of specific target behaviors, and (*c*) a rating of the overall social skill level exhibited by the child during the free-play period. While this rating procedure has not yet been validated against more detailed assessments of social interaction (i.e., direct observation), Walker, McConnell, Walker et al., (1983) report general concordance between therapists' data using this procedure and more detailed assessments of treatment outcome.

These instruments exemplify the type of direct observation procedure that can be successfully used by therapists or aides in clinical settings, without extensive training to target specific skill deficits and/or global response classes for treatment.

Self-Report

Several self-report instruments have been developed that require children to evaluate their feelings, behaviors, and social relationships with peers. In the absence of data indicating deficits in actual social behavior, a target for intervention might be the child's own reported feelings.

The Children's Assertiveness Behavior Scale (CABS) (Wood & Michelson, 1978) and the Self-Report Assertiveness Test for Boys (SRAT-B) (Reardon et al., 1979) are two such examples. Both use paper-and-pencil formats and presume a reading ability level, which may preclude their usefulness for younger populations. Furthermore, such tests confound conceptual knowledge with performance and rest on the assumption that a single response is synonymous with skill level (Hops & Greenwood, 1981).

A standardized interview procedure has been developed recently to assess social competence and peer relations (Bierman & McCauley, 1983). The interview format circumvents problems related to reading level and provides more extensive information about children's behavioral dysfunction.

These and other self-report instruments for assessing children's social skills must be cautiously used because of the well-known limitations associated with self-report data (e.g., reliability, validity). Furthermore, children may not always have the necessary verbal repertoire to understand or report on the determinants of their own behavior (Evans & Nelson, 1977). Further demonstration of the instruments' predictive and experimental validity compared with more objective indexes of social skills (e.g., direct observation) is also required.

Treatment Evaluation

The evaluation phase in a behavioral assessment of social skills deficits provides the therapist with necessary information to determine the effects of a given set of treatment procedures on the identified target behaviors. Two major goals can be identified for this phase of assessment. First, the therapist must be able to determine throughout the course of treatment whether short- and long-term objectives for individual target behaviors are being met. Second, the therapist must be able to assess whether treatment effects are generalizing to other social situations and whether these generalized effects meet the subjective standards of the treatment's participants and consumers (i.e., the referred child, parents, teachers, peers).

Two different procedures provide therapists with the means for achieving these goals. *Continuous monitoring* of the child's behavior on a daily (or other frequent) basis provides information for (*a*) demonstrating mastery of the target behavior in both treatment and generalization settings and (*b*) evaluating the degree to which the referred child's behavior approximates appropriate normative levels. *Posttreatment assessment* evaluates the summative effects of the treatment procedures and provides for the assessment of the long-term, generalized effects of treatment, as well as the perception of referring agents' and significant others' evaluations of the child's current social behavior.

Continuous Monitoring. In their review of assessment procedures for social skills deficits, Hops and Greenwood (1981) noted that "repeated assessment of behavior targeted for treatment provides the *process* data necessary for a precise evaluation of treatment effects for individuals" (p. 381). Continuous monitoring provides an immediate, ongoing basis for evaluating whether treatment goals are being attained and provides an effective method for both planning revisions in the treatment program and evaluating the relative effectiveness of these revisions once they are implemented.

Direct observation measures previously referred to in the Problem Definition and Design sections are examples of the instruments best suited for the continuous monitoring of treatment effects. Daily observations using an interval system (e.g., CSIC) (Hops et al., 1978) or a less formal rating form (e.g., Walker, McConnell, Holmes et al., 1983) can provide inexpensive daily recordings of the effectiveness of treatment. Self-monitoring (McConnell et al., 1984) and daily parent telephone contact (Jones, 1974) can also be considered for assessing the impact of treatment in settings inaccessible to the therapist and for treating older children.

The selection and design of appropriate continuous monitoring procedures must be completed, however, on a case-by-case basis so that (*a*) the resources necessary for this assessment are available throughout the course of treatment, and (*b*) the information gathered is reliable enough to permit the therapist and clients to make ongoing evaluations of progress.

Posttreatment Assessment.   Posttreatment assessment is the final phase of a behavioral assessment of social skills deficits. Posttreatment assessment typically evaluates the summative and long-term effectiveness of treatment as well as the level of satisfaction with this outcome reported by significant social agents.

At one level, posttreatment assessment often repeats the measurement procedures applied during the earlier "problem definition" phase. Parent or teacher reports on behavior checklists or data from direct observation in social situations are collected. These data can then be compared with earlier results as well as with available normative data. The pretreatment to posttreatment comparison of checklist or observational data provides an evaluation of the effects of treatment for the individual child (Hops & Greenwood, 1981).

Comparisons to normative data offer further evidence of the effects of treatment and may provide useful guidelines for determining when to terminate treatment. In their treatment package, Hops et al. (1978) recommend that treatment be continued until the target child is interacting with peers at a level that is one standard deviation *higher* than the normative rate; therapists could use similar guidelines after treatment for determining whether additional booster sessions are necessary (Paine, Hops, Walker, Greenwood, Fleischman, & Guild, 1982).

An additional aspect of posttreatment assessment is an evaluation of the *social* validity of treatment outcomes (Kazdin, 1977; Wolf, 1978). Social validation measures, usually in the form of rating scales, elicit subjective evaluations of posttreatment child behavior from those individuals who referred the child for treatment or have an opportunity to observe the child's behavior after treatment and thus might be considered consumers of the intervention effort. Subjective evaluations might be collected from parents (McMahon & Forehand, 1983), teachers (Walker, McConnell, Holmes et al., 1983), peers (Oden & Asher, 1977), or the referred children themselves.

Summary

In this section, we have described the various phases of a behavioral assessment of social skills deficits. The reader should note, however, that this assessment is not necessarily sequential (i.e., beginning with referral/screening and continuing through posttreatment assessment); nor is this assessment a static process. Rather, the therapists must be prepared to use information gathered at one stage of the process to move quickly and efficiently to another, whether it is earlier or later in the assessment model.

In addition, assessment procedures must be carefully integrated with treatment. As we have discussed, several steps in assessment are closely linked with treatment and are used throughout the course of intervention. We next turn, then, to a discussion of these treatment procedures.

TREATMENT

With increasing recognition of the importance of peer relations to short- and long-term adjustment, clinicians and researchers alike are devoting increasing effort toward the development of intervention techniques to facilitate the social adjustment of young children. Further research is needed to pinpoint the specific behaviors necessary for skillful social interaction, and to delineate more precisely the conditions under which the display of socially appropriate behavior leads to peer acceptance and judgments of social competence. Nevertheless, there is a real-world urgency to intervene on behalf of the child who interacts minimally or inappropriately with his or her social milieu. The result has been a proliferation of intervention procedures based primarily on face validity with varying degrees of success (Hops, 1982).

In the following pages we will review examples of the major existing intervention techniques for remediating social skills deficits, discuss the usefulness of each strategy, and present some guidelines for the practitioner in choosing and implementing the appropriate remediation procedures.

Treatment Components

A variety of intervention procedures has been developed in an attempt to modify the behavioral deficits and excesses in children that contribute to poor social functioning. These procedures, which depend primarily on social learning principles, generally fall into three main categories: (*a*) individual and group reinforcement contingencies, (*b*) modeling procedures, and (*c*) skills training involving the combined use of direct instruction, modeling, behavioral rehearsal, and verbal feedback (Hops, 1982). It is difficult to make useful comparisons among these techniques due to (*a*) differences in methodological and theoretical perspectives underlying each, (*b*) the lack of equivalence among groups across studies, as well as (*c*) the lack of homogeneity within research samples (Hops, 1982; Conger and Keane, 1981). However, methodological, conceptual, and assessment difficulties notwithstanding, outcome research that has incorporated these procedures illustrates that we are headed toward the development and delineation of a working model that can grapple with the complexity of social adjustment in children.

Individual and Group Reinforcement Contingencies

Social Reinforcement. Contingent adult social reinforcement dominated early studies on the modification of children's social behaviors. Allen, Hart, Buell, Harris, and Wolf (1964) demonstrated that teacher praise that was made contingent on the social behavior of a preschool isolate increased the frequency of her interaction with peers. Other studies found that social behavior may be influenced by teacher attention directed at collateral nonsocial behaviors. For example, the crawling behavior of one preschooler was eliminated by praising on-feet behavior and ignoring off-feet behavior. An important side effect of this contingency was an increase in the amount of time this child spent in social interaction with his peer group, due to his increased mobility and similarity to other children. Similarly, Buell, Stoddard, Harris, & Baer (1968) indirectly increased the social play of one motorically and socially deficient preschooler by praising his playing with outdoor equipment. The result was an increase in proximity to his peer group. Moreover, increases in touching, verbalizations, and cooperative play, none of which had been reinforced, were unexpectedly maintained above baseline levels, even during reversal phases. These latter studies emphasize the importance of examining a child's level of competence in nonsocial behaviors, which are likely to be critical antecedents for effective performance in the social arena, and targeting these for intervention if they are found to obstruct the acquisition or performance of effective social skills (Finch & Hops, 1982).

Generally, reinforcement procedures are not used in isolation since adult social reinforcement alone may be insufficient for developing adequate social responding, especially for lower functioning children (Hops et al., 1979). In most studies using contingent reinforcement, praise is generally combined with verbal and physical prompting and priming of the behavior of both targets *and* peers to increase the likelihood that social interaction will occur and, consequently, that praise can be delivered (Hops, 1982, 1983).

A combination of verbal and physical prompts plus contingent verbal praise was used to increase the appropriate social behavior of three behaviorally handicapped preschool boys (Strain, Shores, & Kerr, 1976). Physical prompts included moving the children in closer proximity to their peers and/or physically manipulating them to respond. Verbal prompts included statements designed to elicit social behavior, such as "Let's play with your friends." Results proved more noteworthy for the two children who were more socially responsive. One of these responded positively even when the contingencies were directed at the other child, illustrating the possibility of spillover effects when increasing social interaction. The lowest interactor, however, returned to baseline levels when the conditions were terminated.

It is clear from the above studies that contingent adult social reinforcement can increase the rate of positive social interaction and reduce the rate of inappropriate social responding. However, adult contingent reinforcement may not be the most effective intervention procedure for establishing maintenance and generalization of effects. Successes have been noted generally at the preschool level and under rigorous experimental conditions. More powerful procedures may be required in less structured or controlled settings and for older or more severely deficient children. Adult attention and manipulation can be fruitfully combined with other procedures to maximize effectiveness (Hops, 1982).

Token Reinforcement.   Many studies have investigated the effects of more powerful reinforcers on the social behavior of children. These have ranged from food and tokens with backups of toys, candy, or pleasurable activities to toy components. Primary reinforcers, such as food and candy, have been successfully used to develop social responses in severely retarded or low-functioning children (e.g., Whitman, Mercurio, and Caponigri, 1970). While primary reinforcers can be powerfully used on the spot to shape and strengthen adaptive social behaviors, they are also successfully used as backup reinforcers in token reinforcement programs. Clement and his colleagues (Clement & Milne, 1967; Clement, Roberts, & Lantz, 1970) used token reinforcement within a group psychotherapy setting to increase the social behavior of elementary school boys referred because of shy, withdrawn behavior. Only the group receiving social *and* token reinforcement from the therapist showed increases in social play and proximity to one another during therapy sessions. In contrast, the group receiving only therapist verbal praise actually reduced their level of social behavior during the session.

Walker et al. (1979) conducted a series of three studies in an experimental classroom setting. They were designed to investigate the effects of teacher praise and token reinforcement on three topographic components of social interaction: (*a*) initiations, (*b*) responding to positive initiations, and (*c*) continuing social interactions over time. Three groups of six primary grade children were referred by school counselors because of relatively low social behavior levels. Each child had (*a*) a low rate of observed social interaction and (*b*) a high score on the Walker Problem Behavior Identification Checklist (Walker, 1983). Each group was involved in a different experiment. Experiments 1 and 2 involved differentially reinforcing the topographic components in varying orders. In Experiment 3, all components were reinforced simultaneously within the ongoing social interaction. The results indicated that reinforcing initiations and responding actually decreased overall interactive behavior and produced some artificiality in the children's interactions. On the other hand, measurable increases were noted when children were reinforced for continuing social interactions. The most powerful contingencies, however, occurred in Experiment 3 when children were reinforced for all three components as they naturally occurred. These contingencies seemed to maximally facilitate overall interaction without hampering individual interactive styles. The experiments illustrate the caution that must be taken in treating in isolation individual components of more complex socially skillful behaviors. It may prove to be important to provide training in specific social skill components in a controlled setting and then employ procedures designed to increase the quality and quantity of overall social behavior in the natural setting (Greenwood et al., 1982; Hops, 1983).

In an attempt to extend token systems to the natural setting, Hops and his colleagues (Hops et al., 1979) designed a study in which points were provided to socially withdrawn children contingent on increases in their rate of interaction or time spent in interaction with peers. Individual backup reinforcers for the target children were compared with *group* backups shared by the entire class. The group backup was clearly the more powerful contingency, motivating the peer group to help the child earn points. It was notable that individual backups were extremely slow to take effect and did not produce comparable levels of social behavior in the target child.

The authors conducted another study that examined the effects of different settings on social skills intervention. The individual contingency plus group backup was applied to the same child in the classroom and at recess. Results indicated that the contingencies in operation at recess yielded greater behavior gains and longer maintenance after termination of treatment than when contingencies were applied in the academic setting. It appears that the most powerful token reinforcement procedure for the withdrawn, low-interacting child would consist of individual contingencies paired with a group backup occurring during recess or other free-play periods.

Modeling Procedures

Bandura's (1969) theory of behavior change has led to the therapeutic use of modeling for a variety of problematic behaviors. Most modeling studies of withdrawn or isolate children have used filmed models. In one of the first, O'Connor (1969) exposed six preschool isolate children individually to a 23-minute color film depicting progressively increasing social interaction among children. Dramatic increases in social interaction immediately followed the viewing. A control group, who watched a film about dolphins, showed no such change. Two weaknesses in O'Connor's design were (a) the absence of follow-up data and (b) the film's soundtrack, which may have provided a coaching or instructional component somewhat confounding the effects due to the symbolic modeling. Nevertheless, this study spurred many researchers to study the utility of modeling procedures for the remediation of social skills.

Subsequently, O'Connor (1972) examined the contribution of shaping procedures to symbolic modeling. His findings indicated that, while modeling alone increased social interaction, modeling combined with shaping was no more effective. Noteworthy were the gains achieved in peer interaction, which persisted over three- and six-week follow-ups under both modeling conditions. Evers and Schwarz (1973) attempted to replicate and extend O'Connor's work. They found that modeling, with and without contingent teacher praise, increased positive peer interaction. Furthermore, improvements above postassessment levels resulted for both groups at follow-up. The authors suggested that praise may interfere with or interrupt the ongoing social interactions of children and reduce the utility of modeling. As noted earlier, praise must be appropriately administered in order to ensure therapeutic, rather than disruptive, results.

Gottman (1977b) conducted an investigation on the effects of the original O'Connor film on social isolation. His control group, however, viewed an Alaskan travelogue film rather than O'Connor's (1969) control film. While no experimental-control differences were noted, methodological limitations qualify the interpretation of the results. The results may have been due to (a) differences in control films or (b) lengthy periods between preassessment and postassessments and treatment.

Keller and Carlson (1974) used their own set of videotapes depicting social behaviors assumed to be important components of social interaction, for example, imitation, smiling, laughing, giving tokens, and physical affection. Preschool isolate children in the modeling condition showed a significant increase in giving and receiving reinforcement and in overall peer interaction, while the control group exhibited no changes. However, the effects disappeared at a follow-up assessment conducted three weeks after termination. It is important to note that only those specific behaviors that were initially highest in the subjects' repertoires increased in frequency. There was no impact on those behaviors that occurred infrequently. The authors suggest that symbolic modeling procedures may increase existing social behaviors but do not necessarily build new ones. Perhaps to develop new social repertoires, more direct and explicit training methods may be required. It may be, for example, that children with more serious deficiencies will not benefit from symbolic modeling alone.

The effects of exposure to modeling films, as illustrated in the studies reviewed here, are not entirely clear or consistent. It may be, for example, that the film modeling manipulation alone is not responsible for achieved treatment gains, but rather the coaching or instruction that the film soundtrack provides or a combination of the two. Furthermore, results must be tempered due to methodological concerns, such as differences in subject selection, which resulted in subject populations with differing levels of social skill deficits (Hops & Greenwood, 1981). Studies that identified 20 percent or more of the available population as isolate subjects (e.g., Gottman, 1977b) may have selected children only mildly withdrawn or more responsive to minimum treatments (Hops, 1982). Furthermore, the majority of studies reviewed were conducted with preschool children, thus limiting the generalizability of the findings for older children (Conger & Keane, 1981; Hops, 1982).

Some studies discussed above, with methodological questions aside, have suggested that combining social praise with modeling was no more effective than modeling alone in increasing the social behavior of young children. However, Walker and Hops (1973), in a series of experiments, demonstrated that symbolic modeling combined with token reinforcement could produce more dramatic results. Their three studies compared (a) the O'Connor modeling procedure and token reinforcement directed at a primary grade girl whose rate of initiations to the peer group was greater than theirs to her, (*b*) modeling and reinforcement directed at a peer group whose mean rate of initiations to the low-interacting subject was greater than hers to them, and (*c*) the two procedures directed at both the withdrawn subject *and* her peers in a yoked fashion so that no reinforcement became available unless both had achieved their preset criterion. All three procedures were effective in increasing the interaction rate of the subjects and their respective peer groups. It was the combined procedure in the third experiment, however, that produced the most immediate gains. While these experiments could not tease out the differential impacts of modeling and contingent token reinforcement, they show that their combined effect can produce gains more quickly.

Peers as Behavioral Change Agents

Other cultures traditionally have recognized the utility of peer group assistance in the teaching of academic and social skills (Bronfenbrenner, 1970). Recent evidence indicates that here, too, peers are increasingly used as behavioral change agents in remediating a wide range of problematic behaviors in children (Allen, 1976; Apolloni & Cooke, 1978; Strain, 1981).

Socially skilled peers may be used in training less skilled peers. Strain et al. (1977) and Strain (1977) used socially adept preschool confederates who were instructed, following four training sessions, to get the other children to play with them during specific time periods outside the classroom. Results indicated increases in initiations and gains in overall social behavior for both the targets and trainers. Two of the three subjects in one study (Strain, 1977) also showed generalization to the classroom setting. The differential response to treatment noted was related to initial levels of social involvement. Perhaps those children with levels of social ability extremely lower than their peers require more basic remediation procedures including collateral skills training, such as in language or motor skills, before they can benefit from peer reinforcement and group contingencies. These and other studies (e.g., Morris & Dolker, 1974) provide support for the practical utility of peer trainers who function at higher levels than the targeted subjects.

In contrast, Furman, Rahe, and Hartup (1979) paired withdrawn preschoolers with peers approximately the same age or 15 months younger to evaluate the impact of peer age on the acquisition of social skills by the target children. Each pair was placed in a room for 10 play sessions each of 20 minutes duration over a four- to six-week period. Results indicated that, following treatment, the isolate children in the younger-aged "therapist" group increased their positive interaction rates with children their own age in the regular classroom. Less dramatic changes were noted in those isolates placed with same-aged "therapists." The authors argued that the placement of isolates with younger children provided them with the opportunity to learn and use leadership skills (i.e., initiating and directing social activities), which is an opportunity not available in the classroom with their own age-mates. The results were impressive in terms of cost effectiveness as well as the magnitude of interactional gains. No more than three hours of intervention time were required to increase social interaction at least 50 percent beyond the pretreatment levels to the levels of the normal population.

Clearly, the use of more-skilled children to train their less-skilled peers and the pairing of younger-aged or developmentally equal peers as therapists may provide potentially powerful and cost-effective treatments for establishing social skills in isolate children. Certainly, further research is warranted to replicate and extend these promising findings.

Specific Skills Training

Contingent reinforcement, modeling, coaching, instruction, role playing, and behavioral rehearsal, as we have seen above, have been used to teach children to interact successfully with their peer group. While many of the studies have focused on increasing the frequency of interaction of isolate children, fewer have focused on specific skill components believed to be related to peer acceptance and social competence.

Assertiveness Training. One set of component skills believed to be a prerequisite of competent social functioning falls under the rubric of assertiveness. While the adult social skills literature is replete with assertiveness training studies, interest in this area has only recently been reflected in child research.

As Combs and Slaby (1977) cogently point out, children are faced daily with situations that require assertive behavior yet typically receive little instruction for responding effectively. For example, the inability to refuse to submit to inappropriate demands from peers, particularly aggressive ones, can lead to an increase in aggressive interaction or to further withdrawal of isolate children. Assertiveness training is generally conducted in analogue or laboratory settings in which contrived situations requiring assertive responses are presented. Intervention involves pinpointing the problem and teaching the subject assertive responding using behavioral rehearsal, feedback, modeling, and instructions.

Extrapolating from their work with adults, Bornstein et al. (1977) attempted to change the behavior of four unassertive children found to be consistently low in levels of eye contact, duration of speech, loudness of responding, and ability to make requests. Unfortunately, no normative data were available for assessing whether these deficits were below levels found in nonreferred children, and only subjective clinical judgment was used.

Results of the BAT-R role-play test (see Assessment) indicated that all children changed on component behaviors and on overall assertiveness (as rated by independent judges), with generalization to three untrained scenes. These increases in both trained and untrained responses persisted into the follow-up probes two and four weeks after treatment.

In a related study, Bornstein et al. (1980) attempted to extend their findings to a more severely disturbed population and to assess the degree of generalization to more natural environments. Resting on the assumption that many children exhibiting severely aggressive, antisocial behavior lack appropriate social skills and resort to aggression because they are unable to be appropriately and effectively assertive, the authors treated four highly aggressive children in a similar fashion (Bornstein et al., 1977). Results indicated that the treatment produced gains in each target behavior for each child. Patterns of generalization and maintenance, however, varied substantially across subjects.

The Bornstein et al. (1977, 1980) studies are a good first step in the development of effective assertiveness training procedures for interactionally impaired children. Furthermore, as the authors suggest, their findings are compatible with the hypothesis that hyperaggressive children (as well as isolate children) are deficient in social skills, manifesting both specific deficits and excesses in assertiveness, and can benefit from social skills training. Although results of generalization were not consistently positive, the authors suggest that the fact that there was any generalization with such brief treatment (three 15-30-minute sessions per target behavior), is indicative of the potential power of the procedures. Indeed, as we will discuss later, length of treatment is a critical variable when developing effective social skills treatment programs.

The results of children's assertiveness training programs remain inconclusive. Neglected methodological and theoretical considerations preclude adopting this sort of analogue remediation strategy as a primary one. As discussed earlier in this chapter, it has not yet been convincingly demonstrated that role-play behavior in assessment and training settings corresponds with social behavior in the natural setting (Van Hasselt et al., 1981). Furthermore, normative data bases must be used for assessing specific skill deficits and evaluating treatment. Indeed, successful treatment (and, by extension, social competence) must be judged in relation to a certain normative reference group (e.g., average classmates, agemates).

Problem-solving Training.   Another major approach to social skills remediation involves instruction in interpersonal problem solving. Unlike the majority of treatment strategies discussed above, which have focused on training discrete, observable behaviors, interpersonal problem-solving skills are thought to help the child cope in a variety of situations that may arise in the natural environment (Spivack and Shure, 1974).

The most extensive and comprehensive research in this area has been conducted by Spivack, Shure, and their associates (Spivack & Shure, 1974; Shure and Spivack, 1978), who developed a program for use in classrooms with preschool and kindergarten children. Based on their studies indicating a relationship between the ability to provide alternative solutions to specific inter-personal problems and overall behavioral adjustment (as rated by teachers), Spivack and Shure (1974) developed a program to teach young children to increase the number of alternative solutions they provide to hypothetical inter-personal problem situations. Overall, results indicated an increase on measures of cognitive and affective thinking relative to a no-treatment control group and significant improvements in behavioral adjustment. The treated group main-tained their increases in adjustment in follow-up studies up to two years later, as rated by a new set of teachers who were unaware of the experiment.

Although the Shure and Spivack program of research appears promising, there are several areas of weakness that must be noted (Hops, 1982; Conger & Keane, 1981). First, the research relies solely on one measure of behavioral adjustment, a measure of teacher perception that has not been validated. Sec-ondly, children were divided into somewhat arbitrary dichotomous groups on the basis of face validity. The proportion of children considered aberrant (which, at times, included the inhibited and the impulsive) varied from study to study and may have included children only mildly deficient and, therefore, more likely to respond to minimal treatments (Hops, 1982). Finally, teacher ratings of overall behavioral adjustment may actually be more related to class-room adjustment than to interpersonal competence (Conger & Keane, 1981; Hops, 1982).

While there is much face validity to the cognitive problem-solving approach to social skills intervention, as pioneered by Spivack, Shure, and their associ-ates, their research suffers from the methodological inadequacies outlined above (Conger & Keane, 1981; Urbain & Kendall, 1980). Further, replications with improved designs have not always been successful (Rickel, Eshelman, & Loigman, 1983). The procedures also require replication and extension to more severely withdrawn or interactionally impaired children with comprehensive assessment of both process and outcome variables.

Other Social Skills Training

Treatment procedures designed to train children in sets of specific social skills, other than assertiveness or problem solving, have been included under the heading of *coaching* (Oden & Asher, 1977). The procedures involve the com-bined use of direct instruction, behavioral rehearsal or modeling, and verbal feedback by the trainer. One of the most comprehensive studies with isolate children was carried out by Oden and Asher (1977). They compared coaching with a peer-pairing arrangement and an untreated control group. Each of six coaching sessions, in which the isolate children were individually instructed in a set of skills for playing with other children, was followed by an opportunity to practice these skills with a peer in a game-playing situation and by a feedback session from the instructor. The social skills selected for training were chosen because of their assumed relationship to peer acceptance. These were (*a*) participation in play activities, (*b*) cooperation with peers, (*c*) communication with peers, and (*d*) support and validation of peers. In the peer-pairing condition, children played the same games with a peer partner but received neither instructions nor feedback. The control group was removed from the classroom but engaged solely in solitary play.

Pretreatment to posttreatment gains significantly favored the coaching group, who increased on a "play with" sociometric, but not on a "work with" or "best friends" sociometric. Observation data collected during the game setting revealed no differential treatment effects, showing increases in task participation for both coaching and peer-pairing groups. However, the subjects' behavior in the natural setting was not observed. While follow-up sociometric scores one year later indicated continued gains for the coaching group relative to the peer-pairing and control groups, transformation of the scores to *z* scores to control for changes in peer raters revealed an increase in control group mean scores to the level of the coaching group. Thus, this procedure demonstrated only minimal efficacy for changing peer status in the long run (Hops, 1982). Furthermore, Conger and Keane (1981) point out that the peer-pairing and coaching conditions were not equivalent in terms of adult attention, thus precluding a determination that the gains noted were due to coaching rather than to adult attention per se.

Gottman, Gonso, and Schuler (1976) conducted a coaching study with four girls selected on the basis of a "best friend" sociometric. The two experimental subjects were seen individually by an adult for 30 minutes each day for a week and were instructed in initiating interactions, making friends, and perspective taking. These behaviors had been shown previously to discriminate between popular and unpopular children (Gottman et al., 1975). The results were equivocal. One experimental child improved significantly in social status, and both of the experimental and one of the two control children showed increases in the frequency of positive interaction as measured by direct observation.

LaGreca and Santogrossi (1980) used coaching procedures with videotaped feedback in a four-week skills-training program on a sample of 30 children from grades three through five. These children, who were low on peer acceptance ratings, were assigned to skills training, attention-placebo, or a waiting-list control group. Based on the literature on correlates of peer acceptance (e.g., Hartup, 1970; Oden & Asher, 1977), eight specific skills were selected: (*a*) smiling/laughing, (*b*) greeting others, (*c*) joining ongoing activities, (*d*) extending invitations, (*e*) conversational skills, (*f*) sharing and cooperation, (*g*) verbal complimenting, and (*h*) physical appearance/grooming. The study is unusual in that it involved the use of group training rather than individual training procedures. The study also included a comprehensive assessment including role plays with peers, classroom observations, a verbal test of skill knowledge, a role-play test, and sociometric ratings. Results indicated that the skills-training group improved in skill knowledge, role-play performance, and behavioral observations of initiations to peers, relative to the attention-placebo and waiting-list control groups, but not on total positive social behavior or sociometric acceptance. There was no follow-up measure to assess the durability of the changes obtained. While the authors contend that the lack of change in sociometric ratings may have been due to this measure's insensitivity to the skills-training program, it is possible that the manipulation was not powerful enough to produce more than minimal generalizability to the natural setting.

Ladd (1981) conducted a well-designed study comparing the effects of specific verbal skills training with an attention-control and no-treatment control group on behavioral data and sociometric scores. Thirty-six subjects selected on the basis of (a) relatively low-sociometric acceptance scores and (b) deficits in targeted behaviors demonstrated in the classroom setting were assigned to one of the three groups. The children were trained in pairs for eight, 45- to 50-minute sessions and were taught to ask questions, lead, and offer support to peers. Instructions included guided and self-directed rehearsal and self-evaluation and correction of behavior. Compared to the two other groups, children in the skills-training group increased in the first two behaviors as directly observed in the classroom and in sociometric status as well.

While Ladd's (1981) study is remarkable in its demonstration of changes in both the behavioral and sociometric indicators of social competence, it should be noted that children who were low on both measures were selected. It is also likely that the peer pairing (which allowed opportunities for more realistic practice), the more lengthy treatment phase, the sequential programming of generalization to the normal peer group, and the self-evaluation of behavior (which may serve the children when they are alone among their regular peer group) are features that probably enhanced the effectiveness of the treatment program. Clearly, more research is needed to evaluate the power of each of these features, especially on more severely interactionally impaired children who are more likely to come to the attention of clinicians and other social agents.

Combined Interventions

Broad-based intervention strategies, which combine the most powerful technology available into comprehensive yet practical treatment packages, have also been developed to serve more severely interactionally impaired children. One example of these is the PEERS program (Hops et al., 1979), which is designed to remediate the socially withdrawn behavior of primary grade children by providing them with entry into the peer group mainstream. This is accomplished by (a) arranging the environment so that target children spend more time socially involved in group play activities during recess and in academic work with peers, (b) providing them with specific skills that can be used in successful social interaction, and (c) motivating the peer group to ease their entry. Based on the coaching study of Oden and Asher (1977) and the direct instruction model of Engelmann and Becker (1978), a social skills tutoring component was developed to teach initiating, responding to peers' initiations, and maintaining interactions (see Walker et al., 1979). A peer-pairing arrangement involves the target child and a different peer in an academically related task for 10 minutes per day. Praise and token reinforcement are implemented during recess in which the child receives points for playing and talking with others. The points are traded for rewards to be shared by the entire class, thus motivating the peer group to assist in the intervention. The final component, designed to establish cross-setting generalization, trains the child to report to the teacher what s/he intends to do socially at recess and to report back immediately after. (Studies have indicated that children who are reinforced for reporting accurately, e.g., Risley & Hart, 1968, and for doing what they say they will do, Israel & O'Leary, 1973, actually increase the frequency of the specified behavior.) The individual components are faded systematically until the child is interacting at approximately normal levels under natural conditions.

Although this program appears to have face validity and has demonstrated significant treatment effects (Hops et al., 1979; Paine et al., 1982), generalization and long-term maintenance of gains have received only minimal support (Lewin & Rogers, 1982). Furthermore, as Michelson and Wood point out, the package's main limitation involves the lack of tutoring components directed to more complex social skills (such as assertiveness and requesting behavioral change in others) and to more basic or traditional social skills (such as eye contact, body posture, and smiling) (Michelson & Wood, 1980). It would appear, however, that practitioners could adapt this model to include those skills if they were deemed lacking in a particular target population.

Choosing an Appropriate Intervention Strategy

Confounds in Existing Treatments. A number of methodological and theoretical concerns inherent in the above studies precluded a precise and definitive comparative analysis of the major treatment modalities reviewed. Differences have been noted, for example, in assessment instruments used, length of treatment, and the level of severity in the treated subjects. Furthermore, there appear to be important overlaps across the major treatment procedures in their underlying components. For example, reinforcement contingencies, which are arranged to control the behavior of targeted children and/or their peers, use direct instruction to convey the operating contingencies. Also, when the peer group is involved in the contingency, the competent children provide continuous modeling for the less-competent target children (Hops, 1983). And, as described earlier, the soundtrack of films used in symbolic modeling studies may have provided direct instruction in some cases and, in others, actively induced the children to interact socially by emphasizing its pleasurable aspects.

Maintenance. Clearly, short-term successes have been noted across the major treatment modalities reviewed. However, the durability and generalizability of treatment gains, if assessed at all, appear inconsistent. For example, in the senior author's review of studies of the socially withdrawn/isolate child, no one treatment approach was proven superior to any other in producing long-term treatment gains (Hops, 1982). Nevertheless, we can cull from this rapidly expanding literature (*a*) specific patterns appearing across treatment modalities that are associated with a greater likelihood of occurrence of generalization and maintenance effects and (*b*) some general guidelines for the practitioner for choosing and implementing intervention procedures for the child with social skills deficits.

It is clear that the maintenance and cross-setting generalizability of treatment effects require systematic and extensive programming efforts (Baer, Wolf, & Risley, 1968). Generally, there are two strategies for building in durability and cross-setting generalizability: (*a*) reprogramming the natural environment by changing the behavior of social agents in salient natural settings (e.g., parents, siblings, peers, teachers) to reinforce the target child's new behavior and (*b*) "reprogramming the child" to survive in a nonsupportive environment (Graubard, Rosenberg, & Miller, 1971). Reprogramming the environment involves determining those settings most critical to the child's acquisition and use of social skills and training social agents (e.g., parents or teachers) to apply social and, if needed, token reinforcers to be gradually faded until the child's behavior is maintained by naturally occurring consequences. "Reprogramming the child" refers to teaching the child global strategies for handling a nonresponsive environment. Two frequently cited examples are self-control (Drabman, Spitalnik, & O'Leary, 1973) and problem-solving (Spivack & Shure, 1974) techniques, although their effectiveness is still in some doubt. While desirable, these two strategies for building in persistence of treatment gains demand considerable effort on the part of the clinician and may not be feasible where resources are limited.

A major factor affecting the persistence of treatment gains appears to be the length of treatment. While more research is needed to determine the optimal combination of length and intensity of treatment, studies having the greatest impact over time, regardless of treatment modality or measurement instrument used, are in effect daily for at least two months (Hops, 1982). A second important consideration is the treatment setting. Hops et al. (1979) compared the impact of a token economy and group backup on a kindergarten girl in the classroom and on the playground. Social behavior was found to persist longer on the playground, a likely result of the naturally occurring reinforcement for social behavior in that setting. Treatment in hospital settings or in special self-contained classrooms may not generalize to natural social settings.

Summary

Thus far, we have indicated that the remediation strategy of choice generally involves the appropriate combining of treatment components to achieve maximum effectiveness, since each appears to have a significant functional value for remediating social skill deficits in children (Hops, 1983). To achieve persistence in treatment effects, we advocate lengthier treatments that occur in settings in which social behavior is most likely to occur and is reinforced naturally, coupled with the training of salient social agents in the child's environment to support the newly acquired skills.

Ideally, we begin with a careful *assessment* of each child's specific skill deficits and the situational contexts in which they are manifested. Based on this assessment, a treatment program can be individually tailored to provide training in exactly those skills in which the child shows deficits. For those children lacking specific skills, *coaching and instruction* in a well-controlled setting is the initial treatment of choice. Studies above have indicated that specific behaviors can be increased in the training setting, particularly behaviors that are not present in the child's repertoire at the start of treatment. Such coaching and instruction in a controlled setting is particularly recommended for those molecular behaviors that require repeated practice. In a natural setting, repeated practice may produce artificial behavior and suppress overall interactive levels (Walker et al., 1979).

Once the particular skills have been acquired in the training setting, the child must be afforded *opportunities to practice* these behaviors in the natural environment. At this point, *reprogramming the natural environment* is necessary in those cases in which spontaneous generalization does not occur. The research of the senior author and his colleagues has shown that establishing individual contingencies with backup reinforcers shared by the peer group are powerful incentives to the peers to assist the interactionally impaired child to gain entry into the peer group (Hops et al., 1979; Walker et al., 1981). In the peer group, the new skills can be practiced under controlled conditions until natural contingencies maintaining the behavior are in effect. Certainly, further research is needed to experimentally validate this conceptual model.

CLINICAL CONSIDERATIONS

Our review of the literature on the treatment of social skills deficits presented limited descriptions of available procedures and empirical indications of their effectiveness. However, as clinicians, we are also aware that there are other less specific issues related to clinical experience that may affect the power of treatment. In this section, we will try to consider such issues in providing the reader with some guidelines for use in clinical practice.

Appropriateness of Targeted Skills

We have made clear repeatedly in this chapter that there is little experimental validity on the specific social skills that are directly related to social competence. Consequently, the practitioner is in a bind as to which skills to target for treatment in children with poor social functioning. In other words, how does the clinician identify areas that are problematic and assess a child's ability to function adequately?

Interviews with parents, teachers, and the target children may help to identify potentially problematic settings. Behavioral checklists and rating scales completed by social agents can assist in identifying specific deficits that require remediation. Role-play tests can be helpful; children can demonstrate exactly which responses they have in their repertoires. However, as we indicated earlier, the clinician may have to create role-play situations that sample the child's own experiences. Finally, direct observation of the child during free play, when possible, using codes such as the CSIC (Hops et al., 1979), may provide confirmatory information about appropriate behavioral targets.

Developmental Issues

Consideration of developmental issues is absolutely essential in the selection of target behaviors for assessment and treatment (Achenbach, 1978). The lack of sensitivity to age-related matters is one of the critical weaknesses in extrapolating downward from adult models of social skillfulness (Conger & Keane, 1981). Because many of the studies designed to identify the behavioral correlates of sociometric status were carried out on preschoolers, their findings may not be generalizable to the social behavior and social acceptance of older children.

Indeed, considerable evidence exists to indicate that changes occur in the quantity and quality of social interaction over time and that what may look like a deficit at one age may be unremarkable behavior at another age (O'Connor, 1975; Greenwood et al., 1981). Our research indicates, for example, that the amount of positive social behavior continues to increase from ages three to six in the preschool (Hops & Finch, 1982) and from kindergarten to the fourth grade in elementary school (Hops et al., 1978). To reiterate, the selection of target subjects, skills to be trained, and assessment of outcome *must* be evaluated with reference to norms established for the child's age/grade group, for the peer group at large, or for the children within the same setting (Walker & Hops, 1976).

Normative assessments and treatments are similarly critical when the child presents significant cognitive or other developmental delays. A milieu behavior treatment plan was implemented for one 6-year-old boy on a pediatric rehabilitation ward of a children's hospital. The child was paired with two other six-year-old boys in his bedroom and during social skills training sessions in which sharing, turn taking, and assertiveness were being taught. Because the child was evidencing minimal treatment gains, one of the authors serving as a consultant was called in to provide advice. An assessment indicated that the boy in question was cognitively and developmentally impaired and that his overall functioning was more similar to that of a three-year-old. Educating the milieu counselors about developmental milestones, pairing the child with more developmentally appropriate peers, and focusing on less complex forms of social behavior, such as initiating and responding, produced perceptible behavioral gains within 10 days.

In our experience, it also appears that very young children or cognitively impaired children are less capable of responding to verbally loaded interventions that require cognitive mediation, such as problem-solving training (Combs & Lahey, 1981). Severely impaired children may require training in basic imitation skills before other more complex programs can be initiated (Peck, Cooke, & Apolloni, 1981).

Sex

Sex differences in social behavior also merit consideration when remediating the skill deficits of young children. For example, females prefer more sedentary interaction with fewer peers, whereas males, who are more active, have wider ranging contacts (Mueller, 1972; Rubin, Maioni, & Hornung, 1976). In addition, our own and others' research indicates a stronger relationship between motor skills and popularity among boys than for same-aged girls from kindergarten to seventh grade (Broekhoff, 1977; Steigelman, 1981). Researchers and clinicians need to be cognizant, at the very least, of sex differences as they relate to skills selected for training.[1]

Other Treatment Issues

Failure to achieve desired results should also cause the clinician to reassess other variables that may have influenced the outcome of therapy. These can include a child's motivation or other collateral behaviors that influence social behavior.

Motivation. Our experience with withdrawn, isolate children indicates that they are often difficult to motivate toward behavior change. The use of individual reinforcement contingencies for such children is not always effective (Hops et al., 1979), although it may increase the likelihood of the child's involvement. Failure to respond should force the therapist to examine the power of the reinforcement contingencies in effect. In many cases, more powerful reinforcers are required, such as the group backup used in the PEERS (Hops et al., 1979) and the RECESS (Walker et al., 1978) programs for socially withdrawn and socially aggressive children, respectively. This prompts the peer group to assist in carrying out the treatment plan and, in effect, creates a supportive and reinforcing group atmosphere.

---

[1] We realize that many are concerned with the possible perpetuation of traditional sex roles implied in such treatments. In this time of rapidly changing sex-role norms, it is difficult to identify the specific sex-related behaviors that should be targeted for treatment. Therapists need to remain aware of these issues and make therapeutic decisions on an individual basis, taking into consideration parental consent and important setting variables.

Other Individual Differences.   Even when the clinician has carefully considered normative data in the assessment of the target child's deficits and in the selection of intervention methods and goals, the intervention may fail because individual differences or characteristics unique to the target child were not taken into account. Investigators must strive to achieve the best match between the target child's learning characteristics and the training methodology. For example, if a child has auditory processing problems, information should be relayed through a pairing of verbal instructions with visual cues, such as films or pictures. Similarly, if a child has a short-attention span, the length of training sessions should fall within the child's limits for attention and concentration. Other limitations that the child may present may be critical enough to require a shift in the priority of skills to be trained.

Collateral Skills Training.   As discussed here and elsewhere (Finch & Hops, 1982), our skill deficit model of social competence encompasses three classes of behavior in the child's repertoire. In addition to the specific social skills that enable a child to establish and maintain social contact, there exist important *language and communication skills* presumed to function for the accurate transfer of information among social beings and *motor skills* to engage in choice activities with the peer group. It may be that an intervention that fails to achieve desired results has neglected one or more deficits in these other classes of behavior. For example, a six-year-old boy being treated by one of the authors and exhibiting severe fine and gross motor deficits did not gain entry into his peer group until he could play some games involving skipping and running. Incidentally, he asked to be taught to skip, and once he learned, he was not only able to interact with his peers more successfully, but he also became more cheerful and energetic in school, thus increasing his academic performance. Similar findings were reported by Buell et al. (1968), in which reinforcement of a 3½-year-old withdrawn boy for playing with outdoor equipment had the unexpected positive side effect of increased social interaction with peers.

In summary, clinicians must be aware of a number of variables that may hinder or assist the treatment of socially unskilled youngsters. These include selecting age- and sex-appropriate behaviors for treatment and the recognition of other individual differences. The therapist must be flexible in reassessing and changing the treatment plan dependent on the success of therapy throughout.

CASE STUDY[2]

This case study will illustrate several aspects of the assessment/treatment process. First, a comprehensive assessment phase can help to select appropriate

---

[2] Lewin, L., & Rogers, P. *A comprehensive evaluation of the PEERS program for socially isolate/withdrawn children.* Paper presented at the annual meeting of the Association for Behavior Analysis, Milwaukee, Wisconsin, May 1982.

subjects and to evaluate treatment procedures. Second, school consultants working with teachers can take primary responsibility for remediating socially withdrawn behavior using a comprehensive packaged program. Third, evaluating the relative effectiveness of treatment requires that both short and long-term effects be assessed.

Shirley was a first-grader referred for treatment due to several interactional problems noted by her teacher. She appeared severely withdrawn, rarely initiating interactions with her peers. Moreover, she behaved immaturely, using baby talk and responding to negative attention from her peers.

A two-step screening process was implemented to insure the appropriateness of the referral. First, the teacher completed the *Social Interaction Rating Scale* from the PEERS program (Hops et al., 1979), which is designed to identify socially withdrawn children. Because Shirley met the criterion for social withdrawal, a PEERS program consultant observed her behavior on the playground during free-play periods using the *Consultant Social Interaction Code*. The percent of social behavior she exhibited over a three-day period was more than one standard deviation below the mean established for her grade. Consequently, Shirley met both criteria for inclusion in the intervention program.

To assess the child's social status in the peer group, a nomination picture sociometric instrument was employed. For each of three social referent situations, each peer was individually asked to name two children in response to a positively connoted question (e.g., "Who do you like to play with outside?") and two children in response to a negatively connoted question (e.g., "Who don't you sit next to for stories?"). Two indices of sociometric status were computed: (*a*) social impact (the total number of votes, both positive and negative, received) and (*b*) social preference (the total number of votes minus the number of negative votes received) (Peery, 1979). Since she was low on both social preference and social impact, Shirley was designated an isolate according to Peery's (1979) definition.

Following this multimethod assessment phase, the PEERS program was implemented to include (*a*) social skills tutoring in five components of social interaction: initiating, responding to initiations, maintaining interactions, complementing and praising, and sharing, (*b*) a recess point system in which the target child earned points for social interaction that were traded in for rewards shared by the entire class, and (*c*) teacher-arranged cooperative tasks between the target child and a selection of different classroom peers. On the playground, the program consultant prompted and reinforced the child's and peers' social behavior daily. After the child had reached a preset criterion of social behavior one standard deviation above the grade-level mean, the program components were gradually and systematically withdrawn.

Process evaluation consisted of daily playground observations of social interaction with peers and repeated administration of the picture-sociometric. Figure 14–1 shows the daily interaction rates during Baseline (B), Intervention (I), Fading (F), Short-term follow-up (FU), and One-year follow-up (FU1). Dotted lines represent the mean and ±1 standard deviation for grade-level norms (Hops et al., 1978).

During baseline, Shirley's average percent social behavior was 27.54, approximately one standard deviation below the mean for first graders. During the 14-day PEERS intervention program, her level of social behavior increased to an average of 76.5 percent and remained above the criterion of 1 S.D. above her grade-level mean. In the next phase, fading of program components (such as daily pep talks and rewards) did not change her social behavior, which remained at 81.9 percent. However, with the removal of all the procedures, the child's behavior decreased to baseline levels. During a one-year follow-up in a new classroom with different peers, Shirley's level of social behavior had again increased to above the norms established for second graders.

Figure 14–2 illustrates the sociometric results. During intervention, Shirley's social preference index increased to approximately the 90th percentile, with only a slight increase in impact. During the fading of program components, her impact score increased again slightly, while her preference remained well above baseline, although somewhat diminished at the 65th percentile. At the one-year follow-up assessment, Shirley's social status in the new classroom reflected an increase in social impact as well. Both social preference and impact had increased by 25 percentile points from their baseline levels, thus confirming the results shown in the observation data.

FIGURE 14–1

Daily Percent Positive Social Behavior during Baseline (B), Intervention (I), Fading (F), Short-Term Follow-Up (FU), and One-Year Follow-Up (FU1). (S₁ to S₅ denote sociometric administrations)

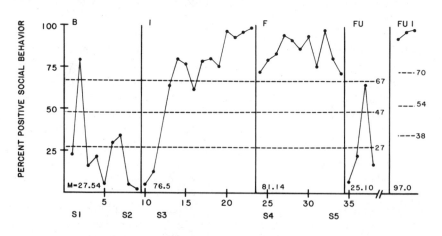

FIGURE 14-2

Social Status as Represented by Social Impact (Vertical Axis) and Social Preference (Horizontal Axis) across Phases

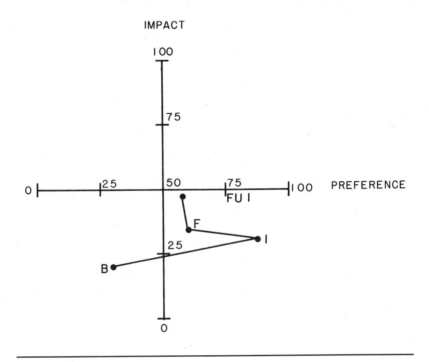

Overall, both the observation and the sociometric data suggest that the PEERS program significantly increased Shirley's level of positive social behavior and her social status. Of concern, however, are the short-term follow-up data, which indicate a return to baseline levels of social behavior. (Unfortunately, concurrent sociometric data is unavailable). Since the intervention program was implemented toward the end of the school year, it is likely that the new reinforcement contingencies placed on Shirley and her peers were not in operation long enough to overcome the problematic interaction patterns with her peers established over the course of the year. A longer intervention coupled with additional efforts to program generalization and maintenance may have insured that the initial gains were maintained under natural conditions.

The long-term observation and sociometric follow-up data suggest that Shirley may very well have incorporated (and rehearsed) the social skills taught during intervention at the end of first grade, thus facilitating her entry into the new second-grade peer group (with whom she had no previous negative interactional patterns) and insuring her social acceptance. Certainly, further replications of the impact of the PEERS program are required (cf. Lewin & Rogers, 1982).

CONCLUSION

Social competence is considered a critical determinant of many forms of personal adjustment. The social skill deficit model assumes that social competence is directly related to the ability to display specific skills in specific situations. Those who have not learned to perform skillfully are likely to be less well adjusted socially, occupationally, and emotionally throughout life. Consequently, a wide variety of assessment instruments and treatment procedures have been developed to increase the skill levels of children who are low in social competence.

Unfortunately, we are still not certain which specific skills comprise social competence. Investigators have attempted to identify them in various ways. As noted by Gottman (1977a), most approaches are the result of armchair discovery based on face validity. Others are downward extrapolations from the adult literature and consist primarily of assertiveness and the accompanying set of behaviors that have been the focus of adult assertiveness training, e.g., eye contact, speech duration. With the press of demands by practitioners for treatment procedures that work has come the development of broad-based treatment approaches that focus primarily on the level of social behavior or interaction rather than its underlying skill components. Many fewer strategies involve identifying skills using validated, external criterion measures of social competence and contrasting the performance of groups at different levels on this criterion. Nevertheless, children across the country are being taught individually or in groups to be assertive, to initiate, to cooperate, and to make friends. Training takes place in schools, hospitals, or office settings, using individual and/or group reinforcement contingencies to increase motivation toward behavior change.

The results of this massive remediation effort are still relatively unclear. The effects vary across different treatment modalities and are confounded by varying assessment procedures. Process data on individual children have rarely been collected to provide information about the necessary conditions for change and how group-designated interventions affect individual subjects within the treatment group. The majority of treated children have been minimally impaired, so it remains unclear whether these procedures have utility for more severely handicapped children. Furthermore, the lack of demonstrated long-term gains casts further doubt on the utility of treatment procedures that have proven successful in the short run.

What implications do these findings have for the practitioner and for the research community? It is clear from our review of the social skills assessment and treatment literature to date that the field is in its infancy. The equivocal nature of the results we found reflects the uneven and somewhat haphazard approach that usually accompanies a new area of interest. What is required now is a more systematic research scheme to (*a*) isolate specific skills associated with validated criteria of social competence, (*b*) combine treatment components that have been shown to be effective across theoretical bases, (*c*) use a multimethod assessment procedure to determine both their short and long-term effectiveness, and (*d*) when necessary, build in procedures that will focus on establishing long-term durability of short-term gains rather than accepting failure as destiny.

The clinician, however, faces a real-world urgency to treat children now, without waiting for research to be completed. Consequently, those in clinical settings must extract from the available literature the assessment instruments and associated treatment procedures that are most suited for each client and the problematic situation, given the availability of time and resources. We hope that we have provided some guidelines in this chapter for achieving this end.

REFERENCES

Achenbach, T. M. The child behavior profile: I. Boys aged 6 - 11. *Journal of Consulting and Clinical Psychology,* 1978, *46,* 478–488.

Achenbach, T. M., & Edelbrock, C. S. Behavioral problems and competencies reported by parents of normal and disturbed children aged four through sixteen. *Monographs of the Society for Research in Child Development,* 1981, *46* (1, Serial No. 188).

Achenbach, T. M., & Edelbrock, C. S. *Manual for the Child Behavior Checklist and Child Behavior Profile.* Burlington, Vt.: Child Psychiatry, University of Vermont, 1982.

Allen, K. E., Hart, B., Buell, J. S., Harris, F. R., & Wolf, M. M. Effects of social reinforcement on isolate behavior of a nursery school child. *Child Development,* 1964, *35,* 511–518.

Allen, V. L. (Ed.). *Children as teachers.* New York: Academic Press, 1976.

American Psychiatric Association. *Diagnostic and statistical manual of mental disorders* (3rd ed.). Washington, D.C.: 1980.

Anderson, S., & Messick, S. Social competency in young children. *Developmental Psychology,* 1974, *10,* 282–293.

Apolloni, R., & Cooke, T. P. Integrated programming at the infant, toddler, and preschool age levels. In M. Guralnik (Ed.), *Early intervention and the integration of handicapped children.* Chicago, Ill.: University Park Press, 1978.

Asher, S. R., & Hymel, S. Children's social competence in peer relations: Sociometric and behavioral assessment. In J. D. Wine & M. D. Smye (Eds.), *Social competence.* New York: Guilford Press, 1981.

Asher, S. R., Singleton, L. C., Tinsley, B. R., & Hymel, S. The reliability of a sociometric method with preschool children. *Developmental Psychology,* 1979, *15,* 443–444.

Asher, S., Oden, S., & Gottman, J. Children's friendships in school settings. In L. Katz (Ed.), *Current topics in early childhood education* (Vol. 1). Hillsdale, N.J.: Lawrence Erlbaum Associates, Inc., 1976.

Baer, D. M., Wolf, M. M., & Risley, T. R. Some current dimensions of applied behavior analysis. *Journal of Applied Behavior Analysis,* 1968, *1,* 91–97.

Bandura, A. *Principles of behavior modification.* New York: Holt, Rinehart, & Winston, 1969.

Becker, W. C., Engelmann, S., Carnine, D. W., & Maggs, A. Direct instruction technology: Making learning happen. In P. Karoly & J. J. Steffen (Eds.), *Improving children's competence: Advances in child behavior analysis and therapy,* (Vol. 1). Lexington, Mass.: Lexington Books, 1982.

Bellack, A. S., & Hersen, M. (Eds.). *Research and practice in social skills training.* New York: Plenum Press, 1979.

Bellack, A. S., & Morrison, R. L. Interpersonal dysfunction. In A. S. Bellack, M. Hersen, & A. E. Kazdin (Eds.), *International handbook of behavior modification and therapy.* New York: Plenum Press, 1982.

Bierman, K. L., & McCauley, E. *A standardized child interview to assess social competence and peer relationships.* Paper presented at the biennial meeting of the Society for Research in Child Development, Detroit, Mich., April 1983.

Biglan, A., Severson, H. H., Bavry, J., & McConnell, S. Social influence and adolescent smoking: A first look behind the barn. *Health Education,* September/ October 1983, *14* (5), pp. 14–18.

Bolstad, O. D., & Johnson, S. M. The relationship between teacher's assessment of students and students' actual behavior in the classroom. *Child Development,* 1977, *48,* 570–578.

Bornstein, M. R., Bellack, A. S., & Hersen, M. Social skills training for unassertive children: A multiple baseline analysis. *Journal of Applied Behavior Analysis,* 1977, *10,* 183–195.

Bornstein, M. R., Bellack, A. S., & Hersen, M. Social skills training for highly aggressive children: Treatment in an inpatient psychiatric setting. *Behavior Modification,* 1980, *4,* 173–186.

Broekhoff, J. Physique types and perceived physical characteristics of elementary school children with low and high social status. In J. Broekhoff (Ed.), *Physical education, sports, and the sciences.* Eugene, Ore.: Microform Publications, 1976.

Broekhoff, J. A search for relationships: Sociological and social-psychological considerations. *The Academy Papers,* 1977, *11,* 45–55.

Bronfenbrenner, U. *Two worlds of childhood: U.S. and U.S.S.R.* New York: Simon & Schuster, 1970.

Bryan, T. S. An observational analysis of classroom behaviors of children with learning disabilities. *Journal of Learning Disabilities*, 1974, *7*, 35–43.

Bryan, T. S., & Bryan, J. H. Social interactions of learning disabled children. *Learning Disabilities Quarterly*, 1978, *1*, 33–38.

Buell, J., Stoddard, P., Harris, F. R., & Baer, D. M. Collateral social development accompanying reinforcement of outdoor play in a preschool child. *Journal of Applied Behavior Analysis*, 1968, *1*, 167–173.

Clement, P. W., & Milne, D. C. Group play therapy and tangible reinforcers used to modify the behavior of 8-year-old boys. *Behaviour Research & Therapy*, 1967, *5*, 301–312.

Clement, P. W., Roberts, P. V., & Lantz, C. E. Social models and token reinforcement in the treatment of shy, withdrawn boys. *Proceedings of the 78th annual convention of the American Psychological Association*, 1970, *5*, 515–516.

Cohen, A. S., & Van Tassel, E. A comparison: Partial and complete paired-comparisons in sociometric measurement of preschool groups. *Applied Psychological Measurement*, 1978, *2*, 31–40.

Cohen, N. J., Sullivan, J. Minde, K., Novak, C., & Helwig, C. Evaluation of the relative effectiveness of methylphenidate and cognitive behavior modification in the treatment of kindergarten-aged hyperactive children. *Journal of Abnormal Child Psychology*, 1981, *9*, 43–54.

Coie, J. D., & Kupersmidt, J. B. A behavioral analysis of emerging social status in boys' groups. *Child Development*, 1983, *54*, 1400–1416.

Combs, M. L., & Lahey, B. B. A cognitive social skills training program: Evaluation with young children. *Behavior Modification*, 1981, *5*, 39–60.

Combs, M. L., & Slaby, D. A. Social skills training with children. In B. Lahey & A. Kazdin (Eds.), *Advances in clinical psychology* (Vol. 1). New York: Plenum Press, 1977.

Conger, J. C., & Keane, S. P. Social skills intervention in the treatment of isolated or withdrawn children. *Psychological Bulletin*, 1981, *90*, 478–495.

Connolly, J., & Doyle, A. Assessment of social competence in preschoolers: Teachers versus peers. *Developmental Psychology*, 1981, *17*, 454–462.

Cowen, E. L., Pederson, A., Babigian, H., Izzo, L. D., & Trost, M. A. Long-term follow-up of early detected vulnerable children. *Journal of Consulting and Clinical Psychology*, 1973, *41*, 438–446.

Cronbach, L. J. *Essentials of psychological testing*. New York: Harper & Row, 1970.

Dodge, K. A. Behavioral antecedents of peer social status. *Child Development*, 1983, *54*, 1386–1399.

Drabman, R. S., Spitalnik, R., & O'Leary, K. D. Teaching self-control to disruptive children. *Journal of Abnormal Psychology*, 1973, *82*, 10–16.

Edelson, J. L., & Rose, S. D. *A behavioral role play test for assessing children's social skills*. Paper presented at the annual meeting of the Association for the Advancement of Behavior Therapy, Chicago, Ill., November 1978.

Eisler, R. M., Hersen, M., Miller, P. M., & Blanchard, E. B. Situational determinants of assertive behaviors. *Journal of Consulting and Clinical Psychology*, 1975, *43*, 330–340.

Emmelkamp, P. M. The current and future status of clinical research. *Behavioral Assessment*, 1981, *3*, 249–253.

Engelmann, S., & Becker, W. C. The direct instruction model. In R. Rhine (Ed.), *Encouraging change in America's schools: A decade of experimentation*. New York: Academic Press, 1978.

Evans, I. M., & Nelson, R. O. Assessment of child behavior problems. In A. R. Ciminero, K. S. Calhoun, & H. E. Adams (Eds.), *Handbook of behavioral assessment*. New York: John Wiley & Sons, 1977.

Evers, W. L., & Schwarz, J. C. Modifying social withdrawal in preschoolers: The effects of filmed modeling and teacher praise. *Journal of Abnormal Child Psychology*, 1973, *1*, 248–256.

Finch, M. Childhood social competence and parental variables: A direct observation study. Unpublished doctoral dissertation, University of Oregon, Eugene, Ore., 1984.

Finch, M., & Hops, H. *Childhood social competence and parental behavior: A direct observation study*. Paper presented at the annual meeting of the Association for Advancement of Behavior Therapy, Toronto, Ontario, November 1981.

Finch, M., & Hops, H. Remediation of social withdrawal in young children: Considerations for the practitioner. *Child and Youth Services*, 1982, *5*, 29–42.

Foster, S., & DeLawyer, D. D. *The nature and recognition of stimulus cues in social situations*. Paper presented at the annual meeting of the Association for Behavior Analysis, Milwaukee, Wis., May 1983.

Foster, S., & Hoier, T. *Traditional and nontraditional methods of assessing children's social skills*. Paper presented at the annual meeting of the Association for Behavior Analysis, Milwaukee, Wis., May, 1983.

Furman, W., Rahe, D. F., & Hartup, W. W. Rehabilitation of socially withdrawn preschool children. *Child Development*, 1979, *50*, 915–922.

Garrett, B., Stevens, T., & Walker, H. M. *RECESS observer training manual*. Eugene, Ore.: University of Oregon, Center at Oregon for Research in the Behavioral Education of the Handicapped, 1978.

Gottman, J. Toward a definition of social isolation in children. *Child Development*, 1977, *48*, 513–517 (a).

Gottman, J. The effects of a modeling film on social isolation in preschool children: A methodological investigation. *Journal of Abnormal Child Psychology*, 1977, *5*, 69–78 (b).

Gottman, J., Gonso, J., & Rasmussen, B. Social interaction, social competence, and friendship in children. *Child Development*, 1975, *46*, 709–718.

Gottman, J., Gonso, J., & Schuler, P. Teaching social skills to isolated children. *Journal of Abnormal Child Psychology,* 1976, *4,* 179–197.

Graubard, P. S., Rosenberg, H., & Miller, M. B. Student applications of behavior modification to teachers and environments or ecological approaches to social deviancy. In E. A. Ramp & B. I. Hopkins (Eds.), *A new direction for education: Behavior Analysis* (Vol. 1). Lawrence, Kan.: University of Kansas, Support and Development Center for Follow-through, 1971.

Greenwood, C. R., Todd, N. M., Hops, H., & Walker, H. M. Behavior change targets in the assessment and behavior modification of socially withdrawn preschool children. *Behavioral Assessment,* 1982, *4,* 273–297.

Greenwood, C. R., Todd, N. M., Walker, H. M., & Hops, H. *SAMPLE (social assessment manual for preschool level).* Eugene, Ore.: Center at Oregon for Research in the Behavioral Education of the Handicapped, University of Oregon, 1978.

Greenwood, C. R., Walker, H. M., & Hops, H. Some issues in social interaction/ withdrawal assessment. *Exceptional Children,* 1977, *43,* 490–499.

Greenwood, C. R., Walker, H. M., Todd, N. M., & Hops, H. *Preschool teachers' assessments of social interaction: Predictive success and normative data* (Report No. 26). Eugene, Ore.: University of Oregon, Center at Oregon for Research in the Behavioral Education of the Handicapped, 1976.

Greenwood, C. R., Walker, H. M., Todd, N. M., & Hops, H. Selecting a cost-effective screening device for the assessment of preschool social withdrawal. *Journal of Applied Behavior Analysis,* 1979, *12,* 639–652.

Greenwood, C. R., Walker, H. M., Todd, N. M., & Hops, H. Normative and descriptive analysis of preschool free play social interaction rates. *Journal of Pediatric Psychology,* 1981, *6,* 343–367.

Gresham, F. M. Multitrait-multimethod approach to multifactored assessment: Theoretical rationale and practical applications. *School Psychology Review,* 1983, *12,* 26–34.

Hartup, W. W. Peer interaction and social organization. In P. H. Mussen (Ed.), *Carmichael's manual of child psychology* (Vol. 2, 3rd ed.). New York: John Wiley & Sons, 1970.

Hartup, W. W. The peer system. In E. M. Hetherington (Ed.), *Handbook of child psychology: Vol. 4. Socialization, personality, and social development.* New York: John Wiley & Sons, 1983.

Hartup, W. W., Charlesworth, R., & Glazer, J. L. Peer reinforcement and sociometric status. *Child Development,* 1967, *38,* 1017–1024.

Hawkins, R. P. The functions of assessment: Implications for the selection and development of devices for assessing repertoires in clinical, educational, and other settings. *Journal of Applied Behavior Analysis,* 1979, *12,* 501–517.

Hersh, R., & Walker, H. M. Great expectations: Making schools effective for all children. *Policy Studies Review,* 1983, *(2)* 1, 147–188.

Hops, H. Social skills training for socially isolated children. In P. Karoly & J. Steffen (Eds.), *Enhancing children's competencies.* Lexington, Mass.: Lexington Books, 1982.

Hops, H. Children's social competence and skill: Current research practices and future directions. *Behavior Therapy,* 1983, *14,* 3–18.

Hops, H., & Finch, M. *A skill deficit view of social competence in preschoolers.* Invited address to the annual meeting of the Association for Behavior Analysis, Milwaukee, Wis., May, 1983.

Hops, H., Finch, M., & Stevens, T. *Stability and validity of the paired-comparison sociometric procedure for preschoolers.* Unpublished manuscript, 1983.

Hops, H., Fleischman, D. H., Guild, J., Paine, S., Street, H., Walker, H. M., & Greenwood, C. R. *Procedures for establishing effective relationship skills (PEERS): Manual for consultants.* Eugene, Ore.: University of Oregon, Center at Oregon for Research in the Behavioral Education of the Handicapped, 1978.

Hops, H., & Greenwood, C. R. Social skills deficits. In E. J. Mash & L. G. Terdal (Eds.), *Behavioral assessment of childhood disorders.* New York: Guilford Press, 1981.

Hops, H., & Lewin, L. Peer sociometric forms. In T. H. Ollendick & M. Hersen (Eds.), *Child behavioral assessment: Principles and procedures.* New York: Pergamon Press, 1984.

Hops, H., & Stevens, T. *PEERS observer training manual.* Eugene, Ore.: University of Oregon, Center at Oregon for Research in the Behavioral Education of the Handicapped, 1978.

Hops, H., Walker, H. M., Fleischman, D. H., Nagoshi, J. T., Omura, R. T., Skindrud, K., & Taylor, J. CLASS: A standardized in-class program for acting-out children. II. Field test evaluations. *Journal of Educational Psychology,* 1978, *70,* 636–644.

Hops, H., Walker, H. M., & Greenwood, C. R. PEERS: A program for remediating social withdrawal in school. In L. A. Hamerlynck (Ed.), *Behavior systems for the developmentally disabled: I. School and family environments.* New York: Brunner/Mazel, 1979.

Israel, A. C., & O'Leary, K. D. Developing correspondence between children's words and deeds. *Child Development,* 1973, *44,* 575–581.

Jones, R. R. *"Observation" by telephone: An economical behavior sampling technique* (Vol. 4, Report No. 1). Eugene, Ore.: Oregon Research Institute, 1974.

Kahn, N. A., & Hoge, R. D. A teacher-judgment measure of social competence: Validity data. *Journal of Consulting and Clinical Psychology,* 1983, *51,* 809–814.

Kane, J. S., & Lawler, E. E., III. Methods of peer assessment. *Psychological Bulletin,* 1978, *85,* 555–586.

Kazdin, A. E. Assessing the clinical or applied importance of behavior change through social validation. *Behavior Modification,* 1977, *1,* 427–452.

Kazdin, A. E. Sociophysiological factors in psychopathology. In A. S. Bellack & M. Hersen (Eds.), *Research and practice in social skills training*. New York: Plenum Press, 1979.

Kazdin, A. E., Esveldt-Dawson, K., & Matson, J. L. Changes in children's social skill performance as a function of preassessment experiences. *Journal of Clinical Child Psychology*, 1982, *11*, 243–248.

Kazdin, A. E., Matson, J. L., & Esveldt-Dawson, K. Social skill performance among normal and psychiatric inpatient children as a function of assessment conditions. *Behaviour Research and Therapy*, 1981, *19*, 145–152.

Keller, M. F., & Carlson, P. M. The use of symbolic modeling to promote social skills in preschool children with low levels of social responsiveness. *Child Development*, 1974, *45*, 912–919.

Kohn, M. *Social competence, symptoms and underachievement in childhood: A longitudinal perspective*. New York: John Wiley & Sons, 1977.

Ladd, G. W. Social skills and peer acceptance: Effects of a social learning method for training social skills. *Child Development*, 1981, *52*, 171–178.

LaGreca, A., & Santogrossi, D. Social skills training with elementary school students: A behavioral group approach. *Journal of Consulting and Clinical Psychology*, 1980, *48*, 220–228.

LeCroy, C. W. Social skills training with adolescents: A review. In C. W. LeCroy (Ed.), *Child and youth services: Social skills training for children and youth* (Vol. 5). New York: The Haworth Press, Inc., 1982.

Lewin, L., & Rogers, P. *A comprehensive evaluation of the PEERS program for socially isolate/withdrawn children*. Manuscript submitted for publication, 1982.

Lewis, M., & Rosenblum, L. A. *Friendship and peer relations*. New York: John Wiley & Sons, 1975.

Lougee, M. D., Grueneich, R., & Hartup, W. W. Social interaction in same- and mixed-age dyads of preschool children. *Child Development*, 1977, *48*, 1353–1361.

Mash, E. J., & Terdal, L. G. Behavior therapy assessment: Diagnosis, design and evaluation. *Psychological Reports*, 1974, *35*, 587–601.

Mash, E. J., & Terdal, L. G. (Eds.). *Behavioral assessment of childhood disorders*. New York: Guilford Press, 1981.

McConnell, S. *Identifying social skills for handicapped boys: Evaluation of teacher rating, peer sociometric, and direct observation measures. Dissertation Abstracts International*, 1983, *43*, 2962–2964.

McConnell, S., Biglan, A., & Severson, H. H. Adolescents' compliance with self-monitoring and physiological assessment of smoking in natural environments. *Journal of Behavioral Medicine*, 1984, *7*, 115–122.

McConnell, S., & Odom, S. L. Sociometrics: Peer-referenced measures and the assessment of social competence. In P. S. Strain, M. J. Guralnick, & H. M.

Walker (Eds.), *Children's social behavior: Development, assessment, and modification.* New York: Academic Press, in press.

McConnell, S., & Walker, H. M. *Social behaviors for survival: A model for selecting settings and preparing students for regular education placement.* Paper presented at the annual meeting of the Association for Behavior Analysis, Milwaukee, Wis., May 1983.

McFall, R. M. A review and reformulation of the concept of social skills. *Behavioral Assessment,* 1982, *4,* 1–33.

McMahon, R. J., & Forehand, R. L. Consumer satisfaction in behavioral treatment of children: Types, issues, and recommendations. *Behavior Therapy,* 1983, *14,* 209–225.

Michelson, L., & Wood, R. Behavior assessment and training of children's social skills. In M. Hersen, R. M. Eisler, & P. M. Miller (Eds.), *Progress in Behavior Modification* (Vol. 9) (pp. 241–292).

Morris, R. J., & Dolker, M. Developing cooperative play in socially withdrawn retarded children. *Mental Retardation,* 1974, *12,* 24–27.

Moses, C., & McConnell, S. *The observer impression assessment scale.* Unpublished manuscript. Eugene, Ore.: University of Oregon, Center on Human Development, 1982.

Mueller, E. The maintenance of verbal exchanges between young children. *Child Development,* 1972, *43,* 930–938.

Mueller, E., & Vandell, O. Infant-infant interaction. In J. D. Osofsky (Ed.), *Handbook of infant development.* New York: Wiley Interscience, 1979.

Nelson, R. O., & Hayes, S. C. Some current dimensions of behavior assessment. *Behavioral Assessment,* 1979, *1,* 1–16.

O'Connor, M. The nursery school environment. *Developmental Psychology,* 1975, *11,* 556–561.

O'Connor, R. D. Modification of social withdrawal through symbolic modeling. *Journal of Applied Behavior Analysis,* 1969, *2,* 15–22.

O'Connor, R. D. The relative efficacy of modeling, shaping, and the combined procedures for the modification of social withdrawal. *Journal of Abnormal Psychology,* 1972, *79,* 327–334.

Oden, S., & Asher, S. R. Coaching children in social skills for friendship making. *Child Development,* 1977, *48,* 495–506.

Paine, S. C., Hops, H., Walker, H. M., Greenwood, C. R., Fleischman, D. H., & Guild, J. J. Repeated treatment effects: A study of maintaining behavior change in socially withdrawn children. *Behavior Modification,* 1982, *6,* 171–199.

Patterson, G. R. Interventions for boys with conduct problems: Multiple settings, treatments, and criteria. *Journal of Consulting and Clinical Psychology,* 1974, *42,* 471–481.

Patterson, G. R. *A social learning approach to family intervention* (Vol. 3). *Coercive family process.* Eugene, Ore.: Castalia, 1982.

Patterson, G. R., & Reid, J. B. Reciprocity and coercion: Two facets of social systems. In C. Neuringer and J. Michael (Eds.), *Behavior modification in clinical psychology.* New York: Appleton-Century-Crofts, 1970.

Peck, C. A., Cooke, T. P., & Apolloni, T. Utilization of peer imitation in therapeutic and instructional contexts. In P. S. Strain (Ed.), *The utilization of classroom peers as behavior change agents.* New York: Plenum Press, 1981.

Peery, J. C. Popular, amiable, isolated, rejected: A reconceptualization of sociometric status in preschool children. *Child Development,* 1979, *50,* 1231–1234.

Pelham, W. E., & Bender, E. Peer relationships in hyperactive children: Description and treatment. *Advances in Learning and Behavioral Disabilities,* 1982, *1,* 365–436.

Pepler, D., Corter, C., & Abramovitch, R. Social relationships among children: Comparison of sibling and peer interaction. In K. H. Rubin and H. S. Ross (Eds.), *Peer relations and social skills in childhood.* New York: Springer-Verlag, 1982.

Putallaz, M. *The importance of the peer group for successful intervention.* Paper presented at the annual meeting of the Association for the Advancement of Behavior Therapy, Los Angeles, Calif., November 1982.

Reardon, R. C., Hersen, M., Bellack, A. S., & Foley, J. M. Measuring social skill in grade school boys. *Journal of Behavioral Assessment,* 1979, *1,* 87–105.

Rickel, A. U., Eshelman, A. K., & Loigman, G. A. Social problem solving training: A follow-up study of cognitive and behavioral effects. *Journal of Abnormal Child Psychology,* 1983, *11,* 15–28.

Risley, T., & Hart, B. Developing correspondence between nonverbal and verbal behavior of preschool children. *Journal of Applied Behavior Analysis,* 1968, *1,* 267–281.

Roff, M. Childhood social interactions and young adult bad conduct. *Journal of Abnormal and Social Psychology,* 1961, *63,* 333–337.

Roff, M., Sells, S. B., & Golden, M. M. *Social adjustment and personality development in children.* Minneapolis: University of Minnesota Press, 1972.

Rolf, J. E., & Hasazi, J. E. Identification of preschool children at risk and some guidelines for primary intervention. In G. W. Albee and J. M. Joffe (Eds.), *Primary Prevention of Psychopathology.* Hanover, N.H.: University Press of New England, 1977.

Rubin, K. H. Fantasy play: Its role in the development of social skills and social cognition. In K. H. Rubin (Ed.), *Children's play: New directions for child development.* San Francisco, Jossey-Bass, 1980.

Rubin, K. H., Maioni, T. L., & Hornung, M. Free-play behaviors in middle and lower class preschoolers: Parten and Piaget revisited. *Child Development,* 1976, *47,* 414–419.

Rubin, K. H., & Ross, H. S. *Peer relations and social skills in childhood.* New York: Springer-Verlag, 1982.

Sherman, H., & Farina, A. Social adequacy of parents and children. *Journal of Abnormal Psychology,* 1974, *83,* 327–330.

Shure, M. B., & Spivack, G. *Problem-solving techniques in childrearing.* San Francisco: Jossey-Bass, 1978.

Singleton, L. C., & Asher, S. R. Peer preference and social integration among third-grade children in an integrated school district. *Journal of Educational Psychology,* 1977, *69,* 330–336.

Snyder, J. J. Reinforcement analysis of interaction in problem and nonproblem families. *Journal of Abnormal Psychology,* 1977, *86,* 528–535.

Spence, S. H., & Marzillier, J. S. Social skills training with adolescent male offenders: I. Short-term effects. *Behaviour Research and Therapy,* 1979, *17,* 7–16.

Spivack, G., & Shure, M. B. *Social adjustment of young children.* San Francisco: Jossey-Bass, 1974.

Steigelman, G. *The role of motor performance in the social status of preschool children.* Unpublished doctoral dissertation, University of Oregon, Eugene, Ore., 1981.

Strain, P. S. An experimental analysis of peer social initiations on the behavior of withdrawn preschool children: Some training and generalization effects. *Journal of Abnormal Child Psychology,* 1977, *5,* 445–455.

Strain, P. S. (Ed.), *The utilization of classroom peers as behavior change agents.* New York: Plenum Press, 1981.

Strain, P. S., McConnell, S. R., & Cordisco, L. K. Selecting and measuring target behaviors in single subject/special education research. *Remedial and Special Education,* 1983, *4* (3), 40–51.

Strain, P. S., Odom, S. L., & McConnell, S. Promoting social reciprocity of exceptional children: Identification, target skill selection, and interventions. *Remedial and Special Education,* 1984, *5,* 21–28.

Strain, P. S., Shores, R. E., & Kerr, M. A. An experimental analysis of "spillover" effects on the social interactions of behaviorally handicapped preschool children. *Journal of Applied Behavior Analysis,* 1976, *9,* 31–40.

Strain, P. S., Shores, R. E., & Timm, M. A. Effects of peer social initiations on the behavior of withdrawn preschool children. *Journal of Applied Behavior Analysis,* 1977, *10,* 289–298.

Strain, P. S., Steele, P., Ellis, R., & Timm, M. A. Long-term effects of oppositional child treatment with mothers as therapists and therapist trainers. *Journal of Applied Behavior Analysis,* 1982, *15,* 163–169.

Tremblay, A., Strain, P. S., Hendrickson, J. M., & Shores, R. E. Social interactions of normally developing preschool children: Using normative data for subject and target behavior selection. *Behavior Modification,* 1981, *5,* 237–253.

Ullman, C. A. Identification of maladjusted school children. *Public Health Monograph No. 7.* Washington, D.C.: Federal Security Agency, 1952.

Ullman, C. A. Teachers, peers, and tests as predictors of adjustment. *Journal of Educational Psychology,* 1957, *48,* 257–267.

Urbain, E. S., & Kendall, P. C. Review of social-cognitive problem-solving interventions with children. *Psychological Bulletin,* 1980, *88,* 109–143.

Van Hasselt, V. B., Hersen, M., & Bellack, A. S. The validity of role play tests for assessing social skills in children. *Behavior Therapy,* 1981, *12,* 202–216.

Van Houten, R. Social validation: The evolution of standards of competency for target behaviors. *Journal of Applied Behavior Analysis,* 1979, *12,* 581–591.

Walker, H. M. *The acting out child: Coping with classroom disruption.* Boston: Allyn & Bacon, 1979.

Walker, H. M. *Walker problem behavior identification checklist: Test and manual.* (2nd ed.). Los Angeles: Western Psychological Services, 1983.

Walker, H. M., Greenwood, C. R., Hops, H., & Todd, N. M. Differential effects of reinforcing topographic components of social interaction: Analysis and systematic replication. *Behavior Modification,* 1979, *3,* 291–321.

Walker, H. M., & Hops, H. The use of group and individual reinforcement contingencies in the modification of social withdrawal. In L. A. Hamerlynck, L. C. Handy, & E. J. Mash (Eds.), *Behavior change: Methodology, concepts, and practice.* Champaign, Ill.: Research Press, 1973.

Walker, H. M., & Hops, H. Use of normative peer data as a standard for evaluating classroom treatment effects. *Journal of Applied Behavior Analysis,* 1976, *9,* 159–168.

Walker, H. M., Hops, H., & Greenwood, C. R. RECESS: Research and development of a behavior management package for remediating social aggression in the school setting. In P. Strain (Ed.), *The utilization of classroom peers as behavior change agents.* New York: Plenum Press, 1981.

Walker, H. M., McConnell, S., & Clarke, J. *Social skills training in school settings: A model for the social integration of handicapped children into unrestrictive settings.* Paper presented at the Banff International Conference on Behavioral Science, Banff, Alberta, Canada, March 1983.

Walker, H. M., McConnell, S., Holmes, D., Todis, B., Walker, J. L., & Golden, N. *A curriculum for children's effective peer and teacher skills (ACCEPTS).* Austin, Tex.: Pro-Ed Publishers, 1983.

Walker, H. M., McConnell, S., Walker, J. L., Clarke, J. Y., Todis, B., Cohen, G., & Rankin, R. Initial analysis of the SBS curriculum: Efficacy of instruction and behavior management procedures for improving the social competence of handicapped children. *Analysis and Intervention in Developmental Disabilities,* 1983, *3,* 105–127.

Walker, H. M., Street, A., Garrett, B., Crossen, J., Hops, H., & Greenwood, C. R. *Reprogramming environmental contingencies for effective social skills (RECESS): Manual for consultants.* Eugene, Ore.: Center at Oregon for Research in the Behavioral Education of the Handicapped, University of Oregon, 1978.

Wanlass, R. L., & Prinz, R. J. Methodological issues in conceptualizing and treating childhood social withdrawal. *Psychological Bulletin*, 1982, *92*, 39–55.

Weinrott, M. R., Corson, J. A., & Wilchesky, M. Teacher mediated treatment of social withdrawal. *Behavior Therapy*, 1979, *10*, 281–294.

Weinrott, M. R., Reid, J. B., Bouske, B. W., & Brummett, B. Supplementing naturalistic observations with observer impressions. *Behavioral Assessment*, 1981, *3*, 151–159.

Whitman, T. L. Mercurio, J. R., & Caponigri, V. Development of social responses in two severely retarded children. *Journal of Applied Behavior Analysis*, 1970, *3*, 133–138.

Wolf, M. M. Social validity: The case for subjective measurement or how behavior analysis is finding its heart. *Journal of Applied Behavior Analysis*, 1978, *11*, 203–214.

Wood, R., & Michelson, L. *Assessment of assertive behavior in elementary school children*. Paper presented at the annual meeting of the Association for the Advancement of Behavior Therapy, Chicago, Ill., 1978.

Zigler, E., & Trickett, P. K. IQ, social competence, and evaluation of early childhood intervention programs. *American Psychologist*, 1978, *33*, 789–798.

15

Conceptualization, Assessment, and Treatment of Depression in Children

Nadine J. Kaslow
University of Wisconsin
School of Medicine

Lynn P. Rehm
University of Houston

INTRODUCTION

Historical Background

Sadness and anergia in children were recognized by physicians as early as the 17th century, and by the middle of the 19th century, cases of melancholia among children were reported (Anthony, 1975). However, until the beginning of the 20th century, affective disorder in childhood was not acknowledged as a clincial entity. It was not until the early 1920s (cf. Bleuler, 1934) that clinicians described depressed children in detail. The early literature on depressive symptoms in children emphasized separation and attachment disorders among these children (Bowlby, 1973; Freud & Burlingham, 1944; Spitz, 1966). Although childhood depression was included in a 1966 report on psychopathological disorders in childhood by the Group for the Advancement of Psychiatry (GAP, 1966), it was not included in the World Health Organization's *Glossary of Mental Disorders* (1974) or in the second version of the *Diagnostic and Statistical Manual* (DSM-II) of the American Psychiatric Association (1968).

Only recently has childhood depression begun to receive a substantial amount of attention by clinicians and researchers. While it has received official recognition, its status as a clinical syndrome of childhood remains unclear. In the recent *Diagnostic and Statistical Manual* (DSM-III; APA, 1980) childhood depression is mentioned. However, it is not listed as a diagnosis in the section entitled "Disorders usually first evident in infancy, childhood, or adolescence." Rather, the DSM-III states that the essential features of Affective Disorder in children are the same as in adults, and therefore, an adult diagnosis is appropriate.

The inclusion of childhood depression in the DSM-III is in part a reflection of recent interest in the topic in psychiatry and psychology. Advances in biological psychiatry and behavioral and cognitive psychology have raised new questions about the existence, etiology, development, course, assessment, and treatment of depression in children. For the first time, a body of empirical work is beginning to develop to enhance our understanding of this phenomena. This recent work will be the central focus of this paper.

Prevalence and Incidence

Good epidemiological data on the prevalence or incidence of depression in children are not available. Those data that are available are difficult to evaluate because of the wide disparity in criteria for evaluating depression as well as the variety of populations sampled. As a result, recent reviews (Carlson & Cantwell, 1979; Kashani, Husain, Shekim, Hodges, Cytryn, & McKnew, 1981; Kashani & Simonds, 1979; Kovacs & Beck, 1977) gives estimates of depression in children ranging from almost zero to 67 percent.

Depression is commonly identified in clinical populations of children. The range of findings is smaller here, especially when studies using the DSM-III criteria are compared. Using DSM-III criteria, Carlson & Cantwell (1979) found a prevalence of Major Depressive Disorder in 27 percent of 102 psychiatric inpatients and outpatients who were between the ages of 7 and 17. Schultz (1982) assessed 62 children from 8 to 12 years old in an outpatient psychiatric clinic. Using data derived from two instruments and two informants (child and mother), she determined that 52 percent of the children met DSM-III criteria for Major Depressive Disorder. Kaslow (1983) assessed another sample of 38 children from the same clinic. Independent structured interviews with the child and each parent yielded an estimate of 42 percent of the children meeting DSM-III criteria. Similar high incidence is reported in studies of inpatient populations (e.g., Carlson & Cantwell, 1982; Robbins, Alessi, Cook, Poznanski, & Yanchyshyn, 1982). Different diagnostic procedures, reports from different informants, and the fact that multiple diagnoses are often made in psychiatric outpatient and inpatient samples of children are factors that may affect the reported rates of depression in children.

There is a scarcity of data on the incidence of depression in the general population. Using DSM-III criteria, Kashani & Simonds (1979) found that only 1.9 percent of school children met the criteria for Major Depressive Disorder, though 17 percent showed sad affect. Based on a sample of nine-year-old children, Kashani, McGee, Clarkson, Anderson, Walton, Williams, Silva, Robins, Cytryn and McKnew (1983) reported the point prevalence of major and minor depressive disorder to be 1.8 percent and 2.5 percent respectively. Using a self-report scale, Kaslow, Rehm, and Siegel (1984) found that 33 percent of elementary school children were at least mildly depressed. A similar finding was reported by Albert and Beck (1975) in a sample of preadolescents. Large-scale epidemiological studies are needed to establish more accurate incidence and prevalence figures.

Sex Ratio and Age

Among adults, depression occurs more frequently in women than in men (Radloff, 1975; Weissman & Kleman, 1977). The data that exist on children are not as clear-cut. There are a number of studies that report a 3 to 1 male to female ratio of depression in children in private practice settings (Ossofsky, 1974), clinic outpatients (Kaslow, 1983; Poznanski & Zrull, 1970), inpatients (McConville, Boag, & Purohit, 1973; Nissen, 1971), and in an educational diagnostic center (Weinberg, Rutman, Sullivan, Penick, & Dietz, 1973). There are studies that report a 1 to 1 sex ratio in outpatients (Connell, 1972; Frommer, 1968) and in a nonpsychiatric sample (Kaslow et al., 1984). There are only a few studies that report a higher rate in females. Frommer, Mendelson & Reid (1972) report a 2 to 1 female to male ratio in their phobic depressive group. Seligman, Peterson, Kaslow, Tanenbaum, Alloy & Abramson (1984) looked at a normal sample of 8- to 13-year-olds and found that girls reported more depressive symptoms than did boys. There is some suggestion that as children enter adolescence there is an increase in the incidence of depression in girls but not in boys (Albert & Beck, 1975; Smucker, Craighead, Wilcoxin-Craighead, & Green, 1983). Using the Kaslow et al. (in press) elementary school children data, Leventon (1982) looked at specific depression scale items and found essentially no sex differences in endorsement in first or fourth graders but some sex differences in eighth graders. Several studies have found increases in children with age (e.g. Makita, 1973; Ossofsky, 1974; Puig-Antich, Blau, Marx, Greenhill, & Chambers, 1978).

In summary, currently available data suggest that depression may be common among clinical samples of children but that its overall incidence in the population may be less than in adults. Depression appears to increase with age, and sex differences in incidence may not appear until adolescence.

DESCRIPTION

Diagnostic Criteria

A distinction in the area of affective disorders in adults has been made between symptom, syndrome, and disorder, and a similar distinction needs to be made in the childhood depression area. The symptom is the single component of sad mood or depressive affect. The syndrome is a group of symptoms that covary in a reliable manner. As an example, Kashani, Barbero, and Bolander (1981) assessed children on a pediatric service and found that 38 percent showed the symptoms of depression, while only 7 percent received the syndromal DSM-III diagnosis. The syndrome of depression may be divided into a variety of depressive disorders distinguished from each other by such factors as course of illness, family pattern of illness, results on laboratory tests, and treatment response (Cantwell & Carlson, 1979). The major subtypes delineated in the DSM-III include major depression single episode, major depression recurrent, dysthymic disorder, and adjustment disorder with depressed mood.

There have been innumerable symptoms mentioned in the literature as being part of the syndrome of childhood depression. There is increasing agreement that some children manifest a syndrome that is phenomenologically similar to adult depression, and thus, the criteria for adult depression are being applied to children. Support for using the DSM-III criteria for a diagnosis of depression in children can be found in the work done by Cytryn, McKnew, and Bunney (1980). They compared the diagnostic criteria of the Children's Depression Inventory (Kovacs & Beck, 1977), the Weinberg criteria (Weinberg et al., 1973), and the DSM-III. They concluded that there is considerable and sufficient similarity between childhood and adult affective disorders, and therefore, the DSM-III is valid for diagnosing childhood affective disorders. Carlson & Cantwell (1982) compared subgroups of children who met DSM-III criteria to those who met the Weinberg et al. (1973) criteria and found that the children did not represent the same group because the DSM-III criteria are more restrictive. They conclude that independent validating measures of depression are necessary before final conclusions can be drawn regarding which criteria are more accurate. In reviewing the findings to date, Puig-Antich (1982a) noted that, while it is feasible and valid to use Research Diagnostic Criteria to make a DSM-III diagnosis of depression, some depressed children may be misdiagnosed.

A number of authors (e.g., Brumback, 1976; Garber, 1981) question whether adult criteria are appropriate for children. As Garber (1981) states, little is known about the reliability and validity of these criteria when they are applied to children, and what is known is not promising. Further, by using adult criteria for diagnosing childhood depression, we make the mistake of treating children like miniature adults and overlook their unique developmental characteristics.

Despite the problems, the current practice is that the following symptoms are necessary for a child to be diagnosed as having a DSM-III diagnosis of major depressive disorder. The child must have a dysphoric mood, which is prominent and relatively persistent, or must have a loss of interest or pleasure in almost all usual activities. Additionally, four out of the following eight symptoms need to be present almost daily for a period of at least two weeks: (1) appetite disturbance or significant weight change; (2) sleep disturbance; (3) psychomotor agitation or retardation; (4) anhedonia; (5) loss of energy or fatigue; (6) feelings of worthlessness, self-reproach, or excessive or inappropriate guilt; (7) diminished ability to think or concentrate or indecisiveness; and (8) suicidal ideation, threats, or attempts.

It is important to note that, although the specification of these symptoms represents an advance over DSM-II, there is, nevertheless, a great deal of clinical judgment involved in evaluating the nature and significance of these symptoms, even in adults. The problem is compounded in diagnosing children by the fact that particular symptoms may be manifested in different fashion by children than they are by adults. For example, appetite disturbances in children may have to be distinguished from changing food preferences. Energy needs vary in normal childhood development.

Based on findings from a number of researchers and clinicians, the DSM-III also discusses the age-specific associated features of depression in children, including separation anxiety in prepubertal children, negativistic or antisocial behavior in adolescent boys, feelings of wanting to leave home, feeling not understood or approved of, restlessness, grouchiness, aggression, sulkiness, social withdrawal, school problems, inattention to personal appearance, increased emotionality, and interpersonal sensitivity. There are a series of symptoms that are considered to be *depressive equivalents*. The more frequently cited depressive equivalents include: enuresis, temper tantrums, disobedience, truancy, running away, delinquency, fire setting, phobias (most notably school phobia), somatization, irritability, learning disabilities, school failures, and eating disorders (for a review, see Kovacs & Beck, 1977). The concept of a depressive equivalent is problematic. It leads to a variety of conceptual and empirical problems with regard to a definition of depression in children, which can be related to the adult disorder. While age-appropriate complaints may be associated with depression in children, some essential core symptoms identifiable specifically as depression should be essential to any definition, even with developmental differences taken into account. That is simply to say that a depressive equivalent symptom is insufficient alone for a diagnosis of depression.

Range of Severity

Like adult depression, depression in children may cover the full range of severity. In critiquing the concept of childhood depression, Lefkowitz and Burton (1978) point out that several studies suggest that depressive symptoms are common in normal children and that apparent depressive syndromes may be relatively transient. As a consequence, Lefkowitz and Burton doubt the existence of a pathological depressive syndrome in children. It is clear, however, that depression in children does exist at serious levels of child psychopathology. Although depression is seldom the presenting complaint and multiple diagnoses are frequently made, the syndrome is present in significant proportions of outpatient (e.g., Kaslow, 1983) and inpatient (e.g., Petti, 1978) populations, as reviewed earlier. Psychotic depressive and manic-depressive syndromes have been reported in children and adolescents (e.g., Carlson, 1983; Chambers, Puig-Antich, Tabrizi, & Davies, 1982). Perhaps even more importantly, depression in children, as in adults, has its own form of morbidity. That is, depression is sometimes implicated in child and adolescent suicide. Statistics suggest that suicide among youth is increasing in the United States (cf. Toolan, 1981). As is the case with adults, not all children who attempt suicide are depressed, but as a contributing factor, the consequences of depression may be quite serious.

Associated Features and Diagnoses

There is a high prevalence of the mixed diagnoses among epidemiological and clinical samples of prepubertal children. Depressive disorders are common in this broad category of children with psychological disorders. Many children who are depressed not only have a variety of other symptoms, but also receive other psychiatric diagnoses (e.g., Kaslow, 1983; Puig-Antich, 1982b), including conduct disorder (e.g., Brumback & Weinberg, 1977; Carlson & Cantwell, 1980; Chiles, Miller & Cox, 1980; Cytryn & McKnew, 1972; Edlebrock & Achenbach, 1980; Ingalls, 1978; Kashani, Cantwell, Shekim & Reid, 1982; Kaslow, 1983; Puig-Antich et al., 1978; Puig-Antich, 1982b), attention deficit disorder (Brumback & Weinberg, 1977; Kaslow, 1983; Zrull, McDermott & Poznanski, 1970), anorexia nervosa (Hendren, 1983), bulimia (Strober, 1981), learning disabilities (Brumback, Dietz-Schmidt & Weinberg, 1977; Brumback & Staton, 1983), and school phobia (Agras, 1959). Psychotic symptoms, including hallucinations and delusions, are also found in some children diagnosed as having major depressive disorder (Chambers, et al., 1982). Future research and clinical work should assess whether a child's depression is primary or secondary (Carlson & Cantwell, 1982a; Welner, 1978). It may be that depressive syndromes in many children in clinical samples are the consequence of other primary problems. The possibility should also be considered that in such samples children receive a diagnosis of depression because they have broad and severe problems in adjustment, among which are a sufficient number of depressive symptoms to meet the DSM-III criteria. Thus, a depressive syndrome should be differentiated from generalized severe psychopathology.

Age of Onset, Course, and Complications

The onset of depression is typically considered to be in early adulthood (DSM-III; APA, 1980). However, there are reports in the literature of depression beginning in infancy, preschool years, elementary school years, and adolescence. There is little information about the course or complications of this disorder in children. The one serious potential complication documented to date is that a percentage of depressed children are also actively suicidal (Carlson &

Cantwell, 1982b; Garfinkel & Golombek, 1974; Renshaw, 1974; Toolan, 1981).

Depression in children of different ages is characterized differently. Depressive behavior (often referred to as *anaclitic depression*) has been observed in infants who are separated from their mothers or in infants who live in emotionally deprived environments. Those infants first respond with angry protest, which is followed by periods of unhappiness, withdrawal, and apathy. They also evidence appetite and sleep disturbance, which is sometimes so extreme that they fail to thrive (Bowlby, 1969; Engel & Reichsman, 1956; Spitz, 1946). Due to the absence of cognitive skills necessary to report depressive thoughts and affect, many authors prefer not to label this infant condition as depression (e.g., Anthony, 1975; Kovacs & Beck, 1977). The relationship between this state in infants and depression, mourning, or a reaction to environmental and emotional deprivation in adults, is questionable.

Children in the early childhood phase (between toddler and kindergarten age) are said to be relatively free of depressive symptoms (Frommer et al., 1972; Poznanski & Zrull, 1970). There are, however, scattered reports of depression in preschool age children (e.g., Bakwin, 1972; Davidson, 1968), and Mahler (1966), who comments on the development of basic moods at this stage of the separation-individuation process, has noted behaviors that seem to indicate a predisposition to depression in later life. Depression during these years appears to be manifested by mood disturbance (irritability, excessive crying or fretfulness, discontentment or anger, grief or sadness), vegetative disturbance (insomnia, loss of appetite), and behavior disturbance (absence of normal play, hyperactivity, temper tantrums) (Mahler, 1966; Ossofsky, 1974). The depressive moods of preschoolers are transient and often occur only in the context of the relationship with the mother (Mahler, 1966). Preschoolers can not abstract and reflect on their inner experience, and thus, it is rare for them to discuss their feelings of sadness (Glasberg & Aboud, 1981). It may be that preschoolers' inability to verbalize how they feel has resulted in the infrequency of the depression diagnosis in children this young (Anthony, 1975).

There has been an increasing amount of attention paid to children in the middle years (6–12 years). Between the ages of six to eight years, depression is typified by feelings of dysphoria, psychosomatic symptoms, difficulties with sleep, appetite, and elimination, and attention-getting behaviors (Arajarvi & Huttunen, 1972; Ling, Oftedal & Weinberg, 1970; Nissen, 1971; Ossofsky, 1974). These symptoms do not necessarily mask the child's depression, but rather they can be viewed as developmentally appropriate concomitant symptoms. Children older than eight years of age who are depressed manifest what has been called a self-esteem or guilt type of depression in which they have low self-esteem, self-deprecatory ideas, and feel guilty and hopeless (McConville et al., 1973; Nissen, 1971). School problems, including underachievement and school phobia, are often presenting complaints when these children are seen at clinics. Depressive symptoms in middle childhood have been found to be stable over time (three to six months) as measured by self, peer, and teacher report (Seligman et al., 1984; Tessiny & Lefkowitz, 1982).

There is little question that adolescents experience depression. What seems to be crucial when dealing clinically with adolescents is to differentiate between the truly depressed adolescent and the individual who is moody and overreacts to environmental stress (Bemporad, 1978a). Some authors assert that depression in adolescents is similar to depression in adults (Carlson & Strober, 1983; Strober, 1983), whereas others argue that a developmental perspective needs to be taken and that adolescent-specific equivalents of depressive disorder can be identified (Easson, 1977; Glaser, 1968). While most adolescent depressions are characterized by their transient nature as much as by their intensity and painful nature, there are some depressed adolescents who become chronic, and their depression is not alleviated by changes in their environment. It is those adolescents who manifest a comprehensive and continuous syndrome that need special attention.

CONCEPTUALIZATION

Depressed Children: Do They Exist? Who Are They?

Most clinicians and researchers agree that youngsters can and do experience feelings of sadness, discouragement, anergia, and even a transient lack of interest in previously enjoyable activities (e.g., Lessing & Zagorin, 1971; Peterson, 1961; Rutter & Graham, 1968). However, there has been an ongoing debate concerning the existence and nature of a depressive syndrome in children. There are four major perspectives in regard to these issues.

The first view is held by the traditional psychoanalytic thinkers who maintain that the young child cannot be depressed because their superego is not sufficiently developed to experience guilt and aggression turned against the self (e.g., Beres, 1966; Rie, 1966; Rochlin, 1959). Further, there are psychoanalysts who conceptualize depression as an emotional response involving a partial or complete collapse of an individual's self-esteem, which results when the person experiences too much discrepancy between what he/she has achieved (real self) and what he/she expects to achieve (ideal self) (Bibring, 1953). According to these theorists, it is not until adolescence that an individual has a stable self-representation, and thus, the major dynamic of low self-esteem is not possible until that time. More current analytic models, which view the ego alone as capable of experiencing depression, do allow for the notion of childhood depression to be seriously considered (Anthony, 1975). Bibring (1953), a major proponent of the ego psychological perspective, defines depression as the emotional indication of a state of helplessness and powerlessness of the ego in which there is a concurrent lowering of self-esteem. Although, as noted above, some theoreticians do not think that children have a stable self-concept, other ego psychologists (Anthony, 1975) assert that helplessness and self-esteem are both within the child's psychological grasp.

The second view essentially states that most children do not express depression directly and that it must be inferred from behaviors and symptoms that mask the underlying depressive feelings (Glaser, 1968; Toolan, 1962). Proponents of this view argue that a child's depressive mood is not sustained because the child cannot tolerate prolonged feelings of sadness. Masking symptoms or depressive equivalents are the child's attempt to defend against the underlying depression. The presence of depressive equivalents is not sufficient for a diagnosis of depression. It is necessary that depressive elements be apparent upon careful interviewing and by analyzing the child's dreams, fantasies, drawings, and responses to projective tests (Cytryn & McKnew, 1974). Many symptoms have been labeled as depressive equivalents, and those most frequently cited include conduct disorders (hyperactivity, aggressiveness, delinquency) (Burks & Harrison, 1962; Lesse, 1974; Toolan, 1962; Zrull et al., 1970), psychological reactions (Malmquist, 1977), somatic complaints (especially headaches, stomachaches, enuresis, encopresis) (Arajarvi & Huttunen, 1972; Cytryn & McKnew, 1974; Frommer, 1968; Ling et al., 1970; Malmquist, 1977; Renshaw, 1974), and school problems (school phobia, poor school performance, learning disability) (Agras, 1959; Glaser, 1968; Hollon, 1970).

The third view was put forth by Lefkowitz and Burton (1978). They assert that childhood depression may not be a distinct clinical syndrome but a condition of childhood development that is transitory in nature and dissipates with time. Their interpretation of data from longitudinal and epidemiological studies was that there are significant variations of the prevalence of depressive symptoms with children's age and that many so-called depressive symptoms are commonly reported in normal children. Based on this, they conclude that these clinical manifestations were neither deviant statistically nor indicative or psychopathology. A number of criticisms have been made about this work (Costello, 1980; Kashani et al., 1981). First, it is important to consider a cluster of symptoms, not just individual symptoms. Secondly, the studies cited as evidence that the prevalence of depressive symptoms was similar in normal children and psychiatric samples were not designed to study affective disorders. Third, their work relies too heavily on a statistical definition of pathology. Finally, it is important to deal with problems that last even briefly to lessen the problematic behavior and possibly to prevent this behavior because of its potential functional relationship to a later, more persistent problem.

The consensus view emerging is that depression in children is similar to depression in adults; however, there are some additional developmentally appropriate symptoms. This is the perspective that has been adopted by the American Psychiatric Association in the DSM-III (APA, 1980). In order for children to be diagnosed as depressed, they need to meet the same criteria as do adults and, thus, are viewed as manifesting the affective (dysphoria, mood change, weepiness, anhedonia), cognitive (low self-esteem, helplessness, hopelessness), motivational (avoidance, anergia, decreased socialization) and vegetative (appetite and sleep disturbance) symptoms that characterize adult depressives. In addition, the developmentally appropriate symptoms that exist in conjunction with the more overt depression symptoms include somatic complaints, difficulties in school, and aggressive or anti-social behavior (Arajarvi & Huttunen, 1972; Brumback et al., 1977; Connell, 1972; Frommer, 1968; McConville et al., 1973; Weinberg et al., 1977). These symptoms are not seen as masking the child's depression but rather as the child's way of expressing him/her self. Although this position gives hints about the different manifestations of depression in children and adults, it lacks a clear-cut developmental perspective—the desirability of which has been emphasized by a number of authors (e.g., Anthony, 1975; Bemporad, 1978a; 1978b; Cole & Kaslow, in press; Malmquist, 1977).

Current theoretical models of depression have been developed primarily in the context of considering adult depression, and very little attention is given to depression in children. Nevertheless, these theories have much to suggest for the child depression literature.

Cognitive-Behavioral Models

Lewinsohn (1974).   Within a behavioral framework, Lewinsohn and his coworkers (1974) view the etiology of depression as a loss or lack of response contingent positive reinforcement. The model assumes that (1) a low rate of response contingent positive reinforcement acts as an eliciting stimulus for some depressive behaviors and (2) the low rate of response contingent positive reinforcement received by a person depends on the number of potentially reinforcing events in the environment, the social skills of the individual to elicit reinforcement from the environment, and the person's ability to experience the pleasurable tone of reinforcement without inhibitory anxiety. The model assumes that low-activity level, inadequate social skills, and anxiety are the central symptoms of depression. A substantial amount of empirical data with adults supports this model (for reviews, see Blaney, 1977; Lewinsohn, 1974).

To date, there has been little attempt to apply this model to depressed children. However, research suggests that children who self-report being more depressed are less popular, although they are aware of what is socially appropriate (Vosk, Forehand, Parker & Rickard, 1982). The one study that examined the relationship between depression and assertion in adolescents found that, contrary to what was predicted, those adolescents who reported themselves as more assertive also reported themselves as being more depressed (Teri, 1982).

Lewinsohn does not directly address the development of depression. One may speculate that depressed parents may restrict the positive events their child may engage in, may not contingently reinforce their child's social behavior; or may be behaviorally and emotionally withdrawn and fail to interact as positively with their children as do nondepressed parents. If a parent is depressed or has poor social skills, the parent may not provide a good model for the child to learn effective social interaction. Children of depressed parents may react to this lack of positive social behavior on the part of their parents by becoming depressed or by acting in such a way to draw attention from their parents. There are some reports, in fact, of social skills deficits and social isolation in children of depressed mothers (Grunebaum, Cohler, Kaufman & Gallant, 1978; Rolf, 1972).

Seligman (1975); Abramson, Seligman & Teasdale (1978). According to Seligman's original learned helplessness model (1975), depressed individuals expect that bad events will occur and that no response in their repertoire will be effective in avoiding them. When an individual learns that outcomes are uncontrollable, he/she becomes depressed, exhibits lowered self-esteem, and has cognitive and motivational deficits that impair problem solving and instrumental responding. Investigators have documented the existence of learned helplessness in depressed adults (Garber & Seligman, 1980). Related research with children reveals that children who endorse more depressive symptoms on the Children's Depression Inventory perform more poorly (e.g., longer latencies, fewer correct reponses) on a block design task, on an anagram task (Kaslow, Tanenbaum, Abramson, Seligman & Peterson, 1983), and on the Matching Familiar Figures Test (Schwartz, Friedman, Lindsay & Narrol, 1982).

In order to accommodate the research findings and to address the inadequacies of the original learned helplessness model, a reformulated model that stresses the role of attributions in helplessness and depression was proposed (Abramson et al., 1978). The causal attributions that people make for negative life events and the degree of importance they attach to them contribute to the development of the expectation of hopelessness and, in turn, depressive symptoms. It is hypothesized that depressed individuals make more internal-stable-global attributions for failure and more external-unstable-specific attributions for success than do their nondepressed counterparts. Research evidence is accumulating, which supports the relationship between attributions and helplessness and depressive deficits in adults (for a review, see Peterson & Seligman, in press).

Nonclinic and clinic samples of depressed children were found to have attributional styles similar to their adult counterparts (Craighead et al., 1981; Friedlander, Philips, Morrison & Traylor, 1981; Kaslow et al., in press; Leon, Kendall & Garber, 1980; Schultz, 1982; Seligman, et al., 1984). Attributional style in children was found to be stable across a three-month time period. While one study found that a child's mood and attributional style correlates significantly with the mother's attributional style but not with that of the father (Seligman et al., 1984), other research has found no relationship between the attributions made by a child and those made by the parents (Kaslow, 1983; Schultz, 1982).

There is some suggestion that depressed adults make two kinds of mis-attributions. Helplessness depressives believe that there is a high degree of response outcome independence in regard to their behavior and, thus, make external attributions of causality. The relevant research with children finds that on the Nowicki-Strickland Locus of Control Scale for Children (Nowicki & Strickland, 1973) depressed children have a more external locus of control than do nondepressed children (Butler, Miezitis, Friedman & Cole, 1980; Lefkowitz & Tessiny, 1980; Moyal, 1977; Tessiny & Lefkowitz, 1982; Tessiny, Lefkowitz & Gordon, 1980). The second type of misattribution is made by individuals with a depressive attributional style, who make excessively internal attributions of causality, while at the same time perceiving themselves as lacking the ability to succeed (Craighead et al., 1981; Foorman, 1982; Friedlander et al., 1981; Kaslow et al., in press; Leon et al., 1980; Seligman et al., 1984; Schultz, 1982). There is some suggestion that depressed individuals make the two types of attributions at different times. Using the Moyal-Miezitis Stimulus Appraisal Scale, Butler and her colleagues (1980) and Moyal (1977) found that depressed children choose less adaptive responses and more helpless, self-blaming, or externalized blaming responses. If this is the case, it is necessary to address the paradox between self-blame and uncontrollability (Abramson & Sacheim, 1978).

Another relevant body of literature is the work done by Dweck and her colleagues with helpless and nonhelpless children (Diener & Dweck, 1978, 1979; Dweck, 1975, 1976; Dweck & Bush, 1976; Dweck, Davidson, Nelson & Enna, 1978; Dweck, Goetz & Strauss, 1978; Dweck & Repucci, 1973). Helpless children attributed their failure to lack of ability (internal-stable), whereas mastery-oriented children attributed their failure to lack of effort (internal-unstable). Helpless children's performance deteriorated after failure, demonstrated negative affect about the task, and expected to do poorly in the future (Diener & Dweck, 1978, 1979; Dweck & Repucci, 1973).

In a discussion of the childhood development of helplessness, Seligman (1975) describes the "dance of development," which occurs in infancy, in which youngsters either acquire a sense of mastery over their environment or a profound sense of helplessness, depending on whether or not they have control of their environment. When an infant's life is filled with powerful synchronies between actions and outcomes, which occurs when there is responsive mothering, he/she develops a sense of mastery. Conversely, if the young child experiences an independence between his/her responses and the outcome, a sense of helplessness develops. Absence of mother, stimulus deprivation, and nonresponsive mothering are all potential factors in an infant's learning of uncontrollability (cf. Spitz, 1946). In addressing the issues of the development of self-esteem, Seligman argues that a sense of worth or high self-esteem cannot be bestowed but must be earned. Individuals need clear and explicit standards to live up to in order to develop high self-esteem (Coopersmith, 1967). It is only when an individual matches his/her ability to a stringent criteria and succeeds that ego strength develops. Although within the attributional reformulation the issue of the development of a depressive attributional style has not been addressed, it may be hypothesized that children learn what factors to attribute their successes and failures to, based on what factors their parents attribute to both their own successes and failures and those they make for their child's performance.

Beck (1967, 1976).   Beck's theory of depression emphasizes the central role of cognitive factors. According to the cognitive model of depression, depressed individuals develop, probably in childhood, a negative view of themselves, the world, and the future (negative cognitive triad). Experiences are filtered through a set of cognitive schema, which is the basis for the cognitive triad and which distort reality in a negative way. The arousal of depressive self-evaluations is associated with systematic errors committed by depressives in interpreting reality, including arbitrary inference, selective abstraction, overgeneralization, magnification and minimization, and personalization (Beck, 1976). The negative cognitive triad is a determinant of the associated affective, motivational, behavioral, and somatic symptoms of depression.

Naturalistic, clinical, and experimental studies have provided substantial support for this model with adults (for a review, see Beck & Rush, 1977). There is evidence that depressed children exhibit a negative view of themselves (e.g., Butler et al., 1980; Kaslow et al., in press; Kazdin, French, Unis & Esveldt-Dawson, 1983b; Lefkowitz & Tessiny, 1980; Moyal, 1977; Tessiny & Lefkowitz, 1982). There is also some indication that depressed children have a more negative view of their future as they report more feelings of hopelessness (Kazdin et al., 1983b).

Although the etiological-developmental aspects of the theory have never been delineated, Beck has speculated that certain unfavorable life circumstances in childhood, such as loss of a parent, continual rejection by peers, or chronic stress, may predispose an individual to becoming depression prone. These experiences may result in the person having a tendency to overreact to similar conditions later in life and to revive the depressive schemas acquired in childhood. Additionally, Beck remarks that individuals who, even as children, tend to set stringent and perfectionistic goals for themselves may also be depression prone. When these individuals face disappointment later in life, they are unable to regulate their negative reaction, and they feel depressed and hopeless. It is the interaction between an individual's specific vulnerability (his/her cognitive structure, which consists of a set of assumptions or beliefs through which the individual construes the world) and a specific stress (typically a loss) that results in the individual becoming depressed. As depression develops and increases in these individuals, the negative distorted thinking replaces objective thinking, and the depressive spiral results.

While Beck assumes that negative cognitions develop in childhood, he does not describe their etiology. One may speculate that one way these cognitions could develop would be through the teachings of a depressed parent, a parent who would model depressive cognitions. Additionally, depressed parents' errors in thinking could lead to distorted perceptions of their child's adjustment and behavior. Recently, Rogers and Forehand (1983) reported a study in which they found that the more depressed the parents were, the more negatively they viewed their children, despite the fact that their children's behavior was comparable to that seen among the children of less depressed parents.

Rehm (1977). Rehm's self-control model of depression encompasses aspects of the models of Beck, Lewinsohn, and Seligman and his colleagues. It derives from and expands Kanfer's self-control model (Kanfer, 1970; Kanfer & Karoly, 1972). Self-control, a three-stage, feedback loop process, includes self-monitoring, self-evaluation, and self-reinforcement. Depressed individuals are hypothesized to have deficits in one or more of these areas. Symptoms of depression are considered to reflect deficits in self-control behavior. Rehm characterizes the self-control deficits evidenced by depressed individuals as follows: (1) selective monitoring or attending to negative events to the exclusion of positive events; (2) selective monitoring of immediate as opposed to delayed consequences of one's behavior; (3) setting overly stringent self-evaluative criteria; (4) failing to make accurate attributions of responsibility for one's behavior; (5) insufficient contingent self-reinforcement; and (6) excessive self-punishment.

Rehm (1982) reviews research evidence for self-monitoring, self-evaluation, and self-reinforcement deficits in depressed adults. Research on depression in children is beginning to demonstrate that depressed children have deficits in various self-control skills. In a group of normal children, those who were more depressed expected to do more poorly, evaluated their performance more negatively, set more stringent criteria for what constituted failure (but not success), perceived their mothers as setting more stringent criteria for failure (but not success), and indicated that punishment was preferable to reward in controlling their behavior (Kaslow et al., in press). The specificity of these deficits to depressed children is unclear, as there is only weak support for depressed clinic children having more self-control deficits than nondepressed clinic children (Kaslow, 1983; Schultz, 1982). Evidence that depressed children have low self-esteem and a depressive attributional style may be construed as evidence for deficits in the self-evaluation and self-attribution components of self-control.

The self-control model provides a framework for studying the etiology of depression. Individuals with adaptive self-control skills are able to cope effectively with depression-inducing stresses in their environment, whereas individuals with poor self-control skills are more susceptible to depression and have a more difficult time overcoming a depression. Rehm posits that maladaptive modeling or reinforcement schedules are in the histories of depressed persons.

Social learning theorists (e.g., Bandura & Walters, 1963) suggest several ways in which parental behavior may influence a child's functioning. Parents serve as potent models whom their children imitate (Bandura, 1969). One may speculate that children of depressed parents imitate their parents' depressive behaviors, including monitoring of negative events, a negative view of themselves and the world, a depressive attributional style, low rates of self-reinforcement, and high rates of self-punishment. Additionally, these children may exhibit depressive behaviors in their interactions with people. For example, like their parents, they may demonstrate little affect, complain a great deal, or remain socially isolated.

According to social learning theory, parents can change the content of their children's behavioral repertoires or modify the frequency with which certain behaviors occur through the use of rewards and punishments. Those discipline practices that seem to be associated with the development of psychopathology in children include high rates of punishment, the use of rewards contingent on approved performance, inconsistency in standards, expectations and the application of rewards and punishments, and excessive indulgence or over-permissiveness (Millon & Millon, 1974). Two of these patterns of parenting—inconsistency and overprotectiveness—are especially likely to be applicable to depressed mothers (Bowlby, 1980; Freud, 1965; Mahler, 1965; Mahler, Pine & Bergman, 1975). According to Millon and Millon, both of these styles of discipline have serious implications for child development.

Children who are raised in environments that are unpredictable and chaotic have problems devising effective strategies for adaptive behavior. In their attempt to avoid conflict, they become behaviorally passive and indecisive. Alternatively, they may imitate their parents' behaviors so that their own behaviors may be characterized as inconsistent and noncommittal. Further, irregular or intermittent reinforcement results in behaviors that are difficult to extinguish. Thus, children whose depressed parents exhibit inconsistent parenting behaviors are likely to develop maladaptive patterns of behavior that persist into adulthood. Overly protective methods of raising children hinder the child in learning and performing age-appropriate self-reliant behaviors. Additionally, these children do not develop a sense of their own competence, which results in their having lower self-esteem. Depressed parents may find it difficult to provide the necessary support and encouragement for their children to develop normal competencies and independence. Thus, social learning theory suggests that children of depressed parents are at risk for the development of maladaptive patterns of behavior, which may occur through the mechanisms of faulty modeling or reinforcement practices.

Family Patterns

The importance of viewing the child within his/her social context (e.g., Brofenbrenner, 1979) and a child's problems within a larger family systems perspective (for a review of models of family theory and therapy, see Gurman &

Kniskern, 1981) has gained increasing attention in the past 15 years. It is only recently that depression in families is being written about, and there are a number of relevant bodies of literature in this area.

Retrospective studies find that depressed adults, in comparison to non-depressed adults, remember their parents as being overprotective, rejecting, intrusive, controlling, and as less than adequate caretakers (e.g., Crook, Raskin & Eliot, 1981; Lamont, Fischoff & Gottlieb, 1976; Parker, 1979). There are a number of explanations for these associations (Parker, 1979). Depressed individuals evaluate their relationships more negatively (Beck, 1967). They may elicit less parental care and/or greater parental overprotection (Lewis & Rosenblum, 1974). Low parental care and/or parental overprotection may make a child vulnerable to becoming depressed.

There is some research that examines the parenting practices of depressed mothers (Weissman & Paykel, 1974). If one juxtaposes the affective, cognitive, and motivational symptoms of depression in adults with the demands of parenthood, then it is not surprising to find that depressed mothers have difficulty being effective parents. Depressed women were found to be less emotionally involved with their children, to have less affection for them, to have difficulties communicating with them, and to evidence an increased amount of hostility towards them. The effect of the mother's depression on the child differs according to the developmental stage of the family (Deykin, Jacobson, Klerman & Solomon, 1966; Weissman, Paykel & Klerman, 1972; Weissman & Siegel, 1972). More specifically, Weissman et al. (1972) report that mothers who experienced a postpartum depression felt helpless and overwhelmed by the amount of attention their newborn required and, in response, became overindulgent, overprotective, or compulsive mothers. Additionally, they set unrealistically high standards for themselves as mothers and felt inadequate when they could not live up to these standards. Depressed mothers of infants were either overconcerned, helpless and guilty, or directly hostile. The mothers of young school-aged children were characterized as being irritable, emotionally uninvolved, or withdrawn. Weissman and Siegel (1972) note that a high degree of impaired communication, resentment, disaffection, and hostility was observed in the depressed mothers toward their adolescent children. "Empty nest" stage mothers, which are those mothers in the stage that marks the termination of child rearing, had difficulties in successfully coping with the termination of child rearing and had problems in adjusting to their role as women when being a mother was not their dominant function (Deykin et al., 1966).

The field of high-risk research has burgeoned in the past 20 years, and a book was recently published on risk, identification, and intervention with children of depressed parents (Morrison, 1983). There are some studies designed to examine children at risk for schizophrenia that have used children of depressed mothers as a control group (e.g., Cohler, Grunebaum, Weiss, Hartman & Gallant, 1976; Gamer, Gallant, Grunebaum & Cohler, 1977; Grunebaum et al., 1978; Rolf & Garmezy, 1974; Sameroff & Zax, 1973; Weintraub, Neale &

Liebert, 1975; Weintraub, Prinz & Neale, 1978). There are some new projects designed to look primarily at children who are at risk for affective disorders (e.g., Anthony, 1975; Conners, Himmelhock, Goyette, Ulrich & Neil, 1979; Foorman, 1982; McKnew, Cytryn, Efron, Gershon & Bunney, 1979; Welner, Welner, McCrary & Leonard, 1977). Children with depressed mothers have difficulties in concentration and attention (Cohler et al., 1976; Gamer et al., 1977; Grunebaum et al., 1978), in academic performance (Weintraub et al., 1975; Weintraub et al., 1978), and in social functioning and competence (Cohler et al., 1976; Grunebaum et al., 1978; Rolf & Garmezy, 1974; Weintraub et al., 1975; Weintraub et al., 1978). Further, the children of depressed mothers evidence a high rate of behavior problems and psychiatric problems, including depression (Conners et al., 1979; Foorman, 1982; McKnew et al., 1979; Welner et al., 1977). Taken together, the studies that examine children of parents with affective disorders suggest that these children are at higher risk for depression than the general population. However, it is by no means the case that all depressed parents have depressed children.

A few studies have considered depressed children as the probands and have looked at their parents (e.g., Brumback et al., 1977; Kaslow, 1983; Ossofsky, 1974; Phillips, 1979; Poznanski & Zrull, 1970; Schultz, 1982). These studies find that a significant number of these children had mothers with depression (40 to 70 percent) and a high incidence of psychopathology in their extended family. This is a higher incidence of depression than is found in parents of normal children (4 percent) or in the parents of nondepressed clinic children (30 to 40 percent). However, it is also not the case that all depressed children have depressed parents.

It is only recently that the depressed person's interpersonal world has been considered. Depressed individuals are said to elicit a type of support and caretaking, which in turn maintains their depression (Coyne, 1976; Feldman, 1975; Rubenstein & Timmins, 1978). There may be a struggle for power or narcissistic primacy that characterizes the depressed family (Hogan & Hogan, 1978). Depressed families may be those families in which there are relationship impasses (Pollack, Kaslow & Harvey, 1982). While there is a wealth of speculations about family patterns associated with childhood depression, it can be seen that empirical evidence is only beginning to accumulate.

ASSESSMENT

Until recently, a major obstacle in studying depression in children has been the lack of a well-developed assessment methodology. Clinical researchers have responded to this problem by developing a number of self-report, parent report, teacher report, peer report, and clinician report instruments to assess the presence and severity of depression in children. Interview schedules that can be used to make a DSM-III diagnosis of depression are also being developed. The current assessment techniques for childhood depression have been detailed elsewhere (Costello, 1981; Kazdin, 1981; Kazdin & Petti, 1982; Kovacs, 1981). Descriptions of the major scales are presented in Table 15–1.

One major issue in regard to assessing and diagnosing depression in children is the question of whose reports are accurate and reliable. It is currently agreed that the diagnosis of major depressive disorder cannot be made with certainty without interviewing the child (Puig-Antich, 1982a). Rutter and Graham (1968) and Herjanic, Herjanic, Brown, and Wheatt (1975) assert that it is possible to obtain reliable information from the child alone. On close examination, it appears that children accurately report factual data (Herjanic et al., 1975; Ovraschel, Puig-Antich, Chambers, Tabrizi & Johnson, 1982) but are less accurate in reporting on issues that entail more subtle discriminations (Garber, 1981). The most controversial child data is in the area of affective expression. Some researchers report that children older than seven years of age are cognitively capable of making judgments about their subjective feelings (e.g., sadness, hopeless, guilt) (Glasberg & Aboud, 1981; Piaget, 1954). However, others assert that youngsters may be limited by their language and cognitive capabilities, or they may deny distressing feelings (Kazdin, 1981). Puig-Antich, Chambers & Tabrizi (1983) note that, although many children report no sadness, they will describe their feelings of dysphoria using a different label. Puig-Antich et al. (1983) discuss the major symptoms of depression, who are the most reliable reporters of each symptom, and the questions that may be asked to elicit the most accurate information.

Given the potential limits in the accuracy of a child's self-report, supplementary data from other informants should be used. Teachers give the best information about school behavior (Garber, 1981; Lefkowitz & Tessiny, 1980; Poznanski, 1982; Puig-Antich, 1983). Peers give useful data about how the child interacts with others and the child's general self-presentation (Lefkowitz & Tessiny, 1980). The parent's perspective is considered to be very important (Carlson & Cantwell, 1979; Garber, 1981; Orvaschel, Weissman, Padian & Lowe, 1981; Poznanski, 1982; Puig-Antich et al., 1983). Parent and child reports have been found to be discrepant in a number of studies (e.g., Garber, 1981; Garber, Greenberg & White, 1980; Kaslow, 1983; Kazdin, French & Unis, 1983a; Kazdin, French, Unis & Esvedlt-Dawson, 1983b; Weissman, Orvaschel & Padian, 1980). Whose report is correct? Kazdin and his colleagues (1983a; 1983b) suggest that when parents and children differ in their reports they may each be accurate. Children are less likely to report certain symptoms than are their parents (e.g., Cytryn et al., 1981; Kazdin et al., 1983a; 1983b; McKnew et al., 1979; Orvaschel et al., 1981; Robbins et al., 1982). Parents either minimize their child's problems because they feel guilty, or they exaggerate their child's problems because of their frustration. Since a high percentage of these parents are depressed, they may either overidentify with their child's problems or withdraw (Poznanski, 1982). In same studies, mother and father reports correlate significantly, but this has not always been found to be the case

TABLE 15-1

Scales for Assessing Depression in Children

scale	author	descriptions	samples and psychometrics reported
Children's Depression Inventory (CDI)	Kovacs & Beck (1977)	27-item self-report. Modified version of Beck Depression Inventory for adults. Measures severity of depression.	Psychiatric, medical and normal children ages 6–17 tested. Item-total correlations, internal consistency, and discriminant validity adequate. Correlates with clinician rating and DSM-III diagnosis.
Short Children's Depression Inventory (SCDI)	Carlson & Cantwell (1979, 1980)	13-item self-report. Modified version of Beck Depression Inventory-short form. Measures severity of depression.	Inpatient and outpatient psychiatric referrals ages 7–17 tested. Correlates with clinician ratings and DSM-III diagnosis.
Children's Depression Scale (CDS)	Lang & Tisher (1978) Tisher & Lang (1983)	66-item self-report. Alternate forms for parents, teachers, and siblings. Subscales for affect, social problems, self-esteem, thoughts of death and illness, guilt, and pleasure.	Psychiatric and normal samples ages 9–16. Internal consistency and discriminant validity are adequate.
Self-Rating Scale (SRS)	Birleson (1981)	18 items	Children 7–13. No psychometric data available.
Kiddie-SADS (K-SADS)	Puig-Antich & Chambers (1978)	Structured interview for depression, other diagnosis and psychiatric history. Modified version of Schedule for Affective Disorders and Schizophrenia. DSM-III compatible revised version. Parent form also.	Psychiatric and normal samples ages 6–16. Interrater reliability high, good convergent validity, but low to moderate inter-informant reliability.
Bellevue Index of Depression (BID)	Petti (1978)	Structured 40-item interview under 19 headings. Assesses severity and duration of symptoms on basis of Weinberg criteria. Parent and child report used.	Inpatient and outpatient samples aged 6–12. Good interrater reliability and adequate convergent validity.
Interview Schedule for Children (ISC)	Kovacs, Betof, Celebre, Mansheim, Petty & Raynak (1977)	Structured interview covering mental status, behavioral observations, and DSM-III diagnoses.	Psychiatric and normal samples ages 8–13. Adequate interrater reliability for most items. Correlates with CDI.

TABLE 15–1 (concluded)

scale	author	descriptions	samples and psychometrics reported
Children's Affective Rating Scale (CARS)	McKnew, Cytryn, Efron, Gershon & Bunney (1979); McKnew & Cytryn (1979)	Clinical interview assessing mood behavior, verbal expression, and fantasy on 10-point scales.	Psychiatric inpatients, medical patients normals, and children of depressed parents ages 5–15. Adequate interrater reliability and concurrent validity.
Children's Depression Rating Scale (CDRS)	Poznanski, Cook, & Carroll (1979); Poznanski, Carroll, Banegas, Cook & Grossman (1982)	Interview assessing severity of depressive symptoms & "expressive communication." Modified from Hamilton Depression Rating Scale. Data from all informants used.	Psychiatric outpatients and medical inpatients ages 6–12. Adequate interrater reliability and item-total correlations. Strong correlations with global clinical ratings.
Diagnostic Interview for Children and Adolescents (DICA)	Herjanic, Herjanic, Brown & Wheatt (1975)	Interview with parent and child forms to assess school progress, social behavior, somatic, and psychiatric symptoms. Parent form also assesses early development, family history, and SES.	Adequate psychometrics.
Personality Inventory for Children-Depression Scale (PIC)	Wirt, Lachar, Klinedinst & Seat (1977)	600-item parent report inventory. 46-item depression scale; symptoms identified by clinicians.	Designed for ages 3–16. Good test-retest reliability. No formal validity data.
Child Behavior Check List (CBCL)	Achenbach (1978); Achenbach & Edelbrock (1978)	Parent and teacher rating scales covering social competence, academic performance, and behavior problems.	Parents and teachers of psychiatric and normal samples ages 4–16. Good test-retest and inter-informant reliability.
Peer Nomination Inventory for Depression (PNIO)	Lefkowitz & Tessiny (1980)	Peer nomination ratings for 13 depression, 4 happiness, and 2 popularity roles.	Given to fourth and fifth graders. Good internal consistency, test-retest, and interrater reliability, and content and concurrent validity.

(Kaslow, 1983). Although there is often a low correlation between informants, informants themselves may be consistent between measures (Lefkowitz & Tessiny, 1980; Poznanski, Cook & Carroll, 1979; Weissman et al., 1981).

One approach that resolves this informant dilemma is to think of depression as a multivariate phenomenon. At least two domains of variables should be considered. First, depression is a syndrome comprised of many related symptoms. Individual cases may vary considerably in the severity, patterning, and significance of specific symptomatic behaviors. The importance of specific target behaviors will be discussed below. Second, informants themselves can be thought of as a salient domain of relevant information. This may be true for adults (Rehm, 1981), but it takes on special significance for children. Children should be assessed not just as individuals independent of their environment, but also in the important contexts of their lives—family, school, and peers. Each context represents a different perspective on the problem. Symptoms may vary in their severity and importance as a function of the perspective of the informant. This may reflect both situational effects (e.g., home versus school) and the values, standards, judgments, and skills of the informant. The child, each parent, teachers, and, most important, the clinician may weigh symptoms quite differently. It may be very important in treatment to take into account the presenting complaints (most salient symptoms) as seen by each informant from their various perspectives. Diagnosis may require a judicious consideration of which symptoms are reported from which perspective.

In general, one cannot discuss assessment instruments apart from the purposes of assessment. Scales for diagnosis versus treatment planning may have different properties. Only three of the scales reviewed, the Kiddie-SADS, the ISC, and the DISC, explicitly yield a DSM-III diagnosis of depression. The BID allows for a diagnosis based on other criteria (Weinberg et al., 1973). Only clinician-perspective interview scales take diagnostic criteria into account. There is no reason why evaluations from other scales could not yield information on the presence or absence of diagnostic criterion symptoms. Nearly all of the scales yield a score indicative of severity of depression. This may be a correlate of a depression diagnosis, but it is not equivalent. A few of the scale developers have suggested cutoff scores for considering depression as mild, moderate, or severe. Apart from the instruments that assess multiple dimensions of psychopathology (e.g., PIC, CBCL), only the Kiddie-SADS and the ISC incorporate explicit means (DSM-III criteria) for making differential diagnoses. Depression severity may be important for treatment planning, but many additional factors (e.g., other forms of psychopathology) may also play a prominent role. Several of the scales yield potentially valuable subscale scores (e.g., CDS, DICA, CBCL). Separate scales for assessing specific treatment targets for therapy will be reviewed below.

In Table 15–1, the scales are grouped in part by the intended user—child/patient, clinician, parent, teacher, sibling and peer. The intended user influences the nature of the scale. Child self-report and peer report scales tend to be short with simple language and concrete items. Clinician scales tend to involve more open-ended questions and involve judgmental ratings on abstract scales. Parent and teacher scales often involve long checklists of specific problem behaviors. Several of the scales have alternate forms for different users (e.g., CDS for child, parent, teacher, and sibling or the Kiddie-SADS, DICA, and ISC for interviewing child and parent). It may be highly desirable to be able to collect parallel data from multiple informants. The CDS gives the broadest informant coverage in questionnaire form. A similar instrument or set of instruments providing parallel assessments by a clinician interviewer could be very useful.

Instruments also may vary as to their intended use for clinical or research applications. Clinical scales should offer a wide coverage of information relevant to treatment planning and decision making. Research scales should identify cases in reliable and replicable fashion. The scales reviewed vary somewhat on their intended use. Of special interest here is the fact that a new scale is currently under development under the auspices of the Center for Epidemiological Studies of the National Institutes of Mental Health. The Diagnostic Interview Schedule for Children (DISC) and its parallel form for interviewing parents (DISC-P) are designed for use in epidemiological research. As such, they provide information for explicit diagnoses in a format usable by persons with less expertise than experienced clinicians. Careful field trials are now underway. If the instrument meets up to its potential, it may become the standard for diagnosis in childhood depression research and may also be influential in clinical practice.

The field of assessment of childhood depression is quite new, as evidenced by the publication dates for the instruments reviewed. With this newness come many problems, but also much potential for the future. None of the instruments reviewed can be considered fully developed in a psychometric sense. More and better data on reliability and validity are needed. Data on construct and discriminant validity are especially important. Does depression in children truly represent a coherent syndrome clearly and usefully distinguishable from other disorders of childhood? Normative data on larger samples of clinical and normal populations are necessary to the clinical application of the instruments. We know little of the clinical utility of the scales (or of the diagnosis of childhood depression). Does it relate to depression in adulthood? Are there differential treatment predictions for the diagnosis? Standard instruments for the diagnosis and severity evaluation of childhood depression would be of great help to research and clinical practice, but the actual process may be one of gradual refinement and redefinition of the construct and of the instruments to assess it.

Finally, it is important to point out that none of the existing instruments for assessing childhood depression take into account the age or developmental level of the child. At the very least, it should be important to establish different norms for different developmental stages of childhood. Scores for six- to eight-year-olds can hardly be expected to be equivalent to scores for 15- to 17-year-olds. Most of the scales reviewed span such an age range. More logically, it might be expected that certain items would vary in their contribution to scores for children at different stages. Concomitant symptoms should also be different at different ages. The field may be beginning to move more in that direction, as evidenced by the recent publication of two depression scales specifically for adolescents (Chiles, Miller & Cox, 1980; Mezzich & Mezzich, 1979). A developmental perspective should be incorporated in future scale constructions for childhood depression.

TREATMENT

Little attention has been paid to treatment of depression in children, and it has been only recently that depression itself has been a focus of therapy with children. There are a number of cognitive-behavioral techniques for treating the symptoms associated with depression in children (enuresis, school phobia, hyperactivity, somatic complaints, aggressiveness and impulsivity, social withdrawal, and poor social skills), and these treatments have been detailed by Petti (1981; 1983a). We recommend that if one or more of these concomitant symptoms are present and primary then initial treatment should focus on alleviating these symptoms. If the child's depression remits with a successful outcome, further treatment may not be indicated. However, if the depression persists when the other symptoms are no longer present, further treatment may be indicated. Further, if the depression-related symptoms persist, it may be the case that the depression needs to be a more focal target of the treatment.

Recently, there have appeared a few studies that focus on treating depression in children. The majority of the reports discuss the use of antidepressants in treating childhood depression. Taken together, the studies suggest that antidepressants, particularly tricyclics (e.g., imipramine, amitryptiline), are effective in 75 percent of the cases, regardless of concomitant symptoms (for a review, see Petti, 1983b). These studies need to be interpreted carefully because they have some serious methodological flaws, and there are few double-blind controlled studies. Further, tricyclics are associated with a number of side effects in children (Klein, Gittelman, Quitkin & Rifkin, 1980), which must be taken into account if one chooses to medicate a child. While MAO inhibitors (e.g., phenelzine) have been used with depressed children (Frommer, 1967), the drug-diet interactions and the potential toxicity of these drugs probably account for their limited use with children. A word is in order about manic-depressive illness and the use of lithium carbonate in children and adolescents (for a review, see Carlson, 1983). The existence of manic-depressive disorder in prepubescent children has been even more controversial than the possibility of a unipolar type illness. Some investigators do report treatment success when lithium carbonate is administered to children exhibiting severe mood swings, characterized by depression combined (or alternating) with irritability, explosive behavior, or intense activity (Connell, 1969; Frommer, 1968; Youngerman & Canino, 1978). Controversies and public concern over the use of psychotropic medications with children may restrain the trend for increased usage of medication in treating children with affective disorders. Further, as Elkins & Rapoport (1983) point out, it may be that children have more immediate response to nondrug therapies than do adults, and they may tend to have fewer symptoms that are primarily drug responsive. However, medications may be appropriate in treatment resistant cases, in severely depressed or suicidal children, and in children with neurovegetative symptoms.

A few case studies have appeared in the literature that describe using traditional psychotherapy to treat depressed children (Bemporad, 1978c; Beres, 1966; Boverman & French, 1979; Furman, 1974; Gilpin, 1976; Sacks, 1979). Bemporad (1978c) stresses the importance of viewing the child's symptoms within a developmental context, and thus, a different focus of therapy may be appropriate for children at different ages. For example, younger children are primarily responsive to their environment; thus, therapy should aim to manipulate the environment. Family involvement is essential. Therapy focuses on diminishing the source of the child's frustration, on helping to build the child's self-esteem, and on increasing areas in which he/she can obtain gratification. As children get older, they internalize their difficulties and develop a more distorted view of themselves. Individual therapy should make the child aware of his/her cognitive distortions, of how they affect his/her behavior, and of the need for the child to be responsible and change his/her behavior. While individual psychotherapy with children is considered by many to be an unnecessary, time-consuming process, and there is little empirical evidence to support its efficacy, the emphasis placed on viewing the child within a developmental perspective should not be ignored.

Reports of using cognitive or behavioral methods for treating depression in children are also rare. Given the efficacy of the cognitive-behavioral treatment for adult depression and for other behavior problems in children, these strategies may prove useful when working with children who are depressed. The following sections will attempt to integrate adult treatment models with related cognitive and behavioral approaches for treating problems in children. The few studies done thus far will be reviewed.

Behavioral Strategies: Case Example

Jack, a nine-year-old male was brought to the clinic by his parents. Data obtained at the initial evaluation revealed that Jack was feeling sad and lonely, he felt isolated from his peers, he did not enjoy any in-school activities, and he was not involved in much activity after school. Further, Jack stated that he was hesitant to approach other children and was reluctant to assert himself. Jack was a good student in school, although he was not feeling interested in his school work. No suicidal ideation was present.

Target Behaviors and Phenomenology

In addition to sad affect, this case suggests prominent symptoms of anhedonia, social withdrawal, and low-activity level. Anhedonia, an inability to experience pleasure, has been identified by Gittelman-Klein (1977) as the essential defining characteristic of childhood depression. Although anhedonia is often assumed to have a biological base, Lewinsohn (e.g., Lewinsohn, Biglan & Zeiss, 1976) asserts that anhedonia is usually a result of social anxiety, and he prescribes desensitization procedures in this instance. We will make the assumption that primary anxiety problems can be differentiated from depression, and the methods for dealing with anxiety in children are reviewed elsewhere in this book. Anhedonia may also be viewed as simply a reflection of low levels of obtained reinforcement from situations because of poor social skills and/or low levels of activity. These latter deficits are the primary targets of behavioral approaches for depression. We assume that the presenting complaints in this case represent low-activity level, which may be based in part on social skills deficits. Assessment and treatment planning from a behavioral position would proceed on this basis.

Assessment of Target Behaviors

Children's Event Schedule (Garber, 1982). Similar to the Pleasant Events Schedule constructed by Lewinsohn and his colleagues (MacPhillamy & Lewinsohn, 1971), Garber devised the Children's Event Schedule, which lists 75 pleasant and 75 unpleasant events that can be rated for how frequently they occur and how enjoyable/aversive they are. The sum of the cross-products reflects the total amount of positive reinforcement or aversiveness experienced by the child. Lewinsohn et al. (1976) suggest that total frequency of positive events may be used to assess activity level, whereas enjoyability ratings can be related to inability to experience pleasure. They suggest cutoff scores for making therapy decisions for adults. Similar guidelines could be adapted for use with children.

Children's Reinforcement Survey Schedule (CRSS; Cautela, 1977). The CRSS, a modified form of the Reinforcement Survey Schedule (RSS; Cautela & Kastenbaum, 1967), is a self-report instrument that assesses the pleasurableness (dislike, like, like very much) of potential reinforcers. There are forms for children of different ages.

Children's Reinforcement Survey (CRS; Clement & Richard, 1970). This survey was designed for use by an informant or by the target child to identify potentially reinforcing events for the child. The scale requests information about the people, places, things, and activities that are (or may be) positively reinforcing to the child. Data obtained from both the CRSS and the CRS could be of use in developing effective behavior increase intervention programs for children who are depressed.

Behavioral Assertiveness Test for Children (BAT-C; Bornstein, Bellack & Hersen, 1977). This behavioral assessment procedure is similar to that used in adult social skills assessment. The BAT-C is a structured role play in which the child is required to interact with an adult who plays the part of a child antagonist in a number of scenes.

Treatment of Target Behaviors

Activity Increase Strategies.   The activity increase strategies utilized by Lewinsohn and his colleagues are based on the assumption that depressed individuals have few person-environment interactions that are positively reinforcing and/or have a high rate of punishing experiences. Depressed individuals emit few behaviors and receive little positive reinforcement from their environment; this in turn leads to feelings of dysphoria and the cycle continues. According to this view, treatment of depressed individuals should focus on restoring an adequate schedule of positive reinforcement. The most common focuses for changing an individual's reinforcement schedule are to alter the frequency, quality, and range of the individual's activities and social interactions.

Since there are no reports in the literature of activity increase programs for treating depressed children, the following is a possible way a program could be conducted. First, data about what events are pleasant and unpleasant for the child and information about what behaviors are either intrinsically reinforcing or have a high probability of external reinforcement should be obtained. If the child is anhedonic and unable to enjoy any activities, it is important to determine what behaviors were enjoyed in the past. Observation that there had been a marked decrease in the involvement in certain activities when the child became depressed would suggest that these activities would be important to target. Second, children could list the behaviors they engaged in daily, rate their moods, and see the correlation between the two. Third, children should be encouraged to increase the number of activities associated with their good moods and those behaviors that they found rewarding in the past. Often, depressed children will refuse to engage in activities because they do not expect to have fun. When this expectation is expressed, the children should be encouraged to try the activity anyway, just as an experiment. Often they will end up having a good time, despite their initial expectations. The way to help children increase the number of positive activities they engage in is by scheduling the activities or by setting up either self-managed or externally managed reinforcement programs. Fourth, children should be helped to decrease those behaviors associated with their depressed mood and those that have been punished in the past. Fifth, children need to be reinforced for their positive activity level. The reinforcement may be intrinsic in simply engaging in the activities, or the child may need adults to give positive reinforcement. For younger children, external reinforcement is particularly important. The reinforcers used may be based on the information obtained from the reinforcement surveys. Sometimes, children like to set up a "reinforcement menu" (Daley, 1976) in which they can choose what they will receive if they do what is required of them. In designing an activity increase program, it is essential that the child be actively involved in the planning, particularly because this will help him/her gain an increased sense of mastery and control over his/her life. Additionally, parents should be included in developing a program, as they can provide information about the child's routines and the feasibility of the schedule, and they can increase the likelihood that the child will participate in the plan by their willingness to be involved.

Social Skills Strategies.   Depressed adults are often deficient in the social skills needed to interact effectively with others (Lewinsohn, Mischel, Chaplin & Barton, 1980; Libet & Lewinsohn, 1973). While there are no systematic studies of social skills deficits in depressed children, there is evidence to suggest that poor interpersonal relationships are associated with a variety of childhood problems (Combs & Slaby, 1977; Gelfand, 1978). As noted earlier, depressed children are often withdrawn socially. Their social withdrawal in combination with their low self-esteem and sensitivity to rejection often result in low rates of assertive behavior. Further, depressed children may lack the social skills that are necessary for obtaining consistent contingent positive reinforcement from significant others in their social environment.

While much has been written about social skills training with children (for a review, see Combs & Slaby, 1977), there has been little attention paid to social skills training with depressed children. Similar to the treatment strategies used with depressed adults to change the quantity and quality of their interpersonal relationships, depressed children may need help in learning to become more assertive, to improve their interpersonal style, to be less withdrawn, and to increase their social activity level. Children who have difficulties being assertive as assessed by the BAT-C may benefit from assertion training in which they are first instructed about the concept of assertion. Then, a list of situations in which it is problematic for the child to be assertive should be devised. The therapist may employ verbal-cognitive approaches to teach relatively specific assertiveness skills and may model some assertive possibilities for the child. After that, the child should be encouraged to rehearse assertive behavior with the therapist. The therapist should give the child feedback on his/her performance and reinforce the child for increased assertive behavior. Finally, transfer to real life situations should be planned and monitored, and feedback should be given.

Another component to the treatment should be to encourage children to increase their involvement in social activities. Goals for increasing social involvement should be set, done by the child, monitored, and reinforced. Since many depressed children are socially withdrawn, those approaches useful for treating social withdrawal in children (Gelfand, 1978) may be employed.

Butler and Miezitis (1980) suggest a number of ways that teachers can help children with social skills problems. These include: (a) having the depressed child sit near and work with children who will be accepting, tolerant, and understanding of him/her, (b) respond to the child as soon as he/she makes an attempt to become involved in classroom activities, (c) model socially appropriate behavior for the child, and (d) respond to the child's nonverbal cues. They stress the importance of interacting with a depressed child, despite the child's attempts to reject others. Once a child feels reassured that someone is interested and accepting, the child will become more sociable.

Four studies have been reported that use social skills training with depressed children. Calpin & Kornblith (1977) worked with four inpatient boys with aggressive behavior and low-average intelligence and who met modified research diagnostic criteria for depression. These children were found to have social skills deficits on the BAT-C. All four children improved in making requests for new bahaviors, affect expression, and overall social skills. At follow-up, three of the four children had maintained their treatment gains. Calpin & Cincirpini (1978) did social skills training with two depressed inpatients who were found to have social skills deficits on the BAT-C. The training program consisted of instruction, modeling, and videotape feedback and focused on specific (e.g., eye contact) and general (e.g., positive peer interactions) social skills. Both children improved at the end of training. However, at follow-up, one child continued to evidence mood swings and oppositional behavior, and target behaviors had returned to their baseline levels. Matson, Esveldt-Dawson, Andrasik, Ollendik, Petti & Hersen (1980) worked with four inpatients who met research diagnostic criteria for depression. The training consisted of instruction, modeling, role playing, information feedback, and social reinforcement. The target behaviors that were trained sequentially included verbal behavior, psychomotor behavior, affect, and eye contact. Social skills training that was done in a group was found to be effective in three of the four children. The treatment gains were maintained at a 15-week follow-up. Using a multiple baseline design, Frame, Matson, Sonis, Fialkov & Kazdin (1982) used instruction, modeling, role play, and feedback to treat four target behavior (inappropriate body position, lack of eye contact, poor speech, and bland affect) in a depressed 10-year-old male. At the end of the treatment and at a 12-week follow-up, the target behaviors had decreased markedly. However, the child's level of depression was not reported at posttreatment.

Taken together, this work suggests that activity increase programs and social skills training may be effective components of treatment programs for depressed children.

Helplessness Strategies: Case Example

Yvette, a 12-year-old female was referred for a psychological evaluation by her pediatrician. She had recently been diagnosed as having juvenile onset diabetes and was feeling sad, helpless, and hopeless, was blaming herself for her physical problems, and was feeling like everything that went bad was her fault. She did not want to try to do anything at school or with her peers because she felt that nothing would turn out well for her.

Target Behaviors and Phenomenology

Yvette's feelings and thoughts appear to have been precipitated by a negative life event that was uncontrollable (Brown & Harris, 1978). She attributed the occurrence of this negative event to something bad about herself, and she expected that she has no control over future events (internal-stable-global attribution for a negative event). These beliefs have led to her having lowered self-esteem and to her feeling helpless, hopeless, and depressed (Abramson et al., 1978). Individuals, both children and adults, feel helpless when they believe that they have little control over the important outcomes in their lives, and they respond by refraining from making adaptive responses. They become passive and apathetic, and they appear to give up. Yvette appears to have made an internal-stable-global attribution to explain why she has diabetes, and this attribution appears to have resulted in her experiencing chronic and generalized symptoms of depression.

Assessment of Target Behaviors

Coddington Life Events Scale (Coddington, 1972).   This scale is designed to assess life events in the child's life. Similar to the Social Readjustment Scale for adults (Holmes & Rahe, 1967), the Coddington scales define stress in terms of events that require readjustment on the part of the child. There are two versions of the scale, one for children up to and including grade six and one for children in grades seven through nine. The parents are asked to indicate whether any of the events listed on the scale happened to their child in the preceding year.

Children's Stressful Life Events Scale (CSLES; Sandler & Block, 1979). The CSLES is designed to yield information about what changes have occurred in the child's life at any point in time and in the past six months and to determine whether or not the event was an undesirable experience for the child. The questionnaire is completed by an informant.

KASTAN-R—Children's Attributional Style Questionnaire (KASTAN-R or CASQ; Kaslow, Tanenbaum & Seligman, 1978).   Based on the reformulated model of helplessness, the KASTAN-R was designed to assess the internality, stability, and globality of the attributions that children make for positive and negative events in their lives. There is a parallel form of this questionnaire for parents to fill out about their child (Parent—KASTAN, Schultz, 1982).

Other relevant assessment measures for self-esteem and hopelessness are detailed elsewhere in the chapter.

Treatment of Target Behaviors

Attribution Retraining. Researchers who espouse the attributional reformulation of the helplessness model have proposed a number of strategies for intervening in a depressive episode (Beach, Abramson & Levine, 1981; Seligman, 1981). They include the following: (a) change the individual's expectations of having no control over important goals to expectations of having control of these goals, (b) modify an individual's unrealistic goals to make them more realistic, (c) decrease the importance of unattainable goals, (d) reduce the estimated likelihood of aversive outcomes and increase the estimated likelihood for desired outcomes, and (e) change an individual's unrealistic attributions to more realistic attributions.

Attribution retraining is the intervention strategy that has received the most attention, and thus, it will be focused on in more detail. It is important when doing attributional retraining with children that the therapist take the child's level of cognitive development into account. Preschoolers have less differentiated perceptions of what is internal versus what is external and do not engage in inferential reasoning. They often make incorrect conclusions about causality based on their level of cognitive development (Sedlak & Kurtz, 1981), and thus, these errors may not be a result of depressive thinking. It may be more difficult to train preschoolers to make different (nondepressive) attributions. By the elementary school years, children's reasoning and behavior patterns are more integrated and stylized. The internal-external differentiation implied in adult depressive thinking is present in these children (Selman & Jurcovic, 1978; Shantz, 1975). Their attributions influence their subsequent behavior and expectations (Dweck & Repucci, 1973; Rholes, Blackwell, Jordan & Walters, 1980) and their beliefs about themselves (Parsons & Ruble, 1977). Elementary school children, if depressed, are capable of exhibiting a "depressive attributional style." For these children, attributional retraining may prove to be useful.

It is interesting to note that different authors propose different goals for attributional retraining. Seligman (1981) proposes that depressed individuals should be retrained to attribute failure to more external, unstable, and specific factors and success to more internal-stable-global factors. Dweck (1975) thinks that individuals should be taught to make more internal-unstable attributions for failure. More specifically, Dweck worked with helpless children to see if they could learn to deal more effectively with failure in an experimental problem-solving situation. She taught them to take responsibility for their failures and to attribute them to lack of effort. When compared to children who had been in a success-only condition, those children who had been taught to handle failure were more persistent and more able to persevere in situations in which reinforcement was delayed.

Facilitating changes in attributional tendencies may be done by modeling more appropriate attributions (Dweck, 1975), by helping the child obtain insight about his/her attributional biases (Ross, Lepper & Hubbard, 1975), by applying the rules of logic to the facts in order to make a more accurate assignment of responsibility (Beck, Rush, Shaw & Emery, 1979), and by challenging inaccurate attributions (Beck et al., 1979; Rehm, 1981).

These techniques appear to be helpful in modifying particular attributions, but there are no explicit techniques for modifying depressive attributional styles, and the strategies used to date have not been successful (Ickes & Layden, 1978). It may be easier to change children's ways of thinking than to change adult's cognitive patterns because children's styles are less crystallized and are continually changing and developing. As Dweck points out, in designing an attributional retraining program for children, it is important to incorporate explicit generalization training to assure changes in other cognitive measures such as self-esteem. Until attribution retraining programs are conducted with depressed children, their efficacy and utility remains a question. However, the relevant work done to date suggests that attributional retraining may prove to be beneficial in the treatment of depressed children.

Cognitive Strategies: Case Example

Sandra, a 13-year-old female was referred for treatment by her school counselor. Her teachers were concerned that, despite the fact that she was performing adequately at school, she frequently made self-deprecatory comments. At the initial interview, Sandra acknowledged feeling sad. She stated that she did not like anything about herself—not her brains, her looks, or her personality. She felt as if things would never get better for her and that she was in a dark tunnel and there was no light at the end. When queried, she admitted to having thoughts about killing herself; however, she claimed that she would not do that because she did not have enough courage.

Target Behaviors and Phenomenology

Sandra's clinical picture highlights three cognitive symptoms observed in depressed children: low self-esteem, hopelessness, and morbid or suicidal thoughts. Children who are depressed often have a low opinion of themselves and do not like themselves. This is a negative subject for many children, and they are often reluctant to discuss it. They frequently try to hide the intensity of their feelings, but their self-descriptions indicate how negatively they view themselves. Children express feelings of hopelessness when they feel that their life is bad and that it will never get better. Frequently, they use a metaphor to describe this experience, such as there being "no light at the end of the tunnel" or "being in a dark room with no door to get out," rather than by explicitly stating that they feel hopeless. Despite many adult's denial that children feel suicidal or attempt to commit suicide, the fact is that many moderately and severely depressed children have suicidal ideations, plans, and actions. When working with depressed children, it is important to inquire about their suicidality, to take it seriously, and to intervene when it is necessary.

Assessment of Target Behaviors

Coopersmith Self-Esteem Inventory (CSEI; Coopersmith, 1967). This 58-item self-report scale assesses the child's self-concept and sense of personal worth. Self-esteem, as reflected in attitudes about oneself, one's parents, home, and school are evaluated.

Piers-Harris Children's Self-Concept Scale (Piers & Harris, 1969). This 80-item self-report scale assesses the child's behavior, intellectual and school status, physical appearance and attributes, anxiety, popularity, happiness, and satisfaction.

Hopelessness Scale (Kazdin, French, Unis, Esveldt-Dawson & Sherick, 1983c). This scale assesses how hopeless the child feels about his/her future. Derived from the Hopelessness Scale for adults (Beck, Weissman, Lester, & Trexler, 1974), Kazdin and his colleagues developed a 17-item, true-false scale that the child completes. Hopelessness, as assessed by this scale, was found to correlate more significantly with suicidality in children, than was depression (Kazdin et al., 1983c).

Means-End Problem Solving Test (MEPS; Shure & Spivak, 1972). The MEPS assesses the child's interpersonal problem-solving abilities. It is an instrument devised to measure children's ability to carefully plan, in sequential fashion, the step-by-step procedures (means) needed in order to achieve an intended goal.

The Preschool Interpersonal Problem Solving Test (PIPS; Shure & Spivak, 1978). The PIPS is a related instrument developed to measure a young child's ability to generate alternative solutions to interpersonal problems.

Treatment of Target Behaviors

Cognitive Therapy. Cognitive therapy, as a way of conceptualizing patients' problems and as a set of cognitive and behavioral intervention strategies, has been detailed by Beck and his colleagues (Beck et al., 1979). The techniques that are employed are designed to help the patient identify, reality test, and modify dysfunctional attitudes and distorted beliefs. The cognitive techniques utilized include the following: (*a*) recognizing the relationship between dysfunctional thoughts and their affect and behavior, (*b*) identifying and recording automatic thoughts, (c) evaluating the accuracy of the perceptions, logic, and conclusions of the automatic thoughts, (d) substituting a more reality-oriented interpretation for distorted cognitions and determining more appropriate responses, and (e) ascertaining, evaluating, and modifying the basic assumptions, rules, and formulas that predispose the patient to depression and that maintain the depression.

Behavioral techniques are often used in the initial stages of therapy, particularly for very depressed patients who need help in becoming mobilized to engage in activities. Behavioral techniques used by cognitive therapists emphasize the evaluation of the negative beliefs that can undermine the therapy, despite the patients' behavioral successes. The specific behavioral techniques utilized may include: activity scheduling, mastery and pleasure techniques, and graded task assignments.

Many therapists and clinical researchers question if children have the cognitive capacity necessary to benefit from cognitive therapy. Emery, Bedrosian & Garber (1983) assert that, while latency age children can understand the techniques of hypothesis testing, they often need help in acquiring new information, in identifying alternative explanations, in testing the hypotheses, and in changing their reality. Parents are useful in helping their child use scientific inquiry to test their beliefs and assumptions and to use the data obtained as evidence for changing their perceptions of reality. The child's intelligence and maturity level need to be taken into account when determining what treatment techniques would be appropriate. Simple procedures, such as direct self-instruction training, are appropriate for children age seven or below. Older children have a developing sense of self from which they can evaluate, have awareness of their internal states, and be better able to reason. Their cognitions can be changed with more Socratic and didactic methods. Elementary school age children have not necessarily developed critical thinking skills (e.g., may not understand the difference between facts and opinions), and thus, disputing and challenging their distorted cognitions may not be effective.

DiGiuseppe (1981) describes some basic principles for doing cognitive therapy with children. He claims that the first step is to provide them with a schema to incorporate a range of social and emotional reactions and to provide a vocabulary for these reactions. Depressed children are sensitive to affective and social cues from their environment, and they need to learn to identify different reactions and to produce a range of reactions. For example, it may be helpful to have a child role play a situation in which he/she feels 10 points worth of depression and a situation in which he/she feels 2 points worth of depression. This will help the child to discriminate between feeling states.

Based on the finding that the ability to generate alternative solutions to interpersonal difficulties is positively related to emotional and behavioral adjustment (Spivak & Shure, 1975), another component of cognitive therapy with children is emotional education and social skills training to teach them problem solving. Interpersonal problem-solving therapy, a cognitive-behavioral treatment program for children, has received a great deal of attention (Spivak, Platt & Shure, 1976). Interpersonal problem-solving therapy is designed to teach the following social problem-solving skills: (a) awareness of the problem, or potential problems, when people interact, (b) generation of numerous alternative solutions to interpersonal problems, (c) means-ends thinking—sequential planning of the step-by-step process necessary to reach a desired goal, (d) consequential thinking—ability to see the consequences for oneself and others that occur as a result of emitting a particular behavior or sequence of behaviors, and (e) cause-effect thinking—understanding that social interaction may be a reciprocal interactive process affected by the feelings or actions of the participants involved.

Beck describes a number of mechanisms of cognitive distortion, such as selective abstraction, arbitrary inference, magnification and minimization. It is assumed that these distoring schemata are acquired early in life. Thus, it is not surprising that depressed children evidence similar cognitive distortions. The cognitive therapist needs to encourage children to empirically test hypotheses about various beliefs, and with some children, the therapist may have to begin by teaching the child the importance of this way of thinking. The child's set of beliefs can be tested by setting up a simple experiment. For example, if a child believes that peers do not like to play with him/her, then the child can try an experiment to see how children respond after the child asks them to play. The results of the experiment will support, question, or discredit the child's perceptions. The therapist also needs to help the child assess the validity of events that occur and the accuracy of his/her self-statements about the events. For example, a depressed child may become upset when a peer says that he/she is stupid or ugly, because the child will then identify him/herself as stupid or ugly. It is important for the child to realize that a peer's statement does not necessarily represent reality, and it may not be the truth.

As DiGiuseppe (1981) points out, sometimes children are faced with negative life situations that are unchangeable. At such times, empirically disputing techniques or problem-solving strategies may not be particularly helpful. Rather, the child can be most helped if he/she learns to perceive the reality of the situation accurately and to develop strategies to cope as effectively as possible with the stress.

To date, there have been no studies that assess the efficacy of cognitive therapy with depressed children. However, there are some projects that are relevant to this discussion. Butler and Miezitis (1980) have a handbook for elementary school teachers and consultants on how to deal with depressed children in the classroom. They provide descriptions of depressive behavior, detailed recommendations, and case study problems. Their program focuses on using cognitive techniques to help children who manifest such depressive behaviors as low self-esteem, self-deprecating remarks, helpless/hopeless behavior, sadness, tearfulness, withdrawn and uncommunicative behavior, aloofness, and standoffishness. Butler, Miezitis, Friedman, and Cole (1980) reported a study on the effect of two school-based intervention programs on depressive symptoms in children in grades five and six. The Role Play Treatment focused on helping depressed children deal with problems that many of them face (e.g., peer relationships, success and failure, rejection and loneliness, guilt and self-blame). The goals of the treatment were (*a*) to make the children aware of their own thoughts and feelings and those of others, (*b*) to teach the children skills that would help them to be more effective in interpersonal situations, and (*c*) to teach them a problem-solving approach to deal with stressful situations. The Cognitive Restructuring Group had the following aims: (*a*) to teach the children to identify negative automatic thoughts and cognitive distortions and to replace them with more rational and logical alternatives, (*b*) to help them to improve their listening skills, and (*c*) to teach them to recognize the relationship between cognition and affect. Children in the two treatment groups did better than those children in the attention placebo and in the control group, with the children in the Role Play Group showing the most improvement in terms of their depressive symptomatology. Recently, Ginsburg, and Twentyman (1983) reported on a project for prevention of depression in children. They described a 10-session group therapy format program that would cover the following topics: (*a*) the identification and expression of feelings, (*b*) the improvement of self-esteem, (*c*) children's increased involvement in pleasurable activities, and (*d*) training in problem-solving skills with a particular emphasis on taking risks in social situations. This program incorporates many of the major cognitive-behavioral treatment strategies discussed so far, and if it proves successful, it may be a model for a broad-based treatment approach. (For a more detailed discussion of cognitive therapy for depressed children, see Emery et al., 1983.)

Self-Control Strategies: Case Example

Don, an 11-year old, was brought to the clinic by his mother who was concerned about his continued sad mood, which appeared to be in response to marital tension. Although Don was typically an above-average student, he was not doing well at school. He did not like doing anything anymore, and he spent his free time at home watching TV or napping. He frequently complained of stomachaches, which had no known organic etiology. At the interview, Don said very little, he appeared hypoactive, and he complained of feeling tired all of the time. He denied feeling sad. He did say that nothing good ever happened in his life, and he felt that he never got praised for anything he did. He stated the reason for staying at home was that he used to want to be a football player, but since he did not make his junior high school team, he had given up.

Target Behaviors and Phenomenology

Some of the depressive behaviors exhibited by Don have been detailed above. Thus, this section will concentrate on those behaviors that have not previously been discussed. First, the reader may note that, although Don's mother stated that he was sad, Don denied feeling sad. It is often the case that children are not able to recognize, label, and report their depressed moods. It should be noted that this is usually more of a problem for younger children. Second, depressed children show a pattern at school similar to that described by Don's mother. Unlike a learning disabled child, depressed children typically performed adequately at school prior to the onset of the depression. Depressed children show variability in their school performance depending on their mood. Lack of interest and difficulty concentrating are two factors that contribute to their poor school performance (Poznanski, 1982). Third, complaints of excessive fatigue are common among depressed children (Poznanski, 1982), and this symptom is more commonly reported by children than by their parents. Fourth, a symptom somewhat related to fatigue is that of psychomotor retardation. Like other moderately depressed children, Don spoke very little and in a monotone voice, and he only spoke in response to questions. His body posture was characteristic of that of a depressive, as he sat slumped down in the chair, with his eyes downcast; he rarely smiled, and he was not very active physically. Fifth, Don complained of stomachaches. Depressed children often have somatic complaints such as stomachaches, headaches, or nonspecific somatic complaints. These children are often seen by pediatricians, and the diagnosis of depression may not be made. It should be noted that not all children with somatic complaints are depressed; however, children who present somatic complaints should be asked about any psychological problems they may be having. Sixth, there were complaints of two self-control deficits typically seen in depressed adults. Don had set a high, not well defined, and possibly unattainable and unrealistic goal for himself (to be a great football player). Instead of setting up subgoals to reach that goal or making a more realistic goal for himself, he gave up as soon as he met an obstacle. Also, Don reported a situation in which he received little positive reinforcement from his environment, and he did not appear to reinforce himself for his own positive behaviors.

Assessment of Target Behaviors

Children's Perceived Self-Control Scale—"Usually That's Me" (CPSCS-UTM; Humphrey, 1982).   The CPSCS is an 11-item scale that assesses children's views of their self-control behavior. Personal self-control, interpersonal self-control, self-evaluation, and consequential thinking are assessed. The scale was designed to reflect the Kanfer-Karoly model of self-control.

Teacher's Self-Control Rating Scale (TSCRS; Humphrey, 1982).   The TSCRS is a 15-item scale that asks teachers questions about a child's self-control behavior. The cognitive-behavioral view of self-control, as delineated by Kanfer & Karoly (1972), provided the framework for the scale. Children's problem recognition, self-regulation, and habit reorganization were assessed.

Both a behavioral/interpersonal and a cognitive/personal self-control factor emerged.

Self-Control Rating Scale (SCRS; Kendall & Wilcox, 1979). The SCRS is a 33-item scale that either teachers or parents complete. The scale is designed to measure both the cognitive (deliberation, problem solving, planning, and evaluation) and behavioral (execution of appropriate behaviors; inhibition of inappropriate behaviors) components of self control.

Self-Control Strategies

Self-control therapy for the treatment of depression (Rehm, 1981) is an outgrowth of the self-control model of depression (Rehm, 1977). The therapy program incorporates aspects of the models of Abramson et al. (1978), Beck et al. (1979), Lewinsohn (1974), and Seligman (1975). The therapy program attempts to remedy the self-monitoring, self-evaluation, self-attribution, and self-reinforcement deficits characteristic of depressed individuals.

The program is didactic in nature, and the sessions are spent with the therapist presenting a rationale for each module of the program and discussing the relevance of the concepts to the difficulties in the participants' lives. Homework assignments are given to help the participants apply the concepts to their daily lives. To date, the therapy program is typically conducted in a group format, however, it can be adapted for use with individuals.

Rehm and his colleagues have written therapy manuals as part of the psychotherapy outcome research, which they have conducted. The following section briefly describes the basic therapy techniques that were utilized in the combined cognitive and behavioral target program of the most recent outcome study.

In the first session, participants are taught that mood in general is related to one's behavior and to their accompanying self-statements. It is also pointed out that depressed individuals frequently do not identify or attend to the positive events (cognitions and activities) that occur in their lives. They typically attend only to the negative events. The homework assignment is to monitor both daily positive and negative events and make a daily mood rating. In the second session, participants graph their mood and events for each day, and the relationship between the two is pointed out. They are instructed to identify those behaviors that seem most related to their mood. For their homework assignment, in addition to self-monitoring mood and behavior, participants are encouraged to increase the positive events in their lives. The focus of the third session is to help the participants discriminate between the immediate and long-term effects of their behavior. Homework for the week includes continued self-monitoring with the additional task of listing a positive delayed effect of at least one positive behavior per day. This will help them attend more to the delayed positive consequences of their daily behavior. The fourth session focuses on attributional retraining. The participants are helped to make more realistic self-statements about both their successes and their failures. The week's homework assignment is to continue to monitor positive events and mood. Additionally, each day they are asked to include at least one positive self-statement about a success and one positive self-statement about a failure. The focus of the fifth and sixth sessions is to teach the participants realistic self-evaluation and goal setting. They are encouraged to set up subgoals as small, individual steps towards reaching their goals—realistic subgoals and goals that are operationally defined, positive, attainable, and in their control. The week's homework is to continue monitoring and to work on goals that they have set for themselves. The seventh and eighth sessions emphasize the importance of overt and covert self-reinforcement. The participants are encouraged to set up a reward menu, which includes rewards that are enjoyable, can be freely administered, and that range from small to large. Rewards can be activities, things, or positive self-statements. The homework is to continue self-monitoring and to reward themselves contingently when they successfully complete a subgoal. The last two sessions are review.

Self-control interventions have been a crucial component of cognitive-behavior therapy. Although much of the early work in this area was done with adults, applications with children began in the mid-70s and has received much attention (Craighead, Wilcoxin-Craighead & Meyers, 1978; Karoly, 1977; Little & Kendall, 1979; Meichenbaum, 1977; Meichenbaum & Asarnow, 1979; Pressley, 1979).

Self-control, the individual's governing of his/her behavior to attain certain ends, requires the behavioral capacity to inhibit inappropriate behaviors and engage in appropriate options (executive function) and in the cognitive skills necessary to generate and evaluate alternative strategies (legislative function) (Little & Kendall, 1977). The process of verbal control of behavior follows the standard developmental sequence: (a) infants have minimal control over themselves, and the verbal instructions of adults has little effect on an infant's motor behavior, (b) toddlers (one to two years old) exhibit orienting and investigatory responses in response to adult's verbal instructions, (c) young preschoolers (three to four years old) can follow instructions given by adults to both initiate new behavior and inhibit their present behavior, and they begin to regulate their own behavior, and (d) older preschoolers (4½ to 5½ years old) respond to their own verbal cues and first learn to initiate responses and then to inhibit them. Thus, by elementary school, children can be taught self-control techniques. Before children can be trained to control or change their behavior, it is necessary to teach them to monitor their own behavior and cognitions and to do so in an accurate manner. There are case reports and studies that demonstrate that children can be taught to self-monitor and that the procedures used also result in significant changes in the target behaviors (e.g., Broden, Hall & Mitts, 1971; Gottman & McFall, 1972; Sagotsky, Patterson & Lepper, 1978). In therapy, it is useful to have children fill out weekly self-monitoring logs in which they record their mood, ongoing activities, and thoughts. Parents may also keep a log of the child's weekly activities in order to assess the accuracy of the child's report. Teaching components of the self-evaluation phase to children has been effective in some studies (Barling, 1980; Spates & Kanfer, 1977), but not all (Sagotsky et al., 1978). Barling (1980) taught young children to self-evaluate appropriately. Spates and Kanfer (1977) report that they were able to teach young children to set goals effectively. However, Sagotsky and colleagues (1978) report that exposure to goal-setting procedures had no effect on academic achievement or study behavior, nor did it enhance the effectiveness of the self-monitoring system. There is little work done on children being taught to reinforce their own behavior. Bolstad and Johnson (1972) found that self-reinforcement is effective with children. However, it is often useful to use external reinforcement for children (Drabman & Lahey, 1974). Once again, it is important that the child be involved in identifying potential rewards. Since depressed children often feel that nothing is rewarding, it is useful to ask them what was rewarding to them when they felt good.

In a complete self-management program, children need to monitor their behavior, accurately evaluate their performance, determine which of their behaviors should be changed, set the goal and direction of such a change, monitor their responses, evaluate the progress made, and then provide the reinforcers for such progress.

While there are no studies that demonstrate how to train depressed children in these skills, children with a variety of problems, including aggressiveness (Camp, Bloom, Herbert & Doornick, 1977), disruptiveness (Kendall & Wilcox, 1980), and hyperactivity (Douglas, Parry, Marton & Garson, 1976), have shown improvements. However, the gains the children make during treatment are often not maintained, and frequently they do not generalize (Goldstein & Kanfer, 1979; Kazdin, 1975).

The major intervention strategy that is popular in the child clinical behavior therapy literature, which falls under the rubric of self-control or self-management techniques, is called *self-instruction training* (Meichenbaum, 1977; Meichenbaum & Goodman, 1971). Self-instruction training has been successful in treating children who are impulsive, aggressive, hyperactive, delinquent, phobic, socially withdrawn, and learning disabled and poor performers in school (for reviews, see Craighead et al., 1978).

According to Meichenbaum (1977), self-instructional training entails teaching individuals to produce internally generated self-statements and to talk to themselves in a self-guiding fashion. The self-instructional training program devised by Meichenbaum and Goodman (1971) was composed of combinations of modeling, overt and covert rehearsal, prompts, feedback, and social reinforcement. The "Think Aloud" programs are designed to teach the following performance-relevant skills: (*a*) problem definition, (*b*) focusing attention and response guidance, (*c*) self-reinforcement involving standard setting and self-evaluation, and (*d*) coping skills and error correcting options. These strategies are similar to the self-monitoring, self-evaluation, and self-reinforcement described previously. (For more details about the strengths and weaknesses of self-instruction training with children, see Cole & Kazdin, 1980; Meichenbaum & Asarnow, 1979.)

Although self-control therapy has not been used specifically to treat depressed children, its efficacy with depressed adolescents (Coats & Reynolds, 1983), with depressed adults (Rehm, 1981), and with children with other behavior problems (Craighead et al., 1978) and the fact that depressed children do have deficits in self-control (Cole & Kaslow, in press) suggest that self-control training may be effective in treating and preventing depression and other problems in children.

CLINICAL CONSIDERATIONS

The therapy strategies reviewed above are suggestive in that very little empirical evidence or even clinical therapy description is currently available to draw upon. Given the breadth of pathological behavior spanned by the concept of childhood depression and its association with other developmental symptoms and disorders, an important clinical consideration would be the problem of sorting out and giving priority to various problematic behaviors that might become targets for intervention. Several recommendations and suggestions can be made. First, depression in children, as in adults, may be secondary to other psychological disorders, from conduct disorder to anorexia nervosa to learning disorders. In such cases, strategies for dealing with depression might be considered as adjunctive therapy, but the first priority in treatment should go toward treating the primary disorder. In our opinion, this would extend to problems that have often been considered as closely associated with depression or even symptoms of so-called masked depression, i.e., enuresis, hyperactivity, school phobia, impulsivity, or aggression.

Once these problems have been dealt with or if depression is the central or sole presenting problem, the next issue would be to make decisions among the various depression therapy strategies. As our examples illustrate, cases sometimes present with suggestive evidence for the prominence of specific deficits. In many (probably most) cases, multiple types of deficits may be suggested (Kaslow & Rehm, 1983), and the deficits identified by the various theories can be logically ordered in sequence of treatment priority. If associated disorders have been dealt with or ruled out, we recommend first evaluating for social skills deficits. Without basic interpersonal skills appropriate to the child's developmental level, other types of intervention are unlikely to significantly reduce depression. Second, we would recommend evaluating activity level toward consideration of a behavioral approach to this problem. Following evaluation of these overt behavioral deficits, we would begin evaluation of cognitive problems with consideration of possible distortions in self-monitoring or self-observation. The inferential distortions may be treated with strategies from the cognitive or self-control models. Next, self-esteem deficits should be evaluated and a variety of cognitive strategies considered. Depressive attributional style would be logically evaluated next and helplessness model interventions considered. Finally, self-reinforcement patterns should be evaluated and these skills taught. Much of this sequence is incorporated into some of the more complex package therapy programs reviewed, such as the Spivak and Shure problem-solving program, Meichenbaum's self-instructional training, or the Rehm self-control therapy program as applied with adults.

Winnett and Bornstein (1983) have suggested an alternative approach to treatment strategy selections in dealing with childhood depression. They suggest a levels-of-treatment approach based on treatment complexity and the developmental capacities of the child. Level I includes contingency management, activity increase and skill training; Level II involves changing self-statements and attributions; Level III encompasses social skill and problem-solving strategies; and Level IV is comprised of self-control procedures.

Clinical consideration may change somewhat with the context of service delivery. In the context of school problems, the teacher may need to become involved as a primary change agent. Butler and Miezitis (1980) have suggested a number of simple and practical interventions for classroom use. Family conflict is a frequent context for childhood depression, and the involvement of parents may be important in various formats. Parents may be included as contingency managers, and they may become involved in more extensive parent training (Gordon, 1970) or family therapy (Gurman & Kniskern, 1981). Parents can be particularly helpful in facilitating their child's use of various cognitive and behavioral strategies. Severely disturbed, treatment resistant, or actively suicidal children may also benefit from antidepressant medication (Puig-Antich & Gittleman, 1982; Petti, 1983a). Inpatient treatment may provide the opportunity for comprehensive treatment programs (multi-model approach), including environmental contingency management, cognitive-behavioral training, family therapy, and antidepressant medication. A program along similar lines has been described by Petti, Bornstein, Delamater & Conners (1980).

CONCLUSIONS

Childhood depression is a new field in several senses. There continues to exist some controversy over its existence as a clinical entity. New theories and models are coming to be applied to considerations of this disorder in childhood. There is a need for greater consideration of developmental factors and familial influences in these models.

Empirical data on childhood depression is only beginning to accumulate. We need good information on the epidemiology, course, and consequences of depression in children. Additionally, better documentation of the syndromal behavior patterns associated with depression versus other disorders of childhood is necessary.

Methods of objectively assessing depression in children are relatively new. Both research and clinical practice would be enhanced by better standardized and psychometrically more sophisticated means of assessment. Problems of method and informant variance need to be addressed systematically. Advances in understanding this form of psychopathology in children may necessarily precede advances in assessment, although the two areas are interdependent.

Reports of treatment are only recently appearing in journals. We can expect a rapid increase in this trend in the new few years. The adaptations of successful adult and child cognitive-behavioral approaches to depressed children are the likely directions this field will follow.

The burgeoning interest in childhood depression may prove to be fadish, but preliminary reports suggest that useful developments in childhood psychotherapy, assessment, and interventions may result. We hope this chapter may contribute toward that end.

REFERENCES

Abramson, L. Y., & Sacheim, H. A. A paradox in depression: Uncontrollability and self-blame. *Psychological Bulletin*, 1983, *84*, 838–851.

Abramson, L. Y., Seligman, M. E. P., & Teasdale, J. Learned helplessness in humans: Critique and reformulation. *Journal of Abnormal Psychology*, 1978, *87*, 49–74.

Achenbach, T. M. The Child Behavior Profile: I. Boys aged 6–11. *Journal of Consulting and Clinical Psychology*, 1978, *46*, 478–488.

Achenbach, T. M., & Edelbrock, C. S. The classification of child psychopathology: A review and analysis of empirical efforts. *Psychological Bulletin*, 1978, *85*, 1275–1301.

Agras, S. The relationship of school phobia to childhood depression. *American Journal of Psychiatry*, 1959, *116*, 533–536.

Albert, N., & Beck, A. T. Incidence of depression in early adolescence: A preliminary study. *Journal of Youth and Adolescence*, 1975, *4*, 301–307.

American Psychiatric Association. *Diagnostic and statistical manual of mental disorders* (2nd ed.). Washington, D.C.: American Psychiatric Association, 1968.

American Psychiatric Association. *Diagnostic and statistical manual of mental disorders* (3rd ed.). Washington, D.C.: American Psychiatric Association, 1980.

Anthony, E. J. Childhood depression. In E. J. Anthony & T. Benedek (Eds.), *Depression and human existence*. Boston: Little, Brown, 1975.

Arajarvi, T., & Huttunen, M. Encopresis and enuresis as symptoms of depression. In A. L. Annell (Ed.), *Depressive states in childhood and adolescence*. Stockholm, Sweden: Almqvist & Wiksell, 1972.

Bakwin, H. Depression—A mood disorder in children and adolescence. *Maryland State Medical Journal*, 1972, June 1972, pp. 55–61.

Bandura, A. *Principles of behavior modification*. New York: Holt, Rinehart & Winston, 1969.

Bandura, A., & Walters, R. *Social learning and personality development*. New York: Holt, Rinehart & Winston, 1963.

Barling, J. Performance standards and reinforcements effects on children's academic performance: A test of social learning theory. *Cognitive Therapy and Research*, 1980, *4*, 409–418.

Beach, S. R. H., Abramson, L. Y., & Levine, F. M. Attributional reformulation of learned helplessness and depression. In J. F. Clarkin & H. I. Glazer (Eds.), *Depression: Behavioral and directive intervention strategies*. New York: Garland STPM Press, 1981.

Beck, A. T. *Depression: Clinical, experimental and theoretical aspects*. New York: Hoeber, 1967. (Republished as Beck, A. T. *Depression: Causes and treatment*. Philadelphia: University of Pennsylvania Press, 1972).

Beck, A. T. *Cognitive therapy and emotional disorders*. New York: International Universities Press, 1976.

Beck, A. T., & Rush, A. J. Cognitive approaches to depression and suicide. In G. Servan (Ed.), *Cognitive deficits in development of mental illness*. New York: Brunner/Mazel, 1977.

Beck, A. T., Rush, A. G., Shaw, B. F., & Emery, G. *Cognitive therapy of depression*. New York: Guilford Press, 1979.

Beck, A. T., Weissman, A., Lester, D., & Trexler, L. The measurement of pessimism: The hopelessness scale. *Journal of Consulting and Clinical Psychology*, 1974, *42*, 861–865.

Bemporad, J. Manifest symptomatology of depression in children and adolescents. In S. Arieti & J. Bemporad (Eds.), *Severe and mild depression: The psychotherapeutic approach*. New York: Basic Books, 1978(a).

Bemporad, J. Psychodynamics of depression and suicide in children and adolescents. In S. Arieti & J. Bemporad (Eds.), *Severe and mild depression: The psychotherapeutic approach*. New York: Basic Books, 1978(b).

Bemporad, J. Psychotherapy of depression in children and adolescents. In S. Arieti & J. Bemporad (Eds.), *Severe and mild depression: A psychotherapeutic approach*. New York: Basic Books, 1978(c).

Beres, D. Superego and depression. In R. M. Lowenstein, L. M. Newman, M. Scherr, & A. J. Solnit (Eds.), *Psychoanalysis—a general psychology*. New York: International Universities Press, 1966.

Bibring, E. The mechanism of depression. In P. Greenacre (Ed.), *Affective disorders*. New York: International Universities Press, 1953.

Birleson, P. The validity of depressive disorder in childhood and the development of a self-rating scale: A research report. *Journal of Child Psychology and Psychiatry*, 1981, *22*, 73–88.

Blaney, P. Contemporary theories of depression: Critique and Comparison. *Journal of Abnormal Psychology*, 1977, *86*, 203–223.

Bleuler, E. *Textbook of psychiatry*. New York: Macmillan.

Bolstad, O. D., & Johnson, S. M. Self-regulation in the modification of disruptive classroom behavior. *Journal of Applied Behavior Analysis*, 1974, *5*, 443–454.

Bornstein, M. R., Bellack, A. S., & Hersen, M. Social skills training for unassertive children: A multiple baseline analysis. *Journal of Applied Behavior Analysis*, 1977, *10*, 183–195.

Boverman, H. & French, A. P. Treatment of the depressed child. In A. French & I. Berlin (Eds.), *Depression in children and adolescents*. New York: Human Sciences Press, 1979.

Bowlby, J. *Attachment and loss: Vol. 1*. New York: Basic Books, 1969.

Bowlby, J. *Attachment and loss: Vol. 2. Separation: Anxiety and anger.* New York: Basic Books, 1978.

Bowlby, J. *Attachment and loss: Vol. 3. Loss: Sadness and depression.* New York: Basic Books, 1980.

Broden, M., Hall, R. V., & Mitts, B. The effect of self-recording on the classroom behavior of two eighth-grade students. *Journal of Applied Behavior Analysis*, 1971, *4*, 191–199.

Bronfenbrenner, U. *The ecology of human development: Experiments by nature and design*. Cambridge, Mass.: Harvard University Press, 1979.

Brown, G. W., & Harris, T. Social origins of depression: *A study of psychiatric disorder in women*. New York: Free Press, 1978.

Brumback, R. A., Letters to the editor: Depressive disorder in childhood. *American Journal of Psychiatry*, 1976, *133*, 455.

Brumback, R. A., Dietz-Schmidt, S. G., & Weinberg, W. A. Depression in children referred to an educational diagnostic center: Diagnosis and treatment and analysis of criteria and literature review. *Diseases of the Nervous System*, 1973, *38*, 529–535.

Brumback, R. A., & Weinberg, W. A. Relationship of hyperactivity and depression in children. *Perceptual and Motor Skills*, 1977, *45*, 247–251.

Brumback, R. A. & Staton, R. D. Learning disability and childhood depression. *American Journal of Orthopsychiatry*, 1983, *53*, 269–281.

Burks, H. L., & Harrison, S. I. Aggressive behavior as a means of avoiding depression. *American Journal of Orthopsychiatry*, 1953, *32*, 416–422.

Butler, L. F., & Miezitis, S. *Releasing children from depression: A handbook for elementary teachers and consultants*. Ontario: OISE Press, 1980.

Butler, L., Miezitis, S., Friedman, R. & Cole, E. The effect of two school-based intervention programs on depressive symptoms in preadolescents. *American Educational Research Journal*, 1980, *17*, 111–119.

Calpin, J. P., & Cincirpini, P. M. *A multiple baseline analysis of social skills training in children*. Paper presented at Midwestern Association for Behavior Analysis, Chicago, May 1978.

Calpin, J. P., & Kornblith, S. J. *Training of aggressive children in conflict resolution skills*. Paper presented at the meeting of the Association for the Advancement of Behavior Therapy, Chicago, 1977.

Camp, B. W., Bloom, G. E., Herbert, F., & Van Doorninck, W. M. "Think aloud": A program for developing self-control in young aggressive boys. *Journal of Abnormal Child Psychology*, 1977, *5*, 157–169.

Carlson, G. A. Bipolar affective disorder in childhood and adolescence. In D. P. Cantwell & G. A. Carlson (Eds.), *Affective disorders in childhood and adolescence: An update*. New York: Spectrum, 1983.

Carlson, G. A., & Cantwell, D. P. A survey of depressive symptoms in a child and adolescent psychiatric population. *American Academy of Child Psychiatry*, 1979, *18*, 587–599.

Carlson, G. A., & Cantwell, D. P. Unmasking masked depression in children and adolescents. *American Journal of Psychiatry*, 1980, *137*, 445, 449.

Carlson, G. A., & Cantwell, D. P. Diagnosis of childhood depression: A comparison of the Weinberg and DSM-III criteria. *Journal of the American Academy of Child Psychiatry*, 1982(a), *21*, 247–250.

Carlson, G. A., & Cantwell, D. P. Suicidal behavior and depression in children and adolescents. *Journal of the American Academy of Child Psychiatry*, 1982(b), *21*, 361–368.

Carlson, G. A., & Strober, M. Affective disorders in adolescence. In D. P. Cantwell & G. A. Carlson (Eds.), *Affective disorders in childhood and adolescence*. New York: Spectrum, 1983.

Cautela, J. R. Children's Reinforcement Survey Schedule (CRSS). In J. R. Cautela (Ed.), *Behavior analysis forms for clinical intervention*. Champaign, Ill.: Research Press, 1977.

Cautela, J. R., & Kastenbaum, R. A reinforcement survey for use in therapy, training, and research. *Psychological Reports*, 1967, *20*, 1115–1130.

Chambers, W. J., Puig-Antich, J., Tabrizi, M. A., & Davies, M. Psychotic symptoms in prepubertal major depressive disorder. *Archives of General Psychiatry*, 1982, *39*, 921–927.

Chiles, J. A., Miller, M. L., & Cox, G. B. Depression in an adolescent delinquent population. *Archives of General Psychiatry*, 1980, *37*, 1179–1184.

Clement, P. W., & Richard, R. C. *Children's Reinforcement Survey*. Unpublished manuscript, Fuller Theological Seminary, Calif., 1970.

Coats, K. I., & Reynolds, W. M. *A comparison of cognitive-behavioral and relaxation therapies for depression with adolescents*. Manuscript submitted for publication, 1983.

Coddington, R. D. The significance of life events as etiologic factors in the diseases of children—II. A study of a normal population. *Journal of Psychosomatic Research*, 1972, *16*, 205–213.

Cohler, B. J., Grunebaum, H. V., Weiss, J. L., Hartman, C. R., & Gallant, D. Child care attitudes and adaptation to the maternal role among mentally ill and well mothers. *American Journal of Orthopsychiatry*, 1976, *46*, 123–134.

Cole, P. M., & Kaslow, N. J. Interactional and cognitive strategies for affect regulation: A developmental perspective on childhood depression. In L. B. Alloy (Ed.), *Cognitive processes in depression*. New York: Guilford Press, in press.

Cole, P. M., & Kazdin, A. E. Critical issues in self-instruction training with children. *Child Behavior Therapy*, 1980, *2*, 1–21.

Combs, M. S., & Slaby, O. A. Social skills training with children. In B. B. Lahey & A. E. Kazdin (Eds.), *Advances in clinical child psychology*. New York: Plenum Press, 1977.

Connell, H. M. Depression in childhood. *Child Psychiatry and Human Development*, 1972, *4*, 71–85.

Conners, C. K., Himmelhock, J., Goyette, G. H., Ulrich, R., & Neil, J. F. Children of parents with affective illness. *Journal of the American Academy of Child Psychiatry*, 1979, *18*, 600–607.

Coopersmith, S. *The antecedents of self-esteem*. San Francisco: W. H. Freeman, 1967.

Costello, C. G. Childhood depression: Three basic but questionable assumptions in the Lefkowitz and Burton critique. *Psychological Bulletin*, 1980, *87*, 185–190.

Costello, C. G. Childhood depression. In J. E. Mash & L. G. Terdal (Eds.), *Behavioral assessment of childhood disorders*. New York: Guilford Press, 1981.

Coyne, J. C. Toward an interactional description of depression. *Psychiatry*, 1976, *39*, 28–40.

Craighead, E., Shmucker, M., & Duchnowski, A. Childhood depression and attributional style. Paper presented in L. P. Rehm (Chair), *Empirical studies of childhood depression*. Symposium conducted at the annual meeting of the American Psychological Association, Los Angeles, August 1980.

Craighead, W. E., Wilcoxin-Craighead, L., & Meyers, A. W. New directions in behavior modification with children. In M. Hersen, R. M. Eisler, & P. M. Miller (Eds.), *Progress in behavior modification* (Vol. 6). New York: Academic Press, 1978.

Crook, T., Raskin, A., & Eliot, J. Parent-child relationships and adult depression. *Child development*, 1981, *52*, 950–951.

Cytryn, L., & McKnew, D. H. Proposed classification of childhood depression. *American Journal of Psychiatry*, 1972, *129*, 149–155.

Cytryn, L., McKnew, D. H., & Bunney, W. E. Diagnosis of depression in children: a reassessment. *American Journal of Psychiatry*, 1980, *137*, 22–25.

Daley, M. F. The "Reinforcement Menu": Finding effective reinforcements. In E. J.

Mash & L. G. Terdal (Eds.), *Behavior therapy assessment: Diagnosis design, and evaluation* (Vol. 2). New York: Springer, 1976.

Davidson, J. Infantile depression in a "normal" child. *Journal of the American Academy of Child Psychiatry,* 1968, *1,* 522–535.

Deykin, E. Y., Jacobson, S., Klerman, G., & Solomon, M. The empty nest: Psychosocial aspects of conflict between depressed women and their grown children. *American Journal of Psychiatry,* 1966, *22,* 1422–1426.

Diagnostic Interview Schedule for Children (DISC). Washington, D.C.: National Institutes of Mental Health, Unpublished manuscript.

Diener, C. I., & Dweck, C. S. An analysis of learned helplessness: Continuous changes in performance, strategy, & achievement cognitions following failure. *Journal of Personality and Social Psychology,* 1978, *36,* 451–462.

Diener, C. I., & Dweck, C. S. *An analysis of learned helplessness: (II) The processing of success.* Unpublished manuscript, University of Illinois, 1979.

DiGiuseppe, R. A. Cognitive therapy with children. In G. Emery, S. Hollon, & R. C. Bedrosian (Eds.), *New directions in cognitive therapy.* New York: Guilford Press, 1981.

Douglas, V. I., Parry, P., Marton, P., & Garson, C. Assessment of a cognitive training program for hyperactive children. *Journal of Abnormal Child Psychology,* 1976, *4,* 389–410.

Drabman, R. S., & Lahey, B. B. Feedback in classroom behavior modification: Effects on the target and her classmates. *Journal of Applied Behavior Analysis,* 1974, *7,* 591–598.

Dweck, C. S. The role of expectations and attributions in the alleviation of learned helplessness. *Journal of Personality and Social Psychology,* 1975, *31,* 674–685.

Dweck, C. S. Children's interpretation of evaluative feedback: The effect of social cues on learned helplessness. In C. S. Dweck, K. T. Hill, W. H. Reed, W. M. Steihman & R. D. Parke (Eds.), The impact of social cues on children's behavior. *Merrill-Palmer Quarterly,* 1976, *22,* 82–123.

Dweck, C. S., & Bush, E. S. Sex differences in learned helplessness: Differential debilitation with peer and adult evaluators. *Developmental Psychology,* 1976, *12,* 147–156.

Dweck, C. S., Davidson, W., Nelson, S., & Enna, B. Sex differences in learned helplessness: II. The contingencies of evaluative feedback in the classroom and III. An experimental analysis. *Developmental Psychology,* 1978, *14,* 268–276.

Dweck, C. S., Goetz, T. E., & Strauss, N. *Sex differences in learned helplessness: (IV) An experimental and naturalistic study of failure generalization and its mediators.* Unpublished manuscript, University of Illinois, 1978.

Dweck, C. S., & Repucci, N. D. Learned helplessness and reinforcement responsibility in children. *Journal of Personality and Social Psychology,* 1973, *25,* 109–116.

Easson, W. H. Depression in adolescence. In S. C. Feinstein & P. L. Giovacchini (Eds.), *Adolescent Psychiatry* (Vol. 5). New York: Jason Aronson, Inc., 1977.

Edelbrock, C., & Achenbach, T. M. A typology of child behavior profiles: Distribution and correlates for disturbed children aged 6–16 years. *Journal of Abnormal Child Psychology,* 1980, *8,* 441–470.

Elkins, R., & Rapoport, J. L. Psychopharmacology of adult and childhood depression: An overview. In D. P. Cantwell & G. A. Carlson (Eds.), *Affective disorders in childhood and adolescence: An update.* New York: Spectrum, 1983.

Emery, G., Bedrosian, R., & Garber, J. Cognitive therapy with depressed children and adolescents. In D. P. Cantwell & G. A. Carlson (Eds.), *Affective disorders in childhood and adolescence: An update.* New York: Spectrum, 1983.

Engel, G., & Reichsman, F. Spontaneous and experimentally induced depression in an infant with gastric fistula. *Journal of the American Psychoanalytic Association,* 1956, *4,* 428–456.

Feldman, L. B. Depression and marital interaction. *Family Process,* 1975, *15,* 389–395.

Foorman, S. *Children at high-risk for depression.* Paper presented at the meeting of the Southwestern Psychological Association, Dallas, Tex., April 1982.

Frame, C., Matson, J. L., Sonis, W. A., Fialkov, M. J., & Kazdin, A. E. Behavioral treatment of depression in a prepubertal child. *Journal of Behavior Therapy and Experimental Psychiatry,* 1982, *3,* 239–243.

Freud, A. *Normality and pathology in childhood.* New York: International Universities Press, 1965.

Freud, A., & Burlingham, D. *Infants without families.* New York: International Universities Press, 1944.

Friedlander, S., Philips, I., Morrison, D., & Traylor, J. *Depression in childhood: An exploratory study.* Paper presented at the American Psychological Association, Los Angeles, Calif., August 1981.

Frommer, E. Treatment of childhood depression with antidepressant drugs. *British Medical Journal,* 1967, *1,* 729–732.

Frommer, E. Depressive illness in childhood. *British Journal of Psychiatry,* 1968, *Special Publication No. 2,* 117–123.

Frommer, E., Mendelson, W. B., & Reid, M. A. Differential diagnosis of psychiatric disturbances in pre-school children. *British Journal of Psychiatry,* 1972, *121,* 71–74.

Furman, E. *A child's parent dies. Studies in childhood bereavement.* New Haven, Conn.: Yale University Press, 1974.

Gamer, E., Gallant, D., Grunebaum, H. U., & Cohler, B. J. Children of psychotic mothers. *Archives of General Psychiatry,* 1977, *34,* 592–597.

Garber, J. Issues in the diagnosis of depression in children. Paper presented in L. P. Rehm (Chair), *Empirical studies of childhood depression.* Symposium presented at the annual meeting of the American Psychological Association, Los Angeles, August 1981.

Garber, J. *The children's events schedule.* Unpublished manuscript, University of Minnesota, Minneapolis, 1982.

Garber, J., Greenberg, E. S., & White, W. *The identification of criteria for the diagnosis of childhood depression.* Paper presented at the annual meeting of the American Psychological Association, Montreal, August 1982.

Garber, J., & Seligman, M. E. P. (Eds.), *Human helplessness: Theory and applications.* New York: Academic Press, 1980.

Garfinkel, B. D., & Golombek, H. Suicide and depression in childhood and adolescence. *Canadian Medical Association Journal,* 1974, *110,* 1278–1281.

Gelfand, D. M. Social withdrawal and negative emotional states: Behavior therapy. In B. B. Wolman, J. Egan, & A. O. Ross (Eds.), *Handbook of treatment of mental disorders in childhood and adolescence.* Englewood Cliffs, N.J.: Prentice-Hall, 1978.

Gilpin, D. C. Psychotherapy of the depressed child. In E. J. Anthony & D. C. Gilpin (Eds.), *Three clinical faces of childhood.* New York: Spectrum, 1976.

Ginsburg, S. D., & Twentyman, C. T. *Prevention of childhood depression.* Unpublished manuscript, University of Rochester, 1983.

Gittelman-Klein, R. Definitional and methodological issues concerning depressive illness in children. In J. G. Schulterbrandt & A. Raskin (Eds.), *Depression in childhood: Diagnosis, treatment, and conceptual models.* New York: Raven Press, 1977.

Glasberg, R., & Aboud, F. E. A developmental perspective on the study of depression: Children's evaluative reactions to sadness. *Developmental Psychology,* 1981, *17,* 195–202.

Glaser, K. Masked depression in children and adolescents. *Annual Progress in Child Psychiatry and Child Development,* 1968, *1,* 345–355.

Goldstein, A. P., & Kanfer, F. H. *Maximizing treatment gains: Transfer enhancement in psychotherapy.* New York: Academic Press, 1979.

Gordon, T. *P.E.T. Parent Effectiveness Training.* New York: Peter H. Wyden, 1970.

Gottman, J. M., & McFall, R. M. Self-monitoring effects in a program for potential high school dropouts: A time series analysis. *Journal of Consulting and Clinical Psychology,* 1972, *39,* 273–281.

Group for the Advancement of Psychiatry. *Psychopathological disorders in childhood: Theoretical considerations and a proposed classification.* New York: Group for the Advancement of Psychiatry, 1966.

Grunebaum, H., Cohler, B. J., Kaufman, C., & Gallant, D. Children of depressed and schizophrenic mothers. *Child Psychiatry and Human Development,* 1978, *8,* 219–228.

Gurman, A. S., & Kniskern, D. P. (Eds.). *Handbook of family therapy.* New York: Brunner/Mazel, 1981.

Hendren, R. L. Depression in anorexia nervosa. *Journal of the American Academy of Child Psychiatry,* 1983, *22,* 59–62.

Herjanic, B., Herjanic, M., Brown, F., & Wheatt, T. Are children reliable reporters? *Journal of Abnormal Child Psychology,* 1975, *3,* 41–48.

Hogan, P., & Hogan, B. K. The family treatment of depression. In F. F. Flach & S. C. Draghi (Eds.), *The nature and treatment of depression.* New York: Wiley & Sons, 1978.

Hollon, T. H. Poor school performance as a symptom of masked depression in children and adolescents. *American Journal of Psychotherapy,* 1970, *25,* 258–263.

Holmes, T. H., & Rahe, R. H. The Social Readjustment Rating Scale. *Journal of Psychosomatic Research,* 1967, *11,* 213–218.

Humphrey, L. L. Children's and teachers' perspectives on children's self-control: The development of two rating scales. *Journal of Consulting and Clinical Psychology,* 1982, *50,* 624–633.

Ickes, W., & Layden, M. A. Attributional styles. In J. Harvey, W. Ickes, & R. Kidd (Eds.), *New directions in attributional research* (Vol. 2). Hillsdale, N.J.: Lawrence Erlbaum Associates, Inc., 1978.

Ingalls, R. P. *A level of care survey in Division for Youth facilities.* Report on New York State Division of Youth/Office of Mental Health Survey of Youth in Facilities. New York: New York State Division of Youth, 1978.

Kanfer, F. H. Self-monitoring: Methodological limitations and clinical applications. *Journal of Consulting and Clinical Psychology,* 1970, *35,* 148–152.

Kanfer, F. H., & Karoly, P. Self-control: A behavioristic excursion into the lion's den. *Behavior Therapy,* 1972, *2,* 398–416.

Kashani, J. H., Barbero, G. J., & Bolander, F. D. Depression in hospitalized pediatric patients. *Journal of the American Academy of Child Psychiatry,* 1981, *20,* 123–124.

Kashani, J. H., Cantwell, D. P., Shekim, W. O., & Reid, J. C. Major depressive disorder in children admitted to an inpatient community mental health center. *American Journal of Psychiatry,* 1982, *139,* 671–672.

Kashani, J. H., Husain, A., Shekim, W. O., Hodges, K. K., Cytryn, L., & McKnew, D. H. Current perspectives on childhood depression: An overview. *American Journal of Psychiatry,* 1981, *138,* 143–153.

Kashani, J. H., McGee, R. O., Clarkson, S. E., Anderson, J. C., Walton, L. A., Williams, S., Silva, P. A., Robins, A. J., Cytryn, L., & McKnew, D. H. Depression in a sample of 9 year-old children: Prevalence and associated characteristics. *Archives of General Psychiatry,* 1983, *40,* 1217–1223.

Kashani, J. H., Simonds, J. F. The incidence of depression in children. *American Journal of Psychiatry,* 1979, *136,* 1203–1205.

Kaslow, N. J. *Depression in children and their parents.* Unpublished doctoral dissertation, University of Houston, 1983.

Kaslow, N. J., & Rehm, L. P. Childhood depression. In R. J. Morris & T. R. Kratochwill (Eds.), *The practice of child therapy: A textbook of methods.* New York: Pergamon Press, 1983.

Kaslow, N. J., Rehm, L. P., & Siegel, A. W. Social and cognitive correlates of depression in children: A developmental perspective. *Journal of Abnormal Child Psychology*, 1984, *12*, 605–620.

Kaslow, N. J., Tanenbaum, R. L., Abramson, L. Y., Peterson, C. P., & Seligman, M. E. P. Problem-solving deficits and depressive symptoms among children. *Journal of Abnormal Child Psychology*, 1983, *11*, 497–502.

Kaslow, N. J., Tanenbaum, R. L., & Seligman, M. E. P. *The KASTAN: A children's attributional style questionnaire*. Unpublished manuscript, University of Pennsylvania, Philadelphia, 1978.

Kazdin, A. E. *Behavior modification in applied settings*. Homewood, Ill.: Dorsey Press, 1975.

Kazdin, A. E. Assessment techniques for childhood depression: A critical appraisal. *Journal of the American Academy of Child Psychiatry*, 1981, *20*, 358–375.

Kazdin, A. E., French, N. H., & Unis, A. S. Child, mother, and father evaluations of depression in psychiatric inpatient children. *Journal of Abnormal Child Psychology*, 1983, *11*, 167–180(a).

Kazdin, A. E., French, N. H., Usin, A. S., & Esveldt-Dawson, K. Assessment of childhood depression: Correspondence of child and parent ratings. *Journal of the American Academy of Child Psychiatry*, 1983, *22*, 157–164(b).

Kazdin, A. E., French, N. H., Unis, A. S., Esveldt-Dawson, K., & Sherick, R. B. Hopelessness, depression, and suicidal intent among psychiatrically disturbed inpatient children. *Journal of Consulting and Clinical Psychology*, 1983, *51*, 504–510(c).

Kazdin, A. E., & Petti, T. A. Self-report and interview measures on childhood and adolescent depression. *Journal of Child Psychology and Psychiatry*, 1982, *23*, 437–457.

Kendall, P. C., & Wilcox, L. E. Self-control in children: Development of a rating scale. *Journal of Consulting and Clinical Psychology*, 1979, *47*, 1020–1029.

Kendall, P. C., & Wilcox, L. E. A cognitive-behavioral treatment for impulsivity: Concrete versus conceptual labeling with nonself-controlled problem children. *Journal of Consulting and Clinical Psychology*, 1980,*48*, 80–91.

Klein, D. F., Gittelman, R., Quitkin, F., & Rifkin, A. *Diagnosis and drug treatment of psychiatric disorders: Adults and children*. Baltimore: Williams & Wilkins, 1980.

Kovacs, M. Rating scales to assess depression in school-aged children. *Acta Paedopsychiatrica*, 1981,*46*, 305–315.

Kovacs, M. *The Children's Depression Inventory: A self-rated depression scale for school-aged children*. Unpublished manuscript, University of Pittsburgh, 1983.

Kovacs, M., & Beck, A. T. An empirical-clinical approach toward a definition of childhood depression. In J. G. Schulterbrandt & A. Raskin (Eds.), *Depression in childhood: Diagnosis, treatment, and conceptual models*. New York: Raven Press, 1977.

Kovacs, M., Betof, N. G., Celebre, J. F., Mansheim, P. A., Petty, L. R., & Raynak, J. T. *Childhood depression: Myth or clinical syndrome?* Paper presented at the American Academy of Child Psychiatry Conference, Houston, 1977.

Lamont, J., Fischoff, S., & Gottlieb, H. Recall of parental behaviors in female neurotic depressives. *Journal of Clinical Psychology,* 1976, *32,* 762–765.

Lang, M., & Tisher, M. *Children's Depression Scale.* Victoria, Australia: The Australian Council for Educational Research, 1978.

Lefkowitz, M. M., & Burton, N. Childhood depression: A critique of the concept. *Psychological Bulletin,* 1978, *85,* 716–726.

Lefkowitz, M. M., & Tessiny, E. P. Assessment of childhood depression. *Journal of Consulting and Clinical Psychology,* 1980, *48,* 43–50.

Leon, G. R., Kendall, P. C., & Garber, J. Depression in children: Parent, teacher, and child perspectives. *Journal of Abnormal Child Psychology,* 1980, *8,* 221–235.

Lesse, S. Depression masked by acting-out behavior patterns. *American Journal of Psychotherapy,* 1974, *28,* 352–361.

Lessing, E. E., & Zagorin, S. W. Dimensions of psychopathology in middle childhood as evaluated by three symptom checklists. *Educational and Psychological Measurement,* 1971, *31,* 175–198.

Leventon, B. *Childhood depression: Symptoms and their relationship to development.* Unpublished thesis, University of Houston, Houston, Tex., 1983.

Lewinsohn, P. M. A behavioral approach to depression. In R. M. Friedman & M. M. Katz (Eds.), *The psychology of depression: Contemporary theory and research.* New York: John Wiley & Sons, 1974.

Lewinsohn, P. M., Biglan, A., & Zeiss, A. M. Behavioral treatment of depression. In P. O. Davidson (Ed.), *Behavioral management of anxiety, depression, and pain.* New York: Brunner/Mazel, 1976.

Lewinsohn, P. M., Mischel, W., Chaplin, W., & Barton, R. Social competence and depression: The role of illusory self-perceptions. *Journal of Abnormal Psychology,* 1980, *89,* 203–213.

Lewis, M., & Rosenblum L. (Eds.). *The origins of fear: The origins of behavior* (Vol. 2). New York: John Wiley & Sons, 1974.

Libet, J., & Lewinsohn, P. M. The concept of social skills with special references to the behavior of depressed persons. *Journal of Consulting and Clinical Psychology,* 1973, *40,* 304–312.

Ling, W., Oftedal, G., & Weinberg, W. Depressive illness in childhood presenting as severe headache. *American Journal of Diseases in Children,* 1970, *120,* 122–124.

Little, V. L., & Kendall, P. C. Cognitive-behavioral interventions with delinquents: Problem-solving, role-taking, and self-control. In P. C. Kendall & S. D. Hollon (Eds.), *Cognitive-behavioral interventions: Theory, research, and procedures.* New York: Academic Press, 1979.

MacPhillamy, D. J., & Lewinsohn, P. M. *Pleasant Events Schedule*. Mimeograph, University of Oregon, 1971.

Mahler, M. S. On early infantile psychosis: The symbiotic and autistic syndromes. *Journal of the American Academy of Child Psychiatry*, 1965, *4*, 554–568.

Mahler, M. S. Notes on the development of basic moods. In R. Lowenstein, L. Newman, M. Schur, & A. Solnit (Eds.), *Psychoanalysis: A general psychology*. New York: International Universities Press, 1966.

Mahler, M., Pine, F., & Bergman, A. *The psychological birth of the human infant*. New York: Basic Books, 1975.

Makita, K. The rarity of depression in childhood. *Acta Paedopsychiatrica*, 1973, *40*, 37–44.

Malmquist, C. P. Childhood depression: A clinical and behavioral perspective. In J. G. Schulterbrandt & A. Raskin (Eds.), *Depression in childhood: Diagnosis, treatment, and conceptual models*. New York: Raven Press, 1977.

Matson, J. L., Esveldt-Dawson, K., Andrasik, F., Ollendik, T. H., Petti, T. A., & Hersen, M. Observation and generalization effects of social skills training with emotionally disturbed children. *Behavior Therapy*, 1980, *11*, 522–531.

McConville, B. J., Boag, L. C., & Purohit, A. P. Three types of childhood depression. *Canadian Psychiatric Association Journal*, 1973, *18*, 133–138.

McKnew, D. H., & Cytryn, L. Urinary metabolites in chronically depressed children. *Journal of the American Academy of Child Psychiatry*, 1979, *18*, 608–615.

McKnew, D. H., Cytryn, L., Efron, A. M., Gershon, E. S., & Bunney, W. E. Offspring of patients with affective disorders. *British Journal of Psychiatry*, 1979, *134*, 148–152.

Meichenbaum, D. *Cognitive behavior modification*. New York: Plenum Press, 1977.

Meichenbaum, D., & Asarnow, J. Cognitive-behavioral modification and metacognitive development: Implications for the classroom. In P. C. Kendall & S. D. Hollon (Eds.), *Cognitive behavioral interventions: Theory, research, and procedures*. New York: Academic Press, 1979.

Meichenbaum, D., & Goodman, J. Training impulsive children to talk to themselves: A means of developing self-control. *Journal of Abnormal Psychology*, 1971, *77*, 115–126.

Mezzich, A. C., & Mezzich, J. E. Symptomatology of depression in adolescence. *Journal of Personality Assessment*, 1979, *43*, 267–275.

Millon, T., & Millon, R. *Abnormal behavior and personality: A biosocial learning approach*. Philadelphia: W. B. Saunders, 1974.

Morrison, H. L. (Ed.). *Children of depressed parents: Risk, identification, and intervention*. New York: Grune and Stratton, 1983.

Moyal, B. R. Locus of control, self-esteem, stimulus appraisal, and depressive symptoms in children. *Journal of Consulting and Clinical Psychology*, 1977, *45*, 951–952.

Nissen, G. *Depressive syndrome im kindes-und jugendalter.* Berlin: Springer-Verlag, 1971.

Nowicki, S., & Strickland, B. A locus of control scale for children. *Journal of Consulting and Clinical Psychology,* 1973, *40,* 148–154.

Orvaschel, H., Puig-Antich, J., Chambers, W., Tabrizi, M. A., & Johnson, R. Retrospective assessment of prepubertal major depression with Kiddie-SADS-E. *Journal of the American Academy of Child Psychiatry,* 1982, *21,* 392–397.

Orvaschel, H., Weissman, M. M., Padian, N., & Lowe, T. L. Assessing psychopathology in children of psychiatrically disturbed parents: A pilot study. *Journal of the American Academy of Child Psychiatry,* 1981, *20,* 112–120.

Ossofsky, H. J. Endogenous depression in infancy and childhood. *Comprehensive Psychiatry,* 1974, *15,* 19–25.

Parker, G. Parental characteristics in relation to depressive disorders. *British Journal of Psychiatry,* 1979, *134,* 138–147.

Parson, J. E., & Ruble, D. N. The development of achievement-related expectancies. *Child Development,* 1977, *48,* 1075–1079.

Peterson, C. P., & Seligman, M. E. P. Causal explanations as a risk factor for depression: Theory and evidence. *Psychological Review,* in press.

Peterson, D. R. Behavior problems in middle childhood. *Journal of Consulting Psychology,* 1961, *25,* 205–209.

Petti, T. A. Depression in hospitalized child psychiatry patients. *Journal of the American Academy of Child Psychiatry,* 1978, *17,* 49–59.

Petti, T. A. Active treatment of childhood depression. In J. F. Clarkin & H. I. Glaser (Eds.), *Depression: Behavioral and directive intervention strategies.* New York: Garland STPM Press, 1981.

Petti, T. A. Behavioral approaches in the treatment of depressed children. In D. P. Cantwell & G. A. Carlson (Eds.), *Affective disorders in childhood and adolescence: An update.* New York: Spectrum, 1983(a).

Petti, T. A. Imipramine in the treatment of depressed children. In D. P. Cantwell & G. A. Carlson (Eds.), *Affective disorders in childhood and adolescence: An update.* New York: Spectrum, 1983(b).

Petti, T. A., Bornstein, M., Delamater, A., & Conners, C. K. Evaluation and multimodal treatment of a depressed prepubertal girl. *Journal of the American Academy of Child Psychiatry,* 1980, *19,* 690–702.

Philips, I. Childhood depression: Interpersonal interactions and depressive phenomena. *American Journal of Psychiatry,* 1979, *136,* 511–515.

Piaget, J. *The construction of reality in the child.* London: Routledge & Kegan Paul, 1954.

Piers, E. V., & Harris, D. B. *The Piers-Harris Children's Self Concept Scale.* Nashville, Tenn.: Counselor Recordings and Tests, 1969.

Piersel, W. C., & Kratochwill, T. R. Self observation and behavior change: Applications to academic and adjustment problems through behavioral consultation. *Journal of School Psychology*, 1979, *17*, 151–161.

Pollack, S. L., Kaslow, N. J., & Harvery, D. M. Symmetry, complementarity, and depression: The evolution of a hypothesis. In F. W. Kaslow (Ed.), *The international book of family therapy*. New York: Brunner/Mazel, 1982.

Poznanski, E. O. The clinical phenomenology of childhood depression. *American Journal of Orthopsychiatry*, 1982, *52*, 308–313.

Poznanski, E. O., Carroll, B. J., Banegas, M. C., Cook, S. C., & Grossman, J. A. The dexamethasone suppression test in prepubertal depressed children. *American Journal of Psychiatry*, 1982, *139*, 321–324.

Poznanski, E. O., Cook, S. C., & Carroll, B. J. A depression rating scale for children. *Pediatrics*, 1979, *64*, 442–450.

Poznanski, E. O., & Zrull, J. P. Childhood depression: Clinical characteristics of overtly depressed children. *Archives of General Psychiatry*, 1970, *23*, 8–15.

Pressley, M. Increasing children's self-control through cognitive interventions. *Review of Educational Research*, 1979, *49*, 319–370.

Puig-Antich, J. Editorial: The use of RDC criteria for major depressive disorder in children and adolescents. *Journal of the American Academy of Child Psychiatry*, 1982, *21*, 291–293(a).

Puig-Antich, J. Major depression and conduct disorder in prepuberty. *Journal of the American Academy of Child Psychiatry*, 1982, *21*, 118–128(b).

Puig-Antich, J., Blau, S., Marx, N., Greenhill, L. L., & Chambers, W. Prepubertal major depressive disorder. *Journal of the American Academy of Child Psychiatry*, 1978, *17*, 695–707.

Puig-Antich, J., & Chambers, W. *Schedule for Affective Disorders and Schizophrenia for School-Age Children (6-16 years)—Kiddie-SADS*. Unpublished manuscript, New York State Psychiatric Institute, New York, 1978.

Puig-Antich, J., Chambers, W. J., & Tabrizi, M. A. The clinical assessment of current depressive episodes in children and adolescents: Interviews with parents and children. In D. P. Cantwell & G. A. Carlson (Eds.), *Affective disorders in childhood and adolescence: An update*. New York: Spectrum, 1983.

Puig-Antich, J., & Gittleman, R. Depression in childhood and adolescence. In E. S. Paykel (Ed.), *Handbook of affective disorders*. London: Churchill, 1981.

Radloff, L. Sex differences in depression. *Sex Roles*, 1975, *1*, 249–265.

Rehm, L. P. A self control model of depression. *Behavior Therapy*, 1977, *8*, 787–804.

Rehm, L. P. A self control therapy program for the treatment of depression. In J. F. Clarkin & H. I. Glazer (Eds.), *Depression: Behavioral and directive intervention strategies*. New York: Garland STPM Press, 1981.

Rehm, L. P. Self-management in depression. In P. Karoly & F. H. Kanfer (Eds.), *Self-management and behavior change: From theory to practice*. New York: Pergamon Press, 1982.

Renshaw, D. C. Suicide and depression in children. *The Journal of School Health*, 1974, *44*, 487–489.

Rholes, W. S., Blackwell, J., Jordan, C., & Walters, C. A developmental study of learned helplessness. *Developmental Psychology*, 1980, *16*, 616–624.

Rickard, K. M., Forehand, R., Wells, K. C., Griest, D. L., & McMahon, R. J. Factors in the referral of children for behavioral treatment: A comparison of mothers of clinic-referred deviant, clinic-referred nondeviant, and nonclinic children. *Behavior Research and Therapy*, 1981, *19*, 201–205.

Rie, H. E. Depression in childhood: A survey of some pertinent contributions. *Journal of the Academy of Child Psychiatry*, 1966, *5*, 653–685.

Robbins, D. R., Alessi, N. E., Cook, S. C., Poznanski, E. O., & Yanchyshyn, G. W. The use of the Research Diagnostic Criteria (RDC) for depression in adolescent psychiatric inpatients. *Journal of the American Academy of Child Psychiatry*, 1982, *21*, 251–255.

Rochlin, G. The loss complex. *Journal of the American Psychoanalytic Association*, 1959, *7*, 299–316.

Rogers, T., & Forehand, R. The role of parent depression in interactions between mothers and their clinic-referred children. *Cognitive Therapy and Research*, 1983, *7*, 315–324.

Rolf, J. E. The academic and social competence of children vulnerable to schizophrenia and other behavior pathologies. *Journal of Abnormal Psychology*, 1972, *80*, 225–243.

Rolf, J. E., Garmezy, N. The school performance of children vulnerable to behavior pathology. In D. F. Ricks, T. Alexander, & M. Roff (Eds.), *Life history research in psychopathology* (Vol. 3). Minnesota: University of Minnesota Press, 1974.

Ross, L., Lepper, M., & Hubbard, M. Perseverance in self-perception and social perception: Biased attributional processes in the debriefing paradigm. *Journal of Personality and Social Psychology*, 1975,*32*, 880–892.

Rubenstein, D., & Timmins, J. F. Depressive dyadic and triadic relationships. *The Journal of Marriage and Family Counseling*, 1978, *4*, 13–24.

Rutter, M., & Graham, P. The reliability and validity of the psychiatric assessment of the child: I. Interview with the child. *The British Journal of Psychiatry*, 1968, *114*, 563–579.

Sacks, J. M. The need for subtlety: A critical session with a suicidal child. *Psychotherapy: Theory, Research, and Practice*, 1977, *14*, 434–437.

Sagotsky, G., Patterson, C. J., & Lepper, M. R. Training children's self-control: A field experiment in self-monitoring and goal-setting in the classroom. *Journal of Experimental Child Psychology*, 1978, *25*, 242–253.

Sameroff, A. J., & Zax, M. Perinatal characteristics of the offspring of schizophrenic women. *The Journal of Nervous and Mental Disease*, 1973, *157*, 191–199.

Sandler, I. N., & Block, M. Life stress and maladaption of children. *American Journal of Community Psychology,* 1979, *1,* 425–440.

Schultz, H. T. *Childhood depression: A cognitive, behavioral, and family perspective.* Unpublished doctoral dissertation, University of Pittsburgh, Pittsburgh, 1982.

Schwartz, M., Friedman, R., Lindsay, P., & Narrol, H. The relationship between conceptual tempo and depression in children. *Journal of Consulting and Clinical Psychology,* 1982, *50,* 488–490.

Sedlak, A. J., & Kurtz, S. T. A review of children's use of causal inference principles. *Child Development,* 1981, *52,* 759–784.

Seligman, M. E. P. *Helplessness: On depression, development, and death.* San Francisco: W. H. Freeman, 1975.

Seligman, M. E. P. A learned helplessness point of view. In L. P. Rehm (Ed.), *Behavior therapy for depression.* New York: Academic Press, 1981.

Seligman, M. E. P., Peterson, C., Kaslow, N. J., Tanenbaum, R. L., Alloy, L. B., & Abramson, L. Y. Explanatory style and depressive symptoms among school children. *Journal of Abnormal Psychology,* 1984, *93,* 235–238.

Selman, R. L., & Jurcovic, G. L. *The child as a budding psychotherapist: What children understand of the introspective processes.* Paper presented at Wheelock/Bank Street Conference on the Development-Interaction Point of View, Boston, June 1978.

Shantz, C. U. The development of social cognition. In E. M. Hetherington (Ed.), *Review of child development research* (Vol. 5). Chicago: University of Chicago Press, 1975.

Shure, M. B., & Spivak, G. Means-ends thinking, adjustment, and social class among elementary-school-aged children. *Journal of Consulting and Clinical Psychology,* 1972, *38,* 348–353.

Shure, M. B., & Spivak, G. *Problem-solving techniques in childrearing.* San Francisco: Jossey-Bass, 1978.

Smucker, M. R., Craighead, W. E., Wilcoxin-Craighead, L., & Green, B. *Psychometric properties of the Children's Depression Inventory.* Unpublished manuscript, Pennsylvania State University, State Park, 1983.

Spates, C. R., & Kanfer, F. H. Self-monitoring, self-evaluation, and self-reinforcement in children's learning: A test of multistage self-regulation model. *Behavior Therapy,* 1977, *8,* 9–16.

Spitz, R. Anaclitic depression. *Psychoanalytic study of the child,* 1946, *5,* 113–117.

Spivak, G., Platt, J. J., & Shure, M. B. *The problem solving approach to adjustment.* San Francisco: Jossey-Bass, 1967.

Spivak, G., & Shure, M. *The social adjustment of young children.* San Francisco: Jossey-Bass, 1975.

Strober, M. The significance of bulimia in juvenile anorexia nervosa: An exploration of possible etiologic factors. *International Journal of Eating Disorders,* 1981, *1,* 28–43.

Strober, M. Clinical and biological perspectives on depressive disorder in adolescence. In D. P. Cantwell & G. A. Carlson (Eds.), *Affective disorders in childhood and adolescence: An update.* New York: Spectrum, 1983.

Teri, L. Depression in adolescence: Its relationship to assertion and various aspects of self-image. *Journal of Clinical Child Psychology,* 1982, *11,* 101–106.

Tessiny, E. P., & Lefkowitz, M. M. Childhood depression: A 6-month follow-up study. *Journal of Consulting and Clinical Psychology,* 1982, *50,* 778–780.

Tessiny, E. P., Lefkowitz, M. M., & Gordon, N. H. Childhood depression, locus of control, and school achievement. *Journal of Educational Psychology,* 1980, *72,* 506–510.

Tisher, M., & Lang, M. The Children's Depression Scale: Review and further developments. In D. P. Cantwell & G. A. Carlson (Eds.), *Affective disorders in childhood and adolescence: An update.* New York: Spectrum, 1983.

Toolan, J. M. Depression in children and adolescents. *American Journal of Orthopsychiatry,* 1962, *32,* 404–414.

Toolan, J. M. Depression and suicide in children: An overview. *American Journal of Psychotherapy,* 1981, *35,* 311–322.

Vosk, B., Forehand, R., Parker, J. B., & Rickard, K. A multimethod comparison of popular and unpopular children. *Developmental Psychology,* 1982, *18,* 571–575.

Weinberg, W. A., Rutman, J., Sullivan, L., Penick, E. C., & Dietz, S. G. Depression in children referred to an educational diagnostic center: Diagnosis and treatment. *The Journal of Pediatrics,* 1973, *83,* 1065–1072.

Weintraub, S., Neale, J. M., & Liebert, D. E. Teacher ratings of children vulnerable to psychopathology. *American Journal of Orthopsychiatry,* 1975, *45,* 838–845.

Weintraub, S., Prinz, R. J., & Neale, J. M. Peer evaluations of the competence of children vulnerable to psychopathology. *Journal of Abnormal Child Psychology,* 1978, *6,* 461–473.

Weissman, M. M., & Klerman, G. L. Sex differences and the epidemiology of depression. *Archives of General Psychiatry,* 1977, *34,* 98–111.

Weissman, M. M., Orvaschel, H., & Padian, N. Children's symptom and social functioning self-report scales: Comparison of mothers' and children's reports. *Journal of Nervous and Mental Disease,* 1980, *168,* 736–740.

Weissman, M. M., & Paykel, E. S. *The depressed woman: A study of social relationships.* Chicago: The University of Chicago Press, 1974.

Weissman, M. M., Paykel, E. S., & Klerman, G. J. The depressed woman as mother. *Social Psychiatry,* 1972, 98–108.

Weissman, M. M., & Siegel, R. The depressed woman and her rebellious adolescent. *Social Casework,* 1972, *53,* 563–579.

Welner, Z. Childhood depression: An overview. *The Journal of Nervous and Mental Disease,* 1978, *166,* 588–593.

Welner, Z., Welner, A., McCrary, M. D., & Leonard, M. A. Psychopathology in children of inpatients with depression: A controlled study. *The Journal of Nervous and Mental Disease,* 1977, *164,* 408–413.

Winnett, R. L., & Bornstein, P. H. *Cognitive behavior therapy for childhood depression: A levels of treatment approach.* Unpublished manuscript, University of Montana, 1983.

Wirt, R. D., Lacahr, D., Klinedinst, J. K., & Seat, P. D. *Multidimensional description of child personality: A manual for the personality inventory for children.* Los Angeles: Western Psychological Services, 1977.

World Health Organization. *Glossary to mental disorders and guide to their classification.* Geneva: World Health Organization, 1974.

Youngerman, J., & Canino, I. A. Lithium carbonate use in children and adolescents. *Archives of General Psychiatry,* 1978, *35,* 216–224.

Zrull, J., McDermott, J., & Poznanski, E. Hyperkinetic syndrome: The role of depression. *Child Psychiatry and Human Development,* 1970, *1,* 33–40.

16

Gender Identity Problems

George A. Rekers
Professor of Family and Child Development
Kansas State University

INTRODUCTION

Children who persistently identify as a member of the opposite sex have been recognized by a growing number of clinicians as manifesting a relatively rare psychological syndrome requiring careful assessment. In the 1960s, a number of clinical reports began to appear in the literature describing a disorder that has variously been referred to as *gender deviance, atypical gender identity, gender dysphoria,* and *gender disturbance* (Bakwin, 1968; Green & Money, 1960; Holeman & Winokur, 1965; Stoller, 1964, 1968). By 1980, the syndrome had received sufficient research attention and clinical recognition to be included in the most recent edition of the *Diagnostic and Statistical Manual of Mental Disorders* (DSM-III; American Psychiatric Association, 1980) as the diagnosis *gender identity disorder of childhood.* The available longitudinal investigations and retrospective studies of adults with gender deviance indicate that gender identity disorders in boys and girls place them at high risk for homosexual orientation in adulthood and possibly for transsexualism and transvestism (Green, 1974, 1979; Money & Russo, 1979; Zuger, 1966, 1978). Early diagnosis and psychological treatment for childhood gender disturbance may be the best preventative strategy for adulthood sexual and gender abnormalities, including homosexual orientation disturbance and potentially also transsexualism and transvestism (Doering, 1981; Green, 1974; Rekers, 1977b, 1978a, 1978b, 1982a, 1982b; Rekers, Bentler, Rosen, & Lovaas, 1977; Rekers & Mead, 1980;

Rekers, Rosen, Lovaas, & Bentler, 1978; Rosen, Rekers, & Bentler, 1978; Stoller, 1968, 1970; Whitam, 1977).

Gender identity disorder in childhood must be differentiated from the kind of episodic and flexible exploration of sex-typed behaviors, which is typical in the normal psychosexual development of many boys and girls (Maccoby, 1966; Maccoby & Jacklin, 1974; Mischel, 1970), and also should be distinguished from *androgyny* (e.g., Bem, 1975; Block, 1977; Serbin, 1980). The clear distinction between the concepts of psychological androgyny and gender identity disorder has been reviewed elsewhere (Doering, 1981; Rekers, 1977; Rekers et al., 1978; Rosen & Rekers, 1980). Deviating from the normal pattern of exploring opposite sex-role behaviors, some children develop a persistent, compulsive and rigidly stereotyped pattern of sex-typed behavior, which is often so extreme as to be a caricature of a cultural sex role. In boys, one extreme is the deviant and excessive hypermasculinity of boys, who are destructive, uncontrolled, interpersonally violent and belligerent, and who lack the expression of gentle and tender emotions as well as other socially sensitive behaviors (Harrington, 1970). Psychological treatment is indicated for these exaggeratedly supermasculine boys. The opposite extreme in boys is the pattern often associated with gender identity disorder, including frequent dressing in girl's clothing and cosmetics, the display of caricatured feminine arm movements, gait or body gestures, the avoidance of play with boys coupled with a preference for predominant play with girls, and often a verbal insistence that they are in fact girls or that they want to grow up to be mothers and to bear children. Such hyperfemininity in boys is a rigid and compulsive pattern that is differentiated from the adaptive flexibility of psychological androgyny and that goes beyond the normal curiosity-induced exploration of feminine stereotypic play in some boys (Green, 1974; Rekers, 1972, 1977a, in press-a; Stoller, 1968). Unfortunately, there are no reliable base-rate data on the occurrence of gender identity disorder in boys, although some investigators have relied on their clinical experience to estimate that 1 in 25,000 to 80,000 boys may display a portion of these feminine sex-role behavior patterns, which distinguish them as deviant from other boys, and that gender identity disorder itself occurs in 1 out of 100,000 to 200,000 boys. These estimates suggest that gender disturbances are rare; however, many cases may go undetected because of the embarrassment of parents or because of reluctance to refer to professionals.

Gender identity disorder in girls can be clinically differentiated from a normal tomboy phase (see extended review of the data and clinical issues by Rekers & Mead, 1980). This deviant pattern includes a chronic rejection of stereotypic feminine toys, female jewelry, cosmetics, and dresses, coupled with a preoccupation with appearing masculine in clothing and toy preferences. One cross-gender identified girl, for example, regularly drew a moustache and beard on her face, avoided play with girls, and adopted male roles in fantasy play, such as play acting shaving her face (Rekers & Mead, 1979a). Such girls also may adopt a masculine appearance in their gestures and mannerisms and in their gait, and they may deliberately and artificially project their voice into lower, gruffer sounds (Rekers & Mead, 1979a, 1980). The girl's expressed desire to be a boy may also include insistence on being called by a boy's name or nickname. One cross-gender identified girl who reached puberty manifested a strong negative reaction to her physical maturation, indicated by her dressing to hide her developing breasts, refusing to wear a bra, and making repeated requests of medical personnel for sex-reassignment surgery and hormonal treatment (Rekers & Mead, 1980). Again, gender identity disorder in girls has been distinguished from the gender-role flexibility of psychological androgyny and from the normal tomboy developmental phase of many normal girls (Green, 1975, 1978; Rekers & Mead 1980; Saghir & Robins, 1973; Stoller, 1975).

In a series of over 150 cases of childhood gender identity disorder over a decade of research, Rekers has received a ratio of 30 to 1 referrals of boys over girls. At the same time, over 90 percent of the clinical reports and research on childhood and adolescent psychosexual disorders reports males cases. However, adulthood cases of gender dysphoria have been reported in the clinical literature at ratios from 5 to 1 to closer to 2 to 1. This suggests that, while gender identity disorders may be less common in females, there may be large numbers of undetected cases of gender identity disorder among young girls that eventuate in adulthood sexual or gender deviance.

DESCRIPTIVE CHARACTERISTICS AND DIMENSIONS OF PSYCHOSEXUAL DISORDERS

In clinical work, it is more helpful to assess a particular child across the several major psychosexual dimensions (Rosen & Rekers, 1980), rather than to assign individual children to the currently limited diagnostic categories of deviancy, which are quite global and inarticulated. Rosen and Rekers (1980) have proposed an alternative approach toward a taxonomic framework for the variables of sex and gender as they relate to psychopathology. For example, the DSM-III makes some unsubstantiated assumptions regarding the interrelationship between gender identity and gender role, for example (see Bentler, Rekers, and Rosen, 1979; Rosen and Rekers, 1980), and assigns children and adolescents to some rather narrow and limited diagnostic categories of psychosexual deviancy, which are not always accurately descriptive of an individual clinical case. It is more useful and accurate to assess a particular child across these seven major psychosexual dimensions (Rekers, 1981):

1. *Physical sex status* is male, female or intersexed (hermaphroditic), depending on the congruity or incongruity across the five variables of genetic constitution, gonads, external sex organ anatomy, internal accessory genital structures, and sex endocrinology. The Tanner Scale provides a further refinement of sex status in terms of the stage of the individual's prepubertal, pubertal, or postpubertal development (Marshall & Tanner, 1969, 1970; Tanner, 1955).

2. *Social sex assignment* is usually initiated by the attending physician at birth and is the sex into which the child is reared. In the case of physically intersexed infants, a given anomoly has been variously socially assigned as either male or female, and this social assignment may be more crucial for psychosexual development than any one of the five physical variables of sex (Money, 1970; Money, Hampson & Hampson, 1955; Zuger, 1970).

3. *Gender identity* is (*a*) normal when a child's self-concept is strongly male or female and matches one's physical sex status, (*b*) ambiguous or un-differentiated in the developmental period of infancy or in the later abnormal condition in which a firm and consistent self-concept as male or female is lacking, (*c*) conflicted when strong feelings of masculine and feminine identity coexist or alternate in a personality, or (*d*) cross-gender or transsexual in people with the strong belief that they are a member of the opposite physical sex than their physical sex status.

4. *Sex-role self-labeling behavior,* sometimes called *orientation,* refers to the person's self-assignment of a sex-role label, such as homosexual, bisexual, heterosexual or a similar label (such as queer or drag queen), which repre-sents the individual's own expectations for his or her gender role and sexual behaviors.

5. *Sexual arousal behavior* is most accurately assessed in children and adolescents in terms of specifying the particular stimulus objects for intra-personally experienced arousal and the magnitude and frequency of such arousal, rather than using general descriptive terms such as heterosexual, homo-sexual, bisexual, or a Kinsey Scale estimate.

6. *Gender role* describes the dimensions of masculine and feminine behav-iors, attitudes, and personality characteristics (Bem, 1974, 1975) in terms of sex-typing as masculine (high on masculine *and* low on feminine), feminine (low on masculine *and* high on feminine), undifferentiated (low on *both* mascu-line and feminine) or androgynous (high on *both* masculine and feminine).

7. *Genital sex behavior* is the history of sexual activity with males, females, both, and/or with animals or inanimate objects (e.g., with fetishism), which may differ from the individual's intrapsychic sexual arousal pattern or from the individual's gender identity or sex-role self-labeling behavior.

In the developmental periods of childhood and adolescence, any incongruity across any two of these seven psychosexual dimensions constitutes a source of psychological conflict with both present and potential future maladjustment. The major types of such psychopathology are gender disorders and sexual behavior disorders.

Range of Severity

Gender behavior disturbance is an incongruity across the dimensions of physical sex status and gender role behavior (Rosen, Rekers & Friar, 1977; Zucker, 1982). This disorder can be present in a child as young as three or four years of age and typically occurs in children with normal physical sex status (as measured by currently available biomedical testing reported by Rekers, Crandall, Rosen, and Bentler, 1979). Social sex assignment is typically congruent with physical sex status, although child rearing may include ambiguous messages to the young child regarding sex status. Gender identity may be normal, ambiguous, or conflicted, and sex-role self-labeling behavior is varied. Sexual arousal to cross-gender clothing may or may not be present, while other sexual arousal or sexual behavior patterns may be absent, unreported, or varied.

The distinguishing features of gender behavior disturbance in boys are any of the following recurring behaviors observed over 12 months or more: (a) taking a female role in play, (b) actual or improvised cross-dressing in feminine garments, (c) use of female cosmetics, (d) feminine-appearing gestures, (e) use of a high feminine-like voice inflection and/or predominantly feminine speech content, or (f) aversion to play activity with boys, coupled with preoccupation with feminine sex-typed activities and games (Rekers, 1972, 1977a, 1979, 1981a, 1984; Rekers, Amaro-Plotkin & Low, 1977; Rekers & Mead, 1979b; Rekers & Milner, 1978, 1979, 1981; Rekers & Rudy, 1978; Rekers, Sanders & Strauss, 1981; Rekers, Sanders, Strauss, Rasbury & Mead, in press; Rekers & Yates, 1976; Rosen et al., 1977).

The major extremes of gender behavior disturbance in boys are the chronic patterns of (a) excessive feminine behavioral rigidity or (b) pathological hypermasculinity (Harrington, 1970). Similarly, the chronic maladaptive patterns of girlhood gender role disturbance include the two extremes of (a) excessive masculine behavioral rigidity and (b) pathological hyperfemininity. But because of the greater gender role flexibility within the range of social acceptance for young girls, the diagnosis of gender behavior disturbance in girls is a more complex process that must distinguish between the normal transient phase of the tomboy role and the chronicity of deviant gender role patterns (see clinical considerations presented by Rekers, 1981b; Rekers & Mead, 1980; Rekers & Milner, 1979).

In adolescence, the gender behavior disturbance is most often observed as the early stages of simple transvestism (e.g., Bentler, 1968).

Gender identity disorder in childhood may first emerge in early childhood as a problem of ambiguous differentiation or conflicted identity and develops to be a cross-gender identification as early as age four or five years. This diagnosis involves an incongruity between physical sex status and gender identity and is also often accompanied with the same characteristics of a gender behavior disturbance (Rekers, 1981b, 1984; Rosen et al., 1977). In boys, gender identity disturbance is usually evidenced by (a) a stated desire to be a girl or a woman, (b) excessive female role taking, often including fantasies of sexual relations with a man, bearing infants, and breast-feeding infants, or (c) a request by the boy to have his penis removed (Greenson, 1966; Rekers, 1972, 1975, 1977a, 1981b; Rekers & Milner, 1978).

Clinical intervention is required for childhood gender disorders (Bates, Skilbeck, Smith & Bentler, 1975; Qualls, 1978; Braun and Rekers, 1981; Rekers, 1977b, 1978a, 1984; Rekers, Bentler, Rosen & Lovaas, 1977; Rekers & Mead, 1980; Rekers, et al., 1978; Rosen et al., 1978; Zuger, 1978). Adolescent cases of transvestism and transsexualism have also been successfully treated with behavior therapy (e.g., Barlow, Reynolds & Agras, 1973; Bentler, 1968).

Sexual Behavior Disorders

Numerous types of sexual behavior problems have been reported that constitute serious maladjustment problems in childhood and adolescence and/or place the individual at high risk for developing a chronic sexual deviation in adulthood (Rekers, 1978b, 1980). The clinician should differentiate these problems from gender identity disorder and diagnose any concurrent sexual behavior disorder with the gender disorder.

From early childhood to late adolescence, clinical assessment and psychotherapeutic intervention have been indicated for *excessive public masturbation* (Bitter-Lebert, 1956; Ferguson & Rekers, 1979; Gilbert, 1916; Levine & Bell, 1956; Rudolf, 1954; Stirt, 1940), *masturbation with ropes or objects* (Coe, 1974; Edmondson, 1972; Resnik, 1972; Shankel & Carr, 1956; Stearns, 1953), *object fetishes* (e.g., Bond & Evans, 1967; McGuire, Carlisle & Young, 1965; Mees, 1966; Salfield, 1957; Strzyewsky & Zierhoffe, 1967), *homosexual behavior* (Barlow, Agras, Abel, Blanchard & Young, 1975; Bentler, 1968; Callahan & Leitenberg, 1973; Canton-Dutari, 1974; Davison, Brierly & Smith, 1971; Gold and Neufeld, 1965; Herman, Barlow & Agras, 1974; Huff, 1970; Larson, 1970; MacCulloch & Feldman, 1967; McConaghy, 1969, 1970), *sexual assault behaviors* (e.g., Atcheson & Williams, 1954; Roberts, McBee & Bettis, 1969; Shoor, Speed, & Bartlett, 1966; Vanden Bergh & Kelly, 1964), *extreme anxiety over the process of puberty* (Brown, 1972; Grover, 1973; Hamelstein, 1974; Rekers & Jurich, 1983), delinquency or truancy involving *sexual acting out or prostitution* of children or adolescents (Craft, 1966; Deisher, 1970; Deisher, Eisner, & Sulzbacher, 1969; Gandy & Deisher, 1970; Ginsburg, 1967; Hackett, 1971; Hartmann, 1973; Mohr and Turner, 1967; Nadler, 1968; Pittman, 1971; Raven, 1963; Reiss, 1963; Roberts, Abrams, & Finch, 1973; Roberts, McBee and Bettis, 1969; Russell, 1971), *exhibitionistic behavior* (Callahan and Leitenbert, 1973; Hackett, 1971; Lowenstein, 1973; MacCulloch, Williams, and Birtles, 1971; Mohrl and Turner, 1967), *promiscuous sexual activity* (e.g., Anant, 1968; Zelnik and Kantner, 1972a, 1972b), *child molesting by an adolescent* (Shoor, Speed, and Bartlet, 1966), *victimization in sexual abuse* (Bender and Blau, 1937; Brunold, 1964; Langsley, Schwartz and Fairbairn, 1968; Mangus, 1932; Schultz, 1972, 1973; Weiss, Rogers, Darwin & Dutton, 1955), and *other sexual adjustment difficulties* (Brown, 1972; Grover, 1973; Hamelstein, 1974; Katzman, 1972; Mangus, 1953; Miller, 1973; Mosse, 1966; Salzman, 1974).

Associated Features

Boys and girls with gender disorders have been behaviorally observed to display a compulsive pattern of cross-sex behaviors coupled with a strong inhibition for same-sex-typed activities (Green, 1974; Green & Money, 1961, 1969; Rekers, Lovaas, & Low, 1974; Rekers & Mead, 1979, 1980; Stoller, 1968a, 1970), in striking contrast to the level of behavioral flexibility in sex-typed behavior that is systematically observed in normal boys and girls (Bates & Bentler, 1973; Rekers & Yates, 1976). A more adaptive psychological state is that in which the biologically mandated and appropriate social distinctions between male and female roles are mastered by the child, with sex-role flexibility and psychological androgyny for those behaviors, characteristics and attitudes which are beyond the basic, legitimate sex-role distinctions (Rekers, 1982b). The gender-disturbed child suffers from a number of associated features to their condition.

Because of the sharp dissonance between rigidly held cross-gender identification and the reality demands of everyday society, the child suffers maladjustment in the peer group, unhappiness, and often social rejection; tragically, many of these children are scapegoated with cruel and insulting labels such as "sissy," "fag," "queer," or "girly" (Green, 1974; Green, Newman, & Stoller, 1972; Rekers & Lovaas, 1974; Rekers, Willis, Yates, Rosen, & Low, 1977; Stoller, 1970). The gender-disturbed child's unhappiness, difficulty in forming close interpersonal peer relationships, detachment, isolation, and withdrawal do not appear to be simply a result of rigidly held social sex-role stereotypes in the peer group. Instead, the gender-disturbed child's personality itself manifests obsessive-compulsive trends, low self-esteem, and negativism. For example, Bates, Skilbeck, Smith, and Bentler (1974) conducted a systematic clinical study of 29 boys with gender disorders and found a lack of social skills and responsiveness, immaturity, and aversiveness in these children. This has paralleled the findings of others (e.g., Green, 1968; Rekers, 1981b; Zuger, 1970a).

Bates and his colleagues (1974) concluded, "certainly this feature of many of the children in the present group offers at least a partial explanation for their rejection by peers, other than for cross-gender behavior" (p. 10). Gender-disturbed girls appear to be relatively less likely than gender-disturbed boys to experience peer ridicule and rejection as a result of opposite sex-typed behavior (Saghir & Robins, 1973). However, many of these girls also suffer social alienation and social ostracism. The excessive physical aggressiveness of pretranssexual girls has been noted as receiving less social tolerance in girls than in boys (Money & Brennan, 1969). Because excessive physical aggression is maladaptive in boys, it is at least equally as maladaptive in the gender-disordered girls. Significant psychopathology has been reported in adolescent gender-disturbed girls, with approximately half of them also receiving concurrent diagnosis of aggressive personality (Kremer & Rifkin, 1969). Studies of adolescent girls with gender disturbance as well as retrospective reports of adults with gender deviance suggest that depression and even suicidal ideation are correlated with female gender disorders (Kenyon, 1968; Kremer & Rifkin, 1969).

Children with gender identity disorders are at high risk for adulthood psychological maladjustment as well (see extensive discussions elsewhere in Rekers, 1977; Rekers, Bentler, Rosen, and Lovaas, 1977; Rekers & Mead, 1980; Rekers et al., 1978; Rosen et al., 1978). Parents who seek treatment for their children with gender identity disorders typically are concerned about the child's overall social and psychological adjustment (Rekers, Bentler, Rosen & Lovaas, 1977).

In a study of boys with gender identity disorder, no abnormalities were detected in their medical history, physical examination, chromosome analysis, and sex chromatin studies (Rekers *et al.*, 1979). Gender identity disorder does not appear to be associated with differences in intelligence or verbal ability, although one controlled study found feminine boys had lower than average scores on a standard test of spatial ability (Finegan, Zucker, Bradley, & Doering, 1982).

THEORETICAL CONCEPTUALIZATION OF GENDER DEVELOPMENT

The sequence of gender development involves a complex interaction among biological, psychological, and social variables and can be conceptualized by analogy as a series of pathways in a relay race (see Money & Ehrhardt's 1972 literature review). The process is initiated when the X or Y sex chromosome supplied by the father's sperm cell is paired with the X chromosome from the mother's ovum. Next, the chromosomal combination (either the XX or the XY) takes a turn in this relay race by passing the program on to the undifferentiated gonad to determine its destiny as a testis or an ovary. Then after the gonad becomes differentiated as male or female, it subsequently passes the program on to the sex hormonal secretions by its own cells. Demonstrating the significance of this sequential relay race, research has discovered that in the total absence of fetal gonadal hormones, the fetus will inevitably develop the female reproductive anatomy regardless of chromosomal status.

After the gonad passes the program on to the secreted sex hormones, those hormones, in turn, are essential for the differentiation of the reproductive structures as male or female, for the shape of the external genitals, and for the patterns of organization in the brain that can influence future behavioral temperament. For example, Money and Ehrhardt (1972) have theoretically localized sex hormonal action as "the hypothalamic pathways that will subsequently influence certain aspects of sexual behavior" (p. 2).

At birth and after, the relay race proceeds in several directions simultaneously. First, at birth the child is socially identified as a boy or a girl, based on external sex anatomy. This transfer of the baton proceeds from genital recognition, to gender role assignment, to immediate major differences in the day-to-day practices of child rearing for boys and girls (see Rekers and Milner, 1979). Secondly, the sex hormones continue to influence physical development along another simultaneous relay race pathway by determining the greater muscle-to-fat ratio in boys, their increased basal metabolism, higher activity level (on the average), and greater aggression (on the average). Third, it has been theorized that the sex hormones have differentiated aspects of the central nervous system, which in turn, passes on the program accounting for behavioral tendencies that are culturally recognized as predominantly boyish or girlish (for example, certain behavioral mannerisms or carrying behaviors may be physically sex specific; see Rekers & Mead, 1979b; Rekers & Rudy, 1978). Furthermore, after birth, these three sources of sex differences inevitably interact both within individual gender development and in terms of the larger cultural expectations for gender stereotypy; for example, there may be biological sex differences observed socially across many individuals that are then culturally identified and elaborated in gender roles, which in turn, become stereotypic expectations reinforced in individuals by differential child rearing practices for boys and girls.

To generalize from all currently available research, the major contributions to gender development and sexual identity formation are derived in this relay race from the consequent day-to-day child-rearing practices differentially received by boys and girls. The most basic of these child-rearing components are (*a*) identification with a role modeling of the parent-figure and peers of the same sex, (*b*) development of complementary role behaviors toward members of the opposite sex, (*c*) differential expectations and social reinforcement for gender role behaviors, and (*d*) the child's recognition of and identification with his or her sexual anatomy and its reproductive function (see Maccoby & Jacklin, 1974; Money & Ehrhardt, 1972). For example, test pairs of hermaphroditic individuals matched chromosomally and gonadally and otherwise physically the same were studied in which one member of each pair had been socially reared as a boy and the other as a girl. Even though it was not possible to specify precise child-rearing variables and detailed cause-and-effect relationships among them, these studies did suggest that socialization aspects of child rearing were stronger variables in gender development and sexual identity formation than any physical variable of sex (Money, Hampson & Hampson, 1955).

While basic gender development occurs in early childhood, a later sequence in the relay race is also of major significance. The onset of hormonal changes in puberty brings about the secondary sexual characteristics and sexual maturity, which psychologically confirm the individual's sense of sexual identity or provide a source of emotional conflict in some individuals with incongruent gender development.

ETIOLOGICAL FACTORS AND FAMILY PATTERNS

In this relay race of gender differentiation, abnormalities along any of these pathways may contribute etiologically to forms of psychopathology. While the individual's socialization experiences are primarily implicated in the etiology of many forms of psychopathology in childhood and adolescence, we must entertain the possibility that some degree of prenatally determined disposition might make certain children more vulnerable to specific psychological disorders (Baker & Stoller, 1968; Green, 1979; Stoller, 1968, 1975), even though we may not be able to measure such variables with current methods of biomedical testing (Doering, 1981). To the extent that some genetic vulnerability factors may be carried by the sex chromosome, there may be a theoretical basis for a relationship between some forms of psychopathology with gender status. Such a biological link may be mediated indirectly through any number of these pathways, which include biological, psychological, social, and interactional variables.

The precise interactions of the variables involved in the etiology of deviant psychosexual development are not yet fully understood (Bentler, 1976; Money, 1970a, 1970b; Money and Ehrhardt, 1972; Rosen, 1969; Zuger, 1970a, 1970b). While no completely reliable scientific data exists on the differential etiology of these various psychosexual abnormalities, investigators in this area have posited plausible developmental theories (for example, Bradley, Steiner, Zucker, Doering, Sullivan, Finegan, and Richardson, 1978). Bentler (1976) has formulated a theory of sexual identity development in the context of a thorough review of the available data.

It is generally held that the main source for gender and sexual behavior deviance can be found in social learning variables (e.g., Ehrhardt, 1979; Meyer-Bahlburg, 1977, 1980), although it has been recognized that there is a theoretical possibility that biological abnormalities could be a potential contributing vulnerability factor (e.g., Dorner, Rhode, Stahl, Krell & Masius, 1975; Ehrhardt & Baker, 1974; Hutt, 1978; Money & Schwartz, 1976). Even though little has been published on the direct study of causes of psychosexual deviation, a body of established findings can be theoretically integrated that will provide a basis for understanding the probable etiology of psychosexual disorders. For example, Rekers, Mead, Rosen and Brigham (1983) conducted a study of fathers, father-substitutes, and older male siblings of 46 boys with gender disturbances. Significantly fewer male role models were found in the family backgrounds of the severely gender-disturbed boys as compared to the mild-to-moderately gender-disturbed boys. This study, in conjunction with the literature on normal sex-role development (see review by Mead & Rekers, 1979), suggests a pattern of father absence may be coupled with other family patterns to contribute etiologically to gender identity disorders.

A substantial body of evidence has accumulated regarding the developmental outcome for children with gender disorders. Childhood gender identity and gender role deviations are strongly predictive of homosexual orientation disturbance, transsexualism, or transvestism in adulthood (Bender & Paster, 1941; Green, 1974, 1979; Green & Money, 1961, 1969; Pauley, 1969; Qualls, 1978; Rekers, 1977b, 1981, in press-a, in press-b, in press-c, Stoller, 1967, 1968a, 1968b, 1970). Retrospective as well as prospective data exist on this question. A number of investigators have found that a majority of adult transsexuals and transvestites make the retrospective report that their cross-gender behavior and identity began in early childhood (Green, 1974; Money & Primrose, 1968; Prince & Bentler, 1972; Walinder, 1967; Zuger, 1966). Effeminate behavior in childhood is also retrospectively reported by adult male homosexuals (Bieber, Dain, Dince, Drellich, Grand, Gundlach, Kremer, Ritkin, Wilbur, & Bieber, 1962; Evans, 1969; Holemon & Winokur, 1965; Whitam, 1977) and adult male transsexuals (Benjamin, 1966; Bentler, 1976; Bentler & Prince, 1970; Green & Money, 1969).

The available prospective longitudinal data indicate that effeminate behavior in boys is fairly predictive of male homosexuality (Bakwin, 1968; Green, 1974, 1979; Lebovitz, 1972; Zuger, 1966, 1970a, 1978; Zuger and Taylor, 1969; Money and Russo, 1978). Furthermore, Zuger's (1978) long-term, 20-year prospective follow-up of a small sample of untreated gender-disturbed boys found 63 percent to be homosexual, 12 percent to be heterosexual, 6 percent to be transvestite, and 6 percent to be transsexual. He also found that 25 percent attempted suicide, and 6 percent actually committed suicide. Overall, the various prospective studies indicate that from 40 percent to 75 percent of gender-disturbed boys develop deviant sexual adult behavior patterns. Based on both the retrospective studies as well as the prospective longitudinal studies, the best scientific prediction is that gender disturbance in boys places them at very high risk for homosexuality, transsexualism, or transvestism as contrasted to normal heterosexual development.

Even though overt sexual behaviors per se are not differential diagnostic criteria for childhood gender disorders, as the gender-disturbed child moves into adolescence, the abnormal sex-role development leads to heterosocial dating deficits, which, in turn, may contribute to the development of deviant sexual patterns, such as homosexual or transvestite arousal patterns or transsexualism. The gender-disordered child is poorly prepared to make a normal heterosexual adjustment. For example, peers typically label the effeminate boy as a homosexual ("fag" or "queer"). The feminine behavioral presentation of these boys results in a greater number of homosexual advances experienced by the gender-disordered boy. Such a child can internalize such social labels and, therefore, be more vulnerable to the temptation of homosexual activity than most same-aged peers.

Feeling different from other normal heterosexual peers can contribute to resignation to a deviant sexual behavior pattern (Rekers, 1982a). Therefore, some gender-disturbed boys may experiment with homosexual behavior that most same-aged peers would reject as unacceptable. Participation in homosexual behavior then constitutes a behavior pattern reinforced by the sexual gratification involved. Other gender-disordered boys may retreat to secluded privacy where solitary masturbation becomes repeatedly paired with cross dressing, often resulting in an atypical, fixated form of transvestite or transsexual fantasy.

Therefore, the etiology of the various psychosexual disorders involves many individual developmental sequences involving early sex typing, early gender identification, childhood gender adjustment, and a chain of choices made in adolescence. Hence, the adulthood sexual dysphoria of the individual results from an accumulation of a long series of psychological, social, and moral developmental experiences (Braun & Rekers, 1981; Rekers, 1982a, 1982b).

Child development research on normal child populations as well as clinical data on children referred for a variety of personality and functional disorders indicate that the nature of sex differences is not merely topological. Three variables are implicated in the etiology of gender disorders in children. First, hormonal factors and the associated neurological and structural differences may predispose the child toward certain responses to his/her environment, although existing research is ambiguous and not definitive in this area. Second, certain temperamental characteristics relatively more common in individual children may contribute to the likelihood of certain types of disturbances that develop as a result of the interaction of the child's temperamental predisposition and the nature of the response of the child's primary caretakers to the temperament of the child. Third, gender identity disturbances that typically occur in children who are otherwise physically normal by current medical testing are significantly influenced by socialization practices of the primary caretakers who model and differentially reinforce culturally accepted behaviors for boys and girls. When the gender role behaviors are inappropriately or inconsistently modeled or reinforced, disturbances may result.

No one variable is sufficient in itself to predict the development of disturbed behavior; however, research strongly indicates these three sets of variables must be addressed in any interactional model that attempts to describe and predict childhood gender identity disorders.

In spite of genuine methodological challenges in efforts to ascertain the precise etiological sequences, profound and significant relationships clearly exist between variables of gender and psychopathology in childhood and adolescent development. Taken separately, *sexuality, gender differences,* and *psychopathology* have been among the most salient and intriguing elements of human experience for study throughout the ages of history. The attempt to understand how these three aspects interact in the development of the human personality from childhood through adolescence to adulthood is perhaps one of the boldest and most complex endeavors of human scholarship. The age-old philosophical questions pertaining to the influences of heredity, environmental determination, and freedom of human moral choices all converge in the study of the development of gender and psychopathology (Schumm & Rekers, 1984).

Perhaps relatively more remains to be discovered than is presently understood on how maleness and femaleness relate to psychological normality and abnormality in developing children.

ASSESSMENT

Experimental intrasubject studies have found that the occurrence of masculine and feminine behaviors in cross-gender identified boys will differ in the various conditions of being alone in the playroom, being with the mother or father, or being with a male or a female examiner (Rekers, 1975). In a clinic setting, the only condition that was reliably correlated with the clinical diagnosis of gender identity disorder was the "alone" condition, in which the child's sex-typed play was observed from behind a one-way mirror. Furthermore, the occurrence and frequency of various masculine and feminine sex-typed behaviors will differ in the child's major living environments, including the home and school classroom settings. The sex-role behavior deviance of gender-disturbed children is characterized by a stimulus specificity and by a response specificity of sex-typed masculine and feminine behaviors (Rekers, 1975). The assessment of gender identity disorder in childhood is complicated by the finding that the occurrence of cross-sex behaviors does not represent a simple function of a generalized response disposition (Rekers, 1977a).

Therefore, it is advisable for the clinician to assess the child's ratio of masculine to feminine sex-typed behaviors in all the child's major in vivo living environments. This multisetting analysis should include a variety of assessment methods, including behavioral observations, interviews of the child, parents, siblings, teachers and relatives, and the use of a variety of psychological assessment procedures. The sources relevant to the assessment process have been reviewed in detail by Rosen et al. (1977), who include the following in the assessment of gender disturbances in children: the situational and temporal contexts of gender identity statements, sex role-play behavior patterns, frequency of cross-dressing behavior, parent-child relationship variables, parental reaction to masculine and feminine sex-role behaviors, characteristics of the physical appearance of the child, presence or absence of other psychological deviance, and the interaction among these various variables.

Because the detailed assessment procedures and diagnostic issues have been reviewed in detail elsewhere (Rekers, 1981b), a briefer clinical summary of assessment issues and procedures will be presented here.

As a practical issue, the clinician should realize that, as children become older, they become increasingly aware of the socially defined sex roles and gain an ability to discriminate masculine and feminine behaviors in their own and others' behaviors. Consequently, children under six years of age are more likely to overtly display deviant sex-role behaviors in the clinic setting, whereas older children may deliberately inhibit the performance of deviant sex-role behaviors in the clinic setting, particularly if they are aware of the reason for referral to the clinician. Because of the cultural taboos associated with cross-sex behavior or identity, the self-conscious older child may not openly reveal verbal or nonverbal indicators of a gender identity disorder. However, some sex-role behaviors may have more diagnostic significance than others in evaluating the older child. For example, intrasubject studies by Rekers and his colleagues (Rekers, 1981b; Rekers, Yates, Willis, Rosen, & Taubman, 1976) indicate that cross-gender identified boys are typically not able to discriminate or suppress their feminine-appearing hand and arm gestures and body mannerisms. In all cases, it is diagnostically helpful to collect data not only in the clinic setting, but also in the home and school settings if possible and if appropriate.

Assessment in the Clinic

It is helpful to interview or observe the child alone as well as conjointly with the mother and father, where possible, to observe mother-child interaction, father-child interaction, and parental responses to this child's sex-typed behaviors. It is useful to ask the child to provide the first names of friends at school and in the home neighborhood because the ratio of male to female names of playmates can be indicative of peer preferences and/or social acceptance of the child. Inquiry into friendship patterns, relationships with peers, favorite games and activities, and any peer relationship difficulties helps to differentiate gender preferences. After rapport has been established, it is appropriate to assess the child's knowledge of the physical differences between the sexes as well as the child's knowledge regarding reproductive anatomy and sexual behavior.

Rekers et al. (1974) describe their procedure whereby a clinician may spend the initial 20 minutes of an interview in a baseline condition in which the clinician limits verbal responses to short, nonleading, and direct answers to the child's questions, which allows later scoring of the 20 minutes of the verbal behavior for sex-typed verbal content and voice inflection. It is possible to assess the taped verbal interaction in terms of the child's speech in neutral, masculine, and feminine categories as well as to assess degree of cross-gender voice inflection (see also Rekers & Mead, 1979, for a similar procedure with gender disturbed girls).

Other questions that have had clinical utility are the following: What are your favorite subjects and activities at school? If you could have three wishes, what would you wish for? How often do you feel like a girl? How often do you feel like a boy? Are you more like your mom or more like your dad? How often do other kids call you names? What do they call you? What are your favorite things to do when you have free time?

Rekers (1972; Rekers & Yates, 1976) developed a behavioral play assessment procedure in which specific sets of masculine and feminine toys are made available for the child to play with in five different social stimulus conditions: while the child is alone in a playroom (but observed from behind one-way mirror), with the mother, the father, male and female clinicians present. This procedure has been replicated and validated by Zucker, Doering, Bradley, and Finegan (1982) who found the procedure to have diagnostic utility. Even without the specific set of masculine and feminine toys used in that procedure, similar toys from a standard clinic playroom could be used, and stop watches could be used to record cumulative seconds of masculine play and cumulative seconds of contact with feminine toys in a free-play situation in which the child is told that he or she can play with any of the toys. The masculine and feminine sex-typed toys used in these studies were articles such as girls' cosmetic articles and apparel, toy jewelry sets, baby dolls and accessories, as well as boys' apparel, football helmet, army helmet and accessories, battery-operated play electric razor, dart guns, and a set of plastic cowboys and Indians. Zucker et al. (1982) found that if one required a child to obtain a 70 to 30 ratio of cross-sex play to same-sex play before considering the pattern deviant, the finding of "false positives" would be rare, although the assessment task may be more vulnerable to instances of "false negatives" (replicating the finding of Rekers & Yates, 1976).

Sex differences have been documented in body gestures and behavioral mannerisms (Birdwhistell, 1970; Jenni, 1976; Jenni & Jenni, 1976; Rekers & Mead, 1979), and the early childhood years have been found to be formative in the development of a child's repertoire of gestures and characteristics of body position and movement (Michael & Willis, 1968). Effeminate-appearing gestures and behavioral mannerisms have been behaviorally defined and systematically observed in gender-disturbed boys (Rekers, 1977a), and the frequency of occurrence of these same gestures have been documented for the normal population of boys and girls in age groups from four to seventeen years of age (Rekers, Amaro-Plotkin, & Low, 1977; Rekers & Rudy, 1978; Rekers et al., 1981). In the clinical evaluation of boys referred for a potential gender identity disorder, it is helpful to make a behavioral assessment of these mannerisms and gestures that were found to occur significantly more frequently in normal girls than in normal boys:

1. *Limp wrist:* operationally defined as flexing the wrist toward the palmar surface of the forearm or upper arm, while the elbow is either flexed or extended.
2. *Arm flutters:* rapid up-and-down movements of the forearm and/or the upper arm, while the wrist remains relaxed.
3. *Flexed elbow:* walking or standing with the arm(s) held such that the angle between the forearm and the upper arm is between 0 and 135° (approximately).
4. *Hand clasp:* touching the hands together in front of the body.
5. *Palming:* touching the palm(s) to the back, front, or sides of the head above the ear level.

One gesture, "hands-on-hips with fingers-forward" (defined as resting the palm or palms on the waist or hips with fingers pointed forward) was found significantly more frequently in 10- to-11-year-old boys than in younger boys and in the girls of all the childhood age groups. Relevant to the assessment procedure, these studies did not discover any significant group differences attributable to the sex of the experimenter present during the assessment procedure. (For further detail in assessing gestures and mannerisms, the clinician is referred to the table of group means and standard deviations for the five feminine gestures and the single masculine gesture in the study by Rekers and Rudy [1978].). In the normal girls comparison group, the frequency of these gestures is generally low so that even a moderate frequency rate for these behaviors would mark a girl and would especially mark a boy who appears different to the point of potentially provoking the peer ridicule that is typically suffered by boys with gender identity disturbance. Clinically, it has been found that the effeminate behavioral mannerisms displayed by gender-disturbed boys are not only at a much higher rate than similar behaviors found in normal girls, but also the performance of these gestures constitute a caricature of femininity that is different from the same clusters of behaviors found in the normal population (Rekers, 1981b). Furthermore, the occurrence of these feminine-appearing mannerisms and gestures are apparently quite stable in gender-disturbed boys, even though they evoke heavy peer criticism and even in cases in which the child desires to change or suppress the occurrence of any behaviors that evoke such peer criticism (Rekers, 1977a). Rekers, Willis, Yates, Rosen, and Low (1977) found that a gender-disturbed boy could not discriminate his sex-typed gestures and mannerisms accurately.

Another quick and useful behavioral observation of the child in the clinic would be to ask the child to carry a book, due to the large sex differences that have been reported for book-carrying behavior in children, adolescence, and adults (Hanaway & Burghardt, 1976; Jenni & Jenni, 1976; Rekers & Mead, 1979b). Normal females generally carry books against their bodies with one or both arms, whereas normal males typically carry their books to their side in one hand. Not only have these sex differences been demonstrated regardless of the grip strength of the individual, the size of the load to be carried, or the book weight, but these sex differences have also been reported to be quite consistent both within individuals and across cultures (Jenni, 1976; Spottswood & Burghardt, 1976).

The interview with the child's parents, both individually and conjointly, provides a developmental history and description of the child, which is necessary to evaluate the severity of the potential gender identity disorder. The age of the onset of the cross-gender behavior is of interpretive importance in that gender identification normally begins to develop around the ages of one and a half to two years and is typically established by age five years. If a pattern of deviant sex-typed behavior did not occur historically until age eight or later, it is relatively less likely that a true gender identity disorder is present, although another form of gender disturbance is possible. In addition to standard developmental inquiry, it is recommended that the clinician obtain information from the parents in the following areas: current and retrospective estimates derived from the parents on the behavior rate frequencies of a large number of feminine, masculine, and neutral sex-typed behaviors; recollection of the parents' early acceptance or nonacceptance or ambivalence toward the child's sex at time of birth and in early childhood; report on the father-child relationship, mother-child relationship, and husband-wife relationship throughout the child's lifetime; a report on their own reactions to sex-typed behaviors in terms of potential positive, negative, or neutral reactions; an assessment of the parents' perceptions of the child's overall behavioral assets, excesses, and deficits; an investigation of the parental attitude toward sex-typed behaviors (some parents report that cross-gender behavior is amusing, is considered innate, or is consciously or unconsciously encouraged).

Clinical psychological tests provide useful assessment information. Screening for deficits in intellectual functioning can determine whether or not a mental deficiency may or may not contribute to the normal sex-role learning process of childhood. Human figure drawings are of potential diagnostic significance because the majority of normal children have been reported to draw a person of their own sex (Jolles, 1952), whereas the drawing of a female figure by boys is moderately predictive of childhood gender disturbance (Green, Fuller, & Rutley, 1972). Another study found that, in response to a draw-a-person instruction, gender-disturbed boys, as contrasted to school-problem boys, were more likely (1) to draw a female figure, (2) to draw their female figure larger than a requested male figure, (3) to draw more articles of clothing on the figures, and (4) to draw figures with enhanced body proportion (Skilbeck, Bates, & Bentler, 1975). Human figure drawing should not be interpreted independently from other data sources, such as in vivo play observations and parent report data, because there is some variability of scores in gender-problem and school-problem comparison groups, even though there does appear to be some construct validity for using the Draw-a-Person Test for diagnosing gender identity disorders.

The Schneidman Make-a-Picture Story Test has been used in a modified format whereby the ratio of the total male to female figures in the stories generated by the child is calculated, and the sex of the main characters in the stories are noted (Rosen et al., 1977). The Family Relations Test (Bene & Anthony, 1957) has also been used to obtain a quantitative measure of the child's reported feelings toward each member of the family. Rosen et al. (1977) recommends noting the correlation between the gender of each family member and the child's incoming and outgoing feelings for them. A gender identity disorder may be more likely to exist in those cases in which this data indicates a lack of involvement with the father coupled with a relatively high degree of involvement and dependence on the mother in the test scores (Rosen et al., 1977;

Rosen & Teague, 1974). In cases in which the parents report sexual behavior, a variety of additional assessment procedures may be considered (see detailed review in Rekers, 1981b).

Assessment in the Home Setting

Parents and external observers can be used to obtain an assessment of the child's gender-role behavior in the home setting. Behavior checklists can be individually designed for a systematic behavioral recording using time-sampling procedures. These checklists can include such sex-typed behaviors as "play with girls," "play with boys," "play with dolls," "cross-dressing," "taking female roles in play," "taking male roles in play," and specifically named feminine or masculine gestures (Rekers & Lovaas, 1974; Rekers et al., 1974; Rekers, Willis, Yates, Rosen, & Low, 1977). The parent can be instructed to make recordings, for example, for 10 minutes at a time at specific times twice or three times daily. External observers can be sent to the home to make simultaneous recordings to assess observer reliability. Over a three-week period, an adequate baseline frequency of these behaviors can be determined. Intrasubject studies have indicated that some sex-typed behaviors are more difficult for the parents to record than trained clinical observers: masculine content versus feminine content in speech, feminine voice inflection, masculine voice inflection, and specific subtypes of sex-typed behavior mannerisms and body gestures as operationally defined above (Rekers et al., 1974; Rekers, Willis, Yates, Rosen & Low, 1977).

Together with the direct observational recordings, two parent-report inventories are useful for diagnostic purposes: the Child Game Participation Questionnaire (based on the data from normal and gender-disturbed boys reported in Bates & Bentler, 1973) and the Child Behavior and Attitude Questionnaire (based on the research on normal and gender-disturbed boys reported in Bates et al., 1973). Those publications provide the questionnaire items and scoring procedures, and the clinical application of that data to the total diagnostic process has been described by Bentler, Rekers and Rosen (1979).

Assessment in the School Setting

The clinician needs to be sensitive to avoid unnecessarily compounding the child's problem by contacts with the school, which might lead to harmful labeling of a child in that setting (Rekers, 1984b). However, if the school has already contacted the parents regarding a potential gender disturbance or has referred the child to the clinician, then it would be useful to send trained behavioral observers to the school setting to make unobtrusive observation of the child's sex-typed behaviors or to train the teacher to make simple time-sampled recordings of behaviors, such as cross-dressing, feminine mannerisms and gestures, feminine and masculine voice inflection, and feminine content in speech versus masculine content in speech. External observers can pose as student teachers to make ratings on an individual child in the classroom, particularly if there is concern regarding adversely labeling a child as gender disturbed for a teacher who may be yet unaware of any potential difficulty. This would require permission and cooperation from school administrators, who might designate to the teacher a list of children who are being observed, with the target child in one set of observed children.

While reliable observational data has been obtained from both teachers and external observers in the school classroom (Rekers et al., 1974; Rekers & Varni, 1977b), an alternative procedure would require the parent to request a teacher conference and to inquire about the child's social adjustment and peer relationships in the school. Included here should be questions regarding the child's level of motivation and actual participation in physical education activities. Gender-disturbed boys, for example, typically dislike and withdraw from physical sports activities.

Differential Diagnosis

The DSM-III diagnostic criteria for gender identity disorder in girls include the following: (1) a persistent insistence that they are really boys or strongly desire to be boys, as distinguished from merely expressing a desire for perceived cultural advantages granted to males; (2) evidence of chronic repudiation of their female anatomies, as evidenced by at least one of the following types of repeated assertions: (a) that they will grow up to actually become men, (b) that they are physically unable to become pregnant, (c) that they will not in fact develop breasts, (d) that they have no vagina, or (e) that they will grow or have a penis; and (3) an onset of this pattern before puberty.

The DSM-III diagnostic criteria for gender identity disorder in boys are the following: (1) a persistent insistence that they are girls or strongly stated desires to be girls; (2) either (a) a preoccupation with feminine stereotyped activities as manifested by cross-dressing, simulated play acting of feminine attire, or a compulsive desire to participate in the games and pastimes of girls, or (b) a persistent repudiation of their male anatomies, as evidenced by at least one of the following repeated assertions: that they will in fact grow up to become women, that their penis or testes will disappear or are disgusting to them or that it would be better not to have a penis or testes; and (c) an onset of this pattern before puberty.

In the current diagnostic system, if these patterns of gender disturbance in boys or girls occur after the onset of puberty in an adolescent child, the diagnosis of "Atypical Gender Identity Disorder" is considered.

The developmental variables that influence diagnostic decisions, the reliability and validity of a diagnostic model, and diagnostic precision are important prerequisites for making treatment decisions. The DSM-III includes a psychosexual disorder for childhood for the first time. While this is a step forward, there are, nevertheless, a number of problems with the diagnostic category as it is described in *DSM-III* (see Bentler, 1976; Bentler et al., 1979; Rekers & Mead, 1980; Rosen et al., 1977; Stoller, 1968a, 1978; Zucker, 1982; Zucker, Finegan, Doering, & Bradley, 1984).

A positive diagnosis for a gender identity disorder should not be based on parental reports alone, but should be based on behavioral assessment data, clinical interview, psychological testing, and, where possible, direct observation of the child in major living environments. The simple rate of occurrence of a given sex-typed behavior, if considered alone, would not necessarily be sufficient to warrant the diagnosis. Instead, the clinical diagnostician should consider the ratio of the frequencies of masculine and feminine sex-typed behaviors, the number of different cross-sex behaviors, the chronicity of the pattern, the situational contexts for the behavior pattern, the child's own verbalized perceptions regarding his or her behavior and identity, the reaction of parents and peers to the child's sex-type behavior in a cultural setting, and the overall psychological adjustment of the child. Clinicians will find it helpful to summarize the accumulated assessment information for an individual child in terms of the outline of the various psychosexual dimensions defined above: physical sex status; social sex assignments; gender identity; sex-role self-labeling behavior; sexual arousal behavior; gender role; and genital sex behavior (see Rosen and Rekers, 1980).

Bentler, Rekers, and Rosen (1979) described a procedure used in a study of 38 gender-disturbed children aged 4 to 12 years of age in which data from a variety of clinical assessment procedures were integrated by three clinicians from psychodynamic, behavioral, and psychometric perspectives. Separate ratings were made on sex-role behavior disturbance and gender identity disturbance. The clinician can combine all assessment information to rate a child on sex-role behavior disturbance ranging from extreme sex-role behavior disturbance, through marked, moderate, mild, to no sex-role behavior disturbance. Similarly, a rating can be made on a scale of gender identity disturbance: (1) profound cross-gender identification, (2) moderate cross-gender identification, (3) gender identity confusion, (4) moderate gender identity confusion, and (5) normal gender identification.

The meaning of the sex-typed behavior to the child is critically important (Rekers, 1977a). For instance, nurturant behavior in a boy is normal and desirable, but if nurturant play acting with a baby doll is accompanied by verbalizations of a female identity, it becomes deviant and maladaptive.

Three diagnostic models have been developed for clinical use with children referred for gender-disturbance: Stoller's (e.g., 1968, 1975) diagnosis of "male childhood transsexualism"; the Rosen et al. (1977) distinction between "cross-gender identification" and "gender behavior disturbance"; and the more recent DSM-III diagnosis of gender identity disorder of childhood. Further research is necessary to assess the differential reliability and validity of these three diagnostic models (Zucker, 1982). However, a number of important distinctions for the practicing clinician can be noted for current clinical practice. First, most cross-gender identified boys and girls appear to know the reality of their anatomical status, although they wish to be biologically the other sex. Some of the younger boys, however, may claim that they are actually girls (Zucker, 1982).

Secondly, although the DSM-III diagnostic criterion number two for boys allows for either a strong preference for stereotypic feminine activities and/or evidence of anatomic dysphoria, the feminine behavior pattern is more often observed. Gender-disturbed boys who do show anatomic dysphoria typically do not deny the fact that they possess male genitals, but they sometimes have been reported by their parents to have repeatedly tucked their penis between their legs to pretend that they have a vagina as though they were girls. One of the most common indicators of an anatomic dysphoria in a boy is his preference to sit rather than to stand when urinating (e.g., Stoller, 1968).

Third, the DSM-III diagnostic criteria for girls is quite different than that for boys in that it does not give this kind of optional pattern in which girls' preoccupation with boys' stereotypic activities could be observed rather than their anatomic dysphoria. Furthermore, the diagnostic system of DSM-III for gender-disturbed girls does not describe *feelings* of aversion for one's sexual anatomy as does the criteria for boys; instead, only statements that deny present reality or future reality of the girl's anatomy or biological capabilities are accepted as evidence of a gender identity disturbance. See Zucker (1982) for a detailed discussion of the problems of the DSM-III diagnostic criteria, particularly those for girls.

The earlier proposal for a diagnosis of cross-gender identification by Rosen et al. (1977) parallels the DSM-III diagnosis of gender identity disorder of childhood. However, Rosen et al. also describe another subgroup of gender-problem boys. In this case, a boy demonstrated a cross-gender behavior pattern without a "strongly and persistently stated desire to be a girl or insistence that he is a girl" (DSM-III, p. 266). There does appear to be another subgroup of gender behavior disorders of children who are disturbed but do not necessarily fit DSM-III diagnostic category of gender identity disorders of childhood (Rekers, 1981b; Zucker, Finegan, Doering, & Bradley, 1984).

Until more diagnostic research and more longitudinal clinical research data are available, the psychodiagnosis of the various childhood gender problems must be rooted in a consideration of the comprehensive assessment collected on the individual child, as compared to the existing data available on the limited prospective studies on untreated child cases followed longitudinally (Green, 1979; Money & Russo, 1979; Zuger, 1978), the data obtained retrospectively from adulthood cases of gender dysphoria and sexual deviation, and developmental theory (see Rekers, 1981b for a detailed review of diagnostic issues and procedures).

TREATMENT

Individual psychotherapy, group therapy, and behavior therapy approaches have been reported for the treatment of childhood gender disorders. Greenson (1966,

1968) presented a summary of his clinical notes of a psychoanalytic treatment of a "transvestite boy" who was five years old at the onset of treatment. Dupont (1968) provided a description of his treatment of a mild transvestite behavior pattern in an eight-year-old boy. In this case, rather than treating the boy or his mother, the clinician met for a single session with the father, who agreed to stop his verbal and physical punishment for the effeminate behavior and give the boy his attention and affection contingent on a normal masculine behavior pattern. Although no systematic data were presented for this uncontrolled case study, Dupont did report that after this single therapy session, the parents observed no further transvestite behavior in the boy during the next 12 years.

Bentler (1968) successfully treated three boys, 11, 13 and 16 years old, with weekly individual therapy sessions. Therapy consisted of systematic verbal disapproval for effeminate behavior, encouragement of conversation about heterosexual dating, social skill rehearsal of social interaction with female peers, encouragement of heterosexual encounters, and direction to change the content of fantasy accompanying masturbation from transvestite to heterosexual themes. After 4 to 12 months of weekly therapy sessions, cross-dressing ceased, masturbation with heterosexual fantasy increased, and masculine interest increased, along with an increase in social dating. No follow-up evaluation is available for these children.

Stoller's (1970) psychotherapy for extremely feminine boys was conceptualized as "re-education" rather than an emphasis on insight. He emphasized the clinical necessity of involving mothers and fathers in the treatment process. Green, Newman, and Stoller (1972) provide additional case material on the boys described by Stoller. These therapists described the psychotherapy procedure involving (1) the development of a close relationship between the therapist and the boy, (2) intervening for parental encouragement of feminine behavior, (3) altering the abnormally close relationship between son and mother, (4) developing a closer and more appropriate father-son relationship, and (5) enhancing the father's role in the family. Five cases were reported of boys, ages 5 to 12 years, and the clinical report indicated treatment success ranging from modest change to considerable shift in gender-role orientation.

Two sets of investigators reported group therapy for childhood gender disturbance in boys. Green (1974; Green & Fuller, 1973) summarized the treatment of several very feminine young boys between the ages of four and nine years who were seen on a weekly basis for one year. Available mothers and fathers were treated in a separate group. No reliability data were obtained on behavioral ratings made by parents before and after treatment, and thus, an empirical evaluation of the results of this treatment is not possible, although the authors discussed their own difficulties in evaluating the treatment success in their anecdotal report.

Bates et al. (1975) conducted group therapy sessions with gender-disturbed boys in which masculine and prosocial behaviors were systematically enforced with structured point-economy systems and individual behavioral charting. Concurrent parents' groups had the goal of increasing parents' cooperative behavior and encouraging the use of behavioral intervention strategies in the home. The results were suggestive, even though no systematic or objective outcome measures were employed.

The only treatment techniques that have demonstrated to have been effective with experimental research have been applications of various behavior therapy procedures by Rekers and colleagues. ABA reversal designs and multiple baseline designs were used in a series of intrasubject experimental studies of the treatment effects (Rekers, 1977a, 1978b, 1983).

Behavior Therapy Procedures

Behavior therapy procedures have been designed in ways to maximize the probability of generalization and maintenance of the therapeutic effects (Rekers, 1977a). Although some of the more complex techniques of behavior shaping and discrimination training for sex-typed gestures and mannerisms require the professional skills of the clinician, many of the other objectives of a social-learning-based therapy can best be accomplished by training the child's parent or teacher to carry out behavioral interventions in the home and school environments. Theoretically, extending treatment to the in vivo living environments of the child will promote greater treatment generalization. If the initial assessment demonstrated that the child's cross-gender play behavior is more predominant in the presence of one parent than the other, then that parent might be appropriately recruited to be one of the main therapists in the home environment.

In play therapy sessions in the clinic, the clinician can demonstrate to the parents (preferably behind a one-way mirror) how to socially reinforce appropriate sex-typed play by attending to it and giving verbal reinforcement as well as how to decrease inappropriate and maladaptive cross-sex-typed play by ignoring it and putting it on "extinction." The therapist then can closely observe and supervise the parents' learning of behavior-shaping skills in the play settings by asking the parents to join in the therapy session in the clinic setting. This procedure requires that a variety of masculine and feminine sex-typed toys be in the playroom. When available, it has been demonstrated that a "bug-in-the-ear" receiver worn by the parent can help the therapist communicate to the parent with the child in the room, while the therapist observes from behind a one-way mirror. The parent can be given a large magazine to hold and can be provided the specific instructions to attend to the child's appropriate sex-typed verbal and play behavior by smiling and complimenting the child's play, but to ignore sex-inappropriate gender behavior by picking up the magazine to read. The parent should be verbally praised for carrying out the procedure correctly and prompting can be gradually faded out. Intrasubject replication designs, using ABA reversal, have demonstrated these procedures are successful in decreasing predominantly feminine play and verbal behavior and in increasing appropriate masculine play in boys (Rekers & Lovaas, 1974; Rekers et al. 1976; Rekers, 1972, 1979).

In a variation of this procedure, Rekers and Varni (1977a, 1977b) taught young gender-disturbed boys to monitor their own gender role behavior using a wrist counter (the type commonly used to keep golf scores). The child was instructed to press the wrist counter only when playing with boys' toys, although he was told he could play with any of the masculine or feminine toys while alone in the playroom. The therapist verbally labeled each toy in the room as being either a boys' or a girls' toy. The "bug-in-ear" device was used in some sessions to reinforce the child for correct observance of these instructions and to prompt him to press the wrist counter. This behavioral cuing procedure was gradually faded out, and the self-reinforcement contingency was found to be effective in decreasing compulsive feminine play behavior. With this self-control procedure, it is possible to let the child take the wrist-counter home with him to use in his normal living surroundings in the same manner.

This same self-monitoring procedure was demonstrated by Rekers and Mead (1979a) to be effective in treating an eight-year-old girl with a cross-gender identification.

In addition to a compulsive pattern of cross-sex play with toys, the clinician needs to intervene for sex-typed speech patterns and cross-gender gestures and mannerisms. Rekers and colleagues (1974) described a procedure in which a highly verbal eight-year-old boy was treated for sex-typed speech. Using an ABA reversal design, a behavior therapist differentially reinforced appropriate masculine speech. When the boy talked about feminine topics (such as dresses, mascara, lipstick, etc.), the therapist withdrew all social attention. If the boy asked the therapist why he was not being attended to, the therapist would simply state disinterest by saying, "I'm not interested in that." With positive interest shown for neutral and masculine speech, appropriate masculine speech content as well as appropriate voice inflection developed.

Normalizing gestures and mannerisms has required much more intensive behavioral treatment. The effeminate gestures in the cross-gender identified boy appear to be exaggerations of feminine standing, sitting, and walking behaviors. A response-cost and verbal-prompt procedure was successfully used to decrease a gender-disturbed boy's flexed elbow and feminine running mannerisms during a game task of throwing a tennis ball at the toy target (Rekers et al., 1976). These gestures were clearly explained to the boy, he was given a number of tokens at the beginning of each play session, and the therapist substracted one token for each instance of flexed elbow and feminine running. Modeling appropriate body movements and asking the child to rehearse masculine-appearing body movements was accomplished, including the use of manual guidance when necessary. In addition, the therapist explained to the parents how to apply these techniques in the home. As a result, the experimental data indicated a decrease in these feminine mannerisms to the degree that the boy ceased to appear effeminate to others.

With another child, a videotaped feedback procedure was used to help the boy discriminate the feminine gestures in his repertoire (Rekers, Willis, Yates, Rosen, & Low, 1977). This procedure was suggested by the boy's expressed desire to learn what it was he was doing to elicit peer ostracism at school. Once he could discriminate the cross-gender behaviors, a response-cost system helped him to cease performing those mannerisms.

Because of skill deficits in athletic games, a specific set of behavior shaping procedures have been developed to shape athletic behaviors in cross-gender identified boys (Rekers et al., 1974; Rekers, Willis et al., 1977; Rekers, 1979). In a park setting, a clinical assistant gradually shaped such skills as throwing a football, socking a playground ball, kicking a kickball, and shooting baskets. Skills were selected based on the type of activity required in the children's physical education classes in school to increase their social adaptation in that setting and to reinforce their self-images as boys. Multiple baseline design studies have indicated that verbal praise and the use of candy as a reinforcement has led to the acquisition of these complex athletic skills (Rekers et al., 1974; Rekers, Willis et al., 1977; Rekers, 1979). The therapy sessions are designed to desensitize the boy's fears, with the goal of helping the boy learn that playing games can become intrinsically enjoyable. Wherever possible, the father was invited to participate in the training sessions, with careful attention given to ensure that the sessions between father and son were nonthreatening, free of punishing remarks, and never too difficult to induce feelings of failure or frustration in the boy.

To overcome the setting-specificity of behavior therapy effects, behavior therapy treatment has been extended to the home environment, after changes in sex-typed behavior have been demonstrated in the clinic and after the mother and/or father have been trained by the therapist in the clinic setting. Parents have been trained to take systematic recordings of gender behavior on a daily behavior checklist form that is individually tailored with descriptions of frequently occurring feminine behaviors and infrequently occurring masculine behaviors in boys. The parent is asked to observe and record the child's behavior for 10-minute intervals at several specific times daily. Observer reliability is assessed by home visits made by clinical assistants.

Parents were then trained to mediate a token reinforcement system, in which a set of backup reinforcers were available for blue poker chip tokens, and red tokens were used to discriminate a response-cost condition whereby red tokens were subtracted from accumulated blue tokens on a one-for-one basis. The specific procedures used have been summarized in detail by Rekers (1977a). Attention is given to one behavior at a time to maximize a feeling of success in the boy and in the parent. Specific adaptive masculine behaviors are agreed on for behavior shaping. Then one feminine behavior at a time is treated by describing the contingency to the child and then by instructing the parent in how to give a red token to the child for each observed incident of that feminine behavior.

It is important to obtain reliable observational data on the boy's sex-typed behavior during the treatment to monitor the child's acquisition of masculine behaviors and to monitor the frequency of feminine behaviors. Similarly, it is important to maintain reliability checks on the parent's observational data. Multiple baseline replication designs have found these techniques to be successful. In Green's (1974) attempt to replicate Rekers' (1972) parent-mediated behavior therapy procedures, careful monitoring of the child's behavior as well as the parent's behavioral treatment behavior was absent. Consequently, Green's partial replication attempt resulted in treatment failures associated with the absence of these experimental control procedures. The independent investigations by Bates and his colleagues (Bates et al., 1975) as well as the intrasubject study investigations of Rekers and colleagues (summarized in Rekers, 1978a, 1983) demonstrate that treatment success does result with the appropriate training and supervision of the parents along with careful behavioral assessment of the child's behavior before, during and after treatment.

Rekers and colleagues (1974) reported an intrasubject study involving contingencies mediated by classroom teachers. Once again, a time-sampling technique was used with a behavior checklist of feminine, masculine, and neutral behaviors of clinical interest. Baseline recordings were obtained with the teacher's data and with reliability checks of an observer who posed as a student teacher in the classroom. A response-cost contingency in a point economy system was found to be effective in reducing the frequency of feminine gesture mannerisms in the school setting. Generalization of the treatment effect was found with feminine speech, which was monitored simultaneously.

Issues in Implementation

Because of the variation in the clinical pattern observed in individual children with gender disturbances, the design of a specific set of treatment procedures must be based on the results of the comprehensive psychological and behavioral assessment of the individual child. For example, if the child has manifested a chronic and persistent desire to be a member of the opposite sex in addition to a preoccupation with cross-sex-typed behaviors and activities, then the treatment objectives would include (1) decreasing the frequency of the cross-sex behavior, (2) increasing the child's repertoire and comfortable performance of appropriate sex-typed behaviors, and (3) normalizing the child's identification with his/her anatomical state. On the other hand, if the child demonstrates a preoccupation with a number of cross-sex-typed behaviors in the absence of a strong cross-gender identity, the therapeutic objectives may be (a) to increase sex-role flexibility, (b) to decrease perhaps only one or two discrete behaviors such as cross-dressing, which elicit social ostracism and place the child at high risk for sexual adjustment difficulties in the future, and (c) to treat any accompanying psychological adjustment problems often correlated with effeminancy in boys, such as passivity, harm avoidance, immaturity, fearfulness, social aversiveness, and social unresponsiveness (see findings of Bates et al., 1974). Other children with gender disturbances may have a specific set of deviant sexual behaviors detected in the clinical assessment (Rekers, 1981b). Treatment for those abnormal behaviors may be part of the individualized treatment plan (Rekers, 1978b).

Any clinical decision to treat children with gender disturbances may involve the complex contemporary set of issues concerning appropriate versus harmful and arbitrary types of social sex-role stereotyping. Some parents and some professionals as well have not investigated the nature of gender disturbances thoroughly enough to be able to differentiate them from simple androgyny or from the harmful social stereotypes of male chauvinism or macho male stereotyping (Rekers, 1982b). A variety of research and clinical investigators have specified the detailed components of a clinical rationale for treatment of childhood gender disturbances (see Bates et al., 1975; Green, 1974; Qualls, 1978; Rekers, Bentler, Rosen & Lovaas, 1977; Stoller, 1970). The professional ethical issues involved have also been discussed in detail (Rosen et al., 1978). The sensitive nature of the clinician's role in promoting the child's adjustment to appropriate sex-role distinctions has been contrasted to the reinforcement of arbitrary sex-role stereotyping (Rekers et al., 1978). And the legitimate implementation of the parents' values and responsibility for their child has been contrasted to the positions taken by social extremists in today's society (Rekers, 1977b; 1978a; 1982a). In some cases, the child may not be requesting that the clinician change their cross-gender identity to match their anatomic status. However, Rosen et al. (1978) have outlined the developmental, legal, and ethical issues involved in protecting children from any inappropriate intrusions on their inalienable dignity and freedom as individuals while being equally conscientious to ensure that children retain their right to possibly very beneficial forms of treatment, in consonance with their parents' request and proper consent for treatment. While we must acknowledge that our contemporary society unfortunately does have many arbitrary sex-role stereotypes, which are not only arbitrary but also harmful to individual development, there is a need for each child to properly identify with his or her own anatomic status and gender role in society and for the child to acquire a variety of the benign and appropriate gender role behaviors.

It is an appropriate clinical goal to reduce the maladaptive sex-role rigidity in the gender-disturbed child in order to increase the life options for that individual (Gray, 1971; Thoresen & Mahoney, 1974, p. 5). It is reasonable for parents and clinicians to collaborate in promoting a child's active sex-role development and satisfaction with anatomic status. For example, parents and clinicians should promote nurturance toward babies in both boys and girls, but clinical treatment is required for the boy who chronically play acts the roles of delivering and breast-feeding babies, while he cross-dresses as a mother.

Nuances of Treatment in Day-to-Day Practice

Related to the finding that father absence is highly correlated with the more severe cases of gender disturbance (Rekers et al., 1983), it is quite common for the gender-disturbed child to be from a mother-headed, single-parent family. Also, because the vast majority of identified cases of gender identity disorder are boys rather than girls, many of these boys could profit from a warm, nurturant, and affectionate relationship with an adult male father-figure. For this reason, the Big Brother program is of particular usefulness for the gender-disturbed child. I have found it helpful as a clinical psychologist to contact the local director of the Big Brother program (with the parent's permission) and to give an especially high recommendation for the gender-disturbed child to be assigned a Big Brother, given the fact that many of these programs have a long waiting list of children to be served. If the child's family is a member of a church, often a Big Brother type of relationship can be arranged within the church family. Because of the role overload on the single-parent, the clinician may need to attend to helping the single-parent family discover various sources of social support in the community (Rekers & Swihart, 1984).

It is often necessary to advise parents of the gender-disturbed child not to overtly punish the child for their gender deviance. Instead, the psychological learning principle of *extinction* can be explained to a parent if they are attempting to decrease the cross-gender behavior. I have observed a number of gender-disordered children who apparently derived some secondary gain from even the negative attention from adults and peers that occurred with their cross-gender behavior. A positive reward system for appropriate gender-behaviors is particularly potent with such children.

Many parents are unskilled, embarrassed, or hesitant to provide appropriate sex education to the child, and this becomes especially important to a gender-disturbed child. The clinician should assist the parents in this role or assist in finding another person who shares the parents' sexual ethical values to provide this sex education. The clinician should be sensitive to working in consonance with the parent's moral values regarding sex education for the child.

CLINICAL CONSIDERATIONS

An experimental study reported by Rosen, Rekers, and Brigham (1982) examined the effects of behavioral treatment of 22 gender-disturbed boys. This study found no support for the apprehension that behavioral treatment of boys with gender problems might yield a macho stereotypic male behavior pattern or self-description. Therefore, parents and clinicians need not fear that behavioral intervention for gender disturbances might result in such unintended side effects. Children treated by Rekers and his colleagues in the early 1970s have been followed longitudinally for posttreatment evaluations, which are made by independent clinicians. In each case thus far, we have found enduring cognitive change in terms of gender identity that followed the change in overt gender behavior, which was accomplished through behavioral treatment procedures. Projective testing, other psychological testing, and behavioral observation of nonverbal and verbal behavior has led to the finding that behavioral treatment does normalize gender identification and that the effects endure into adolescence.

For some parents, one or two discrete behaviors have motivated their request for treatment for the child. For example, the parents may be particularly concerned about their son who cross-dresses, but after that particular behavior has been successfully treated by behavior therapy, the parent's motivation for continued clinical intervention has decreased. Consequently, some children may be withdrawn from treatment before the clinician has ascertained that the underlying gender identity problem has been totally treated. Other parents may withdraw from completing treatment for a variety of other reasons. This situation highlights the necessity of explaining to the parents early in treatment that treatment may take many months to complete, and because of the severity of the gender identity disorder and its implications for the child's future adult adjustment, treatment should be followed through to completion. Special attention should be given to maintaining rapport with the parents and involving parents in the total treatment planning. In fact, at the time of conclusion of the initial assessment phase when diagnostic feedback is provided to the parents, it is often useful to inform the parents that it will be advisable not only to follow a comprehensive treatment program for the child, but also to anticipate the desirability of yearly follow-up checkups through adolescence to determine whether additional treatment is necessary as the child gets older. The parent can be informed that developing children with gender identity disturbances tend to go underground with their disorder as they get older but that this does not necessarily mean that the underlying gender identity problem has gone into remission. In fact, the typical developmental course would be for the child's gender and sexual problems to become more of a private experience, out of the view of the parent. For this reason, early detection in childhood is helpful, but comprehensive treatment and periodic follow-up evaluations will be necessary for this particular disorder.

CASE EXAMPLES

Once the clinician has detected a gender disturbance in a child, a detailed review of one or more intrasubject case studies of treatment procedures would be helpful in formulating an individualized treatment plan for the child. Instead of providing one such case as an illustrative example here, the available detailed intrasubject studies will be indexed for the reader's reference.

Rekers and Mead (1979) reported a self-monitoring procedure combined with a behavioral prompting technique for behavioral treatment of an eight-year-old girl with gender identity disturbance. Ferguson & Rekers (1979) presented a behavioral treatment for excessive public masturbation in a four-year-old girl.

Rekers and Lovaas (1974) presented a behavioral treatment study conducted in the clinic as well as in the home setting for a four-year-old boy with a profound cross-gender identity; this is a primary reference that provides the first detailed behavioral treatment of a gender-disturbed child. Rekers & Varni (1977b) report the therapeutic use of self-regulation strategies to enhance more androgynous play behavior in a four-year-old boy with gender identity confusion; the procedure was conducted in the preschool settings. Rekers et al. (1976) presented the behavioral treatment of a five-year-old, cross-gender identified boy primarily in the clinic setting in which generalization of the treatment effect was accomplished by introducing the treatment in a number of stimulus settings. Rekers and Varni (1977a) behaviorally treated a six-year-old boy with behavioral self-control strategies. Rekers (1979) presented a variation of the treatment procedure reported by Rekers and Lovaas (1974) for a boy for whom a parent was not available to train for administering behavioral procedures in the clinic and the home; in this case, a seven-year-old boy was treated with a therapist in the clinic, and procedures for shaping the child's athletic skills were included in a second study. Rekers et al. (1974) presented a treatment study of an eight-year-old boy with cross-gender identification, who was treated for his high rates of feminine speech in the clinic and for whom the parent was involved in the treatment in the home setting, the teacher was involved in treatment in the school setting, and "concurrent companionship therapy" was included to help provide a Big Brother relationship and to shape athletic behavior skills. Rekers, Willis, Yates, Rosen, and Low (1977) present a comprehensive assessment of cross-gender behaviors in an eight-year-old boy in the home and clinic settings, with detailed procedures for particularly treating effeminate gestures and mannerisms. Rekers & Milner (1978) provide five brief diagnostic cases as examples. Rekers (1978b) surveyed behavioral treatment studies in the literature on a variety of childhood and adolescent sexual behavior problems.

CONCLUSIONS

Over 50 children with gender disturbances have been comprehensively treated by Rekers and his colleagues (1977a, 1983) as well as Bates and his colleagues (1975). Preliminary results after follow-up into adolescent years have indicated permanent changes in gender identity and overall psychological adjustment to the extent that gender identity can be measured by independent clinicians with interview and testing techniques. No other therapeutic intervention approach in childhood has been experimentally demonstrated to have this same effectiveness. Clinicians from a variety of therapeutic approaches can incorporate these behavior therapy techniques in the clinical care of the gender-disturbed child. Although research has not yet addressed the question of the effectiveness of other therapeutic approaches, it is likely that an integrated application of individual psychotherapy, family therapy, and behavior therapy approaches would be helpful in the individualized treatment strategy for a given individual child with gender problems.

REFERENCES

American Psychological Association. *Diagnostic and statistical manual of mental disorders* (3rd ed.). Washington, D.C.: American Psychiatric Association, 1980.

Anant, S. S. Verbal aversion therapy with a promiscuous girl: Case report. *Psychological Reports,* 1968, *22,* 795–796.

Atcheson, J. D., & Williams, D. C. A study of juvenile sex offenders. *American Journal of Psychiatry,* 1954, *111,* 336–370.

Baker, H., & Stoller, R. J. Can a biological force contribute to gender identity? *American Journal of Psychiatry,* 1968, *124,* 1653–1658.

Bakwin, H. Deviant gender-role behavior in children: Relation to homosexuality. *Pediatrics,* 1968, *41,* 620–629.

Barlow, D. H., Agras, W. S., Abel, G. G., Blanchard, E. G., & Young, L. D. Biofeedback and reinforcement to increase heterosexual arousal in homosexuals. *Behaviour Research and Therapy,* 1975, *13,* 45–50.

Barlow, D. H., Reynolds, E. J., & Agras, W. S. Gender identity change in a transsexual. *Archives of General Psychiatry,* 1973, *28,* 569–576.

Bates, J. E., & Bentler, P. M. Play activities of normal and effeminate boys. *Developmental Psychology,* 1973, *9,* 20–27.

Bates, J. E., Bentler, P. M., & Thompson, S. Measurement of deviant gender development in boys. *Child Development,* 1973, *44,* 591–598.

Bates, J. E., Skilbeck, W. M., Smith K. V. R. & Bentler, P. M. Gender role abnormalities in boys: An analysis of clinical ratings. *Journal of Abnormal Child Psychology,* 1974, *2,* 1–16.

Bates, J. E., Skilbeck, W. M., Smith, K. V. R., & Bentler, P. M. Intervention with families of gender-disturbed boys. *American Journal of Orthopsychiatry,* 1975, *45,* 150–157.

Bem, S. L. Sex role adaptability: One consequence of psychological androgyny. *Journal of Personality and Social Psychology,* 1975, *31,* 634–643.

Bem, S. L. The measurement of psychological androgyny. *Journal of Consulting and Clinical Psychology,* 1974, *42,* 155–162.

Bender, L., & Blau, A. The reaction of children to sexual relations with adults. *American Journal of Orthopsychiatry,* 1973, *7,* 500–518.

Bender, L., & Paster, S. Homosexual trends in children. *American Journal of Orthopsychiatry,* 1941, *11,* 730–743.

Bene, E., & Anthony, J. *Manual for the Family Relations Test.* London: National Foundation for Educational Research, 1957.

Benjamin, H. *The transsexual phenomenon.* New York: The Julian Press, 1966.

Bentler, P. M. A note on the treatment of adolescent sex problems. *Journal of Child Psychology and Psychiatry,* 1968, *9,* 125–129.

Bentler, P. M. A typology of transsexualism: Gender identity theory and data. *Archives of Sexual Behavior*, 1976, *5*, 567–584.

Bentler, P. M., & Prince, C. Psychiatric symptomatology in transvestites. *Journal of Clinical Psychology*, 1970, *26*, 434–435.

Bentler, P. M., Rekers, G. A., & Rosen, A. C. Congruence of childhood sex-role identity and behavior disturbances. *Child: Care, Health and Development*, 1979, *5* (4), 267–284.

Bieber, I., Dain, H. J., Dince, P. R., Drellich, M. G., Grand, H. G., Gundlach, R. H., Kremer, M. W., Ritkin, A. H., Wilber, C. B., & Beiber, T. B. *Homosexuality: A psychoanalytic study*. New York: Basic Books, 1962.

Birdwhistell, R. L. *Kinesics and context*. Philadelphia: University of Pennsylvania Press, 1970.

Bitter-Lebert, I. A case of excessive masturbation. *Praxis der Kinderpsychologie und Kinderpsychiatrie*, 1956, *6*, 44–48.

Block, J. H. Another look at sex differentiation in the socialization behaviors of mothers and fathers. In F. Denmark and J. Sherman (Eds.), *Psychology of Women: Future Directions of Research*. New York: Psychological Dimensions, 1977.

Bond, I., & Evans, D. Avoidance therapy: Its uses in two cases of underwear fetishism. *Canadian Medical Association Journal*, 1967, *96*, 1160–1162.

Bradley, S. J., Steiner, B., Zucker, K., Doering, R. W., Sullivan, J., Finegan, J. K., & Richardson, M. Gender identity problems of children and adolescents. *Canadian Psychiatric Association Journal*, 1978, *23*, 1975–1983.

Braun, M., & Rekers, G. A. *The Christian in an Age of Sexual Eclipse*. Wheaton, Ill.: Tyndale House Publishers, 1981.

Brown, F. Sexual problems of the adolescent girl. *Pediatric Clinics of North America*, 1972, *19*, 759–764.

Brunold, H. Observations after sexual traumata suffered in childhood. *Excerpta Criminologica (Netherlands)*, 1964, *4*, 5–8.

Callahan, E. J. & Leitenberg, H. Aversion therapy for sexual deviation: Contingent shock and covert sensitization. *Journal of Abnormal Psychology*, 1973, *81*, 60–73.

Canton-Dutari, A. Combined intervention for controlling unwanted homosexual behavior. *Archives of Sexual Behavior*, 1974, *3*, 367–371.

Coe, J. I. Sexual asphyxias. *Life-Threatening Behavior*, 1974, *4*, 171–175.

Craft, M. Boy prostitutes and their fate. *British Journal of Psychiatry*, 1966, *112*, 1111–1114.

Davidson, K., Brierley, H., & Smith, C. A male monozygotic twinship discordant for homosexuality. *British Journal of Psychiatry*, 1971, *118*, 675–682.

Deisher, R. W. The young male prostitute. *Pediatrics*, 1970, *45*, 153–154.

Deisher, R. W., Eisner, V., & Sulzbacher, S. I. The young male prostitute. *Pediatrics*, 1969, *43*, 936–941.

Doering, R. W. *Parental reinforcement of gender-typed behaviors in boys with atypical gender identity.* Unpublished doctoral dissertation, University of Toronto, 1981.

Dorner, G., Rohde, W., Stahl, F., Krell, L., & Masius, W. G. A neuroendocrine predisposition for homosexuality. *Archives of Sexual Behavior,* 1975, *4,* 1–8.

Dupont, H. Social learning theory and the treatment of transvestite behavior in an eight-year-old boy. *Psychotherapy: Theory, Research, and Practice* 1968, *5,* 44–45.

Edmondson, J. S. A case of sexual asphyxia without fatal termination. *British Journal of Psychiatry,* 1972, *121,* 437–438.

Ehrhardt, A. A. The interactional model of sex hormones and behavior. In H. A. Katchadourian (Ed.), *Human Sexuality.* Berkeley: University of California Press, 1979.

Ehrhardt, A. A., & Baker, S. W. Fetal androgens, human central nervous system differentiation, and behavior sex differences. In R. C. Friedman, R. M. Richart, & R. L. VandeWiele (Eds.), *Sex Differences in Behavior.* New York: John Wiley & Sons, 1974.

Evans, R. B. Childhood parental relationships of homosexual men. *Journal of Consulting and Clinical Psychology,* 1969, *33,* 129–135.

Ferguson, L. N., & Rekers, G. A. Non-aversive intervention for public childhood masturbation. *The Journal of Sex Research,* 1979, *15* (3), 213–223.

Finegan, V. K., Zucker, K. J., Bradley, S. J., & Doering, R. W. Patterns of intellectual functioning and spatial ability in boys with gender identity disorder. *Canadian Journal of Psychiatry,* 1982, *27,* 135–139.

Gandy, P., & Deisher, R. Young male prostitutes: The physician's role in social rehabilitation. *Journal of the American Medical Association.* 1970, *212,* 1661–1666.

Gilbert, J. A. An unusual case of masturbation. *American Journal of Urology and Sexology,* 1916, *12,* 82–87.

Ginsburg, K. N. The "meat-rack": A study of the male homosexual prostitute. *American Journal of Psychotherapy,* 1967, *21,* 170–185.

Gold, S., & Neufeld, I. L. A learning approach to the treatment of homosexuality. *Behaviour Research and Therapy,* 1965, *2,* 201–204.

Gray, S. W. Ethical issues in research in early childhood education. *Children,* 1971, *18,* 83–89.

Green, R. Childhood cross-gender behavior and subsequent sexual preference. *American Journal of Psychiatry,* 1979, *136,* 106–108.

Green, R. Childhood cross-gender identification. *Journal of Nervous and Mental Disease,* 1968, *147,* 500–509.

Green, R. Intervention and prevention: The child with cross-sex identity. In C. B. Qualls, J. P. Wincze, & D. H. Barlow (Eds.), *The prevention of sexual disorders: Issues and approaches.* New York: Plenum Press, 1978.

Green, R. *Sexual identity conflict in children and adults.* New York: Basic Books, 1974.

Green, R. Sexual identity: Research strategies. *Archives of Sexual Behavior,* 1975, *4,* 337–352.

Green, R. & Fuller, M. Group therapy with feminine boys and their parents. *International Journal of Group Psychotherapy,* 1973, *23,* 54–68.

Green, R., Fuller, M., & Rutley, B. IT-scale for children and Draw-A-Person Test: 30 feminine vs. 25 masculine boys. *Journal of Personality Assessment,* 1972, *36,* 349–352.

Green, R., & Money, J. Effeminacy in prepubertal boys: Summary of eleven cases and recommendations for case management. *Pediatrics,* 1961, *27,* 286–291.

Green, R., & Money, J. Incongruous gender role: nongenital manifestations in prepubertal boys. *Journal of Nervous and Mental Disease,* 1960, *131,* 160–168.

Green, R., & Money, J. (Eds.). *Transsexualism and sex reassignment.* Baltimore: The Johns Hopkins Press, 1969.

Green, R., Newman, L. E. & Stoller, R. J. Treatment of boyhood "transsexualism"—An interim report of four years' experience. *Archives of General Psychiatry,* 1972, *26,* 213–217.

Greenson, R. R. A transvestite boy and a hypothesis. *International Journal of Psychoanalysis,* 1966, *47,* 396–403.

Greenson, R. R. Dis-identifying from mother: Its special importance for the boy. *International Journal of Psycho-Analysis,* 1968, *49,* 370–374.

Grover, J. W. Problems of emerging sexuality and their management. *Rhode Island Medical Journal,* 1973, *56,* 274–279; 298.

Hackett, T. P. The psychotherapy of exhibitionists in a court clinic setting. *Seminars in Psychiatry,* 1971, *3,* 297–306.

Hamelstein, H. Youth and their sexual problems. *Journal of Clinical Child Psychology,* 1974, *3,* 31–33.

Hanaway, T. P., & Burghardt, G. M. The development of sexually dimorphic book-carrying behavior. *Bulletin of the Psychonomic Society,* 1976, *7,* 267–270.

Harrington, C. C. *Errors in sex-role behavior in teenage boys.* New York: Teachers College Press, 1970.

Hartmann, L. Some uses of dirty words by children. *Journal of the American Academy of Child Psychiatry,* 1973, *12,* 108–122.

Herman, S. H., Barlow, D. H., & Agras, W. S. An experimental analysis of classical conditioning as a method of increasing heterosexual arousal in homosexuals. *Behavior Therapy,* 1974, *5,* 33–47.

Holemon, E. R., & Winokur, G. Effeminate homosexuality: A disease of childhood. *American Journal of Orthopsychiatry,* 1965, *35,* 48–56.

Huff, F. W. The desensitization of a homosexual. *Behaviour Research and Therapy,* 1970, *8,* 99–102.

Hutt, C. Biological bases of psychological sex differences. *American Journal of Diseases in Childhood*, 1978, *132*, 170–177.

Jenni, M. A. Sex differences in carrying behavior. *Perceptual and Motor Skills*, 1976, *43*, 323–330.

Jenni, D. A., & Jenni, M. A. Carrying behavior in humans: Analysis of sex differences. *Science*, 1976, *194*, 859–860.

Jolles, I. A study of the validity of some hypotheses for the qualitative interpretation of the H-T-P for children of elementary school age. *Journal of Clinical Psychology*, 1952, *8*, 113–118.

Katzman, M. Early sexual trauma. *Sexual Behavior*, 1972, *2*, 13–17.

Kenyon, F. E. Studies in female homosexuality: IV. Social and psychiatric aspects. *British Journal of Psychiatry*, 1968, *114*, 1337–1350.

Kremer, M. W., & Rifkin, A. H. The early development of homosexuality: A study of adolescent lesbians. *American Journal of Psychiatry*, 1969, *126*, 91–96.

Langsley, D. G., Schwartz, M. N., & Fairbairn, R. H. Father-son incest. *Comprehensive Psychiatry*, 1968, *9*, 218–226.

Larson, D. E. An adaptation of the Feldman and MacCulloch approach to treatment of homosexuality by the application of anticipatory avoidance learning. *Behaviour Research and Therapy*, 1970, *8*, 209–210.

Lebovitz, P. S. Feminine behavior in boys: Aspects of its outcome. *American Journal of Psychiatry*, 1972, *128*, 1283–1289.

Levine, M. I., & Bell, A. I. Psychological aspects of pediatric practice. II. Masturbation. *Pediatrics*, 1956, *18*, 803–808.

Lowenstein, L. F. A case of exhibitionism treated by counter-conditioning. *Adolescence*, 1973, *8*, 213–218.

Maccoby, E. E. (Ed.). *The development of sex differences*. Stanford, Calif.: Stanford University Press, 1966.

Maccoby, E. E., & Jacklin, C. N. *The psychology of sex differences*. Stanford, Calif.: Stanford University Press, 1966.

MacCulloch, M. J., & Feldman, M. P. Aversion therapy in management of 43 homosexuals. *British Medical Journal*, 1967, *2*, 594–597.

MacCulloch, M. J., Williams, C., & Birtles, C. J. The successful application of aversion therapy to an adolescent exhibitionist. *Journal of Behavior Therapy and Experimental Psychiatry*, 1971, *2*, 61–66.

Mangus, A. R. Sex crimes against children. In K. M. Bournen (Ed.), *Sexual deviation research*. Sacramento: Assembly of the State of California, March 1932.

Mangus, A. R. Sexual deviation and the family. *Marriage and Family Living*, 1953, *15*, 325–331.

Marshall, W., & Tanner, J. Variations in the pattern of pubertal changes in girls. *Archives of Disease in Childhood*, 1969, *44*, 291–303.

Marshall, W., & Tanner, J. M. Variations in the pattern of pubertal changes in boys. *Archives of Disease in Childhood*, 1970, *45*, 13–23.

McConaghy, N. Penile response conditioning and its relationship to aversion therapy in homosexuals. *Behavior Therapy*, 1970, *1*, 213–221.

McConaghy, N. Subjective and penile plethysmograph responses following aversion-relief and apomorphine aversion therapy for homosexual impulses. *British Journal of Psychiatry*, 1969, *115*, 723–730.

McGuire, R. J., Carlisle, J. M., & Young, B. G. Sexual deviations as conditioned behavior: A hypothesis. *Behaviour Research and Therapy*, 1965, *2*, 185–190.

Mead, S. L., & Rekers, G. A. The role of the father in normal psychosexual development. *Psychological Reports*, 1979, *45*, 923–931.

Mees, H. L. Sadistic fantasies modified by aversive condition and substitution: A case study. *Behaviour Research and Therapy*, 1966, *4*, 317–320.

Meyer-Bahlberg, H. F. L. Neurobehavioral effects of prenatal origin: sex hormones. *Drugs and Chemical Risks to the Fetus and Newborn*. New York: Alan R. Liss, 1980.

Meyer-Bahlburg, H. F. L. Sex hormones and male homosexuality in comparative perspective. *Archives of Sexual Behavior*, 1977, *6*, 297–325.

Michael, G., & Willis, F. N., Jr. The development of gestures as a function of social class, educational level, and sex. *Psychological Record*, 1968, *18*, 515–519.

Miller, W. B. Sexuality, contraception, and pregnancy in high-school population. *California Medicine*, 1973, *119*, 14–21.

Mischel, W. Sex-typing and socialization. In P. H. Mussen (Ed.), *Carmichael's manual of child psychology* (3d ed., Vol. 2). New York: John Wiley & Sons, 1970.

Mohr, J. W., & Turner, R. E. Sexual deviations. Part III: Exhibitionism. *Applied Therapeutics*, 1967, *9*, 263–265.

Money, J. Critique of Dr. Zuger's manuscript. *Psychosomatic Medicine*, 1970, *32*, 463–465 (a).

Money, J. Sexual dimorphism and homosexual gender identity. *Psychological Bulletin*, 1970, *74*, 425–440 (b).

Money, J., & Brennan, J. G. Sexual dimorphism in the psychology of female transsexuals. In R. Green & J. Money (Eds.), *Transsexualism and sex reassignment*. Baltimore: The Johns Hopkins Press, 1969.

Money, J., & Ehrhardt, A. A. *Man and woman, boy and girl: The differentiation and dimorphism of gender identity from conception to maturity*. Baltimore: The Johns Hopkins Press, 1972.

Money, J., Hampson, J. G., & Hampson, J. L. An examination of some basic sexual concepts: Evidence of human hermaphroditism. *Bulletin of the Johns Hopkins Hospital*, 1955, *97*, 301–319.

Money, J., & Primrose, C. Sexual dimorphism and dissociation in the psychology of male transsexuals. *Journal of Nervous and Mental Disease*, 1968, *147*, 472–486.

Money, J., & Russo, A. Homosexual outcome of discordant gender identity/role in childhood: Longitudinal follow-up. *Journal of Pediatric Psychology*, 1978, *4*, 29–41.

Money, J., & Schwartz, M. Fetal androgens in the early treated adreno-genital syndrome of 46XX hermaphroditism: influence on assertive and aggressive types of behaviour. *Aggressive Behaviour,* 1976, *2,* 19–30.

Mosse, H. L. The influence of mass media on the sex problems of teenagers. *Journal of Sex Research,* 1966, *2,* 27–35.

Nadler, R. P. Approach of psychodynamics of obscene telephone calls. *New York State Journal of Medicine,* 1968, *68,* 521–526.

Pauly, I. Adult manifestations of male transsexualism. In R. Green & J. Money (Eds.), *Transsexualism and sex reassignment.* Baltimore: The Johns Hopkins Press, 1969.

Pittman, D. J. The male house of prostitution. *Trans-Action,* 1971, *8,* 21–27.

Prince, C. V., & Bentler, P. M. A survey of 504 cases of transvestism. *Psychological Reports,* 1972, *31,* 903–917.

Qualls, C. B. The prevention of sexual disorders: An overview. In C. B. Qualls, J. P. Wincze, & D. H. Barlow (Eds.), *The prevention of sexual disorders: Issues and approaches.* New York: Plenum Press, 1978.

Raven, S. Boys will be boys: The male prostitute in London. In H. M. Ruitenbeek (Ed.), *Problem of homosexuality in modern society.* New York: E. P. Dutton, 1963.

Reiss, A. J. Social integration of queers and peers. In H. M. Ruitenbeek (Ed.), *Problem of homosexuality in modern society.* New York: E. P. Dutton, 1963.

Rekers, G. A. A priori values and research on homosexuality. *American Psychologist,* 1978, *33,* 510–512 (a).

Rekers, G. A. Assessment and treatment of childhood gender problems. Chapter 7 in B. B. Lahey and A. E. Kazdin (Eds.), *Advances in clinical child psychology* (Vol. 1). New York: Plenum Press, 1977, 267–306 (a).

Rekers, G. A. Atypical gender development and psychosocial adjustment. *Journal of Applied Behavior Analysis,* 1977, *10,* 559–571 (b).

Rekers, G. A. Childhood sexual identity disorders. *Medical Aspects of Human Sexuality,* 1981, *15* (3), 141–142 (a).

Rekers, G. A. Cross-sex behavior. Chapter 26 in Sheridan Phillips, "Behavioral and Developmental Problems in Childhood." In R. A. Hoekelman, S. Blatman, S. B. Friedman, N. M. Nelson, and H. M. Seidel (Eds.), *Principles of Pediatrics: Health Care of the Young* (2nd ed.). C. V. Mosby Publishing Co., 1984 (a).

Rekers, G. A. Ethical issues in child assessment. Chapter 12 in Thomas H. Ollendick and Michael Hersen (Eds.), *Child behavioral assessment: Principles and procedures.* New York: Pergamon Press, 1984, 244–262 (b).

Rekers, G. A. Gender identity disorder of childhood. In David G. Benner (Ed.), *Baker's Encyclopedia of Psychology.* Grand Rapids, Mich.: Baker Book House, in press (a).

Rekers, G. A. *Growing Up Straight: What Every Family Should Know About Homosexuality.* Chicago: Moody Press, 1982 (a).

Rekers, G. A. *Pathological sex-role development in boys: Behavioral treatment and assessment.* (PhD dissertation in psychology, University of California, Los Angeles, 1972). Ann Arbor, Michigan: (University Microfilms, 1972. No. 72–33, 978).

Rekers, G. A. Play therapy with cross-gender identified children. Chapter 20 in Charles E. Schaefer and Kevin J. O'Connor (Eds.), *Handbook of Play Therapy.* New York: John Wiley & Sons, 1983, 369–385.

Rekers, G. A. Psychosexual and gender problems. In E. J. Mash & L. G. Terdal (Eds.), *Behavioral assessment of childhood disorders.* New York: Guilford Press, 1981, 483–526 (b).

Rekers, G. A. Sex-role behavior change: Intrasubject studies of boyhood gender disturbance. *The Journal of Psychology,* 1979, *103,* 255–269.

Rekers, G. A. Sexual problems: Behavior modification. Chapter 17 in B. B. Wolman (Ed.), *Handbook of treatment of mental disorders in childhood and adolescence.* Englewood Cliffs, N.J.: Prentice-Hall, 1978, 268–296 (b).

Rekers, G. A. *Shaping Your Child's Sexual Identity.* Grand Rapids, Mich.: Baker Book House, 1982 (b).

Rekers, G. A. Stimulus control over sex-typed play in cross-gender identified boys. *Journal of Experimental Child Psychology,* 1975, *20,* 136–148.

Rekers, G. A. Therapies dealing with the child's sexual difficulties. In Jean-Marc Samson (Ed.), *Enfance et Sexualite/Childhood and Sexuality.* Montreal & Paris: Les Edition Etudes Vivantes, Inc., 1980, 525–538.

Rekers, G. A. Transsexualism. In David G. Benner (Ed.), *Baker's Encyclopedia of Psychology.* Grand Rapids, Mich.: Baker Book House, in press (b).

Rekers, G. A. Transvestism. In David G. Benner (Ed.), *Baker's Encyclopedia of Psychology.* Grand Rapids, Mich.: Baker Book House, in press (c).

Rekers, G. A., Amaro-Plotkin, H., & Low, B. P. Sex-typed mannerisms in normal boys and girls as a function of sex and age. *Child Development,* 1977, *48,* 275–278.

Rekers, G. A., Bentler, P. M., Rosen, A. C., & Lovaas, O. I. Child gender disturbances: A clinical rationale for intervention. *Psychotherapy: Theory, Research and Practice,* 1977, *14,* 2–11.

Rekers, G. A., Crandall, B. F., Rosen, A. C., & Bentler, P. M. Genetic and physical studies of male children with psychological gender disturbances. *Psychological Medicine,* 1979, *9,* 373–375.

Rekers, G. A., & Jurich, A. P. Development of problems of puberty and sex-roles in adolescence. Chapter 33 in C. Eugene Walker and Michael C. Roberts (Eds.), *Handbook of Clinical Child Psychology.* New York: John Wiley & Sons, 1983, 775–802.

Rekers, G. A. & Lovaas, O. I. Experimental analysis of cross-sex behavior in male children. *Research Relating to Children,* 1971, *28,* 68.

Rekers, G. A., & Lovaas, O. I. Behavioral treatment of deviant sex-role behaviors in a male child. *Journal of Applied Behavior Analysis,* 1974, *7,* 173–190.

Rekers, G. A., Lovaas, O. I., & Low, B. P. The behavioral treatment of a "transsexual" preadolescent boy. *Journal of Abnormal Child Psychology,* 1974, *2,* 99–116.

Rekers, G. A., & Mead, S. Early intervention for female sexual identity disturbance: Self-monitoring of play behavior. *Journal of Abnormal Child Psychology,* 1979, *7*(4), 405–423 (a).

Rekers, G. A., & Mead, S. Female sex-role deviance: Early identification and developmental intervention. *Journal of Clinical Child Psychology,* 1980, *9*(3), 199–203.

Rekers, G. A., & Mead, S. Human sex differences in carrying behaviors: A replication and extension. *Perceptual and Motor Skills,* 1979, *48,* 625–626 (b).

Rekers, G. A., Mead, S. L., Rosen, A. C., & Brigham, S. L. Family correlates of male childhood gender disturbance. *The Journal of Genetic Psychology,* 1983, *142,* 31–42.

Rekers, G. A., & Milner, G. C. Early detection of sexual identity disorders. *Medical Aspects of Human Sexuality,* 1981, *15*(11), 32EE–32FF.

Rekers, G. A., & Milner, G. C. How to diagnose and manage childhood sexual disorders. *Behavioral Medicine,* 1979, *6*(4), 18–21.

Rekers, G. A., & Milner, G. C. Sexual identity disorders in childhood and adolescence. *Journal of the Florida Medical Association,* 1978, *65,* 962–964.

Rekers, G. A., Rosen, A. C., Lovaas, O. I., & Bentler, P. M. Sex-role stereotypy and professional intervention for childhood gender disturbances. *Professional Psychology,* 1978, *9,* 127–136.

Rekers, G. A., & Rudy, J. P. Differentiation of childhood body gestures. *Perceptual and Motor Skills,* 1978, *46,* 839–845.

Rekers, G. A., Sanders, J. A., & Strauss, C. C. Developmental differentiation of adolescent body gestures. *Journal of Genetic Psychology,* 1981, *138*(1), 123–131.

Rekers, G. A., Sanders, J. A., Strauss, C. C., Rasbury, W. C., & Mead, S. L. Differentiation of adolescent activity participation. *The Journal of Genetic Psychology,* in press.

Rekers, G. A., & Swihart, J. J. *Making Up the Difference: How to Strengthen the Single-Parent/Teenager Relationship.* Grand Rapids, Mich.: Baker Book House, 1984.

Rekers, G. A., & Varni, J. W. Self-monitoring and self-reinforcement processes in a pre-transsexual boy. *Behavior Research and Therapy,* 1977, *15,* 177–180 (a).

Rekers, G. A., & Varni, J. W. Self-regulation of gender-role behaviors: A case study. *Journal of Behavior Therapy and Experimental Psychiatry,* 1977, *8,* 427–432 (b).

Rekers, G. A., Willis, T. J., Yates, C. E., Rosen, A. C., & Low, B. P. Assessment of childhood gender behavior change. *Journal of Child Psychology and Psychiatry,* 1977, *18,* 53–65.

Rekers, G. A., & Yates, C. E. Sex-typed play in feminoid boys vs. normal boys and girls. *Journal of Abnormal Child Psychology*, 1976, *4*, 1–8.

Rekers, G. A., Yates, C. E., Willis, T. J., Rosen, A. C., & Taubman, M. Childhood gender identity change: Operant control over sex-typed play and mannerisms. *Journal of Behavior Therapy and Experimental Psychiatry*, 1976, *7*, 51–57.

Resnik, H. L. P. Eroticized repetitive hangings: A form of self-destructive behavior. *American Journal of Psychotherapy*, 1972, *26*, 4–21.

Roberts, R. E., Abrams, L., & Finch, J. R. Delinquent sex behavior among adolescents. *Medical Aspects of Human Sexuality*, 1973, *7*, 162–175.

Roberts, R., McBee, G. W. & Bettis, M. C. Youthful sex offenders: An epidemiologic comparison of types. *Journal of Sex Research*, 1969, *5*, 29–40.

Rosen, A. C. The intersex: Gender identity, genetics, and mental health. In S. Plog & R. Edgerton (Eds.), *Changing perspectives in mental illness*. New York: Holt, Rinehart & Winston, 1969.

Rosen, A. C., & Rekers, G. A. Toward a taxonomic framework for variables of sex and gender. *Genetic Psychology Monographs*, 1980, *102*, 191–218.

Rosen, A. C., Rekers, G. A., & Bentler, P. M. Ethical issues in the treatment of children. *Journal of Social Issues*, 1978, *34*(2), 122–136.

Rosen, A. C., Rekers, G. A., Brigham, S. L. Gender stereotypy in gender-dysphoric young boys. *Psychological Reports*, 1982, *51*, 371–374.

Rosen, A. C., Rekers, G. A., & Friar, L. R. Theoretical and diagnostic issues in child gender disturbances. *The Journal of Sex Research*, 1977, *13*(2), 89–103.

Rosen, A. C., & Teague, J. Case studies in development of masculinity and femininity in male children. *Psychological Reports*, 1974, *34*, 971–983.

Rudolf, G. de M. An experiment in the treatment of masturbation in oligophrenia. *American Journal of Mental Deficiency*, 1954, *58*, 644–649.

Russell, D. H. On the psychopathology of boy prostitutes. *International Journal of Offender Therapy*, 1971, *15*, 49–52.

Saghir, M. T., & Robins, E. *Male and female homosexuality: A comprehensive investigation*. Baltimore: Williams & Wilkins, 1973.

Salfield, D. J. Juvenile fetishism. *Zeitschrift fur Kinderpsychiatrie*, 1957, *24*, 183–188.

Salzman, L. Sexual problems in adolescence. *Contemporary Psychoanalysis*, 1974, *10*, 189–207.

Schultz, L. G. The child sex victim: Social, psychological and legal perspectives. *Child Welfare*, 1973, *52*, 147–157.

Schultz, L. G. Psychotherapeutic and legal approaches to the sexually victimized child. *International Journal of Child Psychotherapy*, 1972, *1*, 115–128.

Schumm, W. R., & Rekers, G. A. Sex should occur only within marriage. Chapter IV-A in Howard Feldman and Andrea Parrot (Eds.), *Current Issues in Human Sexuality*. Beverly Hills, Calif.: Sage Publications, 1984, 105–124.

Serbin, L. Sex-role socialization: a field in transition. In B. B. Lahey and A. E. Kazdin (Eds.), *Advances in Clinical Child Psychology* (Vol. 3). New York: Plenum Press, 1980.

Shankel, L. W., & Carr, A. C. Transvestism and hanging episodes in a male adolescent. *Psychiatric Quarterly,* 1956, *30,* 478–493.

Shoor, M., Speed, M. H., & Bartlett, C. Syndrome of the adolescent child molester. *American Journal of Psychiatry,* 1966, *122,* 783–789.

Skilbeck, W. M., Bates, J. E., & Bentler, P. M. Human figure drawings of gender-problem and school-problem boys. *Journal of Abnormal Child Psychology,* 1975, *3,* 191–199.

Spottswood, P. J., & Burghardt, G. M. The effects of sex, book weight, and grip strength on book-carrying styles. *Bulletin of the Psychonomic Society,* 1976, *8,* 150–152.

Stearns, A. W. Cases of probable suicide in young persons without obvious motivation. *Journal of the Maine Medical Association,* 1953, *44,* 16–23.

Stirt, S. S. Overt mass masturbation in the classroom. *American Journal of Orthopsychiatry,* 1940, *10,* 801–804.

Stoller, R. J. A contribution to the study of gender identity. *International Journal of Psychoanalysis,* 1964, *45,* 220–226.

Stoller, R. J. Male childhood transsexualism. *Journal of the American Academy of Child Psychiatry,* 1968, *7,* 193–209 (a).

Stoller, R. J. Psychotherapy of extremely feminine boys. *International Journal of Psychiatry,* 1970, *9,* 278–280.

Stoller, R. J. *Sex and gender: The development of masculinity and femininity.* New York: Science House, 1968 (b).

Stoller, R. J. *Sex and gender: The transsexual experiment.* New York: Jason-Aronson Inc., 1975.

Strzyewsky, J., & Zierhoffer, M. Aversion therapy in a case of fetishism with transvestic component. *The Journal of Sex Research,* 1967, *3,* 163–167.

Tanner, J. M. *Growth at adolescence.* Oxford: Blackwell Scientific Publications, 1955. (2nd ed., 1962.)

Thoresen, C. E., & Mahoney, M. J. *Behavioral self-control.* New York: Holt Rinehart & Winston, 1974.

Vanden Bergh, R. L., & Kelly, J. F. Vampirism: A review with new observations. *Archives of General Psychiatry,* 1964, *11,* 543–547.

Walinder, J. *Transsexualism: A study of forty-three cases.* Goteborg: Scandinavian University Books, 1967.

Weiss, J., Rogers, E., Darwin, M. R., & Dutton, C. E. A study of girl sex victims. *Psychiatric Quarterly,* 1955, *29,* 1–27.

Whitam, F. L. Childhood indicators of male homosexuality. *Archives of Sexual Behavior,* 1977, *6,* 89–96.

Zelnik, M., & Kantner, J. J. Probability of premarital intercourse. *Social Science Research*, 1972, *1*, 335–341 (a).

Zelnik, M., & Kantner, J. J. Sexuality, contraception, and pregnancy among young unwed females in the United States. In C. Westoff and R. Parke (Eds.), *Demographic and social aspects of population growth*. Washington, D. C.: U.S. Government Printing Office, 1972 (b).

Zucker, K. J. Childhood gender disturbance: Diagnostic issues. *Journal of the American Academy of Child Psychiatry*, 1982, *21* (3), 274–280.

Zucker, K. J., Doering, R. W., Bradley, S. J., & Finegan, J. K. Sex-typed play in gender-disturbed children: A comparison to sibling and psychiatric controls. *Archives of Sexual Behavior*, 1982, *11* (4), 309–321.

Zucker, K. J., Finegan, J. K., Doering, R. W., & Bradley, S. J. Two subgroups of gender-problem children. *Archives of Sexual Behavior*, 1984, *13* (1), 27–39.

Zuger, B. Effeminate behavior present in boys from early childhood: I. The clinical syndrome and follow-up studies. *Journal of Pediatrics*, 1966, *69*, 1098–1107.

Zuger, B. Effeminate behavior present in boys from childhood: Ten additional years of follow-up. *Comprehensive Psychiatry*, 1978, *19*, 363–369.

Zuger, B. Gender role determination: A critical review of the evidence from hermaphroditism. *Psychosomatic Medicine*, 1970, *32*, 449–467 (a).

Zuger, B. The role of familial factors in persistent effeminate behavior in boys. *American Journal of Psychiatry*, 1970, *126*, 1167–1170 (b).

Zuger, B., & Taylor, P. Effeminate behavior present in boys from early childhood. II. Comparison with similar symptoms in noneffeminate boys. *Pediatrics*, 1969, *44*, 375–380.

17

A Conceptual Model for Delivery of Behavioral Services to Behavior Disordered Children in Educational Settings

Hill M. Walker
Special Education and Rehabilitation
University of Oregon

H. Kenton Reavis
Utah State Office of Education
Salt Lake City, Utah

Ginger Rhode
Granite School District
Salt Lake City, Utah

William R. Jenson
Educational Psychology
University of Utah

INTRODUCTION

School systems have played an increasingly active role during the past two decades in serving children with behavior disorders (Noel, 1982). In spite of their greater involvement, however, the public schools have neither a strong history nor an adequate record in serving this population of children. For example, children with minor or minimally disruptive behavior problems have characteristically been accommodated within regular educational settings and generally have not received or been eligible for special therapeutic and remedial

700

services geared to deficits or excesses in behavioral functioning. Similarly, children with *serious* behavior disorders have often been excluded from public schools, assigned to self-contained and isolated settings within the school setting, exposed to home instruction, and/or assigned to external mental health facilities. None of these strategies has served the interests of behavior disordered children especially well. However, they have served the administrative and convenience interests of the public school system extremely well.

Since the passage of Public Law 94-142 in 1975, however, public schools have been *required* to serve the full range of children experiencing behavior disorders within the school setting, to assume responsibility for providing appropriate educational programs for them, and, failing that, to arrange for an appropriate program delivered by an agency external to the school setting. How have the public schools responded to this federal mandate? Large numbers of professionals working in school settings would probably agree that the response has been far less than optimal. The needs of behavior disordered children appear to be the least well met of all the handicapping conditions currently served by public school systems. As a rule, classroom teachers are not well instructed in the competencies necessary to effectively teach and manage such children.

Characteristically, such children place extreme pressures upon the management and instructional skills of teachers in both regular and special education settings (Walker, 1979) and often display behavior patterns (conduct disorders, aggression, noncompliance) that are highly aversive to teachers and peers. Surveys of teachers and other school-based service providers (e.g., counselors, resource specialists, school psychologists) consistently identify the behavior disordered child as representing the highest service priority of the disability categories served (Grosenick & Huntze, 1980). Similarly, the behavior disorders area is frequently rated as the personnel development specialty most in need of professionally trained individuals who are technically skilled and competent (Schofer & Duncan, 1982).

Ironically, the instructional and behavioral technologies exist to effectively accommodate the needs of the great majority of behavior disordered children of school age (Becker, in press; Engelmann & Colvin, 1983; Joyce, Hersh, & McKibbin, 1983; McDowell, Adamson, & Wood, 1982; Paine, Bellamy, & Wilcox, 1984; Reid & Hresko, 1981; Walker, 1979, in press). However, due to complex factors associated with school policy, procedures, and logistics, child services generated by these technologies have not been delivered effectively within public school settings (Morra, 1978; Rehmann & Riggen, 1977; Reynolds, 1983). Partly because of these factors, children experiencing behavior disorders of a moderate or severe magnitude are currently more likely to be exposed to control, containment, and punishment strategies than to therapeutic regimens (Neel & Rutherford, 1981).

The focus of this chapter is on the delivery of effective behavioral services to behavior disordered children within the context of the school setting. The chapter is divided into two major sections.

The first section focuses on service delivery structures, procedures, and practices for behavior disordered children in the school setting and reviews the nature of their operation over the past two decades as well as outcomes associated with them. The second section focuses on a conceptual model that was developed by the authors for delivery of a full range of behavioral services across a continuum of school settings.

SERVICE DELIVERY HISTORICAL FACTORS IN PUBLIC SCHOOLS' ACCOMMODATION OF CHILDREN WITH BEHAVIOR DISORDERS

The public school system in this country has a relatively brief history of providing services and programs for children classified as behavior disordered or emotionally disturbed. Prior to 1960, the mental health system assumed primary responsibility for serving the needs of this population (Paul & Warnock, 1980). The instructional needs and educational development of behavior disordered children were often secondary considerations in the therapeutic treatment processes promulgated by the mental health professions. As a result, academic programs and courses of study were frequently disrupted by mental health treatments administered outside the school setting; for example, assignment to residential or day treatment psychiatric facilities.

In the 1940s and 1950s, intense pressures began to be in evidence for school systems to assume a greater share of the responsibility for accommodating children with behavior disorders (Noel, 1982). These pressures developed primarily because: (a) family relationships were often disrupted by treatments administered in external settings; (b) many behavior disordered children were receiving incomplete and low-quality educational programs; and (c) there was a widespread perception that the mental health system was not sufficiently responsive to the broad array of needs commonly displayed by this population of children.

The failure of mental health approaches to cope effectively with the problems of behavior disordered children was the major impetus for the development of such public school programs. Paul and Warnock (1980), in discussing this development and its role in the shift of responsibility from the mental health professions to the public schools, note the following contributing factors: (a) there was a developing awareness that psychiatric and institutionally based treatments were often inadequate, not relevant to the child's actual behavioral needs, and in some cases, inhumane; (b) there was an insufficient availability of trained mental health personnel; and (c) many questioned the legitimacy of applying the medical disease model to the behavior problems exhibited by most members of this population. In addition, efficacy studies of nonschool-based treatments administered in child guidance clinics that were published in the 1960s and 1970s showed weak or nonexistent effects on child behavior in school (Levitt, 1971). These developments contributed to an emerging consensus among school personnel that mental health services were often not suitable or effective in remediating the problems manifested by behavior disordered children in school settings.

In the late 50s, school programs began developing for the behavior disordered population at an expanding rate. In 1948, for example, only 90 school districts in the United States had formal programs serving this population; by 1958, this figure had increased to 500 (Knoblock, 1963; Mackie, 1969; Noel, 1982). In 1968, Adamson reported that over 35,000 such children were being served within 2,800 programs nationally. The passage of PL 94-142 in 1975 provided a strong incentive for additional program expansion in this area.

Perhaps the most salient factor in the history of public schools' accommodation for behavior disordered children is the extent to which they have been underserved and excluded from available services. Lynn (1983) traces the history of public schools' involvement with all disability categories since 1875. He estimates there were 750,000 behavior disordered children in 1930 who qualified for school-based services—9,040 of them received service of some type. In 1977–78, the incidence figure was 1,026,340, with 288,626 who received service. Clearly, significant numbers of these children are still being denied access to needed services, in spite of the mandate of PL 94-142 regarding a free and appropriate educational program for all handicapped children.

Efficacy studies and surveys of public school programs serving behavior disordered children have been reported with increasing frequency over the last 15 years (Adamson, 1968; Grosenick & Huntze, 1980; Hirshoren & Heller, 1979; Lakin, 1982; Morse, Cutler, & Fink, 1964; Quay, 1963; Vacc, 1972). In a review of the findings of these studies, Noel (1982) notes the following outcomes: (a) public school programs suffer from the absence of a common conceptualization and program orientation; (b) there is no underlying theoretical perspective with a broad consensus among service providers that can serve as a basis for program development; (c) children are frequently isolated from the educational mainstream and served in segregated, self-contained settings; (d) only limited social integration with normal peer groups occurs, in spite of the PL 94-142 mandate relating to serving all handicapped children in the least restrictive educational setting possible; (e) school personnel who staff these programs are frequently noncertified and inadequately prepared to perform the tasks required of them; (f) large numbers of behavior disordered children are not served or are underserved by existing programs; (g) educators have not been able to agree on a logical, functional definition of what constitutes either emotional disturbance or disordered behavior, which, in turn, constrains the processes of screening, identification, program development, and service delivery; (h) internal program evaluation is weak and often nonexistent; and (i) disordered or disturbed child behavior in the school setting is usually not conceptualized in terms of the environmental demands or social context in which it occurs.

This assessment covers program efforts over the last 15 years but, in the authors' view, is highly representative of conditions in the field today. These outcomes suggest strongly that educators have improved little, if at all, on the prior efforts of the mental health professions in impacting upon the ability of behavior disordered children to cope effectively with their environments and to develop academically and socially.

It should be noted that remarkable technological progress has been achieved during this same period of time in the development of instructional and behavior change procedures that can dramatically alter skill deficits and behavior problems of the full range of children experiencing behavior disorders in school (Morgan & Jenson, in press; Paine, Bellamy, & Wilcox, 1984; Walker, 1979, in press; Walker, McConnell, & Clarke, in press). However, school personnel have not, as a rule, been aggressive in adapting, implementing, and delivering these innovative practices to the school setting. Reasons that partially account for this development will be discussed below.

BARRIERS TO EFFECTIVE SERVICE DELIVERY

One could identify a long and complex list of factors that serve as potential barriers to effective service delivery with behavior disordered children. An extensive analysis of such factors is beyond the scope of this chapter. There are, however, some highly salient barriers to service delivery that are germane to school systems and that have been commented on extensively in the professional literature within the recent past. These include the following: (*a*) the philosophical and programmatic values imbedded in the definition and development of school-based educational services for handicapped children; (*b*) teacher referral practices and their impact on children, teachers, and program development; (*c*) the behavioral characteristics of children who are referred and who ultimately access available services; and (*d*) definitional problems with the behavioral criteria used to certify children as behavior disordered.

Philosophical and Programmatic Values

In a very thorough and insightful analysis of the special education delivery system in this country, Lynn (1983) argues that the development of special education services was powerfully shaped by the *regular* educational system and that its inherent priorities, standards, and beliefs strongly influenced the nature and direction of the services that emerged. He identifies the most powerful forces in this regard as (*a*) the convenience needs, priorities, and power of professional educators in the public school system and (*b*) these professionals' concepts of a "normal" child and what a regular classroom should be like. As conceptualized according to these views, the purpose of special education was to maintain a stable, educational environment for normal children by creating special programs and environs for those incompetent, disruptive, or otherwise burdensome children who failed to meet minimal teacher expectations and who disrupt the normal process of education.

Thus, special education services do not have an underlying philosophical base that is grounded in either professional or humanitarian concerns for the accommodation of handicapped children in school settings. Rather, special education services developed as an adjunct or analog system designed for the placement of children who failed to meet requirements for admission to or maintenance within the educational mainstream. This basic value is perhaps most applicable to the treatment of behavior disordered children by the public school system. The dominant concern within this service structure is for simple accommodation or a holding action wherein the child is prevented from disrupting the educational process of other pupils.

Special education has suffered greatly from this philosophical base and school view of its primary function. These factors continue, for example, to plague mainstreaming efforts (Gresham, 1982; Hersh & Walker, 1983), contribute to the underfunding of special education program units, inhibit the development of quality instructional programs, and reinforce the separateness or distinctiveness of special education programming efforts. Unfortunately, special education's basic function as a depository for disruptive children is still highly valued by educators, as evidenced in its powerful reaffirmation as a tactic for coping with school discipline problems in the recently published *President's Commission on Excellence in Education* (1983).

Teacher Referral Practices

Patterns of teacher referral of children to special education are strongly linked to the philosophical base and school view of the purpose of these services as discussed above. Regular teachers have been traditionally encouraged to refer to special education those children who are at variance with their concept of what a "normal" child is. As a general rule, children who fall within +/− one standard deviation of the mean on measures of intellectual, behavioral, sensory, motoric, social, and academic functioning are judged to be within the normal range. Children who fall outside these limits are often more difficult to teach and manage, exert pressure(s) on the teachers' skills and tolerance levels, and are much more likely to be referred. Once referred, such children have a very high probability of being certified as handicapped and of becoming available for specialized placements that are usually external to the regular classroom.

Ysseldyke, Algozzine, and their associates (Ysseldyke, Algozzine, & Epps, 1982; Ysseldyke, Algozzine, Richey, & Graden, 1982; Ysseldyke, Algozzine, Shinn, & McGue, 1982; Ysseldyke, Christenson, Pianta, & Algozzine, 1983) have carefully studied the processes used by educators to refer, classify, and certify children as handicapped. Their findings suggest that: (*a*) once referred, teacher-nominated children are very likely to be certified as handicapped; (*b*) there is a high degree of overlap in the behavioral characteristics and performance deficits of referred, normal, and nonreferred children; and (*c*) the actual performance data relating to the child's deficits or excesses have little influence on the certification decision.

In an intriguing study, Ysseldyke et al. (1982), studied the extent to which data presented at multidisciplinary team meetings supported the decision by the team to either certify or not certify a child as handicapped. They found that such decisions had little or nothing to do with the data presented on measures germane to the referral. Instead, decisions were based much more strongly on such factors as *reason for referral, sex of pupil, appearance,* and *SES*. Given the degree of overlap between normal, nonreferred children and those who are referred and the limited influence of data presented on the child's performance vis-a-vis the referral decision, the authors pose a fair question: Why bother with the data?

The *specific* reasons underlying teacher referrals of children for special services and placements are complex, myriad, and described in great detail in the special education literature. However, it is apparent that both regular and special educators operate under incentive systems associated with the referral process. For example, via referral, regular teachers stand a good chance of ridding themselves permanently of a child with nettlesome behavioral and/or learning characteristics and are thus negatively reinforced for initiating the referral process. Special educators are positively reinforced by this process since referrals validate their existence, contribute to program support, and generate revenues through complex reimbursement formulas. Thus, regular and special education personnel maintain each others' practices very efficiently vis-a-vis the referral process. It is not surprising that such practices have proved remarkably durable over the years. It is also easy to see how a legitimate child's needs and considerations can be submerged within such a powerful incentive system.

The effects of referral practices on teachers, children, and programs are frequently of a deleterious nature. For example, teacher referral of children who are difficult to instruct and manage reduces the heterogeneity of the classroom and deprives the teacher of both the incentive and the opportunity to develop the competencies needed to effectively accommodate them. This is especially true of behavior disordered children. Further, such selective referrals can contribute to a narrowing of the teacher's tolerance level(s) and to an escalation of behavioral standards to a point where normal behavioral diversity is regarded as socially deviant or inappropriate.

The most pernicious effects on children of the indiscriminate referral practices commonly observed in today's schools have been elaborated upon at great length in the mainstreaming literature and are generally regarded as (*a*) *the stigmatizing effects of labeling,* and (*b*) *denial of access to normalized, mainstream environments* (Hunter, 1978; Keogh & Levitt, 1976; MacMillan, Jones, & Meyers, 1976; Sarason & Doris, 1978). Unnecessary removal from the educational mainstream *reduces* rather than increases the target child's ability to function effectively within mainstream classrooms and to cope with the demands of less restrictive settings. The disruption in peer social relationships that occurs in the assignment of such children to special settings is an equally powerful consideration in this regard.

Referral of children to special settings has historically constituted a disincentive in terms of program development activities for handicapped children enrolled in less restrictive settings. Cost-efficient instructional and behavior management programs need to be developed for use by regular teachers with mainstreamed handicapped children—especially behavior disordered children. Even with the advent of federally mandated mainstreaming efforts, there has not been a very strong demand for programming of this type. Conversely, there has been relatively little pressure exerted by regular educators for program development, accountability, and quality within special education. Quality initiatives within special education have been initiated by the field itself via its national leadership (Sontag, Button, & Haggerty, 1982). Such concerns are perhaps secondary to the repository and holding action functions that special education continues to perform for regular education.

Behavioral Characteristics of Referred Children

Several investigators have argued for the validity of bipolar classifications of problematic child behavior (Achenbach & Edelbrock, 1978; Edelbrock, 1979; Ross, 1980). This general approach has great relevance to child behavior disorders in school and the interactions with teacher referral practices and has gained considerable acceptance among professionals (Smith & Wilcots, 1982).

Ross (1980) argues that behavior, which our society defines as deviant or maladaptive, falls into two major classes depending on whether it violates social norms by occurring too frequently or too rarely. This dimension has been variously conceptualized as: (*a*) excessive approach behavior (aggression) versus excessive avoidance (withdrawal), (*b*) conduct problems versus personality problems, and (*c*) internalizing (problems with self) versus externalizing (problems with the environment) (Walker, 1982). In terms of the child behavior disorders commonly observed in school, examples of *externalizing* types would include aggression, hyperactivity, noncompliance, and acting out behavior; *internalizing* types would include social withdrawal/isolation, immaturity, and attention deficits.

As a rule, teachers tend to overrefer children with externalizing behavior disorders and to underrefer those with internalizing disorders. The senior author operated an experimental classroom setting over a nine-year period as part of the CORBEH (Center at Oregon for Research in the Behavioral Education of the

Handicapped) research and development model in behavior disorders (Walker, Hops, & Greenwood, 1984). Children in the elementary age range representing four behavior disorders were accepted as referrals (at different points in time) from 32 elementary schools in the Eugene, Oregon, school district. The behavior disorders were *acting out behavior, low academic survival skills, social withdrawal,* and *social aggression,* with acting out behavior and aggression representing externalizing disorders. Low academic survival skills and social withdrawal were classified as internalizing disorders.

There were dramatic differences among teachers and schools in their willingness to refer these two types of behavior disordered children for three to four months of treatment in the experimental class setting. Although there were sharp differences in the base rates of these four disorders within the general school population, these differences did not completely account for the far greater numbers of referrals of children with externalizing disorders. In many instances, the senior author and his colleagues had to aggressively recruit referrals of socially withdrawn and low survival skills children. This was never the case with the other two disorders; in fact, there were far more referrals of these children than could ever have been accommodated by the facility.

In this context, it should be noted that an impressive literature has developed over the last 8 to 10 years regarding the accuracy of teacher judgment of child behavior. Teacher rankings, ratings, and nominations are quite accurate when validated against criterion measures such as academic achievement, sociometrics, and observation data (Boldstad, 1974; Gresham, in press; Lakin, 1982; Nelson, 1971; Schaefer, 1982; Walker, 1983). This is true across the full range of externalizing and internalizing behavior disorders including social withdrawal (Greenwood, Walker, Todd, & Hops, 1979a), which is an extremely nonsalient, nonaversive disorder. Thus, it is unlikely that the observed higher rate of teacher referrals of disruptive, aggressive children was due exclusively or even substantially to more accurate teacher judgments of same. A more probable explanation concerns the greater salience and general aversiveness of these behavior patterns to teachers.

Recent research by the senior author on the social validation of teacher ratings of adaptive and maladaptive classes of child social behavior supports this view (Hersh & Walker, 1983; Walker, in press; Walker & Rankin, 1983). In these studies, both regular and special education teachers rated aggressive and disruptive forms of child social behavior as most aversive and least acceptable in the classroom setting from among a broad range of child behavior patterns.

Given these outcomes, it is much more likely that children with externalizing behavior disorders will access available school services via the referral process. This is far less true for children with internalizing disorders. In the authors' view, systematic screening procedures need to be in effect within public school systems that give all children an equal chance to be screened and identified for disorders of this type (see Walker, 1978).

The senior author and his colleagues (Greenwood, Walker, Todd, & Hops,

1979b) designed and developed a system called *SAMPLE* (Social Assessment Manual for Preschool Level) for use by teachers in identifying socially withdrawn children at the preschool level. SAMPLE has proven to be a cost-efficient and accurate method for such systematic screening. Other mass screening models of this type are described in Walker (1978, 1982). Additional validated systems of this type are needed to cope with the dual problems of under referral of children with internalizing disorders and their limited access to available school and related services.

Definitional Problems

One of the most pervasive obstacles to effective social policy and program practices in relation to children with behavior disorders or emotional disturbance concerns the field's inability to rationally define its subject matter. That is, what constitutes a behavior disorder or emotional disturbance? In commenting on this issue, Kauffman (1980; 1982) argues that, using existing approaches and criteria, this construct: (*a*) has no objective reliability, (*b*) does not unambiguously distinguish between populations of normal and disturbed/disordered children, and (*c*) becomes whatever professionals choose to make it.

This definitional vagueness and ambiguity has had some disastrous effects on the quality and level of services delivered to behavior disordered children. For example, it has maximized the degrees of freedom for school districts in choosing to identify and serve this population, to not recognize and identify the same, or to use other methods to cope with the problems such children present, for example, expulsion or drug therapy. As Kauffman (1982) notes, mandating and enforcing measurable standards of professional practice in these areas is virtually impossible because of definitional and classification imprecision.

This problem has been compounded by the federal government's adoption of Bower's (1969) definition of the seriously emotionally disturbed child. The definition lists five characteristics or elements that are likely to cause a child to be labeled as deviant. These are: (*a*) an inability to learn, (*b*) an inability to build satisfactory relationships with teachers and peers, (*c*) inappropriate behavior or feelings under normal circumstances, (*d*) a pervasive mood of unhappiness or depression, and (*e*) a tendency to develop physical symptoms or fears associated with personal or school problems (Kauffman, 1982).

Bower's definition has been severely criticized for its vague, subjective, and ambiguous qualities. It is extremely difficult to operationalize in terms of acceptable professional practices and systems, using existing criteria and procedures, cannot reliably distinguish normal from disordered/disturbed children and cannot differentially diagnose children as emotionally disturbed, behavior disordered, or socially maladjusted.

The above barriers to effective service delivery have operated historically within public school systems and are strongly in evidence today. They are the result of policy decisions, institutionalized practices, and long-standing attitudes that will be slow to change. The passage of PL 94-142 has generated counter pressures in relation to many of these barriers. However, they have yet to produce substantive improvements in service delivery for behavior disordered children.

CURRENT STATUS OF SERVICE DELIVERY PRACTICES

The current status of school service delivery practices in relation to behavior disordered children can be described under the following major areas: (a) the degree to which behavior disordered children are being fully served by the school system, (b) the strategy, tactics, and program options used to serve the behavior disordered population, (c) the quality of current programming efforts for behavior disordered children, and (d) the extent to which service delivery practices are responsive to the mandate of PL 94-142.

Service by the School System

In a national survey of needs in the behavior disorders area, Grosenick and Huntze (1980) found data to indicate that approximately three fourths, or 741,000 pupils, of the population of severely behavior disordered children were not being provided special education services. This is a very conservative estimate and refers only to those with severe behavior disorders. A substantially larger number of children with less severe behavior disorders currently receive no school-based services and have no prospect of doing so in the future.

It is estimated that the public schools are directly responsible for 85 to 90 percent of the school-age population, with the remainder assigned to within district mental health facilities or instate/out-of-state special schools (Noel, 1982). As a rule, those pupils involved in such placements have extreme forms or levels of externalizing behavior disorders (e.g., aggression) or bizarre internalizing disorders that challenge community social norms.

It is apparent that public school systems do not have the resources, trained personnel, or established programs to fully serve the behavior disordered population. Kauffman (1982) conservatively estimates that it would cost an additional $2.3 billion annually to fully serve the school-age BD population, with no more than 40 percent of this figure provided by the federal government. Specially trained or certified personnel would not be available in sufficient number to fully staff the programs that would be necessary to accommodate the full range of behavior disordered pupils.

This resource shortage is a joint federal, state, and local school district problem. At present, LEAs (local educational agency) would not be able to generate the revenues necessary to support the required program development and staffing in this area. Without significant state and federal involvement in sharing this financial burden, a long-term solution to the serious problems of underservice in this area will be elusive.

Strategy, Tactics, and Program Options

The strategy and tactics used by school districts to cope with the problems of behavior disordered children vary according to severity level. Walker (in press) and Grosenick (1981) have respectively reviewed the methods used with children in the *mild/moderate* range and those in the *severe* range.

Mild/Moderate Disorders. Four basic strategies are characteristically used by schools to cope with behavior disorders in this severity range. These are: (*a*) counseling and psychotherapy, (*b*) placement on drug therapy programs, (*c*) assignment to resource rooms and self-contained classes serving other handicapping conditions, and (*d*) accommodation in the educational mainstream.

Referral for counseling and psychotherapy has been a very popular alternative for use with the full range of behavior disorders. These techniques are very frequently recommended for remediation of mild/moderate child behavior disorders on the assumption that they will address the fundamental or root causes underlying the disorders. Counseling and psychotherapy, which are indirect forms of treatment, are often inappropriately applied by school personnel with the goal of impacting on the child's problems of overt behavioral functioning. Such techniques do not address the powerful environmental contingencies that support and maintain these behavior patterns. Direct intervention techniques that directly alter these relationships are required for this purpose (Patterson, 1974; Patterson, Cobb, & Ray, 1972; Walker, Greenwood, & Hops, 1981).

The use of drug therapy to control hyperactive, disruptive, and aggressive patterns of child behavior has increased dramatically in the last two decades. O'Leary (1980) estimates that approximately 600 to 700,000 children receive psychostimulant medications annually. Drug therapy is the ultimate control strategy for dealing with child behavior problems and serves the convenience interests of schools and parents more directly than any other available intervention. Drugs can produce powerful suppressive effects achieved at essentially no cost to responsible adult social agents. Evidence suggests that: (*a*) about 70 percent of children are responsive to psychostimulants, such as Ritalin, when the correct dosage is achieved and (*b*) children become more attentive, compliant, and cooperative following exposure (Cantwell & Carlson, 1978; Conners & Wherry, 1979). However, powerful controversies have developed around the pharmacological treatment of children in the last decade or so. There has been strong media and public concern expressed regarding the motives of the producers and dispensers of these drugs (Fox, 1978; Schrag & Divoky, 1975) as well as the possible undesirable side effects associated with their use, which include the *risk of drug dependence in later years, suppression of growth, increased heart rate and blood pressure,* and *impairment of certain cognitive functions* (Bendix, 1974; Cohen, Douglas, & Morgenstern, 1971; Conners, 1973; Knights & Hinston, 1969; Sprague & Slater, 1977; Swanson, Kinsbourne, Roberts, & Zucker, 1978).

Children who have externalizing behavior problems/disorders, but are not certified as emotionally disturbed or behavior disordered, are often assigned to resource rooms or to self-contained classes for other handicapping conditions, such as learning disabled or mild mental retardation. These are usually highly inappropriate placements that are designed to remove the child from the educational mainstream. Although they have little impact on the referral problem(s) they continue to occur at high rates in spite of the passage of PL 94-142.

Accommodation of the behavior disordered child in the educational mainstream with the delivery of appropriate support services in that setting (e.g., behavior management procedures) is probably the least popular of available alternatives. Although effective consultant-based intervention services and programs have been repeatedly demonstrated within the educational mainstream (Grubb & Thompson, 1982; Miller & Sabatino, 1978; Neel, 1981, 1982; Walker, Greenwood, & Hops, 1976, 1981, in press), they are requested and used by teachers at a very low frequency.

Walker (in press) has offered the following reasons as possible explanations for this outcome: (*a*) the teacher's inability to cope with an aversive pattern of child behavior may cause her/him to reject the child and be less than receptive to the use of inclass intervention procedures to deal with the problem, (*b*) teachers may be perceived as too busy or not sufficiently skilled to implement such procedures effectively in the classroom, (*c*) given the possibility of referral and removal to another setting, teachers may be less motivated to consider this procedure, (*d*) once children are placed on drug therapy programs, O'Leary (1980) notes that teachers are reluctant to consider implementing behavioral intervention programs with them, and (*e*) school personnel may have philosophical objections to the intrusiveness and nature of behavior management procedures, for example, reliance on reinforcement procedures.

Whatever the reasons, it is apparent that school systems are not taking advantage of a very powerful approach that is proactive, prescriptive, and therapeutic in application and extremely effective if implemented according to reasonable standards of treatment fidelity. In the authors' view, the necessary behavioral management technology for this task is clearly available and validated. However, school-based delivery systems are not established or operative in a way that allows children to access and benefit from systematic behavior management procedures. A model for achieving this goal will be described in the second section of this chapter.

Severe Disorders. The range of program options normally available to children with severe behavior disorders include the following: (*a*) self-contained classes, (*b*) special schools, (*c*) out-of-district school placements, (*d*) out-of-district residential placements, (e) consultant teachers, and (f) homebound instruction (Grosenick, 1981). In a national survey of school-based programs and services for children with severe behavior disorders, Grosenick and Huntze (1980) reported the following: (a) the great majority of these children are served in self-contained classroom programs, (b) the next most frequent option was out-of-district placements followed by consultant teacher service and homebound instruction, (c) of all children receiving homebound instruction, 41 percent were behavior disordered, and (d) a severe behavior disorder is more likely than any other disability to cause removal from school. In the great majority of cases, these children are exposed to program options that have strong control, containment, and punishment features.

In spite of recent court decisions and the passage of PL 94-142, the use of school "demission" techniques to control rather than to remediate the problems of children with severe behavior disorders is widespread. Grosenick (1981) describes six mechanisms used for this purpose. These are: (a) in-school suspension, (b) continuous suspensions, (c) shortened school day, (d) homebound instruction, (e) alternative school placement, and (f) ignored truancy. Collectively, these techniques have the effect of denying children access to therapeutic services and seriously disrupt the educational process. They are most likely to be abused with older and more seriously disturbed school-age populations. There is widespread agreement among professionals that the use of such techniques is incompatible with an appropriate educational program for behavior disordered children at any level of severity.

Quality of Programming

There has been widespread concern expressed by professionals regarding the quality of programming efforts for handicapped children generally and particularly in relation to programs and services for behavior disordered children of school age. In the Grosenick and Huntze (1980) national survey cited earlier, it was reported that a consensus existed among respondents regarding the poor quality and inappropriate focus of many programs for behavior disordered children. The major reason offered in support of this view was the lack of trained and certified teachers to staff such programs.

A number of other reasons have been offered by professional experts in the field (Apter, 1977; Grosenick, 1981; Kauffman, 1979; Keogh, 1980; Lakin, 1982; Noel, 1982; Paul, 1977, 1980; Walker, 1982). These include the following: (a) a failure to conceptualize disordered/disturbed child behavior in terms of the environmental context in which it occurs (Apter, 1977; Kauffman, 1979; Keogh, 1980; Walker, 1982), (b) a failure to take the behavioral standards and expectations of teachers into account in the definition, assessment, and remediation of behavior disorders (Walker, 1982), (c) the irrelevance of much research-based knowledge to the tasks teachers face in teaching and managing such children and the use of weak methodology in the development of such knowledge (Lakin, 1982), (d) a lack of concern with implementing the most powerful direct instructional and behavioral techniques in the accommodation of such children (Walker, in press), and (e) a tendency to avoid rigorous program evaluation procedures that would provide a basis for documentation of program effects and accountability (Noel, 1982). This state of affairs is somewhat ironic since proven, effective models for remediation of child behavior disorders in resource and self-contained settings have been in existence for some time (Glavin, Quay, & Wherry, 1971; Hewett, 1968; Walker & Buckley, 1972).

In recent years, a number of meta-analysis studies of special education program effectiveness have been reported in the literature (Kavale, 1983). As a rule, these studies show weak effects for much of special education programming. Although there are limitations associated with this methodology as well as the manner in which studies are selected for inclusion and coded, the publication of these findings has generated some intense pressures for accountability and confirmed the worst suspicions of many professionals.

Using meta-analysis techniques, Glass (1983) published a devastating outcome evaluation of the effectiveness of special education for mildly handicapped children who are learning disabled, mentally retarded, speech impaired, and emotionally disturbed. He argues from his findings that, in the behavioral sciences and education, there are a few general interventions of verified effectiveness but that their applications vary so greatly in effectiveness as to be essentially unpredictable. Several researchers have taken strong exception to the conclusions of Glass (see Lakin, 1983); however, he is essentially correct in his observations about the *average* effects of many model programs used in special education. Often, such programs are based on extremely weak instructional and intervention procedures that are applied with abysmally low levels of implementation fidelity.

These two criticisms are especially applicable to many of the program models and strategies used with behavior disordered children. In her review of service delivery practices and programs for behavior disordered children, Noel (1982) found evidence of many new, innovative, and effective model programs that are currently available but that have not been adopted at the school district level where program practices are often of low quality. The following factors may partially account for this outcome: (a) inadequately trained and noncertified teaching personnel who do not discriminate effective program models and practices, (b) a primary focus on behavioral and affective functioning and a corresponding de-emphasis on academic performance, (c) weak or nonexistent attempts to prepare the child for reentry into the educational mainstream, and (d) unconditional acceptance of the holding action function delegated to special educators by the regular educational system. At best, much of current special education programming for behavior disordered children can be classified as having marginal effectiveness.

The Mandate of PL 94-142

Behavior disordered and emotionally disturbed children have been described by Sarason and Doris (1978) as the first to be referred and the last to be mainstreamed. This statement accurately reflects both current and past practices. Reviews of program practices and service options consistently show that this population is served in the most restrictive of available school settings and often referred for placement in even more restrictive nonschool settings (Grosenick, 1981; Grosenick & Huntze, 1980). As noted earlier, many of these children are frequently denied access to the school setting through the abuse of suspension and exclusion mechanisms.

The more aversive and difficult to manage the child's behavior pattern is, the more likely she/he will be exposed to a *control* (drug therapy), *containment* (assignment to a self-contained setting), or *punishment* (excluded from school) strategy (Neel & Rutherford, 1981). Generally, these strategies are incompatible with delivery of an appropriate educational program in the least restrictive setting possible. On the other hand, children with less aversive, less salient behavior disorders are frequently not identified and not referred for services.

The logic or rationale supporting the assignment of behavior disordered children to more restrictive settings is rarely questioned by the school personnel responsible for these practices. Such assignments are made in response to intense pressures from teachers and are often carried out under crisis conditions. Time limits associated with such placements are rarely in evidence and the specification of behavior-exit criteria are equally rare. As a result, the duration of placement is often a function of idiosyncratic factors over which schools have little control.

CONCEPTUAL MODEL RATIONALE AND DESCRIPTION OF A CONCEPTUAL SERVICE DELIVERY MODEL

It is now apparent that mainstreaming, as a social policy, has not been successfully mandated if program practices at the school district level in relation to handicapped children are to be used as the criterion measure of compliance with the law. Tawney (1981) has described the vast discrepancies that exist between educational practices and decision making on a case-by-case basis and the intent or mandate of PL 94-142 as a social policy. It is now widely recognized that large numbers of handicapped children will not access regular classroom environments and that others will do so only for very limited amounts of time.

Hersh and Walker (1983) have described the massive logistical barriers that impinge upon the task of making mainstreaming an effective reality for the majority of handicapped children. These include: (*a*) the technical competence required of regular educators to accommodate the special needs of handicapped children, especially those who are severely handicapped; (*b*) the provision of sufficient diversity, specialization, and individualization of instructional programming to accommodate the needs of handicapped children in less restrictive settings; (*c*) the task of persuading regular educators that a mainstreamed handicapped child is *their* responsibility and that such children are entitled to large amounts of time, energy, and instructional attention to achieve a satisfactory rate of progress; and (*d*) the task of expanding the teacher's tolerance limits for bizarre forms of child social behavior they are not used to seeing and/or are unwilling to accept. Each of these factors has contributed to resistance to effective service delivery for handicapped children enrolled in less restrictive settings. Collectively, they explain or account for numerous mainstreaming failures.

Many handicapped children are not able to meet the performance requirements and behavioral demands (of teachers and peers) that exist in less restrictive settings. Gresham (1982) reviewed research evidence showing that mainstreamed handicapped children rarely achieve satisfactory peer-to-peer social adjustments, have low levels of social participation, and tend not to be accepted by nonhandicapped peers as workers and playmates. Similarly, regular teachers have proven to be quite reactive to the demands and the added burdens imposed by handicapped children who are difficult to teach and manage (Hunter, 1978; Lynn, 1981). Further, Keogh and Levitt (1976) report that regular teachers are very concerned about: (*a*) having control over who is mainstreamed into their classrooms, (*b*) their ability to meet the needs of mainstreamed handicapped children, and (*c*) the availability of adequate support services and technical assistance. The arbitrary placement of handicapped children in such settings without adequate preparation of the setting and the children involved or the provision of the necessary support and technical assistance services is a disservice to all parties. In the great majority of cases, these minimum requirements are not met at the school district level.

In possible anticipation of these outcomes, the National Association for Retarded Citizens (NARC) in 1978 defined mainstreaming as an educational philosophy or principle that is implemented via provision of a variety of classroom and instructional alternatives designed to accommodate the full range of severity levels. The NARC also advocated maximum temporal, social, and instructional interaction between handicapped and nonhandicapped pupils as part of this process.

In the authors' view, an effective service delivery system for serving handicapped pupils, consistent with the mandate of PL 94-142, requires at least three elements. These are (*a*) a range of placement options to accommodate different levels of severity, (*b*) rational and empirically based entry and exit criteria governing placement in such settings, and (*c*) transition strategies to facilitate transfer and integration across settings. The field has responded vigorously to the first of these elements—a large number of placement options have been developed to serve handicapped children representing different disabilities and severity levels. However, adequate development of the other two elements is sorely lacking. This is especially true for children with behavior disorders who are usually assigned to more restrictive settings and retained in those settings for long periods of time (Grosenick, 1981).

The authors have developed a *Comprehensive Behavioral Services Model* (CBSM) that provides a conceptual base for the delivery of services to the full range of behavior disordered children within a continuum of educational settings.

Table 17–1 contains a schematic of the CBSM, which consists of four levels that accommodate: (*a*) child severity level, (*b*) educational setting, and (*c*) type of remediation procedure. Severity levels, settings, and remediation proce-

TABLE 17–1

Comprehensive Behavioral Services Model (CBSM) for a Continuum of Educational Settings

level	child severity level	settings	remediation procedures
I	Mild	Regular classroom	Programs and procedures applied on a class-wide basis by the teacher. No consultant teacher assistance required.
II	Mild-Moderate	Regular classroom	Consultant-based remediation programs/procedures applied on a class-wide or individual basis. Teacher eventually assumes program control under consultant supervision.
III	Moderate	Resource or self-contained classrooms	Direct instruction and direct intervention based model programs containing the following elements: rules, praise, point systems, backup rewards, time-out, cost contingency, parent involvement.
IV	Severe	Special day schools, residential settings, mental health facilities	Intensive, complex, and restrictive intervention procedures. Compliance training level systems, small teacher/pupil ratios, mental health support services, parent involvement, social skills training, careful monitoring and supervision.

Strategies for Facilitating Programming Across Settings
1. Transenvironmental Programming
2. AIMS Assessment System
3. Social Integration Models

dures are correlated within each of the four levels. As one progresses downward through the system levels, child severity levels increase, settings become more restrictive, and remediation procedures become more complex, expensive, and restrictive. Level I and II remediation procedures are designed for use primarily in LRE (least restrictive environment) settings and provide support services for maintaining the child in such settings. Level II procedures usually require a teacher consultant for implementation, while Level I procedures do not. Level III procedures are designed for exclusive use in resource room and self-contained settings and are often standardized in nature. Level IV procedures are the most intensive and complex and are designed for remediation of severe behavioral deficits and excesses characteristic of children assigned to special day schools and residential settings.

Strategies for facilitating transition across and integration into less restrictive settings are a very important part of the CBSM and are required in order for the model to function as envisioned by the authors. Effective programs and models have been demonstrated in this area within the last several years (see Anderson-Inman, Walker, & Purcell, in press; Rhode, Morgan, & Young, 1983; Walker, in press; Walker & Rankin, 1983).

The CBSM rests on the assumption that behavioral technology has developed to the point where effective, validated remediation procedures are available for use in each of the four levels of the system. Standardized behavioral programs are currently available that have been designed for and tested within each of the respective system levels (Paine, Bellamy, & Wilcox, 1984). Proven teacher inservice training procedures are also available for developing competence in the application of such programs (Neel, 1982) within applied settings.

The CBSM relies on the IEP as the central vehicle for coordination of the decisions, resources, and personnel involved in the system's operation. A child study team could function very comfortably within the parameters of this model and would be essential to its effective operation.

The model rests on several key assumptions regarding service delivery, LRE, and transenvironmental programming techniques (Anderson-Inman, Walker, & Purcell, in press). For example, it assumes that a child study team, following a thorough performance/behavioral evaluation, would place the child in the least restrictive setting that was initially judged capable of accommodating the child. The child and teacher would be provided with the necessary support systems and technical assistance to maximize the probability of the child's retention in this setting. The child would be reassigned to a more restrictive setting only after it was clearly demonstrated that she/he was unable to meet the behavioral criteria considered minimally essential for retention in that setting. When such assignments are made, the child's IEP objectives would automatically be adjusted and directed at the specific behavioral requirements and skills required for entry into and maintenance within the next least restrictive placement. At a minimum, these objectives would be reviewed semiannually.

Thus, regardless of the current placement setting, the major focus of all programming efforts directed toward the child would be on preparing her/him to meet the minimal behavioral requirements for the next least restrictive, with the final goal being retention within the regular classroom on a full-time basis.

Special education settings provide opportunities for intensive training in the behavioral skills and competencies required for adjustment to less restrictive settings. Often, the rate of gain or progress can be maximized in these settings if there is a clear focus on preparing the child for either entry or reentry into a less restrictive setting. In this regard, it is extremely important that the critical skills and behavioral requirements that exist in such settings be carefully identified, and the target child's behavioral status on them assessed. Discrepancies between the child's skill or performance level and those specified by the receiving setting(s) would become remediation targets. Walker (in press) has described a model program that focuses on these tasks.

The CBSM also assumes that the target child's behavior would be carefully monitored in relation to these behavioral standards upon entry into and following social integration into a less restrictive setting. Both teacher ratings and direct observations would be necessary to adequately judge the child's behavioral status in this context. The necessary support services and technical assistance strategies should be closely tied to these assessments. The child study team would be the most feasible vehicle for performing these tasks.

Figure 17–1 on page 720 contains a flow chart illustrating decision processes and program options within the CBSM. As noted, the model depends on the careful tracking of pupils, their performance, and the development of specific behavioral criteria to govern successful accommodation to any given educational setting. Walker and his associates have developed an assessment methodology to achieve this goal (Hersh & Walker, 1983; Walker, in press; Walker & Rankin, 1983).

The CBSM targets the regular classroom as the setting in which the majority of behavior disordered children should be served, thus requiring the delivery of appropriate services and technical assistance to children and teachers via a teacher consultant model (Miller & Sabatino, 1978; Walker, Hops, & Greenwood, 1984). Consultant models of this type are both feasible and cost effective (Berry, 1972; Neel, 1982) and are very consistent with the mandate of PL 94–142.

Full and effective implementation of this model would have a dramatic impact on both school district practices in relation to behavior disordered children and the quality of services received by them. Further, it would make it possible for large numbers of such children to access less restrictive settings systematically and to absorb the social and educational benefits associated with them. The professional practices necessary for full implementation of the CBSM are described below.

FIGURE 17-1

Flow Chart of Service Delivery and Placement Processes for Child Behavior Problems/Disorders in LEAs

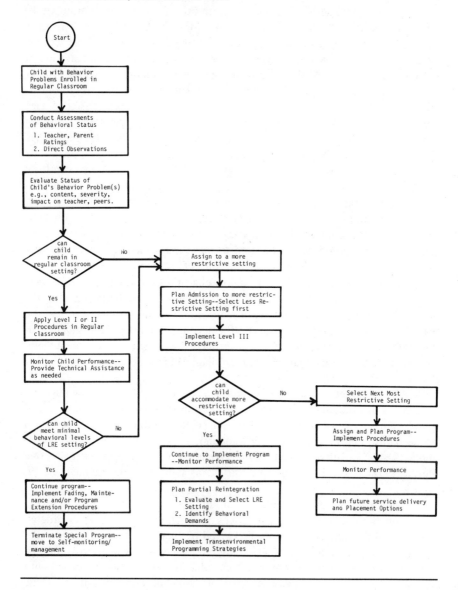

PROFESSIONAL PRACTICES AND IMPLEMENTATION OF THE MODEL

Seven elements or components have to be in place at the school district level in order for the CBSM to operate. These are: (*a*) regularly applied, mass screening-identification procedures; (*b*) the development of empirically based, setting-specific behavioral criteria governing entry/exit criteria for a continuum of school settings; (*c*) instruments and procedures for assessing child status in relation to such criteria; (*d*) remediation procedures and implementation standards for four levels of school placement settings; (*e*) social skills training procedures; (*f*) transenvironmental programming techniques; and (*g*) parent involvement strategies.

Mass Screening-Identification Procedures

Mass screening and identification procedures need to be implemented regularly within regular classrooms to identify children in need of referral for behavioral services. This is particularly true for children experiencing internalizing behavior disorders. Screening-identification models should be defined and structured in such a way as to give each child in these settings an equal chance to be selected for the full range of both internalizing and externalizing behavior disorders.

Walker (1978, 1982) has reviewed research in this area and has described procedures for conducting this task that are cost effective and accurate. Like other model programs developed for this purpose (see Clarfield, 1974; Cowen, Dorr, Clarfield, Kreling, McWilliams, Pokracki, Pratt, Terrel, & Wilson, 1973; Greenwood, Walker, Todd, & Hops, 1979b), they rely heavily on teacher evaluations of child behavior expressed in the form of ratings, rankings, and nominations according to specific criteria. Children who are identified at this level are further screened using more costly, but more sensitive, assessment methods, such as observation and sociometric measures.

A number of validated and reliable teacher checklists/rating scales are available for this purpose. Three of the more popular scales are (*a*) the *Devereaux Rating Scales* (Spivak & Swift, 1966), (*b*) the *Child Behavior Profile* (Achenbach, 1979), and (*c*) the *Walker Problem Behavior Identification Checklist* (Walker, 1970, 1976, 1983). Observation codes suitable for use in classroom settings are also available—some with normative data for use in decision making. These codes can be accessed through the *Mirrors of Behavior* section of most university libraries.

Development of Empirically Based Criteria

The absence of empirically based entry/exit criteria for use in making decisions about placement and transitions has created major obstacles to the mainstreaming process and has contributed to the practice of overretention of behavior disordered children in more restrictive settings, such as self-contained classes and special day or residential programs. Braaten (1982) has presented a valuable conceptual model for the differential evaluation and placement of students that addresses situations, severity levels, and the acute/chronic dimension of behavior disorders. However, his model does not generate information on the behavioral requirements of specific settings. Some limited attempts in this direction have been reported by Wilkes, Bireley, and Schultz (1979) with learning disabled children and by Brown, Branston, Baumgart, Vincent, Falvey, and Schroeder (1979) with severely disabled individuals. The focus of both these efforts was on the development of curricular content to teach the skills and requirements of less restrictive settings.

To date, there have been only informal attempts to develop setting-specific behavioral criteria that can be used for the purposes of placement, as a basis for initiating transenvironmental programming techniques and transition strategies in the transfer of children to less restrictive settings, and as curricular content for preparing target pupils to meet the behavioral requirements that exist in such settings. The senior author has developed and partially validated an assessment system of this type over the past four years called AIMS (Assessments for Integration into Mainstream Settings) (see Hersh & Walker, 1983; Walker, in press; Walker & Rankin, 1983). AIMS consists of four instruments. These are: (*a*) the SBS Inventory of Teacher Social Behavior Standards and Expectations, (*b*) the SBS Checklist of Correlates of Child Handicapping Conditions, (*c*) the Classroom Adjustment Code (CAC), and (*d*) the Social Interaction Code (SIC). The SBS Inventory and Checklist are used to conduct a preassessment of the behavioral requirements and technical assistance needs of teachers in potentially less restrictive placement settings and to produce information that allows one to select settings and to systematically prepare the child to meet the behavioral requirements that exist within them. The CAC and SIC are used for assessing the quality or adequacy of the child's classroom and peer-to-peer social/behavioral adjustments following integration. Normative observational data on ncnhandicapped, mainstreamed, and nonmainstreamed handicapped children are provided to facilitate decision making in this context.

The SBS Inventory is the primary instrument used to identify behavioral criteria for specific settings. Using this instrument, it is possible to develop generic criteria through sampling of a large number of teachers in different settings and also to assess the behavioral standards/expectations of individual teachers on a case-by-case basis. Teachers provide social validation ratings (Kazdin, 1977) on the SBS Inventory in relation to both adaptive and maladaptive classes of child behavior. For example, adaptive items are rated as to whether they are *critical, desirable,* or *unimportant* to a successful classroom adjustment, and maladaptive items are rated along an acceptability dimension of *acceptable, tolerated,* or *unacceptable.* The teacher's technical assistance needs in accommodating mainstreamed handicapped children are also assessed by this instrument.

Through the collection of data on large samples of teachers in different placement settings, the senior author and his colleagues have developed setting-specific behavioral criteria that reflect teachers' behavioral standards/expectations and have also identified a common core of behavioral requirements that appear consistent across settings. In this regard, Conte and McCoy (1980) noted the concern expressed by many professionals working with handicapped children in special settings that the behavioral expectations of professionals who receive such children may be different from those they were exposed to in the sending setting or environment. Research conducted to date (Hersh & Walker, 1983; Walker & Rankin, 1983, in press) indicates a high level of agreement across settings and teachers in the specific content of the *most preferred* and *least preferred* child behavior pinpoints.

Table 17–2 presents summary SBS Inventory item rankings for three groups of teachers (behavior disordered in institutional settings, noncategorical in self-contained settings, and regular) on Section I of the Inventory, which measures adaptive behavior. The items in Table 17–2 are the 10 highest rated behavioral competencies for the three groups of teachers, i.e., those judged to be most critically important to a satisfactory classroom adjustment. Table 17–2 indicates a high degree of overlap in the highest rated or most important items for the three groups of teachers.

TABLE 17–2

Highest Rated Items SBS Inventory Section I

	teacher groups							
	BD (N = 39)			RE (N = 50)			SpE (N = 22)		
item content	Rank	M^a	S.D.	Rank	M	S.D.	Rank	M	S.D.
Complies with teacher commands.	4	2.34	.53	1	2.68	.47	1	2.40	.50
Follows established classroom rules.	2	2.42	.49	2	2.58	.49	2	2.36	.49
Produces work of acceptable quality given skill level.				3	2.48	.50			
Listens carefully to teacher instructions and assignment directions.	9	2.26	.50	4	2.40	.49	9	2.22	.52
Expresses anger appropriately, e.g., not violent or destructive.	1	2.50	.50	5	2.40	.49	3	2.36	.49
Can have normal conversations with peers without becoming hostile.				6	2.38	.53			
Behaves appropriately in nonclassroom settings.	10	2.26	.50	7	2.36	.52			

TABLE 17–2 (concluded)

	BD (N = 39)			RE (N = 50)			SpE (N = 22)		
item content	Rank	M^a	S.D.	Rank	M	S.D.	Rank	M	S.D.
Avoids breaking classroom rule(s) even when encouraged by a peer.				8	2.36	.52			
Does seatwork assignments as directed.				9	2.36	.48	7	2.27	.45
Makes assistance needs known in appropriate manner.	11	2.26	.50	10	2.34	.51	10	2.18	.50
Responds to conventional behavior management techniques.							4	2.36	.58
Observes rules governing movement around the room.	3	2.39	.49				5	2.31	.56
Uses classroom equipment and materials correctly.							6	2.27	.45
Is flexible and can adjust to different instructional situations.	8	2.27	.50				8	2.22	.42
Seeks teacher attention at appropriate times.	5	2.32	.46						
Cooperates with peers in group activities/situations.	6	2.29	.51						
Listens when other children are speaking.	7	2.29	.45						
Copes with failure in appropriate manner.	12	2.26	.55						

^{a} Mean weighted rating

Similarly, Table 17–3 presents the same analysis for the maladaptive items assessed in Section II of the Inventory. There is also a very high level of agreement among the three teacher groups on the least preferred items of Section II. (Section I contains a total of 56 items and Section II has 51 items.)

These findings have been replicated by a number of investigators. They suggest that there is far more agreement than disagreement among teachers in different placement settings serving handicapped children. As such, they create the possibility of developing standardized, generic behavioral criteria that would be extremely valuable in the placement and integration of behavior disordered children.

There was also substantial agreement among the three groups on the level of their behavioral expectations as indicated by the average number of items

TABLE 17-3

Highest Rated Items SBS Inventory Section II

| | teacher groups | | | | | | | | |
| | BD (N = 39) | | | RE (N = 50) | | | SpE (N = 22) | | |
item content	Rank	M^a	S.D.	Rank	M	S.D.	Rank	M	S.D.
Steals.	3	2.92	.27	1	2.98	.14	7	2.81	.39
Self-abusive, for example, biting, head banging.	2	2.95	.22	2	2.98	.14	4	2.90	.29
Behaves inappropriately in class when corrected, for example, shouts back.				3	2.96	.19	8	2.81	.39
Physically aggressive with others.	1	3.00	0	4	2.94	.23	1	2.95	.21
Makes lewd or obscene gestures.				5	2.92	.27			
Engages in inappropriate sexual behavior.	5	2.89	.31	6	2.92	.27	3	2.90	.29
Refuses to obey teacher imposed classroom rules.	6	2.84	.37	7	2.90	.30	5	2.86	.35
Damages others' property.	4	2.92	.29	8	2.90	.30	2	2.95	.21
Has tantrums.				9	2.88	.32			
Ignores teacher warnings or reprimands.				10	2.88	.32	6	2.81	.39
Creates a disturbance during class activities, for example, excessively noisy, bothers other students, out of seat.	7	2.81	.39				9	2.81	.39
Reacts with defiance to instructions or commands.							10	2.77	.42
Verbally aggressive with others.	8	2.79	.41						
Disturbs or disrupts activities of others.	9	2.76	.43						
Does not ask permission to use others' property.	10	2.74	.44						

a Mean weighted rating

checked *critical* and *unacceptable* in Sections I and II. Table 17–4 shows very similar patterns of responding by the three groups on this variable.

Assessment Instruments

With respect to items rated by individual receiving teachers as *critically important* and *unacceptable*, someone knowledgeable about the child's behavior pattern is required to assess the child's behavioral status on these items. The senior author and his colleagues have applied a Likert rating scale to these items

TABLE 17–4

Mean Number of Items and Standard Deviation in Each Scoring Category

scoring category	teacher groups					
	BD (N = 39)		RE (N = 50)		SpE (N = 22)	
	M	S.D.	M	S.D.	M	S.D.
SBS Inventory Section I						
Critical	12.13	16.11	12.78	13.12	9.13	12.62
Desirable	39.55	15.21	39.70	12.30	40.63	12.14
Unimportant	4.24	4.84	3.50	5.80	6.22	8.60
SBS Inventory Section II						
Unacceptable	23.45	11.74	27.96	9.14	25.22	12.76
Tolerated	26.18	11.66	22.22	8.79	25.00	12.35
Acceptable	1.00	1.49	.82	1.73	.77	1.79

* *Note:* Section I: 56 adaptive behavior items; Section II: 51 maladaptive behavior items.

that indicates, for adaptive items, whether the target child is *acceptably skilled, less than acceptably skilled,* or *considerably less than acceptably skilled;* for maladaptive items, it indicates whether the rate or frequency of the maladaptive behavior is *nonexistent, within normal limits,* or *outside normal limits.* This rating format identifies behavioral pinpoints for remediation either prior to or following integration into the target setting. Other teacher rating scales and formats could also be used for this purpose.

Four Levels of School Placement Settings

Model programs and procedures have been developed, tested, and validated for remediation of child behavior disorders in each of the four placement settings contained in the CBSM. Paine, Bellamy, and Wilcox (1984) have described a large number of such programs/procedures for use across a broad range of educational settings. In addition, Millman, Schaefer, and Cohen (1980) have recently described an array of remediation procedures that have proven effective for commonly encountered school behavior problems, such as immaturity, habit disorders, and disturbed peer relationships. Examples of remediation procedures and programs appropriate for use in each of the four CBSM levels are described below.

Level I.   Standardized programs that have proven effective for class-wide applications in regular classroom settings include: (*a*) Assertive Discipline (Cantor, 1976b), (*b*) Precision Teaching (Deno & Mirkin, 1977), (*c*) Group Contingency Procedures (Greenwood, 1981; Walker, 1979), and (*d*) Peer tutoring and remediation strategies (Henderson & Jenson, 1982; Strain, 1981).

Level II.   A number of behavior management programs have been developed for use in regular classroom settings in cooperation with teacher consultants. Examples would include: (*a*) Contingency Contracting (Homme, 1969) and (*b*) The CORBEH (Center at Oregon for Research in the Behavioral Education of the Handicapped) behavior management programs designed for acting out behavior, low academic survival skills, social withdrawal, and social aggression (Walker, Hops, & Greenwood, 1984). These programs can be eventually turned over to teachers for operation with a corresponding reduction in required consultant assistance.

Level III.   Model programs for use in resource and self-contained settings have been reported by Hewett (1968); Walker and Buckley (1972, 1974); Wiederholt, Hammill, and Brown (1978, 1983); and O'Connor (1979). These program models have been widely adopted by school systems and produce powerful effects within the settings in which they are implemented.

Level IV.   Standardized techniques and programs for use with severely behavior disordered children in residential type settings have only recently been developed and reported in the literature. Two examples would include (*a*) Systematic Compliance Training (Engelmann & Colvin, 1983) and (*b*) Level Behavior Management Systems (Morgan & Jenson, in press; Walker, 1983). These are extremely powerful programs that require careful implementation by trained professionals.

Social Skills Training Procedures

Systematic social skills training is of critical importance to the broad range of handicapped children and especially to children with behavior disorders. Reviews of research in this area by Gresham (1981, in press); Michelson and Wood (1980); and Strain, Guralnick, and Walker (in press) indicate that social skills training can improve both social participation and social acceptance. Social skills are an important determinant of social competence (Foster & Ritchey, 1979) and directly influence the quality of peer-to-peer social adjustment. They are a major prerequisite for effective mainstreaming for most handicapped children.

Some excellent social skills training programs are currently available. Examples include (*a*) the ACCEPTS Program (Walker, McConnell, Holmes, Todis, Walker, & Golden, 1983), (*b*) Social Effectiveness Training (Jackson, Jackson, & Monroe, 1983), and (*c*) Skillstreaming the Adolescent (Goldstein, Sprafkin, Gershaw, & Klein, 1980); and Social Skills in the Classroom (Stephens, 1978).

Transenvironmental Programming Techniques

Transenvironmental programming techniques refer to a methodology for matching children to settings in academic, behavioral, social, and ecological domains (see Anderson-Inman, Walker, & Purcell, in press). It consists of assessment, monitoring/tracking, instructional, and behavioral management strategies for use in the effective transitioning of handicapped children from more to less restrictive strategies. Transenvironmental programming attempts to systematically prepare the target child to meet or cope with the demands and performance requirements of LRE settings in these four domains prior to social integration.

Parent Involvement Strategies

Parent involvement is an extremely important component of school-based programs for behavior disordered children (see Jones, 1980; Patterson, 1982; Wilson, 1983). As behavior disorders become more severe and children are treated in more restrictive settings, effective parent involvement becomes ever more imperative. Parent involvement is of two general types: direct training in management techniques and providing for the delivery of school-earned privileges at home.

If the above elements are in place and implemented with reasonable levels of fidelity, the CBSM described herein can provide an effective framework for the delivery of high-quality services to behavior disordered children in a continuum of school settings. Teacher motivation and staff development, however, are not addressed in the CBSM system; these two factors can have a powerful impact on the effectiveness of any service delivery system. Costs are also an issue. The authors have no estimate of the degree to which adoption of the CBSM would increase costs in serving the behavior disordered school population.

A CASE EXAMPLE

During the 1982–83 school year, the authors planned and obtained approval for a partial demonstration of the remediation elements of the CBSM in the state of Utah. The demonstration was implemented during the 1983–84 school year in a cooperative arrangement between the Granite School District of Salt Lake City and the Utah Department of Education.

The demonstration was planned and conducted in two phases. In phase one, the authors conducted an intensive three-day workshop in which participants were exposed to nine remediation programs that collectively spanned the four levels of the CBSM. These included the four CORBEH behavior management programs, the ACCEPTS social skills program, the AIMS assessment system, a compliance training program for severely disturbed pupils, transenvironmental programming, and a model behavior management program for use in resource and self-contained programs. In phase two, the third author, an employee of the Granite School District, provided technical assistance and resource support to the inservice participants who selected one or more of the programs to focus on and implement during the 1983–84 school year.

The inservice training session was held in the Granite School District in August prior to the start of the school year. A total of 25 special educators participated in the training. Three were program specialists, i.e., coordinators, three were teachers of self-contained classrooms for behavior disordered pupils, and 19 were resource teachers. Thirteen were assigned to the elementary level and 12 to the junior/senior high level.

Each of the nine remediation programs was self-contained and packaged in the form of either books, program manuals, or chapters that contained implementation guidelines and instructions. Training focused on acquainting participants with each of the nine programs, their goals, basic features, and appropriate school applications. Training activities involved: (a) lecture, discussion, and question/answer, (b) reading of materials, (c) viewing of videotaped simulations of application procedures, and (d) role-play techniques. At the end of the training session, each participant was asked to select one or more of the programs to focus on during the school year.

Each participant chose a program to master and implement. As a first step, participants familiarized themselves with the program to the point where a conceptual mastery test of the program's content could be passed at a criterion accuracy level of 90 percent. Following conceptual mastery, the participant and the program consultant planned the implementation process. At this point, the participant received ownership of all materials (books, manuals, tests, etc.) relating to the program, with costs absorbed by the district. This proved to be a powerful incentive for achieving program mastery.

The program was then implemented in cooperation with the consultant, who provided supervision, consultation, and technical assistance. Ultimately, the teacher or participant assumed full control of the program and retained it until the program was terminated or faded out. At the end of the training session, participants evaluated the training received and the programs they had been exposed to using a questionnaire format and a Likert scale (1–5) rating procedure. Tables 17–5 and 17–6 on the following pages contain results of this evaluation by *elementary* and *junior/senior high* participants.

Collectively, the participants assigned high ratings to the remediation programs in terms of their relevance, perceived effectiveness, and value. The programs were consistently rated higher by elementary-level participants. This was not unexpected, since the programs had a clear elementary focus and a wider range of applicability at this level. Written comments of the junior/senior high participants consistently indicated that the programs would have to be adapted to be used effectively at that level.

Evaluations of the overall quality of the training session and the manner in which it was conducted were more evenly balanced between the two groups of participants. The results were quite positive, and written comments were

TABLE 17–5

Participants' Evaluation of Inservice Training in CBSM Program Elements

CBSM components	relevance				effectiveness				value			
	elementary		junior/ senior high		elementary		junior/ senior high		elementary		junior/ senior high	
	X̄	S.D.	X̄	S.D.	X̄	S.D.	X̄	S.D.	X̄	S.D.	X̄	S.D.
1. CLASS PASS*	4.91	.28	3.84	.89	4.66	.49	4.09	.83	4.66	.65	4.23	.83
2. PEERS	4.30	.94	3.18	1.47	4.30	.63	3.66	1.41	4.30	.75	3.72	1.48
3. RECESS	4.38	.87	3.07	1.49	4.46	.77	3.70	1.33	4.66	.77	3.45	1.36
4. ACCEPTS	4.15	1.06	4.23	.72	4.58	.79	4.25	.75	4.38	1.26	4.46	.51
5. AIMS	4.53	.66	4.38	1.12	4.38	.65	4.18	1.16	4.41	.66	4.30	1.10
6. Compliance Training	3.07	1.55	2.90	1.30	3.75	1.35	3.62	1.18	3.58	1.31	3.30	1.25
7. Model Program for Self-Contained Behavior Disorders Classroom	3.90	1.13	2.77	1.39	3.90	1.10	3.71	.95	4.10	1.10	3.50	1.06
8. Transenvironmental Programming	4.53	.52	4.54	.68	4.41	.67	4.33	.70	4.69	.48	4.60	.51

* The PASS program was inadvertently omitted from the evaluation form.

TABLE 17-6

Participants' Evaluation of Inservice Training in CBSM Program Elements

inservice training	elementary		junior/ senior high	
	$\overline{X}$	S.D.	$\overline{X}$	S.D.
Content Appropriateness	4.84	.37	4.00	1.15
Organization	4.46	.66	4.38	.87
Format	4.23	.72	4.41	.66
Presentation	4.53	.66	4.69	.48
Clarity	4.69	.48	4.25	.86
Comprehensiveness	4.61	.76	4.00	.81
Rapport	4.69	.63	4.76	.43

strongly supportive of the relevance and appropriateness of the training and the skill outcomes achieved.

As part of the training, participants were exposed to the CBSM model as described herein in order to provide a context for the training session and the goals/objectives of the demonstration project. They were asked two questions relating to this topic as part of the training evaluation. These questions were: (a) interest level in the CBSM service delivery model for bettering statewide services for children with mild to severe behavior disorders and (b) interest level in being a part of the model and its development/demonstration. The participants' average response to question one was as follows: elementary, mean = 4.61, S.D. = .65; junior/senior high, mean = 4.16, S.D. = .71. For question two, the results were: elementary, mean = 4.69, S.D. = .48; junior/senior high, mean = 4.45, S.D. = .82. These data suggest a strong level of interest in the model by these two groups.

Finally, a tally was made of the programs the participants chose to focus on. Participants at the elementary level selected eight of the nine programs one or more times, while junior/senior high participants selected five of nine one or more times. The most popular programs at the elementary level were ACCEPTS (9), CLASS (8), RECESS (6), and PASS (5). At the junior/senior high level, they were ACCEPTS (9), CLASS (7), and PASS (6). These program selections reflect a general teacher concern with social skills training, group classroom management procedures, and the control of disruptive and aggressive behavior.

The results of phase one of the CBSM demonstration were highly encouraging. Follow-up and program implementation are ongoing. Evaluative data are not available as yet on phase two. However, implementation has focused strongly on Level I and II programs in an effort to retain as many behavior disordered children as possible in less restrictive placement settings, for example, resource and regular classrooms.

In a related study within the Granite School District, the senior author has collaborated with district personnel in using the SBS methodology to develop behavioral criteria for mainstreaming handicapped children into the regular classroom setting. The SBS Inventory was completed by the principal and randomly selected first, third, and fifth-grade teachers within 18 elementary schools in the district—a total of 72 professionals. The 16 highest rated adaptive and maladaptive items (from Sections One and Two of the Inventory) were incorporated into a child behavior rating scale for use in determining when to integrate a child into the educational mainstream. The 16 adaptive items are rated in terms of whether the child is *more skilled, as skilled,* or *less skilled* than peers. The 16 maladaptive items are rated in terms of whether the rate or frequency of the behavior is *nonexistent, within normal limits,* or *outside normal limits.* (This work is described in Kukic, Walker, & Grant, in press.) Professionals who have used the scale have found it to be quite useful in providing socially valid exit criteria and in facilitating placement decisions.

CONCLUSIONS AND IMPLICATIONS

A decade ago, a conceptual model of this type would not have been feasible. However, sufficient advances have occurred in the areas of (*a*) mass screening-identification, (*b*) behavioral assessment, (*c*) social skills training, (*d*) development of standardized behavioral programming, (*e*) social validation, and (*f*) social integration models to make a service delivery system of this type both feasible and practicable at the school district level. Although many LEAs would be able to implement only parts of the CBSM, its adoption may prove to be highly cost effective in reversing some of the long-established deleterious practices associated with serving the behavior disordered school-age population.

The CBSM remediation programs described herein require teacher consultant assistance in many instances for effective implementation. The authors are aware that available teacher consultants are in short supply in many LEAs and that teacher consultant services are one of the least often used service options by school districts in accommodating children with severe behavior disorders. However, conventional management procedures are not sufficient to support the retention of such children in less restrictive settings. In the great majority of cases, special programming involving the use of teacher consultants will be required for this purpose. If the practice of assigning and retaining behavior disordered children in less restrictive settings is to be reversed, reallocation of some staffing resources/patterns may be required.

Substantial effort needs to be invested in developing behavior-specific entry/exit criteria for different settings serving the behavior disordered child. Without these criteria, the placement of such children reduces to an arbitrary process, and the duration of placement is often capricious. Further, behavioral programming efforts usually suffer from a weak foundation and lack of focus in their absence.

The authors are aware that numerous obstacles exist in relation to the adoption and effective implementation of the CBSM: for example, costs, availability of trained personnel, logistical barriers, long-established practices serving the convenience needs of schools that are resistant to change, and so forth. However, it is hoped the model will be of value to professionals in their efforts to improve the quality and delivery of services to behavior disordered children in school settings.

REFERENCES

Achenbach, T. The child behavior profile: An empirically based system for assessing children's behavioral problems and competencies. *International Journal of Mental Health,* 1979, *7* (3–4), 26–40.

Achenbach, T., & Edelbrock, C. The classification of child psychopathology: A review and analysis of empirical efforts. *Psychological Bulletin,* 1978, *85,* 275–301.

Adamson, G. Study on programs on the emotionally disturbed. *Exceptional Children,* 1968, *34,* 756–757.

Anderson-Inman, L., Walker, H., Purcell, J. *Promoting the transfer of skills across settings: Transenvironmental programming for handicapped students in the mainstream.* Columbus, Ohio: Charles E. Merrill Publishing, in press.

Apter, S. Applications of ecological theory: Toward a community special education model. *Exceptional Children,* 1977, *43,* 366–373.

Becker, W. Direct instruction. *Proceedings of the XVI Banff Conference on Education.* New York: Brunner/Mazel, in press.

Bendix, S. Drug modification of behavior: A form of chemical violence against children? *Journal of Clinical Child Psychology,* 1974, *2* (3), 17–19.

Berry, K. *Models for mainstreaming.* San Rafael, Calif.: Dimensions Publishing, 1972.

Boldstad, O. *The relationship between teachers' assessment of students and students' actual behavior in the classroom.* Unpublished doctoral dissertation, University of Oregon, 1974.

Bower, E. *Early identification of emotionally handicapped children in school* (2nd ed.). Springfield, Ill.: Charles C Thomas, 1969.

Braaten, S. A model for the differential assessment and placement of emotionally disturbed students in special education programs. In M. Noel & N. Haring (Eds.), *Progress or change: Issues in educating the emotionally disturbed* (Vol. 1). Seattle: University of Washington, 1982.

Brown, L., Branston, M., Baumgart, D., Vincent, L., Falvey, M., & Schroeder, J. Using the characteristics of current and subsequent least restrictive environments in the development of curricular content for severely handicapped students. *American Association for Education of the Severely and Profoundly Handicapped Review*, 1979, *4*, 407–424.

Cantor, L. *Assertive discipline*. Santa Monica, Calif.: Cantor and Associates, 1976.

Cantwell, D., & Carlson, G. Stimulants. In J. S. Wherry (Ed.), *Pediatric psychopharmacology: The use of behavior modifying drugs on children*. New York: Brunner/Mazel, 1978.

Clarfield, S. The development of a teacher referral form for identifying early school maladaption. *American Journal of Community Psychology*, 1974, *2*, 199–210.

Cohen, D., Douglas, V., & Morgenstern, G. The effect of methylphenidate on attentive behavior and autonomic activity in hyperactive children. *Psychopharmacologia*, 1971, *22*, 282.

Conners, C. What parents need to know about stimulant drugs and special education. *Journal of Learning Disabilities*, 1973, *6*, 349–351.

Conners, C., & Wherry, J. Pharmacotherapy of psychopathology in children. In H. C. Quay & J. S. Wherry (Eds.), *Psychopathological disorders of childhood* (2nd ed.). New York: John Wiley & Sons, 1979.

Conte, J. R., & McCoy, L. Teacher and social worker agreement on behavioral expectations of special children. *Exceptional Children*, 1980, *46*, 645–646.

Cowen, E., Dorr, D., Clarfield, S., Kreling, B., McWilliams, S., Pokracki, F., Pratt, D., Terrel, D., & Wilson, A. The AML: A quick screening device for early detection of school maladaption. *American Journal of Community Psychology*, 1973, *1*, 12–35.

Deno, S., & Mirkin, P. *Data-based program modification*. Minneapolis: University of Minnesota, 1977.

Edelbrock, C. Empirical classification of children's behavior disorders: Progress based on parent and teacher ratings. *School Psychology Digest*, 1979, *8*, 355–369.

Engelmann, S., & Colvin, G. *Generalized compliance training*. Austin, Tex.: Pro-Ed Publishers, 1983.

Foster, S. L., & Ritchey, W. L. Issues in the assessment of social competence in children. *Journal of Applied Behavior Analysis*, 1979, *12*, 625–638.

Glass, G. Effectiveness of special education. *Policy Studies Review* [Special issue] 1983, *2* (1), 79–84.

Glavin, J., Quay, A., & Wherry, J. Behavioral and academic gains of conduct problem children in different classroom settings. *Exceptional Children*, 1971, *34*, 441–446.

Goldstein, A. P., Sprafkin, R. P., Gershaw, N. J., & Klein, P. *Skillstreaming the adolescent: A structured learning approach to teaching prosocial skills*. Champaign, Ill.: Research Press, 1980.

Greenwood, C. Group oriented contingencies and peer behavior change. In P. Strain (Ed.), *The utilization of classroom peers as behavior change agents*. New York: Plenum Press, 1981.

Greenwood, C., Walker, H. M., Todd, N., & Hops, H. Selecting a cost-effective device for the assessment of social withdrawal. *Journal of Applied Behavior Analysis*, 1979, *12*, 639–652 (a).

Greenwood, C., Walker, H. M., Todd, N., & Hops, H. *SAMPLE: Social assessment manual for preschool level*. Available from CORBEH, Center on Human Development, University of Oregon, Eugene, Ore., 1979(b).

Gresham, F. Social skills training with handicapped children: A review. *Review of Educational Research*, 1981, *51*, 139–176.

Gresham, F. Misguided mainstreaming: The case for social skills training with handicapped children. *Exceptional Children*, 1982, *48*, 422–433.

Gresham, F. Conceptual issues in the assessment of social competence in children. In P. Strain, M. Guralnick, & H. M. Walker (Eds.), *Children's social behavior: Development, assessment and modification*. New York: Academic Press, in press.

Grosenick, J. Public school and mental health services to severely behavior disordered students. *Behavior Disorders*, 1981, *6*, 183–190.

Grosenick, J. K., & Huntze, S. L. *National needs analysis in behavior disorders: Adolescent behavior disorders*. Columbia: University of Missouri Department of Special Education, 1980.

Grubb, R., & Thompson, M. Delivering related services to the emotionally disturbed: A field based perspective. In N. Haring & M. Noel (Eds.), *Progress or change: Issues in educating the emotionally disturbed* (Vol. 2). Seattle: University of Washington, 1982.

Henderson, H., & Jensen, W. *Management of the behavior of emotionally disturbed children through peer social reinforcement*. Unpublished manuscript, Utah State University, Logan, 1982.

Hersh, R., & Walker, H. M. Great expectations: Making schools effective for all children. *Policy Studies Review*, 1983, [Special issue] *2*(1), 147–188.

Hewett, F. *The emotionally disturbed child in the classroom*. Boston: Allyn & Bacon, 1968.

Hirshoren, A., & Heller, G. Programs for adolescents with behavior disorders: The state of the art. *Journal of Special Education*, 1979, *13*, 275–281.

Homme, C. *Contingency contracting in the classroom*. Champaign: Research Press, 1969.

Hunter, M. Mainstreaming students with exceptional needs: Implications for the school. *UCLA Educator*, 1978, *20*, Spring/Summer, 14–20.

Jackson, N. F., Jackson, D. A., & Monroe, C. *Getting along with others: Teaching social effectiveness to children*. Champaign: Research Press, 1983.

Jones, V. *Adolescents with behavior problems*. Boston: Allyn & Bacon, 1980.

Joyce, B. R., Hersh, R. H., & McKibbin, M. *The structure of school improvement.* New York: Longmans, 1983.

Kauffman, J. An historical perspective on disordered behavior and an alternative conceptualization of exceptionality. In F. H. Wood & K. C. Lakin (Eds.), *Disturbing, disordered or disturbed? Perspectives on the definition of problem behavior in educational settings.* Minneapolis: University of Minnesota Department of Psychoeducational Studies, 1979.

Kauffman, J. Where special education for disturbed children is going: A personal view. *Exceptional Children,* 1980, *46, 522*–527.

Kauffman, J. Social policy issues in special education and related services for emotionally disturbed children and youth. In M. Noel & N. Haring (Eds.), *Progress or change: Issues in educating the emotionally disturbed.* Seattle: University of Washington, 1982.

Kavale, K. Fragile findings, complex conclusions, and meta-analysis in special education. *Exceptional Educational Quarterly,* 1983, *4* (3), 97–106.

Kazdin, A. Assessing the clinical or applied importance of behavior change through social validation. *Behavior Modification,* 1977, *4,* 427–452.

Keogh, B. (Ed.). *Overview of advances in special education* (Vol. 1). Greenwich, Conn.: JAI Press, 1980.

Keogh, B., & Levitt, M. Special education in the mainstream: A confrontation of limitations. *Focus on Exceptional Children,* 1976, *8,* 1–10.

Knights, R., & Hinston, G. The effects of methylphenidate (Ritalin) on motor skills and behavior of children with learning problems. *Journal of Nervous Mental Disorders,* 1969, *48,* 643.

Knoblock, P. Critical factors influencing educational programming for disturbed children. *Exceptional Children,* 1963, *30,* 124–129.

Kukic, S., Walker, H. M., & Grant J. The Granite classroom behavior scale (BCBS): A criterion referenced instrument for guiding placement and programming decisions in school settings. *Behavior Disorders Journal,* in press.

Lakin, K. Research-based knowledge and professional practices in special education for emotionally disturbed children. In C. Smith & B. Wilcots (Eds.), *Current issues in behavior disorders—1982.* Des Moines, Iowa: Department of Public Instruction, 1982.

Lakin, K. A response to Gene Glass. *Policy Studies Review* 1983, [Special issue] *2* (1), 233–240.

Levitt, E. Research in psychotherapy with children. In A. E. Bergin & S. L. Garfield (Eds.), *Handbook of psychotherapy and behavior change. An empirical analysis.* New York: John Wiley & Sons, 1971.

Lynn, L. E., Jr. The emerging system for educating handicapped children. *Policy Studies Review* 1983, Special issue, *2* (1), 21–58.

Mackie, R. *Special education in the United States: Statistics 1948–1966.* New York: Columbia University Teachers College Press, 1969.

MacMillan, D., Jones, R., & Meyers, C. Mainstreaming the mildly retarded: Some questions, cautions and guidelines. *Mental Retardation*, 1976, *14*(1), 86–91.

McDowell, R., Adamson, G., & Wood, F. *Teaching emotionally disturbed children.* Boston: Little, Brown, 1982.

Michelson, L., & Wood, R. Behavioral assessment and training of children's social skills. *Progress in Behavior Modification*, 1980, *9*, 241–291.

Miller, T., & Sabatino, D. An evaluation of the teacher consultant model as an approach to mainstreaming. *Exceptional Children*, 1978, *44*, 86–91.

Millman, H., Schaefer, C., & Cohen, J. *Therapies for school behavior problems.* London: Jossey-Bass, 1980.

Morgan, D., & Jenson, W. *Teaching behaviorally disordered children: Preferred strategies.* New York: McGraw-Hill, in press.

Morra, L. *The individualized educational program* (Monograph series on PL 94–142 implementation). Washington, D.C.: U.S. Office of Education Bureau of Education for the Handicapped, 1978.

Morse, W., Cutler, R., & Fink, A. *Public school classes for the emotionally handicapped: A research analysis.* Washington, D.C.: Council for Exceptional Children, 1964.

National Association for Retarded Citizens. *Mainstreaming mentally retarded students in the public schools.* (April 1978).

Neel, R. How to put the consultant work in consultant teaching. *Behavior Disorders*, 1981, *6*(2), 78–82.

Neel, R. Inservice training for teachers of the emotionally disturbed. In M. Noel & N. Haring (Eds.), *Progress or change: Issues in educating the emotionally disturbed* (Vol. 2). Seattle: University of Washington, 1982.

Neel, R., & Rutherford, R. Exclusion of the socially maladjusted from services under PL 94–142: Why? What should be done about it? In F. Wood (Ed.), *Perspectives for a new decade: Educators' responsibilities for seriously disturbed and behaviorally disordered children and youth.* Reston, Va.: Council for Exceptional Children Publications, 1981.

Nelson, M. Techniques for screening conduct disturbed children. *Exceptional Children*, 1971, *37*, 501–507.

Noel, M. Public school programs for the emotionally disturbed: An overview. In M. Noel & N. Haring (Eds.), *Progress or change: Issues in educating the emotionally disturbed* (Vol. 2). Seattle: University of Washington, 1982.

O'Connor, P. Effects of a short term intervention resource room program on task orientation and achievement. *Journal of Special Education*, 1979, *13*, 375–385.

O'Leary, K. Pills or skills for hyperactive children. *Journal of Applied Behavior Analysis*, 1980, *13*(1), 191–204.

Paine, S., Bellamy, T., & Wilcox, B. (Eds.). *Human services that work.* Baltimore: Paul H. Brookes, 1984.

Patterson, G. R. Intervention for boys with conduct problems: Multiple settings, treatment and criteria. *Journal of Consulting and Clinical Psychology,* 1974, *42,* 471–481.

Patterson, G. R. *Coercive family process.* Eugene, Ore.: Castalia, 1982.

Patterson, G., Cobb, J., & Ray, R. Direct intervention in the classroom: A set of procedures for the aggressive child. In F. W. Clark, D. R. Evans, & L. A. Hamerlynck (Eds.), *Implementing behavioral programs for schools and clinics.* Champaign, Ill.: Research Press, 1972.

Paul, J., & Warnock, N. Special education: A changing field. *The Exceptional Child,* 1980, *27,* 3–28.

President's Commission on Excellence in Education. *A nation at risk: The imperative for education reform.* Washington, D.C.: U.S. Department of Education, 1983.

Quay, H. Some basic considerations in the education of emotionally disturbed children. *Exceptional Children,* 1963, *30,* 27–31.

Rehmann, A., & Roggen, T. (Eds.). *The least restrictive alternative.* Minneapolis: The Minneapolis Public Schools, 1977.

Reid, D., & Hresko, W. *A cognitive approach to learning disabilities.* New York: McGraw-Hill, 1981.

Reynolds, M. (Ed.) Symposium on public policy and educating handicapped persons. *Policy Studies Review.* Lawrence, Kan.: University of Kansas, 1983.

Rhode, G., Morgan, D., & Young, R. Generalization and maintenance of treatment gains of behaviorally handicapped students from resource rooms to regular classrooms using self-evaluation procedures. *Journal of Applied Behavior Analysis,* 1983, *16,* 171–188.

Ross, A. *Psychological disorders of children: A behavioral approach to theory, research and therapy* (2nd ed.). New York: McGraw-Hill, 1980.

Sarason, S., & Doris, J. Mainstreaming: Dilemmas, opposition, opportunities. In M. Reynolds (Ed.), *Futures of education for exceptional children: Emerging structures.* Reston, Va.: Council for Exceptional Children Publications, 1978.

Schaefer, E. Development of adaptive behavior: Conceptual models and family correlates. In M. Begab, H. Garber, & H. C. Haywood (Eds.), *Prevention of retarded development in psychosocially disadvantaged children.* Baltimore: University Park Press, 1982.

Schofer, R., & Duncan, J. *A national survey of comprehensive systems of personnel development: A fourth status study.* Columbia: University of Missouri Department of Special Education, 1982.

Schrag, P., & Divoky, D. *The myth of the hyperactive child.* New York: Pantheon Books, 1975.

Smith, C., & Wilcots, B. (Eds.). *Current issues in behavior disorders—1982.* Des Moines, Iowa: Department of Public Instruction, 1982.

Sontag, E., Button, J., & Hagerty, G. *Quality and leadership in special education.* Paper presented at the meeting of the Division of Personnel Preparation, Washington, D.C., December 1982.

Spivack, G., & Swift, M. The Devereux elementary school behavior rating scales: A study of the nature and organization of achievement related disturbed classroom behavior. *Journal of Special Education,* 1966, *1,* 71–90.

Sprague, R., & Sleater, E. Methylphenidate in hyperactive children: Differences in dose effects on learning and social behavior. *Science,* 1977, *198,* 1274–1276.

Stephens, T. Social skills in the classroom. *Journal of Special Education,* 1978, *13,* 375–385.

Strain, P. (Ed.). *The utilization of classroom peers as behavior change agents.* New York: Plenum Press, 1981.

Strain, P., Guralnick, M., & Walker, H. M. *Children's social behavior: Development, assessment, and modification.* New York: Academic Press, in press.

Swanson, I., Kinsbourne, M., Roberts, W., & Zucker, K. Time-response analysis of the effect of stimulant medication on the learning ability of children referred for hyperactivity. *Pediatrics,* 1978, *61,* 21–29.

Tawney, J. A cautious view of mainstreaming in early education. In *TECSE/ mainstreaming—a challenge for the 1980s.* Aspen Systems Corporation, 1981, 25–36.

Vacc, N. Long term effects of special class intervention for emotionally disturbed children. *Exceptional Children,* 1972, *39,* 15–22.

Walker, H. M. *The Walker Problem Behavior Identification Checklist (WPBIC) Test and Manual.* Los Angeles: Western Psychological Services, 1970.

Walker, H. M. *The Walker Problem Behavior Identification Checklist (WPBIC) Test and Manual* (Rev. ed.). Los Angeles: Western Psychological Services, 1976.

Walker, H. M. The IEP as a vehicle for delivery of special educational and related services to handicapped children. In L. Morra (Ed.), *The individualized educational program* (Monograph series on PL 94–142 implementation). Washington, D.C.: U.S. Office of Education Bureau of Education for the Handicapped, 1978.

Walker, H. M. *The acting out child: Coping with disruptive classroom behavior.* Boston: Allyn & Bacon, 1979.

Walker, H. M. Assessment of behavior disorders in the school setting: Issues, problems and strategies. In M. Noel & N. Haring (Eds.), *Progress or change? Issues in educating the emotionally disturbed* (Vol 1). Seattle: University of Washington, 1982.

Walker, H. M. *The Walker Problem Behavior Identification Checklist (WPBIC) Test and Manual* (2nd rev.). Los Angeles: Western Psychological Services, 1983.

Walker, H. M. Applications of response cost within school settings: Guidelines, outcomes, and issues. *Exceptional Education Quarterly,* 1983, *3*(4), 47–55.

Walker, H. M. *The anti-social child in school: Strategies for remediating aggressive and disruptive child behavior.* Austin, Tex.: Pro-Ed Publishers, in press.

Walker, H. M. The SBS program (Social Behavior Surivival): A systematic approach to the integration of handicapped children into less restrictive settings. *Education and Treatment of Children,* 1984, *6* (4), 421.

Walker, H. M., & Buckley, N. Programming generalization and maintenance of treatment effects across time and across settings. *Journal of Applied Behavior Analysis,* 1972, *5,* 209–224.

Walker, H. M., & Buckley, N. K. *Token reinforcement techniques: Classroom applications for the hard to teach child.* Eugene, Ore.: E-B Press, 1974.

Walker, H. M., Hops, H., & Greenwood, C. R. Competency-based training issues in the development of behavior management packages for specific classroom behavior disorders. *Behavior Disorders,* 1976, *1,* 112–122.

Walker, H. M., Hops, H., & Greenwood, C. R. RECESS: Research and development of a behavior management package for remediating social aggression in the school setting. In P. Strain (Ed.), *The utilization of classroom peers as behavior change agents.* New York: Plenum Press, 1981.

Walker, H. M., Hops, H., & Greenwood, C. R. The CORBEH research and development model: Programmatic issues and strategies. In S. Paine, T. Bellamy, & B. Wilcox (Eds.), *Human services that work.* Baltimore: Paul H. Brookes, 1984.

Walker, H. M., McConnell, S., & Clarke, J. Y. Social skills training in school settings: A model for the social integration of handicapped children into less restrictive settings. In R. J. McMahon & R. D. Peters (Eds.), *Childhood disorders: Behavioral-developmental approaches.* New York: Brunner/Mazel, in press.

Walker, H. M., McConnell, S., Homes, D., Todis, B., Walker, J., & Golden, N. *The Walker social skills curriculum: The ACCEPTS program.* Austin: Pro-Ed Publishers, 1983.

Walker, H. M., McConnell, S., Walker, J., Clarke, J. Y., Todis, B., Cohen, G., & Rankin, R. Initial analysis of the ACCEPTS curriculum: Efficacy of instructional and behavior management procedures for improving the social competence of handicapped children. *Analysis and Intervention in Developmental Disabilities,* 1983, *3,* 105–127.

Walker, H. M., & Rankin, R. Assessing the behavioral expectations and demands of less restrictive settings. *School Psychology Review,* 1983, *12,* 274–284.

Wiederholt, L., Hammill, D., & Brown, L. *The resource teacher: A guide to effective practices.* Austin: Pro-Ed Publishers, 1978.

Wiederholt, L., Hammill, D., & Brown, L. *The resource teacher: A guide to effective practices* (Rev. ed.). Austin: Pro-Ed Publishers, 1983.

Wilkes, H., Bireley, M., & Schultz, J. Criteria for mainstreaming the learning disabled child into the regular classroom. *Journal of Learning Disabilities,* 1979, *12* (4), 46–51.

Ysseldyke, J., Algozzine, B., & Epps, S. A logical and empirical analysis of current practices in classifying students as handicapped. *Exceptional Children*, 1983, *49*, 160–166.

Ysseldyke, J., Algozzine, B., Richey, L., & Graden, J. Declaring students eligible for learning disability services: Why bother with the data? *Learning Disability Quarterly*, 1982, *5*, 37–44.

Ysseldyke, J., Algozzine, B., Shinn, M., & McGue, M. Similarities and differences between underachievers and students classified as learning disabled. *Journal of Special Education*, 1982, *16*, 73–85.

Ysseldyke, J., Christenson, S., Pianta, B., & Algozzine, B. An analysis of teachers' reasons and desired outcomes for students referred for psychoeducational assessment. *Journal of Psychoeducational Assessment*, 1983, *1*, 73–83.

18

A Behavioral Model of Academic Remediation with Learning Disabled Children

Frank A. Treiber
Medical College of Georgia

Benjamin B. Lahey
University of Georgia

INTRODUCTION

History of Learning Disabilities

Throughout the history of formal education there have undoubtedly been children who experienced problems in academic learning despite average intellectual abilities. One of the first descriptions is often attributed to Morgan's (1896) case history of an intelligent 14-year-old boy who encountered severe problems in reading and writing. Some of his difficulties included spelling errors, reversal of the sequences of letters in his name, and problems memorizing the alphabet as a child. Another early account was provided by Orton (1937) in which he described a 16-year-old boy of average intelligence with no apparent sensory deficits and no indications of neurological dysfunction or emotional disturbance, but yet was unable to read whole words. Orton termed this condition *strephosymbolia,* meaning "twisted symbols" due to the individual's frequent reversals of letters and sequences of letters when reading.

Learning disabilities received this type of sporadic attention from a few educators, physicians, and psychologists for many years. Only recently has the public at large and researchers become interested in the area. This is primarily a result of the development of federal funding during the 1960s for school systems in which a variety of special programs were instituted to meet the needs of students experiencing learning problems. While learning disabilities programs are commonplace in public educational systems today, these programs were nonexistent prior to 1960 (McCarthy & McCarthy, 1969). Concurrent with the development of these programs was a significant escalation of research on this topic which continues today.

Definitions of Learning Disabilities

Another outcome of the federally funded special education programs was the need for an acceptable definition of learning disabilities for classification purposes. Learning disabilities have been conceptualized both in a broad sense with reference to terms such as *minimal brain dysfunction* and in a narrow sense in which attention is focused on specific academic deficits in reading, math, writing, and other areas (Sattler, 1981). Definitions incorporated early were typically broad and generally were based on inferred causal events (e.g., brain damage), regardless of whether or not such causes were demonstrated (Hallahan & Kaufman, 1976; Lahey, Delameter, Kupfer, & Hobbs, 1978). One problem with these broad definitions was that they offered little utility in the development of successful remedial programs (Lahey et al., 1981).

A narrower definition frequently used for legal/administrative purposes is stated in Public Law 74–142 (Federal Register, December 29, 1977):

> "Specific learning disability" means a disorder in one or more basic psychological processes involved in understanding or in using language, spoken or written, which may manifest itself in an imperfect ability to listen, think, speak, read, write, spell, or to do mathematical calculations. The term includes such conditions as perceptual handicaps, brain injury, minimal brain dysfunction, dyslexia, and developmental aphasia. The term does not include children who have learning problems which are primarily the result of visual, hearing, or motor handicaps, of mental retardation, of emotional disturbance, or of environmental, cultural, or economic disadvantage.

This definition is based primarily on exclusion (i.e., not due to mental retardation, sensory impairment, emotional disturbance, or economic deprivation) (Lahey et al., 1978). Ross (1976, 1977) has pointed out the circularity of the definition and that when these exclusions are dropped from it one has a diagnostic definition of learning disabilities as problems in learning (disparity between expected and actual academic performance). A consequence of such loosely defined definitions of learning disability is a large number of noncomparable studies, which is in part a result of heterogeneous and ill-defined samples (Lahey, Vosk, & Habif, 1981; Ross, 1976).

An alternative to this approach is to conceptualize a learning disability as a dimension of behavior empirically associated with academic failure (Lahey et al., 1981). A dimensional orientation permits the individual to be placed at some point on a continuum ranging from least to most disabled. The various steps on the continuum can be operationally defined and measured in behavioral terms. One important assumption of the dimensional approach is that learning disabilities are independent of other classifications of maladaptive behavior (e.g., conduct disorder, hyperactivity), but not necessarily unrelated to them. Factor analytic studies by Lahey et al. (1978) and Miller (1972) lend support to this dimensional approach.

Prevalence and Sex Ratio

Due to the lack of a precise operational definition of learning disabilities, decisions about the classification of each child are based on each diagnostician's interpretation of concepts such as "normal intelligence," "lack of economic and cultural disadvantage," and whether any "emotional disturbance" is a by-product or cause of the disorder. Furthermore, some assessors require that other diagnostic criteria be met, such as specific variations in subtest scores on IQ tests or identification of perceptual problems, before a classification of learning disability is made. Thus, classification is unreliable, and estimates of incidence rates vary widely. Incidence rates within general school populations have been found to vary from 1 to 3 percent (National Advisory Committee on Handicapped Children, 1968) to as high as 10 percent (Meier, 1971). While the latter figure seems high, it was based on a sample of 284 students who had been identified using vigorous criteria. Support of this higher incidence rate is provided by Yule (1982) who found about 8 percent of the children followed in the Isle of Wight studies showed reading deficits. In addition, Yule (1982) also reported that boys showed an incidence of reading disorders of as high as 2 or 3 to 1 over girls. Pennington and Smith (1983) reported general incidence rates of reading retardation in educational systems, indicating males over females by a ratio of 3.4 to 1. Support for higher prevalence rates with males is also found with speech and language disorders with the sex ratio of 2.64 to 1 (Ingram, 1959). With prevalence rates so high, it is no wonder that learning disabilities are considered a serious educational, economic, and social issue (Barkley, 1981; Benton & Pearl, 1978).

DESCRIPTION

Diagnostic Classification

As stated earlier, children classified as learning disabled constitute a highly heterogeneous group concerning their etiology, related behavior problems, and specific academic deficits (Benton & Pearl, 1978; Lahey, 1976; Meier, 1971). A number of investigators have made efforts to categorize these children into more homogeneous subgroups based on specific academic patterns. What follows is a brief review of the more commonly employed diagnostic subtypes. For a more thorough discussion the reader is referred to reviews by Benton and Pearl (1978), Lyon and Watson (1981), and Barkley (1981). At this point, we should remember, however, that these subclassification schemes represent attempts to reduce the heterogeneity in the term *learning disabilities* that have not yet received adequate empirical support.

Specific Reading Disorders.   Barkley's (1981) review of the literature identified three kinds of reading problems. The classification scheme developed by Boder (1973) encompasses these subtypes and will be used in the present discussion. *Dysphonetic* disorder is the most frequently reported reading disorder (Boder, 1973). Individuals with this problem typically experience difficulties in vocabulary skills and articulation. For instance, these children read words as whole units and have a small set of words they recognize on sight but have difficulty breaking words into their component parts. Thus, when presented with new words, they will pronounce the initial letters and often replace the entire word with a similarly spelled word.

Boder (1973) reports that the least identified subcategory is termed *dyseidetic* disorder. These children have problems in remembering what letters look like, although they have adequate auditory memory. They typically read in a slow, methodical, choppy manner trying to phonetically pronounce each word. Thus, they experience the most difficulty with irregular words, which cannot be phonetically sounded out. Accordingly, problems in spelling are commonly a result of phonetic-based errors.

The third basic type of reading disability has an incidence rate somewhere between the other two subtypes and has been termed *mixed dysphonetic-dyseidetic* disorder by Boder (1973). This problem is a combination of the two previous disorders and includes those children with the most severe problems, including letter reversals, substitutions, and sequencing difficulties.

Specific Arithmetic Disorders.   Children who experience reading and spelling problems frequently have trouble with arithmetic (Barkley, 1981). One type of disorder involves children who have extreme difficulty with math, but less difficulty with reading. It is believed that these individuals possess deficits in visuospatial skills (Barkley, 1981), since they commonly show poor performance subscales on the Wechsler Intelligence Scale for Children (Rourke, Young, & Flewelling, 1971). Another type of arithmetic disorder involves children who exhibit equal deficits in mathematics, reading, and language. Barkley (1981) notes that little research has been conducted to determine the specific type of academic related deficits these children typically have.

Writing Disorders.   Three basic types of writing disorders are commonly reported and appear to mirror the subtypes of reading disability mentioned earlier (Barkley, 1981). One writing disorder is similar to the dysphonetic reading disorder since the writing deficit is believed to be a result of poor phonetic-analytic skills (Barkley, 1981; Maidoo, 1972). These individuals typically show greater deficiency in spelling rather than writing, with their spelling errors often unsystematic in nature and their writing difficult to read.

The second writing disorder is analogous to the dyseidetic reading disorder in that misspellings are frequently phonetically correct. This disorder is noted by poor visuospatial and word formation abilities (Barkley, 1981) and is noticed most often with math and spelling difficulties than with reading difficulties. Children with the final types of writing disorder have been termed *apraxic writers* (Heilman & Valenstein, 1979). They lack the sensory motor coordination required for writing but generally perform at grade level in reading and arithmetic.

For these diagnostic subcategories to have any value, they must be differentially related to the etiology, prognosis, and/or response to treatment of the specific problem that they define (Lahey et al, 1981). However, little empirical evidence currently exists that supports the use of the diagnostic subtypes previously described. For instance, use of diagnostic subcategories have not been beneficial in the selection of successful treatment programs (Lahey, 1976), with only global behavioral approaches having shown effectiveness across a variety of specific subtypes (Lahey et al., 1977; Novy, Burnett, Powers & Sulzer-Azaroff, 1973; Stromer, 1977). At present, these diagnostic subtypes offer little clinical utility. Further research is needed on the various diagnostic subtypes of learning disabilities until they can provide differential information concerning etiology, prognosis, and response to treatment.

Characteristic Behavior Problems

As mentioned earlier, learning disabled children are heterogenous with respect to a number of areas, especially related behavior problems (Lahey et al., 1981). Nevertheless, several behavior problems have been found to occur at a higher rate with learning disabled children than with other children. Learning disabled students are frequently concomitantly diagnosed as attention deficit disorder with hyperactivity. The overlap between the two classifications has been found to range from 50 percent (Lambert & Sandoval, 1980) to as high as 80 percent (Safer & Allen, 1976). Recent findings (Delameter, Lahey & Drake, 1981) have indicated a number of differences between learning disabled children who are or are not classified as hyperactive. The hyperactive learning disabled were more likely to come from discordant families, to be first born, and to be more easily distracted by extraneous stimuli.

A number of other problems such as social withdrawal, aggression, depression, phobias, and lowered self-confidence have been associated with learning disabilities (Boder, 1973; Rutter, Tizard, Yale, Graham, & Whitmore, 1976). With this assortment of related problems, it is no wonder that when peer sociometric measures are taken that the learning disabled children are perceived in a negative, rejecting manner (Bryan, 1974, 1976; Horowitz, 1981). A number of problems have been associated with extended periods of peer rejection, such as juvenile delinquency (Roff et al., 1972), dropping out of school (Ulman, 1957) and psychiatric disturbance (Cowen et al., 1973). Since learning disabilities are not a transient disorder, this population of children is at risk for such problems.

The determination of the causal chain between learning disabilities and these various behavior problems is often impossible. Three potential causal relationships have been proposed by Sattler (1981). One possibility is that the learning disability results in the development of behavior problems. It is highly likely that a child experiencing continued frustration and disappointment in academics may begin to engage in other attention-getting behaviors incompatible with learning. The second possibility is that children with persistent behavior problems eventually become learning disabled. That is, a hyperactive or conduct-disordered child who is often inattentive and disruptive is not likely to devote quality time to academics. The third possible causal relationship involves another factor, an autonomic abnormality, which is the causative mechanism of both the learning disability and the behavior problem.

THEORIES OF ETIOLOGY

Although learning disabilities are a relatively new area of clinical interest, various theories with concomitant remediation programs have been proposed. However, these theories often lack any empirical support as to the proposed underlying causative mechanisms of the disorder (Vellutino, Steger, Moeyer, Harding, & Niles, 1977; Wong, 1979). As a result, the associated treatment programs are usually unsuccessful in improving the academic performance of these children.

Medical Model Theories

Most of these theories can be categorized into one of two general frameworks: the medical and the behavioral model. Medical model based theories conceptualize learning disabilities as an overtly expressed syndrome of behavior caused by an underlying pathology. The type of pathology frequently alluded to include deficits in perceptual (Fernald, 1943; Frosting & Horn, 1964), perceptual-motor (Barsh, 1967; Kephart, 1971; Lerner, 1971), neurological (Barkley, 1977; Cruickshanck, 1967; Delacatto, 1959) or psycholinguistic (Bush & Giles, 1969; Kirk, McCarthy & Kirk, 1968) processes. All of the medical model based treatment programs operate on the assumption that the underlying deficit or pathology must be remediated before academic achievement (symptomology) can improve (Lahey et al., 1978; Vellutino et al., 1977; Wong, 1979). What follows is a brief overview of the major medical model theories of learning disabilities.

Neuropsychological Theories. The first theories of learning disabilities viewed the disorders as a syndrome of brain damage. These neuropsychological theories were developed after similarities were noted between brain damaged war veterans and learning disabled children. For instance, both groups typically evidenced easy distractibility, short attention spans, memory problems, and high activity levels. Since learning disabled children are not mentally retarded but do show specific deficits in academic performance, it was believed that their problems stemmed from subliminal neurological damage or "minimal" brain damage (Strauss & Lehtinen, 1947; Strauss & Werner, 1942).

Remediation programs based on the minimal brain damages approach included procedures similar to the sensory deprivation technique used in rehabilitation programs for brain injured war veterans (Strauss & Lehtinen, 1947). The basic assumption was that the damaged brain structure prevented the individual from attending to only salient environmental information (e.g., academics) because of an inability to screen out irrelevant stimuli (e.g., other students coughing, sneezing, talking). Therefore, for enhancement of academic performance to occur, it was first necessary to remove all nonsalient stimuli from the classroom. This usually meant that the teacher had to wear plain clothes with no make up or jewelry permitted. The students were often placed in individual cubicles inside a classroom, which was void of any decoration, was soundproofed as much as possible, and had partially opaqued windows. Special instructional programs aimed at improving visual, tactile, and auditory perception were included (Gillingham & Stillman, 1965).

Since investigators were unable to find a definite relationship between learning disabilities and obvious brain injury, the label of "minimal brain damage" was replaced by "minimal brain dysfunction" (Cruickshanck, 1967; Johnson & Mykelbust, 1967). Proponents of this approach conceptualized learning disabilities as being a product of impaired brain functions as opposed to anatomical damage. Johnson and Mykelbust (1967) represent this view in that they maintain learning problems are due to impairment of brain systems involved in auditory, visual, and tactile perception. Their treatment regimen for reading problems included exclusions of reversible letters, structured phonics practice, and multisensory presentation of all academic information.

Perceptual Theories. Another set of theories emphasizes perceptual difficulties as the underlying reason for learning disabilities (Blau & Blau, 1969; Fernald, 1943). Each of the theories proposed specific remediation strategies aimed at alleviating the inferred perceptual deficits. A major tenet of these theories is that the perceptual deficits must be alleviated before remedial academic programs can be implemented.

For example, Frostig and Horne (1964) have developed tests and training programs (e.g., "Frostig Kits") that are frequently used in public school systems. The program involves recognizing and tracing embedded figures, copying abstract forms, and identifying one's position in space. Fernald (1943) used intersensory stimulation in efforts to alleviate perceptual processing problems. For instance, if a child was being taught to read a new sight word, he/she would be presented the word by means of visual, auditory, tactile, and kinesthetic stimulation. This barrage of stimulation was presumed to increase the child's acquisition of information through at least one of the sensory systems.

Perceptual-Motor Theories.   Another group of theorists maintain that learning deficits are a result of problems with perceptual-motor integration. Similar to Piaget's view (1974), they maintain that early sensory motor experiences play a major role in future cognitive development. It is assumed that development follows an invariant sequence with acquisition of sensory motor skills occurring first, which aids perceptual development, which in turn facilitates acquisition of higher order cognitive skills. Therefore, if an individual encounters inadequate sensory motor experiences, then problems with perceptual abilities will probably follow, which in turn would hinder future cognitive development. Following this rationale, many of the treatment programs proposed by these theories involve highly structured sequential sensory-motor training experiences.

As an example, Getman and other developmental optometrists (Getman & Kane, 1964; Getman, Kane, Halgren & McKea, 1964) propose that poorly developed visual perceptual abilities are the cause of learning problems. Their remediation strategies include training in overall body coordination, eye-hand coordination, and form perception and visual memory. Kephart's (1971, 1975) approach is similar in that in order for children to correctly identify the orientation of symbols (i.e., numbers and letters) they must first be able to recognize their own bodily positions in space. Thus, the learning disabled child is given a variety of physical exercises that resemble calisthenics.

One of the most extreme views as to the etiology and treatment of learning problems is that proposed by Delacatto (1959). He maintains that the disability is a consequence of incomplete lateralization of the dominant hemisphere due to inadequate neurological organization. The recommended treatment package includes restriction of sleep positions and forced motor exercises (e.g., crawling, creeping, walking), which supposedly reorganized neural brain structures.

Psycholinguistic Theories.   The final medical model approach views learning disabilities as a consequence of deficits in psycholinguistic functioning. The term *psycholinguistics* is often described by these theorists in such broad terms that it is analogous to the concept of intelligence (Lahey, 1976). Kirk, McCarthy, and Kirk (1968) constructed a test to identify particular linguistic deficits (the Illinois Test of Psycholinguistic Abilities, or ITPA), based on Osgood's (1957) theory of psycholinguistics. The ITPA assesses the following areas: (*a*) auditory and visual modes of communication, (*b*) psycholinguistic processes including input, processing and output, and levels of organization. Concomitantly, a number of remedial programs have been developed that focus on alleviation of specific deficits identified by the ITPA (Bush & Giles, 1969; Karnes, 1968; Kirk & Kirk, 1971).

Behavioral Model

A major conceptual difference between the medical and the behavioral models is that the behavioral approach does not infer underlying pathology as the cause for learning problems. Instead, learning disabilities are viewed as a class of deficient academic behaviors that can be modified through behavioral techniques. Behavioral treatment regimens have successfully altered academic performances in a variety of populations, including mentally retarded (e.g., Bijou, Birnbrauer, Kidder & Tague, 1966; Brown & Perlmutter, 1971; Clark & Walberg, 1979), emotionally disturbed (e.g., Drabman, Spitalnik, & O'Leary, 1973; Hewett, Taylor & Artuso, 1969), disadvantaged and underachieving (e.g., Chadwick & Day, 1971; Miller & Schneider, 1970), and normal children (e.g., Harris & Sherman, 1972; Harris, Sherman, Henderson & Harris, 1973).

With regard to remediation of academic deficits, the behavioral approach is based on three primary tenets (Lahey & Johnson, 1977):

1. Individualization and mastery learning. The child's specific strengths and weaknesses are determined, and remedial approaches progress at the individual's own rate of acquisition of each task that comprise a hierarchy of behaviors.

2. Direct Teaching. General principles of learning (e.g., immediate reinforcement and feedback, repeated practice trials) are employed in the alteration of academic performance rather than in the remediation of some inferred deficit.

3. Emphasis on measurement. One hallmark of the behavioral approach is continuous assessment of academic performance throughout the treatment program. This tactic results in a more effective treatment since immediate feedback of progress is provided, thus permitting modification of the program when necessary. Some of the assessment measures typically used include standardized achievement tests, representative samples of written school work, and direct observation of the child in the classroom setting. A more thorough account of behavioral assessment is provided later.

ASSESSMENT

Psychometric Assessment

As Sattler (1981) notes, there is no standard battery for the assessment of learning disabilities. However, to meet the criteria of most legal definitions, a child minimally must show a discrepancy between intellectual functioning and academic performance. Thus, most psychological evaluations of potentially learning disabled children involve the psychometric assessment of general intelligence and academic achievement.

Intelligence Tests. Three frequently used standardized tests of general intelligence include the Stanford-Binet Intelligence Scale (1973) the Wechsler Intelligence Scale for Children-Revised (WISC-R) (1974), and the McCarthy Scale of Children's Abilities (McCarthy, 1972). Besides providing general information to be used in the general diagnostic classification of learning disabilities, some researchers have attempted to identify specific subscale profiles to further differentiate this population from normals and from children with conduct disorders or other behavior problems (Ackerman et al., 1971; Rourke, 1978).

For instance, some researchers have suggested that a particular pattern of WISC-R subtest scores is associated with reading disabilities (Sattler, 1981). These children are believed to have their lowest subscale scores in arithmetic, coding, information, and digit symbols (ACID). Other investigators have suggested that large differences between verbal and performance IQs on the WISC-R can be used in the differential diagnosis of learning disabilities (Hulesman, 1970; Miller, Stoneburner, & Brecht, 1978; Rourke, Young, & Flowelling, 1971). Dudley-Marling, Kaufman, and Tarver (1981) reviewed 24 studies that had addressed the issues on WISC-R subscale patterns and verbal-performance descrepancies and concluded that neither test reliably characterized learning disabled children. They gave several reasons for their conclusions. First, learning disabled children do not show unusual verbal-performance differences on IQ tests. While many learning disabled children do exhibit such differences, 25 percent of the standardization sample for the WISC-R demonstrated a significant difference in their verbal performance scores. Second, learning disabled children do not show significantly greater subtest scatter compared to normal children, and third, no particular pattern of subtest scores reliably characterizes learning disabled children.

Achievement Tests. A variety of achievement tests have been constructed to assess children's current level of functioning in specific academic areas (e.g., reading recognition, comprehension, and oral abilities). Generally, a wide assortment of these tests are administered to determine the child's strengths and deficits across a variety of academic areas. However, achievement tests should not be the sole indicators of the child's academic performance or of the treatment outcomes. In addition, direct measures of classroom performance should be obtained via observation and collection of daily work samples whenever possible. This allows for an assessment of academic performance in the environment in which it naturally occurs.

Behavioral Assessment

The behavioral approach conceptualizes learning disabilities as a pattern of maladaptive behavior rather than as a symptom of some inferred processing deficit. Since the specific maladaptive behavior of interest is academic, it is primarily academic behavior that is the focus of both the assessment and the consequent treatment efforts. It is probably sufficient to assess "molar" units of academic performance (e.g., writing words, oral reading sentences, solving word problems) as opposed to "molecular" units (e.g., visual discrimination of geometric shapes, phonic discriminations) (Lahey, 1979; Lahey, et al., 1981). However, if this strategy is not effective for a child, then a more molecular assessment would be needed, but only after other reasons for treatment failure has been ruled out (Lahey, 1979). The following methods are suggested for use in the molar assessment of academic behaviors.

Achievement Tests.   Standardized achievement tests can be helpful in assessing a child's academic problems, but only if the instruments are comprised of tasks similar to those encountered in the classroom. For example, the Spache Diagnostic Reading Scales (Spache, 1963) include tasks that are highly similar to those required in the classroom. The same is true for the Arithmetic and Spelling subtests of the Wide Range Achievement Test (Jastak & Jastak, 1965). However, other instruments, such as "cloze" reading tests, which assess comprehension by having a child complete sentences by filling in a missing blank, are not good approximations to behavior typically required in the classroom.

Samples of Written Academic Work.   Excellent direct measures of academic behavior in the classroom can easily be gathered from test papers, workbook pages, penmanship exercises, and other written daily assignments. These written behaviors are excellent sources for determining the student's particular deficits. To obtain an accurate and comprehensive account of the student's academic behaviors, fully inclusive samples should be collected rather than the best or worst examples of the child's work.

Direct Classroom Observation.   A number of relevant academic behaviors can by assessed only through direct observation of ongoing classroom activities. This includes behaviors such as oral reading exercises, small group discussions, and chalkboard activities. Observations of children in the classroom setting provide other important types of information as well. For instance, certain situations in the classroom setting may influence the continued display of behaviors (e.g., talking to classmates, leaving work area) that may interfere with learning and may have treatment implications. These behaviors would be overlooked if direct observations are not included as part of the ongoing assessment. (See Gelfand and Hartmann (1975) for a detailed outline of techniques of unobtrusive observation and systematic recording of target behaviors.)

These three basic components of behavioral assessment provide an individualized approach to the treatment of academic deficits in the learning disabled child. The child's problem areas are observed, operationally defined, and targeted during remediation. In addition, the child's behavioral strengths can be identifed and included in the remedial intervention to increase the likelihood of successful outcome.

TREATMENT

Effectiveness of Medical Model Approaches

As previously stated, each of the medical model theories assumes that learning deficits are overt symptoms of an underlying process deficit. Accordingly, a number of commercially published remedial training kits have been produced to remediate these inferred deficits. These kits have been used extensively in educational settings and have been the subject of many research investigations. The consistent finding, however, has been that these programs have not been successful in modifying learning disabled children's academic performance. For instance, although the early sensory restriction treatment programs (Strauss & Lehtinen, 1947; Strauss & Werney, 1942) have not been as extensively researched as other approaches, the available data are not promising. Halla-han and Kauffman (1976) have surveyed the research literature and concluded that such sensory restriction efforts have no beneficial effect on academic performance.

Similarly, the psycholinguistic remediation strategies (e.g., Kirk & Kirk, 1971) have not fared well when placed under empirical scrutiny. In a review of the literature, Hammill and Larson (1974) found that many of the studies were methodologically flawed, making interpretation impossible. Of those studies that were methodologically sound, they concluded that psycholinguistic train-ing programs were ineffective in altering academic achievement when com-pared to untreated control groups.

Perhaps the most widely researched of the medical model approaches are the perceptual and perceptual-motor training programs, as in the approaches of Frostig, Getman, Kephart, Barsh, and Doman-Delacatto. A number of authors have reviewed this research (Glass & Robins, 1967; Goodman & Hammill, 1973; Hallahan & Kauffman, 1976; Lahey, 1976; Ross, 1976, Spache, 1976; Stone, 1972), and two consistent conclusions have been drawn: (1) a large number of the studies contained flaws in experimental design; and (2) the few methodologically sound experiments did not demonstrate positive effects of the treatments on the academic performance of learning disabled children.

When viewed in terms of general learning principles, it is not surprising that these medical model approaches meet with little success. That is, children are given tasks (e.g., crawling, copying geometric figures, calisthenics) that are not topographically related to the behavior of concern (i. e., writing, math, read-ing), and they do not receive programmed feedback or reinforcement as to their performances on these tasks. The perplexing issue is why these programs continue to be extensively used in efforts to remediate academic deficits. There are three possible reasons for their continued use despite the lack of empirical support. First, some methodologically flawed experiments have been inter-preted as providing support for these approaches. Second, the decision of treatment programs in educational settings is often not based on empirical evidence, and third, educators and other professionals have not been presented with feasible alternatives (Lahey et al., 1978).

Effectiveness of Behavioral Approaches

The behavioral treatment of learning disabilities has been characterized by two basic strategies. The targeted behaviors of initial investigations were those thought to be prerequisites for learning (e.g., attending, nonimpulsivity, low activity levels). It was believed that development of these skills would result in improved academic performances (Madsen, Becker, & Thomas, 1968; O'Leary & Becker, 1967; Wolf, Giles, & Hall, 1968). More recently, however, treatment efforts have focused on direct modification of academic deficits (Lahey, 1976; Lahey et al., 1978).

Modification of Incompatible Behaviors. Learning disabled children are frequently identified as displaying behaviors that are incompatible with learning. Attention deficits, impulsivity, and extreme motor activity are the most frequently cited problems. A brief review of the behavioral treatment programs that have attempted to modify these deterrant behaviors follows.

Attention Deficits. Attention deficits have often been associated with learning problems (Barkley, 1981; Douglas, 1972, Meier, 1971). Behavioral intervention programs have been successful at increasing the attending behaviors of learning disabled children (Drass & Jones, 1971; Novy, Burnett, Powers, & Sulzer-Azaroff, 1973). However, these programs have not consistently resulted in concomitant improved academic performance (Ferritor, Buckholdt, Hamblin & Smith, 1972; Marholin & Steinham, 1977).

The recent evidence that learning disabled children may be no different than normals in their fine-grained overt attentional processes is another reason that this approach does not seem useful. For instance, Lahey, Kupfer, Beggs, and Landon (1982) failed to show differences between learning disabled and normal children in attending eye movements during reading. Findings of this nature seem to indicate that there may be few, if any, overt attentional responses that require assessment or treatment in learning disabled children. If such differences in attending behavior do exist, it does not appear to be helpful to modify them directly; an alternative strategy is obviously needed. A proposal for such a strategy will be presented in a later section.

Impulsivity. Children with academic problems typically respond to academic questions faster and make more errors than normal children (Henry, 1973; Kagan, 1966; Massari & Schack, 1972). Kagan (1966) claims that a large number of errors made by these children are a result of their impulsivity, i.e., responding before they have completed processing pertinent information. Thus, it was hypothesized that, if children with academic difficulties increased the latency of their responses, then improvement in academic performances would follow. Williams and Lahey (1972) directly tested this assumption by separately reinforcing increased response latencies and accuracy of responses in a group of impulsive preschool children. Their findings indicated that reinforcement for accuracy resulted in increased correct responses but had no effect on response latency. Similarly, reinforcement for increased response latency did not improve accuracy of responses. Most importantly, reinforcing children for both longer latencies and accuracy of responses was no more effective than reinforcement for just accurate responses. Thus, it does not seem necessary to reduce impulsive response latencies to enhance academic performance. Rather, direct reinforcement of correct responses appears to be a more useful strategy in the modification of academic behaviors.

Hyperactivity. As mentioned earlier, a large percentage (50–80 percent) of learning disabled children receive concomitant classifications of hyperactivity (Lambert & Sandoval, 1980; Safer & Allen, 1976). In fact, behaviors frequently used in the diagnostic classification of hyperactivity (e.g., distractibility, impulsivity, attention deficits) are commonly associated with learning disabled children (Lahey et al., 1981). Thus, an apparently promising approach to the remediation of academic difficulties would be the reduction of hyperactive behaviors. Behavior therapy programs have been quite successful in eliminating these maladaptive behaviors in children (Kent & O'Leary, 1976; O'Leary et al., 1967). However, none of these studies has looked for corresponding increases in academic performance. Thus, there is no evidence to suggest that modification of hyperactive behavior indirectly benefits academic performance. As we shall see later, however, there is evidence that the opposite is true.

Direct Modification of Academic Deficits. Since the primary diagnostic factor used in the definition of learning disabilities involves academic deficits (Hallahan & Kauffman, 1976; Sattler, 1981), these should be the focus of treatment regimens (Lahey et al., 1981). By directly targeting molar academic behaviors (e.g., reading comprehension, spelling, solutions to arithmetic problems), behavioral programs have been successful in enhancing the academic performance of learning disabled children (Lahey, 1976; Lahey et al., 1978).

Modification of Reading Problems. Reading disorders are frequently observed in learning disabled children (Meier, 1971) and have received much attention from behavioral intervention programs (Haring & Hauck, 1967; Ryback & Staats, 1970; Wadsworth, 1971). For instance, Wadsworth (1971) treated 10 learning disabled third graders in a special education class for a four-month period. Children received points, which were exchangeable for tangible rewards for compliance with classroom rules, completion of workbook assignments, and correct responses during tutoring instruction. After the four-month treatment period, the students were gradually placed back into the regular classroom, and reinforcement was discontinued. The Slosson Oral Reading Test was administered some three months later, and several significant findings were noted. Nine of the 10 children exceeded their predicted achievement, and their mean scores were in close proximity to the appropriate age/grade norm.

Another typical example of the behavioral approach is illustrated in Lahey, McNees and Brown's (1973) work with two sixth-grade children who were experiencing problems with reading comprehension. They showed extreme discrepancies between their oral reading (both at 6.5 grade level) and reading for comprehension (both at 4.5 grade level). An ABAB design was employed with the initial baseline period involving the reading of brief passages (e.g., "This week John saw a girl with an umbrella. The girl was wearing a red dress."). Following each passage, the child was asked a factual question (e.g., "When did John see the girl?"). Only explicit (e.g., this week) or synonym answers (e.g., within the last seven days) were considered accurate. The children were not given feedback during this time. The initial treatment period included delivery of social praise and monetary rewards (pennies), contingent on each correct answer. Incorrect responses were not corrected during this period. Following this, a second identical baseline was implemented, followed by another identical treatment phase.

The children demonstrated correct response rates of 65 to 85 percent during the initial baseline. The initial treatment period resulted in an increase of correct responding to 80 to 100 percent. The percentage of correct response declined during the second baseline, but the institution of the second treatment phase showed increases up to 90 percent or better. In sum, these programs have shown that reinforcement of molar academic behavior is beneficial in enhancing complex reading skills (e.g., comprehension, oral reading) without treating any inferred process deficits (e.g., inadequate memory strategies, poor sequencing skills).

Modification of Mathematic Computations.   Behavioral programs have also focused on remediation of various mathematics problems frequently encountered by learning disabled children (Broughton & Lahey, 1978; Kirby & Shields, 1972; Lovitt & Smith, 1974; Smith, Lovitt, & Kidder, 1972). For instance, Smith and Lovitt (1976) tested seven 8 to 11-year-old learning disabled boys who had difficulty with computational proficiency of addition-carry over and simple digit subtraction. A baseline period was first instituted in which no feedback or reinforcement was given. This phase was followed by a contingent for time treatment period in which varying amounts of free time were earned, based on the total number of correct problems answered during the day. A contingent toy phase followed in which points were earned for correct responses, which later could be exchanged for toys. Finally, a second baseline was implemented. The results indicated significant improvements of percentage correct responding during both treatment phases (median of 19 percent increase for each group) as compared to baseline rates. The contingent free time strategy was slightly more effective in that the largest gains (52 percent) occurred during that treatment phase.

A response-cost procedure was used by Lovitt and Smith (1974) to increase the percentage of correct answers to subtraction problems in an 11-year-old learning disabled girl. The contingency involved a one-minute loss of recess time for each incorrect answer. Implementation of this program quickly resulted in near perfect responding on targeted problems, which was maintained at an acceptable level after the contingency was withdrawn. Subsequently, these findings were corroborated with another 11-year-old learning disabled student. Thus, operant procedures with learning disabled children have been effective in remediating deficits in mathematical computations.

Modification of Other Academic Difficulties.   Certain academic skills such as handwriting and letter recognition, traditionally associated with perceptual motor difficulties, have also been a topic for behavioral treatment programs (Drass & Jones, 1971; Fauke, Burnett, Powers, & Sulzer-Azaroff, 1973; Lahey, Busemeyer, O'Hara & Beggs, 1977). Drass and Jones (1971) used learning disabled children as "tutors" to improve letter recognition skills in learning disabled peers. Children were rewarded with social praise and edibles contingent on repetition of a letter name after the tutor, accurate labeling and tracing of the letter, and correct naming of the letter following a tutor's question. This procedure resulted in a doubling of correct responses within a five-day period.

Lahey et al. (1977) worked with four children with severe perceptual-motor disorders who had extreme problems with handwriting, including orientation and sequencing of letters. Following the completion of each word, immediate feedback was provided, including pennies for accurate answers and corrective information for inaccurate answers. Answers were considered accurate if legible, of correct spatial orientation, and in the correct sequence. The treatment package resulted in dramatic improvements in the legibility and accuracy of their handwriting to trained items as well as generalization to untrained words.

Perhaps the most important study supporting the behavioral approach to the treatment of learning disabled children was conducted by Ayllon, Layman, and Kandel (1975). Their subjects included three children who were diagnosed as both learning disabled and hyperactive. Their hyperactive behaviors had been previously controlled with medication (Ritalin). An initial baseline indicated low levels of activity and poor performances in reading and mathematics while taking Ritalin. A second medication-free baseline followed, which showed large increases in hyperactive behavior and no change in academic performances.

A token economy was then instituted in which students received checks on a note card for correct answers on mathematic problems. These checks were exchanged for an assortment of prizes or free time at the end of the day. This system resulted in significant immediate increases in the children's percentages of correct arithmetic problems with no changes in reading performance observed. Furthermore, their levels of hyperactive behavior in the mathematics class declined to medication baseline levels with no change in activity levels noted in their reading class. Next, the token reinforcement program was implemented in the reading class as well. Corresponding improvements were noted in academic performance as well as with decreases in hyperactive behavior to baseline medication levels. These findings of direct effects on academic performance and indirect benefits for other behavior have been replicated by other investigators (Ayllon & Roberts, 1974; Broughton & Lahey, 1978; Marholin & Steinman, 1977).

Several important implications stem from these findings. First, as shown in the other behavioral studies presented, reinforcement for molar academic responses (e.g., math answers, oral reading, solution of word problems) results in enhanced academic performance. Second, medication is not necessary to control high levels of motor activity, inattentiveness, and disruptive behavior in the classroom. That is, these incompatible behaviors decline significantly when academic responding improves. This latter finding has significant implications since previous investigations, which targeted elimination of these incompatible behaviors through operant techniques (Ferritor, Buckholdt, Hamblin & Smith, 1972) or medication (Rie, Rie, Stewart & Ambriel, 1976), were unsuccessful in indirectly improving academic performance.

PROPOSED BEHAVIORAL MODEL FOR ACADEMIC REMEDIATION

To date, the treatment outcome literature with learning disabled children indicates that medical model approaches, which focus on inferred process deficits, have not been successful in enhancing academic performance. On the other hand, the more direct behavioral approaches have proven effective in the remediation of academic deficits. These findings suggest that deficits in any proposed underlying process either do not exist, are unimportant, or that rewarding correct academic behaviors indirectly alleviates these deficits. In any case, parsimony would suggest that inferred process deficits need not be added to our conceptualization of learning disabilities at this time.

Basic Tenets

Just by knowing that academic deficits can be corrected in operant procedures does not tell us which behaviors should be modified in what manner. Operant treatment regimens have previously centered around two questions: (1) Are all specific academic problems subject to such modification? and (2) Do the effects of modifying academic problems in one area (e.g., reading comprehension) generalize to other specific academic deficits (e.g., oral reading)? This latter issue was tested by Lahey, McNees, and Schnelle (1977) by providing token rewards contingent on accurate responses in one of three different content areas of reading: oral speed, oral accuracy, and comprehension. The findings indicated substantial improvements in those behaviors directly reinforced, but no interdependence across the three areas was noted. That is, improvements in one area did not alter performance in the other two areas. Thus, the evidence indicates that virtually any specific academic behavior can be modified and that these behaviors are generally independent of one another. What is needed at this point is an empirically testable model that specifies which academic behaviors to modify. What follows is a tentative model based on three primary tenets: practicality, functional units of classroom behavior, and use of principles of learning. Although the tenets are diverse in nature, they are quite compatible with one another. The model is outlined below using reading as an example, although any academic area could be substituted.

Practicality.   Teachers, psychologists, and other professionals directly involved in teaching the learning disabled child will be more likely to implement those intervention programs that are less demanding and more feasible, given the restrictive conditions of the educational settings. Remedial strategies will be less likely to be employed if they demand excessive preparation time, one-to-one instruction, or result in decreased effectiveness in the educational progress of others.

Functional Units of Classroom Behavior.   The primary intention of any remedial academic program is to teach individuals academic skills that will make them as functional as possible in the classroom. For instance, some educational settings require the student to answer oral or written questions about prose passages that they have just read. Other classrooms require children to read sentences aloud. Other requirements may include completing questions in programmed instructional workbooks. If these tasks are correctly accomplished, the child is considered to be doing well in reading. These various behaviors (e.g., oral reading, answering workbook questions) would be considered the functional units of reading in these academic settings.

A remedial strategy will be considered beneficial, only if the student's deficiencies are alleviated in these functional units of academic behavior. Thus, from a behavioral approach, the targeted behaviors should be the functional or molar units of reading valued in the classroom. For instance, if an instructor wants the student to correctly answer more written questions from oral readings, then rewards should be made contingent on each correct response. Similarly, if answering workbook questions is desired, then reinforcement should be delivered for each correct answer.

As demonstrated earlier, enhancement of academic achievement is possible through reinforcement of such molar units of academic behavior (e.g., spelling, oral reading), without focusing on inferred process deficits or more molecular units of an academic skill. In some situations, however, it may be necessary to use a more molecular approach and to target aspects of reading that are not functional per se in the classroom but are prerequisite to the functional molar units (e.g., phonics skills). This molecular approach is analogous to the tactic traditionally taken by many reading specialists (Gearhart, 1976; McGinnis, 1963; Minskoff, Wiseman & Minskoff, 1974; Smith, 1981). Their strategy involves a thorough task analysis of the specific academic problem with intervention focused on specific molecular aspects of the deficit. As an example, efforts at improving reading comprehension may be impossible if the child does not know the definitions of some of the words. Or, a student may not show improvements in oral reading if he/she does not know necessary phonics rules or irregular sight words. Thus, it may sometimes be necessary to teach such molecular behaviors (e.g., word definitions, phonics rules) before improvements in the molar units of the behavior can occur. This molecular approach should only be implemented after an effort has been made to remediate the functional units of academic behavior, or if it is apparent that a child's deficits require the additional molecular approach.

Use of Principles of Learning. By definition, learning disabled children encounter more problems than most children in the acquisition of academic skills. Thus, it is mandatory that the teaching approach for these children adhere more closely to the principles of learning than is necessary with other students. It is essential to decrease the size of the unit of behavior to create a greater probability of success, maintain consistent immediate positive reinforcement for correct performance, and provide corrective feedback after incorrect responses.

Assessment and Treatment Phases

A thorough behavioral assessment of the child's academic problems as well as other school-related behaviors (e.g., conduct disorder, attention deficits, social skills deficits) should be conducted for all learning disabled children. After this general assessment is completed, a number of relevant target behaviors should be identified (e.g., oral reading of passages, spelling words read aloud, writing answers to workbook questions). Then these behaviors should be placed in a hierarchy of priorities, based on the areas to be focused on first. The development of this hierarchy should involve the combined efforts of both the teachers and the parents, since cooperation between the two parties increases the likelihood of a successful intervention.

Next, the treatment program should be developed and implemented with specific requirements for success as outlined and with tentative deadlines for completion of the target behaviors. For instance, if reading comprehension is the targeted behavior, then a criterion for success could be to correctly answer a written question in a workbook. The child should receive a reinforcer following each correct response (e.g., a token or checkmark to be exchanged for tangible rewards later). During this treatment phase, the interventionist should attempt to record the antecedent and maintaining events surrounding periods of highest performance. Furthermore, progression to the next targeted behavior on the hierarchy should be made only after adequate generalization of the present skill has been noted.

Another important aspect of the treatment program is that it begins at the student's present academic level rather than grade level. For example, a sixth grader whose reading comprehension is at the 3.5 grade level might show transient improvements in grade-appropriate reading with the initiation of a behavior modification program. However, consistent improvements would not be possible since the child lacks certain prerequisite skills and rules. These skills and rules (e.g., irregular sight words, definitions) should be targeted for modification so the child could handle reading material at the sixth-grade level.

Evaluation Phase

If the child is having difficulty learning the targeted behaviors following the allotted time intervals, then another reassessment should be conducted using the procedures discussed earlier (see Assessment and Treatment Phases). A persistently poor level of performance may be due to insufficient reinforcers or an excessively high criterion for success. If the child shows variations in performance over time, this may be indicative of a number of problems, including environmental factors (e.g., inconsistency in implementation of program), school-related stressors (e.g., social skills deficits), family-related stressors (e.g., extreme parental pressure on academic achievement), and peer reinforcement of incompatible behaviors. Adjustments of the treatment program can be made using information from this assessment. A molecular approach is warranted if the assessment determines that certain skill or rule deficits exist or that no apparent reason is noted for the poor performance.

The discussion of treatment strategies to this point has been based on the assumption that the teacher is willing and able to implement an intervention that, in many cases, may be radically different from the standard remedial curriculum. Obviously, there will be many instances in which this is not the case. Therefore, it is important that consultants be able to arrange for effective interventions that require little involvement of teachers. One such alternative is home-based contingency systems that use daily report cards to give information about the academic and general classroom behavior to parents (or other responsible adults). The parents can then reinforce accurate academic performance at home. The research literature supporting the use of daily report cards is reviewed by Broughton, Barton, and Owen (1981). While this approach is used clinically with diagnosed learning disabled children to improve academic performance with apparent success, there is unfortunately no published research available on this population. Care should be taken, therefore, to carefully monitor its success with learning disabled clients.

Case Study

Application of the model described above can be illustrated with a case study. S.D. was a white male from an upper socioeconomic-level family who was 8 years, 10 months of age at the time of referral. He was a residential student in the Learning Disabilities Program of the Athens Unit of the Georgia Retardation Center. During the four years of its existence, this program served non-retarded learning disabled children who were referred by public school districts in a catchment area comprising half of the state of Georgia. Only severe cases were accepted for this one-year, five-day-per-week residential treatment program.

S.D. was referred because of a total inability to write legible words or letters. His performance on the WISC-R resulted in a Verbal IQ of 80 and a Performance IQ of 46. He consistently failed to complete his classroom assignments, was severely disruptive, and was noncompliant. He interacted reasonably well with other children but stuttered in stressful situations. He had serious problems in both fine and gross motor coordination, leading him to perform very poorly in sports. Perhaps as a consequence, he engaged in a great deal of behavior that appeared to function to avoid both academic and sports tasks.

In the first phase of treatment, S.D. was tutored individually in a separate room near the classroom by a trained graduate student therapist. These sessions were conducted three or four times per week for 15 to 60 minutes. A multiple-baseline design was used across the behaviors of handwriting and shoe tying to evaluate the course of treatment (Lahey, Busemeyer, O'Hara, & Beggs, 1977). During baseline, S.D. was asked to copy from printed cards his full name and 14 common four to six letter words on individual 5 × 8 cards during each session. In addition, he was asked to attempt to tie his shoes four times during each session. No correct responses of either type were emitted during baseline. S.D. eventually complied with the tutors' requests to attempt each of these responses, but baseline sessions were often quite lengthy. S.D. engaged in many avoidance behaviors, including frequently requesting to terminate the session, speaking at length about extraneous topics, refusing for long periods to attempt responses, and kicking the tutor under the table on several occasions. The tutor ignored all of these extraneous behaviors, except for the kicking, which resulted in a two-minute time-out period standing in the corner of the treatment room. At the same time that baseline data were being collected during tutoring, the teacher was asked to collect all written work performed by S.D. in the classroom for later scoring.

During treatment for handwriting, S.D. was given praise and one penny for each correct response. Based on previous research and clinical experience, it was believed that the appropriate functional behavior to modify was actual handwriting (rather than copying abstract forms, etc.) and that treatment should begin with the unit of full, single words. Thus, S.D. was reinforced only for each copied word that was composed of all legible letters that were written in the correct orientation and sequence. Words containing any errors were not scored as correct, and reinforcement was not given. Following incorrect responses, brief corrective feedback was provided, such as "This one is good, except that this letter is backwards; it should be written like this." (demonstrated by tutor) After seven sessions, the percent of correctly written words had risen to over 75 percent. Because it was noticed that S.D. put the pennies he had earned in a wallet containing considerable sums of money, pennies (but not contingent praise) were experimentally dropped at that point. No decrement in performance occurred; instead, performance continued to improve to 14 or more correct responses per 15 trials during the 8th through 10th sessions. As could be predicted on the basis of the findings of Ayllon, Layman, and Kandel (1975), the improvements in academic performance were accompanied by marked and welcome decreases in S.D.'s disruptive behavior.

Two steps were taken at this point to program for generalization to the classroom. First, S.D. was given a new set of 14 words to copy, and when he reached near-perfect performance on the second through fourth sessions, he was given a third new set of words to copy. Similarly, S.D. was copying these words with nearly perfect accuracy after three additional sessions. The second step taken to program generalization involved laying the groundwork, both to transfer the treatment method to the teacher and to increase the unit of S.D.'s handwriting responses. The teacher was asked to discontinue assigning penmanship exercises to S.D. that involved writing sentences. Rather, the teacher gave S.D. one word to copy at a time on classroom paper and provided immediate praise or corrective feedback contingent on performance. One week later, the teacher gave S.D. two words at a time, then three words at a time, and so on, until he was copying full sentences. From baseline performance of 32 percent correctly formed letters, his performance improved to 80 percent correct letters over six months of instruction.

After 28 tutoring sessions, the shoe tying response was targeted to rule out maturation and other time-related confounds as alternative explanations for the improvement in handwriting. This skill was taught using a standard backward chaining procedure. This skill was quickly mastered within five sessions.

Follow-up assessment conducted during the following academic year suggested that S.D.'s treatment gains had been maintained. His handwriting was still sloppy for a child of his age, but it was legible and functional.

CONCLUSIONS

A large but confusing body of literature exists on the topic of learning disabilities, although it only recently has received the full attention of educators, psychologists, and other professionals. Part of the problem with the existing literature is the lack of a clearly specified definition of learning disability. Furthermore, a variety of diagnostic subcategories that have not been empirically validated are frequently used. These problems have partially been responsible for the large number of noncomparable investigations. A dimensional approach to the conceptualization of learning disabilities was proposed as a potential means of alleviating these problems.

Numerous theories abound as to the etiology of learning disabilities, but none of the remedial methods based on medical model theories have been successful in enhancing the academic performance of learning disabled children. However, more direct behavioral treatment strategies have consistently been shown to be effective in the remediation of a wide variety of academic deficiencies evidenced in learning disabled populations. It must be noted, however, that the empirical evaluation of the effectiveness of behavioral remediation strategies is not conclusive. Further research is needed to determine the long-term consequences of such programs and to compare traditional versus behavioral approaches in the treatment of learning disabilities. The clearest conclusion that can be reached from the present literature is that there is a need for more methodologically sound research aimed at the identification of specific subcategories of learning disabilities, the identification of etiological factors, and the development of specific treatment programs for these children.

Nevertheless, at this point, the behavioral approach appears to be the most feasible strategy for the assessment and treatment of learning disabled children. To date, a formal behavioral model does not exist, however, for use in the identification of which academic behaviors should be modified and in what fashion. Such a model was proposed in this chapter, based on the three basic tenets of practicality, incorporation of the principles of learning, and use of functional units of academic behavior. A primary assumption of the model is that it is not necessary to focus on behaviors that are thought to be incompatible with effective learning (e.g., impulsivity, attention deficit) or underlying process deficits (e.g., psycholinguistic skills, eye-hand coordination). Instead, the primary concern of the treatment package is the molar or functional units of deficient academic behavior. At times, a more molecular approach may be warranted if the molar approach is not consistently effective in enhancing academic performance or if certain deficits exist that require this approach (e.g., reading knowledge of irregular sight words, phonics rules).

In addition, since the entire condition of the child must be considered during treatment, not just the child's academic problems, the behavioral approach mandates that other potential problem areas be assessed and treated when appropriate (e.g., conduct disorder, hyperactivity, social skills deficits). Virtually all of these problems are amenable to behavioral intervention (Ross, 1976) so that treatment can proceed concurrently with the academic remediation strategies. Indeed, as suggested by Ayllon, Layman, and Kandel (1975), academic remediation will often result in concomitant improvement in other classroom behavior problems. It is hoped that this proposed model will be empirically tested, with the outcome being the development of treatment protocols effective in enhancing the learning disabled child's academic achievement and other desirable social and school-related behaviors.

REFERENCES

Ackerman, P., Peters, J. E., & Dykman, R. A. Children with specific learning disabilities: WISC profiles. *Journal of Learning Disabilities,* 1971, *4,* 150–166.

Ayllon, T., Layman, D., & Kandel, H. J. A behavioral-education alternative to drug control of hyperactive children. *Journal of Applied Behavior Analysis,* 1975, *8,* 137–146.

Ayllon, T., & Roberts, M. D. Eliminating discipline problems by strengthening academic performance. *Journal of Applied Behavior Analysis,* 1974, *7,* 71–76.

Barkley, R. A. Predicting the response of hyperkinetic children to stimulant drugs: A review. *Journal of Abnormal Child Psychology,* 1977, *4,* 327–348.

Barkley, R. A. Learning disabilities. In E. J. Mash & L. G. Terdal (Eds.), *Behavioral assessment of childhood disorders.* New York: Guilford Press, 1981.

Barsch, R. *Achieving perceptual-motor efficiency.* Seattle, Wash.: Special Child Publication, 1967.

Bijou, D. W., Birnbrauer, J. S., Kidder, J. D., & Taugue, C. Programmed instruction as an approach to teaching of reading, writing, and arithmetic to retarded children. *Psychological Record,* 1966, *16,* 505–522.

Blau, H., & Blau, H. A theory of learning to read by "modality blocking." In J. I. Arena (Ed.), *Successful programming: Many points of view.* Pittsburgh: Association of Children with Learning Disabilities, 1969.

Boder, E. Developmental dyslexia: A diagnostic approach based on three atypical reading-spelling patterns. *Developmental Medicine and Child Neurology,* 1973, *15,* 663–687.

Broughton, S. F., Barton, E. S., & Owen, P. R. Home based contingency systems for school problems. *School Psychology Review,* 1981, *10,* 26–36.

Broughton, S. F., & Lahey, B. B. Direct and collateral effects of positive reinforcement, response cost, and mixed contingencies for academic performance. *Journal of School Psychology,* 1978, *16,* 126–136.

Brown, L., & Perlmutter, L. Teaching functional reading to trainable level retarded students. *Education and Training of the Mentally Retarded,* 1971, *6,* 74–84.

Bryan, T. Peer popularity of learning disabled children. *Journal of Learning Disabilities,* 1974, *1,* 621–626.

Bryan, T. Peer popularity of learning disabled children: A replication. *Journal of Learning Disabilities,* 1976, *9,* 49–53.

Bush, W. J., & Giles, M. T. Aids to psycholinguistic teaching. Columbus, Ohio: Charles E. Merrill Publishing, 1969.

Chadwick, B. A., & Day, R. C. Systematic reinforcement: Academic performance of underachieving students. *Journal of Applied Behavior Analysis*, 1971, *4*, 311–319.

Clark, C. A., & Walberg, H. J. The use of secondary reinforcement in teaching inner-city school children. *Journal of Special Education*, 1979, *3*, 177–185.

Cowen, E. L., Pederson, A., Babigien, H., Izzo, L. D., & Trost, M. A. Long-term follow-up of early detected vulnerable children. *Journal of Consulting and Clinical Psychology*, 1973, *41*, 438–446.

Cruickshanck, W. *The brain-injured child in the home, school, and community.* New York: Syracuse University Press, 1967.

Delacatto, C. *Treatment and prevention of reading problems.* Springfield, Ill.: Charles C Thomas, 1959.

Delamater, A., Lahey, B. B., & Drake, L. Toward an empirical subclassification of "learning disabilities:" A psychophysiological comparison of "Hyperactive" and "nonhyperactive" subgroups. *Journal of Abnormal Child Psychology*, 1981, *9*, 65–77.

Douglas, V. I. Stop, look, and listen: the problem of sustained attention and impulse control in hyperactive and normal children. *Canadian Journal of Behavioral Science*, 1972, *4*, 259–282.

Drabman, R. S., Spitalnik, R., & O'Leary, K. D. Teaching self-control to disruptive children. *Journal of Abnormal Psychology*, 1973, *82*, 10–16.

Drass, S. D., & Jones, R. L. Learning disabled children as behavior modifiers. *Journal of Learning Disabilities*, 1971, *4*, 418–425.

Dudley-Marling, C. C., Kaufman, N. J., & Tarver, S. G. WISC and WISC-R profiles of learning disabled children: A review. *Learning Disability Quarterly*, 1981, *4*, 307–319.

Fauke, B. S., Burnett, J., Powers, M. A., & Sulzer-Azaroff, B. Improvement of handwriting and letter recognition skills: a behavior modification procedure. *Journal of Learning Disabilities*, 1973, *6*, 25–29.

Fernald, G. *Remedial techniques in basic school subjects.* New York: McGraw-Hill, 1943.

Ferritor, D. E., Buckholdt, D., Hamblin, R. L., & Smith, L. The noneffects of contingent reinforcement for attending behavior on work accomplished. *Journal of Applied Behavior Analysis*, 1972, *5*, 7–17.

Frostig, M., & Horne, D. *The Frostig program for the development of visual perception.* Chicago: Follett Education Corporation, 1964.

Gearhart, B. R. *Teaching the learning disabled.* St. Louis: Mosby, 1976.

Gelfand, D. M., & Hartmann, D. R. *Child behavior analysis and therapy.* New York: Pergamon Press, 1975.

Getman, G. N., Kane, E. R., Halgren, M. R., & McKee, G. W. *The physiology of readiness: an action program for the development of perception in children.* Minneapolis: Publications to Accelerate School Success, Inc., 1964.

Gillingham, A., & Stillman, G. *Remedial training for children with specific disability in reading, spelling, and penmanship.* Cambridge, Mass.: Educators Publishing Service, 1965.

Glass, G. V., & Robbins, M. P. A critique of experiments on the role of neurological organization in reading performance. *Reading Research Quarterly,* 1976, *3,* 5–52.

Goodman, L., & Hammill, D. The effectiveness of Kephart-Getman activities in developing perceptual-motor and cognitive skills. *Focus on Exceptional Children,* 1973, *4,* 1–9.

Hallahan, D. P., & Kaufman, J. M. *Introduction to learning disabilities: A psychobehavioral approach.* Englewood Cliffs, N.J.: Prentice-Hall, 1976.

Hammill, D. D., & Larsen, S. The effectiveness of psycholinguistic training. *Exceptional Children,* 1974, *41,* 5–15.

Haring, N. G., & Hauck, M. A. Improved learning conditions in the establishment of reading skills with disabled readers. *Exceptional Children,* 1969, *35,* 341–351.

Harris, L. A., & Sherman, J. A. Effects of homework assignments and consequences on performance in social studies and mathematics. *Journal of Applied Behavior Analysis,* 1972, *7,* 505–519.

Harris, L. A., Sherman, J. A., Henderson, D. G., & Harris, M. S. Effects of peer tutoring on the spelling performance of elementary classroom students. *A new direction for education: Behavior analysis.* Lawrence, Kan.: University of Kansas Support and Development Center for Follow Through, 1973.

Heilman, K. M., & Valenstein, E. (Eds.). *Clinical Neuropsychology.* New York: Oxford University Press, 1979.

Hemry, F. P. Effect of reinforcement conditions on a discrimination learning task for impulsive versus reflective children. *Child Development,* 1973, *44,* 657–660.

Hewett, F. M., Taylor, F., & Artuso, A. The Madison Plan really swings. *Today's Education,* 1968, *59,* 15–17.

Horowitz, E. C. Popularity, decentering ability, and role-taking skills in learning disabled and normal children. *Learning Disability Quarterly,* 1981, *4,* 23–30.

Hulesman, C. B., Jr. The WISC subtest syndrome for disabled readers. *Perceptual and Motor Skills,* 1970, *30,* 535–550.

Jastak, J. F., & Jastak, S. R. *The Wide Range Achievement Test.* (Rev. ed.). Wilmington, Del.: Guidance Association of Delaware, 1965.

Johnson, D., & Myklebust, H. *Learning disabilities: Educational principles and practices.* New York: Grune & Stratton, 1967.

Kagan, J. Reflection-impulsivity: The generality and dynamics of conceptual tempo. *Journal of Abnormal Psychology,* 1966, *71,* 17–24.

Karnes, M. B. *Helping young children develop language skills.* Washington, D.C.: Council for Exceptional Children, 1968.

Kent, R. M., & O'Leary, K. D. A controlled evaluation of behavior modification with conduct problem children. *Journal of Consulting and Clinical Psychology,* 1976, *44,* 586–596.

Kephart, N. *The Slow Learner in the Classroom.* Columbus, Ohio: Charles E. Merrill Publishing, 1971.

Kephart, N. C. The perceptual-motor match. In W. M. Cruickshanck & D. P. Hallahan (Eds.), *Perceptual and learning disabilities in children.* Vol. 1: Psychoeducational practices. Syracuse: Syracuse University Press, 1975.

Kirby, F. D., & Shields, F. Modification of arithmetic response rate and attending behavior in a seventh grade student. *Journal of Applied Behavior Analysis,* 1972, *5,* 79–84.

Kirk, S., & Kirk, W. *Psycholinguistic learning disabilities: Diagnosis and remediation.* Urbana, Ill.: University of Illinois Press, 1971.

Kirk, S. A., McCarthy, J. J., & Kirk, W. D. *Illinois test of psycholinguistic abilities.* Urbana, Ill.: University of Illinois Press, 1968.

Lahey, B. B. Behavior modification with learning disabilities and related problems. In M. Hersen, R. Eisler, & P. Miller (Eds.), *Progress in behavior modification* (Vol. 3). New York: Academic Press, 1976.

Lahey, B. B., *Behavior therapy with hyperactive and learning disabled children.* New York: Oxford University Press, 1979.

Lahey, B. B., Busemeyer, M., O'Hara, C., & Beggs, V. E. Treatment of severe perceptual-motor disorders in children diagnosed as learning disabled. *Behavior Modification,* 1977, *1,* 123–140.

Lahey, B. B., Delamater, A., Kupfer, D. L., & Hobbs, S. A. Behavioral aspects of learning disabilities and hyperactivity. *Education and Urban Society,* 1978, *10,* 477–499.

Lahey, B. B., & Johnson, M. S. *Psychology and instruction.* Glenview, Ill.: Scott, Foresman, 1977.

Lahey, B. B., Kupfer, D. L., Beggs, V. E., & Landon, D. Eye movements of learning disabled children during reading. *Journal of Abnormal Child Psychology,* 1982, *10,* 1–10.

Lahey, B. B., McNees, M. P., & Brown, C. C. Modification of deficits in reading for comprehension. *Journal of Applied Behavior Analysis,* 1973, *6,* 475–480.

Lahey, B. B., Vosk, B. N., & Habif, V. L. Behavioral assessment of learning disabled children: A rationale and strategy. *Behavioral Assessment,* 1981, *3,* 3–14.

Lambert, N., & Sandoval, J. The prevalence of learning disabilities in a sample of children considered hyperactive. *Journal of Abnormal Child Psychology,* 1980, *8,* 33–50.

Lerner, J. W. Children with learning disabilities: Theories, diagnosis and teaching strategy. Boston: Houghton Mifflin, 1971.

Lovitt, T. C., & Smith, D. D. Using withdrawal of positive reinforcement to alter subtraction performance. *Exceptional Children,* 1974, *40,* 357–358.

Madsen, C. H., Becker, W. C., & Thomas, D. R. Rules, praise, and ignoring: Elements of elementary classroom control. *Journal of Applied Behavior Analysis,* 1968, *1,* 139–150.

Marholin, D., & Steinman, W. M. Stimulus control in the classroom as a function of the behavior reinforced. *Journal of Applied Behavior Analysis,* 1977, *10,* 465–478.

Massari, D. J., & Schack, M. L. Discrimination learning by reflective and impulsive children as a function of reinforcement schedule. *Developmental Psychology,* 1972, *6,* 183.

McCarthy, D. *McCarthy scales of children's abilities.* New York: The Psychological Corporation, 1972.

McCarthy, J. J., & McCarthy, J. F. *Learning disabilities.* Boston: Allyn & Bacon, 1969.

Meir, J. H. Prevalence and characteristics of learning disabilities found in second grade children. *Journal of Learning Disabilities,* 1971, *4,* 7–18.

Miller, L. C. School behavior checklist: An inventory of deviant behavior for elementary school children. *Journal of Consulting and Clinical Psychology,* 1972, *38,* 134–144.

Miller, M., Stoneburner, R., & Brecht, R. WISC subtest patterns as discriminators of perceptual disability. *Journal of Learning Disabilities,* 1978, *11,* 449–452.

Morgan, W. P. A case of congenital word-blindness. *British Medical Journal,* 1896, *2,* 1543–1544.

National Advisory Committee on Handicapped Children. Special education for handicapped children: First annual report, Washington, D.C.: U.S. Department of Health, Education, and Welfare, 1968.

Novy, P., Burnett, J., Powers, M., & Sulzer-Azaroff, B. Modifying attending-to-work behavior of a learning disabled child. *Journal of Learning Disabilities,* 1973, *6,* 217–221.

O'Leary, K. D., & Beckery, W. C. Behavior modification of an adjustment class: A token reinforcement program. *Exceptional Children,* 1967, *9,* 637–642.

Orton, S. *Reading, writing, and speech problems in children:* W. W. Norton, 1937.

Osgood, C. *"A behavioral analysis" in contemporary approaches to cognition.* Cambridge, Mass.: Howard University Press, 1957.

Piaget, J. *The construction of reality in the child.* New York: Ballantine Books, 1974.

Rie, H. E., Rie, E. D., Stewart, S., & Ambriel, J. P. Effects of methylphenidate on underachieving children. *Journal of Consulting and Clinical Psychology,* 1976, *44,* 250–260.

Roff, M., Sells, S. B., & Golden, M. M. *Social adjustment and personality development in children.* Minneapolis: The University of Minnesota, 1972.

Ross, A. O. *Psychological aspects of learning disabilities and reading disorders.* New York: McGraw-Hill, 1976.

Ross, A. O. *Learning disability the unrealized potential.* New York: McGraw-Hill, 1977.

Ross, D. M., & Ross, S. A. *Hyperactivity: Research, theory, and action.* New York: John Wiley & Sons, 1976.

Rourke, B. P. Neuropsychological research in reading retardation: A review. In A. Bentton & D. Pearl (Eds.), *Dyslexia: An appraisal of current knowledge.* New York: Oxford University Press, 1978.

Rourke, B. P., Young, G. C., & Flewelling, R. W. The relationships between WISC verbal-performance discrepancies and selected verbal, auditory-perceptual, visual-perceptual, and problem solving abilities in children with learning disabilities. *Journal of Clinical Psychology,* 1971, *27,* 475–479.

Rutter, M., Tizard, J., Yule, W., Graham, P., & Whitmore, K. Research report: Isle of Wight Studies. *Psychological Medicine,* 1976, *6,* 313–332.

Ryback, D., & Staats, A. W. Parents as behavior therapy-technicians in treating reading deficits (dyslexia). *Journal of Behavior Therapy and Experimental Psychiatry,* 1970, *1,* 109–119.

Safer, D. J., Allen, R. P. *Hyperactive children: Diagnosis and management.* Baltimore: University Park Press, 1976.

Sattler, J. M. *Assessment of children's intelligence and special abilities* (2nd ed.). Boston: Allyn & Bacon, 1981.

Smith, D. D. *Teaching the learning disabled.* Englewood Cliffs, N.J.: Prentice-Hall, 1981.

Smith, D. D., & Lovitt, T. C. The differential effects of reinforcement contingencies on arithmetic performance. *Journal of Learning Disabilities,* 1967, *9,* 32–41.

Smith, D. D., Lovitt, T. C., & Kidder, J. S. Using reinforcement contingencies and teaching aids to alter the subtraction performance of children with learning disabilities. In G. Semb (Ed.), *Behavior analysis and education.* Lawrence, Kan.: Kansas University Department of Human Development, 1972.

Spache, G. D. *Diagnostic reading scales.* Monterey, Calif.: CTB/McGraw-Hill, 1963.

Spache, G. D. *Investigating the issues of reading disabilities.* Boston: Allyn & Bacon, 1976.

Stanford-Binet Intelligence Scale. Boston: Houghton Mifflin Co., 1973.

Stone, M. Problems with research designs in studies of sensory-response patterns in remedial reading. *Journal of the Association for the Study of Perception,* 1972, *8,* 8–15.

Strauss, A., & Lehtinen, L. *Psychopathology and education of the brain-injured child.* New York: Grune & Stratton, 1947.

Strauss, A. A., & Werner, H. Disorders of conceptual thinking in the brain-injured child. *Journal of Nervous and Mental Disease,* 1942, *96,* 153–172.

Ullman, C. A. Teachers, peers, and tests as predictors of adjustment. *Journal of Educational Psychology,* 1957, *48,* 257–267.

Vellutino, F. R., Steger, B. M., Moyer, G. C., Harding, C. J., & Niles, J. A. Has the perceptual deficit hypothesis led us astray? *Journal of Learning Disabilities,* 1977, *10,* 54–64.

Wadsworth, H. G. A motivational approach toward the remediation of learning disabled boys. *Exceptional Children,* 1971, *37,* 33–42.

Wechsler, D. *Manual for the Wechsler Intelligence Scale for Children—Revised.* New York: The Psychological Corporation, 1974.

Williams, M., & Lahey, B. B. The functional independence of response latency and accuracy: Implications for the concept of conceptual tempo. *Journal of Abnormal Child Psychology,* 1977, *5,* 371–378.

Wolf, M. M., Giles, D. K., & Hall, R. V. Experiments with token reinforcement in a remedial classroom. *Behaviour Research and Therapy,* 1968, *6,* 51–64.

Wong, B. The role of theory in learning disabilities research. Part 1. An analysis of problems. *Journal of Learning Disabilities,* 1979, *12,* 19–28.

Yule, W. The epidemiology of child psychopathology, In B. B. Lahey & A. E. Kazdin (Eds.), *Advances in Clinical Child Psychology.* New York: Plenum Press, 1981.

19

Behavioral Approaches to Intervention and Assessment with Child-Abusive Families*

John B. Reid
Oregon Social Learning Center
University of Oregon

Because of ever more stringent laws prohibiting physical child abuse, and because of increased public and professional awareness of the extent of this problem, clinicians are more frequently being confronted with the problems of conceptualizing and dealing with child abuse in their daily practices. The purpose of this chapter is fivefold. First, the extent of the problem will be described both in terms of frequency and in terms of critical ages at which children are at highest risk. Second, some relationships between physical abuse and family process variables will be described. Third, a number of general guidelines for working with abusive families will be presented, and fourth, assessment procedures will be discussed. Finally, attempts to use behavioral interventions with abusive families will be reviewed.

THE EXTENT OF THE PROBLEM

It is difficult to describe unambiguously the extent of child abuse in the United States. Depending on the precise definition used and the sampling methods

* The preparation of this manuscript was supported in part by Grant No. 7 RO1 MH 37938, 7 RO1 MH 37940, 2 RO1 MH 37940, and 5 T32 17126 from the National Institute of Mental Health, U.S. Public Health Service. The author is indebted to Kate Kavanagh for critical feedback on earlier drafts, and to Will Mayer and Mary Perry for editorial assistance.

employed, the estimated number of child abuse incidents have ranged from 60,000 to over 6,000,000 each year. The most sophisticated analyses limit the estimated range to between 500,000 and 2,000,000 (Light, 1973; Straus, Gelles, & Steinmetz, 1980). Such population statistics provide the practicing clinician little usable information because only a small fraction (about one fifth) of clear acts of child maltreatment are reported to relevant authorities (American Humane Association, 1981). Incomplete as they may be, a number of findings from analyses of the incidence of child abuse are of direct relevance to clinicians who deal with this problem. First, 96 percent of all cases of child abuse reported in 1980 were perpetrated by parents. Second, it is the very young children who are at the most risk of suffering serious physical abuse and injury. During 1980, 70 percent of the cases of serious physical abuse involved children five years of age or younger. For children killed during child abusive episodes, the average age was 2.8 years. These data have two clear implications for those charged to deal with this phenomenon. First, the highest priorities for the expenditure of clinical energies in this area must be given to prevention, treatment, and assessment in families of infants and young children who are at risk for abuse or reabuse. Second, gruesome as these statistics may be, they indicate that true prevention may be a serious and attainable goal in dealing with this problem. In considering prevention activities in many areas of mental health, we often think of offering a service of some sort to young members of our society in order to prevent a disturbance or problem years or even decades later. Take, for example, efforts to prevent alcoholism. One can think of education efforts or family counseling interventions focused on children and teenagers. The goal is to prevent self-destructive drinking or alcoholism, a disorder that often does not become full blown until middle age (Vaillant, 1983). A similar situation exists in the prevention of smoking. One attempts to prevent serious illnesses that on an actuarial basis, are expected to occur many, many years later. Finally, clinical researchers have been heavily engaged over the last couple of decades in working with youngsters in an attempt to prevent the development of chronic patterns of delinquency during the late teens and early 20s. Such efforts have made us quite humble about the long-term persistence of even powerful intervention programs (Empey, 1978; Reid, 1983a). In the case of the abuse of young children, if the effects of prevention and treatment interventions show only moderate persistence over time, the outcome should be extraordinarily valuable.

It is during infancy and the pre- and primary school years that the child's life experiences are almost totally circumscribed by the interactions he or she has with the immediate family. For example, in research currently being conducted at our center (Patterson, 1983), parents of fourth graders reported that their children were unsupervised (directly or indirectly) for only about one hour per day. Parents of seventh graders reported an average of 1.5 unsupervised hours per day (Patterson, 1983). Because of the facts that in Western culture parents of young children are granted extreme privacy and freedom (Burgess & Richardson, in press) and that broad ranges of discipline and child-rearing strategies are condoned (Stark & McEvoy, 1970), it is the case that many young children are at the mercy of their parents at the time when they are most vulnerable to injury from physical abuse. As the child matures, he or she gradually acquires both the skills and opportunities for self-protection from serious physical injury. At a basic level, an eight- or nine-year-old can more easily run away from an outraged parent than can a two- or three-year-old. As the child develops verbal and social skills, he or she can better anticipate and possibly divert potential escalation in the hostility demonstrated by parents. With increasing verbal skills, the youngster has a chance to mollify an angry parent or perhaps to enlist the aid of a relative or neighbor when the going gets rough. As the child gets older, the rules of society dictate that he or she become increasingly exposed to adults outside the family who have an opportunity to observe the effects of child maltreatment. Moreover, in most states, some of these adults are legally obligated to report and intervene in suspected cases of child abuse (e.g., teachers). Finally, it is the case that, as the child matures, he or she develops increased physical toughness and resilience, which further reduces the possibility that a parental act of anger will lead to physical injury. For example, the throttling of a seven-year-old may lead to tears, the throttling of an infant may lead to bruises on the brain. A swift slap to the face may bloody the nose of a 12-year-old, it may break the nose of a 5-year-old.

Perhaps the most relevant information is the fact that in the vast majority of cases of officially reported child abuse, the child remains in the family home following the detection of physical abuse. In the study conducted by the American Humane Association (1981), only 14 percent of the reported cases of child maltreatment lead to court action of any type, and the proportion of such cases leading to legal action has been steadily decreasing since the mid-1970s. Thus, regardless of the increased public awareness of the problem and despite ever stricter laws concerning the reporting of child abuse, the clinician is usually faced with the task of trying to correct the problem not by placing the child in a safer home, but by rectifying the problems in the child-abusive family. This fact becomes even more salient when we recall that only about one fifth of clear-cut abusive incidents receive any official attention at all.

Relevant to the assessment, prevention, and treatment of child abuse in families of young children, the two key issues that must be faced by clinicians come clearly into focus. First, it is necessary to conceptualize the way in which official or reported child abuse relates to the types of specific intrapersonal and/or social interactional processes in which the problem may be embedded, so that specific foci of treatment or prevention activities can be pinpointed. Second, it is necessary to come up with methods for the assessment of child-abusive family processes, which allow the clinician/researcher access to the clinically important processes that occur in the privacy of abusive-families' settings. Although this is a problem for all family therapists with a behavioral orientation, the situation is particularly acute for those of us who deal with child abuse. In the case of officially reported abuse, families may be particularly resistant to providing the clinician with the day-to-day data that is indispensable to effective treatment. For families entering treatment who have not yet been officially reported, fear, guilt, and perhaps self-deception may impede their ability to give or recall clinically important day-to-day information.

SOME RELATIONSHIPS AMONG OFFICIALLY REPORTED ABUSE, CHILD-ABUSIVE BEHAVIOR, AND FAMILY PROCESS: A CONCEPTUAL MODEL

In thinking about this problem, it is important to keep in mind that official child abuse statistics describe only a small portion of the physical assaults experienced by children in our society. Studies by Erlanger (1974) and by Stark and McEvoy (1970) indicate that 90 percent or more of all parents resort to physical coercion in handling discipline at some time or other. Over 50 percent of the subjects studied by Stark and McEvoy (1970) condoned the use of spanking for children under one year of age. In a large and well-designed survey conducted by Straus, et al. (1980), over 70 percent of the parents surveyed had been physically assaultive toward their children at one time or other. Although most of the physical assaults reported in this study were comprised of spanking and other "normal" types of physical punishment, about one parent in five admitted hitting his or her children with objects, and nearly one in 20 reported engaging in clearly abusive behavior such as beating, biting, and using lethal weapons against their children. Given such high base rates of physical assaultiveness toward children, it is not surprising that those parents whose aggressive behavior toward their children that lead them to official recognition by child-protective agencies do not, compared to nonabusive comparison groups, show excessive or idiosyncratic patterns of psychological or emotional disturbance (Parke & Collmer, 1975). From the literature just reviewed, it seems reasonable to conclude that we live in a culture in which the boundary between discipline and violence is often confused at both the conceptual and behavioral level. Most acts of severe physical abuse occur in the immediate context of discipline confrontations (e.g., Gil, 1969, 1971; Herrenkohl, Herrenkohl, & Egolf, 1983). It is also the case that most clinical researchers, regardless of theoretical persuasion, are in agreement that abusive parents have chronic difficulties in dealing with discipline issues (e.g., Elmer & Gregg, 1967; Reid, Taplin, & Lorber, 1981).

It is our position that a therapeutically useful conceptualization of child abuse in families of young children has the discipline situation as its central focus. Even though child abuse and other patterns of chronic conflict between parents and their children have been found to be embedded within matrices of background stressors, such as social insularity and isolation (e.g., Wahler, Leske, & Rogers, 1979), marital conflict (e.g., Green, 1976; Reid et al., 1981; Straus,

1980), financial stress (e.g., Egeland, Breitenbucher, & Rosenberg, 1980; Garbarino, 1976; Justice & Duncan, 1976), and emotional problems of the parents such as depression (Forehand, Wells, & Griest, 1980; Novaco, 1975; Patterson, 1982a), it is the discipline confrontation that precipitates parental violence in most cases. In our own clinical work with abusive parents, it is not so much the aversive behaviors themselves that depress and anger them, but the frustration of feeling that they cannot handle their children's refusal to desist in aversive behavior or to comply even with everyday requests unless they resort to assaultive behavior. This impression is in accord with the finding reported by Reid et al. (1981) that abusive mothers were able to terminate their children's aversive behavior immediately about 50 percent of the time contrasted with an 85 percent success rate demonstrated by nondistressed parents. This finding is also in line with a laboratory study by Wolfe, Fairbank, Kelly, and Bradlyn (1983) in which child-abusive mothers, as compared to nonabusive mothers, experienced significantly greater increases in both skin conductance and respiration when exposed to videotaped scenes in which children were noncompliant to their parents or showed excessive demands for attention.

It is undoubtedly the case that parents referred because of physical child abuse demonstrate a greater tendency than normals to perceive the behavior of their own children as aversive (Mash, Johnson, & Kovitz, in press). There is also evidence that they demonstrate excessive use of corporal punishment, such as spanking and use of commands and threats, in their day-to-day interactions and that they experience more anger during discipline confrontations (Reid, 1983b). It is our position, however, that the process linking assaultiveness and heavy handedness by parents to their efforts to socialize and manage their children's behavior is not unique to parents who have been labeled or detected as abusive, but is a process common to all parent-child interactions (Reid, Patterson, & Loeber, 1982).

Even in nonabusive homes, child rearing is often a nerve-racking job that is extremely stressful under the best of conditions. Parents who start families usually do so when they are still in the process of working out their marital relationships, when they are beginning careers and earning low pay, and when they have not entirely outgrown their own adolescence. Additionally, it is becoming increasingly common for young parents to have to deal with this difficult period without the help and support of a resident spouse (Glick, 1979). Regardless of the fact that having a family and a child provides the opportunity for numerous wonderful experiences, it exacts a heavy toll as well, and mothers pay most of the bill. A study by Feldman (1971), for example, showed that couples with children reported less satisfaction with their lives and marriages than those without children, and a study by Glenn (1975) demonstrated an increase in mothers' self-ratings of happiness following their children's leaving home. In a survey reported in *Behavior Today* (April 14, 1976), 23 percent of the housewives with children interviewed reported having symptoms such as tension, depression, and headaches; the rate was approximately twice that for the fathers interviewed in the same sample. Halverson and Woldrop (1970) reported that mothers were five times more aversive when interacting with their own children than with other preschool children. After reviewing 12 longitudinal studies in which mood and satisfaction were measured, Rollins and Feldman (1970) found a consistent decline in parental mood and satisfaction over the first 10 years of child rearing. Perhaps most relevant to the present discussion, Bradburn (1969) found that one of the primary sources of tension and concern for parents across socioeconomic levels was child management.

Even in families in which parents report harmonious relationships with their children, children present their parents with extraordinarily high numbers of behaviors that can lead to discipline confrontations. A large number of home observation studies have indicated that youngsters demonstrate misbehavior on the average of every 15 or 20 minutes when they are in the presence of their parents (Fawl, 1963; Forehand, King, Peed, & Yoder, 1975; Minton, Kagan, & Levine, 1971; Reid, 1978). Using systematic daily parent interviews, Chamberlain (1980) found that well over half of a sample of nondistressed parents reported chronic child-management problems such as arguing, defiance, and noncompliance. In thinking about these studies, as well as those discussed earlier, the results of a series of home observation studies conducted at our center (Reid et al., 1981; Reid et al., 1982; Reid, 1983c) are not terribly surprising. Data from these studies show, both for abusive and nonabusive families, strong and consistent correlations between the rates of aversive behavior by the children and the rates of *both* trivial *and* highly aversive behaviors by the parents. Although these relationships were most pronounced in abusive families, the correlations were surprisingly strong for families recruited on the basis of their having harmonious parent-child relationships. In these same studies, it was found that, although abusive parents engaged in higher frequencies of extended discipline confrontations and that any discipline confrontation that lasted over about half a minute was very likely to include a highly aversive parental behavior (hitting, threatening, yelling, or humiliating), *the same* patterns were found in nondistressed families.

On the basis of these and similar data, we have argued for the following conception of child-abusive behavior. The probability of child-abusive behavior is a function of two interrelated factors: the number of actual or potential discipline confrontations faced by the parents as they interact with the child and the parent's ability to quickly terminate or resolve such confrontations without resorting to physical assault. Although these variables are assumed to differentiate abusive from nonabusive families, the relationship is assumed to hold for any family over time. That is, on those days when parents are faced with or create the largest number of discipline confrontations and/or on those days on which they are least able to effectively deal with such discipline problems, the probability that they will engage in abusive, assaultive, or corporal punishment is increased. It is also assumed that any personal characteristics of parent or child or any stressful family, social, or financial factors that increase the probability of discipline confrontations or that decrease the parents' inability to resolve them quickly will, in turn, increase the probability of abusive behavior. This conceptualization, as well as data that support it, have been presented elsewhere (Reid, 1983c; Reid et al., 1981; Reid et al., 1982).

The point of the foregoing brief and selective review is to argue that the day-to-day problems faced by families referred because of child abuse are not qualitatively different from those faced by parents referred for child-management problems in general, with the exception that abusive families are often referred under duress, are usually more apprehensive about giving behavioral information that might be used against them, and may feel that they have to defend their own (often inadequate) theory of child management against a child protective agency that has labeled their approach and perhaps themselves as incompetent, brutal, or unloving (Windell & Windell, 1977). The fact that child-abusive families often present significant marital problems and personal problems for both parent and child and are often under a good deal of environmental stress is not unique to child-abusive families. Such factors must be confronted by therapists who deal with child conduct or management problems in general (e.g., Dumas & Wahler, in press; Margolin & Christensen, 1981). The cup is either half empty or half full. The problems to be confronted in dealing with abusive families are not totally new to therapists who have commonly dealt with run-of-the-mill child-management problems, and the clinical problems involved in dealing with run-of-the-mill child management problems have always been more complex than most of us have described in print. A post hoc content analysis of the case files of 88 sequential families referred to our own center because of child-management problems revealed that 27, or one third, would be considered abusive under state law (Reid, et al., 1981).

WORKING WITH ABUSIVE FAMILIES: SOME GENERAL CONSIDERATIONS

If families or individuals are to engage productively in a treatment program designed to actually change the manner in which they formulate the problems and actually deal with them on a moment-by-moment or day-to-day level, a great deal of openness is required, as well as energy to learn and practice novel patterns of behavior. For a number of problems such as obesity or smoking, which are characterized by daily patterns of habitual and molecular behaviors, a commitment both to deal with the problem and to do what is necessary to correct it is a sine qua non for effective treatment. Most overweight people, for example, do not even enter treatment for obesity, and of those who do enter treatment, only a small fraction complete the treatment process (Stunkard, 1975).

In the case of child abuse and related parent-child problems, it is the case that all but the most grotesque forms of physical abuse are condoned under some situations in our society. As pointed out by a number of clinical investigators (e.g., Conger & Lahey, 1982), most parents referred for child abuse do not agree that they are doing anything wrong but are referred for treatment by someone who does. Unsurprisingly, although such parents are externally motivated to *enter* treatment, very few show the motivation to complete treatment. Wolfe, Aragona, Kaufman, and Sandler (1980) found that only 20 percent of abusive families who were initially referred for, but not forced into, treatment actually completed a multimodal program. For a group of families referred to our center by agencies, compared to group of self-referred families, resistance (microsocially observed from videotapes of treatment sessions) to therapists trying to teach different patterns of parent-child interaction was significantly higher (Chamberlain, Patterson, Reid, Kavanagh, & Forgatch, in press).

In a study just completed at our center that focused on a social learning-parent training strategy, 55 percent of a sample of seriously abusive parents (referred for, but not required to receive, treatment) both agreed to and completed an intensive parent-training program (Reid, 1983b). This figure compares favorably to the 20 percent completion for such clients reported by Wolfe et al. (1980). Of those refusing to or dropping out of treatment, about half reported doing so either on the advice of their attorney or because of their own fear that the intensive behavioral and daily self-report data required by the program would put them at jeopardy for possible termination of parental rights litigation by the courts. In our work with abusive parents who were either self-referred or referred by social service agencies on an unofficial basis, our acceptance/completion rate has run about 75 percent, which is comparable to the rates of attrition we have observed for families referred for general child-management problems. Thus, the motivation for or resistance to treatment demonstrated by child-abusive parents has varied a good deal from study to study. Although client participation in treatment can be increased by having families required by court action to participate (e.g., Wolfe et al., 1980 reported a 76 percent completion rate), the number of child abuse cases actually resulting in court action has decreased steadily over the last several years (American Humane Society, 1981). In our own work, we have attempted to design our therapeutic program so that it would be more attractive to families designated as child abusive and referred by state agencies.

Before engaging a potential client in our program, we make a concerted effort to frame the problem not around the abuse incident itself but in terms of the daily problems the parent is experiencing with the child. In other words, the abusive episode itself is deemphasized as a focus of assessment and treatment, and the daily discipline confrontations or other problems the *parent* is experiencing is the initial focus of the therapeutic interaction. This is not to say that the abusive episode is swept under the rug or that violence is condoned by the therapist; it is to say that any treatment that presupposes intensive involvement by the client must begin by initially addressing those problems perceived to be problems by the client. At the same time, the therapist's role as a professional who must report any future incidence of assaultive or heavy-handed parental discipline is not emphasized. Rather, each family is told (as are all families receiving treatment at our center) that the content of the treatment is protected under professional and legal safeguards for confidentiality and that the only violations of that confidentiality are those prescribed by law, such as the therapist's awareness of serious plans by the client to commit dangerous felonies or a therapist's awareness of current child abuse. The therapist's responsibility to disclose child abuse is presented no differently than are the other regulations and behavioral expectations that go along with the conduct of any family therapy program. Rather than siding with the court or with the parent about the abuse episode that led the parent into therapy, the therapist reformulates the interview into one in which the therapist and client form a mutual contract for change. As in any therapy, the goal is to create an atmosphere in which the clinician works with the client to produce beneficial changes and to create an atmosphere in which the client perceives the therapist to be sensitive to the problems the client is facing at the time of intake.

The therapist's stance during the initial interview can be illustrated by the following examples. Rather than debating whether or not the abusive incident was warranted by the situation or rather than debating whether or not spanking or hitting is a legitimate form of discipline, the therapist attempts to join with the client in ascertaining those situations in which being a parent is most under stress, such as bath time, the early morning rush to school and work, dinner time, or going to the supermarket. Rather than debating whether or not the child protective agency had the right to take the child away from them, the therapist can inquire about the painful and humiliating experience of having their children taken away and having their neighbors interviewed. Rather than responding to the angry parents' protestations that they will not give up spanking, the therapist can talk about the painfulness of feeling that one has to use assaultive discipline techniques on his or her own children over and over again and the need for finding alternative, additional, or adjunctive parental strategies. One really cannot objectively and consistently monitor what parents do with their children in the privacy of their homes on a daily basis. Gaining the cooperation and involvement of the parent is a sine qua non for accurate and candid reporting by the parent; impotent and often authoritatively stated proscriptions against spanking and beating will probably do more to prevent an open and productive therapeutic involvement than to enhance it.

In addition to this general set for client-therapist involvement, it may be productive to talk about specific ways in which the parents may benefit from an involvement with the therapist in terms of their conflicts with the protective services agency. For example, to the extent that the parents are involved actively in a training program, the caseworker may find it less necessary to scrutinize the activity of the family. To the extent that the therapist understands the home situation, the discipline problems faced by the parents, and the progress the parents are making in resolving these problems, the therapist may actually serve as an advocate of the parents in their dealings with caseworkers or probation officers (e.g., Doctor & Singer, 1978). The rationale for each phase of the intervention and for each assessment device should be carefully and completely outlined to the parent. Since the intervention process is a social interactional process between the therapist and family, it is probably necessary for a person who deals with abusive families to deal with a sense of outrage that a parent has physically assaulted or abused or injured a young child and to clarify his or her own professional objectives. That objective is to help the family change and much less to have the parents atone or publicly confess their past sins. Finally, the therapeutic focus must be on the high base rate daily events, which increase the probability of future abusive episodes. This focus should not be unduly clouded by a preoccupation with the dangerous but statistically low base rate reoccurrence of severe abuse that is, in most cases, feared by therapist and parent alike.

ASSESSMENT OF CHILD-ABUSIVE FAMILIES

Although comprehensive assessment is important before, during, and after treatment in any intensive parent training or family intervention, it is critical in work with child-abusive families in which the child is residing in the home. Good assessment procedures not only aid the therapist in making a continuous assessment of the risk of reabuse, but also are indispensable in monitoring the parents' progress in acquiring new child management skills, using nonphysical punishment, and reducing the incidence of problematic child behaviors that lead to discipline confrontations. The choice of assessment modalities and variables is determined, in significant part, by the following factors: the extent to which the procedures will be acceptable to and are seen as treatment-relevant by the family; and the degree to which the assessment procedures directly measure or are highly relevant to the abusive family process. Procedures for directly observing parent-child interaction and for collecting systematic parent report data have proven valuable in the assessment of intervention procedures with abusive families. To this writer's knowledge, there are as yet no assessment procedures that reliably differentiate abusive from nonabusive families when demographic variables are carefully controlled. These issues will be discussed in turn.

The Families' Acceptance of Assessment

Given the potential, the desire, and the ability that abusive parents have to hide, rationalize, and distort the ways in which they deal with their children, they have been found to be surprisingly open in cooperating with a variety of assessment procedures. They will allow themselves to be hooked up to electro-physiological recording devices while watching videotapes (Wolfe et al., 1983); they will provide minute as well as molar parental reaction data while watching their own, as well as other, children (Lorber, Reid, Feldman, & Caeser, 1982; Mash et al., in press); they will provide extensive and fine-grained retrospective data on their lives; they will permit direct observations in their own homes (Burgess & Conger, 1978; Reid, et al., 1981c); and they will provide daily accounts of their children's misbehavior, of their reactions to that behavior, and even on the amount of anger they feel in confronting those situations (Reid, 1983b). In addition, we have found that abusive parents will provide careful data on a wide variety of factors associated with abusive processes, for example, global and daily assessments of stress, mood and personality, marital interaction, and social isolation (Reid, 1983b).

Even though abusive parents can be induced to participate in such potentially useful procedures, some tend to set the tone for collaboration by parents and therapists, while other assessments may increase the feeling of distance between parent and therapist. In a different vein, the measures vary from being obviously useful and relevant in helping parents deal with troublesome interactions with their children to having only a mysterious or clandestine relationship in the eyes of the average client. To the extent that the measurement instruments have an obvious relationship to the treatment procedures to be utilized, needless suspicion by the client or confrontations over compliance to the assessment routine may be avoided. Given that many abusive families may be reluctant to engage in a collaborative relationship with a therapist, fearing that data can be used against them in a subsequent legal action and that they have been put under a broader microscope than is required to effectively resolve the problem, these issues are no small matter.

A convincing rationale should be given to the client that explicitly relates the usefulness of any assessment to the treatment enterprise and that puts the focus of treatment on the day-to-day problems the parents are having with their children rather than on potential flaws in their character or history.

The Specific Relevance of Assessment to Intervention

The choice of assessment procedures should be tied directly to the goals of treatment. In our work (e.g., Reid, 1983b; Reid, et al., 1981), the primary goals have been the reduction of aversive parent-child interactions, the increase of positive exchanges, increased parental reliance on nonphysical discipline, decreased use of spanking, quicker resolution of discipline confrontations, and a reduction in the level of anger experienced by parents during such confrontations. Accordingly, our assessment procedures have emphasized home observations of social interactions between parent and child, systematic parent daily reports of number of problem-child behaviors, type of discipline employed, and the parent's self-rated anger during confrontations.

In treatment approaches in which the primary emphasis is on teaching parents to control their anger during discipline situations, pre and posttreatment assessments of anger (Novaco, 1975) and daily parent counts of angry urges have been employed with success (Nomellini & Katz, 1983). If the goal is to teach a wide variety of positive parenting skills, then parents and their children can be observed in structured situations (in both home and clinic) designed to elicit the parenting behaviors of interest (e.g., Burgess & Conger, 1978; Wolfe et al., 1981). If the goal is to teach parents to deal better with daily situational stress or to improve marital relationships, then a number of standardized assessments and daily report instruments are available (see Jacobson, in press; and Wahler, et al., 1979).

Assessment of Change during Intervention with Abusive Families

Two main types of assessment procedures have been used successfully to measure behavioral changes of abusive families during intervention: direct observation and systematic parent report. These procedures are discussed below.

Direct Observation.   Although somewhat expensive and intrusive, direct observation provides the most straightforward and molecular evaluation of the degree to which relevant behaviors of parents and children actually change during intervention. Techniques have been developed to observe the social interactions of family members in both home and clinic settings. In the case of home observations, coders sequentially record the content and the sequence of parent and child behavior and the reactions to those behaviors by other family members. Although an attempt is made to observe the families during periods of typical social interaction, all major coding systems place some restrictions on the family during observations, such as asking family members to remain in one part of the home, to turn off the television, or to limit outgoing telephone calls (Conger & McLeod, 1977; Reid, 1978; Wahler, House & Stambaugh, 1976). Some coding strategies attempt to increase the chances that important parent-child interactions will occur by requiring that parents and children engage in semistructured activities—such as games—during observational sessions (e.g., Conger & McLeod, 1977).

In the case of observations conducted in the clinic, the parents and the child are observed during structured task or play situations. Although such observations may have somewhat less ecological validity than those conducted in the home, there are some obvious advantages. All families can be observed under the same conditions, and the observational setting will be the same at the beginning and end of treatment, regardless of whether the family moves, refurnishes the house, or takes in an additional family member. The family interaction can be readily video taped for subsequent or fine-grained coding. Such clinic observations have been used in a number of intervention studies with abusive families (e.g., Reid, 1983c; Wolfe et al., 1981).

A number of measures derived from home and clinic observation procedures have been found to be sensitive to behavioral change during intervention with abusive families. Some examples are as follows: reductions in the rate of aversive behavior displayed by parents and children (Crozier & Katz, 1979; Denicola & Sandler, 1980; Reid, et al., 1981; Wahler, 1980; Wolfe & Sandler, 1981); increases in rates of positive behaviors (e.g., Conger & Lahey, 1982; Jeffrey, 1976; Sandler, Van Dercar, & Milhoan, 1978; Wolfe, St. Lawrence, Graves, Brehony, Bradlyn & Kelly, 1982); decreases in parental use of threats and hitting (Reid, 1983b); and decreases in unprovoked aversive behaviors by parents toward their children (Lorber, Reid, & Feldman, 1983).

Systematic Parent Daily Report.   In a number of studies, parents have been given highly specific instructions to report daily data on a number of variables central to child-abusive family process. Unlike global self-reports, these systems require that the parents report or count various behaviors or feelings during relatively short intervals (usually over the course of an hour or day). Though such data are less objective than those produced by direct observation and are subject to bias and distortion, they have demonstrated respectable interparent and test-retest reliability (Chamberlain, 1980; Reid, 1983c) and significant correlations with observation data (Fleischman, 1979; Patterson, 1974; Reid, Rivera, & Lorber, 1979). When used in addition to observation measures in treatment studies, the data have shown similar intervention effects (e.g., Patterson, Chamberlain, & Reid, 1983). Some of the parent daily report variables that have been sensitive to change in intervention studies with child-abusive families are as follow: reductions in angry urges experienced by parents (Nomellini & Katz, 1983); reductions in the level of anger experienced during discipline confrontations (Reid, 1983b); decreases in the rate of spanking (Reid, 1983b); and increases in the use of nonphysical discipline (Reid, 1983b).

As stated previously, parent-report data are less objective than observation data. However, many child behaviors that tend to provoke abuse or harsh parental discipline, such as soiling and stealing (Herrenkohl, et al., 1983), are infrequent events having a low probability of being observed during relatively short observation sessions. Similarly, discipline situations involving serious spanking or hitting by abusive parents, though nearly four times as frequent as in nonabusive families, occur about once every three days (Reid, 1983b). Such events will be sampled inadequately by most observation systems. Thus, imperfect as they may be, daily parent reports are extremely valuable for the monitoring of cases and the evaluation of intervention.

Perhaps the greatest advantage of systematic parent daily report measures is that they can be firmly integrated and individualized in the family intervention process from the very beginning of work with abusive families. Given the specific focus of parent training and other social learning interventions on the identification and modification of specific types of problems that parents have with children, it is quite natural to work with parents during the intake phase on the specific things the child does that frustrate or infuriate the parent and the specific ways the parents react to those behaviors. The parents' endorsement of problem child behaviors from a list of commonly confronted problem behaviors serves not only to make an initial assessment of the severity of the situation, but also to spell out the focuses of the specific treatment intervention. Going through a list of potential problem behaviors with the client produces a mutually agreed upon list of target behaviors to which the parent provides essential input. By producing a list of common behavior problems, the parents may be less likely to feel that the problems they endorse are qualitatively different than those experienced by other families. When the parents are phoned repeatedly and asked which of the problems occurred each day, the assessment is seen as integral to the treatment. Such an assessment strategy allows the therapist to get information on a wide number of discipline problems each day, some trivial and some more severe. Such a strategy also makes commonplace the therapist's inquiry about how discipline is being handled in the home. Rather than putting the therapist in the position of asking precise questions only when his or her suspicion is aroused, the parents are constantly asked for their data on the frequency and nature of the problems they have experienced and their reactions to those problems. Because of its interactive nature, such a procedure can be perceived as an integral aspect of the entire treatment process. After the first few daily phone calls and after the parents learn that they will not be criticized for relating information about discipline confrontations, the data collection is seen as a commonplace and sometimes boring procedure.

Differentiating Abusive from Nonabusive Families

At this time, the classification or diagnosis of families as child abusive is typically accomplished on the basis of self-admission, or from reports of teachers, friends, police, neighbors, spouses, or from child protection agencies. Although there were a number of early studies that reported significant differences between abusive and nonabusive families, parents, and children on a number of clinically relevant dimensions (e.g., psychological, behavioral, and sociological), subsequent research has generally showed such differences to disappear when appropriate demographic and situational differences are controlled (see Gaines, Sandgrund, Green, & Power, 1978; Parke & Collmer, 1975; Starr, 1982; Toro, 1982; and Wolfe, in press). Although this state of affairs has serious implications for efforts to select high-risk families for prevention programs, the problem is probably moot for families referred for treatment because of documented or admitted abuse. Regardless of the manner in which the family has been classified as abusive, the issue is clear: the vast majority of families are referred because a child was beaten, assaulted, or abused during discipline confrontations. Techniques are available to teach parents to handle such situations with less anger and without physical assault. As indicated in the previous section, the choice of assessment seems clear. We should employ devices to assess the magnitude and types of discipline confrontations that are faced or caused by the parents and measures to assess the parents' instrumental and emotional behavior when they discipline or attempt to use positive parenting strategies.

BEHAVIORAL INTERVENTIONS WITH CHILD-ABUSIVE FAMILIES

Over the last 10 years, a number of studies has been reported that describe systematic attempts to teach abusive parents to interact less punitively with their children. The first reported studies represented straightforward applications of parent-training techniques originally designed for families with oppositional children, and most represented single case, or $n = 1$, studies. In addition to providing general information about child development (e.g., Doctor & Singer, 1978; Savino & Sanders, 1973), parents were taught to use positive reinforcement for age-appropriate behaviors (e.g., Hughes, 1974; Tracy & Clark, 1974) to pinpoint and carefully track child behavior (e.g., Doctor & Singer, 1978) and to employ systematic point-incentive systems, time-out, token loss procedures, differential attention, and behavioral contracting procedures (e.g., Christophersen, Kuehn, Grinstead, Barnard, Rainey, & Kuehn, 1976; Mastria, Mastria, & Harkins, 1979; Polakow & Peabody, 1975). In one case, a mother was taught to take a time-out herself when she became angry (Mastria, et al., 1979). The efficacy of the procedures reported in these first studies was documented more by the clinical impressions of the therapists and global self-reports of the clients than by systematic measurement of changes in parent and child behavior. However, these case studies provided most of the ideas and the impetus for more recent and systematic treatment studies. They also provide a wealth of information on clinical techniques and strategies for dealing with abusive families.

During the last several years, the treatment techniques and assessment methodologies have become increasingly sophisticated, multifaceted, and specifically refined for work with abusive families. Although it is not the purpose of this chapter to review the work in detail (a careful review of most of the work has been reported by Isaacs, 1982), a general overview of the techniques employed and the effectiveness of the procedures will be presented here.

Some of the most systematic and comprehensive work to date has been carried out by Wolfe, Sandler, and their colleagues. In an initial study by Sandler, et al. (1978), parent-training techniques similar to those described by Patterson, Reid, Jones, and Conger (1975) were used to train two abusive mothers. Home observation data showed increases in the rates of positive behavior demonstrated by both parents and children.

In a study by Denicola and Sandler (1980), the parent-training procedures were again used, coupled with procedures to teach parents a variety of coping and stress-management skills. Home observations showed increases in parental positive behaviors and decreases in negative behaviors. In another study (Wolfe & Sandler, 1981), parents in three abusive families were taught basic child-management skills. A text on parenting (Becker, 1971), role plays, and behavior rehearsals were used to teach the techniques to the parents. Using a two-variable withdrawal design, an attempt was made to test for the effectiveness of the parent training and of systematically rewarding parents for putting the procedures into practice in their homes. Home observation data clearly indicated reductions in the rates of aversive behavior demonstrated by both the parents and the children. Systematically rewarding the parents for using the techniques did not seem to enhance the treatment effects, which were maintained over a 12-month follow-up period.

In another pilot study (Wolfe, et al., 1982), an abusive parent was instructed as in the previous study but was directly taught to use positive parenting skills. As the mother interacted with her children in the clinic, a bug-in-the-ear device was used to provide coaching and immediate feedback. Observation data collected in both the clinic and the home showed a reduction in her hostile behavior and an increase in her positive behavior toward the children.

Finally, in a carefully controlled study (Wolfe, in press), 16 abusive families were referred either to a parent-training group or to the services normally provided in the community. In the parent-training condition, a group format plus individualized, competency-based training in the home was used. Treatment outcome effects were evaluated by home observations of parenting skills, parents' rating of the number of problematic child behaviors, and case worker ratings. On all three outcome variables, the improvements in the members of the parent-training group were marked and exceeded those of control families. This represents the only study of parent training (of which this writer is aware) that employed an experimental design with an abusive-control group.

Conger and his colleagues have described a multimodal parent-training program for child-abusive parents. In addition to focusing on training parents in pinpointing, recording, positive reinforcement, and nonphysical discipline skills (Patterson, et al., 1975; Wahler, 1975), systematic attempts were made to develop rapport between parent and therapist and to develop techniques to deal with parental stress (Beck, 1976; Meichenbaum, 1977), marital discord (Jacobson, 1978), and pervasive anxiety (Benson, 1975). In an outcome study using a quasi-experimental design (Conger, Lahey, & Smith, 1981), the effects of this intervention for five child-abusive families were compared against a *nonabusive,* untreated control group that was assessed on the same schedule. Home observations as well as a questionnaire measure of physical-emotional distress (Brodman, Erdmann, & Wolff, 1956) were collected before and after treatment. Three observational measures of mother behavior were employed: the proportion of physical behaviors that were clearly positive; the proportion that were clearly negative; and the probability of child compliance given the maternal command. Before treatment, abusive parents experienced a significantly lower command-compliance success rate, a significantly higher proportion of negative physical behaviors, and a nonsignificant tendency to demonstrate a lower proportion of physical positive behaviors. On the pretreatment questionnaire measures, abusive mothers demonstrated significantly more physical/emotional distress and significantly higher depression scores. At the end of treatment, abusive mothers showed significant reductions in depression and negative behavior and a significant increase in positive physical behavior. There was a nonsignificant increase in the effectiveness of commands for abusive parents. In the control group, the only significant pre- to posttreatment change was an increase in the effectiveness of maternal commands. Given the small number of subjects studied in this investigation, the data provide tentative though positive support for the efficacy of parent training and hint that techniques directed at helping abusive parents to better manage anxiety and stress may be viable targets of parent training.

A recent study by Nomellini and Katz (1983) is directly relevant to this issue. Using a multiple baseline design, the efficacy of anger control training was evaluated with three families. The intervention consisted of instructing the parents about the determinants and signs of anger, teaching them methods to self-monitor and control their anger, and providing controlled opportunities to practice these procedures. Three dependent variables were employed: daily home observations, angry urges counted daily by the parents, and the Novaco Anger Scale (1975), administered before and after training. The home observation data showed marked reductions in rates of parent aversive behavior in all three cases. Modest and less consistent increases were observed for rates of positive parent behaviors. The children in two of the three families showed moderately high rates of aversive behavior during baseline. In both cases, the rates decreased notably during intervention. In one of those families, however, a brief program of child-management training was employed. Rates of positive child behavior remained basically unaffected by intervention.

The daily counts of angry urges by the parents showed steady decreases over the course of training in all three families. Treatment effects, as measured by observational and self-monitored measures, persisted over two- to six-month follow-up periods for all families. The pre-post treatment measure of anger proneness showed marked reductions for all three parents. The results of this initial study are quite provocative. The treatment procedures required an average of only 10 hours of therapist time, and the frequency and pervasiveness of parental anger, as well as aversive behavior, was reduced dramatically and persisted in all cases. Although little change in child problem behavior can be attributed specifically to the anger control intervention, the investigators were able to combine it with child-management training when necessary. At the very least, this procedure is a potentially valuable adjunct to parent training in child management.

Wahler (1980) reported on the effects of parent training for a group of abusive mothers in Knoxville, Tennessee. The families were extremely poor, had inadequate housing and few social supports, and were described by Wahler as insular. The intervention procedure consisted of parent training in child management that was conducted in the clinic and supplemented by weekly visits by the therapist. The effectiveness of treatment was evaluated with home observations, supplemented by a measure of social isolation called the Community Interaction Checklist (Wahler, et al., 1979). Data collected during the study showed highly significant mean reductions in the levels of aversive behaviors demonstrated by both mothers and children by treatment termination. Over a year follow-up, however, mean levels of aversive behaviors for both mothers and children returned to pretreatment levels. Correlational analyses demonstrated that, within families, days on which the mothers had few positive social contacts were associated with the highest levels of aversive behavior. A further study (Wahler & Dumas, 1983) showed that two variables accounted for most of the variance in treatment outcome. Low socioeconomic status and high levels of insularity were highly predictive of treatment failure. It is probably the case that parent training, though potent, is not a sufficient condition for insuring long-term benefits when the family is bombarded constantly by environmental stressors. It is interesting to speculate on the effectiveness of parent training with families such as those treated by Wahler, coupled with postintervention visits on a weekly or biweekly schedule by caseworkers or volunteers trained in child-management procedures.

At our center, we have intervened with two samples of child-abusive families. The first group was comprised of a subset from a larger sample who were referred for child-management problems but not for abuse. Post hoc analyses of case files and therapy notes revealed that families in this subset were clearly child-abusive families, as defined by state law. The second sample was comprised of families who each had been referred by the local child protective services agency because of at least one documented incident of physical child abuse.

Our strategy for training parents in child management has been described by Patterson, et al. (1975). Basically, the procedure involves the following steps: instructing the parents to concisely pinpoint positive and aversive child behaviors; teaching them to define and systematically record target behaviors in the home setting; instructing them in the use of positive social reinforcement, differential attention, and point-incentive and point-loss procedures; instructing them in the use of time-out, withdrawal of privileges, and other procedures for the immediate and nonphysical punishment of aversive child behavior; instructing them in contracting and negotiation; and instructing them in other procedures when appropriate, such as dealing with school problems or stealing. Intervention is carried out in the clinic, and the children are often, but not always, included in the sessions. Verbal instruction, modeling, and behavior rehearsal are the primary modes of instruction; parent-training manuals (e.g., Patterson, 1976) and videotapes (e.g., Patterson, 1982b) are often used to supplement training. Between every session, the parents are given assignments to practice the procedures, and this practice is supervised over the phone and during sessions by the therapist. Training in the home is carried out only when the parents experience problems that cannot be solved during clinic or phone contacts. Although intervention is focused on teaching child-management skills, it is not pure, or session-limited, parent training. Problems that *directly interfere* with the instructional goals such as marital discord, poor financial management, stress, or anxiety are dealt with as necessary. Word counts, regularly conducted on therapy tapes, show that between 25 and 40 percent of the content of our intervention sessions regularly deal with noninstructional issues. Families are free to make appointments for booster sessions after intervention is formally concluded. On the average, less than two such sessions are requested by the families (Patterson, 1974).

In the first study (Reid, et al., 1981), 27 families, who were later identified as child abusive, were given our standard intervention. No systematic attempt was made to reduce aversive parent behavior; rather, the emphasis was on the building of positive parenting skills. Pretreatment home observational data showed that the mothers and the children, but not the fathers, in this abusive group demonstrated markedly higher rates of generally aversive behaviors—hitting and threatening in particular—than did their counterparts in either nonabusive families referred for parent training or in a nondistressed comparison group. At treatment termination, significant reductions in the rates of aversive behavior were observed for both mothers and children in the abusive group. It should be noted, however, that the rates were still higher than those displayed by mothers and children in the nondistressed group.

These results encouraged us to initiate a study with officially recognized and serious child abuse cases. The intervention phase of this study has been recently completed, and pre-post treatment but not follow-up data have been analyzed (Reid, 1983b). A quasi-experimental design, similar to that used by Conger et al. (1981), was used. Of the 38 child-abusive families initially contacted, 21 were assessed and completed treatment (a refusal/attrition rate of 45 percent). They were carefully matched on relevant demographic variables to 21 nonabusive families. Families in the untreated, nonabusive control group were assessed on approximately the same schedule as were the child-abusive families.

The serious and often chronically abusive families in this study were more difficult to treat than those in the previous sample. The refusal/attrition rate was nearly twice as high, and the parents initially tended to be hostile, suspicious, and self-righteous. Most importantly, neither they nor their children tended to demonstrate high rates of *generally* aversive behavior on a moment-to-moment basis during the pretreatment home observations. Their rates were nearly identical to their counterparts in the control group. However, the ordinarily low-rate but highly aversive parental behaviors (hits and threats) were observed significantly more frequently for parents in the abuse group. Similarly, daily parent-report data showed that the abusive parents spanked their children more than three times as often, reported significantly more parent-child confrontations, and experienced significantly more anger during discipline occasions.

Whereas data for parents and children in the first study showed them to be generally out of control and aversive in their daily interactions, the seriously abusive parents in the second study showed few problems in their moment-by-moment transactions with their children. From a clinical perspective, it appeared that they were typically quite able to manage the behavior of their children, but they accomplished this by using threats backed up by occasional physical assaults. From the parents' point of view, they had no problem with child management, only with "overrestrictive" child abuse laws. Many of the parents stated that it would be impossible to manage their children without severe discipline.

Accordingly, we modified our clinical approach as described in section three of this chapter. A good deal of time was initially spent in developing a working relationship. The parents' harsh discipline was not directly attacked; rather, the focus was on developing alternative strategies, and the families were assisted in their relationships with case workers when appropriate. In addition, the instructional segment on nonphysical punishment was given immediately after parents learned to pinpoint and track their children's behavior. Using these techniques with these difficult families cost an average of slightly more than 40 hours of therapist time, including telephone calls and home visits. This was nearly twice the amount of time required to treat families in the first study. Though costly, a higher proportion of families who were initially contacted completed treatment compared with most non-court-ordered programs for highly abusive families (e.g., Wolfe, et al., 1980).

The results of the study were quite encouraging. At treatment termination, the observed parental hits and threats showed significant reductions to rates nearly identical to those demonstrated by the control group. The same was true for parent-reported spanking and anger during discipline confrontations. The rates of parent-reported child problem behaviors showed a significant drop, and the observed rates of aversive child behavior remained low. Finally, parent-reported use of systematic, nonphysical discipline, such as time-out and withdrawal of privileges, showed dramatic increases.

Final Comments

It is certainly the case that more research is necessary to demonstrate specific treatment effects for the various approaches and to document the validity of the assessment procedures that are currently in use. Difficult as they may be on both practical and ethical grounds, more studies employing comparison or no-treatment control groups (e.g., Wolfe, et al., 1980) must be conducted. On the positive side, the work reviewed in this chapter demonstrates that it is possible to consistently reduce both the level of potentially dangerous aversive interchanges between parent and child and the level of parental anger in abusive families.

Although more long-term follow-up studies must be carried out to determine the persistence of the treatment effects, it should be recalled that the risk of serious injury due to physical abuse declines sharply as a function of age in even preschool children. If treatment effects persist for only six months to a year, the benefits will still be well worth the effort. In an evaluation of child abuse and neglect demonstration projects (Berkeley Planning Associates, 1977), it was reported that 30 percent of families who received counseling showed a recurrence of abuse or neglect while still in treatment. Although it is conceivable that some investigators did not check, reports of reabuse during the behavioral treatment studies reviewed here have been rare. In our study of 21 severely abusive parents (Reid, 1983c), only one instance of reabuse was reported after referral to the project, and we have at least one-year follow-up for 12 of the families. Similarly, in the study by Wolfe, et al. (1980), no cases of reabuse were reported either during treatment or during a one-year follow-up. Combining parent-training interventions with regular follow-up visits by case workers trained in such techniques is an important next step.

A CASE STUDY

Darby was a single mother, 27 years of age, who sought assistance because she feared that she might seriously injure her nine-year-old daughter. Sophie, her daughter, was described as being extremely noncompliant and defiant, engaging in frequent physical fights with her younger siblings and mother. Sophie was reported to lie and steal frequently, both in the home and the school setting. Darby reported that her attempts to discipline Sophie were typically futile and sometimes seemed to make things worse. In responding to discipline situations, Darby reported that she relied primarily on lecturing; if lecturing was not effective, she would try to make Sophie sit on the couch for a period of time; if that did not work, she would paddle Sophie. On several occasions in the month preceding her coming to the center, she escalated from paddling to hitting with her fists. The event immediately precipitating her request for assistance was a hitting episode that resulted in a serious nosebleed to Sophie. In contrast to her tendency to lose control during serious discipline confrontations, Darby appeared to demonstrate a variety of rather strong, positive parenting skills. For example, she reported using consistent verbal encouragement when Sophie behaved nicely or helped around the house. She was able to get Sophie to do routine chores, such as picking up her own toys and dirty clothes, folding and putting away her own laundry, and helping around the house.

Darby and her family lived under conditions of financial and social stress. The family income, provided by welfare, was less than $500 per month. In addition to Sophie, Darby had three other children—a six-year-old daughter, a five-year-old son, and a six-month-old daughter. Because of her limited financial resources, she could not afford babysitters, money for recreation, transportation, or a telephone. Neither of her two ex-husbands provided any positive social or financial resources. Despite such poverty, she managed to do a remarkably good job in providing the children with food, clothing, and toys, aggressively pursuing such necessities from charitable and community service agencies.

Darby received treatment in the context of a federally funded research program. Before intervention, she participated in a multilevel assessment battery, including a series of home observations; parent daily telephone interviews, during which she reported daily occurrences of child problem behaviors; psychometric testing; and about two hours of structured interview assessment. The home observations showed a rate of aversive behaviors per minutes of .65 for Sophie, .57 per minute for Darby, and .62 for the five-year-old boy. All of these pretreatment rates were well above the rates we have observed for normal control subjects (i.e., approximately .26 per minute; Reid, 1978). The aversive behavior rates of the six-year-old daughter were well within the normal range. The mean number of parent-reported discipline problems per day for Sophie was 12.6, approximately three times that reported for normal control children (Chamberlain, 1980).

Darby was seen for 18 interviews over a five-month period. The first three sessions were focused on developing a working relationship and a common set of treatment goals. Nine sessions were focused on teaching and assisting Darby to implement a set of consistent behavioral rules and expectations, incentive systems, and nonphysical punishment procedures for Sophie. Four sessions were devoted in helping Darby set up a program to deal with Sophie's behavior at school and to generalize her basic home program to include the five-year-old boy. The last two sessions were devoted to wrapping up the intervention and getting Darby to accept independent responsibility and full credit for dealing with her children.

During the first interview, Darby presented her problem as going crazy and losing control during discipline confrontations. She underplayed the significance of the fact that Sophie was quite difficult to manage, that she was attempting to provide a loving home under extremely adverse conditions, and that most of the time she did quite well as a single, socially isolated mother of four young children. In general, she felt that her abusive episodes were the result of psychodynamic or constitutional factors, giving a good deal of importance to the fact that her own father had been arrested for beating her mother. Darby was extremely anxious to learn how she performed on the psychometric tests and expressed the hope and expectation that the therapist would help her to deal with whatever flaws in her personality had led to the abusive episodes.

During the initial sessions, the therapist went over the psychometric tests and indicated there was little evidence to support the idea of psychopathology as a causative factor. Darby's own experience of spousal violence in her home of origin was discussed as just one exemplar that her own developmental history had provided few opportunities for learning and practicing positive methods for handling family problems. Most of the time spent during the initial sessions was devoted to emphasizing the positive factors in her current situation, upon which could be built a more satisfying relationship between Darby and her children. Namely, she was an extremely responsible and resourceful parent when it came to taking care of the physical and social needs of her children. She genuinely experienced intense love towards her children and was already using sound and consistent strategies for reinforcing or encouraging the age-appropriate behavior of her children. Also, she recognized that she needed help and had the courage to seek it out.

Darby obviously needed a good deal of support from the therapist. However, the position was also taken that this woman had some powerful personal resources. It was communicated to Darby that a good deal of work was expected over the course of the training program. Based on her history of successfully dealing with a wide variety of adversities, the therapist expressed confidence that she would be able to help design specific rules and definitions of positive and negative child behaviors, systematically track Sophie's behavior for at least an hour each day, and implement consistent strategies for encouraging Sophie's positive behavior and for mildly punishing her transgressions. It was explained that she already had more knowledge of her child's behavior and of her own reactions than a therapist would ever have, and the basic skill and experience on which to develop an effective parent-child relationship was already in place. The role of the therapist was developed as that of a teacher, consultant, and source of moral support. The therapist consistently adhered to this over the course of intervention.

Following the introductory sessions, Darby was taught a set of general parenting skills specifically developed for Sophie. During session four, she pinpointed three problem behaviors (not minding, stealing, and hitting siblings), two positive child behaviors (compliance to requests and volunteering to help), and one daily chore (picking up her toys). Darby agreed to track and record the occurrence of these behaviors for an hour each day. Using a neighbor's telephone, Darby then contacted the therapist daily to report her data. During these calls, the therapist supported her efforts and corrected misunderstandings about the procedure. With the exception of one day, which was particularly trying, Darby completed her tracking assignments with few problems. Over the course of that week, Sophie's rates of parent-reported problem behaviors showed a moderate decrease, while positive behaviors increased slightly. Darby reported that Sophie was quite interested in the tracking procedure and appeared to adjust her behavior accordingly. This is not an unusual result, but it is typically quite temporary. Therapeutically, the main effect of her immediate behavioral improvement was to encourage Darby that change was indeed possible. Throughout the remainder of the intervention, Darby collected daily data on these and other behaviors, but phone calls were reduced to two to three times a week.

The fifth and sixth treatment sessions were devoted to teaching Darby to construct and implement a point-incentive system. Although the problem behaviors were still tracked on a daily basis, Darby was given specific instructions only about Sophie's reactions to positive behaviors and chores. Each time she noted one of these positive activities, she was to immediately encourage or thank Sophie and paste a star on her chart. At the end of each day, Darby was to go over the chart in a positive way with the child and provide incentives (reading time, special desserts, extra TV, and the privilege of staying up past her bedtime), based on a prearranged point system. During both sessions, Sophie was present so that the therapist could insure her understanding, provide information about rewards, and allow opportunity for behavioral rehearsal. As before, Darby continued to collect data on the targeted behaviors and phoned the therapist every other day. Within three weeks, positive behaviors showed marked increases, and other positive behaviors were added to the incentive system.

Sessions seven, eight, and nine focused on the exclusive use of five-minute time-outs (T.O.) as a reaction to common discipline situations, ignoring mild attention-getting behaviors, and on the development of a program for stealing and lying. The behaviors for which T.O. was to be initially used (i.e., hitting, noncompliance, and defiance) were defined and added to the tracking chart. By this time, Darby was able to develop precise behavioral definitions with little help from the therapist. Following a description and discussion of T.O., Darby viewed a videotape demonstrating its use (Patterson, 1982b). The phone calls during the ensuing week revealed that Darby was unable to implement the procedure effectively. She did not react quickly enough to problem behaviors but let them escalate; she often threatened T.O. without following through; and, when she did try to use the procedure, she allowed arguments to develop about whether or not it was justified, one of which led to a severe spanking. During the phone calls and the next session, Darby was encouraged to use T.O. quickly and every time it was indicated and not to argue but to add minutes to T.O. when Sophie tried to debate or otherwise delay T.O. Over the next week, Darby was able to use the techniques without incident.

During the ninth session, a stealing program was discussed and role played. Each time Darby had a reasonable suspicion that Sophie had taken something that was not hers or had told an instrumental lie, she calmly announced her suspicion and assigned Sophie a half-hour work detail (e.g., pulling weeds). Although the stolen object was confiscated if possible, no attempt was made to lecture or force a confession out of the child. The incident was closed immediately after the work detail was completed. The rationale and specific procedures for this technique have been described by Patterson et al. (1975).

The above procedures had a dramatic effect on Sophie's day-to-day behavior. Parent-reported rates of noncompliance (hitting and defiance) were reduced by about two thirds, positive behaviors continued at a high level, and parent-reported instances of stealing and lying dropped from 3.6 times a week to zero. On the average, Darby used T.O. just over three times a day during the first week and approximately once a day thereafter. Four instances of stealing that occurred were dealt with as prescribed and did not occur again through treatment termination.

Beginning with the 10th session, five-year-old Bill was included in the program. Following the same procedures used with Sophie, Bill's positive and problem behaviors were pinpointed and tracked for a week. A point-incentive system was developed and used for two weeks, and T.O. was initiated in the following week. Although Darby initially resisted the idea of using T.O. with Bill, feeling that it would not work with a boy, she had no problems when it came time to start the procedure. His response to the system was comparable to that demonstrated by Sophie.

During the final two weeks of the program, Darby (with little help from the therapist) developed a list of target problem behaviors that occurred in the school setting. This set of positive and negative behaviors was developed in consultation with Sophie's teacher. Sophie brought a card to school each day, and the teacher indicated whether or not her behavior was acceptable in five target areas. Her school behaviors were incorporated into the point-incentive system used in the home, and Darby encouraged and rewarded her acceptable school behavior. It was during the last two sessions that the therapist extracted himself from the family system. By reviewing Darby's progress, the therapist pointed out that it was she who had been designing and executing the programs during the previous few weeks with little help from him, and Darby became convinced that she could proceed without further therapeutic assistance. After treatment was terminated, the family was reassessed using home observations and the parent daily telephone interview. Total aversive behaviors during home observations was as follows: Sophie, .42; Darby, .38; Bill, .46 per minute. The parent daily telephone interview data, collected only for Sophie, showed a drop of approximately 50 percent to 5.9 problem behaviors per day. Twelve months after termination, the family was again reassessed and further reductions in aversive behaviors were noted: Sophie, .34; Darby, .36; Bill, .13 per minute. Sophie's mean number of parent-reported problem behaviors had shown a further drop to 2.8 per day (stealing and lying were never reported). At a 12-month follow-up, Darby reported that the program had a highly positive effect on her relationships with the children, that she was using T.O. regularly, and that she neither felt out of control nor used severe physical punishment during discipline confrontations.

REFERENCES

Annual Report, 1980: National analysis of official child neglect and abuse reporting. Denver, Colo.: The American Humane Association, 1981.

Beck, A. T. *Cognitive therapy and the emotional disorders.* New York: International Universities Press, 1976.

Becker, W. C. *Parents are teachers.* Champaign, Ill.: Research Press, 1971.

Benson, H. *The relaxation response.* New York: Avon Books, 1975.

Berkeley Planning Associates. *Evaluation of child abuse and neglect demonstration projects 1974–1977: Vol. II. Final Report.* Berkeley, Calif.: Author, 1977.

Bradburn, N. M. *The structure of psychological well-being.* Chicago: Aldine Publishing, 1969.

Brodman, K., Erdmann, A. J., & Wolff, H. G. *Cornell medical index health questionnaire* (Rev. ed.). New York: Cornell University Medical College, 1956.

Burgess, R. L., & Conger, R. D. Family interaction in abusive, neglectful, and normal families. *Child Development,* 1978, *49,* 1163–1173.

Burgess, R. L., & Richardson, R. A. Child abuse during adolescence. In R. M. Lerner & N. Galambos (Eds.), *Experiencing adolescence: A sourcebook for parents, teachers, and teens.* New York: Garland Publishing, in press.

Chamberlain, P. *Standardization of a parent report measure.* Unpublished doctoral dissertation, University of Oregon, 1980.

Chamberlain, P., Patterson, G. R., Reid, J. B., Kavanagh, K., & Forgatch, M. Observation of client resistance. *Behavior Therapy,* in press.

Christophersen, E. R., Kuehn, B. S., Grinstead, J. D., Barnard, J. D., Rainey, S. K., & Kuehn, F. E. A family training program for abuse and neglect families. *Journal of Pediatric Psychology,* 1976, 90–94.

Conger, R. D., & Lahey, B. B. Behavioral intervention for child abuse. *The Behavior Therapist,* 1982, *5,* 49–53.

Conger, R. D., & McLeod, D. Describing behavior in small groups with the DATAMYTE event recorder. *Behavior Research Methods and Instrumentation,* 1977, *9,* 418–424.

Conger, R. D., Lahey, B., & Smith, S. S. *An intervention program for child abuse: Modifying maternal depression and behavior.* Paper presented at the Family Violence Research Conference, University of New Hampshire, July 1981.

Crozier, J., & Katz, R. C. Social learning treatment of child abuse. *Journal of Behavior Therapy and Experiemental Psychiatry,* 1979, *10,* 212–220.

Denicola, J., & Sandler, J. Training abusive parents in child management and self-control skills. *Behavior Therapy,* 1980, *11,* 263–270.

Doctor, R. M., & Singer, E. M. Behavioral intervention strategies with child abusive parents: A home intervention program. *Child Abuse and Neglect,* 1978, *2,* 57–68.

Dumas, J. E., & Wahler, R. G. Predictors of treatment outcome in parent training: Mother insularity and socioeconomic disadvantage. *Behavioral Assessment,* in press.

Egeland, B., Breitenbucher, M., & Rosenberg, D. Prospective study of the significance of life stress in the etiology of child abuse. *Journal of Consulting and Clinical Psychology,* 1980, *48,* 195–205.

Elmer, I. E., & Gregg, G. S. Developmental characteristics of abused children. *Pediatrics,* 1967, *40,* 596–602.

Empey, L. T. *American delinquency: Its meaning and construction.* Homewood, Ill.: Dorsey Press, 1978.

Erlanger, H. Social class and corporal punishment in child rearing: a reassessment. *American Sociological Review,* 1974, *39,* 68–85.

Fawl, C. L. Disturbances experienced by children in their natural habitats. In R. G. Barker (Ed.), *The stream of behavior.* New York: Appleton-Century-Crofts, 1963.

Feldman, H. The effects of children on the family. In A. Michel (Ed.), *Family issues of employed women in Europe and America.* Leiden: Brill, 1971.

Fleischman, M. J. Using parenting salaries to control attrition and cooperation in therapy. *Behavior Therapy,* 1979, *10,* 111–116.

Forehand, R., King, H. E., Peed, S., & Yoder, P. Mother-child interactions: Comparison of a noncompliant clinic group and a nonclinic group. *Behaviour Research and Therapy,* 1975, *13,* 79–84.

Forehand, R., Wells, K., & Griest, D. An examination of the social validity of a parent training program. *Behavior Therapy,* 1980, *11,* 488–502.

Gaines, R., Sandgrund, A., Green, A. H., & Power, E. Etiological factors in child maltreatment: A multivariate study of abusing, neglecting, and normal mothers. *Journal of Abnormal Psychology,* 1978, *87,* 531–540.

Garbarino, J. Some ecological correlates of child abuse: The impact of socioeconomic stress on mothers. *Child Development,* 1976, *47,* 178–185.

Gil, D. G. Physical abuse of children: Findings and implications of a nationwide survey. *Pediatrics,* 1969, *44,* 857–864.

Gil, D. G. Violence against children. *Journal of Marriage and the Family,* 1971, *33,* 637–648.

Glenn, N. D. Psychological well-being in the postparental stage: Some evidence from national surveys. *Journal of Marriage and the Family,* 1975, *37,* 105–110.

Glick, P. C. *Who are the children in one-parent households?* Paper presented at Wayne State University, Detroit, Michigan, 1979.

Green, A. A psychodynamic approach to the study and treatment of child abusing parents. *Journal of Child Psychiatry,* 1976, *15,* 414–429.

Halverson, C. T., & Waldrop, M. F. Maternal behavior toward own and other preschool children: The problem of "owness." *Child Development,* 1970, *41,* 839–845.

Herrenkohl, R. C., Herrenkohl, E. C., & Egolf, B. P. Circumstances surrounding the occurrence of child maltreatment. *Journal of Consulting and Clinical Psychology,* 1983, 51, 424–431.

Hughes, R. C. A clinic's parent-performance training program for child abusers. *Hospital and Community Psychiatry,* 1974, *25,* 779, 782.

Isaacs, C. D. Treatment of child abuse: A review of the behavioral interventions. *Journal of Applied Behavior Analysis,* 1982, *15,* 273–294.

Jacobson, N. S. A component analysis of behavioral marital therapy: The relative effectiveness of behavior exchange and communication/problem-solving training. *Journal of Consulting and Clinical Psychology,* in press.

Jacobson, N. S. Specific and nonspecific factors in the effectiveness of a behavioral approach to the treatment of marital discord. *Journal of Consulting and Clinical Psychology,* 1978, *45,* 92–100.

Jeffrey, M. Practical ways to change parent-child interaction in families of children at risk. In R. E. Helfer & C. H. Kempe (Eds.), *Child abuse and neglect.* Cambridge, Mass.: Ballinger, 1976.

Justice, B., & Duncan, D. F. Life crisis as a precursor to child abuse. *Public Health Reports,* 1976, *91,* 110–115.

Light, R. J. Abused and neglected children in America: A study of alternative policies. *Harvard Educational Review,* 1973, *43,* 563–568.

Lorber, R., Reid, J., & Feldman, D. *The effects of parent training on the tracking behavior of abusive parents.* Paper presented at the meeting of the American Association of Behavior Therapists, Washington, D.C., 1983.

Lorber, R., Reid, J. B., Felton, D., & Caesar, R. *Behavioral tracking skills of child abuse parents and their relationships to family violence.* Paper presented at the meeting of the Association for the Advancement of Behavior Therapy, Los Angeles, November 1982.

Margolin, G., & Christensen, A. *The treatment of families with marital and child problems.* Paper presented at the 15th Annual Convention of the Association for the Advancement of Behavior Therapy, Toronto, Canada, 1981.

Mash, E. J., Johnston, C., & Kovitz, K. A comparison of the mother-child interactions of physically abused and non-abused children during play and task situations. *Journal of Clinical Child Psychology,* in press.

Mastria, E. O., Mastria, M. A., & Harkins, J. C. Treatment of child abuse by behavioral intervention: A case report. *Child Welfare,* 1979, *58,* 253–262.

Meichenbaum, D. H. *Cognitive-behavior modification.* New York: Plenum Press, 1977.

Minton, C., Kagan, J., & Levine, J. A. Maternal control and obedience in the two-year-old child. *Child Development,* 1971, *42,* 1973–1984.

Nomellini, S., & Katz, R. C. Effects of anger control training on abusive parents. *Cognitive Therapy and Research,* 1983, *7,* 57–68.

Novaco, R. W. *Anger control.* Lexington, Mass.: Lexington Books/D. C. Heath and Company, 1975.

Parke, R. D., & Collmer, C. W. Child abuse: An interdisciplinary approach. In E. M. Hetherington (Ed.), *Review of child development research* (Vol. 5). Chicago: University of Chicago Press, 1975.

Patterson, G. R. Intervention for boys with conduct problems: Multiple settings, treatments, and criteria. *Journal of Consulting and Clinical Psychology,* 1974, *42,* 471–481.

Patterson, G. R. *Families: Applications of social learning to family life.* (Rev. ed.). Champaign, Ill.: Research Press, 1976.

Patterson, G. R. Coercive family process. Eugene, Ore.: Castalia 1982(a).

Patterson, G. R. *A videotape for parents.* Eugene, Ore.: Northwest Family and School Consultants, Inc., 1982(b).

Patterson, G. R. *Understanding and prediction of delinquent behavior.* Grant No. 2 RO1 MH 37940, National Institute of Mental Health, United States Public Health Service, 1983.

Patterson, G. R., Chamberlain, P., & Reid, J. B. A comparative evaluation of a parent training program. *Behavior Therapy,* 1982, *13,* 638–650.

Patterson, G. R., Reid, J. B., Jones, R. R., & Conger, R. E. *A social learning approach to family intervention. I. Families with aggressive children.* Eugene, Ore.: Castalia, 1975.

Polakow, R. L., & Peabody, D. L. Behavioral treatment of child abuse. *International Journal of Offender Therapy and Comparative Criminology,* 1975, *19,* 100–103.

Reid, J. B. (Ed.). *A social learning approach to family intervention. II. Observation in home settings.* Eugene, Ore.: Castalia, 1978.

Reid, J. B. *Final Report: Home based treatment for multiple offending delinquents.* Grant No. RO1 MH 37934, National Institute of Mental Health, United States Public Health Service, 1983(a).

Reid, J. B. *Final Report: Child abuse: Developmental factors and treatment.* Grant No. 7 RO1 MH 37938, National Institute of Mental Health, United States Public Health Service, 1983(b).

Reid, J. B. Social-interactional patterns in families of abused and nonabused children. In C. Zahn Waxler, M. Cummings, & M. Radke-Yarrow (Eds.), *Social and biological origins of altruism and aggression.* Cambridge, Mass.: Cambridge University Press, 1983(c).

Reid, J. B., Patterson, G. R., & Loeber, R. The abused child: Victim, instigator, or innocent bystander? In H. C. Howe & D. J. Bernstein (Eds.), *Proceedings from the Nebraska Symposium on Motivation* (Vol. 29). Lincoln, Neb.: University of Nebraska Press, 1982.

Reid, J. B., Rivera, G. H., & Lorber, R. *A social learning approach to the treatment of stealers: An outcome study.* Unpublished manuscript, Oregon Social Learning Center, 1979.

Reid, J. B., Taplin, P. S., & Lorber, R. A social interactional approach to the treatment of abusive families. In R. Stuart (Ed.), *Violent behavior: Social learning approaches to prediction, management, and treatment.* New York: Brunner/Mazel, 1981.

Rollins, B. C., & Feldman, H. Marital satisfaction over the family life cycle. *Journal of Marriage and the Family,* 1970, *32,* 20–28.

Sandler, J., Van Dercar, C., & Milhoan, M. Training child abusers in the use of positive reinforcement practices. *Behaviour Research and Therapy*, 1978, *16*, 169–175.

Savino, A. B., & Sanders, R. W. Working with abusive parents. Group therapy and home visits. *American Journal of Nursing*, 1973, *73*, 482–484.

Stark, R., & McEvoy, J. Middle class violence. *Psychology Today*, 1970, *4*, 52–65.

Starr, R. H. A research-based approach to the prediction of child abuse. In R. H. Starr, Jr. (Ed.), *Child abuse prediction: Policy implications*. Cambridge, Mass.: Ballinger, 1982.

Straus, M. A., Gelles, R. J., & Steinmetz, S. K. *Behind closed doors: Violence in the American family*. New York: Anchor Press, 1980.

Straus, M. A. Social stress and marital violence in a national sample of American families. In F. Wright, C. Bain, & R. W. Rieber (Eds.), *Annals of the New York Academy of Sciences, Vol. 347: Forensic psychology and psychiatry*, 1980.

Stunkard, A. J. Presidential address—1974. From explanation to action in psychosomatic medicine: The case of obesity. *Psychosomatic Medicine*, 1975, *37*(3).

Toro, P. A. Developmental effects of child abuse: A review. *Child Abuse and Neglect*, 1982, *6*, 423–431.

Tracy, J. J., & Clarke, E. H. Treatment for child abusers. *Social Work*, 1974, *19*, 338–342.

Vaillant, G. E. *The natural history of alcoholism*. Cambridge, Mass.: Harvard University Press, 1983.

Wahler, R. G. Some structural aspects of deviant child behavior. *Journal of Applied Behavior Analysis*, 1975, *8*, 27–42.

Wahler, R. G. The insular mother: Her problems in parent-child treatment. *Journal of Applied Behavior Analysis*, 1980, *13*, 207–219.

Wahler, R. G., & Dumas, J. E. "A chip off the old block": Some interpersonal characteristics of coercive children across generations. In P. Strain (Ed.), *Children's social behavior: Development, assessment, and modification*. New York: Academic Press, 1983.

Wahler, R. G., House, A. E., & Stambaugh, E. E. *Ecological assessment of child problems behavior. II. A clinical package for home, school, and institutional settings*. New York: Pergamon Press, 1976.

Wahler, R. G., Leske, G., & Rogers, E. S. The insular family: A deviance support system for oppositional children. In L. A. Hamerlynck (Ed.), *Behavioral systems for the developmentally disabled: I. School and family environments*. New York: Brunner/Mazel, 1979.

Windell, J. O. & Windell, E. A. Parent group training programs in juvenile courts: A national survey. *Family Coordinator*, 1977, *26*, 459–463.

Wolfe, D. A. Parental competence and child abuse prevention. In R. J. McMahon & R. Peters (Eds.), *Childhood disorders: Behavioral-developmental approaches*. New York: Brunner/Mazel, in press.

Wolfe, D. A., Aragona, J., Kaufman, K., & Sandler, J. The importance of adjudication in the treatment of child abusers: Some preliminary findings. *Child Abuse and Neglect,* 1980, *4,* 127–135.

Wolfe, D. A., Fairbank, J. A., Kelly, J. A., & Bradlyn, A. S. Child abusive parents' physiological responses to stressful and non-stressful behavior in children. *Behavioral Assessment,* 1983, *5,* 363–371.

Wolfe, D. A., St. Lawrence, J., Graves, K., Brehony, K., Bradlyn, D., & Kelly, J. A. Intensive behavioral parent training for a child abusive mother. *Behavior Therapy,* 1982, *13,* 438–451.

Wolfe, D. A., & Sandler, J. Training abusive parents in effective child management. *Behavior Modification,* 1981, *5,* 320–335.

PART FOUR

State of the Art in Child
Behavior Therapy

PART FOUR

20

Behavioral-Preventive Interventions with Children: Current Status, Conceptual Issues, and Future Directions

Thomas H. Ollendick
Richard A. Winett
Department of Psychology
Virginia Polytechnic Institute and State University

INTRODUCTION

Although earlier chapters attest to the utility and efficacy of diverse behavioral procedures for a wide array of child behavior problems, these developments are not without their shortcomings. In general, behavioral interventions with children have been characterized by a traditional model of service delivery in which treatment is offered on a one-to-one basis or perhaps on a small group basis to children who already display significant behavioral problems. In this regard, most efforts have been directed toward reducing or eliminating behavioral problems after they occur, not in *preventing* their occurrence (Felner, Jason, Moritsugu, & Farber, 1983). Although Caplan (1964) refers to such practices as *tertiary prevention*, these efforts can be viewed as preventive in name only. Tertiary interventions are designed to reduce or eliminate disabilities associated with particular disorders; accordingly, they are best viewed as habilitative in nature.

The success of behaviorally based tertiary efforts with children notwithstanding, the cost and reach of such interventions have been questioned in recent years (e.g., Felner et al., 1983; Nietzel, Winett, MacDonald, & Davidson,

1977; Rappaport, 1977). As noted nearly 20 years ago by Albee (1967), there will never be enough professionals available to meet the ever increasing demands for services. As new facilities for children open, waiting lists quickly develop (Zax & Cowen, 1976). Further, epidemiological studies show that 25 to 30 percent of elementary school children have identifiable adjustment problems and that 10 to 15 percent of children require direct professional assistance (Werry, 1979). Jason (1983) estimates that, if all psychologists and psychiatrists adopted the traditional one-to-one service delivery mode, they would only reach about 2 percent of those in need of mental health services. In that only one third of child clinicians are behaviorally oriented (Tuma & Pratt, 1982), these projections are even more disconcerting. Our efficacious behavioral treatment procedures are reaching only a very small minority of children in need of services!

In contrast to tertiary interventions, secondary preventive efforts are designed to reduce the duration of disorders and consequently their severity, while primary preventive efforts are aimed at preventing behavioral problems before they occur. In secondary prevention, efforts are directed toward children who show early signs of problematic behavior, and the objective is to shorten the duration and severity of the problem by early and prompt treatment. In primary prevention, emphases are placed on identifying high-risk children who might likely display problematic behavior at some point in time and in determining those environmental conditions that appear to be related to the development of specific behavioral problems. Thus, primary prevention often entails examination of change at institutional and community levels, as well as individual and small group levels. In addition, primary preventive efforts can also be directed toward the promotion of competency-related behavior and settings that maintain such behaviors, in an attempt to inoculate or immunize children to stressful events. Primary and prevention efforts are more truly *preventive* in nature.

Thus, consistent with Reiff (1975), primary, secondary, and tertiary interventions can be focused at individual, group, organization, community, or societal levels. As noted earlier, most child behavior therapy interventions have been focused on tertiary interventions at the individual or small group level. As we shall see shortly, a majority of secondary preventive efforts have also been directed at the individual and small group level. Bloom (1977) refers to these efforts as *person-centered*. In partial contrast, primary preventive efforts at the organization, the community, and the societal level have been described by Bloom as *system-centered* and are designed to modify stressful settings and situations that impinge on individuals and small groups. Factors examined in the system-centered approach include but are not limited to physical characteristics of the setting, the social climate of the setting, availability of support systems, legislative action, and judicial decisions. For the traditional behaviorist, recognition of such global and sometimes nonspecific setting events may be problematic and may require a paradigmatic shift in conceptual thinking (e.g., Wahler & Graves, 1983).

The purpose of the present chapter is twofold: (1) to describe representative primary and secondary preventive efforts that are based on behavioral principles; and (2) to highlight a set of issues, many for which we have no ready solutions, that characterize behavioral-preventive efforts.

BEHAVIORAL APPROACHES TO PREVENTION

Person-Centered Approaches

As noted by Jason (1977, 1981), person-centered approaches based on classical, operant, and vicarious learning principles are as useful in primary and secondary preventive efforts as they are in tertiary habilitative ones. Recent efforts have also witnessed the application of cognitive-behavioral procedures and information-processing tactics in the prevention of child behavior disorders.

A primary preventive model based on the principles of classical conditioning has been proposed by Poser (1970). He has suggested that children be gradually exposed to potentially stressful and anxiety-arousing situations in order to prevent the development of conditioned avoidant responses. Children about to make their first dental visit, for example, might be provided literature on dentists, visit a dental office, and talk with hygienists and dentists. Such experiences, if graded so as not to be anxiety producing, may prevent dental fear from developing. Poser labels this process *antecedent systematic desensitization* and views it as a type of immunization. He maintains that it is the lack of information and the sudden and novel encounter with the stress stimuli that produce the fearful response. If children have been exposed to the stimuli in advance—when unexpected encounters do occur—then they need not produce negative emotional reaction since the children have been preexposed to the relevant stimuli. Such procedures could be used to prevent the occurrence of many fears, including those of bodily injury, tests, and being sent to the principal. Presently, these fears are among the most common in children, as they are observed in one out of every three elementary school children (Ollendick, 1983). They could also be used for less frequently occurring but highly debilitating fear reactions, such as school phobia (Ollendick & Mayer, 1983). To date, they have been successfully used by Poser and King (1975) to prevent dental and snake fears in young children. However, their continued application and evaluation in a preventive mode awaits future research.

Operant techniques have also been used to immunize children against future stressful events (Ollendick, 1974, 1979). For example, Ollendick has proposed an immunization model based on operant principles for helping children deal more constructively with frustration and failure experiences. In this program, efforts are made to help children cope with frustration and failure by programming into their learning environment doses of success and failure. Failure, when experienced along with success, has been shown to increase persistence and tolerance to stress. Through progressively greater exposure to frustrating events associated with failure, tolerance is gradually increased, and children are able to persevere in situations that are not immediately reinforcing. Interestingly, children with extended histories of failure persist longer following increased doses of success, while children with extended histories of success persist longer following failure than success experiences. Such individual differences caution against the large-scale application of such preventive programs to all types of children. To date, this program has been examined only at the individual level and only on a small-scale basis. It, too, awaits further examination before its routine use can be endorsed.

Operant strategies have also been used to build pivotal competencies and strengths in children that will assist them in dealing with future stress and life crises (Cowen, 1977). Frequently, these programs have been directed toward entire classrooms of children in a primary preventive effort. The most frequently targeted pivotal competencies have been related to academic skills and social skills (Kelley, Snowden, & Munoz, 1977). In academic-related programs, patterns of behavior that potentially interfere with academic functioning are targeted for change: roaming around the room, staring into space, not listening while the teacher is giving directions, and talking to other children at inappropriate times. Hops and his colleagues (Cobb & Hops, 1973; Hops & Cobb, 1974) have developed a prevention program to train teachers to use reinforcement contingencies for more appropriate classroom behavior. This program, called *Program for Academic Survival Skills* (PASS), has been used in a number of school settings and has resulted in improved academic achievement as well as classroom deportment. However, its long-term effects as a preventive strategy have not been examined, and one must exercise caution lest one trains children "to be quiet, be docile, and be still" (Winett & Winkler, 1972) in such programs. Continued evidence of academic achievement and prosocial behavior in such programs should militate against such concerns.

Operant strategies have also been used in a number of primary and secondary preventive efforts designed to improve the social skills of children. Most notable among the primary prevention projects is the well-known Rochester Project, conducted by Cowen and his associates (e.g., Cowen, Trost, Lorion, Dorr, Izzo, & Isaacson, 1975). In this project, first-grade children are identified as having problems or *potential* problems (high risk) in social adjustment. Preventive intervention is multifaceted and successive over the first three years of school: teachers are provided mental health consultation, parents are provided discussion groups dealing with child-rearing practices, and the children themselves are involved in after-school group meetings. Unfortunately, while improvement has been noted in teacher ratings (and teachers were aware of which children received treatment), consistent gains have not been noted for academic achievement, peer relationships, and classroom adjustment (Zax & Cowen, 1976). In fact, the identified children continued to experience interpersonal and academic difficulties throughout the study. These disappointing findings prompted the Rochester group to review and expand their intervention strategies to include greater use of paraprofessionals (students and housewives) as aids and adult models and to incorporate cognitive problem-solving strategies in their after-school group meetings with the children (e.g., Gesten, de Apodaca, Rains, Weissberg, & Cowen, 1979; Weissberg, Gesten, Rapkin, Cowen, Davidson, de Apodaca, & McKim, 1981). In general, these changes have resulted in greater improvements on both cognitive problem-solving and behavioral-adjustment measures in the targeted children (Weissberg et al., 1981) than those observed in their earlier efforts.

Operant procedures have also been combined with modeling procedures in secondary preventive efforts designed to increase rates of social interaction in children described as withdrawn. For example, Weinrott, Corson, and Wilchesky (1979) designed a teacher-mediated project to increase prosocial behavior by using symbolic modeling and adult social reinforcement. Previous studies have shown the efficacy of each procedure when used alone with withdrawn children (e.g., O'Conner, 1969, 1972; Walker & Hops, 1973); however, long-term maintenance of change has not been evidenced. In this combined program, targeted children (25 teacher-pupil pairs from grades one to three were studied) were shown to increase social interactions on a behavioral observation measure, to improve on academic attending skills, and to receive less withdrawn ratings on the Walker Problem Behavior Identification Checklist. Control children were not found to evidence these changes. However, at follow-up (two weeks following the completion of treatment), the differences between the targeted and control children were diminished; that is, gains were not maintained over this brief two-week follow-up period. As with the earlier findings, long-term maintenance of change was not demonstrated.

Most primary and secondary behavioral preventive programs today employ integrated strategies based on the principles of operant conditioning, modeling, and cognitive restructuring in anticipation of producing maximal gains. Illustrative of these new programs are those pioneered by the already mentioned Rochester group (Cowen, 1977; Gesten et al., 1979; Weissberg et al., 1981), the Hahneman group (Spivack & Shure, 1974; Spivack, Platt, & Shure, 1976), and the Connecticut group (Allen, Chinsky, Larcen, Lochman, & Selinger, 1976; McClure, Chinsky, & Larcen, 1978). While differences exist among these programs, they are all characterized by providing both primary and secondary preventive programs in the pursuit of what has been called *social problem-solving training*. Based on early work of Ojemann (Ojemann, 1960; Ojemann & Snider, 1964), these researchers have identified four interpersonal cognitive skills that comprise social problem solving: sensitivity to interpersonal problems, ability to generate alternative solutions, ability to understand means-end relationships, and awareness of the effects of one's social acts on others. Such programs have been designed for preschoolers, kindergarteners, adolescents, and for emotionally disturbed and mentally retarded children (e.g., Spivack et al., 1976). In essence, children are taught through instruction, role playing, and reinforcement *how,* not *what,* to think in a variety of social situations. In general, these programs have demonstrated significant changes on self-report, teacher-report, role play, and cognitive problem-solving tasks. They have not, however, demonstrated improvement on behavioral observation measures, nor have the changes observed on the other measures been shown to be maintained over time (Winett, Stefanek, & Riley, 1983). Methodological shortcomings notwithstanding, these social problem-solving programs show clear promise, and the findings are indeed suggestive of their continued utility.

Recently, the first author has initiated a large-scale secondary prevention program aimed at comparing the relative efficacy of different behavioral procedures in the prevention of predelinquent behavior in school-age children. More specifically, we have devised two behavioral intervention packages and are comparing them to a standard attention control condition. The first behavioral strategy consists of social skills training (Bornstein, Bellack, & Hersen, 1977; Ollendick & Hersen, 1979). In this procedure, a number of behavioral strategies are used: instructions, feedback, modeling, role playing, and reinforcement. Essentially, children are taught a set of specific skills to cope with diverse social situations. The second behavioral strategy consists of social problem-solving skills and is modeled after Gesten et al.'s (1979) highly successful program. The same behavioral strategies as used in the social skills groups are employed: instructions, feedback, modeling, role playing, and reinforcement. In contrast to the social skills groups, however, children are taught how to problem solve and are not provided a set of highly specific skills. Children are taught how to generate alternative solutions and how to determine probable consequences to these solutions. Children in the attention control groups meet for the same amount of time and discuss problems in getting along with one's peers. Attempts are made in these latter groups to help the children understand their behavior and accept responsibility for it. However, specific behavioral procedures are not used.

In this program, two subgroups of children have been identified as at risk for predelinquent behavior: the aggressive child and the socially withdrawn child. Though on opposite ends of a behavioral continuum, both types of children display social skill deficits that may lead to predelinquent behavior (Ollendick & Cerny, 1981). While the aggressive child is frequently a rejected sociometric child, the withdrawn child is a neglected one; both are frequently unpopular, at least in the 8- to 10-year-old children in our program. Further, while withdrawn children have been shown to display low rates of positive peer interaction, the aggressive child has been shown to evince high rates of negative social interaction (Ollendick, 1981). It must be reemphasized, however, that children involved in our program are not delinquent; rather, they are identified as at risk children who display behaviors thought to be predictive of later delinquent functioning.

Consistent with principles of multimethod assessment (Ollendick & Hersen, 1984), we obtain self-report (assertion, locus of control, self-efficacy), other-report (teacher rating, sociometric ratings), and simulated (alternating solutions, role-play assertiveness), as well as naturalistic (peer interactions) measures of behavioral change. Further, these measures are obtained prior to intervention, after intervention, and at follow-up intervals of one, two, and three years. Eventually, we plan to track these youngsters into adolescence and obtain measures of truancy, school drop out, and delinquent behavior. Three cohorts of children will be followed.

While our findings are tentative at this time, it appears that the cognitive social problem-solving strategies are more effective for the withdrawn children, while the social skills training strategies are more effective for the aggressive children. It appears that the inhibitive self-statements frequently observed in withdrawn children respond best to our cognitive restructuring procedures, while the clear skill deficits in the aggressive children respond best to social skills training procedures. Further, we are noting significant changes on self-report and simulated measures immediately following treatment but delays in improvement on sociometric ratings and behavioral interaction measures. Some measures are not showing change until the second year of the program. These findings are obviously complex and await our further scrutiny. Nonetheless, in the interim, they clearly affirm the notion that subject differences (aggressive, withdrawn) are important and that prevention programs cannot be indiscriminately applied to children in general.

In sum, a variety of person-centered prevention programs have been developed and evaluated. Short-term effects of these programs appear promising. However, whether or not these programs actually *prevent* subsequent behavioral problems from occurring remains to be empirically demonstrated. As we have noted elsewhere, "claims of prevention have been based more on the intuitive appeal of the model than on actual demonstrable effects" (Ollendick & Cerny, 1981, p. 296). Until such findings are obtained, person-centered behavioral preventive programs remain an admirable goal in need of empirical verification.

System-Centered Approaches

While the above person-centered interventions are largely individual or group focused, behavioral-preventive interventions can also be focused on organizations, communities, and societies (Jason, 1980). Interventions at these levels are generally focused on environmental change in order to bring about positive change in numerous individuals who are affected by those particular settings. Organizational level interventions include the physical characteristics of the setting, its rules and regulations, and its social climate. For children, the one setting in which much effort has already been expended is the school system.

Community level interventions can influence many organizations and people within a given community (e.g., school transportation system, youth programs). Finally, societal level interventions involve attempts to influence policy at a national level (e.g., executive actions, study panels, judicial decisions).

First, we shall examine representative organization level interventions and then turn our attention briefly to community and societal level interventions. As noted by Jason (1983), organization level interventions are aimed at identifying and fostering those environmental stimuli that promote social and academic competencies and that prevent maladaptive behavior from occurring in normal functioning individuals. For example, Risley and his colleagues have found that the physical design of the organization setting, as well as the quality of the resources contained therein, can have potent effects on the academic and social development of children. For instance, Twardosz, Cataldo, and Risley (1974) reported that an open environment in nursery school settings is more conducive to greater exploration and small-group activities than is a standard divided space classroom. Here, it was shown that the architectural units (e.g., partitions) and behavioral settings (instructional area) were related to the functioning of individual children. In a similar vein, Turner and Goldsmith (1976) and Quilitch and Risley (1973) have shown that the social behavior of children can be modified by the types of toys available. In one instance, it was shown that the rate of aggressive interaction could be reliably increased when aggressive toys, such as play guns, were made available, while in the other instance, it was shown that the rate of cooperative play could be increased when group versus individual toys were furnished the children. Cooperative play occurred 78 percent of the time when children were provided with toys that could be used jointly but only 16 percent of the time when children were given toys that required individual use. Apparently, the toy materials themselves served as effective antecedents to positive play interactions among the children.

Further, classic research (Gump, 1975) in the ecological paradigm has consistently shown that the size of a school has specific effects on student interaction patterns. For example, in small schools, more students (i.e., as percent of student body) tend to participate in more extracurricular activities than in large schools. This is because small schools are undermanned, and students are needed for various activities to run properly. Since engagement in a range of extracurricular activities can have social and academic enhancement effects (Gump, 1975), the move across the country to consolidate schools for fiscal reasons may have negative effects on students now and in the future.

Closely related to physical characteristics of the setting and the available resources is the social climate of the organization (Moos, 1979; Trickett & Moos, 1974). Social climate refers to the perceptions and feelings of individuals with respect to the environmental features of their organization. A setting's social climate has a direct effect on the attitude, mood, and behavior of its constituents (Moos, 1979). For example, Moos has shown that children are more satisfied and productive in schools when there are personal student-teacher relationships, innovative teacher methods, student involvement, and clarity regarding rules. Recently, the Department of Justice has become interested in the large-scale application and evaluation of school climate effects on preventing delinquent behavior. Several states have already enacted model programs (e.g., Colorado, New Mexico, and Pennsylvania), while others (e.g., Virginia) are currently developing such programs. The first author is involved in one such program in which the synergistic effects of school climate changes are being evaluated when combined with behavioral-preventive efforts, such as social skills training and cognitive problem-solving strategies. While outcome data on this project are not currently available, the combination of these two efforts is predicted to be more effective than either alone.

As with individual and group preventive efforts, the *real* impact of organizational level change on *preventing* child behavior disorders is unknown. While immediate changes have been noted (e.g., Cowen, 1977; Filipczak, Archer, Neale, & Winett, 1979), long-term effects have not.

In response to these findings, there has been a growing interest over the last decade in merging the scope and values of community psychology with an effective behavioral technology (see review by Jason & Glenwick, 1984). For example, under the general rubric of "behavioral community psychology," examples of applications have included changing medical office practices, such as inappropriate use of X rays by dentists (Greene & Niestat, 1983); changes in fee and other health system practices to promote health practices (Iwata & Becksfort, 1981); efforts to assure more vehicular safety through increases in seat belt use (Geller, Paterson, & Talbott, 1982); large-scale community health programs (Maccoby & Solomon, 1981); municipal-wide efforts to increase use of mass transit (Geller, Winett, & Everett, 1982); and strategies to assure citizen involvement in local policy development (Fawcett, Fletcher, & Mathews, 1980). These are only examples of many ongoing research programs in behavioral community psychology. However exciting these forays are, they are not without their practical and conceptual problems. As Fawcett, Mathews, and Fletcher (1980) point out, behavioral community psychology has yet to find a really "appropriate technology" (borrowing from Shumacher, 1973) that meshes a behavioral approach with some well-documented programmatic characteristics related to initial adoption, continued use, and diffusion of innovations (Rogers & Shoemaker, 1971). Further, within this approach, as with traditional behavior therapy, there still exists the central problem of developing effective, long-term maintenance strategies.

Given these problems and the housing of almost all of this research within a university setting, most projects, with some very notable exceptions (see Geller et al., 1982; Maccoby & Solomon, 1981), remain at the demonstration level. Wide-scale adoption of behavioral community approaches by the public and private sector is very limited (Stolz, 1981). An additional conceptual and methodological point is that most of these programs can be described as mass, aggregate individual change programs. This is because, in the attempt to transfer behavioral psychology to the community, the individual has remained the unit of analysis (e.g., see the critique of the Stanford Heart Disease Preventions projects by Leventhal, Safer, Cleary, & Guttman, 1980), and the conceptualization of institutional and community problems has remained psychological, relatively ignoring such disciplines as sociology, economics, and political science (Rappaport, 1977). However, at their best, these programs provide a glimpse into the potential of larger-scale, behavioral interventions.

Media-Based Approaches

As is evident from our brief overview of behavioral preventive programs, concerted effort has been directed primarily at the individual and small group level. Further, while a cost-benefit analysis of these efforts has not been conducted (see discussion of this issue later), it seems clear that a considerable expenditure of time, effort, and personnel is required for implementation of such programs. Therefore, it is not surprising that researchers have started to more fully explore the role of media in large-scale interventions. As noted by Winett (1981), behaviorists interested in media-based primary prevention can turn to the burgeoning communications literature. Of particular interest is work that is the careful product of a considerable amount of formative research by Palmer (1981), who has described the extensive research involved in developing "Sesame Street" and other programs for the Children's Television Workshop. Other extensive formative research was involved in developing health-spots for children in Spanish-speaking countries. Palmer's report presents a range of strategies for sampling target audience characteristics, level of knowledge, customs, family and cultural aspects of health practices, and acceptable health models. This and additional information was used in the development of the spots, which were, however, first pilot tested for attention, comprehension, information change, and behavioral intention. These steps are analogous to social marketing processes, deemed as essential for tailoring any program to a particular audience (Maccoby & Solomon, 1981). When such steps are taken, media-based efforts seem relatively effective in promoting information and behavior change (Atkin, 1981) and have the obvious advantage of potentially reaching large audience segments.

Perhaps, the best known behavioral, media-based, preventive program for children is represented by the work of Evans and his colleagues (Evans, Roselle, Maxwell, Raines, Dill, Guthrie, Henderson, & Hill, 1981) on smoking prevention. This program is implemented within classrooms, and at its core is a film highly geared to the target audience (e.g., it uses like-aged models) that demonstrates the dangers of smoking but, perhaps more importantly, ways to refuse cigarettes from peers and even parents. Rigorous evaluations have shown that the film, in conjunction with various social influence factors in schools, is effective in reducing the incidence of onset of smoking in early adolescence. Most importantly, what emerges is a general approach, adaptable to different circumstances and problems that combines strategies from social learning theory (Bandura, 1977) and diffusion of innovations theory (Rogers & Shoemaker, 1971). For example, the use of modeling films in a group discussion context, as in Evans et al., is an example of a *media-forum,* an effective intervention with a long history in the social diffusion literature (Rogers & Shoemaker, 1971). This approach has now been shown to be effective in such different areas as teaching children academic and social survival skills (Elias, 1983; Elias & Maher, 1983), training parenting skills (Webster-Stratton, 1981), and informing and motivating adults to conserve energy in their homes (Winett, Leckliter, Love, Chinn, & Stahl, 1983). Two other developments seem noteworthy here: Wright and Houston (1983) are involved in a series of studies investigating, particularly for children, how specific formative features (the syntax, such as pauses, fade outs, etc.) of a program can be used to enhance attention and comprehension; meanwhile, Winett et al. (1983) have shown, through a series of studies, how a program found effective within the media-forum modality can be designed and marketed so as to retain its effectiveness while being broadcast over cable TV.

We have spent a considerable amount of time on this section because we feel that the media approach, which is in essence a mass-aggregate, individual change approach, seems very compatible with the behavioral orientation and the new interest in preventive large-scale change. Two caveats are, however, in order: (1) the behaviorist runs the risk of reinventing the wheel unless the extensive communications literature is first studied and applied; and (2) since American television strictly revolves around profit via delivering a large audience share (Comstock, 1980; with perhaps PBS being an exception), national, media-based, preventive programs must eventually be commercially viable or heavily subsided by government.

MAJOR TENSIONS OF PREVENTIVE INTERVENTIONS

The purpose of this section is to further describe a number of conceptual, methodological, and practical tensions involved in prevention intervention and research. We purposely use the word tension because it connotes being pulled in different directions and because the word suggests that, for many of the issues we will present, the pulls or frictions are *not* resolvable. Our points partly parallel Rappaport's (1981) use of the term *dialectic* to describe similar sorts of problems, which are also within the field of prevention. Finally, we raise each issue separately, but it will be apparent that many of these issues are interrelated.

Level of Conceptualization

The most basic issue we see is the *level* of conceptualization and intervention (Rappaport, 1977). As psychologists, we are most familiar and comfortable with the individual/small group and small-setting level of analysis and intervention. For example, individual behavior change programs for deficits in social skills (Ollendick, 1981), or group contingency approaches to academic problems (Slavin, 1977), or restructuring classrooms (Winett, Battersby, & Edwards, 1975) are our areas of expertise. We have much less experience, for example, in administrative changes at a school district or even a school level and no experience at a community, let alone county or state, level. Yet, when we examine some contemporary issues, such as teacher merit pay or curriculum reform, which are issues that seem to bear directly on quality of education and therefore on social and academic behaviors in schools, these issues *are* being addressed at state and county fiscal levels, and indeed, even at the national political level. The end product or goal, enhanced social behaviors and academic skills, is the same for the behaviorist and the citizen and political groups. We seem to lack the knowledge to approach the problem at an institutional or community level and do not necessarily have the skills needed, or seen as appropriate, for change at higher levels.

To further illustrate this point in another context, we will briefly discuss problems in health and health care. There is a burgeoning psychological literature on treatment and prevention (e.g., Agras, 1982), and clearly, health promotion efforts with children should be the core of preventive efforts. Yet the possibility remains that these efforts will be relatively ineffectual in the face of the contemporary medical system and other dominant social, economic, and political influences on health practices (Navarro, 1976). A more reasonable approach, as some have argued (Roy, 1978), should involve focus on the payment mechanisms, such as in prepayment health maintenance organizations, which can profit by keeping people healthy.

In addition, some writers (e.g., Ryan, 1971) have shown the classic and destructive impact of psychological analysis of essentially social, economic, and political problems, as in "blaming the victim," while others (e.g., Bloom, 1979) have simply stated that when many people display similar problems (e.g., distress caused by divorce) then analysis and intervention should never be focused at the individual level.

These perspectives cannot only give pause to the would-be prevention-minded behaviorist, but also possibly lead to a paralysis of thought and behavior. The limited range of an individual approach is made more microscopic in juxtaposition to larger scale perspectives and the enormity of problems. Implementing individual programs of change in the face of an unsupportive context seems akin to rowing upstream with a broken paddle. Perhaps, though, this is a depiction of the dilemma at its gloomiest.

To wait for all systems to perfectly change to support individual change is to wait for Godot. To assume that all or even most individual problems are solved by system level change is naive and is certainly not consistent with our country's less-than-successful recent history of economic tinkering and social innovation (Reich, 1983). And focusing only at the system level diverts some needed attention from the individual level (Rappaport, 1981).

While we suggest that this tension is ultimately not resolvable, we offer two approaches to the behaviorist: (1) Construct individual interventions within the context of system influences and limitations. This point is excellently illustrated by Wahler's recent work (Wahler & Graves, 1983), which involves teaching mothers behavioral strategies to work with their children. The success of the approach seems to hinge on the mother's interactions with her community/social support systems. (2) Develop more expertise so that interventions can be moved up a notch or embedded within organizational and community systems. For example, the newer Heart Disease Prevention Programs from Stanford are based around individual behavior change procedures that are more carefully delivered within local media and in conjunction with community organizations (Maccoby & Solomon, 1981).

Target Behaviors

A parallel problem to the question of level of analysis and intervention is the issue of *direct* or *indirect* interventions. By direct interventions, we mean change procedures that specifically focus on problem target behaviors. Such interventions may be thought of as more person-centered. On the other hand, indirect interventions seek to change target behaviors without such an explicit focus. These interventions may be thought of as system-centered. For example, in those situations in which there are young children and both parents work full-time outside the home, parents report a great lack of time for any activities aside from work and home and child care (Aldous, 1982). A direct individual approach can involve teaching people to prioritize tasks and activities and use their time more efficiently. Another more indirect approach might analyze the source of the time-scarcity as being within the constraints of inflexible work schedules and propose alterations in work organizations. Interestingly, in this case, both approaches have been tried. King, Winett, and Lovett (1983) found that a simple time management program for working women led to a dramatic increase in use of designated priority time by women working full-time outside the home. In another project (Winett, Neale, & Williams, 1982), allowing more flexible work hours resulted in some minimal (30 minutes), though reportedly meaningful, increase in family time by a similar population. The enhancement and perhaps even preventive potential of either approach for family functioning seems substantial.

While the direct approach may be more effective in terms of immediate behavior change for specific groups of people, this particular approach must be taught over and over again to new groups. It is not cost effective on a large scale. While the indirect approach, flexitime, may be less effective, it is probably more cost effective. Once the relatively cost-free approach is in place, it can help many people and presumably be implemented across many settings (Nollen, 1982).

This example furthers our point about examining levels beyond the individual but also suggests a mechanism for the preventive-minded behaviorist to move up the notch we discussed previously. For working parents, flexibility and other changes at work are necessary, but so is the efficient individual use of time. An ideal work-setting innovation would combine some of the perspectives and skills of the behaviorist with those of the organizational expert (Frederiksen, 1982). The tension remains in actually effecting such mergers of perspectives and skills, given much history showing the lack of cooperation between disciplines (Krasner, 1980).

Timing

Yet another tension, also related to our first point on levels of analysis, is the *timing* of interventions and whether interventions are proactive or reactive. This point, of course, relates to the traditional categorization from public health of primary, secondary, and tertiary prevention (Caplan, 1964). As noted earlier, in primary prevention the goal is to actively intervene on a population basis *before* the onset of the problem. A classic example involves floridation of the water supply to prevent tooth decay and the vaccination of all children for polio. Another example receiving a great deal of current attention is low birth weight, which is related to a host of developmental problems (Matarazzo, 1983). Smoking and drinking (i.e., the fetal alcohol syndrome) and poor nutrition by the pregnant mother are linked to low birth weight, and in most instances, the concomitant infant and childhood problems are preventable. Secondary prevention involves identification and intervention with a specific high-risk population segment and generally means that the problem is in an early onset stage. Hence, in most respects, this is a reactive approach. The first author's project that involves identification and intervention with children experiencing academic and social problems is an example of secondary prevention, as is most of the psychological work in prevention (i.e., Cowen, 1977; Shure & Spivack, 1978). Tertiary prevention is prevention in name only and generally entails reducing the incidence of a specific problem through rehabilitation.

In most instances, true primary prevention involves community and institutional change that may be beyond the reach of most behaviorally trained psychologists. The issue is further complicated by the fact that various problems in living, which are the purview of psychologists, may have multiple and interactive origins (although this may really also be the case with many health problems; Catalano, 1979). However, at the moment, programs that can only promise some form of life enhancement without reducing or eliminating specific problems seem out of favor (Lorion, 1983).

Secondary prevention approaches are not without their problems, either. First, it is not always clear, particularly for child behavior disorders, what are identifiable antecedents *and* whether or not these antecedents are continuous. This is both a psychometric and a developmental issue. The primary characteristic of children is developmental change. Children may move in and out of risk as developmental and contextual factors in their lives change (Bell & Pearl, 1982). For example, hitting, shoving, and pushing one's peers is, to some extent, expected at the preschool level (at least in boys) and is associated with high sociometric status. These very same behaviors at 8 to 10 years of age, at least for middle-class youngsters, are associated with low sociometric status and, accordingly, are used as predictors of later antisocial behavior (Ollendick, 1981). For lower-class children, however, these behaviors are not useful predictors. Clearly, developmental (age) and contextual (social class) factors interact complexly to determine what behaviors and when they are emitted are predictive of later difficulties. Another example may help to clarify this point. Parents who have done what would ordinarily be considered a good job of child rearing may find that their children become school dropouts or drug abusers when they are exposed to a peer group whose values differ from those of the family. It is clear that such children would not have been identified as at risk during their early years and that what constitutes a manifestation of risk changes with age and ecological parameters.

Second, and by no means a trivial point, are the legal, ethical, and treatment issues of identifying dysfunction at an early age but, in doing so, sensitizing the child and significant others so as to make the situation *worse* in the long run. This issue is closely related to the first. For example, West and Farrington (1973) report the results of one long-term predictive study in which the number of false positives (children identified as being at risk) slightly exceeded the number of children who actually became delinquent. In the risk group, based on background factors (low family income, large family, criminality in one parent, and inadequate parental guidance), the correct labeling of 31 future delinquents was achieved at the expense of incorrectly labeling 32. Thus, slightly less than half of the risk children actually became delinquent. This low level of prediction is compounded by the fact that some early prevention programs have reported *adverse* effects of intervention in the area of antisocial behavior (e.g., Gersten, Langner, & Simcha-Fagan, 1979; McCord, 1978). In fact, in a 30-year follow-up of individuals identified as predelinquent in the Cambridge-Sommerville project, individuals in the treatment-prevention groups fared considerably poorer than those in the treatment group. Partially responsible for these findings may be the negative effects of labeling (McCord, 1978). However, we must hasten to add that labeling effects need not necessarily occur if appropriate cautions related to subject selection, group composition, and follow-up are undertaken.

We raise these points not to dissuade behavior therapists from becoming more involved in secondary prevention efforts. In fact, we feel it is in secondary prevention that behavior therapists should find an approach compatible with their skills and knowledge base. These tensions are again raised so that behavior therapists do not blindly enter the fray.

"Paternalism"

We turn now to a series of other somewhat lesser tensions, but issues that are nonetheless significant and capable of becoming dominant dilemmas in the prevention field. A key question raised by Rappaport (1981) is whether prevention despite or perhaps because of its good intentions is inherently paternalistic. After all, the goal of many prevention programs is to have people do what they "should" be doing, and the institutions implementing the prevention programs know what is *best* for the individual, now and in the future. Although this is a bit of a caricature of some prevention programs, there is a grain of truth in this position that applies to most prevention programs. Arguments against paternalistic, controlling prevention programs came at a time when there was considerable political attention given to the overreaching hand of government (i.e., 1980), as in "getting government off the backs of the people." This was also a rallying cry for what was seen as 50 years of more and more sweeping liberal reforms and social planning and engineering that had all but undermined the basic entrepreneurial, free-market mechanisms of the country (e.g., Gilder, 1981).

That some liberal courses have been misdirected and ineffective in the face of new circumstances (e.g., more global economics; Riech, 1983), there is no doubt. However, for many people who have experienced the ravages of unemployment in recent years (see Liem & Ramsay, 1982), we doubt that many see the solution as less and less government and leaving the solutions of national programs to the localities or the workings of the marketplace. Similar arguments about too much government control (i.e., regulatory policy) being the root cause of our economic malice have also been shown to be questionable (Pertschuk, 1982). In other words, economic recession and recent analyses of regulatory policy may have caused a shift back to the idea of the federal government taking a strong, interventionist stance.

Therefore, while we can dismiss some of the extreme claims about the negative effects of government prevention programs, we would not want Rappaport's and other's main points of criticism to be forgotten. Prevention programs *can* become unnecessarily paternalistic and controlling. Prevention programs *can* miss as their major mission *empowering* people so that they have the skills and resources to successfully live in the future. We can return here to a specific point Rappaport (1977) made earlier in characterizing many welfare programs as the "giving enemy" because they more or less permanently assure that people are dependent on government payments to survive. We can also see current unemployment benefits and some welfare programs as a sort of safety-net prevention program (although there are major prevention issues here in terms of loss of health benefits when unemployed and documented negative health effects of job loss; Liem & Ramsay, 1982). However, if it is clear, as it is to some (Reich, 1983), that certain jobs (e.g., on assembly lines) will not be resurrected in the future, then unemployment and welfare payments to some will assure their continued dependency. A systematic and massive effort at training for new job skills that are needed in the future can be an excellent basis for empowerment and can have far more positive individual and societal outcomes than do only maintenance and welfare payments.

The Feasibility of Prevention

Other tensions and issues we wish to discuss are: (1) What are appropriate goals for most prevention programs? (2) What is the feasibility of conducting true prevention research? (3) How applicable is state-of-the-art behavior therapy to preventive interventions? and (4) How can prevention be institutionalized?

The basic idea behind preventive efforts is that it is more effective in the long run to promote some changes now so as to reduce and perhaps even eliminate problems in the future—problems that will be very expensive to treat or that may not really be treatable in the future. We have pointed out that, in the behavioral arena, it has been difficult to make many linkages between present dysfunction and later pathology. How then do we construct and evaluate prevention programs and conduct prevention research? Based on the literature (Price, Ketterer, Bader, & Monahan, 1980), we discuss the first part of this issue using the notion of *proximal* versus *distal goals*—a concept that parallels the problem of linkages between preventable antecedents and later consequences.

For example, there is reasonable evidence that the Type A personality type is linked to increased risk of heart disease (Suinn, 1982) and that this behavioral pattern can be identified fairly early, for example, in junior high (Glass, 1977) and elementary school (Mathews & Siegel, 1983). One health prevention program could entail teaching all sixth graders how to better cope with stress, prioritize their tasks, and become somewhat less competitive. The proximal goals of this program are conveying information, teaching new skills, and effecting behavioral and biochemical change (Baum, Grunberg, & Singer, 1982) in response to certain stimuli. Given the history of behavior therapy, as we will discuss later, the proximal goals themselves are very ambitious. The distal goals are even more so. Cognitive, emotional, and behavioral changes need not only to be maintained, but such changes (away from the Type A personality) must yield demonstrative health outcomes. The distal goals are more than ambitious; given the state of the art, they are incredible! As some writers have done in another context (Solomon, 1981), we can assess the likelihood of this project fulfilling its distal goals by assigning a probability of success to each stage. For example, for the proposed program, we might guess that the likelihood of the children initially gaining the knowledge and skills is 50 percent, but the probability of maintenance into adulthood is low, say 20 percent. The probability of the different personality styles actually significantly affecting health outcomes is also probably low, i.e., 25 percent. When these probabilities are multiplied together, we come to a sobering, although admittedly armchair-based, conclusion: the probability of reaching the distal goal is about .025! Yet, this chain of events represents the rudimentary approach of many behavioral prevention programs.

This example also highlights the enormity of the prevention intervention and research enterprise. Not only do initial interventions have to be successful, but also behavior changes must be maintained. Given that behavior therapists have not demonstrated maintenance of many treatments (Wilson & O'Leary, 1980), one best guess is that over time there must be some continuation of treatment that must be adaptable to changing behavioral and contextual requirements, i.e., the developmental perspective. In terms of research on prevention, we need to emphasize a kind of longitudinal, ecological approach that is the extreme exception in the behavioral sciences (Bronfenbrenner, 1979).

These points *were* meant to be sobering but not devastating. Hopefully, they direct our attention to being more modest in our claims for preventive programs; to pick on higher priority problems and higher probability outcomes; to fully articulate some of the linkages between present and future dysfunction; to become more committed to longitudinal research; and, to more fully explore conceptualization and interventions at a higher level of analysis that may have a greater likelihood of success.

One response to both the problem of direct linkages of present and future events and the developmental dilemma has been to emphasize a more general approach in person-centered prevention programs. For example, many prevention and enhancement programs teach coping skills and problem-solving strategies (e.g., Felner et al., 1983). The basic rationale is to impart skills and strategies that can increase a person's access to material and nonmaterial resources that can be used in many situations and will represent a general style or approach that is adaptable over time. Thus, contemporary literature on prevention has become wedded to this concept, with most publications repeatedly using the term *competencies, coping,* and *support* (Felner et al., 1983), although recent work has recognized the need to make these concepts and strategies much more specific (e.g., Cohen, 1983; Heller & Swindle, 1983). However, many behavioral prevention programs seem to be taking a more general package approach. Perhaps the best examples are the stress management programs, which usually include some form of relaxation training, education about stress, cognitive restructuring, and problem solving. The basic idea is to offer enough different elements to cover most bases, to have something available for everyone, and to provide a program that is replicable and deliverable by paraprofessionals and even through the media (Frederiksen & Brehony, 1979).

As we will discuss in examining the issue of institutionalization of prevention, the goals of new, massive, and hence, more cost-effective delivery systems is a laudatory one and certainly a necessary component of prevention. However, the general package approach is contrary to the roots and successful application of behavior therapy. The key word we use to describe the departure made by behavior therapy from traditional therapies and the areas where it is effective is *specific*. That is, specific designation of target behaviors, specific monitoring of those behaviors, and specific intervention are the hallmarks of behavior therapy. With some exceptions, we do not tend to find success when problems and interventions are diffuse or global (Wilson & O'Leary, 1980). More germane to the point here is the data showing little evidence for the efficacy of any general stress-management program (Frederiksen, Riley, & Winett, 1981), and perhaps only in one or two good examples in the prevention literature has a general problem-solving approach been successful (Bloom, Asher, & White, 1978; Shure & Spivack, 1978).

One approach to this issue is to adopt some of the tactics of social marketing when designing person-centered programs. The most basic concept here is that, through a range of assessment strategies, a program can be designed that is uniquely suited to and acceptable by a particular market segment. For example, in the project described before by King et al. (1983), interview, survey and observation data, and a literature search indicated that a common stress-related problem for women working outside the home who have children is time scarcity. Based on these data and other assessment data indicating the most appropriate type of program format, a time-management program *tailored* to this population was delivered to this particular population. As noted before, the program was successful and seems suitable to be delivered in formats (e.g., media) potentially more cost-effective than its original small group delivery. However, the program could still most likely only be mass delivered to this particular population segment. The approach, and most importantly how it is framed and delivered (although, probably not its basic principles), may not appeal or work with men who also have parental responsibilities, women in higher level career paths, or women without young children. However, the social-marketing perspective is quite compatible with Paul's (1967) early identification of the task at hand: designing particular treatments for particular clients with particular problems.

The enormity of the job of fulfilling this mission, plus all the trappings we have noted with preventive efforts, is also quite sobering. For those who want to pursue the more general approach, we offer encouragement, but the strong caveat of the behavioral and social-marketing literature that the odds against success are strong. This caveat once again suggests that more effective preventive intervention may be found at a higher level of conceptualization and intervention where some organizational and community change may positively and enduringly affect the lives of many people.

As a final warning against putting all the eggs in the person-centered, specificity basket, we note that the extreme specificity of the earlier behavioral approach represented a paradigm that has not only been modified during the last 10 years by the broader social learning model (Bandura, 1977), but also is being supplanted by a very different world view (e.g., Rogers & Kincaid, 1981; Schwartz, 1982). Throughout psychology and, indeed, most of the sciences, earlier mechanistic positions are being replaced by organistic approaches that emphasize interaction, complexity, and systems thinking. As we noted in this chapter, the possibility of changing behavior one at Time A to affect behavior two at Time B may be elusive. What is suggested by contemporary systems thinking is that the task of changing behavior one at Time A, in and of itself, may be more elusive than originally thought!

The final issue we will discuss is the institutionalization of prevention. Many critics have noted that the health care system in this country is slowly turning toward prevention at most and that the great proportion of expenditures now and in the foreseeable future will be for direct treatment (Matarazzo, 1983). What about the prospects for more psychologically based prevention with psychological and health problems? On this score, we once again find much tension within one dominant field—clinical psychology. On the one hand, we see that many clinical programs have adopted the rhetoric and apparently some of the values and activities of the community psychology movement. Broader scale interventions and a focus on prevention and treatment outside the realm of the usual domain of clinical psychology and its traditional delivery system have been apparent (Felner et al., 1983). At least several prominant clinical programs now have noted community psychologists as their directors. These are signs of a genuine paradigm shift and a kind of institutionalization of prevention ideals that would have been fantasy a decade ago.

On the other hand, clinical psychology now has a possibility through third-party payment mechanisms to become more completely embedded in traditional service delivery systems (DeLeon, Vandenbos, & Cummings, 1983). In an insightful and incisive article, Sarason (1981) has shown how the history of clinical psychology has been closely wedded with the availability of funding and *not* conceptual, ideological, or humanitarian concerns. To paraphrase him, never underestimate the power of money on the table! The provision of third-party payments represents a financial bonanza for clinical psychology but perhaps at the high cost of conceptual and intervention innovation. We know of no provision for systematic reimbursement for individual preventive, let alone programmatic, preventive interventions.

CONCLUDING REMARKS

The great resurgence of interest in the rapprochement of behavioral and psychoanalytic paradigms that has coincided with the increased adherence to traditional service delivery systems may not represent, on one level, a substantial conceptual or paradigm shift in the field. If one of the major tasks in prevention is the development and implementation of new service delivery modalities (Rappaport, 1977), then the conceptual integrations of psychotherapeutic thought, which have taken place with the *presumption* of traditional service delivery (or simply ignored the context of intervention), may take energy away from preventive efforts and undermine the field. Conceptual reorientation and, indeed, paradigm shifts are inevitable and vital for any science (Kuhn, 1970).

However, new models and beliefs need to be the servants of current and pressing concerns. Our hope is that part of the search for a new psychological paradigm will address itself to the relationship between new ideas and renewed efforts at prevention.

REFERENCES

Agras, W. S. Behavioral medicine in the 1980's: Nonrandom connections. *Journal of Consulting and Clinical Psychology,* 1982, *50,* 797–803.

Albee, G. W. The relation of conceptual models to manpower needs. In E. L. Cowen, E. A. Gardner, & M. Zax (Eds.), *Emergent approaches to mental health problems.* New York: Appleton-Century-Crofts, 1967.

Aldous, J. (Ed.). *Two paychecks: Life in dual-earner families.* Beverly Hills, Calif.: Sage, 1982.

Allen, G. J., Chinsky, J. M., Larcen, S. W., Lochman, J. E., & Selinger, H. V. *Community psychology and the schools.* New York: John Wiley & Sons, 1976.

Atkin, C. K. Mass media information campaign effectiveness. In R. E. Rice & W. J. Paisley (Eds.), *Public communication campaigns.* Beverly Hills, Calif.: Sage, 1981.

Bandura, A. *Social learning theory.* New York: Prentice-Hall, 1977.

Baum, A., Grunberg, N. E., & Singer, J. E. The use of psychological and neuro-endocrinological measurements in the study of stress. *Health Psychology,* 1982, *1,* 217–236.

Bell, R. Q., & Pearl, D. Implications for early identification of changing risk status in seven categories of risk. *Journal of Prevention in Human Services,* 1982, *1,* 1–18.

Bloom, B. L. *Community mental health: A general introduction.* Monterey, Calif.: Brooks/Cole, 1977.

Bloom, B. L. Prevention of mental disorders: Recent advances in theory and practice. *Community Mental Health Journal,* 1979, *15,* 179–191.

Bloom, B. L., Asher, S. J., & White, S. W. Marital disruption as a stressor: A review and analysis. *Psychological Bulletin,* 1978, *85,* 867–894.

Bornstein, M. R., Bellack, A. S., & Hersen, M. Social skills training for unassertive children: A multiple-baseline analysis. *Journal of Applied Behavior Analysis,* 1977, *10,* 183–195.

Bronfenbrenner, U. *The ecology of human development.* Cambridge, Mass.: Harvard University Press, 1979.

Caplan, G. *Principles of preventive psychiatry.* New York: Basic Books, 1964.

Catalano, R. A. *Health, behavior, and community.* Elmsford, N.Y.: Pergamon Press, 1979.

Cobb, J. A., & Hops, H. Effects of academic survival skills training on low achieving first graders. *Journal of Educational Research*, 1973, *67*, 108–113.

Cohen, S. Social support, stress, and the buffering hypothesis: A theoretical analysis. In A. Baum, J. E. Singer, & S. E. Taylor (Eds.), *Handbook of psychology and health*. (Vol. 4). Hillsdale, N.J.: Lawrence Erlbaum Associates, Inc. 1983.

Comstock, G. *Television in America*. Beverly Hills, Calif.: Sage, 1980.

Cowen, E. L. Baby steps toward primary prevention. *American Journal of Community Psychology*, 1977, *5*, 1–22.

Cowen, E. L., Trost, M. A., Lorion, R. P., Dorr, D., Izzo, L. D., & Isaacson, R. V. *New ways in school mental health: Early detection and prevention of school maladaptation*. New York: Behavioral Publications, 1975.

DeLeon, P. H., Vandenbos, G. R., & Cummings, N. A. Psychotherapy—Is it safe, effective, and appropriate? *American Psychologist*, 1983, *38*, 907–911.

Elias, M. J. Improving coping skills of emotionally disturbed boys through television-based social problem solving. *American Journal of Orthopsychiatry*, 1983, *53*, 61–72.

Elias, M. J., & Maher, C. A. Social and affective development of children: A programmatic perspective. *Exceptional Children*, 1983, *49*, 339–346.

Evans, R. I., Rozelle, R. M., Maxwell, S. E., Raines, B. E., Dill, C. A., Guthrie, T. J., Henderson, A. H., & Hill, P. C. Social modeling films to deter smoking in adolescents: Results of a three-year field investigation. *Journal of Applied Psychology*, 1981, *66*, 399–414.

Fawcett, S. B., Fletcher, R. K., & Mathews, R. M. Behavioral community education. In D. S. Glenwick & L. A. Jason (Eds.), *Behavioral community psychology: Progress and prospects*. New York: Praeger Publishers, 1980.

Fawcett, S. B., Mathews, R. M., & Fletcher, R. K. Behavioral technology for community application: Some promising directions. *Journal of Applied Behavior Analysis*, 1980, *13*, 505–518.

Felner, R. D., Jason, L. A., Moritsugu, J., & Farber, S. S. (Eds.). *Preventive psychology: Theory, research, and practice*. New York: Pergamon Press, 1983.

Filipczak, J., Archer, M. B., Neale, M. S., & Winett, R. A. Issues in multivariate assessment of a large-scale behavioral program. *Journal of Applied Behavior Analysis*, 1979, *12*, 593–614.

Frederiksen, L. W. (Ed.). *Handbook of organizational behavior management*. New York: John Wiley & Sons, 1982.

Frederiksen, L. W., & Brehony, K. Public Broadcasting System series on stress management. Roanoke, Va. WBRA, 1979.

Frederiksen, L. W., Riley, A. W., & Winett, R. A. *Evaluation of a stress management program delivered in a large organizational setting*. Paper presented at the annual meeting of the Association for Advancement of Behavior Therapy, Toronto, 1981.

Geller, E. S., Paterson, L., & Talbott, E. A behavioral analysis of incentive prompts for motivating seat belt usage. *Journal of Applied Behavior Analysis*, 1982, *15*, 403–415.

Geller, E. S., Winett, R. A., & Everett, P. B. *Preserving the environment: New strategies for behavior change*. Elmsford, N.Y.: Pergamon Press, 1982.

Gersten, J. C., Langner, T. S., & Simcha-Fagan, O. Developmental patterns of types of behavioral disturbance and secondary prevention. *International Journal of Mental Health*, 1979, *7*, 132–149.

Gesten, E. L., de Apodaca, R. F., Rains, M., Weissberg, R. P., & Cowen, E. L. Promoting peer-related social competence in schools. In M. W. Kent & J. E. Rolf (Eds.), *Primary prevention of psychopathology* (Vol. 3). Hanover, N.H.: University Press, 1979.

Gilder, G. *Wealth and poverty*. New York: Basic Books, 1981.

Glass, D. C. *Behavior patterns, stress, and coronary disease*. Hillsdale, N.J.: Lawrence Erlbaum Associates Inc., 1977.

Greene, B. F., & Neistat, M. D. Behavior analysis in consumer affairs: Encouraging dental professionals to provide consumers with shielding from unnecessary x-ray exposure. *Journal of Applied Behavior Analysis*, 1983, *16*, 13–27.

Gump, P. V. Ecological psychology and children. In E. M. Hetherington (Ed.), *Review of child development research* (Vol. 5). Chicago: University of Chicago Press, 1975.

Heller, K., & Swindle, R. W. Social network, perceived social support and coping with stress. In R. D. Felner et al. (Eds.), *Preventive psychology: Theory, research, and practice*. Elmsford, N.Y.: Pergamon Press, 1983.

Hops, H., & Cobb, J. A. Initial investigations into academic survival-skill training. *Journal of Educational Psychology*, 1974, *66*, 546–553.

Iwata, B. A., & Becksford, C. M. Behavioral research in preventive dentistry: Educational and contingency management approaches to the problem of patient compliance. *Journal of Applied Behavior Analysis*, 1981, *14*, 111–120.

Jason, L. A. Behavioral community psychology: Conceptualizations and applications. *Journal of Community Psychology*, 1977, *5*, 303–312.

Jason, L. A. Prevention in the schools. In R. Price, R. Ketterer, B. Bader, & J. Monahan (Eds.), *Prevention in mental health: Research, policy and practice*. Beverly Hills, Calif.: Sage, 1980.

Jason, L. A. Prevention and environmental modification in a behavioral community model. *Behavioral Counseling Quarterly*, 1981, *1*, 91–107.

Jason, L. A. Preventive behavioral interventions. In R. D. Felner, L. A. Jason, J. Moritsugu, & S. S. Farber (Eds.), *Preventive psychology: Theory, research and practice*. New York: Pergamon Press, 1983.

Jason, L. A., & Glenwick, D. S. Behavioral community psychology: A review of recent research and applications. In M. Hersen, R. M. Eisler, & P. M. Miller (Eds.), *Progress in behavior modification* (Vol. 17). New York: Academic Press, 1984.

King, A. C., Winett, R. A., & Lovett, S. B. *The effects of support and instruction on home and work behaviors in women from dual-earner families: A secondary prevention program for stress.* Unpublished manuscript, Department of Psychology, Virginia Polytechnic Institute and State University, Blacksburg, Va., 1983.

Kelley, J. G., Snowden, L. R., & Munoz, R. F. Social and community interventions. In M. R. Rosenzweig & L. W. Porter (Eds.), *Annual review of psychology* (Vol. 28). Palo Alto, Calif.: Annual Reviews, 1977.

Krasner, L. *Environmental design and human behavior.* Elmsford, N.Y.: Pergamon Press, 1980.

Kuhn, T. S. *The structure of scientific revolutions* (2nd ed.). Chicago: University of Chicago Press, 1970.

Leventhal, H., Safer, M. A., Cleary, P. D., & Guttman, M. Cardiovascular risk modification by community-based programs for life-style change: Comments on the Stanford study. *Journal of Consulting and Clinical Psychology,* 1980, *48,* 150–158.

Liem, R., & Ramsay, P. Health and social costs of unemployment: Research and policy consideration. *American Psychologist,* 1982, *37,* 1116–1123.

Lorion, R. P. Evaluating preventive interventions: Guidelines for the serious social change agent. Chapter in R. D. Felner et al. (Eds.), *Preventive psychology: Theory, research, and practice.* Elmsford, N.Y., 1983.

Maccoby, N., & Solomon, D. S. Heart disease prevention: Community studies. In R. E. Rice & W. J. Paisley (Eds.), *Public communication campaigns.* Beverly Hills, Calif.: Sage, 1981.

Matarazzo, J. D. *Behavioral immunogens and pathogens in health and illness.* Master lecture delivered at the annual meeting of the American Psychological Association, Anaheim, Calif.: 1983.

Mathews, K. A., & Siegel, J. M. Type A behaviors by children, social comparison, and standards for self-evaluation. *Developmental Psychology,* 1983, *19,* 135–140.

McClure, L. F., Chinsky, J. M., & Larcen, S. W. Enhancing social problem-solving performance in an elementary school setting. *Journal of Educational Psychology,* 1978, *70,* 504–513.

McCord, J. A thirty-year follow-up of treatment effects. *American Psychologist,* 1978, *33,* 284–289.

Moos, R. H. *Evaluating educational environments.* San Francisco: Jossey-Bass, 1979.

Navarro, V. *Medicine under capitalism.* New York: Prodist, 1976.

Nietzel, M. T., Winett, R. A., MacDonald, M. L., & Davidson, W. S. *Behavioral approaches to community psychology.* New York: Pergamon Press, 1977.

Nollen, S. D. *New work schedules in practice: Managing time in a changing society.* New York: Van Nostrand Reinhold, 1982.

O'Connor, R. D. Modification of social withdrawal through symbolic modeling. *Journal of Applied Behavior Analysis*, 1969, *2*, 15–22.

O'Connor, R. D. Relative efficacy of modeling, shaping, and the combined procedures for modification of social withdrawal. *Journal of Abnormal Psychology*, 1972, *79*, 327–334.

Ojemann, R. H. Sources of infection revealed in preventive psychiatry research. *American Journal of Public Health*, 1960, *50*, 329–335.

Ojemann, R. H., & Snider, B. C. The effect of a teaching program in behavioral science on changes in causal behavior scores. *Journal of Educational Research*, 1964, *57*, 255–260.

Ollendick, T. H. Level of *n* achievement and persistence behavior in children. *Developmental Psychology*, 1974, *10*, 457.

Ollendick, T. H. Success and failure: Implications for child psychopathology. In A. J. Finch, Jr., & P. C. Kendall (Eds.), *Clinical treatment and research in child psychopathology*. New York: Spectrum, 1979.

Ollendick, T. H. Assessment of social interaction skills in school children. *Behavioral Counseling Quarterly*, 1981, *1*, 227–243.

Ollendick, T. H. Reliability and validity of the Revised Fear Survey Schedule for Children (FSSC-R). *Behaviour Research and Therapy*, in press, 1983.

Ollendick, T. H., & Cerny, J. A. *Clinical behavior therapy with children*. New York: Plenum Press, 1981.

Ollendick, T. H., & Hersen, M. Social skills training for juvenile delinquents. *Behaviour Research and Therapy*. 1979, *17*, 547–555.

Ollendick, T. H., & Hersen, M. (Eds.). *Child behavioral assessment: Principles and procedures*. New York: Pergamon Press, 1984.

Ollendick, T. H., & Mayer, J. School phobia. In S. M. Turner (Ed.), *Behavioral treatment of anxiety disorders*. New York: Plenum Press, 1983.

Palmer, E. Shaping persuasive messages with formative research. In R. E. Rice & W. J. Paisley (Eds.), *Public communication campaigns*. Beverly Hills, Calif.: Sage, 1981.

Paul, G. L. Strategy of outcome research in psychotherapy. *Journal of Consulting Psychology*, 1967, *31*, 104–118.

Pertschuk, M. *Revolt against regulation: The rise and pause of the consumer movement*. Berkeley: University of California Press, 1982.

Poser, E. G. Toward a theory of behavioral prophylaxis. *Journal of Behavior Therapy and Experimental Psychiatry*, 1970, *1*, 39–45.

Poser, E. G., & King, M. Strategies for the prevention of maladaptive fear responses. *Canadian Journal of Behavioral Science*, 1975, *7*, 279–294.

Price, R. H., Ketterer, R. F., Bader, B. C., & Monahan, J. (Eds.). *Prevention in mental health: Research, policy, and practice*. Beverly Hills, Calif.: Sage, 1980.

Quilitch, H. R., & Risley, T. R. The effects of play materials on social play. *Journal of Applied Behavior Analysis*, 1973, *6*, 573–578.

Rappaport, J. *Community psychology: Values, research, and action.* New York: Holt, Rinehart & Winston, 1977.

Rappaport, J. In praise of paradox: A social policy of empowerment over prevention. *American Journal of Community Psychology*, 1981, *9*, 1–25.

Reich, R. *The next American frontier.* New York: Time-Life Books, 1983.

Reiff, R. Of cabbages and kings. *American Journal of Community Psychology*, 1975, *3*, 187–196.

Rogers, E. M., & Shoemaker, F. F. *Communications of innovations.* New york: Free Press, 1971.

Rogers, E. M., & Kincaid, D. L. *Communication networks: Toward a new paradigm for research.* New York: Free Press, 1981.

Roy, W. R. *Effects of the payment mechanism on the health care delivery system.* Washington, D.C.: U.S. Department of Health, Education & Welfare, 1978.

Ryan, W. *Blaming the victim.* New York: Random House, 1971.

Sarason, S. B. An asocial and a misdirected clinical psychology. *American Psychologist*, 1981, *36*, 827–836.

Schumacher, E. F. *Small is beautiful.* New York: Harper & Row, 1973.

Schwartz, G. E. Testing the biopsychosocial model: The ultimate challenge facing behavioral medicine. *Journal of Consulting and Clinical Psychology*, 1982, *50*, 1040–1053.

Shure, M. B., & Spivack, G. *Problem solving techniques in child rearing.* San Francisco: Jossey-Bass, 1978.

Slavin, R. E. *Using student learning terms to desegregate the classroom.* Center for Social Organization of Schools, Johns Hopkins University, Baltimore, 1977.

Solomon, D. S. A social marketing perspective on campaigns. In R. E. Rice & W. J. Paisley (Eds.), *Public communication campaigns.* Beverly Hills, Calif.: Sage, 1981.

Spivack, G., & Shure, M. B. *Social adjustment of young children.* San Francisco: Jossey-Bass, 1974.

Spivack, G., Platt, J. J., & Shure, M. B. *The problem solving approach to adjustment.* San Francisco: Jossey-Bass, 1976.

Stolz, S. B. Adoption of innovations from applied behavioral research. "Does anybody care?" *Journal of Applied Behavior Analysis*, 1981, *14*, 491–505.

Suinn, R. M. Intervention with Type A behaviors. *Journal of Consulting and Clinical Psychology*, 1982, *50*, 933–949.

Trickett, E., & Moos, R. Personal correlates of contrasting environments: Student satisfaction in high school classrooms. *American Journal of Community Psychology*, 1974, *2*, 1–12.

Tuma, J. M., & Pratt, J. M. Clinical child psychology practice and training: A survey. *Journal of Clinical Child Psychology,* 1982, *11,* 27–34.

Turner, C. W., & Goldsmith, D. Effects of toy guns and airplanes on children's antisocial free play behavior. *Journal of Experimental Child Psychology,* 1976, *21,* 303–315.

Twardosz, S., Cataldo, M. F., & Risley, T. R. Open environment design for infant and toddler day care. *Journal of Applied Behavior Analysis,* 1974, *7,* 529–546.

Wahler, R. G., & Graves, M. G. Setting events in social networks: Ally or enemy in child behavior therapy? *Behavior Therapy,* 1983, *14,* 19–36.

Walker, H. M., & Hops, H. The use of group and individual reinforcement contingencies in the modification of social withdrawal. In L. A. Hamerlynck, L. C. Handy & E. J. Mash (Eds.), *Behavior change: Methodology, concepts and practice.* Champaign, Ill.: Research Press, 1973.

Webster-Stratton, C. Modification of mothers' behaviors and attitudes through a videotape modeling group discussion program. *Behavior Therapy,* 1981, *12,* 634–642.

Weinrott, M. R., Corson, J. A., & Wilchesky, M. Teacher-mediated treatment of social withdrawal. *Behavior Therapy,* 1979, *10,* 281–294.

Weissberg, R. P., Gesten, E. L., Rapkin, B. D., Cowen, E. L., Davidson, E., deApodaca, R. F., & McKim, B. J. Evaluation of a social-problem-solving training program for suburban and inner-city third grade children. *Journal of Consulting and Clinical Psychology,* 1981, *49,* 251–261.

Werry, J. S. Epidemiology. In H. C. Quay & J. S. Werry (Eds.), *Psychopathological disorders of childhood* (2nd ed.). New York: John Wiley & Sons, 1979.

West, D. J., & Farrington, D. P. *Who becomes delinquent.* London: Heinemann, 1973.

Wilson, G. T., & O'Leary, K. D. *Principles of behavior therapy.* New York: Prentice-Hall, 1980.

Winett, R. A. Behavioral community psychology: Integrations and commitments. *The Behavior Therapist,* 1981, *4,* 5–8.

Winett, R. A., Battersby, C. D., & Edwards, S. M. The effects of architectural change, individualized instruction, and group contingencies on the academic performance of social behavior of sixth graders. *Journal of School Psychology,* 1975, *13,* 28–40.

Winett, R. A., Leckliter, I. N., Love, S. Q., Chinn, D. E., & Stahl, B. *Motivating residential energy conservation with special, brief TV programs.* Paper presented at the annual meeting of the American Association for the Advancement of Science, Detroit, 1983.

Winett, R. A., Neale, M. S., & Williams, K. R. The effects of flexible work schedules on urban families with young children: Quasi-experimental, ecological studies. *American Journal of Community Psychology,* 1982, *10,* 49–54.

Winett, R. A., Stefanek, M., & Riley, A. W. Preventive strategies with children and families. In T. H. Ollendick & M. Hersen (Eds.), *Handbook of child psychopathology*, New York: Plenum Press, 1983.

Winett, R. A., & Winkler, R. C. Current behavior modification in the classroom: Be still, be quiet, be docile. *Journal of Applied Behavior Analysis*, 1972, *5*, 499–504.

Wright, J. C. & Houston, A. C. A matter of form: Potentials of television for young viewers. *American Psychologist*, 1983, *38*, 835–843.

Zax, M., & Cowen, E. L. *Abnormal psychology: Changing conceptions.* New York: Holt, Rinehart & Winston, 1976.

21

Characteristics, Trends, and Future Directions in Child Behavior Therapy

Philip H. Bornstein
Alan E. Kazdin
Timothy J. McIntyre

Having spent a significant amount of time reading the preceding chapters of this book, we would like to attempt to make some sense out of this mass of information. Thematically, there are clear, common threads that tie together the field of child clinical behavior therapy. We would like to present our vision of these converging themes with regard both to the present state of the art and to projected future developments. What follows is our best characterization of child behavior therapy, past, present, and future.

THE EMPIRICAL CLINICIAN

The history of the scientist-practitioner model is relatively short but certainly quite arduous. Jointly conceived by the American Psychological Association Committee on Training in Clinical Psychology (Shakow, Hilgard, Kelly, Luckey, Sanford, & Shaffer, 1947) and the 1949 Boulder Conference, the model establishes training clinical psychologists as both scientists and practitioners. Thus, as scientists, psychologists are trained to rigorously evaluate the efficacy of their treatment programs. As practitioners, they implement their various services (e.g., assessment, diagnosis, treatment) in an attempt to reduce human suffering and enhance the lives of their clientele. But, to many, this dual emphasis on science and human service is "schizophrenic" in nature. That is, it is lofty in ideal and simply not bound to the realities of the professional world. Can the empirical scientist function as the warm, empathic clinician? Can the clinician effectively treat his or her clients while simultaneously attempting to discover cause-effect relations? Although questions such as these have remained unanswered over the years, they certainly have created their fair share of controversy and strain.

One can well understand why the clinician-researcher role has been advocated and reaffirmed over the years. First, dual research and clinical functions increase the likelihood of cross-fertilization and effective hybrid developments. Second, via direct client contact, we gain exposure to the most pressing and relevant research questions. Third, "the manifest lack of dependable knowledge in clinical psychology and personality demands that research be considered a vital part of the field of clinical psychology" (Raimy, 1950, p. 80). Clearly, the above reasons are quite substantial, yet the discrepancy between research and practice has continued to exist. The present authors believe this is due to the following:

1. Between-groups research methods may simply be inappropriate to actual clinical practice.
2. Traditional research models often pose methodological impracticabilities and ethical dilemmas on practitioners interested in conducting applied investigations.
3. Reliance on statistical significance has obscured the applicability of treatment effects for individual clients.
4. The majority of clinicians indicate research findings have had little bearing on their actual clinical practice.

But must the research-practice dichotomy continue to exist? We firmly believe that it need not and that it must not. Moreover, clinical behavior therapists have already provided the impetus for the development of alternative research models, which may truly allow for a blending of scientist-practitioner functions. This would include work in the area of single-case research designs (Kazdin, 1982; Wilson & Bornstein, in press), clinical replications (Hersen & Barlow, 1976), quasi-experimental designs (Campbell & Stanley, 1963), program development models (Gottman & Markman, 1978), and deviant case analyses (Ross, 1981). The material presented throughout the preceding chapters of this book attests to the fact that the purpose of clinical behavior therapy with children is to establish cause-effect relationships between an intervention strategy and some problem behavior. Continued application of such models should result in refinement of therapeutic procedures and increased clinical efficacy. Thus, empirical, objective, and systematic approaches to the implementation and evaluation of treatment guards against the research-practice hiatus that has plagued clinical psychology for the past 40 years. As discussed by Jayaratne and Levy (1979), the new breed of clinician-researcher is ". . . one who has (*a*) a clear idea of the independent variable, (*b*) a thorough working knowledge of the client system and its environment, (c) an empirical and objective orientation toward the process of intervention, (*d*) an ability to put research designs and measurement procedures into operation, (*e*) an ability to functionally use empirical feedback that is obtained during intervention, and (*f*) an ability to evaluate, incorporate, and use the research of others" (p. 9). In sum, he or she cannot only specify client, therapist, and treatment characteristics but attempts to determine causal relationships among the above and the behavior under study. It is via the development of such a cumulative corpus of knowledge that we truly provide meaningful treatment for our troubled children. The decade of the empirical clinician is upon us, the methodology is available, the future is now.

CLINICAL UNDERGROUND

Throughout the roughly 100-year history of modern psychotherapy, greater emphasis has been placed on who is correct rather than what is correct (Goldfried, 1980). However, with growing discontent among therapists of all persuasions regarding the absolute efficacy of any one approach, there is increasing interest in pragmatic eclecticism and nonspecific psychotherapeutic factors. Leading behaviorists (Lazarus, 1977; London, 1972; Goldfried, 1982) are also advocating that the time has come to look more dispassionately and pragmatically at clinical practice and to even consider what other orientations may have to offer. Behavior therapy, in keeping with this emerging *Zietgiest,* is beginning to systematically and objectively study aspects of the therapeutic change process that coexist with and complement the application of behavioral techniques. For example, behaviorists are becoming increasingly interested in the contribution of the therapeutic relationship to effective behavior therapy (Wilson & Evans, 1977).

It has long been recognized but not submitted to scientific scrutiny that most behavior therapy procedures require a highly skilled, sensitive, interpersonally adept clinician for intervention purposes. While some self-administered procedures (e.g., bibliotherapy, tape recorded programs) are effective with simple, circumscribed problems, complex clinical disorders, particularly those that involve disturbed relationships, require a socially-skilled, sensitive professional (O'Leary & Wilson, 1975). The significance of the therapist-client relationship was considered less important than technique by early pioneers of behavior therapy (Eysenck, 1959; Lazarus, 1958; Wolpe & Lazarus, 1966). However, Klein, Dittman, Parloff, and Gill (1969) observed the therapy sessions of Wolpe and Lazarus and reported that, while behavioral strategies were in use, strategic application of the therapeutic relationship and clinical judgment were also apparent. Even more importantly, evidence that emerged from behavior therapy studies shows that features of the therapeutic relationship definitely contribute to outcome (Alexander, Barton, Schiavo, & Parsons, 1976; Ford, 1978).

With the wedding of social-learning theory to behavior therapy (Ullmann & Krasner, 1965), the importance of the therapeutic relationship became even more apparent. Within this context, the reciprocal social-influence process occurring between therapist and client was perceived as integral to understanding and effectively practicing behavior therapy (Wilson & Evans, 1977). As a result, contemporary behavior therapists are focusing greater attention on the relationship as a catalyst for modifying client's affective, cognitive, and motoric behavior.

It has become clear that the social-influence process and relationships in general can be fruitfully interpreted using social-psychological and learning-theory principles (Staats, 1975). Consequently, behavior therapists have examined and applied extensive experimental data in an attempt to exploit the therapeutic relationship as a means of achieving treatment goals (Goldstein, 1973). A number of authors have discussed relationship factors from the perspective of the therapist's reinforcement value, role in constructing reinforcement contingencies (Bandura, 1969; Tharp & Wetzel, 1969), and function as a model of appropriate behavior (Bandura, 1971). Empirical examination of the therapist-client relationship from a social-learning perspective is an excellent example of behavior therapy's contribution toward rapprochement. The research technology developed and employed by behaviorists to validate their clinical procedures empirically will undoubtedly play an important part in directing this collaborative effort. In essence, we have already begun utilizing that technology to investigate former "sacred cows" of other approaches (see Wilson & Bornstein, in press).

The hallmark of behavior therapists has been endorsing data-based treatment and employing clinical procedures in accordance with available research. However, behavioral clinicians have not been able to adhere rigidly to these principles, unless they refuse to treat problems without substantive data. Rather, in the absence of empirical evidence, they have been forced to rely on clinical experience. However, a special virtue of behavior therapy has been its accountability. Thus, behavior therapy practitioners will continue to be responsive to data and forsake idiographic clinical experience in the presence of controlled research. Nevertheless, as behavior therapists devote greater attention to relationship and therapeutic process issues, behavior therapy conceptualizations will grow in sophistication. The behavior therapist will be increasingly seen as an active consultant who skillfully assists clients in discovering problem-solving strategies.

CRITICAL SELF-EXAMINATION

The extensive impact of behavior therapy on clinical psychology, psychiatry, social work, medicine, and education has been thoroughly documented (Kazdin

& Wilson, 1978; Thoresen, 1973; Williams & Gentry, 1977). Less attention is being paid to conceptual enemies; instead, the field is critically self-examining successes and failures. A survey of the behavior therapy outcome literature (Kazdin & Wilson, 1978) permits a few conclusions pertinent to this self-examination. First, sweeping claims about the effectiveness of behavior therapy are ridiculous. Behavior therapy is not a monolithic, monomethodological approach. The area incorporates widely diverse methods and techniques with differential efficacy. To draw reasonable conclusions, we must examine the individual literatures for each technique as it is applied to specific problems. In addition, formerly efficacious behavior therapy procedures are now in a state of basic disrepute (e.g., thought stopping) or relative disuse (e.g., semantic desensitization).

As discussed in previous chapters, behavior therapy has proven to be effective with a number of child, adolescent, and adult clinical dysfunctions. The techniques are not a panacea. Evidence for effectiveness varies markedly in quality and availability across diverse techniques. However, more than individual techniques, the self-critical nature of the field has been the central characteristic that is likely to yield empirically based treatments. Wilson and Evans (1977) have aptly summarized the status of behavior therapy in general, and child behavior therapy in particular by noting:

> A brazen confidence has given way to an optimism more cautious; clinical conceptualizations have grown in sophistication; and, an open-minded, empirical approach to unresolved issues is increasingly evident. (p. 544)

EXPANDING EVALUATION CRITERIA

Psychotherapists in general and behavior therapists in particular have long been interested in evaluating the effectiveness of their interventions. Unfortunately, many of the past conclusions drawn have been based on narrowly defined outcome criteria. Consequently, recent investigators have recommended expanding the criteria used to evaluate the differential effectiveness of alternative treatments (Garfield, 1978; Kazdin & Wilson, 1978; Strupp & Hadley, 1977).

Wolf (1978) has suggested that society needs to evaluate treatment on at least three levels:

> (1) The social significance of the *goals*. Are the specific behavioral goals really what society wants?
>
> (2) The social appropriateness of the *procedures*. Do the ends justify the means?
>
> (3) The social importance of the *effects*. Are the consumers satisfied with the results? (p. 207)

Similarly, Kazdin and Wilson (1978) discuss a variety of criteria that may be used to assess relative and comparative efficacy. They divide these into three categories: patient-related criteria, efficiency/cost-related criteria, and consumer-related criteria. Patient-related criteria refers to importance and breadth of change, proportion of clients who improve, and durability of improvements. Cost-related criteria are defined via treatment duration, efficiency, cost of professional expertise, and cost-benefit analyses. Consumer criteria are best exemplified by measures of consumer satisfaction and treatment acceptability. Indeed, it is this latter area of consumer-related criteria that has most recently received considerable attention from clinical behavior therapists (Bornstein & Rychtarik, 1983; McMahon & Forehand, 1983).

Consumer satisfaction surveys have been a standard practice in mental health treatment facilities for the past decade. However, application to the area of child behavior therapy is a relatively recent phenomenon and includes four major areas of evaluation: (1) treatment outcome, (2) satisfaction with therapist, (3) procedures, and (4) format employed. After a thorough review of the literature, McMahon and Forehand (1983) suggested that psychometrically sound consumer satisfaction measures should be "an integral part of every therapist's assessment battery" (p. 222). In addition, they note the obvious absence of assessing target child satisfaction with treatment. Instead, when satisfaction has been assessed, adult participants have been almost the exclusive subjects of such investigations. Consequently, there is a need to develop appropriate consumer satisfaction measures not only for children, but also for children of different ages.

As indicated above, a second aspect of consumer-related criteria pertains to the acceptability of alternative treatments. Kazdin has conducted a series of analogue investigations to assess differential acceptability of varying child treatment approaches (Kazdin, 1980a, 1980b, 1981; Kazdin, French, & Sherick, 1981). In addition to the legal and ethical considerations, acceptable treatments are more likely sought after, implemented, and adhered to than those of lesser acceptability. As a result, child (and adult) participation in the evaluation process is likely to produce indirect benefits that, in the long-run, reflect on treatment outcome and efficacy.

Finally, measures of social validity (Kazdin, 1977) are yet another means by which we can expand the criteria used in psychotherapy evaluation. The two primary ways in which this has been accomplished has been via subjective evaluation and social comparison methods. Subjective evaluation refers to determining the importance of behavior change by assessing the opinions of those who, through expertise or regular interaction with client, are capable of judging changes that result from treatment. Social comparison, on the other hand, compares a client's performance before and after treatment with the behavior of a nondeviant control group. While such global ratings do provide additional evaluation criteria, some caution must be exercised in their interpretation (Ernst, Bornstein, & Weltzien, 1984). In fact, social validity ratings tend to be used as supplementary to more behaviorally specific, primary dependent measures. In any case, they do provide an alternative means by which we might assess the clinical significance of behavior change with children.

MAINTENANCE AND GENERALIZATION

As is evidenced throughout this volume, child behavior therapy has proven highly successful in remediating a wide variety of children's behavior disorders. Yet, the value of these and other accomplishments is limited if changes do not maintain and/or transfer across behaviors and situations. As Kazdin and Wilson (1978) indicate, the dearth of follow-up data in clinical research leads us to question the long-term efficacy of many techniques. In fact, reviews (Kazdin & Wilson, 1978; Keeley, Shemberg, & Carbonell, 1976) have concluded that without more extensive follow-up data definitive conclusions regarding treatment durability cannot be drawn. For example, Stokes and Baer (1977) noted that ignoring long-term assessment and generalization and instead adopting a "train and hope" attitude simply will not work. Thus, the results of Flynn and colleagues (Flynn, Wood, Michelson, & Keen, 1977) become even more disconcerting. These investigators, in reviewing experimental and case study research in *Behavior Therapy* from 1970 to 1977, found that the use of follow-up assessments in behavior therapy were actually declining over time.

Careful attention to the maintenance of behavioral changes should be as much a practice of clinical behavior therapy as is modification of a client's maladaptive behavior. Furthermore, this attention should be an outgrowth of a sound behavioral treatment program. Demonstrations that behaviors return to pretreatment levels when contingencies are withdrawn have prompted several authors to advocate that response maintenance must be systematically programmed into treatment (Stokes & Baer, 1977). Programming of generalization can and probably should occur in at least two ways: (*a*) by implementing procedures during treatment that are removed by the time of termination, and (*b*) by providing events/procedures posttreatment that are different from but complementary to treatment. As Mash and Terdal (1980) indicate, this second alternative highlights the arbitrary boundary between treatment and follow-up.

Unfortunately, until recently, little attention was given either to assessment or to programming of maintenance and generalization (Keeley et al., 1976). Yet, in the last 10 years, a number of potentially powerful techniques have been identified that can be programmed into treatment as a means of increasing the likelihood of maintenance and transfer of training. Introducing behavioral changes that will be maintained by naturally occurring consequences is one such procedure. Baer and his colleagues (Baer, Rowbury, & Goetz, 1976; Stokes & Baer, 1977) labeled this concept *behavioral trap*, referring to the fact that, once developed, a client's behavior is trapped into the system of environmental reinforcers. However, this procedure by itself may result in haphazard maintenance for several reasons: (*a*) the natural environment can be very inconsistent in maintaining the new behavior (Strain, Shores, & Kerr, 1976), and (*b*) the natural network of reinforcers does not always promote or sustain appropriate behavior. Consequently, it is often necessary and desirable to augment natural contingencies via other procedures. Programming naturally occurring reinforcers has been used successfully in this regard. By training parents, relatives, and/or teachers in behavior modification techniques and enlisting their aid in execution, naturally occurring consequences are altered to support new behaviors (Lovaas, Koegel, Simmons, & Long, 1973).

Another method for promoting transfer to the natural environment is gradually fading structured treatment contingencies so that consequences resemble those of the natural environment by the time of termination. This has been successfully demonstrated using psychiatric token economies (Paul & Lentz, 1977), token reinforcement in classrooms (Turkewitz, O'Leary, & Ironsmith, 1975), and "level systems" (Phillips, Phillips, Fixsen, & Wolf, 1971). Reasoning that clients quickly learn to discriminate reinforced from nonreinforced conditions, expanding the breadth of stimuli (i.e., persons, settings, times) that signal the presence of reinforcement has also been used to assist transfer (Stokes, Baer, & Jackson, 1974; Emshoff, Redd, & Davidson, 1976). The research indicates only a few new stimuli need to be introduced to enhance transfer to novel settings or people. Two procedures relevant to this strategy include use of an intermittent reinforcement schedule and a gradual increase of the delay between reinforcement and target behavior occurrence (Kazdin, 1975).

Using peers to aid in transfer and maintenance of appropriate behavior is another strategy worthy of further consideration. Several studies have found that, once learned, new behaviors can be maintained and extended to new situations by the mere presence of peers (Johnston & Johnston, 1972; Stokes and Baer, 1976). Finally, research has also demonstrated that clients themselves can assist transfer and maintenance if taught to establish reinforcement criteria, to evaluate performance, and to appropriately self-reward (Felixbrod & O'Leary, 1974). Thus, we expect that further research regarding clients' self-management abilities is bound to occur in the future. At present, our best recommendation is to combine several of the techniques listed above as a means of programming response maintenance and transfer of training. Several studies have already done this successfully (Jones & Kazdin, 1975; Turkewitz, et al., 1975). Research is needed, however, to examine the critical features of existing techniques and further develop alternative generalization strategies.

BEHAVIORAL ASSESSMENT

Not long ago, behavioral assessment was what one did prior to initiating a behavior modification program. That is, behavioral assessment did not have a life unto itself—it existed as part of some larger, more all-encompassing conceptual scheme. That clearly is no longer the case. Behavioral assessment has come into its own. More importantly, it appears that those of a behavioral persuasion are committed to continue work in the area. While an extended discussion of the future of behavioral assessment is beyond the purview of this chapter, we would like to briefly note some issues of projected concern.[1]

Wade, Baker, and Hartmann (1979) found that nearly half of all behavior therapists responding to a national survey indicated that a major disadvantage of behavioral assessment techniques was their impracticality in applied settings. Similarly, Ford and Kendall (1979) found a variety of obstacles to the employment of naturalistic observation methods. These include time and expense, lack of cooperation from clients, and unavailability or unfeasibility of assessment methods. Quite simply, while quantification remains a priority of the highest order, its attainment is sometimes very difficult in actual practice. Thus, we applaud Nelson's (1981) admonition for the development of realistic and practical dependent measures for use in applied settings. In fact, we expect that scientist-practitioners will expend considerable effort in this regard over the next few years.

Lastly, behavioral assessment is virtually synonymous with tripartite assessment, which is the measurement of behavior across motoric, physiological, and cognitive channels. We anticipate that the use of these multiple measures will continue into the foreseeable future for a variety of reasons. First, since there is no one true measure of a client's problem, tripartite assessment allows us to draw as comprehensive a picture of the individual as possible. Second, since a construct is apt to be comprised of many different components, measurement across response channels is more likely to reveal therapeutic effects when they are obtained. Third, consistency across independent measures of the same construct increases confidence in the validity of our findings. Thus, as we continue to be concerned with the measurement of client response to treatment, we will undoubtedly continue to utilize multiple measures of client performance.

COGNITIVE BEHAVIOR MODIFICATION

According to Mahoney and Arnkoff (1978), "one of the most recent and perhaps surprising developments in clinical psychology has been the emergence of fundamentally cognitive therapies within the boundaries of behavior therapy" (p. 689). Indeed, 20 years ago, the prediction of an impending rapprochement between cognitive psychology and behavior modification would have been operational grounds for institutionalization! Today, however, advocating a cognitive-behavioral approach to treatment is neither alarming nor revolutionary. In fact, as indicated by Bornstein and van den Pol (this volume),

---

[1] For a more elaborate discussion, the interested reader is referred to any of the excellent texts in this area (Ciminero, Calhoun, & Adams, in press; Hersen & Bellack, 1981; Mash & Terdal, 1981; Ollendick & Hersen, 1984).

cognitive-behavior modification is part of the clinical behavior therapy establishment.

Cognitive-behavioral therapy encompasses a wide diversity of principles and procedures, some of which have clearly been developed outside the mainstream of contemporary behavior modification. However, these procedures do share some common fundamental assumptions, which are (*a*) that psychological disturbance is the result of maladaptive or faulty thought patterns; (*b*) that the goal of treatment is to identify dysfunctional thoughts or thought processes and replace them with more adaptive cognitions; and finally, (*c*) that the manner in which we perceive our environment substantially influences and determines our behavior. Although some studies that focused primarily on impulsive, aggressive, and hyperactive children who were treated via cognitive-behavioral techniques provided rather positive results, these findings have not always been replicable. Thus, while the wave of interest in cognitive-behavioral procedures continues to grow, the promise has not yet been fulfilled. In point of fact, Meichenbaum and Cameron (1982) stated ". . . that the current enthusiasm for cognitive-behavioral techniques seems to outstrip the empirical base in the area" (p. 310). It is apparent that via clinical application and research investigation we are becoming more aware of the gaps in our knowledge and limitations of our procedures. Consequently, corrective mechanisms must be implemented so that we learn from our mistakes and increase the effectiveness of our techniques.

In sum, cognition is alive and well in child behavior therapy. As of the mid-1980s, interest has not subsided. To the contrary, the cognitive-behavior modification movement may represent the most significant and influential trend in the clinical practice of behavior therapy. Of equal importance, however, is that behavior therapists appear fully capable of studying thoughts, beliefs, attitudes, and expectations without having compromised their allegiance to a methodological behaviorism. When the cognitive-behavioral techniques of the 1970s and 1980s are long gone, this may be the real and lasting contribution of cognitive behavior modification.

BEHAVIORAL SELF-CONTROL

A quick glance at virtually every chapter in this book attests to the fact that clinical behavior therapists have become increasingly attracted to the broad area of self-control or self-management. Historically, an increasing volume of literature clearly indicates a revolutionary trend in interest away from externally imposed contingencies toward the self-regulation of behavior (Mahoney & Arnkoff, 1978). No doubt, this is most evinced by the contents of this volume and the sheer number of journal articles, tapes, conferences, and books devoted to theory, research, and practice in behavioral self-control.

The increasing popularity of self-control procedures is probably due most to conceptual and practical principles. Conceptually, many clinicians find self-regulation intrinsically appealing on the basis of its congruence with fundamental humanistic values (e.g., independence, self-direction, personal responsibility). Practically speaking, self-management techniques allow for ease of application, access to private events, and heightened likelihood of maintenance/generalization. As has been aptly stated in the past, ". . . many—if not most—treatment programs should have some aspect of self-control built into them . . ." (O'Leary & Wilson, 1975, p. 473).

While even the ancient Greek philosophers believed that thoughts, emotions, and behavior were firmly within our realm of control (see Bornstein, Hamilton, & Bornstein, in press), it is only in the relatively recent past that a scientific technology of self-control has begun to emerge. For example, Kazdin (1974) traces the historical roots of self-monitoring to classical psychophysics and the structuralists' introspective methods. Yet, it is within the past decade that we have truly witnessed a developing trend in the study and application of self-monitoring and other self-administered procedures. In the area of clinical behavior therapy per se, considerable credit must go to Michael Mahoney and Carl Thoresen. Their pioneering texts (Mahoney & Thoresen, *Self-control: Power to the Person;* Thoresen & Mahoney, *Behavioral Self-control,* both published in 1974) provided the area of self-control with state-of-the-art assessment and direction for future research.

Self-management training with children has followed a similar progression. While experiencing rapid growth and considerable success, it has not been without controversy. Namely, two differing theoretical models of self-control have been presented. The Skinnerian model espouses a more radical behavioristic position, stating that all human actions are functionally related to environmental factors. Thus, according to Skinner, individuals may influence their own behavior but ultimate control rests with society.

> When a man controls himself, chooses a course of action, thinks out the solution to a problem, or strives toward an increase in self-knowledge, he is behaving. He controls himself precisely as he would control the behavior of anyone else—through the manipulation of variables of which behavior is a function. (Skinner, 1953, p. 228)

Kanfer, on the other hand, while agreeing that societal contingencies are the ultimate source of behavioral control, places greater emphasis on the role of self-generated cognitive events in interaction with environmental variables. Accordingly, Kanfer (1980) posits self-control via a three-stage process involving self-observation, self-evaluation, and self-reinforcement. Both the Skinner and the Kanfer models have been supported by laboratory research and clinical investigations, but neither has been thoroughly tested. Nevertheless, both have been useful in the development of effective self-control procedures.

A host of such techniques presently abound in the child behavior therapy literature. O'Leary and Dubey (1979) categorized these procedures as self-control via behavioral antecedents (i.e., self-instruction, self-determined criteria), via behavioral consequences (e.g., self-reinforcement, self-punishment), and via innovative self-control procedures (e.g., distraction, restatement of contingencies). The listing of available procedures is virtually endless. At this time, what can be concluded with some assurance is that self-control techniques have successfully enabled target children to modify and improve formerly problematic behaviors. Certainly, a large number of questions remain. However, given that self-change methods are the top-ranked form of intervention predicted to increase over the next 10 years (Prochaska & Norcross, 1983), research efforts should bear on these very questions.

BEHAVIORAL MEDICINE/BEHAVIORAL PEDIATRICS

The field of "behavioral medicine is one of the newest and fastest growing areas of interest in the realm of behavior therapy. Over the last six years, a spokesman organization, the Society of Behavioral Medicine (SBM), has coalesced and published a rapidly growing newsletter *(Behavioral Medicine Update)* and a quarterly journal *(Behavioral Medicine Abstracts)*. The abstracts for this scientific publication come from more than 100 journals of diverse fields and reflect SBM's goal of encouraging and welcoming contributions from many disciplines.

The impact of behavior therapy on behavioral medicine is most evident by virtue of the fact that SBM was spawned in close alliance with the Association for Advancement of Behavior Therapy (Brownell, 1982). At present, behavioral medicine is best connoted as an interdisciplinary field concerned with the clinical application of behavior therapy techniques to medical problems. This will include evaluation, management, treatment, prevention, and rehabilitation of physical health disorders. Topics commonly subsumed under the broad label of *behavioral medicine* include biofeedback, behavioral pediatrics (asthma, seizures, anorexia, enuresis, encopresis), chronic pain, stress-related disorders, hypertension, addictive disorders, obesity, and sexual dysfunctions.

One of the promising features of behavioral medicine resonant in the above definition is that it provides a potential forum in which proponents of medical versus psychological treatments can combine their respective talents. A superb illustration of this is being realized in the treatment of attention deficit disorders (see Barkley, this volume). As Brownell (1982) indicates, when a disorder is not completely understood and two opposing therapeutic camps have formed, there is a natural tendency to square off and fight. Evidence of this process is present in the hyperactivity literature in which advocates of drug versus behavioral therapies have clashed (Gittelman-Klein, Klein, Abikoff, Katz, Gloisten, & Kates, 1976; Sprague & Sleator, 1977; Swanson, Kinsbourne, Roberts, & Zucker, 1978). Behavioral medicine provides a constructive forum in which the relative contributions of both treatments can be evaluated and combined to best fit the psychological, social, and medical needs of the client. As a result, reports are now suggesting that the two approaches combined are more effective than either alone (Pelham, Schnedler, Bologna, & Contreras, 1980; Satterfield, Cantwell & Satterfield, 1979).

Behavioral medicine is indeed a light on the horizon with the potential for making a significant contribution to the treatment of many childhood disorders. It must, however, survive the disillusionment that so often follows in the wake of overly optimistic claims concomitant with new areas of development. This particular movement must also remain interdisciplinary in nature. If this can be accomplished, then behavioral medicine/behavioral pediatrics holds tremendous promise. Given its medical technology, rigorous application of scientific methodology, and efficacious behavior therapy techniques, we may finally be on the brink of psychologically sound health-care provision.

FINAL COMMENTS

It should be evident from our summary perspective of the field that child behavior therapy reflects an orientation that has far-reaching implications. Within the field, individual intervention techniques have emerged to address a myriad of clinical problems. The impact of these techniques, their limitations, and remaining questions have been carefully detailed in previous chapters. But beyond these techniques, there are important themes within the field that are perhaps of even greater significance.

Alternative treatments or orientations may well fade over time. Fadism is not new in psychological therapies. What is new and likely to remain beyond particular orientations is an appreciation, if not an increased demand, for empirical approaches to treatment. There is still no substitute for sound theory or clinical experience. However, there is greater appreciation today than in the past that neither of these is a substitute for empirical evidence. Child behavior therapy has a firm commitment to data as its main contribution. This means that, by any standards, many of the techniques that will be promulgated in upcoming years will be nonbehavioral in nature. Indeed, it is likely, if not certain, that the techniques that produce therapeutic change in children will not all stem from behavioral concepts. The reliance on evidence as the determinant of treatment effectiveness will be the significant contribution. The current techniques will have contributed to this future by modeling empirical methods of treatment evaluation.

REFERENCES

Alexander, J. F., Barton, C., Schiavo, R. S., & Parsons, B. V. Systems-behavioral intervention with families of delinquents: Therapist characteristics, family behavior, and outcome. *Journal of Consulting and Clinical Psychology*, 1976, *44*, 656–664.

Baer, D. M., Rowbury, T. G., & Goetz, E. M. Behavioral traps in the preschool: A proposal for research. *Minnesota Symposium on Child Psychology*. 1976, *10*, 3–27.

Bandura, A. *Principles of behavior modification*. New York: Holt, Rinehart & Winston, 1969.

Bandura, A. Psychotherapy based upon modeling principles. In A. E. Bergin & S. L. Garfield (Eds.), *Handbook of psychotherapy and behavior change: An empirical analysis*. New York: John Wiley & Sons, 1971.

Bornstein, P. H., Hamilton, S. B., & Bornstein, M. T. Self-monitoring procedures. In A. R. Ciminero, K. S. Calhoun, & H. E. Adams (Eds.), *Handbook of behavioral assessment* (2nd ed.). New York: John Wiley & Sons, in Press.

Bornstein, P. H. & Rychtarik, R. G. Consumer satisfaction in adult behavior therapy: Procedures, problems, and future perspectives. *Behavior Therapy*, 1983, *14*, 191–208.

Brownell, K. D. Behavioral medicine. In C. M. Franks, G. T. Wilson, P. C. Kendall, & K. D. Brownell (Eds.), *Annual review of behavior therapy: Theory and practice* (Vol. VIII). New York: Guilford Press, 1982.

Campbell, D. T., & Stanley, J. C. *Experimental and quasi-experimental designs for research*. Chicago: Rand McNally, 1963.

Ciminero, A. R., Calhoun, K. S., & Adams, H. E. *Handbook of behavioral assessment* (2nd ed.). New York: John Wiley & Sons, in Press.

Cone, J. D. Psychometric considerations. In M. Hersen & A. S. Bellack (Eds.), *Behavioral assessment: A practical handbook*. New York: Pergamon Press, 1981.

Emshoff, J. G., Redd, W. H., & Davidson, W. S. Generalization training and the transfer of treatment effects with delinquent adolescents. *Journal of Behavior Therapy and Experimental Psychiatry*, 1976, *7*, 141–144.

Ernst, J., Bornstein, P. H., & Weltzien, R. T. Initial considerations in subjective evaluation research: Does knowledge of treatment affect performance ratings? *Behavioral Assessment*, 1984, *6*, 121–127.

Eysenck, H. J. Learning theory and behavior therapy. *Journal of Mental Science*, 1959, *105*, 61–75.

Felixbrod, J. J., & O'Leary, K. D. Self-determination of academic standards: Toward freedom from external control. *Journal of Educational Psychology*, 1974, *66*, 845–850.

Flynn, J. M., Wood, R., Michelson, L., & Keen, J. *Publication trends in behavior therapy, 1970–1977.* Paper presented at the meeting of the Association for Advancement of Behavior Therapy, Atlanta, December 1977.

Ford, J. D. Therapeutic relationship in behavior therapy: An empirical analysis. *Journal of Consulting and Clinical Psychology.* 1978, *46,* 1302–1314.

Ford, J. D., & Kendall, P. C. Behavior therapists' professional behaviors: Converging evidence of a gap between theory and practice. *The Behavior Therapist,* 1979, *2,* 37–38.

Garfield, S. L. Research problems in clinical diagnosis. *Journal of Consulting and Clinical Psychology.* 1978, *46,* 596–607.

Gittelman-Klein, R., Klein, D. F., Abikoff, H., Katz, J., Gloisten, A. C., & Kates, W. Relative efficacy of methylphenidate and behavior modification: An interim report. *Journal of Abnormal Child Psychology,* 1976, *4,* 361–379.

Goldfried, M. R. Toward the delineation of therapeutic change principles. *American Psychologist,* 1980, *35,* 991–999.

Goldfried, M. R. (Ed.). *Converging themes in psychotherapy.* New York: Springer, 1982.

Goldstein, A. P. *Structured learning therapy. New York: Pergamon Press, 1973.*

Gottman, J. M., & Markman, H. J. Experimental designs in psychotherapy research. In S. L. Garfield & A. E. Bergin (Eds.), Handbook of psychotherapy and behavior change. (2nd ed.). New York: John Wiley & Sons, 1978.

Hersen, M., & Barlow, D. H. *Single-case experimental designs: Strategies for studying behavior change.* New York: Pergamon Press, 1976.

Hersen, M., & Bellack, A. S. *Behavioral assessment: A practical handbook.* New York: Pergamon Press, 1981.

Jayaratne, S., & Levy, R. L. *Empirical clinical practice.* New York: Columbia University Press, 1979.

Johnston, J. M., & Johnston, G. T. Modification of consonant speech-sound articulation in young children. *Journal of Applied Behavior Analysis,* 1972, *5,* 233–246.

Jones, R. T., & Kazdin, A. E. Programming response maintenance after withdrawing token reinforcement. *Behavior Therapy,* 1975, *6,* 153–164.

Kanfer, F. H. Self-management methods. In F. H. Kanfer & A. P. Goldstein (Eds.), *Helping people change: A textbook of methods.* New York: Pergamon Press, 1980.

Kazdin, A. E. Self-monitoring and behavior change. In M. J. Mahoney & C. E. Thoresen (Eds.), *Self-control: Power to the person.* Monterey, Calif.: Brooks/ Cole Publishing, 1974.

Kazdin, A. E. Assessing the clinical or applied significance of behavior change through social validation. *Behavior Modification,* 1977, *1,* 427–452.

Kazdin, A. E. Acceptability of alternate treatments for deviant child behavior. *Journal of Applied Behavior Analysis,* 1980, *13,* 259–273 (a).

Kazdin, A. E. Acceptability of time out from reinforcement procedures for disruptive child behavior. *Behavior Therapy,* 1980, *11,* 329–344 (b).

Kazdin, A. E. Acceptability of child treatment techniques: The influence of treatment efficacy and adverse side effects. *Behavior Therapy,* 1981, *12,* 493–506.

Kazdin, A. E. *Single-case research designs: Methods for clinical and applied settings.* New York: Oxford University Press, 1982.

Kazdin, A. E. *Behavior modification in applied settings* (3rd ed.). Homewood, Ill.: Dorsey Press, 1984.

Kazdin, A. E., French, N. H., & Sherick, R. B. Acceptability of alternative treatments for children: Evaluations by inpatient children, parents, and staff. *Journal of Consulting and Clinical Psychology,* 1981, *49,* 900–907.

Kazdin, A. E., & Wilson, G. T. *Evaluation of behavior therapy: Issues, evidence and research strategies.* Cambridge, Mass.: Ballinger, 1978.

Kazdin, A. E., & Wilson, G. T. Criteria for evaluating psychotherapy. *Archives of General Psychiatry,* 1978, *35,* 407–415.

Keeley, S. M., Shemberg, K. M., & Carbonell, J. Operant clinical intervention: Behavior management or beyond? Where are the data? *Behavior Therapy,* 1976, *7,* 292–305.

Klein, M. H., Dittman, A. T., Parloff, M. B., & Gill, M. M. Behavior therapy: Observations and reflections. *Journal of Consulting and Clinical Psychology,* 1969, *33,* 259–266.

Lazarus, A. A. New methods in psychotherapy: A case study. *South African Medical Journal,* 1958, *32,* 660–664.

Lazarus, A. A. Has behavior therapy outlived its usefulness? *American Psychologist,* 1977, *32,* 550–554.

London, P. The end of ideology in behavior modification. *American Psychologist,* 1972, *27,* 913–920.

Lovaas, O. I., Koegel, R., Simmons, J. Q., & Long, J. S. Some generalization and follow-up measures on autistic children in behavior therapy. *Journal of Applied Behavior Analysis,* 1973, *6,* 131–166.

Mahoney, M. J., & Arnkoff, D. Cognitive and self-control therapies. In S. L. Garfield & A. E. Bergin (Eds.), *Handbook of psychotherapy and behavior change* (2nd ed.). New York: John Wiley & Sons, 1978.

Mahoney, M. J., & Thoresen, C. E. (Eds.) *Self-control: Power to the person.* Monterey, Calif.: Brooks/Cole Publishing, 1974.

Mash, E. J., & Terdal, L. G. Follow-up assessments in behavior therapy. In P. Karoly & J. J. Steffen (Eds.), *Improving the long-term effects of psychotherapy.* New York: Gardner Press, 1980.

Mash, E. J., & Terdal, L. G. (Eds.). *Behavioral assessment of childhood disorders.* New York: Guilford Press, 1981.

McMahon, R. J., & Forehand, R. L. Consumer satisfaction in behavioral treatment of children: Types, issues, and recommendations. *Behavior Therapy*, 1983, *14*, 209–225.

Meichenbaum, D., & Cameron, R. Cognitive-behavior therapy. In G. T. Wilson & C. M. Franks (Eds.), *Contemporary behavior therapy: Conceptual and empirical foundations*. New York: Guilford Press, 1982.

Nelson, R. O. Realistic dependent measures for clinical use. *Journal of Consulting and Clinical Psychology*, 1981, *49*, 168–182.

O'Leary, K. D., & Wilson, G. T. *Behavior therapy: Application and outcome*. Englewood Cliffs, N.J.: Prentice-Hall, 1975.

O'Leary, S. G., & Dubey, D. R. Applications of self-control procedures by children: A review. *Journal of Applied Behavior Analysis*, 1979, *12*, 449–465.

Ollendick, T., & Hersen, M. (Eds.). *Child behavioral assessment: Principles and procedures*. New York: Pergamon Press, 1984.

Paul, G. L., & Lentz, R. J. *Psychosocial treatment of chronic mental patients: Milieu versus social-learning programs*. Cambridge, Mass.: Harvard University Press, 1977.

Pelhem, W. E., Schnedler, R. W., Bologna, N. C., & Contreras, J. A. Behavioral and stimulant treatment of hyperactive children: A therapy study with methylphenidate probes in a within-subject design. *Journal of Applied Behavior Analysis*, 1980, *13*, 221–236.

Phillips, E. L., Phillips, E. A. Fixsen, D. L., & Wolf, M. M. Achievement phase: Modification of the behaviors of pre-delinquent boys within a token economy. *Journal of Applied Behavior Analysis*, 1971, *4*, 45–49.

Prochaska, J. O., & Norcross, J. C. Contemporary psychotherapists: A national survey of characteristics, practices, orientations, and attitudes. *Psychotherapy: Theory, Research, & Practice*, 1983, *20*, 161–173.

Raimy, V. C. (Ed.). *Training in clinical psychology (Boulder conference)*. New York: Prentice-Hall, 1950.

Ross, A. O. Of rigor and relevance. *Professional Psychology*, 1981, *12*, 319–327.

Satterfield, J. H., Cantwell, D. P., & Satterfield, B. T. Multimodality treatment: A one-year follow-up of 84 hyperactive boys. *Archives of General Psychiatry*, 1979, *36*, 965–974.

Shakow, D., Hilgard, E. R., Kelly, E. L., Luckey, B., Sanford, R. N., & Shaffer, L. F. Recommended graduate training program in clinical psychology. *American Psychologist*, 1947, *2*, 539–558.

Skinner, B. F. *Science and human behavior*. New York: Macmillan, 1953.

Sprague, R. L., & Sleator, E. K. Methylphenidate in hyperkinetic children: Differences in dose effects on learning and social behavior. *Science*, 1977, *198*, 1274–1276.

Staats, A. W. Social behaviorism. Homewood, Ill.: Dorsey Press, 1975.

Stokes, T. F., & Baer, D. M. An implicit technology of generalization. *Journal of Applied Behavior Analysis*, 1977, *10*, 349–367.

Stokes, T. F., Baer, D. M., & Jackson, R. L. Programming the generalization of a greeting response in four retarded children. *Journal of Applied Behavior Analysis,* 1974, *7,* 599–610.

Strain, P. S., Shores, R. E., & Kerr, M. M. An experimental analysis of "spillover" effects on the social interaction of behaviorally handicapped preschool children. *Journal of Applied Behavior Analysis,* 1976, *9,* 31–40.

Strupp, H. H., & Hadley, S. W. A tripartite model of mental health and therapeutic outcomes. *American Psychologist,* 1977, *32,* 187–196.

Swanson, J. M., Kinsbourne, M., Roberts, W., & Zucker, K. Time-response analysis of the effect of stimulant medication on the learning ability of children referred for hyperactivity. *Pediatrics,* 1978, *61,* 21–29.

Tharp, R. G., & Wetzel, R. J. *Behavior modification in the natural environment.* New York: Academic Press, 1969.

Thoresen, C. E. (Ed.) *Behavior modification in education: The seventy-second yearbook of the national society for the study of education.* Chicago: University of Chicago Press, 1973.

Thoresen, C. E., & Mahoney, M. J. *Behavioral self-control:* New York: Holt, Rinehart & Winston, 1974.

Turkewitz, H., O'Leary, K. D., & Ironsmith, M. Generalization and maintenance of appropriate behavior through self-control. *Journal of Consulting and Clinical Psychology,* 1975, *43,* 557–583.

Ullmann, L. P., & Krasner, L. (Eds.). *Case studies in behavior modification.* New York: Holt, Rinehart & Winston, 1965.

Wade, T. C., Baker, T. B., & Hartmann, D. P. Behavior therapists self-reported views and practices. *The Behavior Therapist,* 1979, *2,* 3–6

Williams, R. B., Jr., & Gentry, W. D. (Eds.). *Behavioral approaches to medical treatment.* Cambridge, Mass.: Ballinger, 1977.

Wilson, G. L., & Bornstein, P. H. Paradoxical procedures and single-case methodology: Review and recommendations. *Journal of Behavior Therapy and Experimental Psychiatry,* in press.

Wilson, G. T., & Evans, I. M. The therapist-client relationship in behavior therapy. In A. S. Gurman & M. M. Razin (Eds.), *Effective psychotherapy.* New York: Pergamon Press, 1977.

Wolf, M. M. Social validity: The case for subjective measurement or how applied behavior analysis is finding its heart. *Journal of Applied Behavior Analysis,* 1978, *11,* 203–214.

Wolpe, J., & Lazarus, A. A. *Behavior therapy techniques.* New York: Pergamon Press, 1966.

Name Index

O'Tuama, L., 175
Owen, P. R., 761
Owen, Y., 294–95

P

Packard, D., 353, 510
Padian, N., 616, 618
Page, T. J., 141
Paine, S., 558, 560–61, 563–65, 572, 580,
 584, 701, 704, 718, 726
Palkes, H. S., 196
Palmer, E., 814
Palmer, R. L., 310
Parke, R. D., 131, 775, 785
Parker, A., 368–69
Parker, G., 614
Parker, J. B., 608
Parker, L., 413
Parloff, M., 82
Parloff, M. B., 835
Parry, P., 196, 637
Parsons, J. E., 628
Paschalis, A. P., 416
Paster, S., 668
Paternite, C. E., 165, 167, 172–73, 179,
 181–82, 189
Paterson, L., 813
Paterson, M. T., 346
Patterson, C. J., 636–37
Patterson, G. R., 37, 94, 171, 176, 180,
 192, 194, 223–26, 231–32, 236–39,
 245–48, 250–51, 546–47, 559, 711,
 728, 773, 776, 779, 784, 786–87,
 789, 795
Patterson, R. L., 360
Paulauskas, S., 167, 171
Paul, G., 77, 100
Paul, G. L., 280, 823, 840
Paul, J., 702, 713
Pauley, I., 668
Pauls, D. L., 351
Paulsen, K., 162
Paykel, E. S., 614
Peabody, D. L., 786
Pearl, D., 819
Peck, C. A., 581
Pederson, A., 544–45, 555
Pedrini, B. C., 428
Pedrini, D. T., 428
Peed, S., 243, 246, 777
Peery, J. C., 583
Pegram, V., 472, 474–76
Pelham, W. E., 547, 845
Pellegrini, D. S., 96, 103
Pemberton, B. W., 129
Penick, E. C., 601–2, 608, 619
Pennington, B. F., 177
Pennypacker, H. S., 62

Pentecost, J. H., 137
Peoples, A., 353, 510
Pepler, D., 548
Perl, D., 182
Perlman, T., 172
Perlmutter, A. D., 413, 415
Perlmutter, L., 750
Perloff, B. F., 399
Perry, M. A., 286, 291–92
Pertschuk, M., 820
Peters, K. G., 160, 162, 182
Peters, S., 179
Peterson, C., 510
Peterson, C. P., 601, 605, 609–10
Peterson, D. R., 14, 21, 54–55, 606
Peterson, L., 82, 297–98
Peterson, R. F., 398–99, 401
Petti, T. A., 604, 616, 621, 626, 639
Philips, I., 609–10, 615
Phillips, E. A., 840
Phillips, E. L., 840
Piaget, J., 394–95, 616, 749
Pianta, B., 705
Picker, M., 368–69
Pierce, C. M., 414, 420, 422
Piers, E. V., 630
Pincus, J. H., 181, 233
Pine, F., 613
Pinkerton, P., 421, 426
Pinkerton, S., 356
Pittman, D. J., 663
Pitts-Conway, V., 533
Platt, J. J., 25, 632, 809
Platzek, D., 367
Plummer, S., 510, 519
Pokracki, F., 721
Polakow, R. L., 786
Poling, A., 368–69
Polivy, J., 314
Pollack, E., 190
Pollack, S. L., 615
Pollard, S., 161, 175–76, 180, 190, 204
Porter, B., 237–38
Porter, J., 477–78
Porter, R. J., 233, 242
Poser, E. G., 807
Power, E., 785
Powers, M., 746, 754, 757
Poznanski, E. O., 273, 600–601, 604–5,
 607, 615–16, 618, 634
Pratt, D., 721
Pratt, J. M., 806
Pratt, R., 332
President's Commission on Excellence in
 Education, 705
Pressley, M., 636
Price, J. H., 335
Price, M. G., 447

Subject Index

A

ABAB design, 83–85; *see also* Outcome studies
Academic remediation; *see also* Learning disabilities
  behavioral approaches, 754–58
  behavioral model, 758–62
    assessment phase, 760
    described, 758–60
    evaluation, 761–62
    treatment phase, 760–61
  medical models, 753–54
ACCEPTS program, 554, 727
Achenbach Child Behavior Checklist, 168, 186, 202
Achievement tests, 751–52
Activity increase strategies, 624–25
Additives, 176
Aggressive behavior
  assessment of, 241–45
  in attention deficit disorders, 172, 174
  causes of, 231–34, 239–41
  characteristics of, 222, 225–27
  DSM-III syndromes, 219–21, 223
  empirically-derived, 221–25
  and family patterns, 234–39, 241, 244
  prevalence of, 227–28
  treatment of, 245–54
Allergies, 176
Alternating treatment designs; *see also*
  ▪ Outcome studies
  advantages of, 88–90
  disadvantages of, 89
  methodology of, 88
American Association on Mental Deficiency
  Adaptive Behavior Scale, 127, 136
Anorexia nervosa
  causes of, 319–20
  characteristics of, 318–19
  defined, 317
  treatment for, 320–22
Anxiety
  and nightmares, 464–65
  and sleep terrors, 457
  and sleepwalking, 451
Anxiety disorders
  assessment of, 274–78
  causes of, 270–73
  counter conditioning, 279–85

Anxiety disorders—*Cont.*
  defined, 266–68
  diagnosis of, 268–70, 277–78
  DSM-III, diagnosis of, 277–78
  modeling, 285–92
    live, 286–87
    participant, 289–91
    research issues, 291–92
    symbolic, 287–91
  operant procedures, 292–296
  self-control procedures, 296–98
Anxiety hierarchy construction, 280
Applied Behavior Analysis, 64–66
Archival data in evaluation of therapy, 108
Arithmetic disorders, 754, 756–57
Assertive Discipline, 726
Assertiveness training, 572–73
Assessments for Integration into Mainstream
  Settings (AIMS), 722
Attention deficit disorder
  and aggressive behavior, 225
  assessment of, 182–88
  causes of, 174–81
  characteristics of, 162–65, 167–72
  defined, 159, 173, 181–82
  diagnostic criteria, 174
  historical background of, 159–61
  and hyperactivity, 159
  and learning disability, 746
  prevalence of, 161–62
  sensitivity of, 165–66
  treatment of, 188–201
Attention problems
  in learning disabilities, 754
  symptomatic of ADD, 163
Attribution retraining, 628–29
Atypical stereotyped movement disorders
  defined, 347
  treatment, 368–74
Autism
  assessment, 506
  causes of, 505–6
  characteristics, 501–3
  description, 500–501
  diagnosis, 503–4
  vs. schizophrenia, 503–4
  and social skills deficits, 547
  and stereotypy, 352, 368
  target behaviors, 506–9

879

*This book has been set VIP, in 10 and 9 point Times Roman,
leaded 2 points. Part numbers and chapter numbers are 54
point Avant Garde Book. Part titles are 18 point Avant
Garde Book and chapter titles are 16 point Avant Garde
Book. The size of the type page is 27 by 46 picas.*